standard catalog of®
DIE-CAST
VEHICLES
Updated Pricing

Edited by Dan Stearns
Identification and Price Guide

© 2005 by
KP Books

Published by

kp books
An imprint of F+W Publications, Inc.

700 East State Street • Iola, WI 54990-0001
715-445-2214 • 888-457-2873

Our toll-free number to place an order or obtain a free catalog is 800-258-0929.

Library of Congress Catalog Number: 2002105101
ISBN: 0-87349-821-6

Printed in the United States of America

Table of Contents

Foreword

How many people are fortunate enough to work in an environment where you are encouraged to bring your toys to work? And I'm talking about more than just one of those corporate morale-boosting ploys, like "Take Your Toys to Work Day."

Yes, I realize I'm one of the lucky few. A highlight of my job came when I was offered the opportunity to work on the *Standard Catalog of Die-Cast Vehicles*. Most of the die-cast fans here at Krause Publications surround our cubicles with favorite die-casts. They line our reference shelves and perch proudly atop our computers (once they have been secured, of course). I know of several coworkers who often beg Gerry, our maintenance guy, to hunt down more file cabinets in an effort to free up more desk space for that latest die-cast acquisition.

Most of our coworkers are pretty understanding and indulgent. They realize the importance of keeping up with the fluctuations of this market. But for some reason, the housekeeping staff doesn't really love us. Is it presumptuous to expect that each toy and model be lovingly dusted each night? I don't see the problem. But I digress.

I know I'm making our jobs sound like all fun and no work. In truth, putting together this book was rather hard work. Imagine all of the major die-cast collectors at Krause bringing in their collections for the big photo shoot. Yes, it was quite a sight — but think of the security issues!

It's a capital offense here to borrow someone's toys without gaining express written permission. More identification is required to borrow my Revell 1:64-scale Bullitt 1968 Dodge Charger than you would need to rent a Ferrari for the day.

Take for instance the photo shoot for this book cover. While I was busily gathering cars from my desk, editor Dan Stearns was desperately trying to fill the frame with his favorite foreign cars and Matchbox toys. But what about my Ertl 1957 Chrysler 300C? The ensuing fight wasn't pretty, but at least no one was seriously injured.

As Angelo Van Bogart, associate editor of *Old Cars Weekly* and author of the Hot Wheels Hunting column in *Toy Cars & Models*, was preparing his redline Hot Wheels for a close-up, Dan was cheerfully loading up another carrying case with his newly-nabbed "acquisitions."

And poor Karen O'Brien, our expert toy and automotive book editor! As she was pointing out the subtle differences between her three Corgi Batmobiles to a small gathering of die-cast fans, Dan was using the diversion to swipe the dark knight's ride. But I guess you can't blame a guy for trying to "upgrade" his collection, right?

But photo shoot hijackings and good-natured high jinks aside, this book was a huge undertaking. The die-cast market keeps growing and evolving, as evidenced by the increased attention placed on 1:18 and 1:64 in the U.S. The manufacturers that once offered vehicles in various scales are now narrowing their approach to these two extremes. Some are having great success with this strategy, but others are finding it hard to stand out on the shelves amid all of the other lines.

Thankfully, there are 1:18 lines like Trademark Models' Highway 61 and Lane Collectables' Exact Detail. Both companies are building reputations by offering high-detail models of unique subjects. I mean, how many models have you seen of the 1951 Studebaker Champion or the 1970 Olds 4-4-2? Not many. Sure, Hot Wheels made an Olds 442 as a vintage redline car, but do you want to fork over that kind of cash?

Corgi deserves a mention, too. For a company that always catered strictly to the high-end collectibles market, it's rather refreshing to see various castings appear in the kid-friendly Showcase Collection. I've been able to add some nice Corgi models to my shelves at a lower price that I would have paid five years ago.

But whether you prefer large-scale replicas or smaller scaled-to-the-box toys, it's a great time to be a die-cast collector. And kudos to Dan for being the man to fasten his seatbelt, seize the wheel and take us all on a grand adventure.

I don't know where Dan got the energy for this project, but I have suspicions about how he doubled his collection . . .

Merry Dudley is the editor of Toy Cars & Models, *a monthly magazine devoted to model cars of all types and sizes. For more information on* Toy Cars & Models, *visit* www.toycarsmag.com, *or call 800-258-0929 to order a subscription.*

Acknowledgments

Putting together a book—any book—takes a team of people. I've been lucky to have a great team. I'd first like to thank my publisher, Bill Krause, for having infinite patience and incredible enthusiasm for this project. My manager, Don Gulbrandsen, for allowing me to build this project up into the volume it is, and trusting my judgement concerning photo shoots, page layout, design, etc. Kris Kandler and Bob Best, our photographers, put up with almost endless shots of tiny cars and road trips to collections, and my musings about die-cast minutia.

Of course, you couldn't have photo shoots without collections, and many people here generously shared their collection and knowledge with us. Colleague and friend Tom Michael brought in die-cast models without hesitation, and supplied me with ideas, pricing, trends and facts—many of which have percolated throughout this book. He also helped set up the cover shoot, mentioning, "It's easy to tell our cars apart, Dan. Yours are the models people say 'oh, nice' over and mine are the vehicles people 'ooh' and 'ahhhh' over." Thanks, Tom. (I have to admit, it's probably true: Tom's collection of redlines and buttons appears in the color section of this book.)

Another co-worker, George Cuhaj, also brought in his collection to our studio, contributing substantially to our vintage die-cast photos. Angelo Van Bogart, whose article about Redlines colors appears in this book, dug out his models of Johnny Lightnings and Hot Wheels, and cheerfully researched values and facts of each one. Bert Lehman, a fan of most (if not all) things NASCAR, helped me fill in some gaps in our stock car photos. Colin Bruce allowed me to virtually keep some of his models while time slots opened in our photography department. Merry Dudley, editor of *Toy Cars and Models*, thankfully assembled and

wrote the Ertl chapter to this book, tracked down photos and provided much-needed moral support. Karen O'Brien, toy collector extraordinaire, found pricing for new and vintage sections of the book, and without exception, stayed enthusiastic about this project even when I was less so.

Assembling the book, my design and database team were invaluable. Gena Pamperin and Guy Scudella scanned the thousands of images you see in this book. If a picture is worth a thousand words, then they've written a few novels. Stacy Bloch designed all of the intros and non-listing pages of this book, double-checked captions, re-worked the catalog pages until they shined, and overall kept me sane and confident in the final hours before going to press. Her patience was much appreciated. Bonnie Tetzlaff, database wizard and page designer, endured my constant revisions and organizational schemes without complaint. Sandy Morrison, production and database expert, also lent a hand in running out pages of material for this book. Tom Dupuis designed the cover that captured the essence of collecting, and made you pick up this volume in the first place.

And that was just people at work.

Outside this building, my contributors couldn't have been better or more co-operative. Dr. Douglas Sadecky, for instance, took every photograph you'll see of vintage Corgi items, almost all of our vintage Husky and Corgi Junior shots, most of our vintage Dinky shots and photos of almost anything rare in the realm of Matchbox regular wheels. He was the primary force behind the Corgi, Dinky and Husky chapters as well. His good humor and incredible effort made these sections of the book a joy to work on.

Corgi Classics, Inc. was instrumental in allowing us use of their corporate and catalog photography. That same cooperation was granted to us by sister company Lledo, who also allowed us access to their in-house images.

Playing Mantis provided much-needed insight into their newest lines of vehicles, access to images and much-appreciated retail lists.

Kelly Haughey provided retail and release information and images for Matchbox Collectibles, helping round out that chapter.

Another contributor, John Brown, Sr., graciously welcomed us into his home and, allowed us to photograph a significant portion of his epic die-cast collection. Without his help, many

of the photos for Tootsietoy and Matchbox simply wouldn't be present in this book.

Lisa Rockmore of Georgia Marketing and Promotions, happily supplied me with images, retail pricing and a company history, making that chapter a reality.

Carol Pesch of Kyosho went above and beyond in her assistance. She supplied prices, marked-up catalogs and disks of gorgeous images—all of which I wish we would have been able to print in color.

Likewise, Dave Sproul supplied us with much-needed info about Eagle Collectibles, making the chapter more than a simple listing.

Paul's Model Art Minichamps of Aachen, Germany, supplied us with images and support at lightning speed. Their disk arrived via "Luftpost," and was a welcome sight in my mailbox.

Charles Hepperle of Maisto is really responsible for the interesting background and images concerning the Maisto/Zee Toy connection. He was a positive force for this book as well, and his cooperation and efforts supplying us with images for the chapter are much appreciated.

Of course, there wouldn't be a Hot Wheels Numbered Pack chapter without Mike Zarnock. An excerpted portion of his book, "The Ultimate Guide to Hot Wheels Variations", appears here because he cheerfully wants to encourage other collectors. And yes, we do publish his book, too.

Also, our friends at Exact Detail, Eric Trapp and John Berglund win major kudos for sending us photographs and listings for our chapter on those models.

Thanks to Racing Champions/Ertl for allowing us to use their photos as well. Their American Muscle line is one of the reasons behind the current boom in die-cast collecting.

And, of course, much appreciation to everyone I may not have mentioned by name, who had a part in making this book happen. Thank you.

Introduction

Remember when you first collected toy cars? More than likely, it was a matter of running down to the nearest dime store, discounter or supermarket and finding your (newest) favorite Matchbox or Hot Wheels car in the toy aisle. That thrill of discovery is what keeps many of us collecting today. I think it's fair to say we've all experienced that great rush when setting up a whole floor full of toy cars. There's something about seeing the multitude of shapes and colors of many miniature vehicles all lined up in rows that's just plain fun.

In many ways, collectors are like curators of their own museums. They discover objects of interest, track down obscure facts and background histories, and are always ready to give visitors a tour, whenever guests seem interested.

This book, too, aims to be a tour of some of the most popular and well-loved die-cast vehicles.

As such, I've tried to hit upon the high points of many of the leading manufacturers here: Corgi, Dinky, Ertl, Hot Wheels, Johnny Lightning, Lledo, Matchbox, Racing Champions, Tootsietoy and more. In essence, I've tried to make this book a combination of the best of the old and the best of the new.

About Pricing

With the exception of current retail prices (and even those have some flexibility, depending on the retailer) the values in this book are simply a guide. You will find higher or lower prices than the ones shown here at shows, through online dealers and on eBay.

The prices here are a compilation from various dealers, collectors, Krause collectibles experts, auction results and the like. They are averaged out to cover regional differences as much as possible.

About Condition

The range in this book covers excellent, near mint, and mint-in-package models. You could equate the

near mint category to "mint without package," because in many instances, that's what it is. "Excellent" refers to models with very little playwear, a couple of nicks, but for the most part, it's in incredible shape. Beyond this, common sense simply must kick in. There are plenty of models with cruddy boxes that don't add significantly, if at all, to the model's value, but can add to the price you pay. Consider how badly you need that box—there are usually empty boxes you can pair up with loose models in good shape. One word in defense of boxes, though—normally, a box or blister pack (obviously, not "matchable" to a loose model) add about 50% more to the toy's value, and truly can make your purchase an investment.

Most of the vintage toy vehicles carry all three condition categories, "EX," "NM" and "MIP." Some, like Hot Wheels Redlines have "NM" (meaning mint-no-package), and "MIP," for models still in blister packs. New or relatively current models are listed with retail price averages, or current aftermarket averages if they are out-of-production limited edition models.

Corgi Vintage 1956-1971

The first issue of the Batmobile, one of Corgi's most famous cars, issued in 1967.

By Dr. Douglas Sadecky

In 1956, Corgi started as a division of the Mettoy Company based in Northampton, England. Dating back to 1933, Mettoy had produced tin-litho dollhouses, train sets and clockwork mechanical toys. Their first foray into the die-cast market came with Castoys—mechanical vehicles in a larger scale—produced from 1948 to 1958.

Ever in competition with Dinky, Corgi tried to one-up their rival with a variety of gimmicks: spring suspensions, jeweled headlights, chrome plating, detailed engines and multiple mechanical features. The "Corgi Major Toys" were introduced against "Dinky Supertoys."

MARKET UPDATE

Character-related, Chipperfield's Circus, racing and military vehicles remain favorites with collectors—more so than the plain passenger cars, which, as generally British vehicle makes, don't find as ready an audience here in the United States.

Corgi made many versions of the Fordson Power Major Tractor, shown here with the 61-A four furrow plow.

One of Corgi's racing cars, the Vauxhall Formula 1 Grand Prix, 150-A.

In the 1960s, Corgi played it right by getting into licensing agreements with Hollywood and the entertainment industry. Their character toys, including the Batmobile, *The Saint's* Volvo and *The Man From U.N.C.L.E.* cars are highly sought collector's items today.

In 1965, Corgi introduced the Husky line of cars to compete against rivals (notably Matchbox) for the 1:64-scale market. By 1970, the line was changed to Corgi Juniors, and shortly thereafter fitted with "WhizzWheels," the company's answer Hot Wheels.

By 1983, Mettoy declared bankruptcy, and at one time the Corgi name was held by Mattel. In the interim, they continued to produce "collectible" lines of cars as well as die-cast toys. Interestingly, some of the Corgi Junior castings show up later as Hot Wheels vehicles. In 1999, the Hong Kong-based company Zindart purchased Corgi (and Lledo). Since then, their output has been once again become energetic, imaginative and fun.

New to Corgi?

If you're planning to dive into the Corgi market, be aware that mint-in-package examples will be pricey, but worth it. Corgi toys hold their value, and the arrival of re-issues hasn't affected the market for vintage models. Original boxes for gift sets are obviously important, as are the inclusion of accessories, including figures or buildings.

A great model of an American car, the Studebaker Golden Hawk. This vehicle has been replicated by many die-cast companies, old and new, and remains a favorite with collectors.

This Volkswagen 1200 East African Safari model with Rhinoceros is practically a playset. Great detail on everything with this toy—even the packaging.

Two of the Chipperfield's circus vehicles, the crane truck, 1121-A, and the Chipperfield's circus cage wagon, 1123-A.

AGRICULTURAL

(KP Photo by Dr. Douglas Sadecky)

❏ **1-B, Ford Tractor and Beast Carrier,** 1966-72, Gift Set included No. 67 Ford 5000 tractor and No. 58 Beast Carrier
EX $60   NM $90   MIP $150

❏ **2-A, Land Rover and Pony Trailer,** 1958-62, two versions: green No. 438 Land Rover and a red and black No. 102 Pony trailer (1958-62); tan/cream No. 438 Land Rover and a pony trailer (1963-68); value given is for each individual complete set
EX $50   NM $90   MIP $175

❏ **4-B, Country Farm Set,** 1974-75, No. 50 Massey Ferguson tractor, red No. 62 hay trailer w/load, fences, figures
EX $30   NM $45   MIP $75

❏ **5-B, Agricultural Set,** 1967-72, No. 69 Massey-Ferguson tractor, No. 62 trailer, No. 438 Land Rover, No. 484 Livestock Truck w/pigs, No. 71 harrow, No. 1490 skip and churns; w/accessories: four calves, farmhand, dog and six sacks
EX $120   NM $180   MIP $400

❏ **5-C, Country Farm Set,** 1976, same as 4-B but without hay load on trailer
EX $30   NM $45   MIP $75

❏ **7-A, Massey-Ferguson Tractor and Tipping Trailer,** 1959-63, No. 50 tractor and No. 51 trailer, no driver
EX $50   NM $75   MIP $125

❏ **8-A, Combine, Tractor and Trailer,** 1959-62, set of three: No. 1111 combine, No. 50 Massey-Ferguson tractor, and No. 51 trailer
EX $110   NM $185   MIP $350

❏ **9-B, Tractor with Shovel and Trailer,** 1968-73, standard colors, No. 69 Massey-Ferguson Tractor and No. 62 Tipping Trailer
EX $65   NM $100   MIP $165

❏ **13-A, Fordson Tractor and Plow,** 1964-66, No. 60 tractor and No. 61 four-furrow plow
EX $55   NM $85   MIP $140

❏ **15-B, Land Rover & Horse Box,** 1968-77, blue/white Land Rover w/horse trailer in two versions: cast wheels (1968-74) and Whizz Wheels (1975-77); accessories include a mare and a foal; value is for each individual complete set
EX $50   NM $75   MIP $125

❏ **18-A, Fordson Tractor and Plow,** 1961-64, No. 55 Fordson Tractor and No. 56 Four Furrow plow
EX $55   NM $85   MIP $140

❏ **22-A, Agricultural Set,** 1962-66, 1962-64 issue: No. 55 Fordson Tractor, No. 51 Tipping Trailer, No. 438 Land Rover, No. 101 Flat Trailer w/No. 1487 Milk Churns; 1965-66 issue: No. 60 Fordson Tractor, No. 62 Tipping Trailer, No. 438 Land Rover, red No. 100 Dropside Trailer w/No. 1487 Milk Churns
EX $380   NM $900   MIP $1800

❏ **29-A, Massey-Ferguson Tractor and Tipping Trailer,** 1965, No. 50 Massey-Ferguson tractor w/driver, No. 51 trailer
EX $50   NM $75   MIP $125

❏ **32-A, Massey-Ferguson Tractor with Shovel & Trailer,** 1965-66, No. 54 MF tractor w/driver and shovel, No. 62 trailer
EX $30   NM $75   MIP $150

❏ **33-A, Tractor and Beast Carrier,** 1965-66, No. 55 Fordson tractor, figures and No. 58 beast carrier
EX $65   NM $100   MIP $165

❏ **34-A, David Brown Tractor & Trailer,** 1976-79, two-piece set; No. 55 tractor and No. 56 trailer
EX $30   NM $45   MIP $75

❏ **42-A, Agricultural Set,** 1978-80, No. 55 Tractor, No. 56 Tipping Trailer, Silo and mustard yellow conveyor
EX $60   NM $90   MIP $130

❏ **43-A, Silo & Conveyor Belt,** 1978-80, w/yellow conveyor and Corgi Harvesting Co. label on silo
EX $35   NM $50   MIP $85

❏ **47-A, Ford Tractor and Conveyor,** 1966-69, No. 67 tractor, conveyor w/trailer, figures and accessories
EX $60   NM $90   MIP $175

❏ **47-B, Pony Club Set,** 1978-80, brown/white No. 421 Land Rover w/Corgi Pony Club labels, horse box, horse and rider
EX $30   NM $45   MIP $75

❏ **50-A, Massey-Ferguson 65 Tractor,** 1959-66, silver metal or plastic steering wheel, seat and grille, red engine hood, red metal or plastic wheels w/black rubber tires
EX $40   NM $60   MIP $100

❏ **50-B, Massey-Ferguson 50B Tractor,** 1973-77, yellow body, black int. & roof, red plastic wheels w/black plastic tires, windows
EX $15   NM $18   MIP $75

❏ **51-A, Massey-Ferguson Tipping Trailer,** 1959-65, two versions: red chassis w/either yellow or gray tipper and tailgate, red metal or plastic wheels, value is for each
EX $10   NM $18   MIP $35

❏ **53-A, Massey-Ferguson 65 Tractor And Shovel,** 1960-66, two versions: red bonnet w/either cream or gray chassis, red metal or orange plastic wheels; value is for each
EX $55   NM $85   MIP $140

(KP Photo by Dr. Douglas Sadecky)

❏ **54-A, Fordson Power Major Halftrack Tractor,** 1962-64, blue body/chassis, silver steering wheel, seat and grille, three versions: orange cast wheels, gray treads, lights in radiator or on sides of radiator. This bizarre little model can be quite difficult to find--especially with original tracks
EX $90   NM $135   MIP $225

❏ **54-B, Massey-Ferguson Tractor with Shovel,** 1974-81, two versions: either yellow and red or red and white body colors; value is for each
EX $20   NM $30   MIP $50

(KP Photo by Dr. Douglas Sadecky)

❑ **55-A, Fordson Power Major Tractor,** 1961-63, blue body/chassis w/Fordson Power Major decals, silver steering wheel, seat, exhaust, grille and lights. The 61-A Four Furrow Plough makes a nice companion piece to the model
EX $45 NM $65 MIP $110

❑ **55-B, David Brown Tractor,** 1977-82, white body w/black/white David Brown No. 1412 labels, red chassis and plastic engine
EX $15 NM $25 MIP $45

❑ **56-A, Four Furrow Plow,** 1961-63, red frame, yellow plastic parts
EX $15 NM $20 MIP $35

❑ **56-B, Tipping Farm Trailer,** 1977-80, cast chassis and tailgate, red plastic tipper and wheels, black tires, in two versions
EX $10 NM $15 MIP $25

(KP Photo by Dr. Douglas Sadecky)

❑ **57-A, Massey-Ferguson Tractor with Fork,** 1963-67, red cast body and shovel, arms, cream chassis, red plastic wheels, black rubber tires, Massey-Ferguson 65 decals, w/driver
EX $60 NM $90 MIP $150

❑ **58-A, Beast Carrier Trailer,** 1965-71, red chassis, yellow body and tailgate, four plastic calves, red plastic wheels, black rubber tires
EX $24 NM $36 MIP $60

❑ **60-A, Fordson Power Major Tractor,** 1964-66, blue body w/Fordson Power Major decals,

driver, blue chassis and steering wheel, silver seat, hitch, exhaust
EX $50 NM $75 MIP $125

❑ **61-A, Four Furrow Plow,** 1964-70, blue frame w/chrome plastic parts
EX $15 NM $20 MIP $35

❑ **62-A, Tipping Farm Trailer,** 1965-72, red working tipper and tailgates, yellow chassis, red plastic wheels, black tires, w/detachable raves
EX $10 NM $15 MIP $30

❑ **64-A, Jeep FC-150 Pickup with Conveyor Belt,** 1965-69, red body, yellow interior, orange grille, two black rubber belts, shaped wheels, black rubber tires; accessories include farmland figure and sacks
EX $45 NM $65 MIP $130

❑ **66-A, Massey-Ferguson 165 Tractor,** 1966-72, gray engine and chassis, red hood and fenders w/black/white Massey Ferguson 165 decals, white grille, red cast wheels; makes engine sound
EX $35 NM $55 MIP $90

❑ **67-A, Ford 5000 Super Major Tractor,** 1967-73, blue body/chassis w/Ford Super Major 5000 decals, gray cast fenders and rear wheels, gray plastic front wheels, black plastic tires, driver
EX $30 NM $45 MIP $75

(KP Photo by Dr. Douglas Sadecky)

❑ **69-A, Massey-Ferguson 165 Tractor with Shovel,** 1967-73, gray chassis, red hood, fenders and shovel arms, unpainted shovel and cylinder, red cast wheels, black plastic tires, w/figure. This tractor even featured engine noises!
EX $45 NM $65 MIP $120

❑ **71-A, Tandem Disc Harrow,** 1967-72, yellow main frame, red upper frame, working wheels linkage, unpainted linkage and cast discs, black plastic tires
EX $15 NM $20 MIP $45

❑ **72-A, Ford Tractor with Trencher,** 1970-74, blue body/chassis, gray fenders, cast yellow trencher arm and controls, chrome trencher, black control lines
EX $50 NM $75 MIP $125

❑ **73-A, Massey-Ferguson 165 Tractor with Saw,** 1969-73, red hood and fenders, gray engine and seat, cast yellow arm and control, chrome circular saw
EX $55 NM $85 MIP $140

❑ **74-A, Ford 5000 Tractor with Scoop,** 1969-72, blue body/chassis, gray fenders, yellow scoop arm and controls, chrome scoop, black control lines
EX $55 NM $80 MIP $130

(KP Photo by Dr. Douglas Sadecky)

❑ **102-A, Rice Pony Trailer,** 1958-65, cast body and chassis w/working tailgate, horse, in six variations, smooth or shaped hubs, cast or wire drawbar. Shown here is the harder-to-find two-tone cream/red variation
EX $20 NM $30 MIP $50

❑ **112-A, Rice Beaufort Double Horse Box,** 1969-72, long, blue body and working gates, white roof, brown plastic interior, two horses, cast wheels, plastic tires
EX $15 NM $30 MIP $50

❑ **484-A, Dodge Livestock Truck,** 1967-72, tan cab and hood, green body, working tailgate and ramp, five pigs
EX $34 NM $51 MIP $85

❑ **1104-B, Bedford Articulated Horse Box,** 1973-76, cast cab, lower body and three working ramps, yellow interior, plastic upper body, w/horse and Newmarket Racing Stables labels, dark metallic green or light green body w/orange or yellow upper, four horses
EX $32 NM $48 MIP $90

CORGI / VINTAGE

❑ **1105-B, Berliet Articulated Horse Box,** 1976-80, bronze cab and lower semi body, cream chassis, white upper body, black interior, three working ramps, National Racing Stables decals, horse figures, chrome wheels
EX $30   NM $45   MIP $75

❑ **1111-A, Massey-Ferguson Combine,** 1959-63, red body w/yellow metal blades, metal tines, black/white decals, yellow metal wheels
EX $70   NM $105   MIP $175

❑ **1111-B, Massey-Ferguson Combine,** 1968-73, red body, plastic yellow blades, red wheels
EX $60   NM $100   MIP $160

❑ **1112-B, David Brown Combine,** 1978-79, No. 55 Tractor, red and yellow combines, white JF labels
EX $30   NM $45   MIP $75

AIRCRAFT

❑ **12-C, Glider Set,** 1981-83, two versions: white No. 345 Honda, 1981-82; yellow Honda, 1983, value is for individual complete sets
EX $30   NM $45   MIP $75

❑ **19-B, Corgi Flying Club Set,** 1972-77, blue/orange No. 438 Land Rover w/red dome light, blue trailer w/either orange/yellow or orange/white plastic airplane
EX $24   NM $50   MIP $100

❑ **49-A, Flying Club Set,** 1978-80, green and white No. 419 Jeep w/Corgi Flying Club labels, green trailer, blue/white airplane
EX $36   NM $55   MIP $90

❑ **648-A, NASA Space Shuttle,** 1980, white body, two opening hatches, black plastic interior, jets and base, unpainted retracting gear castings, black plastic wheels, w/satalite
EX $30   NM $45   MIP $75

❑ **650-A, Concorde-First Issues,** 1969-72, BOAC decals
EX $20   NM $40   MIP $70

❑ **650-B, Concorde-Second Issues,** 1976-82, BOAC model on display stand
EX $15   NM $20   MIP $35

❑ **651-A, Concorde-First Issues,** 1969-72, Air France decals
EX $20   NM $45   MIP $85

❑ **651-B, Concorde-Second Issue,** 1976-82, Air France model on display stand
EX $15   NM $20   MIP $35

❑ **652-A, Concorde-First Issues,** 1969-72, Air Canada decals
EX $80   NM $120   MIP $200

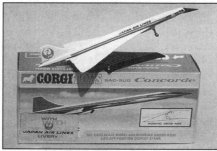
(KP Photo by Dr. Douglas Sadecky)

❑ **653-A, Concorde-First Issues,** 1969-72, Japan Airlines decals. This rare model was probably an import issue. Ironically, the real Concorde was never part of the Japan Air Lines
EX $280   NM $420   MIP $700

❑ **806-A, Lunar Bug,** 1970-72, white body w/red roof, blue interior and wings, clear and amber windows, red working ramp, Lunar Bug labels
EX $25   NM $40   MIP $95

❑ **926-A, Stromberg Jet Ranger Helicopter,** 1978-79, black body w/yellow trim and interior, clear windows, black plastic rotors, white/blue labels
EX $45   NM $65   MIP $125

AUTOMOBILE

❑ **10-A, Rambler Marlin with Kayak and Trailer,** 1968-69, blue No. 263 Marlin w/roof rack, blue/white trailer, w/two kayaks
EX $100   NM $150   MIP $250

❑ **13-B, Tour de France Set,** 1968-72, white and black body, Renault w/Paramount Film roof sign, rear platform w/cameraman and black camera on tripod, plus bicycle and rider
EX $60   NM $90   MIP $200

❑ **13-C, Tour de France Set,** 1981-82, w/white No. 373 Peugeot, red and yellow Raleigh and Total logos, Racing cycles, includes manager figures
EX $25   NM $45   MIP $90

❑ **20-A, Golden Guinea Set,** 1961-63, three vehicle set, gold plated No. 224 Bentley Continental, No. 229 Chevy Corvair and No. 234 Ford Consul
EX $90   NM $150   MIP $325

❑ **31-A, Buick and Cabin Cruiser,** 1965-68, two versions: light blue or dark metallic blue, No. 245 Buick, red boat trailer, dolphin cabin cruiser w/two figures
EX $80   NM $120   MIP $280

(KP Photo by Dr. Douglas Sadecky)

❑ **200-A, Ford Consul,** 1956-61, one-piece body in several colors, clear windows, silver grille, lights and bumpers, smooth wheels, rubber tires
EX $45   NM $65   MIP $120

❑ **200-M, Ford Consul-Mechanical,** 1956-59, same as model 200-A but w/friction motor and blue or green body
EX $55   NM $85   MIP $160

(KP Photo by Dr. Douglas Sadecky)

❑ **201-A, Austin Cambridge,** 1956-61, available in gray, green/gray, silver/green, aqua, green/cream, two-tone green, smooth wheels, shown here with Austin Cambridge-Mechanical
EX $40   NM $60   MIP $120

❑ **201M, Austin Cambridge-Mechanical,** 1956-59, fly-wheel motor, available in orange, cream, light or dark gray, or silver over metallic blue, smooth wheels
EX $50   NM $75   MIP $150

(KP Photo by Dr. Douglas Sadecky)

❑ **202-A, Morris Cowley,** 1959-60, long, one-piece body in several colors, clear windows, silver lights, grille and bumper, smooth wheels, rubber tires. The model on the left is the rare blue version, and the car on the right is the 202-M mechanical flywheel version
EX $45   **NM** $75   **MIP** $140

❑ **202-B, Renault 16TS,** 1970-72, metallic blue body w/Renault decal on working hatch, clear windows, detailed engine, yellow interior
EX $20   **NM** $25   **MIP** $50

❑ **202-M, Morris Cowley-Mechanical,** 1956-59, same as 202-A but w/friction motor, available in off-white or green body
EX $55   **NM** $95   **MIP** $170

(KP Photo by Dr. Douglas Sadecky)

❑ **203-A, Vauxhall Velox,** 1956-60, one-piece body in red, cream, yellow or yellow and red body, clear windows, silver lights, grille and bumpers, smooth wheels, rubber tires
EX $50   **NM** $75   **MIP** $150

❑ **203-M, Vauxhall Velox-Mechanical,** 1956-59, w/friction motor; orange, red, yellow or cream body
EX $60   **NM** $90   **MIP** $170

(KP Photo by Dr. Douglas Sadecky)

❑ **204-A, Rover 90,** 1956-60, one-piece body, silver headlights, grille and bumpers, smooth wheels, rubber tires; multiple colors available. The car on the left is the rare two-tone color scheme and the vehicle on the right is the mechanical version in metallic green
EX $50   **NM** $75   **MIP** $145

❑ **204-M, Rover 90-Mechanical,** 1956-59, w/friction motor and red, green, gray or metallic green body
EX $60   **NM** $90   **MIP** $170

❑ **205-A, Riley Pathfinder,** 1956-61, red or dark blue one-piece body, clear windows, silver lights, grille and bumpers, smooth wheels, rubber tires
EX $45   **NM** $65   **MIP** $125

❑ **205-M, Riley Pathfinder-Mechanical,** 1956-59, w/friction motor and either red or blue body
EX $60   **NM** $95   **MIP** $170

(KP Photo by Dr. Douglas Sadecky)

❑ **206-A, Hillman Husky,** 1956-60, one-piece tan or metallic blue/silver body, clear windows, silver lights, grille and bumpers, smooth wheels. The car on the left is the more rare two-tone version, while the car on the right is the mechanical flywheel version that was only produced for one year in 1959
EX $40   **NM** $70   **MIP** $125

❑ **206-M, Hillman Husky-Mechanical,** 1956-59, same as 206-A but w/friction motor, black base and dark blue, gray or cream body
EX $50   **NM** $100   **MIP** $150

(KP Photo by Dr. Douglas Sadecky)

❑ **207-A, Standard Vanguard,** 1957-61, one-piece red and pale green body, clear windows, silver lights, grille and bumpers, smooth wheels, rubber tires. Pictured with the 207M, the attractive two-tone 207-A version is on the left, and the mechanical version is on the right
EX $50   **NM** $75   **MIP** $125

❑ **207-M, Standard Vanguard-Mechanical,** 1957-59, w/friction motor and yellow or off-white body w/black or gray base, or cream body w/red roof
EX $55   **NM** $90   **MIP** $170

❑ **208-A, Jaguar 2.4 Litre,** 1957-63, one-piece white body w/no interior 1957-59, or yellow body w/red interior 1960-63, clear windows, smooth hubs
EX $50   **NM** $80   **MIP** $130

(KP Photo by Dr. Douglas Sadecky)

❑ **208-M, Jaguar 2.4 Litre-Mechanical,** 1957-59, same as 208-A but w/friction motor and metallic blue body
EX $60   **NM** $90   **MIP** $180

❑ **210-A, Citroen DS19,** 1957-65, one-piece body in several colors, clear windows, silver lights, grille and bumpers, smooth wheels, rubber tires; colors: red, metallic green w/black roof, yellow w/red roof
EX $56   **NM** $84   **MIP** $140

❑ **211-A, Studebaker Golden Hawk,** 1958-60, one-piece body in blue and gold or white and gold, clear windows, silver lights, grille and bumpers, smooth wheels, rubber tires
EX $55   **NM** $85   **MIP** $140

❑ **211-M, Studebaker Golden Hawk-Mechanical,** 1958-59, w/friction motor and white body w/gold trim
EX $70   **NM** $105   **MIP** $175

CORGI / VINTAGE

❑ **211S1, Studebaker Golden Hawk,** 1960-65, first issue: gold plated body, white flashing, shaped hubs
EX $55   NM $85   MIP $140

(KP Photo by Dr. Douglas Sadecky)

❑ **211S2, Studebaker Golden Hawk,** 1960-65, second issue: gold painted body, shaped hubs. The "S" after the catalog number stood for "suspension" which was a new Corgi innovation at the time of the model's release
EX $60   NM $180   MIP $180

(KP Photo by Dr. Douglas Sadecky)

❑ **216-A, Austin A40,** 1959-62, one-piece light blue body with dark blue roof or red body w/black roof and clear windows, smooth wheels, rubber tires
EX $35   NM $50   MIP $100

❑ **216-M, Austin A40-Mechanical,** 1959-60, friction motor, red body w/black roof
EX $55   NM $75   MIP $170

(KP Photo by Dr. Douglas Sadecky)

❑ **217-A, Fiat 1800,** 1960-63, one-piece body in several colors, clear windows, plastic interior, silver lights, grille and bumpers, red taillights, smooth wheels, rubber tires, colors: blue body w/light or bright yellow interior, light tan, mustard, light blue or two-tone blue body
EX $24   NM $40   MIP $80

❑ **218-A, Aston Martin DB4,** 1960-65, red or yellow body w/working hood, detailed engine, clear windows, plastic interior, silver lights, grille, license plate and bumpers, red taillights, rubber tires, smooth or cast spoked wheels; working scoop on early models
EX $45   NM $65   MIP $110

❑ **219-A, Plymouth Sports Suburban,** 1959-63, dark cream body, tan roof, red interior, die-cast base, red axle, silver bumpers, trim and grille and rubber tires
EX $40   NM $60   MIP $100

(KP Photo by Dr. Douglas Sadecky)

❑ **220-A, Chevrolet Impala,** 1960-62, pink body, yellow plastic interior, clear windows, silver headlights, bumpers, grille and trim, suspension, die-cast base w/rubber tires; a second version has a blue body w/red or yellow interior and smooth or shaped hubs
EX $50   NM $75   MIP $125

❑ **222-A, Renault Floride,** 1959-65, one-piece dark red, maroon or lime green body, clear windows, silver bumper, grille, lights and plates, red taillights, smooth or shaped hubs, rubber tires
EX $35   NM $55   MIP $95

❑ **224-A, Bentley Continental,** 1961-66, two-tone green or black and silver bodies, w/red interior, clear windows, chrome grille and bumpers, jewel headlights, red jeweled taillights, suspension, shaped wheels, gray rubber tires
EX $45   NM $65   MIP $110

❑ **225-A1, Austin Seven Mini,** 1961-67, red or yellow body, yellow interior, silver bumpers, grille and headlights, orange taillights
EX $50   NM $75   MIP $125

❑ **225-A2, second issue, Austin Seven Mini,** 1961-67, primrose yellow, red interior, rare
EX $100   NM $200   MIP $325

❑ **228-A, Volvo P-1800,** 1962-65, one-piece body light brown, dark red, pink or dark red body, clear windows, plastic interior, shaped wheels, rubber tires
EX $40   NM $60   MIP $100

(KP Photo by Dr. Douglas Sadecky)

❑ **229-A, Chevrolet Corvair,** 1961-66, either blue or pale-blue body w/yellow interior and working rear hood, detailed engine, clear windows, silver bumpers, headlights and trim, red taillights, rear window blind, shaped wheels, rubber tires
EX $36   NM $55   MIP $90

(KP Photo by Dr. Douglas Sadecky)

❑ **230-A, Mercedes-Benz 220SE Coupe,** 1962-64, cream, black or dark red body, red plastic interior, clear windows, working trunk, silver bumpers, grille and plate, spare wheel in boot
EX $40   NM $60   MIP $100

❑ **231-A, Triumph Herald Coupe,** 1961-66, blue or gold top and lower body, white upper body, red interior, clear windows, silver bumpers, grille, headlights, shaped hubs
EX $35   NM $65   MIP $110

❏ **232-A, Fiat 2100,** 1961-64, light two-tone mauve body, yellow interior, purple roof, clear windows w/rear blind, silver grille, license plates and bumpers, red taillights, shaped wheels, rubber tires
EX $22   **NM** $33   **MIP** $75

❏ **233-A, Trojan Heinkel,** 1962-72, issued in mauve, red, orange or lilac body, plastic interior, silver bumpers and headlights, red taillights, suspension, smooth, spun, or detailed cast wheels
EX $35   **NM** $55   **MIP** $95

❏ **234-A, Ford Consul Classic,** 1961-65, cream or gold body and base, yellow interior, pink roof, clear windows, gray steering wheel, silver bumpers, grille, opening hood
EX $35   **NM** $55   **MIP** $90

❏ **235-A, Oldsmobile Super 88,** 1962-68, three versions: light blue, light or dark metallic blue body w/white stripes, red interior, single body casting
EX $40   **NM** $60   **MIP** $100

(KP Photo by Dr. Douglas Sadecky)

❏ **236-A, Austin A60 Motor School,** 1964-69, light blue body w/silver trim, red interior, single body casting, right-hand drive steering wheel, two figures, steering control on roof; came w/Highway Patrol leaflet
EX $45   **NM** $65   **MIP** $120

(KP Photo by Dr. Douglas Sadecky)

❏ **238-A, Jaguar Mark X Saloon,** 1962-67, several different color versions w/working front and rear hood castings, clear windshields, plastic interior, gray steering wheel. Shown here in silver and blue versions, pictured at the left are the two suitcases that were included with each car
EX $35   **NM** $55   **MIP** $110

❏ **239-A, Volkswagen 1500 Karmann-Ghia,** 1963-68, cream, red or gold body, plastic interior and taillights, front and rear working hoods, clear windshields, silver bumpers; includes spare wheel and plastic suitcase in trunk
EX $35   **NM** $55   **MIP** $90

❏ **240-A, Ghia-Fiat 600 Jolly,** 1963-65, light or dark blue body, red and silver canopy, red seats, two figures, windshield, chrome dash, floor, steering wheels
EX $45   **NM** $85   **MIP** $160

(KP Photo by Dr. Douglas Sadecky)

❏ **241-A, Ghia L64 Chrysler V8,** 1963-69, metallic light blue, green, copper or yellow, plastic interior, hood, trunk and two doors working, detailed engine, clear windshield, shaped or detailed cast wheels
EX $25   **NM** $40   **MIP** $75

❏ **245-A, Buick Riviera,** 1964-68, metallic gold, dark blue, pale blue or gold body, red interior, gray steering wheel, and tow hook, clear windshield, chrome grille and bumpers, suspension, Tan-o-lite headlights, spoked wheels and rubber tires
EX $30   **NM** $45   **MIP** $75

❏ **246-A1, Chrysler Imperial Convertible,** 1965-66, red body w/gray base, working hood, trunk and doors, golf bag in trunk, detailed engine, clear windshield, aqua interior, driver, chrome bumpers
EX $45   **NM** $65   **MIP** $110

❏ **246-A2, Chrysler Imperial Convertible,** 1967-68, metallic blue body w/gray base, working hood, trunk and doors, golf bag in trunk, detailed engine, clear windshield, aqua interior, driver, chrome bumpers
EX $50   **NM** $90   **MIP** $160

❏ **247-A, Mercedes-Benz 600 Pullman,** 1964-69, metallic maroon body, cream interior and steering wheel, clear windshields, chrome grille, trim and bumpers, working windshield operators; includes instruction sheet
EX $40   **NM** $60   **MIP** $100

❏ **248-A, Chevrolet Impala,** 1965-67, tan body, cream interior, gray steering wheel, clear windshields, chrome bumpers, grille, headlights, suspension, red taillights, shaped wheels and rubber tires
EX $50   **NM** $75   **MIP** $125

❏ **251-A, Hillman Imp,** 1963-67, metallic copper, blue, dark blue or gold one-piece bodies, w/white/yellow interior, silver bumpers, headlights
EX $30   **NM** $45   **MIP** $85

❏ **252-A, Rover 2000,** 1963-66, metallic blue w/red interior or maroon body w/yellow interior, gray steering wheel, clear windshields
EX $30   **NM** $45   **MIP** $75

(KP Photo by Dr. Douglas Sadecky)

❏ **253-A, Mercedes-Benz 220SE Coupe,** 1967-68, metallic maroon or blue body, cream plastic interior, medium gray base, clear windows, silver bumpers, headlights, grille and license; accessories include plastic luggage and spare wheel in boot. Except for different exterior colors and the inclusion of luggage, this was exactly the same car as the 230-A
EX $40   **NM** $60   **MIP** $100

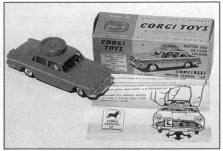

(KP Photo by Dr. Douglas Sadecky)

❏ **255-A, Austin A60 Driving School,** 1964-68, medium blue body w/silver trim, left-hand drive steering wheel, steering control on roof; came w/five language leaflet (US version of No. 236)
EX $45   NM $65   MIP $160

❏ **259-A1, Citroen Le Dandy Coupe,** 1966, metallic maroon body and base, yellow interior, working trunk and two doors, clear windows, plastic interior, folding seats, chrome grille and bumpers, jewel headlights, red taillights, suspension, spoked wheels, rubber tires
EX $50   NM $75   MIP $125

(KP Photo by Dr. Douglas Sadecky)

❏ **259-A2, Citroen Le Dandy Coupe,** 1967-69, metallic dark blue hood, sides and base, plastic aqua interior, white roof and trunk lid, clear windows, folding seats, chrome grille and bumpers, jewel headlights, red taillights, suspension, spoked wheels, rubber tires
EX $70   NM $105   MIP $175

❏ **260-A, Renault 16,** 1969, metallic maroon body, dark yellow interior, chrome base, grille and bumpers, clear windows, opening bonnet and hatch cover, Renault decal
EX $25   NM $35   MIP $60

❏ **262-A, Lincoln Continental,** 1967-69, metallic gold or light blue body, black roof, maroon plastic interior, working hood, trunk and

doors, clear windows; accessories include TV w/picture strips for TV
EX $60   NM $90   MIP $150

❏ **264-A, Oldsmobile Toronado,** 1967-68, metallic medium or dark blue body, cream interior, one-piece body, clear windshield, chrome bumpers, grille, headlight covers, shaped or cast spoked wheels
EX $35   NM $55   MIP $90

❏ **263-A, Rambler Marlin Fastback,** 1966-69, red body, black roof and trim, cream interior, clear windshield, folding seats, chrome bumpers, grille and headlights, opening doors
EX $35   NM $55   MIP $90

❏ **273-A, Rolls-Royce Silver Shadow,** 1970, metallic white upper/dusty blue lower body, working hood, trunk and two doors, clear windows, folding seats, chrome bumpers, Golden Jacks wheels
EX $30   NM $50   MIP $95

❏ **273-B, Honda Ballade Driving School,** 1982-83, red body/base, tan interior, clear windows, tow hook, mirrors, bumpers
EX $10   NM $15   MIP $25

❏ **274-A, Bentley T Series,** 1970-72, red body, cream interior, working hood, trunk and doors, clear windows, folding seats, chrome bumper/grille, jewel headlights, Whizz Wheels
EX $36   NM $55   MIP $90

❏ **275-A, Rover 2000TC,** 1968-70, metallic olive green or maroon one-piece body, light brown interior, chrome bumpers/grille, jewel headlights, red taillights, Golden Jacks wheels
EX $30   NM $45   MIP $75

❏ **275-B, Austin Mini-Metro,** 1981, blue or red body w/plastic interior, working rear hatch and doors, clear windows, folding seats, chrome headlights, orange taillights, black plastic base, grille, bumpers, Whizz Wheels
EX $18   NM $27   MIP $45

❏ **276-A, Oldsmobile Toronado,** 1968-70, metallic copper, metallic blue or red one-piece body, cream interior, Golden jacks, gray tow hook, clear windows, bumpers, grille, headlights
EX $35   NM $55   MIP $90

❏ **276-B, Triumph Acclaim HLS,** 1981-83, metallic peacock blue body/base, black trim, light brown interior, clear windows, mirrors, bumpers, vents, tow hook
EX $15   NM $18   MIP $30

❏ **277-B, Triumph Acclaim Driving School,** 1982, dark yellow body w/black trim, black roof mounted steering wheel steers front wheels, clear windows, mirrors, bumpers
EX $15   NM $25   MIP $40

❏ **278-B, Triumph Acclaim Driving School,** 1982-83, yellow or red body/base, Corgi Motor School labels, black roof mounted steering wheel steers front wheels, clear windows
EX $15   NM $25   MIP $50

❏ **279-A, Rolls-Royce Corniche,** 1979, different color versions w/light brown interior, working hood, trunk and two doors, clear windows, folding seats, chrome bumpers
EX $10   NM $20   MIP $40

❏ **280-A1, Rolls-Royce Silver Shadow,** 1971-73, metallic silver upper and metallic blue lower body, light brown interior, may or may not include hole in trunk for spare tire, Whizz Wheels
EX $25   NM $40   MIP $65

❏ **280-A2, Rolls-Royce Silver Shadow,** 1974-78, metallic blue or gold body, bright blue interior, working hood, trunk and two doors, clear windows, folding seats, spare wheel
EX $25   NM $40   MIP $65

❏ **281-A, Rover 2000TC,** 1971-73, metallic purple body, light orange interior, black grille, one-piece body, amber windows, chrome bumpers and headlights, Whizz Wheels
EX $25   NM $35   MIP $60

❏ **283-A, OSI DAF City Car,** 1971-74, orange/red body, light cream interior, textured black roof, sliding left door, working hood, hatch and two right doors, Whizz Wheels
EX $18   NM $25   MIP $45

❏ **284-A, Citroen SM,** 1971-75, metallic lime gold w/chrome wheels or mauve body w/spoked wheels, pale blue interior and lift-

ing hatch cover, working rear hatch and two doors, chrome inner drs., window frames, bumpers, grille, amber headlights, red taillights, Whizz Wheels
EX $16   NM $24   MIP $40

❑ **285-A, Mercedes-Benz 240D,** 1975-81, silver, blue or copper/beige body, working trunk, two doors, clear windows, plastic interior, two hook, chrome bumpers, grille and headlights, Whizz Wheels
EX $10   NM $15   MIP $25

❑ **287-A, Citroen Dyane,** 1974-78, metallic yellow or green body, black roof and interior, working rear hatch, clear windows, black base and tow bar, silver bumpers, grille and headlights, red taillights, marching duck and French flag decals, suspension, chrome wheels
EX $15   NM $18   MIP $30

❑ **289-A, Volkswagen Polo,** 1976-79, apple green or bright yellow body, black DBP and posthorn (German Post Office) labels, off white interior, black dash
EX $25   NM $40   MIP $65

❑ **289-B, Volkswagen Polo Mail Car,** 1976-80, bright yellow body, black DBP and Posthorn labels, German issue
EX $25   NM $35   MIP $60

❑ **291-A, AMC Pacer,** 1977-78, metallic red body, white Pacer X decals, working hatch, clear windows, light yellow interior, chrome bumpers and wheels
EX $15   NM $20   MIP $50

❑ **293-A, Renault 5TS,** 1980-81, light blue body, red plastic interior, dark blue roof, dome light, S.O.S. Medicine lettering, working hatch and two doors, French issue
EX $20   NM $35   MIP $70

❑ **294-A, Renault Alpine 5TS,** 1980, dark blue body, off white interior, red and chrome trim, clear windows and headlights, gray base and bumpers, black grille, opening doors and hatchback
EX $15   NM $25   MIP $40

❑ **302-C, Volkswagen Polo,** 1979-81, metallic light brown body, off-white interior, black dash, clear windows, silver bumpers, grille and headlights
EX $15   NM $18   MIP $30

❑ **325-B, Chevrolet Caprice Classic,** 1981-82, working doors and trunk, whitewall tires, two versions: light metallic green body w/green interior or silver on blue body w/brown interior
EX $24   NM $36   MIP $60

❑ **332-B, Opel Senator Doctor's Car,** 1980-81,
EX $10   NM $15   MIP $25

❑ **334-B, Ford Escort 13 GL,** 1980, red, blue or yellow body, opening doors
EX $8   NM $15   MIP $25

❑ **338-B, Rover 3500,** 1979, three different body and interior versions, plastic interior, opening hood, hatch and two doors, lifting hatch cover
EX $8   NM $15   MIP $25

❑ **345-B, Honda Prelude,** 1981-82, dark metallic blue body, tan interior, clear windows, folding seats, sunroof, chrome wheels
EX $8   NM $15   MIP $20

❑ **346-A, Citroen 2CV Charleston,** 1981, yellow/black or maroon/black body versions w/opening hood
EX $15   NM $18   MIP $30

❑ **400-A, Volkswagen 1200 Driving School,** 1974-75, metallic red or blue body, yellow interior, gold roof mounted steering wheel that steers, silver headlights, red taillights
EX $25   NM $35   MIP $60

❑ **401-A, Volkswagen Driving School,** 1975-77, metallic blue body, yellow interior, gold roof mounted steering wheel that steers, silver headlights, red taillights
EX $25   NM $40   MIP $70

❑ **424-A, Ford Zephyr Estate Car,** 1960-65, light blue one-piece body, dark blue hood and stripes, red interior, silver bumpers, grille and headlights, red taillights
EX $30   NM $45   MIP $75

❑ **436-A, Citroen ID-19 Safari,** 1963-65, orange body w/red/brown or red/green luggage on roof rack, green/brown interior, working hatch, two passengers, Wildlife Preservation decals
EX $40   NM $70   MIP $120

❑ **440-A, Ford Cortina Estate Car,** 1966-68, 3-1/2" metallic dark blue body and base, brown and cream simulated wood panels, cream interior, chrome bumpers and grille, jewel headlights
EX $35   NM $55   MIP $90

❑ **443-A, Plymouth Suburban Mail Car,** 1963-66, white upper, blue lower body w/red stripes, gray die-cast base without rear axle bulge, silver bumpers and grille, U.S. Mail decals
EX $55   NM $85   MIP $140

(KP Photo by Dr. Douglas Sadecky)

❑ **445-A, Plymouth Sports Suburban,** 1963-65, pale blue body w/silver trim, red roof, yellow interior, gray die-cast base without rear axle bulge, shaped wheels
EX $40   NM $60   MIP $100

❑ **475-A, Citroen Winter Sports Safari,** 1964-67, white body in three versions: two w/Corgi Ski Club decals and either w/or without roof ski rack, or one w/1964 Winter Olympics decals
EX $56   NM $84   MIP $140

❑ **485-A, Austin Mini Countryman,** 1965-69, turquoise body, jeweled headlights, opening rear doors, chrome roofrack w/two surfboards, shaped or cast wheels, w/surfer figure
EX $55   NM $80   MIP $150

(KP Photo by Dr. Douglas Sadecky)

❑ **486-A, Chevrolet Kennel Club Van,** 1967-69, white upper, red lower body, working tailgate

and rear windows, green interior, four dog figures, kennel club decals; shaped spun or detailed cast wheels, rubber tires
EX $56   NM $90   MIP $160

❑ **489-A2, Volkswagen Polo German Auto Club Car,** 1977-79, yellow body, off-white interior, black dash, silver bumpers, grille and headlights, white roof, yellow dome light
EX $25   NM $35   MIP $60

❑ **489-B, Volkswagen Polo Auto Club Car,** 1977-79, yellow body, white roof, yellow dome light, ADAC Strassenwacht labels
EX $15   NM $25   MIP $40

❑ **491-A, Ford Cortina Estate Car,** 1966-69, red body and base or metallic charcoal gray body and base, cream interior, chrome bumpers and grille, jewel headlights
EX $35   NM $55   MIP $90

❑ **499-A, Citroen Winter Olympics Car,** 1967-69, white body, blue roof and hatch, blue interior, red roof rack w/yellow skis, gold sled w/rider, skier, gold Grenoble Olympiade decals on car roof
EX $70   NM $105   MIP $200

❑ **510-A, Citroen Tour de France Car,** 1970-72, red body, yellow interior and rear bed, clear windshield and headlights, driver, black plastic rack w/four bicycle wheels, swiveling team manager figure w/megaphone in back of car, Paramount and Tour de France decals, Whizz Wheels
EX $40   NM $70   MIP $120

❑ **1003-A, Ford Torino Road Hog,** 1981, orange-red body, yellow and gray chassis, gold lamps, chrome radiator shell, windows and bumpers, one-piece body, working horn
EX $15   NM $20   MIP $35

BOAT

❑ **36-A, Olds Toronado and Speedboat,** 1967-70, blue No. 276 Toronado, blue and yellow boat and chrome trailer, w/swordfish decals and three figures
EX $60   NM $90   MIP $165

❑ **37-B, Fiat X 1/9 & Powerboat,** 1979-82, green and white automobile, w/white and gold boat, Carlsberg labels
EX $30   NM $45   MIP $75

❑ **38-C, Powerboat Team,** 1980-81, white/red No. 319 Jaguar w/red/white boat on silver trailer, Team Corgi Carlsberg, Union Jack and #1 labels on boat
EX $25   NM $35   MIP $60

(KP Photo by Dr. Douglas Sadecky)

❑ **104-A, Dolphin Cabin Cruiser,** 1965-68, white hull, blue deck plastic boat w/red/white stripe labels, driver, blue motor w/white cover, gray prop, cast trailer w/smooth wheels, rubber tires
EX $24   NM $40   MIP $80

❑ **1119-A, HDL Hovercraft SR-N1,** 1960-62, blue superstructure, gray base and deck, clear canopy, red seats, yellow SR-N1 decals
EX $60   NM $90   MIP $150

BUS

❑ **11-B, London Set,** 1971-75, orange No. 226 Mini, Policeman, No. 418 London Taxi and No. 468 Outspan Routemaster bus, Whizz Wheels
EX $50   NM $75   MIP $125

❑ **11-C, London Set,** 1980-82, No. 425 London Taxi and No. 469 Routemaster B.T.A. bus in two versions: w/mounted Policeman (1980-81); without Policeman, (1982-on); value is for each individual complete set
EX $25   NM $35   MIP $60

(KP Photo by Dr. Douglas Sadecky)

❑ **35-A, London Set,** 1964-68, No. 418 taxi and No. 468 bus

w/policeman, in two versions: "Corgi Toys" on bus (1964-66); "Outspan Oranges" on bus (1967-68); values for each individual complete set
EX $55   NM $95   MIP $170

❑ **467-A, Routemaster Bus-Promotionals,** 1977, different body and interior versions and promotional labels
EX $15   NM $25   MIP $40

❑ **468-A, London Transport Routemaster Bus,** 1964-75, clear windows w/driver and conductor, released w/numerous advertiser logos, shaped or cast spoked wheels
EX $35   NM $40   MIP $70

❑ **469-A, London Transport Routemaster Bus,** 1975, long, clear windows, interior, some models have driver and conductor, released w/numerous advertiser logos, Whizz Wheels
EX $25   NM $30   MIP $50

❑ **470-B, Open Top Disneyland Bus,** 1977-78, yellow body, red interior and stripe, Disneyland labels, eight-spoked wheels or orange body, white interior and stripe
EX $30   NM $50   MIP $95

❑ **470-C, Green Line Bus,** 1983, green body, white interior and stripe, TDK labels, six spoked wheels
EX $10   NM $15   MIP $25

❑ **471-B, Silver Jubilee London Transport Bus,** 1977, silver body w/red interior, no passengers, labels read "Woolworth Welcomes the World" and "The Queen's Silver
EX $15   NM $18   MIP $30

❑ **701-A, Inter-City Mini Bus,** 1973-79, orange body w/brown interior, clear windows, green/yellow/black decals, Whizz Wheels
EX $8   NM $15   MIP $25

❑ **1004-A, Beep Beep London Bus,** 1981, battery-operated working horn, red body, black windows, BTA decals
EX $26   NM $39   MIP $65

(KP Photo by Dr. Douglas Sadecky)

❏ **1120-A, Midland Red Express Coach,** 1961-62, red one-piece body, black roof w/shaped or smooth wheels, yellow interior, clear windows, silver grille and headlights. Two box variations shown in this photo
EX $70   NM $105   MIP $225

❏ **1168-A, National Express Bus,** 1983, variety of colors and label variations
EX $8   NM $15   MIP $25

CHARACTER

❏ **3-B1, Batmobile, Batboat and Trailer,** 1967-72, first and second versions: red bat hubs on wheels, 1967-72; red tires and chrome wheels, 1972-73
EX $240   NM $360   MIP $650

❏ **3-B2, Batmobile, Batboat and Trailer,** 1973-81, third and fourth versions: 1973; black tires, labels on boat, 1974-76; chrome wheels, boat labels, Whizz Wheels on trailer
EX $120   NM $175   MIP $350

❏ **7-B, Daktari Set,** 1967-75, two versions: No. 438 Land Rover, green w/black stripes, spun or cast spoked wheels, 1968-73; Whizz Wheels, 1974-75, each set
EX $50   NM $75   MIP $150

❏ **8-B, Lions of Longleat,** 1968-74, black/white No. 438 Land Rover pickup w/lion cages and accessories, two versions: cast wheels, 1969-73; Whizz Wheels, 1974, each
EX $60   NM $90   MIP $200

❏ **14-B, Giant Daktari Set,** 1969-73, black and green No. 438 Land Rover, tan No. 503 Giraffe truck, blue and brown No. 484 Dodge Livestock truck, figures
EX $225   NM $350   MIP $650

❏ **21-C, Superman Set,** 1979-81, set of three: No. 265 Supermobile, No. 925 Daily Planet Helicopter and No. 260 Metropolis Police Car
EX $70   NM $120   MIP $225

❏ **22-B, James Bond Set,** 1979-81, set of three: No. 271 Lotus Esprit, No. 649 Space Shuttle and No. 269 Aston Martin
EX $100   NM $200   MIP $400

❏ **23-B, Spider-Man Set,** 1980-81, set of three: No. 266 Spider-Bike, No. 928 Spider-Copter and No. 261 Spider-Buggy
EX $80   NM $160   MIP $350

❏ **36-B, Tarzan Set,** 1976-78, metallic green No. 421 Land Rover w/trailer and Dinghy; cage, five figures and other accessories
EX $100   NM $150   MIP $285

❏ **40-A, Avengers Set,** 1966-69, white Lotus, red or green Bentley; Jonathan Steed and Emma Peel figures w/three umbrellas
EX $260   NM $390   MIP $800

❏ **40-B, Batman Set,** 1976-81, three vehicle set: No. 267 Batmobile, No. 107 Batboat w/trailer and No. 925 Batcopter, Whizz Wheels on trailer
EX $150   NM $300   MIP $800

❏ **41-B, Silver Jubilee Landau,** 1977-80, Landua w/four horses, two footmen, two riders, Queen and Prince figures, and Corgi dog, in two versions
EX $15   NM $25   MIP $50

❏ **107-A1, Batboat,** 1967-72, black plastic boat, red seats, fin and jet, blue windshield, Batman and Robin figures, gold cast trailer, tinplate fin cover, cast wheels, plastic tires, w/plastic towhook for Batmobile
EX $60   NM $90   MIP $175

❏ **107-A2, Batboat,** 1976-80, black plastic boat w/Batman and Robin figures, small Bat logo labels on fin and on side of boat, chain link labels, Whizz Wheels on trailer
EX $30   NM $45   MIP $100

❏ **201-B, Saint's Volvo P-1800,** 1970-72, one-piece white body w/red Saint decal on hood, gray base, clear windows, black interior w/driver, Whizz Wheels
EX $55   NM $95   MIP $200

(KP Photo by Dr. Doug Sadecky)

❏ **258-A, Saint's Volvo P-1800,** 1965-69, three versions of white one-piece body w/silver trim and different colored Saint decals on hood, driver. Pictured here with the 201-B. Note the wheel and hood logo variation between the two cars
EX $55   NM $85   MIP $175

❏ **259-B, Penguinmobile,** 1979-80, white body, black and white lettering on orange-yellow-blue labels, gold body panels, seats, air scoop, chrome engine, w/penguin figure
EX $20   NM $30   MIP $65

❏ **261-A, James Bond Aston Martin DB5,** 1965-68, metallic gold body, red interior, working roof hatch, clear windows, two figures, left seat ejects, spoked wheels, accessory pack
EX $70   NM $150   MIP $300

❏ **261-B, Spider-Buggy,** 1979-81, red body, blue hood, clear windows, dark blue dash, seat and crane, chrome base w/bumper and steps, silver headlights; includes Spider-Man and Green Goblin figures
EX $50   NM $75   MIP $150

❏ **262-B, Captain Marvel Porsche,** 1979-80, white body, gold parts, red seat, driver, red/yellow/blue Captain Marvel decals, black plastic base, gold wheels
EX $20   NM $30   MIP $60

❏ **263-B, Captain America Jetmobile,** 1979-80, 6" white body, metallic blue chassis, black nose cone, red shield and jet, red-white-blue Captain America decals, light blue seats and driver, chrome wheels, red tires
EX $24   NM $36   MIP $60

❏ **264-B, Incredible Hulk Mazda Pickup,** 1979-80, metallic light brown body, gray or red plastic cage, black interior, Hulk label on hood, chrome wheels; includes green and red Hulk figure
EX $20   NM $30   MIP $75

❏ **265-A, Supermobile,** 1979-81, blue body, red, chrome or gray fists, red interior, clear canopy, Superman figure, chrome arms w/removable "striking fists"
EX $30   NM $45   MIP $75

❏ **266-A, Chitty Chitty Bang Bang,** 1968-72, metallic copper body, dark red interior and spoked wheels, four figures, black chassis w/silver running boards, silver

CORGI / VINTAGE

hood, horn, brake, dash, tail and headlights, gold radiator, red and orange wings, handbrake operates side wings
EX $180   NM $270   MIP $425

❑ **266-B, Spider-Bike,** 1979-83, medium blue body, one-piece body, dark blue plastic front body and seat, blue and red Spider-Man figure, amber windshield, black or white wheels
EX $40   NM $60   MIP $85

(KP Photo by Dr. Douglas Sadecky)

❑ **267-A1, Batmobile,** 1966, matte black (rare) or gloss black body, gold hubs, bat logos on door and hubs, maroon interior, black body, plastic rockets, yellow headlights and gold rocket control, blue tinted canopy, working front chain cutter, no tow hook, rubber tires. Although it's difficult to tell from this photo, this is the rare first issue matte black finish with no towhook version of the famous Batmobile
EX $200   NM $300   MIP $550

❑ **267-A2, Batmobile,** 1967-72, same as first issue except for gloss black body, gold towhook
EX $200   NM $300   MIP $500

(KP Photo by Dr. Douglas Sadecky)

❑ **267-C1, Batmobile,** 1973, chrome hubs w/red bat logos on door, maroon interior, red plastic tires, gold tow hook, plastic rockets, yellow headlight and gold rocket control, tinted blue canopy w/chrome support, chain cutter. Made for only one year, this ver-

sion featured red plastic tires and chrome wheels. Also pictured is the back of the rare first-issue window box for this model
EX $140   NM $200   MIP $400

❑ **267-C2, Batmobile,** 1974-79, chrome hubs w/black plastic tires, red bat logos on door, light red interior, gold tow hook, plastic rockets, yellow headlights and gold rocket control, tinted blue canopy w/chrome support
EX $80   NM $120   MIP $200

❑ **267-D, Batmobile,** 1980-81, gloss black body, light red interior, gold towhook, Whizzwheels with 8-spoke chrome hubs
EX $110   NM $80   MIP $175

❑ **268-A, Green Hornet's Black Beauty,** 1967-72, black body, green window/interior, two figures, working chrome grille and panels w/weapons, green headlights, red taillights
EX $175   NM $275   MIP $550

❑ **268-B, Batbike,** 1978-83, black body, one-piece body, black and red plastic parts, gold engine and exhaust pipes, clear windshield, chrome stand, black plastic five-spoked wheels, Batman figure and decals
EX $40   NM $60   MIP $125

❑ **269-B, James Bond Lotus Esprit,** 1977, white body and base, black windshield, grille and hood panel, white plastic roof device that triggers fins and tail, rockets
EX $30   NM $55   MIP $110

(KP Photo by Dr. Douglas Sadecky)

❑ **270-A, James Bond Aston Martin,** 1968-77, metallic silver body, red interior, two figures, working roof hatch, ejector seat, bullet shield and guns, chrome bumpers, spoked wheels. Orginally issued in a rare bubble-pack, the subsequent issues were sold in window boxes. On the left, the rare first issue win-

dow box; on the right, the more commonly seen version
EX $100   NM $150   MIP $325

❑ **271-B, James Bond Aston Martin,** 1978, metallic silver body and die-cast base, red interior, two figures, clear windows, passenger seat raises to eject
EX $30   NM $45   MIP $90

(KP Photo by Dr. Douglas Sadecky)

❑ **272-A, James Bond Citroen 2CV6,** 1981-86, dark yellow body and hood, red interior, clear windows, chrome headlights, red taillights, black plastic grille. This model was available in a window box, or the more difficult to find photo box shown here
EX $15   NM $35   MIP $70

❑ **277-A, Monkeemobile,** 1968-70, red body/base, white roof, yellow interior, clear windows, four figures, chrome grille, headlights, engine, orange taillights
EX $145   NM $225   MIP $450

❑ **290-A, Kojak's Buick Regal,** 1976-81, metallic bronze brown body, off-white interior, two opening doors, clear windows, chrome bumpers, grille and headlights, red taillights; accessories include Kojak and Crocker figures
EX $25   NM $55   MIP $95

❑ **292-A, Starsky and Hutch Ford Torino,** 1977-81, red one-piece body, white trim, light yellow interior, clear windows, chrome bumpers, grille and headlights, orange taillights; includes Starsky, Hutch and Bandit figures
EX $35   NM $55   MIP $100

❑ **320-B, Saint's Jaguar XJS,** 1978-81, white body, red interior, black trim, Saint figure hood label, opening doors, black grille, bumpers and tow hook, chrome headlights
EX $30   NM $45   MIP $85

❑ **336-A, James Bond Toyota 2000GT,** 1967-69, white body, black interior w/Bond and female driver, working trunk and gun rack, spoked wheels, plastic tires, accessory pack
EX $115　　NM $180　　MIP $375

❑ **342-B, Professionals Ford Capri,** 1980-82, metallic silver body and base, red interior, black spoiler, grille, bumpers, tow hook and trim, blue windows, chrome wheels; includes figures of Cowley, Bodie and Doyle
EX $30　　NM $65　　MIP $130

❑ **348-B, Vegas Ford Thunderbird,** 1980-81, orange/red body and base, black interior and grille, opening hood and trunk, amber windshield, white seats, driver, chrome bumper
EX $25　　NM $40　　MIP $85

(KP Photo by Dr. Douglas Sadecky)

❑ **391-A, James Bond Mustang Mach 1,** 1972-73, red and white body w/black hood and opening doors. Because using this model as a Bond vehicle was a last-minute decision, a label was adhered to the right side of the window box. Without this label, no one would know this was a James Bond issue
EX $100　　NM $150　　MIP $300

❑ **434-B, Chevrolet Charlie's Angels Van,** 1977-80, light rose-mauve body w/Charlie's Angels decals, in two versions: either solid or spoked chrome wheels
EX $15　　NM $30　　MIP $55

❑ **435-B, Supervan,** 1978-81, silver van w/Superman labels, working rear doors, chrome spoked wheels
EX $15　　NM $30　　MIP $60

❑ **436-B, Chevrolet Spider-Van,** 1978-80, dark blue body w/Spider-Man decals, in two versions: w/either spoke or solid wheels
EX $26　　NM $39　　MIP $65

❑ **497-A1, Man From U.N.C.L.E. THRUSH-Buster,** 1966-68, plastic interior, blue windows, two figures, two spotlights, dark metallic blue body, w/3-D Waverly ring
EX $80　　NM $130　　MIP $275

(KP Photo by Dr. Douglas Sadecky)

❑ **497-A2, Man From U.N.C.L.E. THRUSH-Buster,** 1968-69, plastic interior, blue windows, two figures, two spotlights, cream body, w/3-D Waverly ring, RARE
EX $100　　NM $350　　MIP $550

❑ **647-A, Buck Rogers Starfighter,** 1980, white body w/yellow plastic wings, amber windows, blue jets, color decal, Buck and Wilma figures
EX $32　　NM $48　　MIP $90

❑ **649-A, James Bond Space Shuttle,** 1979-81, white body w/yellow/black Moonraker labels
EX $30　　NM $50　　MIP $95

❑ **801-A1, Noddy's Car,** 1969-71, first issue: yellow body, red chassis and fenders, figures of Noddy, Big-Ears, and black, gray, or light tan face Golliwog
EX $200　　NM $400　　MIP $600

❑ **801-A2, Noddy's Car,** 1972-73, second issue: same as first issue except Master Tubby is substituted for Golliwog
EX $100　　NM $200　　MIP $350

(KP Photo by Dr. Douglas Sadecky)

❑ **802-A, Popeye's Paddle Wagon,** 1969-72, yellow and white body, red chassis, blue rear fenders, bronze and yellow stacks, white plastic deck, blue lifeboat w/Swee' Pea; includes figures of Popeye, Olive Oyl, Bluto and Wimpey. Produced for a short period, the colorful Paddle-Wagon had multiple working features and contained all of the main characters
EX $195　　NM $300　　MIP $525

❑ **803-A1, Beatles' Yellow Submarine,** 1969, yellow and white hatches, red pinstripes, first issue
EX $200　　NM $500　　MIP $1000

❑ **803-A2, Beatles' Yellow Submarine,** 1969-70, second issue, yellow and white body, working red hatches w/two Beatles in each
EX $180　　NM $270　　MIP $700

❑ **804-A, Noddy's Car,** yellow body, red chassis, Noddy alone, closed trunk w/spare wheel
EX $60　　NM $90　　MIP $175

❑ **805-A, Hardy Boys' Rolls-Royce,** 1970, red body w/yellow hood, roof and window frames, band figures on roof on removable green base
EX $70　　NM $105　　MIP $200

(KP Photo by Dr. Douglas Sadecky)

❑ **807-A, Dougal's Magic Roundabout Car,** 1971-74, yellow body, red interior, clear windows, dog and snail figures, red wheels w/gold trim, Magic Roundabout labels
EX $70　　NM $105　　MIP $175

(KP Photo by Dr. Douglas Sadecky)

❑ **808-A, Basil Brush's Car,** 1971-73, red body, dark yellow chassis, gold lamps and dash, Basil Brush figure, red plastic wheels, plastic tires; w/"Laugh Tapes" and soundbox. Basil Brush could be heard laughing with the aid of laugh tapes and a soundbox that were included with the car
EX $70   NM $105   MIP $200

❑ **809-A, Dick Dastardly's Racing Car,** 1973-76, dark blue body, yellow chassis, chrome engine, red wings, Dick and Muttley figures
EX $40   NM $60   MIP $150

❑ **811-A, James Bond Moon Buggy,** 1972-73, white body w/blue chassis, amber canopy, yellow tanks, red radar dish, arms and jaws, yellow wheels
EX $175   NM $275   MIP $525

❑ **851-A, Magic Roundabout Train,** 1973, red and blue plastic three-piece train; accessories include figures of Mr. Rusty, Basil, Rosaile, Paul and Dougal
EX $70   NM $195   MIP $350

❑ **852-A, Magic Roundabout Musical Carousel,** 1973, plastic roundabout w/Swiss musical movement, w/Dylan, Rosalie, Paul, Florence and Basil figures, rare
EX $275   NM $425   MIP $750

❑ **853-A, Magic Roundabout Playground,** 1973, contains No. 851 Train, No. 852 Carousel, six figures, seesaw, park bench, shrubs and fowers, rare
EX $295   NM $500   MIP $1000

❑ **859-A, Mr. McHenry's Trike,** 1972-74, red and yellow trike and trailer; accessories include Mr. McHenry and Zebedee figures
EX $70   NM $105   MIP $175

❑ **925-A, Batcopter,** 1976-81, black body w/yellow/red/black decals, red rotors, Batman figure, operable winch
EX $30   NM $50   MIP $100

❑ **928-A, Spider-Copter,** 1979-81, blue body w/Spider-Man labels, red plastic legs, tongue and tail rotor, black windows and main rotor
EX $30   NM $45   MIP $85

❑ **929-A, Daily Planet Helicopter,** 1979-81, red and white body, rocket launcher w/ten spare missiles
EX $24   NM $36   MIP $60

❑ **930-A, Drax Jet Helicopter,** 1979-81, white body, yellow rotors and fins, yellow/black Drax labels
EX $35   NM $75   MIP $150

❑ **2030-A, Muppet Vehicles,** Kermit's Car
EX $15   NM $35   MIP $60

❑ **2031-A, Muppet Vehicles,** Fozzie Bear's Truck
EX $15   NM $30   MIP $50

❑ **2032-A, Muppet Vehicles,** Miss Piggy's Sports Coupe
EX $15   NM $30   MIP $50

❑ **2033-A, Muppet Vehicles,** Animal's Percussionmobile
EX $15   NM $30   MIP $50

❑ **9004-A, 1927 Bentley "World of Wooster",** 1967-69, green body, metallic black chassis, cast spoked wheels, figures of Jeeves & Bertie Wooster
EX $50   NM $100   MIP $150

CIRCUS

❑ **12-A, Chipperfield Circus Crane and Cage Wagon,** 1961-65, No. 1121 crane truck, No. 1123 cage wagon and accessories
EX $150   NM $225   MIP $375

❑ **19-A, Chipperfield Circus Land Rover and Elephant Cage,** 1962-68, red No. 438 Range Rover w/blue canopy, Chipperfields Circus decal on canopy, burnt orange No. 607 elephant cage on red bed trailer
EX $90   NM $135   MIP $275

❑ **21-B, Chipperfield Circus Crane and Cage,** 1970-72, No. 1144 crane truck, cage w/rhinoceros, red and blue trailer w/three animal cages and animals; very rare gift set
EX $400   NM $700   MIP $2000

❑ **23-A1, Chipperfield Circus Set, 1st Version,** 1963-65, vehicle and accessory set in two versions: w/No. 426 Booking Office
EX $380   NM $600   MIP $1300

❑ **23-A2, Chipperfield Circus Set, 2nd Version,** 1966, vehicle and accessory set w/#503 Giraffe Truck
EX $340   NM $500   MIP $1000

❑ **30-B, Circus Land Rover and Trailer,** 1978-81, yellow/red No.

421 Land Rover w/Pinder-Jean Richard decals; accessories include blue loudspeakers and figures
EX $30   NM $50   MIP $90

❑ **48-C, Jean Richard Circus Set,** 1978-81, yellow and red Land Rover and cage trailer w/Pinder-Jean Richard decals, No. 426 office van and trailer, No. 1163 Human Cannonball truck, ring and cut-out "Big Top" circus tent
EX $90   NM $135   MIP $275

(KP Photo by Dr. Douglas Sadecky)

❑ **426-A, Chipperfield Circus Karrier Booking Office,** 1962-64, red body, light blue roof, clear windows, tin lithographed interior, circus decals, smooth or shaped wheels, rubber tires
EX $105   NM $165   MIP $325

(KP Photo by Dr. Douglas Sadecky)

❑ **487-A, Chipperfield Circus Land Rover Parade Vehicle,** 1967-69, red body, yellow interior, blue rear and speakers, revolving clown, chimp figures, Chipperfield labels
EX $60   NM $90   MIP $175

❑ **503-A, Chipperfield Circus Bedford Giraffe Transporter,** 1964-71, red "TK" Bedford truck w/blue giraffe box w/Chipperfield decal, two giraffes, shaped, cast, spoked, or detailed wheels
EX $60   NM $90   MIP $175

❑ **511-A, Chipperfield Circus Chevrolet Performing Poodles Van,** 1970-72, blue upper body and tailgate, red lower body and base, clear windshield, pale blue

interior w/poodles in back and ring of poodles and trainer, plastic tires
EX $160   NM $240   MIP $550

(KP Photo by Dr. Douglas Sadecky)

❏ **1121-A, Chipperfield Circus Crane Truck,** 1960-68, red body, embossed Chipperfield blue logo, tinplate boom, blue wheels. Pictured here with Chipperfield Circus Cage Wagon 1123-A, that included a set of polar bears or lions and their appropriate label transfers
EX $80   NM $120   MIP $225

❏ **1123-A, Chipperfield Circus Cage Wagon,** 1961-68, red body, yellow chassis, smooth or spun hubs; includes lions, tigers or polar bears
EX $56   NM $84   MIP $140

(KP Photo by Dr. Douglas Sadecky)

❏ **1130-A, Chipperfield Circus Horse Transporter,** 1962-72, red Bedford "TK" cab, blue upper/red lower horse trailer, three wheel variations; includes six horses
EX $80   NM $120   MIP $235

❏ **1139-A, Chipperfield Circus Menagerie Transporter,** 1968-72, Scammell Handyman MKIII red/blue cab, blue trailer w/three animal cages, two lions, two tigers and two bears
EX $120   NM $180   MIP $375

❏ **1144-A, Chipperfield Circus Scammell Crane Truck,** 1969-72, red upper cab and rear body, light blue lower cab, crane base and winch crank housing, red interior, tow hook, jewel headlights
EX $175   NM $275   MIP $450

❏ **1163-A, Circus Human Cannonball Truck,** 1978-81, red and blue body; w/Marvo figure
EX $30   NM $45   MIP $75

CLASSICS

❏ **9001-A, 1927 Bentley,** 1964-69, green body, metallic black chassis, brown interior, black ragtop, spoked wheels, driver
EX $35   NM $50   MIP $75

(KP Photo by Dr. Douglas Sadecky)

❏ **9002-A, 1927 Bentley,** 1964-69, red body, metallic black chassis, brown interior, black ragtop, red spoked wheels, driver. The red Bentley is slightly harder to find than the green version
EX $30   NM $60   MIP $90

❏ **9011-A, Model T Ford,** 1964-69, black body & chassis, spoked wheels, two figures
EX $20   NM $40   MIP $65

(KP Photo by Dr. Douglas Sadecky)

❏ **9012-A, Model T Ford,** 1964-69, yellow body & spoked wheels, black chassis, two figures
EX $20   NM $40   MIP $65

❏ **9013-A, Model T Ford,** 1964-69, blue body, black chassis, black ragtop, yellow wheels, one figure
EX $20   NM $40   MIP $65

(KP Photo by Dr. Douglas Sadecky)

❏ **9021-A, Daimler 38 1910,** 1964-69, orange-red body, gray and yellow chassis, yellow spoked wheels; w/four figures
EX $20   NM $40   MIP $65

❏ **9031-A, 1910 Renault 12/16,** 1965-69, light purple body & spoked wheels, light black chassis
EX $25   NM $50   MIP $80

❏ **9032-A, 1910 Renault 12/16,** 1965-69, pale yellow body & spoked wheels, light black chassis, black ragtop
EX $25   NM $50   MIP $80

❏ **9041-A, Rolls-Royce Silver Ghost,** 1966-69, silver body/hood, charcoal and silver chassis, bronze interior, gold lights, box and tank, clear windows, dash lights, radiator
EX $15   NM $30   MIP $60

CONSTRUCTION

❏ **2-B, Unimog Dumper & Priestman Cub Shovel,** 1971-73, standard colors, #1145 Mercedes-Benz unimog w/Dumper and 1128 Priestman Cub Shovel
EX $70   NM $135   MIP $200

❏ **27-A, Priestman Shovel and Carrier,** 1963-72, No. 1128 cub shovel and No. 1131 low loader machinery carrier
EX $90   NM $135   MIP $225

❏ **403-B, Thwaites Tusker Skip Dumper,** 1974-79, yellow body, chassis and tipper, driver and seat, hydraulic cylinder, red wheels, black tires two sizes, name labels, Whizz Wheels
EX $10   NM $20   MIP $40

❏ **409-B1, Unimog Dump Truck,** 1971-73, first issue, blue cab, yellow tipper, fenders and bumpers, metallic charcoal gray chassis, red interior, black mirrors, gray tow hook
EX $20   NM $30   MIP $50

❑ **409-B2, Unimog Dump Truck,** 1976-77, second issue, yellow cab, chassis, rear frame and blue tipper, fenders and bumpers, red interior, no mirrors, gray tow hook, hydraulic cylinders
EX $20   NM $30   MIP $50

❑ **409-C, Allis-Chalmers AFC 60 Fork Lift,** 1981, yellow body, white engine hood, w/driver, tan pallets and red containers
EX $15   NM $20   MIP $45

(KP Photo by Dr. Douglas Sadecky)

❑ **458-A, ERF 64G Earth Dumper,** 1958-67, red cab, yellow tipper, clear windows, unpainted hydraulic cylinder, spare tire, smooth wheels, rubber tires
EX $30   NM $45   MIP $85

❑ **459-B, Raygo Rascal Roller,** 1973-78, dark yellow body, base and mounting, green interior and engine, orange and silver roller mounting and castings, clear windshield
EX $15   NM $25   MIP $45

(KP Photo by Dr. Douglas Sadecky)

❑ **494-A, Bedford TK Tipper Truck,** 1968-72, red cab and chassis w/yellow tipper, side mirrors
EX $26   NM $39   MIP $65

❑ **1007-A, Road Repair Unit,** 1982, dark yellow Land Rover w/battery hatch and trailer w/red plastic interior w/sign and open panels, stripe and Roadwork labels
EX $15   NM $25   MIP $40

❑ **1101-B, Warner & Swasey Crane,** 1975-81, yellow cab and body, blue chassis, blue/yellow stripe labels, red interior, black steering wheel, silver knob, gold hook
EX $30   NM $45   MIP $75

❑ **1102-A, Euclid TC-12 Bulldozer,** 1958-62, lime green body w/black or pale gray treads, silver blade surface, gray plastic seat, controls, and stacks; silver grille and lights, painted blue engine sides, black sheet metal base, rubber treads and Euclid decals
EX $80   NM $120   MIP $225

❑ **1102-B, Berliet Fruehauf Dumper,** 1974-76, yellow cab, fenders and dumper; black cab and semi chassis; plastic orange or dark orange dumper body; black interior
EX $30   NM $45   MIP $75

❑ **1103-A, Euclid Caterpillar Tractor,** 1960-63, TC-12 lime green body w/black or pale gray rubber treads, gray plastic seat, driver figure, controls, stacks, silver grille, painted blue engine sides and Euclid decals
EX $50   NM $100   MIP $190

❑ **1103-B, Caterpillar Tractor,** 1960-64, lime green body w/black or gray rubber treads, gray plastic seat, driver figure, controls, stacks
EX $70   NM $105   MIP $250

❑ **1107-A, Euclid TC-12 Bulldozer,** 1963-66, yellow or pale lime-green body, metal control rod, driver, black rubber treads
EX $80   NM $120   MIP $200

❑ **1110-B, JCB 110B Crawler Loader,** 1976-80, white cab, yellow body, working red shovel, red interior w/driver, clear windows, black treads, JCB labels
EX $20   NM $30   MIP $50

❑ **1113-B, Hyster 800 Stacatruck,** 1977, clear windows, black interior w/driver
EX $35   NM $50   MIP $85

❑ **1121-B, Ford Transit Tipper,** 1983, orange cab and chassis, tan tipper, chrome wheels
EX $10   NM $15   MIP $25

❑ **1128-A, Priestman Cub Power Shovel,** 1963-76, orange upper body and panel, yellow lower body, lock rod and chassis, rubber or plastic treads, pulley panel, gray boom, w/figure of driver
EX $40   NM $60   MIP $100

❑ **1145-A, Mercedes-Benz Unimog & Dumper,** 1969-76, yellow cab and tipper, red fenders and tipper chassis, charcoal gray cab chassis, black plastic mirrors or without
EX $25   NM $35   MIP $60

❑ **1152-B, Scania Dump Truck,** 1983, white cab w/green tipper, black/green Barratt labels, black exhaust and hydraulic cylinders, six-spoked Whizz Wheels
EX $7   NM $15   MIP $30

❑ **1153-A, Priestman Cub Crane,** 1972-74, orange body, red chassis and two-piece bucket, unpainted bucket arms, lower boom, knobs, gears and drum castings, clear window, Hi-Grab labels
EX $50   NM $75   MIP $125

❑ **1153-B, Scania Dump Truck,** 1983, yellow truck and tipper w/black Wimpey labels, in two versions: either clear or green windows; six-spoked Whizz Wheels
EX $7   NM $15   MIP $30

❑ **1154-A, Mack-Priestman Crane Truck,** 1972-76, red truck, yellow crane cab, red interior, black engine, Hi Lift and Long Vehicle or Hi-Grab labels
EX $50   NM $75   MIP $125

❑ **1154-B, Giant Tower Crane,** 1981-82, white body, orange cab and chassis
EX $35   NM $50   MIP $85

❑ **1155-A, Skyscraper Tower Crane,** 1975-79, red body w/yellow chassis and booms, gold hook, gray loads of block, black/white Skyscraper labels, black tracks
EX $30   NM $45   MIP $75

❑ **1156-A, Volvo Concrete Mixer,** 1977-81, yellow or orange cab, red or white mixer w/yellow and black stripes, rear chassis, chrome chute and unpainted hitch casings
EX $30   NM $45   MIP $75

EMERGENCY

❑ **18-B, Emergency Set,** 1976-77, three-vehicle set w/figures and accessories, No. 402 Ford Cortina Police car, No. 921 Police Helicopter, No. 481 Range Rover Ambulance
EX $40   NM $60   MIP $100

❑ **19-C, Emergency Set,** 1979-81, No. 339 Land Rover Police Car and No. 921 Police Helicopter w/figures and accessories
EX $30   NM $50   MIP $80

❑ **33-B, German Life Saving Set,** 1980-82, red/white No. 421 Land Rover and lifeboat, white trailer, German labels
EX $30   NM $45   MIP $75

❑ **35-B, Chopper Squad Rescue Set,** 1978-79, blue No. 919 Jeep w/Chopper Squad decal and red/white boat w/Surf Rescue decal, No. 927 Helicopter
EX $40   NM $60   MIP $100

❑ **44-A, Police Land Rover and Horse Box,** 1978-80, white No. 421 Land Rover w/police labels and mounted policeman, No. 112 Horse Box
EX $30   NM $45   MIP $75

❑ **45-B, Canadian Mounted Police Set,** 1978-80, blue No. 421 Land Rover w/Police sign on roof and RCMP decals, No. 102 trailer; includes mounted Policeman
EX $30   NM $50   MIP $100

❑ **209-A, Riley Pathfinder Police Car,** 1958-61, black body w/blue/white Police lettering, unpainted roof sign, gray antenna
EX $50   NM $75   MIP $135

❑ **213-A, Jaguar 2.4 Litre Fire Chief's Car,** 1959-61, red body w/unpainted roof signal/siren, red/white fire and shield decals on doors, in two versions, smooth or spun hubs
EX $60   NM $90   MIP $150

❑ **223-A, Chevrolet State Patrol Car,** 1959-61, black body, State Patrol decals, smooth wheels w/hexagonal panel or raised lines and shaped wheels, yellow plastic interior, gray antenna, clear windows, silver bumpers, grille, headlights and trim, rubber tires
EX $50   NM $75   MIP $125

(KP Photo by Dr. Douglas Sadecky)

❑ **237-A, Oldsmobile Sheriff's Car,** 1962-66, black upper body w/white sides, red interior w/red

dome light and County Sheriff decals on doors, single body casting
EX $50   NM $75   MIP $125

❑ **260-B, Metropolis Police Car,** 1979-81, metallic blue body, off white interior, white roof/stripes, two working doors, clear windows, chrome bumpers, grille and headlights, two roof light bars, City of Metropolis labels
EX $20   NM $30   MIP $50

❑ **284-B, Mercedes-Benz Fire Chief,** 1982-83, light red body, black base, tan plastic interior, blue dome light, white Notruf 112 labels, red taillights, no tow hook, German export model
EX $15   NM $25   MIP $40

❑ **293-A, Renault 5TS,** 1977-80, metallic golden orange body, black trim, tan plastic interior, working hatch and two doors, clear windows and headlights
EX $15   NM $18   MIP $30

❑ **295-A, Renault 5TS Fire Chief,** 1982, red body, tan interior, amber headlights, gray antenna, black/white Sapeurs Pompiers labels, blue dome light, French export issue
EX $15   NM $25   MIP $40

❑ **297-A, Ford Escort Police Car,** 1982, blue body and base, tan interior, white doors, blue dome lights, red Police labels, black grille and bumpers
EX $8   NM $15   MIP $30

❑ **326-A, Chevrolet Caprice Police Car,** 1980-81, black body w/white roof, doors and trunk, red interior, silver light bar, Police decals
EX $20   NM $30   MIP $50

❑ **339-B, Rover 3500 Police Car,** 1980, white body, light red interior, red stripes, white plastic roof sign, blue dome light, red and blue Police and badge label
EX $8   NM $15   MIP $25

❑ **373-A, Volkswagen Police Car/Foreign Issues,** 1970-76, five different versions, one-piece body, red interior, dome light, silver headlights, red taillights, clear windows, Whizz Wheels
EX $60   NM $90   MIP $150

❑ **383-A1, Volkswagen 1200,** 1970-76, dark yellow body, white roof, red interior and dome light,

unpainted base and bumpers, black and white ADAC Strassenwacht labels, Whizz Wheels
EX $60   NM $90   MIP $150

❑ **383-A2, Volkswagen 1200,** 1970-76, seven different color and label versions, plastic interior, one-piece body, silver headlights, red taillights, die-cast base and bumpers
EX $20   NM $45   MIP $85

❑ **395-A, Fire Bug,** 1972-73, orange body, Whizz Wheels
EX $20   NM $30   MIP $50

❑ **402-A, Ford Cortina Police Car,** 1972-76, white body, red or pink and black stripe labels, red interior, folding seats, blue dome light, clear windows, chrome bumpers, Police labels, opening doors
EX $15   NM $25   MIP $45

❑ **405-A, Bedford Fire Tender,** 1956-61, divided windshield, red or green body, each w/different decals, smooth or shaped hubs
EX $60   NM $90   MIP $175

❑ **405-B, Chevrolet Superior Ambulance,** 1978-80, white body, orange roof and stripes, two working doors, clear windows, red interior w/patient on stretcher and attendant, Red Cross decals
EX $30   NM $45   MIP $75

❑ **405M, Bedford Fire Tender-Mechanical,** 1956-59, friction motor, red body w/Fire Dept. decals, divided windshield, silver or black ladder, smooth or shaped hubs
EX $70   NM $115   MIP $185

❑ **406-C, Mercedes-Benz Ambulance,** 1980-81, four different foreign versions, white interior, opening rear and two doors, blue windows and dome lights, chrome bumpers, grille and headlights, various labels; accessories include two attendant figures
EX $15   NM $20   MIP $35

❑ **407-B, Mercedes-Benz Ambulance,** 1981, white body and base, red stripes and taillights, Red Cross and black and white ambulance labels, open rear door, white interior, no figures
EX $15   NM $20   MIP $35

(KP Photo by Dr. Douglas Sadecky)

❑ **412-A, Bedford Utilecon Ambulance,** 1957-60, divided windshield, cream body w/red/white/blue decals, smooth wheels
EX $50 　　NM $75 　　MIP $125

❑ **412-B, Mercedes-Benz Police Car,** 1975-80, white body w/two different hood versions, brown interior, polizei or police lettering, blue dome light
EX $15 　　NM $18 　　MIP $30

❑ **414-B, Coast Guard Jaguar XJ12C,** 1975-77, blue and white body, Coast Guard labels
EX $18 　　NM $27 　　MIP $45

❑ **416-B, Buick Police Car,** 1977-78, metallic blue body w/white stripes and Police decals, chrome light bar w/red lights, orange taillights, chrome spoke wheels, w/two policemen
EX $18 　　NM $27 　　MIP $45

(KP Photo by Dr. Douglas Sadecky)

❑ **419-A1, Ford Zephyr Patrol Car,** 1960-65, white or cream body, blue and white Police red interior, blue dome light, silver bumpers. The car on the left has the common "Police" label, the car on the right, 419-A2, has the rare Dutch "Politie" label on the hood
EX $35 　　NM $50 　　MIP $85

❑ **419-A2, Ford Zephyr Patrol Car,** 1960-65, white or cream body, blue and white Politie/Rijks-politie decals, red interior, blue dome light, silver bumpers; import
EX $70 　　NM $165 　　MIP $275

❑ **422-B, Riot Police Quad Tractor,** 1977-80, white body and chassis, brown interior, red roof w/white panel, gold water cannons, gold spotlight w/amber lens, Riot Police and No. 6 labels
EX $15 　　NM $20 　　MIP $35

❑ **423-A, Bedford Fire Tender,** 1960-62, single windshield version, red body w/either black ladders and smooth wheels or unpainted ladders and shaped wheels
EX $60 　　NM $90 　　MIP $150

❑ **428-B, Renault 5 Police Car,** 1978-79, white body, red interior, blue dome light, black hood, hatch and doors w/white Police labels, orange taillights, aerial
EX $15 　　NM $20 　　MIP $35

❑ **429-A, Jaguar XJ12C Police Car,** 1978-80, white body w/blue and pink stripes, light bar w/blue dome light, tan interior, police labels
EX $15 　　NM $28 　　MIP $45

❑ **430-B, Porsche 924 Police Car,** 1978-80, white body w/different hood and door color versions, blue and chrome light, Polizei white on green panels or Police labels, "1" or "20" labels
EX $15 　　NM $25 　　MIP $40

(KP Photo by Dr. Douglas Sadecky)

❑ **437-A, Cadillac Superior Ambulance,** 1962-68, battery-operated warning lights, red lower/cream upper body or white lower body/blue upper body
EX $60 　　NM $90 　　MIP $150

❑ **439-A, Chevrolet Impala Fire Chief Car,** 1963-65, red body, yellow interior, w/four white doors, w/round either shield or rectangular decals on two doors; includes two fireman
EX $55 　　NM $80 　　MIP $130

(KP Photo by Dr. Douglas Sadecky)

❑ **448-A, Austin Police Mini Van,** 1964-69, dark blue body w/policeman and dog figures, white police decals, opening rear doors, gray plastic antenna
EX $50 　　NM $75 　　MIP $175

❑ **461-A, Police Vigilant Range Rover,** 1972-79, white body, red interior, black shutters, blue dome light, two chrome and amber spotlights, black grille, silver headlights, Police labels, w/police figure
EX $25 　　NM $35 　　MIP $60

(KP Photo by Dr. Douglas Sadecky)

❑ **463-A, Commer 3/4-Ton Ambulance,** 1964-66, in either white or cream body, red interior, blue dome light, red Ambulance decals, shaped wheels
EX $36 　　NM $55 　　MIP $90

(KP Photo by Dr. Douglas Sadecky)

❑ **464-A, Commer 3/4 Ton Police Van,** 1963-68, battery operated working dome light, in several color combinations of dark or light metallic blue or green bodies, various foreign issues. The van on the left has "County Police" labels, horizontal cast bars on the rear side windows, and a metallic blue paint finish. The van on the right has an embossed "Police" logo cast in the sides, vertical lines on the rear side windows, and a dark blue paint finish. Both models have a battery-operated flashing roof light

EX $45   NM $65   MIP $120

(KP Photo by Dr. Douglas Sadecky)

❑ **481-A, Chevrolet Impala Police Car,** 1965-69, black lower body and roof, white upper body, yellow interior w/two policemen, Police and Police Patrol decals on doors and hood

EX $55   NM $80   MIP $130

(KP Photo by Dr. Douglas Sadecky)

❑ **482-A, Chevrolet Impala Fire Chief Car,** 1965-69, w/Fire Chief decal on hood, yellow interior w/driver, red on white body w/either round or rectangular "Fire Chief" decals on doors, spun or cast spoked wheels

EX $55   NM $80   MIP $130

❑ **482-B, Range Rover Ambulance,** 1975-77, two different versions of body sides, red interior, raised roof, open upper and lower doors, black shutters, blue dome light, Ambulance label; includes stretcher and two ambulance attendants

EX $20   NM $30   MIP $50

❑ **483-B, Belgian Police Range Rover,** 1976-77, white body, working doors, red interior, Belgian

Police decal; includes policeman, Emergency signs

EX $22   NM $33   MIP $55

❑ **484-B, AMC Pacer Rescue Car,** 1978-80, chrome roll bars and red roof lights, white w/black engine hood; w/or without Secours decal

EX $10   NM $15   MIP $30

❑ **489-A1, Volkswagen Polo Police Car,** 1976-80, white body, green hood and doors, black dash, silver bumpers, grille and headlights, white roof, blue dome light

EX $15   NM $25   MIP $40

(KP Photo by Dr. Douglas Sadecky)

❑ **492-A, Volkswagen 1200 Police Car,** 1966-69, two different body versions made for Germany, Netherlands and Switzerland, blue dome light in chrome collar, Polizei or Politie decals. Note the opening hood and trunk on this attractive car. The front wheels turn via the roof warning light

EX $40   NM $60   MIP $100

(KP Photo by Dr. Douglas Sadecky)

❑ **506-A, Sunbeam Imp Police Car,** 1968-72, three versions, white or light blue body, tan interior, driver, black or white hood and lower doors, dome light, Police decals, cast wheels. Shown here are two color and box variations

EX $25   NM $45   MIP $85

❑ **509-A, Porsche Targa Police Car,** 1970-75, white body and base, red doors and hood, black roof and plastic interior also comes w/an orange interior, unpainted siren, Polizei labels

EX $25   NM $35   MIP $60

(KP Photo by Dr. Douglas Sadecky)

❑ **513-A, Citroen Alpine Rescue Safari,** 1970-72, white body, light blue interior, red roof and rear hatch, yellow roof rack and skis, clear windshield, man and dog, gold die-cast bobsled, Alpine Rescue decals

EX $80   NM $150   MIP $375

❑ **700-A, Motorway Ambulance,** 1973-79, white body, dark blue interior, red-white-black Accident and Red Cross labels, dark blue windows, clear headlights, red die-cast base and bumpers

EX $10   NM $15   MIP $30

❑ **703-A, Hi-Speed Fire Engine,** 1975-78, red body, yellow plastic ladder

EX $16   NM $24   MIP $40

❑ **921-A, Hughes Police Helicopter,** 1975-80, red interior, dark blue rotors, in several international imprints, Netherlands, German, Swiss, in white or yellow

EX $20   NM $30   MIP $50

❑ **922-A, Sikorsky Skycrane Casualty Helicopter,** 1975-78, red and white body, black rotors and wheels, orange pipes, working rear hatch, Red Cross decals

EX $15   NM $20   MIP $40

❑ **924-A, Bell Rescue Helicopter,** 1976-80, two-piece blue body w/working doors, red interior, yellow plastic floats, black rotors, white N428 decals

EX $20   NM $30   MIP $50

❑ **927-A, Chopper Squad Helicopter,** 1978-79, blue and white body, Sure Rescue decals

EX $20   NM $30   MIP $50

❑ **931-A, Jet Ranger Police Helicopter,** 1980, white body w/chrome interior, red floats and rotors, amber windows, Police labels

EX $25   NM $40   MIP $65

❏ **1001-A, HGB-Angus Fire-streak,** 1980, chrome plastic spotlight and ladders, black hose reel, red dome light, white water cannon, in two interior versions, electronic siren and lights
EX $35   NM $50   MIP $85

❏ **1005-A, Police Land Rover,** 1981, white body, red and blue police stripes, black lettering, open rear door, opaque black windows, blue dome light, working roof light and siren
EX $15   NM $25   MIP $50

❏ **1008-A, Chevrolet Caprice Fire Chief Car,** 1982, red body, red-white-orange decals, chrome roof bar, opaque black windows, red dome light, chrome bumpers, grille and headlights, orange taillights, Fire Dept. and Fire Chief decals, chrome wheels; includes working siren and dome light
EX $28   NM $42   MIP $70

❏ **1103-B, Chubb Pathfinder Crash Truck,** 1974-80, red body w/either "Airport Fire Brigade" or "New York Airport" decals, upper and lower body, gold water cannon unpainted and sirens, clear windshield, yellow interior, black steering wheel, chrome plastic deck, silver lights; w/working pump and siren
EX $60   NM $90   MIP $150

❏ **1118-B, Chubb Pathfinder Crash Tender,** 1981-83, red body, Emergency Unit decals, working water pump
EX $45   NM $65   MIP $110

❏ **1126-B, Simon Snorkel Fire Engine,** 1977-81, red body w/yellow interior, blue windows and dome lights, chrome deck, black hose reels and hydraulic cylinders
EX $30   NM $45   MIP $75

❏ **1127-A, Simon Snorkel Fire Engine,** 1964-76, red body w/yellow interior, two snorkel arms, rotating base, five firemen in cab and one in basket, three styles of wheels
EX $35   NM $55   MIP $100

(KP Photo by Dr. Douglas Sadecky)

❏ **1143-A, American LaFrance Ladder Truck,** 1968-81, first issue: red cab, trailer, ladder rack and wheels; chrome decks and chassis, yellow plastic three-piece operable ladder, rubber tires, six firemen figures, issued 1968-70; second issue: same as first issue except for unpainted wheels, issued 1970-72; third issue: same as earlier issues except for white decks and chassis, silver wheels, plastic tires, issued 1973-81; later issues only had four firemen
EX $60   NM $90   MIP $150

JEEP

❏ **10-C, Jeep and Motorcycle Trailer,** 1982-83, red working No. 441 Jeep w/two blue/yellow bikes on trailer
EX $15   NM $20   MIP $40

❏ **14-A, Tower Wagon and Lamp Standard,** 1961-65, red No. 409 Jeep Tower wagon w/yellow basket, workman figure and lamp post
EX $40   NM $70   MIP $140

❏ **29-C, Jeep & Horse Box,** 1981-83, metallic painted No. 441 Jeep and No. 112 trailer; accessories include girl on pony, three jumps and three hay bales
EX $15   NM $30   MIP $50

❏ **36-C, Off Road Set,** 1983, No. 5 label on No. 447 Jeep, blue boat, trailer
EX $15   NM $20   MIP $45

❏ **409-A, Jeep FC-150 Pickup,** 1959-65, blue body, clear windows, sheet metal tow hook, in two wheel versions: smooth or shaped wheels
EX $35   NM $55   MIP $90

❏ **419-B, Jeep CJ-5,** 1977-79, dark metallic green body, removable white top, white plastic wheels, spare tire
EX $8   NM $15   MIP $30

❏ **441-B, Golden Eagle Jeep,** 1979-82, tan and brown or white and gold body, tan plastic top, chrome plastic base, bumpers and steps, chrome wheels
EX $8   NM $15   MIP $25

❏ **447-B, Renegade Jeep,** 1983, dark blue body w/no top, white interior, base and bumper, white plastic wheels and rear mounted spare
EX $8   NM $15   MIP $25

❏ **448-B, Renegade Jeep with Hood,** 1983, yellow body w/removable hood, red interior, base, bumper, white plastic wheels, side mounted spare, No. 8
EX $8   NM $15   MIP $25

(KP Photo by Dr. Douglas Sadecky)

❏ **470-A, Jeep FC-150 Covered Truck,** 1965-72, four versions: blue body, rubber tires (1965-67); yellow/brown body; rubber tires w/spun hubs (1965-67); blue or yellow/brown body, plastic tires w/cast spoked hubs. The two major color and wheel variations are pictured here
EX $30   NM $45   MIP $75

(KP Photo by Dr. Douglas Sadecky)

❏ **478-A, Jeep FC-150 Tower Wagon,** 1965-69, metallic green body, yellow interior and basket w/workman figure, clear windows, w/either rubber or plastic tires. This was the updated version of the previously released GS14-A which had a red Jeep, smooth wheels and a lamp post
EX $40   NM $60   MIP $100

LAND ROVER

❏ **31-B, Safari Land Rover and Trailer,** 1976-80, black and white No. 341 Land Rover in two versions: w/chrome wheels, 1976; w/red wheels, 1977-80; came w/Warden and Lion figures
EX $20   NM $30   MIP $60

(KP Photo by Dr. Douglas Sadecky)

❏ **406-A, Land Rover 109 WB Pickup,** 1957-62, yellow, green or metallic blue body, spare wheel on hood, clear windows, sheet metal tow hook, smooth hubs, rubber tires
EX $45   **NM** $70   **MIP** $100

(KP Photo by Dr. Douglas Sadecky)

❏ **416-A, RAC Land Rover,** 1959-64, light or dark blue body, plastic interior and rear cover, gray antenna, RAC and Radio Rescue decals
EX $60   **NM** $90   **MIP** $150

❏ **417-A, Land Rover Breakdown Truck,** 1960-65, red body w/silver boom and yellow canopy, revolving spotlight, Breakdown Service labels
EX $35   **NM** $55   **MIP** $90

❏ **421-B, Land Rover 109WB,** 1977-79, working rear doors, tan interior, spare wheel on hood, plastic tow hook
EX $15   **NM** $18   **MIP** $30

❏ **438-A, Land Rover with Canopy,** 1963-77, long, one-piece body w/clear windows, plastic interior, spare wheel on hood, issued in numerous colors
EX $35   **NM** $55   **MIP** $90

(KP Photo by Dr. Douglas Sadecky)

❏ **472-A, Public Address Land Rover,** 1964-66, green No. 438 Land Rover body, yellow plastic rear body and loudspeakers, red interior, clear windows, silver bumper, grille and headlights; includes figure w/microphone and girl figure w/pamphlets
EX $50   **NM** $75   **MIP** $145

❏ **477-A, Land Rover Breakdown Truck,** 1965-77, red body, yellow canopy, chrome revolving spotlight, Breakdown Service labels, shaped hubs or Whizz Wheels
EX $25   **NM** $35   **MIP** $70

LARGE TRUCK

❏ **1-A, Carrimore Car Transporter and Four Cars,** 1957-62, three versions: No. 1101 Bedford Carrimore Transporter w/Riley, Jaguar, Austin Healey and Triumph, 1957-60; No. 1101 Bedford Carrimore Transporter w/four American cars, 1959; No. 1101 Bedford Carrimore Transporter w/Triumph, Mini, Citroen and Plymouth, 1961-62; value is for individual complete sets
EX $300   **NM** $450   **MIP** $800

❏ **20-B, Car Transporter & Cars,** 1970-73, Scammell tri-deck transporter w/six cars: Ford Capri, the Saint's Volvo, Pontiac Firebird, Lancia Fulvia, MGC GT, Marcos 3 Litre, each w/Whizz Wheels; value is for complete set
EX $200   **NM** $400   **MIP** $900

❏ **28-A, Car Transporter and Four Cars,** 1963-66, two versions: No. 1105 Bedford TK Transporter w/Fiat 1800, Renault Floride, Mercedes 230SE and Ford Consul, 1963-65; No. 1105 Bedford TK Transporter w/Chevy Corvair, VW Ghia, Volvo P-1800 and Rover 2000, 1966 only; value is for each individual complete set
EX $200   **NM** $300   **MIP** $700

❏ **41-A, Carrimore Car Transporter and Cars,** 1966, Ford "H" series Transporter and six cars; there are several car variations; sold by mail order only
EX $240   **NM** $360   **MIP** $700

(KP Photo by Dr. Douglas Sadecky)

❏ **48-A, Transporter and Six Cars,** 1966-69, first issue: No. 1138 Ford 'H' Series Transporter w/six cars, No. 252 Rover 2000, blue No. 251 Hillman Imp, No. 440 Ford Cortina Estate, No. 180 Mini w/'wickerwork', metallic maroon No. 204 Mini, and No. 321 Mini Rally ('1966 Monte Carlo Rally') racing No. 2; second issue: same as first issue except No. 251 Hillman is metallic gold, No. 204 Mini is blue, No. 321 Mini is substituted for No. 333 SUN/RAC Rally Mini w/autographs on roof. The Car Transporter gift sets were a good way for Corgi to get rid of their excess stock of automobile models
EX $225   **NM** $365   **MIP** $700

❏ **48-B, Transporter & Six Cars,** 1970-73, Scammell transporter w/six cars: No. 180 Mini DeLuxe, No. 204 Mini, No. 339 Mini Rally, No. 201 The Saint's Volvo, No. 340 Sunbeam Imp, No. 378 MGC GT; includes bag of cones and leaflet
EX $250   **NM** $450   **MIP** $900

❏ **1002-A, BL Roadtrain and Trailers,** 1981, white and orange cab, dark blue freighter semi body w/Yorkie Chocolate labels and tanker semi body w/Gulf label; includes playmat
EX $16   **NM** $24   **MIP** $40

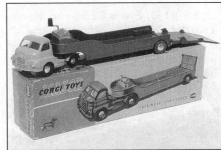

(KP Photo by Dr. Douglas Sadecky)

❏ **1100-A, Bedford Carrimore Low Loader,** 1958-62, red or yellow "S" cab, metallic blue semi

trailer and tailgate; smooth and/or shaped wheels
EX $60   NM $90   MIP $150

❑ **1100-B, Mack Trans Continental Semi,** 1971-73, orange cab body and semi chassis and fenders, metallic light blue semi body, unpainted trailer rests
EX $35   NM $55   MIP $90

❑ **1101-A1, Bedford Car Transporter,** 1957, first issue, black die-cast cab base w/blue "S" cab, yellow semi trailer, blue lettering decals, RARE
EX $100   NM $200   MIP $350

❑ **1101-A2, Bedford Car Transporter,** 1957-62, second issue, red cab, pale green upper and blue lower semi-trailer, white decals, working ramps, clear windshield
EX $70   NM $105   MIP $175

❑ **1105-A, Bedford Car Transporter,** 1962-66, red "TK" cab w/blue lower and light green upper trailer, working ramp, yellow interior, clear windows, white lettering and Corgi dog decals
EX $60   NM $90   MIP $150

❑ **1106-B, Mack Container Truck,** 1972-78, yellow cab, red interior, white engine, red suspension, white ACL labels
EX $30   NM $50   MIP $80

❑ **1107-B, Berliet Container Truck,** 1978, blue cab and semi fenders; white cab chassis and semi flatbed; each w/United States Lines label
EX $30   NM $45   MIP $75

❑ **1108-B, Ford Michelin Container Truck,** 1981, blue cab and trailer, white cab chassis and trailer fenders, yellow containers; includes Michelin Man figure
EX $15   NM $25   MIP $50

❑ **1109-B, Ford Covered Semi-Trailer,** 1979-80, blue cab and trailer, black cab chassis and trailer fenders, yellow covers
EX $15   NM $25   MIP $50

(KP Photo by Dr. Douglas Sadecky)

❑ **1110-A, Bedford Mobilgas Tanker,** 1959-65, red "S" cab and tanker w/Mobilgas decals, shaped wheels, rubber tires
EX $100   NM $150   MIP $250

(KP Photo by Dr. Douglas Sadecky)

❑ **1126-A, Ecurie Ecosse Transporter,** 1961-65, in dark blue body w/either blue or yellow lettering, or light blue body w/red or yellow lettering, working tailgate and sliding door, yellow interior, shaped wheels, rubber tires
EX $70   NM $105   MIP $225

❑ **1129-A, Bedford Milk Tanker,** 1962-65, light blue "S" cab and lower semi, white upper tank, w/blue/white milk decals, shaped wheels, rubber tires
EX $100   NM $150   MIP $275

❑ **1129-B, Mercedes-Benz Semi-Trailer Van,** 1983, black cab and plastic semi trailer, white chassis and airscreen, red doors, red-blue and yellow stripes, white Corgi lettering
EX $15   NM $18   MIP $30

❑ **1130-B, Bedford Tanker,** 1983, red cab w/black chassis, plastic tank w/chrome catwalk, Corgi Chemco decals
EX $15   NM $20   MIP $35

❑ **1131-B, Mercedes-Benz Refrigerator,** 1983, yellow cab and tailgate, red semi-trailer, two-piece lowering tailgate and yellow spare wheel base, red interior, clear window
EX $15   NM $18   MIP $30

(KP Photo by Dr. Douglas Sadecky)

❑ **1132-A, Bedford Carrimore Low Loader,** 1963-65, yellow "TK" cab, red trailer with working ramp, clear windows, red interior, suspension, shaped wheels, rubber tires
EX $90   NM $225   MIP $350

❑ **1137-A, Ford Express Semi-Trailer,** 1965-70, metallic blue cab and trailer, silver roof on trailer, chrome doors marked "Express Service," shaped or detailed cast wheels
EX $60   NM $110   MIP $225

❑ **1140-A, Bedford Mobilgas Tanker,** 1965-66, red "TK" cab and tanker w/red, white and blue Mobilgas decals, shaped wheels, rubber tires
EX $100   NM $175   MIP $350

❑ **1140-B, Ford Transit Wrecker,** 1981, white cab and rear body, red roof, silver bed, "24-hour Service" labels
EX $25   NM $35   MIP $60

❑ **1141-A, Bedford Milk Tanker,** 1966-67, light blue "TK" cab and lower semi, white upper tank w/blue/white milk decals
EX $110   NM $165   MIP $375

❑ **1142-A, Ford Holmes Wrecker,** 1967-74, white upper cab, black roof, red rear body and lower cab, mirrors, unpainted or gold booms
EX $60   NM $90   MIP $200

❑ **1144-B, Berliet Holmes Wrecker,** 1975-78, red cab and bed, blue rear body, white chassis, black interior, two gold booms and hooks, yellow dome light, driver, amber lenses and red/white/blue stripes
EX $30   NM $45   MIP $75

❑ **1144-C, Mercedes-Benz Semi-Trailer,** 1983, red cab and trailer, black chassis
EX $15   NM $18   MIP $30

❑ **1146-A, Scammell Carrimore Tri-deck Car Transporter,** 1970-73, orange lower cab, chassis and lower deck, white upper cab and middle deck, blue top deck, red interior, black hydraulic cylinders, detachable rear ramp
EX $35   NM $60   MIP $130

❑ **1147-A, Scammell Ferrymasters Semi-Trailer Truck,** 1969-72, white cab, red interior, yellow chassis, black fenders, clear windows, jewel headlights, cast step-hub wheels, plastic tires
EX $60   NM $90   MIP $150

❑ **1147-B, Scania Container Truck,** 1983, yellow truck and box w/red Ryder Truck rental labels, clear windows, black exhaust stack, red rear doors, six-spoke Whizz Wheels
EX $7   NM $15   MIP $30

❑ **1148-B, Scania Container Truck,** 1983, blue cab w/blue and white box and rear doors, white deck, Securicor Parcels labels, in red or white rear door colors
EX $7   NM $15   MIP $30

❑ **1149-A, Scania Container Truck,** 1983, white cab and box w/BRS Truck Rental labels, blue windows, red screen, roof and rear doors
EX $7   NM $15   MIP $30

❑ **1150-B, Scania Bulk Carrier,** 1983, white cab, blue and white silos, ladders and catwalk, amber windows, blue British Sugar labels, Whizz Wheels
EX $7   NM $15   MIP $30

❑ **1151-A, Scammell Coop Semi-Trailer Truck,** 1970, white cab and trailer fenders, light blue semi-trailer, red interior, gray bumper base, jewel headlights, black hitch lever, spare wheel
EX $135   NM $210   MIP $350

❑ **1151-B, Mack Exxon Tank Truck,** 1974-75, white cab and tank, red tank chassis and fenders, red interior, chrome catwalk, Exxon labels
EX $15   NM $35   MIP $75

❑ **1151-C, Scania Bulk Carrier,** 1983, white cab, orange and white silos, clear windows, orange screen, black/orange Spillers Flour labels, Whizz Wheels
EX $7   NM $15   MIP $30

❑ **1152-A, Mack Esso Tank Truck,** 1971-75, white cab and tank w/Esso labels, red tank chassis and fenders
EX $20   NM $40   MIP $80

❑ **1157-A, Ford Esso Tank Truck,** 1976-81, white cab and tank, red tanker chassis and fenders, chrome wheels, Esso labels
EX $15   NM $30   MIP $60

❑ **1158-A, Ford Exxon Tank Truck,** 1976-81, white cab and tank, red tanker chassis and fenders, chrome wheels, Exxon labels
EX $15   NM $30   MIP $60

❑ **1159-A, Ford Car Transporter,** 1976-79, metallic lime green or metallic cab and semi, cream cab chassis, deck and ramp
EX $20   NM $30   MIP $60

❑ **1160-A, Ford Gulf Tank Truck,** 1976-78, white cab w/orange chassis, blue tanker body, Gulf labels, chrome wheels
EX $15   NM $25   MIP $40

❑ **1161-A, Ford Aral Tank Truck,** 1977-80, light blue cab and chassis, white tanker body, Aral labels
EX $20   NM $30   MIP $50

❑ **1164-A, Berliet Dolphinarium Truck,** 1980-83, yellow and blue cab and trailer, clear plastic tank; includes two dolphins and a girl trainer
EX $56   NM $84   MIP $175

❑ **1166-A, Mercedes-Benz Tanker,** 1983, tan cab, plastic tank body, black chassis, black and red Guinness labels, w/chrome or black plastic catwalk, clear windows
EX $15   NM $18   MIP $30

❑ **1167-A, Mercedes-Benz Tanker,** 1983, two different versions, white cab and tank, green chassis, chrome or black plastic catwalk, red/white/green 7-Up labels or Corgi Chemo labels
EX $15   NM $18   MIP $30

❑ **1169-A, Ford Guinness Tanker,** 1982, orange, tan, black cab, tan tanker body, Guinness labels
EX $20   NM $30   MIP $50

❑ **1170-A, Ford Car Transporter,** 1982, white cab, red chassis and trailer, white labels and ramps
EX $20   NM $30   MIP $50

MILITARY

❑ **3-A, RAF Land Rover and Thunderbird Missile,** 1958-63, Standard colors, No. 350 Thunderbird Missile on Trolley and 351 RAF Land Rover
EX $100   NM $150   MIP $300

❑ **4-A, RAF Land Rover & Bloodhound,** 1958-61, set of three standard colored, No, 351 RAF Land Rover, No. 1115 Bloodhound Missile, No. 1116 Ramp and No. 1117 Trolley
EX $150   NM $300   MIP $600

❑ **6-A, Rocket Age Set,** 1959-60, set of eight standard models including: No. 350 Thunderbird Missile on Trolley, No. 351 RAF Land Rover, No. 352 RAF Staff Car, No. 353 Radar Scanner, No. 1106 Decca Radar Van and No. 1108 Bloodhound missile w/ramp
EX $325   NM $650   MIP $1400

❑ **9-A, Corporal Missile Set,** 1959-62, No. 1112 missile and No. 1113 ramp, erector vehicle and No. 1118 army truck
EX $340   NM $510   MIP $850

❑ **10-B, Centurion Tank and Transporter,** 1973-78, No. 901 olive tank and No. 1100 transporter
EX $55   NM $80   MIP $140

❑ **17-B, Military Set,** 1975-80, set of three, No. 904 Tiger tank, No. 920 Bell Helicopter, No. 906 Saladin Armored Car
EX $60   NM $90   MIP $150

❑ **350-A, Thunderbird Missile and Trolley,** 1958-62, ice blue or silver missile, RAF blue trolley, red rubber nose cone, plastic tow bar, steering front and rear axles
EX $55   NM $85   MIP $165

❑ **351-A, RAF Land Rover,** 1958-62, blue body and cover, sheet metal rear cover, RAF rondel label, w/or without suspension, silver bumper
EX $60   NM $90   MIP $150

❑ **352-A, Standard Vanguard RAF Staff Car,** 1958-62, blue body, RAF labels
EX $55   NM $85   MIP $140

❑ **353-A, Decca Radar Scanner,** 1959-60, w/either orange or custard colored scanner frame, silver scanner face, w/gear on base for turning scanner
EX $34   NM $51   MIP $85

❑ **354-A, Commer Military Ambulance,** 1964-66, olive drab body, blue rear windows and dome light, driver, Red Cross decals
EX $50   NM $75   MIP $125

❑ **355-A, Commer Military Police Van,** 1964-65, olive drab body, barred rear windows, white MP decals, driver
EX $55   NM $80   MIP $130

❑ **356-A, Volkswagen Military Personnel Carrier,** 1964-66, olive drab body, white decals, driver
EX $55   NM $95   MIP $180

CORGI / VINTAGE

❑ **358-A, Oldsmobile 88 Staff Car,** 1964-66, olive drab body, four figures, white decals
EX $50   NM $75   MIP $125

❑ **359-A, Karrier Field Kitchen,** 1964-66, olive body, white decals, w/figure
EX $60   NM $90   MIP $175

❑ **414-A, Bedford Military Ambulance,** 1961-64, clear front and white rear windows, olive body w/Red Cross decals, w/or without suspension
EX $56   NM $84   MIP $140

❑ **900-A, Tiger Mark I Tank,** 1973-78, tan and green camouflage finish, German emblem, swiveling turret and raising barrel castings, black plastic barrel end, antenna; includes twelve shells, fires shells
EX $30   NM $45   MIP $75

❑ **901-A, Centurion Mark III Tank,** 1974-78, tan and brown camouflage or olive drab body, rubber tracks; includes twelve shells
EX $30   NM $45   MIP $75

❑ **902-A, M60 A1 Medium Tank,** 1974-80, green/tan camouflage body, working turret and barrel, green rollers, white decals
EX $30   NM $45   MIP $75

❑ **903-A, Chieftain Medium Tank,** 1974-80, olive drab body, black tracks, Union Jack labels; includes twelve shells
EX $30   NM $45   MIP $75

❑ **904-A, King Tiger Heavy Tank,** 1974-78, tan and rust body, working turret and barrel, tan rollers and treads, German labels
EX $30   NM $45   MIP $75

❑ **905-A, SU-100 Medium Tank,** 1974-77, olive and cream camouflage upper body, gray lower, working hatch and barrel, black treads, red star and #103 labels; twelve shells included, fires shells
EX $30   NM $50   MIP $80

❑ **906-A, Saladin Armored Car,** 1974-77, olive drab body, swiveling turret and raising barrel castings, black plastic barrel end and tires, olive cast wheels, w/twelve shells, fires shells
EX $30   NM $45   MIP $75

❑ **907-A, Half Track Rocket Launcher & Trailer,** 1975-80, two rocket launchers and single trailer castings, gray plastic roll cage, man w/machine gun, front wheels and hubs
EX $20   NM $35   MIP $55

❑ **907-A, Rocket Launcher and Trailer,** 1975-80, steel blue and red launcher, fires rocket
EX $25   NM $35   MIP $60

❑ **908-A, AMX 30D Recovery Tank,** 1976-80, olive body w/black plastic turret and gun, accessories and three figures
EX $35   NM $50   MIP $80

❑ **909-A, Tractor, Trailer and Field Gun,** 1976-80, tan tractor body and chassis, trailer body, base and opening doors, gun chassis and raising barrel castings, brown plastic interior; twelve shells included, fires shells
EX $30   NM $50   MIP $80

❑ **920-A, Bell Army Helicopter,** 1975-80, two-piece olive/tan camouflage body, clear canopy, olive green rotors, U.S. Army decals
EX $24   NM $36   MIP $60

❑ **923-A, Sikorsky Skycrane Army Helicopter,** 1975-78, olive drab and yellow body w/Red Cross and Army labels
EX $15   NM $20   MIP $40

❑ **1106-A, Decca Airfield Radar Van,** 1959-60, cream body w/four or five orange vertical bands, working rotating scanner and aerial
EX $120   NM $180   MIP $350

❑ **1108-A, Bloodhound Missile and Launching Platform,** 1958-61, white and yellow missile, red rubber nose cone; military green ramp
EX $110   NM $165   MIP $275

❑ **1109-A, Bloodhound Missile on Trolley,** 1959-62, white and yellow missile, red rubber nose cone; military green trolley, rubber tires
EX $120   NM $180   MIP $300

❑ **1112-A, Corporal Missile on Launching Ramp,** 1959-62, white missile, red rubber-nose cone
EX $80   NM $120   MIP $200

❑ **1113-A, Corporal Missile & Erector Vehicle,** 1959-62, white missile, red rubber-nose cone, olive green body on erector body
EX $240   NM $360   MIP $600

❑ **1115-A, Bloodhound Missile,** 1959-62, white and yellow missile, red rubber nose cone
EX $70   NM $105   MIP $175

❑ **1116-A, Bloodhound Launching Ramp,** 1959-62, military green ramp
EX $34   NM $51   MIP $85

❑ **1117-A, Bloodhound Loading Trolley,** 1959-62, military green working lift, red rubber nose cone
EX $40   NM $60   MIP $100

❑ **1118-A, International 6x6 Army Truck,** 1959-63, olive drab body w/clear windows, red/blue decals, six cast olive wheels w/rubber tires
EX $70   NM $105   MIP $225

❑ **1124-A, Corporal Missile Launching Ramp,** 1960-61, sold in temporary pack
EX $36   NM $55   MIP $90

❑ **1133-A, Army Troop Transporter,** 1964-65, olive w/white U.S. Army decals
EX $70   NM $105   MIP $175

(KP Photo by Dr. Douglas Sadecky)

❏ **1134-A, Bedford Army Fuel Tanker,** 1964-65, olive cab and tanker, w/white "U.S. Army" and "No Smoking" decals
EX $140   NM $210   MIP $375

❏ **1135-A, Army Heavy Equipment Transporter,** 1964-65, olive cab and trailer w/white U.S. Army decals w/red or yel. int. and driver
EX $70   NM $105   MIP $325

MISCELLANEOUS

❏ **25-A, Shell or BP Garage Gift Set,** 1963-65, gas station/garage w/pumps and other accessories including five different cars; in two versions: Shell or B.P., rare; value is for each set
EX $295   NM $700   MIP $1500

❏ **490-B, Touring Caravan,** 1975-79, white body w/blue trim, white plastic opening roof and door, pale blue interior, red plastic hitch and awning
EX $15   NM $25   MIP $40

❏ **1401-A, Service Ramp,** 1958-60, metallic blue and silver operable ramp
EX $30   NM $45   MIP $95

MOTORCYCLE

❏ **25-C, Matra & Motorcycle Trailer,** 1980-81, red No. 57 Talbot Matra Rancho w/two yellow and blue bikes on trailer
EX $15   NM $20   MIP $35

❏ **171-A, Red Wheelie Motorcycle,** 1982, red plastic body and fender w/black/white/yellow decals, black handlebars, kickstand and seat, chrome engine, pipes, flywheel-powered rear wheel
EX $10   NM $15   MIP $25

❏ **172-A, White Wheelie Motorcycle,** 1982, white body w/black/white police decals
EX $15   NM $20   MIP $35

❏ **173-A, Cafe Racer Motorcycle,** 1983,
EX $15   NM $18   MIP $30

❏ **681-A, Stunt Motorcycle,** 1971-72, made for Corgi Rockets race track, gold cycle, blue rider w/yellow helmet, clear windshield, plastic tires
EX $70   NM $105   MIP $175

RACING

❏ **5-A, British Racing Cars,** 1959-63, set of three cars, three versions: blue No. 152 Lotus, green No. 151 BRM, green No. 150 Vanwall, all w/smooth wheels, 1959; same cars w/shaped wheels, 1960-61; red Vanwall, green BRM and blue Lotus, 1963, each set
EX $140   NM $210   MIP $475

❏ **6-B, Volkswagen Racing Tender and Cooper,** 1967-69, white No. 490 VW breakdown truck w/racing labels, blue No. 156 Cooper on trailer
EX $50   NM $75   MIP $150

❏ **12-B, Grand Prix Racing Set,** 1968-72, four vehicle set includes: No. 490 Volkswagen Breakdown Truck w/No. 330 Porsche (1969), Porsche No. 371(1970-72), No. 155 Lotus, No. 156 Cooper-Maserati, red trailer
EX $135   NM $210   MIP $425

❏ **15-A, Silverstone Racing Layout,** 1963-66, seven-vehicle set w/accessories; Vanwall, Lotus XI, Aston Martin, Mercedes 300SL, BRM, Ford Thunderbird, Land Rover Truck; second version has a No. 154 Ferrari substituted for Lotus XI, rare
EX $400   NM $900   MIP $1700

❏ **16-A, Ecurie Ecosse Racing Set,** 1961-66, metallic dark or light blue No. 1126 transporter w/three cars in two versions: BRM, Vanwall and Lotus XI, 1961-64; BRM, Vanwall and Ferrari, 1964-66, value is for individual complete set
EX $140   NM $210   MIP $450

❏ **17-A, Land Rover and Ferrari Racer,** 1963-67, red and tan No. 438 Land Rover and red No. 154 Ferrari F1 on yellow trailer
EX $60   NM $90   MIP $150

❏ **25-B, Volkswagen Racing Tender and Cooper Maserati,** 1970-71, two versions: tan or white No. 490 VW breakdown truck, and No. 159 Cooper-Maserati on trailer; value is for each set
EX $50   NM $75   MIP $150

❏ **26-B, Matra and Racing Car,** 1983, black/yellow No. 457 Talbot Matra Rancho and No. 160 Hesketh yellow car w/Team Corgi trailer and labels
EX $15   NM $35   MIP $65

❏ **29-B, Ferrari Daytona and Racing Car,** 1975-77, blue/yellow No. 323 Ferrari and No. 150 Surtees on yellow trailer
EX $25   NM $40   MIP $85

❏ **30-A, Grand Prix Set,** 1973, sold by mail order only; kit version of No. 151 Yardley, No. 154 JPS, No. 152 Surtees and No. 153 Surtees
EX $60   NM $125   MIP $275

❏ **32-B, Lotus Racing Set,** 1976-79, three versions: "3" on No. 301 Elite and "JPS" on No. 154 Lotus racer; "7" on No. 301 Elite and "JPS" on racer; "7" on No. 301 Elite and "Texaco" on No. 154 Lotus racer; value is for each individual complete set
EX $30   NM $45   MIP $95

❏ **37-A, Lotus Racing Team Set,** 1966-69, 490 VW Breakdown Truck, red trailer w/#318 Lotus Elan Open Top, #319 Lotus Elan Hard Top, #155 Lotus Climax; includes pack of cones, sheet of racing number labels
EX $125   NM $200   MIP $375

❏ **38-A, Monte Carlo Rally Set,** 1965-67, three vehicle set, No. 326 Citroen, No. 318 Mini and No. 322 Land Rover rally cars
EX $295   NM $450   MIP $900

❏ **46-A, All Winners Set,** 1966-69, first issue: No. 310 Corvette, No. 312 Jaguar XKE, No. 314 Ferrari 250LM, No. 324 Marcos, No. 325 Mustang; second issue: No. 312 Jaguar XKE, No. 314 Ferrari 250LM, No. 264 Toronado, No. 327 MGB, No. 337 Corvette
EX $100   NM $240   MIP $450

❏ **46-B, Super Karts,** 1982, two carts, orange and blue, Whizz Wheels in front, slicks on rear, silver and gold drivers
EX $15   NM $18   MIP $30

CORGI / VINTAGE

(KP Photo by Dr. Douglas Sadecky)

❑ **150-A, Vanwall Racing Car,** 1957-65, clear windshield, unpainted dash, silver pipes and decals, smooth wheels, rubber tires, in three versions: green body or red body w/silver or yellow seats
EX $35   NM $65   MIP $140

❑ **150-B, Surtees TS9 Racing Car,** 1972-74, black upper engine, chrome lower engine, pipes and exhaust, driver, Brook Bond Oxo-Rob Walker labels, eight-spoke Whizz Wheels
EX $15   NM $20   MIP $40

(KP Photo by Dr. Douglas Sadecky)

❑ **151-A, Lotus Eleven,** 1958-64, red, silver, or light blue/green body, clear windshield and plastic headlights, smooth wheels, rubber tires, racing decals
EX $60   NM $95   MIP $160

❑ **151-B, McLaren M19A Racing Car,** 1972-77, white body, orange stripes, chrome engine, exhaust and suspension, black mirrors, driver, Yardley McLaren #55 labels, Whizz Wheels
EX $15   NM $25   MIP $40

❑ **152-A, BRM Racing Car,** 1958-65, silver seat, dash and pipes, smooth wheels, rubber tires, in three versions: dark green body, 1958-60; light green body w/driver and various number decals 1961-65; light green body, no driver
EX $50   NM $75   MIP $150

❑ **152-B, Ferrari 312 B2 Racing Car,** 1973-75, red body, white fin, gold engine, chrome suspension, mirrors and wheels, Ferrari and #5 labels
EX $16   NM $24   MIP $40

❑ **153-A, Campbell Bluebird,** 1960-65, blue body, red exhaust, clear windshield, driver, in two versions: black plastic wheels, 1960; metal wheels and rubber tires
EX $56   NM $84   MIP $175

❑ **153-B, Surtees TS9B Racing Car,** 1972-74, red body w/white stripes and wing, black plastic lower engine, driver, chrome upper engine, pipes, suspension, eight-spoke wheels
EX $15   NM $20   MIP $40

❑ **154-A, Ferrari Racing Car,** 1963-72, red body, chrome plastic engine, roll bar and dash, driver, silver cast base and exhaust, Ferrari and No. 36 decals, shaped or spoked wheels
EX $24   NM $36   MIP $75

❑ **154-B, Lotus Racing Car,** 1973-82, black body and base, gold cast engine, roll bar, pipes, dash and mirrors, driver, gold cast wheels, in two versions
EX $25   NM $35   MIP $60

❑ **155-A, Lotus-Climax Racing Car,** 1964-69, green body and base w/black/white #1 and yellow racing stripe labels, unpainted engine and suspension, w/driver
EX $25   NM $35   MIP $65

❑ **155-B, Shadow-Ford Racing Car,** 1974-76, black body and base w/white/black #17, UOP and American flag labels, cast chrome suspension and pipes, Embassy Racing label
EX $10   NM $20   MIP $50

❑ **156-A, Cooper-Maserati Racing Car,** 1967-69, blue body w/red/white/blue Maserati and #7 decals, unpainted engine and suspension, chrome plastic steering wheel, roll bar, mirrors and pipes, driver, cast eight-spoke wheels, plastic tires
EX $26   NM $39   MIP $65

❑ **156-B, Shadow-Ford Racing Car,** 1974-77, white body, red stripes, driver, chrome plastic pipes, mirrors and steering wheel, in two versions, Jackie Collins driver figure
EX $10   NM $20   MIP $45

(KP Photo by Dr. Douglas Sadecky)

❑ **158-A, Lotus-Climax Racing Car,** 1969-72, orange/white body w/black/white stripe and #8 labels, unpainted cast rear wing, cast eight-spoke wheels, w/driver
EX $15   NM $25   MIP $50

❑ **158-B, Tyrrell-Ford Racing Car,** 1974-78, dark blue body w/blue/black/white Elf and #1 labels, chrome suspension, pipes, mirrors, Jackie Stewart driver figure
EX $18   NM $25   MIP $50

❑ **159-A, Cooper-Maserati Racing Car,** 1969-72, yellow/white body w/yellow/black stripe and #3 decals, driver tilts to steer car
EX $18   NM $27   MIP $45

❑ **159-B, STP Patrick Eagle Racing Car,** 1974-77, red body w/red, white and black STP and #20 labels, chrome lower engine and suspension, black plastic upper engine; includes Patrick Eagle driver figure
EX $20   NM $30   MIP $50

❑ **160-A, Hesketh-Ford Racing Car,** 1975-78, white body w/red/white/blue Hesketh, stripe and #24 labels, chrome suspension, roll bar, mirrors and pipes
EX $15   NM $18   MIP $30

❑ **161-A, Commuter Dragster,** 1971-73, maroon body w/Ford Commuter, Union Jack and #2 decals, cast silver engine, chrome plastic suspension and pipes, clear windshield, driver, spoke wheels
EX $30   NM $45   MIP $75

❑ **161-B, Tyrrell P34 Racing Car,** 1977, dark blue body and wings w/yellow stripes, #4 and white Elf and Union Jack decals, chrome plastic engine, w/driver in red or blue helmet
EX $20   NM $30   MIP $55

❑ **162-A, Quartermaster Dragster,** 1971-73, long, dark metallic green upper body w/green/yellow/black #5 and Quartermaster labels, light green lower body, w/driver
EX $30   NM $45   MIP $75

❑ **162-B, Tyrrell P34 Racing Car,** 1978-79, without yellow labels, First National Bank labels, w/driver in red or orange helmet
EX $20   NM $30   MIP $55

❑ **163-A, Ford Capri Santa Pod Gloworm,** 1971-76, white and blue body w/red, white and blue lettering and flag decals, red chassis, amber windows, gold-based black engine, gold scoop, pipes and front suspension, w/driver, plastic wheels
EX $18   NM $27   MIP $45

❑ **164-A, Wild Honey Dragster,** 1971-73, yellow body w/red/yellow Wild Honey and Jaguar Powered labels, green windows and roof, black grille, driver, Whizz Wheels
EX $25   NM $40   MIP $65

❑ **165-A, Adams Drag-Star,** 1972-74, orange body, red nose, gold engines, chrome pipes and hood panels, Whizz Wheels
EX $20   NM $30   MIP $45

❑ **166-A, Mustang Organ Grinder Dragster,** 1971-74, yellow body w/green/yellow name, #39 and racing stripe labels, black base, green windshield, red interior, roll bar, w/driver
EX $20   NM $30   MIP $50

❑ **167-A, U.S. Racing Buggy,** 1972-74, white body w/red/white/blue stars, stripes and USA #7 labels, red base, gold engine, red plastic panels, driver
EX $18   NM $25   MIP $50

❑ **169-A, Silver Streak Jet Dragster,** 1973-76, metallic blue body w/Firestone and flag labels on tank, silver engine, orange plastic jet and nose cone
EX $15   NM $25   MIP $45

❑ **170-A, Radio Luxembourg Dragster,** 1972-76, long, blue body w/yellow, white and blue John Wolfe Racing, Radio Luxembourg and #5 labels, silver engine, w/driver
EX $30   NM $45   MIP $85

❑ **190-A, JPS Lotus Racing Car,** 1974-77, black body, scoop and wings w/gold John Player Special, Texaco and #1 labels, gold suspension, pipes and wheels
EX $30   NM $45   MIP $75

❑ **191-A, McLaren M23 Racing Car,** 1974-77, large 1:18-scale red and white body and wings w/red, white and black Texaco-Marlboro #5 labels, chrome pipes, suspension and mirrors, removable wheels
EX $30   NM $60   MIP $110

❑ **201-C, British Leyland Mini 1000,** 1978, red interior, chrome lights, grille and bumper, #8 decal; three variations: silver body w/decals, 1978-82; silver body, no decals; orange body w/extra hood stripes, 1983
EX $16   NM $24   MIP $40

(KP Photo by Dr. Douglas Sadecky)

❑ **227-A, Morris Mini-Cooper,** 1962-65, yellow or blue body and base and/or hood, white roof and/or hood, two versions, red plastic interior, jewel headlights, flag, numbers decals. Even though there are various paint and decal versions of this model, any one of them is valuable
EX $80   NM $150   MIP $300

(KP Photo by Dr. Douglas Sadecky)

❑ **256-A, Volkswagen East African Safari,** 1965-69, light red body, brown interior, working front and rear hood, clear windows, spare wheel on roof steers front wheels, jewel headlights,

w/rhinoceros figure. Although never issued as a gift set, this spectacular little toy could easily have been made into one. A rhinoceros was added as a charging menace to the racing VW
EX $60   NM $130   MIP $285

❑ **281-B, Austin Mini-Metro Datapost,** 1982-83, white body, blue roof, hood and trim, red plastic interior, hepolite and #77 decals, working hatch and doors, clear windows, folding seats, chrome headlights, orange taillights, Whizz Wheels
EX $15   NM $18   MIP $30

❑ **282-A, BMC Mini-Cooper,** 1971-74, white body, black working hood, trunk, two doors, red interior, clear windows, orange/black stripes and #177 decals, suspension, Whizz Wheels
EX $30   NM $45   MIP $95

❑ **291-B, Mercedes-Benz 240D Rally,** 1982, cream or tan body, black, red and blue lettering, "dirt," red plastic interior, clear windows, black radiator guard and roof rack, opening doors, racing #5 label
EX $10   NM $15   MIP $25

❑ **300-C, Ferrari Daytona,** 1979, apple green body, black tow hook, red-yellow-silver-black Daytona #5 and other racing labels, amber windows, headlights, black plastic interior, base, four spoke chrome wheels
EX $15   NM $20   MIP $35

❑ **302-B, Hillman Hunter,** 1969-72, blue body, gray interior, black hood, white roof, unpainted spotlights, clear windshield, red radiator screen, black equipment, Golden Jacks wheels; came w/Kangaroo figure
EX $45   NM $70   MIP $140

❑ **303-A, Mercedes-Benz 300SL Roadster,** 1958-66, blue or white body, yellow interior, plastic interior, smooth, shaped or cast wheels, racing stripes and number, driver
EX $45   NM $75   MIP $140

❑ **303-B, Roger Clark's Capri,** 1970-72, white body, black hood, grille and interior, open doors, folding seats, chrome bumpers, clear headlights, red taillights, Racing #73, label sheet, Whizz Wheels
EX $15   NM $25   MIP $55

CORGI / VINTAGE

(KP Photo by Dr. Douglas Sadecky)

❑ **304-A, Mercedes-Benz 300SL Coupe,** 1959-65, chrome body, red hardtop, red stripe, clear windows, 1959-60 smooth wheels no suspension, 1961-65 racing stripes
EX $45   NM $65   MIP $130

❑ **305-B, Mini-Marcos GT850,** 1972-73, white body, red-white-blue racing stripe and #7 labels, clear headlights, Whizz Wheels, opening doors and hood
EX $20   NM $30   MIP $50

❑ **306-B, Fiat X1/9,** 1980-81, metallic blue body and base, white Fiat #3, multicolored lettering and stripe labels, black roof, trim, interior, rear panel, grille, bumpers and tow hook, chrome wheels and detailed engine
EX $15   NM $20   MIP $35

❑ **307-B, Renault 5 Turbo,** 1981, bright yellow body, red plastic interior, black roof and hood, working hatch and two doors, black dash, chrome rear engine, racing #8 Cibie and other sponsor labels
EX $15   NM $18   MIP $25

❑ **308-B, BMW M1,** 1981, yellow body, black plastic base, rear panel and interior, white seats, clear windshield, multicolored stripes, lettering and #25 decal, Goodyear label
EX $15   NM $20   MIP $35

(KP Photo by Dr. Douglas Sadecky)

❑ **309-A, Aston Martin DB4,** 1962-65, white top w/aqua green sides, yellow plastic interior, racing Nos. 1, 3 or 7
EX $50   NM $75   MIP $125

❑ **312-A, Jaguar E Type Competition,** 1964-68, gold or chrome plated body, black interior, blue and white stripes and black #2 decals, no top, clear windshield, headlights, w/driver
EX $45   NM $65   MIP $130

❑ **312-C, Ford Capri S,** 1982, white body, red lower body and base, red interior, clear windshield, black bumpers, grille and tow hook, chrome headlights and wheels, red taillights, #6 and other racing labels
EX $15   NM $20   MIP $35

(KP Photo by Dr. Douglas Sadecky)

❑ **314-A, Ferrari Berlinetta 250LM,** 1965-72, red body w/yellow stripe, blue windshields, chrome interior, grille and exhaust pipes, detailed engine, #4 Ferrari logo and yellow stripe decals, spoked wheels and spare, rubber tires
EX $30   NM $45   MIP $75

(KP Photo by Dr. Douglas Sadecky)

❑ **315-A, Simca 1000,** 1964-66, chrome plated body, No. 8 and red-white-blue stripe decals, one-piece body, clear windshield, red interior
EX $30   NM $45   MIP $75

❑ **316-B, Ford GT 70,** 1972-73, green and black body, white interior, No. 32 label
EX $10   NM $25   MIP $45

❑ **317-A, Morris Mini-Cooper,** 1964-65, red body and base, white roof, yellow interior, chrome spotlight, No. 37 and Monte Carlo Rally decals
EX $60   NM $125   MIP $250

(KP Photo by Dr. Douglas Sadecky)

❑ **318-A, Lotus Elan S2 Roadster,** 1965-67, working hood, plastic interior w/folding seats, shaped wheels and rubber tires, issued in metallic blue, Exxon "I've got a Tiger in my tank" label on trunk. The ordinary model is powder blue, but shown here is the rare white version of the car
EX $30   NM $50   MIP $110

❑ **318-B, Jaguar XJS Motul,** 1983, black body w/red/white Motul and No. 4, chrome wheels
EX $8   NM $15   MIP $25

❑ **319-B, Lamborghini Miura,** 1973-74, silver body, black interior, yellow/purple stripes and No. 7 label, Whizz Wheels
EX $30   NM $45   MIP $75

❑ **321-A, BMC Mini-Cooper S Rally Car,** 1965-66, red body, white roof, five jewel headlights, Monte Carlo Rally decals w/either No. 52 (1965) or No. 2 (1966); rare w/drivers' autographs on roof
EX $100   NM $275   MIP $500

❑ **321-B, Porsche 924,** 1978-81, red or metallic light brown or green body, dark red interior, opening two doors and rear window, chrome headlights, black plastic grille, racing No. 2
EX $10   NM $25   MIP $50

❑ **322-A1, Rover 2000 Rally,** 1965-66, metallic dark red body, white roof, shaped wheels, No. 136 and Monte Carlo Rally decals
EX $50   NM $95   MIP $175

❑ **322-A2, Rover 2000 Rally,** 1965-66, white body, red interior, black bonnet, No. 21 decal, cast spoked wheels
EX $55   NM $135   MIP $225

(KP Photo by Dr. Douglas Sadecky)

❑ **323-A, Citroen DS 19 Rally,** 1965-66, light blue body, white roof, yellow interior, four jewel headlights, Monte Carlo Rally and No. 75 decals, w/antenna
EX $70   NM $105   MIP $185

❑ **323-B, Ferrari Daytona,** 1973-78, white body w/red roof and trunk, black interior, two working doors, amber windows and headlights, No. 81 and other labels
EX $15   NM $30   MIP $55

❑ **324-B, Ferrari Daytona JCB,** 1973-74, orange body w/No. 33, Corgi and other labels, chrome spoked wheels
EX $15   NM $25   MIP $50

(KP Photo by Dr. Douglas Sadecky)

❑ **328-A, Hillman Imp Rally,** 1966, in various metallic body colors, w/cream interior, Monte Carlo Rally and No. 107 decals
EX $30   NM $65   MIP $110

❑ **330-A, Porsche Carrera 6,** 1967-69, white body, red or blue trim, blue or amber tinted engine covers, black interior, clear windshield and canopy, red jewel taillights, No. 1 or No. 20 decals
EX $30   NM $45   MIP $75

(KP Photo by Dr. Douglas Sadecky)

❑ **333-A, BMC Mini-Cooper S "Sun/RAC" Rally Car,** 1967, red body, white roof w/six jewel headlights, RAC Rally and No. 21 decals
EX $90   NM $180   MIP $350

(KP Photo by Dr. Douglas Sadecky)

❑ **337-A, Corvette Sting Ray,** 1967-69, yellow body, red interior, suspension, No. 13 decals. This car's decorative appearance definitely places it in the 1960's
EX $30   NM $55   MIP $95

❑ **339-A, BMC Mini-Cooper S Rally,** 1967-72, red body, white roof, chrome roof rack w/two spare tires, Monte Carlo Rally and No. 177 decals, w/shaped wheels/rubber tires or cast detailed wheels/plastic tires
EX $40   NM $90   MIP $180

❑ **340-A, Sunbeam Imp Rally,** 1967-68, metallic blue body w/white stripes, Monte Carlo Rally and No. 77 decals, cast wheels
EX $20   NM $45   MIP $85

❑ **340-B, Rover 3500 Triplex,** 1981, white sides and hatch, blue roof and hood, red plastic interior and trim, detailed engine, red-white-black No. 1 label
EX $8   NM $15   MIP $20

❑ **341-B, Chevrolet Caprice Classic,** 1981, white upper body, red sides w/red/white/blue stripes and No. 43 decals, tan interior, STP labels
EX $24   NM $36   MIP $60

❑ **344-A, Ferrari 206 Dino,** 1969-73, black interior and fins, in either red body w/No. 30 label and gold hubs or Whizz Wheels, or yellow body w/No. 23 label and gold hubs or Whizz Wheels
EX $24   NM $36   MIP $60

(KP Photo by Dr. Douglas Sadecky)

❑ **348-A, Psychedelic Ford Mustang,** 1968, light blue body and base, aqua interior, red-orange-yellow No. 20 and flower decals, cast eight spoke wheels, plastic tire
EX $30   NM $50   MIP $100

❑ **371-A, Porsche Carrera 6,** 1970-73, white upper body, red front hood, doors, upper fins and base, black interior, purple rear window, tinted engine cover, racing No. 60 decals
EX $25   NM $35   MIP $60

❑ **376-A, Corvette Sting Ray,** 1970-73, metallic gray body w/black hood, Go-Go-Go labels, Whizz Wheels
EX $40   NM $65   MIP $100

❑ **331-A, Ford Capri 3 Litre GT,** 1973-76, white and black body, racing number 5 label
EX $15   NM $20   MIP $35

❑ **380-B, BMW M1 BASF,** 1983, red body, white trim w/black/white BASF and No. 80 decals
EX $15   NM $18   MIP $30

❑ **381-B, Renault 5 Turbo,** 1983, white body, red roof, red and blue trim painted on, No. 5 lettering, blue and white label on windshield, facom decal
EX $15   NM $18   MIP $25

❑ **384-A, Adams Probe 16,** 1970-73, one-piece body, blue sliding canopy; metallic burgundy, or metallic lime/gold w/and without racing stripes, Whizz Wheels
EX $15   NM $25   MIP $40

❑ **384-B, Volkswagen 1200 Rally,** 1976-77, light blue body, off-white plastic interior, silver headlights, red taillights, suspension, Whizz Wheels
EX $20   NM $30   MIP $50

❑ **386-A, Bertone Barchetta Runabout,** 1971-73, yellow and

black body, black interior, amber windows, die-cast air foil, suspension, red/yellow Runabout decals, Whizz Wheels
EX $15   NM $22   MIP $45

❑ **394-A, Datsun 240Z,** 1973-76, red body w/No. 11 and other labels, two working doors, white interior, orange roll bar and tire rack; one version also has East Africa Rally labels
EX $15   NM $20   MIP $35

❑ **396-A, Datsun 240Z,** 1973-76, white body w/red hood and roof, No. 46 and John Morton labels, Whizz Wheels
EX $15   NM $20   MIP $35

❑ **397-A, Porsche-Audi 917,** 1973-78, white body, red and black No. 6, L and M, Porsche Audi and stripe labels or orange body, orange, two-tone green, white No. 6, racing driver
EX $15   NM $20   MIP $35

SMALL TRUCK

❑ **11-A, ERF Dropside Truck and Trailer,** 1960-64, No. 456 truck and No. 101 trailer w/No. 1488 cement sack load and No. 1485 plank load
EX $60   NM $90   MIP $200

❑ **21-A, Milk Truck and Trailer,** 1962-66, blue and white ERF No. 456 milk truck w/No. 101 trailer and milk churns
EX $60   NM $130   MIP $250

(KP Photo by Dr. Douglas Sadecky)

❑ **24-A, Constructor Set,** 1963-68, one red and one white cab bodies, w/four different interchangeable rear units; van, pickup, milk truck, and ambulance; various accessories include a milkman figure
EX $48   NM $80   MIP $160

❑ **24-B, Mercedes-Benz and Caravan,** 1975-81, truck and trailer in two versions: w/blue No. 285 Mercedes truck and No. 490 Caravan (1975-79); w/brown No.

285 Mercedes and No. 490 Caravan (1980-81); value is for each set
EX $15   NM $30   MIP $50

❑ **28-B, Mazda Pickup and Dinghy,** 1975-78, two versions: red No. 493 Mazda w/"Ford" labels; or w/"Sea Spray" labels, dinghy and trailer
EX $25   NM $35   MIP $60

❑ **405-C, Ford Transit Milk Float,** 1982, white one-piece body, blue hood and roof, tan interior, chrome and red roof lights, open compartment door and milk cases
EX $15   NM $25   MIP $40

❑ **406-B, Mercedes-Benz Unimog 406,** 1970-76, yellow body, red and green front fenders and bumpers, metallic charcoal gray chassis w/olive or tan rear plastic covers, red interior
EX $18   NM $25   MIP $45

❑ **413-B, Mazda Motorway Maintenance Truck,** 1976-78, deep yellow body w/red base, black interior and hydraulic cylinder, yellow basket w/workman figure
EX $18   NM $25   MIP $45

❑ **415-A, Mazda Camper Pickup,** 1976-78, red truck and white camper w/red interior and folding supports
EX $15   NM $25   MIP $451

❑ **431-A, Volkswagen Pickup,** 1964-66, dark yellow body, red interior and rear plastic cover, silver bumpers and headlights, red VW emblem, shaped wheels
EX $45   NM $65   MIP $110

❑ **440-B, Mazda Custom Pickup,** 1979-80, orange body w/red roof, United States flag label
EX $15   NM $18   MIP $30

❑ **452-A, Commer 5-Ton Dropside Truck,** 1956-62, either blue or red cab, both w/cream rear body, sheet metal tow hook, smooth or shaped wheels, rubber tires
EX $40   NM $60   MIP $110

(KP Photo by Dr. Douglas Sadecky)

❑ **453-A, Commer Refrigerator Van,** 1956-60, either light or dark blue cab (pictured here), both w/cream bodies and red/white/blue Wall's Ice Cream decals, smooth wheels
EX $80   NM $120   MIP $225

❑ **454-A, Commer 5-Ton Platform Truck,** 1957-62, either yellow or metallic blue cab w/silver body, smooth or shaped wheels
EX $40   NM $60   MIP $120

❑ **456-A, ERF 44G Dropside Truck,** 1961-64, yellow cab and chassis, metallic blue bed, smooth or shaped wheels
EX $36   NM $55   MIP $110

(KP Photo by Dr. Douglas Sadecky)

❑ **457-A, ERF 44G Platform Truck,** 1958-64, light blue cab w/dark blue flatbed body or yellow cab and blue flatbed, smooth hubs
EX $36   NM $55   MIP $110

(KP Photo by Dr. Douglas Sadecky)

❑ **459-A, ERF 44G Moorhouse Van,** 1958-60, yellow cab, red body, Moorhouse Lemon Cheese decals, smooth wheels, rubber tires
EX $100   NM $150   MIP $295

(KP Photo by Dr. Douglas Sadecky)

❑ **460-A, ERF Neville Cement Tipper,** 1959-66, yellow cab, gray tipper, cement decal, plastic or metal filler caps, w/either smooth or shaped wheels
EX $32   NM $48   MIP $85

❑ **465-A, Commer 3/4-Ton Pickup,** 1963-66, red cab w/orange canopy, yellow interior, Trans-o-Lites
EX $30   NM $45   MIP $75

(KP Photo by Dr. Douglas Sadecky)

❑ **483-A, Dodge Kew Fargo Tipper,** 1967-72, white cab and working hood, blue tipper, red interior, clear windows, black hydraulic cylinders, cast spoked wheels, plastic tires
EX $34   NM $51   MIP $85

❑ **490-A, Volkswagen Breakdown Truck,** 1966-72, tan or white body, red interior and equipment boxes, clear windshield, chrome tools, spare wheels, red VW emblem, no lettering
EX $50   NM $75   MIP $125

❑ **493-A, Mazda B-1600 Pickup Truck,** 1975-78, issued in either blue and white or blue and silver bodies w/working tailgate, black interior, chrome wheels
EX $15   NM $20   MIP $35

❑ **495-A, Mazda 4X4 Open Truck,** 1983, blue body, white roof, black windows, no interior, white plastic wheels
EX $15   NM $20   MIP $35

❑ **702-A, Breakdown Truck,** 1975-79, red body, black plastic boom w/gold hook, yellow interior, amber windows, black/yellow decals, Whizz Wheels
EX $15   NM $18   MIP $30

❑ **1116-B, Shelvoke and Drewry Garbage Truck,** 1979, long, orange or red cab, silver body w/City Sanitation decals, black interior, grille and bumpers, clear windows
EX $15   NM $25   MIP $40

❑ **1117-B, Mercedes-Faun Street Sweeper,** 1980, orange body w/light orange or brown figure, red interior, black chassis and unpainted brushing housing and arm castings
EX $15   NM $25   MIP $40

❑ **1150-A, Unimog with Snowplow (Mercedes-Benz),** 1971-76, 6" four different body versions, red interior, cab, rear body, fender-plow mounting, lower and charcoal upper chassis, rear fenders
EX $30   NM $45   MIP $75

Sports Car

❑ **311-A, Ford Capri,** 1970-72, orange-red or dark red body, gold wheels w/red hubs or Whizz Wheels, two working doors, clear windshield and headlights, black interior, folding seats, black grille, silver bumpers
EX $40   NM $80   MIP $145

❑ **1-C, Ford Sierra and Caravan Trailer,** 1983, blue #299 Sierra, two-tone blue/white #490 Caravan
EX $15   NM $20   MIP $35

❑ **26-A, Beach Buggy & Sailboat,** 1971-76, purple No. 381 buggy, yellow trailer and red/white boat
EX $20   NM $30   MIP $55

❑ **38-B, Mini Camping Set,** 1977-78, cream Mini, w/red/blue tent, grille and two figures
EX $25   NM $40   MIP $65

❑ **200-B, British Leyland Mini 1000,** 1976-78, metallic blue body, working doors, black base, clear windows, white interior, silver lights, grille and bumper, Union Jack decal on roof, Whizz Wheels
EX $18   NM $27   MIP $45

❑ **203-B, De Tomaso Mangusta,** 1970-73, metallic dark green body w/gold stripes and logo on hood, silver lower body, clear front windows, cream interior, amber rear windows and headlights, gray antenna, spare wheel, Whizz Wheels
EX $26   NM $39   MIP $65

❑ **204-B, Morris Mini-Minor,** 1972-73, one-piece body in dark or metallic blue or orange body, plastic interior, silver lights, grille and bumpers, red taillights, Whizz Wheels
EX $30   NM $45   MIP $75

(KP Photo by Dr. Douglas Sadecky)

❑ **214-A, Ford Thunderbird Hardtop,** 1959-65, light green body, cream roof, clear windows, silver lights, grille and bumpers, red taillights, rubber tires
EX $50   NM $80   MIP $130

(KP Photo by Dr. Douglas Sadecky)

❑ **214-M, Ford Thunderbird Hardtop-Mechanical,** 1959, same as 214-A but w/friction motor and pink body and black roof. This model is fairly hard to find
EX $70   NM $120   MIP $215

❑ **215-A, Ford Thunderbird Roadster,** 1959-65, clear windshield, silver seats, lights, grille and bumpers, red taillights, rubber tires, white body
EX $50   NM $75   MIP $125

(KP Photo by Dr. Douglas Sadecky)

❑ **226-A1, Morris Mini-Minor,** 1960-71, light blue or red body w/shaped or smooth wheels, plastic interior, silver bumpers, grille and headlights
EX $40   NM $60   MIP $100

❑ **226-A2, Morris Mini-Minor,** 1960-71, sky blue body w/shaped and/or smooth wheels, plastic interior, silver bumpers, grille and headlights, rare
EX $100   NM $175   MIP $350

❑ **242-A, Ghia-Fiat 600 Jolly,** 1965-66, dark yellow body, red seats, two figures and a dog, clear windshield, silver bumpers and headlights, red taillights, rare
EX $80   NM $175   MIP $325

❑ **249-A, Morris Mini-Cooper Deluxe,** 1965-68, black body/base, red roof, yellow and black wicker work decals on sides and rear, yellow interior, gray steering wheel, jewel headlights
EX $45   NM $65   MIP $120

❑ **271-A, De Tomaso Mangusta,** 1969, white upper/light blue lower body/base, black interior, clear windows, silver engine, black grille, amber headlights, red taillights, gray antenna, spare wheel, gold stripes and black logo decal on hood, suspension, removable gray chassis
EX $32   NM $48   MIP $90

❑ **286-A, Jaguar XJ12C,** 1974-79, five different metallic versions, working hood and two doors, clear windows, tow hook, chrome bumpers, grille and headlights
EX $10   NM $15   MIP $35

❑ **288-A, Minissima,** 1975-79, cream upper body, metallic lime green lower body w/black stripe centered, black interior, clear windows, headlights
EX $15   NM $20   MIP $35

❑ **298-A, Ferrari 308GTS Magnum,** 1982, red body w/solid chrome wheels
EX $24   NM $36   MIP $60

❑ **299-A, Ford Sierra,** 1982, many body color versions w/plastic interior, working hatch and two doors, clear windows, folding seat back, lifting hatch cover
EX $8   NM $15   MIP $25

❑ **300-A1, Austin-Healey,** 1956-63, cream body w/red seats or red body w/cream seats
EX $50   NM $75   MIP $125

❑ **300-A2, Austin Healey,** 1956-63, blue body w/cream seats, shaped hubs, rare
EX $100   NM $215   MIP $350

❑ **300-B, Corvette Sting Ray,** 1970-72, metallic green or metallic red body, yellow interior, black working hood, working headlights, clear windshield, amber roof panel, gold dash, chrome grille and bumpers, decals, gray die-cast base, Golden jacks, cast wheels, plastic tires
EX $40   NM $90   MIP $185

❑ **301-A, Triumph TR2,** 1956-59, cream one-piece body w/red seats, light green body w/white or cream seats, clear windshield, silver grille
EX $70   NM $105   MIP $175

❑ **301-B, Iso Grifo 7 Litre,** 1970-73, metallic blue body, light blue interior, black hood and stripe, clear windshield, black dash, folding seats, chrome bumpers, Whizz Wheels
EX $15   NM $18   MIP $30

❑ **302-A, MGA,** 1957-65, red or metallic green body, cream seats, black dash, clear windshield, silver bumpers, grille and headlights, smooth or shaped wheels
EX $60   NM $90   MIP $150

❑ **303-C, Porsche 924,** 1980-81, bright orange body, dark red interior, black plastic grille, multicolored stripes, swivel roof spotlight
EX $10   NM $15   MIP $25

❑ **304-B, Chevrolet Camaro SS,** 1972-73, blue or turquoise body w/white stripe, cream interior, working doors, white plastic top, clear windshield, folding seats, silver air intakes, red taillights, black grille and headlights, suspension, Whizz Wheels
EX $30   NM $45   MIP $95

❑ **305-A, Triumph TR3,** 1960-62, metallic olive or cream one-piece body, red seats, clear windshield, silver grille, bumpers and headlights, smooth or shaped hubs
EX $60   NM $90   MIP $150

❑ **306-A, Morris Marina 1.8 Coupe,** 1971-73, metallic dark red or lime green body, cream interior, working hood and two doors, clear windshield, chrome grille and bumpers, Whizz Wheels
EX $15   NM $30   MIP $60

❑ **307-A, Jaguar E Type,** 1962-64, maroon or metallic dark gray body, tan interior, red and clear plastic removable hardtop, clear windshield, folded top, spun hubs
EX $45   NM $65   MIP $110

❑ **308-A, BMC Mini-Cooper S,** 1972-76, bright yellow body, red plastic interior, chrome plastic roof rack w/two spare wheels, clear windshield, one-piece body silver grille, bumpers, headlights, red taillights, suspension, Whizz Wheels
EX $45   NM $65   MIP $110

❑ **309-B, Volkswagen Polo Turbo,** 1982, cream body, red interior w/red and orange trim, working hatch and two door castings, clear windshield, black plastic dash
EX $15   NM $18   MIP $30

(KP Photo by Dr. Douglas Sadecky)

❑ **310-A, Corvette Sting Ray,** 1963-68, metallic silver, bronze or red body, two working headlights, clear windshield, yellow interior, silver hood panels, four rotating jewel headlights, suspension, chrome bumpers, w/spoked or shaped wheels, rubber tires. The swivelling jeweled headlights and spoked wheels added real pizzaz to this cool toy
EX $60   NM $90   MIP $175

❑ **310-B, Porsche 92 Turbo,** 1982, black body w/gold trim, yellow interior, four chrome headlights, clear windshield, taillight-license plate decal, opening doors and hatchback
EX $15   NM $20   MIP $35

(KP Photo by Dr. Douglas Sadecky)

(KP Photo by Dr. Douglas Sadecky)

❑ **312-B, Marcos Mantis,** 1971-73, metallic red body, opening doors, cream interior and headlights, silver gray lower body base, bumpers, hood panel, spoked wheels
EX $20   NM $35   MIP $55

❑ **313-A, Ford Cortina GXL,** 1970-73, tan or metallic silver blue body, black roof and stripes, red plastic interior, working doors, clear windshield
EX $30   NM $45   MIP $75

❑ **314-B, Fiat X1/9,** 1975-79, metallic light green or silver body w/black roof, trim and interior, two working doors, rear panel, grille, tow hook and bumpers, detailed engine, suspension, chrome wheels
EX $15   NM $20   MIP $35

❑ **314-C, Jaguar XJS-HE Supercat,** 1982-83, black body w/silver stripes and trim, red interior, dark red taillights, light gray antenna, no tow hook, clear windshield
EX $8   NM $15   MIP $25

❑ **315-C, Lotus Elite,** 1976-78, red body, white interior, two working doors, clear windshield, black dash, hood panel, grille, bumpers, base and tow hook
EX $15   NM $18   MIP $35

(KP Photo by Dr. Douglas Sadecky)

❑ **316-A, NSU Sport Prinz,** 1963-66, metallic burgundy or maroon body, yellow interior, one-piece body, silver bumpers, headlights and trim, shaped wheels
EX $30   NM $45   MIP $75

❑ **319-A, Lotus Elan S2 Hardtop,** 1967-68, cream interior w/folding seats and tan dash, working hood, separate chrome chassis, issued in blue body w/white top or red body w/white top
EX $30   NM $45   MIP $75

❑ **319-C, Jaguar XJS,** 1978-81, metallic burgundy body, tan interior, clear windows, working doors, spoked chrome wheels
EX $10   NM $15   MIP $25

❑ **320-A, Ford Mustang Fastback,** 1965-66, metallic lilac, metallic dark blue, silver or light green body, spoked or detailed cast wheels
EX $30   NM $45   MIP $95

(KP Photo by Dr. Douglas Sadecky)

❑ **324-A, Marcos Volvo 1800 GT,** 1966-69, issued w/either white body w/two green stripes or blue body w/two white stripes, plastic interior w/driver, spoked wheels, rubber tires. The blue version is shown here--the common version is white with racing stripes
EX $25   NM $40   MIP $70

(KP Photo by Dr. Douglas Sadecky)

❑ **325-A, Ford Mustang Fastback,** 1965-69, white body w/double red stripe, blue interior, spun, detailed cast, wire or cast alloy wheels. Shown in the foreground of this photo is an unused number sheet to help jazz up the model
EX $25   NM $45   MIP $85

❑ **327-A, MGB GT,** 1967-69, dark red body, pale blue interior, opening hatch and two doors, jewel headlights, chrome grille and bumpers, orange taillights, spoked wheels, w/suitcase
EX $50   NM $75   MIP $110

❑ **329-A, Ford Mustang Mach 1,** 1973-76, green upper body, white lower body and base, cream interior, folding seat backs, chrome headlights and rear bumper
EX $25   NM $35   MIP $60

❑ **332-A, Lancia Fulvia Zagato,** 1967-69, metallic blue body, metallic green or yellow and black body, light blue interior, working hood and doors, folding seats, amber lights, cast wheels
EX $25   NM $35   MIP $70

❑ **334-A, BMC Mini-Cooper Magnifique,** 1966-70, metallic blue or olive green body w/working doors, hood and trunk, clear windows and sunroof, cream interior w/folding seats, jewel headlights, cast detailed wheels, plastic tires
EX $34   NM $65   MIP $115

❑ **335-A, Jaguar E Type 2+2,** 1968-69, red or blue body and chassis, working hood, doors and hatch, black interior w/folding seats, copper engine, pipes and suspension, spoked wheels
EX $40   NM $60   MIP $120

❑ **338-A, Chevrolet Camaro SS,** 1968-70, metallic gold body w/two working doors, black roof and stripes, red interior, take-off wheels
EX $30   NM $45   MIP $75

❑ **341-A, Mini-Marcos GT850,** 1966-70, metallic maroon body, white name and trim decals, cream interior, open hood and doors, clear windows and headlights, Golden Jacks wheels
EX $30   NM $45   MIP $75

❑ **342-A, Lamborghini Miura P400,** 1970-72, w/red or yellow body, working hood, detailed engine, clear windows, jewel headlights, bull figure, Whizz Wheels
EX $40   NM $60   MIP $100

❑ **343-A, Pontiac Firebird,** 1969-72, metallic silver body and base, red interior, black hood, stripes and convertible top, doors open, clear windows, folding seats, Golden Jacks wheels
EX $50   NM $75   MIP $125

❑ **343-B, Ford Capri 30 S,** 1980-81, Silver or yellow body, black markings, opening doors and hatchback
EX $15   NM $20   MIP $35

❑ **345-A, MGC GT,** 1969, bright yellow body and base, black interior, hood and hatch, folding seats, luggage, jewel headlights, red taillights
EX $50   NM $75   MIP $125

❑ **347-A, Chevrolet Astro I,** 1969-74, dark metallic green/blue body w/working rear door, cream interior w/two passengers, in two versions: gold wheels w/red plastic hubs or Whizz wheels
EX $18   NM $40   MIP $85

(KP Photo by Dr. Douglas Sadecky)

❑ **349-A, Pop Art Mini-Mostest,** 1969, light red body and base, yellow interior, jewel headlights, orange taillights, yellow-blue-purple pop art and "Mostest" decals; very rare. This rare Mini is one of the Holy Grails of any Corgi collection. Very few of these cars were produced in 1969, possibly due to the fact that psychedelia had already passed its prime
EX $1000   NM $1500 MIP $2700

❑ **370-A, Ford Cobra Mustang,** 1982, white, black, red and blue body and chassis, Mustang decal
EX $15   NM $18   MIP $30

❑ **372-A, Lancia Fulvia Zagato,** 1970-72, orange body, black working hood and interior, Whizz Wheels
EX $15   NM $25   MIP $40

❑ **374-A, Jaguar E Type 2+2,** 1970-76, in five versions: red or yellow w/nonworking doors; or w/V-12 engine in yellow body or metallic yellow body, Whizz Wheels
EX $35   NM $55   MIP $90

❑ **375-A, Toyota 2000 GT,** 1970-72, metallic dark blue or purple one-piece body, cream interior, red gear shift and antenna, two red and two amber taillights, Whizz Wheels
EX $15   NM $30   MIP $55

❑ **377-A, Marcos 3 Litre,** 1970-73, working hood, detailed engine, black interior, Marcos label, Whizz Wheels, issued in orange or metallic blue-green
EX $20   NM $30   MIP $55

❑ **378-A, MGC GT,** 1970-73, red body, black hood and base, black interior, opening hatch and two doors, folding seat backs, luggage, orange taillights, Whizz Wheels
EX $50   NM $75   MIP $125

❑ **378-B, Ferrari 308GTS,** 1982, red or black body w/working rear hood, black interior w/tan seats, movable chrome headlights, detailed engine
EX $15   NM $20   MIP $35

❑ **380-A, Alfa Romeo P33 Pininfarina,** 1970-74, white body, gold or black spoiler, red seats, Whizz Wheels
EX $16   NM $24   MIP $45

❑ **381-A, GP Beach Buggy,** 1970-76, metallic blue or orange-red body, two surfboards, flower label, Whizz Wheels
EX $15   NM $20   MIP $35

❑ **382-A, Porsche Targa 911S,** 1970-75, metallic blue, silver-blue or green body, black roof w/or without stripe, orange interior, opening hood and two doors, chrome engine and bumpers, Whizz Wheels
EX $25   NM $35   MIP $60

❑ **382-B, Lotus Elite 22,** 1970-75, dark blue body w/silver trim, Whizz Wheels
EX $15   NM $18   MIP $35

❑ **384-C, Renault 11 GTL,** 1983, light tan or maroon body and base, red interior, opening doors and rear hatch, lifting hatch cover, folding seats, grille
EX $15   NM $25   MIP $40

❑ **385-A, Porsche 917,** 1970-76, red or metallic blue body, black or gray base, blue or amber tinted windows and headlights, opening rear hood, headlights, Whizz Wheels
EX $15   NM $20   MIP $45

❑ **387-A, Corvette Sting Ray,** 1972, either dark metallic blue or metallic mauve-rose body, chrome dash, Whizz Wheels
EX $40   NM $65   MIP $100

❑ **388-A, Mercedes-Benz C-111,** 1971-74, orange main body w/black lower and base, black interior, vents, front and rear grilles, silver headlights, red taillights, Whizz Wheels
EX $15   NM $20   MIP $45

❑ **389-A, Reliant Bond Bug 700 E.S.,** 1971-74, bright orange or lime green body, off white seats, black trim, silver headlights, red taillights, Bug label
EX $15   NM $25   MIP $50

❑ **392-A, Bertone Shake Buggy,** 1972-74, clear windows, green interior, gold engine, four variations: yellow upper/white lower body or metallic mauve upper/white lower body w/spoked or solid chrome wheels
EX $15   NM $22   MIP $45

❑ **393-A, Mercedes-Benz 350SL,** 1972-79, white body, spoke wheels or metallic dark blue body solid wheels, pale blue interior, folding seats, detailed engine
EX $15   NM $30   MIP $60

❑ **457-B, Talbot-Matra Rancho,** 1981-84, red and black, green and black or white and blue body, working tailgate and hatch, clear windows, plastic interior, black bumpers, grille and tow hook
EX $10   NM $15   MIP $25

❑ **801-B, Ford Thunderbird 1957,** 1982, cream body, dark brown, black or orange plastic hardtop, black interior, open hood and trunk, chrome bumpers
EX $10   NM $20   MIP $35

❑ **802-B, Mercedes-Benz 300SL,** 1982, red body and base, tan interior, open hood and two gullwing doors, black dash, detailed engine, clear windows, chrome bumpers
EX $8   NM $15   MIP $25

❑ **803-A, Jaguar 1952 XK120 Rally,** 1983, cream body w/black top and trim, red interior, Rally des Alps and #414 decals
EX $8   NM $15   MIP $25

❑ **803-B, Jaguar XK120 Hardtop,** 1983, red body, black hardtop, working hood and trunk, detailed engine, cream interior, clear windows, chrome wheels
EX $8   NM $15   MIP $25

❑ **805-B, Mercedes-Benz 300SC Hardtop,** 1983, maroon body, tan top and interior, open hood and trunk, clear windows, folding seat backs, top w/chrome side irons
EX $8   NM $15   MIP $25

❑ **806-B, Mercedes-Benz 300SC Convertible,** 1983, black

body, black folded top, white interior, folding seat backs, detailed engine, chrome grille and wheels, lights, bumpers
EX $8   NM $12   MIP $25

❑ **810-B, Ford Thunderbird 1957,** 1983, white body, black interior and plastic top, amber windows, white seats, chrome bumpers, headlights and spare wheel cover
EX $10   NM $20   MIP $35

❑ **811-B, Mercedes-Benz 300SL,** 1983, silver body, tan interior, black dash, clear windows, open hood and two gullwing doors, detailed engine, chrome bumpers
EX $8   NM $15   MIP $25

❑ **1009-A, MG Maestro,** 1983, yellow body, black trim, opaque black windows, black plastic grille, bumpers, spoiler, trim and battery hatch, clear headlights, AA Service label
EX $15   NM $20   MIP $35

TAXI

❑ **221-A, Chevrolet Impala Taxi,** 1960-65, light orange body, base w/hexagonal panel under rear axle and smooth wheels, or two raised lines and shaped wheels, one-piece body, clear windows, plastic interior, silver grille, headlights and bumpers; smooth or shaped spun wheels w/rubber tires
EX $50   NM $75   MIP $125

❑ **327-B, Chevrolet Caprice Taxi,** 1979-81, orange body w/red interior, white roof sign, Taxi and TWA decals
EX $20   NM $30   MIP $50

❑ **373-B, Peugeot 505 STI,** 1981-82, red body and base, red interior, blue-red-white Taxi labels, black grille, bumpers, tow hook, chrome headlights and wheels, opening doors
EX $8   NM $15   MIP $25

❑ **411-B, Mercedes-Benz 240D Taxi,** 1975-80, orange body, orange interior, black roof sign w/red and white Taxi labels, black on door
EX $15   NM $18   MIP $30

❑ **418-A1, Austin London Taxi,** 1960-65, black body w/yellow plastic interior, w/or without driver, shaped or smooth hubs with rubber tires
EX $36   NM $55   MIP $90

❑ **418-A2, Austin London Taxi/Reissue,** 1971-74, updated version w/Whizz Wheels, black or maroon body
EX $15   NM $20   MIP $35

❑ **425-A, Austin London Taxi,** 1978-83, black body w/two working doors, light brown interior, Whizz Wheels
EX $15   NM $20   MIP $35

❑ **430-A, Thunderbird Bermuda Taxi,** 1962-65, white body w/blue, yellow or green plastic canopy w/red fringe, yellow interior, driver, yellow and black labels
EX $50   NM $75   MIP $135

❑ **450-B, Peugeot 505 Taxi,** 1983, cream body, red interior, red, white and blue taxi decals
EX $8   NM $15   MIP $25

❑ **451-A, Ford Sierra Taxi,** 1983, cream body
EX $8   NM $15   MIP $20

❑ **480-A, Chevrolet Impala Yellow Cab,** 1965-67, red lower body, yellow upper, red interior w/driver, white roof sign, red decals
EX $80   NM $120   MIP $200

TRAILER

❑ **100-A, Dropside Trailer,** 1957-65, cream body, red chassis in five versions: smooth wheels 1957-61; shaped wheels, 1962-1965; white body, cream or blue chassis; or silver gray body, blue chassis, each
EX $10   NM $21   MIP $45

(KP Photo by Dr. Douglas Sadecky)

❑ **101-A, Platform Trailer,** 1958-64, in five versions: silver body, blue chassis; silver body, yellow chassis; blue body, red chassis; blue body, yellow chassis
EX $10   NM $20   MIP $45

❑ **109-A, Pennyburn Workmen's Trailer,** 1968-69, blue body w/working lids, red plastic interior, three plastic tools, shaped wheels, plastic tires
EX $15   NM $35   MIP $60

VANS

❑ **403-A, Bedford Daily Express Van,** 1956-59, dark blue body w/white Daily Express decals, divided windshield, smooth wheels, rubber tires
EX $60   NM $90   MIP $150

❑ **403M, Bedford KLG Van-Mechanical,** 1956-59, w/friction motor, red body w/KLG Spark Plugs decals, smooth hubs
EX $70   NM $125   MIP $285

(KP Photo by Dr. Douglas Sadecky)

❑ **404-A, Bedford Dormobile,** 1956-62, two versions and several colors: divided windshield w/cream, green or metallic maroon body; or single windshield w/yellow body/blue roof w/shaped or smooth wheels. Pictured here; the 404-A on the left and the 404M on the right with a mechanical friction motor
EX $50   NM $75   MIP $125

❑ **404M, Bedford Dormobile-Mechanical,** 1956-59, friction motor, dark metallic red or turquoise body, smooth wheels
EX $60   NM $90   MIP $175

❑ **407-A, Karrier Mobile Grocery,** 1957-61, light green body, grocery store interior, red/white Home Service labels, smooth hubs, rubber tires
EX $70   NM $110   MIP $185

(KP Photo by Dr. Douglas Sadecky)

❏ **408-A, Bedford AA Road Service Van,** 1957-62, dark yellow body in two versions: first version with divided windshield, 1957-59 shown; single windshield, 1960-62

EX $50   NM $75   MIP $125

(KP Photo by Dr. Douglas Sadecky)

❏ **411-A, Karrier Lucozade Van,** 1958-62, yellow body w/gray rear door, Lucozade decals, rubber tires, w/either smooth or shaped wheels

EX $70   NM $120   MIP $225

(KP Photo by Dr. Douglas Sadecky)

❏ **413-A, Karrier Butcher Shop,** 1960-64, white body, blue roof, butcher shop interior, Home Service labels, in two versions: w/or without suspension, smooth hubs. Note the meat hanging in the side windows

EX $65   NM $100   MIP $165

(KP Photo by Dr. Douglas Sadecky)

❏ **420-A, Ford Thames Airborne Caravan,** 1962-67, various color versions of body and plastic interior w/table, white blinds, silver bumpers, grille and headlights, two doors

EX $35   NM $55   MIP $95

(KP Photo by Dr. Douglas Sadecky)

❏ **421-A, Bedford Evening Standard Van,** 1960-62, black body/silver roof or black lower body/silver upper body and roof, Evening Standard decals, smooth wheels

EX $55   NM $80   MIP $130

❏ **422-A1, Bedford Corgi Toys Van,** 1962, yellow upper/blue lower body, Corgi Toy decals, rare

EX $100   NM $225   MIP $400

❏ **422-A2, Bedford Corgi Toys Van,** 1960-62, Corgi Toys decals, w/either yellow body/blue roof or blue body/yellow roof

EX $60   NM $105   MIP $200

❏ **423-B, Chevrolet Rough Rider Van,** 1977-78, yellow body w/working rear doors, cream interior, amber windows, Rough Rider decals

EX $15   NM $18   MIP $30

❏ **424-B, Security Van,** 1976-79, black body, blue mesh windows and dome light, yellow/black Security labels, Whizz Wheels

EX $7   NM $15   MIP $25

(KP Photo by Dr. Douglas Sadecky)

❏ **428-A, Karrier Ice Cream Van,** 1963-66, cream upper, blue lower body and interior, clear windows, sliding side windows, Mister Softee decals, figure inside

EX $90   NM $165   MIP $295

❏ **431-B, Chevrolet Vantastic Van,** 1977-80, off white body w/Vantastic decals

EX $10   NM $15   MIP $25

❏ **432-A, Chevrolet Vantastic Van,** 1977-80, black body w/Vantastic decals

EX $10   NM $15   MIP $25

❏ **433-A, Volkswagen Delivery Van,** 1962-64, white upper and red lower body, plastic red or yellow interior, silver bumpers and headlights, red VW emblem, shaped wheels

EX $55   NM $85   MIP $140

❏ **434-A, Volkswagen Kombi Bus,** 1962-66, off-green upper and olive green lower body, red interior, silver bumpers and headlights, red VW emblem, shaped wheels

EX $50   NM $75   MIP $125

(KP Photo by Dr. Douglas Sadecky)

❏ **435-A, Karrier Dairy Van,** 1962-64, light blue body w/Drive Safely on Milk decals, white roof, w/either smooth or shaped wheels

EX $50   NM $75   MIP $145

❏ **437-B, Chevrolet Coca-Cola Van,** 1978-80, red body, white trim, w/Coca Cola logos

EX $15   NM $20   MIP $35

(KP Photo by Dr. Douglas Sadecky)

❑ **441-A, Volkswagen Tobler Van,** 1963-67, light blue body, plastic interior, silver bumpers, Trans-o-lite headlights and roof panel, shaped wheels, rubber tires
EX $55　　NM $85　　MIP $140

❑ **447-A, Ford Wall's Ice Cream Van,** 1965-67, light blue body, dark cream pillars, plastic striped rear canopy, white interior, silver bumpers, grille and headlights. A sidewalk/street display plus a salesman and small boy dress up this non-musical version of the van
EX $80　　NM $160　　MIP $325

(KP Photo by Dr. Douglas Sadecky)

❑ **450-A, Austin Mini Van,** 1964-67, metallic deep green body w/two working rear doors, clear windows
EX $40　　NM $60　　MIP $100

❑ **455-A, Karrier Bantam Two Ton Van,** 1957-60, blue body, red chassis and bed, clear windows, smooth wheels, rubber tires
EX $35　　NM $55　　MIP $95

❑ **462-A, Commer 3/4-Ton Van,** 1970-71, either dark blue body with green roof and Hammonds decals (1971) or white body with light blue roof and CO-OP labels (1970), both w/cast spoked wheels w/plastic tires
EX $45　　NM $90　　MIP $180

❑ **466-A1, Commer 3/4-Ton Milk Float,** 1964-65, white cab w/light blue body
EX $32　　NM $48　　MIP $80

❑ **466-A2, Commer 3/4-Ton Milk Float,** 1970, white cab w/light blue body, w/CO-OP decals
EX $40　　NM $80　　MIP $160

(KP Photo by Dr. Douglas Sadecky)

❑ **471-A1, Karrier Mobile Canteen,** 1965-66, blue body, white interior, amber windows, roof knob rotates figure, working side panel counter, Joe's Diner label. In this photo, the model on the left has the common "Joe's Diner" label, while the van on the right (471-A2) features the rare Belgian-issued "patates frites" label
EX $60　　NM $90　　MIP $150

❑ **471-A2, Karrier Mobile Canteen,** 1965-66, blue body, white interior, amber windows, roof knob rotates figure, working side panel counter, Patates Frites label, Belgium issue
EX $90　　NM $150　　MIP $325

(KP Photo by Dr. Douglas Sadecky)

❑ **474-A, Ford Thames Wall's Ice Cream Van,** 1965-68, light blue body, cream pillar, chimes, chrome bumpers and grille, no figures. This wonderful toy played the Wall's Ice Cream musical tune by turning the hand crank on the rear of the van
EX $55　　NM $110　　MIP $225

❑ **479-A, Commer Mobile Camera Van,** 1967-72, metallic blue lower body and roof rack, white upper body, two working rear doors, black camera on gold tripod, cameraman
EX $60　　NM $105　　MIP $195

❑ **508-A, Commer Holiday Mini Bus,** 1968-69, white upper body w/orange lower body, white interior, clear windshield, silver bumpers, grille and headlights, Holiday Camp Special decal, roof rack, two working rear doors. With bathing suits packed in the roof luggage, a trip to the shore was inevitable in this mod van
EX $30　　NM $75　　MIP $130

❑ **1006-A, Radio Roadshow Van,** 1982, white body, red plastic roof and rear interior, opaque black windows, red-white-black Radio Tele Luxembourg labels, gray plastic loudspeakers and working radio in van
EX $25　　NM $35　　MIP $60

Corgi Classics, Ltd. 1998-2002

The Mini Cooper, a popular release for Corgi is a detailed 1:36-scale model available in a range of colors.

*A*fter 1983, the future of Corgi was uncertain. The company fell into receivership, and only a buyout by management, renaming the company "Corgi Toys Limited," kept the venerable toy name alive.

One year later, the company's focus switched to producing high-quality die-cast models. Sales and Marketing Director, Chris Guest, brought Corgi's product strategy up to 1980s and '90s levels by finding out what the collecting public wanted. Over the next few years, an official Corgi Collector Club was formed—with the emphasis on collectibles rather than off-the-shelf toys.

In 1989, Corgi was sold to Mattel, who gave the company a much-needed infusion of cash. Now Corgi could market their Classics series worldwide.

MARKET UPDATE

The market for any collectible and limited edition die-cast is tricky. Some models seem to have more inherent or widely desired value than others. Licensed vehicles, such as Budweiser trucks or Texaco tankers are of interest to crossover collectors, and many of Corgi's newest series, such as the Vietnam-themed "Unsung Heroes" and "The Definitive Bond Collection" are quite popular.

By 1994, Corgi launched the now-famous "Original Omnibus" series. The 1990s also saw a return to licensed vehicles, including Mr. Bean's Mini, Beatles vehicles, Inspector Morse's Jaguar and others.

The year 1995 saw Corgi back in private hands with a buyout arranged by Chris Guest. By 1997, the French "Heritage Collection" was started, featuring Renaults, Peugeot, and other models. In 1998, the Aviation Archive series—detailed replicas of military and civilian aircraft—was unveiled.

Zindart Limited, a Hong Kong-based firm, acquired Corgi Classics in 1999 (around the same time that Corgi acquired Lledo, which had fallen into receivership.) Interestingly, Corgi and Lledo now share castings, making it fun to track down the elusive Corgi or Lledo version of a particular model, such as a Dodge WC-54 truck or a variation of the Trotter's van.

In Autumn 2001, Corgi released the Showcase collection, sharp-looking die-cast vehicles priced at about $6 each, or about $24 in sets of four. Not produced to any particular scale, these "fit-the-box" models are about four inches long and belong to themed series, such as Fire Heroes fire trucks or Fighter Scramble aircraft.

A re-issue of a famous casting, the Aston Martin DB5 from "Goldfinger." Corgi has been one of the most dynamic companies in acquiring licenses to pop-culture vehicles, including the Green Hornet "Black Beauty," the Starsky and Hutch Ford Gran Torino, the Monkeemobile, and the A-Team van.

From the Corgi Toys series, a police Range Rover with opening doors, tailgate and rear window.

Another from the Showcase collection, a GMC Chicago Fire Department pumper from the Fire Heroes series.

One of the Showcase collection vehicles, the GMC Paragon Oil Tanker, from the Texaco series. A nicely detailed truck with a heavy look and feel, too.

A great-looking model from Corgi, the Texaco Dodge 4x4 from the Showcase series. This casting was used by sister-company Lledo for many years.

Two more views of the wildly popular Mini Cooper. Corgi did a great job with this car, as the interior shot proves. The 1:36-scale size and under $20 price tag make it affordable and easy to display.

The Monkeemobile, a 1:36-scale car from Corgi's "TV and Film" collection. This series has been a favorite with fans of die-cast replicas and pop culture alike.

Another great car in the Texaco Showcase series, a Chevrolet Pickup carrying salt products.

The Renault 1000kg Van from the Heritage Collection, a series of French vehicles, first offered by Corgi in 1997. It's a fun range to choose vehicles from, since most non-American cars collected by die-cast fans are usually British or German. The detail and graphics on these models is outstanding, as usual.

Black Beauty, the Green Hornet's famous car, is another tribute to the 1960s that has gone over very well with collectors. This 1:36-scale model includes a figure of Kato, too.

SHOWCASE: THE TEXAS COMPANY

(Photo Courtesy of Corgi Classics, Inc.)

❏ **CS90001, Model T Ford Tanker- Texaco Petroleum Products,** 2001, Red cab, white roof, black tank, "Texaco" on roof, star graphic on tank and doors
EX n/a   NM n/a   MIP $5

(Photo Courtesy of Corgi Classics, Inc.)

❏ **CS90002, Dodge Airflow - Texaco Motor Oil,** 2001, This model shows a nice use of a former Lledo Days Gone casting
EX n/a   NM n/a   MIP $6

(Photo Courtesy of Corgi Classics, Inc.)

❏ **CS90003, Pontiac Van - Texaco Fire Chief Gasoline,** 2001, Black van with "Fire Chief Gasoline" on panel sides, red wheels, white stripes
EX n/a   NM n/a   MIP $8

(Photo Courtesy of Corgi Classics, Inc.)

❏ **CS90004, GMC Tanker - Texaco Paragon Oil,** 2001, Red cab, green tank with "Paragon" in white type
EX n/a   NM n/a   MIP $6

(Photo Courtesy of Corgi Classics, Inc.)

❏ **CS90005, Scenicruiser - Texas Pipeline,** 2001, Red with Texaco star graphics
EX n/a   NM n/a   MIP $6

(Photo Courtesy of Corgi Classics, Inc.)

❏ **CS90006, Dodge 4 x 4 - Texas Pipeline,** 2001, A nice use of a popular Lledo "Days Gone" casting
EX n/a   NM n/a   MIP $6

(Photo Courtesy of Corgi Classics, Inc.)

❏ **CS90007, Chevrolet Pick-up - Texaco Salt Products,** 2001, Light green body, black fenders, red wheels, Texaco star on sides, salt load in bed
EX n/a   NM n/a   MIP $6

(Photo Courtesy of Corgi Classics, Inc.)

❏ **CS90008, Ford Artic Tanker - Texaco Fire Chief Gasoline,** 2001, Red cab, black fenders, green tanker trailer
EX n/a   NM n/a   MIP $7

SHOWCASE: FIRE HEROES

(Photo Courtesy of Corgi Classics, Inc.)

❏ **CS90009, GMC Fire Pumper - Chicago F.D.,** 2001, Red cab and body, black roof, gray wheels
EX n/a   NM n/a   MIP $8

(Photo Courtesy of Corgi Classics, Inc.)

❏ **CS90010, American La France - Bethpage F.D.,** 2001, Red body, silver-gray wheels
EX n/a   NM n/a   MIP $6

CORGI / CLASSICS

(Photo Courtesy of Corgi Classics, Inc.)

❑ **CS90011, Mack B Open Pumper - Boston F.D.,** 2001, Red body, open cab, ladder and hose details
EX n/a　　　**NM** n/a　　　**MIP** $6

(Photo Courtesy of Corgi Classics, Inc.)

❑ **CS90012, Seagrave Sedan Pumper - San Francisco,** 2001, Red body, silver wheels, blue dome light
EX n/a　　　**NM** n/a　　　**MIP** $6

(Photo Courtesy of Corgi Classics, Inc.)

❑ **CS90013, Chevrolet Car - Fire Chief,** 2001, Red body, black interior, red wheels, silver grille and trim
EX n/a　　　**NM** n/a　　　**MIP** $7

(Photo Courtesy of Corgi Classics, Inc.)

❑ **CS90014, Pontiac Van - Newark F.D.,** 2001, Red body, "Newark Fire Department" on panel sides
EX n/a　　　**NM** n/a　　　**MIP** $6

(Photo Courtesy of Corgi Classics, Inc.)

❑ **CS90015, Ford Fire Pumper - Milwood NYFD,** 2001, Red and white body, red wheels, "MFD" on sides
EX n/a　　　**NM** n/a　　　**MIP** $6

(Photo Courtesy of Corgi Classics, Inc.)

❑ **CS90016, Mack Breakdown Truck - Baltimore FD Recovery,** 2001, White body, red fenders and chassis
EX n/a　　　**NM** n/a　　　**MIP** $7

SHOWCASE: FIGHTER SCRAMBLE

(Photo Courtesy of Corgi Classics, Inc.)

❑ **CS90017, P-51D Mustang - Bomber Escort "Bunnie",** 2001, Silver body, red nose and tail
EX n/a　　　**NM** n/a　　　**MIP** $8

(Photo Courtesy of Corgi Classics, Inc.)

❑ **CS90018, Mitsubishi Zero - Pearl Harbour Gray,** 2001, Light gray, blue stripes on fuselage, red sun graphics, black nose
EX n/a　　　**NM** n/a　　　**MIP** $6

(Photo Courtesy of Corgi)

❑ **CS90019, Supermarine Spitfire - D-8,** 2001, Olive and dark tan camo pattern, RAF markings
EX n/a　　　**NM** n/a　　　**MIP** $7

(Photo Courtesy of Corgi)

❑ **CS90020, B1109 Messerschmitt - Luftwaffe JG-3 "Udet",** 2001, Dark olive green and gray body
EX n/a　　　**NM** n/a　　　**MIP** $7

(Photo Courtesy of Corgi)

❏ **CS90021, P-38 Lightening - Pacific "Little Eva",** 2001, Silver body, blue stripes on tail section
EX n/a   **NM** n/a   **MIP** $6

(Photo Courtesy of Corgi)

❏ **CS90022, F-4U Corsair - US Navy (Pacific),** 2001, Dark blue upper, light blue underbody paint
EX n/a   **NM** n/a   **MIP** $6

SHOWCASE: TOUR OF DUTY: VIETNAM

(Photo Courtesy of Corgi)

❏ **CS90024, Bell Huey Iroquios, U.S. Army Medevac,** 2001, Part of a set of four vehicles, including an M48 Patton tank, a Willys Jeep and an M3 half track. Set of four vehicles price shown
EX n/a   **NM** n/a   **MIP** $22

(Photo Courtesy of Corgi)

❏ **CS90024, M3 Half Track, U.S. Army,** 2001, Dark green with white star graphics, ring-mounted machine gun. Set of four vehicles price shown
EX n/a   **NM** n/a   **MIP** $22

(Photo Courtesy of Corgi)

❏ **CS90024, M48 Patton Tank, U.S. Marine Corps,** 2001, Olive green with painted mud details on treads and body. Set of four vehicles price shown
EX n/a   **NM** n/a   **MIP** $22

(Photo Courtesy of Corgi)

❏ **CS90024, Willys Jeep, U.S. Marine Corps,** 2001, Dark green with painted mud on wheels. Set of four vehicles price shown
EX n/a   **NM** n/a   **MIP** $22

SHOWCASE: PORK CHOP HILL: THE FORGOTTEN HEROES OF KOREA

(Photo Courtesy of Corgi)

❏ **CS90023, WC-54, 4x4 Ambulance,** 2001, Part of a set of four vehicles, including a Willys Jeep, a Bell 47 chopper and an M3 Half Track. Set of four vehicles price shown
EX n/a   **NM** n/a   **MIP** $21

(Photo Courtesy of Corgi)

❏ **CS90023, Bell 47 Chopper,** 2001, Olive green with side-mounted stretchers. Set of four vehicles price shown
EX n/a   **NM** n/a   **MIP** $21

(Photo Courtesy of Corgi)

❏ **CS90023, M3 Half Track,** 2001, Light olive green with ring-mounted machine gun. Set of four vehicles price shown
EX n/a   **NM** n/a   **MIP** $21

(Photo Courtesy of Corgi)

❏ **CS90023, Willys Jeep,** 2001, Light olive-green with white star graphics. Set of four vehicles price shown
EX n/a   **NM** n/a   **MIP** $21

SHOWCASE: THEIR FINEST HOUR

(Photo Courtesy of Corgi)

CORGI / CLASSICS

❏ **CS90025, Morris Van: RAF Airfield Ambulance,** 2001, Blue-gray body with Red Cross marking, and painted mud on tires and chassis. One of a series of four vehicles including: Messerschmitt Bf 109E, Supermarine Spitfire, and AEC Ballast Tractor. Set of four vehicles price shown

EX n/a   NM n/a   MIP $21

(Photo Courtesy of Corgi)

❏ **CS90025, Messerschmitt Bf 109E Luftwaffe,** 2001, Green and gray camo with yellow trim. Set of four vehicle price shown

EX n/a   NM n/a   MIP $21

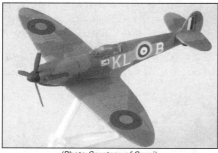

(Photo Courtesy of Corgi)

❏ **CS90025, Supermarine Spitfire Mk1 RAF,** 2001, Tan and olive camo pattern, RAF markings. Set of four vehicles price shown

EX n/a   NM n/a   MIP $21

(Photo Courtesy of Corgi)

❏ **CS90025, AEC "Matador" Ballast Tractor,** 2001, Blue-gray body, generator load in bed, gun cupola on roof. Set of four vehicles price shown

EX n/a   NM n/a   MIP $21

SHOWCASE: FOR KING AND COUNTRY

(Photo Courtesy of Corgi)

❏ **CS90026, Old Bill Bus: British Army Troop Carrier,** 2001, Olive-green double-decker bus with "16th Aux Omnibus" on sides. Part of a four-vehicle series, including: Sopwith Camel, Fokker DR1 and MkIV Tank Male. Set of four vehicles price shown

EX n/a   NM n/a   MIP $21

(Photo Courtesy of Corgi)

❏ **CS90026, Fokker DR1, German Air Force,** 2001, Red and white "Red Baron" colors, with Iron Cross insignia. Set of four vehicles price shown

EX n/a   NM n/a   MIP $21

(Photo Courtesy of Corgi)

❏ **CS90026, MkIV Tank Male: Fray Bentos,** 2001, Brown tank with painted mud and "Fray Bentos" and number "20" on sides. Set of four vehicles price shown

EX n/a   NM n/a   MIP $21

TV & FILM

❏ **CC05901, Bullitt - Ford Mustang with Frank Bullitt Figure,** 2002, Dark green car with Frank Bullit (Steve McQueen figure), 1:36 scale

EX n/a   NM n/a   MIP $28

(Photo Courtesy of Corgi)

❏ **CC99111, Only Fools and Horses Set - Ford Capri & Robin Reliant,** 2002, Lime green Ford Capri, comes with yellow Robin Reliant van, 1:43 scale

EX n/a   NM n/a   MIP $28

(Photo Courtesy of Corgi)

❏ **CC99111, Only Fools and Horses Set - Ford Capri & Robin Reliant,** 2002, Yellow 3-wheeled van, "Trotter's Trading" on sides, part of set with lime green Ford Capri. Set price shown, 1:43 scale

EX n/a   NM n/a   MIP $30

(Photo Courtesy of Corgi)

❏ **CC87503, Scooby Do - Mystery Machine with Shaggy & Scooby Figure,** 2002, Shaggy and Scooby figures included with Mystery Machine set. Price for set shown

EX n/a   NM n/a   MIP $28

(Photo Courtesy of Corgi)

❏ **CC87503, Scooby Doo - Mystery Machine with Shaggy & Scooby Figure,** 2002, Dark blue and lime green Mystery Machine van and Scooby and Shaggy figures, 1:36 scale
EX n/a **NM** n/a **MIP** $28

(Photo Courtesy of Corgi)

❏ **CC01701, Heartbeat - Morris Minor Traveller & Sergeant Oscar Blaketon Figure,** 2002, Dark gray vehicle, silver trim, 1:43 scale
EX n/a **NM** n/a **MIP** $26

(Photo Courtesy of Corgi)

❏ **CC01701, Heartbeat - Morris Minor Traveller & Sergeant Oscar Blaketon Figure,** 2002, Sergeant Oscar Blaketon figure with Heartbeat set. Price for set shown
EX n/a **NM** n/a **MIP** $26

(Photo Courtesy of Corgi)

❏ **CC82217, The Italian Job - Mini & Diorama Scene (Includes one diecast mini),** 2002, Diorama of columned building front with yellow steps and white Mini in background. Inlcudes red Mini die-cast vehicle, 1:36 scale
EX n/a **NM** n/a **MIP** $35

(Photo Courtesy of Corgi)

❏ **CC01601, Last of the Summer Wine - Triumph Herald Convertible & Edie Pegden Figure,** 2002, Red convertible with black interior, includes figure, 1:43 scale
EX n/a **NM** n/a **MIP** $25

(Photo Courtesy of Corgi)

❏ **CC07403, Last of the Summer Wine - Land Rover with Compo in chair Figure,** 2002, Dark green Land Rover pickup with figure in chair tumbling out, 1:43 scale
EX n/a **NM** n/a **MIP** $26

(Photo Courtesy of Corgi)

❏ **CC05301, The Dukes of Hazzard - The General Lee with Bo and Luke Duke Figures,** 2001, Bright red Dodge Charger with Bo and Luke Duke figures, 1:36 scale
EX n/a **NM** n/a **MIP** $27

(Photo Courtesy of Corgi)

❏ **CC05501, Back to the Future - DeLorean with Doc Brown Figure,** 2001, Silver DeLorean with Doc Brown figure. Car features opening gullwing doors, 1:36 scale
EX n/a **NM** n/a **MIP** $25

(Photo Courtesy of Corgi)

❏ **CC05501, Back to the Future - DeLorean with Doc Brown Figure,** 2001, Doc Brown figure included with Back to the Future set
EX n/a **NM** n/a **MIP** $25

(Photo Courtesy of Corgi)

❏ **CC05601, Knight Rider - Pontiac TransAm with Michael Knight Figure,** 2001, Black car features moving pulse/scanner at front of hood, 1:36 scale
EX n/a **NM** n/a **MIP** $24

(Photo Courtesy of Corgi)

❑ **CC87502, The A-Team - Van with BA Baracas Figure,** 2001, Black van with red stripe, rear doors open. Includes Mr. T figure, 1:36 scale
EX n/a   NM n/a   MIP $25

(Photo Courtesy of Corgi)

❑ **18501, Dad's Army - Bedford O Van & Hodges Figure,** 2001, Dark blue van with "W. Hodges" in gold type on panel sides. Includes Mr. Hodges figure, 1:50 scale
EX n/a   NM n/a   MIP $28

(Photo Courtesy of Corgi)

❑ **18501, Dad's Army - Bedford O Van & Hodges Figure,** 2001, Mr. Hodges figure included with set. Price for set shown
EX n/a   NM n/a   MIP $28

(Photo Courtesy of Corgi)

❑ **09002, Dad's Army - Thornycroft Van & Mr Jones Figure,** 2001, Dark blue and white van includes Mr. Jones figure in army fatigues, 1:50 scale
EX n/a   NM n/a   MIP $28

(Photo Courtesy of Corgi)

❑ **09002, Dad's Army - Thornycroft Van & Mr Jones Figure,** 2001, Mr. Jones figure included with set. Price for set with vehicle shown
EX n/a   NM n/a   MIP $28

(Photo Courtesy of Corgi)

❑ **01803, Inspector Morse - Jaguar MkII,** 2001, Deep red/burgundy car with black roof, 1:43 scale
EX n/a   NM n/a   MIP $24

(Photo Courtesy of Corgi)

❑ **00802, Fawlty Towers - Austin 1300 Estate with Basil Fawlty Figure,** 2001, Red car with black interior, black wheels, with gray hubcaps. Includes Basil Fawlty figure, 1:43 scale
EX n/a   NM n/a   MIP $21

(Photo Courtesy of Corgi)

❑ **39902, Marilyn Monroe - Ford Thunderbird with Marilyn Monroe Figure,** 2001, Pink convertible with whitewall tires, white interior, silver trim. Includes Marilyn figure, 1:36 scale
EX n/a   NM n/a   MIP $25

(Photo Courtesy of Corgi)

❑ **39902, Marilyn Monroe - Ford Thunderbird with Marilyn Monroe Figure,** 2001, Marylin figure included with set. Price for set with vehicle shown
EX n/a   NM n/a   MIP $25

(Photo Courtesy of Corgi)

❑ **CC50902, The Green Hornet - Black Beauty with Kato Figure,** 2001, Black car with ejecting scanner in trunk and missile launcher behind grille. Includes Kato figure, 1:36 scale
EX n/a   NM n/a   MIP $27

(Photo Courtesy of Corgi)

❑ **CC50902, The Green Hornet - Black Beauty with Kato Figure,** 2001, Kato figure included with Black Beauty model
EX n/a   NM n/a   MIP $27

(Photo Courtesy of Corgi)

❏ **57404, Return of the Saint - Jaguar XJS,** 2002, White Jaguar XJS, with cream interior, silver wheels. Includes Simon Templar figure, 1:36 scale
EX n/a   **NM** n/a   **MIP** $21

(Photo Courtesy of Corgi)

❏ **CC00401, The Professionals - Ford Capri,** 2002, Silver with opening doors, 1:36 scale
EX n/a   **NM** n/a   **MIP** $16

(Photo Courtesy of Corgi)

❏ **04419, Mr Bean's Mini,** 2001, Yellow and black car with opening doors, includes Mr. Bean figure, 1:36 scale
EX n/a   **NM** n/a   **MIP** $14

(Photo Courtesy of Corgi)

❏ **CC82215, The Italian Job - Mini,** 2001, Red mini with opening doors. Includes driver figure and stack of gold bars, 1:36 scale
EX n/a   **NM** n/a   **MIP** $21

(Photo Courtesy of Corgi)

❏ **CC87501, Charlie's Angels Van,** 2001, Hot pink van with Charlie's Angels' logo on sides. Opening rear doors, 1:36 scale
EX n/a   **NM** n/a   **MIP** $19

❏ **CC52405, The Monkees - Monkeemobile,** 2001, Red with white roof, yellow interior, Monkees' guitar logo on sides, 1:36 scale
EX n/a   **NM** n/a   **MIP** $17

❏ **CC00501, Kojak Buick Regal,** 2002, Metallic brown Buick with opening doors. Includes Kojak figure, 1:36 scale
EX n/a   **NM** n/a   **MIP** $29

(Photo Courtesy of Corgi)

❏ **05201, Only Fools and Horses - Reliant Regal Supervan 3 (Trotters Van),** 2001, Yellow 3-wheeled van with black roof. "Trotter's Independent Trading" on panel sides. Painted dirt appearance, 1:36 scale
EX n/a   **NM** n/a   **MIP** $21

(Photo Courtesy of Corgi)

❏ **00502, Z-Cars - Ford Zephyr,** 2001, Light blue-gray patrol car with blue dome light, "Police" on hood and roof, "Z Car" on front plate. Silver hubs and trim, 1:43 scale
EX n/a   **NM** n/a   **MIP** $21

❏ **CC00201, Starsky and Hutch - Ford Gran Torino,** 2002, Red car with famous white stripe, includes Starsky and Hutch figures, 1:36 scale
EX n/a   **NM** n/a   **MIP** $24

(Photo Courtesy of Corgi)

❏ **05506, The Italian Job Mini Set,** 2001, Includes red, white & blue Minis. Each features opening doors, 1:36 scale
EX n/a   **NM** n/a   **MIP** $40

(Photo Courtesy of Corgi)

❏ **05301, Chitty Chitty Bang Bang,** 2001, Features Caracatus Potts figure and extending wings
EX n/a   **NM** n/a   **MIP** $35

TV & FILM: THE MUPPETS

(Photo Courtesy of Corgi)

❑ **CC06601, The Muppets - Kermit's Car,** 2002, Mustard yellow convertible with Kermit figure as driver
EX n/a   NM n/a   MIP $7

(Photo Courtesy of Corgi)

❑ **CC06602, The Muppets - Fozzie Bear's Car,** 2002, Red truck with "Muppet Show" sign in bed, white tires, Fozzie as driver
EX n/a   NM n/a   MIP $7

(Photo Courtesy of Corgi)

❑ **CC06603, The Muppets - Miss Piggie's Car,** 2002, Pink car with silver trim and heart-shaped grille, white tires. Driver: Miss Piggy
EX n/a   NM n/a   MIP $7

(Photo Courtesy of Corgi)

❑ **CC06604, The Muppets - Animal's Car,** 2002, Black and red steam tractor with drums for wheels and Animal as driver
EX n/a   NM n/a   MIP $7

TV & FILM: THE BEATLES

(Photo Courtesy of Corgi)

❑ **58007, Newspaper Taxi,** 2001, White taxi with newspaper headlines graphics. Opening doors, 1:36 scale
EX n/a   NM n/a   MIP $16

(Photo Courtesy of Corgi)

❑ **42403, Magical Mystery Tour Bus,** 2001, Yellow and blue bus with "Magical Mystery Tour" rainbow-colored type on sides, 1:76 scale
EX n/a   NM n/a   MIP $24

(Photo Courtesy of Corgi)

❑ **35006, AEC Routemaster,** 2001, Dark green and off-white bus with "The Beatles" signage on sides, 1:50 scale
EX n/a   NM n/a   MIP $45

❑ **05404, Mini Yellow Submarine,** 2001, Yellow and white submarine with cartoon-style Beatles figures poking up through the hatches
EX n/a   NM n/a   MIP $18

TV & FILM: THE DEFINITVE BOND COLLECTION

(Photo Courtesy of Corgi)

❑ **05101, BMW 750i - Tomorrow Never Dies,** 2001, Silver car with black trim, firing rockets concealed in sunroof
EX n/a   NM n/a   MIP $17

(Photo Courtesy of Corgi)

❑ **04901, BMW Z3 - Goldeneye,** 2001, Metallic blue, cream interior, front-firing "Stinger" missiles, 1:36 scale
EX n/a   NM n/a   MIP $17

(Photo Courtesy of Corgi)

❑ **05001, BMW Z8 - The World is Not Enough,** 2001, Silver car with black interior and side-firing Stinger missiles, 1:36 scale
EX n/a   NM n/a   MIP $16

(Photo Courtesy of Corgi)

❑ **04801, Aston Martin V8 - The Living Daylights,** 2001, Charcoal-colored car with ejecting side-mounted skis, 1:36 scale
EX n/a   NM n/a   MIP $17

(Photo Courtesy of Corgi)

❑ **05701, Mercedes Saloon - Octopussy,** 2001, Black sedan with removable tires and railroad track display, 1:43 scale
EX n/a   NM n/a   MIP $16

(Photo Courtesy of Corgi)

❑ **04601, Gyrocopter - You Only Live Twice,** 2001, Yellow, black and silver copter with firing missile
EX n/a   NM n/a   MIP $17

❑ **02101, Mustang Mach I - Diamonds are Forever,** 2001, Red body, black chassis and base, opening doors, whitewall tires, silver wheels, 1:43 scale
EX n/a   NM n/a   MIP $16

(Photo Courtesy of Corgi)

❑ **CC99106, The Definitive Bond Film Canister 4 Piece Set (limited Edition),** 2001, Includes a vehicle driven by each Bond actor: "Goldfinger" Aston Martin DB5, "For Your Eyes Only" Lotus Esprit Turbo, "The Living Daylights" Aston Martin Volante and "Goldeneye" BMW Z3. Packaged in movie canister
EX n/a   NM n/a   MIP $80

(Photo Courtesy of Corgi)

❑ **04701, Lotus Esprit Turbo - For Your Eyes Only,** 2001, Red metallic with gold wheels and rear-mounted detachable skis, 1:36 scale
EX n/a   NM n/a   MIP $17

(Photo Courtesy of Corgi)

❑ **65002, Lotus Esprit - The Spy Who Loved Me,** 2001, White body, switches to submersible vehicle, firing surface-to-air missiles, 1:36 scale
EX n/a   NM n/a   MIP $18

❑ **04305, Aston Martin DB5 - Goldfinger,** 2001, Silver body, red interior, front machine guns, rear bullet shield, ejector seat, 1:36 scale
EX n/a   NM n/a   MIP $18

(Photo Courtesy of Corgi)

❑ **CC04101, Stromberg Helicopter - The Spy Who Loved Me,** 2001, Black helicopter with moving rotors and detailed interior
EX n/a   NM n/a   MIP $18

(Photo Courtesy of Corgi)

❑ **CC04401, Moonbuggy - Diamonds are Forever,** 2001, Silver and white buggy with moving mechanical arms and gripping hands, opening driver's hatch and rotating radar dish
EX n/a   NM n/a   MIP $18

(Photo Courtesy of Corgi)

❑ **CC06401, Renault Taxi - A View to a Kill,** 2001, Metallic blue with roof cab light, black trim, silver wheels and detailed interior. Opening rear hatch, 1:36 scale
EX n/a   NM n/a   MIP $18

(Photo Courtesy of Corgi)

❏ **CC06101, Double Deck Bus - Live and Let Die,** 2001, AEC Regent double decker bus in dark green and blue with "San Monique Transport" on sides. Removable upper deck
EX n/a　　**NM** n/a　　**MIP** $18

(Photo Courtesy of Corgi)

❏ **CC04001, Space Shuttle - Moonraker,** 2001, White shuttle with yellow stripes, features opening cargo bay doors, movable satellite, retractable undercarriage, satellite retrieval arm
EX n/a　　**NM** n/a　　**MIP** $18

(Photo Courtesy of Corgi)

❏ **65102, Toyota 2000 GT - You Only Live Twice,** 2001, White convertible with silver wheels and firing rockets from trunk, 1:43 scale,
EX n/a　　**NM** n/a　　**MIP** $17

(Photo Courtesy of Corgi)

❏ **CC85701, Citroen 2CV - For Your Eyes Only,** 2001, Yellow car with black top and opening hood, detailed interior, 1:36 scale,
EX n/a　　**NM** n/a　　**MIP** $18

(Photo Courtesy of Corgi)

❏ **CC99105, BMW Z8 & Diorama - The World Is Not Enough (Limited Edition),** 2001, Includes BMW Z8 car with side-firing missiles in front of diorama showing helicopter and burning buildings
EX n/a　　**NM** n/a　　**MIP** $42

COLLECTIBLES: HAULIERS OF RENOWN

(Photo Courtesy of Corgi)

❏ **CC12901, Scania Topline Curtainside - Eddie Stobart Ltd,** 2002, Dark green, red and white cab and trailer, produced from new tooling. Limited edition, 1:50 scale
EX n/a　　**NM** n/a　　**MIP** $88

(Photo Courtesy of Corgi)

❏ **CC12004, MAN Flatbed Trailer & Container Load - A.R.R. Craib Transport Ltd,** 2002, Light blue with dark blue and white stripes, containers on trailer, 1:50 scale
EX n/a　　**NM** n/a　　**MIP** $89

(Photo Courtesy of Corgi)

❏ **CC12801, Scania T-Cab Feldbinder Tanker - Ian Hayes Transport,** 2002, Blue and white with "Ian Hayes" on tanker section, opening hood and detailed engine, 1:50 scale
EX n/a　　**NM** n/a　　**MIP** $80

(Photo Courtesy of Corgi)

❏ **CC12409, Volvo FH Globetrotter Frdige Trailer - McBurney Transport Ltd,** 2002, Yellow cab with white trailer. Fully tilting cab and detailed engine, 1:50 scale
EX n/a　　**NM** n/a　　**MIP** $80

(Photo Courtesy of Corgi)

❏ **CC12505, Atkinson Borderer Tautliner - Richard Preston & Son Ltd,** 2002, Red cab, yellow and red trailer, red type, 1:50 scale
EX n/a　　**NM** n/a　　**MIP** $80

(Photo Courtesy of Corgi)

❑ **CC12702, ERF ECS Curtainside - Stoford Transport Ltd,** 2002, Dark yellow-orange and red cab and trailer, 1:50 scale
EX n/a   NM n/a   MIP $80

(Photo Courtesy of Corgi)

❑ **CC12802, Scania T-Cab Bulk Tipper - Eddie Stobart Ltd,** 2002, Opening hood with detailed engine, opening tailgate, working telescopic arm and tipper, 1:50 scale
EX n/a   NM n/a   MIP $80

(Photo Courtesy of Corgi)

❑ **CC12211, Scania Curtainside - Fagan & Whalley Ltd,** 2002, Black cab, red trailer with "FW" and "Fagan and Whalley" on sides, 1:50 scale
EX n/a   NM n/a   MIP $80

(Photo Courtesy of Corgi)

❑ **CC12703, ERF cab with ECS Flatbed Trailer - Vaughan Logistics Ltd,** 2002, White cab with blue stripes, blue flatbed trailer, "Vaughn" on front and sides of cab, 1:50 scale
EX n/a   NM n/a   MIP $79

(Photo Courtesy of Corgi)

❑ **CC12410, Volvo FH Bulk Tipper - Knowles Transport Ltd,** 2002, Red and white cab, red tipper trailer, telecscopic hydraulic ram and working tipper section, 1:50 scale
EX n/a   NM n/a   MIP $80

(Photo Courtesy of Corgi)

❑ **CC19901, Blue Curtainside Trailer,** 2001, Blue sides, black rear doors and roof, silver wheels. Fits with any of the cabs in this series, 1:50 scale
EX n/a   NM n/a   MIP $29

COLLECTIBLES: ROAD TRANSPORT HERITAGE

(Photo Courtesy of Corgi)

❑ **CC11504, AEC MkV 8-Wheel Platform Lorry & Tyre Load Spiers of Melksham,** 2002, Realistic tire load on silver flatbed, 1:50 scale
EX n/a   NM n/a   MIP $62

(Photo Courtesy of Corgi)

❑ **CC11607, Albion (LAD) 6-Wheel Dropside Lorry Jack Richards & Son Ltd,** 2002, Yellow body with red type, tan boards lining bed. Type along sides reads, "Leicester, Coventry, Birmingham, Derby, Nottingham, Mansfield", 1:50 scale
EX n/a   NM n/a   MIP $62

(Photo Courtesy of Corgi)

❑ **CC11403, Bedford KM Platform Trailer & Brick Load Knowles Transport Ltd,** 2002, Red and black cab with bricks on flatbed trailer, 1:50 scale
EX n/a   NM n/a   MIP $62

(Photo Courtesy of Corgi)

❑ **CC10601, Leyland Octopus Sheeted Platform Lorry &Trailer Road Services (Caledonian) Ltd,** 2002, Red and white cab, red chassis, 1:50 scale
EX n/a   NM n/a   MIP $76

(Photo Courtesy of Corgi)

❏ **CC10803, Foden S21 Tipper & Gravel Load Sam Longson Ltd,** 2002, Cream cab, silver tipper section with detailed gravel load, 1:50 scale

EX n/a   NM n/a   MIP $62

COLLECTIBLES: HEAVY HAULAGE

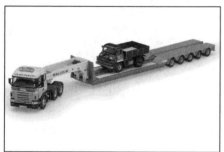

(Photo Courtesy of Corgi)

❏ **CC12210, Scania Low Loader & Thames Trader Tipper W.H.Malcolm Ltd,** 2002, Yellow, light green and blue cab and trailer with Thames Tipper, 1:50 scale

EX n/a   NM n/a   MIP $124

(Photo Courtesy of Corgi)

❏ **CC12506, Atkinson Venturer 2-axle low loader Wynns Heavy Haulage,** 2002, Red, white and black cab, red trailer with yellow "Wynn's" lettering, 1:50 scale

EX n/a   NM n/a   MIP $80

COLLECTIBLES: DIBNAHS CHOICE

(Photo Courtesy of Corgi)

❏ **CC20301, Garret 4CD Showmans Tractor (The Mighty Atom),** 2002, Black tractor with white roof and wheels, removable chimney, real chains, 1:50 scale

EX n/a   NM n/a   MIP $42

(Photo Courtesy of Corgi)

❏ **CC20203, Foden Steam Tanker Anglo American Oil Co.Ltd,** 2002, Black truck with white lettering on tank and cab, 1:50 scale

EX n/a   NM n/a   MIP $52

COLLECTIBLES: LAND ROVER

(Photo Courtesy of Corgi)

❏ **CC07404, Land Rover Canvas Back - Green,** 2002, Dark green body, tan canvas top, painted mud (just like it's been in an English field). Limited edition, 1:43 scale

EX n/a   NM n/a   MIP $21

(Photo Courtesy of Corgi)

❏ **CC07405, Land Rover & Trailer - Rover Mobile Service School,** 2002, Red and cream body and trailer, spare tire on hood, "Mobile Service School" on sides, 1:43 scale

EX n/a   NM n/a   MIP $30

(Photo Courtesy of Corgi)

❏ **CC07406, Land Rover - RAC,** 2002, Dark blue body with white roof, black antenna, silver grille and bumpers, 1:43 scale

EX n/a   NM n/a   MIP $21

COLLECTIBLES: 9 DOUBLE 9 COLLECTION

(Photo Courtesy of Corgi)

❏ **CC13001, Dennis F15 Rear Pumper- Blackburn Fire Brigade,** 2002, Red body, removable individual ladders, 1:50 scale

EX n/a   NM n/a   MIP $56

(Photo Courtesy of Corgi)

❑ **CC06202, Morris J Ambulance - Nottingham City Ambulance Service,** 2002, Cream-colored body, black wheels, green hubs, jewelled headlights, photo-etched wipers, 1:43 scale

EX n/a   **NM** n/a   **MIP** $21

(Photo Courtesy of Corgi)

❑ **US53504, American La France 700 2 Door Pumper - Elkhart, IN,** 2002, Red with silver detailing, 1:50 scale

EX n/a   **NM** n/a   **MIP** $56

(Photo Courtesy of Corgi)

❑ **CC06301, Daimler Conquest Ambulance/Barker - City of Birmingham Ambulance Service,** 2002, White with silver trim, blue dome light, tinted windows, 1:50 scale

EX n/a   **NM** n/a   **MIP** $32

(Photo Courtesy of Corgi)

❑ **CC10304, AEC Pump Ladder - Leicester City Fire Brigade,** 2002, Red and silver engine with Ergomatic cab, revised body tooling, new ladders, 1:50 scale

EX n/a   **NM** n/a   **MIP** $56

(Photo Courtesy of Corgi)

❑ **CC02301, Ford Transit MkI Emergency Tender - Warwickshire County Fire Brigade,** 2002, Red with blue roof lights, "Rescue" on sides, 1:43 scale

EX n/a   **NM** n/a   **MIP** $23

COLLECTIBLES: GOLDEN ELIZABETH II GOLDEN JUBILEE

(Photo Courtesy of Corgi)

❑ **CC25902, Routemaster Bus,** 2002, Black and gold, gold roof, "Golden Jubilee" on sides, 1:50 scale

EX n/a   **NM** n/a   **MIP** $56

(Photo Courtesy of Corgi)

❑ **CC25206, Open Top Tram,** 2002, Black and gold, "Queen Elizabeth II 1952-2002" and "Golden Jubilee" on sides, 1:72 scale

EX n/a   **NM** n/a   **MIP** $32

(Photo Courtesy of Corgi)

❑ **CC09901, State Landau,** 2002, Carriage, towed by four horses on wooden base, 1:40 scale

EX n/a   **NM** n/a   **MIP** $90

(Photo Courtesy of Corgi)

❑ **CC25903, Gold Plated Routemaster Bus,** 2002, , 1:50 scale

EX n/a   **NM** n/a   **MIP** $65

(Photo Courtesy of Corgi)

❑ **CC25207, Gold Plated Fully Closed Tram,** 2002, Gold with black roof, 1:72 scale

EX n/a   **NM** n/a   **MIP** $45

COLLECTIBLES: ORIGINAL OMNIBUS

(Photo Courtesy of Corgi)

❏ **OM43601, Plaxton Palatine - Harris Bus, Grays,** 2002, Bright lime green and bright medium blue body, "Lakeside Lines" on sides, 1:76 scale
EX n/a   NM n/a   MIP $25

(Photo Courtesy of Corgi)

❏ **OM40501, Feltham Tram - London Passenger Transport Board,** 2002, Red with black roof, "The Morning Post" and "Whitbread's Ale & Stout" on sides, 1:76 scale
EX n/a   NM n/a   MIP $40

(Photo Courtesy of Corgi)

❏ **OM43304, Plaxton Excalibur - Elcock Reisen,** 2002, Silver body with red and yellow stripe and "Elcock Reisen" on sides. Posable wheels, 1:76 scale
EX n/a   NM n/a   MIP $27

(Photo Courtesy of Corgi)

❏ **OM45705, AEC Q Double Deck Bus - Westcliff-on-Sea Motor Services Ltd,** 2002, Red and white with black trim, limited edition, 1:76 scale
EX n/a   NM n/a   MIP $30

(Photo Courtesy of Corgi)

❏ **OM45109, MCW Metrobus MkII - West Bromwich Corporation (Heritage),** 2002, Dark green and yellow, details including No Smoking sign and tax disc. Limited edition, 1:76 scale
EX n/a   NM n/a   MIP $31

(Photo Courtesy of Corgi)

❏ **OM43702, AEC 6641T Trolleybus - Cardiff Corporation Transport Dept.,** 2002, Matte gray wartime finish with "Hancock's Amber Ale" on sides. Limited edition, 1:76 scale
EX n/a   NM n/a   MIP $31

(Photo Courtesy of Corgi)

❏ **OM42405, Leyland Leopard/Panorama I - Ribble Motor Services Ltd, Preston,** 2002, Green and dark yellow, chrome grille and trim, photo-etched wipers, made from new tooling. Limited edition, 1:76 scale
EX n/a   NM n/a   MIP $31

(Photo Courtesy of Corgi)

❏ **OM41905, Leyland PD3 Queen Mary Open Top Bus - Southdown Motor Services Ltd,** 2002, Green and yellow, black interior, "Let Southdown Show You" on sides, front and rear windshields on upper deck, photo-etched wipers and radiator. Limited edition, 1:76 scale
EX n/a   NM n/a   MIP $31

(Photo Courtesy of Corgi)

❏ **OM43401, Plaxton Beaver - Stagecoach Ribble,** 2002, Red, white and blue stripe design, black base. Limited edition, 1:76 scale
EX n/a   NM n/a   MIP $23

(Photo Courtesy of Corgi)

❏ **OM40502, Feltham Tram - Leeds City Transport Dept.,** 2002, Red and white with "Say CWS and SAVE" on sides. Comes in special presentation packaging with display plinth, 1:76 scale
EX n/a   NM n/a   MIP $40

(Photo Courtesy of Corgi)

❑ **OM43908, Daimler CW Utility Bus - Belfast Corporation Transport Dept.,** 2002, Red and white with black base, "Craig's Coal" on sides, black wheels and grille. Limited edition, 1:76 scale
EX n/a   NM n/a   MIP $27

(Photo Courtesy of Corgi)

❑ **OM42901, Optare Delta - Metro Coastlines (Blackpool Transport),** 2002, Yellow, black and tan, 1:76 scale
EX n/a   NM n/a   MIP $27

(Photo Courtesy of Corgi)

❑ **OM43504, Blackpool Balloon Tram- Eclipse,** 2002, Black, red and orange, "Eclipse" on sides, 1:76 scale
EX n/a   NM n/a   MIP $37

(Photo Courtesy of Corgi)

❑ **OM44004, Blackpool Brush Railcoach - Mystique,** 2002, Black with "Mystique" in outlined type, and "Appearing and Disappearing Nightly" on sides, 1:76 scale
EX n/a   NM n/a   MIP $34

(Photo Courtesy of Corgi)

❑ **OM40801, Bristol Lodekka FS - Southdown Motor Services Ltd,** 2002, Green and dark yellow, 1:76 scale
EX n/a   NM n/a   MIP $30

(Photo Courtesy of Corgi)

❑ **OM45605, BMMO D9 - Midland Red,** 2002, Red body and wheels, silver trim, "Express Coach Services" on sides. Limited edition, 1:76 scale
EX n/a   NM n/a   MIP $27

(Photo Courtesy of Corgi)

❑ **OM43303, Plaxton Premiere - Blackburn Transport,** 2002, Off-white with green design and compass graphic, "Coachline" in green type, poseable wheels. Limited edition, 1:76 scale
EX n/a   NM n/a   MIP $27

(Photo Courtesy of Corgi)

❑ **OM45706, AEC Q Double Deck Bus- Kingston-upon-Hull Corporation Transport,** 2002, Blue and white with black roof, handrails, photo-etched wipers, removable engine cover. Limited edition, 1:76 scale
EX n/a   NM n/a   MIP $30

(Photo Courtesy of Corgi)

❑ **OM40802, Bristol Lodekka FS6B - Brighton, Hove & District Omnibus Co. Ltd,** 2002, Red and cream body, black wheels, silver grille, "Gilkes Wallpapers" on sides, new tooling. Limited edition, 1:76 scale
EX n/a   NM n/a   MIP $30

(Photo Courtesy of Corgi)

❑ **OM45110, MCW Metrobus MkI - West Midlands Passenger Transport Executive,** 2002, Red and dark yellow with Post Office graphics and "Twice as many goods and services as seats on this bus at your post office" on sides, 1:76 scale
EX n/a   NM n/a   MIP $27

(Photo Courtesy of Corgi)

❑ **OM42602, Bedford OB Coach - Bibby's of Ingleton,** 2002, Green and off-white, silver trim. Limited edition, 1:76 scale
EX n/a   NM n/a   MIP $23

COLLECTIBLES: ORIGINAL OMNIBUS: CARD KITS

(Photo Courtesy of Corgi)

❑ **44902, Victoria Coach Station,** 2001, , 1:76 scale
EX n/a   NM n/a   MIP $23

(Photo Courtesy of Corgi)

❑ **44903, Marton Depot, Blackpool,** 2000, 1:76 scale
EX n/a   NM n/a   MIP $23

(Photo Courtesy of Corgi)

❑ **44904, Southdown Bus Depot/Garage,** 2000, 1:76 scale
EX n/a   NM n/a   MIP $23

(Photo Courtesy of Corgi)

❑ **OM44901, Midland Red Bus/Coach Station,** 2001, 1:76 scale
EX n/a   NM n/a   MIP $12

COLLECTIBLES: TRAMWAY CLASSICS

(Photo Courtesy of Corgi)

❑ **CC25205, Double Deck Closed Tram - Nottingham Corporation Tramways,** 2002, Dark red and yellow, black roof, "Nottingham Evening Post" on sides
EX n/a   NM n/a   MIP $25

(Photo Courtesy of Corgi)

❑ **CC25202, Double Deck Fully Closed Tram - London Transport,** 2001, Red with off-white/yellow trim, "Wisk Washes Cleaner, Faster" on sides, glazed windows, trolley pole, detailed chassis. Limited edition
EX n/a   NM n/a   MIP $28

(Photo Courtesy of Corgi)

❑ **CC25203, Double Deck Fully Closed Tram - Liverpool Corporation Passenger Transport,** 2001, Dark green with yellow trim, black roof, "Phillips Sports" on sides
EX n/a   NM n/a   MIP $25

(Photo Courtesy of Corgi)

❑ **CC25204, Double Deck Fully Closed Tram - Bolton Corporation,** 2001, Dark red/burgundy body with white trim and black roof, "Bolton Corporation" along bottom sides
EX n/a   NM n/a   MIP $25

COLLECTIBLES: CONNOISSEUR CLASSICS

(Photo Courtesy of Corgi)

❑ **CC25901, AEC Routemaster - Metroline,** 2001, Red body, black wheels, "Live Life to the Full" in blue type on left side, "We meet at last, Mr. Bond," on right, 1:50 scale
EX n/a   NM n/a   MIP $45

(Photo Courtesy of Corgi)

❑ **35102, AEC Routemaster Open Top - London Coaches,** 2001, Red body with white open upper deck, detailed figures, 1:50 scale
EX n/a   NM n/a   MIP $42

COLLECTIBLES: MINI MANIA

(Photo Courtesy of Corgi)

❑ **CC82214, Mini 40 - Ian Gunn (Mini Miglia),** 2002, Mustard yellow body, number "6" on hood and doors, "Beechdean" on sides and hood, silver wheels, black grille, 1:36 scale
EX n/a   NM n/a   MIP $16

(Photo Courtesy of Corgi)

❑ **CC82216, Mini Classic - Dave Banwell,** 2002, Dark green body with yellow trim, sponsor graphics, yellow roof with "Total" red and blue logo, silver wheels, "Selby" on sides, 1:36 scale
EX n/a   NM n/a   MIP $16

(Photo Courtesy of Corgi)

❑ **CC99109, The Last Cooper S set,** 2002, Includes three Minis (red, white and blue) on a dashboard-dial stand, with the words "End of an Era" on nameplate in front, 1:36 scale
EX n/a   NM n/a   MIP $76

(Photo Courtesy of Corgi)

❑ **CC86501, The New Mini Cooper - Red,** 2001, Red body, black trim, white roof, five-spoke wheels, opening doors, 1:36 scale
EX n/a   NM n/a   MIP $16

(Photo Courtesy of Corgi)

❑ **CC86502, The New Mini Cooper - Silver,** 2001, Silver body, black roof, seven-spoke wheels, opening doors, 1:36 scale
EX n/a   NM n/a   MIP $16

(Photo Courtesy of Corgi)

❑ **CC86503, The New Mini Cooper - Black,** 2001, Black body, white roof, seven-holed white wheels, opening doors, 1:36 scale
EX n/a   NM n/a   MIP $16

(Photo Courtesy of Corgi)

❑ **CC86504, The New Mini Cooper - Dakar Yellow,** 2001, Deep yellow body, black trim, black roof, white five-spoke wheels, opening doors, 1:36 scale
EX n/a   NM n/a   MIP $16

(Photo Courtesy of Corgi)

❑ **CC86505, The New Mini Cooper - Flamenco Orange,** 2001, Bright red-orange body, black roof, black trim, white five-spoke wheels, opening doors, 1:36 scale
EX n/a   NM n/a   MIP $16

(Photo Courtesy of Corgi)

❑ **CC86506, The New Mini Cooper - British Racing Green,** 2001, Dark green body, white roof, white five-spoke wheels, opening doors, detailed black interior, 1:36 scale
EX n/a   NM n/a   MIP $16

(Photo Courtesy of Corgi)

❏ **CC82206, Mini 40 - Dark Mulberry Red,** 2001, Dark almost purple-red, opening doors, black interior, silver wheels and grille, 1:36 scale
EX n/a   NM n/a   MIP $16

(Photo Courtesy of Corgi)

❏ **CC82207, Mini 40 - Old English White,** 2001, Off-white body, black interior, opening doors, silver grille and wheels, 1:36 scale
EX n/a   NM n/a   MIP $16

(Photo Courtesy of Corgi)

❏ **CC82208, Mini 40 - Island Blue,** 2001, Bright blue body, yellow pinstripe, black interior, opening doors, silver wheels and grille, 1:36 scale
EX n/a   NM n/a   MIP $16

COLLECTIBLES: LEGENDS OF SPEED

(Photo Courtesy of Corgi)

❏ **00201, Bentley Racing Car,** 2001, British Racing Green body with number "1" and Union Jack graphics on sides, silver grille and multi-spoked wheels
EX n/a   NM n/a   MIP $8

❏ **00202, Bugatti Racing Car,** 2001, Blue body, number "3" on sides and tail, black interior
EX n/a   NM n/a   MIP $8

❏ **00203, Mercedes-Benz Racing Car,** 2001, Silver body, black interior, multi-spoked wheels, chrome exhaust pipes on sides
EX n/a   NM n/a   MIP $8

COLLECTIBLES: EDDIE STOBART

(Photo Courtesy of Corgi)

❏ **CC82204, Manx Rally Mini (Plant Bros.),** 2001, Sponsor graphics, number "61" on sides, red trim, silver wheels, black interior, 1:36 scale
EX n/a   NM n/a   MIP $16

(Photo Courtesy of Corgi)

❏ **CC85801, Reliant Regal Van,** 2001, Three-wheeled van in Eddie Stobart dark green and red colors, 1:36 scale
EX n/a   NM n/a   MIP $16

COLLECTIBLES: HEROES UNDER FIRE

(Photo Courtesy of Corgi)

❏ **US50504, Seagrave Safety Sedan Van Pumper: Detroit, MI,** 2002, Red body with silver trim, side-mounted ladders, red roof light. New casting, 6" x 2", 1:50 scale
EX n/a   NM n/a   MIP $32

(Photo Courtesy of Corgi)

❏ **US50503, Seagrave 70th Anniversary, Miami, FL,** 2001, Red with silver running boards, detailed equipment, 6" x 2", 1:50 scale
EX n/a   NM n/a   MIP $40

(Photo Courtesy of Corgi)

❏ **US54905, E-1 Ladder: Anne Arundel County, MD,** 2001, White with yellow stripe, "A.A. County Fire Department" on sides. Fully extendable ladder on pivoting base, realistic pump and panel detail, 8.5" x 11". Limited edition, 1:50 scale
EX n/a   NM n/a   MIP $45

(Photo Courtesy of Corgi)

❏ **US50801, Seagrave K: Jackson, TN,** 2001, Red body with realistic pump and panel design. 6" x 2", 1:50 scale
EX n/a   NM n/a   MIP $40

(Photo Courtesy of Corgi)

❏ **US50802, Seagrave K: NASA, FL,** 2001, White body, silver running boards, realistic hose reels and panel sections. 7.5" x 2", 1:50 scale

EX n/a   NM n/a   **MIP** $40

(Photo Courtesy of Corgi)

❏ **US52208, E-1 Sidemount Pumper: Fairfax County, VA,** 2001, Red and white body, yellow and black hoses. 7.5" x 2", 1:50 scale

EX n/a   NM n/a   **MIP** $45

(Photo Courtesy of Corgi)

❏ **US53803, Mack CF Tower: Philadelphia, PA,** 2001, Red body, white and silver extending ladder on pivoting base. 9" x 2", 1:50 scale

EX n/a   NM n/a   **MIP** $65

(Photo Courtesy of Corgi)

❏ **US50804, Seagrave K: Baltimore, MD,** 2002, White body with red panels and fenders (red fenders are required in Baltimore for all active engines), realistic hoses and pike poles. 6" x 2", 1:50 scale

EX n/a   NM n/a   **MIP** $35

(Photo Courtesy of Corgi)

❏ **US53804, Mack CF Tower: Bethpage, NY,** 2002, Red and white body, white tower/ladder boom with "Bethpage F.D." on sides, fully extending ladder on pivot base, working ground jacks, 9" x 2", 1:50 scale

EX n/a   NM n/a   **MIP** $60

(Photo Courtesy of Corgi)

❏ **US53504, American LaFrance 700 Pumper: Elkhart, IN,** 2002, Red body, side-mounted ladders, red wheels, detailed hoses. New casting, 6.5" x 2", 1:50 scale

EX n/a   NM n/a   **MIP** $56

COLLECTIBLES: CHICAGO FIRE DEPARTMENT

(Photo Courtesy of Corgi)

❏ **US50803, Seagrave J: Engine Co. 54 with Figures,** 2002, Red body with black-roofed cab, silver side-mounted ladders, 6.5" x 2", 1:50 scale

EX n/a   NM n/a   **MIP** $40

(Photo Courtesy of Corgi)

❏ **US50602, Dodge Monaco Battalion Chief's Car with Figures,** 2002, Red car with black roof and red dome lights, number "7" on rear doors, "Chicago Fire Department" on front quarter panels, 5.25" x 1.75", 1:43 scale

EX n/a   NM n/a   **MIP** $21

(Photo Courtesy of Corgi)

❏ **US52007, Mack CF Pumper: Engine Co. 35 with Figures,** 2002, Red body with black-roofed cab, white fire hose, white number "35" on sides, red number "35" on roof, includes firemen carrying ladder, 1:50 scale

EX n/a   NM n/a   **MIP** $36

COLLECTIBLES: VINTAGE BUS LINES

(Photo Courtesy of Corgi)

❑ **US53404, MCI 102 DL3 Greyhound,** 2001, White body with white wheels, black trim, Greyhound logo, 11"x2"
EX n/a   NM n/a   MIP $72

(Photo Courtesy of Corgi)

❑ **US54310, GM Fishbowl: Chicago Transit Authority,** 2001, Silver, green and off-white body, white wheels, 11"x2"
EX n/a   NM n/a   MIP $55

(Photo Courtesy of Corgi)

❑ **US55019, PCC Streetcar: Capital Transit,** 2001, Gray-blue and light gray body, "Capital Transit" in script on sides, 11"x2"
EX n/a   NM n/a   MIP $55

(Photo Courtesy of Corgi)

❑ **US55020, PCC Streetcar: New Jersey Transit,** 2001, White with black trim, blue, magenta and orange stripe, 11"x1.5"
EX n/a   NM n/a   MIP $45

COLLECTIBLES: HEAVY HAULERS

(Photo Courtesy of Corgi)

❑ **US55103, Diamond T980 Girder Trailer and Transformer Load: Gerosa,** 2001, Green, white and red tractor and trailer, gray transformer, "Heavy Hauling" on truck, "Gerosa" on truck and trailer, 21" x 2.5", 1:50 scale
EX n/a   NM n/a   MIP $100

(Photo Courtesy of Corgi)

❑ **US55702, Kenworth W925 with Low Loader and Boiler Load,** 2001, Blue cab and brick red trailer, gray wheels, black boiler, 21" x 2.5", 1:50 scale
EX n/a   NM n/a   MIP $100

(Photo Courtesy of Corgi)

❑ **US50705, Mack LJ Logger: Lifefoot Logging,** 2001, White cab and trailer with blue wheels and trim, "Lifefoot Logging of Republic, WA" on trailer, 14" x 2", 1:50 scale
EX n/a   NM n/a   MIP $60

(Photo Courtesy of Corgi)

❑ **US51401, International Transtar: Girder Trailer,** 2001, Two-tone brown cab with silver trim and wheels towing huge reddish brown girder, 18" x 2.25", 1:50 scale
EX n/a   NM n/a   MIP $100

(Photo Courtesy of Corgi)

❑ **US51402, International Transtar with King Trailer: Texas Pipeline,** 2002, Red and black cab, red trailer hauling gray sub. Sub has "Star Explorer" on conning tower and Texaco star graphic on sides, 21" x 2", 1:50 scale
EX n/a   NM n/a   MIP $100

(Photo Courtesy of Corgi)

❑ **US51403, International Transtar with King Trailer: Sulley Trucking,** 2002, Red and white cab with chrome wheels, airscoops and front bumper, mustard-orange trailer, tilting cab and engine detail, 17.5" x 2.25". New casting, 1:50 scale
EX n/a   NM n/a   MIP $90

(Photo Courtesy of Corgi)

❑ **US55704, Kenworth with Pipe Load and Mutt Escort Vehicle: Texa Pipeline,** 2002, Red cab with black fenders, silver wheels and trim, red trailer section, gray pipe load. Jeep "Mutt" is red with black interior, yellow "Caution" sign in back, black wheels, 1:50 scale
EX n/a   NM n/a   MIP $120

(Photo Courtesy of Corgi)

❑ **US55705, Kenworth W925 with Cold-Cast Porcelain Rock Crusher Load: Interstate Heavy Hauling,** 2002, Black and mustard-yellow cab with Interstate logo on grille, "Oversize Load" sign on top of cab. Black trailer carries yellow and black porcelain rock crusher. 21" x 2.25", 1:50 scale
EX n/a   NM n/a   MIP $128

(Photo Courtesy of Corgi)

❏ **US55706, Kenworth W925 with Culvert Load: Cast Transportation,** 2002, Red cab with black chassis and silver trim, red trailer with six culverts, 13.5" x 2.25", 1:50 scale
EX n/a **NM** n/a **MIP** $60

COLLECTIBLES: BUDWEISER

(Photo Courtesy of Corgi)

❏ **US50706, Mack LJ Hauling a Budweiser Sign,** 2002, Red with red wheels, large sign on red trailer, 11.75" x 2", 1:50 scale
EX n/a **NM** n/a **MIP** $55

(Photo Courtesy of Corgi)

❏ **US52310, Mack B Box Van,** 2002, Red cab and wheels, white van section, black and silver grille, 1:50 scale
EX n/a **NM** n/a **MIP** $35

(Photo Courtesy of Corgi)

❏ **US55022, PCC Streetcar: Budweiser "Ballpark" Destination,** 2002, Red and black with 1950s-era advertising on sides, 11" x 1.5", 1:50 scale
EX n/a **NM** n/a **MIP** $45

COLLECTIBLES: TEXACO

(Photo Courtesy of Corgi)

❏ **US50407, Huey Iroquios: Texas Pipeline,** 2001, Red with silver rotors, "Air Service Operations" and Texaco star on sides, black skids, 10" x 2.25", 1:48 scale
EX n/a **NM** n/a **MIP** $40

(Photo Courtesy of Corgi)

❏ **US51504, American LaFrance 900, Closed Pumper: Texas Pipeline,** 2001, Red with black fenders, front bumper and rear panels, "F1" on roof and rear tarp, 6.5" x 2", 1:50 scale
EX n/a **NM** n/a **MIP** $37

(Photo Courtesy of Corgi)

❏ **53503, Mack B Series Semi with Lowboy and Luffing Shovel,** 2000, Red cab with black fenders, red and black steamshovel on trailer, silver trim, 1:50 scale
EX n/a **NM** n/a **MIP** $76

(Photo Courtesy of Corgi)

❏ **54015, GM 4507 Texaco Crew Bus,** 2000, Red body with black wheels, "Texaco" on front, "The Texas Pipe Line Company" on sides, 1:50 scale
EX n/a **NM** n/a **MIP** $45

(Photo Courtesy of Corgi)

❏ **55610, Diamond T980 Wrecker and Trailer with pipes,** 2000, Red and black wrecker with Texaco star on sides, gray and black trailer with pipe load, red wheels, 1:50 scale
EX n/a **NM** n/a **MIP** $52

(Photo Courtesy of Corgi)

❏ **56204, Diamond T620 Semi with Skirted Tanker,** 2000, Red and black cab with red tanker. "Line Wash" on sides of tanker, 1:50 scale
EX n/a **NM** n/a **MIP** $45

(Photo Courtesy of Corgi)

❏ **55304, Diamond T980 Ballast and 24-wheel Low Loader,** 2000, Red and black cab with red trailer hauling gray "nodding donkey" oil well pump, 1:50 scale
EX n/a **NM** n/a **MIP** $89

(Photo Courtesy of Corgi)

❑ **50201, M35 A1 "Deuce and 1/2" 2.5-ton truck,** 2000, Red and black truck with white roof on cab, Texaco star on doors, 1:50 scale
EX n/a   NM n/a   MIP $45

(Photo Courtesy of Corgi)

❑ **50102, M151 A1 "Mutt" Utility Truck,** 2000, Red Jeep with black seats towing red utility trailer, 1:43 scale
EX n/a   NM n/a   MIP $30

COLLECTIBLES: FORGOTTEN HEROES OF THE KOREAN WAR

(Photo Courtesy of Corgi)

❑ **US51003, M4A3 HVSS POA-CWS-H5 Sherman Flame Tank: USMC,** 2002, Olive tank with painted mud, white star and "F21" on turret, 7" x 2.5", new casting, 1:50 scale
EX n/a   NM n/a   MIP $32

(Photo Courtesy of Corgi)

❑ **US51703, WC51 Weapons Carrier: US Army,** 2002, Olive with tarp partially covering cargo, painted dust on windshield and fenders, white star on hood and sides, 3.75" x 2", 1:43 scale
EX n/a   NM n/a   MIP $30

(Photo Courtesy of Corgi)

❑ **US51902, H13 Bell Helicopter: US Army Medical Service Corps,** 2002, Olive lattice-body, black top rotor, side-mounted stretchers with red cross insignia, 9" x 3", 1:48 scale
EX n/a   NM n/a   MIP $32

COLLECTIBLES: ADVERSARIES

(Photo Courtesy of Corgi)

❑ **US51601, T34/85 Tank: North Korean 109th Tank Regiment,** 2002, Olive body with painted dust, number "316" on turret, 5" x 2.25". This tank is a companion piece to the Forgotten Heroes series, but sold in special "Adversaries" packaging, 1:50 scale
EX n/a   NM n/a   MIP $32

COLLECTIBLES: UNSUNG HEROES

(Photo Courtesy of Corgi)

❑ **50101, M151 A1 "Mutt" Utility Truck: USMC,** 2000, Olive Jeep towing tarp-covered trailer, painted dust, yellow lettering on hood and side of trailer, 1:43 scale
EX n/a   NM n/a   MIP $30

(Photo Courtesy of Corgi)

❑ **50202, M35 A1 "Deuce and 1/2" 2.5 Ton Truck: US Army,** 2000, Olive body with stake sides, no tarp, painted dusty appearance, white star on hood and sides, 1:50 scale
EX n/a   NM n/a   MIP $45

(Photo Courtesy of Corgi)

❑ **50301, M48 A3 "Patton" Main Battle Tank: USMC,** 2000, Dark olive body with painted mud, yellow type says "Eve of Destruction" on barrel, flags on antenna, including Maryland state flag, great detail, 1:50 scale
EX n/a   NM n/a   MIP $47

(Photo Courtesy of Corgi)

❑ **50401, UH-1C "Huey Hog" Gunship Helicopter: US Army,** 2000, Green body, side-mounted rockets, black type "United States Army" on tail, 1:48 scale
EX n/a   NM n/a   MIP $50

COLLECTIBLES: UNSUNG HEROES, SERIES II

(Photo Courtesy of Corgi)

❏ **US50105, M151 Mutt: USAF,** 2001, Green with canvas top, painted mud, white type on hood, "US Air Force". Model of vehicle used by forward Air Controllers calling in strikes, 1:43 scale
EX n/a   NM n/a   MIP $24

(Photo Courtesy of Corgi)

❏ **US50204, M35 A1 2.5-Ton Truck: USMC,** 2001, Olive with painted mud and grime ring-mounted .50-caliber machine gun, sandbags in truck bed, detailed interior. Limited edition, 1:50 scale
EX n/a   NM n/a   MIP $48

(Photo Courtesy of Corgi)

❏ **US50405, UH-1C Huey Medevac Helicopter: US Army,** 2001, Dark olive with Black Horse insignia, red cross and "Blood Sweat & Tears" on nose. 10" x 3.25", 1:48 scale
EX n/a   NM n/a   MIP $50

(Photo Courtesy of Corgi)

❏ **US51101, M113 Armored Cavalry Assault Vehicle: US Army,** 2001, Olive green with painted mud and grime, 4" x 2", 1:50 scale
EX n/a   NM n/a   MIP $35

❏ **US50303, M48 A3 "Patton" Tank: US Army,** 2001, Dark olive with "The War Lord" in chalked-type lettering on barrel, working treads, separately-mounted machine gun, moveable turret. Limited edition, 1:50 scale
EX n/a   NM n/a   MIP $56

(Photo Courtesy of Corgi)

❏ **US51202, Bell AH-1G Huey Cobra Helicopter: USMC,** 2001, Dark green with side-mounted rockets, face painted on nose, 11" x 3", new casting, limited edition, 1:48 scale
EX n/a   NM n/a   MIP $56

COLLECTIBLES: FIREBASE 'NAM

(Photo Courtesy of Corgi)

❏ **US50406, UH-E1 Huey Gunship: USMC,** 2002, Dark green, clean parade-dress finish, side-mounted rockets, moveable rotor blades, 1:48 scale
EX n/a   NM n/a   MIP $50

(Photo Courtesy of Corgi)

❏ **US50104, M151 Mutt Recoilless Rifle and Trailer: US Army,** 2002, Dark olive green, white type, 5.5" x 1.5", moving wheels, detachable trailer, 1:43 scale
EX n/a   NM n/a   MIP $30

(Photo Courtesy of Corgi)

❏ **US50304, M48 A3 Patton Tank: US Army,** 2002, Dark green with light tan covers over spotlight and turret, white lettering on sides, 5.5" x 2.75", rotating turret, moving treads, 1:50 scale
EX n/a   NM n/a   MIP $50

(Photo Courtesy of Corgi)

❏ **US50203, M35 Deuce and a Half, 2.5 Ton Truck: US Army,** 2002, Dark green with canvas covering ammo boxes in bed, 5.5" x 2.75", 1:50 scale
EX n/a   NM n/a   MIP $45

(Photo Courtesy of Corgi)

CORGI / CLASSICS

❑ **US50302, M48 A3 Patton Tank: USMC,** 2002, Dark olive green with yellow lettering, two radio antennas, 5.5" x 2.75", rotating turret, moving treads, 1:50 scale
EX n/a   NM n/a   MIP $50

(Photo Courtesy of Corgi)

❑ **US50404, UH-1C Huey Helicopter: US Army,** 2002, Dark green with yellow triangle insignia and crossed sabers, side-mounted rockets, 10" x 3.25", movable rotor blades, opening cargo doors, 1:48 scale
EX n/a   NM n/a   MIP $50

COLLECTIBLES: CANADIAN COLLECTION

(Photo Courtesy of Corgi)

❑ **US52905, Diamond T620 Box Van: Moosehead,** 2001, Dark blue van with "You'll Like Moosehead Pale Ale" on side panels, silver grille and trim, 5.5" x 2", 1:50 scale
EX n/a   NM n/a   MIP $37

(Photo Courtesy of Corgi)

❑ **US52309, Mack B Box Van: Moosehead,** 2001, Dark blue with Moosehead illustration on sides, silver and black grille silver trim, 5.5" x 2", 1:50 scale
EX n/a   NM n/a   MIP $40

(Photo Courtesy of Corgi)

❑ **US54309, GM 5300 Fishbowl: Gray Coach Lines,** 2001, Silver gray body with greenish gray trim, "Gray Coach Line" shield emblem on sides, 9.5" x 2", 1:50 scale
EX n/a   NM n/a   MIP $35

COLLECTIBLES: FAIRGROUND ATTRACTIONS

(Photo Courtesy of Corgi)

❑ **CC10303, AEC Ergomatic Pole Truck: Fred Harris,** 2001, Red and cream truck with Ergomatic cab, "Harris's Old Tyme Amusements" on sides, silver grille and trim, 1:50 scale
EX n/a   NM n/a   MIP $62

(Photo Courtesy of Corgi)

❑ **CC07401, Land Rover and Trailer: Fred Harris,** 2001, Red Land Rover and Trailer with "Harris's Gallopers" on sides, Union Jack flag on top, red wheels, 1:43 scale
EX n/a   NM n/a   MIP $35

(Photo Courtesy of Corgi)

❑ **CC20401, Galloper Carousel: Fred Harris,** 2001, Yellow platform, canopy reads "Ride For All Ages," Union Jack on top, incredibly detailed horses and engine, 1:50 scale
EX n/a   NM n/a   MIP $144

(Photo Courtesy of Corgi)

❑ **CC10802, Foden S21 8-Wheel Platform & Coldcast Box Back: Fred Harris,** 2001, Red and cream truck with canvas tarp, "Harris's South Down Gallopers" on sides, 1:50 scale
EX n/a   NM n/a   MIP $62

(Photo Courtesy of Corgi)

❑ **CC20103, Fowler Showman's Locomotive: Fred Harris,** 2002, Dark blue with gold pinstripe trim, "Harris's Waltzing Cars, Ashington, Sussex" on sides of canopy, white roof on canopy, black smokestack, 1:50 scale
EX n/a   NM n/a   MIP $62

(Photo Courtesy of Corgi)

❑ **CC10705, Scammell High-wayman Ballast and Caravan: Fred Harris,** 2001, Red, cream and black truck towing black, red and cream wagon, 1:50 scale

EX n/a   NM n/a   MIP $66

(Photo Courtesy of Corgi)

❑ **CC20303, Garrett Showman's Tractor: Fred Harris,** 2001, Red, black and cream tractor, yellow wheels, "Fred Harris & Sons Galloping Horses, Ashington." on canopy sides, gold trim, 1:50 scale

EX n/a   NM n/a   MIP $45

(Photo Courtesy of Corgi)

❑ **CC55104, Diamond T Ballast/Generator and Trailer: Fred Harris,** 2002, Red and cream truck with black ballast section, cream and red trailer with "Harris's Old Tyme Amusements" on sides, 1:50 scale

EX n/a   NM n/a   MIP $60

COLLECTIBLES: COLLECTION HERITAGE (FRENCH)

(KP Photo)

❑ **EX70511, Renault 1000kg: Chambourcy,** 2001, Dark blue and cream van with black wheels, "Chambourcy" on panel sides, black interior, black base, 1:43 scale

EX n/a   NM n/a   MIP $24

COLLECTIBLES: COLLECTION HERITAGE (FRENCH): LA POSTE

(Photo Courtesy of Corgi)

❑ **EX70207, Berliet GLR,** 2002, Two-tone cab and trailer with "Postes" in yellow type on front of cab and sides of trailer, 1:50 scale

EX n/a   NM n/a   MIP $60

(Photo Courtesy of Corgi)

❑ **EX70620, Peugeot DA3: Poste Rurale Jura Transport,** 2002, Dark yellow and green van with roof rack containing mail bags, 1:43 scale

EX n/a   NM n/a   MIP $25

(Photo Courtesy of Corgi)

❑ **EX74003, Citroen Type 55 Bache,** 2002, Yellow truck with blue canvas top over truck bed, blue wheels, airmail graphic on doors, 1:50 scale

EX n/a   NM n/a   MIP $35

COLLECTIBLES: COLLECTION HERITAGE (FRENCH): LES TRANSPORTS ROUTIERS

(Photo Courtesy of Corgi)

❑ **EX70518, Renault 1000kg: Rita,** 2002, Red van with graphic of biscuit on sides and "Rita" in yellow type, silver wheels, black interior, 1:43 scale

EX n/a   NM n/a   MIP $25

COLLECTIBLES: COLLECTION HERITAGE (FRENCH): PINDER

(Photo Courtesy of Corgi)

❑ **EX11404, Bedford TK: Pinder Cuisine,** 2002, Red cab, yellow and red trailer with "Pinder Cuisine" and chef graphics on sides, 1:50 scale

EX n/a   NM n/a   MIP $70

(Photo Courtesy of Corgi)

❑ **EX51704, Dodge with Grizzly Trailer,** 2002, Red Dodge truck towing yellow trailer with "Grizzly" on sides, 1:50 scale

EX n/a   NM n/a   MIP $70

(Photo Courtesy of Corgi)

❏ **EX51705, Dodge with Trailer: Visitez Le Zoo,** 2002, Red and yellow Dodge truck towing yellow trailer with "Pinder" on sides, 1:50 scale
EX n/a NM n/a MIP $70

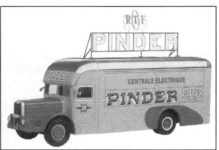

(Photo Courtesy of Corgi)

❏ **EX72013, Bernard Type 110: Centrale Electrique,** 2002, Yellow body with red hood, silver roof. "Pinder" sign on roof, "Pinder" and "Centrale Electrique" on sides, number "28" in blue star graphic on doors, 1:50 scale
EX n/a NM n/a MIP $60

(Photo Courtesy of Corgi)

❏ **EX99114, Pinder Zoo Tents,** 2002, Three red and yellow tents; two with "Zoo-Pinder" on top in red type
EX n/a NM n/a MIP $45

COLLECTIBLES: COLLECTION HERITAGE (FRENCH): TRANSPORTS D'URGENCE

(Photo Courtesy of Corgi)

❏ **EX02401, Volkswagen Van: Pompiers de Cruseilles,** 2002, Red Volkswagen van with blue dome light, black interior, silver hubs, 1:43 scale
EX n/a NM n/a MIP $25

(Photo Courtesy of Corgi)

❏ **EX07402, Land Rover: Pompiers de Marseille,** 2002, Red Land Rover truck with Marseille fire department shield on doors, blue dome light, silver antenna and grille, 1:43 scale
EX n/a NM n/a MIP $25

(Photo Courtesy of Corgi)

❏ **EX70519, Renault 1000kg: La Gendarmerie,** 2002, Dark blue van with blue dome light, "Gendarmerie" in white type on sides, white wheels, black interior, 1:43 scale
EX n/a NM n/a MIP $25

(Photo Courtesy of Corgi)

❏ **EX70618, Peugeot DA3: Police,** 2002, Black and white van with red dome light, black interior, black wheels, silver grille, "Police" in white type along sides, 1:43 scale
EX n/a NM n/a MIP $25

(Photo Courtesy of Corgi)

❏ **EX51706, Dodge: Pompiers de Beziers,** 2002, Red Dodge WC51 truck with red canvas roof on cab, pump unit in truck bed, whitewall tires, 1:43 scale
EX n/a NM n/a MIP $25

(Photo Courtesy of Corgi)

❏ **EX70521, Renault 1000kg: Ambulance Militaire,** 2002, Dark green military ambulance with red cross tampos on sides, French flags on doors, black wheels, black interior, 1:43 scale
EX n/a NM n/a MIP $25

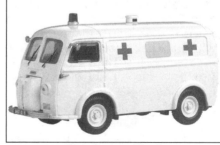

(Photo Courtesy of Corgi)

❏ **EX70619, Peugeot DA3: Ambulance Civile,** 2002, White van body, two red crosses on either side, red dome light, white wheels, silver bumpers, black base, 1:43 scale
EX n/a NM n/a MIP $25

AVIATION ARCHIVE: FALKLANDS (20 YEAR ANNIVERSARY)

(Photo Courtesy of Corgi)

❑ **AA31202, Avro Vulcan B2 - XM597, Falklands (Battle Scarred)**, 2002, Falklands "Black Buck" Campaign, dull gray-green with dark green swirl pattern camo, 1:144 scale

EX n/a   **NM** n/a   **MIP** $58

(Photo Courtesy of Corgi)

❑ **AA31603, Handley Page Victor - K.2, XL551, 55 Sqn, Falklands (Battle Scarred),** 2002, "Black Buck" Campaign, gray-green with dark green swirl pattern camouflage, 1:144 scale

EX n/a   **NM** n/a   **MIP** $58

(Photo Courtesy of Corgi)

❑ **AA33401, Westland Sea King Helicopter HAS 2 - 825 Sqn,** 2002, Detailed interior with pilots, sliding doors, interchangeable undercarriage, flying or static rotors, 1:72 scale

EX n/a   **NM** n/a   **MIP** $58

(Photo Courtesy of Corgi)

❑ **AA32406, BAE Harrier - 809 Squadron, Royal Navy, Falklands (Battle Scarred),** 2002, Green camo pattern, full bomb load. Interchangable undercarriage, detailed armaments, rotating thrust nozzles, 1:72 scale

EX n/a   **NM** n/a   **MIP** $45

(Photo Courtesy of Corgi)

❑ **AA31305, Lockheed Hercules -C130K, XV201, Falklands Campaign (Battle Scarred),** 2002, Number 1312 Flight, gray-green with dark green swirl pattern, 1:144 scale

EX n/a   **NM** n/a   **MIP** $58

AVIATION ARCHIVE: WORLD WAR II (WAR IN THE PACIFIC)

(Photo Courtesy of Corgi)

❑ **AA33101, Mitsubishi A6M2 Zero, Aircraft Carrier Hiryu, 2nd Sentai, 1st Koku Kantai, (Pearl Harbor),** 2001, Light gray (almost white) body, red sun insignia, blue stripes, 6.5" wingspan, 1:72 scale

EX n/a   **NM** n/a   **MIP** $32

(Photo Courtesy of Corgi)

❑ **AA33102, Mitsubishi A6M3-22 Zero, 251st Kokutai, IJNAF, Hiroyoshi Nishizawa,** 2001, Green camo pattern, red sun insignia with white outline, 6.5" wingspan, 1:72 scale

EX n/a   **NM** n/a   **MIP** $32

(Photo Courtesy of Corgi)

❑ **AA33001, Vought F4U-1 Corsair - White 7, Daphne "C" of Capt. James N. Cupp, VMF-213,** 2001, Dull blue-gray with star-in-circle insignia, 6.75" wingspan, 1:72 scale

EX n/a   **NM** n/a   **MIP** $32

(Photo Courtesy of Corgi)

❑ **AA33002, Vought F4U-1A Corsair - "White 29," Ira C. Kepford, VF-17,** 2001, Dark blue-gray, 6.75" wingspan, "29" on sides, 1:72 scale

EX n/a   **NM** n/a   **MIP** $32

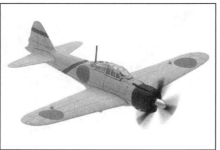

(Photo Courtesy of Corgi)

❑ **AA33103, Mitsubishi A6M2-21 Zero, Tainan NAC, Imperial Japanese Air Force, Saburo Sakai,** 2002, Light gray body with black nose, blue striping and red sun insignia. 6.5" wingspan. Model of Sakai's plane, a Japanese ace with 64 victories by the war's end. Non-limited edition, 1:72 scale

EX n/a   **NM** n/a   **MIP** $24

(Photo Courtesy of Corgi)

❑ **AA33004, F4U-1A Corsair, 86 "Lucybelle," VMF-214, US Marine Corps., Maj. 'Pappy' Boyington (Non-Limited Window Box),** 2002, Dark blue with light blue underside, 6.75" wingspan. Model of plane flown by famous Major "Pappy" Boyington, founder of VMF-214, the "Black Sheep Squadron." In just 84 days, the squadron destroyed or damaged 197 planes, troop transports and ships, and ground installations. Boyington was one of America's top aces in the struggle against the Japanese Empire, 1:72 scale

EX n/a   **NM** n/a   **MIP** $24

AVIATION ARCHIVE: WORLD WAR II (EUROPE AND AFRICA)

(Photo Courtesy of Corgi)

❑ **AA32801, DH Mosquito B IV - DK333/HS-F "Grim Reaper," RAF 109 Sq. No. 8 Group,** 2001, Gray green with olive camo pattern, wingspan, 9.1", 1:72 scale

EX n/a   **NM** n/a   **MIP** $45

(Photo Courtesy of Corgi)

❑ **AA32802, DH Mosquito FB VI - MM403/SB-V, No. 464 Sq. RAAF, No. 140 Wing, No. 2 Group, 2nd TAF,** 2001, Gray with Allied invasion stripes on wings, wingspan: 9.1", 1:72 scale

EX n/a   **NM** n/a   **MIP** $45

(Photo Courtesy of Corgi)

❑ **AA32002, Hawker Hurricane & Fuel Bowser: Night Fighter,** 2001, Dark charcoal color with RAF markings, wingspan: 6.25", 1:72 scale

EX n/a   **NM** n/a   **MIP** $32

(Photo Courtesy of Corgi)

❑ **AA32603, Avro Lancaster - L7578/KM/B - No. 44 (Rhodesia) Sq., RAF (1942),** 2001, Olive with darker green swirl camo pattern, 17" wingspan, 1:72 scale

EX n/a   **NM** n/a   **MIP** $140

(Photo Courtesy of Corgi)

❑ **AA32203, P51D Mustang - "Bunnie" of Capt. Roscoe C. Brown, CO 100 FS/322nd FG,** 2001, Silver body, green nose, red tail, 6.25" wingspan. Model of type flown by the famous Tuskegee Airmen, 1:72 scale

EX n/a   **NM** n/a   **MIP** $40

AVIATION ARCHIVE: WORLD WAR II (EUROPE & AFRICA)

(Photo Courtesy of Corgi)

❑ **AA30701, Hawker Hurricane IIB, BD930 No. 73 Sqn, Western Desert,** 2002, Tan with olive green camo pattern, 6.25" wingspan, removable engine cover shows detailed Rolls-Royce Merlin engine. Non-limited edition, 1:72 scale

EX n/a   **NM** n/a   **MIP** $24

(Photo Courtesy of Corgi)

❏ **AA33003, Corsair I - JT172, No.1835 Sqn, Royal Navy Fleet Air Arm,** 2002, Two-tone gray camouflage pattern, Royal Navy insignia, 6.75" wingspan, limited edition, 1:72 scale

EX n/a   **NM** n/a   **MIP** $34

(Photo Courtesy of Corgi)

❏ **AA99110, DH Mosquito & Supermarine Spitfire MkII - Photo Reconnaissance Unit,** 2002, Gray and green camo pattern Mosquito, (9.1" wingspan) and tan Supermarine Spitfire (6" wingspan). Limited edition, 1:72 scale

EX n/a   **NM** n/a   **MIP** $80

(Photo Courtesy of Corgi)

❏ **AA30201, Avro Lancaster - NX611, DX-C, "Just Jane",** 2002, Clear cockpit and turret canopies, moving guns and propellers, interchangeable undercarriage. Non-limited edition, 1:144 scale

EX n/a   **NM** n/a   **MIP** $32

(Photo Courtesy of Corgi)

❏ **AA32501, Junkers JU 87 Stuka - T6-HL, 3 Staffel, Stukageschwader 2, "Immelmann," St. Malo, France, August 1940,** 2002, Green with light blue underbelly, yellow trim, Breslau coat of arms, (3. Staffel's home base in 1937). Very detailed--red triangle emblem next to Staffel insignia stands for 87-octane fuel. New casting, 1:72 scale

EX n/a   **NM** n/a   **MIP** $37

(Photo Courtesy of Corgi)

❏ **AA32604, Avro Lancaster I - No. 106 Sqn, Syerston, Guy Gibson, November 1944,** 2002, A model of British pilot Guy Gibson's plane, the "Admiral Prune," with a 17" wingspan. Rotating gun turrets and propellers, opening bomb bay doors, interchangeable undercarriage. Limited edition, 1:72 scale

EX n/a   **NM** n/a   **MIP** $144

(Photo Courtesy of Corgi)

❏ **AA32803, DH Mosquito NFII - No.23 Sqn, RAF (Night-fighter),** 2002, Deep blue body, black props, 9.1" wingspan. Limited edition, 1:72 scale

EX n/a   **NM** n/a   **MIP** $35

(Photo Courtesy of Corgi)

❏ **AA32502, Junkers JU 87R R-2 Stuka - Tropical,** 2002, Tan and green desert camo pattern, snake painted on fuselage (may have been flown by Hubert Polz with these markings), 6-1/2" wingspan. Assigned to 6./StG2, Tmimi/Libya, July 1941, 1:72 scale

EX n/a   **NM** n/a   **MIP** $32

(Photo Courtesy of Corgi)

❏ **AA31902, Supermarine Spitfire MkVB - EP706/T-L, Sqn Leader Maurice Stephens, No. 249 Sq., Takali,** 2002, Tan and olive green body, 6-1/4" wingspan. Removable engine cover, detailed engine, interchangeable landing gear, detailed pilot. Non-limited edition, 1:72 scale

EX n/a   **NM** n/a   **MIP** $24

AVIATION ARCHIVE: BOMBERS

(Photo Courtesy of Corgi)

❏ **AA31103, B-17 Flying Fortress - "Yankee Doodle" 414th Sq. 97th Bomb Group,** 2001,

Olive and dark green RAF camo pattern, US star-in-circle markings, 8.5" wingspan, 1:144 scale

EX n/a   **NM** n/a   **MIP** $45

(Photo Courtesy of Corgi)

❑ **AA31303, C-130E Hercules - Royal Australian Air Force 37 Sq., 1993,** 2001, Gray and white with blue tail. Yellow type on tail reads, "50th Anniversary." Wingspan: 11", 1:144 scale

EX n/a   **NM** n/a   **MIP** $54

(Photo Courtesy of Corgi)

❑ **AA31802, B-29A Superfortress "Hawg Wild" preserved at IWM, Duxford,** 2001, Silver with dark camo underbody, "Y" on tail, orange tips on wings and tail, 11.25" wingspan, 1:144 scale

EX n/a   **NM** n/a   **MIP** $54

AVIATION ARCHIVE: VIETNAM, UNSUNG HEROES

(Photo Courtesy of Corgi)

❑ **AA31304, Lockheed Hercules - 16th Special Operations Sq. Gunship, 8 TFW, Thailand,** 2002, Tan, olive green and dark green camo pattern, weathered appearance, 11" wingspan, 1:144 scale

EX n/a   **NM** n/a   **MIP** $36

(Photo Courtesy of Corgi)

❑ **AA33204, F4C Phantom - USAF 12 TFW, "Annette," Cam Ranh Bay AFB, 1968-69,** 2002, Tan, olive green and dark green camo pattern. Model of plane F4 flown by First Lieutenant Buck Shuler, Jr., and named after his wife. Wingspan: 7", 1:72 scale

EX n/a   **NM** n/a   **MIP** $30

(Photo Courtesy of Corgi)

❑ **AA33502, Boeing B-52D, 083, 7th Bomb Wing, SAC - "Diamond Lil",** 2002, Tan, olive green and dark green camo pattern. Model of plane flown from Utapoa Royal Thai Naval Airfield, 1972. 15.5" wingspan, 1:144 scale

EX n/a   **NM** n/a   **MIP** $80

AVIATION ARCHIVE: MILITARY AIR POWER

(Photo Courtesy of Corgi)

❑ **AA32704, Hawker Hunter FGA Mk.9,** 2002, Camo pattern and checkerboard design insignia. Comes with poseable display stand, 1:72 scale

EX n/a   **NM** n/a   **MIP** $37

(Photo Courtesy of Corgi)

❑ **AA30002, Douglas R4D-5 "Que Sera Sera," 12418--US Navy Sq. VX-6,** 2002, White, silver and orange. Model of first aircraft to land at the South Pole, October 31, 1956. Limited edition, 1:144 scale

EX n/a   **NM** n/a   **MIP** $32

(Photo Courtesy of Corgi)

❑ **AA32304, English Electric Lightning F3 - No 11 Sqn, RAF Binbrook, 1954,** 2002, Dark blue-gray with silver trim. Limited edition, 1:72 scale

EX n/a   **NM** n/a   **MIP** $37

(Photo Courtesy of Corgi)

❑ **US51902, Bell H-13D "Sioux" MASH Helicopter - US Army,** 2002, Green frame with externally-mounted stretchers. Limited edition, 1:48 scale

EX n/a   **NM** n/a   **MIP** $52

(Photo Courtesy of Corgi)

❑ **AA33203, F-4J Phantom II - US Navy Blue Angels Aerobatic Team, 1969-73,** 2002, Blue and yellow body, "Blue Angels" in script on intakes, non-limited edition, 7" wingspan, 1:72 scale
EX n/a   NM n/a   MIP $32

(Photo Courtesy of Corgi)

❑ **AA33501, Boeing B52C - 54-2672, 7th Bomb Wing, Carswell Air Force Base, Fort Worth,** 2002, Silver with white underside (on the real aircraft, it meant to reflect nuclear radiation and heat). New casting, 15.5" wingspan, 1:144 scale
EX n/a   NM n/a   MIP $80

(Photo Courtesy of Corgi)

❑ **AA33402, Sikorsky SH-3D Sea King - HS-4 Sqn., U.S. Navy**

❑ **1969 Apollo Recovery,** 2002, White and silver body with sliding door, winch, moving or static rotors, base with Apollo capsule. Rotor "wingspan," 10.25". Non-limited edition, 1:48 scale
EX n/a   NM n/a   MIP $68

(Photo Courtesy of Corgi)

❑ **AA32705, Hawker Hunter GA.11, No. 738 Sqn. 'Rough Diamonds' Aerobatic Team, Royal Navy, Brawdy,** 2002, Dark blue body with orange trim and wingtips. Limited edition, 1:72 scale
EX n/a   NM n/a   MIP $37

AVIATION ARCHIVE: JETS

(Photo Courtesy of Corgi)

❑ **AA32404, Harrier GR.1 - XV741 - 1969 Transatlantic Air Race,** 2001, Gray underside, green and olive camo pattern, 4.25" wingspan, interchangeable landing gear, 1:72 scale
EX n/a   NM n/a   MIP $39

(Photo Courtesy of Corgi)

❑ **AA32405, BA Sea Harrier FRS.1, ZD578 50th Anniversary of 899 Sq., Royal Navy, 1992,** 2001, Dark gray, interchangeable landing gear, 4.25" wingspan, 1:72 scale
EX n/a   NM n/a   MIP $39

(Photo Courtesy of Corgi)

❑ **AA33201, F-4N Phantom II - 151000 - US Navy, VF-111 "Sundowners" Sq., 1975,** 2001, Light gray with blue, "Sundowners" insignia on tail, "USS Coral Sea" on fuselage, 7" wingspan, 1:72 scale
EX n/a   NM n/a   MIP $45

(Photo Courtesy of Corgi)

❑ **AA33202, F-4J (UK) Phantom F.Mk.3 - ZE361 - No. 74 Sq., RAF 1986,** 2001, Dark gray, black tail, 7" wingspan, interchangeable landing gear, 1:72 scale
EX n/a   NM n/a   MIP $45

AVIATION ARCHIVE: AIRLINERS OF THE WORLD

(Photo Courtesy of Corgi)

❑ **AA30505, Vickers Viscount 700: Capital Airlines N7443 - 1956,** 2001, White with red markings, silver wings, 7.5" wingspan, includes steps, 1:144 scale
EX n/a   NM n/a   MIP $45

(Photo Courtesy of Corgi)

CORGI / CLASSICS

❑ **AA30504, Vickers Viscount 800: Northeast Airlines - G-AOYH - 1972,** 2001, White, yellow and silver with "Northeast" on sides, 7.5" wingspan, 1:144 scale
EX n/a   **NM** n/a   **MIP** $76

(Photo Courtesy of Corgi)

❑ **AA32904, 707-327C - N7099 - Braniff International Airways, 1966,** 2001, Dark blue fuselage, silver wings, white tail, 12" wingspan, includes steps, 1:144 scale
EX n/a   **NM** n/a   **MIP** $76

(Photo Courtesy of Corgi)

❑ **AA32906, 707-321 - Pan American World Airways N412PA, 1965,** 2001, White, silver and blue, "Pan American" on sides, PanAm world logo on tail, steps included. 12" wingspan, 1:144 scale
EX n/a   **NM** n/a   **MIP** $76

(Photo Courtesy of Corgi)

❑ **AA31504, Bristol Britannia 300 - Cunard Eagle Airways - G-ARKA, 1961,** 2002, Silver and white body, comes with steps, 1:144 scale
EX n/a   **NM** n/a   **MIP** $52

(Photo Courtesy of Corgi)

❑ **AA32905, Boeing 707-336, BOAC, G-AXGW - 1970,** 2002, White and silver body, 1:144 scale
EX n/a   **NM** n/a   **MIP** $68

(Photo Courtesy of Corgi)

❑ **AA30505, Vickers Viscount 700 - Capital Airlines N7443 - 1956,** 2002, White body, "Capital Airlines" on fuselage, 1:144 scale
EX n/a   **NM** n/a   **MIP** $50

(Photo Courtesy of Corgi)

❑ **AA32907, Boeing 707-323C--American Airlines,** 2002, Polished chrome finish, 12" wingspan, poseable display stand, steps, 1:144 scale
EX n/a   **NM** n/a   **MIP** $70

(Photo Courtesy of Corgi)

❑ **AA30506, Vickers Viscount 803 - KLM,** 2002, White and silver body, "KLM--Royal Dutch Airlines" on fuselage. Includes steps. Limited edition, 1:144 scale
EX n/a   **NM** n/a   **MIP** $45

AVIATION ARCHIVE: AIR FORCE ONE

(Photo Courtesy of Corgi)

❑ **AA30402, VC-121A Constellation 48-610 "Columbine",** 2001, "Silver, with "United States Air Force" on fuselage. President Eisenhower adopted this plane as his transport, the first to be called "Air Force One.", 1:144 scale
EX n/a   **NM** n/a   **MIP** $62

(Photo Courtesy of Corgi)

❑ **AA32901, VC-137C - Air Force One President Carter,** 2001, White, silver and blue, "USAF" on right wingtip, "United States of America" on fuselage, 12" wingspan, 1:144 scale
EX n/a   **NM** n/a   **MIP** $80

TOYS: MANCHESTER UNITED

(Photo Courtesy of Corgi)

❏ **TY88001, Manchester United - Football on Wheels,** 2002
EX n/a   NM n/a   MIP $15

(Photo Courtesy of Corgi)

❏ **TY82218, Manchester United - Mini,** 2002, Red, white and black with opening doors
EX n/a   NM n/a   MIP $17

(Photo Courtesy of Corgi)

❏ **TY85901, Manchester United - LTI Taxi,** 2002, Opening doors
EX n/a   NM n/a   MIP $16

(Photo Courtesy of Corgi)

❏ **TY84102, Manchester United - Team Coach,** 2002, Red, white and black. Opening passenger doors and luggage compartment
EX n/a   NM n/a   MIP $12

(Photo Courtesy of Corgi)

❏ **TY81708, Manchester United - Transit Van,** 2002, Opening rear doors
EX n/a   NM n/a   MIP $11

(Photo Courtesy of Corgi)

❏ **TY82218, Manchester United - Megastore,** 2002, Volvo cab. Red, white and black
EX n/a   NM n/a   MIP $16

TOYS: SUPERHAULERS

(Photo Courtesy of Corgi)

❏ **TY86608, Scania Cab & Fuel Tanker - BP,** 2002, Green, yellow and white cab and tanker, silver wheels, 1:64 scale
EX n/a   NM n/a   MIP $17

(Photo Courtesy of Corgi)

❏ **TY86608, Scania Cab & Fuel Tanker - BP,** 2002, Detail showing cab and trailer attachment, 1:64 scale
EX n/a   NM n/a   MIP $17

(Photo Courtesy of Corgi)

❏ **TY87004, DAF '95 Cab & Skeletal Trailer - P&O Nedlloyd,** 2002, Blue cab, dark gray container, opening rear doors, coupling trailer, black chassis, 1:64 scale
EX n/a   NM n/a   MIP $17

(Photo Courtesy of Corgi)

❏ **TY86706, Volvo Rigid Truck - Wiseman Dairies,** 2002, Black cab, white and black Holstein graphics and "Wiseman Dairies" on bed section, 1:64 scale
EX n/a   NM n/a   MIP $10

(Photo Courtesy of Corgi)

❏ **TY86611, Scania Cab & Curtainside - Knights of Old,** 2002, Blue cab and trailer, red chassis, "Knights of Old" and knight jousting graphics on trailer, 1:64 scale
EX n/a   NM n/a   MIP $17

(Photo Courtesy of Corgi)

❑ **TY86903, Renault Premium & Curtainside - City Truck Group,** 2002, White cab and trailer, black chassis, "City" graphic and "Driven by our Customers" on trailer, 1:64 scale
EX n/a　　NM n/a　　MIP $17

(Photo Courtesy of Corgi)

❑ **TY86609, Scania Cab & Car Transporter - ECM,** 2002, Blue with light blue and white stripes, 1:64 scale
EX n/a　　NM n/a　　MIP $17

(Photo Courtesy of Corgi)

❑ **TY99103, Truck Set - Royal Mail,** 2002, Includeds two Ford Transit vans, one ERF rigid truck and one ERF cab and container. Red, 1:64 scale
EX n/a　　NM n/a　　MIP $32

(Photo Courtesy of Corgi)

❑ **TY86602, Scania Cab & Fuel Tanker - ESSO,** 2001, White cab and tanker, Tiger graphic, "Esso" and "Pricewatcher" on sides, 1:64 scale
EX n/a　　NM n/a　　MIP $17

(Photo Courtesy of Corgi)

❑ **TY86902, Renault Cab & Fuel Tanker - Shell,** 2001, White and yellow cab and tanker, green chassis, 9" length, 1:64 scale
EX n/a　　NM n/a　　MIP $17

❑ **TY87002, DAF '95 Cab & Curtainside - Dukes Transport,** 2001, Red cab and trailer, 1:64 scale
EX n/a　　NM n/a　　MIP $17

(Photo Courtesy of Corgi)

❑ **59512, Scania Cab & Curtainside - Omega,** 2001, Opening door, coupling trailer, dark blue with silver lettering, "Omega" graphics, 1:64 scale
EX n/a　　NM n/a　　MIP $17

(Photo Courtesy of Corgi)

❑ **59513, ERF Rigid Truck - Royal Mail,** 2001, Red with yellow stripe, crown graphics and "Royal Mail" on sides, black base, 1:64 scale
EX n/a　　NM n/a　　MIP $9

(Photo Courtesy of Corgi)

❑ **59570, ERF Cab & Container - Royal Mail,** 2001, Red with yellow stripe, 1:64 scale
EX n/a　　NM n/a　　MIP $17

(Photo Courtesy of Corgi)

❑ **59511, Volvo Cab & Curtainside - Kit Kat,** 2001, Red and white, silver wheels, opening rear door, coupling trailer, "Kit Kat" graphics on sides
EX n/a　　NM n/a　　MIP $17

(Photo Courtesy of Corgi)

❑ **65803, Renault Cab & Car Transporter - Richard Lawson Auto Logistics,** 2001, Red, white, silver and dark blue, 12.2", includes three cars, 1:64 scale
EX n/a　　NM n/a　　MIP $17

(Photo Courtesy of Corgi)

❑ **TY86601, Scania Race Transporter - Castrol Honda,** 2001, White cab and trailer with Honda motorcycle graphics and "Castrol Honda" on sides, 1:64 scale
EX n/a　　NM n/a　　MIP $17

(Photo Courtesy of Corgi)

❑ **TY86801, DAF Race Transporter - DUCATI,** 2001, Red racing graphics, opening rear doors, coupling trailer, 11" length, silver wheels, 1:64 scale

EX n/a   NM n/a   MIP $17

(Photo Courtesy of Corgi)

❑ **59568, Scania Cab & Container - TNT,** 2001, Orange, white and black, silver wheels, opening rear doors, coupling trailer, 1:64 scale

EX n/a   NM n/a   MIP $17

Toys: Eddie Stobart

(Photo Courtesy of Corgi)

❑ **TY86705, Volvo Cab & Skeletal Trailer,** 2002, Removeable containers, opening container doors, de-coupling trailer. Limited edition, 1:64 scale

EX n/a   NM n/a   MIP $18

(Photo Courtesy of Corgi)

❑ **TY99108, Truck Set,** 2002, Includes cargo box van, forklift truck, short wheelbase lorry and Mercedes 207D van, 1:64 scale

EX n/a   NM n/a   MIP $32

(Photo Courtesy of Corgi)

❑ **TY87001, DAF '95 Cab & Curtainside,** 2001, Opening rear door, 1:64 scale

EX n/a   NM n/a   MIP $16

(Photo Courtesy of Corgi)

❑ **59503, Scania Cab & Curtainside,** 2001, Green, white and red, opening rear door, coupling trailer, 1:64 scale

EX n/a   NM n/a   MIP $16

(Photo Courtesy of Corgi)

❑ **59504, Volvo Cab & Curtainside,** 2001, 1:64 scale

EX n/a   NM n/a   MIP $16

❑ **59516, Volvo Rigid Truck & Close Couple Trailer,** 2001, Opening rear doors, 1:64 scale

EX n/a   NM n/a   MIP $16

(Photo Courtesy of Corgi)

❑ **59538, Renault Premium Cab & Curtainside,** 2001, Opening rear doors, coupling trailer, 1:64 scale

EX n/a   NM n/a   MIP $16

(Photo Courtesy of Corgi)

❑ **59502, ERF Cab & Curtainside,** 2001, 1:64 scale

EX n/a   NM n/a   MIP $16

(Photo Courtesy of Corgi)

❑ **58112, Ford Transit Van Personnel Carrier,** 2001, Silver spoked hubs, opening rear doors. These small-size vans seem almost like a return to Corgi Jrs.-style die-cast toys, 1:64 scale

EX n/a   NM n/a   MIP $8

(Photo Courtesy of Corgi)

❏ **58401, Mercedes 207D Van,** 2001, "Roadside Maintenance" on sides, opening rear and side doors, 1:64 scale

EX n/a   **NM** n/a   **MIP** $7

(Photo Courtesy of Corgi)

❏ **66201, 1:64 Scale Ford Transit Van,** 2001, 1:64 scale

EX n/a   **NM** n/a   **MIP** $3

(Photo Courtesy of Corgi)

❏ **56702, Fork Lift Truck,** 2001, Includes figure and pallet, features operating lift

EX n/a   **NM** n/a   **MIP** $8

(Photo Courtesy of Corgi)

❏ **59601, Ford Cargo Box Van,** 2001, Opening roller shutter

EX n/a   **NM** n/a   **MIP** $11

(Photo Courtesy of Corgi)

❏ **59508, Scania Rigid Truck,** 2001, Opening rear doors, 1:64 scale

EX n/a   **NM** n/a   **MIP** $11

(Photo Courtesy of Corgi)

❏ **60023, 4 Piece Set & Mat,** 2001

EX n/a   **NM** n/a   **MIP** $30

(Photo Courtesy of Corgi)

❏ **58304, Ford Escort Van,** 2001, "Roadside Maintenance" on sides, green and white, silver hubs

EX n/a   **NM** n/a   **MIP** $7

TOYS: CHITTY CHITTY BANG BANG

❏ **TY87801, Miniature Chitty Chitty Bang Bang,** 2002,

EX n/a   **NM** n/a   **MIP** $7

TOYS: FORD TRANSIT

(Photo Courtesy of Corgi)

❏ **TY81706, Ford Transit Van - James Irlam,** 2002, Red with yellow and white lettering on sides, black base, 1:64 scale

EX n/a   **NM** n/a   **MIP** $3

(Photo Courtesy of Corgi)

❏ **TY81707, Ford Transit Van - Tarmac,** 2002, White with yellow and black graphics and "Tarmac" on hood and sides. Black base, 1:64 scale

EX n/a   **NM** n/a   **MIP** $3

(Photo Courtesy of Corgi)

❏ **66202, Ford Transit Van - TNT,** 2001, Orange, white and black, 1:64 scale

EX n/a   **NM** n/a   **MIP** $3

(Photo Courtesy of Corgi)

❏ **66203, Ford Transit Van - Royal Mail,** 2001, Red with "Royal Mail" crown graphics, 1:64 scale

EX n/a   **NM** n/a   **MIP** $3

(Photo Courtesy of Corgi)

❑ **66204, Ford Transit Van - RAC,** 2001, Red with silver "RAC" lettering, 1:64 scale
EX n/a   **NM** n/a   **MIP** $3

(Photo Courtesy of Corgi)

❑ **66207, Ford Transit Van - Transco,** 2001, Light blue with red markings and "Transco" on sides. Black base, 1:64 scale
EX n/a   **NM** n/a   **MIP** $3

(Photo Courtesy of Corgi)

❑ **TY81703, Ford Transit Van - AA,** 2001, Yellow with black lettering and checkerboard graphics, 1:64 scale
EX n/a   **NM** n/a   **MIP** $3

(Photo Courtesy of Corgi)

❑ **TY81701, Ford Transit Van - Michelin,** 2001, Dark blue with yellow and Michelin Man graphics on sides, black base, "Michelin" on hood and doors, 1:64 scale
EX n/a   **NM** n/a   **MIP** $3

TOYS: CONSTRUCTION

(Photo Courtesy of Corgi)

❑ **TY87901, Cement Mixer - The Concrete Company,** 2002, White Mercedes cab, green chassis, silver wheels, white and dark blue drum
EX n/a   **NM** n/a   **MIP** $11

(Photo Courtesy of Corgi)

❑ **TY88101, Tower Crane,** 2001, Red and white with exendable boom
EX n/a   **NM** n/a   **MIP** $19

(Photo Courtesy of Corgi)

❑ **64801, Dumper Truck - Wimpey,** 2001, Tipping dumper, black seat and steering wheel, includes figure, 3.1"
EX n/a   **NM** n/a   **MIP** $8

(Photo Courtesy of Corgi)

❑ **66801, Mercedes Tipper - Tarmac,** 2001, White with work-

ing tipper section, black and orange graphics
EX n/a   **NM** n/a   **MIP** $11

(Photo Courtesy of Corgi)

❑ **66401, Loader - KS Plant Hire,** 2001, Yellow, with black cab, bucket and treads. Operating bucket, 6.8"
EX n/a   **NM** n/a   **MIP** $11

(Photo Courtesy of Corgi)

❑ **64901, Big Bin - Biffa,** 2001, White Mercedes cab with operating red bin skip section, white "Biffa" type on sides, silver wheels
EX n/a   **NM** n/a   **MIP** $11

(Photo Courtesy of Corgi)

❑ **66402, KS Plant - Mobile Crane,** 2001, Detail showing operating boom and stabilizers

(Photo Courtesy of Corgi)

CORGI / CLASSICS

❏ **66402, KS Plant - Mobile Crane,** 2001, Yellow with black stripes, operating winch and "K.S. Plant Ltd." on boom, 8.3"
EX n/a   NM n/a   MIP $11

(Photo Courtesy of Corgi)

❏ **TY86001, Road Roller - Wimpey,** 2001, Yellow body, silver engine trim, red engine, rolling roller, 4.9"
EX n/a   NM n/a   MIP $8

(Photo Courtesy of Corgi)

❏ **66301, Cement Truck - Blue Circle,** 2001, Yellow body, black cab, operating cement drum, "Blue Circle" graphics on drum and hood, 8.3"
EX n/a   NM n/a   MIP $11

TOYS: WORKING LIFE

(Photo Courtesy of Corgi)

❏ **60031, Land Rover, Road Drill & Figure - Transco,** 2001, Light blue vehicle and trailer, orange stripes. Includes figure
EX n/a   NM n/a   MIP $18

(Photo Courtesy of Corgi)

❏ **58603, Refuse Truck - Biffa,** 2001, White cab, red garbage section with rotating compactor and lifting crusher
EX n/a   NM n/a   MIP $11

(Photo Courtesy of Corgi)

❏ **58903, Streetsweeper - MHS Highway Hire,** 2001, Yellow and white, operating mobile arm, rotating road-sweeping brush
EX n/a   NM n/a   MIP $11

TOYS: EMERGENCY SERVICES

(Photo Courtesy of Corgi)

❏ **TY82701, Land Rover - Coastguard,** 2002, Dark blue and yellow, silver wheels, opening rear doors
EX n/a   NM n/a   MIP $8

(Photo Courtesy of Corgi)

❏ **TY82701, Land Rover - Coastguard,** 2002, Detail of opening rear doors on Coastguard Land Rover

(Photo Courtesy of Corgi)

❏ **65901, Volvo Fire Engine - City Fire Brigade,** 2001, Red and silver with removeable ladder, 5.9"
EX n/a   NM n/a   MIP $11

(Photo Courtesy of Corgi)

❏ **57601, Range Rover - Metropolitan Police,** 2001, Yellow and dark blue checkerboard design on silver and white body, blue dome lights, opening tailgate, rear window and driver and passenger doors, silver wheels, 4.8"
EX n/a   NM n/a   MIP $8

(Photo Courtesy of Corgi)

❏ **57801, BMW 525 - Hampshire Police,** 2001, Opening doors, hood and detailed engine
EX n/a   NM n/a   MIP $8

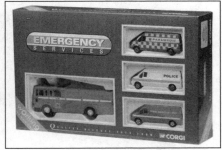

(Photo Courtesy of Corgi)

❏ **60026, Motorway Emergency Services Set,** 2001, Includes three Ford Transit vans and one Volvo fire engine. Set of four vehicles price shown
EX n/a   NM n/a   MIP $23

(Photo Courtesy of Corgi)

❏ **60026, Motorway Emergency Services Set,** 2001, Ford Transit Van: Paramedic, checkerboard graphics, part of set. Set of four vehicles price shown, 1:64 scale
EX n/a   NM n/a   MIP $23

(Photo Courtesy of Corgi)

❏ **60026, Motorway Emergency Services Set,** 2001, Ford Transit Van: Fire van, red, part of set. Four vehicle set price shown, 1:64 scale
EX n/a   NM n/a   MIP $23

(Photo Courtesy of Corgi)

❏ **60026, Motorway Emergency Services Set,** 2001, Volvo fire truck with removable ladders, part of set. Four vehicle set price shown
EX n/a   NM n/a   MIP $23

(Photo Courtesy of Corgi)

❏ **60026, Motorway Emergency Services Set,** 2001, Ford Transit Van: Police van. Set of four vehicles price shown, 1:64 scale
EX n/a   NM n/a   MIP $23

TOYS: THE GREAT OUTDOORS

(Photo Courtesy of Corgi)

❏ **59102, Mercedes with Caravan Set,** 2001, Red Mercedes with opening doors and gray caravan trailer with opening door and operating awning, 9.8"
EX n/a   NM n/a   MIP $12

(Photo Courtesy of Corgi)

❏ **57904, Land Rover,** 2001, Green body, off-white roof and wheels, spare on hood, opening rear doors
EX n/a   NM n/a   MIP $9

(Photo Courtesy of Corgi)

❏ **TY82802, Range Rover,** 2002, Dark green body, opening tailgate and rear window, opening driver and passenger doors
EX n/a   NM n/a   MIP $8

TOYS: NOBBY IN TOYLAND

(Photo Courtesy of Corgi)

❏ **69001, Noddy,** 2001, Yellow, with red fenders, character from British children's television show
EX n/a   NM n/a   MIP $10

(Photo Courtesy of Corgi)

❑ **69002, Mr Sparks,** 2001, Black tow truck with "Toyland Garage" on sides
EX n/a   NM n/a   MIP $10

(Photo Courtesy of Corgi)

❑ **69003, Mr Milko,** 2001, White milk truck with blue fenders, milk bottles in back
EX n/a   NM n/a   MIP $10

(Photo Courtesy of Corgi)

❑ **69004, Big Ears,** 2001, Gnome figure in red fire truck
EX n/a   NM n/a   MIP $10

(Photo Courtesy of Corgi)

❑ **69005, Mr Plod,** 2001, Black police paddy wagon with white fenders and "Gobbo" figure in back
EX n/a   NM n/a   MIP $10

(Photo Courtesy of Corgi)

❑ **69006, Gobbo,** 2001, Red car with green fenders, Gobbo figure at wheel
EX n/a   NM n/a   MIP $10

TOYS: LONDON SCENE

(Photo Courtesy of Corgi)

❑ **66101, 1:64 Scale LTI Taxi - Black,** 2001, Opening passenger doors, 1:64 scale
EX n/a   NM n/a   MIP $4

(Photo Courtesy of Corgi)

❑ **66002, 1:36 Scale LTI Taxi - Dial a Cab,** 2001, "Dial a Cab" graphics on doors, fold-down seat, opening rear doors, wheelchair ramp, 3", 1:36 scale
EX n/a   NM n/a   MIP $8

(Photo Courtesy of Corgi)

❑ **66001, 1:36 Scale LTI Taxi - Black,** 2001, Opening rear doors, fold-down seat, key wheelchair ramp, 1:36 scale
EX n/a   NM n/a   MIP $8

(Photo Courtesy of Corgi)

❑ **TY82303, Routemaster - Guide Friday,** 2001, Gold body with black open top, "The Dublin Tour" on sides, 1:64 scale
EX n/a   NM n/a   MIP $9

(Photo Courtesy of Corgi)

❑ **32403, Open Top Routemaster - London Transport,** 2001, Red body with off-white plastic seats in open upper deck
EX n/a   NM n/a   MIP $8

(Photo Courtesy of Corgi)

❑ **59902, Concorde,** 2001, White, "British Airways" on fuselage, moving nose cone, 7.2"
EX n/a   NM n/a   MIP $8

(Photo Courtesy of Corgi)

❑ **TY82301, Routemaster Bus - London Route,** 2001, Red body
EX n/a   NM n/a   MIP $8

(Photo Courtesy of Corgi)

❑ **60029, Gift Set - Routemaster & 1:64 Scale LTI Taxi,** 2001, Red Routemaster bus with "The London Standard" on sides, 4.7", black LTI Taxi, 3", 1:64 scale
EX n/a   NM n/a   MIP $11

(Photo Courtesy of Corgi)

❑ **32602, Plaxton Paramount - National Express,** 2001, White with red and blue stripe, opening passenger door and luggage compartment
EX n/a   NM n/a   MIP $11

(Photo Courtesy of Corgi)

❑ **32605, Plaxton Paramount - British Airways Holidays,** 2001, Opening passenger door and luggage compartment
EX n/a   NM n/a   MIP $11

(Photo Courtesy of Corgi)

❑ **4410, 1:36-Scale Mini - Union Jack (Red),** 2001, Red body, white roof with Union Jack, opening doors, gray wheels, black interior, 1:36 scale
EX n/a   NM n/a   MIP $8

(Photo Courtesy of Corgi)

❑ **4413, 1:36-Scale Mini - Union Jack (Green),** 2001, British Racing Green body with white roof and Union Jack, opening doors, silver wheels, grille and trim, 1:36 scale
EX n/a   NM n/a   MIP $8

TOYS: SEIRBHISI BOTHAR NA HEIREANN (IRISH ROAD SERVICES)

(Photo Courtesy of Corgi)

❑ **TY86301, Volvo Fire Engine - Irish Fire Brigade,** 2001, Red and silver body, removeable ladder, black base, 5.9"
EX n/a   NM n/a   MIP $11

(Photo Courtesy of Corgi)

❑ **TY82801, Range Rover - Garda,** 2001, White body with yellow stripe, blue "Garda" on hood and doors, opening tailgate, rear window and doors, silver wheels, black base, blue roof lights
EX n/a   NM n/a   MIP $8

(Photo Courtesy of Corgi)

❑ **TY82303, Guide Friday - Dublin Tour,** 2001, Gold and black body with open upper deck, "The Dublin Tour" on sides, 4.7"
EX n/a   NM n/a   MIP $9

(Photo Courtesy of Corgi)

❑ **TY82302, Routemaster - City Tour Bus,** 2001, Dark green with "Ireland" on sides, white interior, 4.7", 1:64 scale
EX n/a   NM n/a   MIP $8

(Photo Courtesy of Corgi)

❑ **TY84101, Plaxton Paramount Coach - Bus Eireann,** 2001, White with red stripes, opening passenger doors and luggage compartment
EX n/a   NM n/a   MIP $11

TOYS: ROAD RESCUE

(Photo Courtesy of Corgi)

CORGI / CLASSICS

❏ **57605, Range Rover - RAC,** 2001, Red, with silver "RAC" type, opening tailgate, driver and passenger doors, rear window
EX n/a   **NM** n/a   **MIP** $8

(Photo Courtesy of Corgi)

❏ **58204, Ford Transit Wrecker - RAC,** 2001, Operating winch
EX n/a   **NM** n/a   **MIP** $8

(Photo Courtesy of Corgi)

❏ **58118, Ford Transit Van 1:36 Scale - RAC,** 2001, Red, with "RAC" in silver lettering. Opening rear doors
EX n/a   **NM** n/a   **MIP** $8

(Photo Courtesy of Corgi)

❏ **58202, Ford Transit Wrecker - AA,** 2001, Yellow, with black lettering, checkerboard graphics along bottom, operating winch
EX n/a   **NM** n/a   **MIP** $8

Dinky Toys

The Automobile Association patrol motorcycle, (270/44B) was a much-used casting. Naturally, (the Automobile Association being a British institution) the decal and color of the vehicle depended mainly on which country it was being sold in at the time. The motorcycle is shown here next to the Robot Traffic Signal, (773).

By Dr. Douglas Sadecky

Meccano, Dinky's parent company, was founded in 1900 by Frank Hornby. In 1933, he began producing "Model Miniatures," a line of vehicles originally intended to accompany Hornby model trains. Later these models became known as Dinky Toys, and were a favorite with British children and collectors. Roughly made in 1:43/1:48-scale (all items were intended for train layouts) the company made road signs, accessories and figures, too.

Postwar toys, as with Tootsietoy, were generally re-issues of prewar castings, so dating the models from this time can be tricky. After 1947, the metal required for toy production was again available. During the same year, Dinky Supertoys were launched—stand-alone toys not necessarily intended for model railroad use.

When Hot Wheels rolled onto the scene, Dinky responded with "Speedwheels," a lighter wheel and axle system that became standard to their line.

By the 1950s, models in the Dinky range expanded dramatically. Their licensing agreements in the 1970s led to some famous releases, most notably ships and vehicles from Thunderbirds, Space 1999 and Star Trek.

By 1979, even though they still released new models, Mecanno shut down it's original Binns Road, Liverpool factory. The name "Dinky" was acquired by Matchbox in the 1980s (while under ownership of Universal Toys) and launched the 1:43-scale line of collectible "Dinky Matchbox" vehicles. These models are sharp-looking and generally affordable in mint condition today, and provide crossover appeal to Matchbox and Dinky collectors.

Dinky catalogs are great resources for any collector. They provide vehicle measurements and often, original retail pricing that makes you say, "If only I had a time machine..." Early editions were generally black and white, but by the late 1950s, sharp, vibrant color illustrations were the order of the day.

The Foden Diesel 8-Wheel Wagon (501) was part of the Dinky Supertoy range.

Another in the Dinky Supertoy range, the Mighty Antar with Propeller (986). The propeller looks heavy, but was actually made of plastic.

Military vehicles were especially well-made by Dinky. Shown here are the Reconnaissance Car, (152B), the Medium Gun, (692) and the French-made AMX Tank, (F80C/817).

The Superior Cadillac Ambulance, (288) was a long-used casting. Shown here, one of the last, circa 1978. It featured heavy construction, an opening rear door, and a patient on a stretcher.

Two major oil companies represented by these models, Mobil and Esso. On the left, the Mobilgas Tanker, (440) and on the right, the French-made Panhard Esso Tanker, (F32C). Generally, each casting was identical, but given the decals of either brand.

AIRCRAFT

❏ **60a, Atalanta (Imperial Airways Liner),** 1934-41, gold, G-ABTI
EX $150   NM $375   MIP $500

❏ **60a, Arc-en-Ciel,** 1935-40
EX $200   NM $375   MIP $450

❏ **60a/800, Mystere IV,** 1957-63
EX $30   NM $75   MIP $110

❏ **60b, Leopard Moth,** 1934-41, light green, G-ACPT
EX $50   NM $140   MIP $180

❏ **60b/61d, Potez 58,** 1935-40
EX $100   NM $260   MIP $350

❏ **60b/801, Vautour,** 1957-63
EX $30   NM $80   MIP $125

❏ **60c, Percival Gull,** 1934-41, white, blue wing tips
EX $70   NM $150   MIP $225

❏ **60c, Henriot 180T,** 1935-40
EX $110   NM $170   MIP $225

(KP Photo by Dr. Douglas Sadecky)

❏ **60c/892, Super G Constellation Lockheed,** 1956-63, Wingspan, 7-3/4"
EX $90   NM $200   MIP $350

❏ **60d, Vickers Jockey,** 1934-41, red, cream wing tips
EX $75   NM $110   MIP $150

❏ **60d, Breguet Corsair,** 1935-40
EX $100   NM $200   MIP $300

❏ **60d/802, Sikorsky S58 Helicopter,** 1957-61
EX $45   NM $135   MIP $190

❏ **60e, General Monospar,** 1934-41, silver, blue wing tips
EX $75   NM $225   MIP $300

❏ **60e, Dewoitine 500,** 1935-40
EX $100   NM $200   MIP $300

❏ **60e/803, Viscount,** 1957-60
EX $75   NM $125   MIP $195

❏ **60f, Autogyro,** 1934-41, gold, blue rotor, w/pilot
EX $90   NM $180   MIP $250

❏ **60f, Cierva Autogyro,** 1935-40
EX $100   NM $200   MIP $250

(KP Photo by Dr. Douglas Sadecky)

❏ **60f/891, Caravelle S.E. 210,** 1959-62
EX $45   NM $170   MIP $230

❏ **60g, D.H. Comet Racer,** 1935-40, silver, G-ACSR
EX $60   NM $125   MIP $225

❏ **60g, D.H. Comet Racer,** 1946-49, yellow, G-RACE
EX $50   NM $110   MIP $155

❏ **60h, Singapore Flying Boat,** 1936-41, silver, RAF roundels
EX $100   NM $300   MIP $400

❏ **60m, Singapore Flying Boat,** 1936-41, four-engine, silver, G-EUTG
EX $125   NM $400   MIP $550

❏ **60n, Fairy Battle,** 1937-41, silver, "Fairy Battle Bomber" under wing
EX $40   NM $100   MIP $140

❏ **60p, Gloster Gladiator,** 1937-40, silver, RAF roundels, no words under wing
EX $90   NM $175   MIP $225

❏ **60r, Empire Flying Boat,** 1945-49, silver, G-ADUV, hollowed out front to hull
EX $90   NM $175   MIP $250

❏ **60r, Empire Flying Boat,** 1937-41, silver, G-ADUV, solid front to hull
EX $150   NM $325   MIP $450

❏ **60s, Fairy Battle,** 1937-41, camouflaged, one roundel, light variation
EX $50   NM $125   MIP $200

❏ **60t, Douglas DC3,** 1938-41, silver, PH-ALI
EX $125   NM $300   MIP $650

❏ **60v, Whitley Bomber,** 1937-41, silver, RAF roundels
EX $95   NM $150   MIP $225

❏ **60w, Clipper III Flying Boat,** 1938-41, silver, NC16736
EX $150   NM $250   MIP $400

❏ **60w, Clipper III Flying Boat,** 1945-49, silver, no registration
EX $75   NM $175   MIP $250

❏ **60x, Empire Flying Boat,** 1938-40, Atlantic Flying Boat, blue, cream wings, G-AZBP
EX $350   NM $600   MIP $1000

❏ **61a/64, Dewoitine D338,** 1937-46
EX $225   NM $350   MIP $500

❏ **61b, Potez 56,** 1937-40
EX $125   NM $200   MIP $270

❏ **61d, Potez 58 Sanitaire,** 1937-40
EX $110   NM $175   MIP $250

❏ **61e, Hanriot 180M,** 1937-40
EX $90   NM $150   MIP $225

❏ **62A, Spitfire,** 1945-49, silver, large canopy, roundels red, white, and blue
EX $30   NM $75   MIP $125

❏ **62B, Bristol Blenheim,** 1945-48, medium bomber; silver, red, and blue roundels
EX $35   NM $95   MIP $120

❏ **62B, Bristol Blenheim**
EX $60   NM $85   MIP $130

❏ **62b/62d, Bristol Blenheim,** 1940-41, silver, roundels w/outer yellow ring
EX $60   NM $140   MIP $175

❏ **62e/62a, Spitfire,** 1940-41, silver, small canopy, roundels red, white, and blue
EX $35   NM $150   MIP $200

❏ **62g, Boeing Flying Fortress,** 1939-41, silver, USAAC stars on wings
EX $100   NM $200   MIP $300

❏ **62g, Boeing Flying Fortress,** 1945-48, "Long Range Bomber" under wings
EX $50   NM $125   MIP $225

❏ **62h, Hawker Hurricane,** 1939-41, silver, no undercarriage
EX $30   NM $70   MIP $115

❏ **62k, Airspeed Envoy,** 1938-40, King's Aeroplane, red, blue, and silver, G-AEXX
EX $70   NM $200   MIP $300

❏ **62m, Airspeed Envoy,** 1938-41, silver, G-ACVI
EX $55   NM $175   MIP $250

DINKY

❏ **62m, Airspeed Envoy,** 1945-49, light transport, red, G-ATMH
EX $40   NM $125   MIP $200

❏ **62n, Junkers JU90 Airliner,** 1938-40, silver, D-AIVI
EX $90   NM $250   MIP $325

❏ **62P, A.W. Ensign,** 1945-49, A.W. Airliner, silver, G-ADSV
EX $65   NM $145   MIP $175

❏ **62p, Armstrong Whitworth Ensign,** 1938-41, silver, G-ADSR
EX $90   NM $175   MIP $250

❏ **62R, D.H. Albatross,** 1945-49, four-engine liner; gray, G-ATPV
EX $75   NM $170   MIP $250

❏ **62r, D.H. Albatross,** 1939-41, silver, G-AEVV
EX $75   NM $275   MIP $400

❏ **62S, Hawker Hurricane,** 1945-49, three-blade prop; red, white, and blue roundels
EX $40   NM $95   MIP $130

❏ **62t, Whitley Bomber,** 1937-41, camouflaged, light variation
EX $95   NM $300   MIP $350

❏ **62w, D.H. Albatross,** 1939-41, Frobisher Class Liner, silver, G-AFDI
EX $75   NM $275   MIP $400

❏ **62x, A.W. Ensign,** 1945-49, forty-seat airliner, olive/dark green, G-AZCA
EX $95   NM $275   MIP $350

❏ **62y, Junkers JU89,** 1938-41, high speed monoplane, green/dark green, D-AZBK
EX $100   NM $275   MIP $350

❏ **62Y, Junkers JU89,** 1945-49, high speed monoplane, silver, G-ATBK
EX $70   NM $160   MIP $225

❏ **63, Mayo Composite,** 1939-41
EX $200   NM $450   MIP $750

❏ **63b, Mercury Seaplane,** 1939-41, silver, G-ADHJ
EX $50   NM $100   MIP $175

❏ **64a, Amiot 370,** 1939-48
EX $70   NM $130   MIP $200

❏ **64b, Bloch 220,** 1939-48
EX $75   NM $150   MIP $250

❏ **64c, Potez 63,** 1939-48
EX $150   NM $250   MIP $400

❏ **64d, Potez 662,** 1939-40
EX $125   NM $250   MIP $400

❏ **66a, Atalanta,** 1940, camouflaged, dark variation
EX $200   NM $450   MIP $650

❏ **66b, Leopard Moth,** 1940, camouflaged, dark
EX $70   NM $225   MIP $300

❏ **66c, Percival Gull,** 1945-48, Light Tourer, light green
EX $65   NM $125   MIP $150

❏ **66c, Percival Gull,** 1940, camouflaged, dark
EX $100   NM $225   MIP $275

❏ **66d, Vickers Jockey,** 1940, camouflaged, dark
EX $75   NM $175   MIP $225

❏ **66e, General Monospar,** 1940, camouflaged, dark
EX $90   NM $300   MIP $350

❏ **66f, Autogyro,** 1940, Army cooperation, silver, RAF roundels
EX $125   NM $250   MIP $350

❏ **67a, Junkers JU89 Heavy Bomber,** 1941, black, German cross
EX $100   NM $400   MIP $600

❏ **68a, A.W. Ensign,** 1940, camouflaged, dark variation
EX $150   NM $300   MIP $450

❏ **68b, D.H. Albatross,** 1940, camouflaged, dark variation
EX $150   NM $300   MIP $450

❏ **700, Spitfire II,** 1979, chrome
EX $65   NM $165   MIP $250

❏ **700, Empire Flying Boat,** 1937-41, MAIA, silver, G-AVKW
EX $150   NM $275   MIP $350

❏ **700, Mercury Seaplane,** 1949-57, silver, G-AVKW
EX $35   NM $75   MIP $110

❏ **701, Short Shetland Flying Boat,** 1947-49, silver, G-AGVD
EX $200   NM $550   MIP $750

❏ **701/733, Lockheed P-80 Shooting Star,** 1947-62, silver, USAF stars
EX $10   NM $20   MIP $30

(KP Photo by Dr. Douglas Sadecky)

❏ **702/999, D.H. Comet Airliner,** 1954-65, silver wings, G-ALYX, wingspan 7-1/8"
EX $45   NM $105   MIP $200

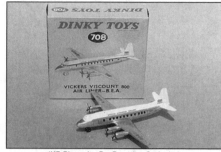
(KP Photo by Dr. Douglas Sadecky)

❏ **708, Vickers Viscount,** 1956-65, British European Airways, G-AOJA, wingspan 5-7/8"
EX $40   NM $125   MIP $200

❏ **708, Vickers Viscount,** 1956-65, Air France, F-BGNL
EX $40   NM $125   MIP $200

❏ **70a/704, Avro York,** 1946-59, silver, G-AGJC
EX $45   NM $155   MIP $200

❏ **70b/730, Hawker Tempest II,** 1946-55, silver, RAF roundels, flat spinner
EX $15   NM $45   MIP $75

❏ **70c/705, Vickers Viking,** 1947-63, silver, G-AGOL, flat spinners
EX $15   NM $40   MIP $65

❏ **70d/731, Twin Engined Fighter,** 1946-55, silver, no registration
EX $10   NM $25   MIP $35

(KP Photo)

❏ **70e/732, Gloster Meteor,** 1946-62, silver, RAF roundels
EX $10   NM $25   MIP $35

❏ **710, Beechcraft Bonanza,** 1965-76
EX $20   NM $55   MIP $80

❏ **712, Beechcraft T42A,** 1972-77
EX $30   NM $75   MIP $110

□ 715, Bristol 173 Helicopter, 1956-63, turquoise, red rotors, G-AUXR
EX $20   NM $60   MIP $95

□ 715, Beechcraft Baron, 1968-76
EX $25   NM $60   MIP $90

□ 716, Westland Sikorsky Helicopter, 1957-63, red/cream, G-ATWX
EX $30   NM $75   MIP $125

□ 717, Boeing 737, 1970-75
EX $20   NM $45   MIP $90

□ 718, Hawker Hurricane IIc, 1972-75
EX $50   NM $95   MIP $155

□ 719, Supermarine Spitfire II, 1969-78, motorized
EX $60   NM $95   MIP $175

□ 721, Junkers JU87B Stuka, 1969-80
EX $40   NM $75   MIP $145

□ 722, Hawker Harrier, 1970-80
EX $25   NM $65   MIP $95

□ 723/728, Hawker Siddeley HS 125, 1970-75
EX $20   NM $50   MIP $75

□ 724/736, Sea King Helicopter, 1971-79, motorized
EX $15   NM $35   MIP $85

□ 725/727/73, M.D. F-4 Phantom, 1972-77
EX $70   NM $125   MIP $175

□ 726, ME BI 109, 1972-76, motorized
EX $50   NM $100   MIP $175

□ 729, MRCA Tornado, 1974-76
EX $35   NM $90   MIP $155

□ 731, SEPCAT Jaguar, 1973-76
EX $25   NM $70   MIP $115

□ 732, Bell 47 Police Helicopter, 1974-80
EX $10   NM $30   MIP $55

□ 734, Supermarine Swift, 1955-63, green/gray camouflage
EX $10   NM $45   MIP $85

□ 734, Republic P47 Thunderbolt, 1975-78, motorized
EX $75   NM $175   MIP $250

□ 735, Gloster Javelin, 1956-65, green/gray camouflage, wingspan, 3-1/4"
EX $15   NM $50   MIP $90

□ 736, Hawker Hunter, 1955-63, green/gray camouflage
EX $15   NM $45   MIP $85

□ 737, P1B Lightning, 1959-69, silver, RAF roundels
EX $20   NM $55   MIP $100

□ 738, D.H. Sea Vixen, 1960-65, gray, white undersides
EX $30   NM $65   MIP $110

□ 739, Mitsubishi A65M Zero, 1975-78, motorized
EX $75   NM $150   MIP $225

□ 741, Spitfire II, 1978-80, non-motorized
EX $40   NM $80   MIP $135

□ 749/707/99, Vulcan Bomber, 1955-56, silver, RAF roundels
EX $500   NM $1500   MIP $4000

□ 749/992, Avro Vulcan Delta Wing Bomber, 1955-56
EX $800   NM $1500   MIP $4500

□ 804, Nord Noratlas, 1960-64
EX $125   NM $250   MIP $400

□ 997, S.E. Caravelle Airliner, 1962-69, Air France, F-BGNY, starboard wing
EX $70   NM $150   MIP $250

(KP Photo by Dr. Douglas Sadecky)

□ 998, Bristol Brittania, 1959-65, silver, blue line, CF-CZA. Canadian Pacific shown
EX $50   NM $250   MIP $500

BUSES AND TAXIS

□ 29F/280, Observation Coach, 1954-60
EX $50   NM $75   MIP $100

(KP Photo)

□ 40H/254, Austin Taxi with Driver, 1951-62, Pictured here with Robot Traffic Signal, 773 (which is 2-3/4" H and approx. $35 MIP)
EX $65   NM $95   MIP $140

□ F1400, Peugeot 404 Taxi, 1967-71
EX $50   NM $75   MIP $100

□ F24XT, Ford Vedette Taxi, 1956-59
EX $60   NM $95   MIP $150

□ F29D, Autobus Parisien, 1948-51
EX $80   NM $135   MIP $200

□ F29F/571, Autocar Chausson, 1956-60
EX $70   NM $120   MIP $200

□ 266, Plymouth Plaza Taxi, 1960-67
EX $65   NM $100   MIP $155

□ 283, B.O.A.C. Coach, 1956-63
EX $55   NM $80   MIP $115

□ 284, Austin/London Taxi, 1972-79
EX $25   NM $35   MIP $75

□ 289, Routemaster Bus, 1964-80, Tern Shirts
EX $75   NM $100   MIP $150

□ 297, Silver Jubilee Bus, 1977
EX $25   NM $35   MIP $70

□ 953, Continental Touring Coach, 1963-66
EX $135   NM $200   MIP $350

CARS

□ 24C, Town Sedan, 1934-40
EX $85   NM $130   MIP $200

□ 27D/344, Estate Car, 1954-61
EX $45   NM $70   MIP $115

□ 281, Pathe News Camera Car, 1967-70
EX $70   NM $105   MIP $180

□ 30B, Rolls-Royce, 1946-50
EX $65   NM $100   MIP $125

□ 32/30A, Chrysler Airflow, 1935-40
EX $130   NM $250   MIP $450

□ 36A, Armstrong Siddeley, 1937-40, blue or brown
EX $85   NM $130   MIP $225

□ 57/005, Ford Thunderbird, 1965-67, (Hong Kong)
EX $50   NM $70   MIP $100

□ 105, Triumph TR-2, 1957-60, gray
EX $60   NM $85   MIP $135

DINKY

(KP Photo)

❏ **105, Triumph TR-2,** 1957-60, yellow, pictured here with 773 Robot Traffic Signal
EX $75   NM $120   MIP $200

❏ **106/140A, Austin Atlantic Convertible,** 1954-58, blue
EX $60   NM $95   MIP $150

❏ **115, Plymouth Fury Sports,** 1965-69
EX $35   NM $55   MIP $80

(KP Photo)

❏ **122, Volvo 265 DL Estate,** 1977-79, Blue, with opening rear hatch and brown plastic interior, black grille
EX $12   NM $22   MIP $45

❏ **129, Volkswagen 1300 Sedan,** 1965-76
EX $20   NM $35   MIP $75

❏ **131, Cadillac Eldorado,** 1956-62
EX $60   NM $95   MIP $135

❏ **145, Singer Vogue,** 1962-67
EX $50   NM $75   MIP $100

❏ **148, Ford Fairlane,** 1962-66, pale green
EX $60   NM $120   MIP $200

❏ **148, Ford Fairlane,** 1962-66, South African Issue, bright blue
EX $150   NM $300   MIP $700

❏ **153, Standard Vanguard,** 1954-60
EX $60   NM $85   MIP $120

❏ **157, Jaguar XK 120,** 1954-62, white
EX $120   NM $200   MIP $400

(KP Photo by Dr. Douglas Sadecky)

❏ **157, Jaguar XK 120,** 1959-62, gray-green, yellow or red
EX $95   NM $210   MIP $375

❏ **157, Jaguar XK 120,** 1954-62, turquoise, cerise
EX $80   NM $125   MIP $250

❏ **157, Jaguar XK 120,** 1954-62, yellow/gray
EX $80   NM $125   MIP $250

❏ **161, Mustang Fastback,** 1965-73
EX $35   NM $55   MIP $75

❏ **187, Volkswagen Karmann-Ghia,** 1959-64
EX $45   NM $80   MIP $125

(KP Photo)

❏ **191, Dodge Royal Sedan,** 1959-64, available in various color schemes
EX $80   NM $120   MIP $160

❏ **198, Rolls-Royce Phantom V,** 1962-69
EX $50   NM $75   MIP $100

❏ **212, Ford Cortina Rally Car,** 1967-69
EX $35   NM $55   MIP $75

❏ **231, Maserati Race Car,** 1954-64
EX $45   NM $75   MIP $110

❏ **238, Jaguar D-Type,** 1957-65
EX $60   NM $86   MIP $125

❏ **241, Lotus Racing Car,** 1963-70
EX $20   NM $30   MIP $50

❏ **342, Austin Mini-Moke,** 1967-75
EX $20   NM $30   MIP $55

(KP Photo)

❏ **F24Y/540, Studebaker Commander,** 1959-61, another in the line of French-made Dinky toys
EX $75   NM $95   MIP $160

❏ **F521/24B, Peugeot 403 Sedan,** 1959-61
EX $50   NM $90   MIP $135

❏ **F522/24C, Citroen DS-19,** 1959-68
EX $60   NM $90   MIP $135

❏ **F524/24E, Renault Dauphine,** 1959-62
EX $50   NM $80   MIP $125

❏ **F535/24T, Citroen 2 CV,** 1959-63
EX $50   NM $70   MIP $90

❏ **F545, DeSoto Diplomat,** 1960-63, orange
EX $25   NM $85   MIP $160

❏ **F545, DeSoto Diplomat,** 1960-63, green
EX $70   NM $130   MIP $200

❏ **F547, Panhard PL17,** 1960-68
EX $45   NM $80   MIP $120

❏ **F550, Chrysler Saratoga,** 1961-66
EX $70   NM $100   MIP $190

❏ **F565, Ford Thunderbird,** South African Issue, blue
EX $120   NM $250   MIP $600

CHARACTER & TV RELATED

❏ **100, Lady Penelope's Fab 1,** 1966-76, shocking pink version
EX $115   NM $200   MIP $340

❏ **100, Lady Penelope's Fab 1,** 1966-76, pink version
EX $80   NM $135   MIP $220

❏ **102, Joe's Car,** 1969-75
EX $60   NM $90   MIP $140

❏ **106, Prisoner Mini-Moke,** 1967-70
EX $120   NM $210   MIP $345

❏ **350, Tiny's Mini-Moke,** 1970-73
EX $60   NM $85   MIP $120

❏ **357, Klingon Battle Cruiser,** 1976-79
EX $30   NM $45   MIP $70

❏ **361, Galactic War Chariot,** 1979-80
EX $30   NM $45   MIP $70

(KP Photo)

❏ **371/803, U.S.S. Enterprise,** 1980
EX $40   NM $60   MIP $110

(KP Photo by Dr. Douglas Sadecky)

❏ **477, Parsley's Car Morris Oxford,** 1970-72, Cut-out stand-up figures of Parsley's friends were included for additional play
EX $65   NM $115   MIP $145

❏ **485, Santa Special Model T Ford,** 1964-68
EX $65   NM $100   MIP $150

❏ **F1406, Renault Sinpar,** 1968-71
EX $80   NM $135   MIP $220

CONSTRUCTION

❏ **437, Muir Hill Two-Wheel Loader,** 1962-78
EX $30   NM $40   MIP $60

❏ **561, Blaw Knox Bulldozer**
EX $45   NM $75   MIP $115

❏ **963, Road Grader,** 1973-75
EX $30   NM $45   MIP $70

(KP Photo)

❏ **965, Euclid Dump Truck,** 1955-69, with lever-operated tipping bed. Part of the "Dinky Supertoys" range
EX $55   NM $80   MIP $125

❏ **971, Coles Mobile Crane,** 1955-66
EX $40   NM $70   MIP $110

❏ **984, Atlas Digger**
EX $30   NM $45   MIP $70

❏ **F595, Salev Crane,** 1959-61
EX $65   NM $100   MIP $175

❏ **F830, Richier Road Roller,** 1959-69
EX $75   NM $100   MIP $150

EMERGENCY VEHICLES

❏ **Fire Chief Land Rover**
EX $35   NM $50   MIP $85

❏ **25H/25, Streamlined Fire Engine,** 1946-53
EX $75   NM $100   MIP $175

❏ **30F, Ambulance**
EX $100   NM $160   MIP $275

(KP Photo by Dr. Douglas Sadecky)

❏ **32E, Berliet Fire Pumper,** Included two detachable hose reels as accessories. French-made Dinky toy
EX $75   NM $95   MIP $120

❏ **244, Plymouth Police Car,** 1977-80
EX $25   NM $35   MIP $50

❏ **251, USA Police Car (Pontiac)**
EX $35   NM $50   MIP $85

(KP Photo)

❏ **255, Mersey Tunnel Police Land Rover,** 1955-61
EX $60   NM $85   MIP $135

❏ **263, Superior Criterion Ambulance,** 1962-68
EX $50   NM $75   MIP $100

❏ **268, Range Rover Ambulance,** 1974-78
EX $25   NM $35   MIP $50

(KP Photo by Dr. Douglas Sadecky)

❏ **276, Airport Fire Tender with Flashing Light,** 1962-69
EX $32   NM $65   MIP $100

(KP Photo by Dr. Douglas Sadecky)

❏ **277, Superior Criterion Ambulance,** 1962-68, The roof beacon warning light actually flashed with the aid of a small battery
EX $40   NM $75   MIP $110

❏ **278, Vauxhall Victor Ambulance,** 1964-70
EX $55   NM $85   MIP $115

DINKY

DINKY

(KP Photo)

❑ **288, Superior Cadillac Ambulance,** 1971-79, opening rear hatch with plastic patient on stretcher
EX $15   NM $28   MIP $60

❑ **955, Commer Fire Engine,** 1955-69
EX $60   NM $85   MIP $135

❑ **956, Bedford Fire Escape,** 1969-74
EX $75   NM $110   MIP $175

❑ **F25D/562, Citroen Fire Van,** 1959-63
EX $80   NM $110   MIP $250

(KP Photo by Dr. Douglas Sadecky)

❑ **F32D/899, Delahaye Fire Truck,** 1955-70, the white tires really enhance this French-made Dinky toy
EX $120   NM $190   MIP $375

❑ **F501, Citroen DS19 Police Car,** 1967-70
EX $75   NM $95   MIP $175

❑ **F551, Ford Police Car,** 1960s
EX $50   NM $100   MIP $150

FARM

❑ **27A/300, Massey-Harris Tractor**
EX $50   NM $75   MIP $120

❑ **27G/342, Moto-Cart,** 1954-60
EX $35   NM $50   MIP $75

❑ **37N/301, Field Marshall Tractor,** 1954-65
EX $60   NM $85   MIP $150

(KP Photo)

❑ **105A, Garden Roller,** 1948-54
EX $15   NM $25   MIP $35

❑ **305, David Brown Tractor,** 1966-75
EX $60   NM $120   MIP $200

❑ **324, Hayrake,** 1954-71
EX $30   NM $40   MIP $60

MILITARY

❑ **25WM/60, Bedford Military Truck**
EX $80   NM $125   MIP $250

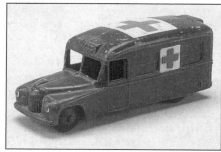
(KP Photo)

❑ **30HM/624, Daimler Ambulance,** a popular casting available in military and civilian variations
EX $80   NM $125   MIP $250

❑ **30SM/625, Austin Covered Truck**
EX $85   NM $135   MIP $275

(KP Photo)

❑ **152B, Reconnaisance Car,** This model was produced in pre- and post-war periods
EX $40   NM $60   MIP $100

❑ **161A, Searchlight,** prewar
EX $125   NM $250   MIP $500

❑ **601, Austin Paramoke**
EX $25   NM $35   MIP $50

❑ **612, Commando Jeep**
EX $25   NM $35   MIP $50

❑ **618, AEC with Helicopter**
EX $50   NM $85   MIP $125

❑ **620, Berliet Missile Launcher**
EX $75   NM $100   MIP $175

❑ **621, Three Ton Army Wagon,** 1954-63
EX $50   NM $85   MIP $125

❑ **622, 10 Ton Army Truck,** 1954-63
EX $20   NM $40   MIP $80

❑ **626, Military Ambulance**
EX $25   NM $45   MIP $75

❑ **630, Ferret Armoured Car**
EX $25   NM $35   MIP $50

❑ **651, Centurian Tank**
EX $30   NM $50   MIP $75

❑ **660, Tank Transporter**
EX $75   NM $100   MIP $175

(KP Photo)

❑ **661, Recovery Tractor,** 1957, Tow hook has working reel
EX $60   NM $90   MIP $140

(KP Photo by Dr. Douglas Sadecky)

❑ **666, Missile Erecting Vehicle,** 1959, with Corporal Missile and Launching Platform
EX $100   NM $155   MIP $240

(KP Photo by Dr. Douglas Sadecky)

❑ **667, Missile Servicing Platform,** 1960, this vehicle made a nice companion to the 666 Missile Erecting Vehicle. A nicely detailed toy, it had a short production run
EX $95   NM $130   MIP $270

❑ **677, Armoured Command Vehicle**
EX $50   NM $85   MIP $125

(KP Photo)

❑ **692, 5.5 Medium Gun,** 1955
EX $15   NM $30   MIP $50

(KP Photo)

❑ **F80C/817, AMX Tank**
EX $50   NM $75   MIP $100

❑ **F80F/820, Military Ambulance**
EX $50   NM $75   MIP $100

❑ **F806, Berliet Wrecker**
EX $60   NM $90   MIP $140

❑ **F810, Dodge Command Car**
EX $40   NM $60   MIP $85

❑ **F816, Jeep**
EX $50   NM $75   MIP $115

❑ **F823, GMC Tanker**
EX $125   NM $250   MIP $500

❑ **F883, AMX Bridge Layer**
EX $75   NM $110   MIP $200

MISCELLANEOUS

(KP Photo by Dr. Douglas Sadecky)

❑ **796, Healey Sports Boat on Trailer,** 1960-62
EX $25   NM $35   MIP $55

MOTORCYCLES AND CARAVANS

❑ **Caravane Caravelair**
EX $75   NM $150   MIP $250

❑ **30G, Caravan,** postwar
EX $40   NM $60   MIP $85

❑ **30G, Caravan,** prewar
EX $55   NM $85   MIP $150

❑ **37B, Police Motorcyclist,** 1938-40
EX $50   NM $75   MIP $125

❑ **37B, Police Motorcyclist,** 1946-48
EX $30   NM $45   MIP $70

❑ **42B, Police Motorcycle Patrol,** 1936-40
EX $50   NM $75   MIP $125

❑ **42B, Police Motorcycle Patrol,** 1946-53
EX $30   NM $45   MIP $70

❑ **188, 4-Berth Caravan w/ Transparent Roof,** 1963-69
EX $25   NM $45   MIP $85

❑ **190, Caravan,** 1956-64
EX $30   NM $45   MIP $60

(KP Photo by Dr. Douglas Sadecky)

❑ **270/44B, A.A. Motorcycle Patrol,** 1946-64, the decal on the sidecar changed depending in which country the motorcycle was sold
EX $30   NM $45   MIP $70

❑ **271, Touring Secours Motorcycle Patrol,** 1960s, Swiss version
EX $70   NM $110   MIP $200

TRUCKS

❑ **Leland Tanker,** Corn Products
EX $700   NM $1200   MIP $3000

❑ **14A/400, B.E.V. Truck,** 1954-60
EX $15   NM $30   MIP $70

❑ **22C, Motor Truck,** red, blue
EX $150   NM $350   MIP $650

❑ **22C, Motor Truck,** red, green, blue
EX $80   NM $120   MIP $200

❑ **25B, Covered Wagon,** green, gray
EX $65   NM $115   MIP $160

❑ **25B, Covered Wagon,** Carter Paterson
EX $150   NM $300   MIP $750

❑ **25D, Petrol Wagon,** Power
EX $150   NM $300   MIP $500

❑ **25F, Market Gardeners Wagon,** yellow
EX $65   NM $115   MIP $160

❑ **25R, Forward Control Wagon,** 1948-53
EX $45   NM $65   MIP $90

❑ **30W/421, Electric Articulated Vehicle**
EX $60   NM $85   MIP $120

❑ **33a, Mechanical Horse,** 1935-41
EX $35   NM $60   MIP $100

❑ **280, Midland Bank,** 1966-68
EX $60   NM $85   MIP $120

❑ **408/922, Big Bedford,** maroon, fawn
EX $80   NM $120   MIP $200

❑ **408/922, Big Bedford,** blue, yellow
EX $90   NM $135   MIP $210

(KP Photo)

DINKY

❑ **419/933, Leyland Cement Wagon,** 1956-59, one of Dinky's foreign vehicles, this toy was made in Argentina
EX $90   NM $130   MIP $220

❑ **422/30R, Thames Flat Truck,** 1951-60
EX $45   NM $75   MIP $110

❑ **431, Guy Warrior 4 Ton,** 1958-64
EX $150   NM $270   MIP $450

❑ **440, Studebaker Mobilgas Tanker,** 1954-61
EX $70   NM $100   MIP $175

❑ **449, Chevrolet El Camino,** 1961-68
EX $35   NM $65   MIP $100

(KP Photo by Dr. Douglas Sadecky)

❑ **449/451, Johnston Road Sweeper,** 1970s, as the toy was pushed forward, a spring coil turned the brushes in a sweeping motion
EX $25   NM $50   MIP $75

(KP Photo)

❑ **501, Foden Diesel 8-Wheel Wagon,** 1948-52, Dark cab and bed, red fenders and chassis. Various color variations were available. Pictured here is the first-version cab, updated in 1952. Part of the Dinky Supertoy range
EX $160   NM $220   MIP $435

❑ **503/903, Foden Flat Truck w/ Tailboard 1,** red/black
EX $140   NM $210   MIP $450

❑ **503/903, Foden Flat Truck w/Tailboard 1,** gray/blue
EX $140   NM $210   MIP $450

❑ **503/903, Foden Flat Truck w/ Tailboard 2,** blue/yellow, orange or blue
EX $90   NM $150   MIP $275

(KP Photo by Dr. Douglas Sadecky)

❑ **881, Pinder Circus Truck and Wagon,** 1969-71, A French-made Dinky toy. This photo shows the animals and decorative labels still in the package
EX $110   NM $235   MIP $375

(KP Photo by Dr. Douglas Sadecky)

❑ **882, Pinder Circus Peugeot and Caravan,** 1969-71, The Peugeot and Caravan are the only other vehicles produced in the Pinder Circus livery by Dinky. It would have been interesting to see what other circus vehicles would have been produced had sales been better. Again, this is a French-produced model
EX $110   NM $240   MIP $380

❑ **935, Leyland Octapus Flat Truck w/ Chassis,** 1964-66
EX $500   NM $1000   MIP $1600

❑ **936, Leyland Eight-Wheeled Test Chassis,** 1964-69
EX $65   NM $125   MIP $175

❑ **941, Foden Mobilgas Tanker,** 1954-57
EX $145   NM $350   MIP $750

❑ **942, Foden Regent Tanker,** 1954-57
EX $135   NM $300   MIP $550

❑ **944, Leland Tanker,** 1963-69, Shell/BP
EX $125   NM $215   MIP $450

(KP Photo by Dr. Douglas Sadecky)

❑ **948, McLean Tractor-Trailer,** 1961-67
EX $95   NM $190   MIP $280

❑ **974, A.E.C. Hoynor Transporter,** 1969-75
EX $60   NM $90   MIP $130

(KP Photo by Dr. Douglas Sadecky)

❑ **982, Pullmore Car Transporter with 794 Loading Ramp,** 1954-63, the 794 loading ramp cam separately packaged in the Transporter box and was used to unload the cars
EX $85   NM $140   MIP $190

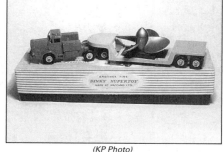

(KP Photo)

❑ **986, Mighty Antar With Propeller,** 1959-64, the propeller included with this model is made of plastic
EX $150   NM $300   MIP $425

❑ **F32AB, Panhard SNCF Semi Trailer,** 1954-59
EX $100   NM $165   MIP $280

❑ **F32AJ, Panhard Kodak Semi Trailer,** 1952-54
EX $140   NM $250   MIP $450

(KP Photo)

❑ **F32C, Panhard Esso Tanker,** 1954-59, this toy was a French-made vehicle as part of the Dinky Supertoys line
EX $75   NM $120   MIP $170

❑ **F33C/579, Simca Glass Truck,** yellow, green
EX $100   NM $150   MIP $250

❑ **F33C/579, Simca Glass Truck,** gray, green
EX $75   NM $120   MIP $170

❑ **F35A/582, Citroen Wrecker,** 1959-71
EX $75   NM $120   MIP $250

❑ **F36A/897, Willeme Log Truck,** 1956-71
EX $75   NM $120   MIP $200

(KP Photo)

❑ **F36B/896, Willeme Semi Trailer Truck,** 1959-71, another French-made Dinky toy
EX $95   NM $140   MIP $235

❑ **F38A/895, Unic Bucket Truck,** 1957-65
EX $75   NM $120   MIP $225

(KP Photo by Dr. Douglas Sadecky)

❑ **F39A/984, Unic Auto Transporter,** 1959-68, French-made Dinky toy, part of the Supertoys line. Ramp raises and lowers with a lever on the side of the trailer
EX $100   NM $200   MIP $300

❑ **F561, Renault Estafette**
EX $50   NM $85   MIP $150

❑ **F586, Citroen Milk Truck,** 1961-65
EX $145   NM $275   MIP $600

❑ **F898, Berliet Transformer Carrier,** 1961-65
EX $100   NM $200   MIP $450

VANS

❑ **28B, Pickfords Delivery Van,** 1934-35, type 1
EX $300   NM $500   MIP $1000

❑ **28B, Pickfords Delivery Van,** 1934-35, type 2
EX $200   NM $375   MIP $600

❑ **28E, Ensign Delivery Van,** 1934, type 1
EX $300   NM $500   MIP $1000

❑ **28N, Atco Delivery Van,** 1935-40, type 2
EX $200   NM $375   MIP $850

❑ **28N, Atco Delivery Van,** 1935-40, type 3
EX $135   NM $200   MIP $350

❑ **31B/451, Trojan Dunlop Van,** 1952-57
EX $70   NM $110   MIP $185

(KP Photo by Dr. Douglas Sadecky)

❑ **260, Royal Mail Van,** 1955-61
EX $50   NM $100   MIP $150

❑ **273, Mini Minor Van,** 1960s, R.A.C.
EX $65   NM $115   MIP $150

❑ **274, Mini Minor Van,** Joseph Mason Paints
EX $150   NM $300   MIP $500

❑ **417, Ford Transit Van,** 1978-80
EX $15   NM $20   MIP $30

❑ **470, Austin Van,** 1954-56, Shell/BP
EX $60   NM $110   MIP $175

❑ **471, Austin Van,** 1955-63, Nestle's
EX $60   NM $110   MIP $175

❑ **472, Austin Van,** 1957-60, Raleigh
EX $60   NM $110   MIP $175

❑ **482, Bedford Van,** 1956-58, Dinky Toys
EX $60   NM $115   MIP $200

❑ **514, Guy Van,** Lyons
EX $275   NM $550   MIP $1600

❑ **514, Guy Van,** Spratts
EX $135   NM $300   MIP $575

(KP Photo)

❑ **514, Guy Van,** Slumberland
EX $145   NM $315   MIP $590

❑ **923, Bedford Van,** 1955-59, Heinz
EX $100   NM $165   MIP $300

❑ **967, BBC-TV Control Room,** 1959-64
EX $60   NM $125   MIP $185

(KP Photo by Dr. Douglas Sadecky)

❑ **968, BBC-TV Camera Truck,** 1959-64
EX $60   NM $125   MIP $185

DINKY

(KP Photo by Dr. Douglas Sadecky)

❑ **969, BBC TV Extending Mast Vehicle,** 1959-64
EX $60   **NM** $125   **MIP** $185

(KP Photo by Dr. Douglas Sadecky)

❑ **987, ABC-TV Mobile Control Room,** 1962-69, A camera and cameraman was also included with this van
EX $65   **NM** $130   **MIP** $210

(KP Photo by Dr. Douglas Sadecky)

❑ **988, ABC-TV Transmitter Van,** 1962-69, this was the companion vehicle to the 987 ABC TV Mobile Control Room
EX $65   **NM** $130   **MIP** $210

❑ **F561, Citroen Cibie Delivery Van,** 1960-63
EX $90   **NM** $150   **MIP** $350

❑ **F571, Saviem Race Horse Van,** 1969-71
EX $125   **NM** $225   **MIP** $400

Eagle Collectibles

A view of four Plymouth Prowlers in 1:43-scale by Eagle.

Eagle Collectibles produce 1:43 and 1:18-scale cars of almost every variety, from 1940 Ford Coupe Street Rods to Series II Land Rover Trucks. Eagle's process from concept to market is about 15 months. Wisely, they generally seek out making models of cars that haven't been represented by other die-cast manufacturers. They are, at present, the only firm making 1:18-scale Land Rovers, and the only company outside of Minichamps that produces many European road cars, like the Saab Sonett.

After taking hundreds of photographs and measurements of the real vehicle, plans of the scale model are drawn to keep the proportions accurate. Then, a 1:12-scale mock-up is created to see how well the 90 or more parts will fit together. At this stage, Eagle also figures out which materials are best for sections of the car—whether a piece should be plastic, die-cast or photoetched. Then the manufacturing begins.

MARKET UPDATE

Eagle Collectibles are generally accessible models. Many toy and hobby stores carry the brand, but it can be a challenge to locate non-American representations, like Renault Clio rally cars and "Polizei" Volkswagens. The prices for most 1:18-scale models average about $30, and 1:43-scale vehicles retail for about $20, sometimes less.

Two 1:18-scale 1965 Shelby 350 Mustangs, with opening doors and hoods.

Another 1:43-scale vehicle: A Plymouth Belvedere driven by Paul Goldsmith.

Porsche 911 Carrera RS "Bosch" No. 10 East African Safari, 1973. Limited to only 2,000 pieces.

Detail of the 911 No. 10 Safari.

Dodge Viper GTS, San Diego County Sheriff car in 1:43-scale.

More 1:43-scale Dodge Vipers from the Twin Stryker Series.

Two Land Rovers: The West Sussex Fire Brigade Pickup and the Dorset Fire Brigade vehicle. Highly-detailed Series II Land Rovers in 1:18-scale are nice to see on the market.

'40 DELUXE COUPE

❑ **1940 Deluxe Ford Coupe,** 2000, Green-gray body, silver grille, bumpers and hubcaps, whitewall tires, opening hood, doors and trunk, 1:18 scale, Model No. 3816

EX n/a   NM n/a   MIP $31

❑ **1940 Deluxe Ford Coupe,** 2000, Folkstone gray body, silver grille, bumpers and hubcaps, whitewall tires, opening hood, doors and trunk, 1:18 scale, Model No. 3811

EX n/a   NM n/a   MIP $31

❑ **1940 Deluxe Ford Coupe,** 2000, Burgundy body, silver grille, bumpers and hubcaps, whitewall tires, opening hood, doors and trunk, 1:18 scale, Model No. 3810

EX n/a   NM n/a   MIP $31

❑ **1940 Deluxe Ford Coupe,** 2000, Dark metallic blue body, silver grille, bumpers and hubcaps, whitewall tires, opening hood, doors and trunk, 1:18 scale, Model No. 3808

EX n/a   NM n/a   MIP $31

❑ **1940 Deluxe Ford Coupe,** 2000, Cream body, silver grille, bumpers and hubcaps, whitewall tires, opening hood, doors and trunk, 1:18 scale, Model No. 3803

EX n/a   NM n/a   MIP $31

❑ **1940 Deluxe Ford Coupe,** 2000, Red body, silver grille, bumpers and hubcaps, whitewall tires, opening hood, doors and trunk, 1:18 scale, Model No. 3802

EX n/a   NM n/a   MIP $31

(Eagle Photo)

❑ **1940 Deluxe Ford Coupe,** 2000, Black body, silver grille, bumpers and hubcaps, whitewall tires, opening hood, doors and trunk. Shown here with Folkstone Gray and Cream models, (#3811 and 3803), 1:18 scale, Model No. 3801

EX n/a   NM n/a   MIP $31

(Eagle Photo)

❑ **1940 Deluxe Ford Coupe: North Carolina Highway Patrol,** 2000, Dark green body with black hood, police shield graphic on doors, silver grille, bumpers and hubcaps, whitewall tires, opening hood, doors and trunk. Shown here with Folkstone Gray and Cream models, (#3811 and 3803), 1:18 scale, Model No. 3815

EX n/a   NM n/a   MIP $31

'40 DELUXE COUPE/ HOT ROD

❑ **1940 Deluxe Ford Coupe Hot Rod,** 2000, Bright green with scallop graphics, black running boards, no bumpers, black interior, 1:18 scale, Model No. 3814

EX n/a   NM n/a   MIP $31

❑ **1940 Deluxe Ford Coupe Hot Rod,** 2000, Purple with yellow and orange flame graphics, black running boards, no bumpers, black interior, 1:18 scale, Model No. 3812

EX n/a   NM n/a   MIP $31

❑ **1940 Deluxe Ford Coupe Hot Rod,** 2000, Bright blue with magenta scallops graphics, silver and blue wheels, black running boards, no bumpers, black interior, 1:18 scale, Model No. 3805

EX n/a   NM n/a   MIP $31

❑ **1940 Deluxe Ford Coupe Hot Rod,** 2000, Metallic gold with gold flame graphics, silver and black wheels, opening doors and hood, no bumpers, dual exhaust, 1:18 scale, Model No. 3817

EX n/a   NM n/a   MIP $31

❑ **1940 Deluxe Ford Coupe Hot Rod,** 2000, Yellow with red flame graphics, silver and black wheels, opening doors and hood, no bumpers, dual exhaust, 1:18 scale, Model No. 3807

EX n/a   NM n/a   MIP $31

❑ **1940 Deluxe Ford Coupe Hot Rod,** 2000, Black with yellow flames graphics, silver and black wheels, opening doors and hood, no bumpers, dual exhaust, 1:18 scale, Model No. 3806

EX n/a   NM n/a   MIP $31

(Eagle Photo)

❑ **1940 Deluxe Ford Coupe Hot Rod,** 2000, Red with yellow flames graphics, silver and black wheels, opening doors and hood, no bumpers, dual exhaust. Shown here with others in the series, (#3806, #3807 and #3817), 1:18 scale, Model No. 3804

EX n/a   NM n/a   MIP $31

911 CARRERA RSR 3.0L

(Eagle Photo)

❑ **Porsche Carrera RSR: Street Version,** 2000, Silver body, silver multi-spoked wheels, detailed interior, 1:43 scale, Model No. 1137

EX n/a   NM n/a   MIP $20

❑ **Porsche Carrera RSR: Street Version,** 2000, Pink body, black wheels, detailed interior, 1:43 scale, Model No. 3678

EX n/a   NM n/a   MIP $20

❑ **Porsche Carrera RSR: Street Version,** 2000, Red body, silver wheels, detailed interior, 1:43 scale, Model No. 3677

EX n/a   NM n/a   MIP $20

911S/911 2.4L/911 RS

(Eagle Photo)

❑ **Porsche 911 2.4L, 1973,** 2000, Signal yellow body (a dark orange-yellow), silver, five-spoke wheels, silver trim. Shown here with olive version, (#3695), 1:43 scale, Model No. 1096
EX n/a   NM n/a   MIP $20

(Eagle Photo)

❑ **Porsche 911 2.4L, 1973,** 2000, Red body with silver five-spoke wheels, black interior, silver trim. Shown here with silver-gray version, (#1130), 1:43 scale, Model No. 1019
EX n/a   NM n/a   MIP $20

❑ **Porsche 911 2.4L, 1973,** 2000, Silver-gray body with silver five-spoke wheels, gray interior, 1:43 scale, Model No. 1130
EX n/a   NM n/a   MIP $20

(Eagle Photo)

❑ **Porsche 911 2.4L, 1973,** 2001, Black body with silver five-spoke wheels, silver-gray trim, 1:43 scale, Model No. 3682
EX n/a   NM n/a   MIP $20

❑ **Porsche 911 2.4L, 1973,** 2001, Olive green body with silver five-spoke wheels, silver-gray trim, 1:43 scale, Model No. 3695
EX n/a   NM n/a   MIP $20

❑ **Porsche 911 Carrera RS 2.7L, 1973,** 2000, White with blue Carrera stripes, blue and silver wheels, black interior, 1:43 scale, Model No. 1090
EX n/a   NM n/a   MIP $20

❑ **Porsche 911 Carrera RS 2.7L, 1973,** 2000, Blue with black Carrera stripes, black and silver wheels, black interior, 1:43 scale, Model No. 1094
EX n/a   NM n/a   MIP $20

(Eagle Photo)

❑ **Porsche 911 Carrera RS 2.7L, 1973,** 2001, Red with black Carrera stripes, black and silver wheels, black interior. Shown here with white and blue versions, (#1090 and #1094), 1:43 scale, Model No. 3694
EX n/a   NM n/a   MIP $20

❑ **Porsche 911 S no. 105, Tour de France, 1973,** 1999, Dark-yellow body with blue bumpers, "Galla" and number "105" with sponsor labels, black interior, silver five-spoke wheels, 1:43 scale, Model No. 1131
EX n/a   NM n/a   MIP $20

❑ **Porsche 911 S no. 80, Monte Carlo Rallye, 1972,** 1998, Orange body with red stripes, five-spoke silver wheels, black interior, number "80", sponsor labels including "Shell", 1:43 scale, Model No. 1044
EX n/a   NM n/a   MIP $20

911S/911 2.4L/911 RS SC 3.0L

❑ **Porsche 911 SC 3.0L "Esso" no. 9, Monte Carlo, 1980,** 2001, Limited edition of 2500 pieces, 1:43 scale, Model No. 3700
EX n/a   NM n/a   MIP $20

(Eagle Photo)

❑ **Porsche 911 SC 3.0L "Gitane" no. 3, Monte Carlo, 1978,** 2001, Blue body with number "3" on sides, "Gitanes" and "Michelin" sponsor labels, gray multi-spoked wheels. Limited edition to 2500 pieces, 1:43 scale, Model No. 3699
EX n/a   NM n/a   MIP $20

❑ **Porsche 911 SC 3.0L "Kenwood" no. 16, Tour de Corse, 1982,** 2001, Limited edition of 2500 pieces, 1:43 scale, Model No. 3710
EX n/a   NM n/a   MIP $20

CHEVROLET CORVETTE "GRAND SPORT"

❑ **Corvette "Grand Sport" Coupe no. 2, 12 Hours Sebring, 1964,** 2000, Blue body with white stripe, number "2" on hood, sides and rear, silver wheels, Goodyear tires. Drivers: AJ Foyt and J. Canon, 1:43 scale, Model No. 2001
EX n/a   NM n/a   MIP $20

❑ **Corvette "Grand Sport" Coupe no. 2, 12 Hours Sebring, 1965,** 2000, Blue and white body with number "2" on sides, hood and rear, silver wheels, 1:43 scale, Model No. 2010
EX n/a   NM n/a   MIP $20

❑ **Corvette "Grand Sport" Coupe no. 3, 12 Hours Sebring, 1964,** 2000, Blue body with red and white stripe on hood, roof and trunk. Number "3" on hood, sides and rear. Silver spoked wheels, Firestone tires. Drivers: Johnson and Morgan, 1:43 scale, Model No. 2002
EX n/a   NM n/a   MIP $20

❑ **Corvette "Grand Sport" Coupe no. 4, 12 Hours Sebring, 1964,** 2000, White body with blue light covers, number "4" on hood, sides and rear, silver wheels, Firestone tires, black interior, 1:43 scale, Model No. 2010
EX n/a   NM n/a   MIP $20

❑ **Corvette "Grand Sport" Coupe no. 50, Nassau Speed Week, 1963,** 2000, Blue body with circle number "50" on hood and sides. White stripe on hood. Chrome wheels, Goodyear tires, 1:43 scale, Model No. 2009
EX n/a   NM n/a   MIP $20

❑ **Corvette "Grand Sport" Coupe no. 65, Nassau Speed Week, 1963,** 2000, Blue body with circle number "65" on hood and sides. Black stripe on hood. Chrome wheels, Goodyear tires, 1:43 scale, Model No. 2008
EX n/a   NM n/a   MIP $20

(Eagle Photo)

❑ **Corvette "Grand Sport" Coupe no. 67, Road America, 1967,** 2000, White body with number "67" on hood, sides and rear, silver wheels, Goodyear tires. Drivers: Jall and Penske, 1:43 scale, Model No. 2006
EX n/a   NM n/a   MIP $20

❑ **Corvette "Grand Sport" Coupe no. 80, Nassau Speed Week, 1963,** 2000, Blue body with circle number "80" hood and sides. Red stripe on hood. Chrome wheels, Goodyear tires. Driver: John Mecom, 1:43 scale, Model No. 2003
EX n/a   NM n/a   MIP $20

❑ **Corvette "Grand Sport" Roadster, no. 10, 12-hours Sebring, 1966,** 2000, Blue body, yellow pipes, number "10" on sides, hood and trunk, silver wheels, Firestone tires, 1:43 scale, Model No. 2005
EX n/a   NM n/a   MIP $20

❑ **Corvette "Grand Sport" Roadster, no. 12, Bridgehampton, 1966,** 2000, White body, wide blue stripe, number "12" on hood, sides and rear, 1:43 scale, Model No. 2004
EX n/a   NM n/a   MIP $20

DELUXE CONVERTIBLE/ COUPE 1941

(Eagle Photo)

❑ **Chevrolet Deluxe Convertible 1941,** 2000, Black body, red interor, light-tan covertible roof cover, silver trim, whitewall tires, 1:18 scale, Model No. 4352
EX n/a   NM n/a   MIP $31

❑ **Chevrolet Deluxe Convertible 1941,** 2000, Red body, light-brown interior, silver trim, whitewall tires, 1:18 scale, Model No. 4351
EX n/a   NM n/a   MIP $31

(Eagle Photo)

❑ **Chevrolet Deluxe Convertible 1941,** 2000, Beige body, red interior, silver trim, whitewall tires. Each of the 1941 Chevrolets in this series are hand-assembled from 150 pieces. Pictured here with red model (#4351), 1:18 scale, Model No. 4350
EX n/a   NM n/a   MIP $31

❑ **Chevrolet Deluxe Convertible 1941, soft top,** 2000, Dark gray body, black soft top roof, silver trim, whitewall tires, 1:18 scale, Model No. 4355
EX n/a   NM n/a   MIP $31

❑ **Chevrolet Deluxe Convertible 1941, soft top,** 2000, Dark blue body, dark blue soft top roof, silver trim, whitewall tires, 1:18 scale, Model No. 4354
EX n/a   NM n/a   MIP $31

❑ **Chevrolet Deluxe Convertible 1941, soft top,** 2000, Reed green body, black soft top roof, silver trim, whitewall tires. The three color variations in the series are shown in this photo, 1:18 scale, Model No. 4353
EX n/a   NM n/a   MIP $31

❑ **Chevrolet Deluxe Coupe 1941,** 2000, blue-gray body, silver trim, whitewall tires. Opening hood shows detailed engine on each of these convertibles and coupes, 1:18 scale, Model No. 4358
EX n/a   NM n/a   MIP $31

(Eagle Photo)

❑ **Chevrolet Deluxe Coupe 1941,** 2000, Dark green body, silver trim, whitewall tires. Two of the models from the series are shown here, 1:18 scale, Model No. 4357
EX n/a   NM n/a   MIP $31

❑ **Chevrolet Deluxe Coupe 1941,** 2000, Two-tone color, dark gray and burgundy body, silver trim, whitewall tires, 1:18 scale, Model No. 4356
EX n/a   NM n/a   MIP $31

DODGE CHARGER DAYTONA

(Eagle Photo)

❑ **Dodge Charger Daytona Street Legal,** 1998, Dark blue, gray and white, silver five-spoke wheels, white interior. Shown here with white and red model, (#1407), 1:43 scale, Model No. 1408
EX n/a   NM n/a   MIP $20

EAGLE / CHEVROLET

❑ **Dodge Charger Daytona Street Legal,** 1998, Metallic brown and white, silver five-spoke wheels, brown interior, 1:43 scale, Model No. 1411
EX n/a   **NM** n/a   **MIP** $20

(Eagle Photo)

❑ **Dodge Charger Daytona Street Legal,** 1998, Bright blue and white, silver five-spoke wheels, black interior. Shown here with metallic brown and white version, (#1411), 1:43 scale, Model No. 1409
EX n/a   **NM** n/a   **MIP** $20

❑ **Dodge Charger Daytona Street Legal,** 1998, White and red body, silver five-spoke wheels, black interior, 1:43 scale, Model No. 1407
EX n/a   **NM** n/a   **MIP** $20

(Eagle Photo)

❑ **Dodge Charger Daytona Street Legal,** 2000, Silver body with black stripe and spoiler, black interior, silver five-spoke wheels, 1:43 scale, Model No. 1412
EX n/a   **NM** n/a   **MIP** $20

❑ **Dodge Charger Daytona Street Legal,** 2001, Light yellow body with black stripe and spoiler, black interior, silver five-spoke wheels. Limited edition: 2500 pieces, 1:43 scale, Model No. 1415
EX n/a   **NM** n/a   **MIP** $20

❑ **Dodge Charger Daytona, Chrysler Race Engineering Car,** 1998, Bright blue body with white stripe and spoiler, number "88" on sides, roof and trunk, blue wheels, black interior. Modeled after the first car to break 200 miles, driver; Buddy Baker, 1:43 scale, Model No. 1402
EX n/a   **NM** n/a   **MIP** $20

❑ **Dodge Charger Daytona, no. 06, 1970 Daytona 500,** 2000, White body with red stripe and spoiler, silver wheels, number "06" on sides and roof, 1:43 scale, Model No. 1414
EX n/a   **NM** n/a   **MIP** $20

(Eagle Photo)

❑ **Dodge Charger Daytona, no. 30,** 2002, Bright blue body with yellow stripe and spoiler, black roof, number "30" on sides, roof and trunk, black wheels, black interior. Driver; Dave Marcis, 1:43 scale, Model No. 1418
EX n/a   **NM** n/a   **MIP** $20

❑ **Dodge Charger Daytona, no. 31, 1970 World 600,** 2001, Yellow and blue body with number "31" on sides, roof and trunk. Driver, Jim Vandiver. Limited edition to 2500 pieces, 1:43 scale, Model No. 1417
EX n/a   **NM** n/a   **MIP** $20

(Eagle Photo)

❑ **Dodge Charger Daytona, no. 42, 1970 National 500,** 2001, Hot pink and orange body, number "42" on hood, sides and roof, driver: Marty Robbins. Limited edition to 2500 pieces. Shown here with 1970 World 600 Dodge Charger Daytona, (#1417), 1:43 scale, Model No. 1416
EX n/a   **NM** n/a   **MIP** $20

(Eagle Photo)

❑ **Dodge Charger Daytona, no. 71, 1970 Talladega,** 1998, Red body with white stripe and spoiler, white number "71" on sides, roof and back, black wheels, Goodyear tires, red rollbar. Shown here with Daytona Chrysler Engineering car, (#1402), 1:43 scale, Model No. 1401
EX n/a   **NM** n/a   **MIP** $20

❑ **Dodge Charger Daytona, no.6,** 1998, Red body with black roof, orange stripe and spoiler, black interior, silver wheels, outline number "6" on doors, yellow "6" on roof. Driver, Buddy Baker, 1:43 scale, Model No. 1405
EX n/a   **NM** n/a   **MIP** $20

(Eagle Photo)

❑ **Dodge Charger Daytona, Street Legal no. 99,** 1998, Dark blue body with white spoiler and roofline, white wheels. Number "99" on doors, roof and trunk, Dow logo on hood and sides. Driver, Richard Brickhouse. Shown here with Daytona 500 no. 06 and Daytona no. 6 (#1414 and 1405), 1:43 scale, Model No. 1404
EX n/a   **NM** n/a   **MIP** $20

DODGE RAM 2500 PICKUP

❑ **Dodge Ram 2500 V10 Magnum,** 2001, Dark-gray and light-silver body, silver wheels, gray interior, 1:43 scale, Model No. 3652
EX n/a   **NM** n/a   **MIP** $20

❑ **Dodge Ram 2500 V10 Magnum,** 2001, Dark chestnut and light-silver body, silver wheels, gray interior, 1:43 scale, Model No. 3656
EX n/a   **NM** n/a   **MIP** $20

(Eagle Photo)

❑ **Dodge Ram 2500 V10 Magnum,** 2001, Deep amethyst and light-silver body, silver wheels, gray interior. Shown here with dark-gray/light silver version, (#3652), 1:43 scale, Model No. 3655
EX n/a   NM n/a   MIP $20

(Eagle Photo)

❑ **Dodge Ram 2500 V10 Magnum,** 2001, Emerald-green and light-silver body, silver wheels, beige interior, black bed, 1:43 scale, Model No. 3654
EX n/a   NM n/a   MIP $20

❑ **Dodge Ram 2500 V10 Magnum,** 2001, Red and light-silver body, silver wheels, gray interior, black bed, 1:43 scale, Model No. 3654
EX n/a   NM n/a   MIP $20

DODGE VIPER GTS-R RACING

❑ **Dodge Viper GTS-R no. 40 Rent a Car, Le Mans 1994,** 2001, Red with gold spoked wheels, white number "40" and French flag on sides and hood, 1:43 scale, Model No. 3609
EX n/a   NM n/a   MIP $20

(Eagle Photo)

❑ **Dodge Viper GTS-R no. 41 Rent a Car, Le Mans 1994,** 2001, Yellow with gold spoked wheels, white number "41" and French flag on sides and hood. Shown with red number "40" Rent a Car, (#3609), 1:43 scale, Model No. 3610
EX n/a   NM n/a   MIP $20

❑ **Dodge Viper GTS-R no. 5 Presentation,** 1998, White with blue stripes, gray multi-spoked wheels, number "5" on doors, 1:43 scale, Model No. 3603
EX n/a   NM n/a   MIP $20

❑ **Dodge Viper GTS-R no. 52, Team Oreca 1997,** 1999, FIA GT2 Championship winner. White with blue stripes, "Warsteiner" windshield decal, number "52" on doors, silver-gray multi-spoked wheels, black interior, 1:43 scale, Model No. 3616
EX n/a   NM n/a   MIP $20

(Eagle Photo)

❑ **Dodge Viper GTS-R no. 53, Team Oreca 1998,** 1999, FIA GT2 Championship second. White, blue and red body with American flag design on roof, number "53" on doors and hood. Silver-gray multi-spoked wheels. Shown here with Viper 1997 Team Oreca number "52" (#3616), 1:43 scale, Model No. 3663
EX n/a   NM n/a   MIP $20

❑ **Dodge Viper GTS-R no. 61, Team Oreca 1997,** 1999, Le Mans. Drivers: White body, blue stripes, silver-gray multi-spoked wheels, number "61" on hood and sides, 1:43 scale, Model No. 3617
EX n/a   NM n/a   MIP $20

❑ **Dodge Viper GTS-R no. 62, Team Oreca 1997,** 1998, Le Mans. Drivers: Dupuy/Archer. White body, blue stripes, silver-gray multi-spoked wheels, number "62" on hood and sides, 1:43 scale, Model No. 3614
EX n/a   NM n/a   MIP $20

(Eagle Photo)

❑ **Dodge Viper GTS-R no. 63, Team Oreca 1997,** 1998, Le Mans. Drivers: J. Bell/Beretta. White body, blue stripes, silver-gray multi-spoked wheels, number "63" on hood and sides. Shown here with other 1997 Team Oreca Vipers, (#3614 and #3617), 1:43 scale, Model No. 3615
EX n/a   NM n/a   MIP $20

(Eagle Photo)

❑ **Dodge Viper GTS-R no. 98 Daytona 1996,** 1998, White with black stripes, "Exxon" windshield decal, number "98" on doors and hood. Shown here with GTS-R no. "5," (#3603), 1:43 scale, Model No. 3606
EX n/a   NM n/a   MIP $20

(Eagle Photo)

❑ **Dodge Viper GTS-R Taisan Team 1997,** 1999, Black and red body with "STP Taisan" and "34" on sides and hood. Silver-gray spoked wheels, "Advan" on spoiler. Shown here with Taisan Team 1998 Viper, (#3664), 1:43 scale, Model No. 3618
EX n/a   NM n/a   MIP $20

❑ **Dodge Viper GTS-R Taisan Team 1998,** 1999, Blue and red body with "STP Taisan" and "55," silver-gray multi-spoked wheels, 1:43 scale, Model No. 3664
EX n/a   NM n/a   MIP $20

DODGE VIPER RT/10-GTS

❑ **Dodge Viper Coupe GTS 1998,** 1998, Red body with white stripes, silver five-spoke wheels, black interior, 1:43 scale, Model No. 3628
EX n/a   NM n/a   MIP $20

(Eagle Photo)

❑ **Dodge Viper Coupe GTS 1999,** 1999, Black body with silver stripes, silver five-spoke wheels, black interior, 1:43 scale, Model No. 3631
EX n/a   NM n/a   MIP $20

❑ **Dodge Viper Coupe GTS 2001,** 2001, Steel-gray body with silver stripes, silver five-spoke wheels, black interior, 1:43 scale, Model No. 3706
EX n/a   NM n/a   MIP $20

(Eagle Photo)

❑ **Dodge Viper Coupe GTS 2001,** 2001, Yellow body with black stripes, silver five-spoke wheels, black interior. Shown here with steel-gray/silver stripes model, (#3706), 1:43 scale, Model No. 3704
EX n/a   NM n/a   MIP $20

❑ **Dodge Viper Coupe RT/10 1996,** 1998, White body with blue stripes, silver five-spoke wheels, 1:43 scale, Model No. 3620
EX n/a   NM n/a   MIP $20

❑ **Dodge Viper Coupe RT/10 1996,** 1998, Blue body with white stripes, silver five-spoke wheels, 1:43 scale, Model No. 3624
EX n/a   NM n/a   MIP $20

❑ **Dodge Viper Coupe RT/10 1996,** 1998, Black body with removable softtop, silver stripes, silver five-spoke wheels, 1:43 scale, Model No. 3621
EX n/a   NM n/a   MIP $20

(Eagle Photo)

❑ **Dodge Viper Coupe RT/10 1998,** 1998, Silver body with blue stripes, open top, silver, five-spoke wheels, black interior. Shown here with 1996 Vipers, black with silver stripes and white with blue stripes (#3621 and #3620), 1:43 scale, Model No. 3627
EX n/a   NM n/a   MIP $20

❑ **Dodge Viper Coupe RT/10 2001,** 2001, Deep saphire blue, open top, silver, five-spoke wheels, black interior, 1:43 scale, Model No. 3705
EX n/a   NM n/a   MIP $20

DODGE VIPER SPECIAL EDITION

❑ **Dodge Viper "ACR",** 2001, Red body, silver-gray multi-spoked wheels, black and red interior, "Viper GTS ACR" on front quarter panels, 1:43 scale, Model No. 3667
EX n/a   NM n/a   MIP $20

(Eagle Photo)

❑ **Dodge Viper "Twin Stryker Turbo",** 2001, American flag decoration, gray multi-spoked wheels, black interior. Pictured here with red Viper "ACR," (#3667), 1:43 scale, Model No. 3674
EX n/a   NM n/a   MIP $20

(Eagle Photo)

❑ **Dodge Viper GTS: San Diego County Sheriff,** 2001, Black body with San Diego County Sheriff stars on doors and hood, five-spoke silver wheels, 1:43 scale, Model No. 3865
EX n/a   NM n/a   MIP $20

FORD MUSTANG MACH III/GT 40

❑ **Ford GT 40, no. 95, 3rd place, 24-hours Daytona, 1966,** 2001, White and black body, number "95" on hood, sides and rear, 1:43 scale, Model No. 3696
EX n/a   NM n/a   MIP $20

(Eagle Photo)

❑ **Ford GT 40, no. 97, 2nd place, 24-hours Daytona, 1966,** 2001, White and black body, number "97" on hood, sides and rear. Shown here with number "95" GT 40, (#3696), 1:43 scale, Model No. 3693
EX n/a   NM n/a   MIP $20

❑ **Ford Mustang Mach III,** 1998, Black body, black interior, silver five-spoke wheels, 1:43 scale, Model No. 1049
EX n/a   NM n/a   MIP $20

❑ **Ford Mustang Mach III,** 1998, Yellow body, black interior, silver five-spoke wheels, 1:43 scale, Model No. 1050
EX n/a   NM n/a   MIP $20

(Eagle Photo)

❑ **Ford Mustang Mach III: Detroit Auto Show Presentation,** 1997, Red body, red and black interior, silver five-spoke wheels, 1:43 scale, Model No. 1005
EX n/a   NM n/a   MIP $20

GT 40

(Eagle Photo)

❑ **Ford GT 40 MKII, no. "3," Le Mans 1966, Shelby American, Inc.,** 2000, Red body with white stripes, gold and silver wheels, number "3" in white circle on front, rear and sides. Opening doors and rear hood, 1:18 scale, Model No. 3168
EX n/a NM n/a MIP $31

❑ **Ford GT 40 MKII, no. "6," Le Mans 1966, Mario Andretti & Lucien Biandri,** 2000, Dark blue body with yellow flare on hood, white stripes on front, roof and rear hood, and on lower panels. Number "6" in circles on front, sides and rear of car, 1:18 scale, Model No. 3171
EX n/a NM n/a MIP $31

❑ **Ford GT 40 MKII, no. "68," Le Mans 1969, Kelleners & Joest,** 2000, White body with German flag stripe (black, red and gold) on front, roof and rear hood. Number "68" in circle on front, sides and rear of car, 1:18 scale, Model No. 3172
EX n/a NM n/a MIP $31

(Eagle Photo)

❑ **Ford GT 40 MKII, no. "8," Le Mans 1966,** 2000, Yellow body with black stripes, circle number "8" on front, sides and rear hood, red and gray wheels. Photo shows this model with Ford GT 40 no. "6" 1969 Le Mans winner (#3008), 1:18 scale, Model No. 3164
EX n/a NM n/a MIP $31

❑ **Ford GT 40 Street Version,** 2000, Green and black body with black stripe running from front to rear hood. Silver wheels, 1:18 scale, Model No. 3174
EX n/a NM n/a MIP $31

(Eagle Photo)

❑ **Ford GT 40 Street Version,** 2000, Silver gray body with black and yellow stripes running from front, roof and rear hood, silver wheels. Both street versions in the series are shown here, 1:18 scale, Model No. 3173
EX n/a NM n/a MIP $31

❑ **Ford GT 40, no. "1," Le Mans 2nd place, 1966,** 2000, Light blue body, opening doors and rear hood, number "1" on front, rear and sides, 1:18 scale, Model No. 3039
EX n/a NM n/a MIP $31

(Eagle Photo)

❑ **Ford GT 40, no. "2," Le Mans 1st place, 1966,** 2000, Black body, opening doors and rear hood, number "2" on front, sides and rear. Shown here with the second and third place winners, (#3039 & #3040), 1:18 scale, Model No. 3019
EX n/a NM n/a MIP $31

❑ **Ford GT 40, no. "5," Le Mans 3rd place, 1966,** 2000, Brown-bronze body, opening doors and rear hood, number "5" on front, sides and rear, 1:18 scale, Model No. 3040
EX n/a NM n/a MIP $31

❑ **Ford GT 40, no. "6," 1969 Le Mans winner,** 2000, Light blue body with orange stripe, opening doors and rear hood, number "6" on front, rear and sides, 1:18 scale, Model No. 3008
EX n/a NM n/a MIP $31

HOT RODS: '32 FORD STREET RODS

(Eagle Photo)

❑ **'32 Ford Street Rod,** 2000, Black with red interior, lift-off hood, chrome wheels and pipes, detailed engine, 1:43 scale, Model No. 1202
EX n/a NM n/a MIP $20

(Eagle Photo)

❑ **'32 Ford Street Rod,** 2001, Metallic bright green with orange flames graphics, chrome wheels and pipes, 1:43 scale, Model No. 1220
EX n/a NM n/a MIP $20

(Eagle Photo)

❑ **'32 Ford Street Rod Pickup: "Pete and Jake's Hot Rod Repair",** 2001, Light pink body with "Pete and Jake's Hot Rod Repair" on doors and bed cover. Whitewall tires, chrome, five-spoke wheels, white interior, 1:43 scale, Model No. 1219
EX n/a NM n/a MIP $20

❑ **'32 Ford Street Rod: "Eat My Dust",** 2001, White body with red flame graphics, chome wheels and "Eat My Dust" on trunk, 1:43 scale, Model No. 1212
EX n/a NM n/a MIP $20

EAGLE / FORD

EAGLE / FORD

(Eagle Photo)

❑ **'32 Ford Street Rod: "Nostalgic" Dry Lake Racers,** 2001, Red and white body with "So-Cal Speedshop" on sides, chrome wheels and pipes, lift-off hood. Shown here with "Eat My Dust" street rod, (#1212), 1:43 scale, Model No. 1215
EX n/a   NM n/a   MIP $20

LAND ROVER FREELANDER

❑ **Freelander Hard Back, 1998,** 1998, White gold (metallic finish with a touch of gold) body, black trim, silver-gray wheels, gray interior, 1:43 scale, Model No. 1506
EX n/a   NM n/a   MIP $20

(Eagle Photo)

❑ **Freelander Hard Back, 1998,** 1998, Metallic purple body, black trim, silver-gray wheels, gray interior. Shown here with green and white gold versions, (#1504 and #1506), 1:43 scale, Model No. 1505
EX n/a   NM n/a   MIP $20

❑ **Freelander Hard Back, 1998,** 1998, Metallic light green bod-y, black trim, silver-gray wheels, gray interior, 1:43 scale, Model No. 1504
EX n/a   NM n/a   MIP $20

(Eagle Photo)

❑ **Freelander Hard Back, commercial delivery version,** 2001, White body with black trim, closed "commercial-style" rear side windows, gray five-spoked wheels. Shown here with blue version, (1508), 1:43 scale, Model No. 1507
EX n/a   NM n/a   MIP $20

❑ **Freelander Hard Back, commercial delivery version,** 2001, Oxford blue body with black trim, closed "commercial-style" rear side windows, gray five-spoked wheels, 1:43 scale, Model No. 1508
EX n/a   NM n/a   MIP $20

(Eagle Photo)

❑ **Freelander Open Back,** 2001, Icelandic blue (light metallic blue) body, blue-gray interior, gray five-spoked wheels, black trim, 1:43 scale, Model No. 1509
EX n/a   NM n/a   MIP $20

(Eagle Photo)

❑ **Freelander Open Back, 1998,** 1998, Light silver body, gray five-spoked wheels, gray interior. Shown here with red and black versions, (#1501 and #1502), 1:43 scale, Model No. 1503
EX n/a   NM n/a   MIP $20

❑ **Freelander Open Back, 1998,** 1998, Bright red body, gray five-spoked wheels, gray interior, 1:43 scale, Model No. 1502
EX n/a   NM n/a   MIP $20

❑ **Freelander Open Back, 1998,** 1998, Black body, gray five-spoked wheels, gray interior, 1:43 scale, Model No. 1501
EX n/a   NM n/a   MIP $20

LAND ROVER SERIES III-109

❑ **Land Rover Series III-109 Softtop,** 2001, Gray-blue body with black softtop, spare on hood, 1:43 scale, Model No. 1521
EX n/a   NM n/a   MIP $20

(Eagle Photo)

❑ **Land Rover Series III-109 Softtop,** 2001, British racing green body with tan softtop, spare on hood, 1:43 scale, Model No. 1520
EX n/a   NM n/a   MIP $20

MERCURY 1949 COUPE/HOD ROD

(Eagle Photo)

❑ **Mercury Club Coupe,** 2000, Light green body with dark green top, silver trim and hubcaps, whitewall tires, 1:43 scale, Model No. 1558
EX n/a   NM n/a   MIP $20

(Eagle Photo)

❏ **Mercury Club Coupe,** 2000, Red body, silver hubs, bumper and trim, whitewall tires, 1:43 scale, Model No. 1551
EX n/a   NM n/a   MIP $20

(Eagle Photo)

❏ **Mercury Club Coupe,** 2000, Black body, silver hubs, bumper and trim, whitewall tires, 1:43 scale, Model No. 1550
EX n/a   NM n/a   MIP $20

❏ **Mercury Fire Chief's Car,** 2000, Red body with black roof, red dome light, "Bureau of Fire" on doors, whitewall tires, 1:43 scale, Model No. 1553
EX n/a   NM n/a   MIP $20

❏ **Mercury Hot Rod,** 2000, Yellow body with red flames, whitewall tires, silver hubcaps, silver trim, 1:43 scale, Model No. 1557
EX n/a   NM n/a   MIP $20

❏ **Mercury Hot Rod,** 2000, Black body with yellow flames, whitewall tires, silver hubcaps, silver trim, 1:43 scale, Model No. 1556
EX n/a   NM n/a   MIP $20

❏ **Mercury Hot Rod,** 2000, Silver body with bright green scallop design, five-spoke wheels, 1:43 scale, Model No. 1555
EX n/a   NM n/a   MIP $20

(Eagle Photo)

❏ **Mercury Hot Rod,** 2000, Purple body with yellow flames graphics, five-spoke wheels, silver trim, 1:43 scale, Model No. 1554
EX n/a   NM n/a   MIP $20

(Eagle Photo)

❏ **Mercury Police Cruiser,** 2000, Black and white body, police shield on doors, "Highway Patrol" on hood, whitewall tires, silver hubcaps, bumpers and trim. Shown here with Fire Chief's Car, (#1553), 1:43 scale, Model No. 1552
EX n/a   NM n/a   MIP $20

MG-MGB Mᴋ II

❏ **MGB Mk II "LE" Limited Edition,** 1999, Gold body with silver trim, yellow and black interior, silver-spoked wheels, 1:43 scale, Model No. 1066
EX n/a   NM n/a   MIP $20

(Eagle Photo)

❏ **MGB Mk II "LE" Limited Edition,** 1999, Blue-black with silver trim, yellow and black interior, silver-spoked wheels. Shown here with bronze/gold version, (#1066), 1:43 scale, Model No. 1065
EX n/a   NM n/a   MIP $20

❏ **MGB Mk II 1967 Roadster, left-hand drive,** 1997, British racing green body, also available as right-hand drive model, (#1053), 1:43 scale, Model No. 1021
EX n/a   NM n/a   MIP $20

(Eagle Photo)

❏ **MGB Mk II 1967 Roadster, left-hand drive,** 1997, Red body with silver-spoked wheels and trim, black interior. Also available in right-hand drive version, (#1056). Shown here with right-hand drive British racing green version, (#1053), 1:43 scale, Model No. 1020
EX n/a   NM n/a   MIP $20

❏ **MGB Mk II 1967 Roadster, left-hand drive,** 1998, Light blue body, blue interior with white trim, whitewall tires, 1:43 scale, Model No. 1060
EX n/a   NM n/a   MIP $20

❏ **MGB Mk II British Police Car,** 1998, White body with "Police" and trunk. Silver trim, including bumper-mounted lights, black interior, 1:43 scale, Model No. 1064
EX n/a   NM n/a   MIP $20

(Eagle Photo)

❏ **MGB Mk II British Police Car,** 1998, Black body with "Police" in white on hood, in gold lettering on trunk. Silver wheels and trim, black interior. Shown here with white version, (#1064), 1:43 scale, Model No. 1063
EX n/a   NM n/a   MIP $20

❏ **MGB, no. 102, 1000 kms Nurburgring, 1967,** 2001, Number "102" on hood, sides and trunk, silver-spoked wheels. Real version of car placed 3rd in 2L GT category. Limited edition to 1500 pieces, 1:43 scale, Model No. 3691
EX n/a   NM n/a   MIP $20

EAGLE / MG

(Eagle Photo)

❑ **MGB, no. 30, Silverstone 1967,** 2001, Number "30" on hood, sides and trunk, racing stripes on hood and trunk, silver-spoked wheels. Shown here with number "120" edition, (#3691). Also limited edition to 1500 pieces, 1:43 scale, Model No. 3692
EX n/a   NM n/a   MIP $20

MG-MGF

❑ **MGF 1.8L VVC Hardtop,** 1998, Metallic dark-blue body with black roof, silver-gray five-spoke wheels, black interior, 1:43 scale, Model No. 1075
EX n/a   NM n/a   MIP $20

❑ **MGF 1.8L VVC Hardtop,** 1998, Metallic light-gray body with black roof, silver-gray five-spoke wheels, red interior, 1:43 scale, Model No. 1074
EX n/a   NM n/a   MIP $20

(Eagle Photo)

❑ **MGF 1.8L VVC Hardtop,** 1998, Burgundy body with black roof, silver-gray five-spoke wheels. Shown here with light gray and dark metallic blue versions, (#1074 and #1075), 1:43 scale, Model No. 1076
EX n/a   NM n/a   MIP $20

(Eagle Photo)

❑ **MGF 1.8L VVC Roadster,** 1998, Red with silver-gray five-spoked wheels, 1:43 scale, Model No. 1070
EX n/a   NM n/a   MIP $20

(Eagle Photo)

❑ **MGF 1.8L VVC Roadster,** 1998, Orange body with silver-gray five-spoked wheels. Shown here with British racing green version, (#1071), 1:43 scale, Model No. 1073
EX n/a   NM n/a   MIP $20

(Eagle Photo)

❑ **MGF 1.8L VVC Roadster,** 1998, Purple body with silver-gray five-spoked wheels, 1:43 scale, Model No. 1072
EX n/a   NM n/a   MIP $20

❑ **MGF 1.8L VVC Roadster,** 1998, British racing green body with silver-gray five-spoked wheels, 1:43 scale, Model No. 1071
EX n/a   NM n/a   MIP $20

MODEL T DELIVERY TRUCK/TOURING CARS

❑ **Ford Model "T" Delivery Truck: Dreyer's Ice Cream,** 2000, Brown and white with "Dreyer's Ice Cream" on sides, gold grille and headlights, 1:18 scale, Model No. 4305
EX n/a   NM n/a   MIP $31

❑ **Ford Model "T" Delivery Truck: Ford Service,** 2000, White with light silver hood and running boards, Ford oval and "Goods and Services" on sides, 1:18 scale, Model No. 4306
EX n/a   NM n/a   MIP $31

❑ **Ford Model "T" Paddy Wagon,** 2000, Black body with "Police Department" and "New York Police Department" on sides, gold headlights and grille, steerable wheels, opening rear doors, 1:18 scale, Model No. 4304
EX n/a   NM n/a   MIP $31

❑ **Ford Model "T" Touring,** 2000, Red with gold headlights and grille, black interior, 1:18 scale, Model No. 4302
EX n/a   NM n/a   MIP $31

(Eagle Photo)

❑ **Ford Model "T" Touring,** 2000, Dark blue with gold headlights and grille, black interior, 1:18 scale, Model No. 4303
EX n/a   NM n/a   MIP $31

(Eagle Photo)

❑ **Ford Model "T" Touring,** 2000, Black car with gold headlights and grille. Shown here with red model (#4302), 1:18 scale, Model No. 4301
EX n/a   NM n/a   MIP $31

MUSTANG 1994/ DREAM CAR

(Eagle Photo)

❑ **Ford Mustang "Shinoda Boss" Cobra Convertible with roll bar,** 2000, Saphire blue body with silver stripes and "Boss" lettering on hood and doors, silver wheels, opening hood, trunk and doors, gray interior, 1:18 scale, Model No. 3144

EX n/a   NM n/a   MIP $31

❑ **Ford Mustang "Shinoda Boss" Coupe,** 2000, Orange body with black stripes and "Boss" lettering on hood and doors, silver wheels, opening hood, trunk and doors, black interior, 1:18 scale, Model No. 3145

EX n/a   NM n/a   MIP $31

❑ **Ford Mustang "Shinoda Boss" Coupe,** 2000, Black body with silver stripes and "Boss" lettering on hood and doors, silver wheels, opening hood, trunk and doors, black interior, 1:18 scale, Model No. 3143

EX n/a   NM n/a   MIP $31

❑ **Ford Mustang "Shinoda Boss" Coupe,** 2000, Yellow body with black stripes and "Boss" lettering on hood and doors, silver wheels, opening hood, trunk and doors, black interior, 1:18 scale, Model No. 3130

EX n/a   NM n/a   MIP $31

❑ **Ford Mustang Coupe Dream Car,** 2000, Blue with flag stripe, black interior, silver wheels, opening hood, doors and trunk, 1:18 scale, Model No. 3158

EX n/a   NM n/a   MIP $31

❑ **Ford Mustang Coupe Dream Car,** 2000, Red with gold stripe, black interior, silver wheels, opening hood, doors and trunk, 1:18 scale, Model No. 3157

EX n/a   NM n/a   MIP $31

❑ **Ford Mustang Coupe Dream Car,** 2000, White with blue stripes, black interior, silver wheels, opening hood, doors and trunk, 1:18 scale, Model No. 3156

EX n/a   NM n/a   MIP $31

❑ **Ford Mustang Coupe Dream Car,** 2000, Blue with white stripes, black interior, silver wheels, opening hood, doors and trunk, 1:18 scale, Model No. 3155

EX n/a   NM n/a   MIP $31

❑ **Ford Mustang Graphic Convertible with roll bar,** 2000, Orange with black stripes and design on hood, black interior, silver wheels, opening hood, doors and trunk. Shown here with "Graphic" convertible, (#3138), 1:18 scale, Model No. 3138

EX n/a   NM n/a   MIP $31

(Eagle Photo)

❑ **Ford Mustang Graphic Coupe,** 2000, Black with gold striping and design on hood, black interior, silver wheels, opening hood, doors and trunk. Shown here with "Graphic" convertible, (#3138), 1:18 scale, Model No. 3135

EX n/a   NM n/a   MIP $31

MUSTANG 350 GT 350 1966 "HERTZ"/CUSTOM

❑ **Ford Mustang GT 350 1966 "Hertz",** 2000, Ivy-green body with gold stripes, opening doors, hood and trunk, silver five-spoke wheels, black interior, 1:18 scale, Model No. 3175

EX n/a   NM n/a   MIP $31

❑ **Ford Mustang GT 350 1966 "Hertz",** 2000, Dark blue body with gold stripes, opening doors, hood and trunk, silver five-spoke wheels, black interior, 1:18 scale, Model No. 3179

EX n/a   NM n/a   MIP $31

(Eagle Photo)

❑ **Ford Mustang GT 350 1966 "Hertz",** 2000, Red body with blue stripes (custom colors), opening doors, hood and trunk, silver five-spoke wheels, black interior. Pictured here with black and gold model, (#3118), 1:18 scale, Model No. 3159

EX n/a   NM n/a   MIP $31

❑ **Ford Mustang GT 350 1966 "Hertz",** 2000, White body with gold stripes, opening doors, hood and trunk, silver five-spoke wheels, black interior, 1:18 scale, Model No. 3154

EX n/a   NM n/a   MIP $31

❑ **Ford Mustang GT 350 1966 "Hertz",** 2000, Red body with gold stripes, opening doors, hood and trunk, silver five-spoke wheels, black interior, 1:18 scale, Model No. 3124

EX n/a   NM n/a   MIP $31

❑ **Ford Mustang GT 350 1966 "Hertz",** 2000, Black body with gold stripes, opening doors, hood and trunk, silver five-spoke wheels, black interior, 1:18 scale, Model No. 3118

EX n/a   NM n/a   MIP $31

❑ **Ford Mustang GT 350 1966 Custom,** 2000, Black with gold stripe, opening trunk, hood and doors, silver five-spoked wheels, black interior, 1:18 scale, Model No. 3167

EX n/a   NM n/a   MIP $31

❑ **Ford Mustang GT 350 1966 Custom,** 2000, Light pink with white stripe, opening trunk, hood and doors, silver five-spoked wheels, black interior, 1:18 scale, Model No. 3166

EX n/a   NM n/a   MIP $31

❑ **Ford Mustang GT 350 1966 Custom,** 2000, Bright green with yellow stripes, opening trunk, hood and doors, silver five-spoked wheels, black interior, 1:18 scale, Model No. 3153

EX n/a   NM n/a   MIP $31

❑ **Ford Mustang GT 350 1966 Custom,** 2000, Bright blue with dark blue stripes, opening trunk, hood and doors, blue and silver five-spoked wheels, black interior, 1:18 scale, Model No. 3152

EX n/a   NM n/a   MIP $31

EAGLE / FORD

MUSTANG 350 GT 65/FASTBACK

❏ **Ford Mustang Fastback,** 2000, Yellow body, silver five-spoked wheels, opening hood, doors and trunk, 1:18 scale, Model No. 3178
EX n/a   NM n/a   MIP $31

❏ **Ford Mustang Fastback,** 2000, Dark green body, silver five-spoked wheels, opening hood, doors and trunk, 1:18 scale, Model No. 3169
EX n/a   NM n/a   MIP $31

(Eagle Photo)

❏ **Ford Mustang Fastback,** 2000, Light blue body, silver five-spoked wheels, opening hood, doors and trunk. Pictured here with dark green model, (#3169), 1:18 scale, Model No. 3170
EX n/a   NM n/a   MIP $31

❏ **Ford Mustang GT 350 1965 "Shelby",** 2000, Dark blue with white stripes, opening hood, doors and trunk. Black interior, detailed engine, silver five-spoke wheels, 1:18 scale, Model No. 3128
EX n/a   NM n/a   MIP $31

(Eagle Photo)

❏ **Ford Mustang GT 350 1965 "Shelby",** 2000, Red with white stripes, opening hood, doors and trunk. Black interior, detailed engine, silver five-spoke wheels, 1:18 scale, Model No. 3116
EX n/a   NM n/a   MIP $31

(Eagle Photo)

❏ **Ford Mustang GT 350 1965 "Shelby",** 2000, White with dark blue stripes, opening hood, doors and trunk. Black interior, detailed engine, silver five-spoke wheels. Pictured here with the dark blue version from the same series, (#3128), 1:18 scale, Model No. 3101
EX n/a   NM n/a   MIP $31

PLYMOUTH BELVEDERE

(Eagle Photo)

❏ **1964 Plymouth Belvedere Hardtop: Racing Version,** 2001, Red body with gold number "25" on doors, white on roof, "Paul Goldsmith" driver, white "400 H.P." on hood, black wheels, Goodyear tires, silver grille and bumpers, 1:43 scale, Model No. 1456
EX n/a   NM n/a   MIP $20

(Eagle Photo)

❏ **1964 Plymouth Belvedere Hardtop: Racing Version,** 2001, White body with red number "54" on doors and roof, "J. Pardue" driver, blue "400 H.P." on hood, black wheels, Goodyear tires, silver grille and bumpers, 1:43 scale, Model No. 1455
EX n/a   NM n/a   MIP $20

❏ **1964 Plymouth Belvedere Hardtop: Street Version,** 2001, White body with opening doors, black interior, silver hubcaps, grille and bumpers, 1:43 scale, Model No. 1452
EX n/a   NM n/a   MIP $20

(Eagle Photo)

❏ **1964 Plymouth Belvedere Hardtop: Street Version,** 2001, Red body with opening doors, red interior, silver hubcaps, grille and bumpers. Shown here with black and white versions, (#1450 & #1452), 1:43 scale, Model No. 1451
EX n/a   NM n/a   MIP $20

❏ **1964 Plymouth Belvedere Hardtop: Street Version,** 2001, Black body with opening doors, red interior, silver hubcaps, grille and bumpers, 1:43 scale, Model No. 1450
EX n/a   NM n/a   MIP $20

PLYMOUTH PROWLER

❏ **Plymouth Prowler Hot Rod,** 2001, Bright yellow with red scallop design, silver five spoke wheels, red interior, 1:43 scale, Model No. 3675
EX n/a   NM n/a   MIP $20

❏ **Plymouth Prowler Open Top, 1999,** 2000, Purple body, gray, five-spoked wheels, black interior, 1:43 scale, Model No. 3640
EX n/a   NM n/a   MIP $20

❏ **Plymouth Prowler Open Top, 1999,** 2000, Yellow body, gray, five-spoked wheels, black interior, 1:43 scale, Model No. 3642
EX n/a   NM n/a   MIP $20

(Eagle Photo)

❏ **Plymouth Prowler Open Top, 2000 "Black Tie" Edition,** 2001, Silver with black hood, stripes and trunk, silver five-spoked wheels. Limited edition of 2000 pieces. Shown here with "Woodward Edition" (#3673) and 1999 open top in black, (#3644), 1:43 scale, Model No. 3702
EX n/a   NM n/a   MIP $20

❑ **Plymouth Prowler Open Top, 2000 "Woodward" Edition,** 2001, Red with black hood, stripes and trunk, silver five-spoked wheels, 1:43 scale, Model No. 3673
EX n/a   NM n/a   MIP $20

(Eagle Photo)

❑ **Plymouth Prowler Open Top, 2001,** 2001, Metallic orange body, silver five-spoked wheels, black interior, limited edition of 3,000 pieces, 1:43 scale, Model No. 3703
EX n/a   NM n/a   MIP $20

❑ **Plymouth Prowler Softtop, 1999,** 2000, Purple body with black softtop roof, gray bumpers, light silver-gray wheels, 1:43 scale, Model No. 3641
EX n/a   NM n/a   MIP $20

❑ **Plymouth Prowler Softtop, 1999,** 2000, Black body with black softtop roof, gray bumpers, light silver-gray wheels, 1:43 scale, Model No. 3645
EX n/a   NM n/a   MIP $20

❑ **Plymouth Prowler Softtop, 1999,** 2000, Red body with black softtop roof, gray bumpers, light silver-gray wheels, 1:43 scale, Model No. 3647
EX n/a   NM n/a   MIP $20

PORSCHE 911

❑ **911 Carrera RS 2.4L 1972,** 2001, Red body with opening hood, doors and front trunk, five-spoked silver wheels, 1:18 scale, Model No. 3205
EX n/a   NM n/a   MIP $31

❑ **911 Carrera RS 2.4L 1972,** 2001, Dark metallic blue body with opening hood, doors and front trunk, five-spoked silver wheels, 1:18 scale, Model No. 3214
EX n/a   NM n/a   MIP $31

(Eagle Photo)

❑ **911 Carrera RS 2.4L 1972,** 2001, Signal yellow (light-orange) body with opening hood, doors and front trunk, five-spoked silver wheels. Shown here with others in the series, (#3210, #3205 & #3214), 1:18 scale, Model No. 3207
EX n/a   NM n/a   MIP $31

❑ **911 Carrera RS 2.4L 1972,** 2001, Metallic-silver body with opening hood, doors and front trunk, five-spoked silver wheels, 1:18 scale, Model No. 3210
EX n/a   NM n/a   MIP $31

(Eagle Photo)

❑ **911 Carrera RS 2.4L 1972,** 2001, Olive-green body with opening hood, doors and front trunk, five-spoked silver wheels, 1:18 scale, Model No. 3217
EX n/a   NM n/a   MIP $31

❑ **911 Carrera RS 2.7L 1973,** 2000, Gulf blue, 1:18 scale, Model No. 3215
EX n/a   NM n/a   MIP $31

❑ **911 Carrera RS 2.7L 1973,** 2000, Gulf orange, 1:18 scale, Model No. 3211
EX n/a   NM n/a   MIP $31

❑ **911 Carrera RS 2.7L 1973,** 2000, Red with black stripes, 1:18 scale, Model No. 3216
EX n/a   NM n/a   MIP $31

(Eagle Photo)

❑ **911 Carrera RS 2.7L 1973,** 2000, Tour de France 1973 model, white with "Le Grand Bazar" and caricature faces of racing team on sides and hood, 1:18 scale, Model No. 3212
EX n/a   NM n/a   MIP $31

❑ **911 Carrera RS 2.7L 1973,** 2000, Viper-green with black & silver spoked wheels, black interior, 1:18 scale, Model No. 3206
EX n/a   NM n/a   MIP $31

❑ **911 Carrera RS 2.7L 1973,** 2000, Blue-black with red and silver spoked wheels, black interior, 1:18 scale, Model No. 3204
EX n/a   NM n/a   MIP $31

(Eagle Photo)

❑ **911 Carrera RS 2.7L 1973,** 2000, Yellow body with green spoked wheels, "Carrera" along bottom sides, 1:18 scale, Model No. 3203
EX n/a   NM n/a   MIP $31

(Eagle Photo)

❑ **911 Carrera RS 2.7L 1973,** 2000, White with red spoked wheels, opening hood, doors and trunk, black interior "Carrera" along bottom on sides, 1:18 scale, Model No. 3203
EX n/a   NM n/a   MIP $31

❑ **911 Carrera RS 2.8L no. "48," Le Mans 1973,** 2000, Equipe Sonauto BP Racing. Yellow with black interior, circle number "48", 1:18 scale, Model No. 3209
EX n/a   NM n/a   MIP $31

❑ **911 S, no. "80," Le Mans 1972,** 2000, Orange with sponsor graphics and round "80", 1:18 scale, Model No. 3208
EX n/a   NM n/a   MIP $31

PORSCHE 911: LIMITED EDITION

(Eagle Photo)

❑ **Porsche 911 Carrera RS "Bosch" no. 10, East African Safari, 1973,** 1999, Dark yellow body with "Bosch" and number "10" on sides and roof, "Carrera" stripe along bottom, chrome five-spoke wheels. Drivers: B. Waldegaard & H. Thorszelius. Limited to 2000 pieces, 1:43 scale, Model No. 1601
EX n/a   NM n/a   MIP $31

(Eagle Photo)

❑ **Porsche 911 Carrera RS "Kuhne & Nagel" no. 19, East African Safari, 1974,** 1999, White body with blue "Kuhne & Nagel" and "Nakufreight" stripe. Number "19" on doors and roof. Limited to 2000 pieces, 1:43 scale, Model No. 1602
EX n/a   NM n/a   MIP $31

(Eagle Photo)

❑ **Porsche 911 Carrera RS 2.2L, "Facit & Lakeroll" no. 1, East African Safari, 1971,** 2001, Green and black body with number "1" on sides and roof, silver and gray five-spoked wheels. Drivers: Anderson & H. Thorszelius. Limited production to 2000 pieces, 1:43 scale, Model No. 1608
EX n/a   NM n/a   MIP $31

PORSCHE 917 RACING

❑ **Porsche 917 K, no. "12," Brands Hatch 1970,** 2000, Shell Racing Team, Hemmenn and Atwood. Dark blue body with white stripes, number "12" on front, sides and rear, black wheels, Goodyear tires, black interior, 1:18 scale, Model No. 3912
EX n/a   NM n/a   MIP $31

❑ **Porsche 917 K, no. "19," Le Mans 1971,** 2000, Gulf Racing Team, Miller and Atwood. Light blue body with orange striping on bottom sides and top, black wheels, number "19" and Gulf logos on front, sides and rear, 1:18 scale, Model No. 3910
EX n/a   NM n/a   MIP $31

❑ **Porsche 917 K, no. "2," 1000 kms, Monza 1971 winner,** 2000, Light blue with orange stripe and Gulf logos, number "2" on front, sides and rear, 1:18 scale, Model No. 3903
EX n/a   NM n/a   MIP $31

❑ **Porsche 917 K, no. "2," 1970 Daytona,** 2000, Gulf Racing Team, light blue with orange stripe, black wheels, black interior, Gulf logos, 1:18 scale, Model No. 3904
EX n/a   NM n/a   MIP $31

❑ **Porsche 917 K, no. "22," 1974 Le Mans,** 2000, This car set up the never-broken record with 5335,313 km. It driven by Marko and Van Lennep and was the 24-hour Le Mans winner, Martini racing team, 1:18 scale, Model No. 3901
EX n/a   NM n/a   MIP $31

❑ **Porsche 917 K, no. "23," 1970 Le Mans,** 2000, Porsche Konstrucktionen Team, driven by Hermann and Attwood. Red body with Shell, Goodyear and Porsche graphics, circle number "23" on hood, sides and rear, 1:18 scale, Model No. 3902
EX n/a   NM n/a   MIP $31

❑ **Porsche 917 K, no. "3 ," nine-hour Kylamai,** 2000, Martini Racing Team, driven by Siffert and Ahrens. Yellow-orange body with red curved striping and number "2" on front, sides and rear, 1:18 scale, Model No. 3908
EX n/a   NM n/a   MIP $31

❑ **Porsche 917 K, no. "3," 1970 Daytona,** 2000, Porsche Salzburg (Porsche Austria team), white with red stripes on sides and hood, number "3" on front, sides and rear. Driven by K. Amres and V. Elford, 1:18 scale, Model No. 3907
EX n/a   NM n/a   MIP $31

❑ **Porsche 917 K, no. "3," 1971 12 Hours Sebring Winner,** 2000, Silver with blue and red stripes, "Martini Racing Team," number "3" on front, sides and rear, black wheels, Firestone tires, 1:18 scale, Model No. 3905
EX n/a   NM n/a   MIP $31

❑ **Porsche 917 K, no. "4," Monza 1971,** 2000, Martini Racing Team, driven by H. Marka and Van Lennep. Light blue with circle number "4" on front, sides and rear, 1:18 scale, Model No. 3914
EX n/a   NM n/a   MIP $31

❑ **Porsche 917 K, no. "55," 1000 Km Nurburgring 1971,** 2000, Team Auto USDAU, pale yellow body with green stripes, circle number "55," Shell and Firestone sponsor graphics, 1:18 scale, Model No. 3911
EX n/a   NM n/a   MIP $31

❑ **Porsche 917 K, no. "57," 1971 Le Mans,** 2000, Zitro Racing Cars, white with blue stripes, "Zitro" and number "57" on hood, sides and rear, 1:18 scale, Model No. 3906
EX n/a   NM n/a   MIP $31

PORSCHE 934 TURBO

(Eagle Photo)

❏ **Porsche 934 Turbo "Denver" no. 70, Le Mans, 1981,** 2001, Pink body, "Denver" on hood and roof, number "70" on hood and sides, gold and chrome multi-spoked wheels, 1:43 scale, Model No. 2303
EX n/a　　NM n/a　　MIP $20

(Eagle Photo)

❏ **Porsche 934 Turbo "Lois" no. 84, Le Mans, 1979,** 2001, Gray body, "Lois" emblems on stripes, number "84," multi-spoked gold and silver wheels, 1:43 scale, Model No. 2304
EX n/a　　NM n/a　　MIP $20

(Eagle Photo)

❏ **Porsche 934 Turbo "Lubrifilm Racing" no. 82, Le Mans, 1979,** 2001, White body, black stripes, red and yellow diamond pattern over wheelwells, "Lubrifilm Racing" and "82" on sides and front. Fourth-place winner in 1979 Le Mans, 1:43 scale, Model No. 2302
EX n/a　　NM n/a　　MIP $20

PORSCHE 962 C RACING

❏ **Porsche 962 C, "Blaupunkt" 1989 Le Mans 3rd place, no. "9",** 2000, White body with number "9" on sides, front and rear, racing team; Wollek and Stuck, 1:18 scale, Model No. 4705
EX n/a　　NM n/a　　MIP $35

❏ **Porsche 962 C, "Coke" 1986 12-hour Sebring winner, no. "5",** 2000, Red body with white Coca-Cola stripe on sides, "Coke" on hood. Racing team: Wollek and Foyt, 1:18 scale, Model No. 4707
EX n/a　　NM n/a　　MIP $35

❏ **Porsche 962 C, "Dunlop" 1988 Le Mans 2nd place, no. "17",** 2000, Orange and red body with white wheels, "Shell" and "Dunlop," number "17" on sides, front and rear of car. Racing team, Bell, Stuck and Ludwig, 1:18 scale, Model No. 4704
EX n/a　　NM n/a　　MIP $35

❏ **Porsche 962 C, "Havoline" 1988 Le Mans 3rd place, no. "9",** 2000, White body with number "9" on sides, front and rear, racing team; Wollek and Stuck, 1:18 scale, Model No. 4705
EX n/a　　NM n/a　　MIP $35

❏ **Porsche 962 C, "Primagaz" 1987 Le Mans 2nd place, no. "72",** 2000, White body with red sides, "Primagaz" and number "72," racing team, Yver, Dryver, Laessig, 1:18 scale, Model No. 4703
EX n/a　　NM n/a　　MIP $35

❏ **Porsche 962 C, "Rothmans" 1986 Le Mans winner, no. "1",** 2000, White body with dark blue sides, white wheels, circle number "1", team Stuck, Bell and Hollbert, 1:18 scale, Model No. 4701
EX n/a　　NM n/a　　MIP $35

❏ **Porsche 962 C, "Rothmans" 1987 Le Mans winner, no. "17",** 2000, White body with dark blue sides, white wheels, circle number "17," team Stuck, Bell and Hollbert, 1:18 scale, Model No. 4702
EX n/a　　NM n/a　　MIP $35

❏ **Porsche 962 C, "Swap Shop" 1985 24-hour Daytona winner, no. "5",** 2000, Red body with green and red "Swap Shop" letting, white wheels, 1:18 scale, Model No. 4708
EX n/a　　NM n/a　　MIP $35

RENAULT 5 GT TURBO

(Eagle Photo)

❏ **Renault Super 5 GT no. 17, Tour de Corse, 1989,** 2001, Silver with number "17" on sides, sponsor graphics. Drivers: Oreille/Thimonier. Limited edition to 3000 pieces, 1:43 scale, Model No. 2462
EX n/a　　NM n/a　　MIP $20

❏ **Renault Super 5 GT no. 19, Monte Carlo Rally, 1989,** 2001, White with yellow stripes and number "19" on sides, sponsor graphics. Drivers: Oreille/Thimonier. Limited edition to 3000 pieces, 1:43 scale, Model No. 2461
EX n/a　　NM n/a　　MIP $20

❏ **Renault Super 5 GT no. 9, Ivory Coast Rally, 1989,** 2001, Silver with yellow stripes and number "9" on sides, sponsor graphics. Drivers: Oreille/Thimonier. Limited edition to 3000 pieces, 1:43 scale, Model No. 2460
EX n/a　　NM n/a　　MIP $20

❏ **Renault Super 5 GT Turbo Phase 2,** 2001, White with silver stripe graphic along bottom, silver-gray hubs, limited edition to 3000 pieces, 1:43 scale, Model No. 2450
EX n/a　　NM n/a　　MIP $20

❏ **Renault Super 5 GT Turbo Phase 2,** 2001, Metallic bright blue with silver stripe graphic along bottom, silver-gray hubs, limited edition to 3000 pieces, 1:43 scale, Model No. 2454
EX n/a　　NM n/a　　MIP $20

(Eagle Photo)

❏ **Renault Super 5 GT Turbo Phase 2,** 2001, Red with silver stripe graphic along bottom, silver-gray hubs, limited edition to 3000 pieces, 1:43 scale, Model No. 2453
EX n/a　　NM n/a　　MIP $20

RENAULT 5 MAXI TURBO

(Eagle Photo)

❏ **Renault 5 Maxi Turbo no. "1" "Philips" Tour de France winner, 1985,** 2001, Blue car with orange-red trim, "Philips" and number "1" on sides. Driver: Ragnotti. Shown here with "Diac" Tour de Corse 1986 car, (#1758), 1:43 scale, Model No. 1752
EX n/a   **NM** n/a   **MIP** $20

❏ **Renault 5 Maxi Turbo no. "1" "Region Picardie" Quercy, 1988,** 2001, White with blue trim, white wheels, black interior. Number "1" on sides, 1:43 scale, Model No. 1757
EX n/a   **NM** n/a   **MIP** $20

❏ **Renault 5 Maxi Turbo no. "11" "Diac" Tour de Corse, 1986,** 2001, Black, white and pink car with "Diac" and number "11" on sides. Black interior, white wheels, 1:43 scale, Model No. 1758
EX n/a   **NM** n/a   **MIP** $20

(Eagle Photo)

❏ **Renault 5 Maxi Turbo no. "20" "Conseil General du Gard," Rally Garrigues, 1986,** 2001, White and yellow body with green trim, number "20" on sides. Shown here with "Fouya" Rally Cross 1987 winner, (#1756), 1:43 scale, Model No. 1755
EX n/a   **NM** n/a   **MIP** $20

❏ **Renault 5 Maxi Turbo no. "3" "Philips" Tour de Corse 1985 winner,** 2001, Blue body with red trim, white wheels, number "3" on sides, 1:43 scale, Model No. 1750
EX n/a   **NM** n/a   **MIP** $20

(Eagle Photo)

❏ **Renault 5 Maxi Turbo no. "5" Rally Costa Brava, 1986,** 2001, White, yellow and black body with number "5" on sides. Driver: Carlos Sainz. Shown here with "Region Picardie" number "1" car, 1988, (#1757), 1:43 scale, Model No. 1754
EX n/a   **NM** n/a   **MIP** $20

❏ **Renault 5 Maxi Turbo no. "6" "Fouya" Rally Cross winner, 1987,** 2001, Red, white and blue stars and stripes paint scheme, "Fouya" and number "6" on sides, 1:43 scale, Model No. 1756
EX n/a   **NM** n/a   **MIP** $20

(Eagle Photo)

❏ **Renault 5 Maxi Turbo Presentation Version,** 2001, White, black and yellow body, no numbering, close in paint to Costa Brava, 1986 car, number "5" (#1754). Shown here with Philips Tour de Corse 1985 winner (#1750), 1:43 scale, Model No. 1759
EX n/a   **NM** n/a   **MIP** $20

RENAULT ATLES

(Eagle Photo)

❏ **Renault Atles Tractor,** 2001, Orange and black tractor with cab details, and white wheels, 1:32 scale, Model No. 2200
EX n/a   **NM** n/a   **MIP** $25

RENAULT CLIO I

(Eagle Photo)

❏ **Renault Clio "Williams",** 2001, Dark metallic blue body with gold "Williams" lettering, and gold hubs, 1:43 scale, Model No. 2505
EX n/a   **NM** n/a   **MIP** $20

(Eagle Photo)

❏ **Renault Clio 16S,** 2001, Black body, gray, multi-spoked hubs. Shown here with yellow version, (#2550), 1:43 scale, Model No. 2551
EX n/a   **NM** n/a   **MIP** $20

❏ **Renault Clio 16S,** 2001, Light yellow body, multi-spoked hubs, 1:43 scale, Model No. 2550
EX n/a   **NM** n/a   **MIP** $20

❏ **Renault Clio 16S,** 2001, White body, multi-spoked hubs, 1:43 scale, Model No. 2501
EX n/a   **NM** n/a   **MIP** $20

(Eagle Photo)

❑ **Renault Clio 16S,** 2001, Red body, multi-spoked hubs. Shown here with white version, (#2501), 1:43 scale, Model No. 2500
EX n/a   **NM** n/a   **MIP** $20

RENAULT CLIO MAXI

(Eagle Photo)

❑ **Renault Clio Maxi "Belga" no. "10" Boucle Spa, 1995,** 2001, Silver and red body, red graphics with "Belga" and number "10" on sides. Championnat de Belgique, driver: Munster. Limited edition to 1500 pieces. Shown here with number "17" Tour de Corse car, (#1776), 1:43 scale, Model No. 1778
EX n/a   **NM** n/a   **MIP** $20

❑ **Renault Clio Maxi "Diac" no. "17" Tour de Corse, 1995,** 2001, "Diac" and number "17" on sides, white multi-spoked wheels, driver: Ragnotti. Limited edition to 3000 pieces, 1:43 scale, Model No. 1776
EX n/a   **NM** n/a   **MIP** $20

(Eagle Photo)

❑ **Renault Clio Maxi "Diac" no. "21" Tour de Corse, 1995,** 2001, Silver body with blue and yellow graphics, "Diac" on hood and sides, number "21" on sides. Limited to 2500 pieces. Shown with Clio Maxi "Renault," RAC Rally 1995, number "25," driver: Ragnotti, 1:43 scale, Model No. 1777
EX n/a   **NM** n/a   **MIP** $20

❑ **Renault Clio Maxi "Renault" no. "25" RAC Rally, 1995,** 2001, Number "25" and "Renault" on sides, limited edition of 2500 pieces. Driver: Jordan, 1:43 scale, Model No. 1782
EX n/a   **NM** n/a   **MIP** $20

(Eagle Photo)

❑ **Renault Clio Maxi no. "14" Monte Carlo, 1995,** 2001, Silver body with blue and yellow triangle graphics, "Diac" and number "14" on sides, silver multi-spoked wheels, limited edition to 3000 pieces. Driver: Ragnotti, 1:43 scale, Model No. 1779
EX n/a   **NM** n/a   **MIP** $20

(Eagle Photo)

❑ **Renault Clio Maxi: Street Version,** 2001, Silver body, white multi-spoked wheels. Shown here with "Version Presentation," (#1775), 1:43 scale, Model No. 1780
EX n/a   **NM** n/a   **MIP** $20

❑ **Renault Clio Maxi: Version Presentation,** 2001, Yellow with black stripes, silver multi-spoked wheels. Limited edition of 2000 pieces, 1:43 scale, Model No. 1775
EX n/a   **NM** n/a   **MIP** $20

RENAULT R5 TURBO

❑ **Renault R5 Turbo no. "1" "Elf",** 2001, Blue car with red and white stripes, "Elf" and number "1" on hood and sides, black and silver wheels. Driver: Ragnotti, 1:43 scale, Model No. 1720
EX n/a   **NM** n/a   **MIP** $20

❑ **Renault R5 Turbo no. "15" Tour de Corse, 1984,** 2001, Black, white and pink body with "Diac" on "15", silver spoked wheels, sponsor graphics, 1:43 scale, Model No. 1721
EX n/a   **NM** n/a   **MIP** $20

(Eagle Photo)

❑ **Renault R5 Turbo no. "2" Coupe Europe, 1982, "Elf",** 2001, Black, with red arrow graphics and "Elf" and number "2" on hood and sides. Driver: Ragnotti. Shown here with two other versions, (#1720 and #1715), 1:43 scale, Model No. 1717
EX n/a   **NM** n/a   **MIP** $20

❑ **Renault R5 Turbo no. "41" Coupe Europe, 1981, "Europecar",** 2001, Orange with white and black stripes, number "41" and French flag graphics, orange wheels. Driver: Gouhier, 1:43 scale, Model No. 1715
EX n/a   **NM** n/a   **MIP** $20

(Eagle Photo)

❑ **Renault R5 Turbo no. "598" Tour Italy, 1979,** 2001, Yellow, red and black body with number "598" on sides, silver wheels. Shown here with Tour de Corse car number "15" car, (#1721), 1:43 scale, Model No. 1706
EX n/a   **NM** n/a   **MIP** $20

(Eagle Photo)

❏ **Renault R5 Turbo, no. "14" Rasoir Philips, Monte Carlo, 1983,** 2001, Blue and orange body with "Philips" and number "14" on sides, 1:43 scale, Model No. 1707
EX n/a   NM n/a   MIP $20

RENAULT R5 TURBO/TURBO 2

(Eagle Photo)

❏ **Renault R5 Turbo 1,** 2000, Red with red and silver wheels, some black trim, "Turbo" on doors, 1:43 scale, Model No. 1701
EX n/a   NM n/a   MIP $20

❏ **Renault R5 Turbo 1,** 2000, Metallic silver with black trim, silver and black wheels, gray interior, "Turbo" on doors, 1:43 scale, Model No. 1710
EX n/a   NM n/a   MIP $20

❏ **Renault R5 Turbo 1,** 2000, Blue with black trim, silver and blue wheels, blue interior, "Turbo" on doors, 1:43 scale, Model No. 1702
EX n/a   NM n/a   MIP $20

❏ **Renault R5 Turbo 1,** 2001, Metallic silver and blue body with blue interior, silver and blue wheels, "Turbo" in blue type on doors, 1:43 scale, Model No. 1725
EX n/a   NM n/a   MIP $20

❏ **Renault R5 Turbo 2,** 2000, Red with black trim, black and silver wheels, "Turbo 2" in outline type on doors, 1:43 scale, Model No. 1712
EX n/a   NM n/a   MIP $20

❏ **Renault R5 Turbo 2,** 2000, Glossy black body with black and silver wheels, "Turbo 2" on doors, 1:43 scale, Model No. 1714
EX n/a   NM n/a   MIP $20

❏ **Renault R5 Turbo 2,** 2000, Pearl white with black trim, silver and black wheels, "Turbo 2" in outlined letters on doors, 1:43 scale, Model No. 1713
EX n/a   NM n/a   MIP $20

❏ **Renault R5 Turbo 2,** 2001, Burgundy with black trim, silver wheels, "Turbo 2" in white type on doors, 1:43 scale, Model No. 1724
EX n/a   NM n/a   MIP $20

RENAULT SPORT CLIO V6/V6 "TROPHY"

(Eagle Photo)

❏ **Renault Sport Clio V6: Street Version,** 2001, Dark metallic purple body with silver-gray multi-spoked wheels, 1:43 scale, Model No. 1826
EX n/a   NM n/a   MIP $20

❏ **Renault Sport Clio V6: Street Version,** 2001, Metallic-blue body with opening hood, doors and hatch, silver-spoked wheels, 1:18 scale, Model No. 4503
EX n/a   NM n/a   MIP $35

❏ **Renault Sport Clio V6: Street Version,** 2001, Red body with opening hood, doors and hatch, silver-spoked wheels, 1:18 scale, Model No. 4501
EX n/a   NM n/a   MIP $35

(Eagle Photo)

❏ **Renault Sport Clio V6: Street Version,** 2001, Black body with opening hood, doors and hatch, silver-spoked wheels. Shown here with Light-gray and red models (#4500 and 4501), 1:18 scale, Model No. 4502
EX n/a   NM n/a   MIP $35

(Eagle Photo)

❏ **Renault Sport Clio V6: Street Version,** 2001, Light-gray body with opening hood, doors and hatch, silver-spoked wheels, 1:18 scale, Model No. 4500
EX n/a   NM n/a   MIP $35

(Eagle Photo)

❏ **Renault Sport Clio V6: Trophy 2000 no. "11" "Papagayo",** 2001, Red body with white hood and "Papagayo Beach Resort" graphic. Number "11" on sides and roof, gray multi-spoked wheels. Limited edition of 1500 pieces, 1:43 scale, Model No. 1812
EX n/a   NM n/a   MIP $20

(Eagle Photo)

❏ **Renault Sport Clio V6: Trophy 2000 no. "2" Clio Trophy Cup winner, 2000,** 2001, Yellow body with silver-gray multi-spoked wheels, driver's side netting, number "2" on sides and roof, driver: L. Rangoni. Limited to 1500 pieces, 1:43 scale, Model No. 1824
EX n/a   NM n/a   MIP $20

❏ **Renault Sport Clio V6: Trophy 2000 no. "24" "Renault Catalunya",** 2001, Silver and black body with silver-gray multi-spoked wheels, number "24" on sides and roof. Limited to 1500 pieces, 1:43 scale, Model No. 1815
EX n/a   NM n/a   MIP $20

(Eagle Photo)

❑ **Renault Sport Clio V6: Trophy 2000 no. "41" "Hop Va",** 2001, Red body with orange trim and wheels, driver's side netting, number "41" on sides. Limited edition of 1500 pieces. Shown here with number "24" Renault Catalunya" (#1815), 1:43 scale, Model No. 1823
EX n/a   NM n/a   MIP $20

(Eagle Photo)

❑ **Renault Sport Clio V6: Trophy 2000 no. "81" "Autosport",** 2001, Multi-colored body with "Autosport" and "81" on sides, silver-gray multi-spoked wheels, netting on driver's side door. Limited edition of 3600 pieces, 1:43 scale, Model No. 1811
EX n/a   NM n/a   MIP $20

(Eagle Photo)

❑ **Renault Sport Clio V6: Trophy 2000 Winner, no. 2,** 2001, Yellow body with sponsor graphics including "Grundig" and "Fina." Driver: L. Rangoni, 1:18 scale, Model No. 4504
EX n/a   NM n/a   MIP $35

(Eagle Photo)

❑ **Renault Sport Clio V6: Trophy 2000 Winner, no. 24,** 2001, Silver and black body with "Renault Catalunya" on sides. Driver: E. Codony, 1:18 scale, Model No. 4506
EX n/a   NM n/a   MIP $35

❑ **Renault Sport Clio V6: Trophy 2000 Winner, no. 81,** 2001, Multi-colored boey with "81" and "Autosport" on sides, silver wheels, 1:18 scale, Model No. 4505
EX n/a   NM n/a   MIP $35

SAAB SONNETT III 1972-1974

❑ **Saab Sonnett III, 1972,** 2001, Emerald-green body, silver wheels, red interior, black grille. Limited edition to 1500 pieces, 1:43 scale, Model No. 3752
EX n/a   NM n/a   MIP n/a

❑ **Saab Sonnett III, 1972,** 2001, Orange body, silver wheels, red interior, black grille. Limited edition to 1500 pieces, 1:43 scale, Model No. 3754
EX n/a   NM n/a   MIP $20

❑ **Saab Sonnett III, 1974,** 2001, California Burgundy body, silver wheels, red interior, black grille. Limited edition to 1500 pieces, 1:43 scale, Model No. 3755
EX n/a   NM n/a   MIP $20

SERIES III/109

❑ **Land Rover Series III, 109 Hardtop,** 2000, Beige body with brown top, spare wheel and tire on hood, gray grille and bumpers, opening doors, 1:18 scale, Model No. 4402
EX n/a   NM n/a   MIP $35

❑ **Land Rover Series III, 109 Pickup,** 1999, Red body with white hood and cab, white wheels, fold-out windshield, spare tire on hood, 1:18 scale, Model No. 4405
EX n/a   NM n/a   MIP $35

❑ **Land Rover Series III, 109 Pickup,** 2000, Gray-blue body, beige wheels, silver-gray bumpers and trim, 1:18 scale, Model No. 4406
EX n/a   NM n/a   MIP $35

(Eagle Photo)

❑ **Land Rover Series III, 109 Pickup,** 2001, Light-brown body, light-brown wheels, fold-out windshield, spare tire on hood. Shown here with softtop model in British racing green, (#4403), 1:18 scale, Model No. 4408
EX n/a   NM n/a   MIP $35

❑ **Land Rover Series III, 109 Softtop,** 1999, British racing green body, tan softtop, white wheels, opening doors, 1:18 scale, Model No. 4403
EX n/a   NM n/a   MIP $35

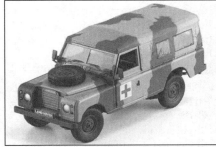

(Eagle Photo)

❑ **Land Rover Series III, 109 Softtop, Military Medic,** 2000, Temperate camouflage green, green wheels, red cross graphics on doors, spare on hood, 1:18 scale, Model No. 4404
EX n/a   NM n/a   MIP $35

SERIES III/109- SERIES II/109

(Eagle Photo)

❑ **Land Rover Series II, Pickup,** 2000, Light-gray body with black interior, fold-down windshield, green wheels, spare on opening hood. Shown here with Series III softtop, (#4403), 1:18 scale, Model No. 4421
EX n/a **NM** n/a **MIP** $35

❑ **Land Rover Series II, Pickup,** 2000, Light-green body with black interior, fold-down windshield, green wheels, spare on opening hood, 1:18 scale, Model No. 4422
EX n/a **NM** n/a **MIP** $35

(Eagle Photo)

❑ **Land Rover Series II, Pickup,** 2001, Yellow pickup with "West Sussex Fire Brigade" on doors, ladder, hose and fire gear in back, spare on hood. Shown here with "Dorset Fire Brigade" model (#4412), 1:18 scale, Model No. 4414
EX n/a **NM** n/a **MIP** $35

❑ **Land Rover Series II, Road Patrol,** 2000, Blue hardtop with white roof and "RAC Motorway Patrol" and "Mobile Service Unit" on sides. Opening hood and doors, spare on hood, 1:18 scale, Model No. 4420
EX n/a **NM** n/a **MIP** $35

(Eagle Photo)

❑ **Land Rover Series III, 109 Pickup, Towtruck,** 2000, Black body with yellow type, "Keith Motors, LTD" on doors, silver-gray towing boom, black wheels, red roof light, 1:18 scale, Model No. 4411
EX n/a **NM** n/a **MIP** $35

❑ **Land Rover Series III, 109 Police Patrol,** 2000, White hardtop with orange and blue police stripe, "Police" on side panels, white wheels, spare on hood, blue roof light, 1:18 scale, Model No. 4409
EX n/a **NM** n/a **MIP** $35

❑ **Land Rover Series III, Dorset Fire Brigade,** 2001, Red hardtop with "Dorset Fire Brigade" and shield graphic on sides, red wheels, opening doors and hood, 1:18 scale, Model No. 4412
EX n/a **NM** n/a **MIP** $35

TRIUMPH TR2-TR3

(Eagle Photo)

❑ **Triumph TR2 Convertible,** 2001, Signal red with black interior, red wheels, silver trim and hubcaps. Shown here with dark yellow version, (#3683), 1:43 scale, Model No. 3684
EX n/a **NM** n/a **MIP** $20

❑ **Triumph TR2 Convertible,** 2001, Dark yellow with burgundy interior, yellow wheels with silver hubcaps, silver trim, 1:43 scale, Model No. 3683
EX n/a **NM** n/a **MIP** $20

❑ **Triumph TR3 Convertible,** 1999, Light yellow body, black interior, silver bumpers, 1:43 scale, Model No. 1084
EX n/a **NM** n/a **MIP** $20

(Eagle Photo)

❑ **Triumph TR3 Convertible,** 1999, Salvador blue body, beige interior, silver bumpers. Shown here with light yellow version, (#1083), 1:43 scale, Model No. 1084
EX n/a **NM** n/a **MIP** $20

(Eagle Photo)

❑ **Triumph TR3 Hardtop,** 1999, Beige with red top, silver spoked wheels, silver trim, 1:43 scale, Model No. 1093
EX n/a **NM** n/a **MIP** $20

(Eagle Photo)

❑ **Triumph TR3 no. 96 Tour de Corse, 1957,** 2000, Red body with black softtop, white number "96" on doors, silver-spoked wheels, black interior, 1:43 scale, Model No. 1085
EX n/a **NM** n/a **MIP** $20

(Eagle Photo)

❑ **Triumph TR3A Convertible, rapid response vehicle,** 1998, Red body and interior, silver-gray trim, including hood-mounted siren. Part of the historic Rochester, NY Fire Department lineup. Shown here with TR3A hardtop in metallic blue and white, (#1128), 1:43 scale, Model No. 1097
EX n/a **NM** n/a **MIP** $20

❑ **Triumph TR3A Convertible, right-hand drive,** 1997, British racing green with black interior, silver-spoked wheels, silver bumpers, silver luggage rack and trim, 1:43 scale, Model No. 1058
EX n/a **NM** n/a **MIP** $20

(Eagle Photo)

❑ Triumph TR3A Convertible, right-hand drive, 1997, Red with black interior, silver-spoked wheels, silver trim on seats. Shown here with British racing green version, (#1058), 1:43 scale, Model No. 1057
EX n/a   NM n/a   MIP $20

❑ Triumph TR3A Hardtop, 1999, Metallic blue and white body, silver-spoked wheels and trim, whitewall tires, 1:43 scale, Model No. 1128
EX n/a   NM n/a   MIP $20

(Eagle Photo)

❑ Triumph TR3A Hardtop, left-hand drive, 1997, Silver exterior, red interior with silver trim, silver-spoked wheels. Shown here with black version, (#1008), 1:43 scale, Model No. 1009
EX n/a   NM n/a   MIP $20

❑ Triumph TR3A Hardtop, left-hand drive, 1997, Black exterior, red interior with silver trim, silver-spoked wheels, 1:43 scale, Model No. 1008
EX n/a   NM n/a   MIP $20

❑ Triumph TR3A no. 25, Le Mans, 1959, 1998, British racing green body with white front, number "25" on sides, hood and trunk, white interior, 1:43 scale, Model No. 1081
EX n/a   NM n/a   MIP $20

(Eagle Photo)

❑ Triumph TR3A no. 26, Le Mans, 1959, 1998, British racing green body with yellow front, number "26" on sides, hood and trunk, white interior, 1:43 scale, Model No. 1082
EX n/a   NM n/a   MIP $20

(Eagle Photo)

❑ Triumph TR3A no. 27, Le Mans, 1959, 1998, British racing green body with red front, number "27" on sides, hood and trunk, white interior. Shown here with number "25" car, (#1081), 1:43 scale, Model No. 1089
EX n/a   NM n/a   MIP $20

VOLKSWAGEN BEETLE 1303

❑ Volkswagen Beetle 1303 convertible, 1997, Black with black interior, white folded softtop, silver trim and hubs, 1:43 scale, Model No. 1025
EX n/a   NM n/a   MIP $20

❑ Volkswagen Beetle 1303 coupe, 2001, Yellow body with silver hubs, bumpers and trim, black running boards, 1:43 scale, Model No. 1022
EX n/a   NM n/a   MIP $20

❑ Volkswagen Beetle 1303 coupe, 2001, Cream-colored body, black interior, silver hubs, bumpers and trim, 1:43 scale, Model No. 1023
EX n/a   NM n/a   MIP $20

❑ Volkswagen Beetle 1303 coupe, "Champion", 2001, White body with red polka dots, "Champion" on sides, white softtop, black interior, 1:43 scale, Model No. 3676
EX n/a   NM n/a   MIP $20

❑ Volkswagen Beetle 1303 coupe, hot rod, 2001, Yellow with white scallop design, painted bumpers, silver hubs, black interior, 1:43 scale, Model No. 3687
EX n/a   NM n/a   MIP $20

(Eagle Photo)

❑ Volkswagen Beetle 1303 coupe, hot rod, 2001, Pink with purple scallop design, painted bumpers, purple interior, purple wheels with silver hubcaps. Shown here with white and yellow version, (#3687), 1:43 scale, Model No. 3688
EX n/a   NM n/a   MIP $20

(Eagle Photo)

❑ Volkswagen Beetle 1303 coupe, special edition, 2000, White body with cloverleaf design, "eye" tv graphic on doors. This model was the first prize in Germany's first tv lottery, "A Place in the Sun", 1:43 scale, Model No. 1126
EX n/a   NM n/a   MIP $20

❑ Volkswagen Beetle 1303, coupe, 2000, Orange body, silver-gray hubs, bumpers and trim, black interior, 1:43 scale, Model No. 1111
EX n/a   NM n/a   MIP $20

(Eagle Photo)

❑ **Volkswagen Beetle 1303, coupe,** 2000, Apple-green body, silver-gray hubs, bumpers and trim, black interior. Shown here with orange version (#1111), 1:43 scale, Model No. 1112

EX n/a   NM n/a   MIP $20

(Eagle Photo)

❑ **Volkswagen Beetle 1303, coupe,** 2001, Purple and white body, purple wheel with silver hubs, bumpers and trim, black running boards, 1:43 scale, Model No. 3686

EX n/a   NM n/a   MIP $20

❑ **Volkswagen Beetle 1303, coupe: ADAC Road Patrol Car,** 1998, Yellow body with white roof, black running boards, "ADAC Strassenwacht" on sides and on hood with eagle design, red roof light, 1:43 scale, Model No. 1110

EX n/a   NM n/a   MIP $20

(Eagle Photo)

❑ **Volkswagen Beetle 1303, coupe: Fire Brigade,** 1998, Red body with white fenders, black interior, fire brigade markings on

doors, blue roof light, 1:43 scale, Model No. 1109

EX n/a   NM n/a   MIP $20

❑ **Volkswagen Beetle 1303, coupe: Polizei,** 1998, Green and white body, silver bumpers, hubs and trim, blue roof light, "Polizei" ("Police" in German) on sides, 1:43 scale, Model No. 1108

EX n/a   NM n/a   MIP $20

❑ **Volkswagen Beetle 1303, softtop,** 1997, Light blue with black softtop. Silver hubs, bumpers and trim. Black interior, 1:43 scale, Model No. 1027

EX n/a   NM n/a   MIP $20

(Eagle Photo)

❑ **Volkswagen Beetle 1303, softtop,** 1998, Gold with white softtop. Silver hubs, bumpers and trim. Beige interior. Shown here with light blue and silver versions, (#1027 and #1114), 1:43 scale, Model No. 1107

EX n/a   NM n/a   MIP $20

❑ **Volkswagen Beetle 1303, softtop,** 2000, Silver body with black softtop. Silver hubs, bumpers and trim. Black interior, whitewall tires, 1:43 scale, Model No. 1114

EX n/a   NM n/a   MIP $20

WILLYS COUPE 1941

(Eagle Photo)

❑ **1941 Willys Coupe: Drag Racer,** 2001, Blue, white and red with "2D" on doors. Shown here with other drag racers in the series, (#1909 and #1908), 1:43 scale, Model No. 1906

EX n/a   NM n/a   MIP $20

❑ **1941 Willys Coupe: Drag Racer: Campbell Racing,** 2001, Red with white and yellow flames, chrome wheels. The real version, driven by Sue Campbell, was the 1998 Goodguys Hot Rod Nationals winner, 1:43 scale, Model No. 1909

EX n/a   NM n/a   MIP $20

❑ **1941 Willys Coupe: Drag Racer: Wright Racing,** 2001, Blue with purple and light blue metallic flames, chrome wheels, metallic light blue spoiler. Driver: Gary Wright. The actual car was the Super Chevy Editor's Choice winner for 2000, 1:43 scale, Model No. 1909

EX n/a   NM n/a   MIP $20

❑ **1941 Willys Coupe: Hot Rod,** 2001, Dark blue (called "dark silver") with bright blue scallops, chrome wheels and grille, black interior, 1:43 scale, Model No. 1902

EX n/a   NM n/a   MIP $20

❑ **1941 Willys Coupe: Hot Rod,** 2001, White with silver and yellow flames, chrome wheels and grille, 1:43 scale, Model No. 1903

EX n/a   NM n/a   MIP $20

(Eagle Photo)

❑ **1941 Willys Coupe: Hot Rod,** 2001, Yellow with chromed engine, chrome wheels, silver bumpers. Shown here with rose red version, (#1904), 1:43 scale, Model No. 1905

EX n/a   NM n/a   MIP $20

❑ **1941 Willys Coupe: Hot Rod,** 2001, Rose red with chromed engine, chrome wheels, silver bumpers, 1:43 scale, Model No. 1904

EX n/a   NM n/a   MIP $20

❑ **1941 Willys Coupe: Street Version,** 2001, Metallic electric blue body, chrome wheels, black interior, 1:43 scale, Model No. 1901

EX n/a   NM n/a   MIP $20

Ertl Die-Cast

Domino's Pizza promotional Chevette by Ertl. A funky choice for a casting and concept.

By Merry Dudley

Most die-cast enthusiasts know the history of Ertl, but it bears repeating. In 1945, Fred Ertl Sr., a molder, found himself unemployed due to a strike at the foundry where he worked in Dubuque, Iowa. When Ertl's son Joe broke his old Arcade toy tractor, Ertl set out to repair it using his knowledge of molds. He enjoyed the project and began to make other molds of different types of tractors. The entire family helped with the assembly and detailing of the toys.

As the story goes, a neighbor saw Ertl's work and was impressed with the craftsmanship. He struck a bargain to purchase as many toys as the Ertl family could produce to be sold in Roshek's department store in Dubuque. The family business took off. Fred Ertl Jr. remembers that the family could make 150 tractors on a good day.

Within two years, Ertl bought a building in Dubuque and set up business. A new factory was built in July 1959 in Dyersville, Iowa, where the company still maintains an office.

In 1982, Ertl bought AMT, the renowned plastic model manufacturer. That year also marked the launch of The Replica, a printed newsletter that remained part of the company's collector club until 2002 when it became an online-only webzine.

But the biggest change occurred when the company was acquired by Racing Champions in 1999 to create Racing Champions/Ertl.

MARKET UPDATE

Ertl toys and models of every vintage have found homes within the hearts of collectors, and their popularity continues to grow. Some of the early die-casts command a nice premium, while newer releases remain steady at prices just above original retail prices.

The American Muscle 1:18-scale releases of the last 10 years have gathered quite a following. Expect to pay higher prices for limited-edition examples that have been detailed by companies like Supercar Collectibles, Campbell Collectibles, Performance Years Enterprises and various collector car clubs.

The Early Die-Cast Days

Many collectors find the early 1980s a confusing time for Ertl products. This isn't surprising, but here is some information that has been gathered from early issues of The Replica and The Ertl Collectors Handbook (1989), both printed by the company.

Before the release of the standardized Replica series in 1982, Ertl issued several 1:64-scale cars under various series names, most notably American Classics (1978), European Classics, International Cars or Cars of the World (1977) and Fun Truckin' Vehicles (1979-80).

The first 12 cars were all produced in Hong Kong. Cars #13-18 were originally manufactured in Hong Kong, but the tooling was transferred to Taiwan in 1981. While early versions sported various opening features, most of these extras were removed by 1982.

Numbers and original casting dates are as follows:

1. Porsche 911, 1977 2. Mazda RX7, 1982 (Originally designed in 1979 but was not produced until the introduction of the Replica series in 1982.)
3. Mercedes Benz 350SL, 1977
4. Porsche 917, 1977
5. Mercedes Benz 450SE, 1977
6. BMW Turbo, 1977

7. Volkswagen 1200LS, 1977 8. 1982 Ford EXP, 1982
9. Ford Mark IV, 1977; replaced by Jaguar XJ12, 1980
10. Datsun 280ZX Turbo, 1982. (Originally designed in 1979 as a 280Z but was not produced until the introduction of the Replica series in 1982 when it was redesigned to replicate the 280ZX Turbo.)
11. BMW Turbo, 1977, replaced by Porsche 930 Turbo, 1980

12. Fiat Abarth, 1977, replaced by Ferrari Dino 246GT, 1980

13. 1957 Chevy two-door hardtop, 1979

14. 1950 Mercury two-door coupe, 1979

15. 1955 Chevy Nomad station wagon, 1979
16. 1950 Ford convertible, 1979

17. 1956 Ford Crown Victoria hardtop, 1979

18. 1951 Chevy sedan, 1979

19. 1932 Ford Coupe street car, 1981
20. 1934 Ford Sedan street car, 1981
21. 1940 Ford Coupe street car, 1981
22. 1957 Chevy convertible street rod, 1981
23. 1923 Ford T-Bucket street rod, 1981
24. 1913 Ford Model T van street rod, 1981
25. 1932 Ford five-window coupe, 1978

26. 1957 Ford Thunderbird, 1978. (Originally part of American Classics series.)
27. 1976 Chevy Camaro, 1981
28. 1963 Corvette Stingray, 1978 (American Classics series)
29. Pontiac Turbo Firebird, 1978. (Originally part of American Classics series as a 1977 Firebird; changed in 1980 to the Turbo model.)
30. Chevy Stepside pickup, 1979 (Fun Truckin' Vehicles series)

31. Jeep CJ7, 1980 (Fun Truckin' Vehicles series)
32. 1982 Turbo Firebird, 1982
33. 1982 Chevy Mini Truck, 1982
34. 1982 Camaro, 1982
35. 1964-1/2 Ford Mustang, 1982
36. 1980 Bonneville police car, 1981

Although many of the cars were issued earlier, the Replica series of 1982 included 36 different castings. How can you tell if your car was made before 1982? It may be tough, but most cars made before that time did not have the car's number and production date code molded onto the chassis.

The New Ertl

Over the past few years, the company has diversified into action figures based on video game properties, licensed preschool toys and an ever-growing list of vehicles based on movies and television programs. In 2000, the company teamed with Ford to release the Precision 100 line of high-quality 1:18-scale die-cast models of important Ford vehicles, such as the 1964-1/2 Mustang, 1913 Model T Speedster, 1957 Thunderbird and 1964 Thunderbolt.

An Explanation of Early Production Codes

The early codes give plenty of information about each car. For example, a number 32 in a circle would represent the 1982 Pontiac Firebird. The production date code "1242Z" would mean that the car was made on the 124th day of 1982. The letter Z is the location code, or the country of origin for the toy.

Despite the best of intentions, the production code does not always appear on the base because of the problems associated with switching production to Taiwan. In these cases, the production code would have appeared on the packaging.

Fun Fact

In 1981, Ertl won the Toy of the Year Award for its Dukes of Hazzard series, beating out the popular Rubik's Cube.

That year, Ertl sold more than 20 million Dukes of Hazzard vehicles, including the General Lee, Daisy's Jeep, Boss Hogg's Cadillac, Roscoe's Police Car and Cooter's pickup. The replicas were made in either 1:64 or 1:25-scale.

1:18-SCALE

❑ **Drive-In Theater set,** 2000, 1:18 scale, Model No. 32174
EX n/a NM n/a MIP $15

(Photo courtesy Racing Champions Ertl)

❑ **Gas Station set,** 2000, 1:18 scale, Model No. 32172
EX n/a NM n/a MIP $15

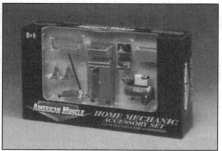

(Photo courtesy Racing Champions Ertl)

❑ **Home Mechanic set,** 2000, 1:18 scale, Model No. 32173
EX n/a NM n/a MIP $15

10 FASTEST

❑ **1966 Shelby Cobra,** 2001, Red body, tan interior, white side pipes, 1:18 scale, Model No. 32760
EX n/a NM n/a MIP $35

(Photo courtesy Racing Champions Ertl)

❑ **1973 Pontiac Trans Am,** 2001, Cameo White body, blue interior, folding front bucket seats, plated gauge cluster, Formula steering wheel, LS2 455 Super Duty engine, 1:18 scale, Model No. 32755
EX n/a NM n/a MIP $35

10 FASTEST MOPARS

❑ **1969 Dodge Super Bee,** 2002, 1:18 scale, Model No. 33010
EX n/a NM n/a MIP $30

❑ **1969 Plymouth GTX hardtop,** 2002, 1:18 scale, Model No. 33011
EX n/a NM n/a MIP $30

❑ **1970 Plymouth Barracuda 440,** 2001, Black body, white stripes, black vinyl top, black interior, 1:18 scale, Model No. 33007
EX n/a NM n/a MIP $35

❑ **1971 Dodge Challenger R/T,** 2001, Bright Red body, white stripes, black spoiler, white/black interior, 1:18 scale, Model No. 33008
EX n/a NM n/a MIP $35

(Photo courtesy Racing Champions Ertl)

❑ **1971 Plymouth Cuda,** 2001, Curious Yellow body, white billboard stripes, Mopar valve covers, white interior, woodgrain dash, plated shifter, five-spoke wheels, 1:18 scale, Model No. 32751
EX n/a NM n/a MIP $35

❑ **1971 Plymouth Hemi Cuda,** 2001, Evening Blue body, white vinyl top, black/white interior, black spoiler, 1:18 scale, Model No. 33009
EX n/a NM n/a MIP $35

AIRWOLF

❑ **Airwolf Helicopter,** 1985, From TV series; also part of three-vehicle set (#1230FO), Model No. 1231
EX n/a NM n/a MIP $6

❑ **Santini Helicopter,** 1985, From TV series; also part of three-vehicle set (#1230FO), Model No. 1233
EX n/a NM n/a MIP $6

❑ **Santini Jeep,** 1985, From TV series; also part of three-vehicle set (#1230FO), Model No. 1232
EX n/a NM n/a MIP $6

AMERICAN CLASSICS

❑ **1932 Ford Coupe,** 1979, Beige body; also part of six-car set (#1702) in 1978, 1:64 scale, Model No. 1613
EX n/a NM n/a MIP $10

❑ **1932 Ford five-window coupe,** 1978, mentioned in 1978 Ertl catalog; set of six with display case, 1:64 scale, Model No. 1741
EX n/a NM n/a MIP $10

❑ **1957 Chevy,** 1979, Yellow body; also part of six-car set (#1702) in 1978, 1:64 scale, Model No. 1614
EX n/a NM n/a MIP $20

❑ **1957 Chevy Bel Air,** 1978, mentioned in 1978 Ertl catalog; set of six with display case, 1:64 scale, Model No. 1741
EX n/a NM n/a MIP $10

❑ **1957 Ford Thunderbird,** 1978, mentioned in 1978 Ertl catalog; set of six with display case, 1:64 scale, Model No. 1741
EX n/a NM n/a MIP $10

❑ **1957 Ford Thunderbird,** 1979, Blue body; also part of six-car set (#1702) in 1978, 1:64 scale, Model No. 1615
EX n/a NM n/a MIP $10

❑ **1963 Corvette Stingray,** 1979, Red body; also part of six-car set (#1702) in 1978, 1:64 scale, Model No. 1617
EX n/a NM n/a MIP $20

❑ **1963 Corvette Stingray split-window coupe,** 1978, mentioned in 1978 Ertl catalog; set of six with display case, 1:64 scale, Model No. 1741
EX n/a NM n/a MIP $10

❑ **Ford Mustang Mach I,** 1978, mentioned in 1978 Ertl catalog; set of six with display case, 1:64 scale, Model No. 1741
EX n/a NM n/a MIP $10

❑ **Mustang Mach I,** 1979, Maroon body; also part of six-car set (#1702) in 1978, 1:64 scale, Model No. 1616
EX n/a NM n/a MIP $20

❑ **Pontiac Firebird Trans Am,** 1978, mentioned in 1978 Ertl catalog; set of six with display case, 1:64 scale, Model No. 1741
EX n/a NM n/a MIP $10

❑ **Pontiac Trans Am,** 1979, Black body; also part of six-car set (#1702) in 1978, 1:64 scale, Model No. 1618
EX n/a NM n/a MIP $10

AMERICAN GRAFFITI

❏ **1932 Ford Deuce coupe,** 2000, Yellow body, black interior, 1:18 scale, Model No. 32078
EX n/a   NM n/a   MIP $25

(Photo courtesy Racing Champions Ertl)

❏ **1934 Ford hot rod,** 2001, Primer body, detailed engine, plated tri-carbs, suicide doors, black interior, custom shifter and steering wheel, 1:18 scale, Model No. 32859
EX n/a   NM n/a   MIP $25

(Photo courtesy Racing Champions Ertl)

❏ **1951 Mercury Coupe,** 2000, Maroon body, 1:18 scale, Model No. 32081
EX n/a   NM n/a   MIP $25

(Photo courtesy Racing Champions Ertl)

❏ **1955 Chevy,** 2000, Black body, black interior, 1:18 scale, Model No. 32080
EX n/a   NM n/a   MIP $25

(Photo courtesy Racing Champions Ertl)

❏ **1958 Chevy Impala,** 2000, White body, red accents, 1:18 scale, Model No. 32079
EX n/a   NM n/a   MIP $25

❏ **1962 Corvette,** 2001, White body, black interior, 1:18 scale, Model No. 33022
EX n/a   NM n/a   MIP $25

(Photo courtesy Racing Champions Ertl)

❏ **1962 Corvette custom,** 2001, White body, light blue stripes and cove, plated wheel covers, whitewall tires, 1:18 scale, Model No. 32860
EX n/a   NM n/a   MIP $25

BATMAN

❏ **Batmissile,** 1992, From "Batman Returns" movie (1992), 1:64 scale, Model No. 2478
EX n/a   NM n/a   MIP $6

❏ **Batmobile,** 1988, From "Batman" movie (1989), 1:64 scale, Model No. 1064FO
EX n/a   NM n/a   MIP $6

❏ **Batmobile,** 1989, "Special Edition 1989" behind cockpit, blistercard marked with gold foil decal, exclusive promotion for Warner Bros. And DC Comics, limited to 1,500, 1:64 scale, Model No. 1064FA
EX n/a   NM n/a   MIP $8

❏ **Batmobile,** 1989, Plastic Batman figure molded in driver's seat, 1:43 scale, Model No. 2575EO
EX n/a   NM n/a   MIP $8

❏ **Batmobile,** 1992, From "Batman Returns" movie (1992), 1:64 scale, Model No. 1064
EX n/a   NM n/a   MIP $6

❏ **Batmobile and Jokermobile,** 1989, 1:64 scale, Model No. 2497FO
EX n/a   NM n/a   MIP $6

❏ **Batmobile with Batman figure,** 1992, From "Batman Returns" movie (1992), 1:64 scale, Model No. 2477
EX n/a   NM n/a   MIP $6

❏ **Batmobile, Jokermobile, Batwing,** 1989, Plastic bodies, die-cast chassis; set of three, 1:128 scale, Model No. 2498FO
EX n/a   NM n/a   MIP $18

❏ **Batskiboat,** 1992, From "Batman Returns" movie (1992), 1:64 scale, Model No. 2479
EX n/a   NM n/a   MIP $6

❏ **Batwing,** 1990, 1:43 scale, Model No. 2495EO
EX n/a   NM n/a   MIP $8

❏ **Jokermobile,** 1989, Plastic Joker figure molded in driver's seat, 1:48 scale, Model No. 2494EO
EX n/a   NM n/a   MIP $8

❏ **Penguin's Duck Vehicle,** 1992, From "Batman Returns" movie (1992), 1:64 scale, Model No. 2480
EX n/a   NM n/a   MIP $6

BLADE RUNNER

❏ **Bryant's Police Spinner,** 1982, also sold as part of four-car set (#1891), 1:64 scale, Model No. 1873
EX n/a   NM n/a   MIP $50

❏ **Deckard's Chase Spinner,** 1982, also sold as part of four-car set (#1891), 1:64 scale, Model No. 1872
EX n/a   NM n/a   MIP $50

❏ **Deckard's Ground Car,** 1982, also sold as part of four-car set (#1891), 1:64 scale, Model No. 1871
EX n/a   NM n/a   MIP $50

❏ **Rachel's Spinner,** 1982, also sold as part of four-car set (#1891), 1:64 scale, Model No. 1874
EX n/a   NM n/a   MIP $50

BLUEPRINT REPLICAS

❏ **1988 Camaro IROC,** 1988, Blue body, 1:43 scale, Model No. 2653EO
EX n/a   NM n/a   MIP $12

❏ **1988 Corvette,** 1988, Red body, 1:43 scale, Model No. 2650EO
EX n/a   NM n/a   MIP $12

❏ **1988 Ford Mustang GT,** 1988, Charcoal gray body, 1:43 scale, Model No. 2652EO
EX n/a   NM n/a   MIP $12

❏ **1988 Pontiac Fiero GT,** 1988, Burgundy body, 1:43 scale, Model No. 2651EO
EX n/a   NM n/a   MIP $12

BULLITT

(Photo courtesy Racing Champions Ertl)

❑ **1968 Ford Mustang,** 2002, Dark green body, black interior, plated valve covers and air cleaner, plated center console, steering wheel and dashboard trim, 1:18 scale, Model No. 33118
EX n/a   NM n/a   MIP $30

CARS

(Photo courtesy Racing Champions Ertl)

❑ **1913 Ford Model T speedster,** 2001, Red body, black seats, 1:18 scale, Model No. 32401
EX n/a   NM n/a   MIP $30

❑ **1932 Ford "High Tech" Rod,** 1996, Yellow body, black interior, open chrome engine, 1:18 scale, Model No. 7238DO
EX n/a   NM n/a   MIP $30

❑ **1932 Ford "High Tech" street rod,** 1998, Meadow Green Metallic body, red/orange flames, light green pearl interior, 1:18 scale, Model No. 7850DP
EX n/a   NM n/a   MIP $30

❑ **1932 Ford "Newstalgia" Rod,** 1996, Black body, red interior, 1:18 scale, Model No. 7239DO
EX n/a   NM n/a   MIP $30

❑ **1932 Ford "Newstalgia" street rod,** 1998, Big League Blue body, white hood and body scallops, white interior, 1:18 scale, Model No. 7851DP
EX n/a   NM n/a   MIP $35

❑ **1932 Ford Highboy,** 2002, Best of the Best series, 1:18 scale, Model No. 32961
EX n/a   NM n/a   MIP $30

(Photo courtesy Racing Champions Ertl)

❑ **1932 Ford hot rod,** 2000, Black body, black interior, 1:18 scale, Model No. 32310
EX n/a   NM n/a   MIP $30

❑ **1934 Ford hot rod,** 2000, Red body, black interior, 1:18 scale, Model No. 32311
EX n/a   NM n/a   MIP $30

❑ **1934 Ford hot rod,** 2001, Black body, flames on suicide doors, red/black interior, plated tri-carbs amd va;ve cpvers, 1:18 scale, Model No. 32852
EX n/a   NM n/a   MIP $30

❑ **1934 Ford three-window coupe street rod,** 1997, Metallic Orange body, tan interior, fenders and hood, 1:18 scale, Model No. 7278DP
EX n/a   NM n/a   MIP $35

(Photo courtesy Racing Champions Ertl)

❑ **1934 Ford three-window coupe street rod,** 1997, "Newstalgia," light blue body, dark interior, no fenders, open engine, 1:18 scale, Model No. 7277DP
EX n/a   NM n/a   MIP $35

(Photo courtesy Racing Champions Ertl)

❑ **1935 Auburn 815,** 2000, Silver/maroon body, 1:18 scale, Model No. 32397
EX n/a   NM n/a   MIP $30

(Photo courtesy Racing Champions Ertl)

❑ **1935 Auburn Boattail Speedster,** 2000, Cigarette Cream body, red striping, 1:18 scale, Model No. 17138
EX n/a   NM n/a   MIP $30

(Photo courtesy Racing Champions Ertl)

❑ **1935 Duesenberg SSJ,** 2000, Clark Gable car, silver/red body, 1:18 scale, Model No. 7962DP
EX n/a   NM n/a   MIP $40

❑ **1935 Duesenberg SSJ,** 2000, Gary Cooper car, silver/gray body, 1:18 scale, Model No. 7963DP
EX n/a   NM n/a   MIP $35

(Photo courtesy Racing Champions Ertl)

❑ **1937 Cord 812 convertible,** 2000, Cream body, 1:18 scale, Model No. 32159
EX n/a   NM n/a   MIP $30

(Photo courtesy Racing Champions Ertl)

❑ **1937 Cord 812 convertible,** 2000, Maroon body, 1:18 scale, Model No. 32158
EX n/a   NM n/a   MIP $30

❑ **1937 Lincoln Zephyr,** 2002, Maroon body, 1:18 scale, Model No. 32890
EX n/a   NM n/a   MIP $30

(Photo courtesy Racing Champions Ertl)

❑ **1940 Ford,** 1999, Black body, black interior, small-block mill, chrome oil cap and air intakes, 1:18 scale, Model No. 32302
EX n/a   NM n/a   MIP $30

❑ **1940 Ford Custom,** 2000, Blue body, red/yellow flames, 1:43 scale, Model No. 32248
EX n/a   NM n/a   MIP $8

❑ **1940 Ford Deluxe Coupe,** 1999, Mandarin Maroon body, 1:18 scale, Model No. 7936DP
EX n/a   NM n/a   MIP $30

(Photo courtesy Racing Champions Ertl)

❑ **1949 Mercury,** 2000, James Dean car; black body, 1:18 scale, Model No. 32482
EX n/a   NM n/a   MIP $30

❑ **1949 Mercury coupe,** 1997, Black body, 1:18 scale, Model No. 7122DP
EX n/a   NM n/a   MIP $35

❑ **1949 Mercury custom,** 1997, Purple body, white/yellow flames, 1:18 scale, Model No. 7123DP
EX n/a   NM n/a   MIP $30

(Photo courtesy Racing Champions Ertl)

❑ **1949 Mercury Custom,** 2000, Maroon body, gray interior, 1:43 scale, Model No. 32244
EX n/a   NM n/a   MIP $8

(Photo courtesy Racing Champions Ertl)

❑ **1949 Mercury police car,** 2001, Florida Highway Patrol, black body, roof-mounted torpedo light with red lens, spotlight on front fender, 1:18 scale, Model No. 32818
EX n/a   NM n/a   MIP $30

(Photo courtesy Racing Champions Ertl)

❑ **1951 Mercury,** 2000, Black body with flames, triple carburetor, chrome grille fender skirts, red/white interior, 1:18 scale, Model No. 32314
EX n/a   NM n/a   MIP $30

(Photo courtesy Racing Champions Ertl)

❑ **1951 Mercury,** 2000, Teal body, chrome front bumper, triple carburetor, custom striping on sides, teal/white interior, 1:18 scale, Model No. 32315
EX n/a   NM n/a   MIP $30

❑ **1951 Mercury,** 2000, Primer Gray body, chrome grille and hubcaps, beehive oil filter, dual carburetor, scroll striping on hood and trunk, simulated leopard skin upholstery, 1:18 scale, Model No. 32313
EX n/a   NM n/a   MIP $30

❑ **1952 MG TD,** 1998, Reno Red body, red interior, 1:18 scale, Model No. 7795DO
EX n/a   NM n/a   MIP $30

❑ **1952 MG TD,** 1998, Authentic Woodland Green body, beige interior, 1:18 scale, Model No. 7886DO
EX n/a   NM n/a   MIP $30

❑ **1955 Chevy 3100,** 2002, Best of the Best series, 1:18 scale, Model No. 32956
EX n/a   NM n/a   MIP $30

❑ **1955 Chevy Bel Air,** 1998, Gypsy Red body, 1:18 scale, Model No. 7846DP
EX n/a   NM n/a   MIP $30

❑ **1955 Chevy Bel Air,** 1999, Onyx Black body, white top, includes continental kit, 1:18 scale, Model No. 32074
EX n/a   NM n/a   MIP $30

❑ **1955 Chevy Bel Air,** 2000, Black body, black interior, 1:43 scale, Model No. 32252
EX n/a   NM n/a   MIP $8

❑ **1955 Chevy Bel Air convertible,** 2001, Black body and interior, plated side spear, white convertible boot, folding seat blacks, plated dual exhaust tips, 1:18 scale, Model No. 32850
EX n/a   NM n/a   MIP $30

❑ **1955 Chevy Bel Air hardtop,** 1996, Harvest Gold/India Ivory body, 265cid V8 engine, 1:18 scale, Model No. 7254DO
EX n/a   NM n/a   MIP $30

❑ **1955 Chevy Bel Air hardtop,** 1996, Gypsy Red/India Ivory body, 265cid V8 engine, 1:18 scale, Model No. 8110DO
EX n/a   NM n/a   MIP $30

❑ **1955 Chevy Bel Air hardtop,** 1997, Neptune Green/Shoreline Beige body, light interior, 1:18 scale, Model No. 7256DP
EX n/a   NM n/a   MIP $30

(Photo courtesy Racing Champions Ertl)

❑ **1956 Ford Sunliner,** 1998, Raven Black/Fiesta Red body, red/black interior, 1:18 scale, Model No. 7258DP
EX n/a   NM n/a   MIP $30

❑ **1956 Ford Sunliner,** 1998, Mandarin Orange/Colonial White body, orange/white interior, 1:18 scale, Model No. 7259DP
EX n/a   NM n/a   MIP $30

(Photo courtesy Racing Champions Ertl)

❑ **1956 Ford Sunliner,** 2000, Vermillion red/white body, 1:18 scale, Model No. 32076
EX n/a   NM n/a   MIP $30

❑ **1956 Plymouth,** 2000, 1:64 scale, Model No. 32362
EX n/a   NM n/a   MIP $6

❑ **1957 Chevy Bel Air,** 2000, Black/white body, 1:43 scale, Model No. 32126
EX n/a   NM n/a   MIP $8

(Photo courtesy Racing Champions Ertl)

❑ **1957 Chevy Bel Air,** 2000, Matador Red body, white roof, red/black interior, Ramjet V8 engine, 1:18 scale, Model No. 32917
EX n/a   NM n/a   MIP $30

❑ **1957 Chevy Bel Air,** 2001, Onyx Black body, white top, red/black interior, 1:18 scale, Model No. 32947
EX n/a   NM n/a   MIP $30

❑ **1957 Chevy Bel Air convertible,** 1991, Blue body, 1:18 scale, Model No. 7480
EX n/a   NM n/a   MIP $29

❑ **1957 Chevy Bel Air convertible,** 1991, Matador Red body, Continental kit, fender skirts, 1:18 scale, Model No. 7490
EX n/a   NM n/a   MIP $29

❑ **1957 Chevy Bel Air convertible,** 1992, Black body, 283cid engine, 1:18 scale, Model No. 7388
EX n/a   NM n/a   MIP $30

❑ **1957 Chevy Bel Air convertible,** 1993, Harbor Blue body, 1:18 scale, Model No. 7498DO
EX n/a   NM n/a   MIP $30

❑ **1957 Chevy Bel Air hardtop,** 1994, Surf Green body, ivory top, 1:18 scale, Model No. 7331DO
EX n/a   NM n/a   MIP $30

❑ **1957 Chevy Bel Air hardtop,** 1994, Matador Red body, ivory top, 1:18 scale, Model No. 7330DO
EX n/a   NM n/a   MIP $30

❑ **1957 Chevy Bel Air hardtop,** 1997, Tropical Turquoise/India Ivory body, 1:18 scale, Model No. 7901DP
EX n/a   NM n/a   MIP $30

❑ **1957 Chevy Bel Air hardtop,** 1997, Dusk Pearl/India Ivory body, 1:18 scale, Model No. 7900DP
EX n/a   NM n/a   MIP $30

(Photo courtesy Racing Champions Ertl)

❑ **1957 Chevy Bel Air police car,** 2002, Colma, Calif., Fire Department, roof-mounted bulb, black interior, opening hood, 1:64 scale, Model No. 33044
EX n/a   NM n/a   MIP $7

(Photo courtesy Racing Champions Ertl)

❑ **1957 Chevy Bel Air police car,** 2002, Colma, Calif., Fire Department, roof-mounted bulb, front fender-mounted spotlight, black interior, 1:18 scale, Model No. 33044
EX n/a   NM n/a   MIP $30

(Photo courtesy Racing Champions Ertl)

❑ **1957 Chevy convertible,** 2000, Black body, 1:18 scale, Model No. 32415
EX n/a   NM n/a   MIP $30

❑ **1957 Chevy convertible,** 2001, Pearl White body, white interior, orange/yellow flames, plated side pipes, dice hanging from mirror, 1:18 scale, Model No. 32851
EX n/a   NM n/a   MIP $30

(Photo courtesy Racing Champions Ertl)

❏ **1957 Chevy hardtop,** 2000, Red body, 1:18 scale, Model No. 32414
EX n/a   NM n/a   MIP $30

❏ **1957 Chrysler 300C,** 2000, Dark green metallic body, 1:64 scale, Model No. 32351
EX n/a   NM n/a   MIP $6

(Photo courtesy Racing Champions Ertl)

❏ **1957 Chrysler 300C,** 2000, Black body, 1:64 scale, Model No. 32349
EX n/a   NM n/a   MIP $6

❏ **1957 Chrysler 300C,** 2000, Black body, tan interior, chrome wheels, grille and trim. Part of the "American Muscle" series, 1:43 scale, Model No. 32127
EX n/a   NM n/a   MIP $10

❏ **1957 Chrysler 300C,** 2000, 1:18 scale, Model No. 32503
EX n/a   NM n/a   MIP $30

❏ **1957 Chrysler 300C,** 2000, Red body, 1:64 scale, Model No. 32350
EX n/a   NM n/a   MIP $6

(Photo courtesy Racing Champions Ertl)

❏ **1957 Chrysler 300C,** 2001, Black body, tan interior, 392cid V8, 1:18 scale, Model No. 32503
EX n/a   NM n/a   MIP $35

(Photo courtesy Racing Champions Ertl)

❏ **1957 Ford Thunderbird,** 2001, Starmist Blue body, Colonial White removable top, moveable gearshift on floor, photoetched radio speaker grille, light blue interior, 1:18 scale, Model No. 32889
EX n/a   NM n/a   MIP $30

❏ **1957 Mercury Turnpike Cruiser,** 2000, Red body, 1:43 scale, Model No. 32128
EX n/a   NM n/a   MIP $8

❏ **1958 Chevy Impala,** 2000, Cashmere Blue body, Arctic White roof, blue interior, fender skirts, continental kit, 1:18 scale, Model No. 32286
EX n/a   NM n/a   MIP $30

❏ **1958 Chevy Impala,** 2000, Cay Coral body, Arctic White roof, Coral interior, continental kit, fender skirts, 1:18 scale, Model No. 32288
EX n/a   NM n/a   MIP $30

❏ **1958 Chevy Impala,** 2000, Glen Green body and roof, green interior, 1:18 scale, Model No. 32287
EX n/a   NM n/a   MIP $30

❏ **1958 Chevy Impala,** 2000, Onyx Black or Cashmere Blue/Arctic White body, 1:18 scale, Model No. 36054
EX n/a   NM n/a   MIP $30

❏ **1958 Chevy Impala,** 2000, Silver Blue body and roof, blue interior, 1:18 scale, Model No. 32289
EX n/a   NM n/a   MIP $30

❏ **1958 Chevy Impala,** 2000, Onyx Black body, black roof and interior, 1:18 scale, Model No. 32285
EX n/a   NM n/a   MIP $30

(Photo courtesy Racing Champions Ertl)

❏ **1958 Chevy Impala,** 2000, Gold body and interior, 1:18 scale, Model No. 32291
EX n/a   NM n/a   MIP $29

❏ **1958 Chevy Impala,** 2000, Turquoise body and interior, Arctic White roof, fender skirts, 1:18 scale, Model No. 32290
EX n/a   NM n/a   MIP $30

❏ **1958 Chevy Impala,** 2000, Glen Green/Arctic White, Arctic White/Cay Coral or Silver Blue body, 1:18 scale, Model No. 36054A
EX n/a   NM n/a   MIP $30

❏ **1958 Chevy Impala,** 2000, Tropic Turquoise/Arctic White, Anniversary Gold or Snowcrest White body, 1:18 scale, Model No. 36054B
EX n/a   NM n/a   MIP $30

❏ **1958 Chevy Impala,** 2000, White body and interior, fender skirts, continental kit, 1:18 scale, Model No. 32292
EX n/a   NM n/a   MIP $30

(Photo courtesy Racing Champions Ertl)

❏ **1958 Chevy Impala,** 2001, Two-car set (1:18 and 1:64); Fathom Blue body, Snowcrest White roof, stainless steel rocker, blackened grille, opening hood and trunk, 1:18/1:64 scale, Model No. 32821
EX n/a   NM n/a   MIP $40

(Photo courtesy Racing Champions Ertl)

❏ **1958 Chevy Impala police car,** 2001, Michigan State Police, blue body, roof-mounted red light, 1:18 scale, Model No. 32819
EX n/a   NM n/a   MIP $30

(Photo courtesy Racing Champions Ertl)

❑ **1958 Chevy Impala SS,** 2000, Cay Coral body, continental kit, white roof, opening hood and trunk, 1:64 scale, Model No. 32333
EX n/a   NM n/a   MIP $6

❑ **1958 Plymouth Belvedere,** 2000, Copper body, 1:18 scale, Model No. 32619
EX n/a   NM n/a   MIP $30

❑ **1958 Plymouth Belvedere,** 2000, Red body, 1:18 scale, Model No. 32618
EX n/a   NM n/a   MIP $28

❑ **1958 Plymouth Belvedere,** 2000, Midnight Blue body, 1:18 scale, Model No. 32617
EX n/a   NM n/a   MIP $30

❑ **1958 Plymouth Belvedere,** 2000, Misty Green body and interior, 1:18 scale, Model No. 32615
EX n/a   NM n/a   MIP $30

❑ **1958 Plymouth Belvedere,** 2000, Arctic Turquoise body and interior, 1:18 scale, Model No. 32614
EX n/a   NM n/a   MIP $30

❑ **1958 Plymouth Belvedere,** 2000, Black body and interior, 1:18 scale, Model No. 32616
EX n/a   NM n/a   MIP $30

❑ **1958 Plymouth Fury,** 2000, Red body, 1:18 scale, Model No. 32612
EX n/a   NM n/a   MIP $30

❑ **1958 Plymouth Fury,** 2001, Buckskin Beige body, beige/brown interior, plated whip antennas and astray on back of front seat, fender skirts, 1:18 scale, Model No. 36612
EX n/a   NM n/a   MIP $30

(Photo courtesy Racing Champions Ertl)

❑ **1960 Chevelle COPO,** 2001, Liberty Blue body, white stripe, black interior, folding seat backs, plated shifter on center console, plated Rally wheels, 1:18 scale, Model No. 32977
EX n/a   NM n/a   MIP $30

❑ **1960 Ford Starliner,** 2000, Skymist Blue body, medium blue interior, dark blue accents, 1:18 scale, Model No. 32296
EX n/a   NM n/a   MIP $28

❑ **1960 Ford Starliner,** 2000, Monte Carlo Red, Yosemite Yellow/white or Platinum body, 1:18 scale, Model No. 36053B
EX n/a   NM n/a   MIP $30

❑ **1960 Ford Starliner,** 2000, Meadowvale Green body, medium green interior, dark green accents, 1:18 scale, Model No. 32297
EX n/a   NM n/a   MIP $28

❑ **1960 Ford Starliner,** 2000, Corinthian White body, medium blue interior, dark blue accents, 1:18 scale, Model No. 32295
EX n/a   NM n/a   MIP $30

❑ **1960 Ford Starliner,** 2000, Orchid Gray body, lavender interior, fender skirts, plated wheel covers, 1:18 scale, Model No. 32294
EX n/a   NM n/a   MIP $30

❑ **1960 Ford Starliner,** 2000, Black body, red interior, plated outer wheels and center caps, 1:18 scale, Model No. 32293
EX n/a   NM n/a   MIP $30

❑ **1960 Ford Starliner,** 2000, Black body, chrome bumpers and wheels with center caps, 1:64 scale, Model No. 32359
EX n/a   NM n/a   MIP $7

(Photo courtesy Racing Champions Ertl)

❑ **1960 Ford Starliner,** 2000, Platinum Metallic body, plated bumpers and wheels with center caps, 1:64 scale, Model No. 32358
EX n/a   NM n/a   MIP $6

❑ **1960 Ford Starliner,** 2000, Black or Orchid Gray/white body, 1:18 scale, Model No. 36053
EX n/a   NM n/a   MIP $30

❑ **1960 Ford Starliner,** 2000, Skymist Blue body, white roof, chrome bumpers and wheels with center caps, 1:64 scale, Model No. 32357
EX n/a   NM n/a   MIP $8

❑ **1960 Ford Starliner,** 2000, Corinthian White, Skymist Blue/white or Meadowvale Green body, 1:18 scale, Model No. 36053A
EX n/a   NM n/a   MIP $30

(Photo courtesy Racing Champions Ertl)

❑ **1960 Ford Starliner,** 2000, Monte Carlo Red, fender skirts, chrome plated continental kit, full wheel covers, 1:64 scale, Model No. 32355
EX n/a   NM n/a   MIP $6

(Photo courtesy Racing Champions Ertl)

❑ **1960 Ford Starliner police car,** 2001, Ohio State Highway Patrol, black body, single roof-mounted red bulb, whip antenna, mounted spotlight, 1:18 scale, Model No. 32816
EX n/a   NM n/a   MIP $30

(Photo courtesy Racing Champions Ertl)

❏ **1961 Chevy Impala SS 409,** 2001, Roman Red body, white roof, clear display case, 1:64 scale, Model No. 32651

EX n/a **NM** n/a **MIP** $5

(Photo courtesy Racing Champions Ertl)

❏ **1961 Chevy Impala SS 409,** 2001, White body, black interior, plated shifter, 1:64 scale, Model No. 32680

EX n/a **NM** n/a **MIP** $6

(Photo courtesy Racing Champions Ertl)

❏ **1961 Chevy Impala SS 409,** 2001, Sateen Silver body, black interior, plated shifter, 1:64 scale, Model No. 32681

EX n/a **NM** n/a **MIP** $6

(Photo courtesy Racing Champions Ertl)

❏ **1961 Chevy Impala SS 409,** 2001, Jewel Blue body, black interior, plated shifter, 1:64 scale, Model No. 32682

EX n/a **NM** n/a **MIP** $6

❏ **1961 Corvette coupe,** 1999, Jewel Blue body, white coves, 1:18 scale, Model No. 7834DP

EX n/a **NM** n/a **MIP** $30

❏ **1962 Corvette convertible,** 1999, Roman Red body, red interior, 1:18 scale, Model No. 7835DP

EX n/a **NM** n/a **MIP** $30

(Photo courtesy Racing Champions Ertl)

❏ **1962 Pontiac Catalina 421SD,** 2002, Ensign Blue body and interior, steel wheels, plated handles and cranks, front bench seat with folding backs, plated steering wheel and center shifter, separate pedals, 1:18 scale, Model No. 32990

EX n/a **NM** n/a **MIP** $30

(Photo courtesy Racing Champions Ertl)

❏ **1962 Pontiac Catalina 421SD,** 2002, Mandalay Red body, black interior, plated handles and cranks, front bench seat with folding backs, plated steering wheel and center shifter, separate pedals, steel wheels with center hubcap, 1:18 scale, Model No. 32991

EX n/a **NM** n/a **MIP** $30

(Photo courtesy Racing Champions Ertl)

❏ **1962 Pontiac Catalina SD 421,** 2002, Belmar Red Metallic body, black interior, plated center manual shifters and horn rings, plated dual carbs, flexible wiring, 1:18 scale, Model No. 32938

EX n/a **NM** n/a **MIP** $30

(Photo courtesy Racing Champions Ertl)

❏ **1962 Pontiac Catalina SD 421,** 2002, Starlight Black body, black interior, plated center manual shifters and horn rings, plated dual carbs, flexible wiring, 1:18 scale, Model No. 32939

EX n/a **NM** n/a **MIP** $30

❏ **1963 Chevy Impala 409,** 2000, 1:64 scale, Model No. 32340

EX n/a **NM** n/a **MIP** $6

❏ **1963 Corvette Stingray coupe,** 1994, Tuxedo Black body, red interior, 1:18 scale, Model No. 7365DO

EX n/a **NM** n/a **MIP** $30

❏ **1963 Corvette Stingray coupe,** 1994, Daytona Blue body, black interior, 1:18 scale, Model No. 7321DO

EX n/a **NM** n/a **MIP** $30

(Photo courtesy Racing Champions Ertl)

❏ **1963 Ford Galaxie,** 2001, Black body and interior, 1:64 scale, Model No. 32688

EX n/a **NM** n/a **MIP** $5

(Photo courtesy Racing Champions Ertl)

❑ **1963 Ford Galaxie,** 2001, Red body, black roof, red interior, clear display case, 1:64 scale, Model No. 32653

EX n/a   NM n/a   MIP $6

(Photo courtesy Racing Champions Ertl)

❑ **1963 Ford Galaxie,** 2001, White body, tan interior, 1:64 scale, Model No. 32686

EX n/a   NM n/a   MIP $5

(Photo courtesy Racing Champions Ertl)

❑ **1963 Ford Galaxie,** 2001, Glacier Blue body and interior, 1:64 scale, Model No. 32687

EX n/a   NM n/a   MIP $5

(Photo courtesy Racing Champions Ertl)

❑ **1963 Pontiac Catalina Super Duty,** 2001, Starlight Black body, black interior, plated shifter and steering wheel, 1:64 scale, Model No. 32684

EX n/a   NM n/a   MIP $6

(Photo courtesy Racing Champions Ertl)

❑ **1963 Pontiac Catalina Super Duty,** 2001, Ensign Blue body, blue interior, plated shifter and steering wheel, 1:64 scale, Model No. 32683

EX n/a   NM n/a   MIP $6

(Photo courtesy Racing Champions Ertl)

❑ **1963 Pontiac Catalina Super Duty,** 2001, Burgundy Metallic body, clear plastic display case, 1:64 scale, Model No. 32652

EX n/a   NM n/a   MIP $5

(Photo courtesy Racing Champions Ertl)

❑ **1963 Pontiac Catalina Super Duty,** 2001, Mandalay Red body, black interior, plated shifter and steering wheel, 1:64 scale, Model No. 32685

EX n/a   NM n/a   MIP $7

(Photo courtesy Racing Champions Ertl)

❑ **1964 Chevy Impala convertible lowrider,** 2000, Emerald Green, simulated padded upholstery and engine cover, swiveling front seats, gold air cleaner, hydraulic control box with cord, 1:18 scale, Model No. 32308

EX n/a   NM n/a   MIP $30

(Photo courtesy Racing Champions Ertl)

❑ **1964 Chevy Impala convertible lowrider,** 2000, Orange metallic body, orange interior, yellow pinstripes, gold side spears and spinner wheel covers, removable hydraulic control box, 1:18 scale, Model No. 32305

EX n/a   NM n/a   MIP $30

(Photo courtesy Racing Champions Ertl)

❑ **1964 Chevy Impala police car,** 2001, Ankeny, Iowa, Patrol, black body, white door, roof-mounted red light, mounted spotlight, dog dish rims, 1:18 scale, Model No. 32817

EX n/a   NM n/a   MIP $30

(Photo courtesy Racing Champions Ertl)

❑ **1964 Chevy Impala sedan lowrider,** 2000, Blue body, fender skirts, gold accents on front and rear bumpers, blue/pink pinstripes, chain-link steering wheel, 1:18 scale, Model No. 32304

EX n/a   NM n/a   MIP $30

(Photo courtesy Racing Champions Ertl)

❑ **1964 Chevy Impala sedan lowrider,** 2000, Candy Apple Red body, gold accents, chain-link steering wheel, console-mounted hydraulic controls, 1:18 scale, Model No. 32307
EX n/a   NM n/a   MIP $30

(Photo courtesy Racing Champions Ertl)

❑ **1964 Chevy Impala SS,** 2000, Light blue body, blue interior; also Tuxedo Black 409 version, 1:43 scale, Model No. 32249
EX n/a   NM n/a   MIP $8

❑ **1964 Chevy Impala SS convertible,** 1999, Palomar Red body, gray interior, 1:18 scale, Model No. 7837DP
EX n/a   NM n/a   MIP $30

❑ **1964 Chevy Impala SS hardtop,** 1999, Tuxedo Black body, red interior, 1:18 scale, Model No. 7838DP
EX n/a   NM n/a   MIP $30

❑ **1964 Ford Thunderbolt,** 2001, Yellow body, black interior, 1:64 scale, Model No. 32691
EX n/a   NM n/a   MIP $6

❑ **1964 Ford Thunderbolt,** 2001, Red body, black interior, 1:64 scale, Model No. 32689
EX n/a   NM n/a   MIP $6

❑ **1964 Ford Thunderbolt,** 2001, Black body, black interior, 1:64 scale, Model No. 32690
EX n/a   NM n/a   MIP $6

❑ **1964 Ford Thunderbolt,** 2001, White body, black interior, clear display case, 1:64 scale, Model No. 32654
EX n/a   NM n/a   MIP $8

❑ **1964 Ford Thunderbolt,** 2002, White body, white interior, 427 engine, soft intake hoses and plug wires, removable hood pins, dash-mounted plated tach, die-cast tow bars, opening trunk with battery, 1:18 scale, Model No. 33057
EX n/a   NM n/a   MIP $30

❑ **1964 Pontiac GTO,** 1995, Aquamarine Metallic body, 389cid V8, 1:12 scale, Model No. 7308CO
EX n/a   NM n/a   MIP $45

(Photo courtesy Racing Champions Ertl)

❑ **1964-1/2 Ford Mustang,** 2000, Rangoon Red body, red interior, 1:18 scale, Model No. 32400
EX n/a   NM n/a   MIP $30

❑ **1964-1/2 Ford Mustang convertible,** 1994, Rangoon Red body, black interior, opening doors, hood and trunk, 289cid Hi Po V8, detailed interior, 1:12 scale, Model No. 8776CO
EX n/a   NM n/a   MIP $45

❑ **1965 Chevelle SS 396,** 2001, Black body, red striping, black interior, opening hood and trunk, plated air cleaner and valve covers, 1:64 scale, Model No. 32655
EX n/a   NM n/a   MIP $7

❑ **1965 Chevelle SS396,** 2001, Saffron Yellow body, black interior, 1:64 scale, Model No. 32693
EX n/a   NM n/a   MIP $7

❑ **1965 Chevelle SS396,** 2001, Black body, black interior, 1:64 scale, Model No. 32692
EX n/a   NM n/a   MIP $6

❑ **1965 Pontiac GTO,** 2000, Tiger Gold body, black interior, plated air cleaner, valve covers, bumpers and wheels, clear display case, 1:64 scale, Model No. 32366
EX n/a   NM n/a   MIP $7

❑ **1965 Pontiac GTO,** 2000, Burgundy Red body, tan interior, plated air cleaner, valve covers, bumpers and wheels, 1:64 scale, Model No. 32369
EX n/a   NM n/a   MIP $7

❑ **1965 Pontiac GTO,** 2000, Starlight Black body, dark red interior, plated air cleaner, valve covers, bumpers and wheels, 1:64 scale, Model No. 32368
EX n/a   NM n/a   MIP $7

(Photo courtesy Racing Champions Ertl)

❑ **1965 Pontiac GTO,** 2001, Montero Red body, plated valve covers and tri-carbs, 1:64 scale, Model No. 32370
EX n/a   NM n/a   MIP $6

❑ **1965 Shelby Cobra,** 2001, Red body, black interior, flat black exhaust, 1:18 scale, Model No. 32951
EX n/a   NM n/a   MIP $30

(Photo courtesy Racing Champions Ertl)

❑ **1965 Shelby Cobra 427,** 2001, Black body, yellow stripes, flexible yellow engine wiring, black interior, two dash-mounted tachs, 1:18 scale, Model No. 32984
EX n/a   NM n/a   MIP $30

(Photo courtesy Racing Champions Ertl)

❑ **1965 Shelby GT 500,** 2001, Red body, gold stripes, plated Cobra air cleaner and valve covers, black interior, folding bucket seats, plated steering wheel, dash-mounted tach, 1:18 scale, Model No. 32985
EX n/a   NM n/a   MIP $30

❑ **1965 Shelby GT 500,** 2001, Red body, gold stripes, plated Cobra air cleaner and valve covers, black interior, folding front bucket seats, plated steering wheel, dash-mounted tach, 1:18 scale, Model No. 32958
EX n/a   NM n/a   MIP $30

(Photo courtesy Racing Champions Ertl)

❏ **1966 Chevy Nova SS,** 2001, Lemonwood Yellow body, Firestone tires, 1:18 scale, Model No. 32931
EX n/a   **NM** n/a   **MIP** $30

❏ **1966 Chevy Nova SS,** 2001, Mist Blue body, opening trunk, 1:18 scale, Model No. 32979
EX n/a   **NM** n/a   **MIP** $30

(Photo courtesy Racing Champions Ertl)

❏ **1966 Chevy Nova SS,** 2002, Black body, opening trunk, 1:18 scale, Model No. 32978
EX n/a   **NM** n/a   **MIP** $30

(Photo courtesy Racing Champions Ertl)

❏ **1966 Chevy Nova SS,** 2002, Red body, redline tires, 1:18 scale, Model No. 32930
EX n/a   **NM** n/a   **MIP** $30

(Photo courtesy Racing Champions Ertl)

❏ **1966 Chevy Nova SS Pro Stock,** 2001, Blue body, silver radiator, plated carbs, silver exhaust with pipes, blackwall tires, black trunk tubs, 1:18 scale, Model No. 33134
EX n/a   **NM** n/a   **MIP** $30

(Photo courtesy Racing Champions Ertl)

❏ **1966 Chevy Nova SS Pro Stock,** 2001, White body with decals, gold carbs, flat white headers, no exhaust pipes, dash-mounted tach, white letter rear tires, silver trunk tubs, 1:18 scale, Model No. 33133
EX n/a   **NM** n/a   **MIP** $30

(Photo courtesy Racing Champions Ertl)

❏ **1966 Dodge Charger,** 2001, Silver body, black striping and wing, black interior, 1:64 scale, Model No. 32656
EX n/a   **NM** n/a   **MIP** $8

❏ **1966 Pontiac GTO,** 1997, Starlight Black body, 1:18 scale, Model No. 7292DP
EX n/a   **NM** n/a   **MIP** $35

❏ **1966 Pontiac GTO,** 1997, Tiger Gold body, 1:18 scale, Model No. 7291DP
EX n/a   **NM** n/a   **MIP** $35

❏ **1966 Pontiac GTO,** 2000, Black body, white interior, 1:43 scale, Model No. 32250
EX n/a   **NM** n/a   **MIP** $8

(Photo courtesy Racing Champions Ertl)

❏ **1966 Pontiac GTO,** 2001, Carousel Red body, black tiger stripes, 389cid V8 with Tri-Power intake, black interior with plated center console and steering wheel, front Hurst five-spoke wheels with Firestone tires, rear M&H Racemaster slicks, 1:18 scale, Model No. 32974
EX n/a   **NM** n/a   **MIP** $29

(Photo courtesy Racing Champions Ertl)

❏ **1966 Pontiac GTO Royal Bobcat Hurst Edition,** 2001, Barrier Blue body, white interior, red fender liners, gold Hurst Wheels, Firestone white letter tires, plated shifter, Ram Air tub, sport steering wheel, limited to 2,500 from Performance Years Enterprises, 1:18 scale, Model No. 29169
EX n/a   **NM** n/a   **MIP** $30

❏ **1966 Shelby Cobra,** 2001, Red body, brown interior, 427 Cobra, plated shifter and steering wheel, 1:18 scale, Model No. 32760
EX n/a   **NM** n/a   **MIP** $30

(Photo courtesy Racing Champions Ertl)

❏ **1967 Baldwin-Motion Corvette/Ko-Motion,** 2002, Maroon body with race graphics, black interior, 427 Turbo-Jet, dash-mounted tach, plated shifter and side pipes, 1:18 scale, Model No. 33128
EX n/a   **NM** n/a   **MIP** $30

❏ **1967 Buick GS,** 2001, 1:64 scale, Model No. 32657
EX n/a   **NM** n/a   **MIP** $7

(Photo courtesy Racing Champions Ertl)

❑ **1967 Buick GS 400,** 2002, Black body, black interior, simulated hood scoops, 400 stock engine, plated center console with automatic shifter and tach, plated five-spoke wheels, 1:18 scale, Model No. 33086

EX n/a   NM n/a   MIP $30

(Photo courtesy Racing Champions Ertl)

❑ **1967 Buick GS 400,** 2002, White body, black vinyl roof, black flooring, white upholstery, plated hood scoop, painted front fender louvers, plated center console with tach, simulated white mesh speakers on doors, 1:18 scale, Model No. 32964

EX n/a   NM n/a   MIP $30

(Photo courtesy Racing Champions Ertl)

❑ **1967 Buick GS 400,** 2002, Red body, black interior, simulated hood scoops, 400 stock engine, plated center console with automatic shifter and tach, plated five-spoke wheels, 1:18 scale, Model No. 33085

EX n/a   NM n/a   MIP $30

❑ **1967 Camaro SS,** 1999, Madera Maroon body, 1:43 scale, Model No. 32104

EX n/a   NM n/a   MIP $8

❑ **1967 Chevelle SS,** 1998, Bolero Red body, black stripes, 1:18 scale, Model No. 7246DP

EX n/a   NM n/a   MIP $30

(Photo courtesy Racing Champions Ertl)

❑ **1967 Chevelle SS,** 1998, Marina Blue, red stripes, 1:18 scale, Model No. 7245DP

EX n/a   NM n/a   MIP $30

(Photo courtesy Racing Champions Ertl)

❑ **1967 Corvette coupe,** 2000, Ermine White body, 1:18 scale, Model No. 32274

EX n/a   NM n/a   MIP $30

❑ **1967 Corvette coupe,** 2000, Sunfire Yellow body, 1:18 scale, Model No. 32273

EX n/a   NM n/a   MIP $30

❑ **1967 Corvette coupe,** 2000, Marina Blue body, 1:18 scale, Model No. 32272

EX n/a   NM n/a   MIP $30

❑ **1967 Corvette coupe,** 2000, Elkhart Blue or Silver Pearl body, 1:18 scale, Model No. 36122

EX n/a   NM n/a   MIP $30

❑ **1967 Corvette coupe,** 2000, Tuxedo Black body, L-78 engine, hood without insert, triangle air cleaner, plated side exhausts, 1:18 scale, Model No. 32276

EX n/a   NM n/a   MIP $30

(Photo courtesy Racing Champions Ertl)

❑ **1967 Corvette coupe,** 2000, Marlboro Maroon body, Saddle interior, black stripes, L-71 engine, Rally wheels, 1:18 scale, Model No. 32513

EX n/a   NM n/a   MIP $30

❑ **1967 Corvette coupe,** 2000, Marine Blue, Sunfire Yellow or Ermine White body, 1:18 scale, Model No. 36122A

EX n/a   NM n/a   MIP $6

❑ **1967 Corvette coupe,** 2000, Rally Red or Lynndale Blue body, 1:18 scale, Model No. 36122B

EX n/a   NM n/a   MIP $30

❑ **1967 Corvette coupe,** 2000, Rally Red, L-88 engine, hood with insert for L-88 air cleaner, plated exhausts, 1:18 scale, Model No. 32275

EX n/a   NM n/a   MIP $30

❑ **1967 Corvette L-71 convertible,** 1991, Red body, 1:18 scale, Model No. 7489

EX n/a   NM n/a   MIP $30

❑ **1967 Corvette L-71 roadster,** 1992, Black body, red interior, finned aluminum sheels, 1:18 scale, Model No. 7445

EX n/a   NM n/a   MIP $30

❑ **1967 Corvette L-88 convertible,** 1991, Ermine White body, black interior, 1:18 scale, Model No. 7491

EX n/a   NM n/a   MIP $30

❑ **1967 Ford Mustang GT,** 1999, Wimbledon White body, blue stripes, 1:18 scale, Model No. 7294DP

EX n/a   NM n/a   MIP $30

(Photo courtesy Racing Champions Ertl)

❑ **1967 Ford Mustang GT,** 2000, Lime Gold body, black interior and stripes, 289cid Hi-Po engine, stock wheels, 1:18 scale, Model No. 32517

EX n/a   NM n/a   MIP $28

❑ **1967 Pontiac Firebird 400,** 1999, Plum Mist body, 1:43 scale, Model No. 32093

EX n/a   NM n/a   MIP $8

❑ **1967 Shelby GT350,** 1999, Yellow body, black stripes, 1:43 scale, Model No. 32092

EX n/a   NM n/a   MIP $8

(Photo courtesy Racing Champions Ertl)

ERTL / AMERICAN MUSCLE

❏ **1967 Shelby GT350,** 2000, Red body, Rally stripes, black interior, Mag Star wheels with raised white letter tires, 1:18 scale, Model No. 32553
EX n/a   NM n/a   MIP $30

❏ **1967 Shelby GT350,** 2000, Dark Moss Gray body, 1:18 scale, Model No. 32560
EX n/a   NM n/a   MIP $30

❏ **1967 Shelby GT350,** 2000, Raven Black body, Rally stripes, black interior, 10-spoke wheels with raised white letter tires, 1:18 scale, Model No. 32554
EX n/a   NM n/a   MIP $30

❏ **1967 Shelby GT350,** 2000, Wimbledon White body, 1:18 scale, Model No. 32561
EX n/a   NM n/a   MIP $30

❏ **1967 Shelby GT350,** 2000, Bronze Metallic body, Rally and LeMans stripes, black interior, mag Star wheels with raised white letter tires, 1:18 scale, Model No. 32555
EX n/a   NM n/a   MIP $30

❏ **1967 Shelby GT350,** 2000, Brittany Blue body, 1:18 scale, Model No. 32562
EX n/a   NM n/a   MIP $30

❏ **1967 Shelby GT350,** 2000, Wimbledon White body, blue Rally and LeMans stripes, white interior, 10-spoke wheels with raised white letter tires, 1:18 scale, Model No. 32552
EX n/a   NM n/a   MIP $30

❏ **1967 Shelby GT350,** 2001, Medium Metallic Gray body, Rally and LeMans stripes, black interior, 10-spoke wheels with raised white letter tires, 1:18 scale, Model No. 32556
EX n/a   NM n/a   MIP $30

(Photo courtesy Racing Champions Ertl)

❏ **1967 Shelby GT350,** 2001, Bare metal chase car, Rally and LeMans stripes, black interior, 10-spoke wheels, raised white letter tires, 1:18 scale, Model No. 32763
EX n/a   NM n/a   MIP $30

❏ **1968 AMC AMX,** 2000, Frost White body, black striping, red interior, automatic transmission, plated side pipes, mag wheels, 1:18 scale, Model No. 32279
EX n/a   NM n/a   MIP $28

❏ **1968 AMC AMX,** 2000, Frost White body, 1:18 scale, Model No. 36051A
EX n/a   NM n/a   MIP $30

(Photo courtesy Racing Champions Ertl)

❏ **1968 AMC AMX,** 2000, Classic Black body, white stripes, red interior, automatic transmission, lower body molding, mag wheels, 1:18 scale, Model No. 32277
EX n/a   NM n/a   MIP $30

❏ **1968 AMC AMX,** 2000, Caravelle Blue body, white striping, tan interior, four-speed transmission, plated side pipes, mag wheels, 1:18 scale, Model No. 32282
EX n/a   NM n/a   MIP $30

❏ **1968 AMC AMX,** 2000, Caravelle Blue body, 1:18 scale, Model No. 36051B
EX n/a   NM n/a   MIP $30

❏ **1968 AMC AMX,** 2000, Matador Red body, white striping, black interior, automatic transmission, lower body molding, mag wheels, 1:18 scale, Model No. 32283
EX n/a   NM n/a   MIP $28

(Photo courtesy Racing Champions Ertl)

❏ **1968 Baldwin-Motion Chevelle,** 2002, Black body, black interior, red striping, black vinyl roof, plated mesh air cleaner and valve covers, plated floor shifter, plated side pipes and five-spoke rims, 1:18 scale, Model No. 32987
EX n/a   NM n/a   MIP $30

❏ **1968 Chevelle SS 396,** 2000, Seafrost Green body, 1:18 scale, Model No. 32494
EX n/a   NM n/a   MIP $30

❏ **1968 Chevelle SS 396,** 2000, Fathom Blue body, 1:18 scale, Model No. 32493
EX n/a   NM n/a   MIP $30

❏ **1968 Chevelle SS 396,** 2000, Matador Red body, 1:18 scale, Model No. 32492
EX n/a   NM n/a   MIP $30

❏ **1968 Chevelle SS 396,** 2001, Butternut Yellow body, black interior, plated automatic shifter, black vinyl roof, Rally wheels, 1:18 scale, Model No. 32488
EX n/a   NM n/a   MIP $30

❏ **1968 Chevelle SS 396,** 2001, Ash Gold body, gold interior, black air cleaner, plated automatic shifter, Rally wheels, 1:18 scale, Model No. 32489
EX n/a   NM n/a   MIP $30

❏ **1968 Chevelle SS 396,** 2001, Cordovan Maroon body, Parchment interior, plated air cleaner, plated stick shifter, Rally wheels, 1:18 scale, Model No. 32490
EX n/a   NM n/a   MIP $30

❏ **1968 Chevelle SS 396,** 2001, Bare metal chase car, 1:18 scale, Model No. 32761
EX n/a   NM n/a   MIP $30

❏ **1968 Chevelle SS 396,** 2001, Ermine White body, red interior, black air cleaner, plated automatic shifter, dog dish wheels, 1:18 scale, Model No. 32491
EX n/a   NM n/a   MIP $30

❏ **1968 Chevelle SS 396,** 2001, Tuxedo Black body, black interior, plated stick shifter and dog dish wheels, 1:18 scale, Model No. 32487
EX n/a   NM n/a   MIP $30

(Photo courtesy Racing Champions Ertl)

❏ **1968 Chevelle SS396,** 2001, Black body, red stripes, opening hood and trunk, plated air cleaner and valve covers, plated shifter, 1:64 scale, Model No. 32658
EX n/a   NM n/a   MIP $6

(Photo courtesy Racing Champions Ertl)

❑ **1968 Dodge Charger R/T,** 2001, Bronze Poly body, black interior, black vinyl roof, black rear deck stripes, 426 Hemi engine, 1:18 scale, Model No. 32768
EX n/a   NM n/a   MIP $30

❑ **1968 Dodge Charger R/T,** 2001, Racing Green body, black interior, 440 Magnum engine, 1:18 scale, Model No. 32766
EX n/a   NM n/a   MIP $30

(Photo courtesy Racing Champions Ertl)

❑ **1968 Dodge Charger R/T,** 2001, Red body, black interior, black vinyl roof, black rear deck stripes, 426 Hemi engine, 1:18 scale, Model No. 32765
EX n/a   NM n/a   MIP $30

(Photo courtesy Racing Champions Ertl)

❑ **1968 Dodge Charger R/T,** 2001, Burgundy body, white interior, white rear deck stripes, 426 Hemi engine, 1:18 scale, Model No. 32767
EX n/a   NM n/a   MIP $30

(Photo courtesy Racing Champions Ertl)

❑ **1968 Dodge Charger R/T,** 2001, White body, tan interior, no rear deck stripes, 440 Magnum engine, 1:18 scale, Model No. 32764
EX n/a   NM n/a   MIP $30

❑ **1968 Ford Mustang CJ428,** 1999, Acapulco Blue body, black stripes, 1:18 scale, Model No. 7295DP
EX n/a   NM n/a   MIP $30

(Photo courtesy Racing Champions Ertl)

❑ **1968 Ford Mustang CJ428,** 2000, Wimbledon White body, black interior and stripes, 428 Cobra Jet engine, GT wheels, 1:18 scale, Model No. 32518
EX n/a   NM n/a   MIP $30

(Photo courtesy Racing Champions Ertl)

❑ **1968 Ford Mustang CJ428,** 2000, White body, TASCA Ford markings, 1:18 scale, Model No. 32648
EX n/a   NM n/a   MIP $30

❑ **1968 Hurst Oldsmobile,** 2000, Ebony Black body, 1:18 scale, Model No. 32549
EX n/a   NM n/a   MIP $30

❑ **1968 Hurst Oldsmobile,** 2000, Silver Green body, 1:18 scale, Model No. 32551
EX n/a   NM n/a   MIP $30

(Photo courtesy Racing Champions Ertl)

❑ **1968 Hurst Oldsmobile,** 2000, Silver body, black stripes, 1:18 scale, Model No. 32547
EX n/a   NM n/a   MIP $30

❑ **1968 Olds 442,** 2001, Ocean Turquoise body, black interior, Goodyear Wide Treads, 1:18 scale, Model No. 32559
EX n/a   · NM n/a   MIP $30

(Photo courtesy Racing Champions Ertl)

❑ **1968 Olds 442,** 2001, Bare metal chase car, 1:18 scale, Model No. 32548
EX n/a   NM n/a   MIP $30

❑ **1968 Olds 442,** 2001, Provincial White body, red interior, redline tires, 1:18 scale, Model No. 32557
EX n/a   NM n/a   MIP $30

❑ **1968 Olds 442,** 2001, Cordovan Maroon body, black interior, Goodyear Wide Treads, 1:18 scale, Model No. 32558
EX n/a   NM n/a   MIP $30

❑ **1968-1/2 Ford Mustang CJ 428,** 2000, Sun Lit Gold body black interior, 1:18 scale, Model No. 32409
EX n/a   NM n/a   MIP $30

(Photo courtesy Racing Champions Ertl)

❑ **1968-1/2 Ford Mustang Cobra Jet,** 2000, Dyno Don Nicholson, white body; limited edition from Supercar Collectibles, 1:18 scale, Model No. 29141
EX n/a   NM n/a   MIP $30

❑ **1969 AMC AMX,** 2000, Big Bad Blue body, black striping, charcoal interior, four-speed transmission, plated side pipes, mag wheels, 1:18 scale, Model No. 32280
EX n/a   NM n/a   MIP $8

❏ **1969 AMC AMX,** 2000, Shirley Shahan's "Drag-On-Lady" Super Stock drag car, red/white/blue body, race day graphics; limited edition from Supercar Collectibles, 1:18 scale, Model No. 29136
EX n/a   NM n/a   MIP $30

❏ **1969 AMC AMX,** 2000, Frost White body, blue striping, Charcoal interior, automatic transmission, plated side pipes, mag wheels, 1:18 scale, Model No. 32284
EX n/a   NM n/a   MIP $30

❏ **1969 AMC AMX,** 2000, Matador Red or white body, 1:18 scale, Model No. 36051B
EX n/a   NM n/a   MIP $30

❏ **1969 AMC AMX,** 2000, Hunter Green body, silver striping, Saddle Brown interior, automatic transmission, lower body molding, mag wheels, 1:18 scale, Model No. 32281
EX n/a   NM n/a   MIP $30

(Photo courtesy Racing Champions Ertl)

❏ **1969 AMC AMX,** 2000, Matador Red body, red interior, white stripes, standard engine and wheels, 1:18 scale, Model No. 32512
EX n/a   NM n/a   MIP $30

❏ **1969 AMC AMX,** 2000, Big Bad Orange body, black striping, charcoal interior, four-speed transmission, plated side pipes, mag wheels, 1:18 scale, Model No. 32278
EX n/a   NM n/a   MIP $30

❏ **1969 AMC AMX,** 2000, Big Bad Blue or Hunter Green body, 1:18 scale, Model No. 36051A
EX n/a   NM n/a   MIP $30

❏ **1969 AMC AMX,** 2001, Playboy Pink body, black interior, 1:18 scale, Model No. 32948
EX n/a   NM n/a   MIP $30

(Photo courtesy Racing Champions Ertl)

❏ **1969 Baldwin-Motion Camaro,** 2000, Gold body, cowl induction hood, Baldwin-Motion spoiler, black interior, side pipes, SS wheels with redline tires, 1:18 scale, Model No. 32473
EX n/a   NM n/a   MIP $30

❏ **1969 Baldwin-Motion Camaro,** 2000, Black body, L88 hood with hood pins, stock spoiler, black interior, stock exhaust, American wheels with redline tires, 1:18 scale, Model No. 32472
EX n/a   NM n/a   MIP $30

❏ **1969 Baldwin-Motion Camaro,** 2000, LeMans Blue, L88 hood with hood pins, stock spoiler, black interior, side pipes, Cragar wheels with raised white letter tires, 1:18 scale, Model No. 32471
EX n/a   NM n/a   MIP $30

❏ **1969 Baldwin-Motion Camaro,** 2000, Rally Green, L88 hood, Baldwin-Motion spoiler, white interior, side pipes, Rally wheels with raised white letter tires, 1:18 scale, Model No. 32470
EX n/a   NM n/a   MIP $30

❏ **1969 Baldwin-Motion Camaro,** 2000, Hugger Orange body, L88 hood with hood pins, Baldwin-Motion spoiler, Black interior, side pipes, SS wheels with raised white letter tires, 1:18 scale, Model No. 32474
EX n/a   NM n/a   MIP $30

❏ **1969 Baldwin-Motion Camaro,** 2001, Garnet Red body, red interior, white stripes, rear-deck spoiler, plated beehive air cleaner, 1:18 scale, Model No. 32806
EX n/a   NM n/a   MIP $30

(Photo courtesy Racing Champions Ertl)

❏ **1969 Baldwin-Motion Camaro 454,** 2002, Butternut Yellow body, black striping, black interior, plated rear fender louvers, plated "motion" valve covers and

mesh air cleaner, plated steering wheel and floor-mounted manual shifter, yellow traction bars, plated Rally rims, 1:18 scale, Model No. 32986
EX n/a   NM n/a   MIP $35

❏ **1969 Baldwin-Motion Chevy Nova,** 2000, Forest Green body, black vinyl top, bucket seats, Rally wheels, redline tires, 1:18 scale, Model No. 32477
EX n/a   NM n/a   MIP $35

❏ **1969 Baldwin-Motion Chevy Nova,** 2000, Black body, red bumble bee striping, black vinyl top, Torque wheels, plated mesh air cleaner, bench seats, plated shifter, silver headers, blackwall tires, 1:18 scale, Model No. 32476
EX n/a   NM n/a   MIP $35

❏ **1969 Baldwin-Motion Chevy Nova,** 2000, Garnet Red body, white bumble bee striping, bucket seats, Cragar wheels, raised white letter tires, mesh air cleaner, 1:18 scale, Model No. 32478
EX n/a   NM n/a   MIP $35

(Photo courtesy Racing Champions Ertl)

❏ **1969 Baldwin-Motion Chevy Nova,** 2000, Dusk Blue body, white bumble bee striping, Cragar wheels, plated air cleaner, bucket seats, center console with plated shifter, silver exhaust manifolds, raised white letter tires, 1:18 scale, Model No. 32475
EX n/a   NM n/a   MIP $35

(Photo courtesy Racing Champions Ertl)

❑ **1969 Baldwin-Motion Chevy Nova,** 2000, Butternut Yellow body, black arrow striping, bench seats, Torque wheels, raised white letter tires, side exhausts, 1:18 scale, Model No. 32479
EX n/a   NM n/a   MIP $35

(Photo courtesy Racing Champions Ertl)

❑ **1969 Baldwin-Motion Nova,** 2001, Dover White body, black interior, black stripes, 427 engine, 1:18 scale, Model No. 32807
EX n/a   NM n/a   MIP $37

❑ **1969 Camaro RS Z28,** 2001, Daytona Yellow body, black stripes, black/white houndstooth interior, Endura bumper, Cragar S/S wheels, black vinyl roof, limited to 2,500 from Super Toy Cars, 1:18 scale, Model No. 29165P
EX n/a   NM n/a   MIP $30

❑ **1969 Camaro RS Z28,** 2001, Fathom Green body, black/white houndstooth interior, Endura bumper, Cragar S/S wheels, black vinyl roof, limited to 500 from Super Toy Cars, 1:18 scale, Model No. 26195PM
EX n/a   NM n/a   MIP $30

❑ **1969 Camaro SS 396,** 1994, Hugger Orange body, white SS stripes, black interior, 1:18 scale, Model No. 7456DO
EX n/a   NM n/a   MIP $30

❑ **1969 Camaro SS 396,** 1995, Daytona Yellow, black "hockey stick" stripes, black interior, 1:18 scale, Model No. 7367DO
EX n/a   NM n/a   MIP $30

❑ **1969 Camaro SS 396 convertible,** 1999, Roman Red body, black interior, 1:18 scale, Model No. 32009
EX n/a   NM n/a   MIP $30

❑ **1969 Camaro SS 396 convertible,** 1999, Rallye Green body, black interior, 1:18 scale, Model No. 32008
EX n/a   NM n/a   MIP $30

(Photo courtesy Racing Champions Ertl)

❑ **1969 Camaro SS convertible,** 2000, LeMans Blue body, white interior and stripes, 396cid engine, Rally wheels, 1:18 scale, Model No. 32519
EX n/a   NM n/a   MIP $30

❑ **1969 Camaro Z/28,** 1994, Garnet Red body, white stripes, black interior, 1:18 scale, Model No. 7455DO
EX n/a   NM n/a   MIP $30

❑ **1969 Camaro Z28,** 1995, Tuxedo Black body, white stripes, black interior, 1:18 scale, Model No. 7366DO
EX n/a   NM n/a   MIP $30

(Photo courtesy Racing Champions Ertl)

❑ **1969 Chevelle SS,** 2001, Monaco Orange body, black interior and stripes, 1:18 scale, Model No. 32929
EX n/a   NM n/a   MIP $30

(Photo courtesy Racing Champions Ertl)

❑ **1969 Chevelle SS,** 2001, Daytona Yellow body, black interior and stripes, black vinyl roof, 1:18 scale, Model No. 32928
EX n/a   NM n/a   MIP $30

❑ **1969 Chevy Camaro COPO,** 2001, Silver body, black vinyl top, blak stripes and interior, Rally wheels, 1:18 scale, Model No. 32950
EX n/a   NM n/a   MIP $30

(Photo courtesy Racing Champions Ertl)

❑ **1969 Chevy Camaro COPO,** 2001, White body, black vinyl top, 427cid Turbo Jet engine, black interior with folding front seat backs, yellow traction bars, tampo graphics, plated Rally wheels, 1:18 scale, Model No. 32976
EX n/a   NM n/a   MIP $30

❑ **1969 Chevy Camaro RS Z28,** 2001, Hugger Orange body, black stripes, black hood stripes, black interior, 1:18 scale, Model No. 32941
EX n/a   NM n/a   MIP $30

❑ **1969 Chevy Camaro SS 396,** 2001, Daytona Yellow body, black stripes, black interior, plated five-spoke sport wheels, 1:18 scale, Model No. 32921
EX n/a   NM n/a   MIP $30

❑ **1969 Chevy Nova,** 2000, Cortez Silver body, 1:18 scale, Model No. 36052B
EX n/a   NM n/a   MIP $30

❑ **1969 Chevy Nova SS,** 1999, Tuxedo Black body, bucket seats, rally wheels, blackwall tires, 1:18 scale, Model No. 32226
EX n/a   NM n/a   MIP $30

❑ **1969 Chevy Nova SS,** 1999, LeMans Blue body, white stripe, bench seats, sport wheels, redline tires, 1:18 scale, Model No. 32227
EX n/a   NM n/a   MIP $30

❑ **1969 Chevy Nova SS,** 1999, Classic White body, black stripe, bucket seats, rally wheels, redline tires, detailed battery, washer fluid container and chassis, 1:18 scale, Model No. 32224
EX n/a   NM n/a   MIP $30

(Photo courtesy Racing Champions Ertl)

❑ **1969 Chevy Nova SS,** 1999, Cortez Silver body, black stripe, bucket seats, sport wheels, redline tires, 1:18 scale, Model No. 32229
EX n/a   **NM** n/a   **MIP** $30

❑ **1969 Chevy Nova SS,** 2000, Black body, 1:64 scale, Model No. 32354
EX n/a   **NM** n/a   **MIP** $7

(Photo courtesy Racing Champions Ertl)

❑ **1969 Chevy Nova SS,** 2000, Hugger Orange body, black hood louvers, silver gas tank, white oil filter, 1:64 scale, Model No. 32356
EX n/a   **NM** n/a   **MIP** $7

❑ **1969 Chevy Nova SS,** 2000, LeMans Blue body, 1:64 scale, Model No. 32353
EX n/a   **NM** n/a   **MIP** $6

❑ **1969 Dodge Charger,** 2000, Black body, black interior, 1:43 scale, Model No. 32253
EX n/a   **NM** n/a   **MIP** $8

(Photo courtesy Racing Champions Ertl)

❑ **1969 Dodge Charger 500,** 2001, Red body, 440 Magnum engine, blackwall tires, 1:18 scale, Model No. 32955
EX n/a   **NM** n/a   **MIP** $30

(Photo courtesy Racing Champions Ertl)

❑ **1969 Dodge Charger 500,** 2001, White body, black interior, 426cid Hemi engine, Hemi logo on doors, redline tires, 1:18 scale, Model No. 32944
EX n/a   **NM** n/a   **MIP** $30

(Photo courtesy Racing Champions Ertl)

❑ **1969 Dodge Charger 500,** 2002, Medium Metallic Green body, white stripe around rear deck, black interior, bucket seats, center console, 440 engine, 1:18 scale, Model No. 32963
EX n/a   **NM** n/a   **MIP** $30

❑ **1969 Dodge Charger Daytona,** 1995, Charger Red, white stripe and rear spoiler, black interior, 1:18 scale, Model No. 7390DO
EX n/a   **NM** n/a   **MIP** $30

❑ **1969 Dodge Charger Daytona,** 1995, Black body, red stripe and rear spoiler, red interior, 1:18 scale, Model No. 7389DO
EX n/a   **NM** n/a   **MIP** $30

❑ **1969 Dodge Charger R/T,** 2000, Hemi Orange body, 1:18 scale, Model No. 32259
EX n/a   **NM** n/a   **MIP** $30

❑ **1969 Dodge Charger R/T,** 2000, Hemi Orange, Charger White or bright blue body, 1:18 scale, Model No. 36104B
EX n/a   **NM** n/a   **MIP** $30

❑ **1969 Dodge Charger R/T,** 2000, Silver, red or yellow body, 1:18 scale, Model No. 36104A
EX n/a   **NM** n/a   **MIP** $30

❑ **1969 Dodge Charger R/T,** 2000, Bright Blue body, 1:18 scale, Model No. 32261
EX n/a   **NM** n/a   **MIP** $30

(Photo courtesy Racing Champions Ertl)

❑ **1969 Dodge Charger R/T,** 2000, Cream body, black top, black interior and stripes, 440 Magnum engine, dog-dish wheels, 1:18 scale, Model No. 32510
EX n/a   **NM** n/a   **MIP** $30

❑ **1969 Dodge Charger R/T,** 2000, White body, 1:18 scale, Model No. 32260
EX n/a   **NM** n/a   **MIP** $30

(Photo courtesy Racing Champions Ertl)

❑ **1969 Dodge Charger R/T,** 2001, Bronze body, black interior and striping, black vinyl roof, 440 Magnum, plated shifter, woodgrain dash, painted steel wheels with center hubcaps, 1:18 scale, Model No. 32641
EX n/a   **NM** n/a   **MIP** $30

❑ **1969 Dodge Coronet,** 2000, Performance Red body, black top and interior, 1:18 scale, Model No. 32075
EX n/a   **NM** n/a   **MIP** $30

(Photo courtesy Racing Champions Ertl)

❑ **1969 Dodge Coronet R/T,** 2001, Black body, black interior,

white striping, black vinyl roof, 426 Hemi, flexible wiring, plated five-spoke wheels, 1:18 scale, Model No. 32642
EX n/a   NM n/a   MIP $30

❑ **1969 Dodge Coronet Super Bee,** 1999, Performance Red body, 426cid Hemi V8, rally wheels with Firestone Redlines, 1:18 scale, Model No. 32075
EX n/a   NM n/a   MIP $30

❑ **1969 Dodge Daytona,** 1997, Jade Green body, black stripe and rear spoiler, 1:18 scale, Model No. 7781DP
EX n/a   NM n/a   MIP $30

❑ **1969 Dodge Daytona,** 2000, Yellow/Black body, spoiler, redline tires, 1:64 scale, Model No. 32338
EX n/a   NM n/a   MIP $6

❑ **1969 Dodge Daytona,** 2000, Red/White body, spoiler, redline tires, 1:64 scale, Model No. 32339
EX n/a   NM n/a   MIP $6

(Photo courtesy Racing Champions Ertl)

❑ **1969 Dodge Daytona,** 2001, Two-car set (1:18 and 1:64); Black body, white wraparound stripes on rear deck, opening hood, 426 Hemi, five-spoke wheels, redline tires, 1:18/1:64 scale, Model No. 32822
EX n/a   NM n/a   MIP $40

(Photo courtesy Racing Champions Ertl)

❑ **1969 Dodge Daytona,** 2002, Silver body, white rear end and wing, black floors, white uphol-stery, plated shifter, 426 Hemi, plated air cleaner, 1:18 scale, Model No. 33012
EX n/a   NM n/a   MIP $30

❑ **1969 Dodge Super Bee,** 1996, Blue body, white stripes, 1:18 scale, Model No. 7271DO
EX n/a   NM n/a   MIP $30

❑ **1969 Dodge Super Bee,** 1996, Yellow body, black stripes, 1:18 scale, Model No. 7270DO
EX n/a   NM n/a   MIP $29

(Photo courtesy Racing Champions Ertl)

❑ **1969 Dodge Super Bee,** 2001, Silver body, black vinyl roof and bumble bee stripes, black interior, front bench seat, plated shifter and five-spoke wheels, redline tires, 1:18 scale, Model No. 32754
EX n/a   NM n/a   MIP $30

❑ **1969 Ford Mustang Mach I,** 2000, Indian Fire Poly body, 1:18 scale, Model No. 32268
EX n/a   NM n/a   MIP $30

❑ **1969 Ford Mustang Mach I,** 2000, Calypso Coral body, 1:18 scale, Model No. 32264
EX n/a   NM n/a   MIP $30

❑ **1969 Ford Mustang Mach I,** 2000, Silver Jade Ply body, 1:18 scale, Model No. 32265
EX n/a   NM n/a   MIP $30

(Photo courtesy Racing Champions Ertl)

❑ **1969 Ford Mustang Mach I,** 2000, Acapulco Blue body, 1:18 scale, Model No. 32267
EX n/a   NM n/a   MIP $30

❑ **1969 Ford Mustang Mach I,** 2000, Calypso Coral, Vermillion or Gulf Stream Aqua body, 1:18 scale, Model No. 36056A
EX n/a   NM n/a   MIP $30

❑ **1969 Ford Mustang Mach I,** 2000, Acapulco Blue, Indian Fire Poly or Wimbledon White body, 1:18 scale, Model No. 36056B
EX n/a   NM n/a   MIP $30

❑ **1969 Ford Mustang Mach I,** 2000, Gulfstream Aqua body, 1:18 scale, Model No. 32266
EX n/a   NM n/a   MIP $28

❑ **1969 Ford Mustang Mach I,** 2000, Wimbledon White body, 1:18 scale, Model No. 32269
EX n/a   NM n/a   MIP $30

(Photo courtesy Racing Champions Ertl)

❑ **1969 Ford Mustang Mach I,** 2000, Black body, opening hood, 1:64 scale, Model No. 32329
EX n/a   NM n/a   MIP $6

❑ **1969 Ford Mustang Mach I,** 2000, 1:43 scale, Model No. 32551
EX n/a   NM n/a   MIP $8

(Photo courtesy Racing Champions Ertl)

❑ **1969 Ford Mustang Mach I,** 2000, Champagne Gold body, black interior, black/gold stripes, 428 Cobra Jet engine, styled steel wheels, 1:18 scale, Model No. 32511
EX n/a   NM n/a   MIP $30

(Photo courtesy Racing Champions Ertl)

❏ **1969 Ford Mustang Mach I,** 2001, Two-car set (1:18 and 1:64); Candy Apple Red body, Cobra Jet engine, opening hood, black interior, gold stripes, louvered rear windows, rear deck spoilers, plated GT wheels, 1:18/1:64 scale, Model No. 32820

EX n/a   NM n/a   **MIP $40**

(Photo courtesy Racing Champions Ertl)

❏ **1969 Ford Mustang Mach I,** 2001, Black body, black interior, 428 Cobra Jet engine, scooped hood, bucket seats, plated shifter, 1:18 scale

EX n/a   NM n/a   **MIP $35**

(Photo courtesy Racing Champions Ertl)

❏ **1969 Hurst AMX,** 2001, Red, white and blue body, "Pete's Patriot" markings, 1:18 scale, Model No. 32647

EX n/a   NM n/a   **MIP $30**

❏ **1969 Hurst Olds,** 1996, White body, gold stripes, 1:18 scale, Model No. 7260DO

EX n/a   NM n/a   **MIP $29**

❏ **1969 Mercury Cougar Eliminator,** 2000, 1:64 scale, Model No. 32344

EX n/a   NM n/a   **MIP $6**

(Photo courtesy Racing Champions Ertl)

❏ **1969 Mercury Cougar Eliminator,** 2000, White body, black interior, Cobra 428 engine, Eliminatory stripes, 1:64 scale, Model No. 32348

EX n/a   NM n/a   **MIP $7**

(Photo courtesy Racing Champions Ertl)

❏ **1969 Mustang Mach I,** 2000, Meadowlark Yellow body, opening hood, 1:64 scale, Model No. 32330

EX n/a   NM n/a   **MIP $7**

❏ **1969 Mustang Mach I,** 2000, Calypso Coral, opening hood, 1:64 scale, Model No. 32336

EX n/a   NM n/a   **MIP $7**

❏ **1969 Mustang Mach I,** 2000, Silver Jade Poly, opening hood, 1:64 scale, Model No. 32331

EX n/a   NM n/a   **MIP $6**

(Photo courtesy Racing Champions Ertl)

❏ **1969 Olds 4-4-2 W-32,** 2000, Nassau Blue body, white interior, 1:18 scale, Model No. 32480

EX n/a   NM n/a   **MIP $28**

❏ **1969 Oldsmobile 4-4-2,** 1996, Black body, white stripes, 1:18 scale, Model No. 8113DO

EX n/a   NM n/a   **MIP $30**

❏ **1969 Oldsmobile 4-4-2,** 1998, Aztec Gold body, black stripes, black interior, 1:18 scale, Model No. 7848DP

EX n/a   NM n/a   **MIP $30**

❏ **1969 Plymouth GTX convertible,** 1997, Spinnaker White body, black stripes, red interior, 1:18 scale, Model No. 7249DP

EX n/a   NM n/a   **MIP $35**

❏ **1969 Plymouth GTX convertible,** 1998, Crimson Red body, black stripes, tan interior, 1:18 scale, Model No. 7248DP

EX n/a   NM n/a   **MIP $30**

❏ **1969 Plymouth GTX convertible,** 1999, Black body, 1:18 scale, Model No. 32020

EX n/a   NM n/a   **MIP $30**

(Photo courtesy Racing Champions Ertl)

❏ **1969 Plymouth GTX coupe,** 2000, Ralleye Green body, black interior, black/red stripes, 440 Magnum engine, Cragar wheels, 1:18 scale, Model No. 32520

EX n/a   NM n/a   **MIP $30**

(Photo courtesy Racing Champions Ertl)

❏ **1969 Plymouth GTX street machine,** 1999, Gold body, flat black hood stripes, black interior, plated center console, dual exhausts, custom wheels, 1:18 scale, Model No. 32031

EX n/a   NM n/a   **MIP $30**

❏ **1969 Plymouth Roadrunner,** 1994, Jamaica Blue body, black hood stripes, 426cid Hemi, 1:18 scale, Model No. 7384DO

EX n/a   NM n/a   **MIP $30**

❏ **1969 Plymouth Roadrunner,** 1994, Sunfire Yellow body, black hood stripes, 426cid Hemi, 1:18 scale, Model No. 7368DO

EX n/a   NM n/a   **MIP $30**

❏ **1969 Plymouth Roadrunner,** 2001, Jamaica Blue body, flat black hood stripes, black interior, 1:18 scale, Model No. 32922

EX n/a   NM n/a   **MIP $30**

❏ **1969 Pontiac GTO,** 1992, Turquoise body, 400cid V8, chrome wheel trim rings, 1:18 scale, Model No. 7466

EX n/a   NM n/a   **MIP $30**

(Photo courtesy Racing Champions Ertl)

❑ **1969 Pontiac GTO,** 2002, Champagne body, Parchment interior and vinyl top, plated center shifter, plated door and window handles, plated five-spoke wheels with thin whitewalls, 1:18 scale, Model No. 32962
EX n/a NM n/a MIP $30

(Photo courtesy Racing Champions Ertl)

❑ **1969 Pontiac GTO,** 2002, Paladium Silver body, black vinyl roof, black interior, double-bulge hood, plated valve covers and dual-snorkel air cleaner, bucket seats, plated shifter, Arnie Beswick signature on roof, 1:18 scale, Model No. 32989
EX n/a NM n/a MIP $30

(Photo courtesy Racing Champions Ertl)

❑ **1969 Pontiac GTO "Royal Bobcat",** 2000, Carousel Red body, white interior, white stripes, hood-mounted tach, Ram Air IV engine, Ontario license plates; limited edition from The Collectors Guild, 1:18 scale
EX n/a NM n/a MIP $30

❑ **1969 Pontiac GTO Judge,** 1992, Carousel Red body, Judge markings, rear wing spoiler, d-port exhaust manifolds, Ram Air III 400cid V8, hood-mounted tach, hidden headlights, 1:18 scale, Model No. 7467
EX n/a NM n/a MIP $30

❑ **1969 Pontiac GTO Judge,** 1994, Midnight Green body, black interior, 1:18 scale, Model No. 7328DO
EX n/a NM n/a MIP $30

(Photo courtesy Racing Champions Ertl)

❑ **1969 Pontiac GTO Judge,** 2000, Arnie Beswick car, orange body, Beswick graphics, limited to 4,000 from Red Alert Racing Collectibles, 1:18 scale
EX n/a NM n/a MIP $30

(Photo courtesy Racing Champions Ertl)

❑ **1969 Pontiac GTO Judge,** 2000, Liberty Blue body, rear spoiler, 400 Ram Air III V8 engine, white interior, 1:18 scale, Model No. 32916
EX n/a NM n/a MIP $30

(Photo courtesy Racing Champions Ertl)

❑ **1969 Shelby GT 500 convertible,** 2002, Green body, white stripes, beige upholstery, 1:18 scale, Model No. 32997
EX n/a NM n/a MIP $32

(Photo courtesy Racing Champions Ertl)

❑ **1969 Shelby GT350,** 2000, Grabber Blue body, white stripes, 1:18 scale, Model No. 32073
EX n/a NM n/a MIP $32

❑ **1969 Shelby GT350,** 2002, Best of the Best series, 1:18 scale, Model No. 32955
EX n/a NM n/a MIP $32

❑ **1969 Shelby GT-500,** 1995, Grabber Yellow, black stripes and interior, 1:18 scale, Model No. 7351DO
EX n/a NM n/a MIP $32

❑ **1969 Shelby GT-500,** 1995, Candy Apple Red body, gold stripes, black interior, 1:18 scale, Model No. 7350DO
EX n/a NM n/a MIP $32

❑ **1969 Shelby GT-500,** 1997, Onyx Black body, red stripes, 1:18 scale, Model No. 7778DP
EX n/a NM n/a MIP $32

❑ **1969 Triumph TR6,** 1997, Carman Red body, 1:18 scale, Model No. 7884DO
EX n/a NM n/a MIP $30

❑ **1969 Triumph TR6,** 1997, Blue body, 1:18 scale, Model No. 7898DO
EX n/a NM n/a MIP $30

(Photo courtesy Racing Champions Ertl)

❑ **1969 Yenko Nova 427,** 2000, Rally Green body, white Yenko stripes, 427 engine, body-colored wheels, chrome dog dish hubcaps; limited edition from Supercar Collectibles, 1:18 scale, Model No. 29137
EX n/a NM n/a MIP $30

❑ **1970 Baldwin Motion Chevelle SS,** 2000, Sunflower Yellow/black body, 1:18 scale, Model No. 32396

EX n/a   NM n/a   MIP $6

(Photo courtesy Racing Champions Ertl)

❑ **1970 Baldwin-Motion Camaro,** 2001, Black body and interior, red stripes, rear-deck spoiler, plated beehive air cleaner, 1:18 scale, Model No. 32808

EX n/a   NM n/a   MIP $37

❑ **1970 Baldwin-Motion Camaro,** 2002, Best of the Best series, 1:18 scale, Model No. 32957

EX n/a   NM n/a   MIP $30

(Photo courtesy Racing Champions Ertl)

❑ **1970 Baldwin-Motion Camaro,** 2002, White body with race graphics, Phase III scooped hood, black interior, plated floor shifter, dash-mounted tach, 1:18 scale, Model No. 32972

EX n/a   NM n/a   MIP $30

(Photo courtesy Racing Champions Ertl)

❑ **1970 Baldwin-Motion Chevelle,** 2001, Forest Green body, black interior, white stripes, plated beehive air cleaner, 1:18 scale, Model No. 32809

EX n/a   NM n/a   MIP $35

(Photo courtesy Racing Champions Ertl)

❑ **1970 Baldwin-Motion Chevelle SS,** 2000, Hugger Orange body, black interior and stripes, 454 Phase III engine, Rally wheels, 1:18 scale, Model No. 32514

EX n/a   NM n/a   MIP $30

(Photo courtesy Racing Champions Ertl)

❑ **1970 Bladwin-Motion Camaro RS/SS,** 2000, Black Cherry body, black interior, white stripes, 454cid big-block engine, Cragar wheels, 1:18 scale, Model No. 32516

EX n/a   NM n/a   MIP $30

❑ **1970 Buick GS Stage 1,** 2002, Fire Red body, red/white interior, white vinyl roof, one for each Canadian province or territory from The Collector's Guild, limited to 2,500 for each version, 1:18 scale

EX n/a   NM n/a   MIP $30

❑ **1970 Buick GS Stage 1,** 2002, Glacier White or Diplomat Blue body, black vinyl tops, black interiors, limited to 350 of each color from G.S. Collectibles, 1:18 scale

EX n/a   NM n/a   MIP $30

❑ **1970 Buick GSX,** 1994, Saturn Yellow body, black stripes, 1:18 scale, Model No. 7603DO

EX n/a   NM n/a   MIP $30

(Photo courtesy Racing Champions Ertl)

❑ **1970 Camaro SS,** 2000, Tuxedo Black body, tan interior, 350cid small-block, stock wheels, 1:18 scale, Model No. 32515

EX n/a   NM n/a   MIP $30

(Photo courtesy Racing Champions Ertl)

❑ **1970 Camaro SS,** 2001, Cortez Silver body, black interior, 350cid V8, limited to 1,500, 1:18 scale, Model No. 32411

EX n/a   NM n/a   MIP $45

(Photo courtesy Racing Champions Ertl)

❑ **1970 Camaro Z28,** 2000, Astro Blue body, white stripes, blue entire, bucket seats, plated shifter, 1:64 scale, Model No. 32363

EX n/a   NM n/a   MIP $7

❑ **1970 Camaro Z28,** 2000, Cranberry Red body, white stripes, plated bumpers, grille, valve covers, Z28 Rally wheels, 1:64 scale, Model No. 32360

EX n/a   NM n/a   MIP $6

❑ **1970 Camaro Z28,** 2000, Cortez Silver, black stripes, plated bumpers, grille, valve covers, Z28 Rally wheels, 1:64 scale, Model No. 32361

EX n/a   NM n/a   MIP $8

❑ **1970 Challenger R/T,** 2001, Sublime body, black vinyl roof, black interior, 1:18 scale, Model No. 32946

EX n/a   NM n/a   MIP $30

❑ **1970 Chevelle,** 2000, Orange body, black interior, mag wheels, Goodyear Wide Tread F70-14 tires, 1:18 scale, Model No. 32242

EX n/a   NM n/a   MIP $30

❏ **1970 Chevelle 454 LS-6,** 1992, Astro blue body; also black body, white stripes, four-speed manual transmission, bench seat, 1:18 scale, Model No. 7487
EX n/a   NM n/a   MIP $30

❏ **1970 Chevelle Baldwin-Motion,** 2000, Sunflower Yellow body, 454cid engine, chrome side pipes, 1:18 scale, Model No. 32070
EX n/a   NM n/a   MIP $30

❏ **1970 Chevelle S,** 2001, Fathom Blue body, white stripes, black interior, 1:18 scale, Model No. 32923
EX n/a   NM n/a   MIP $30

❏ **1970 Chevelle SS 454,** 1994, Fathom Blue body, white SS stripes, black interior, 1:18 scale, Model No. 7323DO
EX n/a   NM n/a   MIP $30

❏ **1970 Chevelle SS 454,** 1994, Sunflower Yellow body, black stripes, black interior, 1:18 scale, Model No. 7322DO
EX n/a   NM n/a   MIP $30

❏ **1970 Chevelle SS 454 LS-6 automatic,** 1992, Cranberry Red body, black interior and stripes, front bucket seats, 1:18 scale, Model No. 7486
EX n/a   NM n/a   MIP $30

(Photo courtesy Racing Champions Ertl)

❏ **1970 Chevelle SS454,** 2000, Black body, white stripes, brown interior, 1:43 scale, Model No. 32245
EX n/a   NM n/a   MIP $8

❏ **1970 Chevelle street machine,** 2001, Black body, flames, black interior, 1:18 scale, Model No. 32942
EX n/a   NM n/a   MIP $30

❏ **1970 Chevy El Camino,** 1996, Blue body, white stripes, 1:18 scale, Model No. 7263DO
EX n/a   NM n/a   MIP $32

❏ **1970 Chevy El Camino,** 1996, Red body, black stripes, 1:18 scale, Model No. 7262DO
EX n/a   NM n/a   MIP $30

❏ **1970 Chevy El Camino SS,** 1999, Black body, white stripes, 1:18 scale, Model No. 32035
EX n/a   NM n/a   MIP $30

❏ **1970 Chevy Nova,** 2000, Black Cherry or Sunflower Yellow body, 1:18 scale, Model No. 36052B
EX n/a   NM n/a   MIP $30

(Photo courtesy Racing Champions Ertl)

❏ **1970 Chevy Nova SS,** 1999, Sunflower Yellow body, black stripe, bucket seats, sport wheels, raised white letter tires, 1:18 scale, Model No. 32231
EX n/a   NM n/a   MIP $30

(Photo courtesy Racing Champions Ertl)

❏ **1970 Chevy Nova SS,** 1999, Cranberry Red body, black stripe, bucket seats, sport wheels, raised white letter tires, detailed battery, washer fluid container and chassis, 1:18 scale, Model No. 32234
EX n/a   NM n/a   MIP $30

❏ **1970 Chevy Nova SS,** 1999, Hugger Orange body, black stripe, bucket seats, sport wheels, raised white letter tires, 1:18 scale, Model No. 32228
EX n/a   NM n/a   MIP $30

❏ **1970 Chevy Nova SS,** 1999, Black Cherry body, white stripe, bench seats, rally wheels, raised white letter tires, 1:18 scale, Model No. 32230
EX n/a   NM n/a   MIP $30

❏ **1970 Chevy Nova SS,** 2000, Black Cherry, chrome Rally SS wheels, clear display case, 1:64 scale, Model No. 32351
EX n/a   NM n/a   MIP $6

(Photo courtesy Racing Champions Ertl)

❏ **1970 Chevy Nova SS,** 2001, Astro Blue body, white pinstripes, 396cid, simulated air louvers, plated valve covers, limited to 1,500, 1:18 scale, Model No. 32412
EX n/a   NM n/a   MIP $40

❏ **1970 Chevy SS Nova,** 1999, Cranberry Red body, 1:43 scale, Model No. 32095
EX n/a   NM n/a   MIP $8

❏ **1970 Dodge Challenger R/T,** 1997, Plum Crazy Puple body, 1:18 scale, Model No. 7251DP
EX n/a   NM n/a   MIP $35

❏ **1970 Dodge Challenger R/T,** 1999, Bright Red body, 1:18 scale, Model No. 32016
EX n/a   NM n/a   MIP $30

(Photo courtesy Racing Champions Ertl)

❏ **1970 Dodge Challenger R/T,** 2001, Bright Blue body, black/white houndstooth upholstery, 440 Six Pack engine, plated shifter, door inserts, 1:18 scale, Model No. 32643
EX n/a   NM n/a   MIP $30

(Photo courtesy Racing Champions Ertl)

❏ **1970 Dodge Challenger R/T,** 2001, Bright White body, black vinyl roof, black/white houndstooth seat inserts, 1:18 scale, Model No. 32753
EX n/a   NM n/a   MIP $30

(Photo courtesy Racing Champions Ertl)

❏ **1970 Dodge Challenger R/T SS/D,** 2001, White/orange/black body, 426 Hemi with two four-barrels, four-speed transmission, Challenger T/A hood, limited to 2,500 from Performance Years Enterprises, 1:18 scale
EX n/a   NM n/a   MIP $30

❏ **1970 Dodge Challenger T/A,** 1997, Moulin Rouge body, black stripes, 1:18 scale, Model No. 7252DP
EX n/a   NM n/a   MIP $35

❏ **1970 Dodge Challenger T/A,** 1999, Top Banana body, black hood and stripes, 1:18 scale, Model No. 32017
EX n/a   NM n/a   MIP $30

(Photo courtesy Racing Champions Ertl)

❏ **1970 Dodge Challenger T/A,** 2000, Moulin Rouge body, black stripes, opening hood with black scoop, black interior, 340 Six-Pack, 1:18 scale, Model No. 32915
EX n/a   NM n/a   MIP n/a

❏ **1970 Dodge Challenger T/A,** 2000, Go Mango body, flat black T/A striping, scooped hood, 340cid Six Pack, 1:18 scale, Model No. 32410
EX n/a   NM n/a   MIP $30

(Photo courtesy Racing Champions Ertl)

❏ **1970 Dodge Challenger T/A,** 2001, Sublime Green body, flat-black T/A striping, 340cid Six Pack engine, limited to 1,500, 1:18 scale, Model No. 32413
EX n/a   NM n/a   MIP $45

(Photo courtesy Racing Champions Ertl)

❏ **1970 Dodge Challenger T/A,** 2002, Diamond in the Rough series; missing door, houndstooth upholstery, 1:18 scale, Model No. 32963
EX n/a   NM n/a   MIP $30

❏ **1970 Ford Mustang 429 fastback,** 1991, Orange body, black interior, 1:18 scale, Model No. 7485
EX n/a   NM n/a   MIP $30

❏ **1970 Ford Mustang Boss 302,** 1994, Grabber Orange body, black interior, shaker hood, 1:18 scale, Model No. 7326DO
EX n/a   NM n/a   MIP $30

❏ **1970 Ford Mustang Boss 302,** 2001, Grabber Blue body, black stripes, shaker hood, black interior, 1:18 scale, Model No. 32924
EX n/a   NM n/a   MIP $30

❏ **1970 Ford Mustang Boss 302 fastback,** 1991, Yellow body, black stripes, black interior, 1:18 scale, Model No. 7484
EX n/a   NM n/a   MIP $40

❏ **1970 Ford Mustang Boss 429,** 2002, Best of the Best series, 1:18 scale, Model No. 32958
EX n/a   NM n/a   MIP $30

(Photo courtesy Racing Champions Ertl)

❏ **1970 Ford Torino,** 2002, Diamond in the Rough series, 1:18 scale, Model No. 32962
EX n/a   NM n/a   MIP $30

❏ **1970 Ford Torino Cobra,** 1999, Grabber Blue body, 1:43 scale, Model No. 32094
EX n/a   NM n/a   MIP $8

❏ **1970 Ford Torino Cobra,** 2001, Bare metal chase car, 1:18 scale, Model No. 37622
EX n/a   NM n/a   MIP $30

❏ **1970 Ford Torino Cobra,** 2001, Maroon Metallic body, black interior, Shaker hood, Shaker air cleaner, rear window shade, Magnum 500 wheels, 1:18 scale, Model No. 32499
EX n/a   NM n/a   MIP $30

❏ **1970 Ford Torino Cobra,** 2001, Grabber Yellow body, black interior, Cobra hood, plated air cleaner, rear window shade, Magnum 500 wheels, 1:18 scale, Model No. 32495
EX n/a   NM n/a   MIP $30

❏ **1970 Ford Torino Cobra,** 2001, Wimbledon White body, Vermillion interior, Cobra hood, plated air cleaner, Magnum 500 wheels, 1:18 scale, Model No. 32498
EX n/a   NM n/a   MIP $30

❏ **1970 Ford Torino Cobra,** 2001, Grabber Blue body, black interior, Shaker hood, Shaker air cleaner, Magnum 500 wheels, 1:18 scale, Model No. 32496
EX n/a   NM n/a   MIP $30

❏ **1970 Ford Torino Cobra,** 2001, Grabber Green Metallic body, black interior, Shaker hood, Shaker air cleaner, rear window shade, Magnum 500 wheels, 1:18 scale, Model No. 32497
EX n/a   NM n/a   MIP $30

❏ **1970 Mustang Boss 302,** 1994, Grabber Blue body, black interior, shaker hood, 1:18 scale, Model No. 7325DO
EX n/a   NM n/a   MIP $30

❑ **1970 Olds 4-4-2,** 1999, Astro Blue body, 1:43 scale, Model No. 32105
EX n/a   NM n/a   MIP $8

❑ **1970 Plymouth AAR Cuda,** 1994, Lime Twist Green body, black hood and graphics, black interior, 1:18 scale, Model No. 7379DO
EX n/a   NM n/a   MIP $30

❑ **1970 Plymouth AAR Cuda,** 1996, Vitamin C Orange body, black stripes and interior, 1:18 scale, Model No. 7268DO
EX n/a   NM n/a   MIP $30

❑ **1970 Plymouth Cuda,** 2002, Best of the Best series, 1:18 scale, Model No. 32959
EX n/a   NM n/a   MIP $30

❑ **1970 Plymouth Hemi Cuda,** 1994, Moulin Rouge body, black interior, 1:18 scale, Model No. 7375DO
EX n/a   NM n/a   MIP $30

❑ **1970 Plymouth Hemi Cuda,** 1996, Plum Crazy Purple body, white stripes, 1:18 scale, Model No. 7267DO
EX n/a   NM n/a   MIP $30

❑ **1970 Plymouth Hemi Cuda,** 2001, Vitamin C body, black interior, Shaker hood, Hemi engine, hockey stick graphics, rear window louvers, 1:18 scale, Model No. 32759
EX n/a   NM n/a   MIP $30

❑ **1970 Pontiac Trans Am,** 1998, Cameo White body, blue stripes, 1:18 scale, Model No. 7843DP
EX n/a   NM n/a   MIP $30

❑ **1970 Pontiac Trans Am,** 1998, Lucerne Blue body, white stripes, 1:18 scale, Model No. 7844DP
EX n/a   NM n/a   MIP $30

(Photo courtesy Racing Champions Ertl)

❑ **1970 Shelby GT 500,** 2002, Gray body, black stripes, black floors, white upholstery, 428 Cobra Jet engine with plated distributor, five-scooped hood, 1:18 scale, Model No. 32996
EX n/a   NM n/a   MIP $30

❑ **1970-1/2 Baldwin Motion Phase III Camaro,** 1999, Cranberry Red body, white stripes, 1:18 scale, Model No. 7129DP
EX n/a   NM n/a   MIP $30

❑ **1970-1/2 Chevy Camaro Z28,** 1999, Citrus Green body, black stripes, 1:18 scale, Model No. 7128DP
EX n/a   NM n/a   MIP $30

(Photo courtesy Racing Champions Ertl)

❑ **1970-1/2 Chevy Camaro Z28,** 2001, White body, black interior, black vinyl roof, 350cid engine, plated valve covers, bucket seats, simulated woodgrain dash, 1:18 scale
EX n/a   NM n/a   MIP $30

❑ **1971 Buick GSX,** 1994, Regal Black body, gold stripes, 1:18 scale, Model No. 7604DO
EX n/a   NM n/a   MIP $30

❑ **1971 Dodge Challenger,** 2000, Citron Yellow body, black interior and striping, black vinyl roof, 1:18 scale, Model No. 32798
EX n/a   NM n/a   MIP $32

❑ **1971 Dodge Challenger,** 2000, Gunmetal Metallic body, black interior and striping, black vinyl roof, 1:18 scale, Model No. 32799
EX n/a   NM n/a   MIP $30

❑ **1971 Dodge Challenger,** 2000, Black body and interior, white striping, white vinyl roof, 1:18 scale, Model No. 32801
EX n/a   NM n/a   MIP $30

❑ **1971 Dodge Challenger,** 2000, Plum Crazy body, black interior and striping, black vinyl roof, 1:18 scale, Model No. 32802
EX n/a   NM n/a   MIP $30

❑ **1971 Dodge Challenger,** 2000, Go Green body, black interior and striping, black vinyl roof, 1:18 scale, Model No. 32800
EX n/a   NM n/a   MIP $30

❑ **1971 Dodge Challenger R/T,** 2001, Hemi Orange body, white stop, white stripe, black interior, 1:18 scale, Model No. 32940
EX n/a   NM n/a   MIP $28

❑ **1971 Dodge Charger R/T,** 2000, Charger Red body, Rally wheels, louvered rear window, 1:64 scale, Model No. 32523
EX n/a   NM n/a   MIP $7

(Photo courtesy Racing Champions Ertl)

❑ **1971 Dodge Charger R/T,** 2001, Green Go body, 1:64 scale, Model No. 32371
EX n/a   NM n/a   MIP $6

(Photo courtesy Racing Champions Ertl)

❑ **1971 Dodge Charger R/T,** 2001, Citron Yellow body, 1:64 scale, Model No. 32372
EX n/a   NM n/a   MIP $6

(Photo courtesy Racing Champions Ertl)

❑ **1971 Dodge Charger R/T,** 2001, Hemi Orange body, 1:64 scale, Model No. 32522
EX n/a   NM n/a   MIP $6

❑ **1971 Ford Torino Cobra,** 2000, Light Pewter body, 1:18 scale, Model No. 32502
EX n/a   NM n/a   MIP $30

❑ **1971 Ford Torino Cobra,** 2000, Medium Yellow/gold body, 1:18 scale, Model No. 32501
EX n/a   NM n/a   MIP $30

❑ **1971 Ford Torino Cobra,** 2000, Bright Red body, 1:18 scale, Model No. 32500
EX n/a   NM n/a   MIP $30

(Photo courtesy Racing Champions Ertl)

❑ **1971 Plymouth AAR Cuda,** 2000, Lime Twist Green body, flat black hood, black louvered window, black striping and interior, opening hood, 340 V8 engine, 1:18 scale, Model No. 32918
EX n/a   NM n/a   MIP $30

(Photo courtesy Racing Champions Ertl)

❑ **1971 Plymouth Cuda,** 2000, Orange body, black stripes, black interior, 1:43 scale, Model No. 32246
EX n/a   NM n/a   MIP $8

(Photo courtesy Racing Champions Ertl)

❑ **1971 Plymouth Cuda,** 2000, White body, 383 engine, factory mags, chrome bumpers, no rear spoiler or louvers; limited edition from Supercar Collectibles, 1:18 scale, Model No. 29030
EX n/a   NM n/a   MIP $30

(Photo courtesy Racing Champions Ertl)

❑ **1971 Plymouth Cuda,** 2000, Purple body, 440 six-barrel, go-wing, vinyl top, body-colored grille and bumper; limited edition from Supercar Collectibles, 1:18 scale, Model No. 29030
EX n/a   NM n/a   MIP $30

(Photo courtesy Racing Champions Ertl)

❑ **1971 Plymouth Cuda,** 2000, B-5 Blue body, white billboards, dog dish hubcaps, 340 engine; limited edition from Supercar Collectibles, 1:18 scale, Model No. 29027
EX n/a   NM n/a   MIP $30

(Photo courtesy Racing Champions Ertl)

❑ **1971 Plymouth Cuda,** 2001, Toreador Red body, black interior, black vinyl roof and rear-deck spoiler, scooped hood, 440 Six Pack, 1:18 scale
EX n/a   NM n/a   MIP $30

(Photo courtesy Racing Champions Ertl)

❑ **1971 Plymouth Duster,** 2002, Sassy Grass Green body, blacked-out hood, black vinyl top, black stripes and spoiler, black interior, 1:18 scale, Model No. 33079
EX n/a   NM n/a   MIP $30

(Photo courtesy Racing Champions Ertl)

❑ **1971 Plymouth Duster,** 2002, True Blue body, dual scooped hood, white vinyl top, white stripes, white interior, 1:18 scale, Model No. 33078
EX n/a   NM n/a   MIP $30

(Photo courtesy Racing Champions Ertl)

❑ **1971 Plymouth Duster 340,** 2002, Lemon Twist body, black vinyl top, dual-scoop hoood, 340 engine, black interior and spoiler, 1:18 scale, Model No. 32980
EX n/a   NM n/a   MIP $30

(Photo courtesy Racing Champions Ertl)

❑ **1971 Plymouth Duster 340,** 2002, Red body, flat black hood, 340cid Wedge engine, stock wheels, 1:18 scale, Model No. 32981
EX n/a   NM n/a   MIP $30

(Photo courtesy Racing Champions Ertl)

❏ **1971 Plymouth GTX 440,** 2002, Butterscotch body, white vinyl top, no spoiler, 1:18 scale, Model No. 33081
EX n/a   NM n/a   MIP $30

(Photo courtesy Racing Champions Ertl)

❏ **1971 Plymouth GTX 440,** 2002, Green Go body, black vinyl top and interior, rear spoiler, 1:18 scale, Model No. 33080
EX n/a   NM n/a   MIP $30

(Photo courtesy Racing Champions Ertl)

❏ **1971 Plymouth Hemi Cuda,** 2000, Curious Yellow body, rear window louver, go-wing, rallye wheels; limited edition from Supercar Collectibles, 1:18 scale, Model No. 29026
EX n/a   NM n/a   MIP $30

(Photo courtesy Racing Champions Ertl)

❏ **1972 Pontiac Trans Am,** 2001, White body, blue stripes, 455 HO engine, black interior with folding front seats, plated dashboard and five-spoke wheels with gold rim inserts, "Boss Bird" and sponsor tampos, 1:18 scale, Model No. 32975
EX n/a   NM n/a   MIP $32

❏ **1973 Pontiac Trans Am,** 1995, Buccaneer Red body, black/orange Firebird hood decal, 1:18 scale, Model No. 7300DO
EX n/a   NM n/a   MIP $30

❏ **1973 Pontiac Trans Am,** 1995, Cameo White body, blue/black Firebird hood decal, 455cid Super Duty V8, 1:18 scale, Model No. 7301DO
EX n/a   NM n/a   MIP $30

❏ **1973 Pontiac Trans Am,** 2001, Valencia Gold body, black interior, 1:18 scale, Model No. 32953
EX n/a   NM n/a   MIP $30

❏ **1973 Pontiac Trans Am,** 2002, Buccaneer Red body, black interior, folding front bucket seats, Formula steering wheel, Arnie Beswick's signature on roof, 1:18 scale, Model No. 32988
EX n/a   NM n/a   MIP $30

❏ **1980 Chevy, Darrell Waltrip Mountain Dew,** 1982, 1:64 scale, Model No. 1946
EX n/a   NM n/a   MIP $8

❏ **1983 Ford Thunderbird, Bill Elliott #9,** 1986, 1:64 scale, Model No. 9408
EX n/a   NM n/a   MIP $8

❏ **1986 Ford Thunderbird, Bill Elliott,** 1987, 1:64 scale, Model No. 9466
EX n/a   NM n/a   MIP $8

❏ **1988 Chevy Monte Carlo,** 1988, White body; shipped undecaled by Ertl but offered for sale by company in Pennsylvania with its own set of waterslide decals to represent a NASCAR racer, 1:64 scale, Model No. 9363
EX n/a   NM n/a   MIP $6

❏ **1988 Chevy Monte Carlo stock car,** 1988, Black body; shipped undecaled by Ertl but offered for sale by company in Pennsylvania with its own set of waterslide decals to represent a NASCAR racer, 1:64 scale, Model No. 9796
EX n/a   NM n/a   MIP $6

❏ **1996 Camaro Z28 convertible,** 1996, Bright Red body, 1:18 scale, Model No. 7232DO
EX n/a   NM n/a   MIP $30

❏ **1996 Chevy Camaro Z28 convertible,** 1996, Mystic Teal Metallic body, tan interior, 1:18 scale, Model No. 7231DO
EX n/a   NM n/a   MIP $30

❏ **1996 Pontiac Trans Am,** 1996, Cyclamen Metallic purpple body, tan interior, 1:18 scale, Model No. 7208DO
EX n/a   NM n/a   MIP $30

❏ **1996 Pontiac Trans Am,** 1996, Cayenne Red Metallic body, 1:18 scale, Model No. 7209DO
EX n/a   NM n/a   MIP $30

❏ **1998 Land Rover Freelander,** 1998, Beluga Black body, 1:18 scale, Model No. 7897DO
EX n/a   NM n/a   MIP $30

❏ **1998 Land Rover Freelander,** 1998, Charleston Green body, 1:18 scale, Model No. 7885DO
EX n/a   NM n/a   MIP $30

❏ **1998 Pontiac Trans Am,** 1998, Bright Red body, gray interior, 1:18 scale, Model No. 7831DP
EX n/a   NM n/a   MIP $30

❏ **1998 Pontiac Trans Am,** 1998, Black body, 1:18 scale, Model No. 7832DP
EX n/a   NM n/a   MIP $30

(Photo courtesy Racing Champions Ertl)

❏ **Baldwin-Motion Drag Cobra,** 2002, Orange/brown body with graphics, flip-forward hood, removable roof, 1:18 scale, Model No. 33096
EX n/a   NM n/a   MIP $30

❏ **Big Blocks,** 2000, Three-car set: 1965 Pontiac GTO, 1971 Dodge Charger, 1969 Ford Mustang Mach I, 1:64 scale, Model No. 32663D
EX n/a   NM n/a   MIP $15

(Photo courtesy Racing Champions Ertl)

❑ **Bladwin-Motion King Cobra,** 2002, Black body, cream top, scooped hood with plated hood locks, 427 engine, plated dual carbs and valve covers, flexible wiring, 1:18 scale, Model No. 33059

EX n/a   NM n/a   MIP $30

❑ **Bobby Allison Gatorade,** 1982, 1:64 scale, Model No. 1944

EX n/a   NM n/a   MIP $6

❑ **Cale Yarborough Valvoline,** 1980, First licensed cars from Ertl, 1:64 scale, Model No. 1912

EX n/a   NM n/a   MIP $8

❑ **Cale Yarborough Valvoline,** 1982, 1:64 scale, Model No. 1943

EX n/a   NM n/a   MIP $8

❑ **Camaro,** 1982, White/red body, #98; three-piece set with yellow Chevrolet pickup and red plastic trailer, 1:64 scale, Model No. 1785

EX n/a   NM n/a   MIP $6

❑ **Camaro Z28,** 1997, White body, red stripes, tan interior, 1:18 scale, Model No. 7296DP

EX n/a   NM n/a   MIP $30

❑ **Chevy Camaro Z28,** 1998, Quasar Blue Metallic body, tan interior, 1:18 scale, Model No. 7207DP

EX n/a   NM n/a   MIP $30

❑ **Chevy Caprice,** 1982, Yellow/red body, #31; three-piece set with white Chevrolet pickup and red plastic trailer, 1:64 scale, Model No. 1785

EX n/a   NM n/a   MIP $18

❑ **Chevy Lumina, Dale Earnhardt Goodwrench,** 1992, opening hoods, detailed motors, full roll cage, vent windows, 1:18 scale, Model No. 7356

EX n/a   NM n/a   MIP $45

❑ **Chevy Lumina, Dale Jarrett Interstate Batteries,** 1992, opening hoods, detailed motors, full roll cage, vent windows, 1:18 scale, Model No. 7447

EX n/a   NM n/a   MIP $45

❑ **Chevy Lumina, Darrell Waltrip Western Auto,** 1993, opening hoods, detailed motors, full roll cage, vent windows, 1:18 scale, Model No. 7355

EX n/a   NM n/a   MIP $45

❑ **Chevy Lumina, Derrike Cope Purolater,** 1993, opening hoods, detailed motors, full roll cage, vent windows, 1:18 scale, Model No. 7349

EX n/a   NM n/a   MIP $45

❑ **Chevy Lumina, Ernie Irvan Kodak,** 1992, opening hoods, detailed motors, full roll cage, vent windows, 1:18 scale, Model No. 7450

EX n/a   NM n/a   MIP $45

(Photo courtesy Racing Champions Ertl)

❑ **Class of 1957: Chevy Bel Air,** 2000, Part of a three-car set: Chevy Bel Air (#36126), Chrysler 300C (#36127), Mercury Turnpike Cruiser (#36128). Set price shown, 1:43 scale, Model No. 32001; 36001

EX n/a   NM n/a   MIP $32

(Photo courtesy Racing Champions Ertl)

❑ **Class of 1957: Chrysler 300C,** 2000, Part of three-car set: Chevy Bel Air (#36126), Chrysler 300C (#36127, Mercury Turnpike Cruiser (#36128). Set price for all three shown, 1:43 scale, Model No. 36001

EX n/a   NM n/a   MIP $32

(Photo courtesy Racing Champions Ertl)

❑ **Class of 1957: Mercury Turnpike,** 2000, Part of three-car set: Chevy Bel Air (#36126), Chrysler 300C (#36127), Mercury Turnpike Cruiser (#36128). Set price shown., 1:43 scale, Model No. 36001

EX n/a   NM n/a   MIP $32

❑ **Class of 1967,** 1999, Three-car set: Shelby GT350, Pontiac Firebird 400, Chevy Camaro, 1:43 scale, Model No. 32002

EX n/a   NM n/a   MIP $30

❑ **Class of 1969,** 2000, Three-car set: Mustang Mach I, Dodge Daytona, Mercury Cougar, 1:64 scale, Model No. 32663A

EX n/a   NM n/a   MIP $15

❑ **Class of 1969,** 2001, Three-car set: Mustang Mach I, Dodge Daytona, Mercury Cougar, 1:64 scale

EX n/a   NM n/a   MIP $15

❑ **Class of 1970,** 1999, Three-car set: Ford Torino Cobra, Chevy SS Nova, Olds 4-4-2, 1:43 scale, Model No. 32003

EX n/a   NM n/a   MIP $30

❑ **Darrell Waltrip Gatorade,** 1980, First licensed cars from Ertl, 1:64 scale, Model No. 1912

EX n/a   NM n/a   MIP $8

❑ **Darrell Waltrip Mountain Dew,** 1980, First licensed cars from Ertl, 1:64 scale, Model No. 1912

EX n/a   NM n/a   MIP $6

❑ **Darrell Waltrip Mountain Dew,** 1982, pullback motor, 1:43 scale, Model No. 1720

EX n/a   NM n/a   MIP $8

❑ **Early Muscle,** 2000, Three-car set: 1957 Chrysler 300C, 1958 Plymouth Belvedere, 1960 Ford Starliner, 1:64 scale, Model No. 32663B

EX n/a   NM n/a   MIP $15

❑ **Ford Thunderbird, Bill Elliott/Harry Melling #9,** 1989, Red/white body, deep dish gold-plated wheels, 1:64 scale, Model No. 9670YO

EX n/a   NM n/a   MIP $6

❑ **Ford Thunderbird, Geoff Bodine Motorcraft,** 1993, opening hoods, detailed motors, full roll cage, vent windows, 1:18 scale, Model No. 7357

EX n/a   NM n/a   MIP $40

❑ **Ford Thunderbird, Mark Martin Valvoline,** 1993, opening hoods, detailed motors, full roll cage, vent windows, 1:18 scale, Model No. 7457

EX n/a   NM n/a   MIP $40

❑ **Formula One racer,** 1982, Blue body with white markings, #2; three-piece set with blue Chevrolet pickup and white plastic trailer, 1:64 scale, Model No. 1785

EX n/a   NM n/a   MIP $11

❑ **Harry Gant Skoal Bandit,** 1982, radio controlled, 1:20 scale, Model No. 4756

EX n/a   NM n/a   MIP $30

❑ **Harry Gant Skoal Bandit,** 1982, pullback motor, 1:43 scale, Model No. 1721

EX n/a   NM n/a   MIP $10

❑ **Harry Gant Transporter,** 1982, Graphic #33 Skoal Bandit car on trailer, Model No. 3420

EX n/a   NM n/a   MIP $10

❑ **Kings of the Street,** 2000, Three-car set: 1962 Pontiac SD421, 1963 Ford Galaxie, 1964 Ford Fairlane Thunderbolt, 1:64 scale, Model No. 32663F

EX n/a   NM n/a   MIP $15

❑ **Plymouth Prowler,** 1995, Candy Magenta body, 1:18 scale, Model No. 7394DO

EX n/a   NM n/a   MIP $40

❑ **Pontiac Grand Prix, Kyle Petty Mello Yello,** 1992, opening hoods, detailed motors, full roll cage, vent windows, 1:18 scale, Model No. 7448

EX n/a   NM n/a   MIP $45

❑ **Pontiac Grand Prix, Michael Waltrip Pennzoil,** 1992, opening hoods, detailed motors, full roll cage, vent windows, 1:18 scale, Model No. 7348

EX n/a   NM n/a   MIP $45

❑ **Pontiac Grand Prix, Richard Petty STP,** 1992, opening hoods, detailed motors, full roll cage, vent windows, 1:18 scale, Model No. 7461

EX n/a   NM n/a   MIP $45

❑ **Pontiac Trans Am,** 1997, 25th anniversary edition, white body, black stripes and top, gray interior, 1:18 scale, Model No. 7211DP

EX n/a   NM n/a   MIP $30

❑ **Pony Cars,** 2000, Three-car set: 1970 Camaro SS, 1969 Ford Mustang Mach I, 1969 Mercury Cougar, 1:64 scale, Model No. 32663E

EX n/a   NM n/a   MIP $15

❑ **Richard Petty STP,** 1980, First licensed cars from Ertl, 1:64 scale, Model No. 1912

EX n/a   NM n/a   MIP $8

❑ **Richard Petty STP,** 1982, 1:64 scale, Model No. 1942

EX n/a   NM n/a   MIP $6

❑ **Richard Petty STP,** 1982, pullback motor, 1:43 scale, Model No. 1719

EX n/a   NM n/a   MIP $10

❑ **Shelby Cobra 427 S/C,** 1994, Red body, white stripes, black interior, 1:18 scale, Model No. 7369DO

EX n/a   NM n/a   MIP $30

❑ **Shelby Cobra 427 S/C,** 1994, Blue body, white stripes, black interior, 1:18 scale, Model No. 7386DO

EX n/a   NM n/a   MIP $30

❑ **Super Sports,** 2000, Three-car set: 1964 Chevy Impala SS, 1969 Chevy Nova SS, and 1970 Camaro SS, 1:64 scale, Model No. 32663C

EX n/a   NM n/a   MIP $15

CARS OF THE '50S

❑ **1950 Ford,** 1979, Red body, black top; red body, white top (1982), 1:64 scale, Model No. 1708

EX n/a   NM n/a   MIP $10

❑ **1950 Mercury,** 1979, Maroon body, brown interior, 1:64 scale, Model No. 1708

EX n/a   NM n/a   MIP $10

❑ **1951 Chevy,** 1979, Green body, white interior; green body, tan interior (1982), 1:64 scale, Model No. 1708

EX n/a   NM n/a   MIP $10

❑ **1955 Chevy Nomad,** 1979, Blue body, black interior; blue body, tan interior (1982), 1:64 scale, Model No. 1708

EX n/a   NM n/a   MIP $10

❑ **1956 Ford Crown Victoria,** 1979, Black body, tan/white interior, 1:64 scale, Model No. 1708

EX n/a   NM n/a   MIP $10

❑ **1957 Chevy,** 1979, Yellow body, dark interior, 1:64 scale, Model No. 1708

EX n/a   NM n/a   MIP $10

CARS OF THE WORLD

❑ **Alfa Romeo Coupe 33,** 1977, Red body, 1:64 scale, Model No. 1701

EX n/a   NM n/a   MIP $10

❑ **Alfa Romeo Coupe 33,** 1978, Red body, speed wheels, opening hoods and doors, 1:64 scale, Model No. 1612

EX n/a   NM n/a   MIP $10

❑ **BMW Turbo,** 1977, Orange body, 1:64 scale, Model No. 1701

EX n/a   NM n/a   MIP $10

❑ **BMW Turbo,** 1978, Orange/red body, speed wheels, opening hoods and doors, 1:64 scale, Model No. 1604

EX n/a   NM n/a   MIP $10

❑ **Ferrari Dino 246 GT,** 1977, Yellow body, 1:64 scale, Model No. 1701

EX n/a   NM n/a   MIP $10

❑ **Fiat Abarth,** 1977, Blue body, 1:64 scale, Model No. 1701

EX n/a   NM n/a   MIP $10

❑ **Fiat Abarth,** 1978, Blue metallic body, speed wheels, opening hoods and doors, 1:64 scale, Model No. 1601

EX n/a   NM n/a   MIP $10

❑ **Ford Mk IV,** 1977, White body, 1:64 scale, Model No. 1701

EX n/a   NM n/a   MIP $10

❑ **Ford Mk IV,** 1978, White body, speed wheels, opening hoods and doors, 1:64 scale, Model No. 1602

EX n/a   NM n/a   MIP $10

❑ **Jaguar XJ10,** 1977, Maroon body, 1:64 scale, Model No. 1701

EX n/a   NM n/a   MIP $10

❑ **Maserati Merak SS,** 1977, Red body, 1:64 scale, Model No. 1701

EX n/a   NM n/a   MIP $10

❑ **McLaren M8A,** 1977, Orange body, 1:64 scale, Model No. 1701

EX n/a   NM n/a   MIP $10

❑ **McLaren M8A,** 1978, Yellow body, speed wheels, opening hoods and doors, 1:64 scale, Model No. 1608

EX n/a   NM n/a   MIP $10

❑ **Mercedes Benz 350SK,** 1977, Dark red body, 1:64 scale, Model No. 1701

EX n/a   NM n/a   MIP $10

ERTL / AUTOMOBILES

❏ **Mercedes Benz 450SE,** 1977, Cream body, 1:64 scale, Model No. 1701
EX n/a   NM n/a   MIP $10

❏ **Mercedes Benz C111,** 1977, Light green body, 1:64 scale, Model No. 1701
EX n/a   NM n/a   MIP $10

❏ **Mercedes Benz C111,** 1978, Metallic red body, speed wheels, opening hoods and doors, 1:64 scale, Model No. 1605
EX n/a   NM n/a   MIP $10

❏ **Mercedes-Benz 359SL,** 1978, Metallic orange body, speed wheels, opening hoods and doors, 1:64 scale, Model No. 1606
EX n/a   NM n/a   MIP $10

❏ **Mercedes-Benz 450SE,** 1978, Silver body, speed wheels, opening hoods and doors, 1:64 scale, Model No. 1609
EX n/a   NM n/a   MIP $10

❏ **Porsche 911,** 1977, Yellow body, 1:64 scale, Model No. 1701
EX n/a   NM n/a   MIP $10

❏ **Porsche 911,** 1978, Yellow body, speed wheels, opening hoods and doors, 1:64 scale, Model No. 1603
EX n/a   NM n/a   MIP $10

❏ **Porsche 917,** 1977, Green body, 1:64 scale, Model No. 1701
EX n/a   NM n/a   MIP $10

❏ **Porsche 917,** 1978, Silver body, speed wheels, opening hoods and doors, 1:64 scale, Model No. 1607
EX n/a   NM n/a   MIP $10

❏ **Porsche 930 Turbo,** 1977, White body, 1:64 scale, Model No. 1701
EX n/a   NM n/a   MIP $10

❏ **Rolls Royce Silver Shadow,** 1977, Blue body, 1:64 scale, Model No. 1701
EX n/a   NM n/a   MIP $10

❏ **Rolls Royce Silver Shadow,** 1978, Metallic blue body, speed wheels, opening hoods and doors, 1:64 scale, Model No. 1610
EX n/a   NM n/a   MIP $10

❏ **Volkswagen 1200LS,** 1977, Red body, 1:64 scale, Model No. 1701
EX n/a   NM n/a   MIP $10

❏ **Volkswagen 1200LS,** 1978, Red body, speed wheels, opening hoods and doors, 1:64 scale, Model No. 1611
EX n/a   NM n/a   MIP $10

CHOPPER SQUADRON

❏ **Air Ambulance Casualty Helicopter,** 1986, Model No. 1085
EX n/a   NM n/a   MIP $10

❏ **Black Widow Attack Helicopter,** 1986, Model No. 1083
EX n/a   NM n/a   MIP $10

❏ **Commando Transport Helicopter,** 1986, Camouflage body, Model No. 1084
EX n/a   NM n/a   MIP $10

CITGO

❏ **Ford Thunderbird,** 1987, White body with red, blue and orange decals, 1:64 scale, Model No. 9183
EX n/a   NM n/a   MIP $6

CLASSIC VEHICLES

❏ **1912 Buick Touring Car,** 1990, Red body and fenders in "Classic Vehicles" series (1990), 1:43 scale, Model No. 2516
EX n/a   NM n/a   MIP $15

❏ **1913 Ford Model T van,** 1990, White body, "St. Mary's Hospital" markings, 1:43 scale, Model No. 2502
EX n/a   NM n/a   MIP $15

❏ **1914 Chevy,** 1990, Orange body, 1:43 scale, Model No. 2543
EX n/a   NM n/a   MIP $15

❏ **1923 Ford Model T sedan,** 1990, Green body, New York taxi markings, 1:43 scale, Model No. 2519
EX n/a   NM n/a   MIP $15

❏ **1930 Chevy Barrel truck,** 1992, Red cab, black fenders, brown box, tan tarp, 1:43 scale, Model No. 2861
EX n/a   NM n/a   MIP $15

❏ **1930 Chevy Delivery truck,** 1992, Blue Chicago Police truck, 1:43 scale, Model No. 2518
EX n/a   NM n/a   MIP $15

❏ **1930 Chevy Stake truck,** 1994, Red body, black fenders, "Orville's" markings, 1:43 scale, Model No. 2503EP
EX n/a   NM n/a   MIP $12

❏ **1930 Packard Boattail Speedster,** 1990, Silver/black body, 1:43 scale, Model No. 2542
EX n/a   NM n/a   MIP $15

❏ **1930-31 Chevy Stake truck,** 1990, Yellow body, "W.J. Kennedy Dairy" markings, 1:43 scale, Model No. 2503
EX n/a   NM n/a   MIP $12

❏ **1932 Ford Panel Delivery truck,** 1994, Turquoise body, cream fenders and hubs, "Daisy's Floral Gifts" markings, 1:43 scale, Model No. 2504EP
EX n/a   NM n/a   MIP $12

❏ **1932 Ford Roadster,** 1990, Yellow body, 1:43 scale, Model No. 2501
EX n/a   NM n/a   MIP $15

❏ **1934 Ford Panel Delivery,** 1990, Red body, "Chicago Fire Dept." markings, 1:43 scale, Model No. 2504
EX n/a   NM n/a   MIP $15

❏ **1938 Ford Panel,** 1994, Tan body and wheels, brown fenders, "Delaney's Bakery" markings, 1:43 scale, Model No. 2824EP
EX n/a   NM n/a   MIP $15

❏ **1940 Ford Woody Station Wagon,** 1990, White/black police car, 1:43 scale, Model No. 2517
EX n/a   NM n/a   MIP $15

❏ **1940 Ford Woody Wagon,** 1994, Blue body, brown/tan body, black roof, "Wilson's" markings, 1:43 scale, Model No. 2517EP
EX n/a   NM n/a   MIP $12

❏ **1947 International KB-12,** 1992, Yellow body and wheels, black fenders, "Cruise Cartage Company" markings, 1:43 scale, Model No. 2627
EX n/a   NM n/a   MIP $12

❏ **1948 Diamond T semi cab,** 1992, Red body, black fenders, "J.T. Wilson" markings, 1:43 scale, Model No. 2594
EX n/a   NM n/a   MIP $15

❏ **1948 Jaguar XK-120,** 1992, British Racing Green body, cream interior, 1:43 scale, Model No. 2850
EX n/a   NM n/a   MIP $15

❏ **1949 Ford coupe,** 1990, Beige/yellow body in "Classic Vehicles" series (1990; EF suffix), 1:43 scale, Model No. 2803EF
EX n/a   NM n/a   MIP $12

❏ **1950 Chevy Panel,** 1994, Blue two-tone body, "Deli Supply" markings, 1:43 scale, Model No. 2825EP
EX n/a   NM n/a   MIP $15

❏ **1950 Chevy truck,** 1992, Red body, "HW" markings, 1:43 scale, Model No. 2625
EX n/a   NM n/a   MIP $12

❏ **1951 GMC Panel,** 1994, Blue two-tone body, "Deli Supply" markings, 1:43 scale, Model No. 2826EP
EX n/a   NM n/a   MIP $15

❏ **1952 Cadillac sedan,** 1990, Blue body, white top, 1:43 scale, Model No. 2541
EX n/a   NM n/a   MIP $12

❏ **1952 Cadillac sedan,** 1994, Green body, white roof, 1:43 scale, Model No. 2541EP
EX n/a   NM n/a   MIP $15

❏ **1955 Chevy Cameo pickup,** 1994, Metallic brown body, tinted windows, crates and barrels in bed, 1:43 scale, Model No. 2154EO
EX n/a   NM n/a   MIP $15

❏ **1955 Chevy Cameo pickup,** 1994, White body, red trim and cover, tinted windows, 1:43 scale, Model No. 2155EO
EX n/a   NM n/a   MIP $15

❏ **1955 Chevy Cameo wrecker,** 1994, Red body, brown boom, chrome hook and details, tinted windows, 1:43 scale, Model No. 2159EO
EX n/a   NM n/a   MIP $15

❏ **1957 Chevy,** 1990, Yellow body with white top, 1:43 scale, Model No. 2540
EX n/a   NM n/a   MIP $15

❏ **1957 Chevy,** 1994, Light blue/white body, 1:43 scale, Model No. 2540EP
EX n/a   NM n/a   MIP $15

❏ **1957 Ford Thunderbird,** 1990, White body and top, 1:43 scale, Model No. 2802EF
EX n/a   NM n/a   MIP $12

❏ **1957 Ford Thunderbird,** 1994, Black body, white top and interior, 1:43 scale, Model No. 2802EP
EX n/a   NM n/a   MIP $15

❏ **1960 Chevy truck,** 1992, Blue/gray body, "Gerald E. Orv Trucking" markings, 1:43 scale, Model No. 2628
EX n/a   NM n/a   MIP $15

❏ **1960 Corvette,** 1994, Purple/white body, white interior, 1:43 scale, Model No. 2588EP
EX n/a   NM n/a   MIP $15

❏ **1960 Corvette convertible,** 1990, Mint green/white body; light blue/white body (1992), 1:43 scale, Model No. 2588EF
EX n/a   NM n/a   MIP $12

❏ **1961 Ferrari 250GT,** 1990, Red body; first European car added to Classic Vehicles collection, 1:43 scale, Model No. 2853EF
EX n/a   NM n/a   MIP $15

❏ **1964-1/2 Ford Mustang,** 1990, Red body; pink body (1994), 1:43 scale, Model No. 2586EF
EX n/a   NM n/a   MIP $12

❏ **1965 Cobra 427,** 1990, Blue body, white stripes, 1:43 scale, Model No. 2851EF
EX n/a   NM n/a   MIP $15

❏ **1968 Pontiac GTO,** 1990, Red body, 1:43 scale, Model No. 2589EF
EX n/a   NM n/a   MIP $12

❏ **1968 Pontiac GTO,** 1994, Red body, white interior, 1:43 scale, Model No. 2589EP
EX n/a   NM n/a   MIP $15

❏ **1968 Shelby Mustang GT,** 1990, White body, blue stripes, 1:43 scale, Model No. 2804EF
EX n/a   NM n/a   MIP $15

❏ **1969 Chevy Camaro,** 1990, Yellow body, black stripes, 1:43 scale, Model No. 2809EF
EX n/a   NM n/a   MIP $12

❏ **Checker Cab,** 1994, Yellow body, taxi graphics, 1:43 scale, Model No. 2587EF
EX n/a   NM n/a   MIP $15

CLASSICS

❏ **1935 Auburn 851 boattail speedster,** 1999, Rich Maroon body, 280cid Lycoming supercharged straight eight engine, wire wheels, wide whitewalls, 1:18 scale, Model No. 7995DP
EX n/a   NM n/a   MIP $30

❏ **1935 Auburn 851 boattail speedster,** 1999, Starlight Black body, 280cid Lycoming supercharged straight eight engine, wire wheels, wide whitewalls, 1:18 scale, Model No. 7994DP
EX n/a   NM n/a   MIP $30

COLLECTOR'S CLUB

❏ **1982 Pontiac Firebird,** 1982, Red body, T tops, "00" molded into the chassis; mailed to new members of Ertl Replica Collector's Club, 1:64 scale, Model No. 2000
EX n/a   NM n/a   MIP $12

COMMERCIAL AIRLINE

❏ **Boeing 707,** 1978, Silver body, blue, red and white markings, American Airlines, Model No. 1510
EX n/a   NM n/a   MIP $12

❏ **Boeing 727,** 1978, Blue body, gray wings, Braniff, Model No. 1510
EX n/a   NM n/a   MIP $12

❏ **Boeing 747,** 1978, White body, blue, black and green markings, PanAm, Model No. 1510
EX n/a   NM n/a   MIP $13

❏ **Douglas DC-10,** 1978, White body, orange and black markings, United Air Lines, Model No. 1510
EX n/a   NM n/a   MIP $12

❏ **Douglas DC-9,** 1978, White body, blue and black markings, Eastern Air Lines, Model No. 1510
EX n/a   NM n/a   MIP $14

❏ **Lockheed L-1011 Tristar,** 1978, White body, red markings, TWA, Model No. 1510
EX n/a   NM n/a   MIP $12

COMMERCIAL JETS

❏ **American Airline DC-10,** 1988, 1:370 scale, Model No. 2394EO
EX n/a   NM n/a   MIP $11

❏ **Continental DC-9,** 1988, 1:250 scale, Model No. 2393EO
EX n/a   NM n/a   MIP $10

❏ **TWA 737,** 1988, 1:230 scale, Model No. 2392EO
EX n/a   NM n/a   MIP $7

❏ **United 747,** 1988, 1:470 scale, Model No. 2390EO
EX n/a   NM n/a   MIP $10

CONVOY (1978)

❏ **Mack Rig, "Rubber Duck",** 1979, Black cab with sleeper, silver tanker with movie logo, rubber duck hood ornament, steerable front end with I-beam axle and tandem rear axles, detachable trailer, 9-1/2 inches, 1:64 scale, Model No. 1440
EX n/a   NM n/a   MIP $10

CRISCO

❑ **Ford Thunderbird,** 1987, 1:64 scale, Model No. 1329
EX n/a   NM n/a   MIP $6

CROWN PETROLEUM

❑ **1989 Buick Grand National,** Model No. 9663GO
EX n/a   NM n/a   MIP $6

CRUISIN' SERIES DISPLAYS

❑ **1932 Ford "Newstalgia",** 1997, Drive-in movie scene, flames on car, movie speakers, male and female figures; changed to Skyvue Drive-In with 1969 Plymouth GTX convertible (1999), 1:18 scale, Model No. 7907BO
EX n/a   NM n/a   MIP $30

❑ **1932 Ford High Tech Rod,** 1998, Starlight Drive-In scene with car, includes a couple, movie speaker and food tray, 1:18 scale, Model No. 7907KO
EX n/a   NM n/a   MIP $30

❑ **1932 Ford Roadster,** 1998, Doin' It Yourself scene with blue Ford, includes car's owner, tools and toolboxes, tripod to pull the engine, 1:18 scale, Model No. 7912KP
EX n/a   NM n/a   MIP $30

❑ **1940 Ford Woody Wagon, 1965 Ford Mustang,** 1998, Flamingo Beach scene with cars; only black Ford Woody in 1999, 1:43 scale, Model No. 7913KO
EX n/a   NM n/a   MIP $10

❑ **1949 Ford coupe police car, 1951 GMC Panel truck,** 1999, Silver Diner scene with cars, includes diner and two figures, 1:43 scale, Model No. 27173
EX n/a   NM n/a   MIP $10

❑ **1949 Ford Coupe, 1952 Cadillac,** 1998, Esquire Theatre scene with pink/white Cadillac, dark blue Ford, 1:43 scale, Model No. 7905KO
EX n/a   NM n/a   MIP $10

❑ **1950 Chevy Panel Van, 1952 Cadillac,** 1997, Starlight Drive-In scene with cars, 1:43 scale, Model No. 7905BO
EX n/a   NM n/a   MIP $10

❑ **1955 Chevy Bel Air,** 1997, Ted's Drive-in scene with dark green/light green Chevy, driver and waitress figures, Bruce Kaiser illustrated print, 1:18 scale, Model No. 7906BO
EX n/a   NM n/a   MIP $30

❑ **1955 Chevy Stepside pickup,** 1997, Oscar's Gas Station scene with dark blue Chevy; includes vintage gas pumps, driver and gas station attendant figures, 1:18 scale, Model No. 7909BO
EX n/a   NM n/a   MIP $30

❑ **1956 Ford Sunliner,** 1999, Why Me scene with car, includes gas station, two people and a Texaco gas station attendant, gas pump, tire rack, oilcan rack, 1:18 scale, Model No. 27178
EX n/a   NM n/a   MIP $30

❑ **1957 Chevy Bel Air, 1955 Tow Truck,** 1997, Wally's Service Station scene with green/white Chevy, red truck, 1:43 scale, Model No. 7903BO
EX n/a   NM n/a   MIP $10

❑ **1957 Chevy convertible,** 1999, Coming Home scene with car, includes two women, two Air Force pilots, background with jet and flight line, 1:18 scale, Model No. 27177
EX n/a   NM n/a   MIP $30

❑ **1959 Corvette, 1969 Pontiac GTO,** 1998, Life's a Drag scene with red/white Corvette and light blue GTO, inspired by Bruce Kaiser illustration. Includes cold-cast "Christmas tree" starting lights and box, 1:43 scale, Model No. 7914KO
EX n/a   NM n/a   MIP $10

❑ **1966 Pontiac GTO,** 1998, Honest Al's Used Car Lot scene with red GTO, includes sales building, Honest Al in plaid coat and white shoes, 1:18 scale, Model No. 7911KO
EX n/a   NM n/a   MIP $30

❑ **1967 Shelby GT350,** 1999, Cruisin' scene with Speed Shop, figures and props, 1:43 scale, Model No. 27174
EX n/a   NM n/a   MIP $10

❑ **Cobra 427, 1957 Thunderbird,** 1997, Johnny's Restaurant scene with black/white Cobra, white T-bird (named Dolly's Restaurant, 1998), 1:43 scale, Model No. 7904BO
EX n/a   NM n/a   MIP $10

CUSTOM POSIES

❑ **Extremeliner,** 1999, 1:24 scale, Model No. 32083
EX n/a   NM n/a   MIP $20

❑ **Orange Krisp,** 1999, Bright Orange Metallic body, 1:24 scale, Model No. 32086
EX n/a   NM n/a   MIP $20

❑ **Sweptback Coupe,** 1999, Pearl Yellow body, 1:24 scale, Model No. 32085
EX n/a   NM n/a   MIP $20

CUSTOM STREET RODS

❑ **1914 Chevy Roadster,** 1989, Jacked-up rear end, racing slicks, chrome trim, 1:43 scale, Model No. 2841
EX n/a   NM n/a   MIP $15

❑ **1932 Ford Panel Truck,** 1989, Jacked-up rear end, racing slicks, chrome trim, 1:43 scale, Model No. 2844
EX n/a   NM n/a   MIP $15

❑ **1932 Ford Roadster,** 1989, Jacked-up rear end, racing slicks, chrome trim, 1:43 scale, Model No. 2842
EX n/a   NM n/a   MIP $15

❑ **1957 Chevy,** 1989, Jacked-up rear end, racing slicks, chrome trim, 1:43 scale, Model No. 2843
EX n/a   NM n/a   MIP $15

DAZED AND CONFUSED

❑ **1970 Chevelle SS 454,** 2001, Black body, white stripes, black interior, 1:18 scale, Model No. 33018
EX n/a   NM n/a   MIP $30

DAZED AND CONFUSED (1993)

❑ **1958 Plymouth Fury,** 2002, 1:18 scale, Model No. 33027
EX n/a   NM n/a   MIP $30

DICK TRACY (1990)

❑ **1936 Ford,** 1990, Dick Tracy's car, 1:64 scale, Model No. 2679
EX n/a   NM n/a   MIP $10

❑ **1936 Ford Fordor police car,** 1990, 1:64 scale, Model No. 2676
EX n/a   NM n/a   MIP $10

❑ **1937 Plymouth,** 1990, Tess' car, 1:64 scale, Model No. 2678
EX n/a   NM n/a   MIP $10

❑ **1937 Plymouth, 1936 Ford Fordor police car, 1939 Chevy, 1936 Ford,** 1990, Four-car set, 1:128 scale, Model No. 2672
EX n/a   NM n/a   MIP $28

❑ **1939 Chevy,** 1990, Itchy and Flattop's car, 1:64 scale, Model No. 2677
EX n/a   NM n/a   MIP $10

DIE-CAST KITS

❑ **1932 Ford Roadster,** 2000, Black body, red flames, 1:24 scale, Model No. 30284
EX n/a   NM n/a   MIP $12

❑ **1940 Ford Sedan Delivery,** 2000, Yellow body, black running boards, 1:64 scale, Model No. 30308
EX n/a   NM n/a   MIP $6

❑ **1940 Ford Woody,** 2000, Blue body, wood sides, 1:64 scale, Model No. 30298
EX n/a   NM n/a   MIP $6

❑ **1941 Willys Gasser,** 2000, Gold body, black top, black interior, chrome motor; packaged in window box or blister pack, 1:64 scale, Model No. 36297A
EX n/a   NM n/a   MIP $6

❑ **1949 Mercury (chopped),** 2000, 1:24 scale, Model No. 36296
EX n/a   NM n/a   MIP $12

❑ **1962 Chevy,** 2000, Silver body, 1:24 scale, Model No. 36296
EX n/a   NM n/a   MIP $12

❑ **1964 Chevy Impala custom,** 2000, Yellow body, black stripes, 1:64 scale, Model No. 30297
EX n/a   NM n/a   MIP $6

❑ **1964 Pontiac GTO,** 2000, Aqua Green body, 1:24 scale, Model No. 30285
EX n/a   NM n/a   MIP $15

❑ **1967 Corvette L71 convertible,** 1997, Black body, red stripe, red interior, 1:18 scale, Model No. 6597CO
EX n/a   NM n/a   MIP $15

❑ **1968 AMC Javelin,** 2000, Purple body, 1:24 scale, Model No. 30283
EX n/a   NM n/a   MIP $12

❑ **1968 AMC Javelin,** 2000, Red/white/blue body, 1:24 scale, Model No. 36296
EX n/a   NM n/a   MIP $12

❑ **1969 Camaro,** 2000, Yellow body, black stripes and top, black interior, chrome engine; packaged in window box or blister pack, 1:64 scale, Model No. 36297A
EX n/a   NM n/a   MIP $6

❑ **1969 Chevy Camaro,** 2000, Blue body, 1:64 scale, Model No. 30311
EX n/a   NM n/a   MIP $6

❑ **1969 Chevy Camaro Z28,** 1997, Hugger Orange body, white stripes, 1:18 scale, Model No. 6590CO
EX n/a   NM n/a   MIP $15

❑ **1969 Mercury Cougar Eliminator,** 2000, Yellow body, hood scoop, rear deck spoiler, Eliminator stripes, 1:64 scale, Model No. 30299
EX n/a   NM n/a   MIP $6

❑ **1970 Chevelle SS,** 2000, Red body, white stripes, 1:64 scale, Model No. 31000
EX n/a   NM n/a   MIP $6

❑ **1970 Dodge Super Bee,** 2000, Purple body, white interior, chrome engine; packaged in window box or blister pack, 1:64 scale, Model No. 36297A
EX n/a   NM n/a   MIP $6

❑ **1970 Plymouth Superbird,** 2000, Red body, black roof, white markings, 1:64 scale, Model No. 30310
EX n/a   NM n/a   MIP $6

❑ **1978 Pontiac Trans Am,** 2000, Gold body, black Firebird decal, 1:64 scale, Model No. 30309
EX n/a   NM n/a   MIP $6

❑ **1987 Buick Grand National,** 2000, Black body, black interior; packaged in window box or blister pack, 1:64 scale, Model No. 36297A
EX n/a   NM n/a   MIP $6

❑ **Posies Extremeliner,** 2000, 1:24 scale, Model No. 32050
EX n/a   NM n/a   MIP $12

❑ **Posies Orange Krisp,** 2000, Bright Orange Metallic body, 1:24 scale, Model No. 32052
EX n/a   NM n/a   MIP $12

❑ **Posies Sweptback Coupe,** 2000, Pearl Yellow body, 1:24 scale, Model No. 32051
EX n/a   NM n/a   MIP $12

❑ **Shelby Cobra 427 S/C,** 1997, Yellow body, black interior, 1:18 scale, Model No. 6589CO
EX n/a   NM n/a   MIP $15

DOMINO'S

❑ **Chevette: Domino's Promo,** 1988, White body with red and blue stripes, Domino's Pizza logo on sides, "Fast, Friendly, Free Delivery", 1:64 scale
EX n/a   NM n/a   MIP $8

EUROPEAN CLASSICS

❑ **1948 Jaguar XK-120,** 1991, Ivory body; crème body, tan interior, 1:18 scale, Model No. 7482
EX n/a   NM n/a   MIP $35

❑ **1948 Jaguar XK-120,** 1991, Green body; silver body, red interior, 1:18 scale, Model No. 7492
EX n/a   NM n/a   MIP $30

❑ **1948 Jaguar XK-120,** 1992, British Racing Green, tan interior, #38, 1:18 scale, Model No. 7446
EX n/a   NM n/a   MIP $45

❑ **1948 Jaguar XK-120,** 1992, die-cast kit; silver body, red interior, 1:18 scale, Model No. 7479
EX n/a   NM n/a   MIP $45

❑ **1956 Austin Healey 100-Six,** 1992, die-cast kit, 1:18 scale, Model No. 7462
EX n/a   NM n/a   MIP $45

❑ **1956 Austin Healey 100-Six,** 1992, Blue and white body, 1:18 scale, Model No. 7459
EX n/a   NM n/a   MIP $45

❑ **1960 Mercedes 190 SL,** 1992, die-cast kit, 1:18 scale, Model No. 7463
EX n/a   NM n/a   MIP $45

❑ **1960 Mercedes 190 SL convertible,** 1992, Black body, red interior, 1:18 scale, Model No. 7464
EX n/a   NM n/a   MIP $45

❑ **1960 Mercedes 190 SL hardtop,** 1992, Red body, black interior, 1:18 scale, Model No. 7465
EX n/a   NM n/a   MIP $45

❑ **1961 Austin Healey 3000,** 1992, Red body, 1:18 scale, Model No. 7460
EX n/a   NM n/a   MIP $45

❏ **1966 Ferrari 275 GTB-4,** 1991, Silver body; white body, black interior (1992), 1:18 scale, Model No. 7493
EX n/a   NM n/a   MIP $30

❏ **1966 Ferrari 275 GTB-4,** 1991, Red body, 1:18 scale, Model No. 7483
EX n/a   NM n/a   MIP $30

❏ **1966 Ferrari 275 GTB-4,** 1992, Yellow body, black interior, 1:18 scale, Model No. 7378
EX n/a   NM n/a   MIP $45

❏ **1966 Ferrari 275 GTB-4,** 1992, die-cast kit; red body, 1:18 scale, Model No. 7494
EX n/a   NM n/a   MIP $45

❏ **Ford Mk IV,** 1978, White body, speed wheels, opening hood and doors; part of set of six with display case, 1:64 scale, Model No. 1740
EX n/a   NM n/a   MIP $10

❏ **Mercedes Benz 450SE,** 1978, Silver body, speed wheels, opening hood and doors; part of set of six with display case, 1:64 scale, Model No. 1740
EX n/a   NM n/a   MIP $10

❏ **Mercedes Benz C111,** 1978, Red metallic body, speed wheels, openings hoods and doors; part of set of six with display case, 1:64 scale, Model No. 1740
EX n/a   NM n/a   MIP $10

❏ **Porsche 911,** 1978, Yellow body, speed wheels, opening hood and doors; part of set of six with display case, 1:64 scale, Model No. 1740
EX n/a   NM n/a   MIP $10

❏ **Rolls Royce Silver Shadow,** 1978, Metallic blue body, speed wheels, opening hood and doors; part of set of six with display case, 1:64 scale, Model No. 1740
EX n/a   NM n/a   MIP $10

❏ **Volkswagen 1200LS,** 1978, Red body, speed wheels, opening hood and doors; part of set of six with display case, 1:64 scale, Model No. 1740
EX n/a   NM n/a   MIP $10

FALL GUY

❏ **GMC Fleetside Pickup,** 1982, From TV series; pullback motor, 1:43 scale, Model No. 1722
EX n/a   NM n/a   MIP $7

❏ **GMC Fleetside Pickup,** 1982, From TV series; show logo on hood, brushguard, roll bar, speed wheels, 1:64 scale, Model No. 1875
EX n/a   NM n/a   MIP $7

FOLGERS

❏ **1984 Buick Regal,** 1987, Red body, 1:64 scale, Model No. 9305
EX n/a   NM n/a   MIP $6

❏ **Buick Regal,** 1986, Red body, 1:64 scale, Model No. 9410
EX n/a   NM n/a   MIP $6

FORCE ONE

❏ **AV-8B Harrier,** 1989, military markings, 1:75 scale, Model No. 1168EO
EX n/a   NM n/a   MIP $7

❏ **F-18A Hornet,** 1989, military markings, 1:91 scale, Model No. 1035EO
EX n/a   NM n/a   MIP $6

❏ **F-4 Phantom II,** 1989, military markings, 1:96 scale, Model No. 1036EO
EX n/a   NM n/a   MIP $7

FORCE ONE ARMORED SUPPORT

❏ **Apache Helicopter,** 1987, Model No. 1142
EX n/a   NM n/a   MIP $6

❏ **Armored Personnel Carrier,** 1987, Model No. 1145
EX n/a   NM n/a   MIP $6

❏ **M-1 Abrahms Tank,** 1987, Model No. 1143
EX n/a   NM n/a   MIP $6

FORCE ONE MILITARY AIRCRAFT

❏ **A-10 Thunderbolt,** 1987, 1:100 scale, Model No. 1160
EX n/a   NM n/a   MIP $6

❏ **F-14 Tomcat,** 1987, 1:100 scale, Model No. 1161
EX n/a   NM n/a   MIP $6

❏ **F-15 Eagle,** 1987, 1:100 scale, Model No. 1162
EX n/a   NM n/a   MIP $6

❏ **F-16 Falcon,** 1987, 1:100 scale, Model No. 1163
EX n/a   NM n/a   MIP $6

❏ **Stealth Fighter, Air Force,** 1987, 1:100 scale, Model No. 1164
EX n/a   NM n/a   MIP $6

FORCE ONE SQUADRON

❏ **B-1 Bomber,** 1988, with display stand, 1:100 scale, Model No. 1169EO
EX n/a   NM n/a   MIP $7

❏ **USAF SR-71 Blackbird,** 1988, with display stand, 1:100 scale, Model No. 1165EO
EX n/a   NM n/a   MIP $7

FORMULA ONE

❏ **Brabham BT45B,** 1980, Red body, Champion, #3; part of six-car set, 1:64 scale, Model No. 1736
EX n/a   NM n/a   MIP $6

❏ **Formula One Racer,** 1980, Blue/white body, Elf, #2; part of six-car set, 1:64 scale, Model No. 1736
EX n/a   NM n/a   MIP $6

❏ **Lotus 77,** 1980, Yellow body, Texaco, #6; part of six-car set, 1:64 scale, Model No. 1736
EX n/a   NM n/a   MIP $6

❏ **Lotus 78,** 1980, Black body, #5; part of six-car set, 1:64 scale, Model No. 1736
EX n/a   NM n/a   MIP $6

❏ **McLaren M23B,** 1980, White body, Gulf, #10; part of six-car set, 1:64 scale, Model No. 1736
EX n/a   NM n/a   MIP $6

❏ **McLaren M26,** 1980, White/red body, Marlboro, #11; part of six-car set, 1:64 scale, Model No. 1736
EX n/a   NM n/a   MIP $6

FUN TRUCKIN'

❏ **Chevy Van,** 1980, Blue body, 1:64 scale, Model No. 1704
EX n/a   NM n/a   MIP $10

❏ **Dodge Street Van,** 1980, Red body, 1:64 scale, Model No. 1704
EX n/a   NM n/a   MIP $12

❏ **Ford Van,** 1980, Silver body, purple/pink markings, 1:64 scale, Model No. 1768
EX n/a   NM n/a   MIP $10

❏ **GMC Stepside pickup,** 1980, Yellow body, red markings, 1:64 scale, Model No. 1769
EX n/a   NM n/a   MIP $12

❏ **IH Scout Traveler,** 1980, Brown body, white top, 1:64 scale, Model No. 1752
EX n/a   NM n/a   MIP $12

❏ **Jeep CJ-7,** 1980, Orange/red body, black top, 1:64 scale, Model No. 1766
EX n/a   NM n/a   MIP $10

GONE IN 60 SECONDS

❏ **1969 Pontiac GTO,** 2001, Midnight Green body, black vinyl top, black interior, 1:18 scale, Model No. 33019
EX n/a   NM n/a   MIP $30

GONE IN 60 SECONDS (2000)

❏ **1970 Ford Mustang Boss 302,** 2002, 1:18 scale, Model No. 33028
EX n/a   NM n/a   MIP $30

GRAND NATIONAL STOCKERS

❏ **Buick Regal, Cale Yarborough Hardee's,** 1983, Also appeared in "Pow-R-Pull" series in 1984 with pullback motor, 1:64 scale, Model No. 4078
EX n/a   NM n/a   MIP $6

❏ **Buick Regal, Kyle Petty 7-Eleven,** 1983, Also appeared in "Pow-R-Pull" series in 1984 with pullback motor, 1:64 scale, Model No. 4079
EX n/a   NM n/a   MIP $6

❏ **Buick Regal, Richard Petty STP,** 1983, Also appeared in "Pow-R-Pull" series in 1984 with pullback motor, 1:64 scale, Model No. 4076
EX n/a   NM n/a   MIP $6

❏ **Dodge Challenger, Darrell Waltrip Pepsi,** 1983, Replaced by Dale Earnhardt's Wrangler Jeans Machine in "Pow-R-Pulls" series in 1984 with pullback motor, 1:64 scale, Model No. 4077
EX n/a   NM n/a   MIP $6

GREASE

(Photo courtesy Racing Champions Ertl)

❏ **1932 Ford hot rod,** 2001, Black body, flames, black interior, removable hood, V8 engine, moon rims, 1:18 scale, Model No. 32849
EX n/a   NM n/a   MIP $30

(Photo courtesy Racing Champions Ertl)

❏ **1960 Ford Starliner hot rod,** 2001, Black body, white interior, 342cid V8, plated floor shifter and mag wheels, 1:18 scale, Model No. 32848
EX n/a   NM n/a   MIP $30

HAPPY DAYS

❏ **1957 Chevy Bel Air,** 2002, From TV series, 1:18 scale, Model No. 33031
EX n/a   NM n/a   MIP $30

HARDCASTLE AND McCORMICK

❏ **Coyote,** 1984, From TV series, 1:64 scale, Model No. 1437
EX n/a   NM n/a   MIP $6

HO SCALE

❏ **GMC General,** 1981, Silver cab, light blue/pink markings, 1:87 scale, Model No. 1910
EX n/a   NM n/a   MIP $15

❏ **Kenworth,** 1981, Red cab, yellow/orange markings, 1:87 scale, Model No. 1910
EX n/a   NM n/a   MIP $15

❏ **Kenworth, GMC cabs,** 1981, Kenworth and GMC General (#1910); set of two cabs with Exxon tanker, 7-3/4 inches, 1:87 scale, Model No. 1907
EX n/a   NM n/a   MIP $20

❏ **Mack COE,** 1981, Black cab, yellow/white markings, 1:87 scale, Model No. 1910
EX n/a   NM n/a   MIP $15

❏ **Peterbilt,** 1981, Blue cab, light blue markings, 1:87 scale, Model No. 1910
EX n/a   NM n/a   MIP $15

❏ **Peterbilt, Mack cabs,** 1981, Peterbilt and Mack COE (#1910); set of two cabs with Pepsi container trailer, 7-3/4 inches, 1:87 scale, Model No. 1907
EX n/a   NM n/a   MIP $20

HOT RODS

❏ **1932 Ford,** 2000, 1:18 scale, Model No. 36287
EX n/a   NM n/a   MIP $30

❏ **1932 Ford five-window coupe,** 2000, Red body, tan interior, 1:18 scale, Model No. 36290
EX n/a   NM n/a   MIP $30

❏ **1934 Ford,** 2000, 1:18 scale, Model No. 36290
EX n/a   NM n/a   MIP $30

❏ **1940 Ford,** 2000, 1:18 scale, Model No. 36287
EX n/a   NM n/a   MIP $30

❏ **1949 Mercury,** 2000, 1:18 scale, Model No. 36290
EX n/a   NM n/a   MIP $30

❏ **1951 Mercury,** 2000, 1:18 scale, Model No. 36291
EX n/a   NM n/a   MIP $30

INDY 500 PACE CARS

(Photo courtesy Racing Champions Ertl)

❏ **1955 Chevy Bel Air,** 1999, Gypsy Red/Ivory body, pace car graphics, 1:18 scale, Model No. 7124DP
EX n/a   NM n/a   MIP $32

❏ **1964-1/2 Ford Mustang convertible,** 1998, Wimbledon White body, blue racing stripes, Indy 500 graphics, 1:12 scale, Model No. 7125CO
EX n/a   NM n/a   MIP $45

❏ **1969 Camaro convertible,** 1998, White body, orange stripes and interior, Indy 500 graphics, 1:18 scale, Model No. 7100DP
EX n/a   NM n/a   MIP $30

INDY WINNERS

❑ **Penske PC9,** 1981, Blue body, yellow/white markings, Bobby Unser, Norton, #11, 5 inches, 1:43 scale, Model No. 1555
EX n/a **NM** n/a **MIP** $15

❑ **Penske PC9,** 1981, Blue body, red markings, Rick Mears, Gould, #1, 5 inches, 1:43 scale, Model No. 1555
EX n/a **NM** n/a **MIP** $15

❑ **Penske PC9,** 1981, Brown body, white markings, Bill Alsup, #12, 5 inches, 1:43 scale, Model No. 1555
EX n/a **NM** n/a **MIP** $15

❑ **Penske PC9,** 1981, Blue body, white/red markings, Mario Andretti, Essex, 5 inches, 1:43 scale, Model No. 1555
EX n/a **NM** n/a **MIP** $15

❑ **Penske PC9,** 1982, White body, green/red markings, Josele Garza, "Mexico" markings, 1:43 scale, Model No. 1555
EX n/a **NM** n/a **MIP** $15

INTERNATIONAL CLASSICS

❑ **BMW 733,** 1981, Metallic blue body, opening doors and hood, speed wheels, 1:43 scale, Model No. 1550
EX n/a **NM** n/a **MIP** $15

❑ **BMW Sports Wagon,** 1981, Silver body, opening doors and hatch, speed wheels, 1:43 scale, Model No. 1546
EX n/a **NM** n/a **MIP** $15

❑ **Mercedes-Benz 350SE,** 1981, Metallic red body, opening doors and hood, speed wheels, 1:43 scale, Model No. 1545
EX n/a **NM** n/a **MIP** $15

❑ **Porsche 924,** 1981, Yellow body, opening doors and hatch, speed wheels, 1:43 scale, Model No. 1548
EX n/a **NM** n/a **MIP** $15

❑ **VW Beetle,** 1981, Gold body, opening doors, speed wheels, 1:43 scale, Model No. 1547
EX n/a **NM** n/a **MIP** $15

❑ **VW Rabbit,** 1981, Red body, opening hatch, hood and doors, speed wheels, 1:43 scale, Model No. 1549
EX n/a **NM** n/a **MIP** $15

JOHN FORCE

(Photo courtesy Racing Champions Ertl)

❑ **1967 Ford Shelby GT 350,** 2002, Red body, yellow/white flames, "11-Time Champion" graphics, 1:18 scale, Model No. 77448
EX n/a **NM** n/a **MIP** $30

(Photo courtesy Racing Champions Ertl)

❑ **1967 Ford Shelby GT 350,** 2002, White body, yellow/black flames, "11-Time Champion" graphics, 1:18 scale, Model No. 77448
EX n/a **NM** n/a **MIP** $30

JOHN FORCE CARS

(Photo courtesy Racing Champions Ertl)

❑ **1961 Corvette,** 2001, Black body, white side cove, black interior and roof, plated air cleaner, etched valve covers, John Force signature on roof, 1:18 scale, Model No. 32892
EX n/a **NM** n/a **MIP** $30

(Photo courtesy Racing Champions Ertl)

❑ **1966 Pontiac GTO,** 2001, Tiger Gold body, black interior, black vinyl roof, plated tri-carbs and valve covers, plated console and Hurst shifter, 1:18 scale, Model No. 32893
EX n/a **NM** n/a **MIP** $30

(Photo courtesy Racing Champions Ertl)

❑ **1969 Plymouth,** 2001, Toreador Red body, flat black stripes, black interior, black vinyl roof, Air Grabber hood, redline tires, plated five-spoke wheels, 1:18 scale, Model No. 32894
EX n/a **NM** n/a **MIP** $30

❑ **1970 Ford Mustang Boss,** 2001, Black body, black interior, Larry Shinoda-inspired white graphics, Shaker hood, 302cid engine, Holley four-barrel carb, plated shifter, 1:18 scale, Model No. 32896
EX n/a **NM** n/a **MIP** $30

KNIGHT RIDER

❑ **Knight Rider Firebird,** 1986, From TV series; black body; originally only available in Great Britain, 1:64 scale, Model No. 1377
EX n/a **NM** n/a **MIP** $6

LAND ROVERS

❑ **Automobile Service Land Rover,** 1988, Yellow body, tow hitch, removable top; sold only in Europe and Australia, 1:64 scale, Model No. 1193
EX n/a **NM** n/a **MIP** $10

❑ **Farm Land Rover,** 1988, Green body, brown soft-top effect, tow hitch, removable top; sold only in Europe and Australia, 1:64 scale, Model No. 1195
EX n/a   NM n/a   MIP $10

❑ **Police Land Rover,** 1988, White body, orange and black markings, tow hitch, removable top; sold only in Europe and Australia, 1:64 scale, Model No. 1194
EX n/a   NM n/a   MIP $10

❑ **Royal Marines Land Rover,** 1988, Army green body, tow hitch, removable top; sold only in Europe and Australia, 1:64 scale, Model No. 1199
EX n/a   NM n/a   MIP $10

LOWRIDERS

❑ **1964 Chevy Impala,** 2000, Orange body, yellow accents, orange interior, 1:18 scale, Model No. 36288
EX n/a   NM n/a   MIP $30

MADE IN AMERICA

❑ **1984 Corvette,** 1984, Silver body; special yellow version released (Collector "01") and limited to 7,500, 1:64 scale, Model No. 1387
EX n/a   NM n/a   MIP $10

❑ **1984 Pontiac Firebird,** 1984, 1:64 scale, Model No. 1389
EX n/a   NM n/a   MIP $10

❑ **Dodge Shelby Charger,** 1984, 1:64 scale, Model No. 1388
EX n/a   NM n/a   MIP $10

❑ **Pontiac Fiero,** 1984, 1:64 scale, Model No. 1399
EX n/a   NM n/a   MIP $10

MATT HOUSTON

❑ **Cadillac convertible,** 1983, From TV series; black body, white interior, white "Matt Houston" on side, 1:64 scale, Model No. 1435AO
EX n/a   NM n/a   MIP $6

❑ **Excalibur,** 1983, From TV series; white body, black interior, red "Houston" markings on side, 1:64 scale, Model No. 1620
EX n/a   NM n/a   MIP $6

❑ **Ford Bronco,** 1983, From TV series; white body, black top, red "Matt Houston" markings on side, 1:64 scale, Model No. 1621
EX n/a   NM n/a   MIP $6

❑ **Helicopter,** 1983, From TV series; yellow body, gray blades, red "Matt Houston" on side, 1:100 scale, Model No. 1436SO
EX n/a   NM n/a   MIP $6

❑ **Maserati,** 1983, From TV series; blue/gray body, tan interior, white "Matt Houston" on side, 1:64 scale, Model No. 1435AO
EX n/a   NM n/a   MIP $8

MIGHTY CORPS.

❑ **Crawler,** 1986, Camouflage body, military decals, Model No. 1031
EX n/a   NM n/a   MIP $6

❑ **Hauler,** 1986, Camouflage body, military decals, Model No. 1033
EX n/a   NM n/a   MIP $6

❑ **Road Grader,** 1986, Camouflage body, military decals, Model No. 1034
EX n/a   NM n/a   MIP $6

❑ **Wheel Loader,** 1986, Camouflage body, military decals, Model No. 1032
EX n/a   NM n/a   MIP $6

MIGHTY MOVER TRUCKS

❑ **Ford LTL 9000 cab with tanker,** 1987, Blue body, 1:64 scale, Model No. 1184EO
EX n/a   NM n/a   MIP $8

❑ **Mack COE with livestock trailer,** 1987, White and silver, 1:64 scale, Model No. 1188EO
EX n/a   NM n/a   MIP $8

❑ **Navistar International cab with grain trailer,** 1987, Red body, 1:64 scale, Model No. 1187EO
EX n/a   NM n/a   MIP $8

MIGHTY MOVERS OF THE WORLD

❑ **IH 350 Hauler,** 1979, Yellow/white body, working dumpster, 2-1/2 inches, 1:80 scale, Model No. 1852
EX n/a   NM n/a   MIP $12

❑ **IH 560 Wheel Loader,** 1979, Yellow/white body, articulated frome, moving bucket, 4-3/4 inches, 1:80 scale, Model No. 1850
EX n/a   NM n/a   MIP $12

❑ **IH Backhoe/Loader,** 1979, Yellow/white body, moving backhoe and front-end loader, 3 inches, 1:64 scale, Model No. 1853
EX n/a   NM n/a   MIP $12

❑ **IH Excavatory 640,** 1981, Yellow/white/black body, moving bucket and boom, body pivots 360 degrees, rubber track, 5-7/8 inches, 1:64 scale, Model No. 1854
EX n/a   NM n/a   MIP $10

❑ **IH Scraper 412B,** 1981, Yellow/white cab, articulated body (90 degrees), rubber elevator, scraper pivots down, 5-7/8 inches, 1:64 scale, Model No. 1855
EX n/a   NM n/a   MIP $10

❑ **IH TD-20E Crawler,** 1979, Yellow body, rolling rubber tracks, lifting front blade, 3-1/2 inches, 1:64 scale, Model No. 1851
EX n/a   NM n/a   MIP $10

MILITARY

❑ **Air Force F-15, Air Force F-16,** 1991, each 1-1/2 inches long, Model No. 791
EX n/a   NM n/a   MIP $7

❑ **Air Force F-15, Russian Mig 29,** 1991, each 1-1/2 inches long, Model No. 792
EX n/a   NM n/a   MIP $7

❑ **BAC Jaguar,** 1978, Camouflage body, RAF, Model No. 1511
EX n/a   NM n/a   MIP $10

❑ **Boeing 747-200B Air Force One,** 1989, 1:470 scale, Model No. 1499FO
EX n/a   NM n/a   MIP $10

❑ **Grumman F-11F Tiger,** 1978, Blue body, Blue Angels, Model No. 1511
EX n/a   NM n/a   MIP $10

❑ **Lockheed F-104 Starfighter,** 1978, Dark Camouflage body, German Air Force, Model No. 1511
EX n/a   NM n/a   MIP $11

❑ **Marines F-18, Marines Harrier,** 1991, each 1-1/2 inches long, Model No. 293
EX n/a   NM n/a   MIP $7

❑ **McDonnell F-4E Phantom,** 1978, Camouflage body, Model No. 1511
EX n/a   NM n/a   MIP $10

❑ **Mig 21,** 1978, Silver body, Soviet Air Force, Model No. 1511
EX n/a   NM n/a   MIP $11

❑ **Navy F-18, Navy F-14,** 1991, each 1-1/2 inches long, Model No. 794
EX n/a   **NM** n/a   **MIP** $7

❑ **Saab Draken,** 1978, Dark camouflage body, Sweden, Model No. 1511
EX n/a   **NM** n/a   **MIP** $10

MILLENNIUM

(Photo courtesy Racing Champions Ertl)

❑ **1935 Auburn 851,** 2000, Emerald Green anodized finish, #1 in series, 1:18 scale, Model No. 32232
EX n/a   **NM** n/a   **MIP** $30

❑ **1936 Duesenberg SSJ,** 2000, Silver anodized finish, #10 in series, 1:18 scale, Model No. 32243
EX n/a   **NM** n/a   **MIP** $30

(Photo courtesy Racing Champions Ertl)

❑ **1940 Ford,** 2000, Burgundy anodized finish, #2 in series, 1:18 scale, Model No. 32233
EX n/a   **NM** n/a   **MIP** $30

❑ **1949 Mercury,** 2000, Black anodized finish, #3 in series, 1:18 scale, Model No. 32234
EX n/a   **NM** n/a   **MIP** $30

(Photo courtesy Racing Champions Ertl)

❑ **1955 Chevy convertible,** 2000, Copper anodized finish, #4 in series, 1:18 scale, Model No. 32235
EX n/a   **NM** n/a   **MIP** $30

(Photo courtesy Racing Champions Ertl)

❑ **1963 Corvette,** 2000, Red anodized finish, #5 in series, 1:18 scale, Model No. 32236
EX n/a   **NM** n/a   **MIP** $30

(Photo courtesy Racing Champions Ertl)

❑ **1965 Shelby Cobra,** 2000, Blue anodized finish, #6 in series, 1:18 scale, Model No. 32237
EX n/a   **NM** n/a   **MIP** $30

(Photo courtesy Racing Champions Ertl)

❑ **1967 Ford Mustang GT,** 2000, Yellow anodized finish, #7 in series, 1:18 scale, Model No. 32239
EX n/a   **NM** n/a   **MIP** $30

❑ **1969 Olds 4-4-2,** 2000, Gold or red anodized finish, #8 in series, 1:18 scale, Model No. 32240
EX n/a   **NM** n/a   **MIP** $30

(Photo courtesy Racing Champions Ertl)

❑ **1970 Chevelle,** 2000, Orange anodized finish, #9 in series, 1:18 scale, Model No. 32242
EX n/a   **NM** n/a   **MIP** $30

NASA

❑ **747 Shuttle Package,** 1979, Removable space shuttle on 747 jumbo jet with retractable landing gear, 6 inches, 1:500 scale, Model No. 1513
EX n/a   **NM** n/a   **MIP** $15

❑ **Columbia Space Shuttle,** 1985, 3 inches long, Model No. 1535
EX n/a   **NM** n/a   **MIP** $6

❑ **Shuttle,** 1985, pullback motor, 4.75 inches long, Model No. 1534
EX n/a   **NM** n/a   **MIP** $6

❑ **Shuttle Package,** 1985, Space shuttle riding on 747 jumbo jet, Model No. 1513
EX n/a   **NM** n/a   **MIP** $12

❑ **Space Shuttle "Enterprise",** 1979, Opening cargo doors, removable three-section space lab payload, retractable landing gear, 7-1/4 inches, 1:196 scale, Model No. 1514
EX n/a   **NM** n/a   **MIP** $12

❑ **Space Shuttle Orbiter,** 1979, Launching pad, two detachable booster rockets, 6 inches, 1:500 scale, Model No. 1515
EX n/a   **NM** n/a   **MIP** $9

❑ **Space Shuttle Orbiter,** 1985, 3 inches long, Model No. 1515
EX n/a   **NM** n/a   **MIP** $8

❑ **U.S. Space Shuttle,** 1985, Opening cargo door, retractable landing gear, 7.5 inches long; includes decal sheet for Columbia, Challenger, Discovery or Atlantis customs, Model No. 1514
EX n/a   **NM** n/a   **MIP** $8

PERFORMANCE SPORT

❑ **1979 Corvette,** 1979, Silver body, red interior, opening hood and doors, movable seats, detailed chrome engine, 1:25 scale, Model No. 1676
EX n/a   NM n/a   MIP $25

❑ **Chevy Stepside Pickup,** 1979, Brown body and interior, opening hood and doors, movable seats, chrome engine, 1:25 scale, Model No. 1677
EX n/a   NM n/a   MIP $25

❑ **Jeep CJ7,** 1979, Yellow body, black top, opening hood and doors, movable seats, chrome engine, 1:25 scale, Model No. 1675
EX n/a   NM n/a   MIP $25

❑ **Pontiac Trans Am,** 1979, Black body, black interior, T-tops, gold wheels, opening hood and doors, movable seats, detailed chrome engine, 1:25 scale, Model No. 1678
EX n/a   NM n/a   MIP $25

POW-R-PULL

❑ **1964 Ford Mustang,** 1983, Pullback motor; packaged with jump ramp, start sign, four plastic pylons, 1:64 scale, Model No. 1767
EX n/a   NM n/a   MIP $6

❑ **1983 Ford Thunderbird,** 1983, Pullback motor; packaged with jump ramp, start sign, four plastic pylons, 1:64 scale, Model No. 1735
EX n/a   NM n/a   MIP $6

❑ **1983 Mustang,** 1983, Pullback motor; packaged with jump ramp, start sign, four plastic pylons, 1:64 scale, Model No. 1711
EX n/a   NM n/a   MIP $6

❑ **1984 Corvette,** 1983, Pullback motor; packaged with jump ramp, start sign, four plastic pylons, 1:64 scale, Model No. 1710
EX n/a   NM n/a   MIP $6

❑ **Cale Yarborough's Hardee's,** 1983, pullback motor, 1:64 scale, Model No. 4020
EX n/a   NM n/a   MIP $6

❑ **Camaro,** 1983, Pullback motor; packaged with jump ramp, start sign, four plastic pylons, 1:64 scale, Model No. 1732
EX n/a   NM n/a   MIP $6

❑ **Coyote,** 1984, From "Hardcastle and McCormick" TV series; with pullback motor, 1:48 scale, Model No. 3227
EX n/a   NM n/a   MIP $6

❑ **Dale Earnhardt's Wrangler,** 1983, pullback motor, 1:64 scale, Model No. 4020
EX n/a   NM n/a   MIP $6

❑ **Darrell Waltrip's Pepsi Challenger,** 1983, pullback motor, 1:64 scale, Model No. 4020
EX n/a   NM n/a   MIP $6

❑ **Pontiac Firebird,** 1983, Pullback motor; packaged with jump ramp, start sign, four plastic pylons, 1:64 scale, Model No. 1731
EX n/a   NM n/a   MIP $6

❑ **Richard Petty's STP,** 1983, pullback motor, 1:64 scale, Model No. 4020
EX n/a   NM n/a   MIP $6

❑ **Van,** 1983, From "The A Team" TV series; pullback motor, 1:48 scale, Model No. 3225
EX n/a   NM n/a   MIP $6

PROSHOP DIE CAST

❑ **Dodge Avenger Funny Car,** 2000, Kendall, Frank Manzo; hinged body reveals blown engine and undercarriage, 1:24 scale, Model No. 32391
EX n/a   NM n/a   MIP $20

❑ **Dodge Avenger Funny Car,** 2000, Valvoline, Bob Newberry; hinged body reveals blown engine and undercarriage, 1:24 scale, Model No. 32392
EX n/a   NM n/a   MIP $20

❑ **Dodge Avenger Funny Car,** 2000, Pioneer, Cory Lee; hinged body reveals blown engine and undercarriage, 1:24 scale, Model No. 32390
EX n/a   NM n/a   MIP $20

❑ **Ford Thunderbird,** 2000, McDonald's, Bill Elliott, #94, 1:18 scale, Model No. 32381
EX n/a   NM n/a   MIP $30

❑ **Top Fuel Dragster,** 2000, Exide, Tony Schumacher; removable top cover, 1:24 scale, Model No. 32394
EX n/a   NM n/a   MIP $20

❑ **Top Fuel Dragster,** 2000, Jerzees, Bob Vandergriff; removable top cover, 1:24 scale, Model No. 32393
EX n/a   NM n/a   MIP $20

PULLERS

❑ **Intimidator,** 1986, pullback motor, 1:64 scale, Model No. 4089
EX n/a   NM n/a   MIP $10

❑ **Kenworth,** 1986, pullback motor, 1:64 scale, Model No. 4086
EX n/a   NM n/a   MIP $10

❑ **Tennessee Thunder,** 1986, pullback motor, 1:64 scale, Model No. 4088
EX n/a   NM n/a   MIP $10

RACING

❑ **Chevy Lumina,** 1992, Dale Jarrett #18 Interstate, black/green body, race markings, 1:18 scale, Model No. 7474
EX n/a   NM n/a   MIP $30

❑ **Chevy Lumina,** 1992, Ernie Irvan #4 Kodak, yellow body, race markings, 1:18 scale, Model No. 7450
EX n/a   NM n/a   MIP $45

❑ **Chevy Monte Carlo,** 1996, Western Auto, Darrell Waltrip #17, 1:18 scale, Model No. 7281DO
EX n/a   NM n/a   MIP $35

❑ **Chevy Monte Carlo,** 1996, Kellogg's Corn Flakes, Terry Labonte #5, 1:18 scale, Model No. 7219DO
EX n/a   NM n/a   MIP $35

❑ **Chevy Monte Carlo,** 1996, Budweiser, #25, 1:18 scale, Model No. 7217DO
EX n/a   NM n/a   MIP $35

❑ **Chevy Monte Carlo,** 1996, Kellogg's Corn Flakes, special edition silver body, #5, 1:18 scale, Model No. 7116DP
EX n/a   NM n/a   MIP $35

❑ **Chevy Monte Carlo,** 1998, Western Auto's Parts America, #17, 1:18 scale, Model No. 7370DP
EX n/a   NM n/a   MIP $30

❑ **Chevy Monte Carlo,** 1998, Kodak Film, 1:18 scale, Model No. 7335DP
EX n/a   NM n/a   MIP $30

❑ **Chevy Monte Carlo,** 1998, Kellogg's Monte Carlo, #5, 1:18 scale, Model No. 7362DP
EX n/a   NM n/a   MIP $30

ERTL / AMERICAN MUSCLE

❑ **Chevy Monte Carlo,** 1999, Kodak, #4, 1:18 scale, Model No. 7916DP
EX n/a   NM n/a   MIP $30

❑ **Chevy Monte Carlo,** 1999, Kellogg's, 1:18 scale, Model No. 7917DP
EX n/a   NM n/a   MIP $45

❑ **Chevy Monte Carlo,** 1999, Coors, 1:18 scale, Model No. 7918DP
EX n/a   NM n/a   MIP $30

❑ **Chevy Monte Carlo,** 1999, Valvoline, 1:18 scale, Model No. 7924DP
EX n/a   NM n/a   MIP $30

❑ **Chevy Monte Carlo,** 1999, STP, 1:18 scale, Model No. 7922DP
EX n/a   NM n/a   MIP $30

❑ **Chevy Monte Carlo,** 1999, Cheerios, 1:18 scale, Model No. 7923DP
EX n/a   NM n/a   MIP $30

❑ **Chevy SuperTruck,** 1996, Sears Die-Hard, Mike Chase #1, 1:18 scale, Model No. 7364DP
EX n/a   NM n/a   MIP $35

❑ **Chevy SuperTruck,** 1996, AC Delco, Ken Schrader #52, 1:18 scale, Model No. 7287DO
EX n/a   NM n/a   MIP $35

❑ **Chevy SuperTruck,** 1996, DuPont Auto Refinish, #24, 1:18 scale, Model No. 7289DO
EX n/a   NM n/a   MIP $35

❑ **Chevy SuperTruck,** 1996, GM Goodwrench, Mike Skinner #3, 1:18 scale, Model No. 7286DO
EX n/a   NM n/a   MIP $35

❑ **Chevy SuperTruck,** 1996, Quaker State, 1:18 scale, Model No. 7363DP
EX n/a   NM n/a   MIP $40

❑ **Dallara,** 1998, IRL, Buddy Lazier, Cinergy, #91, 1:43 scale, Model No. 7090EO
EX n/a   NM n/a   MIP $10

❑ **Dallara,** 1998, Buddy Lazier, 1:43 scale, Model No. 7315KO
EX n/a   NM n/a   MIP $8

❑ **Dallara,** 1998, Roberto Guerrero, 1:43 scale, Model No. 7314KO
EX n/a   NM n/a   MIP $10

❑ **Dallara,** 1998, Guthrie, 1:43 scale, Model No. 7311KO

❑ **Dallara,** 1998, IRL, John Paul Jr., Klipsch, #18, 1:43 scale, Model No. 7091EO
EX n/a   NM n/a   MIP $10

❑ **Dallara,** 1998, IRL, Jim Guthrie, Jacuzzi, #27, 1:43 scale, Model No. 7085EO
EX n/a   NM n/a   MIP $10

❑ **Dallara,** 1998, IRL, Roberto Guerrero, Pennzoil, #21, 1:43 scale, Model No. 7086EO
EX n/a   NM n/a   MIP $10

❑ **Ford SuperTruck,** 1996, Ortho Lawn and Garden Care, Tobey Butler #21, 1:18 scale, Model No. 7288DO
EX n/a   NM n/a   MIP $35

❑ **Ford SuperTruck,** 1996, QVC, #07, 1:18 scale, Model No. 7118DP
EX n/a   NM n/a   MIP $35

❑ **Ford SuperTruck,** 1996, Raybestos, Butch Miller #98, 1:18 scale, Model No. 7285DO
EX n/a   NM n/a   MIP $30

❑ **Ford Thunderbird,** 1995, Red body, Budweiser markings, Bill Elliott #11, 1:18 scale, Model No. 7358DO
EX n/a   NM n/a   MIP $40

❑ **Ford Thunderbird,** 1995, Blue, white and red body, Valvoline markings, Mark Martin #6, 1:18 scale, Model No. 7357DO
EX n/a   NM n/a   MIP $30

❑ **Ford Thunderbird,** 1996, Valvoline, Mark Martin #6, 1:18 scale, Model No. 7283DO
EX n/a   NM n/a   MIP $35

❑ **Ford Thunderbird,** 1996, Quality Care, 1:18 scale, Model No. 7806DP
EX n/a   NM n/a   MIP $35

❑ **Ford Thunderbird,** 1996, Raybestos, Jeff Burton #8, 1:18 scale, Model No. 7221DO
EX n/a   NM n/a   MIP $35

❑ **Ford Thunderbird,** 1996, McDonald's, Bill Elliott #94, 1:18 scale, Model No. 7220DO
EX n/a   NM n/a   MIP $35

❑ **Ford Thunderbird,** 1996, Family Channel, Ted Musgrave #16, 1:18 scale, Model No. 7360DO
EX n/a   NM n/a   MIP $35

❑ **Ford Thunderbird,** 1996, Valvoline, #6, 1:18 scale, Model No. 7222DO
EX n/a   NM n/a   MIP $35

❑ **Ford Thunderbird,** 1998, Valvoline, 1:18 scale, Model No. 7373DP
EX n/a   NM n/a   MIP $30

❑ **Ford Thunderbird,** 1998, McDonald's, 1:18 scale, Model No. 7799DP
EX n/a   NM n/a   MIP $35

❑ **Ford Thunderbird,** 1998, Family Channel, #16, 1:18 scale, Model No. 7798DP
EX n/a   NM n/a   MIP $30

❑ **Ford Thunderbird,** 1998, Exide Batteries, #99, 1:18 scale, Model No. 7810DP
EX n/a   NM n/a   MIP $30

❑ **Ford Thunderbird,** 1998, Quality Care, #88, 1:18 scale, Model No. 7806DP
EX n/a   NM n/a   MIP $30

❑ **G-Force,** 1998, IRL, Robbie Buhl, Quaker State, #3, 1:43 scale, Model No. 7095EO
EX n/a   NM n/a   MIP $10

❑ **G-Force,** 1998, IRL, Davey Hamilton, Power Team, #14, 1:43 scale, Model No. 7096EO
EX n/a   NM n/a   MIP $10

❑ **G-Force,** 1998, IRL, Tony Stewart, Glidden, #2, 1:43 scale, Model No. 7097EO
EX n/a   NM n/a   MIP $10

❑ **G-Force,** 1998, Stewart, 1:43 scale, Model No. 7318KO
EX n/a   NM n/a   MIP $8

❑ **G-Force,** 1998, Buhl, 1:43 scale, Model No. 7317KO
EX n/a   NM n/a   MIP $8

❑ **G-Force,** 1998, IRL, Arie Luyendyk, Nortel, #5, 1:43 scale, Model No. 7094EO
EX n/a   NM n/a   MIP $8

❑ **G-Force,** 1998, Arie Luyendyk, 1:43 scale, Model No. 7316KO
EX n/a   NM n/a   MIP $8

❑ **Pontiac Grand Prix,** 1992, Richard Petty #43 STP, blue/red body, race markings, 1:18 scale, Model No. 7461
EX n/a   NM n/a   MIP $40

❑ **Pontiac Grand Prix,** 1992, Kyle Petty #42 Mello Yello, black body, flourescent race markings, 1:18 scale, Model No. 7448
EX n/a   NM n/a   MIP $45

❑ **Pontiac Grand Prix,** 1996, Pennzoil, 1:18 scale, Model No. 7800DP
EX n/a   NM n/a   MIP $35

❏ **Pontiac Grand Prix,** 1996, Hooter's, 1:18 scale, Model No. 7112DP
EX n/a   NM n/a   MIP $35

❏ **Pontiac Grand Prix,** 1998, Skittles, #36, 1:18 scale, Model No. 7371DP
EX n/a   NM n/a   MIP $30

❏ **Reynard,** 1998, CART, Gil de Ferran, Valvoline, #5, 1:18 scale, Model No. 7213DP
EX n/a   NM n/a   MIP $30

❏ **Reynard,** 1998, CART, Alex Zanardi, Target, #4, 1:18 scale, Model No. 7265DP
EX n/a   NM n/a   MIP $30

❏ **Reynard,** 1998, CART, Bobby Rahal, Miller Lite, 1:18 scale, Model No. 7272DP
EX n/a   NM n/a   MIP $30

❏ **Reynard,** 1998, CART, Jimmy Vasser, Target, #1, 1:18 scale, Model No. 7216DP
EX n/a   NM n/a   MIP $30

❏ **Swift,** 1998, CART, Christian Fittipaldi, Kmart, #11, 1:18 scale, Model No. 7793DP
EX n/a   NM n/a   MIP $30

❏ **Swift,** 1998, CART, Michael Andretti, Kmart, #6, 1:18 scale, Model No. 7794DP
EX n/a   NM n/a   MIP $30

READY TO RUMBLE

❏ **1934 Ford street rod,** 1998, Green body, green interior; red body, yellow flames, black interior (1999), 1:18 scale, Model No. 7726DP
EX n/a   NM n/a   MIP $30

❏ **1957 Chevy,** 1996, Purple Pearl, chrome engine, "Blown and Wild" base that actives sounds, lights and rumbling action, 1:18 scale, Model No. 7156DO
EX n/a   NM n/a   MIP $35

❏ **1957 Chevy,** 1996, Red body, yellow flames, chrome engine, "Blown and Wild" base that actives sounds, lights and rumbling action, 1:18 scale, Model No. 7399DO
EX n/a   NM n/a   MIP $35

❏ **1957 Chevy street rod,** 1998, Turquoise body, hot magenta scallops, turquoise interior, 1:18 scale, Model No. 7929DP
EX n/a   NM n/a   MIP $30

❏ **Corvette Engines,** 1999, Set of three, including 1957 283cid fuel-injected small-block V8, 1960s 427cid big-block V8, 1990s Hi-Tech 350cid dual-overhead cam LS1, 1:12 scale, Model No. 7987DP
EX n/a   NM n/a   MIP $25

❏ **Harley-Davidson Evolution,** 1999, Black display base; push button activates rumbling sounds, 1:4 scale, Model No. 7966CP
EX n/a   NM n/a   MIP $25

❏ **Harley-Davidson Vintage Engines,** 1999, Set of three, including Knucklehead, Shovelhead and Panhead, 1:6 scale, Model No. 7965CP
EX n/a   NM n/a   MIP $25

REPLICA

❏ **1913 Ford Model T van street rod,** 1982, Metallic maroon and black body, speed wheels, large rear tires, chrome exhaust pipe, chrome radiator, two-color tampo; first appeared in 1981; made in Taiwan, 1:64 scale, Model No. 1931
EX n/a   NM n/a   MIP $15

❏ **1923 Ford Model T bucket street rod,** 1982, Bright red and black body, speed wheels, exposed chrome V8 engine, running boards, open front windows, large rear tires, simulated storage compartment on rear, two color tampo; first appeared in 1981; made in Taiwan, 1:64 scale, Model No. 1929
EX n/a   NM n/a   MIP $15

❏ **1932 Ford coupe five-window,** 1982, Beige and black body, speed wheels, extended bumper with spare tire, fender-mounted headlights, running boards; first appeared in 1978 with opening doors; made in Hong Kong, 1:64 scale, Model No. 1932
EX n/a   NM n/a   MIP $15

❏ **1932 Ford coupe street rod,** 1982, Bright red body, speed wheels, large rear tires, chopped roof, exposed chrome V8 engine, tinted windows, two-color tampo; first appeared in 1981; made in Taiwan, 1:64 scale, Model No. 1923
EX n/a   NM n/a   MIP $15

❏ **1934 Ford sedan street rod,** 1982, Metallic silver body, speed wheels, chopped roof, exposed chrome V8 engine, tinted windows, two-color tampo; first appeared in 1981; made in Taiwan, 1:64 scale, Model No. 1924
EX n/a   NM n/a   MIP $15

❏ **1940 Ford coupe street rod,** 1982, Maroon body, speed wheels, sunroof, tinted windows, two-color tampo; first appeared in 1981; made in Taiwan, 1:64 scale, Model No. 1927
EX n/a   NM n/a   MIP $15

❏ **1950 Ford convertible,** 1982, Blue, beige or red body, 1:64 scale, Model No. 1919
EX n/a   NM n/a   MIP $10

❏ **1950 Mercury two-door coupe,** 1982, Maroon or red body, 1:64 scale, Model No. 1913
EX n/a   NM n/a   MIP $10

❏ **1951 Chevy sedan,** 1982, Light green, black or dark green body, 1:64 scale, Model No. 1922
EX n/a   NM n/a   MIP $15

❏ **1955 Chevy Nomad station wagon,** 1982, Blue or gold body, 1:64 scale, Model No. 1914
EX n/a   NM n/a   MIP $12

❏ **1956 Ford Crown Victoria hardtop,** 1982, Black body, 1:64 scale, Model No. 1921
EX n/a   NM n/a   MIP $10

❏ **1957 Chevy convertible street rod,** 1982, Metallic green body, tinted windows, continental kit and fender flares, two color tampo; first appeared in 1981; made in Taiwan, 1:64 scale, Model No. 1928
EX n/a   NM n/a   MIP $15

❏ **1957 Chevy two-door hardtop,** 1982, Orange or white body, 1:64 scale, Model No. 1911
EX n/a   NM n/a   MIP $10

❏ **1957 Ford Thunderbird,** 1982, Azure Blue body, speed wheels, opening hood with detailed engine; first appeared in "American Classics" series in 1978 with opening doors; made in Hong Kong, 1:64 scale, Model No. 1933
EX n/a   NM n/a   MIP $15

❏ **1963 Corvette Stingray,** 1982, Red body, speed wheels; first appeared in "American Classics" series in 1978 with opening hood; made in Hong Kong, 1:64 scale, Model No. 1935
EX n/a   NM n/a   MIP $15

ERTL / AUTOMOBILES

❑ **1964-1/2 Ford Mustang,** 1982, Yellow body, speed wheels, tinted windows; made in Hong Kong, 1:64 scale, Model No. 1889
EX n/a   NM n/a   MIP $12

❑ **1976 Camaro,** 1982, Orange (#55) or light blue body, speed wheels, hood scoop, rear spoiler, two-color decals; first appeared in 1981; made in Hong Kong and Taiwan. Also sold through Hardee's restaurants as Hardee's Road Runner #90, 1:64 scale, Model No. 1878
EX n/a   NM n/a   MIP $15

❑ **1980 Pontiac Bonneville police car,** 1982, Gold body, speed wheels, light bar, sheriff decal; also white body with blue light bar (1982); also appeared in "The Dukes of Hazzard" and "Smokey and the Bandit II" series (gold body, sheriff's decal, red lights); made in Hong Kong, Singapore, U.S., 1:64 scale, Model No. 1728
EX n/a   NM n/a   MIP $15

❑ **1980 Pontiac Firebird Turbo,** 1982, Black body, speed wheels, gold Firebird decal; first appeared in "American Classics" series in 1978 as a 1977 Firebird with opening doors and die-cast chassis; changed to a 1980 Firebird in 1980. 1977 Firebird was sold as the "Smokey and the Bandit II" car; made in Hong Kong., 1:64 scale, Model No. 1936
EX n/a   NM n/a   MIP $15

❑ **1982 Camaro,** 1982, Red body, speed wheels, T bar roof, rear spoiler, tinted windows; made in Hong Kong, 1:64 scale, Model No. 1882
EX n/a   NM n/a   MIP $12

❑ **1982 Chevy Mini Truck,** 1982, Yellow or black body, speed wheels; made in Hong Kong, 1:64 scale, Model No. 1886
EX n/a   NM n/a   MIP $12

❑ **1982 Ford EXP,** 1982, Metallic blue body, light blue and black accents, speed wheels, tinted windows, 1:64 scale, Model No. 1825
EX n/a   NM n/a   MIP $10

❑ **1982 Pontiac Firebird Turbo,** 1982, Daytona Blue body, speed wheels, tinted windows, T-bar roof, rear spoiler, bucket seats; also issued as the Replica Series

"00" car; made in Hong Kong, 1:64 scale, Model No. 1884
EX n/a   NM n/a   MIP $12

❑ **BMW Turbo,** 1982, Orange/red or silver body, speed wheels, opening hood; first appeared in 1977; dropped from line in 1981 but returned in 1982 as part of Replica series, 1:64 scale, Model No. 1895
EX n/a   NM n/a   MIP $10

❑ **Chevy Stepside Pickup,** 1982, Yellow body, speed wheels, side decals, rear hitch; first appeared in "Fun Truckin' Vehicles" series in 1979 with opening doors; also sold as Bell Telephone pickup and Dekalb Seed Corn pickup; made in Hong Kong, 1:64 scale, Model No. 1938
EX n/a   NM n/a   MIP $12

❑ **Datsun 280 ZX Turbo,** 1982, Black or orange body, speed wheels, tinted windows, T sunroof; originally designed in 1979 as a 280Z but never released, 1:64 scale, Model No. 1888
EX n/a   NM n/a   MIP $12

❑ **Ferrari Dino 246GT,** 1982, Yellow body, speed wheels, opening trunk; first appeared in "Cars of the World" series in 1980 (replaced Fiat Abarth), 1:64 scale, Model No. 1909
EX n/a   NM n/a   MIP $10

❑ **Jaguar XJ10,** 1981, Maroon or black body, chrome wheels and bumpers, 1:64 scale, Model No. 1898
EX n/a   NM n/a   MIP $12

❑ **Jaguar XJ12,** 1982, Black body, speed wheels, opening hood with detailed engine; first appeared in "Cars of the World" series in 1980 (replaced Ford Mark IV), 1:64 scale, Model No. 1898
EX n/a   NM n/a   MIP $10

❑ **Jeep CJ7,** 1982, Red and black body, speed wheels, removable roof, rear hitch; first appeared in "Frun Truckin' Vehicles" series in 1980; also sold as "Daisy's Jeep"; made in Hong Kong and Singapore, 1:64 scale, Model No. 1937
EX n/a   NM n/a   MIP $12

❑ **London Taxi,** 1988, Maroon body, 1:43 scale, Model No. 2552
EX n/a   NM n/a   MIP $15

❑ **London Taxi,** 1988, Green body, 1:43 scale, Model No. 2553
EX n/a   NM n/a   MIP $15

❑ **London Taxi,** 1989, Black body, white interior, chrome wheels and grille, "For Hire" label on front roof sign, 1:43 scale, Model No. 2531
EX n/a   NM n/a   MIP $15

❑ **Mazda RX7,** 1982, Silver or blue body, speed wheels, bucket seats, console with stick shift, tinted windows; originally designed in 1979 but not released until 1982, 1:64 scale, Model No. 1880
EX n/a   NM n/a   MIP $10

❑ **Mercedes Benz 350SL,** 1982, Red body, speed wheels, opening hood, detailed engine; first appeared in "Cars of the World series in 1977, 1:64 scale, Model No. 1892
EX n/a   NM n/a   MIP $10

❑ **Mercedes Benz 450SE,** 1982, Black body, speed wheels, opening hood, detailed engine; first appeared in "Cars of the World" sereis in 1977, 1:64 scale, Model No. 1894
EX n/a   NM n/a   MIP $10

❑ **Pontiac Firebird,** 1984, Black body, gold wheel inserts, 1:64 scale, Model No. 1577
EX n/a   NM n/a   MIP $15

❑ **Porsche 911,** 1982, Yellow body, jeweled headlights, unpainted base, made in Hong Kong; first appeared in 1977 with speed wheels, opening trunk, rhinestone headlights in "Cars of the World" series, 1:64 scale, Model No. 1890
EX n/a   NM n/a   MIP $12

❑ **Porsche 917,** 1982, Green body, speed wheels, back-opening hood, no engine; first appeared with back-opening hood and detailed engine in Cars of the World series in 1977, 1:64 scale, Model No. 1893
EX n/a   NM n/a   MIP $10

❑ **Porsche 930 Turbo,** 1982, White body, Martini logo, #38, speed wheels, racing decals; first appeared in "Cars of the World" series in 1980 (replaced BMW Turbo), 1:64 scale, Model No. 1908
EX n/a   NM n/a   MIP $15

❑ **Volkswagen 1200LS,** 1982, Red body, speed wheels, opening hood; first appeared in "Cars of the World" series in 1977, 1:64 scale, Model No. 1896
EX n/a   NM n/a   MIP $10

RIPTIDE

❑ **1960 Corvette,** 1984, From TV series; red body; also part of three-vehicle set, 1:64 scale, Model No. 1077
EX n/a   NM n/a   MIP $15

❑ **Pickup,** 1984, From TV series; red body; also part of three-vehicle set, 1:64 scale, Model No. 1078
EX n/a   NM n/a   MIP $15

❑ **Screamin' Mimi Helicopter,** 1984, From TV series; pink body; also part of three-vehicle set, Model No. 1076
EX n/a   NM n/a   MIP $15

ROCKY III (1982)

❑ **Maserati Quattroporte,** 1982, movie logo decal on the hood, 1:64 scale, Model No. 1836
EX n/a   NM n/a   MIP $8

SEARS

❑ **1912 Buick,** 1986, Black body; sold as part of six-car set, 1:43 scale, Model No. 2530
EX n/a   NM n/a   MIP $10

❑ **1913 Ford Model T,** 1986, Green body; sold as part of six-car set, 1:43 scale, Model No. 2530
EX n/a   NM n/a   MIP $10

❑ **1923 Ford Fordor,** 1986, Brown body; sold as part of six-car set, 1:43 scale, Model No. 2530
EX n/a   NM n/a   MIP $10

❑ **1932 Ford Panel Truck,** 1986, Beige body; sold as part of six-car set, 1:43 scale, Model No. 2530
EX n/a   NM n/a   MIP $10

❑ **1932 Ford Roadster,** 1986, Navy blue body; sold as part of six-car set, 1:43 scale, Model No. 2530
EX n/a   NM n/a   MIP $10

❑ **1940 Ford Woody,** 1986, Red body; sold as part of six-car set, 1:43 scale, Model No. 2530
EX n/a   NM n/a   MIP $10

SIMON & SIMON

❑ **1982 Camaro Z-28,** 1984, From TV series; red body, T-bar roof, mag wheels, show logo on side, 1:64 scale, Model No. 1438FO
EX n/a   NM n/a   MIP $6

SIX PACK (1982)

❑ **Camaro,** 1982, also sold as part of three-piece gift set (#1431), 1:64 scale, Model No. 1556
EX n/a   NM n/a   MIP $6

❑ **Ford Thunderbird,** 1982, also sold as part of three-piece gift set (#1431), 1:64 scale, Model No. 1725
EX n/a   NM n/a   MIP $6

SMOKEY AND THE BANDIT

(Photo courtesy Racing Champions Ertl)

❑ **1977 Pontiac Trans Am,** 2002, Black body, gold accents, open T-top, tan interior, gold painted gauge cluster, CB radio with flexible cable, 1:18 scale, Model No. 33121
EX n/a   NM n/a   MIP $30

SMOKEY AND THE BANDIT II (1980)

❑ **GMC cab and trailer,** 1981, Silver cab, blue markings, Western mural decal on trailer, 1:87 scale, Model No. 1906
EX n/a   NM n/a   MIP $10

❑ **Pontiac Trans Am,** 1982, also sold as part of a two-car blister set (#1790), 1:64 scale, Model No. 1883
EX n/a   NM n/a   MIP $10

SPECIAL

❑ **F-117A Stealth Fighter,** 1989, 1:110 scale, Model No. 1048EO
EX n/a   NM n/a   MIP $6

❑ **F-16 Falcon,** 1989, USAF, Thunderbirds, Model No. 1488EO
EX n/a   NM n/a   MIP $6

❑ **F-18 Hornet,** 1989, Blue/yellow body, U.S. Navy, Blue Angels, Model No. 1489EO
EX n/a   NM n/a   MIP $8

SPEED RACER

(Photo courtesy Racing Champions Ertl)

❑ **Mach 5,** 2002, From TV series; white body, red graphics and interior, #5 on side, spring-loaded periscope, ion jacks, homing robot, plastic Chim Chim figure, 1:18 scale, Model No. 33141
EX n/a   NM n/a   MIP $30

STAR TREK

❑ **Enterprise,** 1984, Model No. 1372
EX n/a   NM n/a   MIP $10

❑ **Excelsior,** 1984, Model No. 1373
EX n/a   NM n/a   MIP $10

❑ **Klingon Bird of Prey,** 1984, Model No. 1374
EX n/a   NM n/a   MIP $10

STOCK RODS

(Photo courtesy Racing Champions Ertl)

❑ **1971 Plymouth Barracuda,** 2002, Caterpillar, Ward Burton, #22; black/yellow/red version, 1:18 scale, Model No. 77435
EX n/a   NM n/a   MIP $30

(Photo courtesy Racing Champions Ertl)

ERTL / RACING

❑ **1971 Plymouth Barracuda,** 2002, Caterpillar, Ward Burton, #22; white/yellow/red version, 1:18 scale, Model No. 77435
EX n/a   NM n/a   MIP $30

STREET MACHINES

❑ **1955 Chevy,** 2000, 1:18 scale, Model No. 36293
EX n/a   NM n/a   MIP $30

❑ **1955 Chevy pickup,** 2000, 1:18 scale, Model No. 36286
EX n/a   NM n/a   MIP $30

❑ **1969 Chevy Camaro,** 1998, Lime green body, green/white interior, 1:18 scale, Model No. 7981DP
EX n/a   NM n/a   MIP $30

❑ **1969 Plymouth GTX,** 2000, Gold body, black stripes, black interior, 1:18 scale, Model No. 36286
EX n/a   NM n/a   MIP $30

❑ **1969 Pontiac GTO,** 1998, Pink/purple body, white interior, 1:18 scale, Model No. 7978DP
EX n/a   NM n/a   MIP $30

❑ **1970 Chevelle,** 1998, Purple body, gray stipes and hood, purple interior, 1:18 scale, Model No. 7979DP
EX n/a   NM n/a   MIP $30

❑ **1970 Cuda,** 1998, Purple body, white stripes, 1:18 scale, Model No. 7982DP
EX n/a   NM n/a   MIP $30

STREET RODS

❑ **1913 Ford Model T van,** 1982, Metallic brown body, Vandit markings, chrome speed wheels, oversized tires, street rod engines; part of six-car Street Rods set, 1:64 scale, Model No. 1838
EX n/a   NM n/a   MIP $15

❑ **1923 Ford Model T bucket,** 1982, Red body, yellow interior, checkerboard pattern on sides, chrome engine, chrome speed wheels, oversized tires; part of six-car Street Rods set, 1:64 scale, Model No. 1838
EX n/a   NM n/a   MIP $15

❑ **1932 Ford,** 1981, Red body, yellow flames, chrome speed wheels, oversized tires, street rod engines; part of six-car Street Rods set, 1:64 scale, Model No. 1838
EX n/a   NM n/a   MIP $10

❑ **1934 Ford,** 1981, Silver body, green markings, chrome speed wheels, oversized tires, street rod engines; part of six-car Street Rods set, 1:64 scale, Model No. 1838
EX n/a   NM n/a   MIP $10

❑ **1940 Ford,** 1981, Red body, yellow markings, chrome speed wheels, oversized tires, street rod engines; part of six-car Street Rods set, 1:64 scale, Model No. 1838
EX n/a   NM n/a   MIP $15

❑ **1940 Ford,** 1999, Midnight Blue body, yellow/red flames, 1:18 scale, Model No. 7937DP
EX n/a   NM n/a   MIP $30

❑ **1940 Ford Custom,** 1999, Metallic Green body, tan/gray interior, 1:18 scale, Model No. 32097
EX n/a   NM n/a   MIP $30

❑ **1955 Chevy Nomad,** 1981, Blue body, yellow/red flames, speed wheels (replaced by 1913 Ford Model T van in 1982), 1:64 scale, Model No. 1838
EX n/a   NM n/a   MIP $10

❑ **1957 Chevy convertible,** 1981, Black body, tan interior, tinted windshield, chrome speed wheels, oversized tires, street rod engines; part of six-car Street Rods set, 1:64 scale, Model No. 1838
EX n/a   NM n/a   MIP $10

❑ **1957 Chevy two-door hardtop,** 1981, Red body, yellow/red flames, speed wheels (replaced by 1923 Ford Model T Bucket in 1982), 1:64 scale, Model No. 1838
EX n/a   NM n/a   MIP $15

STROKER ACE (1983)

❑ **Cadillac convertible,** 1983, Red body, white interior, yellow "Chicken Pit" markings, 1:64 scale, Model No. 1502FO
EX n/a   NM n/a   MIP $6

❑ **Ford Thunderbird stock car,** 1983, Red body, #7, yellow "Chicken Pit" markings, 1:64 scale, Model No. 1502FO
EX n/a   NM n/a   MIP $6

❑ **Tractor/trailer,** 1983, Red cab, red trailer with yellow "Clyde Torkle's Chicken Pit" markings and logo, 1:87 scale, Model No. 1502FO
EX n/a   NM n/a   MIP $10

SUPER-SIZE MINIATURES

❑ **1913 Ford Model T Delivery Van,** 1981, Yellow body, green top and fenders, rubber tires, yellow spoke wheels; Country Time lemonade markings (1982), 1:25 scale, Model No. 1640
EX n/a   NM n/a   MIP $25

❑ **1932 Ford Roadster,** 1980, Metallic brown body, black fenders, opening doors, rim wheels; white body, black top and fenders (1981); beige body, brown top and interior (1982), 1:25 scale, Model No. 1682
EX n/a   NM n/a   MIP $25

❑ **1963 Corvette,** 1981, Yellow body, split-window, opening hood with 327 engine, chrome bumper and wheels, 1:25 scale, Model No. 1782
EX n/a   NM n/a   MIP $25

❑ **1965 Ford Mustang,** 1981, Dark blue body, white interior, opening doors and hood, 289 engine, moving seats; red body, black interior (1982), 1:25 scale, Model No. 1783
EX n/a   NM n/a   MIP $25

❑ **1970 Dodge Charger,** 1981, From "The Dukes of Hazzard" TV series; Confederate flag on roof, "01" decal, 1:25 scale, Model No. 1781
EX n/a   NM n/a   MIP $25

❑ **Camaro Z28,** 1980, Metallic brown/red body, blue interior, gold bucket seats, sunroof, tinted windows; blue body, light blue interior (1981), 1:25 scale, Model No. 1680
EX n/a   NM n/a   MIP $25

❑ **Chevy Stepside Pickup,** 1980, Metallic brown body, tan interior, black bed cover, tilt-back seats, opening doors and tailgate, chrome engine, bumper and wheels; metallic green body (1982), 1:25 scale, Model No. 1677
EX n/a   NM n/a   MIP $25

❑ **Chevy, Darrell Waltrip Gatorade Super Stock Car,** 1980, White body, green graphics, #88, opening hood, movable seats, chrome engine and wheel covers, 1:25 scale, Model No. 1683
EX n/a   NM n/a   MIP $25

❏ **Chevy, Richard Petty STP Super Stock Car,** 1980, Petty blue body, red graphics, #43, opening hood, detailed engine, bucket seats, 1:25 scale, Model No. 1679
EX n/a   NM n/a   MIP $25

❏ **Corvette Stingray,** 1980, Silver body, red interior, folding bucket seats, opening doors and hood, chrome V8 engine; blue body (1982), 1:25 scale, Model No. 1676
EX n/a   NM n/a   MIP $25

❏ **Ford Bronco,** 1980, Green body, opening doors, movable seats, removable hardtop, chrome wheels; Red body, black top (1981); white body, red/orange markings, black top (1982), 1:25 scale, Model No. 1681
EX n/a   NM n/a   MIP $25

❏ **Formula Turbo Firebird,** 1981, Dark red body, black interior, opening hood, trunk and doors, folding bucket seats, chrome V8 engine and wheels, 1:25 scale, Model No. 1678
EX n/a   NM n/a   MIP $25

❏ **Jeep CJ7,** 1980, Yellow body, removable black top, "Renegade" on hood with red and orange markings, chrome engine, wheels and spare tire, 1:25 scale, Model No. 1675
EX n/a   NM n/a   MIP $25

❏ **Pontiac Trans Am,** 1980, Red body, black interior, black/gold eagle on hood, opening trunk, doors and hood, chrome V8 engine, 1:25 scale, Model No. 1678
EX n/a   NM n/a   MIP $25

❏ **Trans Am Turbo,** 1981, From "Smokey and the Bandit II" movie (1980); black body, gold eagle on hood, opening hood, chrome turbo-charged engine, folding bucket seats, 1:25 scale, Model No. 1644
EX n/a   NM n/a   MIP $25

THE A TEAM

❏ **Jeep,** 1983, From TV series, 1:64 scale, Model No. 1824
EX n/a   NM n/a   MIP $8

❏ **Van,** 1983, From TV series, 1:64 scale, Model No. 1823
EX n/a   NM n/a   MIP $8

THE BLUES BROTHERS (1980)

❏ **Bluesmobile,** 1981, Black and white body, gold star on doors, silver base, 1:64 scale
EX n/a   NM n/a   MIP $8

THE CANNONBALL RUN (1981)

❏ **1980 Chevy Caprice two-door, Hawaiian Tropic Stocker,** 1982, 1:64 scale, Model No. 1867
EX n/a   NM n/a   MIP $10

❏ **Ambulance,** 1982, 1:64 scale, Model No. 1869
EX n/a   NM n/a   MIP $10

❏ **Ferrari,** 1982, 1:64 scale, Model No. 1868
EX n/a   NM n/a   MIP $10

❏ **Rolls-Royce,** 1982, 1:64 scale, Model No. 1866
EX n/a   NM n/a   MIP $10

THE DUKES OF HAZZARD

❏ **1970 Dodge Charger, "General Lee",** 1981, From TV series; orange body, Confederate flag on roof, "01" on sides; part of four-car set, 1:64 scale, Model No. 1570
EX n/a   NM n/a   MIP $9

❏ **1970 Dodge Charger, "General Lee",** 1982, From TV series; orange body, Confederate flag on roof, "01" on sides; part of two-car set (#1572), 1:64 scale, Model No. 1581
EX n/a   NM n/a   MIP $8

❏ **1970 Dodge Charger, "General Lee",** 1999, From TV series; orange body, Confederate flag on roof, "01" on sides, 1:25 scale, Model No. 7967DO
EX n/a   NM n/a   MIP $20

(Photo courtesy Racing Champions Ertl)

❏ **1970 Dodge Charger, "General Lee",** 2000, From TV series; orange body, Confederate flag on roof, "01" on sides, 1:18 scale, Model No. 32485
EX n/a   NM n/a   MIP $30

❏ **1970 Dodge Charger, 1970 Cadillac convertible, 1980 Pontiac Bonneville,** 1999, From TV series; set of three cars, including General Lee, Boss Hogg's Cadillac and Sheriff's car, 1:64 scale, Model No. 7068EO
EX n/a   NM n/a   MIP $15

❏ **Boss Hogg's 1970 Cadillac,** 1982, From TV series; white body, "Boss Hogg" on side; also part of two-car set (#1572), 1:64 scale, Model No. 1567
EX n/a   NM n/a   MIP $8

❏ **Daisy's Jeep,** 1981, From TV series; white body, eagle on hood; part of four-car set, 1:64 scale, Model No. 1570
EX n/a   NM n/a   MIP $8

(Photo courtesy Racing Champions Ertl)

❏ **Ford Mustang,** 2001, Blue exterior, flames on hood, "00" on sides, opening doors, folding seatbacks, plated center console, functional steering wheel, 1:18 scale, Model No. 33043
EX n/a   NM n/a   MIP $30

(Photo courtesy Racing Champions Ertl)

❏ **Ford Mustang,** 2001, Blue exterior, flames on hood, "00" on sides, 1:64 scale, Model No. 33043
EX n/a   NM n/a   MIP $6

❏ **Sheriff's car, 1980 Pontiac Bonneville, "The Dukes of Hazzard",** 1981, From TV series; white body, Hazzard County decals, blue lights; pair packaged in four-car set, 1:64 scale, Model No. 1570
EX n/a   **NM** n/a   **MIP** $6

THE FAST AND THE FURIOUS (2001)

❏ **1996 Pontiac Trans Am,** 2001, Black body, gray interior, 5.7 Liter V8 engine, 1:18 scale, Model No. 33021
EX n/a   **NM** n/a   **MIP** $30

THE MONKEES

(Photo courtesy Racing Champions Ertl)

❏ **Monkeemobile,** 2002, From TV series; red body, removable white T-bucket convertible top, plated engine, plated center console, dash tach, plated horns on front wheelwells, 1:18 scale, Model No. 33150
EX n/a   **NM** n/a   **MIP** $30

THE MUNSTERS

(Photo courtesy Racing Champions Ertl)

❏ **Munsters Koach,** 2002, From TV series; black body, Bobby Barr funnel racing headers, casket handles, ooga horn, plated spoke wheels, A/l knock-off hubs, 1:18 scale, Model No. 33036
EX n/a   **NM** n/a   **MIP** $30

THRIFTWAY

❏ **Ford Thunderbird,** 1987, White body, 1:64 scale, Model No. 9193
EX n/a   **NM** n/a   **MIP** $6

TOY FAIR

❏ **1912 Buick Touring Car,** 1987, Maroon body; 1987 American Toy Fair, Toy Fair decal, gold "Buyer's Limited Edition" lettering on rear, limited to 1,000, 1:43 scale, Model No. 2539
EX n/a   **NM** n/a   **MIP** $10

❏ **1912 Buick Touring Car,** 1987, Maroon body; 1987 Toy Fair in Canada, Great Britain and West Germany, Toy Fair decal, gold "Buyer's Limited Edition" lettering on rear, limited to 500, 1:43 scale, Model No. 2539
EX n/a   **NM** n/a   **MIP** $10

❏ **1913 Ford Model T Van,** 1985, 1985 American Toy Fair, Buyer's Limited Edition I, limited to 1,000 pieces, 1:43 scale, Model No. 2525
EX n/a   **NM** n/a   **MIP** $10

❏ **1913 Ford Model T Van,** 1986, 1986 Canadian Toy Fair, Buyer's Limited Edition I, 1:43 scale, Model No. 2533
EX n/a   **NM** n/a   **MIP** $10

❏ **1913 Ford Model T Van,** 1986, 1986 American Toy Fair, Buyer's Limited Edition II, 1:43 scale, Model No. 2532
EX n/a   **NM** n/a   **MIP** $10

❏ **1952 Cadillac,** 1988, Black body, 1988 Toy Fair in Canada, Great Britain and West Germany, limited to 500, 1:43 scale, Model No. 2560
EX n/a   **NM** n/a   **MIP** $10

❏ **1952 Cadillac,** 1988, Black body, 1988 American Toy Fair, white lettering, limited to 1,000, 1:43 scale, Model No. 2560
EX n/a   **NM** n/a   **MIP** $10

❏ **Checker Cab,** 1989, Yellow body, 1989 Canadian Toy Fair, limited to 500, 1:43 scale, Model No. 2573MA
EX n/a   **NM** n/a   **MIP** $10

❏ **Checker Cab,** 1989, Yellow body, 1989 American Toy Fair, limited to 1,000, 1:43 scale, Model No. 2573YA
EX n/a   **NM** n/a   **MIP** $10

❏ **London Taxi,** 1989, Maroon body, 1989 Nremberg Toy Fair, limited to 500, 1:43 scale, Model No. 2574MI
EX n/a   **NM** n/a   **MIP** $10

❏ **London Taxi,** 1989, Maroon body, 1989 British Toy Fair, limited to 200, 1:43 scale, Model No. 2574YI
EX n/a   **NM** n/a   **MIP** $10

TOYS R US

❏ **1940 Ford Woody,** 1986, Navy blue body; sold as part of three-car set, 1:43 scale, Model No. 2810
EX n/a   **NM** n/a   **MIP** $10

❏ **1952 Cadillac,** 1986, Black body; sold as part of three-car set, 1:43 scale, Model No. 2810
EX n/a   **NM** n/a   **MIP** $10

❏ **1957 Chevy Bel Air,** 1986, Light blue body; sold as part of three-car set, 1:43 scale, Model No. 2810
EX n/a   **NM** n/a   **MIP** $10

TRUCKS

❏ **1955 Chevy Cameo Carrier pickup,** 1994, Bombay Ivory body, Commercial Red interior, trim and bed, 1:18 scale, Model No. 7340DO
EX n/a   **NM** n/a   **MIP** $40

(Photo courtesy Racing Champions Ertl)

❏ **1955 Chevy pickup street machine,** 1999, Red body, gray interior, chrome shifter and steering wheel, custom wheels, 1:18 scale, Model No. 32032
EX n/a   **NM** n/a   **MIP** $30

❏ **1955 Chevy Stepside pickup,** 1994, Ocean Green body, black interior, 1:18 scale, Model No. 7339DO
EX n/a   **NM** n/a   **MIP** $40

❏ **1955 Chevy Stepside pickup,** 1997, Commercial Red body, tan interior, 1:18 scale, Model No. 7788DP
EX n/a   **NM** n/a   **MIP** $30

❏ **1956 Ford F100 Custom,** 1999, Bright Orange body, black bed and running board, 1:18 scale, Model No. 32030
EX n/a   NM n/a   MIP $30

❏ **1956 Ford F100 custom pickup,** 1997, Starlight Purple body, gray interior and bed, 1:18 scale, Model No. 7770DP
EX n/a   NM n/a   MIP $35

❏ **1956 Ford F100 stock,** 1997, Vermillion Red body, red interior, 1:18 scale, Model No. 7771DP
EX n/a   NM n/a   MIP $35

❏ **1956 Ford F100 Stock,** 1999, Black body, black interior, 1:18 scale, Model No. 32034
EX n/a   NM n/a   MIP $30

❏ **1957 Chevy pickup,** 1998, Ivory body, Indian Turquoise contrasts, 1:18 scale, Model No. 7854DP
EX n/a   NM n/a   MIP $30

❏ **1957 Chevy pickup,** 1998, Ivory body, Omaha Orange contrasts, white interior, 1:18 scale, Model No. 7853DP
EX n/a   NM n/a   MIP $30

❏ **1970 Chevy El Camino,** 1998, Red body, black stripes, 1:18 scale, Model No. 7862DP
EX n/a   NM n/a   MIP $30

❏ **1970 Chevy El Camino,** 1998, Silver body, black stripes, 1:18 scale, Model No. 7856DP
EX n/a   NM n/a   MIP $30

❏ **1978 Dodge Li'l Red Express truck,** 1994, Red body, gold and woodgrain decoration, 1:18 scale, Model No. 7385DO
EX n/a   NM n/a   MIP $40

❏ **1978 Dodge Warlock pickup,** 1994, Black body, gold markings, black interior, 1:18 scale, Model No. 7383DO
EX n/a   NM n/a   MIP $40

❏ **1995 Dodge Ram,** 1995, Flame Red and silver body, 1:18 scale, Model No. 7333DO
EX n/a   NM n/a   MIP $40

❏ **1995 Dodge Ram,** 1995, Black and silver body, 1:18 scale, Model No. 7334DO
EX n/a   NM n/a   MIP $40

(Photo courtesy Racing Champions Ertl)

❏ **1995 Dodge Ram 2500,** 2001, Gold body, camouflage bottom, Advantage Timber markings, 1:18 scale, Model No. 13312
EX n/a   NM n/a   MIP $30

(Photo courtesy Racing Champions Ertl)

❏ **1995 Dodge Ram 2500,** 2001, Brown body, silver bottom, Mossy Oak markings, 1:18 scale, Model No. 13313
EX n/a   NM n/a   MIP $30

(Photo courtesy Racing Champions Ertl)

❏ **1997 Ford F150,** 2001, U.S. Border Patrol, white body, green stripe, red roof-mounted bulb, plated hood-mounted spotlight, side mirrors, whip antenna, 1:18 scale, Model No. 33053
EX n/a   NM n/a   MIP $30

❏ **1997 Ford F-150,** 1997, Moonlight Blue/Saddle Tan Metallic body, 1:18 scale, Model No. 7225DP
EX n/a   NM n/a   MIP $35

❏ **1997 Ford F-150,** 1998, Bright red body, black interior, 1:18 scale, Model No. 7858DP
EX n/a   NM n/a   MIP $30

❏ **1997 Ford F-150,** 1998, Moonlight Blue/Saddle Tan Metallic body, 1:18 scale, Model No. 7225DP
EX n/a   NM n/a   MIP $30

(Photo courtesy Racing Champions Ertl)

❏ **1997 Ford F-150,** 2001, White body, black bottom, Triton Boats markings, 1:18 scale, Model No. 13315
EX n/a   NM n/a   MIP $30

❏ **1997 Ford F-150 Styleside pickup,** 1996, Pacific Green body, 1:18 scale, Model No. 7224DO
EX n/a   NM n/a   MIP $35

❏ **1997 Ford F-150 Styleside pickup,** 1996, Toreador Red body, 1:18 scale, Model No. 7223DO
EX n/a   NM n/a   MIP $35

(Photo courtesy Racing Champions Ertl)

❏ **2000 Ford Harley-Davidson F150 pickup,** 2000, Black body, 1:18 scale, Model No. 32389
EX n/a   NM n/a   MIP $30

❏ **2001 Ford Harley-Davidson Super Crew F150,** 2001, Black body, black interior, tinted sunroof and rear passenger windows, 1:18 scale, Model No. 32782
EX n/a   NM n/a   MIP $30

❏ **2002 Harley-Davidson Ford F150 Super Crew pickup,** 2002, Gray Metallic body, crew cab, supercharged engine, gray interior with bucket seats, 1:18 scale, Model No. 33140
EX n/a   NM n/a   MIP $30

❏ **Dodge Ram,** 1997, Emerald Green/Silver body, 1:18 scale, Model No. 7729DP
EX n/a   NM n/a   MIP $35

/ SPORTSMAN

(Photo courtesy Racing Champions Ertl)

❏ **Dodge Ram pickup,** 2002, Ward Burton #22 Caterpillar, yellow/black body, opening hood and doors, beige interior, black door inserts and speakers, opening tailgate, 1:18 scale, Model No. 77443
EX n/a   NM n/a   MIP $35

(Photo courtesy Racing Champions Ertl)

❏ **Ford F150 pickup,** 2002, John Force 11-Time Champion, white/black/green body, opening hood, doors and tailgate, flexible engine wiring, functional steering, 1:18 scale, Model No. 77442
EX n/a   NM n/a   MIP $37

TRUCKS OF THE WORLD

❏ **"Eagle" Flatbed Trailer,** 1978, Red cab and trailer, silver I-beam load, 10-5/8 inches, Model No. 1412
EX n/a   NM n/a   MIP $20

❏ **"Eagle" Grain Trailer,** 1978, Red cab, gray trailer, removable yellow plastic tarp, rear and hopper doors open, 10-1/2 inches, Model No. 1413
EX n/a   NM n/a   MIP $20

❏ **"Eagle" Tanker,** 1978, Red cab, white tanker, spare tire, 10-5/8 inches, Model No. 1414
EX n/a   NM n/a   MIP $20

❏ **"Eagle" Van Trailer,** 1978, Blue cab, white trailer with Ertl graphics, trailer doors open, 10-5/8 inches, Model No. 1411
EX n/a   NM n/a   MIP $20

❏ **Ford CLT 9000 Cab with flatbed trailer,** 1978, White cab with black and gold markings, red trailer with silver I-beam load, Model No. 1450
EX n/a   NM n/a   MIP $20

❏ **Ford CLT 9000 Cab with grain trailer,** 1978, White cab with black and gold markings, gray trailer with removable yellow plastic tarp, Model No. 1451
EX n/a   NM n/a   MIP $20

❏ **IH Paystar 5000 Gravel Trailer,** 1978, Green cab, white hood, gray/green trailer which raises, tailgate opens, trailer disconnects, 7-3/8 inches, Model No. 1403
EX n/a   NM n/a   MIP $20

❏ **IH Paystar 5000 Logger,** 1978, Blue cab, white hood, three removable plastic logs, trailer unhooks, 8-1/2 inches, Model No. 1404
EX n/a   NM n/a   MIP $20

❏ **IH Paystar 5000 Mixer,** 1978, Red body, white hood, white drum which rotates, 6 inches, Model No. 1401
EX n/a   NM n/a   MIP $20

❏ **IH Paystar 5000 Wrecker,** 1978, Red cab, white hood, white wrecker, twin boom unit, hand crank for wrecker hook, 5-1/2 inches, Model No. 1402
EX n/a   NM n/a   MIP $20

❏ **IH Transtar II Flatbed,** 1978, Dark blue COE, red trailer with silver I-beam load, trailer pivots and detaches from tractor, 9-5/8 inches, Model No. 1416
EX n/a   NM n/a   MIP $20

❏ **IH Transtar II Grain Trailer,** 1978, Dark blue COE, gray trailer with removable yellow plastic tarp, rear and hopper doors open, 9-5/8 inches, Model No. 1417
EX n/a   NM n/a   MIP $20

❏ **IH Transtar II Tanker,** 1978, Dark blue COE, white tanker, spare tire, 9-5/8 inches, Model No. 1418
EX n/a   NM n/a   MIP $20

❏ **IH Transtar II Van,** 1978, Dark blue COE, white trailer with Ertl graphics, trailer doors open, 9-5/8 inches, Model No. 1415
EX n/a   NM n/a   MIP $20

TWO-LANE BLACKTOP (1971)

❏ **1955 Chevy Bel Air,** 2002, 1:18 scale, Model No. 33030
EX n/a   NM n/a   MIP $30

❏ **1969 Dodge Daytona,** 2001, Light bronze body, black stripe, black interior, five-spoke sport wheels, 1:18 scale, Model No. 33020
EX n/a   NM n/a   MIP $30

VANISHING POINT (1971)

❏ **1970 Dodge Challenger R/T,** 2001, White body, black interior, 1:18 scale, Model No. 33017/33029
EX n/a   NM n/a   MIP $30

VINTAGE

❏ **1956 Ford,** 2000, Fireball Roberts, #22, 1:18 scale, Model No. 32125
EX n/a   NM n/a   MIP $30

❏ **1956 Ford,** 2000, Glen Wood, #22, 1:18 scale, Model No. 32124
EX n/a   NM n/a   MIP $30

❏ **1956 Ford,** 2000, Joe Wetherly, #12, 1:18 scale, Model No. 32123
EX n/a   NM n/a   MIP $30

❏ **1956 Ford,** 2000, White/orange body, Curtis Turner, #26, 1:18 scale, Model No. 32122
EX n/a   NM n/a   MIP $30

❏ **1957 Chevy,** 1999, Fireball Roberts, #22, 283cid V8, hood and trunk tie-downs, 1:18 scale, Model No. 7997DP
EX n/a   NM n/a   MIP $30

❏ **1957 Chevy convertible,** 1999, Fireball Roberts, #22, 1:18 scale, Model No. 7998DP
EX n/a   NM n/a   MIP $30

VINTAGE VEHICLES

❏ **1912 Buick Touring Car,** 1986, Red body, black fenders, 1:43 scale, Model No. 2516
EX n/a   NM n/a   MIP $20

❏ **1913 Ford Model T van,** 1984, Dark blue body, yellow trim, white rubber tires, "TA-PAT-CO Horse Collar Pads" markings, 1:43 scale, Model No. 2502
EX n/a   NM n/a   MIP $20

❏ **1914 Chevy Royal Mail,** 1987, Green body, chrome trim, identifying license plate, collector's print, 1:43 scale, Model No. 2543
EX n/a   NM n/a   MIP $20

❏ **1923 Ford Model T sedan,** 1986, Black body, 1:43 scale, Model No. 2519
EX n/a   NM n/a   MIP $20

❏ **1930 Chevy Delivery truck,** 1986, Orange body, 1:43 scale, Model No. 2518
EX n/a   NM n/a   MIP $20

❏ **1930 Packard Boattail Speedster,** 1987, Burgundy body, whitewall tires, chrome trim, identifying license plate, collector's print, 1:43 scale, Model No. 2542
EX n/a   NM n/a   MIP $20

❏ **1930-31 Chevy Stake truck,** 1984, Black and tan body, "Carl Jones, Prop., Livestock Truck & Transportation" markings, 1:43 scale, Model No. 2503
EX n/a   NM n/a   MIP $20

❏ **1932 Ford Roadster,** 1984, Brown and cream body, 1:43 scale, Model No. 2501
EX n/a   NM n/a   MIP $20

❏ **1934 Ford Panel Delivery,** 1984, Dark green and black body, "Perfection Oil Burning Stoves" markings, 1:43 scale, Model No. 2504
EX n/a   NM n/a   MIP $20

❏ **1940 Ford Woody Station Wagon,** 1986, Brown body and sides, "Whispering Pines Lodge" markings; black body, brown sides with "Moser Manufacturing" markings (1988); brown body, black fenders, brown sides in with "Moser Manufacturing" markings (1989; limited to 5,000), 1:43 scale, Model No. 2517
EX n/a   NM n/a   MIP $20

❏ **1949 Ford Coupe,** 1989, Dark green body, 1:43 scale, Model No. 2803
EX n/a   NM n/a   MIP $20

❏ **1952 Cadillac,** 1987, Pink body, white top, whitewall tires, chrome trim, identifying license plate, collector's print, 1:43 scale, Model No. 2541
EX n/a   NM n/a   MIP $20

❏ **1957 Chevy,** 1987, Red body, whitewall tires, chrome trim, identifying license plate, collector's print, 1:43 scale, Model No. 2540
EX n/a   NM n/a   MIP $20

❏ **1957 Ford Thunderbird,** 1989, Light blue body, white top, 1:43 scale, Model No. 2802
EX n/a   NM n/a   MIP $20

❏ **1958 Austin FX3 London Taxi,** 1988, Black, maroon, or dark green body; no collector print; original release sold only in Europe and Australia, 1:43 scale, Model No. 2551
EX n/a   NM n/a   MIP $20

❏ **1959 Checker Cab,** 1988, Yellow body, chrome trim, soft vinyl tires, 1:43 scale, Model No. 2587EO
EX n/a   NM n/a   MIP $20

❏ **1960 Corvette convertible,** 1988, Red/white body, chrome trim, soft vinyl tires, 1:43 scale, Model No. 2588EO
EX n/a   NM n/a   MIP $20

❏ **1964-1/2 Ford Mustang,** 1988, Beige or white body, chrome trim, soft vinyl tires, 1:43 scale, Model No. 2586EO
EX n/a   NM n/a   MIP $20

❏ **1968 Pontiac GTO,** 1988, Dark green body, chrome trim, soft vinyl tires, 1:43 scale, Model No. 2589EO
EX n/a   NM n/a   MIP $20

❏ **1968 Shelby Mustang GT,** 1989, Red body, 1:43 scale, Model No. 2804
EX n/a   NM n/a   MIP $20

❏ **1969 Camaro,** 1989, Metallic blue, 1:43 scale, Model No. 2809
EX n/a   NM n/a   MIP $20

WORK AND RECREATION VEHICLES

❏ **Chevy Van,** 1978, Blue body, white and light blue markings, opening doors, 1:64 scale, Model No. 1626
EX n/a   NM n/a   MIP $12

❏ **Dodge Street Van,** 1978, Red body, white markings, opening doors, 1:64 scale, Model No. 1625
EX n/a   NM n/a   MIP $12

❏ **Ford Van,** 1978, Silver body, purple and pink markings, opening doors, 1:64 scale, Model No. 1627
EX n/a   NM n/a   MIP $12

❏ **GMC Stepside Pickup,** 1978, Yellow body, red and orange markings, opening doors, 1:64 scale, Model No. 1628
EX n/a   NM n/a   MIP $12

WORLD WAR II

❏ **Douglas A-20J Havoc,** 1978, Camouflage body, Model No. 1512
EX n/a   NM n/a   MIP $10

❏ **Messerschmitt ME 262A Sturmvogel,** 1978, Gray/silver body, Model No. 1512
EX n/a   NM n/a   MIP $10

❏ **Mitsubishi A6M-5 Zero,** 1978, Black body, red "zero" on wings and tail, Model No. 1512
EX n/a   NM n/a   MIP $10

❏ **North American P-51 Mustang,** 1978, Camouflage body, Model No. 1512
EX n/a   NM n/a   MIP $10

❏ **Republic P-47 Thunderbolt,** 1978, Dark green body, Model No. 1512
EX n/a   NM n/a   MIP $10

❏ **Supermarine V Spitfire,** 1978, Dark camouflage body, Royal Air Force, Model No. 1512
EX n/a   NM n/a   MIP $10

WRANGLER

❏ **Ford Thunderbird,** 1983, Also sold as part of four-vehicle set (#1482), 1:64 scale, Model No. 1485
EX n/a   NM n/a   MIP $10

❏ **Helicopter,** 1983, Also sold as part of four-vehicle set (#1482), Model No. 1540
EX n/a   NM n/a   MIP $10

❏ **Jeep,** 1983, Also sold as part of four-vehicle set (#1482), 1:64 scale, Model No. 1486
EX n/a   NM n/a   MIP $10

❏ **Pickup,** 1983, Also sold as part of four-vehicle set (#1482), 1:64 scale, Model No. 1487
EX n/a   NM n/a   MIP $10

Exact Detail Replicas

One of Exact Detail's sharpest models—a 1970 Indy Pace Car Olds 4-4-2.

Soon after being founded, in the early 1990s as an offshoot of Lane Automotive, Lane Collectables Division began commissioning its own exclusive, limited production collectables called the Exact Detail Series. The first Exact Detail project, based on the 1965-66 Ford Mustang fastback, yielded several stunning replications of the famous Shelby G.T. 350. These models quickly sold out and the company knew it had a hit. Their second model was the 1967-68 Chevrolet Camaro—also a favorite with collectors. The company is constantly offering new variations of these models, but they're not taking the easy way—each new entry has completely new bumpers, grilles and interiors, so they're not just sequels of the same first hit vehicle.

Each time a new vehicle is going to be modeled, the actual car is studied, photographed and measured. Car owners are consulted for additional insight. When the model is assembled, it's built by hand, using a process not unlike the construction of the real thing.

MARKET UPDATE

Exact Detail models are truly limited editions, so they sell out quickly and are soon available only on the secondary market. The replicas are some of the best 1:18-scale vehicles around, and definitely fall into the "high-end" category.

The first model of the Shelby G.T. 350—Camee Edelbrock's #27. This model was a huge success for Exact Detail, and is currently only available on the secondary market.

1965-66 Shelby G.T. 350 1:18 Series

The 1965-66 Shelby G.T. 350 was Exact Detail's first mold, presented as Camee Edelbrock's #27 Shelby G.T. 350, now available only in the secondary market. several other equally popular versions followed, such as the famous G.T. 350H series and a select group of Shelby R-Models.

First Release

Camee Edelbrock's #27 1966 Shelby G.T. 350
Part #101
Release Date: January, 1999
Production Run Limited to 2,500 Cars
Color: Guardsman Blue with White LeMans Stripes and Racing Graphics
Original Issue Price $79.95

Second Release

1966 Supercharged Shelby G.T. 350
Part #102
Release Date: May, 1999
Production Run Limited to 3,120 Cars
Color: Candyapple Red with White LeMans stripes
Original Issue Price $79.95

Third Release

1966 Shelby G.T. 350H
Part #103
Release Date: July, 1999
Production Run Limited to 5,004 Cars
Color: Black with Gold LeMans stripes
Original Issue Price $79.95

Fourth Release

Christi Edelbrock's 1966 Shelby G.T. 350
Part #104
Release Date: October, 1999
Production Run Limited to 3,000 Cars
Color: Wimbledon White with Blue LeMans stripes and Racing Graphics
Original Issue Price $79.95

Fifth Release

1966 Shelby G.T. 350H
Part #105
Release Date: January, 2000
Production Run Limited to 2,500 Cars
Color: Wimbledon White with Gold Le Man stripes
Original Issue Price $79.95

Sixth Release

1965 Shelby G.T. 350
Part #106
Release Date: March, 2000
Production Run Limited to 3,000 Cars
Color: Wimbledon White with Blue Le Mans stripes
Original Issue Price $79.95

Seventh Release

1966 Shelby G.T. 350S
Part #107
Release Date: June 2000
Production Run Limited to 2,500 Cars
Color: Ivy Green Metallic
Original Issue Price $79.95

Eighth Release A

1966 Shelby G.T. 350H
Part # 108B
Release Date: November, 2000
Production Run Limited to 1,750 Cars
Color: Guardsman Blue Metallic with Inca Gold Metallic Stripes
Original Issue Price $79.95

Eighth Release B

1966 Shelby G.T. 350H
Part # 108R
Release Date: December, 2000
Production Run Limited to 1,750 Cars
Color: Candyapple Red with Inca Gold Metallic Stripes
Original Issue Price $79.95

Eighth Release C

1966 Shelby G.T. 350H
Part # 108G
Release Date: January, 2001
Production Run Limited to 1,750 Cars
Color: Ivy Green Metallic with Inca Gold Metallic Stripes
Original Issue Price $79.95

Ninth Release

1965 Shelby R-Model/Driver: Jerry Titus
Part #109
Release Date: April, 2001
Production Run Limited to 2,800 Cars
Color: White with Blue Stripes / #61B graphics
Original Issue Price $89.95

Tenth Release

1965 Shelby R-Model/Essex Wire
Part# 110
Release Date: July, 2001/Debuting at SAAC26
Production Run Limited to 2,502 Cars
Color: White with black and orange stripe
Original Issue Price $89.95

Eleventh Release

Dan Gerber's 1965 Shelby G.T. 350 R-Model
Part# 111
Release Date: July, 2002
Production Run Limited to 2,250 Cars
Color: Red, white, and blue with racing graphics
Original Issue Price $89.95

Another sold-out vehicle for Exact Detail, the Shelby American Automobile Club 25th Anniversary model. Only 750 pieces were made.

Promo Release

SAAC-25 1965 Shelby G.T. 350
PART#107 PROMO
Release Date: June 2000
Production Run Limited to 750 CARS
Color: Silver with Blue Le Mans Stripes
Stock Availability: Sold Out—only available on the secondary market.
Original Issue Price $89.95

This model was one of Exact Detail's first Camaros, the 1967 "Grumpy's Toy" super stocker.

1967-68 Chevrolet Camaro 1:18 Series

Exact Detail's second tooling project was the 1967-68 Chevrolet Camaro, debuting in 2000. Like the Shelby series, each model is unique with different hoods, bumpers, grilles, wheels, and tires.

First Release

1967 Camaro Z-28
Part #201
Release Date: January, 2000
Production Run Limited to: 3,000 Cars
Color: Bolero Red with Black Stripes and Black Vinyl Top
Original Issue Price $79.95

Second Release

1967 Camaro rs/ss
Part #202
Release Date: June, 2000
Production Run Limited to: 2,500 Cars
Color: Nantucket Blue
Original Issue Price $79.95

Third Release

1967 Camaro SS396
Part #203
Release Date: September, 2000
Production Run Limited to: 2,500 Cars
Color: Tuxedo Black with White Stripe and Black Vinyl Top
Original Issue Price $79.95

Fourth Release A

1967 Nickey Chevrolet Camaro SS/RS - Street Prepared
Part #204S
Release Date: June, 2001
Production Run Limited to: 1,500 Cars
Color: Tahoe Turquoise with White stripe
Original Issue Price $79.95

Fourth Release B

1967 Nickey Chevrolet Camaro SS/RS - Drag Prepared
Part #204D
Release Date: June, 2001
Production Run Limited to: 1,500 Cars
Color: Tahoe Turquoise with White stripe
Original Issue Price $89.95

Fifth Release

1967 Grumpy's Toy Super Stock Drag Camaro
Part #205
Release Date: June, 2001
Production Run Limited to: 5,004 Cars
Color: White with drag racing graphics
Original Issue Price $89.95

Sixth Release

1967 Yenko Camaro SS427
Part# 206SC
Release Date: August, 2001
Production Run Limited to 2,754 Cars
Color: Deepwater blue metallic with white stripe
Original Issue Price $79.95

Seventh Release

1968 Yenko Camaro SS/RS 427
Part# 207SC
Release Date: July, 2001
Production Run Limited to 2,754 Cars
Color: Matador Red with black hockey stick stripes
Original Issue Price $79.95

Eighth Release A

1968 Nickey Chevrolet Camaro SS/RS
Street Prepared
Part #208S
Release Date: Sept 2001
Production Run Limited to: 1,500 Cars
Color: Butternut Yellow with Black vinyl top
Original Issue Price $79.95

Eighth Release B

1968 Nickey Chevrolet Camaro SS/RS
Drag Prepared
Part #208D
Release Date: Sept 10, 2001
Production Run Limited to: 1,500 Cars
Color: Butternut Yellow with Black vinyl top
Original Issue Price $89.95

Ninth Release A

1967 Nickey Chevrolet Camaro SS 427
Street Prepared
Part #209S
Release Date: Nov. 2001
Production Run Limited to: 1,000 Cars
Color: Bolero Red
Original Issue Price $79.95

Ninth Release B

1967 Nickey Chevrolet Camaro SS 427
Drag Prepared
Part #209D
Release Date: Nov. 2001
Production Run Limited to: 1,000 Cars
Color: Bolero Red
Original Issue Price $79.95

Another highly-detailed car, Dave Strickler's Old Reliable 1968 Camaro.

Tenth Release

1968 Dave Strickler's Old Reliable Super Stock Camaro
Part #210
Release Date: Dec, 2001
Production Run Limited to: Not to exceed 4,000 Cars
Color: Corvette Bronze with drag racing graphics
Original Issue Price $89.95

Eleventh Release

Little Hoss 1967 Z/28 Stock Eliminator
Camaro
Part #211
Release Date: June, 2002
Production Run Limited to: 2,000 Cars
Color: Royal Plum with white stripes
Original Issue Price $89.95

Promo Release

1967 Camaro SS396
Part #HC2001
Release Date: DEC. 2001
Production Run Limited to: 720 Cars
Color: Red
Original Issue Price N/A

1970-72 Oldsmobile 442 and Cutlass 1:18 Series

Until Exact Detail's replicas came along, no manufacturer had ever offered a model of the 1970, 1971, or 1972 Cutlass Supreme or 4-4-2 in 1:18-scale.

First Release

1970 Oldsmobile 442 Indy Pace Car
Part #301
Release Date: Nov, 2001
Production Run Limited to: 3,750 Cars
Color: Porcelain White with Indy graphics
Original Issue Price $99.95

Second Release

'71 Olds Cutlass Supreme SX
Part # 302
Release Date: April, 2002
Production Run Limited to: 2,000 Cars
Color: Triple Black
Original Issue Price $99.95

Promo Release

1970 Oldsmobile 442 Convertible
Part #301Z
Release Date: Nov, 2001
Production Run Limited to: 650 Cars
Color: Aegean Aqua with white stripes
Original Issue Price $99.95

GMP
Georgia Marketing & Promotions

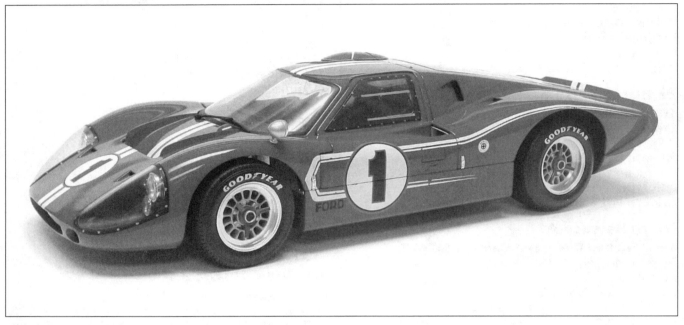

An incredibly detailed model, the 1:12-scale Foyt/Gurney No. 1 LeMans Mk. IV. It features steerable wheels, opening doors, removable engine covers—even rubber hoses and belts.

Georgia Marketing & Promotions, or "GMP" as it's commonly known, was created during NASCAR's boom time in 1991. GMP President Tom Long traveled to Charlotte, North Carolina to work out contracts and licensing agreements with the Busch Series of vehicles, which Long noticed were underrepresented.

Agreements to produce 1:64-scale transporters for various teams were forthcoming, but Ertl, Long's main supplier, had to back out of the agreement due to conflicts with another business.

However, Long soon met with Stan Gill of RCI, who told him about a new transporter casting, and wondered if Long would be interested. It turned out to be fortuitous for GMP (at the time known as "Peachstate Motorsports").

By autumn of 1992, a new shipment of Harry Gant/Mac Tools transporters arrived, and the first release of 10,000 pieces sold out quickly. Models in 1:18-scale were followed closely, including replicas of winged sprint cars, muscle cars and classic LeMans racers. Currently, the company has over 40 different families of molds, and some models contain over 400 parts.

MARKET UPDATE

GMP models are high-end replicas, and could really be considered automotive sculpture. While most of their vehicles are 1:18-scale, they do produce pieces in 1:64, 1:43 and 1:25th-scales as well. The models are limited in production, so they do sell out even at the pre-order stage, making scarcity an issue. Keeping a watch at shows or online auctions is probably a good way to gauge the popularity or rarity of the replica you're looking for.

Detail of the Foyt/Gurney LeMans with engine covers and wheels removed.

Close-up of front-end detail of the Foyt/Gurney LeMans.

A 1:18-scale model of Don Garlits' Swamp Rat from 1957—the first dragster to make 170 mph. Realistic features on this car even include spark plug wires!

Parnelli Jones' '66 T-70 Ford 4 Cam Spyder 1:18-scale car in metallic blue. A great-looking model.

Another Don Garlits dragster—the Swamp Rat III in 1:18-scale.

A Georgia State Patrol Mustang in 1:18-scale with opening hood, doors, trunk and a detailed engine right down to the fan belt!

The Al Unser/Johnny Lightning 1:18-scale racer from the Vintage Dirt Champs series.

The No. 4 Bruce McClaren M8B High Wing in 1:18-scale.

1:12 DIRT CHAMP

❑ **#1 Bobby Unser/Bardhal,** 2000, Black and yellow large check pattern body, black pipes, black interior, silver wheels, Goodyear tires, "Bardhal" white type reversed out of black square on hood. These 1:12-scale models have incredible detail and include: steering arms, drag link, torsion arms, steering box, oil lines, fuel lines, electrical wiring, spark plug wires and coolant lines, 1:12 scale, Model No. 7903
EX n/a　　NM n/a　　MIP $270

❑ **Don Branson/Wynn's Special,** 2002, Yellow body with silver roll bar, chrom pipes, clear windshield, black and chrome wheels, red number "4" on tail, red "Wynn's Special" on hood, red interior, 1:12 scale, Model No. 7905
EX n/a　　NM n/a　　MIP $270

❑ **Mario Andretti 4 Cam Ford/Vel's Parnelli Jones,** 2002, White with white roll cage, silver and gold wheels, exposed silver engine, red stripe and red and blue number "2" on tail, various sponsor graphics. Lift-off hood shows extremely detailed engine. Due to pre-order, this model is also sold-out, price below reflects suggested retail only, 1:12 scale, Model No. 7904
EX n/a　　NM n/a　　MIP $320

1:12-SCALE FORD GT40 ENDURANCE CARS

(Georgia Marketing & Promotions)

❑ **#1 Foyt/Gurney LeMans 1967 MK IV,** 2002, Model of 1967 LeMans winning red and white car. Each vehicle in this series is incredibly detailed with a working suspension, steerable wheels, opening compartments including doors, front and rear body panels,

rear body panel hatch and fuel doors, removable carburetor covers, linkage covers and removable wheels and tires, 1:12 scale, Model No. 12072
EX n/a　　NM n/a　　MIP $445

❑ **#2 McLaren/Amon 1966 LeMans MK IIB,** 2002, Black and silver model with number "2" on sides and hood, and like the others in the series, will be comprised of over 350 separated pieces, 1:12 scale, Model No. 13022
EX n/a　　NM n/a　　MIP $490

❑ **#6 Ickx/Oliver 1969 LeMans MK I,** 2002, Orange and blue model of the winning car, 1:12 scale, Model No. 12073
EX n/a　　NM n/a　　MIP $460

1:18 '84-'92 MUSTANG SERIES

(Georgia Marketing & Promotions)

❑ **1985 Mustang GT,** 2001, Black with dark charcoal interior. Each car in the Mustang series includes: opening doors, hood and trunk, highly detailed chassis, rubber fan belts and hoses, engine wiring, individual numbering and serialization, Model No. 8061
EX n/a　　NM n/a　　MIP $95

❑ **1987 Mustang LX,** 2002, Canyon Red, Model No. 8063
EX n/a　　NM n/a　　MIP $95

1:18 '84-'92 POLICE MUSTANG SERIES

❑ **1988 Georgia State Patrol,** 2002, Blue body with white roof, black wheels and small silver hubcaps. "Georgia State Patrol" and "State Trooper" in white. Each of the Police Mustangs features: opening doors, hood and trunk, real rubber fan belts and hoses, engine wiring, individual numbering and serialization, Model No. 9061
EX n/a　　NM n/a　　MIP $95

❑ **1989 Florida Highway Patrol,** 2002, Black body with white roof, roof lights, "State Trooper" lettering on front quarter panels, Model No. 9063

❑ **1992 Texas Highway Patrol,** 2002, Black body with white roof, no roof lights, Texas Patrol graphics on doors, Model No. 9062

1:18 BUICK SERIES

❑ **'86 Regal "T" Type,** 2002, Designers Series WH1, black and silver exterior, white spoked wheels, gray interior, Model No. 8008
EX n/a　　NM n/a　　MIP $60

❑ **'87 Buick Turbo T,** 2001, Gray metallic. Each vehicle in the Buick series features; accurate, detailed chassis and engines, posable wheels, individual numbering and serialization, Model No. 8006
EX n/a　　NM n/a　　MIP $60

1:18 CHEVY CAMARO TRANS-AM

❑ **1967 Mark Donohue/Team Penske,** 2002, 1:18 scale, Model No. 13021
EX n/a　　NM n/a　　MIP $80

❑ **1968 Mark Donohue/ Sunoco Team Penske,** 2002, 1:18 scale, Model No. 13022
EX n/a　　NM n/a　　MIP $80

❑ **1969 Mark Donohue/Sunoco Team Penske,** 2002, Model No. 13023
EX n/a　　NM n/a　　MIP $80

GMP

1:18 FORD FAIRLANE REPLICAS

❑ **1966 Ford Fairlane 390,** 2002, GTA, Raven Black with red stripes, Model No. 8082
EX n/a   **NM** n/a   **MIP** $110

❑ **1966 Ford Fairlane 427,** 2002, 500, Wimbledon White with dual carbs, Model No. 8083
EX n/a   **NM** n/a   **MIP** $110

❑ **1967 Ford Fairlane 427,** 2001, 500 XL, Candy Apple Red hardtop. Standard features for each of the cars in this series include: opening doors, hood and trunk, highly detailed chassis, real rubber fan belts, hoses and engine wiring, working suspension, steerable front wheels, adjustable front seats, door windows that roll up and down with a hand crank, and a rotating drive shaft. Each car is individually numbered and serialized, Model No. 8081
EX n/a   **NM** n/a   **MIP** $110

1:18 GTO SERIES

❑ **'71 Judge Convertible,** 2002, Cameo White body, silver wheels, Goodyear tires. GTO's in this series have extremely detailed engines, opening doors (with handles, just like a real door!) opening hood and trunk, real rubber fan belts and hoses, engine wiring, working suspensions, separate die-cast chassis, individual numbering and serialization, 1:18 scale, Model No. 8042
EX n/a   **NM** n/a   **MIP** $120

❑ **'72 GTO with rare ducktail spoiler,** 2002, Cardinal Red body, silver five-spoked wheels, Model No. 8043
EX n/a   **NM** n/a   **MIP** $120

1:18 MUSCLE CARS

❑ **'32 Ford Roadster,** 2001, Hot Rod Red, 1:18 scale, Model No. 7030TO
EX n/a   **NM** n/a   **MIP** $38

❑ **'67 Chevy Camaro,** 2001, Belero Red, 1:18 scale, Model No. 201
EX n/a   **NM** n/a   **MIP** $75

❑ **'69 Camaro,** 2001, LeMans Blue, Cannaday's, 1:18 scale, Model No. 7063
EX n/a   **NM** n/a   **MIP** $50

❑ **'69 GTX Hardtop,** 2001, Alpine White, 1:18 scale, Model No. 29013
EX n/a   **NM** n/a   **MIP** $40

❑ **'70 El Camino,** 2001, Forest Green, 1:18 scale, Model No. 7028TO
EX n/a   **NM** n/a   **MIP** $38

❑ **'70 Shelby GT-500,** 2001, Competition Red, 1:18 scale, Model No. 7043
EX n/a   **NM** n/a   **MIP** $40

1:18 NOVA SERIES

❑ **'68 Dick Harrell Drag Nova,** 2002, Red body with silver wheels, "Fred Gibbs" graphics on doors, and "Dick Harrell" on sides in white type, 1:18 scale, Model No. 8026
EX n/a   **NM** n/a   **MIP** $60

❑ **'68 Pro Street,** 2001, Black body, black interior, silver five-spoke hubs, 1:18 scale, Model No. 8025
EX n/a   **NM** n/a   **MIP** $60

❑ **'69 Nova, SS396,** 2001, Fathom Green body, silver five-spoke wheels, Goodyear tires, black interior. Each car in this series features: highly detailed engines and chassis, posable wheels and individual numbering and serialization, 1:18 scale, Model No. 8021
EX n/a   **NM** n/a   **MIP** $55

1:18 VINTAGE DIRT CHAMPS

❑ **#2 Mario Andretti/STP,** 2000, Red body with STP logo on hood, silver wheels, black interior, silver number "2" on tail, Firestone tires. Each of the vintage series include: detailed engines, fuel lines, detailed brakes, spark plug wires, full frame, differing noses and suspensions, rotating break calipers and narrow and wide tires, 1:18 scale, Model No. 7624
EX n/a   **NM** n/a   **MIP** $90

(Georgia Marketing & Promotions)

❑ **Al Unser/Johnny Lightning,** 2001, Blue with yellow Johnny Lightning (lightning bolt) graphic on hood, yellow number "1" on tail, red pipes, dull silver finish wheels, Firestone tires, 1:18 scale, Model No. 7626
EX n/a   **NM** n/a   **MIP** $90

(Georgia Marketing & Promotions)

❑ **Bobby Marshman/Econo,** 2000, Blue body with red number "5" on tail and hood, black interior, silver wheels with Firestone tires, 1:18 scale, Model No. 7625
EX n/a   **NM** n/a   **MIP** $90

❑ **Jim Hurtubise/Sterling Plumbing,** 2002, Red body with gold and silver wheels, Firestone tires, silver detailing, white nose with number "56" and green "56" on tail, 1:18 scale, Model No. 7628
EX n/a   **NM** n/a   **MIP** $90

1:18 VINTAGE FRONT ENGINE RAIL DRAGSTERS

(Georgia Marketing & Promotions)

❑ **C. Swingle '61 Swamp Rat III,** 2002, Model of the record setting racer that topped off at 198.66 mph, 1:18 scale, Model No. 14003
EX n/a   **NM** n/a   **MIP** $110

GMP

GMP

(Georgia Marketing & Promotions)

❑ **Don Garlits' '57 Swamp Rat I,** 2001, First dragster to go over 170 mph! Black body with blue and white flame graphics, spoked front wheels, large whitewall rear tires, "Don's Speed Shop" on hood. These models have highly detailed engines, drivelines, sparkplug wires, die-cast frame, aluminum body panels and individual numbering and serialization, 1:18 scale, Model No. 14001
EX n/a   NM n/a   MIP $110

❑ **Don Garlits' '59 Swamp Rat I Blown Hemi,** 2002, Model of the world record setter at 182.56 mph!, 1:18 scale, Model No. 14002
EX n/a   NM n/a   MIP $110

1:18 VINTAGE MIDGETS

(Georgia Marketing & Promotions)

❑ **Duke Nalon/ Bowes Seal Fast,** 2000, Black and white body with red number "44" on tail of car and red "Seal Fast" circle graphics on hood. Chrome wheels and detail trim, 1:18 scale, Model No. 7644
EX n/a   NM n/a   MIP $80

(Georgia Marketing & Promotions)

❑ **Lloyd Axel/ Foster's Auto Supply,** 2000, White body with red interior, number "5" on tail, chrome detailing. This model is sold out, so suggested retail shown below may be less than current aftermarket value, 1:18 scale, Model No. 7645
EX n/a   NM n/a   MIP $80

❑ **Rodger Ward/Edelbrock V8-60,** 2000, Red and white with number "27" on rear of car, chrome wheels, trim and exhaust pipes, 1:18 scale, Model No. 7643
EX n/a   NM n/a   MIP $80

1:18 VINTAGE SPRINT

❑ **#2 Jud Larson/A.J. Watson,** 2000, Red with black seat and interior, chrome wheels, Firestone tires, chrome detailing, racer's names on hood, 1:18 scale, Model No. 7610
EX n/a   NM n/a   MIP $70

1:18 WINGED SPRINTS

❑ **#1 Billy Pauch/Zemco,** 2001, The 1:18-scale winged sprint cars feature removable wings, differing hood styles (including snorkel hood) fuel and oil pump lines, valve covers, plug and distributor wires, water hoses, oil reservoir and filter, 1:18 scale, Model No. 7010
EX n/a   NM n/a   MIP $70

❑ **#104 Jeff Swindell/104+ Octane,** 2001, 1:18 scale, Model No. 7016
EX n/a   NM n/a   MIP $70

❑ **#11 Steve Kinser/Aristocrat,** 2001, 1:18 scale, Model No. 7017
EX n/a   NM n/a   MIP $70

❑ **#11H Greg Hodnet/Vivarin,** 2001, 1:18 scale, Model No. 7015
EX n/a   NM n/a   MIP n/a

❑ **#1A Bobby Allen/Shark Car,** 2001, Blue body with shark eyes and mouth graphics on hood, black roll cage, silver wings, Goodyear tires, 1:18 scale, Model No. 7021
EX n/a   NM n/a   MIP $73

❑ **#2 Andy Hillenburg/STP,** 2001, 1:18 scale, Model No. 7011
EX n/a   NM n/a   MIP $70

❑ **#2 Brad Furr/Sanmina,** 2002, Red body with number "2" on red wings, Hoosier tires, 1:18 scale, Model No. 7032
EX n/a   NM n/a   MIP $75

❑ **#22 Jac Haudens- child/Radioactive Wild Child,** 2001, 1:18 scale, Model No. 7022
EX n/a   NM n/a   MIP $73

❑ **#40 NARC Budweiser/40th Anniversary,** 2001, 1:18 scale, Model No. 7110
EX n/a   NM n/a   MIP $80

❑ **#63 Jack Hewitt/Hampshire,** 2001, 1:18 scale, Model No. 7020
EX n/a   NM n/a   MIP $73

❑ **Sammy Swindell/Nance,** 2001, Silver with "Nance" graphics, gold and chrome wheels, Goodyear tires, 1:18 scale, Model No. 7028
EX n/a   NM n/a   MIP $75

1:18-SCALE LOLA CAN-AM

❑ **#21 Mario Andretti Lola T-70 Ford 4 Cam,** 2001, 1:18 scale, Model No. 12006M
EX n/a   NM n/a   MIP $90

❑ **#6 Mark Donohue Parsons Lola Coupe,** 2000, Dark blue with number "6" on sides and hood, silver and black wheels, Goodyear tires, Sunoco and Goodyear logo graphics. The Can-Am models all feature accurate interiors and chassis, removable hoods and detailed engine, detailed wheels and brakes, individual numbering and posable wheels, 1:18 scale, Model No. 12003
EX n/a   NM n/a   MIP $75

(Georgia Marketing & Promotions)

❑ **#6 Mark Donohue Penske '67 T-70 Spyder,** 2000, Blue body with number "6" on doors and hood, yellow front wheels, chrome spoked rear wheels, Firestone tires, 1:18 scale, Model No. 12005
EX n/a   NM n/a   MIP $90

❑ **#7 Mark Donohue/Nassau Trophy Race Winner,** 2002, Dark blue with number "7" on sides and hood, chrome six-spoke wheels, yellow "Sunoco Special" type and Pepsi Cola graphics on hood, 1:18 scale, Model No. 12007

EX n/a   NM n/a   MIP $90

❏ **John Surtees 1966 Lola T-70 Spyder,** 2000, Red, with number "7" on sides and hood, opening hood, detailed engine, silver and red wheels with Firestone tires, 1:18 scale, Model No. 12004

EX n/a   NM n/a   MIP $90

(Georgia Marketing & Promotions)

❏ **Parnelli Jones '66 T-70 Ford 4 Cam Spyder,** 2001, Light metallic blue, number "21" on doors and hood, six-spoke chrome wheels, white air scoop, 1:18 scale, Model No. 12006P

EX n/a   NM n/a   MIP $90

1:18-SCALE McCLAREN CAN-AM

❏ **#4 Bruce McClaren M8B High Wing,** 2002, Orange body, black pipes, chrome wheels, number "4" on sides and hood, white high wing, silver highlights, "Gulf Oil" graphics on front panels, 1:18 scale, Model No. 12024

EX n/a   NM n/a   MIP $100

❏ **#48 Dan Gurney M8D,** 2001, Orange body, low rear spoiler, black pipes, four-spoke chrome wheels, Goodyear tires, number "48" on sides, hood and spoiler, 1:18 scale, Model No. 12025

EX n/a   NM n/a   MIP $100

1:18-SCALE TRANS-AM

❏ **#1 Dorsey Schroeder/Whistler Mustang (1990),** 2000, Red body with white trim and "Whistler 1" graphics, gold-spoked and silver-rimmed wheels with Goodyear tires, 1:18 scale, Model No. 13002

EX n/a   NM n/a   MIP $75

❏ **#11 Scott Pruett/Motorcraft IMSA Mustang (1986),** 2000, White body with "Motorcraft Quality Parts" and number "11" graphics. Gold-spoked and silver-rimmed wheels with Goodyear tires. Each model in this series features accurate detailing on the interior and chassis, removable hoods to show engine detail, posable wheels, intricately-crafted wheels and brakes, 1:18 scale, Model No. 13001

EX n/a   NM n/a   MIP $75

(Georgia Marketing & Promotions)

❏ **#7 Bruce Jenner/7-11 Mustang,** 2000, Blue and white body with "7-11," "Citgo" graphics on sides and hood, gold-spoked and silver-rimmed wheels, Goodyear tires, 1:18 scale, Model No. 13004

EX n/a   NM n/a   MIP $90

1:25 WINGED SPRINTS

❏ **#11 Steve Kinser/Quakerstate,** 2001, Muddy version, Model No. 7319

EX n/a   NM n/a   MIP $45

❏ **#19 Stevie Smith/Ingersoll-Rand,** 2001, 1:25 scale, Model No. 7310

EX n/a   NM n/a   MIP $40

❏ **#1F Dean Jacobs/Frigidaire,** 2001, 1:25 scale, Model No. 7302

EX n/a   NM n/a   MIP $40

❏ **#1W Danny Lasoki/Conn West,** 2001, 1:25 scale, Model No. 7307

EX n/a   NM n/a   MIP $40

❏ **#23S Frankie Kerr/Shoff Motorsports,** 2001, 1:25 scale, Model No. 7309

EX n/a   NM n/a   MIP $40

❏ **#2M Brent Keading,** 2001, 1:25 scale, Model No. 7308

EX n/a   NM n/a   MIP $40

❏ **#35 Tyler Walker/Air Sep,** 2001, 1:25 scale, Model No. 7315

EX n/a   NM n/a   MIP $40

❏ **#77 Fred Rahmer/Hamilton Motorsports,** 2001, 1:25 scale, Model No. 7311

EX n/a   NM n/a   MIP $40

❏ **#8H Joe Gaerte/Holbrook Motorsports,** 2001, 1:25 scale, Model No. 7316

EX n/a   NM n/a   MIP $40

❏ **#U2 Keith Kauffman/U2,** 2001, 1:25 scale, Model No. 7312

EX n/a   NM n/a   MIP $40

1:43 LOLA T-70 3-CAR BOX SET

❏ **John Surtees Lola T-70 Spyder Box Set,** 2002, Three highly-detailed 1:43-scale models in wooden presentation box, 1:43 scale, Model No. 12402

EX n/a   NM n/a   MIP $70

(Georgia Marketing & Promotions)

❏ **Penske/Sunoco 3-Car Set,** 2002, Set of three, 1:43 scale cars in wood presentation case: #6 Lola Coupe and #7 and #16 T-70 Spyders, 1:43 scale, Model No. 12401

EX n/a   NM n/a   MIP $70

1:50 WINGED SPRINTS

❏ **#11H Greg Hodnet/Vivarin,** 2001, 1:50 scale, Model No. 7704

EX n/a   NM n/a   MIP $13

❏ **#15 Donny Schatz/Petro,** 2001, 1:50 scale, Model No. 7703

EX n/a   NM n/a   MIP $13

❏ **#19 Stevie Smith/Ingersoll-Rand,** 2001, Standard features for the 1:50-scale winged sprints include: removable wings, chassis detail, engine detail, decorative box and a serialized certificate with room for the driver's signature, 1:50 scale, Model No. 7702

EX n/a   NM n/a   MIP $13

GMP

GMP

❏ **#1A Bobby Allen/Shark Car,** 2001, 1:50 scale, Model No. 7714
EX n/a   NM n/a   MIP $13

❏ **#2 Andy Hillenburg/Luxaire,** 2001, 1:50 scale, Model No. 7711
EX n/a   NM n/a   MIP $13

❏ **#22 Jac Haudenschild,** 2001, 1:50 scale, Model No. 7709
EX n/a   NM n/a   MIP $13

❏ **#23 Kasey Kahne/Speed Racer,** 2001, 1:50 scale, Model No. 7719
EX n/a   NM n/a   MIP $13

❏ **#29 Doug Wolfgang/Weikert's Livestock,** 2001, Model No. 7710
EX n/a   NM n/a   MIP $13

❏ **#63 Jack Hewitt/Hampshire,** 2001, 1:50 scale, Model No. 7712
EX n/a   NM n/a   MIP $13

❏ **#77 Fred Rahmer/Hamilton Motorsports,** 2001, 1:50 scale, Model No. 7708
EX n/a   NM n/a   MIP $13

❏ **#83 Danny Lasoki/Beef Packers,** 2001, 1:50 scale, Model No. 7705
EX n/a   NM n/a   MIP $13

❏ **Amoco Knoxville 40th Anniversary,** 2001, 1:50 scale, Model No. 7716
EX n/a   NM n/a   MIP $13

❏ **Jac Haudenschild/Radioactive Wild Child,** 2001, 1:50 scale, Model No. 7713
EX n/a   NM n/a   MIP $13

1:64 NASCAR TRANSPORTERS

❏ **#99 Jeff Burton/Citgo,** 2002, 1:64 scale, Model No. 3131
EX n/a   NM n/a   MIP $55

❏ **Bill Elliott/McDonald's,** 2001, Only 2004 of these models were produced. All transporters features include: all die-cast construction, silk screened or pad printed graphics, individual numbers and serialization, 1:64 scale, Model No. 3119
EX n/a   NM n/a   MIP $50

❏ **Chad Little/John Deere,** 2001, 2256 total production, 1:64 scale, Model No. 3121
EX n/a   NM n/a   MIP $50

❏ **Jeff Burton/Exide,** 2001, 1440 models produced, 1:64 scale, Model No. 3123
EX n/a   NM n/a   MIP $50

❏ **Jeremy Mayfield/Mobile 1,** 2001, Limited production of 996 pieces, 1:64 scale, Model No. 3127
EX n/a   NM n/a   MIP $50

❏ **Johnny Benson/Cheerio's,** 2001, Limited production of 1008, 1:64 scale, Model No. 3126
EX n/a   NM n/a   MIP $50

❏ **Mark Martin/Viagra,** 2001, 1:64 scale, Model No. 3129
EX n/a   NM n/a   MIP $55

❏ **Rick Mast/Remington,** 2001, Only 1800 produced, 1:64 scale, Model No. 3120
EX n/a   NM n/a   MIP $50

❏ **Todd Bodine/Tabasco,** 2001, Limited edition of 1144 pieces, 1:64 scale, Model No. 3124
EX n/a   NM n/a   MIP $50

ACCESSORIES

❏ **2-post Service Floor Lift with Base,** 2002, 1:18 scale, Model No. 9013
EX n/a   NM n/a   MIP $40

❏ **2-post Service Floor Lift with Base,** 2002, 1:24 scale, Model No. 9016
EX n/a   NM n/a   MIP $40

❏ **Buick Garage Accessories,** 2000, Buick-branded garage accessories, including battery charger, arc welder, engine stand, tool chest, air compressor and gas welder, 1:18 scale, Model No. 9011
EX n/a   NM n/a   MIP $25

❏ **Can-Am Tire and Wheel Set,** 2001, 1:18 scale, Model No. 9009
EX n/a   NM n/a   MIP $15

❏ **Chevy Rally/Super Sport Tire and Wheel Set,** 2000, 1:18 scale, Model No. 9007
EX n/a   NM n/a   MIP $15

❏ **Garage Accessories Package,** 2001, Includes: air compressor, gas welder, arc welder, battery charger, engine stand and tool chest, 1:18 scale, Model No. 9010
EX n/a   NM n/a   MIP $20

(Georgia Marketing & Promotions)

❏ **Nostalgic Corvette 1:18 Trailer and Tool set,** Includes red tandem trailer, air compressor, gas welder, tool chest, arc welder, battery charger and engine stand. Shown here with the modern "Corvette Racing" set, (#2605-1), 1:18 scale, Model No. 2605-1
EX n/a   NM n/a   MIP $40

❏ **Nova/Muscle Car Wheel and Tire Set,** 2001, Includes super sport and drag tires and wheels for 1:18-scale vehicles, 1:18 scale, Model No. 9006
EX n/a   NM n/a   MIP $15

❏ **Shop Tools,** 2002, Includes: welder, air compressor, battery charger, tool box, 1:24 scale, Model No. 9015
EX n/a   NM n/a   MIP $18

❏ **Shop Tools Set,** 2002, Includes: welder, air compressor, battery charger and tool box, 1:18 scale, Model No. 9012
EX n/a   NM n/a   MIP $20

❏ **Tandem trailer with tire rack,** Includes removable ramps that raise and lower, optional tire rack and three different hitch options, 1:24 scale, Model No. 2602
EX n/a   NM n/a   MIP $20

❏ **Tandem trailer with tire rack,** Black and gray. Comes with optional tire rack, removable ramps that lower and raise and three different hitch options, 1:18 scale, Model No. 2601
EX n/a   NM n/a   MIP $25

❏ **Tandem trailer with tire rack,** Includes three different hitch options, removable ramps and optional tire rack, 1:43 scale,
EX n/a   NM n/a   MIP $18

❏ **Team Corvette 1:18 Trailer/Tools Set,** Includes yellow tandem trailer, tool chest, engine stand, battery charger, arc welder, gas welder and air compressor, 1:18 scale, Model No. 2605-2
EX n/a   NM n/a   MIP $40

❏ **Vintage Midget Kit,** 2001, 1:18 scale, Model No. 7661
EX n/a   NM n/a   MIP $30

❏ **Vintage Sprint Car Kit,** 2001, 1:18 scale, Model No. 7121
EX n/a   NM n/a   MIP $30

Number 22, the Talbot Lago. Vintage vehicles by Hot Wheels always look sharp. This casting has been reissued a number of variations, but this was the first.

By Michael Zarnock

©2002 Michael Zarnock

Hello all you Die-Cast Car Collectors! My name is Michael Zarnock and I'm the author of *The Ultimate Guide To Hot Wheels Variations,* another collector guide published by the Krause Family. The staff at Krause asked me to lend a hand to The Standard Catalog of Die-Cast vehicles and I was more than happy to help.

Let me start by telling you a little about myself and how I got to where I am today. As a child I was fascinated with cars, all kinds of cars. My dad was a body man and I would go with him sometimes to the shop. I saw a lot of cars and trucks as I was growing up. I collected all types of toy cars as far back as I can remember. I was always trying to soup-up my Matchbox and Slot cars to make them look as real as the cars I saw on the street. I used to read *Hot Rod*

magazine and would drool at all the California Custom cars. You have to remember that this was a time when seeing Super Bee Six-Pack's, Hemi Roadrunner's, Big Block Corvette's and the occasional A/C Cobra driving down the road or parked in a neighbors driveway was commonplace. This was a time when you could go down to the local car dealer and buy a brand new 12-second quarter mile car right off the lot. To me, it was the greatest time to be a 10-year-old boy who was in love with American muscle cars. You never forget that deep rumbling sound or feeling the ground shake when one of them went by. It was and still is a very special thing that anyone who loves cars and horsepower should get to experience.

One day back in 1968, I was riding my "Stingray" bicycle with the tall sissy bar and redline slick rear

The First Non-Series Numbered Pack vehicle, "Old Number 5." Adding this vehicle MIP to your collection could set you back about $180.

tire down to the local shopping center to look at the models. I walked into a local department store named "W.T. Grants" and saw a new display of diecast cars. Well, when I saw "Hot Wheels with California Custom Styling," I went nuts! All these way cool cars with mag wheels and red line tires already on them. Blowers popping out of the hood, sidepipes or Zoomies, and trick paint. I was in Hod Rod heaven and I have been hooked on them ever since.

A lot of people ask me: "What is your favorite car?" That's like asking which one of your kids do you love best? I like most of the "real" looking cars— the cars that you can see out there on the street. I like a lot of the new cars Mattel is putting out. The '56 Ford Panel is way cool. The Mustang Mach, '70 RoadRunner, Tow Trucks and anything that can carry another vehicle (of course), A/C Cobra, '57 T-Bird, Corvettes, '65 Mustang, and the list goes on.

Another question they ask is how I would compare Hot Wheels to other die-cast cars and I really can't give a straight answer. I'm sure that there are other diecast carmakers that make their cars in closer scale or more detail, but then so do Mattel with their new "Collectibles" line. I guess it's all in what you like and what you're looking to get from it.

I'm also a package collector. I like the different styles of the packages from the many eras of Hot

Wheels. Like I said before, it's all about the memories for me. Hot Wheels are something that can get me away from the stress of the everyday adult world where everyone at work and home depend on you to be the pillar of strength. Hot Wheels relax me and bring me back to the easygoing childhood I once knew. So, I would guess you could tell I keep everything in the original package. My thoughts are: "Preserve the toy, preserve the boy." Hot Wheels have always brought me pleasure. Whether it's just looking at the cars that trigger those great memories from my childhood, or playing with them today with my boys. I would say Hot Wheels give me a calming effect that brings me back to when the most important thing I had to do was clean my room and mow the lawn to get my allowance so I could buy another new Hot Wheels car. I'm sure it's that way with a lot of other people as well. It becomes one of the few constant things in your life when the rest of the world is changing at such a rapid pace. For me, Hot Wheels have been a consistency for the past 30 plus years.

As with most of us over the years, we have stopped and started our collecting as life permits. During my most recent collecting period, I have gotten into the Collector Number Packages or "Collector Numbers" as they are called by those

Notice some of the packaging changing over time: the Mercedes 500 SL, Collector #815.

The Oshkosh Snowplow, number 42, a nice hefty model. This casting is still used by Hot Wheels, but no longer includes the plastic plow.

The Bulldozer, number 34. Hot Wheels construction vehicles are generally well-detailed toys, as this photo attests.

who are obsessed with them. Hopefully this book will give you insight to a better understanding about the largest obsession in Hot Wheels collecting since Red Lines.

The best thing I like about Collector Numbers is that you actually have a chance to have some sort of complete collection. What I mean is that there are actually a definite number of packages that can be collected. It gives you a goal to set and that goal is possible to meet.

The words "Collector Numbers" and "Blue Cards" have become a type of package now and have brought upon their own meaning.

Let's define what a "Collector Number" package really is. There has been a lot of confusion as to what is actually a "Collector Number" package. In this section of the book we will be talking about the Collector Numbers from 1 to 1121, produced by Mattel from 1989 to 1999. Packages that were readily available from any store that sold Hot Wheels.

Number 30, the '80s Corvette.

Hydroplane, number 346, from the 1995 Model Series.

Another construction vehicle, the Oshkosh Cement Mixer, number 144.

Limited Edition cars or cars from clubs with Collector Numbers on the package are not included—only cars that were released by Mattel for retail sale to mass merchandisers.

In the year 2000, Mattel started the Collector Numbers over at #1 and did it again in 2001. We will get to those numbers later on in another edition. There were also packages produced before 1989 with small black collector numbers in a circle. These packages are known as "Experimental Packs", and are not considered "Collector Numbers" as we are talking about. There was also a checklist of cars with numbers on the backs of those packages.

Some people include the Experimental Packs in the "Collector Numbers" category because the numbers for those cars are pretty much the same as the "Blue Card" collector number packages.

Now I know you're saying, "Hey, I thought they were all blue cards? They're Blue aren't they?" NO! That is another misconception. This whole Collector Number and Blue Card craze was all started with the same card.

In 1989 Mattel developed the "All Blue Card" with large white Collector Numbers in the lower right hand corner. This was after the Experimental Pack that was also blue, light blue. Some people take it that any card that is blue, any shade of blue is a "Blue Card" It's not! Each card has its own name.

In 1995 Mattel came out with the "Series Cards". These cards were changed to Blue and White.

Some people call these cards "Blue Cards". They are not. These are "Blue & White cards". The cards changed to blue on the top half and white on the lower half, with blue "Collector Numbers" in the lower right hand corner. Like I said earlier, just because there is some blue on the card, does not mean it's a "Blue Card".

The Blue & White cards carried on the "Collector Numbers". The series cards have the collector number on the back of the card with the "Series" name on the front. The cars that were not part of any "Series" still had the Collector Number on the front of the card in

the same place that the "Blue Cards" did, but the number changed to Blue. Later on they changed to having the collector number on the right side of the car name that was in the banner in the center of the card.

In 1995 there were reissues of cars with "Collector Numbers" on the new "Blue & White" cards. Same car, same number, new packaging. Some cars stayed the same, others changed color or wheels, but one thing did stay the same, the "Collector Number". Of course cars that are on all Blue Cards do go for a little more than the same car on a Blue and White card. The older the package, the more the value.

1995 is also when many Variations started showing up too. In the first few series alone there were at least three variations of each car. That's when things got really crazy. There were all new cards, all new Series Cars along with Collector Number reissues and different wheels, colors, windows, you name it and it was happening. It was enough to make a guy spend his lunch hour and his lunch money buying any different variation of Hot Wheels he or she could find.

But, alas, due to a limited amount of space in this book, we are only able to list one of each of the Collector Numbers and had to leave out the variations. If you would like to see what variations are out there of these cars, all you need to do is pick up my book called *The Ultimate Guide To Hot*

The Lamborghini Countach, number 60.

Wheels Variations, also by Krause Publications. In there you will find over 1100 color photos and more than 2000 detailed variations. There has never been a more complete listing of Collector Number Variations published anywhere. If you're into Hot Wheels Variations or think you might want to start collecting Variations, that is a book that will be invaluable to you as a collector.

The prices in this book are for packaged cars in mint condition and are taken from actual sales. Whether it be from that auction site we all know about, or at toy shows or at some Hot Wheels Club meeting. Now remember, these prices are not written in stone. There have been cars sold for less, but what I have chosen to do is put down the highest price I have ever seen the car sell for. As time goes on, most prices go up and have proved to do so.

I have been collecting, selling, trading and watching in this hobby for a long time. I have seen how most people take all the sales they know about and average them to put a value on a car. That doesn't work when we have an abundance of one car in one area of the country and only a handful in another. If there are a ton where YOU are, then you know not to pay a lot for it. But if you have never seen one, then you know it's rare. It's all in how bad you want it and what you're willing to pay for it. Now, this brings me to how these prices come about. Simply put, supply and demand. If the demand is great and the supply is small, the price will be high. If the demand is small, no mater how small the supply, the price will be low.

The most important things I can tell you are these. Know what you're getting, ask questions, do your homework, read, read and read some more until you know what you're doing and most of all, use your head! That is what the guides are for. To guide you in the right direction. You may not always agree with the pricing, but you can't ague with a full color picture and detailed description.

Best of luck and most of all.....Have Fun!
Michael

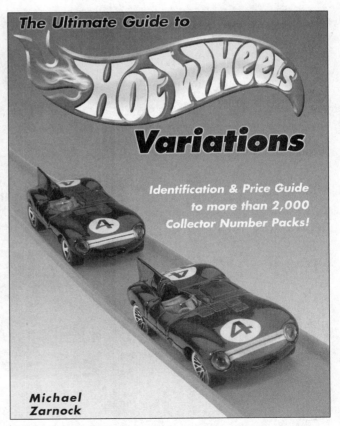

NON-SERIES COLLECTOR NUMBER PACKS

(KP Photo)

❑ **1, Old Number 5,** Red enamel, matching red metal Malaysia base, louvres on hood, tan interior, red, yellow & black tampo on hood w/"No. 5" & "Fire Dept." twice, black plastic ladder on each side, bw
EX n/a   **NM** n/a   **MIP** $180

(Photo by Frank Veres)

❑ **2, Sol-Aire CX4,** a. Black with yellow, orange and blue stripe tampo, "33" on top and side, metal Malaysia base and interior, yellow tint window, uh
EX n/a   **NM** n/a   **MIP** $32

(KP Photo)

❑ **3, Wheel Loader,** Yellow enamel, yellow Malaysia base, black interior, alw, yct
EX n/a   **NM** n/a   **MIP** $10

(Photo by Frank Veres)

❑ **4, XT-3,** Purple with white, yellow and red flame tampo, black canopy and purple painted Malaysia base, asw, bw
EX n/a   **NM** n/a   **MIP** $12

❑ **5, Good Humor Truck,** a. White with red and blue tampos, large rear window, black plastic Malaysia base, blue int., clear window, asw, bw
EX n/a   **NM** n/a   **MIP** $15

(KP Photo)

❑ **6, Blazer 4X4,** a. Black with yellow, red and white tampo, metal Malaysia base, yellow int., yellow tint window, alw, ct
EX n/a   **NM** n/a   **MIP** $60

(KP Photo)

❑ **7, Troop Convoy,** Olive with green, brown and tan camouflage on cover, alw, bbw
EX n/a   **NM** n/a   **MIP** $300

(Photo by Frank Veres)

❑ **8, Vampyra,** a. Dark purple with white, orange and red wing tampo, metal Malaysia base, chrome engine, bw
EX n/a   **NM** n/a   **MIP** $25

(Photo by Frank Veres)

❑ **10, Baja Breaker,** White with black, red and yellow tampo, metal base, red interior, clear window, asw, ct
EX n/a   **NM** n/a   **MIP** $250

(Photo by Frank Veres)

❑ **11, '31 Doozie,** Maroon with no tampo, tan top, metal Malaysian base, maroon interior, blue tint window, asw, ww
EX n/a   **NM** n/a   **MIP** $117

(Photo by Frank Veres)

❑ **12, Roll Patrol,** Olive with tan green and brown camouflage on hood, clear window, alw, bbw
EX n/a   **NM** n/a   **MIP** $500

(Photo by Frank Veres)

❑ **15, Peterbilt Tank Truck,** Yellow metal cab, metal Malaysia base, silver metallic painted metal tank with red "Shell" and yellow "Shell" logo outlined in red on side, alw, bw

EX n/a   **NM** n/a   **MIP** $60

(KP Photo)

❑ **16, Earth Mover,** Yellow enamel, matching yellow painted Metal Malaysia base, black seat, alw, yct

EX n/a   **NM** n/a   **MIP** $104

(KP Photo)

❑ **17, Suzuki Quadracer,** Yellow plastic, black tinted metal base, blue seat, black handlebars, yct

EX n/a   **NM** n/a   **MIP** $56

(Phot by Frank Veres)

❑ **18, Mercedes 540K,** Black enamel, tan plastic top, metal Malaysia base, tan int., clear window, asw, bw

EX n/a   **NM** n/a   **MIP** $103

(Phot by Frank Veres)

❑ **19, Shadow Jet,** Yellow w/red "Intercooled" tampo on rear wing, blue "F-3" tampo on top, metal Malaysia base, yellow int., smoked canopy, bw

EX n/a   **NM** n/a   **MIP** $140

(Phot by Frank Veres)

❑ **20, Rocketank,** Olive w/olive painted metal base

EX n/a   **NM** n/a   **MIP** $25

❑ **21, Nissan Hardbody,** a. White with red & blue tampo, black Malaysia base, black int., clear window, alw, ct

EX n/a   **NM** n/a   **MIP** $165

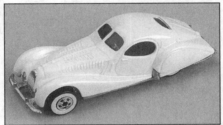
(Photo by Frank Veres)

❑ **22, Talbot Lago,** White w/metal Malaysia base, chrome int., smoked window, ww

EX n/a   **NM** n/a   **MIP** $25

❑ **23, '80's Firebird,** a. Black w/black base, red int., clear window, asw, bw

EX n/a   **NM** n/a   **MIP** $84

(Photo by Frank Veres)

❑ **24, Hiway Hauler,** a. Red cab, black int./red tint window w/metal Malaysia base, long Pepsi tampo on white box, alw, bw

EX n/a   **NM** n/a   **MIP** $30

❑ **26, '65 Mustang Convertible,** a. Turquoise with black side tampo, metal Malaysia base, tan int., clear window, ww

EX n/a   **NM** n/a   **MIP** $30

(Photo by Frank Veres)

❑ **27, Command Tank,** Olive w/light green, tan & brown camouflage on top & sides, tan star on side, olive base

EX n/a   **NM** n/a   **MIP** $25

❑ **28, '37 Bugatti,** a. Yellow with red cove & yellow fenders, metal Malaysia base chrome int., blue tint window, asw, bw

EX n/a   **NM** n/a   **MIP** $75

❑ **29, Tail Gunner,** a. Olive green with light green, tan & brown camouflage, olive painted Malaysia base, black window, alw, bct

EX n/a   **NM** n/a   **MIP** $125

(Photo by Frank Veres)

❑ **30, '80's Corvette,** Blue with blue painted base, red, white & yellow tampo w/88 & Corvette on sides, tan & red int. w/tan bag in back, clear window, alw, gho

EX n/a   **NM** n/a   **MIP** $631

❑ **31, Classic Cobra,** a. Red w/metal Malaysia base, black int., clear window, alw, bw

EX n/a   **NM** n/a   **MIP** $7

(Photo by Frank Veres)

❑ **32, Sharkruiser,** a. Gray with gray painted Malaysia base, chrome engine, sho
EX n/a   NM n/a   MIP $15

(Photo by Frank Veres)

❑ **33, Camaro Z28,** a. Purple with yellow, green & orange side tampo, black plastic Malaysia base, black window, bw
EX n/a   NM n/a   MIP $11

(KP Photo)

❑ **34, Bulldozer,** Yellow metal body, yellow plastic Malaysia base, black rubber treads, black plastic rollers
EX n/a   NM n/a   MIP $33

❑ **35, Ferrari Testarossa,** a. Red enamel, matching red painted Malaysia base, black & red int., clear window, uh
EX n/a   NM n/a   MIP $10

(KP Photo)

❑ **36, Baja Bug,** White with red & orange flames, purple "Blazin' Bug," metal Malaysia base, red int., bw
EX n/a   NM n/a   MIP $125

(Photo by Frank Veres)

❑ **37, Hot Bird,** a. Black w/yellow bird tampo on hood, red & yellow stripe on roof & trunk, metal Malaysia base, red int., blue tint window, gho
EX n/a   NM n/a   MIP $22

(Photo by Frank Veres)

❑ **38, Dump Truck,** a. Yellow enamel, metal Malaysia base, yellow metal dump box, yct
EX n/a   NM n/a   MIP $16

❑ **39, Monster Vette,** a. Yellow w/red & purple flames on hood & side, metal Malaysia base, black int., smoked window, alw, ct
EX n/a   NM n/a   MIP $30

(Photo by Frank Veres)

❑ **40, Power Plower,** Black w/orange, red & purple stripe, "Midnight Removal" on door, metal Malaysia base, red int., smoked window, asw, ct
EX n/a   NM n/a   MIP $84

(KP Photo)

❑ **42, Oshkosh Snowplow,** a. Orange metal cab, box & fenders, orange plastic plow blade, metal Malaysia base, orange int., alw, oct
EX n/a   NM n/a   MIP $35

(Photo by Frank Veres)

❑ **43, Tall Ryder,** a. Mf. silver, black plastic between metal Malaysia base, red & yellow stripe, yellow & blue "Tall Rider" tampo on side, black window, alw, ct
EX n/a   NM n/a   MIP $46

(KP Photo)

❑ **44, Classic Caddy,** a. Blue w/black plastic fenders, metal Malaysia base, tan int., ww
EX n/a   NM n/a   MIP $15

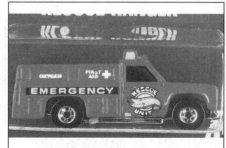

(Photo by Frank Veres)

❏ **45, Rescue Ranger,** Red enamel, chrome Malaysia base, white & black "Rescue Unit" w/red & yellow HW on door, yellow "Emergency" in black panel on rear w/white "Oxygen" & "First Aid+," yellow insert, black int., smoked window, alw, bw
EX n/a   **NM** n/a   **MIP** $20

(Photo by Frank Veres)

❏ **46, Rig Wrecker,** White enamel w/"Steves Towing" tampo, chrome Malaysia base, chrome int., clear window, bw
EX n/a   **NM** n/a   **MIP** $101

❏ **47, '57 Chevy,** a. Turquoise, chrome Malaysia base, blue tint int. & window, uh
EX n/a   **NM** n/a   **MIP** $100

(Photo by Frank Veres)

❏ **49, Gulch Stepper,** a. Red with black plastic between a metal Malaysia base, yellow, white & blue stripe tampo, "Pennzoil" on side, black window, alw, ct
EX n/a   **NM** n/a   **MIP** $54

(KP Photo)

❏ **50, Rolls Royce Phantom II,** Met. blue, metal Malaysia base, black int., tan top, clear window, ww
EX n/a   **NM** n/a   **MIP** $405

(Photo by Frank Veres)

❏ **51, '40s Woodie,** Yellow enamel fenders & hood, light brown wood sides, chrome engine & grille, black painted roof, blue tint window, black int., asw, bw
EX n/a   **NM** n/a   **MIP** $2400

(Photo by Frank Veres)

❏ **52, Delivery Truck,** White enamel, "Larry's Mobile Tune-up," blue, red & yellow tampo, black plastic Malaysia base, red int., clear window, asw, bw
EX n/a   **NM** n/a   **MIP** $32

(Photo by Frank Veres)

❏ **53, Zombot,** a. Gold chrome w/purple chrome gun, metal Malaysia base, sho
EX n/a   **NM** n/a   **MIP** $15

(KP Photo)

❏ **54, Nissan 300 ZX,** a. Met. red w/yellow 300 ZX tampo on hood, yellow stripe on roof, metal base, tan int., clear window, uh
EX n/a   **NM** n/a   **MIP** $33

(Photo by Frank Veres)

❏ **55, Road Roller,** Yellow enamel, black plastic Malaysia base, black inserts & rollers
EX n/a   **NM** n/a   **MIP** $25

❏ **56, Bronco 4-Wheeler,** a. White w/white cap, red, yellow & blue stripe tampo, w/ "Built Ford Tough" on side, red & yellow flames on hood, red motorcycle on rear, red int., smoked window, asw, ct
EX n/a   **NM** n/a   **MIP** $55

(Photo by Frank Veres)

❏ **57, 3-Window '34,** Purple w/purple fenders, black running boards, metal base, light green, dark blue & red side tampo, chrome int., clear window, bw
EX n/a   **NM** n/a   **MIP** $35

❏ **58, Blown Camaro Z28,** a. Turquoise w/dark blue & white stripes, yellow Z28, white "Camaro" on side, white & blue stripe w/yellow "Z28" on hood, gray int., blue tint window, gho
EX n/a   **NM** n/a   **MIP** $65

(Photo by Frank Veres)

❑ **59, Sheriff Patrol,** a. Mf. blue w/both doors white, black & yellow "Sheriff" on front door w/yellow & black star, "Sheriff 701" on roof, metal Malaysia base, black int., blue tint window, asw, bw
EX n/a   NM n/a   MIP $15

(Photo by Frank Veres)

❑ **60, Lamborghini Countach,** White w/white painted Malaysia base, light blue & red stripes on side, red int., smoked window, uh
EX n/a   NM n/a   MIP $13

(KP Photo)

❑ **62, Alien,** a. Dark red plastic & mf. Silver, unpainted metal Malaysia base, metal int., smoked canopy, uh
EX n/a   NM n/a   MIP $7

(Photo by Frank Veres)

❑ **63, Radar Ranger,** a. Mf. silver w/red, black & blue tampo, metal Malaysia base, chrome radar dish, black int., clear window, alw, cts
EX n/a   NM n/a   MIP $40

❑ **65, VW Bug,** a. Turquoise w/yellow, orange & magenta

tampo on roof & side, metal Malaysia base, tan int., clear window, bw
EX n/a   NM n/a   MIP $41

(Photo by Frank Veres)

❑ **66, Custom Corvette,** Met. dark red w/yellow, white & blue side stripe tampo, yellow & blue stripe on hood & trunk, blue "Corvette" on hood & sides, black Malaysia base, tan int., blue tint window, uh
EX n/a   NM n/a   MIP $45

(Photo by Frank Veres)

❑ **67, '32 Delivery,** Yellow w/yellow fenders, orange, red & blue stripe tampo on sides, "Delivery" tampo in blue, metal base, yellow int., clear window, bw
EX n/a   NM n/a   MIP $35

❑ **68, T-Bucket,** a. Yellow w/red & blue flames, metal Malaysia base, red int./clear window, bw
EX n/a   NM n/a   MIP $10

(KP Photo, Tom Michael collection)

❑ **69, Ferrari F40,** a. Red w/yellow "Ferrari F40" on hood, "F40"

& stripe on sides, metal Malaysia base, tan int., clear window, uh
EX n/a   NM n/a   MIP $10

(Photo by Frank Veres)

❑ **70, Chevy Stocker,** a. Black w/light red, yellow stripe on side, white & red "3" on door, side tampo includes red & blue "V" (Valvoline) in white circle & "Union," gray int., clear window, bw
EX n/a   NM n/a   MIP $15

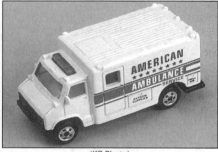

(KP Photo)

❑ **71, Ambulance,** a. White w/blue "American" & stars side tampo, red & blue stripe on sides, black "Oxygen Supplies" & "First Aid" side tampos, black Malaysia base, white int., blue tint window, asw, bw
EX n/a   NM n/a   MIP $5

(KP Photo)

❑ **72, School Bus,** a. Yellow w/thick black stripe on side, black Malaysia base, black int., clear window, asw, bw
EX n/a   NM n/a   MIP $9

(Photo by Frank Veres)

❑ **73, Street Roader,** a. White w/red, blue & black tampo on hood & sides, black int., clear window, alw, ct

EX n/a   **NM** n/a   **MIP** $15

(KP Photo)

❑ **74, GT Racer,** a. Purple w/orange, dark blue & white stripe tampo, w/dark blue "5" on hood & sides, "Bell" & "V" tampo on sides, chrome pipes & rear wing, metal base, metal int., dark smoked window, uh

EX n/a   **NM** n/a   **MIP** $20

(KP Photo)

❑ **75, Pontiac Banshee,** a. Red w/dark red roof bar, dark smoked window, metal Malaysia base, asw, uh

EX n/a   **NM** n/a   **MIP** $10

(KP Photo)

❑ **76, Kenworth Big Rig,** a. Black w/dark red, orange, blue side tampo, black Malaysia base, gray window, alw, bw

EX n/a   **NM** n/a   **MIP** $8

❑ **77, Bywayman,** a. Maroon w/yellow & black eagle tampo, white "Eagle" & stars tampo on sides, metal base, red int., dark smoked window, asw, ct

EX n/a   **NM** n/a   **MIP** $20

(Photo by Frank Veres)

❑ **78, Peterbilt Cement Truck,** Red enamel, metal Malaysia base, white plastic barrel, alw, bw

EX n/a   **NM** n/a   **MIP** $100

(KP Photo)

❑ **79, Big Bertha,** Olive w/green, tan & brown camouflage on top

EX n/a   **NM** n/a   **MIP** $11

(Photo by Frank Veres)

❑ **80, Porsche 959,** a. Met. red with orange & yellow tampos, metal base, tan int., clear window, asw, uh

EX n/a   **NM** n/a   **MIP** $15

❑ **81, Ratmobile,** a. White plastic w/metal Malaysia base, chrome engine, asw, uh

EX n/a   **NM** n/a   **MIP** $5

(KP Photo)

❑ **82, Fire Eater,** a. Red w/black & yellow tampos, blue insert, blue tint int. & window, chrome Malaysia base, alw, bw

EX n/a   **NM** n/a   **MIP** $8

(KP Photo)

❑ **83, Tank Gunner,** Olive w/green, brown & tan camouflage on sides & hood/tan star on hood, alw bbw

EX n/a   **NM** n/a   **MIP** $103

(KP Photo)

❑ **84, Probe Funny Car,** "Motorcraft" red w/white tampos, metal base, smoked window, bw

EX n/a   **NM** n/a   **MIP** $30

❑ **86, Propper Chopper,** a. White w/red, blue & yellow tampo, yellow triangle, blue base & int., blue tint window

EX n/a   **NM** n/a   **MIP** $65

(KP Photo)

❑ **87, Purple Passion,** a. Purple met. w/green & dark blue scallop tampo on hood & sides, chrome Malaysia base, red int., clear window, ww
EX n/a **NM** n/a **MIP** $14

(Photo by Frank Veres)

❑ **88, T-Bird Stocker,** a. "Motorcraft" red w/white tampos on hood & sides, black base, black int., clear window, bw
EX n/a **NM** n/a **MIP** $25

❑ **89, Mini Truck,** a. Turquoise w/magenta, blue & yellow stripes, turquoise plastic Malaysia base, blue int., clear window, sho
EX n/a **NM** n/a **MIP** $200

❑ **92, Mercedes 380 SEL,** a.Black w/black Malaysia base, tan int., clear window, asw, gho
EX n/a **NM** n/a **MIP** $40

(Photo by Frank Veres)

❑ **94, Auburn 852,** a. Red w/red fenders, red int., clear window, metal Malaysia base, ww
EX n/a **NM** n/a **MIP** $20

(Photo by Frank Veres)

❑ **95, '55 Chevy,** a. White w/orange, yellow & magenta side tampo, dark magenta window, gray Malaysia base, bw
EX n/a **NM** n/a **MIP** $16

(Photo by Frank Veres)

❑ **98, Nissan Custom "Z",** a. Met. red w/yellow "300ZX" tampo on hood, yellow stripe on roof, metal base, tan int., clear window, uh
EX n/a **NM** n/a **MIP** $12

(Photo by Frank Veres)

❑ **99, Ford Stake Bed Truck,** Mf. blue w/yellow stake rack, yellow, red & white door tampo, chrome Malaysia base, chrome int., clear window, asw, bw
EX n/a **NM** n/a **MIP** $9

(Photo by Frank Veres)

❑ **100, Peterbilt Dump Truck,** a. Red w/red plastic dump box, metal Malaysia base, clear window & int., alw, bw
EX n/a **NM** n/a **MIP** $5

(KP Photo)

❑ **102, Surf Patrol,** a. Yellow w/red tampos, thick white "Rescue" tampo, metal Malaysia base, light red int., clear window, asw, ct
EX n/a **NM** n/a **MIP** $3

(KP Photo)

❑ **103, Range Rover,** White w/blue & red side stripe, black Malaysia base, tan int., clear window, ct
EX n/a **NM** n/a **MIP** $8

❑ **104, Turbo Streak,** a. Day-glo red w/painted rear wing & front spoiler, blue & pink "Tune-up Masters" tampo, unpainted metal Malaysia base, bw
EX n/a **NM** n/a **MIP** $75

(Photo by Frank Veres)

❑ **105, Peugeot 205 Rallye,** White w/red, yellow, blue, & black tampos, w/"2" tampo on hood & sides, metal Malaysia base, gray int., clear window, alw, bw
EX n/a **NM** n/a **MIP** $91

(Photo by Frank Veres)

❑ **106, VW Golf,** a. White w/pink, green & blue tampos, pink Malaysia base & int., clear window, asw, bw
EX n/a **NM** n/a **MIP** $50

❑ **108, Ramp Truck,** a. White w/dark blue, yellow & red tampos, metal Malaysia base, clear window, asw, bw

EX n/a   NM n/a   MIP $41

(KP Photo)

❑ **110, Trailbuster,** a. Turquoise w/pink, yellow & black tampo, metal Malaysia base, pink int., clear window, asw, ct

EX n/a   NM n/a   MIP $25

(Photo by Frank Veres)

❑ **111, Street Beast,** Turquoise & white w/blue & pink tampos, metal Malaysia base, turquoise int., clear window, ww

EX n/a   NM n/a   MIP $5

(Photo by Frank Veres)

❑ **112, Limozeen,** White w/pink, orange & blue side tampos, chrome Malaysia base, white int., smoked window, ww

EX n/a   NM n/a   MIP $15

❑ **113, Speed Shark,** a. Maroon w/white, pink & yellow tampos, chrome window, chrome Malaysia base, pink int., bw

EX n/a   NM n/a   MIP $45

❑ **114, Pontiac Fiero 2M4,** a. Red w/metal Malaysia base, black int., clear window, asw, uh

EX n/a   NM n/a   MIP $8

(KP Photo)

❑ **115, Roll Patrol,** Olive w/green, tan & brown camouflage on hood, olive painted Malaysia base, black int., clear window, alw, bct

EX n/a   NM n/a   MIP $27

(KP Photo)

❑ **116, Mazda MX-5 Miata,** a. Red w/yellow, pink & green "Miata" tampo on hood, red painted Malaysia base, tan int., clear window, asw, bw

EX n/a   NM n/a   MIP $10

(KP Photo)

❑ **117, Ferrari Classic,** a. Yellow w/black "7" in dark yellow circle, magenta "Ferrari" tampos on hood & sides, chrome base & pipes, black int., clear window, bw

EX n/a   NM n/a   MIP $17

❑ **118, Ferrari 348,** a. Yellow w/red, turquoise & white hood tampo, black Malaysia base, black & yellow int., clear window, uh

EX n/a   NM n/a   MIP $6

(Photo by Frank Veres)

❑ **122, Toyota MR2 Rally,** a. White w/red, orange & yellow tampos, black Malaysia base, chrome lights, red int., clear window, asw, sho

EX n/a   NM n/a   MIP $22

(Photo by Frank Veres)

❑ **123, Lamborghini Diablo,** Red w/red painted Malaysia base, yellow "Diablo" tampo, tan int., smoked window, uh

EX n/a   NM n/a   MIP $6

❑ **125, Zender Fact 4,** a. Mf. silver w/yellow "Fact 4" on front & on sides, white "Zender" on front, black Malaysia base, black int., clear window, uh

EX n/a   NM n/a   MIP $15

(KP Photo)

❑ **126, Chevy Lumina,** a. Red w/pink, yellow & blue stripes on side, black Malaysia base, tan int., clear window, w/black painted top, black pillar on side of windshield, asw-bw

EX n/a   NM n/a   MIP $8

(Photo by Frank Veres)

❑ **127, Power Plower,** a. Mf. purple w/dark blue, yellow & orange tampos on hood & sides, metal Malaysia base, yellow int., clear window, asw, ct

EX n/a　　NM n/a　　MIP $20

(Photo by Frank Veres)

❑ **128, Baja Breaker,** Met purple w/yellow tampo on sides, blue tint metal China base

EX n/a　　NM n/a　　MIP $3

(Photo by Frank Veres)

❑ **129, Suzuki Quadracer,** a. White w/blue seat, black handlebars, black tint metal Malaysia base, alw, yct

EX n/a　　NM n/a　　MIP $12

(Photo by Frank Veres)

❑ **131, Nissan Hardbody,** a. Black w/light green, blue & pink

tampos on hood, roof & sides, "10" in green on hood, "10" in pink on door, blue tint window, black plastic Malaysia base, pink int., front end, roll bar, alw, ct

EX n/a　　NM n/a　　MIP $12

❑ **133, Shadow Jet,** a. Purple met., w/green "Inter Cooled" tampo on rear wing, "F-3" in yellow, metal Malaysia base, purple int., yellow tint canopy, bw

EX n/a　　NM n/a　　MIP $14

(Photo by Frank Veres)

❑ **134, Mercedes 540K,** White w/tan top, red int., clear window, metal Malaysia base, asw, bw

EX n/a　　NM n/a　　MIP $12

❑ **135, '32 Ford Delivery,** a. White w/turquoise fenders, turquoise, pink & blue tampo side tampo, metal Malaysia base, turquoise int., clear window, bw

EX n/a　　NM n/a　　MIP $7

(Photo by Frank Veres)

❑ **136, '56 Flashsider,** a. Turquoise w/pink, yellow & blue side tampo, chrome Malaysia base, black window, sho

EX n/a　　NM n/a　　MIP $35

(Photo by Frank Veres)

❑ **137, Goodyear Blimp,** Gray w/black "Goodyear" on side, white gondola w/black window tampo

EX n/a　　NM n/a　　MIP $9

(Photo by Frank Veres)

❑ **140, Flashfire,** a. Black w/green, yellow & pink side tampo, black Malaysia base, red int. & side insert, yellow tint canopy, sho

EX n/a　　NM n/a　　MIP $15

(Photo by Frank Veres)

❑ **141, Shock Factor,** a. Black metal body w/red plastic engine, driver & side pods, metal Malaysia base, red, blue & yellow tampos on sides & wing, ct

EX n/a　　NM n/a　　MIP $45

(Photo by Frank Veres)

❑ **142, Hiway Hauler,** a. Red cab, white box w/blue Kool-Aid tampo, thin red ribbon, yellow "Wacky Warehouse," chrome Malaysia base, black window, alw, bw

EX n/a　　NM n/a　　MIP $15

(KP Photo)

❑ **143, Recycling Truck,** a. Orange metal cab, orange plastic box w/yellow & blue "Recycler" tampo on side, box closed at top, black plastic Malaysia base, black window, alw, bw
EX n/a   **NM** n/a   **MIP** $10

(KP Photo)

❑ **144, Oshkosh Cement Mixer,** White plastic body, red barrel, blue painted fenders & blue plastic Malaysia base, blue painted seat, asw, bw
EX n/a   **NM** n/a   **MIP** $6

(KP Photo)

❑ **145, Tractor,** a. Yellow metal body & bucket, yellow plastic base, cab & hydraulics, ytt
EX n/a   **NM** n/a   **MIP** $10

(KP Photo)

❑ **146, Bulldozer,** Yellow metal body, yellow plastic base & blade, one-piece black treads & rollers, black seat & grille
EX n/a   **NM** n/a   **MIP** $8

(KP Photo)

❑ **147, Tank Truck,** a. Red w/matching red plastic Malaysia base, chrome window & tank w/blue "Unical 76" the "76" is in an orange circle, asw, bw
EX n/a   **NM** n/a   **MIP** $6

❑ **148, Porsche 930,** a. Mf. green w/pink, yellow & blue tampos, metal Malaysia base, rose tint int. & window, asw, bw
EX n/a   **NM** n/a   **MIP** $50

(KP Photo)

❑ **149, BMW 850i,** a. Blue w/white, pink & yellow tampos on hood & sides, blue plastic Malaysia base, tan int., clear window, asw, uh
EX n/a   **NM** n/a   **MIP** $5

❑ **150, BMW 323,** a. Black w/white "M3" & red & blue slash tampo on side, "BMW" on rear plate, black plastic Malaysia base, tan int., clear window, alw, bw
EX n/a   **NM** n/a   **MIP** $8

(Photo by Frank Veres)

❑ **151, Ford Aerostar,** Met. purple w/yellow tampo on side, metal Malaysia base, chrome window, bw
EX n/a   **NM** n/a   **MIP** $6

❑ **153, Thunderstreak,** a. Dark blue & dark green w/"Hot Wheels" logo on side pod, red stripe w/white "1" on front, metal Malaysia base, bw (The green #153 cars are supposed to be leftovers from the "Zip-Lock" promotion with a re-paint.)
EX n/a   **NM** n/a   **MIP** $7

(Photo by Frank Veres)

❑ **154, '59 Cadillac,** Pearl white w/chrome Malaysia base, red int./clear window, ww
EX n/a   **NM** n/a   **MIP** $7

(Photo by Frank Veres)

❑ **155, Turboa,** a. Yellow w/green tampo, blue tint metal Malaysia base, uh
EX n/a   **NM** n/a   **MIP** $5

❑ **156, Rodzilla,** a. Purple body w/light purple plastic Malaysia base, yellow eyes, white teeth, sho
EX n/a   **NM** n/a   **MIP** $15

(Photo by Frank Veres)

❑ **157, '57 Chevy,** a. Yellow w/red flames over white w/blue stripe on sides, blue tint int., & window, uh
EX n/a   **NM** n/a   **MIP** $26

(KP Photo)

❑ **158, Mercedes-Benz Unimog,** White metal cab & box, metal Malaysia base, white plastic rear box cover w/red, green & black tampo, red plastic fenders & int., clear window, alw, ct
EX n/a   **NM** n/a   **MIP** $10

(Photo by Frank Veres)

❑ **159, Big Bertha,** Light gray painted metal body & treads, brown & black camouflage, white star on rear gray plastic turret & Malaysia base
EX n/a   **NM** n/a   **MIP** $12

(Photo by Frank Veres)

❑ **160, Command Tank,** White painted body, dark gray, light gray & black camouflage, white plastic treads, base & turret
EX n/a   **NM** n/a   **MIP** $7

❑ **161, Roll Patrol,** a. Light gray, white, black & brown camouflage, light gray painted Malaysia base, black int., clear window, asw, ct
EX n/a   **NM** n/a   **MIP** $12

(Photo by Frank Veres)

❑ **162, '65 Mustang Conv.,** a. Red w/yellow side tampo, metal Malaysia base, tan int., clear window, ww
EX n/a   **NM** n/a   **MIP** $15

(Photo by Frank Veres)

❑ **163, Talbot Largo,** Mf. red, metal Malaysia base, orange tint window & int., ww
EX n/a   **NM** n/a   **MIP** $15

(Photo by Frank Veres)

❑ **164, Mercedes 540K,** a. Mf. blue, metal Malaysia base, light blue top, red int., clear window, asw, bw
EX n/a   **NM** n/a   **MIP** $6

(Photo by Frank Veres)

❑ **165, Suzuki Quadracer,** a. Bright pink body, blue seat, black handlebars, black tinted metal Malaysia base, alw, ct
EX n/a   **NM** n/a   **MIP** $9

❑ **166, Vampyra,** a. Black w/yellow, green & pruple wing tampo, green & yellow eyes, metal Malaysia base, sho
EX n/a   **NM** n/a   **MIP** $40

(Photo by Frank Veres)

❑ **167, '80's Firebird,** a. Orange w/purple & pink lightning bolt tampos on side & hood, black Malaysia base, purple int., clear window, asw, bw
EX n/a   **NM** n/a   **MIP** $6

(Photo by Frank Veres)

❑ **168, GT Racer,** Black w/yellow, pink, purple & red stripes on sides, roof & hood, "5" on sides & hood, metal Malaysia base, silver window, bw
EX n/a   **NM** n/a   **MIP** $8

(Photo by Frank Veres)

❑ **169, Sol-Aire CX4,** a. Candy blue, pink, purple & orange tampos, "2" on front & sides, black plastic Malaysia base, black int., clear window, sho
EX n/a   **NM** n/a   **MIP** $15

(Photo by Frank Veres)

❑ **170, Chevy Stocker,** Mf. pink, metal Malaysia base, yellow int., yellow tint window, bw
EX n/a   **NM** n/a   **MIP** $7

(KP Photo, Tom Michael collection)

❏ **171, VW Bug,** a. Met. purple, metal Malaysia base, orange, green & yellow tampos on roof, hood & sides, red int., clear window, bw
EX n/a **NM** n/a **MIP** $9

(Photo by Frank Veres)

❏ **172, Mazda MX-5 Miata,** a. Yellow w/pink, blue & black side tampos, yellow painted Malaysia base, pink int., clear window, asw, bw
EX n/a **NM** n/a **MIP** $5

(Photo by Frank Veres)

❏ **174, Limozeen,** Mf. lt. Blue, chrome Malaysia base, light yellow int., clear window, ww
EX n/a **NM** n/a **MIP** $7

(Photo by Frank Veres)

❏ **175, Ferrari 348,** a. Pearl white, pink, red & purple tampo on hood & roof, red & white int., black plastic Malaysia base, clear window, sho
EX n/a **NM** n/a **MIP** $15

(Photo by Frank Veres)

❏ **176, Lamborghini Diablo,** a. Mf. blue, light blue rear wing & bumper, metal Malaysia base, red int., red tint window, uh
EX n/a **NM** n/a **MIP** $10

(Photo by Frank Veres)

❏ **177, Zender Fact 4,** a. Mf. purple, orange plastic Malaysia base, orange int., clear window, sho
EX n/a **NM** n/a **MIP** $15

(Photo by Frank Veres)

❏ **178, Hot Bird,** Mf. black, metal Malaysia base, pink int., rose tint window, uh
EX n/a **NM** n/a **MIP** $10

(Photo by Frank Veres)

❏ **179, Porsche 959,** a. Met. purple w/yellow, pink & gray tampos, gray "5" on sides, metal Malaysia base, chrome window, asw, sho
EX n/a **NM** n/a **MIP** $15

(Photo by Frank Veres)

❏ **181, Pontiac Fiero 2M4,** a. Light green mf., metal Malaysia base, light yellow int., clear window, sho
EX n/a **NM** n/a **MIP** $15

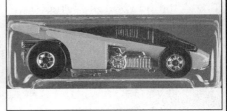

(Photo by Frank Veres)

❏ **182, Shadow Jet,** a. Green w/green "Inter Cooled" on rear wing, blue "F-3" metal Malaysia base, smoked canopy, green int., bw
EX n/a **NM** n/a **MIP** $8

(Photo by Frank Veres)

❏ **183, VW Golf,** a. Mf. dark green, chrome Malaysia base, yellow int., yellow tint window, asw, bw
EX n/a **NM** n/a **MIP** $30

(Photo by Frank Veres)

❏ **184, Mercedes 380 SEL,** a. Mf. blue, metal Malaysia base, yellow int., yellow tint window, asw, sho
EX n/a **NM** n/a **MIP** $15

(Photo by Frank Veres)

❑ **185, Propper Chopper,** a. White, w/black, yellow & red side tampo, thin yellow "Police," gray rotors, black Malaysia base, tail & int., blue tint window
EX n/a **NM** n/a **MIP** $7

❑ **186, Ford Aerostar,** a. White w/red, yellow & blue "Speedie Pizza" tampo w/phone #, metal Malaysia base, chrome window, bw
EX n/a **NM** n/a **MIP** $12

(Photo by Frank Veres)

❑ **187, Ramp Truck,** a. Yellow metal cab, white plastic ramp w/blue, red & yellow tampo, metal Malaysia base, black window, asw, bw
EX n/a **NM** n/a **MIP** $5

❑ **188, Hummer,** a. Light brown metal body w/matching gun on roof, brown, orange & black camouflage everywhere, black star on hood, black plastic Malaysia base, black window, asw, ct
EX n/a **NM** n/a **MIP** $9

(Photo by Frank Veres)

❑ **189, Gleamer Patrol,** a. Dark chrome texture, metal Malaysia base, tan int., smoked window, asw, bw
EX n/a **NM** n/a **MIP** $8

(KP Photo, Tom Michael collection)

❑ **190, '57 T-Bird,** a. Light gold chrome texture, metal Malaysia base, black int., smoked window, bw
EX n/a **NM** n/a **MIP** $8

❑ **191, Aeroflash,** a. Dark pink chrome texture, metal Malaysia base, black window, uh
EX n/a **NM** n/a **MIP** $8

(Photo by Frank Veres)

❑ **192, Corvette Stingray,** a. Green chrome texture, metal Malaysia base, black int., smoked window, bw
EX n/a **NM** n/a **MIP** $25

(Photo by Frank Veres)

❑ **193, Porsche 959,** a. Pink chrome texture, metal Malaysia base, dark smoked window, asw, uh
EX n/a **NM** n/a **MIP** $8

(KP Photo)

❑ **194, Goodyear Blimp,** a. Gray w/red & light yellow "Hot Wheels" tampo, white gondola w/black tampo windows
EX n/a **NM** n/a **MIP** $5

(Photo by Frank Veres)

❑ **195, Troop Convoy,** Light gray w/brown, white & black camouflage on top of canopy, white star & "US ARMY" on hood, alw, bbw
EX n/a **NM** n/a **MIP** $8

(Photo by Frank Veres)

❑ **196, 3-Window '34,** a. White w/pink fenders, black running boards & int., pink, orange & black lines & star side tampo, metal Malaysia base, asw-bw
EX n/a **NM** n/a **MIP** $40

(KP Photo)

❑ **197, Corvette Split Window,** a. Light blue w/red, magenta & yellow tampo on hood, roof & trunk, chrome (1 rivet) Malaysia base, red int., clear window, ww
EX n/a **NM** n/a **MIP** $5

(Photo by Frank Veres)

❏ **198, Path Beater,** a. Day-glo yellow w/orange, blue & white side tampo, blue tint metal Malaysia base, w/smaller front bumper gray int., roll bar & bed, blue tint window, asw, ct

EX n/a   NM n/a   MIP $15

(Photo by Frank Veres)

❏ **199, Double Demon,** a. Bright yellow plastic body, green tampo, chrome insert, metal Malaysia base, alw, uh

EX n/a   NM n/a   MIP $6

❏ **200, Custom Corvette,** A. White pearl w/red side tampo, yellow, red & black tampo on hood, black Malaysia base, red int., clear window, uh

EX n/a   NM n/a   MIP $5

(Photo by Frank Veres)

❏ **201, Oshkosh Snowplow,** a. Orange plastic cab & box, orange metal fenders, int., & hood, metal Malaysia base, alw oct

EX n/a   NM n/a   MIP $5

(Photo by Frank Veres)

❏ **202, '93 Camaro,** a. Purple enamel w/yellow & orange "Camaro" tampo on side, black

plastic Malaysia base, clear window, white int., alw, uh

EX n/a   NM n/a   MIP $10

❏ **203, Jaguar XJ220,** A. Met. silver, black Malaysia base, black int., clear window, uh

EX n/a   NM n/a   MIP $5

❏ **204, Oscar Mayer Wiener-mobile,** a. Dark red plastic hot dog, two-piece matching tan Malaysia base, dark smoked window, bbw

EX n/a   NM n/a   MIP $5

(KP Photo)

❏ **205, Treadator,** a. Red metal body w/orange plastic scoops, chrome fenders, engine & canopy, black treads & Malaysia base

EX n/a   NM n/a   MIP $5

(KP Photo)

❏ **206, Pipe Jammer,** a. Yellow w/black painted Malaysia base, chrome int., uh

EX n/a   NM n/a   MIP $6

(KP Photo)

❏ **207, Vector "Avtech" WX-3,** a. Dark pearl lavender w/matching

top, black plastic Malaysia base, tan int., smoked window, uh

EX n/a   NM n/a   MIP $8

❏ **208, Avus Qualtro,** a. Met. silver w/black plastic Malaysia base, red int., clear window, alw, uh

EX n/a   NM n/a   MIP $3

(Photo by Frank Veres)

❏ **209, Lexus SC400,** Met. black w/black plastic Malaysia base, white int., clear window, alw, uh

EX n/a   NM n/a   MIP $5

(KP Photo)

❏ **210, Viper RT/10,** a. Red w/black plastic Malaysia base, black int., smoked window, alw, uh

EX n/a   NM n/a   MIP $5

❏ **211, Twin Mill II,** a. Day-glo yellow, black plastic Malaysia base, black window, alw, uh

EX n/a   NM n/a   MIP $40

(Photo by Frank Veres)

❏ **212, Silhouette II,** a. Met purple w/chrome Malaysia base, white int., clear window, uh

EX n/a   NM n/a   MIP $7

(Photo by Frank Veres)

❏ **213, '57 Chevy,** a. Aqua w/orange, yellow & magenta stripe tampo on side, "Chevy emblem" on door, chrome Malaysia base, blue tint window & int., uh

EX n/a   **NM** n/a   **MIP** $12

(Photo by Frank Veres)

❑ **214, Swingfire,** a. Dark met. Blue & white, white & yellow tampo on hood & top of fenders, metal Malaysia base, white int., clear window, ww

EX n/a   **NM** n/a   **MIP** $6

❑ **215, Auburn 852,** a. Lt. red w/black fenders, metal Malaysia base, black int./clear window, asw, ww

EX n/a   **NM** n/a   **MIP** $10

(Photo by Frank Veres)

❑ **216, Fat Fendered '40,** Purple enamel w/metal Malaysia base, yellow tampo on side outlined in red, black int., clear window, asw, bw

EX n/a   **NM** n/a   **MIP** $20

(Photo by Frank Veres)

❑ **217, '40's Woodie,** a. Turquoise & black w/magenta & yellow stripes on hood & rear fender, metal Malaysia base, yellow int., clear window, bw

EX n/a   **NM** n/a   **MIP** $6

(Photo by Frank Veres)

❑ **218, Street Roader,** Met. light green w/blue, magenta & orange tampo on hood & sides, metal Malaysia base, gray int., smoked window, alw-ct

EX n/a   **NM** n/a   **MIP** $70

(Photo by Frank Veres)

❑ **219, Gulch Stepper,** Day-glo yellow w/orange, red & black side tampo, metal Malaysia base, black window, alw-ct

EX n/a   **NM** n/a   **MIP** $6

(Photo by Frank Veres)

❑ **220, Bywayman,** a. Pearl white w/pink & orange tampo w/gray stripe on hood & sides, metal Malaysia base, black int., clear window, asw, ct

EX n/a   **NM** n/a   **MIP** $12

(Photo by Frank Veres)

❑ **221, Range Rover,** a. Met. black w/orange stripe & white

"Range Rover" on sides, gray Malaysia base, tan int., clear window, asw, ct

EX n/a   **NM** n/a   **MIP** $5

(Photo by Frank Veres)

❑ **222, Blazer 4X4,** a. Mf. blue w/metal Malaysia base, yellow int./blue tint window, alw, ct

EX n/a   **NM** n/a   **MIP** $11

(Photo by Frank Veres)

❑ **223, Baja Bug,** Mf. red w/metal Malaysia base, black int., bw

EX n/a   **NM** n/a   **MIP** $31

❑ **224, Zombot,** a. Lt. blue chrome body, purple chrome gun, metal Malaysia base, uh

EX n/a   **NM** n/a   **MIP** $9

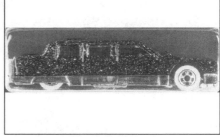

(Photo by Frank Veres)

❑ **225, Limozeen,** a. Mf. black, chrome Malaysia base, bright red int., clear window, ww

EX n/a   **NM** n/a   **MIP** $12

❑ **226, Ferrari 348,** a. Day-glo pink w/yellow, white & black tampo on hood, white & black stripe on roof, black plastic Malaysia base, black & red int., clear window, uh

EX n/a   **NM** n/a   **MIP** $6

(KP Photo)

❑ **227, Lamborghini Diablo,** a. Yellow w/black "Diablo" on side, metal Malaysia base, gray int., red tint window, uh

EX n/a   **NM** n/a   **MIP** $5

❑ **228, Zender Fact 4,** a. Met. blue w/white "Zender" on front, yellow "Fact 4" on top of fender, black Malaysia base, gray int., smoked window, uh

EX n/a   **NM** n/a   **MIP** $6

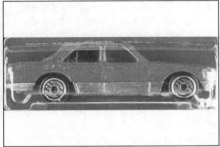

(Photo by Frank Veres)

❑ **229, Mercedes 380 SEL,** Mf. pink w/metal Malaysia base, black int., smoked window, asw, uh

EX n/a   **NM** n/a   **MIP** $11

(Photo by Frank Veres)

❑ **230, XT-3,** a. Pearl white w/matching painted Malaysia base, black nose & int., yellow, white & red flames, red tint canopy, bw

EX n/a   **NM** n/a   **MIP** $6

❑ **231, Mini Truck,** a. Day-glo orange w/blue, white & black tampos, orange Malaysia base, blue int., clear window, uh

EX n/a   **NM** n/a   **MIP** $5

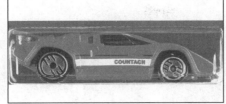

(Photo by Frank Veres)

❑ **232, Lamborghini Countach,** a. Red w/separate wing casting, red painted Malaysia base, white & black stripe side tampos, black int., dark smoked window, uh

EX n/a   **NM** n/a   **MIP** $8

❑ **233, Toyota MR2 Rally,** a. Black w/orange, purple & lavender stripes on hood & sides, black Malaysia base, red int., clear window, asw, uh

EX n/a   **NM** n/a   **MIP** $100

❑ **234, Nissan Custom "Z",** a. Met. purple w/yellow stripes on roof & hood, "300 ZX" on hood twice, metal Malaysia base, black int., clear window, uh

EX n/a   **NM** n/a   **MIP** $6

(Photo by Frank Veres)

❑ **235, Turbo Streak,** a. Day-glo yellow w/red "Hot Wheels" logo on side, metal Malaysia base, chrome engine, bw

EX n/a   **NM** n/a   **MIP** $10

(Photo by Frank Veres)

❑ **236, Ford Aerostar,** Black w/aqua, yellow, purple & red tampo on side, metal Malaysia base, chrome window, bw

EX n/a   **NM** n/a   **MIP** $8

❑ **237, Ford Stake Bed Truck,** a. Red cab w/bright yellow & white tampo, yellow plastic stake rack, chrome Malaysia base, chrome int., clear window, asw, bw

EX n/a   **NM** n/a   **MIP** $8

(Photo by Frank Veres)

❑ **238, Hiway Hauler,** a. Purple cab, white box w/dark green, dark blue & dark purple tampo, chrome Malaysia base, black window, alw, bw

EX n/a   **NM** n/a   **MIP** $30

❑ **239, Mercedes Unimog,** a. Light brown metal cab & box w/brown, orange & black camouflage, green rear box cover, tan plastic fenders & int., clear window, alw, ct

EX n/a   **NM** n/a   **MIP** $14

❑ **242, 1993 Camaro,** a. Blue "enamel" w/white on sides, red & yellow "Hot Wheels" logo, black "1" & "25th Anniversary" logo on side, red stripe on bottom, "Jack Baldwin" twice in white on roof w/red Chevy Bow tie, "Hot Wheels" in yellow w/2 logos on rear spoiler, "Camaro" in white on clear windsheild, gray Malaysia base, white int., alw, uh

EX n/a   **NM** n/a   **MIP** $150

❑ **244, No Fear Race Car,** a. Black w/red "No Fear" on nose, rear wing, side body & pod, "Racer" & # 1 on side body, "1" & "Hot Wheels" logo on nose, "Goodyear" in white on front wing, black painted Malaysia base, black plastic driver, bw

EX n/a   **NM** n/a   **MIP** $5

(KP Photo)

❑ **245, Driven To The Max,** a. Day-glo orange w/blue & red "Driven To The Max" on sides, red "Hot Wheels" logo on side by driver, gray plastic wing & driver, metal Malaysia base, large rear bw
EX n/a **NM** n/a **MIP** $5

(KP Photo)

❑ **246, Shadow Jet II,** a. Black tint chrome w/mf. Black painted Malaysia base, white "Hot Wheels" logo on rear, chrome driver, clear canopy, uh
EX n/a **NM** n/a **MIP** $4

(Photo by Frank Veres)

❑ **247, Rigor Motor,** Dark red met. w/metal Malaysia base, white skulls & radiator, chrome int., clear canopy, bw
EX n/a **NM** n/a **MIP** $3

❑ **248, Splittin' Image II,** a. Dark met. blue w/blue plastic Malaysia base, white "Hot Wheels" logo on front fender top, chrome canopy, engine & headlights, uh
EX n/a **NM** n/a **MIP** $12

(KP Photo)

❑ **249, Fuji Blimp,** White plastic w/dark green stripe, white gondola w/green & red "Fuji Film" tampo
EX n/a **NM** n/a **MIP** $4

❑ **250, Talbot Lago,** a. Mf. black w/metal Malaysia base, chrome int., clear window, ww
EX n/a **NM** n/a **MIP** $5

(Photo by Frank Veres)

❑ **251, Gulch Stepper,** a. Red w/black & yellow tampo on roof & sides, black window, tire on hood & spacer between body & base, metal Malaysia base, alw, ct
EX n/a **NM** n/a **MIP** $10

(Photo by Frank Veres)

❑ **252, Street Roader,** a. White w/pink & dark blue tampo on sides & hood, "Suzuki" in grille, metal Malaysia base, blue int. & spacer between body & base, blue tint window, alw, ct
EX n/a **NM** n/a **MIP** $10

❑ **253, Mercedes 380 SEL,** a. Maroon w/metal Malaysia base, tan int., red "Hot Wheels" logo in rear clear window, asw, uh
EX n/a **NM** n/a **MIP** $5

❑ **254, Sol-Aire CX-4,** a. Mf. blue, white sides w/red & yellow "Hot Wheels" logo & red "1", white plastic Malaysia base, white int., clear window, guh
EX n/a **NM** n/a **MIP** $7

(Photo by Frank Veres)

❑ **255, BMW 850i,** a. Dark met. blue w/black Malaysia base, red int., red "Hot Wheels" logo in rear smoked window, asw, uh

(Photo by Frank Veres)

❑ **256, 80's Firebird,** Fluorescent red w/green, blue & yellow ribbons on sides, green bird on hood, black plastic Malaysia base, light yellow int., black window, asw, bw
EX n/a **NM** n/a **MIP** $11

❑ **257, 3-Window '34,** a. Mf. silver w/yellow, orange & red flames, gray fenders, running boards & int., metal Malaysia base, tinted window, asw, bw
EX n/a **NM** n/a **MIP** $15

❑ **258, Blazer 4x4,** a. Light blue pearl w/pearl blue, magenta & black tampos on hood & sides, metal Malaysia base, gray int., blue tint window, red HW logo on side window, alw, ct
EX n/a **NM** n/a **MIP** $10

❑ **259, Lumina Minivan/Taxi,** a. Yellow w/black squares & "taxi" tampo on hood & sides, yellow plastic Malaysia base, black int., clear window, asw, bw
EX n/a **NM** n/a **MIP** $5

❑ **260, Twinmill II,** a. Dark blue w/red & white stripes on roof & hood, chrome engines, gray plastic Malaysia base, red window, alw, uh
EX n/a **NM** n/a **MIP** $20

(KP Photo)

❑ **261, Cybercruiser,** a. Mf. purple w/purple chrome driver & engine, metal Malaysia base, uh
EX n/a **NM** n/a **MIP** $5

❑ **262, 1993 Camaro,** a. Met. blue w/white on sides, red & yellow "Hot Wheels" logo, black "1" & "25th Anniversary" logo on side, red stripe on bottom, "Jack Baldwin" twice in white on roof w/red Chevy Bow tie, "Hot Wheels" in yellow w/2 logos on rear spoiler, "Camaro" in white on clear windshield, gray Malaysia base, white int., alw, guh

EX n/a   **NM** n/a   **MIP** $8

(Photo by Frank Veres)

❑ **263, Mean Green Passion,** Green w/olive & blue flames on hood & sides, chrome Malaysia base, tan int., clear window, alw, ww

EX n/a   **NM** n/a   **MIP** $15

❑ **264, Lexus SC400,** a. Dark met. red w/black plastic Malaysia base, white-ish int., clear window, asw, uh

EX n/a   **NM** n/a   **MIP** $10

(KP Photo)

❑ **265, Oldsmobile Aurora,** a. Pearl turquoise, gray plastic Malaysia base, gray int., clear window, asw, bw

EX n/a   **NM** n/a   **MIP** $15

❑ **266, '59 Caddy,** a. Lavender pearl, chrome Malaysia base, white int., ww

EX n/a   **NM** n/a   **MIP** $10

(KP Photo)

❑ **267, Olds 442 W-30,** a. Yellow w/black stripes on hood scoops, chrome Malaysia base, black int., red "Hot Wheels" logo in rear clear window, asw, bw

EX n/a   **NM** n/a   **MIP** $5

❑ **268, GM Lean Machine,** a. Neon yellow plastic w/black painted Malaysia base, black canopy, uh

EX n/a   **NM** n/a   **MIP** $8

❑ **269, Oshkosh Cement Mixer,** a. Yellow plastic body & Malaysia base, yellow painted fenders, black barrel, bw

EX n/a   **NM** n/a   **MIP** $4

(Photo by Frank Veres)

❑ **270, Chevy Stocker,** a. Mf. pink w/metal Malaysia base, yellow tint window, guh

EX n/a   **NM** n/a   **MIP** $5

(Photo by Frank Veres)

❑ **271, Funny Car,** Lt. met. blue w/red & yellow over white "Hot Wheels" logo on hood & sides, white "F/C 1" & "Goodyear" tampo on sides w/racing decals, metal Malaysia base, bw

EX n/a   **NM** n/a   **MIP** $3500

(Photo by Frank Veres)

❑ **273, Tail Gunner,** White w/gray, blue & black camouflage on roof, hood & sides, metal Malaysia base, gray int., front end & guns on rear bed, dark smoked window, wct

EX n/a   **NM** n/a   **MIP** $8

❑ **274, Super Cannon,** a. Olive w/green, light green, tan & yellow camouflage, olive Malaysia base, black plastic guns & front window, wbw

EX n/a   **NM** n/a   **MIP** $4

❑ **440, Monte Carlo Stocker,** a. Dark blue met, race team tampos, white "1" on roof & door, gray & red stripe on bottom side, white int., clear window, gray plastic Malaysia base, yellow letter alw, b7sp

EX n/a   **NM** n/a   **MIP** $3

(Photo by Frank Veres)

❑ **441, Chevy Stocker,** Black w/red & white "1" on roof & door, white "Chevrolet" on rear fender & hood, racing decals & "Hot Wheels" logo on side, red int., clear window, metal Malaysia base, 7sp

EX n/a   **NM** n/a   **MIP** $5

❑ **442, Ferrari F40,** a. Pearl white, large yellow & black Ferrari logo on hood, tan int., smoked window, red logo on rear plate, metal Malaysia base, 5sp

EX n/a   **NM** n/a   **MIP** $3

❑ **443, Ferrari 348,** a. Met. black, yellow & black Ferrari logo on hood, red int., yellow "Hot Wheels" logo on rear clear window, black plastic Malaysia base, 5sp

EX n/a   **NM** n/a   **MIP** $8

(Photo by Frank Veres)

❑ **444, Aeroflash,** White w/yellow, green & blue tampo, day-glo orange painted Malaysia base & int., orange tint window, red logo behind rear wheel, g7sp

EX n/a   **NM** n/a   **MIP** $2

❑ **445, Jaguar XJ220,** a. Met. green, gray plastic Malaysia base, gray int., red logo on rear clear window, 5sp

EX n/a   NM n/a   MIP $3

(Photo by Frank Veres)

❑ **446, '32 Ford Delivery,** a. Very dark blue (almost black), white "Ford" on side, black int., clear window, white logo on rear, 3sp

EX n/a   NM n/a   MIP $20

❑ **447, '63 Split-Window,** a. Met. green, chrome Malaysia base, tan int., red logo on clear windshield, asw, 3sp

EX n/a   NM n/a   MIP $4

(KP Photo, Tom Michael collection)

❑ **448, '67 Camaro,** a. Yellow w/black stripes on hood & trunk, black int., yellow logo on rear smoked window, metal no origin base, 5sp

EX n/a   NM n/a   MIP $7

❑ **449, Camaro Z-28,** a. Day-glo orange, black painted Malaysia base, black int., smoked window, orange "Camaro" on windshield, orange logo on rear window, 3sp

EX n/a   NM n/a   MIP $5

❑ **450, Corvette Stingray,** a. Pearl white, metal Malaysia base, blue tint window & int., blue logo on rear fender, 3sp

EX n/a   NM n/a   MIP $3

(Photo by Frank Veres)

❑ **451, 3-Window '34,** a. Day-glo pink, pink fenders & running boards, pink int., black logo on rear, rose tint window, metal Malaysia base, 3sp

EX n/a   NM n/a   MIP $15

(Photo by Frank Veres)

❑ **452, Ferrari 250,** a. Met. green, green plastic base, yellow & black Ferrari logo on nose, dark tan int., chrome pipes, clear window, red logo in white box on rear, 5sp

EX n/a   NM n/a   MIP $15

❑ **453, Audi Avus,** a. Red w/black plastic Malaysia base, white int., smoked canopy w/red & black painted markings, white logo on rear, alw, 5sp

EX n/a   NM n/a   MIP $10

❑ **454, Zender Fact 4,** a. White pearl w/blue "Zender" on nose, gold "Fact 4" on top of fender, gray int., blue tint window, gray plastic Malaysia base, blue logo on rear spoiler, 5sp

EX n/a   NM n/a   MIP $3

❑ **455, '65 Mustang Convertible,** a. Mf. gold w/white side stripe, white int., smoked window, metal Malaysia base, no logo, asw, 3sp

EX n/a   NM n/a   MIP $4

❑ **457, Pontiac Banshee,** a. Met. black, metal China base, neon yellow int., clear canopy w/black band, red logo windshield, asw, 5sp

EX n/a   NM n/a   MIP $3

(Photo by Frank Veres)

❑ **458, Speed Shark,** Met. lavender, chrome China base, purple int., purple tint window, white log on rear spoiler, 5sp

EX n/a   NM n/a   MIP $3

(Photo by Frank Veres)

❑ **460, Zombot,** Black over silver, day-glo orange China base, orange plastic gun, 2 red logos on bottom of feet, 5sp

EX n/a   NM n/a   MIP $3

(Photo by Frank Veres)

❑ **461, Enforcer,** Pearl purple, silver painted windows, gray plastic guns & rockets, metal China base, silver logo on nose, alw, 5sp

EX n/a   NM n/a   MIP $3

❑ **462, '80s Firebird,** a. Met. blue, blue plastic China base, white int., red logo on clear windshield, asw, 5sp

EX n/a   NM n/a   MIP $3

❑ **463, Fiero 2M4,** a. Day-glo yellow, black Fiero logo on hood, black stripe on side, black int., clear window, red logo in front of rear wheel, asw, 5sp

EX n/a   NM n/a   MIP $3

(Photo by Frank Veres)

❑ **464, Blazer 4X4,** a. Met. dark blue, blue tint metal China base, yellow int., blue tint window, no logo, alw, ct

EX n/a   NM n/a   MIP $3

(Photo by Frank Veres)

❏ **467, Peugeot 405,** a. Met. dark green, green plastic China base, white plastic spacer between body & base, white int., red logo in rear clear window, asw 5sp

EX n/a   NM n/a   MIP $4

(Photo by Frank Veres)

❏ **468, GT Racer,** a. Day-glo orange, black window, large "Hot Wheels" logo on black rear wing, metal China base, 5sp

EX n/a   NM n/a   MIP $5

(Photo by Frank Veres)

❏ **469, Hot Bird,** a. Mf. gold, metal China base, white int., tinted window, red logo on rear plate, 5sp

EX n/a   NM n/a   MIP $5

(Photo by Frank Veres)

❏ **470, Turbo Streak,** a. White body, met. dark blue side pods, white painted China base, large "Hot Wheels" logo on white rear wing, 5sp

EX n/a   NM n/a   MIP $4

(Photo by Frank Veres)

❏ **471, Velocitor,** a. Dark met. blue w/large "Hot Wheels" logo on hood, red int. & spacer between

body & white painted China base, clear window, 5sp

EX n/a   NM n/a   MIP $4

(Photo by Frank Veres)

❏ **472, Buick Stocker,** a. Day-glo yellow, black painted China base, black int., red logo on clear windshield, 5sp

EX n/a   NM n/a   MIP $3

(Photo by Frank Veres)

❏ **473, Street Beast,** a. Pearl teal w/matching painted China base, gray int. & rear louvers, red logo on tinted windshield, 5sp

EX n/a   NM n/a   MIP $3

(Photo by Frank Veres)

❏ **474, VW Golf,** a. Met. black, black plastic China base, red int., yellow logo in clear back window, asw, 5sp

EX n/a   NM n/a   MIP $5

(Photo by Frank Veres)

❏ **475, Fork Lift,** Yellow, black cage & seat, yellow forks, metal China base, red logo on side, large bw front/ medium 5sp rear

EX n/a   NM n/a   MIP $5

(Photo by Frank Veres)

❏ **477, Double Demon,** Day-glo green plastic body, magenta chrome insert, black painted China base w/green logo on side, alw-5sp

EX n/a   NM n/a   MIP $3

(KP Photo)

❏ **478, Dragon Wagon,** Day-glo yellow w/orange eyes, pearl teal painted China base, red logo on rear, alw, 5sp

EX n/a   NM n/a   MIP $3

(Photo by Frank Veres)

❏ **479, Computer Warrior,** Black over blue, day-glo orange China base, chrome engine 2 red logos on bottom of feet, 5sp

EX n/a   NM n/a   MIP $3

(Photo by Frank Veres)

❏ **481, Tall Ryder,** a. Pearl green, chrome spacer between body & metal China base, chrome window, white logo on rear, alw, cts

EX n/a   NM n/a   MIP $4

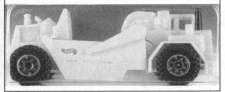

(Photo by Frank Veres)

❑ **482, Earth Mover,** Yellow plastic cab, yellow painted China frame, black seat & exhaust, red logo on side, alw, cts

EX n/a   NM n/a   MIP $5

(Photo by Frank Veres)

❑ **483, Thunder Roller,** Met dark red, chrome China base, tan int., clear window, red logo on front bumper, large bw rear, large 5sp front

EX n/a   NM n/a   MIP $5

(KP Photo)

❑ **484, Grizzlor,** a. White plastic body, orange plastic engine, metal China base red logo on rear, 5sp

EX n/a   NM n/a   MIP $3

(Photo by Frank Veres)

❑ **485, Evil Weevil,** Light orange plastic body w/light green eyes, unpainted metal exhaust, day-glo orange painted China vase, no logo, alw, 5sp

EX n/a   NM n/a   MIP $3

(Photo by Frank Veres)

❑ **486, Command Tank,** Pearl purple w/flat black camouflage & "Nite Force" tampo on side, black plastic turret, rear door & China base, silver logo on side rear

EX n/a   NM n/a   MIP $5

(Photo by Frank Veres)

❑ **487, Troop Convoy,** a. Met. gray metal cab, day-glo orange plastic roof & rear bed, black canopy, black painted China base, gold logo on hood, alw-5sp

EX n/a   NM n/a   MIP $15

(Photo by Frank Veres)

❑ **488, Sting Rod,** Met. dark gray, orange plastic guns & rockets, day-glo orange painted China base, red logo on nose, alw, ct

EX n/a   NM n/a   MIP $3

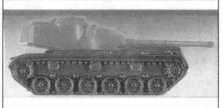

(Photo by Frank Veres)

❑ **489, Big Bertha,** a. Met. dark gray, day-glo orange plastic turret, gray plastic China base, gold logo on front

EX n/a   NM n/a   MIP $12

(Photo by Frank Veres)

❑ **491, Rocket Shot,** a. Met. gray body & tracks, day-glo orange plastic top w/gray rocket, gray plastic China base, silver logo on front

EX n/a   NM n/a   MIP $10

(Photo by Frank Veres)

❑ **492, Swingfire,** a. Day-glo orange metal body, gray plastic int. & China base, silver logo on front, 5sp

EX n/a   NM n/a   MIP $10

(Photo by Frank Veres)

❑ **493, Porsche 911 Targa,** a. Day-glo yellow, black plastic China base & int., yellow in rear clear window, alw-5sp

EX n/a   NM n/a   MIP $8

(KP Photo)

❑ **494, Mercedes 500SL,** Met. dark gray, black painted China base, red int., yellow on clear windshield, asw, 5sp

EX n/a   NM n/a   MIP $2

❏ **496, Ferrari 308GTS,** a. Red w/black plastic China base, black int., yellow logo on tinted windshield, asw, 5sp
EX n/a   NM n/a   MIP $3

❏ **497, Ferrari Testarossa,** a. Pearl white, black plastic China base & int., red logo on clear windshield, asw-5sp
EX n/a   NM n/a   MIP $3

(KP Photo)

❏ **498, BMW 850i,** a. Mf. silver, red int., black plastic China base, yellow logo on rear clear window, asw, 5sp
EX n/a   NM n/a   MIP $3

(KP Photo)

❏ **499, Corvette Coupe,** a. Met. dark green, red int., black plastic China base, red logo on rear clear window w/painted black top, asw, 5sp
EX n/a   NM n/a   MIP $6

(Photo by Frank Veres)

❏ **502, Chevy Nomad,** a. Met. red, tan int. w/open steering wheel, clear window, gold logo on rear, metal Malaysia base, g7sp
EX n/a   NM n/a   MIP $7

❏ **503, '80s Corvette,** a. Dark red pearl, gray int., clear window w/black painted top, black logo on rear, metal Malaysia base, asw, 3sp
EX n/a   NM n/a   MIP $3

❏ **504, Camaro Z-28,** a. Pearl white, black painted Malaysia base, blue tint window, no int., gold logo behind rear wheel, 3sp
EX n/a   NM n/a   MIP $3

❏ **505, 1993 Camaro,** a. Met. black, tan int., clear window, black plastic Malaysia base, yellow logo on rear, alw, 5sp
EX n/a   NM n/a   MIP $3

(Photo by Frank Veres)

❏ **506, Nissan 300ZX,** Met. purple w/matching painted China base, gold tampos on side & hood, purple int., clear window, gold logo on front right of hood, asw, 5sp
EX n/a   NM n/a   MIP $3

(Photo by Frank Veres)

❏ **507, Peugeot 205 Rallye,** Black, blue & purple body with silver "205" tampo on door, silver "Hot Wheels" logo in front of rear wheel, orange painted metal China base, alw, 5sp
EX n/a   NM n/a   MIP $30

(KP Photo)

❏ **523, 1970 Plymouth Barracuda,** Sublime w/black side stripe, black hood scoop, chrome base China base, black int., tinted window, black logo behind front wheel, asw, 5sp
EX n/a   NM n/a   MIP $7

(Photo by Frank Veres)

❏ **524, GMC Motor Home,** Race team met. blue w/large logo on side, gray plastic India base, white int., clear window, bw
EX n/a   NM n/a   MIP $25

(Photo by Frank Veres)

❏ **525, Trailbuster Jeep,** Black enamel w/red side stripes, red over white logo on side rear, metal India base, black int., clear window, alw, bw
EX n/a   NM n/a   MIP $4

(Photo by Frank Veres)

❏ **526, Neet Streeter,** Yellow enamel w/magenta & black side tampo, black hood scoop, black int., metal India base, red logo on side, bw
EX n/a   NM n/a   MIP $5

(Photo by Frank Veres)

❑ **527, Second Wind,** White w/blue "6" in red circle & red logo on side, blue plastic India base & int., blue tint window, bw
EX n/a   NM n/a   MIP $3

(Photo by Frank Veres)

❑ **528, Beach Blaster,** White w/purple & red side tampo, gray plastic India base, red int., clear window, red logo behind rear wheel, bw
EX n/a   NM n/a   MIP $2

(Photo by Frank Veres)

❑ **577, Police Cruiser,** a. Black enamel, white doors w/gold & red "Auto City Police" tampo, gold "Emergency" on rear fender, red logo on rear door, white & gold "96" & blue lights on roof, gold & white logo & gold "Police" on trunk, tan int., smoked window, black plastic Malaysia base, asw, b7sp
EX n/a   NM n/a   MIP $4

❑ **590, Porsche 911,** a. Red enamel, black int., smoked window, metal Malaysia base, black logo on nose, asw, t/b
EX n/a   NM n/a   MIP $3

❑ **591, Porsche 959,** a. Silver blue pearl, black int., smoked window, metal Malaysia base, blue logo on rear spoiler, asw, t/b
EX n/a   NM n/a   MIP $3

❑ **592, Porsche 930,** a. Pearl blue, black int., smoked window, metal Malaysia base, white logo on nose, asw, t/b
EX n/a   NM n/a   MIP $3

(Photo by Frank Veres)

❑ **593, Skullrider,** a. Dark pink chrome body, black int. & engine, metal Malaysia base, black logo behind passengers head, 5sp
EX n/a   NM n/a   MIP $4

(Photo by Frank Veres)

❑ **594, GM Ultralite,** a. White & black enamel w/gray "SAPD" & police logo on sides, black, gray & white tampo on hood, no logo, black painted windows. This is the same as the "Demo man" series car except for the wheels. Notice the "Warner" name on the black plastic Malaysia base, 7sp (I would say that there were some painted bodies hanging around from the Demo Man Series that ended up here.)
EX n/a   NM n/a   MIP $10

(Photo by Frank Veres)

❑ **595, Corvette Sting Ray III,** a. Dark met. purple, purple plastic Malaysia base, gray int., clear window, no logo, 5sp
EX n/a   NM n/a   MIP $5

❑ **596, Pontiac Salsa,** a. Orange enamel, chrome Malaysia base, silver mf. window, light gray int., no logo, alw, 3sp
EX n/a   NM n/a   MIP $25

(Photo by Frank Veres)

❑ **597, Buick Wildcat,** a. Candy red or blood red, black engine, black window, black plastic Malaysia base, no logo, alw, 7 sp. (Another car I think was left over from the "Demo Man" series.)
EX n/a   NM n/a   MIP $20

(Photo by Frank Veres)

❑ **598, Turboa,** Butterscotch pearl, red, silver & black tampo, gold chrome seat, engine & pipes, metal China base, red logo on back of head, 5sp
EX n/a   NM n/a   MIP $2

(Photo by Frank Veres)

❑ **599, Camaro Wind,** White enamel w/yellow, orange & red flames on nose & sides, pink chrome window, engine & side pipes, metal China base, red logo behind side window, bbs
EX n/a   NM n/a   MIP $4

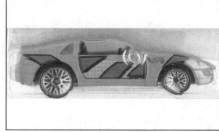

(Photo by Frank Veres)

❑ **600, Nissan Custom "Z",** a. Light blue enamel w/magenta, silver & black tampo on side, magenta logo behind front wheel, metal China base, black int., clear window, bbs
EX n/a   NM n/a   MIP $4

(Photo by Frank Veres)

❏ **601, Commando,** Brown pearl, black & gold side tampo, gold logo on door, metal China base, black int., clear window, alw, cts

EX n/a　　**NM** n/a　　**MIP** $6

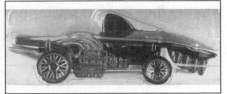

(Photo by Frank Veres)

❏ **602, Sharkruiser,** Black enamel, gray painted China base, red chrome engine, seat & teeth, silver logo above front wheel, bbs

EX n/a　　**NM** n/a　　**MIP** $3

(Photo by Frank Veres)

❏ **603, BMW 325i,** Yellow enamel w/red & black tampos on hood & sides, gray painted China base, black logo behind front wheel, black int., clear window, asw, bbs

EX n/a　　**NM** n/a　　**MIP** $2

❏ **604, Ferrari 308 GTS,** a. Yellow & black enamel w/black & yellow Ferrari logo on hood, black int., black plastic China base, clear windshield w/yellow logo, asw, 5sp

EX n/a　　**NM** n/a　　**MIP** $6

(Photo by Frank Veres)

❏ **605, Mercedes 2.6,** Met. gold, red painted taillights, silver

painted grille, black plastic China base, black int., clear window, gold logo in rear window, asw, bbs

EX n/a　　**NM** n/a　　**MIP** $2

(Photo by Frank Veres)

❏ **606, Mercedes 300TD,** Met. dark green, red painted taillights, silver painted grille, gray plastic China base, gray int., red logo in rear clear window, asw, 5sp

EX n/a　　**NM** n/a　　**MIP** $3

❏ **607, Fat Fendered '40,** Aqua w/yellow, orange & purple side tampo, black int., metal China base, white logo in clear side window, asw, 5sp. (The #607 along with the #216 Fat Fendered '40 are very heavy & were bought up by the guys in Puerto Rico for racing. I expect these to become very hard to find still in the package.)

EX n/a　　**NM** n/a　　**MIP** $12

(Photo by Frank Veres)

❏ **608, Porsche 911 Targa,** Mf. silver, black painted door handle, black plastic China base, black int., red logo in rear clear window, 5sp

EX n/a　　**NM** n/a　　**MIP** $2

(Photo by Frank Veres)

❏ **609, Jaguar XJ40,** Dark blue, red painted taillights, silver painted rear plate & front grille, white int., white logo in rear blue tint window, black plastic China base, asw, bbs

EX n/a　　**NM** n/a　　**MIP** $3

(Photo by Frank Veres)

❏ **610, Land Rover MkII,** Orange enamel w/blue & white side tampos, black int., clear window, no logo, black plastic China base, alw, 5sp

EX n/a　　**NM** n/a　　**MIP** $10

(Photo by Frank Veres)

❏ **611, Fire-Eater II,** Red enamel, silver tampos on side, gray plastic China base & ladder, dark blue tint window, silver logo on side, asw, 5sp

EX n/a　　**NM** n/a　　**MIP** $2

(Photo by Frank Veres)

❏ **612, '57 T-Bird,** Aqua enamel, chrome bumpers, white int., red logo in clear windshield, metal China base, bw

EX n/a　　**NM** n/a　　**MIP** $10

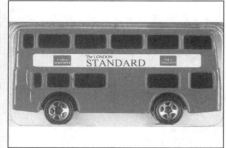

(Photo by Frank Veres)

❑ **613, London Bus,** Red enamel, white side strip w/red & black tampos, black plastic China base & window, gold logo on rear, asw, 5sp

EX n/a   NM n/a   **MIP** $9

(Photo by Frank Veres)

❑ **615, Ford XR4Ti,** Mf. silver w/butterscotch & purple side tampos, purple "4" & blue "Ford" oval on hood, purple logo behind front wheel, red int. & taillights, clear window & headlights, black plastic China base, asw-5sp

EX n/a   NM n/a   **MIP** $2

(Photo by Frank Veres)

❑ **616, 80's Corvette,** White enamel, yellow & blue side tampo w/gray #2 & Corvette, blue int./black dashboard, black painted top, gold logo in rear clear window, black plastic China base, asw, bbs

EX n/a   NM n/a   **MIP** $4

(Photo by Frank Veres)

❑ **617, Flame Stopper II,** Red enamel, red & white side tampos, gray plastic China base & boom w/bucket, dark smoked window, black logo on door, asw, 5sp

EX n/a   NM n/a   **MIP** $2

(KP Photo, Tom Michael collection)

❑ **618, Chevy Stocker,** White enamel, silver & blue side stripe w/red & blue tampos, silver & blue tampo on hood w/red & blue "Huffman Racing," purple int., clear window, red logo behind rear wheel, metal China base, asw-5sp (Another car bought up by the guys in Puerto Rico, most of these have been taken out of the package & are going to be hard to find.)

EX n/a   NM n/a   **MIP** $20

(Photo by Frank Veres)

❑ **619, London Taxi,** Yellow enamel w/black & white squared side stripe, black "London Cab Co." on rear fender, red "See City of Hot Wheels" on side, black logo behind front wheel, black int., clear window, metal China base, asw, 5sp

EX n/a   NM n/a   **MIP** $7

(KP Photo, Tom Michael collection)

❑ **620, Ford Transit Wrecker,** Light blue enamel w/white & red tampos, white plastic China base & boom, black hook & window, red logo behind rear wheel, asw, 5sp

EX n/a   NM n/a   **MIP** $5

(Photo by Frank Veres)

❑ **622, City Police,** Black enamel, white & yellow side stripe w/black tampos & "City of "Hot Wheel's" logo black tampo on white roof w/blue light, gold "Police" on trunk, dark gray int. & bumpers, black China base, red logo above rear wheel, alw, b5sp

EX n/a   NM n/a   **MIP** $3

(Photo by Frank Veres)

❑ **623, Mustang Cobra,** a. Pearl dark pink w/black stripe on hood, black "Mustang 5.0" on door, thin gold stripe on side, gold logo above 5.0 behind front wheel, black int., clear window, black plastic China base, asw, bbs

EX n/a   NM n/a   **MIP** $2

(Photo by Frank Veres)

❑ **624, Assault Crawler,** Olive w/brown, green & tan camouflage, olive plastic China base black enamel w/black plastic fenders, black int., silver logo in rear clear window, metal China base, asw, 5sp

EX n/a   NM n/a   **MIP** $5

(Photo by Frank Veres)

❑ **625, Classic Packard,** Black enamel w/black plastic fenders, black int., silver logo in rear clear window, metal China base, asw, 5sp
EX n/a   NM n/a   MIP $5

(Photo by Frank Veres)

❑ **641, Wheel Loader,** a. Orange & black, white logo on cab door, metal China base, gray seat, engine & scoop, alw, cts
EX n/a   NM n/a   MIP $4

(Photo by Frank Veres)

❑ **642, Forklift,** a. White enamel, blue plastic cage, black plastic forks, small blue logo between wheels on side, metal China base, rear 5sp-front bw
EX n/a   NM n/a   MIP $5

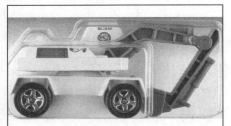

(Photo by Frank Veres)

❑ **643, Digger,** a. Yellow enamel w/black "E 32" & City of "Hot Wheels" logo on side, black logo on side, gray plastic boom & scoop, yellow painted China base, (no "Hot Wheels" flame on base above Digger), alw, 5sp
EX n/a   NM n/a   MIP $5

(Photo by Frank Veres)

❑ **700, Shock Factor,** Yellow enamel & blue plastic, black, red & white tampos on side & rear wing, black logo on side by scoop, metal China base, blue plastic driver, alw, bw
EX n/a   NM n/a   MIP $3

(Photo by Frank Veres)

❑ **702, Lumina Van,** a. Dark green met, three thin silver w/"Lumina" on sides, black plastic China base, tan int., smoked window, silver logo on rear fender, bbs
EX n/a   NM n/a   MIP $4

(Photo by Frank Veres)

❑ **712, Tipper,** a. Blue enamel, black plastic China base, white tip box w/yellow & black w/small "BD" tampo in blue, black & white logo on box side, black int., smoked window, asw, 5sp
EX n/a   NM n/a   MIP $2

❑ **714, Talbot Lago,** Blue enamel w/black fenders, black painted metal base, bbs
EX n/a   NM n/a   MIP $180

(Photo by Frank Veres)

❑ **715, 1996 Mustang GT,** White enamel, metal China base, thin black stripe w/yellow & orange tampos trimmed in black on sides, yellow logo in tampo behind front wheel, silver painted headlights, red int., clear window, asw, 5sp
EX n/a   NM n/a   MIP $30

(Photo by Frank Veres)

❑ **761, Flame Stopper,** Red enamel, black plastic Malaysia base, white stripe below doors w/gold & black "Fire Dept" & "City of Hot Wheel's" logo, gold & black "31" behind black rear window, white logo behind rear wheel, gray plastic boom w/part number on side, alw, ct/b
EX n/a   NM n/a   MIP $2

(Photo by Frank Veres)

❑ **765, Oshkosh P-Series,** a. Light met. blue, white plastic cab & box, gray plastic plow blade, blue tint metal Malaysia base, met. blue seats, white logo on hood, alw, ct/b
EX n/a   NM n/a   MIP $4

(Photo by Frank Veres)

❑ **767, Mercedes 380 SEL,** Pearl white w/met. gold painted Malaysia base, tan int., red logo in rear clear window, gold chrome grille & headlights, asw, t/b
EX n/a   **NM** n/a   **MIP** $2

(Photo by Frank Veres)

❑ **768, Lamborghini Countach,** Black enamel, black plastic Malaysia base, red int., clear window, gold logo in front window, asw, 5dot
EX n/a   **NM** n/a   **MIP** $2

(Photo by Frank Veres)

❑ **770, Lexus SC400,** a. Met. blue, black plastic Malaysia base, white int., smoked window, white logo on rear plate, asw, bbs
EX n/a   **NM** n/a   **MIP** $5

❑ **771, '56 Flashsider,** a. Yellow pearl w/pink & blue side tampo, black window, chrome Malaysia base, pink logo on rear fender, 5dot
EX n/a   **NM** n/a   **MIP** $3

(Photo by Frank Veres)

❑ **773, Hot Wheels 500,** Day-glo yellow, blue tint metal Malaysia base, black, white & orange tampos on side pod, side of front wing, nose & rear deck, black plastic driver, yellow letter b/7sp
EX n/a   **NM** n/a   **MIP** $3

(Photo by Frank Veres)

❑ **774, Ramp Truck,** Dark met. green w/large logo on roof, met. gray ramp w/yellow, blue & red tampo on side, metal China base, smoked window, asw, 5sp
EX n/a   **NM** n/a   **MIP** $3

(Photo by Frank Veres)

❑ **778, Speed Blaster,** a. Met. blue w/red & white side tampo, white logo & C778 in front of rear wheel, chrome window & engine, black plastic Malaysia base, 3sp
EX n/a   **NM** n/a   **MIP** $4

❑ **779, Big Chill,** a. Blue enamel w/white flames on sides, logo on front between chrome driver & white skis, white plastic Thailand base w/black front wheel
EX n/a   **NM** n/a   **MIP** $8

❑ **780, '58 Corvette Coupe,** a. Aqua enamel w/chrome engine through hood, silver painted headlights, aqua plastic Malaysia base, smoked window, chrome int., exhaust, bumpers & grille, white box w/red & white logo on trunk, 5dot
EX n/a   **NM** n/a   **MIP** $6

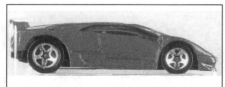

(Photo by Frank Veres)

❑ **781, Lamborghini Diablo,** a. Met. red, black painted Malaysia base, tan int., tinted window, red met. plastic rear wing & bumper, gold logo on windshield, 5sp
EX n/a   **NM** n/a   **MIP** $3

❑ **782, Radar Ranger,** Met. gold w/black & white tampos, blue tint metal Malaysia base, chrome radar dish, black logo on front

right, black insert & seat, clear canopy, alw, ct/b
EX n/a   **NM** n/a   **MIP** $3

(Photo by Frank Veres)

❑ **783, Twin Mill II,** Silver pearl w/magenta & black side tampo, chrome engine, black plastic Malaysia base, black window, magenta logo in front of rear wheel, alw, bbs
EX n/a   **NM** n/a   **MIP** $3

❑ **784, Ferrari Testarossa,** a. Met. silver w/yellow & black Ferrari logo on hood, black painted Malaysia base, black int., clear window, black logo on rear plate, 5dot (red car on card)
EX n/a   **NM** n/a   **MIP** $5

(Photo by Frank Veres)

❑ **787, '57 Chevy,** Met. purple metal body w/blue tint metal engine through hood, black & red side tampo w/red "'57" & white "Chevy," chrome Thailand base, black int., smoked window, white logo on rear fender, t/b
EX n/a   **NM** n/a   **MIP** $4

(Photo by Frank Veres)

❑ **788, Mercedes 540K,** a. Met. purple w/light blue stripe on side, light blue top & tampo on door, metal Malaysia base, black int., clear window, asw, bbs
EX n/a   **NM** n/a   **MIP** $4

(Photo by Frank Veres)

❑ **791, Treadator,** a. Met. blue w/white scoops & nose, black plastic Thailand base & treads, chrome canopy, engine & fenders, white logo on front left window
EX n/a   **NM** n/a   **MIP** $3

(Photo by Frank Veres)

❑ **792, Camaro Race Car,** White pearl w/orange squares on sides and black outlined "4" & "Bousquette Racing," black square w/orange outlined "4" on roof, black w/white "Bousquette Racing" twice on hood, white & orange logo on rear fender, black plastic Malaysia base, black int., clear window, alw, 5sp
EX n/a   **NM** n/a   **MIP** $3

(Photo by Frank Veres)

❑ **793, Auburn 852,** Black enamel w/met. gold plastic fenders & int., gold tampo on hood & behind seat, gold logo on rear deck, gold chrome headlights, grille & windshield frame w/tinted window, metal Malaysia base, asw, gbbs
EX n/a   **NM** n/a   **MIP** $6

(Photo by Frank Veres)

❑ **795, Tractor,** Silver pearl, black plastic cab & hydraulics, black plastic Malaysia base, black logo on nose, c/tt rear-ct/b frt
EX n/a   **NM** n/a   **MIP** $3

(Photo by Frank Veres)

❑ **796, '96 Camaro Convertible,** White enamel w/orange stripes on sides, hood & trunk, gray plastic India base, orange int., smoked window, white & orange logo on rear fender above rear tire, alw, w5sp
EX n/a   **NM** n/a   **MIP** $3

❑ **797, Dodge Ram 1500,** a. Red enamel w/red plastic rear cap, white tampos on front & rear fenders w/"Dodge Ram X-Tra" between, light yellow plastic bumpers, int. & spacer between body and white plastic Malaysia base, smoked window, alw, 5dot
EX n/a   **NM** n/a   **MIP** $4

(Photo by Frank Veres)

❑ **798, Propper Chopper,** Blue enamel w/gold, black, blue & white POLICE tampos, black plastic tail, rotors, hook, int. & China base, blue tint window gold & white logo on side rear by tail
EX n/a   **NM** n/a   **MIP** $3

❑ **802, Flashfire,** a. Met. gold w/pink, green & yellow side tampos, gold chrome engine, light gold Thailand base, black rear

spoiler, side panel, exhaust & int., smoked canopy, no logo, 5dot
EX n/a   **NM** n/a   **MIP** $5

(Photo by Frank Veres)

❑ **803, '40s Woodie,** Pearl white hood & fenders w/black & gold pinstripes on side of hood, chrome engine through hood, tan wood grain plastic body, white enamel roof w/orange, black & gold pinstripes, orange & white logo on front of roof, smoked window, black int., metal Malaysia base, 5sp
EX n/a   **NM** n/a   **MIP** $8

(Photo by Frank Veres)

❑ **808, Driven to the Max,** Pearl white w/magenta & dark blue tampos, magenta & dark blue logo on side, white "Hot Set-Up" on side, blue tint metal engine & Thailand base, hot pink plastic driver & spoiler, 5sp
EX n/a   **NM** n/a   **MIP** $3

(Photo by Frank Veres)

❑ **812, GM Lean Machine,** Met. green & met. gold plastic body, metal Malaysia base, gold seat, smoked canopy w/white logo, t/b
EX n/a   **NM** n/a   **MIP** $3

(Photo by Frank Veres)

❏ **813, Ferrari 355,** a. Black enamel w/yellow & black Ferrari logo on hood & door, metal Malaysia base, yellow int., yellow tint window, white "Hot Wheels" logo on rear fender, asw, 3sp
EX n/a   NM n/a   MIP $90

❏ **814, Speed-A-Saurus,** a. Glossy teal plastic dinosaur, orange painted Malaysia base, gold tint chrome engine & exhaust, magenta logo on left rear tail, large rear 5sp
EX n/a   NM n/a   MIP $3

(Photo by Frank Veres)

❏ **815, Mercedes 500 SL,** Met. green w/red, gold & black stripes on hood & sides, black plastic Thailand base, tan int., smoked window, gold chrome headlights & grille, gold logo on front fender behind wheel, alw, 3sp
EX n/a   NM n/a   MIP $3

(Photo by Frank Veres)

❏ **816, Ferrari 308,** a. Met. bronze w/yellow & black Ferrari logo on hood, black painted metal Malaysia base, yellow "Hot Wheels" logo on rear plate, tan int., smoked window, 5dot
EX n/a   NM n/a   MIP $3

(Photo by Frank Veres)

❏ **817, Porsche 928,** Pearl white, metal Malaysia base, red logo on nose, black window, bbs
EX n/a   NM n/a   MIP $3

(Photo by Frank Veres)

❏ **818, Porsche Carrera,** a. Met. red, metal Malaysia base, tan int., smoked window, yellow logo on rear fender, g5sp
EX n/a   NM n/a   MIP $3

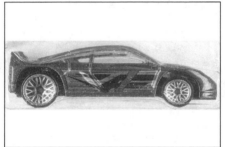

(Photo by Frank Veres)

❏ **820, Zender Fact 4,** Met. green w/gold & black tampos on hood & sides, black plastic China base, gold logo on clear windshield, black int., bbs
EX n/a   NM n/a   MIP $3

(Photo by Frank Veres)

❏ **821, '96 Mustang Convertible,** White enamel, metal China base (same as #715), thin black stripe w/yellow & orange tampos trimmed in black on sides, yellow logo in tampo behind front wheel, silver painted headlights, red int., clear window, asw, 5sp
EX n/a   NM n/a   MIP $4

(Photo by Frank Veres)

❏ **822, Camaro Z28,** Met. teal, metal no origin base, gray int., clear window, yellow logo behind rear wheel, 3sp
EX n/a   NM n/a   MIP $5

(Photo by Frank Veres)

❏ **823, Sol-Aire CX4,** Met. blue, white sides w/large "Hot Wheels" logo & red "1," large logo & red bow tie on nose, white "1" on top of right front fender, yellow "Hot Wheels" on rear wing, yellow "Goodyear" behind rear wheel, white int., clear window, white plastic Malaysia base, gbbs
EX n/a   NM n/a   MIP $4

(KP Photo)

❏ **827, Radio Flyer Wagon,** a. Red enamel w/white "Radio Flyer" side tampo, white "Hot Wheels" logo on rear, chrome motor, metal Malaysia base, black seat & handle, 5sp
EX n/a   NM n/a   MIP $5

(Photo by Frank Veres)

❏ **829, Porsche Carrera,** Met. silver w/red "Hot Wheels" logo behind front wheel, metal Malaysia base, red int., clear window, t/b
EX n/a   NM n/a   MIP $3

(Photo by Frank Veres)

❑ **834, Ferrari Testarossa,** a. Black enamel, gloss black painted India base, yellow "Ferrari" w/yellow & black Ferrari logo on hood, tan & black int., clear window, yellow "Hot Wheels" logo on rear deck, bw

EX n/a   NM n/a   MIP $3

(Photo by Frank Veres)

❑ **835, Baja Bug,** a. Dark met. blue w/large logo on sides & white "Nithia" on door, metal India base, white int., all medium bw

EX n/a   NM n/a   MIP $5

(Photo by Frank Veres)

❑ **837, Radio Flyer Wagon,** Met. blue w/white "Radio Flyer" side tampo, smaller white "Hot Wheels" logo on rear, chrome motor, metal China base, white seat & handle, 5sp

EX n/a   NM n/a   MIP $4

(Photo by Frank Veres)

❑ **850, Rail Rodder,** Gray plastic body, gold tint chrome engines &

drivers, yellow & black side tampos w/green fade "Rail Rodder," black logo & "Engine 5" on cab side, metal Malaysia base, b5sp

EX n/a   NM n/a   MIP $3

(Photo by Frank Veres)

❑ **851, Treadator,** a. Light blue pearl w/white plastic scoops & nose, silver & black tampo on tail, silver logo on side by scoop, light day-glo green plastic Thailand base & treads, chrome canopy, engine, exhaust & fenders

EX n/a   NM n/a   MIP $5

(Photo by Frank Veres)

❑ **852, Rigor Motor,** a. Pearl purple w/gold "Rigor Motors Racing" on side, gold tint engine, fuel tank & seat, yellow tint canopy, white plastic skulls & radiator, metal Malaysia base, all medium g5sp

EX n/a   NM n/a   MIP $7

❑ **853, Camaro Z28,** a. Day-glo yellow plastic body w/blue, red, white & black side tampo, large black & white "4" on side w/red & white logo behind front wheel, metal Malaysia base, black window, 5dot

EX n/a   NM n/a   MIP $5

(Photo by Frank Veres)

❑ **854, Porsche 959,** a. White enamel, metal Malaysia base, pink & black tampo on door & front fender w/large black "2," black "High Bank Racing" & red logo on rear fender, black int., smoked window, asw, t/b

EX n/a   NM n/a   MIP $5

(Photo by Frank Veres)

❑ **855, Ferrari F50,** Purple pearl w/silver, red & black side tampo, black plastic Malaysia base, silver logo on rear fender by spoiler, smoked window, black int., asw, t/b

EX n/a   NM n/a   MIP $3

(Photo by Frank Veres)

❑ **856, Porsche 930,** a. Met. red w/orange, white & black tampo on side, white logo behind rear wheel, metal Thailand base, black int., smoked window, asw, 3sp

EX n/a   NM n/a   MIP $4

(Photo by Frank Veres)

❑ **857, T-Bird Stocker,** Orange plastic body w/magenta, silver, black & white side tampo, black logo behind front wheel, black painted Thailand metal base, black window, 5dot

EX n/a   NM n/a   MIP $3

(Photo by Frank Veres)

❑ **858, Hummer,** a. White plastic body, black zebra stripes & orange "Hummer Racer," yellow "Jungle" w/orange outline, red tinted window, black logo on rear, black painted Malaysia base, asw, ct/b

EX n/a   NM n/a   MIP $6

(Photo by Frank Veres)

❑ **859, Bronco,** Red enamel w/white plastic bed cap, black plastic motorcycle on rear, black & white side tampo, white logo above tampo on door, blue tint metal Thailand base, black int., smoked window, asw, ct/b
EX n/a   NM n/a   MIP $5

(Photo by Frank Veres)

❑ **860, Road Rocket,** White plastic w/dark blue top, light green & silver tampo on side w/silver logo, metal Thailand base, 3sp
EX n/a   NM n/a   MIP $3

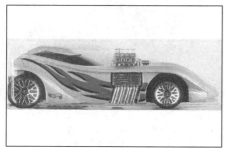

(Photo by Frank Veres)

❑ **861, Twin Mill II,** Met. gold w/magenta & black side tampo, chrome engines, black window, magenta logo in front of rear wheel, black plastic Malaysia base, large bbs rear, small bbs front
EX n/a   NM n/a   MIP $3

(Photo by Frank Veres)

❑ **862, Pontiac Salsa,** Met. red w/yellow & blue side tampo, dark blue logo on side above tampo, black int., black window, chrome Malaysia base, alw, 5dot
EX n/a   NM n/a   MIP $3

(Photo by Frank Veres)

❑ **863, Oshkosh Cement Mixer,** Day-glo yellow plastic body, silver painted metal fenders, black plastic Malaysia base, black plastic barrel w/yellow, green & black tampos, asw, 3sp
EX n/a   NM n/a   MIP $4

(Photo by Frank Veres)

❑ **864, Tank Truck,** a. Very dark met. burgundy (looks black), white, orange & blue tampo on cab side, chrome tank w/red & blue stripes & chrome lettering, chrome outline logo in red stripe by exhaust stack, chrome window, headlights & grille, black plastic Malaysia base, asw, 5dot
EX n/a   NM n/a   MIP $5

(Photo by Frank Veres)

❑ **865, Ford F150,** White enamel, orange side tampo w/large orange "M," small black "M" & logo on rear fender, small black "M" in orange dot behind front wheel, chrome bumpers, bed & int., smoked window, black plastic Malaysia base, alw, 3sp
EX n/a   NM n/a   MIP $3

(Photo by Frank Veres)

❑ **866, Ferrari 250,** a. Met. gold, black plastic Thailand base, black circle w/white "16" on door & black "Classic Racer," yellow & black Ferrari logo on nose, black "Hot Wheels" logo in middle of rear fender behind wheel, chrome grille & side pipes, black int., smoked window, bbs
EX n/a   NM n/a   MIP $4

❑ **867, '97 Corvette,** a. Met. blue w/red, white, silver & black side tampos, red "Hot Wheels" logo middle of door above tampo, red tampo, white bow tie & silver lettering on hood, silver & white box w/black "1" on door & hood, white int., tinted window, red plastic Thailand base, alw, 5sp
EX n/a   NM n/a   MIP $4

❑ **868, Range Rover,** a. Met. green, chrome Thailand base, red w/white outline & blue tampos, misc. decals on side w/white "Hot Wheels" logo on door, gold Land Rover logo on door & hood, tan int., smoked window, asw, ct/b
EX n/a   NM n/a   MIP $4

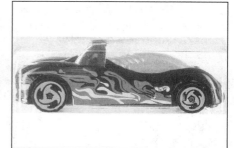

(Photo by Frank Veres)

❑ **869, Power Pipes,** Black plastic body, orange painted Thailand base, brown & yellow side tampo, white logo behind front wheel, gold tint chrome scoops & int., orange tint canopy, ot/b
EX n/a   NM n/a   MIP $3

(Photo by Frank Veres)

❑ **870, Chevy Stocker,** Purple plastic body, black painted Malaysia metal base, orange, gray & white side tampo, two skulls on front fender, one skull on rear fender, gray logo on right upper side of door, black window, gt/b
EX n/a　　NM n/a　　MIP $3

(Photo by Frank Veres)

❑ **871, Olds 442,** Met. blue w/white sides & large "Hot Wheels" logo & misc. racing decals, white "1" on rear fender above wheel, white "Richard" on door above logo, white int., smoked window, chrome Thailand base, asw, 5sp
EX n/a　　NM n/a　　MIP $4

❑ **872, Rig Wrecker,** a. White enamel w/black diamond tampo on side, red & blue tampo on door, red "1" w/black outline on side w/black "Pit Crew" and black "Tow Rig" w/red outline, red & yellow "Hot Wheels" logo on side by fuel tank, red plastic boom, black plastic Thailand base, chrome int., grille & exhaust stacks, smoked window, asw, 5dot
EX n/a　　NM n/a　　MIP $5

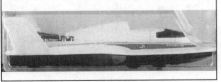
(Photo by Frank Veres)

❑ **873, Hydroplane,** White enamel w/red & black "Harbor Patrol" on pontoons, red tampo w/"City of Hot Wheels" logo on pontoons, white numbers on left pontoon only, large dark blue "Hot Wheels" logo on top of rear wing, chrome engine, black int., smoked canopy, black plastic Malaysia base
EX n/a　　NM n/a　　MIP $3

❑ **874, Pit Crew Truck,** a. Pearl gray w/red, blue & white side tampos, gold logo behind rear wheel above blue stripe, red plastic Thailand base & int., blue tint window, asw, 5dot
EX n/a　　NM n/a　　MIP $3

(Photo by Frank Veres)

❑ **875, Police Car,** Black enamel, white roof w/black "01" & red lights, white "State Police" & stripe on side w/"City of Hot Wheels" logo on door, red & white "Hot Wheels" logo behind front fender, black plastic Thailand base, gray int., tinted window, asw, 5sp
EX n/a　　NM n/a　　MIP $5

(Photo by Frank Veres)

❑ **876, Bywayman,** a. Red enamel w/silver, black & gold side tampos, silver logo behind rear wheel, metal Thailand base, white int., roll bar & bed, tinted window, asw, ct/b
EX n/a　　NM n/a　　MIP $3

(Photo by Frank Veres)

❑ **877, Chevy 1500,** Gray plastic body, black painted metal India base, red, yellow, black & white side tampos, white "Powercharger," black "Racing" on rear fender, white "Hot Wheels" logo behind rear wheel, black int. & bed cover, clear window, asw, t/b
EX n/a　　NM n/a　　MIP $3

❑ **881, '95 Camaro,** a. Black enamel w/red, yellow & white side tampo, white "Buckle Up & Hold On" tampo on rear fender, red logo behind rear wheel, red int., smoked window, black plastic India base, alw, 3sp
EX n/a　　NM n/a　　MIP $3

(Photo by Frank Veres)

❑ **884, Gulch Stepper,** Pearl yellow, blue tint metal Thailand base, magenta side tampo w/black & white "Gulch Stepper" & cactus, black window & spacer between body & base, white logo on rear fender, alw-ct/b
EX n/a　　NM n/a　　MIP $3

(Photo by Frank Veres)

❑ **889, Mercedes 380 SEL,** Black enamel, met. gold painted Malaysia base, gold chrome grille & headlights, thin gold stripe on side w/"Custom 380 SL" on rear fender, gold logo behind rear wheel on fender, tan int., tinted window, asw, gbbs
EX n/a　　NM n/a　　MIP $3

(Photo by Frank Veres)

❑ **890, BMW M Roadster,** White enamel w/two wide black stripes on hood & trunk, black on side w/white outline "Roadster" & red "Nicholas Leasing," black logo behind rear wheel, metal Malaysia base, red int., smoked window, 3sp
EX n/a　　NM n/a　　MIP $3

(Photo by Frank Veres)

❑ **894, Toyota MR2,** White enamel, black plastic Thailand base, red & gray on side w/large black "TOYOTA" & misc. racing decals, red tampo on roof w/black "TOYOTA" twice and "Saferoil" over red "36," red & gray tampo on hood w/black "TOYOTA," "Chosen Performance" & "4t" tampo, black logo behind rear wheel, light gray int., smoked window, asw, bbs
EX n/a   NM n/a   MIP $3

❑ **899, '56 Flashsider,** a. Silver pearl, chrome Thailand base, large dark red "Hot Wheels" logo on side, small dark blue flames on both fenders, dark blue "Adrian" & red "My other Hot Wheels is a car" on door, red & blue stripe on bottom of cab, red & blue # 42 on lower left corner of door, red "Hot Wheels" & dark blue "Fan" on rear fender, black window, 5sp
EX n/a   NM n/a   MIP $7

❑ **908, Ford F Series CNG Pickup,** a. Met. purple, black plastic Malaysia base, light green, orange & yellow tampos on hood, roof & side, white logo high on rear fender by taillight, chrome int., bumpers & bed, smoked window, alw, 3sp
EX n/a   NM n/a   MIP $15

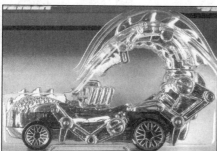

(Photo by Frank Veres)

❑ **991, Rodzilla,** Chrome plastic body, white teeth & eyes, metal China base, gold chrome engine, red "Hot Wheels" logo on rear arm (fender brace), gbbs
EX n/a   NM n/a   MIP $3

(Photo by Frank Veres)

❑ **992, Ferrari F51 2M,** Red enamel, black painted metal Malaysia base, larger yellow & black Ferrari emblem on hood, black "Hot Wheels" logo on rear plate, tan int., smoked window, 5sp
EX n/a   NM n/a   MIP $3

(Photo by Frank Veres)

❑ **993, Ferrari 348,** Yellow enamel, black plastic Malaysia base, larger yellow Ferrari emblem on hood, black & yellow int., smoked window, 5sp
EX n/a   NM n/a   MIP $3

(Photo by Frank Veres)

❑ **994, Way 2 Fast,** Met. black, met. gold painted metal Malaysia base, black, orange, white & gold tampos on roof & side, gold "Hot Wheels" logo on roof in curve of tampo, chrome int. & engines, g5sp
EX n/a   NM n/a   MIP $3

(Photo by Frank Veres)

❑ **995, Porsche 911,** Yellow enamel, metal Malaysia base, black "Hot Wheels" logo on door, black int., smoked window, 5sp
EX n/a   NM n/a   MIP $3

(Photo by Frank Veres)

❑ **996, '32 Ford Delivery,** Pearl light blue body, black plastic fenders, chrome head lights & radiator, silver & dark blue tampo on side, black "Hot Wheels Delivery" in silver rectangle in side panel, black "Hot Wheels Delivery" in silver tampo on rear, metal Malaysia base, silver "Hot Wheels" logo on door, black int., blue tint window, bbs
EX n/a   NM n/a   MIP $3

(Photo by Frank Veres)

❑ **997, Jaguar D-Type,** a. Red enamel w/matching painted metal Malaysia base, green tinted tampo w/black stripes down the center from the nose to the tail, black ring & "27" in white circle outlined in green tint on hood, side has green tint tampo w/black stripes & "JAGUAR D-TYPE" and black ring & "27" in white circle outlined in green tint, white "Hot Wheels" logo below side stripe in front of rear wheel along with two other racing decals, black "Hot Wheels" logo on rear also, gray int., smoked window, alw-bbs
EX n/a   NM n/a   MIP $5

(Photo by Frank Veres)

❑ **998, Firebird Funny Car,** Met. red, metal Malaysia base, black & white side tampo w/silver "MARTIN Racing" & misc. racing decals, small "Hot Wheels" logo above tampo behind front wheel, black & white tampo on hood w/black "Martin" & white "Racing" & misc. racing decals, smoked window, g5sp
EX n/a   NM n/a   MIP $5

❏ **999, Hot Seat,** a. Chrome plastic body (bowl), metal Malaysia base, gold "Hot Wheels" logo below white toilet paper roll on rear of side (pun intended), red plastic seat & plunger, 5sp
EX n/a   NM n/a   MIP $5

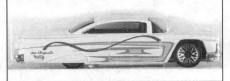
(Photo by Frank Veres)

❏ **1000, '59 Impala,** a. Pearl white, gold tint plastic Malaysia base, yellow & gold tampo on side w/dark red ribbon & "59 Impala," gold "Hot Wheels" logo below "59 Impala" on rear fender, small yellow, gold & dark red pinstripe tampo on hood, black int., smoked window, gbbs
EX n/a   NM n/a   MIP $3

(Photo by Frank Veres)

❏ **1001, Slideout,** Met. blue body, white plastic Malaysia base, yellow plastic rear push bar, engine, front wing & top wing, black & yellow "27" on rear, yellow stripe on rear side of roll cage, black triangle tampo w/two white racing decals & yellow "Hot Wheels" logo on side, yellow & black splochy stripe on body above engine, dark blue & white "27" & splotchy stripe w/Rman Racing on side of top wing, 5sp
EX n/a   NM n/a   MIP $3

(Photo by Frank Veres)

❏ **1003, Ferrari F40,** Black enamel, larger yellow & black Ferrari emblem on front, yellow "Hot Wheels" on rear plate, metal

Malaysia base, red int., smoked window, 5sp
EX n/a   NM n/a   MIP $4

(Photo by Frank Veres)

❏ **1004, Dairy Delivery,** White enamel w/black cow spots & red "Got Milk?" on side, gold "Hot Wheels" logo in black spot left of "Got Milk?," chrome Malaysia base, black int., clear window, 5sp
EX n/a   NM n/a   MIP $4

(Photo by Frank Veres)

❏ **1005, Mercedes-Benz Unimog,** Red enamel cab & box, black plastic fenders, int. & rear box cover, white "Hot Wheels" logo on center of hood, metal Malaysia base, clear windows, large ct/b
EX n/a   NM n/a   MIP $3

(Photo by Frank Veres)

❏ **1006, Dodge Viper RT/10,** Met. blue, black plastic Malaysia base, small Dodge emblem between two wide white stripes on hood & trunk, white "Hot Wheels" logo & "Viper R/T 10" on front fender behind front wheel, orange tampo-ed directional lights in front bumper, black int., smoked window, 5sp
EX n/a   NM n/a   MIP $4

(Photo by Frank Veres)

❏ **1007, Tow Jam,** Met. green, chrome Malaysia base, black, yellow & green outlined flame tampo on hood & side, small green & black "Hot Wheels" logo on rear of roof, metal boom w/black plastic sling, black window, 3sp
EX n/a   NM n/a   MIP $3

(Photo by Frank Veres)

❏ **1008, Chaparral 2,** Red enamel, white painted metal Malaysia base, two wide white stripes from nose to tail, white "Hot Wheels" logo on door, gray injection & exhaust, black int., clear window, bbs/2
EX n/a   NM n/a   MIP $3

(Photo by Frank Veres)

❏ **1009, Peterbilt Dump Truck,** Dark blue enamel, white plastic dump box, white "Hot Wheels" logo on hood, metal Malaysia base, blue tint window & int., alw-5sp
EX n/a   NM n/a   MIP $4

(Photo by Frank Veres)

❏ **1010, Ford Stake Bed Truck,** Teal enamel, gray stake bed, chrome Malaysia base, int., exhaust stacks & grille, silver "Hot

Wheels" logo on door, blue tint window, asw-5dot

EX n/a   **NM** n/a   **MIP** $4

(Photo by Frank Veres)

❏ **1011, Oshkosh Cement Truck,** Black plastic body, barrel & Malaysia base, met. burgundy painted fenders & seat, gold "Hot Wheels" logo on front bumper, asw, t/b

EX n/a   **NM** n/a   **MIP** $4

(Photo by Frank Veres)

❏ **1012, Flame Stopper,** White enamel, black plastic Malaysia base, brown & yellow over black airplane tampo w/light green & black "Airport" & black "Fire & Rescue Team" on cab doors, small red "Hot Wheels" logo, flame in circle & "Emergency" w/two thin stripes on cab behind window, black boom w/rivets & part number, black window, alw, ct/b

EX n/a   **NM** n/a   **MIP** $3

(Photo by Frank Veres)

❏ **1013, Mercedes 500 SL,** Silver pearl, black plastic Malaysia base, red "Hot Wheels" logo on rear plate, chrome grille & headlights, black int., smoked window, alw, bbs

EX n/a   **NM** n/a   **MIP** $3

(Photo by Frank Veres)

❏ **1014, '67 Camaro,** Gray pearl, metal Malaysia base, black, yellow, red & white tampos w/"Stunt 99" on hood & side, gray "Hot Wheels" logo on hood, black int., blue tint window, 5sp

EX n/a   **NM** n/a   **MIP** $5

(Photo by Frank Veres)

❏ **1015, Mercedes C-Class,** Yellow enamel, black plastic Malaysia base, dark blue "Hot Wheels" logo on rear fender, red int., clear window, asw, bbs

EX n/a   **NM** n/a   **MIP** $2

(Photo by Frank Veres)

❏ **1018, '32 Ford Coupe,** a. White pearl, black plastic China base, blue-tint white, dark blue & magenta flames on roof & side, chrome engine & radiator, magenta "Hot Wheels" logo above rear tire, black int., clear window, 5sp

EX n/a   **NM** n/a   **MIP** $4

(Photo by Frank Veres)

❏ **1022, '63 T-Bird,** Met. gold, metal Thailand base, black side tampo, black & white tampo on hood, "Hot Wheels" logo on rear fender near taillight, white int., tinted window, bbs

EX n/a   **NM** n/a   **MIP** $3

(Photo by Frank Veres)

❏ **1024, Shelby Cobra 427 S/C,** White enamel, metal Thailand base, black, rose & orange flames on tops of front fenders, trunk & side, black on nose, hood & cowl w/white scoop, black "47" in white circle & "Celebrity Tour De Milan" tampo on hood, black "Celebrity," white "Hollywood Tour" in orange rectangle and white "47" in black circle on rear fender, white & black "Hot Wheels" logo on rear deck, black int., smoked window, alw, 5sp

EX n/a   **NM** n/a   **MIP** $4

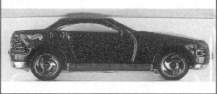

(Photo by Frank Veres)

❏ **1025, Mercedes SLK,** a. Mf. dark blue, metal India base, white "Hot Wheels" logo on rear fender by taillight, white int., tinted window, asw, t/b

EX n/a   **NM** n/a   **MIP** $4

(Photo by Frank Veres)

❏ **1026, Dodge Caravan,** Pearl orange, black plastic Malaysia base, black & yellow "METRO HOTEL" w/pink "SHUTTLE" on side, black & silver tampo w/3 small airplanes from fender to fender, black white Handicapped decal & silver "Hot Wheels" logo behind rear fender, black stripe on bottom, white int., dark smoked window, alw, 5sp

EX n/a   **NM** n/a   **MIP** $9

❑ **1027, Customized C3500,** Pearl magenta, black plastic Thailand base, large yellow lightning tampo across hood & roof, large yellow lightning tampo across side w/black outlined "Jerry's Electric" & white "24 HR. Service since 1999," "i" in "Electric" is a white lightning bolt, white "How Am I Driving?" over rear wheel, yellow "Hot Wheels" logo on box between cab & rear fender, black int. blue tint window, 5sp
EX n/a   NM n/a   MIP $7

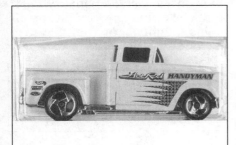

(Photo by Frank Veres)

❑ **1028, '56 Flashsider,** Yellow enamel, chrome Thailand base, brown & black tampo on hood & side, white & black "Hot Rod" on door, black & orange "HANDYMAN" on front fender, two black & white decals & "Hot Wheels" logo on rear fender behind rear wheel, black & yellow "Hot Wheels" logo on rear of bed cover, black window, 3sp
EX n/a   NM n/a   MIP $5

(Photo by Frank Veres)

❑ **1029, '40s Ford Truck,** Red enamel, chrome China base, black, yellow & white "Pizza on Wheels" tampo on door over seven thin white pinstripes, black & white check stripe from door to hood, black "Fast Delivery" on rear fender over tire, black "Hot Wheels" logo on rear fender behind tire, white int., roll bar, tubs & rear wing, yellow tint window, 5sp
EX n/a   NM n/a   MIP $4

(Photo by Frank Veres)

❑ **1030, Porsche 959,** Gray pearl, metal china base, black & white "959" on door, red & black "Twin Turbo" on rocker panel, red & yellow Porsche emblem on hood w/red & black "Twin Turbo," red "Hot Wheels" logo on rear fender by taillight, black int., blue tint window, asw-5dot
EX n/a   NM n/a   MIP $3

(Photo by Frank Veres)

❑ **1031, Aeroflash,** Green plastic body w/black painted Malaysia base, black, brown & white tampos on tops of front fenders & top rear, black & brown "3" & white "Hot Wheels" logo on rear, black int., clear window, 3sp
EX n/a   NM n/a   MIP $4

(Photo by Frank Veres)

❑ **1032, Ford GT-90,** Yellow enamel, metal China base, side has black & white tampos on it w/yellow, black & red circle, black "15" above black stripe on side, black & white "Hot Wheels" logo behind front wheel, yellow "COLLISION PATROL" in black stripe on rocker panel, black & yellow tampo w/black "15" on nose, black int., clear window, asw-3sp
EX n/a   NM n/a   MIP $2

(Photo by Frank Veres)

❑ **1035, 1970 Plymouth Barracuda,** Met. purple, chrome China base, black side w/silver dots & white outline Octopus on door, "PURPLE OCTOPUS beach rentals" tampo on rear fender above wheel, white & black "Hot Wheels" logo on rear fender behind rear wheel, black int. & hood scoop, smoked window, asw, 3sp
EX n/a   NM n/a   MIP $3

(Photo by Frank Veres)

❑ **1037, Roll Patrol Jeep,** Yellow enamel, metal Thailand base, black, silver & pearl blue tampo on hood & side, gray "Mudcat" over rear wheel, gray "13" w/black outline on front fender high behind front wheel, "JT Motorsport" & two other decals on rocker panel, black "Hot Wheels" logo behind rear wheel, tan int., tinted window, asw-ct/b
EX n/a   NM n/a   MIP $25

(Photo by Frank Veres)

❑ **1038, Dodge Viper RT/10,** Mf. silver, black plastic China base, red, white & blue flag tampo w/black & white "Team Benjamin" on side & hood, red, white & black "27" on hood & rear fender, black "World of Racing Federation" on rear fender above "27" & below "27" on hood, black "Hot Wheels" logo on rocker panel behind front wheel, black int., clear window, alw, 3sp
EX n/a   NM n/a   MIP $3

(Photo by Frank Veres)

❏ **1040, Panoz GTR-1,** Pearl green, black plastic China base, red, white & blue stripe tampos on side, hood & tops of front fenders, small blue & white "17" on hood & behind front wheel, misc. racing decals on tops of front fenders, white "WRF" & small "World of Racing Federation" on tops of rear fenders, white "Hot Wheels" logo on rear fender low behind rear wheel, black int. & rear wing, clear window, 3sp
EX n/a　　**NM** n/a　　**MIP** $3

(Photo by Frank Veres)

❏ **1041, Super Comp Dragster,** Pearl gray w/black plastic Thailand fenders, chrome base & fuel tank, red & white tampo on side w/purple & white lettering, purple "Hot Wheels" logo on side behind chrome headers, brown & white "WRF" & small "World of Racing Federation" on side in front of headers, red & purple Oriental writing on top of body next to driver & rear deck, purple "Power," red "Speed" & white "Attitude" on rear deck, black roll cage & wheelie bars, 5sp
EX n/a　　**NM** n/a　　**MIP** $3

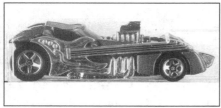
(Photo by Frank Veres)

❏ **1042, Twang Thang,** Met. green, black plastic China base, white & gold flames on hood & rear deck, gold "Hot Wheels" logo in center of rear deck, gold chrome guitars on each side connected over the hood, chrome int., engine & headers, green tint window, 5sp
EX n/a　　**NM** n/a　　**MIP** $3

(Photo by Frank Veres)

❏ **1043, Rail Rodder,** a. White plastic body, metal Malaysia base, blue tint white, dark blue & light blue "Ice Breaker" tampo on side, blue tint white, dark blue & light blue "Engine 32 below" on side of cab, light blue "Hot Wheels" logo on side before "Ice Breaker" tampo, light blue chrome engines, stack & drive wheels, tiny dark blue chrome front wheels, b5sp
EX n/a　　**NM** n/a　　**MIP** $4

(Photo by Frank Veres)

❏ **1044, Whatta Drag,** Black enamel, gray painted China base & headers, black "6" in white circle on right front & roof, misc. racing decals on left front, orange painted headlights, gold chrome engine, rear suspension & wing, gold plastic air scoop, large "Hot Wheels" logo on top of wing, red tint window, 5dot
EX n/a　　**NM** n/a　　**MIP** $3

(Photo by Frank Veres)

❏ **1045, Dodge Ram 1500,** Black enamel, light gray China base, silver "Federal Drug Enforcement" on side of rear box w/silver "Hot Wheels" logo and white "Drug Sniffing" & red "K9," silver & white "Federal Drug Enforcement" emblem on door w/"1037" large silver & white "Federal Drug Enforcement" emblem on hood, light gray int., box bed, bumpers & grille, clear window, alw, 5sp
EX n/a　　**NM** n/a　　**MIP** $5

(Photo by Frank Veres)

❏ **1046, Police Cruiser,** White enamel, black plastic Thailand base & bumpers, flag tampo on side w/red "Hot Wheels" logo on door, white "Hot Wheels Police Force" in blue stripe below large black "POLICE" on door, red "02" high on front fender behind wheel, black int., blue tint window, headlights & light bar on roof, asw, 3sp
EX n/a　　**NM** n/a　　**MIP** $5

(Photo by Frank Veres)

❏ **1047, Olds Aurora,** Black enamel w/white doors, black plastic Thailand base, "Highway Patrol" & "To Protect & Serve" in gold on doors, black & gold police emblem on rear door, large white "39" & small gold "Hot Wheels" logo on roof, gold "unit" & white "L91" on rear fender, small white "POLICE" half on door & half on front fender, tan int., clear window, asw-5dot
EX n/a　　**NM** n/a　　**MIP** $5

(Photo by Frank Veres)

❏ **1048, Rescue Ranger,** a. White enamel, chrome China base, black "BOMB SQUAD" w/red & black tampo on door, red "Caution" & black "Explosive Materials" on front fender above wheel, black with red pinstripe tampo on side of box w/white "Squad 3649," large black "BOMB SQUAD" w/red "Emergency Detonation Team" on side, small "Hot Wheels" logo on side behind door, small red & black "Caution" tampo below "Hot Wheels" logo, black "Safety Kit" & tampo behind rear wheel, red insert, blue tint window & int., alw, 5sp
EX n/a　　**NM** n/a　　**MIP** $15

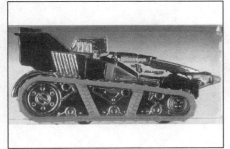

(Photo by Frank Veres)

❑ **1049, Treadator,** Black enamel, purple plastic side scoops & nose, blue Thailand base & treads, white w/light blue, black & purple tampos on side of driver's compartment, chrome canopy, engine, headers, fenders & track drives

EX n/a **NM** n/a **MIP** $3

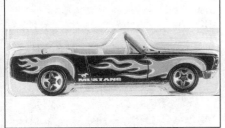

(Photo by Frank Veres)

❑ **1051, '65 Mustang,** Black enamel, metal China base, yellow & orange flames outlined in red on front fender to door, rear fender and hood, white "Mustang" & horse on rocker panel in front of rear wheel, red & yellow "Hot Wheels" logo on front of hood in flame, tan int., tinted window, asw-g5sp

EX n/a **NM** n/a **MIP** $4

(Photo by Frank Veres)

❑ **1052, Rigor Motor,** Red enamel, metal China base, black & yellow "Thorny Graves" on top & side over white, red & black roses tampo, chrome engine, fuel tank & seat, black skull headlights & radiator, black "Hot Wheels" logo below skulls, smoked canopy, 5sp

EX n/a **NM** n/a **MIP** $3

(Photo by Frank Veres)

❑ **1053, Hydroplane,** Black enamel, black plastic China base, white & gold tampo w/two red pinstripes on top of pontoons, white "7" in black circle on front of left pontoon, red & yellow over white "Hot Wheels" logo on top of rear wing, chrome int. & engine, yellow tint canopy

EX n/a **NM** n/a **MIP** $3

(Photo by Frank Veres)

❑ **1054, Porsche 959,** Black enamel, metal China base, gold "Hot Wheels" logo on nose, white int., clear window, asw-bbs

EX n/a **NM** n/a **MIP** $2

(Photo by Frank Veres)

❑ **1055, School Bus,** Black enamel, black plastic China base, silver, black & light purple tampo on roof w/white, yellow & black 5-spoke wheel & flame tampo, black, silver & light purple tampo on side w/large white "Hot Wheels" logo behind rear wheel, white "Graphics" outlined in light green in front of rear wheel, black int., red tint window, asw, 5dot

EX n/a **NM** n/a **MIP** $2

(Photo by Frank Veres)

❑ **1056, Corvette Stingray,** Tan plastic body, metal China base, orange, white & black tampo on hood & side, black "Stingray" on rear of hood by windshield, white "Hot Wheels" logo on bottom of door in front of rear wheel, smoked window w/black lines, gbbs

EX n/a **NM** n/a **MIP** $3

(Photo by Frank Veres)

❑ **1057, Thunderstreak,** Met. red, blue plastic side pods, metal China base, light green "Thunderstreak" over black on side pod & top of rear wing, misc. silver racing decals on side pod w/small silver "Hot Wheels" logo, blue plastic driver, yellow lettering, b5sp

EX n/a **NM** n/a **MIP** $3

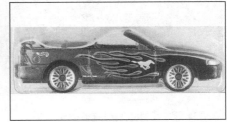

(Photo by Frank Veres)

❑ **1058, '96 Mustang,** Met. dark red, metal China base, black & gold flames on hood & side, white horse in flame on door, small white "Mustang" & horse in flames on hood, white "Mustang" & gold "96" above black stripe on rocker panel in front of rear wheel, white "Hot Wheels" logo high on rear fender, black int., smoked window, asw-gbbs

EX n/a **NM** n/a **MIP** $3

(Photo by Frank Veres)

❑ **1059, Dodge Ram 1500,** Met. light green, gray plastic China base, pale green stripes on side with black & white check tampo from front fender well to top center of rear fender, chrome int., box bed, bumpers & spacer between body & base, light green "Hot Wheels" logo on rear fender above bumper, tinted window, alw, 5dot
EX n/a   **NM** n/a   **MIP** $4

(Photo by Frank Veres)

❑ **1060, Ramp Truck,** Black enamel, metal China base, yellow plastic ramp w/yellow, red & blue "24 HR. Emergency Towing" tampo, large gold "Hot Wheels" logo on roof, black window, asw, 5dot
EX n/a   **NM** n/a   **MIP** $4

(Photo by Frank Veres)

❑ **1061, Rescue Ranger,** White enamel, red plastic China base, red & gold stripe on side w/gold & black "Fire Dept." on box and "51" on front fender, "City of Hot Wheels" logo on door w/gold "Emergency," gold "Oxygen Supply" & "First Aid" w/small black "+" on top doors on box, white "Hot Wheels" logo in red stripe on side rear, red plastic insert, red tint window & int., alw, 5dot
EX n/a   **NM** n/a   **MIP** $4

(Photo by Frank Veres)

❑ **1062, Rail Rodder,** Dark blue plastic body, metal Malaysia base, orange & white "Rail Rodder" w/light green & white "RXR" & stripes on side, small white "Hot Wheels" logo & "Engine 5" on side of cab, gold chrome engines & wheel drivers, small gold 5sp front wheels & b5sp rear
EX n/a   **NM** n/a   **MIP** $3

(Photo by Frank Veres)

❑ **1063, 1970 Plymouth Barracuda,** Orange enamel, chrome China base, white stripe on side w/orange "426" on rear fender, white "Hot Wheels" logo on front fender below stripe, behind front wheel, black int. & hood scoop, tinted window, asw, 3sp
EX n/a   **NM** n/a   **MIP** $4

(Photo by Frank Veres)

❑ **1064, Lakester,** Met. silver w/matching painted China base, blue, black & green tampo on side w/black "93005" & green & black "Alien X plorer," black "Hot Wheels" logo above "X plorer", chrome engines & int., green tint canopy, alw, 5sp
EX n/a   **NM** n/a   **MIP** $2

(Photo by Frank Veres)

❑ **1065, Firebird,** White enamel, gray plastic China base, silver, blue & red tampo on side w/red & blue "1" & "Huffman Racing" along with misc. racing decals, blue & white tampo on hood w/red & blue "Huffman Racing," red "Hot Wheels" logo on side behind rear wheel, black int., smoked window, alw, yellow letter black 5sp
EX n/a   **NM** n/a   **MIP** $4

(Photo by Frank Veres)

❑ **1066, Mustang Cobra,** Met. gold, black plastic India base, black striped tampo on side w/gold "Mustang" in cove on door, black "Hot Wheels" logo high on door above stripes, black int., clear window, asw, 5sp
EX n/a   **NM** n/a   **MIP** $3

(Photo by Frank Veres)

❑ **1067, Express Lane,** Orange plastic body, metal China base, engine & push handle, red & black "Floyd$ Market" tampo over yellow on side, red seat & butterfly steering wheel, black "Hot Wheels" logo on rear, 5sp
EX n/a   **NM** n/a   **MIP** $3

(Photo by Frank Veres)

❏ **1068, Dodge Concept Car,** Met. silver, metal China base, black & gold stripes on side w/black & gold stripes on rocker panel, white "Dodge" in front of rear wheel on rocker panel, black panel w/gold stripes on hood & trunk, tampo on hood has white "Dodge" on each side, black "Hot Wheels" logo on rear fender above rear wheel, black int., tinted window, g/bbs
EX n/a   NM n/a   MIP $2

(Photo by Frank Veres)

❏ **1069, '40 Ford (Pickup),** a. Yellow enamel, black plastic China base, dark red & black over gold "Haulin' 40" tampo on roof, red, gold & black tampos on both fenders, red & black stripes on side of running board, black int., roll bar, tubs, rear wing, wheelie bars, scoop & grille, black "Hot Wheels" logo on rear fender behind wheel, smoked window, 5dot
EX n/a   NM n/a   MIP $10

(Photo by Frank Veres)

❏ **1070, '32 Ford (Coupe),** Met. red, gray plastic China base, silver, white & black tampo on side w/gray & black "Frankie's Garage," chrome engine & grille, black "Hot Wheels" logo on lower part of side by headers, black int., clear window, 5dot
EX n/a   NM n/a   MIP $4

(Photo by Frank Veres)

❏ **1071, Panoz GTR-1,** Black enamel, black plastic China base, red, white & silver tampo on door, white "Power" & "Atittude," red "Speed" on side of front fender, white "Samurai Racing" on top of left front fender, red & silver sword tampo on top of right front fender, silver, red & white Samurai warrior tampo on hood with two white swiggles, white "Hot Wheels" logo on rear fender behind rear wheel white "Honor," red int. & rear wing, clear window, 3sp
EX n/a   NM n/a   MIP $2

(Photo by Frank Veres)

❏ **1073, Ford GT-90,** Red enamel, metal China base, white, gold & black tampo on side, white painted headlights, gold stripe below rear window, silver "FORD GT-90" on rocker panel in front of rear wheel, black "Hot Wheels" logo in center front by windshield, black int., smoked window, asw-t/b
EX n/a   NM n/a   MIP $2

(Photo by Frank Veres)

❏ **1074, Blimp,** Black plastic balloon, red plastic tail, red enamel metal Malaysia gondola, large red & yellow over white "Hot Wheels" logo on side
EX n/a   NM n/a   MIP $3

(Photo by Frank Veres)

❏ **1075, Scorchin' Scooter,** Red enamel, blue tint metal Malaysia base, black tampos w/white "Duncans" & gold & black "Motorcycles" on tank & side of rear fender, black tampo w/gold & white "Tall Dude Shocks" on side of front fender, black, white & gold tampo on side of tank, white "Hot Wheels" logo on rear fender below "Motorcycles" black plastic forks & handlebars, black painted seat, black spoked wheel w/chrome rim
EX n/a   NM n/a   MIP $5

(Photo by Frank Veres)

❏ **1076, '59 Eldorado,** a. Met. blue w/white cove & silver pinstripe, chrome Malaysia base, black "Eldorado" on front fender behind front wheel, white pinstriping on hood & trunk, silver HJW logo on rear fender behind rear wheel, white int., blue tint window, bbs
EX n/a   NM n/a   MIP $9

(Photo by Frank Veres)

❏ **1077, '57 Chevy,** Red enamel metal body, chrome Malaysia base, white & gold tampos on side w/white & gold flames on rear fender, thin white pinstripe on side with gold "Custom Rod," white & gold tampo on roof w/thin white pinstripes, white "Hot Wheels" logo above rear wheel, blue tint metal engine, black int., black window, g/bbs
EX n/a   NM n/a   MIP $4

(Photo by Frank Veres)

❑ **1078, Camaro Z28,** Met. blue, metal Malaysia base, red & white flag tampo on side w/white & gold stars, red & white flag tampo on hood w/white & gold stars on both sides, large white "3" over gold "30" tampo on roof, small white "3" over gold "30" tampo on rear roof pillar, white "Hot Wheels" logo on front fender above flag tampo, black window, 3sp

EX n/a   NM n/a   MIP $3

(Photo by Frank Veres)

❑ **1079, '63 Corvette,** Pearl gray, black plastic Malaysia base, black panels w/yellow pinstripes & light green & white tampos on hood, roof & side, yellow "Hot Wheels" logo on rear fender behind rear wheel, black int., clear window, asw-5dot

EX n/a   NM n/a   MIP $3

(Photo by Frank Veres)

❑ **1080, Humvee,** a. Green pearl plastic body, metal Malaysia base, black, silver & yellow tampo on side w/black "Hummer" above rear wheel, yellow circle w/black "B" & silver "Man" tampo on side of front fender and center of hood, silver "HUMVEE" on rear deck, no "Hot Wheels" logo, gray window, asw-ct/b

EX n/a   NM n/a   MIP $3

(Photo by Frank Veres)

❑ **1081, Power Plower,** Met. green, metal Thailand base, white & orange "Oak Bros" light green pinstripes & tree w/white "Mulching" & "earth pros" on door, white "Landscaping" & "Tree Trimming" with light green & white leaf, & orange, white & brown acorn on side of box, white "Bio Recycling" & light green pinstripes on side of front fender, white "Hot Wheels" logo high, behind rear wheel, light green int., roll bar & bed, yellow tint window, asw-ct/b

EX n/a   NM n/a   MIP $3

(Photo by Frank Veres)

❑ **1082, Jaguar XJ220,** Met. gold, black plastic Malaysia base, black & light blue tampos on side & hood, large black "Jaguar XJ220" above rear wheel, small white "Jaguar" & emblem behind front wheel, white circle emblem in center on front of hood, white "Hot Wheels" logo behind rear wheel, gold int., smoked window, g3sp

EX n/a   NM n/a   MIP $2

(Photo by Frank Veres)

❑ **1083, Blown Camaro,** a. Met. teal, metal Malaysia base, thin silver stripes on left side hood w/silver & black "Blown," gold & black "Camaro" & black & silver "650" w/small gold & silver squares, side has thin silver pinstripes w/gold & silver squares, large black & silver "650," silver & black "Brown" w/gold & black "Camaro," black stripe on rocker panel & bottom of

rear fender, thin black stripes going diagonal under silver stripes on door, small "Hot Wheels" logo high behind rear wheel, black int., smoked window, bbs

EX n/a   NM n/a   MIP $3

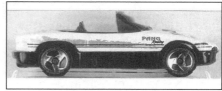

(Photo by Frank Veres)

❑ **1084, Mazda MX-5 Miata,** White enamel, black painted Malaysia base, thick silver splotch on side w/thin purple & black pinstripes, purple "PANG" & black "Racing" on front fender above stripes, large purple over silver "PANG" & black over silver "Racing" with purple over silver "OFFICIAL PACE CAR" on hood, thin purple & black stripes on hood & trunk over silver splotches, black "CAR 23" on trunk w/silver over purple "Hot Wheels" logo, black int., smoked window, asw-3sp

EX n/a   NM n/a   MIP $2

(Photo by Frank Veres)

❑ **1085, Porsche 928,** Pearl gold, metal Malaysia base, black "Hot Wheels" logo on nose, black window, 5dot

EX n/a   NM n/a   MIP $2

(Photo by Frank Veres)

❑ **1086, Toyota MR2,** Pearl purple, black plastic Malaysia base, silver diagonal stripes on door & roof, white, black & orange "4" on roof & door, white, black & orange "MR2" & white & black "Racing" on rear fender, thin silver pinstripe through center of side, "Hot Wheels" logo on front fender high behind wheel, gray int., clear window, asw-3sp

EX n/a   NM n/a   MIP $2

(Photo by Frank Veres)

❏ **1087, Rig Wrecker,** Yellow enamel, chrome Malaysia base, gray, white & black tampo on side, white & black "Finish Towing" on door w/small black "Radio Dispatched" & three blue & white stripes, "City of Hot Wheels," small gray www.hotwheels.com, black "24 Hour Service," and small blue "Hot Wheels" logo high on side by black plastic exhaust stack, large white & blue "Finish Line" w/blue "Towing" & small white "Moving The Community Since 1999" above rear wheels, black outlined doors w/blue "TOOLS" & "CABLES" blue plastic boom & lights above roof, black int. & grille, clear window, asw-5dot
EX n/a   **NM** n/a   **MIP** $5

(Photo by Frank Veres)

❏ **1088, Speed Machine,** Black enamel, metal Malaysia base, red outlined eagle on small white & orange circle w/orange & yellow flames on front, orange & yellow flames on side w/white "SPEED SEEKER" & "Hot Wheels" logo, white int., yellow tint canopy, g5dot
EX n/a   **NM** n/a   **MIP** $3

(Photo by Frank Veres)

❏ **1089, 25th Anniversary silver Lamborghini Countach,** Pearl, black plastic Malaysia base, white "Hot Wheels" logo in lower left side of windshield, black int., clear window, asw-5dot
EX n/a   **NM** n/a   **MIP** $3

(Photo by Frank Veres)

❏ **1090, '97 Corvette,** Black enamel, black plastic Malaysia base, white & light red tampo on side w/misc. racing decals, silver "CORVETTE" above rear wheel, black "1" in white & silver "World Racers" tampo on door, red "Hot Wheels" logo high on door, bronze stripe tampo on hood w/large white Bow Tie & small "CORVETTE," silver "USA 1" & black "1" in white & silver "World Racers" tampo, "Heraldawest" twice on front bumper in white, white int., blue tint window, alw, 3sp
EX n/a   **NM** n/a   **MIP** $3

(Photo by Frank Veres)

❏ **1091, X-Ploder,** a. Black plastic body, metal Malaysia base, yellow & orange flames on side, orange "Hot Wheels" logo in front of rear wheel, chrome engine & driver, red tint canopy, t/b
EX n/a   **NM** n/a   **MIP** $7

❏ **1092, '58 Corvette,** a. Black enamel, black plastic Malaysia base, aqua engine compartment (some of these were repaints of the aqua cars & you can still see the aqua paint under the hood), chrome int., exhaust, bumpers & grille, red "Hot Wheels" logo in white box on trunk, smoked window, silver painted headlights, bbs
EX n/a   **NM** n/a   **MIP** $15

(Photo by Frank Veres)

❏ **1093, BMW 850i,** Met. gold, met. gold plastic Malaysia base, black "Hot Wheels" logo on nose, black int. & taillights, smoked window, asw-bbs
EX n/a   **NM** n/a   **MIP** $2

(Photo by Frank Veres)

❏ **1094, Ferrari F355 Berlinetta,** Red enamel, metal Malaysia base, larger yellow & black Ferrari horse logo on hood w/green & white stripe above, small yellow & black Ferrari horse logo on door close to front fender, black "Hot Wheels" logo high behind rear wheel, black int., clear window, asw-5sp
EX n/a   **NM** n/a   **MIP** $4

(Photo by Frank Veres)

❏ **1095, Mercedes SLK,** Met. gray, black painted India base, red "Hot Wheels" logo high behind rear wheel, black int., smoked window & headlights, asw-t/b
EX n/a   **NM** n/a   **MIP** $2

(Photo by Frank Veres)

❏ **1096, Avus Quattro,** Chrome body, black plastic Malaysia base, smoked canopy w/black & met. silver tampos, black int., black "Hot Wheels" logo top rear, alw, 5sp
EX n/a   **NM** n/a   **MIP** $2

(Photo by Frank Veres)

❑ **1097, '31 Doozie,** Met. red, metal Malaysia base, black plastic fenders, top & int., gray "Hot Wheels" logo on side of fender-mounted spare tire, clear window, alw, bbs

EX n/a   NM n/a   MIP $3

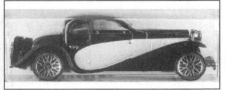

(Photo by Frank Veres)

❑ **1098, '37 Bugatti,** Black enamel w/yellow cove, metal Malaysia base, chrome int., grille & headlights, small "Hot Wheels" logo above cove in front of rear wheel, clear window, alw, bbs

EX n/a   NM n/a   MIP $3

(Photo by Frank Veres)

❑ **1099, Road Rocket,** Red plastic body, black plastic top, metal Malaysia base, black tampo n side w/red & black "Hot Wheels" logo behind front wheel, chrome engine & roll bar, red int., bbs

EX n/a   NM n/a   MIP $2

(Photo by Frank Veres)

❑ **1100, Power Pipes,** a. White plastic body, red painted metal Malaysia base, red & yellow tampo on side w/red "Hot Wheels" logo behind front wheel, gold chrome scoops & int., red tint canopy, 5dot

EX n/a   NM n/a   MIP $2

(Photo by Frank Veres)

❑ **1101, Radar Ranger,** Teal enamel, metal Malaysia base, large white & black "radar ranger" w/small "mission control" & "11" tampo on side, small white & black "radar ranger" w/small "mission control" & "11" tampo on top of right pod, black circle w/white "6" & "recon. vehcile" on side by canopy & front of right pod, black "Hot Wheels" logo on front of right pod, white plastic radar dish & white insert, clear canopy, alw, ct/b

EX n/a   NM n/a   MIP $3

(Photo by Frank Veres)

❑ **1102, Mini Truck,** Black enamel, black plastic Malaysia base, gold chrome engine, shifter, front grille, exhaust & speakers in rear bed, gold "Hot Wheels" logo on front of hood, red int., smoked window, gbbs

EX n/a   NM n/a   MIP $2

(Photo by Frank Veres)

❑ **1103, 1980 Corvette,** Met. gold, metal Malaysia bae, black roof, smoked window, black int., black "Hot Wheels" logo on rear plate, asw, bbs

EX n/a   NM n/a   MIP $4

(Photo by Frank Veres)

❑ **1104, Twang Thang,** Pearl orange, purple plastic Malaysia base, purple plastic guitars on side, (no color on strings or hardware) gold chrome engine, exhaust & int., smoked window, black "Hot Wheels" logo on nose, g5sp

EX n/a   NM n/a   MIP $3

(Photo by Frank Veres)

❑ **1105, Mustang Mach 1,** Met. blue, black plastic Malaysia base, thin white, wide silver & thin orange stripes on hood & side, black rocker panel w/two thin white stripes & "MACH 1" behind front wheel, small white "Mustang" above "MACH 1" on lower front fender, black int., hood scoop, tach, grille, rear window louvers & spoiler, white "Hot Wheels" logo high on rear fender behind wheel, clear window, bbs

EX n/a   NM n/a   MIP $4

❑ **1106, Go Kart,** a. Lt. orange enamel painted metal Malaysia body, metal chassis & engine, black plastic seat, black panel w/pink & black "Hot Wheels" logo & "123 racing," orange "MJ engineering," 5dot

EX n/a   NM n/a   MIP $8

❑ **1107, Chrysler Thunderbolt,** Dark met. blue, black plastic Malaysia base, silver flames outlined in white on side w/black & white "Lucero," silver "36" outlined in white on front fender above flame behind wheel, lower portion of side has wide black stripe w/one silver pinstripe on top, two silver pinstripes below black stripe on rocker panel w/silver "thunderstreak" in front of rear wheel, four triangles above Thunderstreak in black stripe, white int., smoked window, asw, 3sp (very hard to find)

EX n/a   NM n/a   MIP $5

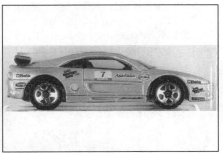

(Photo by Frank Veres)

❏ **1115, Ferrari F335 Challenge,** a. Silver pearl, metal Malaysia base, pearl green, white enamel & red enamel stripes on hood & roof misc. racing decals on side, small rectangle yellow & black Ferrari horse logo on hood, no "Hot Wheels" logo, black int., smoked rear spoiler & window, asw, 5sp
EX n/a   **NM** n/a   **MIP** $3

(Photo by Frank Veres)

❏ **1118, Ferrari 456M,** Red enamel, metal Malaysia base, small rectangle yellow & black Ferrari horse logo on hood w/green & white stripes above it, yellow "Hot Wheels" logo on rear of trunk, tan int., clear window, asw, 5sp
EX n/a   **NM** n/a   **MIP** $3

(Photo by Frank Veres)

❏ **1119, Ferrari F355 Spider,** Red enamel, metal Malaysia base, green & white stripe over yellow & black Ferrari logo on hood & front fender behind front wheel, small black lettering in front of rear wheel, no "Hot Wheels" logo, tan int., clear window, asw, 5sp
EX n/a   **NM** n/a   **MIP** $5

(Photo by Frank Veres)

❏ **1120, Ferrari F50,** a. Red enamel, black painted Malaysia base, w/"Ferrari F50" green & white stripe over yellow & black rectangle Ferrari logo on hood, small triangle yellow & black rectangle Ferrari logo w/green & white stripe above it on front fender behind front wheel, small black lettering in front of rear wheel, no "Hot Wheels" logo, black int. & rear grille, clear window, asw, 5sp
EX n/a   **NM** n/a   **MIP** $3

(Photo by Frank Veres)

❏ **1121, Chevy 1500,** Orange plastic body, met. silver painted India base, black, white & red Bull's Eye tampo on side w/black & white "2" behind rear wheel, small white "Hot Wheels" logo on rear fender by taillight, black int., roll bar & bed cover, tinted window, asw, 5dot
EX n/a   **NM** n/a   **MIP** $3

RACE TEAM SERIES

(Photo by Frank Veres)

❏ **275, #1-Lumina Stocker,** a. Light blue met. w/red & yellow "Hot Wheels" logo over white on hood, white "1" on hood, roof & doors, red bow tie on hood & trunk, racing decals & yellow "Hot Wheels" on sides, white int., clear window, uh
EX n/a   **NM** n/a   **MIP** $5

(KP Photo)

❏ **276, #2-Hot Wheels 500,** a. Light blue met. w/metal Malaysia base, white w/red stripe & "Hot Wheels" logo on nose, "Goodyear" twice on front spoiler, "Hot Wheels" in yellow on side pod, large "Hot Wheels" logo on sides & rear white painted wing, gray plastic driver, bw
EX n/a   **NM** n/a   **MIP** $5

(Photo by Frank Veres)

❏ **277, #3-Side Splitter,** a. Lt. met. blue w/red & yellow over white "Hot Wheels" logo on hood & sides, white F/C 1 & "Goodyear" tampo on sides w/racing decals, metal Malaysia base, bw (This is the same car that is in the "271" Package for $3500. See what packaging does for prices!)
EX n/a   **NM** n/a   **MIP** $8

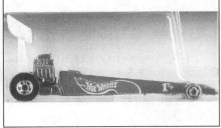

(Photo by Frank Veres)

❏ **278, #4-Dragster,** a. Light met. blue w/white on top & small red stripes, white "1", "T/F" & large red & yellow "Hot Wheels" logo on sides metal Malaysia base & engine, white plastic rear wing & driver, bw
EX n/a   **NM** n/a   **MIP** $5

KRACKLE CAR SERIES

(Photo by Frank Veres)

❑ **280, #1-Sharkruiser,** a. Blue & yellow met. cracked paint w/lime plastic teeth, engine & int., red "Hot Wheels" logo between exhaust, metal Malaysia base, uh
EX n/a **NM** n/a **MIP** $5

(Photo by Frank Veres)

❑ **281, #2-Turboa,** a. Purple & red met. cracked paint, metal Malaysia base, red plastic int., uh
EX n/a **NM** n/a **MIP** $5

❑ **282, #3-'63 Split,** a. Aqua & orange met. cracked paint w/chrome Malaysia 1 rivet base, white int., black "Hot Wheels" logo on front orange tint window, asw, bw
EX n/a **NM** n/a **MIP** $7

❑ **284, #4-Flashfire,** a. Purple & yellow met. cracked paint w/black plastic Malaysia base, purple chrome engine, yellow int. & side insert, yellow tint canopy w/red "Hot Wheels" logo, uh
EX n/a **NM** n/a **MIP** $5

STEEL STAMP SERIES

❑ **285, #1-Steel Passion,** a. Met. black w/rose & silver cove tampo, gold side stripe, rose, gold & silver tampo on hood, red int., tinted window, gold logo on side, ww
EX n/a **NM** n/a **MIP** $8

❑ **287, #2-Zender Fact 4,** a. Met. dark burgundy (almost black) w/rose & blue specs, gold side stripe, black plastic Malaysia base, white int., smoked window, gold logo on top of rear spoiler, uh
EX n/a **NM** n/a **MIP** $5

❑ **289, #3-'56 Flashsider,** a. Met. burgundy w/gold, rose & light blue side tampo, chrome window & Malaysia base, gold logo on side, uh
EX n/a **NM** n/a **MIP** $6

❑ **290, #4-'57 Chevy,** a. Dark met. blue w/rose, silver & light blue side tampo, rose logo in rear window, chrome Malaysia base, blue tint window & int., uh
EX n/a **NM** n/a **MIP** $6

PEARL DRIVER SERIES

❑ **292, #2-Pearl Passion,** a. Pearl lavender w/chrome Malaysia base, light yellow int., tinted window, green logo on side above rear wheel, ww
EX n/a **NM** n/a **MIP** $8

❑ **293, #3-VW Bug,** a. Pearl pink, metal Malaysia base, gray int., clear window, red logo in white circle on rear, bw
EX n/a **NM** n/a **MIP** $7

(Photo by Frank Veres)

❑ **295, #1-Talbot Lago,** a. Pearl blue, metal Malaysia base, chrome int., blue tint window, red logo in white circle on rear, ww
EX n/a **NM** n/a **MIP** $8

❑ **296, #4-Jaguar XJ220,** a. Pearl white, black plastic Malaysia base, white int., white logo on rear smoked window, uh
EX n/a **NM** n/a **MIP** $5

DARK RIDER SERIES

(Photo by Frank Veres)

❑ **297, #1-Splittin' Image,** a. Black met., black plastic Malaysia base, red logo on top front fender, black tint chrome engine & canopy, black tint 6sp
EX n/a **NM** n/a **MIP** $10

❑ **298, #2-Twin Mill II,** a. Black met., black plastic Malaysia base, black tint chrome engines, black window, red logo on rear, black tint 6sp
EX n/a **NM** n/a **MIP** $10

(Photo by Frank Veres)

❑ **299, #3-Silhouette II,** a. Black met., black tint chrome Malaysia base, black int., clear window, red logo on rear, black tint chrome engine, black tint chrome 6 sp
EX n/a **NM** n/a **MIP** $10

(Photo by Frank Veres)

❑ **300, #4-Rigor Motor,** a. Black met., black met. painted Malaysia base, black tint chrome engine & int., clear canopy, white skulls & radiator, red logo on rear, black tint 6sp
EX n/a **NM** n/a **MIP** $10

ROARIN' RODS SERIES

❑ **302, #4-Mini Truck,** a. Tan w/black tampos, tan int. & bed, chrome speakers in bed, chrome engine, tan base, black logo on side, smoked window, uh
EX n/a **NM** n/a **MIP** $5

(Photo by Frank Veres)

❑ **303, #1-Street Roader,** a. Orange w/black tampos on hood & sides, black int., dark smoked window, metal Malaysia base, black logo on side, alw, oct
EX n/a **NM** n/a **MIP** $25

❏ **304, #2-Roll Patrol,** a. White w/black tampos on hood & sides, black int., dark smoked window, black tint metal Malaysia base, black logo on side, asw, yct
EX n/a   NM n/a   MIP $4

❏ **305, #3-Classic Cobra,** a. Neon yellow w/silver tampos, metal Malaysia base, olive int., silver logo on side, smoked window, alw, 7sp
EX n/a   NM n/a   MIP $10

HOT HUBS SERIES

(Photo by Frank Veres)

❏ **307, #1-Cyber Cruiser,** Burgundy mf., metal Malaysia base, purple chrome driver & engine, black logo in white box on rear, blue swirl wheel w/orange tire
EX n/a   NM n/a   MIP $7

(Photo by Frank Veres)

❏ **308, #2-Vampyra,** a. Purple w/yellow & red eyes, black tint metal Malaysia base, gold tint chrome engine, gold logo on side of wing, green 6sp wheel w/black tire
EX n/a   NM n/a   MIP $9

❏ **310, #3-Shadow Jet,** Day-glo green mf. w/purple "Inter Cooled" tampo on rear wing, red "F-3" tampo on top, red logo on top, yellow nose, metal Malaysia base, green int., yellow tint canopy, yellow swirl wheel w/purple fire
EX n/a   NM n/a   MIP $9

(Photo by Frank Veres)

❏ **311, #4-Suzuki Quadracer,** a. Yellow w/purple seat, black handlebars, black tint Malaysia base, red logo on rear fender, yellow swirl wheel w/black tire, alw
EX n/a   NM n/a   MIP $10

SPEED GLEAMER SERIES

(Photo by Frank Veres)

❏ **312, #1-3-Window '34,** Aqua chrome w/aqua running boards, int. & fenders, metal Malaysia base, gold logo in rear blue tinted window, 7 sp
EX n/a   NM n/a   MIP $4

❏ **313, #2-T-Bucket,** a. Purple pearl, black tint metal Malaysia base, red logo in white box on rear, blue tint chrome engine, white int., clear window, 5sp
EX n/a   NM n/a   MIP $35

❏ **315, #3-Ratmobile,** a. Black plastic rat body w/gray painted Malaysia base, red logo on chrome engine, asw, uh
EX n/a   NM n/a   MIP $3

❏ **316, #4-Limozeen,** a. Mf. gold w/gold chrome Malaysia base, white int., smoked window, red logo on rear, ww
EX n/a   NM n/a   MIP $15

REAL RIDER SERIES

(Photo by Frank Veres)

❏ **317, #1-Dump Truck,** Day-glo yellow w/yellow dump box, black int. & window, metal Malaysia base, red logo in white box on rear, day-glo yellow wheel w/"Real Rider" rubber tire
EX n/a   NM n/a   MIP $30

(Photo by Frank Veres)

❏ **318, #2-Mercedes Unimog,** Met. silver metal cab & box, day-glo orange plastic fenders, int. & rear box cover, metal Malaysia base, red logo in white box on rear, orange wheels w/knobby "Real Rider" rubber tires
EX n/a   NM n/a   MIP $25

(Photo by Frank Veres)

❏ **320, #3-'59 Caddy Convertible,** Pearl rose, white int., chrome Malaysia base, red logo on clear windshield, chrome wheels w/white wall "Real Rider" tires
EX n/a   NM n/a   MIP $45

(Photo by Frank Veres)

❏ **321, #4-Corvette Stingray,** Met. green, metal Malaysia base, gold logo on rear fender behind wheel, clear window & int., gray wheels w/Goodyear "Real Rider" tires
EX n/a   NM n/a   MIP $75

SILVER SERIES

(Photo by Frank Veres)

❑ **322, #1-Fire Eater,** a. Chrome w/yellow & black tampos, red insert, blue tint window & int., chrome Malaysia base, alw, bw
EX n/a **NM** n/a **MIP** $15

(Photo by Frank Veres)

❑ **323, #2-Rodzilla,** a. Chrome body w/white eyes & teeth, gold chrome engine, metal Malaysia base, red logo on top rear arm, uh
EX n/a **NM** n/a **MIP** $4

(Photo by Frank Veres)

❑ **325, #3-Propper Chopper,** Chrome w/yellow & black "Police" side tampo, black Malaysia base, int. & tail, blue tint window gray rotors, red logo on side
EX n/a **NM** n/a **MIP** $3

❑ **328, #4-School Bus,** a. Chrome w/thick black stripe & "School Bus" on side, "Emergency Exit" on rear door, black logo on rear, black plastic Malaysia base, white int., clear window, asw, bw
EX n/a **NM** n/a **MIP** $10

PHOTO FINISH SERIES

(Photo by Frank Veres)

❑ **331, #1-Aerostar,** White w/orange photo on side, metal Malaysia, silver window, no logo, 7sp
EX n/a **NM** n/a **MIP** $7

(Photo by Frank Veres)

❑ **332, #2-Flying Aces Blimp,** White w/"Hot Wheels" city photo on side, black gondola, no logo
EX n/a **NM** n/a **MIP** $7

(Photo by Frank Veres)

❑ **333, #3-Tank Truck,** Candy blue, white tank w/orange & dark blue photo on side, chrome Malaysia base, chrome window, no logo, asw, 7sp
EX n/a **NM** n/a **MIP** $7

(Photo by Frank Veres)

❑ **335, #4-Hiway Hauler,** Pearl green, white box w/NYC photo on side, chrome Malaysia base, black window, asw, 7sp
EX n/a **NM** n/a **MIP** $7

RACING METALS SERIES

(Photo by Frank Veres)

❑ **336, #1-Race Truck,** Dark tint chrome w/red & white tampos on side & hood, yellow "Hot Wheels" on smoked windshield, red int., bed & roll bar, black painted metal Malaysia base, asw, ct
EX n/a **NM** n/a **MIP** $5

❑ **337, #2-Ramp Truck,** a. Chrome cab, metal Malaysia base, purple ramp w/large red & yellow "Hot Wheels" logo & blue lettering, dark smoked window, asw, 7sp
EX n/a **NM** n/a **MIP** $5

(Photo by Frank Veres)

❑ **338, #3-Camaro Racer,** a. Light blue tint chrome, gray Malaysia base, large "Hot Wheels" logo on sides & hood, "Jack Baldwin" in white on roof, red bow tie on roof & hood, two "Hot Wheels" logos on rear spoiler w/yellow "Hot Wheels," white int., clear window, alw, 5sp
EX n/a **NM** n/a **MIP** $8

(Photo by Frank Veres)

❑ **340, #4-Dragster,** Light blue tint chrome w/large red & yellow "Hot Wheels" logo on sides, white on top of nose w/red stripe, white int. & rear wing, metal engine & Malaysia base, 5sp
EX n/a **NM** n/a **MIP** $5

1995 MODEL SERIES

❑ **341, #3-'58 Corvette,** a. Dayglo pink, pink plastic Malaysia base, chrome int. & engine, red logo in white box on trunk, bw
EX n/a   **NM** n/a   **MIP** $5

(Photo by Frank Veres)

❑ **342, #2-Mercedes SL,** a. Red w/matching plastic Malaysia base, tan int., clear window, red logo in white box on rear, alw, uh
EX n/a   **NM** n/a   **MIP** $5

(KP Photo)

❑ **343, #1-Speed Blaster,** a. Met. blue, chrome Malaysia base & window, red logo in white box on rear, uh
EX n/a   **NM** n/a   **MIP** $10

❑ **344, #8-Camaro Conv.,** a. Met. teal, black plastic Malaysia base, gray int., red logo on clear windshield, alw, uh
EX n/a   **NM** n/a   **MIP** $7

(KP Photo)

❑ **345, #4-Speed-a-Saurus,** a. Green plastic, metal Malaysia base, chrome engine, bw
EX n/a   **NM** n/a   **MIP** $3

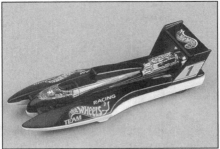

(KP Photo)

❑ **346, #6-Hydroplane,** Met. blue, white plastic Malaysia base, chrome int., clear canopy, large "Hot Wheels" logo on top of rear wing & each side, red "1" over white on rear wing side
EX n/a   **NM** n/a   **MIP** $3

❑ **347, #5-Power Rocket,** a. Bronze plastic body, metal Malaysia base, gray int., blue tint canopy, silver logo on side, uh
EX n/a   **NM** n/a   **MIP** $30

(KP Photo)

❑ **348, #7-Dodge Ram,** a. Met. dark green, gray plastic Malaysia base, green cap, chrome int., smoked window, red logo in white box on rear, alw, 5sp
EX n/a   **NM** n/a   **MIP** $4

❑ **349, #9-Power Pipes,** a. Dark blue plastic body, silver painted metal Malaysia base, red logo in white box on rear, chrome int., purple canopy, 3sp
EX n/a   **NM** n/a   **MIP** $3

❑ **350, #10-Ferrari 355,** a. Yellow w/metal Malaysia base, black int., clear window, red logo on rear, asw, 3sp
EX n/a   **NM** n/a   **MIP** $3

(Photo by Frank Veres)

❑ **351, #11-Power Rocket,** a. Purple mf. plastic body w/orange stripe tampo & silver lettering, metal Malaysia base, chrome driver & engine, orange logo behind rear wheel, extended tip on engine front, 5sp
EX n/a   **NM** n/a   **MIP** $7

(KP Photo)

❑ **352, #12-Big Chill,** a. White, black plastic Malaysia base, chrome canopy, black treads, metal rollers, pink ski
EX n/a   **NM** n/a   **MIP** $12

1995 TREASURE HUNT SERIES

(Photo by Frank Veres)

❑ **353, #1-Olds 442,** Met. blue w/white scoops, chrome Malaysia base, white int., clear window, red, "Hot Wheels" logo in rear window, chrome wheel red line, "Real Rider" tires
EX n/a   **NM** n/a   **MIP** $70

(Photo by Frank Veres)

❑ **354, #2-Gold Passion,** Mf. gold, gold chrome Malaysia base, black cove w/gold pinstripe, lavender tampo on door to rear fender, black, gold & lavender tampo on hood, black "Hot Wheels" logo on rear fender skirt, white int., clear window, gold wheel "Real Rider" tires
EX n/a   **NM** n/a   **MIP** $75

❏ **355, #3-'67 Camaro,** a. White enamel, orange "SS" stripes on hood & trunk, metal Malaysia base, orange int., clear window, chrome wheel "Real Rider" tires
EX n/a   **NM** n/a   **MIP** $400

(Photo by Frank Veres)

❏ **356, #4-'57 T-Bird,** Met. dark purple, chrome Malaysia base, clear window & int., white "Hot Wheels" logo in rear window, white line "Real Rider" tires
EX n/a   **NM** n/a   **MIP** $65

(Photo by Frank Veres)

❏ **357, #5-VW Bug,** Day-glo green, metal Malaysia base, purple int., clear window, red logo in white box on rear, purple swirl wheel w/chrome rim
EX n/a   **NM** n/a   **MIP** $125

(Photo by Frank Veres)

❏ **358, #6-'63 Split-Window,** Met. blue, chrome Malaysia base, white int., red "Hot Wheels" logo on front clear window, chrome wheel white line "Real Rider" tires
EX n/a   **NM** n/a   **MIP** $75

(Photo by Frank Veres)

❏ **359, #7-Stutz Blackhawk,** Met. black, metal Malaysia base, red int., gold logo in front clear window, chrome wheel red line "Real Rider" tire
EX n/a   **NM** n/a   **MIP** $50

(Photo by Frank Veres)

❏ **360, #8-Rolls-Royce,** Dark met. red w/tan plastic top, metal Malaysia base, dark red logo in white oval on rear, red int., clear window, red 6sp wheel w/chrome rim
EX n/a   **NM** n/a   **MIP** $50

(Photo by Frank Veres)

❏ **361, #9-Classic Caddy,** Met. light green body w/olive plastic fenders, metal Malaysia base, tan int., clear window, red logo on front fender, gold 6sp
EX n/a   **NM** n/a   **MIP** $50

❏ **362, #10-Classic Nomad,** Met. teal, metal Malaysia base, white int., red "Hot Wheels" logo in front clear window, chrome swirl wheel
EX n/a   **NM** n/a   **MIP** $60

(Photo by Frank Veres)

❏ **363, #11-Classic Cobra,** Dark met. green, metal Malaysia base, two wide gold stripes on hood & trunk, tan int., clear window, gold chrome 6sp
EX n/a   **NM** n/a   **MIP** $70

(Photo by Frank Veres)

❏ **364, #12-'31 Doozie,** Yellow enamel w/black plastic fenders, top & int., metal Malaysia base, red logo on side, clear window, yellow 6sp
EX n/a   **NM** n/a   **MIP** $50

1996 First Editions

(Photo by Frank Veres)

❏ **367, #2-Chevy 1500 Pickup,** a. Silver w/metal Malaysia base, silver int., smoked window, large "Hot Wheels" logos on hood & bed, orange, blue & black side tampos, orange number on roof & door, yellow letter alw, b7sp
EX n/a   **NM** n/a   **MIP** $12

❏ **369, #7-Road Rocket,** Light green plastic body w/transparent blue plastic top, metal Malaysia base, blue "Hot Wheels" logo on side, gbbs (You might notice here that there are 2 cars with the same "Collector Number". I have no idea why it happened, it's just one of those Mattel Mysteries.)
EX n/a   **NM** n/a   **MIP** $2

(KP Photo)

❏ **369, #8-Turbo Flame,** a. Pearl white plastic body, w/large "Hot Wheels" logo on sides, metal Malaysia base, orange tint window, chrome engine, 5sp
EX n/a   **NM** n/a   **MIP** $6

(KP Photo)

(KP Photo)

❑ **380, #1-Dodge Ram 1500,** a. Red w/yellow & black "4" on roof & door, yellow & black Ram tampo on hood, silver "Dodge" tampo on rear fender, yellow & silver "Hot Wheels" logo in front of rear wheel, red int., red plastic Malaysia base, yellow letter alw, b7sp

EX n/a   **NM** n/a   **MIP** $3

❑ **370, #5-Rail Rodder,** a. Black plastic w/chrome engines & drivers (wheels), "Hot Wheels" logo on orange & dark red side stripe, greenish yellow "Rail rodder" tampo, metal Malaysia base, small rear b5sp

EX n/a   **NM** n/a   **MIP** $8

❑ **375, #10-Dog Fighter,** a. Met. red, yellow, red & white side tampo, tan propeller chrome engine, seat & suspension, red logo on tail, black painted Malaysia base, 5sp

EX n/a   **NM** n/a   **MIP** $3

❑ **381, #2-Ford LTL,** a. Mf. silver, red plastic Malaysia base, white, red & blue tampos on sleeper sides, blue window, yellow letter large b7sp (This was supposed to be the Ford LTL, but for some reason it did not make it into production and they used the Kenworth T600 instead.)

EX n/a   **NM** n/a   **MIP** $10

(Photo by Frank Veres)

(KP Photo, Tom Michael collection)

❑ **382, #3-'56 Flashsider,** a. Met. black, gray & red "1" & stripe on sides w/racing decals, gray & red "1" on roof, white Chevrolet on hood w/large red bow tie, white Chevrolet twice & small red bow tie on bed cover, chrome Malaysia base, red logo on rear, chrome window, yellow letter b7sp

EX n/a   **NM** n/a   **MIP** $9

❑ **371, #7-Road Rocket,** Light green plastic body w/transparent blue plastic top, metal Malaysia base, blue "Hot Wheels" logo on side, red "Hot Wheels" logo on top of rear wing, gbbs

EX n/a   **NM** n/a   **MIP** $10

❑ **376, #11-Twang-Thang,** Silver mf., red transparent guitars w/chrome strings on side, chrome int., clear window, blue logo on rear, pearl plastic Malaysia base, 5sp

EX n/a   **NM** n/a   **MIP** $2

❑ **383, #4-Nissan Truck,** a. Met. dark blue, chrome Malaysia base, red & white tampos, yellow front end, int. & roll bar, clear window, alw, ct

EX n/a   **NM** n/a   **MIP** $125

❑ **377, #12-Ferrari F50,** a. Red w/yellow Ferrari on rear spoiler (snuck out in a US package), asw, 7sp

EX n/a   **NM** n/a   **MIP** $30

FLAMETHROWER SERIES

(Photo by Frank Veres)

❑ **378, #1-'96 Mustang,** a. Met. red, metal Malaysia base, red logo on rear spoiler, silver met. headlights, tan int., clear window, asw, 3sp

EX n/a   **NM** n/a   **MIP** $7

(Photo by Frank Veres)

❑ **372, #6-VW Bus Funny Car,** Met. blue, large "Hot Wheels" logo on side w/yellow "Fahrvergnugen," metal China base, orange int., clear window, 5sp/front.

EX n/a   **NM** n/a   **MIP** $65

❑ **382, #3-'70 Dodge Daytona,** a. Red enamel, chrome Malaysia base, tan int., gold logo in front of rear wheel, clear window, asw, gbbs

EX n/a   **NM** n/a   **MIP** $3

❑ **384, #1-'57 T-Bird,** a. Pearl white w/chrome Malaysia base, copper & green flames, 2 flames on rear fender, 5 flames on trunk, gold "Hot Wheels" logo in rear window, clear window & int., 7sp

EX n/a   **NM** n/a   **MIP** $8

❑ **373, #4-Street Cleaver,** a. Yellow plastic body, yellow painted Malaysia base, chrome engine, 5sp

EX n/a   **NM** n/a   **MIP** $4

RACE TRUCK SERIES

❑ **374, #9-Radio Flyer Wagon,** a. Red w/white "Radio Flyer" tampo on sides, black seat, metal Malaysia base, white logo on rear, chrome engine, 5sp

EX n/a   **NM** n/a   **MIP** $4

(KP Photo)

(Photo by Frank Veres)

❑ **385, #2-Hydroplane,** a. Yellow w/yellow, red & blue flames on sides & rear wing, chrome engine & int., black plastic Malaysia base, smoked canopy

EX n/a   **NM** n/a   **MIP** $3

(Photo by Frank Veres)

❑ **386, #3-Range Rover,** a. Red w/gold & magenta flames on hood, roof & side, chrome Malaysia base, red logo in rear window, tan int., clear window, ct

EX n/a   **NM** n/a   **MIP** $5

❑ **387, #4-Oshkosh Snowplow,** a. Black plastic cab & box, yellow & blue flames on door, top of box, hood & top of rear fenders, black enamel metal nose, fenders & int., metal Malaysia base, black tint chrome alw, ct

EX n/a   **NM** n/a   **MIP** $4

SPACE SERIES

(Photo by Frank Veres)

❑ **388, #1-Radar Ranger,** Pearl white w/orange, blue & red tampos, red logo on nose, black painted Malaysia base, chrome dish, orange int., clear canopy, alw, ct

EX n/a   **NM** n/a   **MIP** $3

(Photo by Frank Veres)

❑ **389, #2-GM Lean Machine,** a. Pearl white & blue w/metal Malaysia base, orange, blue & red tampos, red logo on rear, black canopy, 5sp

EX n/a   **NM** n/a   **MIP** $3

(Photo by Frank Veres)

❑ **390, #3-Alien,** Pearl white & blue, orange, blue & red tampos, red logo by rear tire, black window, metal Malaysia base, 5sp

EX n/a   **NM** n/a   **MIP** $3

❑ **391, #4-Treadator,** a. Light blue pearl w/orange scoops & nose, red "Hot Wheels SA" & logo on front wing, black plastic Malaysia base, blue chrome engine & canopy

EX n/a   **NM** n/a   **MIP** $4

RACE TEAM SERIES II

❑ **392, #1-Ramp Truck,** a. Met. blue, white ramp w/large "Hot Wheels" logo & blue lettering on side, metal Malaysia base, clear window, asw, 5sp

EX n/a   **NM** n/a   **MIP** $3

(Photo by Frank Veres)

❑ **393, #2-Baja Bug,** Met. blue w/large "Hot Wheels" logo on hood & side, yellow "Hot Wheels" on roof, white int., metal Malaysia base, 5sp

EX n/a   **NM** n/a   **MIP** $5

(Photo by Frank Veres)

❑ **394, #3-'57 Chevy,** Met. blue w/metal engine sticking out of hood, white sides & large "Hot Wheels" logo & red "1", white bow tie & "Hot Wheels" logo on trunk, blue tint window & int., chrome Malaysia base, 5sp

EX n/a   **NM** n/a   **MIP** $4

(Photo by Frank Veres)

❑ **395, #4-Bywayman,** a. Met. blue w/large "Hot Wheels" logos on hood & sides, white bow tie on hood, metal Malaysia base, white int. & roll bar, clear window, asw, ct

EX n/a   **NM** n/a   **MIP** $4

MOD BOD SERIES

❑ **396, #1-Hummer,** a. Pink plastic body w/green, magenta & yellow tampos, purple met. painted Malaysia base, logo above rear wheel, green tint window, asw, ct

EX n/a   **NM** n/a   **MIP** $4

(Photo by Frank Veres)

❑ **397, #2-School Bus,** Purple w/orange, green & yellow tampos on roof & sides, yellow plastic Malaysia base, orange int., clear window, asw, 7sp

EX n/a   **NM** n/a   **MIP** $4

(Photo by Frank Veres)

❑ **398, #3-VW Bug,** Light blue w/magenta, green & yellow tampos on sides, roof & hood, metal Malaysia base, green int., clear window, 7sp

EX n/a   **NM** n/a   **MIP** $5

❑ **399, #4-'67 Camaro,** a. Bright green w/red stripes, large logos on sides & roof, red int. w/open steering wheel, clear window, metal Malaysia base, 5sp
EX n/a   NM n/a   MIP $7

DARK RIDER SERIES II

(Photo by Frank Veres)

❑ **400, #1-Big Chill,** a. Met. black, black plastic Malaysia base, black tint chrome engine & canopy, black treads, metal rollers, gray logo on side, black ski
EX n/a   NM n/a   MIP $3

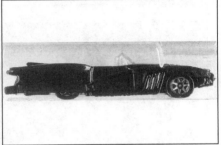

(Photo by Frank Veres)

❑ **401, #2-Street Beast,** Met. black w/black painted Malaysia base, black int., clear window, gray logo on trunk, black tint 7sp
EX n/a   NM n/a   MIP $3

(Photo by Frank Veres)

❑ **402, #3-Thunderstreak,** Met. black & black tint side pods, black painted Malaysia base, black driver, gray logo on nose, black tint 7sp
EX n/a   NM n/a   MIP $3

(Photo by Frank Veres)

❑ **403, #4-Power Pistons,** Black tint chrome, black painted Malaysia base, black int., clear canopy, gray logo in front of rear wheel, black tint 7sp
EX n/a   NM n/a   MIP $3

SPORTS CAR SERIES

(Photo by Frank Veres)

❑ **404, #1-Porsche 930,** Mf. silver w/red, white & black tampos, metal Malaysia base, black int., smoked window, alw, 7sp
EX n/a   NM n/a   MIP $3

(Photo by Frank Veres)

❑ **405, #2-Custom Corvette,** a. Pearl purple w/green & yellow tampos on hood, sides & trunk, football on hood, yellow helmet on sides, black Malaysia base, red logo on smoked windshield, gray int., 5sp
EX n/a   NM n/a   MIP $45

(Photo by Frank Veres)

❑ **406, #3-Cobra 427 S/C,** a. Pearl white w/black, red & blue tampos, metal Malaysia base, black int., clear window blue logo behind driver, alw, 5sp
EX n/a   NM n/a   MIP $55

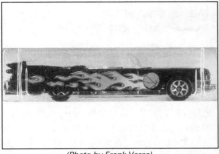

(Photo by Frank Veres)

❑ **407, #4-'59 Caddy,** a. Met. black w/yellow & orange flames on sides, "Slam Dunk" tampo on hood w/ball & net, white int., red logo on clear windshield, 7sp
EX n/a   NM n/a   MIP $3

SPLATTER PAINT SERIES

(Photo by Frank Veres)

❑ **408, #1-Rescue Ranger,** a. Dayglo orange w/blue splatters, orange plastic Malaysia base, blue insert & lights on roof, blue int., red logo on blue tint windshield, alw, t/b (The Rescue Ranger is another one of the cars that the guys from "Puerto Rico" were buying up. They are real heavy & were used for racing.)
EX n/a   NM n/a   MIP $7

(KP Photo)

❑ **409, #2-Side Splitter Funny Car,** White w/red & yellow splatters, metal Malaysia base, clear window, 5sp
EX n/a   NM n/a   MIP $5

(Photo by Frank Veres)

❑ **410, #3-'55 Chevy,** a. Yellow w/red splatters, red plastic Malaysia base, red logo on magenta tint windshield, t/b
EX n/a   **NM** n/a   **MIP** $7

(Photo by Frank Veres)

❑ **411, #4-'80s Camaro,** White w/blue & black splatters, metal Malaysia base, white int., red logo on clear windshield, 5sp
EX n/a   **NM** n/a   **MIP** $2

STREET EATERS SERIES

(Photo by Frank Veres)

❑ **412, #1-Speed Machine,** a. Light pearl green w/red yellow & black tampos, red int., red tint canopy, yellow logo on rear, metal Malaysia base, 7sp
EX n/a   **NM** n/a   **MIP** $10

(Photo by Frank Veres)

❑ **413, #2-Silhouette II,** a. Pearl purple w/red, green & white tampos, red int., orange tint canopy, red logo on rear, red plastic Malaysia base, chrome engine, 5sp
EX n/a   **NM** n/a   **MIP** $4

(Photo by Frank Veres)

❑ **414, #3-Propper Chopper,** a. Blue enamel w/red, orange & white tampos, orange Malaysia base, blue rotors & tail, orange int., clear window, white logo on side
EX n/a   **NM** n/a   **MIP** $15

(Photo by Frank Veres)

❑ **415, #4-Roll Patrol,** a. Light brown w/red, white & black tampos, orange painted Malaysia base, light orange int., black logo on side, black roll bar, clear window, asw, yct
EX n/a   **NM** n/a   **MIP** $10

FAST FOOD SERIES

❑ **416, #1-Pizza Vette,** a. White w/pepperoni tampos, black window, black painted Malaysia base, logo behind front wheel, 3sp
EX n/a   **NM** n/a   **MIP** $3

(KP Photo)

❑ **417, #2-Pasta Pipes,** White w/orange & yellow tampos, chrome int., black painted Malaysia base, blue tint canopy, logo on rear, 3sp
EX n/a   **NM** n/a   **MIP** $3

(KP Photo)

❑ **418, #3-Sweet Stocker,** White w/red, orange, green & purple candy tampos, black painted Malaysia base, yellow int., yellow tint window, red logo on trunk, asw, 3sp
EX n/a   **NM** n/a   **MIP** $20

❑ **419, #4-Crunch Chief,** a. White w/red, orange, green & purple tampos, black painted Malaysia base, no int., yellow tint window, logo behind front wheel, 3sp
EX n/a   **NM** n/a   **MIP** $4

SILVER SERIES II

(Photo by Frank Veres)

❑ **420, #1-Dump Truck,** a. Chrome cab, chrome dump box, red logo on top of box, metal Malaysia base, black grille, ct/b
EX n/a   **NM** n/a   **MIP** $20

❑ **421, #2-'40s Woodie,** Chrome w/metal Malaysia base, black int., gold logo in side clear window, 5sp
EX n/a   **NM** n/a   **MIP** $3

(Photo by Frank Veres)

❑ **422, #3-'57 Chevy,** Chrome w/metal Malaysia base, no int., black logo in rear orange tint window, 5sp
EX n/a   **NM** n/a   **MIP** $5

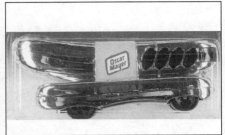

(Photo by Frank Veres)

❑ **423, #4-Oscar Mayer Wienermobile,** Chrome hot dog w/yellow band, red & white "Oscar Mayer" tampo, dark smoked window, chrome Malaysia base, b5sp
EX n/a   NM n/a   MIP $5

FIRE SQUAD SERIES

❑ **424, #1-Ambulance,** a. Day-glo green w/yellow & black "Fire Dept." & "City of Hot Wheels" logo w/white background in center, black "Hot Wheels" logo behind rear wheel, white int. & rear doors, chrome Malaysia base, smooth rear step, asw, 5sp
EX n/a   NM n/a   MIP $8

(Photo by FrankVeres)

❑ **425, #2-Rescue Ranger,** Yellow w/red & black tampo on door, black outline "Fire Dept" on hood, red rear insert & lights on roof, black int., chrome Malaysia base, black logo on side behind door, smoked window, alw, 5sp
EX n/a   NM n/a   MIP $3

❑ **426, #3-Flame Stopper,** a. Yellow w/black plastic Malaysia base, red & black side tampos, black logo on rear door, black window, black boom, alw, yct
EX n/a   NM n/a   MIP $50

❑ **427, #4-Fire Eater,** a. Red w/yellow & black tampos, blue insert, blue tint window & int., chrome Malaysia base, black logo on front door, asw, 5sp
EX n/a   NM n/a   MIP $4

1996 TREASURE HUNT SERIES

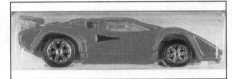

(Photo by Frank Veres)

❑ **428, #1-'40's Woodie,** a. Day-glo yellow w/tan wood, black int., metal Malaysia base, gold logo in side rear smoked window, yellow wheel w/yellow rim, whitewall "Real Rider" tires
EX n/a   NM n/a   MIP $40

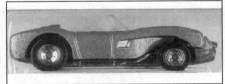

(Photo by Frank Veres)

❑ **429, #10-Lamborghini Countach,** a. Day-glo orange w/matching painted Malaysia base, tan int., clear window, c6sp
EX n/a   NM n/a   MIP $30

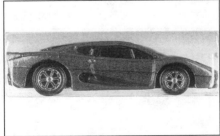

❑ **430, #3-Ferrari 250,** Met. gray, red stripe on hood & trunk, gray plastic Malaysia base, gold logo in white box on rear plate, red int., clear window, chrome wheel "Real Rider" tires
EX n/a   NM n/a   MIP $35

(Photo by Frank Veres)

❑ **431, #4-Jaguar XJ 220,** Met. green, black plastic Malaysia base, gold logo on rear smoked window, g6sp
EX n/a   NM n/a   MIP $30

(Photo by Frank Veres)

❑ **432, #5-'59 Caddy,** Red enamel, chrome Malaysia base, tan int., silver side stripe & "Eldorado" tampo gold logo on clear windshield, chrome wheel whitewall "Real Rider" tire
EX n/a   NM n/a   MIP $50

(Photo by Frank Veres)

❑ **433, #6-Dodge Viper RT/10,** a. White enamel w/2 blue stripes on hood & trunk, black int. & Malaysia base, gold logo on clear windshield, w6sp
EX n/a   NM n/a   MIP $60

(Photo by Frank Veres)

❑ **434, #7-'57 Chevy,** Met. purple w/chrome Malaysia base, purple tint window & int., gold logo in rear window, chrome wheel "Goodyear" "Real Rider" tires
EX n/a   NM n/a   MIP $60

(Photo by Frank Veres)

❑ **435, #8-Ferrari 355,** Pearl white w/metal Malaysia base, tan int., clear window, gold logo on rear plate, gold star wheel
EX n/a   NM n/a   MIP $30

1997 FIRST EDITIONS

(Photo by Frank Veres)

❑ **436, #9-'58 Corvette,** Mf. silver w/red cove, chrome bumpers, gray plastic Malaysia base, red int., clear windshield, gold logo in white box on trunk, chrome wheel whitewall "Real Rider" tires
EX n/a **NM** n/a **MIP** $60

(Photo by Frank Veres)

❑ **437, #2-Auburn 852,** Gold w/black flakes, gold fenders & int., clear window, gold logo in white box on trunk, metal Malaysia base, gold chrome wheel whitewall "Real Rider" tires
EX n/a **NM** n/a **MIP** $35

(Photo by Frank Veres)

❑ **438, #11-Dodge Ram 1500,** Met. maroon w/maroon cap, dark gray plastic Malaysia base, gray int., clear window, gold logo in white box on rear, chrome wheel "Real Rider" tires
EX n/a **NM** n/a **MIP** $35

(Photo by Frank Veres)

❑ **439, #12-'37 Bugatti,** Met. blue w/metal Malaysia base, red int., clear window, gold logo in white oval on trunk, c6sp
EX n/a **NM** n/a **MIP** $25

(KP Photo, Tom Michael collection)

❑ **509, #1-Firebird Funny Car,** Dark met. blue w/large "Hot Wheels" logo on hood & sides, white 1 f/c tampo on side w/racing decals, metal Malaysia base & int., clear window, 5sp
EX n/a **NM** n/a **MIP** $5

(Photo by Frank Veres)

❑ **510, #12-25th Countach,** Pearl yellow, black plastic Malaysia base, black int., gold logo on clear windshield, asw, 5dot
EX n/a **NM** n/a **MIP** $3

(KP Photo)

❑ **512, #3-Excavator,** White w/dark blue side tampo, gray plastic boom & bucket, black plastic Malaysia base & tracks
EX n/a **NM** n/a **MIP** $25

(Photo by Frank Veres)

❑ **513, #2-Ford 150 Pickup Truck,** Red, chrome int., bed & bumpers, gray plastic Malaysia base, smoked window, red logo in white box on rear plate, alw, 5sp
EX n/a **NM** n/a **MIP** $3

(KP Photo)

❑ **514, #7-Way 2 Fast,** a. Orange enamel w/black & white squares & red logo on roof, metal Malaysia base "no tm," chrome int., 5sp
EX n/a **NM** n/a **MIP** $5

(Photo by Frank Veres)

❑ **515, #11-'97 Corvette,** a. Met. green, black plastic Malaysia base, tan int., logo stamped in rear smoked window, alw, bbs
EX n/a **NM** n/a **MIP** $3

(KP Photo)

❑ **516, #10-Mercedes C-Class,** Black enamel w/silver #3 on roof & rear door, silver "Mercedes Benz" on rear fender, silver logo on front lower door, gray plastic Malaysia base & int., clear window, asw, gbbs
EX n/a **NM** n/a **MIP** $3

(Photo by Frank Veres)

❑ **517, #5-'59 Chevy Impala,** a. Light pearl purple w/gray & black stripe & orange tampo on side, chrome Malaysia base, white int., clear window, gray logo on fender skirt, g7sp
EX n/a **NM** n/a **MIP** $35

❑ **518, #6-BMW Z3 Roadster,** a. Mf. silver w/dark blue, light blue & red stripe on door, red logo on door, red int., clear window, metal Malaysia base, asw, 5sp

EX n/a   NM n/a   MIP $6

(Photo by Frank Veres)

❑ **519, #9-Scorchin' Scooter,** a. Met. purple w/orange, blue & silver flames, black painted seat, metal engine & pipes, gray forks & handle bars, chrome wheel w/black spokes

EX n/a   NM n/a   MIP $5

(Photo by Frank Veres)

❑ **520, #4-Saltflat Racer,** a. Light red plastic body, chrome engine & int., clear window, silver painted Malaysia base w/racing decals on front fender, 5sp

EX n/a   NM n/a   MIP $4

PHANTOM RACERS SERIES

❑ **529, #1-Power Rocket,** a. Transparent green body w/white logo on side, pink transparent canopy, chrome int., metal Malaysia base, chrome engine, 3sp

EX n/a   NM n/a   MIP $10

❑ **530, #2-Power Pistons,** a. Transparent red body w/white logo in front of rear wheel, gray int., clear canopy, metal Malaysia base, 3sp

EX n/a   NM n/a   MIP $3

(Photo by Frank Veres)

❑ **531, #3-Power Pipes,** Transparent blue body, purple tint canopy,

chrome int., red logo in white box on rear, metal Malaysia base, 3sp

EX n/a   NM n/a   MIP $3

❑ **532, #4-Road Rocket,** a. Transparent orange body, lime transparent top, chrome engine, white logo behind front wheel, 3sp

EX n/a   NM n/a   MIP $4

RACE TEAM SERIES III

(Photo by Frank Veres)

❑ **533, #1-Hummer,** a. Dark blue pearl plastic body w/small antenna, 2 large "Hot Wheels" logos on roof, red "1" & racing decals on sides, metal Malaysia base, gray windows, asw, t/b

EX n/a   NM n/a   MIP $3

❑ **534, #2-Chevy 1500 Pickup,** a. Met. blue w/large logo on hood & sides, white on sides w/red lettering & racing decals, white int., smoked window, metal Malaysia base, asw, 3sp

EX n/a   NM n/a   MIP $9

(Photo by Frank Veres)

❑ **535, #3-3-window '34,** Met. blue w/white on side & large "Hot Wheels" logo, white & orange flames on hood, blue int. & running boards, smoked window, metal Malaysia base, 5sp

EX n/a   NM n/a   MIP $130

(Photo by Frank Veres)

❑ **536, #4-'80s Corvette,** a. Met. blue w/large logo on hood & sides, white on sides w/red "1" & racing decals, clear window

w/transparent blue painted roof, white int., metal Malaysia base, asw, 5sp

EX n/a   NM n/a   MIP $3

HEAT FLEET SERIES

❑ **537, #1-Police Cruiser,** a. Light green enamel w/orange & purple flames on hood & sides, dark purple Malaysia base, light purple int., clear window, purple logo behind rear wheel, asw, 3sp

EX n/a   NM n/a   MIP $10

❑ **538, #2-School Bus,** a. Dark green enamel w/orange & purple flames on roof & sides, red logo on rear of roof, black plastic Malaysia base, clear window, white int., asw, 3sp

EX n/a   NM n/a   MIP $5

❑ **539, #3-Peterbilt Tank Truck,** a. Maroon met. metal cab w/flames on hood, black plastic tank w/flames & red logo on side, chrome Malaysia base & window, asw, 5sp

EX n/a   NM n/a   MIP $3

❑ **540, #5-Ramblin' Wrecker,** a. Black enamel w/flames on sides, red plastic boom, chrome Malaysia base & int., smoked window, yellow logo on side rear, asw, 7sp

EX n/a   NM n/a   MIP $5

BIFF! BAM! BOOM! SERIES

❑ **541, #1-Mini Truck,** a. Red enamel w/white, yellow & black tampos, black logo on side rear, black plastic Malaysia base & int., smoked window, 3sp

EX n/a   NM n/a   MIP $3

❑ **542, #2-Limozeen,** a. Pearl blue w/silver & magenta tampos, white int., magenta logo on front fender, smoked window, chrome Malaysia base, 5dot

EX n/a   NM n/a   MIP $30

❑ **543, #4-VW Bug,** a. Met. green w/yellow, white, red & black tampos, black logo in front of rear wheel, black int., clear window, 5sp

EX n/a   NM n/a   MIP $5

(Photo by Frank Veres)

❑ **544, #3-Range Rover,** Pearl purple w/orange, black, light blue & white tampos, black logo behind rear wheel, gray int., clear window, chrome Malaysia base, asw, ct/b
EX n/a　　**NM** n/a　　**MIP** $3

QUICKSILVER SERIES

(Photo by Frank Veres)

❑ **545, #1-Chevy Stocker,** a. Red plastic body w/yellow, white & black tampo on hood & sides, metal Malaysia base, black window, white logo behind rear wheel, asw-3sp
EX n/a　　**NM** n/a　　**MIP** $2

(Photo by Frank Veres)

❑ **546, #2-Aeroflash,** a. Purple plastic body w/white, red "7" & black tampos on hood & roof, white painted Malaysia base, white window, white logo on rear, 3sp
EX n/a　　**NM** n/a　　**MIP** $2

(Photo by Frank Veres)

❑ **547, #3-Ferrari 308,** Pearl white plastic body w/blue, lavender & black tampos, black painted Malaysia base, black window, light blue logo on nose, 5dot
EX n/a　　**NM** n/a　　**MIP** $2

(Photo by Frank Veres)

❑ **548, #4-T-Bird Stock Car,** a. Blue plastic body w/orange, yellow & black tampos, metal Malaysia base, black window, white logo behind rear wheel, 5sp
EX n/a　　**NM** n/a　　**MIP** $2

SPEED SPRAY SERIES

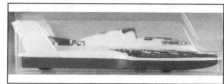

(Photo by Frank Veres)

❑ **549, #1-Hydroplane,** White w/aqua, yellow & black tampo on sides & top, blue plastic Malaysia base, chrome int., clear canopy black logo on top of scoop
EX n/a　　**NM** n/a　　**MIP** $3

(Photo by Frank Veres)

❑ **550, #2-Street Roader,** White w/brown mud tampo & red "Dirty Dog" on door & hood, red int. & spacer between body & metal Malaysia base, clear window, red logo on side rear, alw, ct/b
EX n/a　　**NM** n/a　　**MIP** $3

(Photo by Frank Veres)

❑ **551, #3-XT-3,** Blue enamel w/white tampo on sides, white painted Malaysia base, orange tint canopy, orange nose tip, metal engine, white logo on side, 5sp
EX n/a　　**NM** n/a　　**MIP** $3

(Photo by Frank Veres)

❑ **552, #4-Funny Car,** Pearl magenta w/white, yellow & black tampos on side, metal Malaysia base, clear window, black logo behind rear wheel, 5sp
EX n/a　　**NM** n/a　　**MIP** $4

SPY PRINT SERIES

(Photo by Frank Veres)

❑ **553, #1-Stealth,** a. Purple plastic body, white on side w/red & black tampos, metal Malaysia base, purple tint window, chrome int., black logo over front wheel, 3sp
EX n/a　　**NM** n/a　　**MIP** $3

❑ **554, #2-Alien,** a. Blue enamel w/white plastic top, black, blue & red tampos, white & blue int., smoked canopy, metal Malaysia base, red logo on front left, 3sp
EX n/a　　**NM** n/a　　**MIP** $3

❑ **555, #3-Sol-Aire CX4,** a. Dark maroon met., white sides w/black & green tampos, black window, black plastic Malaysia base, black logo behind rear wheel, 3sp
EX n/a　　**NM** n/a　　**MIP** $3

(Photo by Frank Veres)

❑ **556, #4-Custom Corvette,** Black enamel w/yellow, red & white tampos, gray int., smoked window, black plastic Malaysia base, red & white logo on nose, 3sp
EX n/a　　**NM** n/a　　**MIP** $2

STREET BEAST SERIES

(Photo by Frank Veres)

❏ **557, #1-Mercedes-Benz Unimog,** Black enamel cab & box, red plastic fenders & int., tan rear box cover w/black logo & black & red tampo, clear window, metal Malaysia base, alw, ct/b
EX n/a **NM** n/a **MIP** $2

(Photo by Frank Veres)

❏ **558, #2-Jaguar XJ220,** a. Orange enamel w/black & gold tampos on side & hood, black int., clear window, black plastic Malaysia base, black logo behind rear wheel, yt/b
EX n/a **NM** n/a **MIP** $2

(Photo by Frank Veres)

❏ **559, #3-Blown Camaro,** a. Day-glo yellow pearl w/black & pearl tampos on hood & sides, metal Malaysia base, black int., clear window, logo on hood, ot/b
EX n/a **NM** n/a **MIP** $3

(Photo by Frank Veres)

❏ **560, #4-Corvette Stingray,** White enamel w/yellow, red & black tampos on hood & roof, blue tint window & int., metal Malaysia base, black logo on roof, yt/b
EX n/a **NM** n/a **MIP** $3

WHITE ICE SERIES

(Photo by Frank Veres)

❏ **561, #1-Speed Machine,** Pearl white, metal Malaysia base, white int., red tint window, black logo on rear, 3sp
EX n/a **NM** n/a **MIP** $2

(Photo by Frank Veres)

❏ **562, #2-Shadow Jet,** a. Pearl white, metal Malaysia base, white int., yellow tint canopy, yellow plastic nose, light gold tint chrome engines & fuel tanks, black "Hot Wheels" logo on top behind canopy, 5sp
EX n/a **NM** n/a **MIP** $2

(Photo by Frank Veres)

❏ **563, #3-Splittn' Image II,** Pearl white, white plastic Malaysia base, blue tint chrome canopy, engine & headlights, gray plastic side pipes, black logo behind left headlight, 3sp
EX n/a **NM** n/a **MIP** $2

(Photo by Frank Veres)

❏ **564, #4-Twin Mill II,** Pearl white, white plastic Malaysia base, red tint window, white int., pink chrome engines, black logo on rear, alw, 5sp
EX n/a **NM** n/a **MIP** $2

DEALER'S CHOICE SERIES

(Photo by Frank Veres)

❏ **565, #1-Silhouette II,** a. Pearl blue w/white & red tampos on side, white tampos on hood, gold int. & engine, clear canopy, black plastic Malaysia base, gold logo behind front wheel, 5dot
EX n/a **NM** n/a **MIP** $2

❏ **566, #2-Street Beast,** a. White & gold w/black, gold & red tampos on hood & sides, gold int., clear window, red logo behind seats, metal Malaysia base, 5dot
EX n/a **NM** n/a **MIP** $2

❏ **567, #3-Baja Bug,** a. Met. red w/white, black & red tampo on side, white & black tampo on hood, metal Malaysia base, white int., white logo on door above spade, 5sp
EX n/a **NM** n/a **MIP** $5

(Photo by Frank Veres)

❏ **568, #4-'63 Corvette,** a. Black enamel w/red, white & gold tampo on hood, red & white tampo on side, red "Q" & heart on roof, red plastic Malaysia base w/"'63 Corvette," red int., clear window, red logo on right side hood, asw, 5dot
EX n/a **NM** n/a **MIP** $3

ROCKIN' RODS SERIES

(Photo by Frank Veres)

❏ **569, #1-Twang Thang,** Met. dark red w/black & white tampo on nose, magenta tampo behind chrome seats, chrome engine, black plastic Malaysia base, black guitars on side w/chrome strings, white logo behind front wheel, 5sp
EX n/a **NM** n/a **MIP** $2

❑ **570, #2-Ferrari 355,** a. Black enamel w/pearl green, purple, white & orange tampos, purple int., clear window, metal Malaysia base, red & white logo in front of rear wheel, asw, 3sp

EX n/a   **NM** n/a   **MIP** $3

(Photo by Frank Veres)

❑ **571, #3-Turbo Flame,** a. Purple plastic body, w/red, yellow, black & white tampo on side, black painted Malaysia base, yellow tint window, yellow logo on side up by chrome engine, 5sp

EX n/a   **NM** n/a   **MIP** $5

❑ **572, #4-Porsche 930,** a. Pearl dark green w/brown, yellow & white tampos, metal Malaysia base, black int., smoked window, brown & white logo behind rear wheel, asw, 3sp

EX n/a   **NM** n/a   **MIP** $50

BLUE STREAK SERIES

(Photo by Frank Veres)

❑ **573, #1-Olds 442,** Dark candy blue, large silver logo on trunk, chrome Malaysia base, black int., blue tint window, asw, 3sp

EX n/a   **NM** n/a   **MIP** $5

(Photo by Frank Veres)

❑ **574, #2-Nissan Truck,** Candy blue, black plastic Malaysia base, black int. & roll bar, blue tint window, chrome engine, large silver "Hot Wheels" logo on hood, alw, t/b

EX n/a   **NM** n/a   **MIP** $20

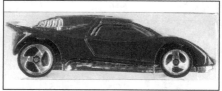

(KP Photo)

❑ **575, #3-'55 Chevy,** a. Candy blue, chrome Malaysia base, black window, large silver "Hot Wheels" logo on trunk, 3sp

EX n/a   **NM** n/a   **MIP** $5

(Photo by Frank Veres)

❑ **576, #4-Speed Blaster,** a. Candy blue, chrome Malaysia base, chrome window & engine, large "Hot Wheels" logo on hood, 3sp

EX n/a   **NM** n/a   **MIP** $20

1997 TREASURE HUNT SERIES

(Photo by Frank Veres)

❑ **578, #1-'56 Flashsider,** Met. green w/orange & lavender tampo on hood, chrome Malaysia base & window, black bed cover, orange logo on rear, 5sp

EX n/a   **NM** n/a   **MIP** $25

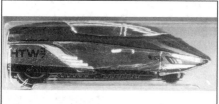

(Photo by Frank Veres)

❑ **579, #2-Silhouette II,** White enamel, white plastic Malaysia base & int., blue tint canopy, blue tint chrome engine, red logo on rear, w3sp

EX n/a   **NM** n/a   **MIP** $15

(Photo by Frank Veres)

❑ **580, #3-Mercedes 500SL,** Black enamel w/silver luggage rack tampo on trunk, silver "SL500" tampo on side, silver logo on rear, black plastic Malaysia bae, clear window, white int., alw, 5sp

EX n/a   **NM** n/a   **MIP** $15

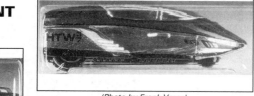

(Photo by Frank Veres)

❑ **581, #4-Street Cleaver,** Black plastic w/red & gold tampo w/gold logo, gold painted Malaysia base, gold tint chrome engine, alw-5sp

EX n/a   **NM** n/a   **MIP** $20

(Photo by Frank Veres)

❑ **582, #5-GM Lean Machine,** Met. burgundy & chrome, black tampos, chrome canopy, black painted Malaysia base, black logo on side, 5sp

EX n/a   **NM** n/a   **MIP** $12

❑ **583, #6-Hot Rod Wagon,** Yellow enamel, gold tint chrome engine & rear wing, black seat & handle, metal Malaysia base, red logo on rear, y5sp

EX n/a   **NM** n/a   **MIP** $35

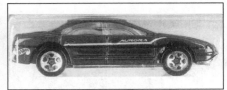

(Photo by Frank Veres)

❑ **584, #7-Olds Aurora,** Pearl purple w/silver stripe & "Aurora" on side, small silver tampo on hood, gray int., clear window, chrome Malaysia base, silver logo behind rear wheel, asw, 5sp
EX n/a   NM n/a   MIP $11

(Photo by Frank Veres)

❑ **585, #8-Dogfighter,** Met. green w/gold & black tampos on sides, yellow plastic Malaysia base, orange prop, gold tint chrome engine & suspension, black logo on tail, 5sp
EX n/a   NM n/a   MIP $20

(Photo by Frank Veres)

❑ **586, #9-Buick Wildcat,** Mf. silver w/red stripes, met. black window, gray plastic Malaysia base, chrome engine, red & white logo on rear, alw, 3sp
EX n/a   NM n/a   MIP $15

(Photo by Frank Veres)

❑ **587, #10-Blimp,** Blue plastic w/large "Hot Wheels" logo on side, white gondola w/black window & "T.H. 97" tampo
EX n/a   NM n/a   MIP $12

(Photo by Frank Veres)

❑ **588, #11-Avus Quattro,** Gold pearl, black "Avus" on side, black "Audi" logo on hood, red "Hot Wheels" logo in front of rear wheel, white int., smoked canopy w/gold & black, black plastic Malaysia base, alw, t/b
EX n/a   NM n/a   MIP $12

(Photo by Frank Veres)

❑ **589, #12-Rail Rodder,** White pearl plastic body, red flames w/one orange flame at the end w/red logo on side, pink tint chrome engines & smoke stack, chrome drivers (wheels), metal Malaysia base, b5sp
EX n/a   NM n/a   MIP $25

1999 FIRST EDITIONS

(Photo by Frank Veres)

❑ **912, #10-Porsche 911 GT3 CUP,** a. Gray pearl, black plastic Malaysia base, side has yellow w/pearl green outlined in red and misc. racing decals w/red "8 Cup" in silver circle, white "Hot Wheels" logo behind rear wheel, yellow plastic rear wing, orange int., blue tint window & head lights, asw, bbs
EX n/a   NM n/a   MIP $10

(Photo by Frank Veres)

❑ **649, #1-1936 Cord,** a. Met. dark red, chrome Malaysia base, casting still on top of window plastic inside, looks like a dome light, purple int., clear window, silver logo on bottom of front fender behind wheel, bbs
EX n/a   NM n/a   MIP $10

❑ **656, #3-'38 Phantom Corsair,** a. Black enamel, metal Malaysia base, gray int., clear window, gray logo behind front wheel, ww5sp
EX n/a   NM n/a   MIP $15

(Photo by Frank Veres)

❑ **675, #7-Pontiac Rageous,** a. Met. red, black plastic Malaysia base, gray int., smoked window with black painted roof, small silver "Rageous" on front door, silver logo on rear fender, alw-3sp
EX n/a   NM n/a   MIP $3

(Photo by Frank Veres)

❑ **676, #25-Porsche 911 GT1-98,** a. White enamel, black plastic Malaysia base, orange, purple & gray tampos w/misc. racing decals, black logo behind rear wheel, black rear window & int., clear window, asw, bbs
EX n/a   NM n/a   MIP $2

(Photo by Frank Veres)

❑ **680, #24-Baby Boomer,** Candy blue w/orange, yellow & white flames on sides, chrome engine & fuel tanks, gray injection & belts, metal Malaysia base, white logo on side rear, 5sp
EX n/a **NM** n/a **MIP** $2

(Photo by Frank Veres)

❑ **683, #9'Tee'd Off,** a. White pearl, metal Malaysia base, white pearl plastic top w/magenta "Miller CC" and pearl green & white "Country Club" tampo, gold "Hot Wheels" logo above "Miller" on top, gray int., chrome engine, 5sp
EX n/a **NM** n/a **MIP** $15

(Photo by Frank Veres)

❑ **909, #2-'99 Mustang,** a. Dark purple pearl, black plastic Malaysia base, small Mustang logo on front fender by door, silver "MUSTANG" on rear bumper, silver "Hot Wheels" logo on rear fender above tire, red int., clear window, 5sp
EX n/a **NM** n/a **MIP** $31

❑ **910, #6-Monte Carlo Concept Car,** a. Red enamel, silver mf. painted Malaysia base, gray int/smoked window, black logo on rear fender, asw, 5sp
EX n/a **NM** n/a **MIP** $3

(Photo by Frank Veres)

❑ **911, #5-Olds Aurora GT3,** a. White enamel w/met. blue on trunk & side, red stripe below blue on rear fender & door, hood has dark blue "11," large "Hot Wheels" logo outlined in pearl blue w/"Leading The Way" & Aurora logo, side has large "Hot Wheels" logo coming off front wheel well, white "11" & misc. racing decals, black rear spoiler, int. & Malaysia base, clear window, asw, gbbs
EX n/a **NM** n/a **MIP** $20

(Photo by Frank Veres)

❑ **913, #13-Popcycle,** a. Met. burgundy w/orange stripe & "Hot Wheels" logo, metal Malaysia base, chrome engine, chrome "Stingray" bicycle under orange tint canopy, 3sp
EX n/a **NM** n/a **MIP** $15

❑ **914, #8-Semi-Fast,** a. Red plastic, metal Malaysia base & lower grille, yellow & black stripes w/black circle & white "17" on cab & body, black vents on side w/black "Hot Wheels" logo & "Jones" tampos behind front wheel, "Champion & Goodyear" tampos below stripe on cab, smoked window, gray engine & int., 5sp
EX n/a **NM** n/a **MIP** $8

❑ **915, #4-1970 Chevelle SS,** a. Met. blue, wide white "SS" stripes on hood & trunk, metal Malaysia base, white int., blue & white logo on trunk in stripe, blue tint window, 5sp
EX n/a **NM** n/a **MIP** $16

(Photo by Frank Veres)

❑ **916, #14-Phaeton,** Met. teal w/thin silver over gold stripes on side, tan plastic top & int., metal Malaysia base, tinted window, silver logo in front of rear wheel over exhaust, 5sp
EX n/a **NM** n/a **MIP** $3

(Photo by Frank Veres)

❑ **917, #12-Track T,** a. Black enamel, metal Malaysia base, seat & engine, yellow & red flames outlined in green on hood, silver painted grille, tan plastic cover, dash & steering wheel, silver "Hot Wheels" logo on trunk, 5sp
EX n/a **NM** n/a **MIP** $4

(Photo by Frank Veres)

❑ **918, #15-Screamin' Hauler,** a. Met. purple, metal Malaysia base & int., chrome engines, blue tint window, silver logo on rear, 5sp
EX n/a **NM** n/a **MIP** $3

❑ **919, #11-Fiat 500C,** a. Purple w/thin gold stripe on side, metal Malaysia base, gray plastic roll cage & rear wing, chrome engine, exhaust & windshield, gold logo on side by engine, 5sp
EX n/a **NM** n/a **MIP** $5

(Photo by Frank Veres)

❏ **921, #16-Ford GT-40, a.** Met. blue, gray plastic Malaysia base, white racing stripe on center of trunk, roof & hood, white circle & black "59" on hood & door, white racing stripe on lower side w/"FORD," white logo on rear fender, gray int., blue tint window, thin rear 5sp
EX n/a   NM n/a   MIP $5

(Photo by Frank Veres)

❏ **922, #17-Jeepster,** Red enamel, metal Malaysia base, black plastic fenders, bumpers, & int., black & silver "Jeepster" tampo behind front wheel, silver logo on door below handle, smoked window w/silver painted trim, alw, 5sp
EX n/a   NM n/a   MIP $3

(Photo by Frank Veres)

❏ **923, #18-Turbolence, a.** Black enamel, gold "Dayla" tampo twice by gold chrome engine, gold "1" w/purple outline on nose, gold "Hot wheels" logo on rear, gold chrome int., metal Malaysia base, alw, g5dot
EX n/a   NM n/a   MIP $2

(Photo by Frank Veres)

❏ **924, #19-Pikes Peak Tacoma,** Yellow w/white roof, hood & grille, yellow painted side vent, black & red "TOYOTA Express Lube" and yellow, black & red "Pennzoil" logo on hood, red & black "1" & black "Hot Wheels" logo on rear fender, "PENNZOIL" & misc. racing decals on side, black plastic Malaysia base, int. & bed cover, clear window, asw, gbbs
EX n/a   NM n/a   MIP $3

❏ **925, #20-Shadow Mk IIa, a.** Black enamel, gray plastic Malaysia base & int., met. silver painted rear wing w/gray & black "Shadow" tampo, side has white "101" & misc. racing decals, white "Hot Wheels" logo behind front wheel, 5sp
EX n/a   NM n/a   MIP $3

(Photo by Frank Veres)

❏ **926, #26-Mercedes CLK-LM, a.** Pearl gray, black plastic Malaysia base, silver "Hot Wheels" logo on black rear wing, black int., clear window, asw, gbbs
EX n/a   NM n/a   MIP $3

(Photo by Frank Veres)

❏ **927, #22-'56 Ford Truck,** Light pearl blue, gray plastic Malaysia base, blue flames w/magenta outline & "Genuine Ford Parts" tampo on side, chrome int. & engine, blue tint window, 5sp
EX n/a   NM n/a   MIP $5

(Photo by Frank Veres)

❏ **928, #23-Chrysler Pronto,** Pearl yellow, black plastic Malaysia base, black roof, dark smoked window, gray int., silver painted headlights & emblem on grille, black "Hot Wheels" logo in front of rear wheel, 5sp
EX n/a   NM n/a   MIP $3

(Photo by Frank Veres)

❏ **1113, #21-360 Modena, a.** Red enamel, small yellow Ferrari logo on hood, black plastic Malaysia base, no "Hot Wheels" logo on rear plate, black int., clear window, asw, 5sp
EX n/a   NM n/a   MIP $10

1998 First Editions

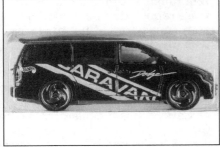

(Photo by Frank Veres)

❏ **633, #4-Dodge Caravan, a.** Dark met. burgundy, yellow, black & white side tampo, gray plastic Malaysia base, white int., smoked window, white logo on rear fender, alw, t/b
EX n/a   NM n/a   MIP $5

(KP Photo)

❑ **634, #3-Dodge Sidewinder,** a. Day-glo orange, gray plastic Malaysia base, purple int. & bed cover, smoked window, white logo behind rear wheel, 5sp

EX n/a **NM** n/a **MIP** $3

(Photo by Frank Veres)

❑ **635, #8-'65 Impala,** Purple pearl w/yellow & orange tampos on hood & sides, tan int., clear window, orange logo in front of rear wheel, chrome Malaysia base, gbbs

EX n/a **NM** n/a **MIP** $4

(Photo by Frank Veres)

❑ **636, #7-'32 Ford,** a. The very first releases of the #7-'32 Ford were reported to have a driver by some collectors. What they saw was the casting post still inside. The post is where they break the body from the mold. This car is on the older Card with the rear of the Porsche & the card reads, "# 7 of 48 Cars" & has the blister from the Slideout. Shortly after, the post was cleaned out & it got it's own blister. a. (48 on card) black enamel w/int post, the flames on the first few were yellow w/most of the flame being red & trimmed in aqua, red int., clear window, black plastic Malaysia base, aqua logo in front of rear wheel, 5sp

EX n/a **NM** n/a **MIP** $15

(KP Photo)

❑ **637, #1-Escort Rally,** a. Pearl white w/pearl blue, red & black side tampos, pearl blue nose w/black & white headlights, white & yellow lettering, red int., smoked window, gray plastic Malaysia base w/"Ford Rally," asw, bbs

EX n/a **NM** n/a **MIP** $10

(KP Photo)

❑ **638, #6-Jaguar D-Type,** a. Dark blue pearl w/matching painted Malaysia base, white circle w/black "4" on front & rear, two white stripes on nose, white logo on rear, gray int., clear window, 5sp

EX n/a **NM** n/a **MIP** $2

(Photo by Frank Veres)

❑ **639, #5-Jaguar XK8,** a. (48 on card) Pearl green w/black & white side tampo, white int., clear window, white logo behind rear wheel, gray plastic Malaysia base, bbs

EX n/a **NM** n/a **MIP** $100

(Photo by Frank Veres)

❑ **640, #2-Slideout,** Pearl purple, black & white tampo on rear roll bar, orange & white "6" & racing decals in sides, white & black "6" & racing decals on side of top wing, orange wings, engine & rear push bar, orange logo on side below racing decals, gray plastic Malaysia base, 5sp

EX n/a **NM** n/a **MIP** $5

(Photo by Frank Veres)

❑ **644, #9-'63 T-Bird,** a. Met. teal w/silver side trim, metal Malaysia base, white int., clear window, silver logo on rear fender, 5dot

EX n/a **NM** n/a **MIP** $3

❑ **645, #10-Dairy Delivery,** a. Pearl white, dark pink & teal side tampos, teal logo in front of rear wheel, aqua int., gray plastic Malaysia base, clear window, 5sp

EX n/a **NM** n/a **MIP** $4

❑ **646, #11-Mercedes SLK,** a. Yellow enamel w/white side paint, black logo on rear fender, black int., smoked window, metal Malaysia base, asw, 5dot

EX n/a **NM** n/a **MIP** $12

(Photo by Frank Veres)

❑ **647, #12-Lakester,** Red enamel w/matching painted Malaysia base, yellow & orange "61" on top w/white lettering, black, yellow & white racing decals on sides, chrome engines, exhaust & int., clear canopy, alw, 5sp

EX n/a **NM** n/a **MIP** $3

(Photo by Frank Veres)

❑ **648, #13-Hot Seat,** a. White plastic w/black plastic seat & plunger, blue tint metal Malaysia engine & base, black logo on rear (no pun intended), 5sp

EX n/a　　　NM n/a　　　MIP $3

(Photo by Frank Veres)

❑ **650, #23-Solar Eagle III,** Yellow plastic w/blue solar cells on top, black & red tampos on side & nose, black canopy, no logo, black mf. Malaysia base, black window

EX n/a　　　NM n/a　　　MIP $2

(Photo by Frank Veres)

❑ **651, #21-Go Kart,** Day-glo green w/black & orange tampo, white logo on side pod, metal chassis, day-glo painted metal Malaysia base, black seat, 5sp

EX n/a　　　NM n/a　　　MIP $5

(Photo by Frank Veres)

❑ **652, #15-Pikes Peak Celica,** a. Yellow enamel w/black, red & white tampos on hood & roof, purple & red side tampo w/black & white "Pennzoil," black "No Fear" & purple "Toyota Express Lube," black plastic Malaysia base, red int., dark smoked window, white logo on hood by windshield, asw, gbbs

EX n/a　　　NM n/a　　　MIP $7

(Photo by Frank Veres)

❑ **653, #16-Iroc Firebird,** a. Met. gold, black & white tampos, gray plastic China base, light tan int., tinted window, no logo, yellow. letter b5sp

EX n/a　　　NM n/a　　　MIP $2

(Photo by Frank Veres)

❑ **654, #20-'40 Ford Pickup,** a. Light pearl blue, yellow, red tampo w/purple outline on door & rear fender, red & white logo on door, chrome Malaysia base, gray int., roll bar, tubs & wing, blue tint window, 5sp

EX n/a　　　NM n/a　　　MIP $20

(Photo by Frank Veres)

❑ **655, #22-Super Comp Dragster,** a. Black enamel, 3 decals on side including logo, black plastic fenders w/Malaysia, "1" or "2" under running board, gray roll cage, int. & wheelie bar, chrome exhaust & base, 5sp

EX n/a　　　NM n/a　　　MIP $8

(Photo by Frank Veres)

❑ **657, #19-Panoz GTR-1,** a. White enamel, black plastic China base, dark red & silver stripes on top of hood & rear fenders, dark red "66" & Panoz logo on hood,

light blue panel w/red "66" on door, larger red "Hot Wheels" logo behind rear wheel, misc. racing decals behind front wheel, blue int., clear window, bbs

EX n/a　　　NM n/a　　　MIP $5

❑ **658, #25-Tow Jam,** a. Red enamel, large "Hot Wheels" logo on roof, logo covers almost all of the roof, metal boom, black sling, chrome Malaysia base, black window, 3sp

EX n/a　　　NM n/a　　　MIP $50

(Photo by Frank Veres)

❑ **659, #24-Tail Dragger,** a. Met. purple w/pearl pink & blue pinstripe tampos on hood & sides, metal Malaysia base, pearl blue logo in front of rear wheel, white int., clear window, bbs

EX n/a　　　NM n/a　　　MIP $4

❑ **661, #17-'70 Roadrunner,** a. Light Hemi Orange, short black stripe on trunk w/silver logo, the stripe on the trunk ran short of the rear window, black stripe on hood didn't come to the windshield either. Hood has black stripe w/silver "426 HEMI" & hood pins, chrome Malaysia base, black int., clear window, 5sp

EX n/a　　　NM n/a　　　MIP $5

(Photo by Frank Veres)

❑ **662, #33-Bad Mudder,** a. White enamel, "No Roof Tampo," dark blue wedge w/white oval & red outlined "8" on side, light blue pearl stripes, light red stripes & red, blue & black racing decals on sides, no logo, two decals side by side above "Chi Motors," light blue pearl "Goodyear" on front fender, large "Ford" oval on door, black int., black plastic Malaysia base, asw, ct/b

EX n/a　　　NM n/a　　　MIP $80

(Photo by Frank Veres)

❏ **663, #26-Customized C3500,** a. Met. teal w/long thin blue, magenta & white stripe down sides, magenta logo on side behind cab, thin black stripes above rocker panel, gray plastic Malaysia base & int., smoked window, 5dot

EX n/a   NM n/a   MIP $15

(Photo by Frank Veres)

❏ **664, #27-Super Modified,** a. Black enamel w/magenta, orange, yellow, & white tampo on front w/white, black & red lettering, white logo on nose, metal engine & Malaysia base, chrome rear wing & roll cage, pink seat, front wing & rear push bar, bbs/2

EX n/a   NM n/a   MIP $3

(Photo by Frank Veres)

❏ **665, #18-Mustang Cobra,** a. Black enamel, gray plastic Malaysia base, side tampos include; green wedge on side w/thin yellow stripe & orange "Mustang" & "OSO," misc. racing decals, yellow & green over white "11," "Cosen" tampo missing from rear fender, hood tampos include; green wedge w/thin yellow stripe, orange "Mustang," white "Team OSO," yellow & green over white "11", white Ford oval, "Team OSO" & "Hot Wheels" logo on trunk, gray int., clear window, asw, gbbs

EX n/a   NM n/a   MIP $10

❏ **667, #34-At-A-Tude,** a. Met. blue w/yellow stripes & black, red & white racing decals on sides, black logo in front of rear wheel on door, black plastic Malaysia base, chrome int., orange tint window, large rear bbs/small front bbs

EX n/a   NM n/a   MIP $4

(Photo by Frank Veres)

❏ **668, #14-Ford GT-90,** White enamel, small black Ford oval & GT90 tampos on side, black logo in front of rear wheel, metal Malaysia base, blue int., smoked window, 3sp

EX n/a   NM n/a   MIP $2

(Photo by Frank Veres)

❏ **669, #28-Chaparral 2,** a. White enamel, black "66" in black circle on nose, gray plastic injection & exhaust, red logo on side in front of rear wheel, black painted metal Malaysia base, black int., clear window, bbs/2

EX n/a   NM n/a   MIP $3

(Photo by Frank Veres)

❏ **670, #29-Mustang Mach I,** a. Day-glo orange, black stripe on hood, black int. & rear louvers, blue tint window, black plastic Malaysia base, black logo on rear fender, 5sp

EX n/a   NM n/a   MIP $40

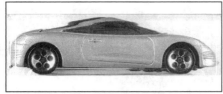

(Photo by Frank Veres)

❏ **671, #32-Chrysler Thunderbolt,** a. Silver pearl, black plastic Malaysia base, white int., purple tint window, purple logo on trunk, asw, 5dot

EX n/a   NM n/a   MIP $2

(Photo by Frank Veres)

❏ **672, #35-Dodge Concept Car,** a. Pearl orange w/silver logo on trunk, silver painted headlights, metal Malaysia base, smoked window, black int., 5sp

EX n/a   NM n/a   MIP $300

(Photo by Frank Veres)

❏ **673, #36-Whatta Drag,** Met. Red w/yellow & green roof tampo, red & white logo on roof, chrome engine, rear wing & suspension, gray scoop, metal Malaysia base, chrome int., orange tint window, 3sp

EX n/a   NM n/a   MIP $3

(Photo by Frank Veres)

❏ **674, #30-Sweet 16 II,** Dark met. purple w/matching painted metal Malaysia base, purple tint window, chrome engine, int. & front wheel drive unit, silver logo on rear, 5sp

EX n/a   NM n/a   MIP $3

(Photo by Frank Veres)

❑ **677, #31-Callaway C-7,** a. Silver pearl, black & red lettering on hood, black lettering on sides & rear, orange dot above front wheel, black painted headlights, black plastic rear wing, front cowl, int. & Malaysia base, black logo behind rear wheel, clear window, 5sp

EX n/a   NM n/a   MIP $4

(Photo by Frank Veres)

❑ **678, #37-Express Lane,** a. Red plastic, white side tampo w/red "Express Lane," black seat & steering wheel, white logo on rear plate, metal engine & Malaysia base, 5sp

EX n/a   NM n/a   MIP $3

❑ **681, #38-Cat-A-Pult,** a. Red enamel w/faint white stripe down hood, white oval w/black "64" on nose, red logo above oval on hood, metal Malaysia base, black int., orange tint window, asw, 5sp

EX n/a   NM n/a   MIP $25

(Photo by Frank Veres)

❑ **682, #39-Fathom This,** a. White enamel, black & white props, red "Experimental" tampo & "Hot Wheels" logo on top of white plastic pontoons, orange windows

EX n/a   NM n/a   MIP $4

❑ **684, #40-Double Vision,** a. Met. red w/white & black tampos, white logo on rear fender behind wheel, gray engines w/chrome Super Chargers, gray plastic Malaysia base & seat, clear canopy, gbbs

EX n/a   NM n/a   MIP $2

TATTOO MACHINES

(KP Photo, Tom Michael collection)

❑ **685, #1-'57 T-Bird,** Light pearl blue, white & black tampo on hood & sides, black logo on rear fender by taillight, chrome Malaysia base, blue tint window & int., 3sp

EX n/a   NM n/a   MIP $2

❑ **686, #2-'93 Camaro,** a. Dayglo green w/black & white side tampo, black & white logo on side in front of rear wheel, black plastic Malaysia base, white int., smoked window, alw, 3sp

EX n/a   NM n/a   MIP $2

(KP Photo, Tom Michael collection)

❑ **687, #3-Stutz Blackhawk,** a. Met. red w/white & black side tampos, red & white logo behind rear wheel, metal Malaysia base, white int., tinted window, asw, 3sp

EX n/a   NM n/a   MIP $2

❑ **688, #4-Corvette Stingray,** a. Orange enamel, yellow sides w/black & orange tampos, metal Malaysia base, black int., smoked window, black logo behind front tire, 3sp

EX n/a   NM n/a   MIP $2

TECHNO BITS SERIES

(Photo by Frank Veres)

❑ **689, #1-Shadow Jet II,** a. Black plastic, orange side tampo w/thin yellow outline, white & light green tampos on side over the orange, white, orange, light green, & yellow tampos on front, orange & white logo on side toward rear, metal Malaysia base, chrome int., green tint window, b5sp

EX n/a   NM n/a   MIP $3

❑ **690, #2-Power Pistons,** a. Purple plastic w/yellow, black & gray side tampos, gold int., yellow tint window, metal Malaysia base, 3sp

EX n/a   NM n/a   MIP $2

❑ **691, #3-Shadow Jet,** a. Met. blue w/gold & silver tampos on top, silver, black & gold tampo on side pod, red & silver logo on top of rear wing, gold chrome engine & exhaust, black int., black plastic nose, smoked canopy, metal Malaysia base, 5sp

EX n/a   NM n/a   MIP $6

(Photo by Frank Veres)

❑ **692, #4-Radar Ranger,** Dayglo green w/black, purple & white tampos, black plastic radar dish, purple plastic insert, purple & yellow logo behind canopy on side, red tint canopy, black painted Malaysia base, ct/b

EX n/a   NM n/a   MIP $2

TROPICOOL SERIES

(Photo by Frank Veres)

❏ **693, #1-Ice Cream Truck,** a. White enamel w/black plastic Malaysia base, yellow, red, green & black stripes, "Rasta Fruits & Veggies" & Rasta Dude w/green & yellow hat on side, white logo in red stripe behind rear wheel, green int., clear window, asw, 5sp
EX n/a   **NM** n/a   **MIP** $10

❏ **694, #2-Baja Bug,** a. White enamel, metal Malaysia base, dark red, black, yellow & green stripes w/Rasta Dude on door, yellow & red tampo w/Rasta Dude on hood, "Bug'n Taxi" in white in side & hood, red int., black & white logo on side behind door, large rear 5sp
EX n/a   **NM** n/a   **MIP** $7

❏ **695, #3-Classic Caddy,** a. Red enamel w/yellow, white, red & green side tampo, black plastic fenders, light gray int., smoked window, white tampo w/large logo behind side window, metal Malaysia base, asw, bbs
EX n/a   **NM** n/a   **MIP** $3

(Photo by Frank Veres)

❏ **696, #4-Corvette Convertible,** a. Day-glo green w/blue, white & black side tampo, black plastic Malaysia base w/o "Custom Corvette," blue int., smoked window, blue logo on rear fender, 3sp
EX n/a   **NM** n/a   **MIP** $6

LOW 'N COOL SERIES

(Photo by Frank Veres)

❏ **697, #1-Mini Truck,** Day-glo yellow, black plastic Malaysia base, light green & yellow tampos outlined in orange & dark blue on hood & sides, black int. & rear bed, smoked window, chrome engine, shifter & rear speakers, dark blue logo on rear fender behind wheel, g3sp
EX n/a   **NM** n/a   **MIP** $2

(Photo by Frank Veres)

❏ **698, #2-'59 Impala,** a. Pearl green w/dark purple & black side tampo, white logo on rear fender, white int., smoked window, chrome Malaysia base, gbbs
EX n/a   **NM** n/a   **MIP** $4

(Photo by Frank Veres)

❏ **699, #3-'59 Caddy,** a. Rose pearl w/yellow & blue tampos on sides & hood, chrome Thailand base, white int., smoked window, yellow logo on front fender by headlight, gbbs
EX n/a   **NM** n/a   **MIP** $5

(Photo by Frank Veres)

❏ **716, #4-Limozeen,** Black mf. w/pearl tampo & gold stripe on side, gold tint chrome Malaysia base, white int., smoked window, gold logo on rear fender, gbbs
EX n/a   **NM** n/a   **MIP** $4

BIOHAZARD SERIES

(Photo by Frank Veres)

❏ **717, #1-Hydroplane,** a. Dark day-glo green, yellow "Biohazard Removal" tampo on pontoons, yellow w/black over brown Biohazard Removal logo on pontoons, black over brown (mostly black) designs on pontoons, black behind canopy w/yellow "Unit 4" & red "Hot Wheels" logo, black plastic Thailand base, chrome int., clear canopy
EX n/a   **NM** n/a   **MIP** $25

(Photo by Frank Veres)

❏ **718, #2-Flame Stopper,** a. Day-glo pink, yellow w/black over brown biohazard removal, yellow "Caution High Pressure Foam Flow" over black rectangle behind rear wheel, black window, black plastic boom w/rivets, black plastic Thailand base w/long headlights, alw, yct/b
EX n/a   **NM** n/a   **MIP** $3

(Photo by Frank Veres)

❏ **719, #3-Recycling Truck,** a. Day-glo yellow metal cab, black window, day-glo yellow plastic waste container with black & red over yellow side tampo, thin white lettering outlined in black, red over black logo on side, this tampo is very hard to read, black plastic Malaysia base, asw, t/b
EX n/a   **NM** n/a   **MIP** $5

(Photo by Frank Veres)

❏ **720, #4-Rescue Ranger,** a. Black enamel, dark red, yellow &

white side tampos, day-glo yellow plastic insert, chrome Malaysia base, yellow tint window & interior, alw, 5sp

EX n/a   NM n/a   MIP $4

DASH 4 CASH SERIES

❑ **721, #1-Jaguar XJ220,** a. Silver w/black on sides, black stripes on hood & roof, magenta outlined tampo on hood, silver "Fast Cash" & magenta outlined tampo on sides, silver & black logo on rear fender behind rear wheel, light purple int., clear window, black plastic Malaysia base, bbs

EX n/a   NM n/a   MIP $5

❑ **722, #2-Ferrari F40,** a. Light yellow gold, metal Malaysia base, black & with tampos on hood & sides, white logo on front fender, tan int., tinted window, gbbs

EX n/a   NM n/a   MIP $4

(Photo by Frank Veres)

❑ **723, #3-Audi Avus,** Black enamel, white, dark red & yellow side tampos, gold & black tampos on smoked canopy, dark red logo in front of rear wheel, white int., black plastic Thailand base, alw, gbbs

EX n/a   NM n/a   MIP $3

❑ **724, #4-Dodge Viper,** a. White pearl, black plastic Thailand base, pearl blue side tampo, red & black tampo & red & white logo on hood, red int., smoked window, alw, t/b

EX n/a   NM n/a   MIP $3

RACE TEAM SERIES IV

(Photo by Frank Veres)

❑ **725, #1-'67 Camaro,** a. Met. blue w/white sides & large "Hot Wheels" logo, red # 1 on rear fender, white "1" & yellow "Hot Wheels" on roof, dark red stripe below white on rear fender, white bow tie in front of rear wheel, white int., tinted window, metal no origin base, 5sp

EX n/a   NM n/a   MIP $5

(Photo by Frank Veres)

❑ **726, #2-Mercedes C-Class,** Met. blue w/white sides & large "Hot Wheels" logo, large logo on hood w/white "1," red "1" on rear fender, dark red stripe below white on rear fender, white "Bridgestone" on rear post above rear tire, white int., smoked window, black plastic Thailand base, asw, 5sp

EX n/a   NM n/a   MIP $3

(Photo by Frank Veres)

❑ **727, #3-Shelby Cobra 427 S/C,** Met. blue w/white sides & large "Hot Wheels" logo, red "1" on rear fender, dark red stripe below white on rear fender, white "Ford" above logo on door, yellow "Hot Wheels" above trunk, large logo on hood, white "1" on nose, white int., smoked window, metal Malaysia base, alw, 5sp

EX n/a   NM n/a   MIP $3

(Photo by Frank Veres)

❑ **728, #4-'63 Corvette,** Met. blue w/white sides & large "Hot Wheels" logo, red "1" on rear fender, dark red stripe below white on rear fender, white "Goodyear" above logo on door, yellow "Hot Wheels" & large white # 1 on roof, large logo & small "1" on hood, white int., tinted window, chrome 2-rivet Malaysia base, asw, 5sp

EX n/a   NM n/a   MIP $8

ARTISTIC LICENSE SERIES

(Photo by Frank Veres)

❑ **729, #1-Alien,** a. White enamel & white plastic, black, yellow & red tampos on side & front, thin yellow "Alien" in black box on side, thin white "Alien" in red box on front, black logo in front of rear wheel, metal Thailand base, white int., tinted canopy, 3sp

EX n/a   NM n/a   MIP $8

(Photo by Frank Veres)

❑ **730, #2-'57 Chevy,** a. Gray plastic body w/chrome engine through hood, orange, black, red & white girl tampo on sides, white dotted stripe on roof & trunk, black & white logo on rear fender, dark smoked window, metal Malaysia base, t/b

EX n/a   NM n/a   MIP $3

❑ **731, #3-VW Bug,** a. Pearl white, metal Malaysia base, red, dark blue, light green & black tampos on roof & sides, red & white logo on rear of roof, black int., blue tint window, 5dot

EX n/a   NM n/a   MIP $4

❑ **732, #4-1970 Barracuda,** a. Black enamel, white tampos on hood & sides, orange & blue over white twist on trunk, orange & blue twist w/orange logo on door, day-glo dark orange int. & hood scoop, smoked window, chrome Malaysia base, asw, 3sp

EX n/a   NM n/a   MIP $3

MIXED SIGNALS SERIES

(Photo by Frank Veres)

❑ **733, #1-Street Roader,** Pearl white w/yellow, red & black street sign tampos on sides, yellow int. & spacer between body & metal Malaysia base, black logo above rear wheel, smoked window, alw, ct/b

EX n/a   NM n/a   MIP $2

(Photo by Frank Veres)

❏ **734, #2-'80s Corvette,** Met. green w/black, white & yellow road sign tampos on sides, black int., smoked window w/black top, black logo above rear wheel, metal Malaysia base, asw, bbs
EX n/a NM n/a MIP $2

(Photo by Frank Veres)

❏ **735, #3-Nissan Truck,** Pearl orange w/yellow, red, black & white road sign tampos on sides, black int. & roll bar, clear window, chrome engine, black plastic Malaysia base, white logo above rear wheel, alw, ct/b
EX n/a NM n/a MIP $2

(Photo by Frank Veres)

❏ **736, #4-School Bus,** a. Yellow enamel w/black, red, white & green road sign tampos on sides, black int., clear window, black logo on rear door, black plastic Malaysia base, asw, 5dot
EX n/a NM n/a MIP $3

FLYN' ACES SERIES

(Photo by Frank Veres)

❏ **737, #1-1970 Dodge Daytona Charger,** a. Met. green w/white stripes on hood, red stripe on nose & top of rear wing, white,

gold, black & red tampos on sides, red & black over white logo on rear fender, black int., clear window, tan Malaysia base, asw, 5dot
EX n/a NM n/a MIP $3

(Photo by Frank Veres)

❏ **738, #2-Dogfighter,** a. Black enamel w/white, gold, red & yellow tampos on tail, yellow plastic Malaysia base & prop, chrome seat, engine & suspension, dark red logo on tail, 5dot
EX n/a NM n/a MIP $3

❏ **739, #3-Sol-Aire CX4,** a. Yellow enamel w/black, red & white tampos on nose & rear wing, black & gray stripes w/red & white logo on side, red, white, gold & black tampos on side, black plastic Malaysia base, black int., clear window, 5sp
EX n/a NM n/a MIP $3

(Photo by Frank Veres)

❏ **740, #4-XT-3,** Met. gray w/red, black, green & white tampos, orange painted Malaysia base, black canopy & nose, blue tint metal engine, red & white logo in front of engine on top of side pod, 5sp
EX n/a NM n/a MIP $2

SUGAR RUSH SERIES

(Photo by Frank Veres)

❏ **741, #1-Mazda MX-5 Miata,** a. Orange enamel w/matching orange painted Thailand base, yellow & black "Reese's" tampo on hood, trunk & sides, yellow & black

logo on rear fender, bright yellow headlights & gas cap, black int., smoked window, asw, 5sp
EX n/a NM n/a MIP $5

❏ **742, #2-Funny Car,** White enamel w/brown sides & gray "Hershey's" tampo, small white "Milk Chocolate" & gray logo behind rear wheel, brown stripe w/brown "Milk Chocolate" twice on hood, black window, metal Malaysia base, 5sp
EX n/a NM n/a MIP $5

(Photo by Frank Veres)

❏ **743, #3-'95 Camaro,** Dark met. blue, white stripe on side & hood w/red "Crunch," white "Nestles" on hood, trunk & side, white "Milk Chocolate with Crisped Rice" on door & rear spoiler, red & white logo on front fender behind wheel, black int., clear window, black plastic Malaysia base, alw, 5sp
EX n/a NM n/a MIP $4

(Photo by Frank Veres)

❏ **744, #4-'96 Mustang Convertible,** Yellow enamel w/dark blue stripe on hood & rear spoiler, dark blue, yellow & white "Butterfinger" tampo on sides, dark blue logo behind rear wheel, black int., clear window, metal China base, asw, 5sp
EX n/a NM n/a MIP $5

(Photo by Frank Veres)

❏ **969, #1-'70 Roadrunner,** Yellow enamel, chrome Malaysia base, brown stripe on side w/"Nestle" & "Oh Henry!," red "Oh" on side & trunk, brown "Hot Wheels" logo on rear fender, black int., clear window, 5dot
EX n/a NM n/a MIP $4

(Photo by Frank Veres)

❑ **970, #2-Jaguar XK8,** Red enamel, black plastic Malaysia base, white, brown & yellow "100 GRAND" tampo on side & hood, yellow "Nestle" on trunk by boot, yellow "Hot Wheels" tampo on rear fender, tan int., smoked window & head lights, gbbs
EX n/a　　**NM** n/a　　**MIP** $3

❑ **971, #3-Pikes Peak Celica,** White enamel, black plastic Malaysia base & rear wing, magenta & light blue tampo on side, roof & hood, light green & magenta tampo over "Tarts" on hood & side, magenta "Hot Wheels" logo above rear wheel, black int., clear window, asw, bbs
EX n/a　　**NM** n/a　　**MIP** $3

❑ **972, #4-Dodge Concept Car,** a. White enamel, metal Malaysia base, two blue stripes on trunk, hood & side, red & blue "Nestle Baby Ruth" on hood & side, blue "Hot Wheels" logo on rear fender, blue int., clear window, 5dot
EX n/a　　**NM** n/a　　**MIP** $3

TECH TONES SERIES

(Photo by Frank Veres)

❑ **745, #1-Buick Wildcat,** Black enamel w/green met. inlay, light green plastic Malaysia base, silver painted window, chrome engine, white logo on rear, 3sp
EX n/a　　**NM** n/a　　**MIP** $3

(Photo by Frank Veres)

❑ **746, #2-Silhouette II,** a. Black enamel w/magenta met. inlay, purple plastic Malaysia base, white int., clear canopy, pink chrome engine, white logo on rear canopy, 5dot
EX n/a　　**NM** n/a　　**MIP** $5

(Photo by Frank Veres)

❑ **747, #3-Speed Machine,** Black enamel w/met. gold inlay, metal Malaysia base, gold int., clear canopy, white logo on rear, t/b
EX n/a　　**NM** n/a　　**MIP** $3

(Photo by Frank Veres)

❑ **748, #4-Avus Quattro,** Black enamel w/dark red met. inlay, dark red plastic Malaysia base, white int., clear canopy w/red & black tampos, red logo on rear of canopy, alw, gbbs
EX n/a　　**NM** n/a　　**MIP** $3

1998 TREASURE HUNT SERIES

(Photo by Frank Veres)

❑ **749, #1-Twang Thang,** Black enamel w/blue chrome quitars, chrome engine, exhaust & int., clear window, pearl blue "Treasure Hunt '98" & logo on nose, black plastic Malaysia base, 5sp
EX n/a　　**NM** n/a　　**MIP** $15

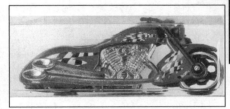

(Photo by Frank Veres)

❑ **750, #2-Scorchin' Scooter,** Met. red w/yellow & black tampo on sides, yellow & black logo on front fender by axle, metal Malaysia engine, black forks, chrome rim w/black spokes
EX n/a　　**NM** n/a　　**MIP** $40

❑ **751, #3-Kenworth T600A,** a. Dark purple pearl, silver, orange & purple tampo w/silver logo on side of sleeper, chrome Malaysia base, black window, alw, 3sp
EX n/a　　**NM** n/a　　**MIP** $25

(Photo by Frank Veres)

❑ **752, #4-3-Window '34,** Orange enamel w/yellow orange & red tampo on sides, orange plastic fenders, black running boards & int., yellow & orange logo in front of rear window, clear window, chrome engine & grille, metal Malaysia base, 5dot
EX n/a　　**NM** n/a　　**MIP** $35

(Photo by Frank Veres)

❑ **753, #5-Turbo Flame,** Chrome w/green, yellow & black side tampo, yellow & black logo behind front wheel, black engine, green tint canopy & rear, chrome int., black painted Malaysia base, 5sp

EX n/a　　**NM** n/a　　**MIP** $15

(Photo by Frank Veres)

❑ **754, #6-Saltflat Racer,** Black plastic body, gold painted Thailand base, gold chrome engine, front drive, int. & roll bar, red & black tampo on front fender, red tint window, red & white logo on front fender, 5sp

EX n/a　　**NM** n/a　　**MIP** $15

(Photo by Frank Veres)

❑ **755, #7-Street Beast,** Red enamel & white plastic, black & gold tampos, white int., red tint window, black logo on rear fender, metal Malaysia base, gbbs

EX n/a　　**NM** n/a　　**MIP** $15

(Photo by Frank Veres)

❑ **756, #8-Road Rocket,** Chrome body w/clear top, black "TH-" & red "98" on side, black & red logo on clear rear wing, black roll bar & engine, metal Malaysia base, 3sp

EX n/a　　**NM** n/a　　**MIP** $15

(Photo by Frank Veres)

❑ **757, #9-Sol-Aire CX4,** Pearl white w/flag tampo on sides, blue w/white stars on nose, flag tampo on top of rear engine cover, blue plastic Malaysia base & int., clear canopy, blue logo behind rear wheel, wbbs

EX n/a　　**NM** n/a　　**MIP** $15

(Photo by Frank Veres)

❑ **758, #10-'57 Chevy,** Met. green metal body & metal engine through hood, gold, black & silver tampo on sides, white & silver logo in front of rear wheel, yellow tint window & int., gold tint Thailand base, 3sp

EX n/a　　**NM** n/a　　**MIP** $35

(Photo by Frank Veres)

❑ **759, #11-Stingray III,** Silver pearl w/black stripes & Corvette logo on hood, black & white tampo on sides, black & white logo on door, black plastic Malaysia base, red int., smoked window, 3sp

EX n/a　　**NM** n/a　　**MIP** $25

(Photo by Frank Veres)

❑ **760, #12-Way 2 Fast,** Mf. olive w/metal Thailand base, orange stripes & white circle w/gold & orange "1" on roof, orange stripe & white circle w/gold & orange "1" on side, gold "Treasure Hunt 98" on roof twice & once on side, white "Treasure Hunt Special" behind rear wheel, orange logo in front of rear wheel, chrome int. & engine, gold plastic radiator shell, 5sp

EX n/a　　**NM** n/a　　**MIP** $20

1999 TREASURE HUNT SERIES

(Photo by Frank Veres)

❑ **929, #1-Mercedes 540K,** Red enamel, metal Malaysia base, gold over black stripe on top of door, black panels w/gold pinstriping on hood & trunk, gold "TR" on trunk, chrome grille & headlights, black plastic top, clear window, asw, 5sp

EX n/a　　**NM** n/a　　**MIP** $25

(Photo by Frank Veres)

❑ **930, #2-T-Bird Stocker,** Blue enamel, gray plastic Malaysia base, black & yellow side tampo w/white & red "12," white "T. HUNTER" on rear fender w/misc. racing decals on side, large white & red "12" on roof, black hood w/white "T. HUNTER" & misc. racing decals, yellow logo on rear fender, yellow int., clear window, asw, 5sp

EX n/a　　**NM** n/a　　**MIP** $10

❑ **931, #3-'97 Corvette,** Pearl lavender, black plastic Thailand base, red & white stripe over gold on hood & side, "Nineteen 98" in black on rocker panel, yellow int., smoked window, alw, 5dot

EX n/a　　**NM** n/a　　**MIP** $25

(Photo by Frank Veres)

❑ **932, #4-Rigor Motor,** Day-glo yellow, black painted metal Malaysia base & exhaust, black, orange & silver flames on top behind chrome engine, white skulls, chrome fuel tank & int., yellow tint canopy, black logo on rear, g5sp

EX n/a　　**NM** n/a　　**MIP** $15

(Photo by Frank Veres)

❑ **933, #5-Ferrari F512M,** a. Yellow enamel, metal Malaysia base, silver "Ferrari" on rear of engine cover, yellow & black rectangle "Ferrari" emblem on front, white & red "TH" emblem on rear plate, red & silver painted taillights, silver & black painted lights in front bumper, black int., clear window, chrome star wheel
EX n/a **NM** n/a **MIP** $20

(Photo by Frank Veres)

❑ **934, #6-'59 Impala,** Met. purple, gold tint chrome Malaysia base, pearl purple, red, gold & black tampo on side & hood, "99 Treasure Hunt" in gold & black on door, gold logo on rear fender, white int., smoked window, gbbs
EX n/a **NM** n/a **MIP** $20

(Photo by Frank Veres)

❑ **935, #7-Hot Wheels 500,** Black enamel, metal Malaysia base, large orange & white "1" w/"Treasure Hunt" logo & orange name on side, orange tampo on nose w/black & white "1," orange "Treasure Hunt ninety-nine" on front wing, red & white "Hot Wheels" logo on rear wing, black plastic driver, orange letter "Treasure Hunt ninety-nine" with black 7sp wheels
EX n/a **NM** n/a **MIP** $15

(Photo by Frank Veres)

❑ **936, #8-Jaguar D-Type,** Met. black w/matching painted Malaysia base, red & gold stripe on side, gold, red & black over white "TH" on hood, gold plastic int. & side pipes, clear window, alw, 5sp
EX n/a **NM** n/a **MIP** $15

(Photo by Frank Veres)

❑ **937, #9-'32 Ford Delivery,** Met. gold, purple plastic fenders & int., clear window, black panels w/red pinstripe & yellow tampos on sides, white & red "T. HUNTER" on door, black panel on roof w/yellow pinstripe & red diamond pattern, black panels w/red pinstripe on hood & cowl, gold chrome headlights & grille, metal Malaysia base, yellow logo on bottom right of door, g5sp
EX n/a **NM** n/a **MIP** $15

(Photo by Frank Veres)

❑ **938, #10-Hot Seat,** Clear plastic, metal Malaysia base, black seat & plunger, 5sp
EX n/a **NM** n/a **MIP** $15

(Photo by Frank Veres)

❑ **939, #11-Mustang Mach I,** Met. green, black plastic Malaysia base, silver stripe on side, black "TH" tampo on rear fender, black int., rear spoiler, hood scoop & rear window louvers, clear window, 5sp
EX n/a **NM** n/a **MIP** $25

(Photo by Frank Veres)

❑ **940, #12-Express Lane,** Purple plastic body, "Hot Wheels" logo on side w/gold "Treasure Hunt," black plastic seat & butterfly steering wheel, metal Malaysia base, engine & pushbar, g5sp
EX n/a **NM** n/a **MIP** $20

BUGGIN' OUT SERIES

(Photo by Frank Veres)

❑ **941, #1-Treadator,** a. Red enamel, yellow plastic side scoops & nose, chrome fenders, drive wheels, engine, exhaust & canopy, yellow, silver & black Ant tampo on side of rear wing, yellow, silver & black "Anteater" tampo on top of rear wing, black plastic Thailand base & treads, yellow logo on side between scoop & exhaust
EX n/a **NM** n/a **MIP** $3

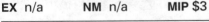

(Photo by Frank Veres)

❑ **942, #2-Shadow Jet II,** Gray plastic body, metal Malaysia base, green, yellow & black tampo on side & top, green & yellow "Stinger" below tampo, yellow "Hot Wheels" logo behind rear wheel, yellow int., green tint canopy, 5sp
EX n/a **NM** n/a **MIP** $3

(Photo by Frank Veres)

❑ **943, #3-Radar Ranger,** Met. purple, metal Malaysia base, yellow, black & white spider web & spider tampo on side & top of right side pod, black radar dish, blue plastic inserts & seat, blue tint canopy, alw, ct/b

EX n/a   **NM** n/a   **MIP** $3

❑ **944, #4-Baja Bug,** a. Light met. blue, metal Malaysia base, light yellow, orange & black tampos on front & side, light yellow logo in front of rear wheel, orange int., 5sp

EX n/a   **NM** n/a   **MIP** $6

X-RAY CRUISER SERIES

❑ **945, #1-Mercedes C-Class,** a. Met. black, black plastic Malaysia base, silver & very light purple tampos, silver & purple logo on rear fender, white int., yellow int. window, asw, gbbs

EX n/a   **NM** n/a   **MIP** $8

(Photo by Frank Veres)

❑ **946, #2-Lamborghini Diablo,** Met. teal, teal plastic rear wing, black painted Malaysia base, silver & black tampos on side & front, gray int., smoked window, 5sp

EX n/a   **NM** n/a   **MIP** $3

❑ **947, #3-'67 Camaro,** a. Blue enamel, metal Malaysia base, yellow, red & white tampos on hood, roof & sides, red & yellow flames on side, white logo on rear roof pillar above wheel, white int., tinted window, 5sp

EX n/a   **NM** n/a   **MIP** $7

(Photo by Frank Veres)

❑ **948, #4-Jaguar XJ220,** Yellow enamel, black plastic Malaysia base, black tampos on front & sides, blue int., clear window, black logo behind rear wheel, 3sp

EX n/a   **NM** n/a   **MIP** $3

(Photo by Frank Veres)

❑ **1114, #1-'63 Corvette,** Black met., gold chrome Malaysia 2 rivet base, silver & gold tampos on hood & sides, silver logo on rear fender, tan int., clear window, g5sp

EX n/a   **NM** n/a   **MIP** $6

STREET ART SERIES

(Photo by Frank Veres)

❑ **949, #1-Mini Truck,** Met. black, black plastic base, orange, gold & white tampos on hood & side, white & black "Mini Truck" on hood & door, black & white, "Hot Wheels" logo on side behind door, chrome engine, exhaust, grille & speakers, black int., clear window, t/b

EX n/a   **NM** n/a   **MIP** $3

(Photo by Frank Veres)

❑ **950, #2-Propper Chopper,** Met. green, black plastic Malaysia base, rotors & tail, green, black & gold tampos, white & black logo above rear window, black int., yellow tint window

EX n/a   **NM** n/a   **MIP** $4

❑ **951, #3-Ambulance,** a. Met. purple, chrome Malaysia base, blue, white, green & black tampos on side, black & white "Speedy" & large white & green "Hot Wheels" logo on side, purple int. & rear doors, orange tint window & light bar on roof, asw, 5sp

EX n/a   **NM** n/a   **MIP** $4

(Photo by Frank Veres)

❑ **952, #4-School Bus,** a. Yellow enamel, black plastic Malaysia base, no rear door, orange, black & gold tampo on side, orange logo behind rear wheel, yellow int., red tint window, asw, 5dot

EX n/a   **NM** n/a   **MIP** $8

PINSTRIPE POWER SERIES

(Photo by Frank Veres)

❑ **953, #1-3-Window '34,** Dark met. purple, light purple plastic fenders, black plastic running

boards & int., gold & silver pinstripe tampo on side, silver logo behind side window, chrome engine grille & headlights, metal Malaysia base, blue tint window, 5sp
EX n/a   **NM** n/a   **MIP** $5

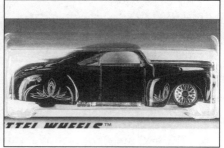
(Photo by Frank Veres)

❑ **954, #2-Tail Dragger,** Black enamel, metal Malaysia base, silver & gold pinstripe tampos on hood, fenders & trunk, gold logo on rear fender, tan int., clear window, bbs
EX n/a   **NM** n/a   **MIP** $4

(Photo by Frank Veres)

❑ **955, #3-'65 Impala,** Met. light green, gold tint chrome Malaysia base, silver & gold pinstripe tampos on hood & side, gold logo on rear fender, tan int., smoked window, asw, gbbs
EX n/a   **NM** n/a   **MIP** $4

(Photo by Frank Veres)

❑ **956, #4-Auburn 852,** Black enamel & silver met., white plastic fenders, gold & black pinstripe tampos on hood & trunk, black logo on trunk behind seat, metal Malaysia base, chrome headlights, grille & steering wheel, white int., clear window, asw, bbs
EX n/a   **NM** n/a   **MIP** $3

GAME OVER SERIES

(Photo by Frank Veres)

❑ **957, #1-Lean Machine,** Black enamel & purple plastic, metal Malaysia base, yellow, green, black & silver side tampos, green logo on top behind black canopy, 5sp
EX n/a   **NM** n/a   **MIP** $3

(Photo by Frank Veres)

❑ **958, #2-Shadow Jet,** Yellow enamel, metal Malaysia base, pearl blue, red, white & black tampos on side top rear, two black "Hot Wheels" logos on rear wing, chrome engine & fuel tank, yellow int., smoked canopy, 5sp
EX n/a   **NM** n/a   **MIP** $3

(Photo by Frank Veres)

❑ **959, #3-Speed Blaster,** a. Light green enamel, day-glo yellow plastic Malaysia base, green "Dino," yellow "HUNT" on side w/green, yellow, gold & black tampo, green, yellow, gold & black tampo on hood & roof, gold tint chrome window & rear engine, gt/b
EX n/a   **NM** n/a   **MIP** $2

(Photo by Frank Veres)

❑ **960, #4-Twin Mill II,** Pearl pink, black plastic Malaysia base, yellow & black tampo on side & top of front fenders, black & white "FINAL FIGHT IV FIGHT2DAFINISH" tampo on side w/black & white men w/blue boxing gloves, yellow & black "FF IV" on nose, roof has black & white over yellow man with blue boxing gloves and black "Hot Wheels" logo, chrome engine, alw-bbs
EX n/a   **NM** n/a   **MIP** $3

SURF 'N FUN SERIES

(KP Photo)

❑ **961, #1-'40s Woodie,** Met. purple fenders & hood, tan plastic body, black roof w/yellow, orange & white tampo, black over white tampo on top of front fenders, right front fender has yellow & orange flower tampo, chrome engine & grille, metal Malaysia base, white "Hot Wheels" logo on roof by windshield, black int., blue tint window, 5sp
EX n/a   **NM** n/a   **MIP** $4

(Photo by Frank Veres)

❑ **962, #2-VW Bug,** Light pearl blue, metal Malaysia base, white, light green & dark blue tampo on roof & side, "Olas del Sol" in white on roof & side in tampo, white "Hot Wheels" logo on side between rear fender & door, white int., smoked window, 5sp

EX n/a   NM n/a   MIP $5

(Photo by Frank Veres)

❑ **963, #3-'55 Chevy,** Met. red, chrome Malaysia base, white, light blue & dark blue wave tampo on side & hood, "Ride Yourself Wild" tampo on roof, "Ride Yourself Wild," "Macon" & "Spike Surfboards" tampos on side, light blue "Hot Wheels" logo on front fender above wheel, black window, 3sp

EX n/a   NM n/a   MIP $4

(Photo by Frank Veres)

❑ **964, #4-Chevy Nomad,** a. Pearl white, metal Malaysia base, long black & gold racing stripe in center of hood that goes over the hood almost to the grille, gold & black "West Side" with emblem on hood & rear fender, black & gold racing stripe down side w/"Spike Surfboards" over red & black flames, black "Hot Wheels" logo on rear fender by rear pillar, white int., smoked window, g5sp

EX n/a   NM n/a   MIP $8

X-TREME SPEED SERIES

(Photo by Frank Veres)

❑ **965, #1-Dodge Sidewinder,** White enamel, black plastic Malaysia base, purple, light green & dark blue tampos on hood & side, purple logo on driver's side rear fender, purple int. & bed cover, smoked window, 5sp

EX n/a   NM n/a   MIP $3

❑ **966, #2-Callaway C7,** a. Light green enamel, black plastic Malaysia base, yellow, white & black side

tampo, black tampo in center of hood, black int., rear wing, cowl & headlights, clear window, white "Hot Wheels" logo on driver's side rear fender, t/b

EX n/a   NM n/a   MIP $3

(Photo by Frank Veres)

❑ **967, #3-Porsche Carrera,** Silver pearl, metal Malaysia base, black, red & white tampos on hood & side, white "Hot Wheels" logo on rear fender above rear tire, white int., tinted window, g5sp

EX n/a   NM n/a   MIP $3

(Photo by Frank Veres)

❑ **968, #4-Mazda MX-5 Miata,** Blue enamel w/matching painted metal Malaysia base, black, yellow & pearl light green tampos on hood & side, pearl light green tampo on trunk, black "Hot Wheels" logo on hood, day-glo green int., clear window, asw, bbs

EX n/a   NM n/a   MIP $3

MEGA GRAPHICS SERIES

(Photo by Frank Veres)

❑ **973, #1-Funny Car,** Day-glo yellow, metal Malaysia base, black & gray tampo on side w/black & orange "3" and orange & gray "Team Bousquette" black over day-glo yellow on hood, orange "Hot Wheels" logo on hood next to blower, yellow tint window, 5sp

EX n/a   NM n/a   MIP $5

❑ **974, #2-Mustang Cobra,** a. Pearl white black plastic Malaysia base, black, silver & orange tampos on roof, hood & side, orange

"Hot Wheels" logo on right side of roof by windshield, black int., clear window, asw, t/b

EX n/a   NM n/a   MIP $3

(Photo by Frank Veres)

❑ **975, #3-Turbo Flame,** Black plastic body, red painted Malaysia base, yellow, gold & red tampos on side & behind gold chrome engine, red "Hot Wheels" logo above front wheel, black int., yellow tint canopy & rear, g5sp

EX n/a   NM n/a   MIP $3

(Photo by Frank Veres)

❑ **976, #4-Firebird Funny Car,** Dark purple met. (looks black), blue tint metal Malaysia base, side has large white, pearl rose & orange "Hot Wheels" logo over wide white stripes, large black, white & pearl rose "1" w/orange & black "F/C" and orange "Team Handy," two white panels on hood w/large black, white & pearl rose "1" and orange & black "F/C," orange "Team Handy" w/white "Racing" on nose, smoked window, b5sp

EX n/a   NM n/a   MIP $5

TERRORIFIC SERIES

(Photo by Frank Veres)

❑ **977, #1-At-A-Tude,** Met. green, black plastic Malaysia base & rear wing, light green w/black outline "Freaks Of Horror" & Wolfman face w/white lightning bolts on hood & side, orange lettering & swirl on side, black "Hot Wheels" logo below orange swirl on hood left of Wolfman face, chrome int. & engine, green tint window, b5sp

EX n/a   NM n/a   MIP $3

(Photo by Frank Veres)

❏ **978, #2-Cat-A-Pult,** Orange enamel, metal Malaysia base, green & black "Hunchback of Los Angeles" tampo on hood & side, black "Hot Wheels" logo in front of rear wheel, black int., smoked window, asw, 5sp
EX n/a   NM n/a   MIP $3

❏ **979, #3-Sweet 16 II,** a. Black enamel, metal Malaysia base, purple, red, white & black side tampo, purple, white & black tampo on hood, red "Hot Wheels" logo above rear tire, gold tint chrome engine & front drive, yellow tint canopy, 5sp
EX n/a   NM n/a   MIP $4

(Photo by Frank Veres)

❏ **980, #4-Splittin' Image II,** Met. gold, black plastic Malaysia base, red, green & black side tampos, small "Hot Wheels" logo in front of rear wheel, pink tint chrome canopy, engine & exhaust, 3sp
EX n/a   NM n/a   MIP $3

CLASSIC GAMES SERIES

(Photo by Frank Veres)

❏ **981, #1-Super Modified,** Pearl light blue, metal Malaysia base & engine, purple & white "Ker Plunk" on top panel & side, orange, purple & light green tampos on top panel, white "Hot Wheels" logo on side behind rear tire, purple "Classic Games" on orange oval behind front wheel, black int., roll cage, rear push bar, rear & front wings, gbbs2
EX n/a   NM n/a   MIP $3

(Photo by Frank Veres)

❏ **982, #2-Silhouette II,** Silver-blue pearl, black plastic Malaysia base, magenta & white "Toss Across" tampo on side, magenta & light blue stripes on hood, chrome engine, magenta "Hot Wheels" logo behind front wheel, white int., blue tint canopy, 5dot
EX n/a   NM n/a   MIP $2

❏ **983, #3-Sol-Aire CX4,** White enamel, black plastic Malaysia base, blue & red "Skip-Bo" tampos on top of rear wing & side, Skip-Bo emblem on nose & in front of rear wheel, blue "Hot Wheels" logo behind rear wheel, black int., blue tint window, 3sp
EX n/a   NM n/a   MIP $2

(Photo by Frank Veres)

❏ **984, #4-Escort Rally,** Red enamel, gray plastic Malaysia base, yellow, white & purple "UNO" on hood & door, yellow, red, black & white side tampos, yellow "Hot Wheels" logo on rear fender behind rear wheel, black int., clear window & rear spoiler, asw, bbs
EX n/a   NM n/a   MIP $8

CAR-TOON FRIENDS SERIES

(Photo by Frank Veres)

❏ **985, #1-Saltflat Racer,** Purple plastic body, silver painted Malaysia base, black & white "Natasha Fatale" tampos on top & side, red & white "Hot Wheels" logo above red dynomite stick on side, chrome int., roll bar, engine & front drive, clear canopy, 5sp
EX n/a   NM n/a   MIP $3

(Photo by Frank Veres)

❏ **986, #2-XT-3,** Orange enamel, black painted Malaysia base, white, black & gray "Rocky" tampos on top & side, blue tint metal engine, black "Hot Wheels" logo on left side top panel, black canopy & nose, g5sp
EX n/a   NM n/a   MIP $3

❏ **987, #3-Double Vision,** a. Black enamel, black plastic Malaysia base, red, white & yellow tampos w/picture of Bullwinkle on side, yellow stripe around white & orange "Bullwinkle" behind engines, gray engines, chrome blowers white "Hot Wheels" logo above front wheel, gray seat, clear canopy, gbbs
EX n/a   NM n/a   MIP $3

(KP Photo, Tom Michael collection)

❏ **988, #4-Lakester,** White & black enamel, black painted Malaysia base, black & white picture of Boris on top w/orange "Hot Wheels" logo, white & orange "The Bomb" w/black bomb on side, chrome engine & int., red tint canopy, alw-5sp
EX n/a   NM n/a   MIP $2

Hot Wheels Redlines 1968-1977

Surf's Up! The Deora, (#6210), was one of the original sixteen models in Hot Wheel's introductory year.

It's tough to imagine the world of die-cast cars before Hot Wheels. Until then, miniature vehicles were realistic, detailed, frequently British and…. Slow. Mattel changed all that in 1968 when sixteen new (and fast) cars hit the market.

Ruth Handler, Mattel's co-founder, knew that die-cast cars were popular, but wondered how her company could improve on them. Jack Ryan, head of Research and Development, was put in charge of the project. His team consisted of Harvey LaBranch, Howard Newman and Harry Bradley (replaced by Ira Gilford in 1967). The group designed sixteen cars that changed the world forever.

Based on popular and customized cars of the period, Hot Wheels cars featured thin axles and lightweight "mag" wheels that zoomed down the bright orange tracks (wisely marketed right away when the cars were released) so familiar to die-cast fans, (i.e. kids) across the country.

Mattel must have known they had a hit, because soon enough, they were backlogged with orders for months. These original cars, called "redlines" (but described in the 1967 catalog as "Red Stripe Slicks") because of the stripe around their tires, have become wildly popular and extremely pricey—especially mint-in-pack examples.

There seems to be some overlap in vintage redlines collecting and current numbered pack collectors. Newer collectors will save up for a nice (if slightly expensive) redlines model, and redlines collectors have been known to pick up a new model off the pegs, especially when it's a re-issue of a favorite old casting.

Condition, naturally, is key here. There are plenty of redlines-era Hot Wheels with bent or dished axles, massively chipped paint, and missing decals. (Mostly in my collection.) Therefore, the pricing structure for this section is near mint (no pack) or mint-in-package.

Also, bear in mind that the original "Spectraflame" colored models (a kind of chromed paint) are the most valuable. After 1973, Mattel used a duller, but longer-lasting, enamel paint.

Hot Wheels collectors are everywhere—they're probably in your school or workplace—but a quick scan online can help locate clubs near you. And, even online exchanges can help you find elusive pieces to round out your collection.

This Ford J-Car, (#6214), shows some playwear, and the classic bowed axles that so many redlines have as a result of cruising down orange racetracks.

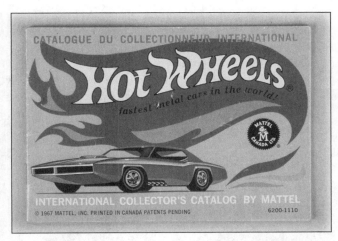

A Canadian edition of the 1967 introductory catalog. The first sixteen redlines were shown as illustrations rather than photos, common in the late 1960s.

While not the holy grail of VW Buses, this side-loading Volkswagen Beach Bomb, (#6274), is still a nice item to find. Originally packaged with decal sheets, so you customize your own surfin' machine.

The Moving Van, (#6455), was part of the "Heavyweights" series. The castings for these beauties feel pretty substantial—even when accompanied by plastic (or mostly plastic) trailers.

This Twinmill, (#6258), also shows the bowed axles so common on not-so-mint early Hot Wheels.

Opening features, like hoods and doors, are always a favorite. This Custom Barracuda, (#6211), shows off a realistic engine. Many of these early models had detailed underbodies and suspensions as well.

The color of Hot Wheels money

By Angelo Van Bogart

All colors aren't equal, at least in the world of Redline Hot Wheels collecting. And, even when a desirable car in an equally desirable color does surface, the overall condition of the car and its paint play an extremely important in the car's value to a collector. The advent of the Internet auction trading pool has added a fresh level of convenience in searching for rare, vintage cars, as well as selling them. This too, also allowed collectors to become even pickier when it comes to finding cars to add to their collection, so determining values and condition has become more important than ever. That, presumably, is why you are holding this book in your hands.

Ironically, it seems big boys and girls prefer their Hot Wheels in pink, unusual for a toy considered so masculine. Plus, they typically have no problem paying for it, often doling out money that would buy several examples of the same casting in the same condition. Why? The feminine color was obviously not very popular with boys when the cars were new, and many long-time collectors believe few Hot Wheels were painted pink. Of course, most castings have a color that will attract a premium, but it tends to vary; what is common in one casting may be rare for a different casting. For instance, the price of a magenta Evil Weevil is one of the castings highest, but an Old in the same color fetches one of the castings lowest values.

Now, before you pull out your wallet and lay out a small fortune for that pink Redline Olds, an understanding of grading the spectraflame paint's condition is critical. Time can be devastating to the highly metallic, sometimes almost chrome-like, paint surface of the early Redline Hot Wheels. That's just the start, too. The presence and condition of decals on cars that should have them also affect the car's value. Heck, even the manner in which these decals (crooked or even incorrectly) have been applied to the car weighs heavily on the car's value. It is not out of the question to find these cars with a value that is 70 to 80 percent that of a Mint loose example.

Time punishes Hot Wheels' trademark paint with chipping, flecking, and toning, but only the first can be credited to the love and play of children. The latter two are found on cars that have never even left their packages in past (or less) 35 years. Toning, characterized by dark splotches, affects nearly every color applied to the Hot Wheels casting, regardless of whether the car ever left its package. The same goes is true for the flaw collectors call "flecking," the pin-sized chips that flake off the spectraflame-painted cars. Hot Wheels suffering these flaws, even to an average degree, usually find themselves with half the value of a mint-in-pack example, sometimes more. Missing paint, especially in severe circumstances, is definitely the most value-affecting flaw; expect to pay only 10 to 30 percent of the Mint price when a car is missing 50 percent or more of its paint. These cars also tend to have other flaws to their bases, wheels, and glass, which must also account for this low pricing.

A defect that seems to be isolated to one color, at least in my experience, is corrosion to light blue Olds 442 castings. When this happens, the paint does the opposite of toning and the car's finish develops white splotches. These cancerous spots are like leprosy to collectors who typically fear the damage cannot be reversed, even in an expensive restoration. These cars tend to fetch, on average, about 20 to 30 percent the value of a Mint example of the same color.

Because value is so dependent on a Redline car's condition, and so many flaws can develop through time, some collectors take matters into their own hands and restore cars back to new condition. While there definitely is room for these enthusiasts in the collecting field, especially the talented artisans, these cars are not nearly as valuable as examples in equally mint, or even lesser, condition, so beware for collectors trying to pass off restored cars as counterfeits. Look for clues of disassembly, such as poor alignment and tampered rivets, and flaws, and you will be able to get what you pay for.

As with any large purchase, research is the key to a pleasant transaction. Use these tips to know what to look for and make your Redline purchase an intelligent one that your pocketbook won't regret.

Angelo Van Bogart is an associate editor of Old Cars Weekly and writes the "Hot Wheels Hunting" column in Toy Cars and Models magazine. He is currently hunting some great old Redlines models to add to his collection.

The Sand Drifter, (#7651), was a later-era redlines, appearing in 1975. Notice the enamel color—a cost-saving measure introduced by Mattel in 1973.

The enamel-painted Sweet Sixteen, (#6007), was another example of a souped-up older car. This one even kept a redline wheel to spare!

Another favorite with collectors, the Classic Cord, (#6472), included a removable roof—often missing on examples found today.

Short Order, (#6176), had an extending plastic tailgate, which is usually missing on playworn models today. An interesting hod rod version of a vintage Ford pickup.

Snorkel, (#6020), another truck in the Heavyweights series, was a 1971 release.

S'cool Bus, (#6468), was (and still is) an extremely popular model—leading to quite a few re-releases since its introduction in 1971.

The Custom AMX, (#6267), an early Redlines with an opening hood and detailed engine. Hot Wheels' muscle cars are some of the most actively collected models, and little wonder. They are very accurate replicas of the real thing, and to think—they were once considered "just toys!"

Volkswagen Beetles are just the perfect platform for customization, as many real and die-cast models show. One of the coolest modified bugs is the "Evil Weevil," (#6471), a 1971 release.

REDLINES

❑ **Alive '55,** 1973, assorted, Model No. 6968
EX n/a　　**NM** $125　　**MIP** $600

❑ **Alive '55,** 1974, blue, Model No. 6968
EX n/a　　**NM** $90　　**MIP** $350

❑ **Alive '55,** 1974, green, Model No. 6968
EX n/a　　**NM** $50　　**MIP** $110

❑ **Alive '55,** 1977, chrome, red-line, Model No. 9210
EX n/a　　**NM** $15　　**MIP** $55

(KP Photo)

❑ **Ambulance,** 1970, assorted, Model No. 6451
EX n/a　　**NM** $30　　**MIP** $75

(KP Photo)

❑ **American Hauler,** 1976, blue metal cab, white plastic box with American-flag style graphics and "American Hauler" lettering, Model No. 9118
EX n/a　　**NM** $30　　**MIP** $70

(KP Photo)

❑ **American Tipper,** 1976, red metal cab, white plastic tipper bed with American flag graphics, Model No. 9089
EX n/a　　**NM** $25　　**MIP** $65

(KP Photo)

❑ **American Victory,** 1975, light blue with American flag design and number "9" on sides, silver interior and exposed engine, Model No. 7662
EX n/a　　**NM** $20　　**MIP** $60

(KP Photo)

❑ **AMX/2,** 1971, assorted colors, rear engine covers lift up. Name changed to "Xploder" in 1973, Model No. 6460
EX n/a　　**NM** $40　　**MIP** $150

(KP Photo)

❑ **Backwoods Bomb,** 1975, Light blue body with green striping along the sides, plastic camper shell on bed, silver base, Model No. 7670
EX n/a　　**NM** $40　　**MIP** $125

❑ **Baja Bruiser,** 1974, yellow, magenta in tampo, Model No. 8258
EX n/a　　**NM** $300　**MIP** $1200

❑ **Baja Bruiser,** 1974, orange, Model No. 8258
EX n/a　　**NM** $30　　**MIP** $90

❑ **Baja Bruiser,** 1974, yellow, blue in tampo, Model No. 8258
EX n/a　　**NM** $300　**MIP** $1200

❑ **Baja Bruiser,** 1976, light green, Model No. 8258
EX n/a　　**NM** $400　**MIP** $1300

❑ **Baja Bruiser,** 1977, blue, red-line or blackwall, Model No. 8258
EX n/a　　**NM** $25　　**MIP** $85

(KP Photo)

❑ **Beatnik Bandit,** 1968, assorted, Model No. 6217
EX n/a　　**NM** $15　　**MIP** $65

(KP Photo)

❑ **Boss Hoss,** 1970, chrome, Club Kit, Model No. 6499
EX n/a　　**NM** $50　　**MIP** $160

(KP Photo)

❑ **Boss Hoss,** 1971, assorted, Model No. 6406
EX n/a　　**NM** $125　**MIP** $300

(KP Photo)

❑ **Brabham-Repco F1,** 1969, assorted colors, long tailpipe on silver engine, Model No. 6264
EX n/a   **NM** $20   **MIP** $65

(KP Photo)

❑ **Breakaway Bucket,** 1974, dark blue with orange designs, Model No. 8263
EX n/a   **NM** n/a   **MIP** $120

(KP Photo)

❑ **Bugeye,** 1971, assorted, Model No. 6178
EX n/a   **NM** $30   **MIP** $75

❑ **Buzz Off,** 1973, assorted, Model No. 6976
EX n/a   **NM** $110   **MIP** $500

❑ **Buzz Off,** 1974, blue, Model No. 6976
EX n/a   **NM** $30   **MIP** $90

❑ **Buzz Off,** 1977, gold plated, redline or blackwall, Model No. 6976
EX n/a   **NM** $15   **MIP** $30

(KP Photo)

❑ **Bye-Focal,** 1971, assorted, with opening hood. Called "Show-Off" in 1973, Model No. 6187
EX n/a   **NM** $125   **MIP** $400

(KP Photo)

❑ **Carabo,** 1970, assorted, Model No. 6420
EX n/a   **NM** $35   **MIP** $80

❑ **Carabo,** 1974, yellow, Model No. 7617
EX n/a   **NM** $500   **MIP** $1400

(KP Photo)

❑ **Carabo,** 1974, Light green with blue and red stripes, opening gull-wing style doors, Model No. 7617
EX n/a   **NM** $35   **MIP** $100

(KP Photo)

❑ **Cement Mixer,** 1970, assorted colors for cab and chassis, orange plastic cement mixer with Hot Wheels logo. Part of the "Heavy-weights" series, Model No. 6452
EX n/a   **NM** $30   **MIP** $100

(KP Photo)

❑ **Chaparral 2G,** 1969, assorted, Model No. 6256
EX n/a   **NM** $20   **MIP** $75

❑ **Chief's Special Cruiser,** 1977, red, redline, Model No. 7665
EX n/a   **NM** $25   **MIP** $65

(KP Photo)

❑ **Classic '31 Ford Woody,** 1969, assorted, Model No. 6251
EX n/a   **NM** $30   **MIP** $90

(KP Photo)

❑ **Classic '32 Ford Vicky,** 1969, assorted, Model No. 6250
EX n/a   **NM** $30   **MIP** $95

❑ **Classic '36 Ford Coupe,** 1969, blue, Model No. 6253
EX n/a   **NM** $20   **MIP** $60

(KP Photo)

❑ **Classic '36 Ford Coupe,** 1969, assorted, Model No. 6253
EX n/a   **NM** $35   **MIP** $100

(KP Photo)

HOT WHEELS / REDLINES

❑ **Classic '57 T-Bird,** 1969, assorted, Model No. 6252
EX n/a   **NM** $30   **MIP** $110

(KP Photo)

❑ **Classic Cord,** 1971, assorted colors, opening hood, detachable plastic soft-top roof (often missing), Model No. 6472
EX n/a   **NM** n/a   **MIP** $100

(KP Photo)

❑ **Classic Nomad,** 1970, assorted, Model No. 6404
EX n/a   **NM** $55   **MIP** $150

(KP Photo)

❑ **Cockney Cab,** 1971, assorted, Model No. 6466
EX n/a   **NM** $50   **MIP** $210

(KP Photo)

❑ **Cool One,** 1976, Magenta body, "Cool One" letting on front,

lightning tampo on body. Available as blackwalls variation, Model No. 9120
EX n/a   **NM** $30   **MIP** $60

(KP Photo)

❑ **Custom AMX,** 1969, assorted, Model No. 6267
EX n/a   **NM** $100   **MIP** $225

(KP Photo)

❑ **Custom Barracuda,** 1968, assorted, Model No. 6211
EX n/a   **NM** $80   **MIP** $400

(KP Photo)

❑ **Custom Camaro,** 1968, assorted, Model No. 6208
EX n/a   **NM** $100   **MIP** $450

(KP Photo)

❑ **Custom Charger,** 1969, Assorted body colors, white plastic interior, opening hood, Model No. 6268
EX n/a   **NM** $100   **MIP** $250

(KP Photo)

❑ **Custom Continental Mark III,** 1969, assorted, Model No. 6266
EX n/a   **NM** $35   **MIP** $80

(KP Photo)

❑ **Custom Corvette,** 1968, assorted, Model No. 6215
EX n/a   **NM** $90   **MIP** $300

(KP Photo)

❑ **Custom Cougar,** 1968, assorted, Model No. 6205
EX n/a   **NM** $80   **MIP** $275

(KP Photo)

❑ **Custom El Dorado,** 1968, assorted, Model No. 6218
EX n/a   **NM** $50   **MIP** $145

(KP Photo)

❏ **Custom Firebird,** 1968, assorted, Model No. 6212
EX n/a　　**NM** $50　　**MIP** $250

(KP Photo)

❏ **Custom Fleetside,** 1968, assorted, Model No. 6213
EX n/a　　**NM** $60　　**MIP** $250

(KP Photo)

❏ **Custom Mustang,** 1968, assorted, Model No. 6206
EX n/a　　**NM** $85　　**MIP** $450

(KP Photo)

❏ **Custom Mustang,** 1968, assorted w/open hood scoops or louvered windows, Model No. 6206
EX n/a　　**NM** $400　　**MIP** $1400

(KP Photo)

❏ **Custom Police Cruiser,** 1969, Black and white paint scheme on a Plymouth with "Police" and star tampos, red dome light. A nice companion car to the the 6469 Fire Chief Cruiser, Model No. 6269
EX n/a　　**NM** $65　　**MIP** $205

(KP Photo)

❏ **Custom T-Bird,** 1968, assorted, with opening hood, Model No. 6207
EX n/a　　**NM** $50　　**MIP** $165

(KP Photo)

❏ **Custom VW Bug,** 1968, Beetle with oversized engine, sunroof, assorted colors, Model No. 6220
EX n/a　　**NM** $30　　**MIP** $125

(KP Photo)

❏ **Demon,** 1970, assorted colors. Called "Prowler" in 1973, Model No. 6401
EX n/a　　**NM** $25　　**MIP** $50

(KP Photo)

❏ **Deora,** 1968, assorted, Model No. 6210
EX n/a　　**NM** $60　　**MIP** $375

❏ **Double Header,** 1973, assorted, Model No. 5880
EX n/a　　**NM** $120　　**MIP** $450

(KP Photo)

❏ **Double Vision,** 1973, assorted finishes, flip-up plastic canopy over the seats, rear engine, Model No. 6975
EX n/a　　**NM** $110　　**MIP** $400

(KP Photo)

❏ **Dump Truck,** 1970-72, metal cab and chassis, unpainted base, plastic dump truck bed, part of the Heavyweights series, Model No. 6453
EX n/a　　**NM** $25　　**MIP** $50

HOT WHEELS / REDLINES

HOT WHEELS / REDLINES

(KP Photo)

❏ **Dune Daddy,** 1973, assorted, Model No. 6967
EX n/a   **NM** $110   **MIP** $400

(KP Photo)

❏ **El Rey Special,** 1974, Green with yellow and red "Dunlop" and number "1" tampos. Silver metal base, Model No. 8273
EX n/a   **NM** $50   **MIP** $120

❏ **El Rey Special,** 1974, light green, Model No. 8273
EX n/a   **NM** $75   **MIP** $175

❏ **El Rey Special,** 1974, dark blue, Model No. 8273
EX n/a   **NM** $225   **MIP** $900

(KP Photo)

❏ **Evil Weevil,** 1971, assorted, Model No. 6471
EX n/a   **NM** $75   **MIP** $150

(KP Photo)

❏ **Ferrari 312P,** 1970, assorted, Model No. 6417
EX n/a   **NM** $30   **MIP** $60

❏ **Ferrari 312P,** 1973, assorted, Model No. 6973
EX n/a   **NM** $300   **MIP** $1100

(KP Photo)

❏ **Ferrari 512-S,** 1972, assorted, featured opening rear hood and cockpit, Model No. 6021
EX n/a   **NM** $75   **MIP** $250

(KP Photo)

❏ **Fire Chief Cruiser,** 1970, red Plymouth Fury--matches Custom Police Cruiser, #6269, Model No. 6469
EX n/a   **NM** $30   **MIP** $85

(KP Photo)

❏ **Fire Engine,** 1970, red, Model No. 6454
EX n/a   **NM** $25   **MIP** $100

(KP Photo)

❏ **Ford J-Car,** 1968, assorted, Model No. 6214
EX n/a   **NM** $20   **MIP** $70

(KP Photo)

❏ **Ford MK IV,** 1969, assorted, Model No. 6257
EX n/a   **NM** $15   **MIP** $60

(KP Photo)

❏ **Fuel Tanker,** 1971, White cab and chassis, with plastic fuel tanker section and removable fuel hoses. Part of the "Heavyweights" series, Model No. 6018
EX n/a   **NM** $75   **MIP** $200

(KP Photo)

❏ **Funny Money,** 1972, gray armored car body on funny car chassis, orange plastic bumper (usually missing), "Funny Money" labels, Model No. 6005
EX n/a   **NM** $70   **MIP** $335

(KP Photo)

❑ **Grass Hopper,** 1971, assorted, shown here without white plastic canopy, Model No. 6461
EX n/a　　**NM** $45　　**MIP** $100

(KP Photo)

❑ **Grass Hopper,** 1974, light green, Model No. 7621
EX n/a　　**NM** $40　　**MIP** $100

❑ **Grass Hopper,** 1975, light green, no engine, Model No. 7622
EX n/a　　**NM** $90　　**MIP** $350

❑ **Gremlin Grinder,** 1975, green, Model No. 7652
EX n/a　　**NM** $35　　**MIP** $85

(KP Photo)

❑ **Gremlin Grinder,** 1976, chrome, Model No. 9201
EX n/a　　**NM** $20　　**MIP** $40

(KP Photo)

❑ **Gun Bucket,** 1976, Olive green body with redlines wheels in front, white "Army," star and number tampos on hood, black plastic anti-aircraft gun and treads. Also comes in blackwalls wheels variation, Model No. 9090
EX n/a　　**NM** $25　　**MIP** $60

❑ **Gun Slinger,** 1975, olive, Model No. 7664
EX n/a　　**NM** $25　　**MIP** $50

(KP Photo)

❑ **Hairy Hauler,** 1971, assorted, with lifting front canopy, Model No. 6458
EX n/a　　**NM** $20　　**MIP** $65

(KP Photo)

❑ **Heavy Chevy,** 1970, chrome, Club Kit, Model No. 6189
EX n/a　　**NM** $75　　**MIP** $300

❑ **Heavy Chevy,** 1970, assorted, Model No. 6408
EX n/a　　**NM** $65　　**MIP** $200

❑ **Heavy Chevy,** 1974, light green, Model No. 7619
EX n/a　　**NM** $200　　**MIP** $750

❑ **Heavy Chevy,** 1974, yellow, Model No. 7619
EX n/a　　**NM** $90　　**MIP** $200

❑ **Heavy Chevy,** 1977, chrome, redline or blackwall, Model No. 9212
EX n/a　　**NM** $40　　**MIP** $120

❑ **Hiway Robber,** 1973, assorted, Model No. 6979
EX n/a　　**NM** $75　　**MIP** $250

(KP Photo)

❑ **Hood,** 1971, assorted, Model No. 6175
EX n/a　　**NM** $35　　**MIP** $120

(KP Photo)

❑ **Hot Heap,** 1968, assorted, Model No. 6219
EX n/a　　**NM** $20　　**MIP** $65

(KP Photo)

❑ **Ice T,** 1971, yellow, with "Ice T" on plastic roof, Model No. 6184
EX n/a　　**NM** $40　　**MIP** $200

(KP Photo)

❑ **Ice T,** 1973, Body in assorted colors, black plastic interior, plastic roof (mostly in white), silver base. Blackwall wheels variations also produced at the same time, Model No. 6980
EX n/a　　**NM** $200　　**MIP** $650

❏ **Ice T,** 1974, yellow with hood tampo, Model No. 6980
EX n/a   NM $200   MIP $525

❏ **Ice T,** 1974, light green, Model No. 6980
EX n/a   NM $25   MIP $75

❏ **Indy Eagle,** 1969, gold, Model No. 6263
EX n/a   NM $75   MIP $240

(KP Photo)

❏ **Indy Eagle,** 1969, assorted colors with tinted plastic windshield and silver rear engine and tailpipes, Model No. 6263
EX n/a   NM $15   MIP $40

(KP Photo)

❏ **Jack Rabbit Special,** 1970, white, Model No. 6421
EX n/a   NM $25   MIP $75

❏ **Jack-in-the-Box Promotion,** 1970, white, Jack Rabbit w/decals, Model No. 6421
EX n/a   NM $300   MIP n/a

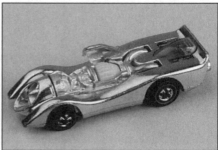
(KP Photo)

❏ **Jet Threat,** 1971, assorted, Model No. 6179
EX n/a   NM $45   MIP $185

❏ **King Kuda,** 1970, chrome, Club Kit, Model No. 6411
EX n/a   NM $75   MIP $300

(KP Photo)

❏ **King 'Kuda,** 1970, assorted, Model No. 6411
EX n/a   NM $25   MIP $100

(KP Photo)

❏ **Large Charge,** 1975, green, Model No. 8272
EX n/a   NM $30   MIP $80

❏ **Letter Getter,** 1977, white, redline, Model No. 9643
EX n/a   NM $175   MIP $550

(KP Photo)

❏ **Light My Firebird,** 1970, Convertible in assorted finishes, with decal number on doors and exposed silver engine in front. Brown plastic interior, Model No. 6412
EX n/a   NM $35   MIP $75

(KP Photo)

❏ **Lola GT 70,** 1969, assorted, Model No. 6254
EX n/a   NM $20   MIP $60

(KP Photo)

❏ **Lotus Turbine,** 1969, Assorted colors, plastic interior, Model No. 6262
EX n/a   NM $20   MIP $60

❏ **Lowdown,** 1976, light blue, Model No. 9185
EX n/a   NM $30   MIP $75

❏ **Lowdown,** 1977, gold plated, redline or blackwall, Model No. 9185
EX n/a   NM $15   MIP $30

❏ **Mantis,** 1970, assorted, Model No. 6423
EX n/a   NM $20   MIP $60

❏ **Maserati Mistral,** 1969, assorted, Model No. 6277
EX n/a   NM $50   MIP $125

(KP Photo)

❏ **Maxi Taxi,** 1976, Oldsmobile 442 body in yellow with checkboard and "Maxi Taxi" tampo on sides, black plastic interior. Also in a blackwalls variation, Model No. 9184
EX n/a   NM $25   MIP $60

(KP Photo)

❑ **McClaren M6A,** 1969, assorted, Model No. 6255
EX n/a   NM $20   MIP $65

(KP Photo)

❑ **Mercedes 280SL,** 1969, assorted, Model No. 6275
EX n/a   NM $25   MIP $85

❑ **Mercedes 280SL,** 1973, assorted, Model No. 6962
EX n/a   NM $100   MIP $450

❑ **Mercedes C-111,** 1972, assorted, Model No. 6169
EX n/a   NM $80   MIP $250

❑ **Mercedes C-111,** 1973, assorted, Model No. 6978
EX n/a   NM $300   MIP $1200

(KP Photo)

❑ **Mercedes C-111,** 1974, red, with stars and stripes tampo, Model No. 6978
EX n/a   NM $55   MIP $100

(KW6414)

❑ **Mighty Maverick,** 1970, assorted, Model No. 6414
EX n/a   NM $45   MIP $130

(KP Photo)

❑ **Mighty Maverick,** 1975, light green, Model No. 9209
EX n/a   NM $300   MIP $750

❑ **Mighty Maverick,** 1975, blue, Model No. 7653
EX n/a   NM $50   MIP $100

(KP Photo)

❑ **Mighty Maverick,** 1976, chrome, part of the "Super Chromes" series. Called "Street Snorter" in 1973, Model No. 9209
EX n/a   NM $25   MIP $50

(KP Photo)

❑ **Mod-Quad,** 1970, assorted, Model No. 6456
EX n/a   NM $20   MIP $75

❑ **Mongoose,** 1973, red/blue, Model No. 6970
EX n/a   NM $400   MIP $1400

(KP Photo)

❑ **Mongoose Funny Car,** 1970, red, Model No. 6410
EX n/a   NM $50   MIP $210

(KP Photo)

❑ **Mongoose II,** 1971, metallic blue, Model No. 5954
EX n/a   NM $75   MIP $350

❑ **Mongoose Rail Dragster,** 1971, blue, two pack, Model No. 5952
EX n/a   NM $75   MIP n/a

❑ **Monte Carlo Stocker,** 1975, yellow, Model No. 7660
EX n/a   NM $45   MIP $120

(KP Photo)

❑ **Motocross I,** 1975, red plastic seat and tank, unpainted gray die-cast body, Model No. 7668
EX n/a   NM $100   MIP $200

(KP Photo)

❑ **Moving Van,** 1970, assorted, another vehicle in the "Heavy-weights" series, Model No. 6455
EX n/a   NM $50   MIP $125

❑ **Mustang Stocker,** 1975, yellow w/red in tampo, Model No. 9203
EX n/a   NM $300   MIP $900

❏ **Mustang Stocker,** 1975, white, Model No. 7664
EX n/a   NM $400   MIP $1200
(KP Photo)

❏ **Mustang Stocker,** 1975, yellow with magenta and orange tampo with "Ford" and "450 HP", Model No. 7664
EX n/a   NM $80   MIP $135

❏ **Mustang Stocker,** 1976, chrome, Model No. 9203
EX n/a   NM $40   MIP $90

❏ **Mustang Stocker,** 1977, chrome, redline or blackwall, Model No. 9203
EX n/a   NM $40   MIP $90

(KP Photo)

❏ **Mutt Mobile,** 1971, assorted. The dogs in back are an especially nice touch, Model No. 5185
EX n/a   NM $80   MIP $185

❏ **Neet Streeter,** 1976, blue, Model No. 9244
EX n/a   NM $30   MIP $75

(KP Photo)

❏ **Nitty Gritty Kitty,** 1970, assorted, Model No. 6405
EX n/a   NM $30   MIP $90

(KP Photo)

❏ **Noodle Head,** 1971, assorted, Model No. 6000
EX n/a   NM $55   MIP $165

❏ **Odd Job,** 1973, assorted, Model No. 6981
EX n/a   NM $100   MIP $600

(KP Photo)

❏ **Odd Rod,** 1977, yellow plastic bucket around seats, clear plastic hood with flame graphics, redline or blackwall version available, Model No. 9642
EX n/a   NM $30   MIP $50

❏ **Odd Rod,** 1977, plum, blackwall or redline, Model No. 9642
EX n/a   NM $200   MIP $400

❏ **Olds 442,** 1971, assorted, Model No. 6467
EX n/a   NM $400   MIP $800

(KP Photo)

❏ **Open Fire,** 1972, modified AMC Gremilin with oversized engine and six wheels, assorted colors, Model No. 5881
EX n/a   NM $100   MIP $450

(KP Photo)

❏ **Paddy Wagon,** 1970, blue, with plastic covering over bed, Model No. 6402
EX n/a   NM $25   MIP $75

❏ **Paddy Wagon,** 1973, blue, Model No. 6966
EX n/a   NM $30   MIP $120

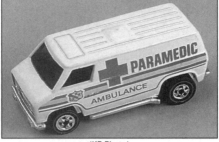
(KP Photo)

❏ **Paramedic,** 1975, white with yellow and red stripes and "Paramedic" lettering, Model No. 7661
EX n/a   NM $30   MIP $65

(KP Photo)

❏ **Peepin' Bomb,** 1970, assorted, Model No. 6419
EX n/a   NM $20   MIP $80

(KP Photo)

❏ **Pit Crew Car,** 1971, white, Model No. 6183
EX n/a   NM $30   MIP $350

(KP Photo)

❏ **Poison Pinto,** 1976, Light green body with Skull and Crossbones and "Poison Pinto" lettering tampo on side panels. A late-era redlines, also available with blackwalls wheels, Model No. 9240
EX n/a   NM $25   MIP $65

❏ **Police Cruiser,** 1974, white, Model No. 6963
EX n/a   NM $45   MIP $125

(KP Photo)

❏ **Porsche 911,** 1975, yellow, with blue and red stripes on hood and roof, Model No. 7648
EX n/a   NM $40   MIP $75

❏ **Porsche 911,** 1975, orange, Model No. 6972
EX n/a   NM $25   MIP $65

❏ **Porsche 911,** 1977, chrome, redline or blackwall, Model No. 9206
EX n/a   NM $20   MIP $40

❏ **Porsche 917,** 1970, assorted, Model No. 6416
EX n/a   NM $25   MIP $75

❏ **Porsche 917,** 1973, assorted, Model No. 6972
EX n/a   NM $300   MIP $950

❏ **Porsche 917,** 1974, red, Model No. 6972
EX n/a   NM $175   MIP $500

❏ **Porsche 917,** 1974, orange, Model No. 6972
EX n/a   NM $40   MIP $75

(KP Photo)

❏ **Power Pad,** 1970, assorted, Model No. 6459
EX n/a   NM $30   MIP $125

❏ **Prowler,** 1973, assorted, Model No. 6965
EX n/a   NM $200   MIP $1000

❏ **Prowler,** 1974, light green, Model No. 6965
EX n/a   NM $500   MIP $1000

(KP Photo)

❏ **Python,** 1968, assorted, Model No. 6216
EX n/a   NM $20   MIP $75

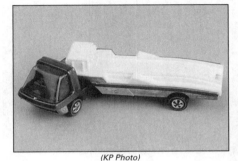

(KP Photo)

❏ **Racer Rig,** 1971, red/white, part of the "Heavyweights" series, Model No. 6194
EX n/a   NM $100   MIP $375

(KP Photo)

❏ **Ranger Rig,** 1975, medium green with yellow lettering and design, Model No. 7666
EX n/a   NM $20   MIP $75

❏ **Rear Engine Mongoose,** 1972, red, Model No. 5699
EX n/a   NM $200   MIP $600

(KP Photo)

❏ **Rear Engine Snake,** 1972, yellow, Model No. 5856
EX n/a   NM $200   MIP $600

(KP Photo)

❏ **Red Baron,** 1970, red, Model No. 6400
EX n/a   NM $25   MIP $80

(KP Photo)

❏ **Red Baron,** 1973, red, note no Iron Cross on the helmet, Model No. 6964
EX n/a   NM $30   MIP $200

❏ **Rock Buster,** 1976, yellow, Model No. 9088
EX n/a   NM $20   MIP $35

(KP Photo)

❏ **Rocket Bye Baby,** 1971, assorted, Model No. 6186
EX n/a   NM $60   MIP $200

(KP Photo)

❑ **Rodger Dodger,** 1974, Magenta Dodge Charger with flame tampos on hood and roof, exposed silver engine, red plastic exhaust pipes, Model No. 8259
EX n/a　　**NM** $40　　**MIP** $125

❑ **Rodger Dodger,** 1974, blue, Model No. 8259
EX n/a　　**NM** $200　　**MIP** $550

❑ **Rodger Dodger,** 1977, gold plated, blackwall or redline, Model No. 8259
EX n/a　　**NM** $30　　**MIP** $80

❑ **Rolls-Royce Silver Shadow,** 1969, assorted, opening hood shows detailed engine, Model No. 6276
EX n/a　　**NM** $30　　**MIP** $125

(KP Photo)

❑ **Sand Crab,** 1970, assorted, Model No. 6403
EX n/a　　**NM** $20　　**MIP** $60

❑ **Sand Drifter,** 1975, green, Model No. 7651
EX n/a　　**NM** $150　　**MIP** $375

(KP Photo)

❑ **Sand Drifter,** 1975, yellow, with flame tampo on hood, black plastic interior and covering over bed, Model No. 7651
EX n/a　　**NM** $45　　**MIP** $85

(KP Photo)

❑ **Sand Witch,** 1973, assorted, Model No. 6974
EX n/a　　**NM** $125　　**MIP** $450

(KP Photo)

❑ **S'Cool Bus,** 1971, yellow, with lift-up funny car body and silver chassis, Model No. 6468
EX n/a　　**NM** $175　　**MIP** $750

(KP Photo)

❑ **Scooper,** 1971, assorted, Model No. 6193
EX n/a　　**NM** $100　　**MIP** $325

(KP Photo)

❑ **Seasider,** 1970, assorted, Model No. 6413
EX n/a　　**NM** $60　　**MIP** $135

(KP Photo)

❑ **Second Wind,** 1977, white with yellow and red striping and number "5" on hood. Can feature either blackwall or redline wheels, Model No. 9644
EX n/a　　**NM** $35　　**MIP** $90

(KP Photo)

❑ **Shelby Turbine,** 1969, assorted, Model No. 6265
EX n/a　　**NM** $20　　**MIP** $55

(KP Photo)

❑ **Short Order,** 1971, assorted, with extending plastic tailgate, Model No. 6176
EX n/a　　**NM** $50　　**MIP** $125

(KP Photo)

❑ **Show Hoss II,** 1977, yellow funny car Mustang II body lifts up over silver base, black plastic roll-

cage, redline or blackwalls versions available, Model No. 9646
EX n/a   **NM** $300   **MIP** $600

❏ **Show-Off,** 1973, assorted, Model No. 6982
EX n/a   **NM** $140   **MIP** $400

❏ **Sidekick,** 1972, assorted, Model No. 6022
EX n/a   **NM** $80   **MIP** $200

(KP Photo)

❏ **Silhouette,** 1968, Body in assorted colors, plastic dome canopy over seats, exposed front engine, Model No. 6209
EX n/a   **NM** $20   **MIP** $90

❏ **Sir Sidney Roadster,** 1974, yellow, Model No. 8261
EX n/a   **NM** $50   **MIP** $90

❏ **Sir Sidney Roadster,** 1974, light green, Model No. 8261
EX n/a   **NM** $325   **MIP** $650

(KP Photo)

❏ **Sir Sidney Roadster,** 1974, Orange body with brown plastic roof and exposed silver engine. Red flame tampos, silver metal base, Model No. 8261
EX n/a   **NM** $375   **MIP** $700

(KP Photo)

❏ **Six Shooter,** 1971, assorted, Model No. 6003
EX n/a   **NM** $75   **MIP** $225

(KP Photo)

❏ **Sky Show Fleetside (Aero Launcher),** 1970, assorted, Model No. 6436
EX n/a   **NM** $400   **MIP** $850

❏ **Snake,** 1973, white/yellow, Model No. 6969
EX n/a   **NM** $600   **MIP** $1500

(KP Photo)

❏ **Snake Funny Car,** 1970, assorted, Model No. 6409
EX n/a   **NM** $60   **MIP** $300

❏ **Snake II,** 1971, white, Model No. 5953
EX n/a   **NM** $60   **MIP** $275

(KP Photo)

❏ **Snake Rail Dragster,** 1971, white, part of a two-pack, Model No. 5951
EX n/a   **NM** $75   **MIP** $1250

(KP Photo)

❏ **Snorkel,** 1971, assorted, Model No. 6020
EX n/a   **NM** $90   **MIP** $200

(KP Photo)

❏ **Special Delivery,** 1971, blue, Model No. 6006
EX n/a   **NM** $45   **MIP** $250

(KP Photo)

❏ **Splittin' Image,** 1969, assorted, Model No. 6261
EX n/a   **NM** $25   **MIP** $75

(KP Photo)

❏ **Spoiler Sport,** 1977, light green van with tropical island scene on side panels, redline wheels. Blackwalls variations also exist, Model No. 9641
EX n/a   **NM** $25   **MIP** $50

(KP Photo)

❑ **Steam Roller,** 1974, white body with stars and stripes graphics, three stars reversed out of red stripe on hood; the more common model, Model No. 8260
EX n/a   **NM** $25   **MIP** $70

❑ **Steam Roller,** 1974, white body with red white and blue graphics, seven stars on front, Model No. 8260
EX n/a   **NM** $100   **MIP** $300

❑ **Street Rodder,** 1976, black, Model No. 9242
EX n/a   **NM** $40   **MIP** $85

❑ **Street Snorter,** 1973, assorted, Model No. 6971
EX n/a   **NM** $110   **MIP** $400

(KP Photo)

❑ **Strip Teaser,** 1971, assorted, Model No. 6188
EX n/a   **NM** $65   **MIP** $200

❑ **Sugar Caddy,** 1971, assorted, Model No. 6418
EX n/a   **NM** $45   **MIP** $120

❑ **Super Van,** 1975, Toys-R-Us, Model No. 7649
EX n/a   **NM** $100   **MIP** $350

(KP Photo)

❑ **Super Van,** 1975, Magenta body with dirt bike in yellow circel tampo on side panels, Model No. 7649
EX n/a   **NM** $110   **MIP** $270

❑ **Superfine Turbine,** 1973, assorted, Model No. 6004
EX n/a   **NM** $400   **MIP** $1100

❑ **Sweet 16,** 1973, assorted, Model No. 6007
EX n/a   **NM** $125   **MIP** $650

(KP Photo)

❑ **Swingin' Wing,** 1970, assorted, Model No. 6422
EX n/a   **NM** $25   **MIP** $75

(KP Photo)

❑ **T-4-2,** 1971, assorted, Model No. 6177
EX n/a   **NM** $50   **MIP** $175

(KP Photo)

❑ **Team Trailer,** 1971, white/red, detailed plastic interior and opening door on trailer, Model No. 6019
EX n/a   **NM** $95   **MIP** $250

(KP Photo)

❑ **TNT-Bird,** 1970, assorted, Model No. 6407
EX n/a   **NM** $60   **MIP** $125

(KP Photo)

❑ **Top Eliminator,** 1974, blue lift-up funny car body on silver chassis, with green light tan and orange "Hot Wheels" graphics and stripes on sides, Model No. 7630
EX n/a   **NM** $50   **MIP** $165

(KP Photo)

❑ **Torero,** 1969, assorted, Model No. 6260
EX n/a   **NM** $20   **MIP** $75

(KP Photo)

❑ **Torino Stocker,** 1975, red, Model No. 7647
EX n/a   **NM** $35   **MIP** $95

(KP Photo)

❑ **Tough Customer,** 1975, olive, with rotating turret and white numbering tampos, Model No. 7655
EX n/a   NM $30   MIP $60

(KP Photo)

❑ **Tow Truck,** 1970, assorted, Model No. 6450
EX n/a   NM $30   MIP $80

(KP Photo)

❑ **Tri-Baby,** 1970, assorted, interesting engine casting under opening rear hood, Model No. 6424
EX n/a   NM $25   MIP $85

❑ **T-Totaller,** 1977, black, Red Line, six-pack only, Model No. 9648
EX n/a   NM $500   MIP $1000

❑ **Turbofire,** 1969, assorted, Model No. 6259
EX n/a   NM $15   MIP $75

(KP Photo)

❑ **Twinmill,** 1969, assorted, Model No. 6258
EX n/a   NM $15   MIP $50

❑ **Twinmill II,** 1976, orange, Model No. 8240
EX n/a   NM $15   MIP $45

❑ **Vega Bomb,** 1975, green, Model No. 7658
EX n/a   NM $250   MIP $800

(KP Photo)

❑ **Vega Bomb,** 1975, orange, this model is right on the cusp of the Redlines era--blackwall versions (like this one as #7654) were becoming a more common sight, Model No. 7658
EX n/a   NM $40   MIP $120

(KP Photo)

❑ **Volkswagen,** 1974, orange enamel with bug graphic on roof, Model No. 7620
EX n/a   NM $30   MIP $125

❑ **Volkswagen,** 1974, orange w/stripes on roof, Model No. 7620
EX n/a   NM $100   MIP $400

(KP Photo)

❑ **Volkswagen Beach Bomb,** 1969, surf boards on side raised panels, Model No. 6274
EX n/a   NM $115   MIP $400

❑ **Volkswagen Beach Bomb,** 1969, surf boards in rear window, Model No. 6274
EX n/a   NM $7000   MIP n/a

(KP Photo)

❑ **Warpath,** 1975, white, with stars and stripes tampo, opening plastic engine covers, Model No. 7654
EX n/a   NM $60   MIP $115

(KP Photo)

❑ **Waste Wagon,** 1971, assorted, part of the "Heavyweights" series of highly-detailed trucks, Model No. 6192
EX n/a   NM $90   MIP $250

(KP Photo)

❑ **What-4,** 1971, assorted, Model No. 6001
EX n/a   **NM** $50   **MIP** $150

(KP Photo)

❑ **Whip Creamer,** 1970, assorted, with slide-back plastic canopy, Model No. 6457
EX n/a   **NM** $25   **MIP** $60

❑ **Xploder,** 1973, assorted, Model No. 6977
EX n/a   **NM** $100   **MIP** $500

❑ **Z Whiz,** 1977, white, redline, Model No. 9639
EX n/a   **NM** $1500   **MIP** n/a

❑ **Z Whiz,** 1977, gray, redline, Model No. 9639
EX n/a   **NM** $35   **MIP** $70

Chitty Chitty Bang Bang, by Husky. A strength of the lineup was a strong showing in television and movie vehicles.

By Dr. Douglas Sadecky

Husky Toys were produced by the Mettoy Company from 1964 until 1969 to directly compete with Lesney's Matchbox cars. The Mettoy Company was enjoying great success with their Corgi Toys diecast vehicles and felt there was room for competition on the smaller 1:64 scale toys. The Husky range included many of the same categories as the Corgi Toys and in a fair number of cases, the Husky models were miniature versions of their Corgi counterparts. Some of the Huskys had chrome plating on their bodies and/or chassis, which was eye appealing but could not hold up under play conditions. The Husky models were even fitted with gray plastic wheels similar to the Matchbox series. These solid gray wheels eventually gave way to metal wheels with black plastic tires. Husky vehicles were sold exclusively in Woolworth Stores in the U.S. and U.K. Because these new toys were selling well, Mettoy in 1968 expanded the Husky range to include Accessories, Majors, Twin Packs, and Extras. The Majors were larger scale Huskys similar to the Major series in the Corgi Toys range. Twin Packs were two or more vehicles aimed at selling multiple toys. Some of these multipacks were called gift sets just like the

MARKET UPDATE

Husky models are nicely detailed toys that appeal to many diecast collectors but are still overlooked by many. Because demand is not as high as Hot Wheels or Matchboxs, a collector can put together a nice collection of Husky Toys at a fraction of the cost of the competitor models. One of the biggest problems inherent to the Husky regular series is the flaking or tarnishing of the chrome plating. Even unopened models on their original blistercards are not immune to this problem. The Husky Extras are in greatest demand because of the character affiliation that appeals to several categories of collectors and the extreme detail of these little toys. The gift sets are highly sought after, as these are hard to find in their original packaging. Prices will probably not significantly escalate soon, but now is the time to get in on the ground floor as these Husky Toys have been slowly increasing in value. The original packaging is essential to bring full book value, especially on the gift sets and Extras.

gift sets in the Corgi Toys series. The Extras were slightly more money, but worth every penny since this series was devoted to television, movie, and character vehicles such as the Batmobile, Monkeemobile, and Chitty Chitty Bang Bang to name but a few. By the end of 1969, the exclusivity contract with Woolworth's expired, and Mettoy decided to wisely rename the series Corgi Juniors to give name affiliation to their larger counterparts, Corgi Toys. When Mattel introduced Hot Wheels in 1968, Mettoy had to scramble to compete with the new competition and introduced Whizzwheels for both the Corgi and Corgi Juniors lines. Since time was of the essence, many of the models had Corgi Juniors labels adhered over the Husky name embossed on the chassis until new tool dies could be manufactured. Solid black transitional wheels were used on many of the early Corgi Juniors until the new Whizzwheels became available. Corgi Juniors were produced in great numbers from 1970 until the late 1980's. Many of the regular Huskys and Extras were carried over into the new Corgi Juniors line but with the new modifications. The regular series Huskys were sold on red and white blistercards and eventually yellow and white blistercards.

An especially nice Jaguar E-type casting by Husky. It's easy to identify this as a model from the later sixties, because of its metal wheels and black tires. Earlier Husky toys featured solid gray plastic wheels.

The Citroen Safari Ambulance is a favorite with collectors. It was available in civilian and military versions.

Ford Wrecker by Husky. Notice the chromed towing boom—nice enough in the store, but the plating didn't hold up so well to hard play.

Sunbeam Alpine by Husky. A sharp-looking European sports car.

An unusual combination—a Guy Warrior tanker truck with Shell and BP decals.

Aveling-Barford Dump Truck. Notice the chipped chrome on the plow—normal for chromed parts on Husky. As with the tow truck, these parts looked nice when new, but tended to chip considerably with play wear.

Aston Martin DB6. While not the miniature James Bond version, this model is still popular with collectors.

The BM Volvo Farm Tractor looks perfect parked next to older Matchbox farm equipment. It's style and color make it stand out from the myriad Fords and John Deere models.

This Ford Camper casting is the same as the Ford Wrecker. The only change is what sits in the truck bed. Again, the chrome on this model has seen some wear.

ERF Cement Lorry by Husky. Many construction toys see pretty tough play wear, so finding examples in good shape like this one can be a challenge.

Studebaker Wagonaire Ambulance and Jaguar Fire Chief Car. Although both cars are unpackaged examples, the ambulance still has its plastic stretcher—almost always long-separated from these models

Buick Electra by Husky. Interesting choice of model for Husky, since this car already looked (and, in fact, was) old by the time they produced the toy.

The Guy Warrior Milk Truck with oval tank. These castings were used for milk and gasoline trucks in two variations: square and oval tanks.

HUSKY / CORGI JUNIORS

REGULAR

(KP Photo, Tom Michael collection)

❑ **1-A, Jaguar Mark X (smaller casting),** 1964-67, Blue body, yellow-cream interior, silver base
EX $10   NM $20   MIP $40

❑ **1-B, Jaguar Mark X (larger casting),** 1967-69
EX $7   NM $15   MIP $30

(KP Photo, Chad Elmore collection)

❑ **2-A, Citroen Safari with Boat (smaller casting),** 1964-67, Gold metallic body, white interior, red plastic boat
EX $10   NM $20   MIP $40

❑ **2-B, Citroen Safari with Boat (larger casting),** 1967-69
EX $7   NM $15   MIP $30

❑ **3-A, Mercedes-Benz 220,** 1964-69
EX $7   NM $15   MIP $30

❑ **3-B, Volkswagen 1200 Police Car (smaller casting),** 1969-69
EX $10   NM $20   MIP $40

(KP Photo, Tom Michael collection)

❑ **3-C, Volkswagen 1200 Police Car (larger casting),** 1965-67, White with black hood and doors, "Police" in white type on doors, gray wheels, black tires, unpainted base, blue dome light, red plastic interior

❑ **4-A, Jaguar Mark X Fire Chief's Car (smaller casting),** 1964-67
EX $10   NM $20   MIP $40

❑ **4-B, Jaguar Mark X Fire Chief's Car (larger casting),** 1967-69
EX $7   NM $15   MIP $30

❑ **5-A, Lancia Flaminia,** 1964-68
EX $7   NM $10   MIP $30

❑ **5-B, Willys Jeep,** 1968-69
EX $7   NM $15   MIP $30

(KP Photo by Dr. Douglas Sadecky)

❑ **6-A, Citroen Safari Ambulance,** 1964-67, White body, red cross emblems on hood, blue dome light and windows
EX $10   NM $20   MIP $40

❑ **6-B, Ferrari Berlinetta 250GT,** 1967-69
EX $10   NM $20   MIP $40

❑ **7-A, Buick Electra,** 1964-68, Red body, yellow interior, black wheels, silver base, bumper and grille
EX $10   NM $20   MIP $40

(KP Photo by Dr. Douglas Sadecky)

❑ **7-B, Duple Vista 25 Coach,** 1968-69, Greenish-blue and white body, red interior, silver wheels, black tires
EX $10   NM $20   MIP $40

(KP Photo by Dr. Douglas Sadecky)

❑ **8-A, Ford Thunderbird Convertible,** 1964-66, Pictured here with the 8-B Ford Thunderbird Hardtop
EX $10   NM $20   MIP $40

❑ **8-B, Ford Thunderbird Hardtop,** 1966-68
EX $10   NM $18   MIP $35

❑ **8-C, Tipping Farm Trailer,** 1968-69
EX $6   NM $12   MIP $25

(KP Photo by Dr. Douglas Sadecky)

❑ **9-A, Buick Electra Police Car,** 1964-68, Dark blue body, yellow interior, silver base, bumpers and grille, "Police" labels on sides
EX $10   NM $20   MIP $40

❑ **9-B, Cadillac Eldorado,** 1968-69
EX $7   NM $15   MIP $30

(KP Photo by Dr. Douglas Sadecky)

❑ **10-A, Guy Warrior Coal Truck,** 1964-69, The truck on the left is the earlier release with solid black plastic wheels while the truck on the right is a later version with orange paint and metal wheels with black plastic tires
EX $10   NM $20   MIP $40

(KP Photo by Dr. Douglas Sadecky)

❑ **11-B, Forward Control Land Rover,** 1964-69, This version was a later release which had a metallic green finish as opposed to the earlier olive green edition
EX $10   NM $18   MIP $35

(KP Photo by Dr. Douglas Sadecky)

❑ **12-A, Volkswagen Tower Truck,** 1964-67, Assorted colored body, red plastic tower, silver base, no interior
EX $10   NM $18   MIP $35

(KP Photo by Dr. Douglas Sadecky)

❑ **12-B, Ford Tower Truck,** 1968-69, Red telescopic tower in truck bed. Husky used this casting for many of their Ford Trucks including the camper and tow truck
EX $7   NM $15   MIP $30

❑ **13-A, Guy Warrior Sand Truck,** 1964-69
EX $10   NM $18   MIP $35

(KP Photo, Tom Michael collection)

❑ **14-A, Guy Warrior Tanker (Shell decals),** 1964-66, Yellow body, black wheels, metal base, "Shell" decals on sides
EX $10   NM $20   MIP $40

❑ **14-B, Guy Warrior Tanker (Esso decals),** 1966-69
EX $7   NM $15   MIP $30

❑ **15-A, Volkswagen Pickup Truck,** 1965-67
EX $10   NM $18   MIP $35

(KP Photo by Dr. Douglas Sadecky)

❑ **15-B, Studebaker Wagonaire TV Camera Car,** 1967-69, A nicely detailed camera and cameraman accompanied this model
EX $12   NM $25   MIP $50

(KP Photo by Dr. Douglas Sadecky)

❑ **16-A, Aveling-Barford Dump Truck,** 1965-69, Two color variations shown
EX $5   NM $10   MIP $20

❑ **17-A, Guy Warrior Milk Tanker (oval tank),** 1965-67
EX $10   NM $20   MIP $40

(KP Photo by Dr. Douglas Sadecky)

❑ **17-B, Guy Warrior Milk Tanker (square tank),** 1967-68, Square and oval tank variations
EX $7   NM $18   MIP $30

(KP Photo by Dr. Douglas Sadecky)

❑ **18-A, Jaguar Mark X (smaller plated casting),** 1965-67, Represented here are the smaller scale plated Jaguar and two color and wheel variations of the 1-B Jaguar
EX $12   NM $25   MIP $50

❑ **18-B, Jaguar Mark X (larger plated casting),** 1967-69
EX $12   NM $25   MIP $50

(KP Photo by Dr. Douglas Sadecky)

❑ **19-A, Commer Walk-Thru Van,** 1965-69, Two color variations are represented in this photo
EX $7   NM $15   MIP $30

❑ **19-B, Sport Boat on Trailer,** 1969-70
EX $5   NM $10   MIP $20

❑ **20-A, Ford Thames Van,** 1965-69
EX $10   NM $20   MIP $40

HUSKY / CORGI JUNIORS

❑ **20-B, Volkswagen 1300,**
1968-69
EX $10   NM $20   MIP $40

❑ **21-A, Military Land Rover Forward Control Truck,** 1965-68
EX $10   NM $18   MIP $35

(KP Photo by Dr. Douglas Sadecky)

❑ **21-B, Jaguar E Type 2+2,**
1968-69
EX $12   NM $25   MIP $50

(KP Photo, Tom Michael collection)

❑ **22-A, Citroen Safari Military Ambulance,** 1965-68, Dark green body, red cross emblem on hood, blue windows and dome light, silver base
EX $7   NM $15   MIP $30

(KP Photo by Dr. Douglas Sadecky)

❑ **22-B, Aston Martin DB6,**
1968-69
EX $12   NM $25   MIP $50

❑ **23-A, Guy Warrior U.S. Army Tanker,** 1965-67
EX $10   NM $20   MIP $40

(KP Photo by Dr. Douglas Sadecky)

❑ **23-B, Loadmaster Shovel,**
1967-69
EX $5   NM $10   MIP $20

❑ **24-A, Ford Zephyr Estate Car,** 1966-69
EX $10   NM $20   MIP $40

(KP Photo by Dr. Douglas Sadecky)

❑ **25-A, S&D Refuse Wagon,**
1966-69, The truck on the left was issued first with black plastic wheels while the truck on the right is a later version with black plastic tires
EX $7   NM $15   MIP $30

(KP Photo by Dr. Douglas Sadecky)

❑ **26-A, Sunbeam Alpine,**
1966-69
EX $12   NM $25   MIP $50

❑ **27-A, Bedford TK 7-Ton Lorry,** 1966-69
EX $7   NM $15   MIP $30

(KP Photo by Dr. Douglas Sadecky)

❑ **28-A, Ford Wrecker,** 1966-69, When Husky models were repackaged as Corgi Juniors, the Corgi Company didn't have enough time to retool the bases, so a Corgi label was applied to the base to identify the new toys
EX $7   NM $15   MIP $30

(KP Photo by Dr. Douglas Sadecky)

❑ **29-A, ERF Cement Lorry,**
1966-69
EX $7   NM $15   MIP $30

❑ **29-B, ERF Simon Snorkel Fire Engine,** 1970-71
EX $7   NM $15   MIP $30

❑ **30-A, Studebaker Wagonaire Ambulance,** 1966-69, Studebaker ambulance is shown here with 4-B Jaguar Fire Chief Car. Notice the patient on stretcher--normally missing on loose versions of the ambulance
EX $7   NM $15   MIP $30

❑ **31-A, Oldsmobile Starfire Coupe,** 1966-69
EX $7   NM $15   MIP $30

❑ **32-A, Volkswagen Luggage Elevator Truck,** 1966-69
EX $7   NM $15   MIP $30

(KP Photo by Dr. Douglas Sadecky)

❑ **33-A, Farm Livestock Trailer,** 1967-69
EX $4   NM $7   MIP $15

(KP Photo, Tom Michael collection)

❑ **34-A, BM Volvo 400 Farm Tractor,** 1967-69, Red body, yellow wheels, silver-painted grille and headlights, black-painted stack
EX $6   NM $12   MIP $25

(KP Photo by Dr. Douglas Sadecky)

❑ **35-A, Ford Camper,** 1966-69, The chrome on the camper back had a lot of eye-appeal but impractical for play wear. This model is a testament
EX $7   NM $15   MIP $30

❑ **36-A, Simon Snorkel Fire Engine,** 1967-69
EX $6   NM $12   MIP $25

❑ **37-A, NSU RO80,** 1969
EX $6   NM $12   MIP $25

❑ **38-A, Rice Beaufort Horse Box Trailer,** 1968-69
EX $5   NM $10   MIP $20

(KP Photo, Tom Michael collection)

❑ **39-A, Jaguar XJ6 4.2,** 1968-69, Yellow body, red plastic interior, gray wheels with black tires, unpainted base, opening trunk
EX $12   NM $25   MIP $50

❑ **40-A, Ford Transit Caravan,** 1968-69
EX $6   NM $12   MIP $25

EXTRAS

(KP Photo by Dr. Douglas Sadecky)

❑ **1001-A, James Bond Aston Martin DB6,** 1968-69, Complete with miniature ejector seat
EX $65   NM $125   MIP $200

(KP Photo by Dr. Douglas Sadecky)

❑ **1002-A, Batmobile,** 1968-69, Corgi Junior model with "Whizzwheels"
EX $75   NM $140   MIP $225

(KP Photo by Dr. Douglas Sadecky)

❑ **1003-A, Batboat on Trailer,** 1968-69
EX $75   NM $140   MIP $225

(KP Photo by Dr. Douglas Sadecky)

❑ **1004-A, Monkeemobile,** 1968-69, The first early version illustrated the Monkee's faces on the top of the header card where this simply shows a vehicle shot
EX $75   NM $140   MIP $225

❑ **1005-A, The Man From U.N.C.L.E. Car,** 1968-69
EX $75   NM $140   MIP $225

(KP Photo by Dr. Douglas Sadecky)

❑ **1006-A, Chitty Chitty Bang Bang,** 1968-69, This Husky version featured orange side wings and yellow front and rear tail wings. The color of the wings was exactly the opposite for the Corgi Juniors version
EX $75   NM $140   MIP $225

ACCESSORIES

❑ **1561, Triangular Traffic Signs,** 1968-69
EX $12   NM $25   MIP $45

❑ **1562, Circular Traffic Signs,** 1968-69
EX $12   NM $25   MIP $45

❑ **1571, Pedestrian Figures,** 1968-69
EX $10   NM $18   MIP $35

❑ **1572, Workmen Figures,** 1968-69
EX $10   NM $18   MIP $35

HUSKY / CORGI JUNIORS

❑ **1573, Garage Personnel,** 1968-69
EX $10   NM $18   MIP $35

❑ **1574, Public Servants,** 1968-69
EX $10   NM $18   MIP $35

❑ **1580, Husky Collector Case,** 1968-69
EX $10   NM $18   MIP $35

MAJORS

❑ **2001-A, Four Car Garage,** 1968-69
EX $12   NM $25   MIP $45

❑ **2002-A, Hoynor Mark II Car Transporter,** 1967-69
EX $18   NM $35   MIP $65

❑ **2003-A, Ford Low Loader With Loadmaster Shovel,** 1968-69
EX $18   NM $35   MIP $65

❑ **2004-A, Ford Removals Van,** 1968-69
EX $18   NM $35   MIP $65

TWIN PACKS

❑ **3001-A, Garage and Three Vehicles,** 1968-69
EX $35   NM $55   MIP $105

❑ **3002-A, Batmobile & Batboat,** 1968-69
EX $100   NM $200   MIP $325

❑ **3003-A, Car Transporter and Five Cars,** 1968-69, This Corgi Juniors car transporter shows all-black Whizzwheels to compete against Mattel's Hot Wheels
EX $75   NM $140   MIP $225

❑ **3004-A, Garage and Two Cars,** 1968-69
EX $35   NM $55   MIP $105

❑ **3005-A, Holiday Time Set,** 1968-69
EX $75   NM $140   MIP $225

(KP Photo by Dr. Douglas Sadecky)

❑ **3006-A, Service Station Set,** 1968-69, Includes three vehicles
EX $35   NM $55   MIP $105

(KP Photo)

❑ **3008-A, Crime Busters Set,** 1968-69, Set includes Batmobile and Batboat, Man from U.N.C.L.E. car and James Bond Aston Martin DB6
EX $185   NM $285   MIP $600

Topper Johnny Lightning 1969-1971

A selection of Johnny Lightning cars made by Topper.

Topper Johnny Lightnings cars were obvious competitors to Mattel's Hot Wheels. Henry Orenstein, President of Topper Toys, knew a winner when he saw it, and there was no denying that Hot Wheels had taken the toy world by storm.

Topper Toys already had many successful toy series by the time they entered the world of die-cast cars. Suzy Homemaker, Johnny Eagle (toy guns), Johnny Toymaker were already established brands among American kids. The inclusion of die-cast cars just completed the process.

The wheels were the key—and indeed, early Topper Johnny Lightning wheels looked an awful lot like Hot Wheels "redlines." The first wheels were made of Celcon, mounted on plastic bushings, and lubricated. Estimated by the company set high "scale mph" for the cars. In fact, the 1970 Topper Catalog claims "Scale speeds greater than 1200 mph!"

MARKET UPDATE

Only 47 models were produced before Topper was forced to declare bankruptcy in 1971, making a complete series of vehicles a tempting target for any die-cast collector. However, prices for mint-in-pack examples are quite high—especially for models with mirror finishes. Also, new collectors will want to be aware of differences between Topper and Playing Mantis Johnny Lightning cars—although the baseplates and packaging are clearly labeled. Plus, even the Commemorative series, produced by Playing Mantis to honor original Topper cars, are not exact reproductions.

Smart marketing came early for Johnny Lightnings in the form of sponsorship of Al Unser in the 1970 Indy 500. Unser's win brought a lot of people over to the toys, and they were serious competition for Mattel's Hot Wheels. Even Sports Illustrated chronicled their competition in a December 1970 article citing the intense rivalry between the Hot Wheels and Johnny Lightning camps. Topper capitalized on its fame by partnering with General Mills in a very successful cereal promotion.

One of Topper's first series vehicles (known as the "great eight"), a Jaguar XKE, with opening doors—a feature later dropped from the lineup.

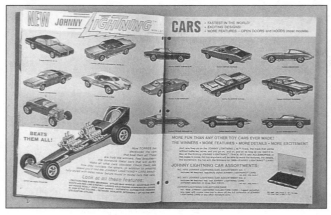

Catalog shot from 1970—notice the vehicles in the new lineup—some would only see existence as a toy 20 years later under the aegis of "Playing Mantis Johnny Lightning."

Another close second to Hot Wheels—plastic racetracks. Topper even produced air compressors to fuel their "Jet Power" series of Johnny Lightning cars.

COLLECTOR'S TIP

When the original Johnny Lightning "great eight" (El Dorado, GTO, El Camino, Thunderbird, Toronado, Ferrari, Mako Shark and XKE) cars were made with a thin strip of metal for fitting opening doors. The process of putting these doors on the cars was eliminated halfway through 1969 and the molds were changed giving the cars a unibody with sealed doors. However, the each car's rarity is a two-fold issue. First, when a car was produced before the model change, and secondly, how long those molds were in use.

Distinguishing the three separate production runs among the first eight cars is easy. The Eldorado, for instance, is generally thought of as the first car built out of the gates for Topper. For this reason, collectors know it is the most abundant model of the first five "Detroits" or American cars. It seems that the molds were retired for this car shortly after the switch to closed doors, so closed-door models are some of the most rare.

The four remaining Detroits had a short production run that started after the El Dorado and intersected about halfway through this transition period. That means the GTO, El Camino, Thunderbird and Toronado are fairly evenly split between open- and closed-door styles with perhaps a sixty/forty split between open and closed-door models.

The remaining members of the "great eight," the Ferrari, Mako Shark and XKE, were introduced right before the mold change and had a long career in the Johnny Lightning lineup, so opening-door models are quite rare. Closed-door versions of these cars are quite common.

Generally speaking, Detroit cars are the most favored by collectors. However, new collectors may want to look at any opening-door model in good condition as a smart investment.

Two examples of a model that literally made it to the drawing boards back in 1970, now produced by Playing Mantis—"Tow'd."

How fast is legal for die-cast cars? An opening page from Topper's 1970 dealer catalog claims, "Scale speeds greater than 1200 M.P.H."

A variation of the Custom Turbine, without a painted interior. One of the more outrageous cars produced by Topper.

The Nucleon, however, is probably the most unusual vehicle in the Topper lineup. The plastic canopies are often missing on played-with examples.

A car made famous by Al Unser and Johnny Lightning—the Indy car from 1970. A newer version of this car is currently produced by Playing Mantis in the "Ad Rods" series.

A shot of the Topper Toy Factory from their 1965 catalog— four years before the Johnny Lightning series was born.

A clever re-use of the Ferrari casting, the Frantic Ferrari.

The Custom Ferrari, with opening doors and hood.

JOHNNY LIGHTNING / TOPPER

(KP Photo)

❏ **'32 Roadster,** 1969, Varied chromed color body, rumble seat in back flips up. This model has missing windshield, common to play worn examples
EX $25   **NM** $60   **MIP** $125

❏ **A.J. Foyt Indy Special,** 1970, blackwall tires
EX $40   **NM** $60   **MIP** $250

(KP Photo, Tom Michael collection)

❏ **Al Unser Indy Special,** 1970, Chrome blue finish, Lightning number "2" decal, black wall tires
EX $100   **NM** $200   **MIP** $500

❏ **Baja,** 1970,
EX $45   **NM** $125   **MIP** $200

(KP Photo, Tom Michael collection)

❏ **Big Rig,** 1971, Originally included add on extras called "Customs;" prices reflect fully accessorized car. Called the "Track Bac" in the 1970 Topper Toys catalog
EX $65   **NM** $150   **MIP** $275

❏ **Bubble,** 1970, Jet Powered
EX $45   **NM** $75   **MIP** $150

(Photo courtesy Dennis Seleman)

❏ **Bug Bomb,** 1970, Various chromed color schemes, two silver engines, blackwall tires. This example is missing the rear engine
EX $40   **NM** $90   **MIP** $225

❏ **Condor,** 1970, blackwall tires
EX $150   **NM** $200   **MIP** $1200

❏ **Custom Camaro,** 1968-69, Prototype, only one known to exist
EX n/a   **NM** $6000   **MIP** n/a

❏ **Custom Charger,** 1968-69, Prototype, only one known to exist. A Version of this car is now available by Playing Mantis as part of the "Lost Toppers" series
EX n/a   **NM** $6000   **MIP** n/a

❏ **Custom Continental,** 1968-69, Prototype, only six known to exist. Another casting re-released by Playing Mantis
EX n/a   **NM** $4000   **MIP** n/a

❏ **Custom Dragster,** 1969, Mirror finish
EX $150   **NM** $250   **MIP** $1000

(KP Photo)

❏ **Custom Dragster,** 1969, Version with a plastic canopy, Topper-style redlines wheels, unpainted base. While versions were made without a canopy, the example here is simply missing one
EX $60   **NM** $150   **MIP** $200

❏ **Custom Dragster,** 1969, Without canopy
EX $35   **NM** $75   **MIP** $125

❏ **Custom El Camino,** 1969, With sealed doors
EX $110   **NM** $300   **MIP** $500

❏ **Custom El Camino,** 1969, Mirror finish
EX $200   **NM** $350   **MIP** $1125

(Photo courtesy Dennis Seleman)

❏ **Custom El Camino,** 1969, With opening doors, surfboards on back, Topper-style redlines wheels
EX $150   **NM** $275   **MIP** $500

❏ **Custom Eldorado,** 1969, With sealed doors
EX $150   **NM** $300   **MIP** $1000

❏ **Custom Eldorado,** 1969, With opening doors
EX $150   **NM** $275   **MIP** $350

❏ **Custom Ferrari,** 1969, With opening doors, mirror finish
EX $300   **NM** $450   **MIP** $1000

(KP Photo)

❏ **Custom Ferrari,** 1969, With sealed doors
EX $40   **NM** $80   **MIP** $130

❏ **Custom Ferrari,** 1969, With opening doors
EX $150   **NM** $275   **MIP** $500

❏ **Custom GTO,** 1969, With opening doors
EX $200   **NM** $450   **MIP** $1500

❏ **Custom GTO,** 1969, Mirror finish
EX $200   **NM** $475   **MIP** $1100

❏ **Custom GTO,** 1969, With sealed doors
EX $200   **NM** $450   **MIP** $1700

❏ **Custom Mako Shark,** 1969, With opening doors
EX $125   NM $350   MIP $500

❏ **Custom Mako Shark,** 1969, With sealed doors
EX $40   NM $75   MIP $225

(Photo Courtesy Dennis Seleman)

❏ **Custom Mako Shark,** 1969, With opening doors, mirror finish
EX $200   NM $500   MIP $1800

❏ **Custom Mustang,** 1968-69, Prototype, only one known to exist
EX n/a   NM $6000   MIP n/a

❏ **Custom Spoiler,** 1970, Black-wall tires
EX $35   NM $65   MIP $150

❏ **Custom T-Bird,** 1969, With opening doors
EX $100   NM $250   MIP $475

❏ **Custom T-Bird,** 1969, Mirror finish
EX $200   NM $400   MIP $5000

❏ **Custom T-Bird,** 1969, With sealed doors
EX $150   NM $300   MIP $800

❏ **Custom Toronado,** 1969, Mirror finish
EX $450   NM $600   MIP $2000

❏ **Custom Toronado,** 1969, With sealed doors
EX $300   NM $500   MIP $1500

❏ **Custom Toronado,** 1969, With opening doors
EX $225   NM $400   MIP $1000

(KP Photo, Tom Michael collection)

❏ **Custom Turbine,** 1969, With unpainted interior, Topper redline-style wheels
EX $30   NM $60   MIP $125

❏ **Custom Turbine,** 1969, Mirror finish
EX $150   NM $225   MIP $500

❏ **Custom Turbine,** 1969, Red, black, white painted interior
EX $50   NM $150   MIP $200

(KP Photo, Tom Michael collection)

❏ **Custom XKE,** 1969, With opening doors, unpainted base, opening hood, blackwalls tires
EX $150   NM $275   MIP $475

(KP Photo, Tom Michael collection)

❏ **Custom XKE,** 1969, With sealed doors, unpainted base, full window plastic all-around, opening hood, blackwalls tires
EX $35   NM $80   MIP $110

❏ **Custom XKE,** 1969, With opening doors, mirror finish
EX $300   NM $450   MIP $800

❏ **Double Trouble,** 1970, Black-wall tires
EX $75   NM $180   MIP $1500

❏ **Flame Out,** 1970, Black wall tires
EX $60   NM $125   MIP $350

❏ **Flying Needle,** 1970, Jet Powered
EX $45   NM $100   MIP $225

(KP Photo)

❏ **Frantic Ferrari,** 1970, Unpainted base, silver exposed engine, various finishes
EX $35   NM $45   MIP $90

❏ **Glasser,** 1970, Jet Powered
EX $40   NM $75   MIP $150

❏ **Hairy Hauler,** 1971, Came with add-on extras called "Customs;" prices reflect fully accessorized cars
EX $65   NM $150   MIP $275

❏ **Jumpin' Jag,** 1970, Blackwall tires
EX $35   NM $80   MIP $175

(KP Photo)

❏ **Leapin' Limo,** 1970, Blackwall tires, large silver and black plastic engine. Example here shows Topper packaging, duplicated to an extent by Playing Mantis with the Commemorative series
EX $50   NM $125   MIP $400

❏ **Mad Maverick,** 1970, Black-wall tires
EX $75   NM $150   MIP $450

❏ **Monster,** 1970, Jet Powered
EX $40   NM $74   MIP $150

❏ **Movin' Van,** 1970, Blackwall tires
EX $35   NM $65   MIP $90

(KP Photo, Tom Michael collection)

❑ **Nucleon,** 1970, Blackwall tires
EX $35   NM $80   MIP $225

❑ **Parnelli Jones Indy Special,**
1970, Blackwall tires
EX $40   NM $80   MIP $250

❑ **Pipe Dream,** 1971, Came with
add-on extras called "Customs;"
prices reflect fully accessorized cars
EX $65   NM $150   MIP $275

(KP Photo, Tom Michael collection)

❑ **Sand Stormer,** 1970, Blackwall tires
EX $20   NM $35   MIP $90

❑ **Sand Stormer,** 1970, Black
roof, blackwall tires
EX $50   NM $100   MIP $200

❑ **Screamer,** 1970, Jet Powered
EX $45   NM $75   MIP $200

❑ **Sling Shot,** 1970, Blackwall
tires
EX $50   NM $95   MIP $250

❑ **Smuggler,** 1970, Blackwall
tires
EX $35   NM $75   MIP $150

(KP Photo)

❑ **Stiletto,** 1970, Blackwall tires,
various paint schemes. The example
shown is pretty rough. The casting
was re-released by Playing Mantis as
part of the "Topper Series"
EX $60   NM $85   MIP $300

❑ **TNT,** 1970, Blackwall tires
EX $40   NM $75   MIP $175

❑ **Triple Threat,** 1970, Blackwall
tires
EX $40   NM $90   MIP $200

❑ **Twin Blaster,** 1971, Came with
add-on extras called "Customs;"
prices reflect fully accessorized cars
EX $65   NM $150   MIP $275

(KP Photo)

❑ **Vicious Vette,** 1970, Blackwall
tires
EX $35   NM $80   MIP $225

❑ **Vulture w/wing,** 1970, Blackwall tires
EX $75   NM $130   MIP $500

❑ **Wasp,** 1970, Blackwall tires
EX $80   NM $100   MIP $400

❑ **Wedge,** 1970, Jet Powered
EX $45   NM $75   MIP $200

❑ **Whistler,** 1970, Blackwall tires
EX $75   NM $125   MIP $300

❑ **Wild Winner,** 1971, Came
w/add on extras called "Customs;"
prices reflect fully accessorized
cars
EX $60   NM $125   MIP $250

Johnny Lightning: Playing Mantis

The Chrysler Atlantic, a "red card" car from Johnny Lightning. The vehicles from the red card series are all-metal, but don't feature rubber tires, opening hoods or any extras. However, they are sharp little cars that typically sell for less than any of the other Johnny Lightning vehicles.

Johnny Lightning cars by Playing Mantis made their first appearance in 1994, one year after company president Tom Lowe purchased a die-cast collection that included some great old Topper cars. Upon learning that the copyright had long run out on Topper's "Johnny Lightning" product name, Lowe applied for it and sent off some vintage cars to have replicas made.

Much as they had been nearly 20 years earlier, the vehicles were an instant hit. Although the first castings were really commemoratives of the vintage Topper lineup, it didn't take long before Playing Mantis released all-new vehicles.

Presently, the differing series of vehicles that Johnny Lightning produces is staggering. Anyone new to collecting the models may be surprised at the volume of variations. The same model car can appear in many guises and colors—sometimes within different releases of the same series.

But the best part of collecting Johnny Lightnings is that they genuinely seem to favor an "out-of-package" experience. Many of the cars feature opening hoods, rubber tires, great tampo detail, collector card or stickers—even miniature model kit boxes.

MARKET UPDATE

With the exception of some of the White Lightning models, most of the Johnny Lightning cars retail for around $5 a piece—often less. At that price, anyone can afford to take them out of a pack and enjoy them. Plus, the series that Johnny Lightning creates are just plain fun. Want a Monkeemobile or a Bluesmobile? Just look at Hollywood on Wheels. How about some of the best-detailed (and most affordable) die-cast military vehicles around? Well, check out the Lightning Brigade—they have everything from modern tanks and humvees to World War II-era Dodge WC-54s and Willys Jeeps. For most Johnny Lightnings collectors, the White Lightning versions of their favorite cars can be the toughest to find, and naturally, the priciest. Expect to pay anywhere from $10 to $40 and even $100 for each model.

From the American Graffiti series, a 1957 Lincoln Premier, featuring rubber tires and an opening hood. Some of Johnny Lightning's best 1950s cars naturally come from this series.

From the Surf Rods series: The "Lava Mamas" Studebaker pickup.

The Monopoly series is another Johnny Lightning group that just begs to be removed from the pack. After all, how else can you play monopoly with the custom game pieces included with every car?

The "Hollywood on Wheels" series includes some of the great TV and movie cars like the Green Hornet's "Black Beauty."

The Ghostbusters' car, from the Fright'ning Lightnings series, 1996. Great detail on this model.

From JL Direct, the '60s VW Van, "Moon and Sun," part of a two-vehicle set that was available to club members in the Winter 2001-2002 catalog.

Another example from the "Hollywood on Wheels" series—the Partridge Family Bus, winner of the Toy Cars and Models reader's award in 1999.

Launched in 2002, the Volkswagen series combines old and new. This is the 1998 New Beetle.

Some of the best military die-cast vehicles are found in Johnny Lightning's "Lightning Brigade" series. This WC-54 is seen in Army and Navy colors.

The Beep Heap is a 2002 release and part of the "Topper Lost Lightnings" series. It is based on promotional drawings seen in old Topper catalogs in 1970. Since this toy (and many planned at the same time) never made it into production, Playing Mantis has brought it to life.

This Studebaker pickup is an example of one of Johnny Lightning's "White Lightning" vehicles. In this case, it features a pearl-white finish and rubber tires, but sometimes the difference is more subtle—white wheels. White Lightnings represent some of the pricer models in Johnny Lightning's lineup, and if you're planning to sell any, you'll want to keep them "in-pack."

Bad Bird from the "Lightning Speed" series. This casting of a modified 1962 T-Bird features hard plastic ridged wheels, much like those found on old Topper Johnny Lightnings.

The Austin Healey Sprite from the "British Invasion" series, a set of classic British sports cars.

The Racing Viper driven by Bobby Archer from the "Classic Gold 2" series. Excellent exterior detail and rubber tires on this model. As with all Johnny Lightnings cars, it features a metal body and base, giving it a substantial weight and feel.

.COM RACERS

(KP Photo)

❏ **Bikini.com,** 1999, Mustang Trans-Am, white, light blue and purple swirl design, orange rims, 1:64 scale

EX n/a   NM n/a   MIP $5

(KP Photo)

❏ **CBS Sports,** 1999, Chevy Monte Carlo race car with yellow stripe along bottom with "cbs.sportsline.com" and number "69" on sides and roof. Black rims, "Goodyear" tires and opening hood, 1:64 scale

EX n/a   NM n/a   MIP $4

(KP Photo)

❏ **eBay,** 1999, Viper GTS-R, white with dark blue, yellow and red color patches, "eBay" on hood and roof, number "12" on hood and sides, 1:64 scale, Model No. 188

EX n/a   NM n/a   MIP $4

(KP Photo)

❏ **Playing Mantis Internet Car,** 1999, Firebird dragster with small front wheels, large rear wheels,

red rims. Black, green, yellow and white body, Playing Mantis on hood, sides and trunk, 1:64 scale, Model No. 062

EX n/a   NM n/a   MIP $4

(KP Photo)

❏ **Y2K VW Bus,** 1999, Orange and blue with either spoked or razor-style chrome wheels, "Y2K Bus" along sides, 1:64 scale

EX n/a   NM n/a   MIP $8

(KP Photo)

❏ **Yahoo!,** 1999, IRL Car, dark blue-green and yellow with "Yahoo!" ovals on sides and front, "Do You Yahoo?" on spoiler. Yellow rims, small number "99" on nose and sides, 1:64 scale, Model No. 184

EX n/a   NM n/a   MIP $4

AD RODS

❏ **'00 Chevy Silverado,** 2001, Dark bronze mist, real wheels rubber tires, photo card, 1:64 scale

EX n/a   NM n/a   MIP $5

❏ **'00 Dodge Ram 2500,** 2001, Shelby red, real wheels, includes miniature reproduction of ad campaign for the truck, "Ever notice how the sheep follow the Ram?" print ad, 1:64 scale

EX n/a   NM n/a   MIP $5

❏ **'34 Ford Coupe,** 2002, Daytona yellow, real wheels, chrome rims, photo card, 1:64 scale, Model No. 567

EX n/a   NM n/a   MIP $5

❏ **'65 Pontiac GTO Convertible,** 2002, Butternut yellow, black

interior, real wheels, chrome rims, photo card, 1:64 scale, Model No. 209

EX n/a   NM n/a   MIP $5

❏ **'67 Camaro,** 2002, Red body, black stripes on hood, black roof, silver rims, photo card, 1:64 scale

EX n/a   NM n/a   MIP $5

❏ **'67 Mercury Cougar,** 2002, White body, silver chrome rims, opening hood, photo card, 1:64 scale

EX n/a   NM n/a   MIP $5

❏ **'68 Ford Mustang,** 2002, Dark metallic body, silver rims, photo card, 1:64 scale

EX n/a   NM n/a   MIP $5

❏ **'69 Camaro RS/SS,** 2002, Rally green body, real wheels, chrome rims, photo card, 1:64 scale, Model No. 537

EX n/a   NM n/a   MIP $5

(KP Photo)

❏ **'70 Al Unser Indy Car,** 2001, Johnny Lightning blue with yellow "lightning bolt" and number "2" on sides and hood, real wheels "Firestone" rubber tires. Includes an repro illustrated ad from 1970, 1:64 scale

EX n/a   NM n/a   MIP $5

❏ **'71 Camaro RS,** 2002, Emerald green body with red stripes running from hood to trunk, real wheels, chrome rims, photo card, 1:64 scale, Model No. 538

EX n/a   NM n/a   MIP $5

❏ **'71 Plymouth Road Runner,** 2002, Mahogany body, real wheels, chrome rims, photo card, 1:64 scale, Model No. 487

EX n/a   NM n/a   MIP $5

❏ **'71 Plymouth Satellite,** 2002, Bright blue body, black interior, silver painted, photo card, 1:64 scale

EX n/a   NM n/a   MIP $5

❏ **'77 Chevy Camaro Z28,** 2001, Brown Firemist, real wheels rubber tires, photo card, 1:64 scale

EX n/a   NM n/a   MIP $5

❏ **'78 Chevy Corvette,** 2001, Moonglow silver, real wheels rubber tires, photo card, 1:64 scale
EX n/a   NM n/a   MIP $5

❏ **'78 Ford Mustang Cobra II,** 2001, Snow white with red stripes, real wheels rubber tires, photo card, 1:64 scale
EX n/a   NM n/a   MIP $5

❏ **'80 Corvette,** 2002, Yellow body, silver chrome wheels, photo card, 1:64 scale
EX n/a   NM n/a   MIP $5

❏ **'88 Ford Mustang,** 2002, Starlight black body, real wheels, chrome rims, photo card, 1:64 scale, Model No. 728
EX n/a   NM n/a   MIP $5

❏ **Absorber Rumbur,** 2002, Orange and black body, silver chrome five-spoke wheels, photo card, 1:64 scale
EX n/a   NM n/a   MIP $5

AMERICAN BLUE

❏ **'66 Ford Galaxy 300,** Kissimmee Police, 1:64 scale
EX n/a   NM n/a   MIP $5

❏ **'66 Ford Galaxy 300,** Missouri State Highway Patrol, 1:64 scale
EX n/a   NM n/a   MIP $5

❏ **'77 Dodge Royal Monaco,** Chicago Police Department, white with blue stripes, 1:64 scale
EX n/a   NM n/a   MIP $5

❏ **'77 Dodge Royal Monaco,** Mount Prospect Police Department, black and white. Available through a mail-in offer, 1:64 scale
EX n/a   NM n/a   MIP $5

❏ **'95 Caprice,** New Hampshire State Police. Green and gold metallic, 1:64 scale
EX n/a   NM n/a   MIP $5

❏ **'95 Caprice,** Key West Police, white body, 1:64 scale
EX n/a   NM n/a   MIP $5

❏ **'95 Caprice,** California Highway Patrol, 1:64 scale
EX n/a   NM n/a   MIP $5

❏ **'95 Corvette ZR-1,** Baltimore Police, bonus car, 1:64 scale
EX n/a   NM n/a   MIP $5

❏ **'97 Camaro,** South Carolina State Police. White pearl finish, 1:64 scale
EX n/a   NM n/a   MIP $5

❏ **'97 Camaro,** Nevada Highway Police, 1:64 scale
EX n/a   NM n/a   MIP $5

❏ **'97 Camaro,** Oregon State Police, 1:64 scale
EX n/a   NM n/a   MIP $5

❏ **'97 Chevy Tahoe,** Michigan State Police. Royal Blue body, 1:64 scale
EX n/a   NM n/a   MIP $5

(KP Photo)

❏ **'97 Chevy Tahoe,** Wisconsin State Police. Blue and white body, "Traffic Patrol," photo card. Each photo card in this series includes info about a missing child on the back., 1:64 scale
EX n/a   NM n/a   MIP $5

❏ **'97 Chevy Tahoe,** Spring Grove Police, 1:64 scale
EX n/a   NM n/a   MIP $5

❏ **'97 Crown Victoria,** New Orleans Police Department. White body. Photo card, 1:64 scale
EX n/a   NM n/a   MIP $5

❏ **'97 Crown Victoria,** New Orleans Harbor Patrol, green and white, 1:64 scale
EX n/a   NM n/a   MIP $5

❏ **'97 Crown Victoria,** Detroit Police, 1:64 scale
EX n/a   NM n/a   MIP $5

❏ **'97 Crown Victoria,** Georgia State Police, 1:64 scale
EX n/a   NM n/a   MIP $5

❏ **'98 Hummer,** Black body, S.P.O.C. in West Virginia, 1:64 scale
EX n/a   NM n/a   MIP $5

❏ **Dodge Royal Monaco,** New York State Police, yellow and blue body, 1:64 scale
EX n/a   NM n/a   MIP $5

❏ **Ford Galaxy 300,** Cook County Sheriff's Office, red and white body, 1:64 scale
EX n/a   NM n/a   MIP $5

AMERICAN CHROME

❏ **'53 Buick Super,** 2000, Sky blue body, rubber whitewall tires, chrome rims, 1:64 scale, Model No. 140
EX n/a   NM n/a   MIP $5

❏ **'53 Buick Super,** 2000, Red-orange body, whitewall "real wheels" rubber tires, 1:64 scale
EX n/a   NM n/a   MIP $5

❏ **'53 Buick Super,** 2001, Mint green, white interior, real wheels rubber tires, opening hood, 1:64 scale
EX n/a   NM n/a   MIP $5

❏ **'53 Buick Super,** 2001, Butternut yellow, real wheels rubber tires, chrome rims, 1:64 scale, Model No. 140
EX n/a   NM n/a   MIP $5

❏ **'53 Buick Super,** 2001, Gunpowder gray body, black interior, real wheels rubber tires, 1:64 scale
EX n/a   NM n/a   MIP $5

❏ **'55 Chrysler C-300,** 2000, White body, opening hood, silver rims, rubber tires, 1:64 scale
EX n/a   NM n/a   MIP $5

❏ **'55 Chrysler C-300,** 2000, Red body, real wheels rubber tires, opening hood, chrome rims, 1:64 scale, Model No. 141
EX n/a   NM n/a   MIP $5

❏ **'55 Chrysler C-300,** 2001, Cameo white body with "Chrysler 300" on doors, real wheels rubber tires, opening hood, 1:64 scale
EX n/a   NM n/a   MIP $5

(KP Photo)

❏ **'55 Chrysler C-300,** 2001, Starlight black body, real wheels, chrome rims, opening hood, 1:64 scale, Model No. 141
EX n/a   NM n/a   MIP $5

❏ **'55 Ford Crown Victoria,** 2000, Blue and white body, whitewall rubber tires, silver rims, 1:64 scale
EX n/a   NM n/a   MIP $5

(KP Photo)

❑ **'55 Ford Crown Victoria,** 2000, Black and Crocus yellow body, real wheels, chrome rims, silver painted trim, 1:64 scale, Model No. 142
EX n/a   NM n/a   MIP $5

❑ **'55 Ford Crown Victoria,** 2001, Tropical rose and Cameo white body, white interior, real wheels rubber tires, 1:64 scale
EX n/a   NM n/a   MIP $5

❑ **'55 Ford Crown Victoria,** 2001, Cascade green body, Cameo white, real wheels, chrome rims, 1:64 scale, Model No. 142
EX n/a   NM n/a   MIP $5

❑ **'55 Ford Crown Victoria,** 2001, Red-orange body, Cameo white roof, real wheels, chrome rims, 1:64 scale, Model No. 142
EX n/a   NM n/a   MIP $5

(KP Photo)

❑ **'57 Lincoln Premier,** 2000, Cameo white body with black roof, "real wheels" rubber whitewall tires, chrome rims, opening hood, 1:64 scale, Model No. 143
EX n/a   NM n/a   MIP $6

(KP Photo, Angelo Van Bogart collection)

❑ **'57 Lincoln Premier,** 2000, Tan body with black roof, black interior, silver painted trim, whitewall "real wheels" rubber tires, chrome rims, 1:64 scale
EX n/a   NM n/a   MIP $6

(KP Photo, Angelo Van Bogart collection)

❑ **'57 Lincoln Premier,** 2000, Turquoise with black roof, whitewall "real wheels" tires, opening hood, chrome rims, 1:64 scale
EX n/a   NM n/a   MIP $6

❑ **'57 Lincoln Premier,** 2001, Bright Seascape blue, real wheels rubber tires, opening hood, chrome rims, 1:64 scale
EX n/a   NM n/a   MIP $6

❑ **'57 Lincoln Premier,** 2001, Bermuda coral, real wheels, chrome rims, 1:64 scale, Model No. 143
EX n/a   NM n/a   MIP $6

❑ **'58 Chevy Impalla,** 2000, Brown metallic body, rubber tires, 1:64 scale
EX n/a   NM n/a   MIP $5

❑ **'58 Chevy Impalla,** 2000, Starlight black body, real wheels rubber tires, chrome rims, 1:64 scale, Model No. 144
EX n/a   NM n/a   MIP $5

❑ **'58 Chevy Impalla,** 2000, Green, marine and white body, real wheels, chrome rims, 1:64 scale, Model No. 144
EX n/a   NM n/a   MIP $5

❑ **'58 Chevy Impalla,** 2001, Matador red body, rubber tires, silver rims, white interior, 1:64 scale
EX n/a   NM n/a   MIP $5

❑ **'58 Chevy Impalla,** 2001, Metallic gold body, real wheels, chrome rims, 1:64 scale, Model No. 144
EX n/a   NM n/a   MIP $5

AMERICAN GRAFFITI

❑ **'23 Ford T-Bucket,** 2001, Red-orange body, black interior, chrome engine, real wheels, chrome rims, 1:64 scale, Model No. 562
EX n/a   NM n/a   MIP $5

❑ **'32 Ford Coupe,** 2001, Daytona yellow, black roof, real wheels, chrome rims, 1:64 scale, Model No. 564
EX n/a   NM n/a   MIP $5

(KP Photo)

❑ **'37 Ford Coupe,** 2001, Starlight black, real wheels rubber tires with thin whitewalls, black interior, silver painted grille and trim, opening hood, chrome rims, 1:64 scale, Model No. 565
EX n/a   NM n/a   MIP $5

❑ **'40 Ford Truck,** 2002, Maize yellow body, real wheels rubber tires, chrome rims, 1:64 scale, Model No. 412
EX n/a   NM n/a   MIP $5

(KP Photo)

❑ **'41 Willys,** 2001, Satin pearl body with darker pearl outlines, real wheels rubber tires with thin whitewalls, chrome rims, silver painted grille and headlights, black interior, 1:64 scale, Model No. 439
EX n/a   NM n/a   MIP $6

❑ **'49 Custom Mercury,** 2001, Bronze, real wheels rubber tires, chrome rims, 1:64 scale, Model No. 751
EX n/a   NM n/a   MIP $5

❑ **'55 Chevy Cameo Truck,** 2002, Red orange body with silver painted grille, real wheels, chrome rims, 1:64 scale, Model No. 414
EX n/a   NM n/a   MIP $5

(KP Photo)

❑ **'55 Chevy Nomad,** 2001, Navajo Tan, (gold) real wheels rubber tires, silver-painted rims, grille and details, gold interior, opening hood, 1:64 scale, Model No. 242

EX n/a   NM n/a   MIP $5

(KP Photo)

❏ **'55 Custom Chevy,** 2001, Starlight black body, off-white interior, real wheels rubber tires, large wheels in rear, smaller in front, chrome rims, 1:64 scale, Model No. 305

EX n/a   NM n/a   MIP $5

❏ **'56 Chevy Bel-Air,** 2002, Sunburst yellow, real wheels, chrome rims, 1:64 scale, Model No. 151

EX n/a   NM n/a   MIP $5

❏ **'56 Ford Thunderbird,** 2001, Antique white, real wheels, chrome rims, 1:64 scale, Model No. 290

EX n/a   NM n/a   MIP $6

❏ **'57 Chevy 210 Coupe,** 2002, Pearl white, real wheels, chrome rims, 1:64 scale, Model No. 427

EX n/a   NM n/a   MIP $5

(KP Photo)

❏ **'57 Chevy Bel-Air,** 2001, Sierra gold body with white roof, silver and gold painted grille, brown interior, real wheels with thin whitewalls, chrome rims, 1:64 scale, Model No. 427

EX n/a   NM n/a   MIP $5

❏ **'57 Chevy Corvette,** 2001, Pearl white, real wheels, chrome rims, 1:64 scale, Model No. 166

EX n/a   NM n/a   MIP $4

❏ **'58 Austin Healey Sprite,** 2001, Daytona yellow, real wheels, chrome rims, 1:64 scale, Model No. 093

EX n/a   NM n/a   MIP $5

(KP Photo)

❏ **'58 Chevy Impala,** 2001, Cameo white body, silver and gold painted trim, real wheels rubber tires, chrome rims, opening hood, white interior, 1:64 scale, Model No. 144

EX n/a   NM n/a   MIP $5

❏ **'61 Ford Galaxie,** 2002, Cameo white, real wheels rubber tires, chrome rims, 1:64 scale, Model No. 781

EX n/a   NM n/a   MIP $5

❏ **'62 Chevy Corvette Convertible,** 2002, Cameo white, red interior, real wheels rubber tires, chrome rims, 1:64 scale, Model No. 167

EX n/a   NM n/a   MIP $5

AMERICAN HEROES - FIRE AND RESCUE

❏ **'80's Crown Victoria Fire Chief,** 2002, Red body, white roof, red dome lights, 1:64 scale

EX n/a   NM n/a   MIP $5

❏ **ATF Bureau '61 Galaxie,** 2002, Green body and wheels, rubber tires, 1:64 scale

EX n/a   NM n/a   MIP $5

❏ **CHP Dodge Monaco,** 2002, Black and white body, California Highway Patrol emblems on doors, 1:64 scale

EX n/a   NM n/a   MIP $5

❏ **Hummer Underwater Rescue,** 2002, Orange body, gray roof, 1:64 scale

EX n/a   NM n/a   MIP $5

❏ **Port Authority NY/NY Chevy Tahoe,** 2002, , 1:64 scale

EX n/a   NM n/a   MIP $5

AMERICA'S FINEST

❏ **'95 Caprice,** Honolulu Police Department, White body. Photo card, 1:64 scale

EX n/a   NM n/a   MIP $6

❏ **'95 Caprice,** St. Louis Metropolitan Police, White Lightning, 1:64 scale

EX n/a   NM n/a   MIP $15

❏ **'97 Camaro,** Contra Costa County, CA, 1:64 scale

EX n/a   NM n/a   MIP $6

❏ **'97 Camaro,** Texas Highway Patrol, black and white body, White Lightning, 1:64 scale

EX n/a   NM n/a   MIP $20

❏ **'97 Crown Victoria,** North Carolina Highway Patrol, metallic silver and black, 1:64 scale

EX n/a   NM n/a   MIP $6

❏ **'97 Crown Victoria,** Indiana State Police, DWI and Seatbelt Enforcement Cruiser. Red, white and blue body. An exclusive mail-in car, 1:64 scale

EX n/a   NM n/a   MIP $12

❏ **'97 Crown Victoria,** Niles Township Police, White Lightning, 1:64 scale

EX n/a   NM n/a   MIP $20

❏ **'97 Tahoe,** Mesquite, Texas Police Department, white body, 1:64 scale

EX n/a   NM n/a   MIP $10

❏ **'97 Tahoe,** Michigan State Police, White Lightning, 1:64 scale

EX n/a   NM n/a   MIP $20

ANNIVERSARY CARS

❏ **'56 Chevy Bel Air,** 2001, Cascade green, rubber tires, chrome rims, photo card & coin, 1:64 scale, Model No. 151

EX n/a   NM n/a   MIP $5

❏ **'66 Chevelle SS 396,** 2001, Snow white body, black interior, rubber tires, chrome rims, photo card & coin, 1:64 scale, Model No. 212

EX n/a   NM n/a   MIP $5

❏ **'70 AMC Rebel Machine,** 2000, White body with gray interior, wide blue stripe on hood, red stripe along sides and on trunk, blue stripe on trunk, rubber tires, silver Cragar rims, 1:64 scale

EX n/a   NM n/a   MIP $5

❏ **'70 Buick GSX,** 2000, Yellow body, chrome wheels, rubber tires, photo card, stand and coin, 1:64 scale

EX n/a   NM n/a   MIP $5

❑ **'70 Camaro RS,** 2000, Red body, black interior, Cragar rims, silver painted grille, 1:64 scale
EX n/a   NM n/a   MIP $5

❑ **'70 Camaro Z28,** 2000, Green metallic body, chrome wheels, rubber tires, 1:64 scale
EX n/a   NM n/a   MIP $5

❑ **'70 Challenger R/T,** 2000, Red body, black airscoop on hood, silver five-spoke Cragar rims, rubber tires, black interior, opening hood, 1:64 scale
EX n/a   NM n/a   MIP $5

❑ **'70 Chevelle SS,** 2001, Red body, black stripes on hood and trunk, silver trim, silver base, 1:64 scale
EX n/a   NM n/a   MIP $5

❑ **'70 Cobra 429,** 2000, Yellow body, black hood, chrome Cragar rims, rubber tires. Like all cars in the Anniversary series, it also comes with a display stand, metal coin and a miniature magazine "Ad Card", 1:64 scale
EX n/a   NM n/a   MIP $5

❑ **'70 Corvette,** 2001, Red body, red interior, rubber ties, silver wheels, opening hood, 1:64 scale
EX n/a   NM n/a   MIP $5

❑ **'70 Mustang Boss 302,** 2000, Orange body, black stripe on hood and sides, black louvers and spoiler, black interior, 1:64 scale
EX n/a   NM n/a   MIP $5

❑ **'70 Olds 4-4-2 Pace Car,** 2000, White body, chrome wheels, rubber tires, photo card, stand and coin, 1:64 scale
EX n/a   NM n/a   MIP $5

❑ **'70 Superbee,** 2001, Lime green body, engine shows through hood, rubber tires, silver chrome Cragar wheels, 1:64 scale
EX n/a   NM n/a   MIP $5

❑ **'70 Superbird,** 2000, Yellow body with black roof, black interior, silver wheels, "Plymouth" in black type on sides under spoiler, 1:64 scale
EX n/a   NM n/a   MIP $5

❑ **'71 Dodge Demon 340,** 2001, Mopar butterscotch body, black roof, black hood, rubber tires, chrome rims, photo card & coin, 1:64 scale, Model No. 231
EX n/a   NM n/a   MIP $5

❑ **'71 Javelin AMX,** 2001, Copper, real wheels, chrome rims, photo card & coin, 1:64 scale, Model No. 219
EX n/a   NM n/a   MIP $5

❑ **'76 Chevy Camaro RS,** 2001, White with starlight black separated by orange stripe, rubber tires, photo card & coin, 1:64 scale, Model No. 539
EX n/a   NM n/a   MIP $5

❑ **'91 GMC Syclone,** 2001, Starlight black, real wheels, chrome rims, photo card & coin, 1:64 scale, Model No. 419
EX n/a   NM n/a   MIP $5

ART CARS

(KP Photo)

❑ **'32 Ford Hi Boy,** 2001, Bright glossy blue, white plastic interior, silver chrome engine, shifter and five spoke wheels, hard tires, photo card. This vehicle is part of the Scott Williamson "Photodesign" subseries, 1:64 scale
EX n/a   NM n/a   MIP $5

❑ **'34 Ford Victoria,** 2001, Snow white body, chrome wheels, hard tires, photo card. Another vehicle in the Scott Williamson "Photodesign" subseries, 1:64 scale
EX n/a   NM n/a   MIP $5

❑ **'54 Chevy Corvette,** 2001, Slate blue body, chrome wheels, hard tires, photo card. In the Lucinda Lewis "Car Culture" subseries, 1:64 scale
EX n/a   NM n/a   MIP $5

❑ **'55 Chevy Bel Air Convertible,** 2001, Matador red body, real wheels rubber tires, photo card, 1:64 scale
EX n/a   NM n/a   MIP $5

❑ **'55 Ford Crown Victoria,** 2001, Tropical rose rose body, real wheels rubber tires, photo card, 1:64 scale
EX n/a   NM n/a   MIP $5

❑ **'61 Chevy Corvette,** 2001, Tor-Red body, hard tires, chrome wheels, photo card. Another vehicle in the Lucinda Lewis "Car Culture" subseries. Other photos by Lewis can be seen in the books "American Cars" and "Roadside America", 1:64 scale
EX n/a   NM n/a   MIP $5

❑ **'63 Chevy Corvette,** 2001, Roman red body, chrome wheels, hard tires, photo card. A part of the Lucinda Lewis "Car Culture" subseries, 1:64 scale
EX n/a   NM n/a   MIP $5

❑ **'66 Jaguar E-Type Roadster,** 2001, Shelby red body, chrome wheels, hard tires, photo card. A vehicle in the Scott Williamson "Photodesign" subseries, 1:64 scale
EX n/a   NM n/a   MIP $5

❑ **'69 Chevy Camaro Z28/RS,** 2001, Calypso coral, real wheels rubber tires, photo card, 1:64 scale
EX n/a   NM n/a   MIP $5

❑ **'70 Plymouth Road Runner,** 2001, Hemi orange, real wheels rubber tires, photo card, 1:64 scale
EX n/a   NM n/a   MIP $5

❑ **'70 Plymouth Superbird,** 2001, Hemi orange body, real wheels rubber tires, photo card, 1:64 scale
EX n/a   NM n/a   MIP $5

❑ **'71 Plymouth Duster 340,** 2001, Sunburst yellow, real wheels rubber tires, photo card, 1:64 scale
EX n/a   NM n/a   MIP $5

BASSIN' USA

❑ **'00 Chevy Silverado Ext. Cab w/trailer:Tom Mann, Jr:,** 2001, Medium green metallic truck with light green trailer, two-tone green boat, hard wheels, chrome rims, photo card, 1:64 scale
EX n/a   NM n/a   MIP $8

❑ **'00 Chevy Silverado Ext. Cab w/trailer: Bernie Schultz,** 2001, Bright blue body, black interior, orange trailer, purple and orange boat, hard tires, photo card, 1:64 scale, Model No. 051
EX n/a   NM n/a   MIP $8

❑ **'00 Chevy Silverado Ext. Cab w/trailer: Denny Brauer,** 2001, Starlight black truck & trailer, purple, blue and black boat, hard wheels, five-spoke chrome rims, photo card, 1:64 scale

EX n/a   NM n/a   MIP $8

❏ **'00 Chevy Silverado w/trailer: Kevin VanDam,** 2001, Candyapple red truck with red trailer, silver and red boat, chrome five spoke wheels, hard tires, photo card, 1:64 scale

EX n/a   NM n/a   MIP $8

❏ **'00 Chevy Silverado w/trailer: Paul Elias,** 2001, Bright metallic blue truck and light blue trailer, hard wheels, chrome rims, photo card, 1:64 scale

EX n/a   NM n/a   MIP $8

❏ **'00 Chevy Silverado w/trailer: Skeet Reese,** 2001, Bright yellow truck with white interior, black trailer with black and yellow boat, silver five spoke wheels, 1:64 scale

EX n/a   NM n/a   MIP $8

BATTLE OF THE BULGE

(KP Photo)

❏ **WWII CCKW 6x6 GMC Tanker,** 2002, Olive drab body and tank section, silver toned star-in-circle designs on doors, hood and rear, taillight tampos, real wheels, green rims, Model No. 067

EX n/a   NM n/a   MIP $6

(KP Photo)

❏ **WWII CCKW 6x6 Troop Transporter,** 2002, Olive drab body, opening hood, silver-tinted white star-in-circle design on hood, black and olive grille, real wheels rubber

tires, olive rims, very realistic detail, Model No. 067

EX n/a   NM n/a   MIP $6

❏ **WWII M-16 Half Track,** 2002, Olive drab, real wheels, star-in-circle design on hood, anti-aircraft guns in truck bed, olive green rims, 1:64 scale, Model No. 070

EX n/a   NM n/a   MIP $6

❏ **WWII WC54 Ambulance,** 2002, Olive drab, real wheels, white star design on hood and doors, red cross on sides and roof, 1:64 scale, Model No. 069

EX n/a   NM n/a   MIP $6

❏ **WWII Willys MB Jeep,** 2002, Olive drab, thin jeep tires, black machine gun mounted in back, , Model No. 065

EX n/a   NM n/a   MIP $6

(KP Photo)

❏ **WWII Willys MB Jeep with top,** 2002, Olive drab body and roof, silver-tinted white star-in-circle design on opening hood, thin jeep tires, green rims. The "Battle of the Bulge" series can also be counted as round 3 of the Lightning Brigade series, , Model No. 065

EX n/a   NM n/a   MIP $6

BRITISH INVASION

❏ **'58-'60 MGA 1500,** 2001, Jorgensen blue body, black interior, real wheels rubber tires, chrome rims, photo card, 1:64 scale, Model No. 090

EX n/a   NM n/a   MIP $5

❏ **'58-'60 MGA TWIN CAM,** White body, real wheels rubber tires, chrome rims, photo card, 1:64 scale

EX n/a   NM n/a   MIP $5

❏ **'58-'60 MGA Twin Cam,** Red body, black interior, opening hood, rubber tires, silver chrome rims, photo card, 1:64 scale

EX n/a   NM n/a   MIP $5

❏ **'58-'61 Austin Healey Sprite,** 2001, Rally green, real wheels, chrome rims, photo card, 1:64 scale, Model No. 093

EX n/a   NM n/a   MIP $5

(KP Photo)

❏ **'58-'61 Austin-Healey Sprite,** Mint green body, opening hood, silver rims, rubber tires, photo card, 1:64 scale

EX n/a   NM n/a   MIP $5

❏ **'58-'61 Austin-Healey Sprite,** White body, silver and black painted grille, rubber tires, photo card, 1:64 scale

EX n/a   NM n/a   MIP $5

❏ **'58-'61 Triumph TR3A,** Red body, silver wheels, rubber tires, photo card, 1:64 scale

EX n/a   NM n/a   MIP $5

❏ **'58-'61 Triumph TR3A,** Black body, tan interior, chrome rims, rubber tires, photo card, 1:64 scale

EX n/a   NM n/a   MIP $5

❏ **'61 Jaguar Convertible,** Black body, silver trim, chrome rims, rubber tires, photo card, 1:64 scale

EX n/a   NM n/a   MIP $5

❏ **'61 Jaguar Convertible,** 2001, Cameo white, tan interior, clear windshield, real wheels, chrome rims, photo card, 1:64 scale, Model No. 784

EX n/a   NM n/a   MIP $5

❏ **'62 Sunbeam Alpine,** Light blue body, black interior, rubber tires, chrome rims, photo card, 1:64 scale

EX n/a   NM n/a   MIP $5

❏ **'62 Sunbeam Alpine,** Royal blue body, black interior, rubber tires, chrome five-spoke rims, photo card, 1:64 scale

EX n/a   NM n/a   MIP $5

(KP Photo)

JOHNNY LIGHTNING / PLAYING MANTIS

❑ **'62 Sunbeam Alpine,** 2001, British green, real wheels, chrome rims, photo card, 1:64 scale, Model No. 651
EX n/a   NM n/a   MIP $5

❑ **'62-'69 MGB,** 2001, Candyapple red body, black interior, real wheels rubber tires, chrome rims, photo card, 1:64 scale, Model No. 091
EX n/a   NM n/a   MIP $5

❑ **'62-'71 MGB,** Antique white body, rubber tires, chrome rims, 1:64 scale
EX n/a   NM n/a   MIP $5

❑ **'62-'71 MGB,** British racing green body, silver chrome rims, 1:64 scale
EX n/a   NM n/a   MIP $5

❑ **'68-'61 Triumph TR3A,** 2001, Light yellow body, tan interior, opening hood, real wheels, chrome rims, photo card, 1:64 scale, Model No. 092
EX n/a   NM n/a   MIP $5

BUFFY THE VAMPIRE SLAYER

❑ **'57 Chevy Bel-Air Convertible: Xander,** 2001, Matador red body, red interior, opening hood, whitewall rubber tires, chrome rims, photo card, 1:64 scale
EX n/a   NM n/a   MIP $5

❑ **'59 DeSoto: Spike,** 2001, Starlight black with gray trim, painted gray rims, real wheels rubber tires, photo card, 1:64 scale
EX n/a   NM n/a   MIP $5

❑ **'63 Citroen: Giles,** 2001, Gray metallic body, painted rims, real wheels rubber tires, photo card, 1:64 scale
EX n/a   NM n/a   MIP $5

(KP Photo, Angelo Van Bogart collection)

❑ **'67 Plymouth GTX: Angel,** 2001, Starlight black convertible with top down, real wheels rubber tires, photo card, 1:64 scale
EX n/a   NM n/a   MIP $7

BUFFY THE VAMPIRE SLAYER & ANGEL

❑ **'57 Chevy Bel-Air Convertible: Xander,** 2001, Skyline light blue body, white interior, opening hood, real wheels, chrome rims, photo card, 1:64 scale, Model No. 241
EX n/a   NM n/a   MIP $5

(KP Photo)

❑ **'59 DeSoto: Spike,** 2001, Starlight black body, chrome rims, thin whitewalls, rubber tires, photo card, 1:64 scale, Model No. 031
EX n/a   NM n/a   MIP $5

(KP Photo)

❑ **'63 Citroen: Giles,** 2001, Quicksilver flat body, real wheels rubber tires, photo card, 1:64 scale, Model No. 032
EX n/a   NM n/a   MIP $5

(KP Photo)

❑ **'67 Plymouth GTX: Angel,** 2001, Starlight black covertible body with top up, black rims, real wheels rubber tires, photo card, 1:64 scale, Model No. 033
EX n/a   NM n/a   MIP $7

CAMAROS

❑ **'67 Camaro,** Red body, mail-in offer bonus car, 1:64 scale
EX n/a   NM n/a   MIP $8

❑ **'67 Camaro RS/SS,** Red body, silver chrome wheels, 1:64 scale
EX n/a   NM n/a   MIP $6

❑ **'67 Camaro RS/SS,** Red body, chrome wheels, 1:64 scale
EX n/a   NM n/a   MIP $5

❑ **'67 Coupe Camaro,** , 1:64 scale
EX n/a   NM n/a   MIP $5

❑ **'68 Camaro RS/SS,** White body, 1:64 scale
EX n/a   NM n/a   MIP $6

❑ **'68 Camaro RS/SS,** Metallic blue body, silver chrome wheels, 1:64 scale
EX n/a   NM n/a   MIP $6

❑ **'68 Camaro Z-28,** Blue body, chrome wheels, 1:64 scale
EX n/a   NM n/a   MIP $6

❑ **'69 Camaro RS,** Black body, silver chrome wheels, 1:64 scale
EX n/a   NM n/a   MIP $6

❑ **'69 Camaro RS/SS 396,** Black body, chrome wheels, 1:64 scale
EX n/a   NM n/a   MIP $5

❑ **'69 COPO Camaro,** 1:64 scale
EX n/a   NM n/a   MIP $5

❑ **'70 Camaro RS/SS,** Metallic blue body, 1:64 scale
EX n/a   NM n/a   MIP $5

❑ **'72 Camaro RS,** Green body, chrome wheels, 1:64 scale
EX n/a   NM n/a   MIP $4

❑ **'73 RS Camaro,** 1:64 scale
EX n/a   NM n/a   MIP $4

❑ **'76 Camaro LT,** Red body, chrome wheels, 1:64 scale
EX n/a   NM n/a   MIP $4

❑ **'76 Coupe Camaro,** 1:64 scale
EX n/a   NM n/a   MIP $4

❑ **'77 Camaro Z28,** White body, silver chrome wheels, 1:64 scale
EX n/a   NM n/a   MIP $5

❑ **'77 Camaro Z28,** 1:64 scale
EX n/a   NM n/a   MIP $4

❑ **'82 Camaro Z28,** Black body, silver wheels, 1:64 scale
EX n/a   NM n/a   MIP $4

❑ **'82 Camaro Z28,** Metallic silver and blue body, 1:64 scale
EX n/a   NM n/a   MIP $4

❑ **'87 IROC-Z Camaro,** 1:64 scale
EX n/a   NM n/a   MIP $4

❑ **'89 Camaro IROC-Z,** Black body, chrome wheels, 1:64 scale
EX n/a   NM n/a   MIP $3

CAMAROS II - 35TH ANNIV.

❏ **'02 35th Anniversary T-Top,** 2002, Orange body, photo card, 1:64 scale
EX n/a   NM n/a   MIP $6

❏ **'67 Sports Coupe,** 2002, Maroon body, photo card, 1:64 scale
EX n/a   NM n/a   MIP $5

❏ **'69 Hardtop,** 2002, Turquoise body, photo card, 1:64 scale
EX n/a   NM n/a   MIP $5

❏ **'70 Camaro RS,** 2002, Gold body, photo card, 1:64 scale
EX n/a   NM n/a   MIP $5

❏ **'75 Rally Sports,** 2002, Red body, photo card, 1:64 scale
EX n/a   NM n/a   MIP $5

❏ **'87 IROC-Z,** 2002, White body, photo card, 1:64 scale
EX n/a   NM n/a   MIP $5

CARTOON NETWORK CARS

(KP Photo)

❏ **Dick Dastardly's Mean Machine,** 1998, Dark purple body with light puple nose and tail, black fenders, silver rims, gray tires, brown interior. Includes animation cel, 1:64 scale
EX n/a   NM n/a   MIP $4

(KP Photo)

❏ **Flintstone's Sports Car,** 1998, Dark brown body with light brown interior, nose and tail. Hole in bottom of body for Fred's feet, silver rims, gray tires, 1:64 scale
EX n/a   NM n/a   MIP $4

❏ **Penelope Pitstop's Compact Pussycat,** 1998, Orange and yellow body, striped umbrella, gray tires, 1:64 scale
EX n/a   NM n/a   MIP $4

❏ **Speed Buggy,** 1998, Orange body, yellow interior, silver wheels, gray tires. This model is generally not found on the pegs like others in the series, 1:64 scale
EX n/a   NM n/a   MIP $7

CLASSIC GOLD

❏ **'33 Custom Willys,** 1998, Cherry red body with "Blood, Sweat and Tears" tampos on sides, "Ansen" and "B&M" sponsor graphics, silver wheels, real wheels rubber tirs, photo card, 1:64 scale
EX n/a   NM n/a   MIP $5

❏ **'33 Custom Willys,** 1998, Blue body with "USA Racing" and various sponsor graphics on sides, silver wheels, "Goodyear" rubber tirs, photo card, 1:64 scale
EX n/a   NM n/a   MIP $5

❏ **'33 Custom Willys,** 1998, Pale orange and white body with flame design, sunroof, silver five-spoke wheels, rubber tires, photo card, 1:64 scale
EX n/a   NM n/a   MIP $5

❏ **'56 Chevy Bel-Air,** 1998, Matador red hood and sides, white roof and trunk, silver wheels, rubber tires, clear windows, 1:64 scale
EX n/a   NM n/a   MIP $5

❏ **'56 Chevy Bel-Air,** 1998, Nassau blue and white, silver wheels, rubber tires, clear windows, 1:64 scale
EX n/a   NM n/a   MIP $5

(KP Photo, Angelo Van Bogart collection)

❏ **'56 Chevy Bel-Air,** 1998, Deep brown and white, silver wheels, rubber tires, clear windows, 1:64 scale
EX n/a   NM n/a   MIP $5

❏ **'63 Impala,** 1998, White body, rubber tires, chrome wheels, photo card, 1:64 scale
EX n/a   NM n/a   MIP $5

❏ **'63 Impala,** 1998, Tuxedo black body, rubber tires, chrome wheels, photo card, 1:64 scale
EX n/a   NM n/a   MIP $5

❏ **'63 Impala,** 1998, Dark metallic red body, rubber tires, chrome wheels, photo card, 1:64 scale
EX n/a   NM n/a   MIP $5

❏ **'66 Shelby GT-350,** 1998, Red body with white stripes running from hood to trunk, rubber tires, silver wheels, opening hood, photo card, 1:64 scale
EX n/a   NM n/a   MIP $5

❏ **'66 Shelby GT-350,** 1998, Wimbledon white body with blue stripes, rubber tires, silver wheels, opening hood, photo card, 1:64 scale
EX n/a   NM n/a   MIP $5

❏ **'66 Shelby GT-350,** 1998, Ivy green body with gold stripes, rubber tires, silver wheels, photo card, 1:64 scale
EX n/a   NM n/a   MIP $5

❏ **'69 Camaro,** 1998, Red body, silver wheels, rubber tires, photo card, 1:64 scale
EX n/a   NM n/a   MIP $5

❏ **'69 Camaro,** 1998, Dusk blue body, silver wheels, rubber tires, photo card, 1:64 scale
EX n/a   NM n/a   MIP $5

❏ **'69 Camaro,** 1998, Orange body, silver chrome wheels, rubber tires, photo card, 1:64 scale
EX n/a   NM n/a   MIP $5

❏ **'69 Hurst SC/Rambler,** 1998, Pro Street white body with opening hood, rubber tires, chrome wheels, photo card, 1:64 scale
EX n/a   NM n/a   MIP $5

❏ **'69 Hurst SC/Rambler,** 1998, Pro Street white body with opening hood, rubber tires, chrome wheels, photo card, 1:64 scale
EX n/a   NM n/a   MIP $5

❏ **'69 Hurst SC/Rambler,** 1998, Rogue white body with hood scoop and opening hood, rubber tires, chrome wheels, photo card, 1:64 scale
EX n/a   NM n/a   MIP $5

❏ **'70 Cougar XR-7,** 1998, Grabber green convertible body, real wheels rubber tires, chrome rims, photo card, 1:64 scale
EX n/a   NM n/a   MIP $5

❑ **'70 Cougar XR-7,** 1998, Grabber orange convertible body, real wheels rubber tires, chrome rims, photo card, 1:64 scale
EX n/a   NM n/a   **MIP** $5

❑ **'70 Cougar XR-7,** 1998, Bright red convertible body, silver chrome wheels, rubber tires, photo card, 1:64 scale
EX n/a   NM n/a   **MIP** $5

❑ **'70 Olds 442,** 1998, Ebony black body, rubber tires, silver wheels, photo card, 1:64 scale
EX n/a   NM n/a   **MIP** $5

❑ **'70 Olds 442,** 1998, Twilight blue body, silver wheels, rubber tires, photo card, 1:64 scale
EX n/a   NM n/a   **MIP** $5

❑ **'70 Olds 442,** 1998, Rally red body, rubber tires, silver wheels, photo card, 1:64 scale
EX n/a   NM n/a   **MIP** $5

❑ **'74 Olds Cutlass,** 1998, Saturn gold body, rubber tires, photo card, 1:64 scale
EX n/a   NM n/a   **MIP** $5

❑ **'74 Olds Cutlass,** 1998, Beige body, silver wheels, rubber tires, photo card, 1:64 scale
EX n/a   NM n/a   **MIP** $5

❑ **'74 Olds Cutlass,** 1998, Nordic blue body, rubber tires, photo card, 1:64 scale
EX n/a   NM n/a   **MIP** $5

❑ **'80s Buick T-Type,** 1998, Black body, silver five-spoke wheels, rubber tires, photo card, 1:64 scale
EX n/a   NM n/a   **MIP** $5

❑ **'80s Buick T-Type,** 1998, Black body with silver trim, silver five-spoke wheels, rubber tires, photo card, 1:64 scale
EX n/a   NM n/a   **MIP** $5

❑ **'80s Buick T-Type,** 1998, Silver body, silver five-spoke wheels, rubber tires, photo card, 1:64 scale
EX n/a   NM n/a   **MIP** $5

CLASSIC GOLD 2

❑ **"Clark's Service" Ford Tow Truck,** 2001, Roman red, real wheels rubber tires, red tow boom, red emergency lights, photo card, 1:64 scale
EX n/a   NM n/a   **MIP** $5

❑ **'41 Willys Gasser,** 2000, Daytona yellow with purple and pink tampo design on rear quarter panel, chrome wheels, rubber tires, silver-painted grille and headlights, rubber tires, photo card, 1:64 scale
EX n/a   NM n/a   **MIP** $5

❑ **'41 Willy's Pro Stock,** Candyapple red body, silver wheels, rubber tires, photo card, 1:64 scale
EX n/a   NM n/a   **MIP** $5

❑ **'41 Willy's Pro Street,** Starlight black body, rubber tires, photo card, 1:64 scale
EX n/a   NM n/a   **MIP** $5

❑ **'49 Mercury,** 2000, Roman red body, silver rims, whitewall rubber tires, photo card, 1:64 scale
EX n/a   NM n/a   **MIP** $5

❑ **'56 Chevy Bel-Air,** 2000, Hemi-orange body with rubber tires, silver wheels, photo card, 1:64 scale
EX n/a   NM n/a   **MIP** $5

❑ **'57 Chevy Bel Air,** 2001, Cobalt blue body with white roof and trim, real wheels rubber tires, chrome rims and bumpers, photo card, 1:64 scale, Model No. 427
EX n/a   NM n/a   **MIP** $5

❑ **'59 El Camino,** White and red body, silver rims, rubber whitewall tires, photo card, 1:64 scale
EX n/a   NM n/a   **MIP** $5

❑ **'63 Chevy Nova,** 2001, Sunset Pearl (metallic blue) body, real wheels rubber tires, silver-painted headlights, photo card, 1:64 scale
EX n/a   NM n/a   **MIP** $5

❑ **'64 Pontiac GTO,** 2002, Nocturne blue body, silver-painted trim, real wheels rubber tires, chrome rims, photo card, 1:64 scale, Model No. 096
EX n/a   NM n/a   **MIP** $5

❑ **'65 Mustang Convertible,** Sunset orange body, opening hood, real wheels rubber tires, photo card, 1:64 scale
EX n/a   NM n/a   **MIP** $5

❑ **'67 Camaro RS Convertible,** 2001, Snow white body, black interior, two black stripes running from hood to trunk, real wheels rubber tires, opening hood, photo card, 1:64 scale
EX n/a   NM n/a   **MIP** $5

❑ **'67 Corvette Roadster,** 2000, Red body with white roof, chrome wheels, rubber tires, photo card, 1:64 scale
EX n/a   NM n/a   **MIP** $5

❑ **'67 Pontiac GTO,** Black body, opening hood, silver wheels, silver-painted trim, rubber tires, photo card, 1:64 scale
EX n/a   NM n/a   **MIP** $5

❑ **'68 Chevy Camaro,** 2002, Glacier blue body, white roof, white stripe on front, real wheels rubber tires, chrome rims, photo card, 1:64 scale, Model No. 536
EX n/a   NM n/a   **MIP** $5

❑ **'68 Chevy Camaro RS/SS,** 2002, Sunset orange body, exposed engine, real wheels, chrome rims, photo card, 1:64 scale, Model No. 536
EX n/a   NM n/a   **MIP** $5

❑ **'69 AMX,** 1998, Mail-in offer car: Orange body, rubber tires, photo card, 1:64 scale
EX n/a   NM n/a   **MIP** $5

❑ **'69 AMX,** 2000, Bright "Big Bad Green" body with black stripes running from hood to trunk, silver chrome wheels, black grille, rubber tires, photo card, 1:64 scale
EX n/a   NM n/a   **MIP** $5

❑ **'69 AMX Javelin,** Aztec copper body, silver wheels, rubber tires. Bonus car from mail-in offer, 1:64 scale
EX n/a   NM n/a   **MIP** $5

❑ **'69 Camaro RS/SS,** 2001, Snow white body with black roof, opening hood, real wheels rubber tires, chrome rims, photo card, 1:64 scale, Model No. 537
EX n/a   NM n/a   **MIP** $5

❑ **'69 Charger RT/SE,** 2002, Yellow body with black roof and stripe, silver five-spoke wheels, rubber tires, photo card, 1:64 scale
EX n/a   NM n/a   **MIP** $5

❑ **'69 Chevy Nova SS,** 2002, Candyapple red body, real wheels rubber tires, chrome rims, photo card, 1:64 scale, Model No. 098
EX n/a   NM n/a   **MIP** $5

❑ **'69 Ford Mustang Mach 1,** 2001, Champagne body, opening black hood, real wheels rubber tires, photo card, 1:64 scale
EX n/a   NM n/a   **MIP** $5

❑ **'69 Mercury Cougar,** British Racing Green body, silver wheels, rubber tires, opening hood, photo card, 1:64 scale
EX n/a　　NM n/a　　MIP $5

❑ **'70 Chevelle SS,** 2000, Quick-silver body with real wheels rubber tires, five-spoke silver wheels, photo card, 1:64 scale
EX n/a　　NM n/a　　MIP $5

❑ **'70 Mercury Cyclone GT,** 2002, Tor-Red body, black roof, real wheels rubber tires, chrome rims, photo card, 1:64 scale, Model No. 097
EX n/a　　NM n/a　　MIP $5

❑ **'70 Montego,** 2002, Intense blue pearl body, real wheels rubber tires, photo card, 1:64 scale
EX n/a　　NM n/a　　MIP $5

❑ **'70 Olds 442,** 2000, Black and gold convertible body, chrome wheels, opening hood, rubber tires, photo card, 1:64 scale
EX n/a　　NM n/a　　MIP $5

❑ **'71 Boss Mustang,** Metallic blue body, silver wheels, rubber tires, photo card, 1:64 scale
EX n/a　　NM n/a　　MIP $5

❑ **'71 Challenger Convertible,** Silver body, rubber tires, chrome wheels, photo card, 1:64 scale
EX n/a　　NM n/a　　MIP $5

❑ **'71 Chevy El Camino,** 2001, Hemi orange body with two black stripes on hood, real wheels rubber tires, silver rims, photo card, 1:64 scale
EX n/a　　NM n/a　　MIP $5

❑ **'71 Chevy Nova,** 2001, Calypso Coral (red-orange) body, silver five-spoke wheels, rubber tires, opening hood, photo card, 1:64 scale
EX n/a　　NM n/a　　MIP $5

❑ **'71 Ford Mustang Mach 1,** 2000, Sunburst yellow body with black stripe, silver wheels, rubber tires, photo card, 1:64 scale
EX n/a　　NM n/a　　MIP $5

❑ **'71 Plymouth Cuda Convertible,** 2001, Glacier blue body, blue interior, blue rims, real wheels rubber tires, photo card, 1:64 scale
EX n/a　　NM n/a　　MIP $5

❑ **'72 Chevy Nova SS,** 2002, Seafoam turquoise with wide

black stripes on hood and trunk, real wheels rubber tires, chrome rims, photo card, 1:64 scale, Model No. 098
EX n/a　　NM n/a　　MIP $5

❑ **'72 Olds 422 Convertible,** Atlantic blue body, real wheels rubber tires, photo card, 1:64 scale
EX n/a　　NM n/a　　MIP $5

❑ **'72 Plymouth Road Runner,** 2002, Orange body, opening hood with scoops, silver wheels, rubber tires, photo card, 1:64 scale
EX n/a　　NM n/a　　MIP $5

❑ **'73 Camaro Z28,** 2001, Goofy Grape (lilac purple) body with exposed engine and no hood, silver wheels, rubber tires, photo card, 1:64 scale
EX n/a　　NM n/a　　MIP $5

❑ **'73 Dodge Charger,** 2001, Sherwood green body, white roof, real wheels rubber tires, chrome rims, photo card, 1:64 scale, Model No. 232
EX n/a　　NM n/a　　MIP $5

❑ **'74 Ford Torino,** Metallic brown body, rubber tires, photo card, 1:64 scale
EX n/a　　NM n/a　　MIP $5

❑ **'76 Camaro,** 2001, Blue body with wide white stripe on hood and trunk, real wheels rubber tires, chrome rims, photo card, 1:64 scale, Model No. 539
EX n/a　　NM n/a　　MIP $5

❑ **'77 Ford Mustang Cobra II,** 2000, Starlight black body with silver-painted headlights, chrome wheels, rubber tires, photo card, 1:64 scale
EX n/a　　NM n/a　　MIP $5

❑ **'78 Ford Mustang II King Cobra,** 1998, Red body, rubber tires, chrome wheels, photo card, 1:64 scale
EX n/a　　NM n/a　　MIP $5

❑ **'78 Mustang II King Cobra,** Red body, real wheels rubber tires, photo card, 1:64 scale
EX n/a　　NM n/a　　MIP $5

❑ **'79 Corvette,** 2001, Navy blue body, white interior, real wheels rubber tires, chrome rims, photo card, 1:64 scale, Model No. 466
EX n/a　　NM n/a　　MIP $5

❑ **'79 Dodge Midnight Express,** Starlight black body, rubber tires, photo card, 1:64 scale
EX n/a　　NM n/a　　MIP $5

❑ **'92 Camaro RS,** 2001, Black and white police car with "Highway Patrol" lettering and shield on doors, real wheels rubber tires, five-spoke chrome wheels, photo card, 1:64 scale
EX n/a　　NM n/a　　MIP $5

❑ **'95 Chevrolet Impala SS,** 2000, Wineberry body with silver chrome wheels, rubber tires, photo card, 1:64 scale
EX n/a　　NM n/a　　MIP $5

❑ **'96 Dodge Viper,** Red body, silver wheels, rubber tires, photo card, 1:64 scale
EX n/a　　NM n/a　　MIP $5

❑ **'96 Dodge Viper GTS,** GTS Blue, silver rims, real wheels rubber tires, photo card, 1:64 scale
EX n/a　　NM n/a　　MIP $5

❑ **'97 Chevy Caprice Taxi,** Yellow Cab markings, silver wheels, rubber tires, photo card, 1:64 scale
EX n/a　　NM n/a　　MIP $5

❑ **'97 Chevy Tahoe,** White body, rubber tires, chrome rims, photo card, 1:64 scale
EX n/a　　NM n/a　　MIP $5

❑ **'97 Chevy Tahoe,** Blue metallic body, rubber tires, photo card, 1:64 scale
EX n/a　　NM n/a　　MIP $5

❑ **'97 Dodge Ram SS/T,** 2001, Starlight black body with yellow/orange stripes running up hood and roof, real wheels rubber tires, chrome rims, photo card, 1:64 scale
EX n/a　　NM n/a　　MIP $5

❑ **'97 Impala SS,** Black body, rubber tires, photo card, 1:64 scale
EX n/a　　NM n/a　　MIP $5

❑ **'99 Plymouth Prowler,** 2001, Yellow body with red and orange stripes, black interior, real wheels rubber tires, chrome rims, photo card, 1:64 scale, Model No. 162
EX n/a　　NM n/a　　MIP $5

❑ **'99 Pontiac Firebird,** 2001, White body with two wide blue stripes running from hood to trunk, white interior, rubber tires, photo card, 1:64 scale
EX n/a　　NM n/a　　MIP $5

❑ **Austin Healey,** 2002, Bright blue body, black interior, silver rims, photo card, 1:64 scale
EX n/a　　NM n/a　　MIP $5

❑ **Boothill Express,** 2000, Red and black with silver engine and five-spoke wheels, rubber tires, photo card, 1:64 scale
EX n/a   NM n/a   MIP $5

❑ **Dodge A-100 Truck: Dodge Fever,** 2001, Red, white and blue body with "Dodge Fever" on center white stripe, silver wheels, exposed engine in truck bed, real wheels rubber tires, photo card, 1:64 scale
EX n/a   NM n/a   MIP $5

❑ **Dodge Viper,** 2002, White and blue body, real wheels rubber tires, photo card, 1:64 scale
EX n/a   NM n/a   MIP $5

(KP Photo)

❑ **Racing Viper GTS: Bobby Archer,** 2000, Metallic twilight blue body with red and white "swoop" on sides, number "32" on sides, front and rear, "Viper Speed Racing" on hood, sides and roof, "Dodge" in yellow lettering on roof, silver five-spoke wheels, real wheels rubber tires, photo card, 1:64 scale
EX n/a   NM n/a   MIP $5

❑ **Shelby Cobra Terlingua,** 2002, Black body with yellow stripe on hood, sponsor decals, silver five-spoke wheels, photo card, 1:64 scale
EX n/a   NM n/a   MIP $5

CLASSIC PLASTIC

❑ **'66 Volkswagen Beetle,** 2002, Candyapple red body, silver spoked wheels, includes miniature model kit box, 1:64 scale
EX n/a   NM n/a   MIP $5

❑ **'70 Dodge Challenger F/C Ram-Rod,** 2001, Cherry red, real wheels, chrome rims, miniature Model Kit Box, 1:64 scale, Model No. 345
EX n/a   NM n/a   MIP $5

❑ **'71 Ford Mustang F/C Boss Hoss,** 2002, Pacific blue, real wheels, chrome rims, miniature Model Kit Box, 1:64 scale, Model No. 347
EX n/a   NM n/a   MIP $5

❑ **'71 Plymouth Cuda Sox & Martin,** 2002, Snow white body, silver wheels, rubber tires, miniature Model Kit Box, 1:64 scale, Model No. 330
EX n/a   NM n/a   MIP $5

❑ **'72 AMC Javelin AMX,** 2002, McLaren yellow, real wheels, chrome rims, Miniature Model Kit Box, 1:64 scale, Model No. 219
EX n/a   NM n/a   MIP $5

❑ **Aurora Black Beauty,** 2002, Black body, includes miniature model kit box, 1:64 scale
EX n/a   NM n/a   MIP $5

❑ **Aurora Sad Sack '27,** 2002, Yellow and orange Ford roadster with miniature model kit box, 1:64 scale
EX n/a   NM n/a   MIP $5

❑ **Aurora Vega Funny Car,** 2002, , 1:64 scale
EX n/a   NM n/a   MIP $5

❑ **Badman,** 2001, , 1:64 scale
EX n/a   NM n/a   MIP $5

❑ **Boothill Express,** 2001, 1:64 scale
EX n/a   NM n/a   MIP $5

❑ **Draggin' Dragon,** 2001, 1:64 scale
EX n/a   NM n/a   MIP $5

❑ **Haulin' Hearse,** 2001, Light yellow, real wheels, chrome rims, miniature Model Kit Box, 1:64 scale, Model No. 508
EX n/a   NM n/a   MIP $5

❑ **Hemi Under Glass,** 2001, 1:64 scale
EX n/a   NM n/a   MIP $5

❑ **Hurst Hairy Olds,** 2001, 1:64 scale
EX n/a   NM n/a   MIP $5

❑ **Jo-Han '69 AMX,** 2002, Dark blue with white stripes running from hood to trunk, miniature model kit box, 1:64 scale
EX n/a   NM n/a   MIP $5

❑ **Jo-Han '69 SC/Rambler,** 2002, White body with red stripes on sides, blue stripe running from hood to trunk, miniature model kit box, 1:64 scale
EX n/a   NM n/a   MIP $5

❑ **Jo-Han '70 Rebel Machine,** 2002, White body with red and blue tampos, "Rebel" on sides, miniature model kit box, 1:64 scale
EX n/a   NM n/a   MIP $5

❑ **Plymouth Superbird Sox & Martin,** 2001, Snow white body, rubber tires, chrome rims, Miniature Model Kit Box, 1:64 scale, Model No. 201
EX n/a   NM n/a   MIP $5

❑ **Vampire Van,** 2001, 1:64 scale
EX n/a   NM n/a   MIP $5

COMMEMORATIVE

❑ **Bug Bomb,** White Lightnings edition, 1993, 1:64 scale
EX n/a   NM n/a   MIP $10

❑ **Bug Bomb,** 1994, Chocolate brown body, silver engines, front and rear, Topper-style redlines hard wheels, 1:64 scale
EX n/a   NM n/a   MIP $5

❑ **Bug Bomb,** 1994, Slate blue body, two silver engines, (black plastic exhaust pipes on rear engine) Topper-style redlines hard wheels, collector coin, 1:64 scale
EX n/a   NM n/a   MIP $4

❑ **Bug Bomb,** 1994, Red body, two large silver engines, black exhaust pipes, unpainted base, 1:64 scale
EX n/a   NM n/a   MIP $5

❑ **Bug Bomb,** 1994, Hot pink body, two silver plastic engines, unpainted base, Topper-style redlines wheels, collector coin, 1:64 scale
EX n/a   NM n/a   MIP $5

❑ **Bug Bomb,** 1994, Black body, silver exposed engines in front and rear, Topper-style redlines hard tires, collector coin, 1:64 scale
EX n/a   NM n/a   MIP $5

❑ **Bug Bomb,** 1994, Red-orange body, two silver engines, unpainted base, Topper-style redlines wheels, collector coin, 1:64 scale
EX n/a   NM n/a   MIP $5

❑ **Bug Bomb,** 1994, Bright yellow body, silver exposed engines front and back, unpainted base, collector coin, 1:64 scale
EX n/a   NM n/a   MIP $5

❑ **Bug Bomb,** 1994, Sky blue body, two silver plastic engines,

unpainted base, collector coin, 1:64 scale
EX n/a   **NM** n/a   **MIP** $5

❑ **Bug Bomb,** 1994, Light metallic purple body, front and rear engines, unpainted base, collector coin, 1:64 scale
EX n/a   **NM** n/a   **MIP** $5

❑ **Bug Bomb,** 1994, Emerald green body, silver exposed engines front and back, (rear engine with black exhaust pipes), hard redline-style wheels, 1:64 scale
EX n/a   **NM** n/a   **MIP** $5

❑ **Custom '32 Roadster,** White Lightnings edition, 1:64 scale
EX n/a   **NM** n/a   **MIP** $10

❑ **Custom '32 Roadster,** 1994, Black body, Topper-style redline hard wheels, exposed silver engine, collector coin, 1:64 scale
EX n/a   **NM** n/a   **MIP** $5

❑ **Custom '32 Roadster,** 1994, Emerald green body, silver engine, clear windshield, Topper-style redlines wheels, collector coin with production number, 1:64 scale
EX n/a   **NM** n/a   **MIP** $5

❑ **Custom '32 Roadster,** 1994, Slate blue body, exposed silver engine, unpainted base, collector coin, 1:64 scale
EX n/a   **NM** n/a   **MIP** $5

❑ **Custom '32 Roadster,** 1994, Bright yellow body, clear windshield, Topper-style redlines hard tires, collector coin, 1:64 scale
EX n/a   **NM** n/a   **MIP** $5

❑ **Custom '32 Roadster,** 1994, Hot pink body, Topper-style redlines hard tires, 1:64 scale
EX n/a   **NM** n/a   **MIP** $4

❑ **Custom '32 Roadster,** 1994, Cherry red body, clear windshield, exposed engine, unpainted base, collector, 1:64 scale
EX n/a   **NM** n/a   **MIP** $5

❑ **Custom '32 Roadster,** 1994, Chocolate brown body, unpainted base, exposed engine, 1:64 scale
EX n/a   **NM** n/a   **MIP** $5

❑ **Custom '32 Roadster,** 1994, Sky blue body, clear windshield, Topper-style redlines hard wheels, collector coin, 1:64 scale
EX n/a   **NM** n/a   **MIP** $5

❑ **Custom '32 Roadster,** 1994, Red-orange body, clear windshield, silver engine, Topper-style redlines wheels, collector coin, 1:64 scale
EX n/a   **NM** n/a   **MIP** $5

❑ **Custom '32 Roadster,** 1994, Light purple body, hard redline-style wheels, unpainted base, 1:64 scale
EX n/a   **NM** n/a   **MIP** $5

❑ **Custom Camaro,** 1:64 scale
EX n/a   **NM** n/a   **MIP** $4

❑ **Custom Charger,** 1:64 scale
EX n/a   **NM** n/a   **MIP** $4

❑ **Custom Continental,** 1:64 scale
EX n/a   **NM** n/a   **MIP** $4

❑ **Custom Continental,** White Lightnings edition, 1:64 scale
EX n/a   **NM** n/a   **MIP** $12

❑ **Custom Dragster,** 1:64 scale
EX n/a   **NM** n/a   **MIP** $4

❑ **Custom El Camino,** White Lightnings edition, 1:64 scale
EX n/a   **NM** n/a   **MIP** $12

❑ **Custom El Camino,** 1994, Bright yellow body, unpainted base, Topper-style hard wheels, collector coin, 1:64 scale
EX n/a   **NM** n/a   **MIP** $5

❑ **Custom El Camino,** 1994, Hot pink body, unpainted base, Topper-style hard wheels, collector coin, 1:64 scale
EX n/a   **NM** n/a   **MIP** $5

❑ **Custom El Camino,** 1994, Slate blue body, unpainted base, Topper-style hard wheels, collector coin, 1:64 scale
EX n/a   **NM** n/a   **MIP** $4

❑ **Custom El Camino,** 1994, Light purple body, unpainted base, Topper-style hard wheels, collector coin, 1:64 scale
EX n/a   **NM** n/a   **MIP** $5

❑ **Custom El Camino,** 1994, Emerald green body, unpainted base, Topper-style hard wheels, collector coin, 1:64 scale
EX n/a   **NM** n/a   **MIP** $5

❑ **Custom El Camino,** 1994, Black body, unpainted base, redline-style hard wheels, collector coin, 1:64 scale
EX n/a   **NM** n/a   **MIP** $4

❑ **Custom El Camino,** 1994, Champagne body, unpainted base, Topper-style hard wheels, collector coin, 1:64 scale
EX n/a   **NM** n/a   **MIP** $4

❑ **Custom El Camino,** 1994, Charcoal body, unpainted base, Topper-style hard wheels, collector coin, 1:64 scale
EX n/a   **NM** n/a   **MIP** $4

❑ **Custom El Camino,** 1994, Cherry red body, unpainted base, Topper-style hard wheels, collector coin, 1:64 scale
EX n/a   **NM** n/a   **MIP** $4

❑ **Custom El Camino,** 1994, Chocolate brown body, unpainted base, Topper-style hard wheels, collector coin, 1:64 scale
EX n/a   **NM** n/a   **MIP** $4

❑ **Custom GTO,** , 1:64 scale
EX n/a   **NM** n/a   **MIP** $4

❑ **Custom GTO,** White Lightnings edition, 1:64 scale
EX n/a   **NM** n/a   **MIP** $12

❑ **Custom GTO,** 1994, Green body, unpainted base, redline Topper-style wheels, collector coin, 1:64 scale
EX n/a   **NM** n/a   **MIP** $5

❑ **Custom GTO,** 1994, Hot pink body, Topper-style redline hard wheels, unpainted base, collector coin, 1:64 scale
EX n/a   **NM** n/a   **MIP** $4

❑ **Custom GTO,** 1994, Slate blue body, unpainted base, redline-style hard tires, collector coin, 1:64 scale
EX n/a   **NM** n/a   **MIP** $4

❑ **Custom GTO,** 1994, Yellow body, unpainted base, Topper-style redlines hard tires, 1:64 scale
EX n/a   **NM** n/a   **MIP** $4

❑ **Custom GTO,** 1994, Light purple body, unpainted base, Topper-style redlines hard wheels, collector coin, 1:64 scale
EX n/a   **NM** n/a   **MIP** $5

❑ **Custom GTO,** 1994, Champagne body, unpainted base, Topper-style redlines hard tires, collector coin, 1:64 scale
EX n/a   **NM** n/a   **MIP** $5

❑ **Custom GTO,** 1994, Dark blue body, unpainted base, Topper-style redlines hard wheels, collector coin with production number, 1:64 scale
EX n/a   **NM** n/a   **MIP** $4

❏ **Custom GTO,** 1994, Cherry red body, unpainted base, Topper-style redlines wheels, collector coin, 1:64 scale
EX n/a   NM n/a   MIP $5

❏ **Custom GTO,** 1994, Chocolate brown body, unpainted base, Topper-style redline wheels, collector coin, 1:64 scale
EX n/a   NM n/a   MIP $5

❏ **Custom GTO,** 1994, Black body, unpainted base, hard redline-style wheels, collector coin, 1:64 scale
EX n/a   NM n/a   MIP $4

❏ **Custom L,** 1:64 scale
EX n/a   NM n/a   MIP $4

❏ **Custom Mako Shark,** 1:64 scale
EX n/a   NM n/a   MIP $6

❏ **Custom Mako Shark,** White Lightnings edition, 1:64 scale
EX n/a   NM n/a   MIP $15

❏ **Custom Mustang,** 1:64 scale
EX n/a   NM n/a   MIP $4

❏ **Custom Mustang,** White Lightnings edition, 1:64 scale
EX n/a   NM n/a   MIP $15

❏ **Custom Spoiler,** 1:64 scale
EX n/a   NM n/a   MIP $4

❏ **Custom Spoiler,** White Lightnings edition, 1:64 scale
EX n/a   NM n/a   MIP $10

❏ **Custom Stiletto,** 1:64 scale
EX n/a   NM n/a   MIP $4

❏ **Custom T-Bird,** 1:64 scale
EX n/a   NM n/a   MIP $4

❏ **Custom T-Bird,** White Lightnings edition, 1:64 scale
EX n/a   NM n/a   MIP $15

(KP Photo, Angelo Van Bogart collection)

❏ **Custom T-Bird,** 1995, Light metallic green body, white interior, silver wheels. A re-release of original Topper model, 1:64 scale
EX n/a   NM n/a   MIP $4

❏ **Custom Toronado,** 1:64 scale
EX n/a   NM n/a   MIP $4

❏ **Custom Toronado,** White Lightnings edition, 1:64 scale
EX n/a   NM n/a   MIP $10

❏ **Custom Turbine,** 1:64 scale
EX n/a   NM n/a   MIP $4

❏ **Custom Turbine,** White Lightnings edition, 1:64 scale
EX n/a   NM n/a   MIP $10

❏ **Custom XKE,** White Lightnings edition, 1:64 scale
EX n/a   NM n/a   MIP $10

❏ **Custom XKE,** 1994, Light purple body, opening hood, Topper-style redline hard wheels, unpainted base, collector coin, 1:64 scale
EX n/a   NM n/a   MIP $5

❏ **Custom XKE,** 1994, Hot pink body, opening hood, hard Topper-style redline wheels, collector coin, 1:64 scale
EX n/a   NM n/a   MIP $4

❏ **Custom XKE,** 1994, Emerald green body, opening hood, unpainted base, 1:64 scale
EX n/a   NM n/a   MIP $5

❏ **Custom XKE,** 1994, Charcoal body, opening hood, unpainted base, Topper-style redlines hard tires, collector coin, 1:64 scale
EX n/a   NM n/a   MIP $5

❏ **Custom XKE,** 1994, Chocolate body, opening hood, Topper-style redlines hard wheels, collector coin, 1:64 scale
EX n/a   NM n/a   MIP $5

❏ **Custom XKE,** 1994, Black body, opening hood, Topper-style redlines hard wheels, unpainted base, collector coin with production number, 1:64 scale
EX n/a   NM n/a   MIP $4

❏ **Custom XKE,** 1994, Yellow body, unpainted base, Topper-style redline wheels, opening hood, collector coin, 1:64 scale
EX n/a   NM n/a   MIP $4

❏ **Custom XKE,** 1994, Cherry red body, opening hood, unpainted base, Topper-style redlines wheels, collector coin, 1:64 scale
EX n/a   NM n/a   MIP $5

❏ **Custom XKE,** 1994, Teal body, unpainted base, opening hood, Topper-style hard wheels, collector coin, 1:64 scale
EX n/a   NM n/a   MIP $5

❏ **Custom XKE,** 1994, Slate blue body, opening hood, hard redline-style wheels, unpainted base, collector coin, 1:64 scale
EX n/a   NM n/a   MIP $4

❏ **Flame Out,** 1:64 scale
EX n/a   NM n/a   MIP $4

❏ **Mad Maverick,** 1:64 scale
EX n/a   NM n/a   MIP $4

❏ **Movin' Van,** 1994, Chocolate brown body, "Movin' Van" tampo on panel section, silver exposed engine, black plastic exhaust pipes, collector coin, 1:64 scale
EX n/a   NM n/a   MIP $5

❏ **Movin' Van,** 1994, Hot pink body, prominent unpainted base, small Topper-style redlines wheels all-around, "Movin' Van" in oval on panel sides, collector coin, 1:64 scale
EX n/a   NM n/a   MIP $5

❏ **Movin' Van,** 1994, Black body, unpainted base, small Topper-style redlines hard wheels, "Movin' Van" in oval on sides, collector coin, 1:64 scale
EX n/a   NM n/a   MIP $5

❏ **Movin' Van,** 1994, Cherry red body, small Topper-style redline wheels, unpainted base, "Movin' Van" in white type in oval design on panels, 1:64 scale
EX n/a   NM n/a   MIP $5

❏ **Movin' Van,** 1994, Emerald green body, large unpainted base, small Topper-style redlines wheels, collector coin, 1:64 scale
EX n/a   NM n/a   MIP $5

❏ **Movin' Van,** 1994, Slate blue body, small Topper style redlines all around, large unpainted base, collector coin, 1:64 scale
EX n/a   NM n/a   MIP $5

❏ **Movin' Van,** 1994, Yellow-orange body, unpainted base, Topper-style redlines hard tires, collector coin, 1:64 scale
EX n/a   NM n/a   MIP $5

❏ **Movin' Van,** 1994, Light purple body, "Movin' Van" in white type in black oval on sides, small redline-style wheels, 1:64 scale
EX n/a   NM n/a   MIP $5

❏ **Movin' Van,** 1994, Light green body, unpainted base, small Topper-style redlines wheels, collector coin with production number, 1:64 scale

EX n/a NM n/a MIP $5

❑ **Movin' Van,** 1994, Yellow body, "Movin' Van" tampos on sides, small redline-style wheels, unpainted base, collector coin, 1:64 scale

EX n/a NM n/a MIP $5

❑ **Nucleon,** 1:64 scale

EX n/a NM n/a MIP $4

❑ **Nucleon,** White Lightnings edition, 1:64 scale

EX n/a NM n/a MIP $10

❑ **Sand Stormer,** 1:64 scale

EX n/a NM n/a MIP $4

❑ **T.N.T.,** 1:64 scale

EX n/a NM n/a MIP $4

❑ **T.N.T.,** White Lightnings edition, 1:64 scale

EX n/a NM n/a MIP $10

❑ **The Wasp,** White Lightnings edition, 1:64 scale

EX n/a NM n/a MIP $10

❑ **The Wasp,** 1994, Teal body, rear-mounted silver plastic engine, unpainted base, collector coin, 1:64 scale

EX n/a NM n/a MIP $5

❑ **The Wasp,** 1994, Light purple body, clear windshield, rear-mounted silver engine, Topper-style redline wheels, collector coin with production number, 1:64 scale

EX n/a NM n/a MIP $5

❑ **The Wasp,** 1994, Chocolate brown body, unpainted base, small Topper-style hard wheels, clear windshield, silver plastic engine, collector coin, 1:64 scale

EX n/a NM n/a MIP $5

❑ **The Wasp,** 1994, Yellow-orange body, unpainted base, clear windshield, rear-mounted silver plastic engine, collector coin, 1:64 scale

EX n/a NM n/a MIP $5

❑ **The Wasp,** 1994, Black body, silver exposed engine, clear windshield, collector coin, 1:64 scale

EX n/a NM n/a MIP $5

❑ **The Wasp,** 1994, Bright yellow body, rear-mounted silver engine, clear windshield, Topper-style redlines hard wheels, collector coin, 1:64 scale

EX n/a NM n/a MIP $5

❑ **The Wasp,** 1994, Slate blue body, unpainted base, clear windshield, Topper-style redline wheels, collector coin, 1:64 scale

EX n/a NM n/a MIP $5

❑ **The Wasp,** 1994, Emerald green body, clear windshield, silver rear-mounted engine, Topper-style redlines hard tires, collector coin with production number, 1:64 scale

EX n/a NM n/a MIP $5

❑ **The Wasp,** 1994, Hot pink body, clear windshield, Topper-style redline wheels, collector card, 1:64 scale

EX n/a NM n/a MIP $5

❑ **The Wasp,** 1994, Cherry red body, unpainted base, clear windshield, hard redline-style tires, collector coin, 1:64 scale

EX n/a NM n/a MIP $5

❑ **Triple Threat,** 1:64 scale

EX n/a NM n/a MIP $4

❑ **Triple Threat,** White Lightnings edition, 1:64 scale

EX n/a NM n/a MIP $10

❑ **Vicious Vette,** White Lightnings edition, 1:64 scale

EX n/a NM n/a MIP $15

❑ **Vicious Vette,** 1994, Dark blue body, unpainted base, Topper-style redlines wheels, silver plastic engine, collector coin, 1:64 scale

EX n/a NM n/a MIP $4

❑ **Vicious Vette,** 1994, Light green body, silver plastic engine with black plastic exhaust, unpainted base, Topper-style redlines wheels, collector coin, 1:64 scale

EX n/a NM n/a MIP $5

❑ **Vicious Vette,** 1994, Emerald green body, exposed silver engine with black plastic exhaust pipes, hard redline-style wheels, collector coin, 1:64 scale

EX n/a NM n/a MIP $5

❑ **Vicious Vette,** 1994, Slate blue body, silver plastic engine with black plastic exhaust pipes, Topper-style redlines wheels, unpainted base, collector coin, 1:64 scale

EX n/a NM n/a MIP $5

❑ **Vicious Vette,** 1994, Cherry red body, silver exposed engine, Topper-style redlines hard wheels, unpainted base, collector coin, 1:64 scale

EX n/a NM n/a MIP $5

❑ **Vicious Vette,** 1994, Bright yellow body, silver exposed engine with black plastic exhaust pipes, hard Topper-style redline wheels, collector coin, 1:64 scale

EX n/a NM n/a MIP $4

❑ **Vicious Vette,** 1994, Chocolate brown body, exposed silver engine with black exhaust pipes, Topper-style redlines hard wheels, plastic collector coin with production number, 1:64 scale

EX n/a NM n/a MIP $5

❑ **Vicious Vette,** 1994, Light metallic purple body, silver engine, Topper redline-style hard wheels,, 1:64 scale

EX n/a NM n/a MIP $4

❑ **Vicious Vette,** 1994, Black body, silver exposed engine with black plastic exhaust pipes, Topper-style redlines wheels, collector coin, 1:64 scale

EX n/a NM n/a MIP $5

❑ **Vicious Vette,** 1994, Hot pink body, hard redline-style wheels, unpainted base, 1:64 scale

EX n/a NM n/a MIP $5

CORVETTE COLLECTION

❑ **'53 Corvette,** First Shots edition, 1:64 scale

EX n/a NM n/a MIP $10

❑ **'53 Corvette,**

EX n/a NM n/a MIP $4

❑ **'54 Corvette Nomad,** White Lightnings edition

EX n/a NM n/a MIP $120

(KP Photo, Angelo Van Bogart collection)

❑ **'54 Corvette Nomad,** 1996, Light brown body, white roof, silver wheels, 1:64 scale

EX n/a NM n/a MIP $8

❑ **'57 Corvette Roadster,**

EX n/a NM n/a MIP $4

❑ **'57 Corvette Roadster,** White Lightnings edition

EX n/a NM n/a MIP $65

❏ **'62 Corvette Convertible,** , 1:64 scale
EX n/a   NM n/a   MIP $4

❏ **'62 Corvette Convertible,** White Lightnings edition
EX n/a   NM n/a   MIP $65

❏ **'63 Corvette Sting Ray,** First Shots edition, 1:64 scale
EX n/a   NM n/a   MIP $10

❏ **'63 Corvette Sting Ray,**
EX n/a   NM n/a   MIP $4

❏ **'63 Grand Sport,** First Shots edition, 1:64 scale
EX n/a   NM n/a   MIP $10

❏ **'63 Grand Sport,**
EX n/a   NM n/a   MIP $4

❏ **'65 Corvette Sting Ray Coupe,** First Shots edition, 1:64 scale
EX n/a   NM n/a   MIP $10

❏ **'65 Corvette Sting Ray Coupe,**
EX n/a   NM n/a   MIP $4

❏ **'65 Mako Shark II,** 1:64 scale
EX n/a   NM n/a   MIP $5

❏ **'65 Mako Shark II,** White Lightnings edition
EX n/a   NM n/a   MIP $60

❏ **'67 Corvette 427 Sting Ray,** , 1:64 scale
EX n/a   NM n/a   MIP $4

❏ **'67 Corvette 427 Sting Ray,** White Lightnings edition
EX n/a   NM n/a   MIP $65

❏ **'70 Corvette Sting Ray Coupe,** First Shots edition, 1:64 scale
EX n/a   NM n/a   MIP $10

❏ **'70 Corvette Sting Ray Coupe,**
EX n/a   NM n/a   MIP $4

❏ **'80 Aerovette,**
EX n/a   NM n/a   MIP $5

❏ **'80 Aerovette,** White Lightnings edition
EX n/a   NM n/a   MIP $45

❏ **'82 Corvette,** 1:64 scale
EX n/a   NM n/a   MIP $5

❏ **'82 Corvette,** White Lightnings edition
EX n/a   NM n/a   MIP $75

❏ **'95 Corvette ZR-1,** White Lightnings edition
EX n/a   NM n/a   MIP $95

(KP Photo, Angelo Van Bogart collection)

❏ **'95 Corvette ZR-1,** 1996, Jet black body, painted silver highlights and trim, chrome wheels, black interior, 1:64 scale
EX n/a   NM n/a   MIP $5

❏ **'98 Corvette Convertible,** First Shots edition, 1:64 scale
EX n/a   NM n/a   MIP $10

❏ **'98 Corvette Convertible,**
EX n/a   NM n/a   MIP $4

❏ **Corvette Indy,**
EX n/a   NM n/a   MIP $4

❏ **Corvette Sting Ray III,**
EX n/a   NM n/a   MIP $4

COVER CARS

❏ **'56 Chevy Nomad,** 2002, Red body, photo card, 1:64 scale
EX n/a   NM n/a   MIP $5

❏ **'62 Corvette Roadster,** 2002, Red body, photo card, 1:64 scale
EX n/a   NM n/a   MIP $5

❏ **'63 Corvette Coupe,** 2002, Silver body, photo card, 1:64 scale
EX n/a   NM n/a   MIP $5

❏ **'65 Mustang Rag Top,** 2002, Blue body, photo card, 1:64 scale
EX n/a   NM n/a   MIP $5

❏ **'69 Camaro,** 2002, Blue body, photo card, 1:64 scale
EX n/a   NM n/a   MIP $5

❏ **'71 Mustang 429 CJ,** 2002, Red body, photo card, 1:64 scale
EX n/a   NM n/a   MIP $5

COVER CARS - SUPER CHEVY

❏ **'57 Chevy Nomad,** 2002, Torred, real wheels, chrome rims, photo card, 1:64 scale, Model No. 244
EX n/a   NM n/a   MIP $4

❏ **'61 Chevy Corvette,** 2002, Candyapple red, real wheels, chrome rims, photo card, 1:64 scale, Model No. 167
EX n/a   NM n/a   MIP $4

❏ **'67 Chevy Camaro RS/SS,** 2002, Blue Fire, real wheels, painted rims, photo card, 1:64 scale, Model No. 535
EX n/a   NM n/a   MIP $4

❏ **'69 Chevy Nova,** 2002, Gold Poly, real wheels, chrome rims, photo card, 1:64 scale, Model No. 098
EX n/a   NM n/a   MIP $4

❏ **'70 Chevelle SS,** 2002, Black cherry, real wheels, chrome rims, photo card, 1:64 scale, Model No. 206
EX n/a   NM n/a   MIP $4

❏ **'70 Chevy Camaro RS/SS,** 2002, Aspen green, real wheels, chrome rims, photo card, 1:64 scale, Model No. 538
EX n/a   NM n/a   MIP $4

COVER CARS— MUSTANG ILLUSTRATED

❏ **'65 Mustang Convertible,**
EX n/a   NM n/a   MIP $5

❏ **'67 GTA,**
EX n/a   NM n/a   MIP $5

❏ **'68 Mustang GT,**
EX n/a   NM n/a   MIP $5

❏ **'68 Shelby GT 350,**
EX n/a   NM n/a   MIP $5

❏ **'69 Mach 1,**
EX n/a   NM n/a   MIP $5

❏ **'69 Mach 1,**
EX n/a   NM n/a   MIP $5

❏ **'72 Mustang,**
EX n/a   NM n/a   MIP $5

❏ **'73 Mach 1,**
EX n/a   NM n/a   MIP $5

❏ **'77 Cobra II,**
EX n/a   NM n/a   MIP $5

❏ **'88 GT,**
EX n/a   NM n/a   MIP $5

❏ **'94 Boss,**
EX n/a   NM n/a   MIP $5

❏ **Ford Mustang Convertible,**
EX n/a   NM n/a   MIP $5

COVER CARS— SUPER CHEVY

❏ **'54 Corvette,**
EX n/a   NM n/a   MIP $5

❏ **'57 Chevelle,**
EX n/a   NM n/a   MIP $5

❑ **'57 Chevy,**
EX n/a   NM n/a   MIP $5

❑ **'61 Convertible Corvette,**
EX n/a   NM n/a   MIP $5

❑ **'61 Corvette,**
EX n/a   NM n/a   MIP $5

❑ **'63 Corvette Grand Sport,**
EX n/a   NM n/a   MIP $5

❑ **'63 Impala Z-11,**
EX n/a   NM n/a   MIP $5

❑ **'63 Nova SS,**
EX n/a   NM n/a   MIP $5

❑ **'66 Malibu,**
EX n/a   NM n/a   MIP $5

❑ **'67 Camaro RS/SS,**
EX n/a   NM n/a   MIP $5

❑ **'68 Camaro SS,**
EX n/a   NM n/a   MIP $5

❑ **'68 Chevelle,**
EX n/a   NM n/a   MIP $5

❑ **'69 Camaro RS/SS 396,**
EX n/a   NM n/a   MIP $5

❑ **'69 Z-28,**
EX n/a   NM n/a   MIP $5

❑ **'72 Camaro RS,**
EX n/a   NM n/a   MIP $5

❑ **'98 Corvette (Pace car),**
EX n/a   NM n/a   MIP $5

CUSTOMIZING KIT

❑ **'23 Ford T-Bucket/'23 Ford T-Bucket,** 2001, Includes two Shelby red bodies, chrome wheels, hard tires, "real wheels" rubber tires and engines. Enough for two complete models, 1:64 scale
EX n/a   NM n/a   MIP $12

❑ **'27 Ford T-Bucket/'27 Ford T-Bucket,** 2001, Includes two Starlight black bodies, chrome wheels, hard wheels or rubber tires. Enough for two domplete vehicles, 1:64 scale
EX n/a   NM n/a   MIP $12

❑ **'64 Pontiac GTO,** 2002, Kit contains two white bodies, (one with black painted roof), axles with hard tires, or wheels for Real Wheels, hoods, interiors and base plates, 1:64 scale
EX n/a   NM n/a   MIP $12

❑ **'67 Camaro/'68 Camaro,** 2001, Includes parts for two cars, including bodies, wheels, tires, (choose hard tires or "real wheels" rubber tires) interiors and hood. Also contains a decal sheet to personalize the kit even further, 1:64 scale
EX n/a   NM n/a   MIP $12

(KP Photo)

❑ **'67 Camaro/'68 Camaro Convertible,** 2001, Includes parts for two cars, including white bodies, black and white interior, various rims, hoods and decals. Up to 96 variations are possible, 1:64 scale
EX n/a   NM n/a   MIP $12

❑ **'67/'68 Pontiac Firebird,** 2002, Kit contains two Starlight black bodies, rubber tires or hard wheels options, hoods, interiors, baseplates, chrome rims, 1:64 scale
EX n/a   NM n/a   MIP $12

❑ **'70 Plymouth Hemi Cuda,** 2001, Includes two orange bodies (one with black-painted roof) three hoods, hard tires or rubber tires options, decal sheet, interiors, baseplates. Enough parts for two complete cars with 28 possible variations, 1:64 scale
EX n/a   NM n/a   MIP $12

❑ **'70 Plymouth Road Runner GTX,** 2001, Two glacier blue bodies, two hoods, hard tires or rubber tires options, decal sheet, interiors, baseplates. Enough parts for two complete cars, 1:64 scale
EX n/a   NM n/a   MIP $12

DIORAMAS

❑ **American Graffiti: Paradise Road,** 2002, Set includes Starlight black '55 Custom Chevy, and Daytona yellow '32 Ford Coupe with real wheels rubber tires. Miniature figures and Paradise Road racing scene part of package, 1:64 scale
EX n/a   NM n/a   MIP $11

❑ **Austin Powers,** 2002, Set includes Austin Powers' Shaguar with Union Jack graphics and Felicity Shagwell's '65 Vette Convertible with American flag design, 1:64 scale
EX n/a   NM n/a   MIP $11

❑ **Back To The Future,** 2002, Includes Dr. E. Brown's Step Van in Cameo white and DeLorean in Moonglow silver. Both vehicles have real wheels rubber tires, 1:64 scale
EX n/a   NM n/a   MIP $11

(KP Photo)

❑ **James Bond: Goldfinger,** 2001, Set includes gray Aston Martin DB5, and Starlight black '55 Chrysler C-300, Oddjob, James Bond and female figure. Both vehicles have real wheels rubber tires, 1:64 scale
EX n/a   NM n/a   MIP $13

❑ **Mearle's Drive Inn,** 2002, Includes white '58 Chevy Impala and Daytona yellow '32 Ford coupe with diner backdrop and figures, 1:64 scale
EX n/a   NM n/a   MIP $11

❑ **Monkees,** 2001, Includes red and white VW bus and '66 GTO Monkee Mobile. Set features miniature figures and surf background. Vehicles ride on rubber tires, 1:64 scale
EX n/a   NM n/a   MIP $12

❑ **Speed Racer,** 2001, Includes Speed Racer Mach 5 with white body, and "number 5" on hood and sides, and yellow Racer X Shooting Star. Both vehicles ride real wheels rubber tires, 1:64 scale
EX n/a   NM n/a   MIP $13

❑ **Starsky and Hutch,** 2001, Set includes '74 Ford Torino in candyapple red with white stripe and '69 Lincoln Continental Custom in Starlight black. Miniature figures included. Both vehicles have real wheels rubber tires. Interestingly, the Continental is the same casting as the proposed Topper "Custom Continental Mark III" as seen in the 1970 Topper Toys catalog, 1:64 scale

EX n/a   NM n/a   MIP $11

DRAGSTERS USA

❑ **Blue Max,** '71 Mustang, 1:64 scale

EX n/a   NM n/a   MIP $4

❑ **Chi-Town Hustler,** '72 Charger, 1:64 scale

EX n/a   NM n/a   MIP $4

❑ **Color Me Gone,** '72 Challenger, 1:64 scale

EX n/a   NM n/a   MIP $4

(KP Photo, Angelo Van Bogart collection)

❑ **Drag-On Lady,** 1995, '69 AMX, 1:64 scale

EX n/a   NM n/a   MIP $5

❑ **Fast Orange—Whit Bazemore,** '94 Daytona, 1:64 scale

EX n/a   NM n/a   MIP $3

(KP Photo)

❑ **Hawaiian: Roland Leong,** 1995, 71 Charger, light blue with white, "Hawaiian" in yellow bamboo-style lettering on sides, gray metal base, plastic photo button included, 1:64 scale

EX n/a   NM n/a   MIP $4

❑ **Kendall GT-1—Chuck Etchells,** '96 Avenger, 1:64 scale

EX n/a   NM n/a   MIP $3

❑ **King of the Burnouts—Spurlock,** '95 Avenger, 1:64 scale

EX n/a   NM n/a   MIP $3

❑ **L.A.P.D.,** '92 Camaro, 1:64 scale

EX n/a   NM n/a   MIP $4

❑ **Mantis,** '97 Firebird, 1:64 scale

EX n/a   NM n/a   MIP $3

❑ **Mooneyes—Kenji Okazaki,** '95 Avenger, 1:64 scale

EX n/a   NM n/a   MIP $3

❑ **Motown Shaker,** '71 Vega, 1:64 scale

EX n/a   NM n/a   MIP $4

❑ **Otter Pops—Ed McCulloch,** '91 Olds, 1:64 scale

EX n/a   NM n/a   MIP $3

❑ **Pioneer—Tom Hoover,** '95 Daytona, 1:64 scale

EX n/a   NM n/a   MIP $3

❑ **Revellution,** '71 Demon, 1:64 scale

EX n/a   NM n/a   MIP $4

❑ **Rug Doctor—Jim Epler,** '94 Olds, 1:64 scale

EX n/a   NM n/a   MIP $3

❑ **Sentry Gauges—Bruce Larson,** '90 Olds, 1:64 scale

EX n/a   NM n/a   MIP $3

(KP Photo, Angelo Van Bogart collection)

❑ **Sox 'N Martin,** 1995, '71 Cuda, tan metallic, black roof, red stripe on sides, 1:64 scale

EX n/a   NM n/a   MIP $4

❑ **Western Auto—Al Hofmann,** '95 Firebird, 1:64 scale

EX n/a   NM n/a   MIP $3

DRAGSTERS USA, VINTAGE CARS

❑ **Barry Setzer,** '71 Vega, 1:64 scale

EX n/a   NM n/a   MIP $5

❑ **Bob Banning,** '72 Challenger, 1:64 scale

EX n/a   NM n/a   MIP $5

❑ **Don Garlits,** '71 Charger, 1:64 scale

EX n/a   NM n/a   MIP $5

(KP Photo)

❑ **Gene Snow,** '72 Charger body, red, with "The Snowman" graphics on sides, silver rims, hard tires, plain metal base, 1:64 scale

EX n/a   NM n/a   MIP $5

❑ **Jungle Jim,** '71 Vega, 1:64 scale

EX n/a   NM n/a   MIP $5

❑ **Mantis,** '71 Vega, 1:64 scale

EX n/a   NM n/a   MIP $5

❑ **Mr. Norm's,** '72 Charger

EX n/a   NM n/a   MIP $5

❑ **Ramchargers,** '71 Duster, 1:64 scale

EX n/a   NM n/a   MIP $5

❑ **Trojan Horse,** '71 Mustang

EX n/a   NM n/a   MIP $5

❑ **Wildman,** '72 Charger

EX n/a   NM n/a   MIP $5

❑ **Wonder Wagon,** '71 Vega, 1:64 scale

EX n/a   NM n/a   MIP $5

EVEL KNIEVEL

❑ **Harley Davidson 750 XR,**

EX n/a   NM n/a   MIP $5

❑ **Triumph T-120 Bonneville 650,**

EX n/a   NM n/a   MIP $5

❑ **X-2 Sky Cycle,** Red, white and blue rocket cycle

EX n/a   NM n/a   MIP $6

FRIGHT'NING LIGHTNINGS

❑ **Boothill Express,** 1996, Black, red and gold, 1:64 scale

EX n/a   NM n/a   MIP $5

(KP Photo, Angelo Van Bogart collection)

❑ **Christine,** 1996, Black 1958 Plymouth Fury, silver wheels, silver metal base, gray interior, red painted taillights, 1:64 scale

EX n/a   NM n/a   MIP $5

❑ **Drag-U-La,** , 1:64 scale

EX n/a   NM n/a   MIP $18

(KP Photo)

❏ **Drag-U-La,** 1999, Gold body with small spoked wheels in front, large wheels in back, rubber tires, silver plastic "pipe organ" engine, collector card showing Grampa Munster and car, 1:64 scale
EX n/a   NM n/a   MIP $6

(KP Photo, Angelo Van Bogart collection)

❏ **Elvira Macabre Mobile,** 1996, Black Ford Thunderbird, silver wheels, black interior, 1:64 scale
EX n/a   NM n/a   MIP $5

(KP Photo)

❏ **Ghostbusters: Collector's Edition,** 1996, White body with yellow and black stripes along sides, silver wheels, "We're Back" in green type along roof rack, rubber "Firestone" tires, 1:64 scale
EX n/a   NM n/a   MIP $10

(KP Photo, Angelo Van Bogart collection)

❏ **Haulin' Hearse,** 1996, Red body with black plastic top, "Hau-

lin' Hearse" on sides, silver five-spoke wheels, 1:64 scale
EX n/a   NM n/a   MIP $5

❏ **Heavenly Hearse,** 1:64 scale
EX n/a   NM n/a   MIP $15

(KP Photo)

❏ **Heavenly Hearse,** 1999, Purple body, black roof, "Heavenly Hearse" and flower graphics on sides, roof and hood, silver six-spoke wheels, rubber tires, collector card, 1:64 scale
EX n/a   NM n/a   MIP $5

❏ **Meat Wagon,** 1999, Silver body with red cross tampos, 1:64 scale, Model No. 511
EX n/a   NM n/a   MIP $15

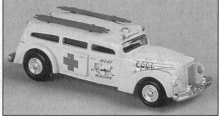

(KP Photo)

❏ **Meat Wagon,** 1999, White body with red cross tampos on sides, "Meat Wagon" on doors, "Quiet Zone" near engine, "Be Patient" over rear door, silver painted grille and details, red painted lights, rubber "real wheels" tires, 1:64 scale, Model No. 511
EX n/a   NM n/a   MIP $8

❏ **Munster's Coach,** 1:64 scale
EX n/a   NM n/a   MIP $18

(KP Photo)

❏ **Munster's Koach,** 1999, Black body with red interior, gold engine, silver exhaust pipes, photo card showing Munsters family and car, 1:64 scale
EX n/a   NM n/a   MIP $6

❏ **Mysterion,** 1:64 scale
EX n/a   NM n/a   MIP $7

❏ **Surf Hearse,** 1:64 scale
EX n/a   NM n/a   MIP $15

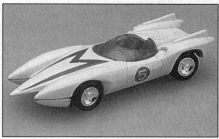

(KP Photo)

❏ **Surf Hearse,** 1999, Magenta-red body with silver plastic engine, black canopy, rubber tires, collector card, 1:64 scale
EX n/a   NM n/a   MIP $5

❏ **Undertaker,** 1:64 scale
EX n/a   NM n/a   MIP $15

(KP Photo)

❏ **Undertaker,** 1999, Green body, white plastic roof, small spoked wheels in front, large wheels in back, silver engine, collector card, 1:64 scale
EX n/a   NM n/a   MIP $5

❏ **Vampire Van,** 1:64 scale
EX n/a   NM n/a   MIP $5

FUNNY CAR LEGENDS

❏ **Al Vandewoude's Flying Dutchman,** '68 Charger
EX n/a   NM n/a   MIP $5

❏ **Blue Max,** '74 Mustang
EX n/a   NM n/a   MIP $4

❏ **Bruce Larson's USA-1,** '70 Camaro, 1 scale
EX n/a   NM n/a   MIP $5

❑ **Bunny Burkett,** '94 Daytona
EX n/a   NM n/a   MIP $4

❑ **Connie Kalitta,** '73 Mustang
EX n/a   NM n/a   MIP $4

❑ **Cruz Pedregon "McDonald's",** '91 Olds
EX n/a   NM n/a   MIP $4

❑ **Dicky Harrell,** '71 Vega
EX n/a   NM n/a   MIP $4

❑ **Don Schumacher's "Stardust",** '70 Cuda
EX n/a   NM n/a   MIP $5

❑ **Dunn and Reath Satellite,** '73 Satellite
EX n/a   NM n/a   MIP $4

❑ **Gene Snow's Rambunctious,** '70 Challenger
EX n/a   NM n/a   MIP $4

❑ **Gordon Mineo, Flash Gordon,** '75 Monza
EX n/a   NM n/a   MIP $4

❑ **Jim Green's "Green Elephant",** '74 Vega
EX n/a   NM n/a   MIP $5

❑ **Jim Murphy's "Holy Smokes",** '73 Satellite
EX n/a   NM n/a   MIP $4

❑ **Jungle Jim,** '75 Monza
EX n/a   NM n/a   MIP $5

❑ **Kosty Ivanof,** '78 Corvette
EX n/a   NM n/a   MIP $4

❑ **Larry Arnold's "Kingfish",** '70 Cuda
EX n/a   NM n/a   MIP $4

❑ **Lew Arrington's "Brutus",** '73 Mustang
EX n/a   NM n/a   MIP $4

❑ **Malcom Durham,** '70 Camaro
EX n/a   NM n/a   MIP $4

❑ **Mr. Norms Charger,** '68 Charger
EX n/a   NM n/a   MIP $4

❑ **Radice Wise,** '74 Vega
EX n/a   NM n/a   MIP $4

❑ **Ramchargers,** '70 Challenger
EX n/a   NM n/a   MIP $4

❑ **Shirl Greer's "Chain Lightning",** '74 Mustang
EX n/a   NM n/a   MIP $5

❑ **Tom Hoover's "Showtime",** '78 Corvette

❑ **Tom Hoover's "White Bear Dodge",** '72 Charger
EX n/a   NM n/a   MIP $4

FUTURE PRO STOCKS

❑ **Dynagear—Steve Schmidt,** '96 Olds
EX n/a   NM n/a   MIP $5

❑ **Mama Rosa's Pizza—Osborne,** '96 Olds
EX n/a   NM n/a   MIP $5

❑ **Six Flags—Tom Martino,** '96 Firebird
EX n/a   NM n/a   MIP $5

❑ **Splitfire—Jim Yates,** '96 Firebird
EX n/a   NM n/a   MIP $5

❑ **Summit—Mark Pawuk,** '96 Firebird
EX n/a   NM n/a   MIP $5

❑ **Super Clean—Larry Morgan,** '96 Olds
EX n/a   NM n/a   MIP $5

GTO

❑ **'64 Pontiac GTO Hardtop,** 2001, Dark blue body, opening hood, hard tires, chrome, five-spoke wheels, 1:64 scale
EX n/a   NM n/a   MIP $5

❑ **'64 Pontiac GTO Hardtop,** 2001, Cameo white body, opening hood, hard tires, chrome wheels, 1:64 scale
EX n/a   NM n/a   MIP $5

❑ **'64 Pontiac GTO Hardtop,** 2001, Lime gold body, chrome wheels, hard tires, opening hood, red interior, 1:64 scale
EX n/a   NM n/a   MIP $5

(KP Photo)

❑ **'65 Pontiac GTO Ragtop,** 2001, Citrus orange body with black tiger stripes, chrome five spoke wheels, hard tires, black interior, 1:64 scale
EX n/a   NM n/a   MIP $5

❑ **'65 Pontiac GTO Ragtop,** 2001, Glacier blue body, hard tires, chrome wheels, blue interior, 1:64 scale
EX n/a   NM n/a   MIP $5

❑ **'65 Pontiac GTO Ragtop,** 2001, Evening orchid body, white interior, hard tires, chrome rims, 1:64 scale
EX n/a   NM n/a   MIP $5

❑ **'67 Pontiac GTO Hardtop,** 2001, Nocturne blue body, white interior, chrome rims, hard tires, opening hood, 1:64 scale
EX n/a   NM n/a   MIP $5

❑ **'67 Pontiac GTO Hardtop,** 2001, White body, opening hood, chrome five-spoke wheels, hard tires, 1:64 scale
EX n/a   NM n/a   MIP $5

❑ **'67 Pontiac GTO Hardtop,** 2001, Aspen green, hard tires, chrome rims, opening hood, 1:64 scale
EX n/a   NM n/a   MIP $5

❑ **'69 Pontiac GTO Super Stock,** 2001, Citrus orange with black tiger stripes, chrome rims, opening hood, hard tires, 1:64 scale
EX n/a   NM n/a   MIP $5

❑ **'69 Pontiac GTO Super Stock,** 2001, Bright red body, chrome five-spoke wheels, 1:64 scale
EX n/a   NM n/a   MIP $5

❑ **'69 Pontiac GTO Super Stock,** 2001, Bronze body, hard tires, chrome wheels, opening hood, 1:64 scale
EX n/a   NM n/a   MIP $5

❑ **'71 Pontiac GTO,** 2001, Teal body, chrome rims, white interior, hard tires, 1:64 scale
EX n/a   NM n/a   MIP $5

❑ **'71 Pontiac GTO,** 2001, Maverick red body, chrome five-spoke wheels, hard tires, 1:64 scale
EX n/a   NM n/a   MIP $5

❑ **'71 Pontiac GTO Judge,** 2001, Cameo white body, hard tires, chrome rims, 1:64 scale
EX n/a   NM n/a   MIP $5

❑ **'71 Pontiac GTO Pro Street,** 2001, Maverick red, chrome rims, hard tires, light gray interior, 1:64 scale
EX n/a   NM n/a   MIP $5

(KP Photo)

❏ **'71 Pontiac GTO Pro Street,** 2001, Light metallic green body, hard tires, chrome five-spoke wheels, black interior, 1:64 scale
EX n/a   NM n/a   MIP $5

❏ **'71 Pontiac GTO Pro Street,** 2001, Citrus orange with black tiger stripes, chrome wheels, hard tires, opening hood, 1:64 scale
EX n/a   NM n/a   MIP $5

HOLIDAY MUSCLE 2

❏ **'64 Pontiac GTO,** 2001, Purple chrome body, real wheels rubber tires, 1:64 scale
EX n/a   NM n/a   MIP $5

❏ **'67 Mercury Cougar,** 2001, Orange chrome finish, real wheels rubber tires, 1:64 scale
EX n/a   NM n/a   MIP $5

❏ **'67 Olds Cutlass 442,** 2001, Green chrome body, real wheels rubber tires, 1:64 scale
EX n/a   NM n/a   MIP $5

(KP Photo, Angelo Van Bogart collection)

❏ **'67 Pontiac GTO,** 2000, Deep red chrome finish, silver wheels, hard tires, 1:64 scale
EX n/a   NM n/a   MIP $6

❏ **'68 Pontiac Firebird 400 H.O.,** 2001, Light Citron chrome finish, real wheels, 1:64 scale
EX n/a   NM n/a   MIP $5

❏ **'69 Dodge Charger R/T,** 2001, Red chrome finish, real wheels, 1:64 scale
EX n/a   NM n/a   MIP $5

❏ **'69 Dodge Daytona,** 2001, Light blue chrome finish, real wheels, 1:64 scale
EX n/a   NM n/a   MIP $5

❏ **'70 Mercury Cyclone Spoiler,** 2001, Blue chrome finish, real wheels rubber tires, 1:64 scale
EX n/a   NM n/a   MIP $5

❏ **'70 Plymouth Hemi Cuda,** 2001, Fuschia chrome finish, real wheels rubber tires, 1:64 scale
EX n/a   NM n/a   MIP $5

❏ **'70 Plymouth Road Runner,** 2001, Light green chrome finish, real wheels, 1:64 scale
EX n/a   NM n/a   MIP $5

❏ **'71 Plymouth Duster 340,** 2001, Ice blue chrome finish, real wheels rubber tires, 1:64 scale
EX n/a   NM n/a   MIP $5

❏ **'71 Plymouth Road Runner,** 2001, Gold chrome finish, real wheels, 1:64 scale
EX n/a   NM n/a   MIP $5

❏ **'72 Chevy Nova,** 2001, Silver chrome body, real wheels, 1:64 scale
EX n/a   NM n/a   MIP $5

HOLLYWOOD ON WHEELS

❏ **Andy Griffith Police Cruiser,** 1998, Black and white body, photo card, 1:64 scale
EX n/a   NM n/a   MIP $5

(KP Photo)

❏ **Austin Powers (Felicity) '65 Corvette Convertible,** 2001, Red, white & blue flag graphics, real wheels rubber tires, white and black plastic interior, "CIA 1" license plate, chrome rims, photo card packaging, 1:64 scale, Model No. 149
EX n/a   NM n/a   MIP $4

(KP Photo)

❏ **Austin Powers Jaguar XKE,** 1999, Austin Powers "Shaguar" with Union Jack graphics, silver rims, opening hood, black interior, photo card, 1:64 scale
EX n/a   NM n/a   MIP $6

❏ **Back to the Future,** 1998, Silver-gray Delorean, photo card, 1:64 scale
EX n/a   NM n/a   MIP $6

(KP Photo)

❏ **Black Beauty,** 2001, Starlight black, real wheels, (rubber tires) chrome five-spoke rims, black interior, photo card, 1:64 scale, Model No. 148
EX n/a   NM n/a   MIP $5

(KP Photo)

❏ **Black Beauty: Target Exclusive,** 2001, Chrome green body and wheels, rubber tires, black roof, silver base, 1:64 scale, Model No. 148
EX n/a   NM n/a   MIP $5

(KP Photo)

❏ **Blues Brothers,** 1998, Black and white with star emblem and "P1" on doors, black wheels. Interestingly, the car says "State Police," even though the Bluesmobile was an old Mount Prospect police car. ("They were practically giving them away"), 1:64 scale
EX n/a   NM n/a   MIP $4

(KP Photo)

❏ **Blues Brothers 2000,** 1998, Black and white Crown Victoria, black wheels, "K-9" on roof, photo card, 1:64 scale, Model No. 783
EX n/a   NM n/a   MIP $4

(KP Photo)

❏ **Dragnet,** 1998, Metallic gold, with silver grille and base, 1:64 scale
EX n/a   NM n/a   MIP $4

(KP Photo)

❏ **Mod Squad Woody,** 2001, Starlight black body with paneling, real wheels rubber tires, chrome rims, 1:64 scale, Model No. 146
EX n/a   NM n/a   MIP $5

❏ **Monkee Mobile,** 1998, Red with white roof, photo card, 1:64 scale
EX n/a   NM n/a   MIP $5

❏ **Nash Bridges '71 Hemi Cuda,** 1999, Nash Bridges, dark yellow body, photo card, 1:64 scale
EX n/a   NM n/a   MIP $4

(KP Photo)

❏ **Partridge Family,** 1998, Multi-colored Mondrian-style graphics over white body, "The Partridge Family" along sides, red rims, 1:64 scale
EX n/a   NM n/a   MIP $7

❏ **Partridge Family Bus,** 2001, Multicolored bus with red and blue rims and a different interior to mark it from the first round release, 1:64 scale, Model No. 777
EX n/a   NM n/a   MIP $6

❏ **Scooby Doo Mystery Machine,** 2001, Real wheels, bulbous lime green and blue body with "Mystery Machine" on sides, lime green rims, photo card, 1:64 scale, Model No. 150
EX n/a   NM n/a   MIP $6

❏ **Starsky & Hutch,** 1998, Red Gran Torino with familiar stripe on sides, 1:64 scale
EX n/a   NM n/a   MIP $5

(KP Photo)

❏ **Supercar,** 2001, Red and white Supercar with yellow wings and nose, photo card, 1:64 scale, Model No. 163
EX n/a   NM n/a   MIP $6

❏ **Walker, Texas Ranger Dodge Ram,** 1999, Walker Texas Ranger, metallic dark gray body, photo card, 1:64 scale
EX n/a   NM n/a   MIP $4

HOT RODS

❏ **'23 T-Bucket,** 2001, Light green, hard tires, chrome rims, 1:64 scale, Model No. 562
EX n/a   NM n/a   MIP $4

❏ **'27 T-Roadster,** 2001, Orange, real & hard tires, chrome rims, 1:64 scale, Model No. 563
EX n/a   NM n/a   MIP $4

❏ **'29 Crew Cab,**
EX n/a   NM n/a   MIP $5

❏ **'32 Ford HiBoy,** 2001, Evening orchid, hard tires, chrome rims, 1:64 scale, Model No. 564
EX n/a   NM n/a   MIP $4

❏ **'33 Ford Delivery,** 2001, Vampire red, hard tires, chrome rims, 1:64 scale, Model No. 566
EX n/a   NM n/a   MIP $4

❏ **'34 Ford Coupe,** 2001, Signal amber, hard tires, chrome rims, 1:64 scale, Model No. 567
EX n/a   NM n/a   MIP $4

❏ **'37 Ford Coupe,** 2001, Starlight black, hard tires, chrome rims, 1:64 scale, Model No. 565
EX n/a   NM n/a   MIP $4

❏ **'62 Bad Bird,**
EX n/a   NM n/a   MIP $5

❏ **'66 Pro Street,**
EX n/a   NM n/a   MIP $5

❏ **'69 Pro Street,**
EX n/a   NM n/a   MIP $5

❏ **'72 Goin' Goat,**
EX n/a   NM n/a   MIP $5

❏ **'86 Beastmobile,**
EX n/a   NM n/a   MIP $5

(KP Photo, Angelo Van Bogart collection)

❏ **Bumongous,** 1997, Metallic magenta body, black roof, silver wheels, black interior
EX n/a   NM n/a   MIP $5

❏ **Flathead Flyer,**
EX n/a   NM n/a   MIP $5

❏ **Frankenstude,**
EX n/a   NM n/a   MIP $5

(KP Photo, Angelo Van Bogart collection)

❏ **Rumblur,** 1997, Dark blue, chrome wheels, clear windows, silver grille and headlights, 1:64 scale
EX n/a   NM n/a   MIP $5

HOT RODS 2

❏ **'23 T-Bucket,** 2001, Cameo white, hard tires
EX n/a   NM n/a   MIP $5

❏ **'27 T Roadster,** 2001, Surf green, hard tires
EX n/a   NM n/a   MIP $5

❑ **'32 Hi Boy,** 2001, Passion Pearl, hard tires

EX n/a   NM n/a   MIP $5

❑ **'33 Delivery,** 2001, Dandelion yellow, hard tires

EX n/a   NM n/a   MIP $5

❑ **'34 Coupe,** 2001, Starlight black, hard tires

EX n/a   NM n/a   MIP $5

❑ **'37 Coupe,** 2001, Chianti red, hard tires

EX n/a   NM n/a   MIP $5

HUMMERS

❑ **Army National Guard,** 1:64 scale

EX n/a   NM n/a   MIP $4

❑ **Army Reserve Hummer,** 1:64 scale

EX n/a   NM n/a   MIP $5

❑ **Atlantic Beach Rescue Hummer,** Red with white and silver trim, ambulance body, red rims, photo card, 1:64 scale

EX n/a   NM n/a   MIP $5

(KP Photo)

❑ **ATR Rescue Hummer,** Red body, white stripes, yellow "ATR" and "Rescue" lettering, red rims, photo card, 1:64 scale

EX n/a   NM n/a   MIP $5

❑ **Civilian - 2dr pickup,** Tan body, looks almost like a "Lightning Brigade" issue, 1:64 scale

EX n/a   NM n/a   MIP $5

(KP Photo)

❑ **Civilian Hummer,** Four-door wagon, black body, "Hummer"

stripe along bottom, photo card, 1:64 scale

EX n/a   NM n/a   MIP $5

❑ **Civilian Hummer,** Four-door wagon, silver, bonus car, mail-in-offer, 1:64 scale

EX n/a   NM n/a   MIP $5

❑ **Civilian Hummer,** Four-door wagon (Red bonus car) with white rims, 1:64 scale

EX n/a   NM n/a   MIP $5

❑ **Gatorade Hummer,** Yellow body, light green splash graphics on sides, "Gatorade" logo on doors, 1:64 scale

EX n/a   NM n/a   MIP $5

(KP Photo)

❑ **M1025A2 Tow Missile Carrier,** Light and dark green camouflage body, green rims, black TOW on roof, photo card, 1:64 scale

EX n/a   NM n/a   MIP $5

(KP Photo)

❑ **Rod Hall's Off-Road Racing Hummer,** Red truck body with roll cage and spares in truck bed, silver rims, rubber "BF Goodrich" tires, "Rod Hall" and number "862" on sides, photo card, 1:64 scale

EX n/a   NM n/a   MIP $5

❑ **St. Joseph County Sheriff Hummer,** White body with police graphics, 1:64 scale

EX n/a   NM n/a   MIP $5

❑ **Tom Wamberg Race Hummer,** Blue, white and red American flag design on body, silver rims, rubber tires, 1:64 scale

EX n/a   NM n/a   MIP $5

❑ **US Marines Humvee,** Red body, not an official military-style vehicle, 1:64 scale

EX n/a   NM n/a   MIP $5

HURST MUSCLE

❑ **'69 Hurst Olds,** 2000, White body with gold stripe running from opening hood to trunk, black interior, black grille, silver wheels, rubber "Goodyear" tires, 1:64 scale

EX n/a   NM n/a   MIP $5

❑ **'69 SC/Rambler,** 2000, White body with blue stripe running from hood to trunk, red stripe on sides, opening hood with scoop, silver wheels, rubber "Goodyear" tires, black grille, 1:64 scale

EX n/a   NM n/a   MIP $5

❑ **'72 Hurst Olds,** 2000, White convertible body with two white gold stripes on hood and trunk, gold stripes on sides, black interior, silver wheels, rubber tires, 1:64 scale

EX n/a   NM n/a   MIP $5

❑ **'74 Hurst Olds,** 2000, White convertible body with gold stripe running from hood to trunk, gold stripes on sides, black interior, silver wheels, rubber "Goodyear" tires, black grille, 1:64 scale

EX n/a   NM n/a   MIP $5

❑ **Hurst Hairy Olds,** 2000, Gold body with black stripes running from hood to trunk, black interior, "Hurst Hairy Oldsmobile" on sides, silver wheels, silver engine sticking up through hood, rubber "Goodyear" tires, 1:64 scale

EX n/a   NM n/a   MIP $5

❑ **Hurst Hemi Under Glass,** 2000, Gold body with black stripe running from hood to trunk, silver wheels, rubber "Goodyear" tires, "Hurst Hemi Under Glass" on sides, "Mopar" on hood, 1:64 scale

EX n/a   NM n/a   MIP $5

INDY PACE CARS

❑ **'55 Chevy Bel Air Conv. Pace Car,** 2001, Red-orange, rubber tires, chrome rims, photo card, 1:64 scale, Model No. 239

EX n/a   NM n/a   MIP $6

❑ **'64 1/2 Ford Mustang Convertible Pace Car,** 2001, Cameo white, rubber tires, chrome rims, photo card, 1:64 scale, Model No. 653

EX n/a   **NM** n/a   **MIP** $6

❏ **'64-1/2 Mustang,**
EX n/a   **NM** n/a   **MIP** $6

❏ **'67 Chevy Camaro Conv. Pace Car,** 2001, Snow white, rubber tires, chrome rims, photo card, 1:64 scale, Model No. 535
EX n/a   **NM** n/a   **MIP** $6

❏ **'68 Torino,**
EX n/a   **NM** n/a   **MIP** $6

❏ **'69 Camaro,**
EX n/a   **NM** n/a   **MIP** $6

(KP Photo, Angelo Van Bogart collection)

❏ **'70 Olds 442,** 1996, Light metallic green, silver five-spoke wheels, "Official Pace Car" on sides, 1:64 scale
EX n/a   **NM** n/a   **MIP** $6

❏ **'71 Challenger,**
EX n/a   **NM** n/a   **MIP** $6

❏ **'71 Dodge Challenger Conv. Pace Car,** 2001, Hemi orange, rubber tires, chrome rims, photo card, 1:64 scale, Model No. 480
EX n/a   **NM** n/a   **MIP** $6

❏ **'72 Olds,**
EX n/a   **NM** n/a   **MIP** $6

❏ **'73 Cadillac Eldorado,** 1999, White with red interior, silver mag wheels, "Official Pace Car" in red type on sides, 1:64 scale
EX n/a   **NM** n/a   **MIP** $6

(KP Photo, Angelo Van Bogart collection)

❏ **'74 Hurst Olds,** 1996, Reef blue body, "Official Pace Car" on sides, black interior, silver wheels, 1:64 scale
EX n/a   **NM** n/a   **MIP** $6

(KP Photo, Angelo Van Bogart collection)

❏ **'75 Buick Century,** 1996, White with red, white and blue graphics on sides, silver wheels, 1:64 scale
EX n/a   **NM** n/a   **MIP** $5

❏ **'77 Olds Delta 88,**
EX n/a   **NM** n/a   **MIP** $6

(KP Photo, Angelo Van Bogart collection)

❏ **'77 Olds Delta 88,** 1996, White with black on hood and sides, "Official Pace Car" on sides, black interior, gray base, 1:64 scale
EX n/a   **NM** n/a   **MIP** $5

❏ **'78 Corvette,**
EX n/a   **NM** n/a   **MIP** $4

❏ **'79 Mustang,**
EX n/a   **NM** n/a   **MIP** $6

❏ **'82 Camaro,**
EX n/a   **NM** n/a   **MIP** $6

❏ **'92 Allante,**
EX n/a   **NM** n/a   **MIP** $4

❏ **'93 Chevy Camaro Z-28 Pace Car,** 2001, Black/white, rubber tires, white/silver rims, photo card, 1:64 scale, Model No. 368
EX n/a   **NM** n/a   **MIP** $6

❏ **'96 Dodge Viper Pace Car,** 2001, GTS blue, rubber tires, chrome rims, photo card, 1:64 scale, Model No. 188
EX n/a   **NM** n/a   **MIP** $6

❏ **'96 Viper GTS,**
EX n/a   **NM** n/a   **MIP** $6

❏ **'98 Corvette Convertible,**
EX n/a   **NM** n/a   **MIP** $6

INDY RACE CARS

❏ **'69 Andretti,**
EX n/a   **NM** n/a   **MIP** $6

❏ **'70 A. Unser,**
EX n/a   **NM** n/a   **MIP** $6

❏ **'74 Rutherford,**
EX n/a   **NM** n/a   **MIP** $6

❏ **'75 B. Unser,**
EX n/a   **NM** n/a   **MIP** $6

❏ **'77 A.J. Foyt,**
EX n/a   **NM** n/a   **MIP** $6

❏ **'78 A. Unser,**
EX n/a   **NM** n/a   **MIP** $6

❏ **'79 Mears,**
EX n/a   **NM** n/a   **MIP** $6

❏ **'92 A. Unser Jr.,**
EX n/a   **NM** n/a   **MIP** $6

JAMES BOND

❏ **'57 Chevy Convertible,** 2001, Starlight black, real wheels whitewalls rubber tires, chrome rims, photo card, 1:64 scale, Model No. 241
EX n/a   **NM** n/a   **MIP** $6

❏ **'64 Aston Martin,** Goldeneye
EX n/a   **NM** n/a   **MIP** $7

❏ **'64 Aston Martin,** Thunderball, silver body, chrome rims, photo card
EX n/a   **NM** n/a   **MIP** $6

❏ **'64 Aston Martin,** 2001, Real wheels, chrome rims, photo card, 1:64 scale, Model No. 652
EX n/a   **NM** n/a   **MIP** $6

❏ **'64 Aston Martin DB5,** 2001, Moonglow silver body, chrome rims, real wheels, 1:64 scale
EX n/a   **NM** n/a   **MIP** $6

❏ **'65 Ford Mustang Convertible,** 2001, Jorgensen blue with white top (up), real wheels, opening hood, chrome rims, photo card, 1:64 scale, Model No. 653
EX n/a   **NM** n/a   **MIP** $6

❏ **'67 Toyota 2000 GT,** 2001, Snow white body, real wheels rubber tires, 1:64 scale
EX n/a   **NM** n/a   **MIP** $6

❏ **'69 Mercury Cougar,** 2001, Calypso coral (red) body, real wheels rubber tires, opening hood, 1:64 scale
EX n/a   **NM** n/a   **MIP** $6

❏ **'71 Ford Mustang Mach 1,** 2001, Calypso coral body, real wheels rubber tires, 1:64 scale
EX n/a   **NM** n/a   **MIP** $6

❑ **'81 Lotus Turbo Esprit,** 2001, Snow white body, black trim, red interior, real wheels rubber tires, 1:64 scale
EX n/a   NM n/a   **MIP** $6

❑ **'87 Aston Martin,** The Living Daylights
EX n/a   NM n/a   **MIP** $6

❑ **'95 Corvette,** 2001, Moonglow silver body with black roof, rubber tires, chrome rims, photo card, 1:64 scale, Model No. 170
EX n/a   NM n/a   **MIP** $6

❑ **'99 BMW Z8,** 2001, Silver body, white painted headlights, real wheels rubber tires, gray-silver rims, 1:64 scale
EX n/a   NM n/a   **MIP** $6

❑ **BMW Z-3,** 2001, Goldeneye, Aegean blue body, black interior, real wheels, gray rims, photo card, 1:64 scale, Model No. 659
EX n/a   NM n/a   **MIP** $7

❑ **BMW Z-8,** 2001, The World Is Not Enough, silver body, black interior, real wheels, chrome rims, photo card, 1:64 scale, Model No. 660
EX n/a   NM n/a   **MIP** $5

❑ **Ford Mustang Convertible,** Goldfinger, white convertible body, red interior, black folded down roof, silver chrome wheels
EX n/a   NM n/a   **MIP** $7

❑ **Ford Mustang Mach 1,** Diamonds are Forever, red body, chrome wheels
EX n/a   NM n/a   **MIP** $6

❑ **Lotus Espirit,** For Your Eyes Only, red Lotus Esprit with black trim, chrome wheels, painted headlights, photo card
EX n/a   NM n/a   **MIP** $5

❑ **Lotus Espirit,** The Spy Who Loved Me, white Lotus Esprit with black trim
EX n/a   NM n/a   **MIP** $6

❑ **Mercury Cougar Convertible,** On Her Majesty's Secret Service, red body, black interior, chrome rims, photo card
EX n/a   NM n/a   **MIP** $6

❑ **Sunbeam,** Dr. No, blue convertible body, chrome rims, black interior, photo card
EX n/a   NM n/a   **MIP** $10

❑ **Toyota 2000GT Convertible,** You Only Live Twice, white body, chrome wheels, photo card
EX n/a   NM n/a   **MIP** $6

JL COLLECTION

❑ **'00 Ford F-250 Supercab,** 2001, Candyapple red body, silver and black painted grille, rubber tires, chrome rims, 1:64 scale, Model No. 052
EX n/a   NM n/a   **MIP** $6

❑ **00 GMC 2500 Van,** 2001, Burgundy body, red interior, chrome rims, 1:64 scale, Model No. 703
EX n/a   NM n/a   **MIP** $6

❑ **'34 Ford Coupe,** 2001, Starlight black body, rubber tires, chrome rims, silver painted grille, 1:64 scale
EX n/a   NM n/a   **MIP** $6

(KP Photo)

❑ **'60s Studebaker pickup,** 2001, White body with stars and stripes paint scheme, white interior, opening hood, silver-painted headlights and grille, "Hoosier" rubber tires, silver wheels, 1:64 scale
EX n/a   NM n/a   **MIP** $5

❑ **'63 Chevy Impala,** 2001, Quicksilver body, opening hood, chrome rims, rubber tires, 1:64 scale
EX n/a   NM n/a   **MIP** $6

❑ **'65 Ford Mustang Convertible,** 2001, Saddle bronze, opening hood, real wheels rubber tires, 1:64 scale
EX n/a   NM n/a   **MIP** $6

❑ **'67 Chevy Camaro Convertible,** 2001, Metallic gold body, chrome rims, opening hood, 1:64 scale
EX n/a   NM n/a   **MIP** $6

❑ **'67 Toyota 2000 GT Convertible,** 2001, Candyapple red body, silver painted grille, black interior, rubber tires, 1:64 scale
EX n/a   NM n/a   **MIP** $6

❑ **'68 Chevy Camaro Z-28,** 2001, Rally green with two white stripes on hood an trunk, chrome rims, 1:64 scale, Model No. 536
EX n/a   NM n/a   **MIP** $6

❑ **'69 Mercury Cougar Convertible,** 2001, Seafoam turquoise body, chrome rims, opening hood, black interior, 1:64 scale
EX n/a   NM n/a   **MIP** $6

❑ **'70 Cougar Convertible,** 2001, Glacier blue body, red interior, rubber tires, chrome rims, 1:64 scale, Model No. 001
EX n/a   NM n/a   **MIP** $6

❑ **'70 Plymouth GTX,** 2001, Rally green body, real wheels rubber tires, 1:64 scale
EX n/a   NM n/a   **MIP** $6

❑ **'71 Plymouth Satellite Sebring,** 2001, Citron yellow body, real wheels rubber tires, silver painted trim, opening hood, 1:64 scale
EX n/a   NM n/a   **MIP** $6

❑ **'79 Ford Mustang,** 2001, Orange body, real wheels rubber tires, 1:64 scale
EX n/a   NM n/a   **MIP** $6

❑ **'83 Lagonda,** 2001, Red body and spoiler, rubber tires, chrome rims, 1:64 scale
EX n/a   NM n/a   **MIP** $6

❑ **'87 Aston Martin,** 2001, Snow white body, rubber tires, chrome spoked wheels, 1:64 scale
EX n/a   NM n/a   **MIP** $6

❑ **'95 Chevy Caprice,** 2001, Bright Cobalt blue body, chrome rims, rubber tires, 1:64 scale
EX n/a   NM n/a   **MIP** $6

❑ **'97 Chevy Tahoe,** 2001, Moonglow silver body, chrome wheels, 1:64 scale, Model No. 367
EX n/a   NM n/a   **MIP** $6

❑ **Lotus Esprit,** 2001, Starlight black body, red interior, chrome rims, 1:64 scale
EX n/a   NM n/a   **MIP** $6

JL DIRECT

(KP Photo)

❏ **'60s VW Van: Hippie Peace Bus,** 2000, Red body with white peace symbols on roof and sides, multi-colored designs, green wheels, plain black rubber tires. Available in the Winter 2001-2002 collector's catalog as part of a two-vehicle set, 1:64 scale
EX n/a NM n/a MIP $8

(KP Photo)

❏ **'60s VW Van: Sun and Moon,** 2000, Dark blue front with moon and stars, yellow and orange in back with sun and rays. Silver wheels, silver-painted headlights, plain rubber tires. Available as part of two vehicle set with the "Peace" van, 1:64 scale
EX n/a NM n/a MIP $8

(KP Photo)

❏ **Polarlights.com Car,** 2000, Blue and white "Meat Wagon" with "PolarLights" oval on sides, hood and rear, silver chrom rims, rubber tires, silver painted grille and trim, two white surfboards in back, 1:64 scale, Model No. 511
EX n/a NM n/a MIP $6

JL TOPPER 4

❏ **Custom Dragster,** 2001, KR Aqua, real wheels, chrome rims, photo card, 1:64 scale, Model No. 245
EX n/a NM n/a MIP $6

❏ **Custom Dragster,** 2001, Apricot, real wheels, chrome rims, photo card, 1:64 scale, Model No. 245
EX n/a NM n/a MIP $6

❏ **Custom L,** 2001, Bronze, real wheels, chrome rims, photo card, 1:64 scale, Model No. 246
EX n/a NM n/a MIP $6

❏ **Custom L,** 2001, Medium violet, real wheels, chrome rims, photo card, 1:64 scale, Model No. 246
EX n/a NM n/a MIP $6

❏ **Custom Stiletto,** 2001, Cobalt blue, real wheels, chrome rims, photo card, 1:64 scale, Model No. 247
EX n/a NM n/a MIP $6

❏ **Custom Stiletto,** 2001, Lt. Green, real wheels, chrome rims, photo card, 1:64 scale, Model No. 247
EX n/a NM n/a MIP $6

❏ **Flame Out,** 2001, Cherry red, real wheels, chrome rims, photo card, 1:64 scale, Model No. 299
EX n/a NM n/a MIP $6

❏ **Flame Out,** 2001, KR orange, real wheels, chrome rims, photo card, 1:64 scale, Model No. 299
EX n/a NM n/a MIP $6

❏ **Mad Maverick,** 2001, Dark Irish pearlcoat, real wheels, chrome rims, photo card, 1:64 scale, Model No. 248
EX n/a NM n/a MIP $6

❏ **Mad Maverick,** 2001, Green marine, real wheels, chrome rims, photo card, 1:64 scale, Model No. 248
EX n/a NM n/a MIP $6

(KP Photo)

❏ **Sand Stormer,** 2000, Blue metallic, hard tires, chrome five spoke wheels, silver engine, photo card, 1:64 scale, Model No. 300
EX n/a NM n/a MIP $6

❏ **Sand Stormer,** 2001, KR purple, real wheels, chrome rims, photo card, 1:64 scale, Model No. 300
EX n/a NM n/a MIP $6

JOHNNY LIGHTNING RED CARD SERIES

❏ **'41 Willy's Coupe,** 1:64 scale
EX n/a NM n/a MIP $5

❏ **'57 Chevy,** 1:64 scale
EX n/a NM n/a MIP $8

❏ **'57 Vette Gasser,** 1:64 scale
EX n/a NM n/a MIP $6

❏ **'69 SuperBee,** 1:64 scale
EX n/a NM n/a MIP $5

❏ **'72 GTO,** 1:64 scale
EX n/a NM n/a MIP $5

❏ **'73 Trans Am,** 1:64 scale
EX n/a NM n/a MIP $5

(KP Photo)

❏ **'81 Z-Car,** 1999, Teal or gold with black bumpers, silver wheels, 1:64 scale
EX n/a NM n/a MIP $3

(KP Photo, Angelo Van Bogart collection)

❏ **Bad Man,** 1996, Yellow '55 Chevy with "Bad Man" on sides, black stripe with "396", 1:64 scale
EX n/a NM n/a MIP $5

❏ **Bad News,** 1:64 scale
EX n/a NM n/a MIP $5

❏ **Cheetah,** 1:64 scale
EX n/a NM n/a MIP $5

(KP Photo)

❏ **Chrysler Atlantic,** 1999, Purple metallic body, painted headlights, silver wheels, 1:64 scale
EX n/a NM n/a MIP $3

(KP Photo)

❏ **Dan Fink Speedwagon,** 1999, Purple body, black roof, silver wheels, 1:64 scale
EX n/a   NM n/a   MIP $4

❏ **Li'l Van,** 1:64 scale
EX n/a   NM n/a   MIP $5

❏ **Shelby 427 Cobra,** 1:64 scale
EX n/a   NM n/a   MIP $5

KISS RACING DREAMS

❏ **Ace Frehley,** '97 Firebird, 1:64 scale
EX n/a   NM n/a   MIP $5

❏ **Gene Simmons,** '94 Daytona, 1:64 scale
EX n/a   NM n/a   MIP $5

❏ **Paul Stanley,** '91 Olds, 1:64 scale
EX n/a   NM n/a   MIP $5

❏ **Peter Criss,** '96 Avenger, 1:64 scale
EX n/a   NM n/a   MIP $5

LIGHTNING BRIGADE

❏ **6x6 Fuel Tanker,** 2001, Olive drab body with white star, opening hood, rubber tires, , Model No. 067
EX n/a   NM n/a   MIP $6

❏ **7th Army Half Track,** 2001, Light green body with darker green pattern on top, white circle design on hood, sides and front, anti-aircraft gun in truck bed, black treads, tan roller wheels, Model No. 070
EX n/a   NM n/a   MIP $6

❏ **CUCV-II Carrier Cargo/Trooper,** 2001, Desert sand body, tan interior, tan painted rims, black trim
EX n/a   NM n/a   MIP $6

❏ **CUCV-II Carrier Cargo/Trooper,** 2001, Flat green with dark green camo pattern, tan interior
EX n/a   NM n/a   MIP $6

❏ **CUCV-II Command Tahoe,** 2001, Light sand and dark green camouflage paint, rubber tires, , Model No. 367
EX n/a   NM n/a   MIP $6

❏ **Desert Storm M1A1 Tank,** 2000, Gulf armor sand-colored body, black arrow emblem on sides, black treads, black machine gun on turret, Model No. 066
EX n/a   NM n/a   MIP $6

(KP Photo)

❏ **Desert Storm M998 Cargo Humvee,** 2000, Sand-colored body, black wheels, open bed, painted headlights, sand-colored rims
EX n/a   NM n/a   MIP $6

❏ **M1A1 Tank,** 2001, Sand color with olive and dark green camo pattern, mine plow on front
EX n/a   NM n/a   MIP $6

❏ **M1A1 Tank,** 2001, Olive drab body with snow painted along top of treads and sides, Model No. 066
EX n/a   NM n/a   MIP $6

❏ **M1A1 Tank w/Mine Plow,** 2001, Tan with darker green camouflage pattern with mine plow in front, black gun, Model No. 066
EX n/a   NM n/a   MIP $6

❏ **WC54 Military Police truck,** 2001, Olive drab body, white star-in-circle design, rubber tires, "Military Police" on sides and above windshield, Model No. 069
EX n/a   NM n/a   MIP $6

❏ **Willys Jeep w/top,** 2001, Olive drab body, tan top, rubber tires, opening hood, silver painted headlights, Model No. 065
EX n/a   NM n/a   MIP $6

❏ **WWII Anti-aircraft Half Track,** 2000, Olive body, white stars on grille, hood and sides, black treads, Model No. 070
EX n/a   NM n/a   MIP $6

❏ **WWII CCKW 6x6,** 2001, Dark olive drab body with olive drab canvas over truck bed, opening hood, white stars on hood and doors
EX n/a   NM n/a   MIP $6

❏ **WWII CCKW 6x6,** 2001, Plain olive drab with no star designs, opening hood
EX n/a   NM n/a   MIP $6

❏ **WWII GMC 6x6 Truck,** 2000, Light olive drab, opening hood, white stars on hood and doors, open stakeside truck bed
EX n/a   NM n/a   MIP $6

❏ **WWII M-16 Half Track,** 2001, Flat olive drab, white stars on hood and sides, anti-aircraft gun in truck bed, Model No. 070
EX n/a   NM n/a   MIP $6

❏ **WWII M2A1 Half Track,** 2001, White winter camouflage pattern, black treads, green painted rims, , Model No. 070
EX n/a   NM n/a   MIP $6

❏ **WWII MB Willys Jeep,** 2001, Flat olive drab body, no top, olive rims, opening hood, Model No. 065
EX n/a   NM n/a   MIP $6

❏ **WWII MB Willys Jeep,** 2001, Olive drab body, no top, white star-in-circle on opening hood, "Military Police" in yellow type on windshield, Model No. 065
EX n/a   NM n/a   MIP $6

❏ **WWII WC-54 Ambulance,** 2000, Olive drab, real wheels tires, olive rims, white star-in-circle design, Model No. 069
EX n/a   NM n/a   MIP $8

(KP Photo)

❏ **WWII WC-54 Ambulance,** 2001, Olive drab, real wheels, white star design on hood and doors, red cross designs on sides and roof, Model No. 069
EX n/a   NM n/a   MIP $8

❏ **WWII WC-54 Ambulance,** 2001, Ford blue body and rims, red cross emblems on roof and sides, Model No. 069

EX n/a   NM n/a   MIP $8

❑ **WWII Willys Scout Jeep,** 2000, Olive drab, thin Jeep wheels, olive rims, opening hood with white star, black machine gun in back, , Model No. 065

EX n/a   NM n/a   MIP $6

LIGHTNING SPEED

(KP Photo, Angelo Van Bogart collection)

❑ **1996 Dodge Ram,** 2001, Green body, black cover, silver wheels, 1:64 scale, Model No. 413

EX n/a   NM n/a   MIP $5

❑ **'29 Crew Cab,** 2001, Metallic light purple body, silver wheels, Racer's Edge hard tires, "Johnny Lightning" sticker, 1:64 scale

EX n/a   NM n/a   MIP $5

❑ **'29 Crew Cab,** 2001, Metallic light purple body, silver wheels, Racer's Edge hard tires, "Johnny Lightning" sticker, 1:64 scale

EX n/a   NM n/a   MIP $5

❑ **'50 Ford,** 2001, Seafoam metallic body, silver wheels, Racer's Edge hard tires, "Johnny Lightning" sticker, 1:64 scale

EX n/a   NM n/a   MIP $5

❑ **'59 El Camino,** 2001, Metallic green body, silver wheels, Racer's Edge hard tires, 1:64 scale

EX n/a   NM n/a   MIP $5

❑ **'60's VW Bus,** 2001, Tan and bronze body, silver rims. All of the vehicles in this series feature the hard "Racer's Edge" tires, which have a raised lip on the inside edge, intended for higher track speeds, 1:64 scale

EX n/a   NM n/a   MIP $7

(KP Photo)

❑ **'62 Bad Bird,** 2001, Modified Ford Thunderbird body, metallic gold-green, silver wheels, Racer's Edge hard tires, 1:64 scale

EX n/a   NM n/a   MIP $5

❑ **'72 Camaro,** 2001, Metallic purple body, silver wheels, Racer's Edge hard tires. These tires are quite similar to the original versions on old Topper Johnny Lightning cars that allowed them to race at "...scale speeds greater than 1200 mph...", 1:64 scale

EX n/a   NM n/a   MIP $5

❑ **'76 Chevy Camaro,** 2001, White body, silver wheels, Racer's Edge hard tires, "Johnny Lightning" sticker, 1:64 scale

EX n/a   NM n/a   MIP $5

❑ **'78 Li'l Red Express,** 2001, Metallic mustard yellow body, silver wheels, Racer's Edge hard tires, 1:64 scale

EX n/a   NM n/a   MIP $5

❑ **'87 Mustang GT,** 2001, Starlight black body, silver wheels, Racer's Edge hard tires, "Johnny Lightning" sticker, 1:64 scale

EX n/a   NM n/a   MIP $5

(KP Photo)

❑ **'95 Caprice,** 2000, Red body, silver wheels, "Racer's Edge" hard tires, black plastic interior, red and clear dome lights. Looks like a fire chief car withouth the insignia, 1:64 scale

EX n/a   NM n/a   MIP $5

❑ **'97 Camaro,** 2001, Metallic silver body, chrome wheels, Racer's Edge hard tires, "Johnny Lightning" sticker in pack, 1:64 scale

EX n/a   NM n/a   MIP $5

LOST IN SPACE

(KP Photo)

❑ **Jupiter II,** 1998, Silver die-cast body, clear plastic observation bubble on top, plastic landing pads

EX n/a   NM n/a   MIP $5

(KP Photo)

❑ **Robot B-9,** 1998, Gray and silver die-cast body with clear plastic "bubble head", detailed torso, roller wheels on base

EX n/a   NM n/a   MIP $6

(KP Photo)

❑ **Space Chariot,** 1998, Metal chassis with static treads (hidden wheels on base), clear plastic body with red and gray interior, detailed radar and gear on roof, gray-painted grille, 1:64 scale

EX n/a   NM n/a   MIP $5

(KP Photo)

❑ **Space Pod,** 1998, Silver and red die-cast body with black-painted windows, gray plastic landing gear, and silver and gray plastic radar and antenna

EX n/a   NM n/a   MIP $5

LOST TOPPERS

(KP Photo)

❏ **Beep Heap,** 2002, Cameo white, hard wheels, chrome rims, illustration trading card, 1:64 scale, Model No. 074
EX n/a   NM n/a   MIP $5

❏ **Commuter,** 2002, Red chrome, hard wheels, chrome rims, illustration trading card, 1:64 scale, Model No. 071
EX n/a   NM n/a   MIP $4

❏ **Custom Camaro,** 2002, Blue chrome body, hard wheels, chrome rims, illustrations trading card, 1:64 scale, Model No. 119
EX n/a   NM n/a   MIP $5

(KP Photo)

❏ **Custom Charger,** 2002, Daytona yellow, hard wheels, chrome rims, opening hood, illustrations card, 1:64 scale, Model No. 120
EX n/a   NM n/a   MIP $5

(KP Photo)

❏ **Skinni Mini,** 2002, Chrome green body, hard wheels, silver exposed engine, chrome rims. KB Toys exclusive, 1:64 scale, Model No. 072
EX n/a   NM n/a   MIP $5

❏ **Skinni Mini,** 2002, Orange body, hard wheels, silver exposed engine, chrome rims, 1:64 scale, Model No. 072
EX n/a   NM n/a   MIP $5

(KP Photo)

❏ **Tow'd,** 2002, Black body, black plastic stacks and tow hook, unpainted base, red dome light, silver engine, white-painted headlights, hard tires, chrome rims, illustration trading card, 1:64 scale, Model No. 073
EX n/a   NM n/a   MIP $5

(KP Photo)

❏ **Tow'd,** 2002, Light green, hard wheels, chrome rims, black plastic tow hook, illustration trading card, 1:64 scale, Model No. 073
EX n/a   NM n/a   MIP $5

MAGMAS

❏ **'68 Camaro,** 1999, Blue-green body, opening hood, silver chrome wheels and engine, 1:43 scale
EX n/a   NM n/a   MIP $8

❏ **'70 A. Unser Indy,** 1999, Dark blue with yellow Johnny Lightning bolt designs on hood and sides, number "2" on hood and sides, 1:43 scale
EX n/a   NM n/a   MIP $7

❏ **'70 Challenger Trans Am,** 1999, Sublime body, black stripe on sides, black opening hood, silver chrome engine and wheels, black grille, 1:43 scale
EX n/a   NM n/a   MIP $7

❏ **'71 Mustang Boss 351,** 1999, Bright Grabber blue body, silver engine and wheels, opening hood, black interior, silver stripe along sides, 1:43 scale
EX n/a   NM n/a   MIP $7

❏ **'71 Mustang Mach 1,** 1999, Bright red body, silver gray hood and spoiler, chrome wheels, black louvers, black interior, 1:43 scale
EX n/a   NM n/a   MIP $7

❏ **'71 Plymouth Roadrunner,** 1999, Plum Crazy (purple) body, with black stripe on sides, wide stripe on hood, silver engine and wheels, 1:43 scale
EX n/a   NM n/a   MIP $7

(KP Photo)

❏ **Donkey Kong,** 2000, Pontiac Grand Prix, mostly blue body with Donkey Kong imagery and number "64", silver wheels, "Goodyear" tires, 1:43 scale
EX n/a   NM n/a   MIP $8

❏ **Drag-u-la,** 1999, Gold casket-shaped body with small spoked wheels in front, large wheels in rear. Clear plastic canopy, 1:43 scale
EX n/a   NM n/a   MIP $8

❏ **Smash Brothers,** 2000, Ford Taurus stock car, 1:43 scale
EX n/a   NM n/a   MIP $8

❏ **T'rantula,** 1999, Green dragster body with chrome engine and rims, small spoked wheels in front, large wheels in rear, 1:43 scale
EX n/a   NM n/a   MIP $7

(KP Photo)

❑ **Yoshi's Story,** 2000, Ford Taurus stock car, mostly blue with Yoshi graphics on sides and hood, silver wheels, "Goodyear" tires, 1:43 scale
EX n/a   NM n/a   MIP $8

(KP Photo)

❑ **Zelda,** 2000, Pontiac Grand Prix body with Zelda image and sponsor graphics, "Goodyear" tires, 1:43 scale
EX n/a   NM n/a   MIP $8

MODERN MUSCLE

❑ **'00 Chevy Monte Carlo,** 2000, Cranberry red body, chrome rims, painted headlights and grille, 1:64 scale, Model No. 236
EX n/a   NM n/a   MIP $4

❑ **'00 Chevy Monte Carlo SS,** 2001, Starlight black body, hard tires, crhome rims, 1:64 scale, Model No. 236
EX n/a   NM n/a   MIP $6

❑ **'00 Dodge Viper,** 2000, Steel gray body, painted headlights, chrome rims, 1:64 scale, Model No. 234
EX n/a   NM n/a   MIP $4

❑ **'00 Dodge Viper RT/10 Roadster,** 2001, Shelby red body, hard tires, chrome rims, photo card, opening hood, 1:64 scale, Model No. 234
EX n/a   NM n/a   MIP $6

❑ **'00 Firebird,** 2001, Graphite metallic body, hard wheels, chrome rims, photo card, 1:64 scale, Model No. 233
EX n/a   NM n/a   MIP $6

❑ **'00 Ford Mustang,** 2000, Sunburst gold body, chrome rims, black grille, photo card, 1:64 scale, Model No. 235
EX n/a   NM n/a   MIP $4

❑ **'00 Ford Mustang Convertible,** 2001, Sunburst yellow body, black interior, chrome rims, hard tires, opening hood, photo card, 1:64 scale, Model No. 235
EX n/a   NM n/a   MIP $6

❑ **'00 Jaguar XK8,** 2000, Anthracite black body, chrome rims, black interior, 1:64 scale, Model No. 237
EX n/a   NM n/a   MIP $4

❑ **'00 Jaguar XK8,** 2001, Blue fire body, tan interior, chrome rims, hard tires, 1:64 scale, Model No. 237
EX n/a   NM n/a   MIP $6

❑ **'00 Jaguar XK8,** 2001, Phoenix red body, brown interior, hard wheels, chrome rims, photo card, 1:64 scale, Model No. 237
EX n/a   NM n/a   MIP $6

❑ **'00 Mazda Miata,** 2001, Snow white body, red interior, chrome rims, hard tires, photo card, 1:64 scale, Model No. 238
EX n/a   NM n/a   MIP $6

❑ **'00 Miata,** 2000, Bright red body, black interior, tan folded-down top, chrome rims, 1:64 scale, Model No. 238
EX n/a   NM n/a   MIP $4

❑ **'00 Miata MX5,** 2001, Burgundy body, tan interior, hard wheels, chrome rims, photo card, 1:64 scale, Model No. 238
EX n/a   NM n/a   MIP $6

❑ **'00 Monte Carlo SS,** 2001, Snow white body, hard wheels, chrome rims, photo card, 1:64 scale, Model No. 236
EX n/a   NM n/a   MIP $6

❑ **'00 Mustang,** 2001, Cobalt blue body, black interior, hard wheels, chrome rims, photo card, 1:64 scale, Model No. 235
EX n/a   NM n/a   MIP $6

❑ **'00 Pontiac Firebird,** 2001, Emerald green, hard tires, chrome rims, opening hood, photo card, 1:64 scale, Model No. 233
EX n/a   NM n/a   MIP $6

❑ **'00 Pontiac Firebird Trans-Am,** 2000, White body, black roof, tan interior, chrome rims, 1:64 scale, Model No. 233
EX n/a   NM n/a   MIP $4

❑ **'00 Viper RT/10 Roadster,** 2001, Starlight black, hard wheels, chrome rims, photo card, 1:64 scale, Model No. 234
EX n/a   NM n/a   MIP $6

MONOPOLY

❑ **'00 BMW Z-3,** 2001, Boardwalk, in "Park Place blue," hard tires, 1:64 scale
EX n/a   NM n/a   MIP $5

❑ **'33 Ford Delivery Truck,** 2001, Get Out of Jail, Monopoly green, hard tires, 1:64 scale
EX n/a   NM n/a   MIP $5

(KP Photo)

❑ **'33 Willys,** 2000, Vintage Monopoly, cream and black body, silver painted headlights, chrome wheels, 1:64 scale
EX n/a   NM n/a   MIP $5

❑ **'33 Willys: KB Toys Exclusive,** 2000, Vintage Monopoly, golden chrome, 1:64 scale
EX n/a   NM n/a   MIP $5

(KP Photo)

❑ **'40 Ford,** 2000, Reading Railroad designs on doors, brown painted sideboards on bed, "Reading Railroad" on opening hood, silver wheels, silver gamepiece included with toy, 1:64 scale
EX n/a   NM n/a   MIP $5

(KP Photo)

❑ **'57 Chevy,** 2000, Illinois Ave., red body with Illinois Ave. card

graphic on hood, white trim, black interior, chrome wheels, 1:64 scale
EX n/a   NM n/a   MIP $5

❑ **'57 Lincoln Premier,** 2001, Income Tax, Moonglow silver body, hard tires, 1:64 scale
EX n/a   NM n/a   MIP $5

(KP Photo)

❑ **'60's VW Van,** 2001, Free Parking. Snow white and red, includes metal game piece, 1:64 scale
EX n/a   NM n/a   MIP $7

(KP Photo)

❑ **'60's VW Van: KB Toys Exclusive,** 2001, Free Parking. Chrome red and snow white body, green "Free Parking" diamond on sides, chrome red VW van game piece included, 1:64 scale
EX n/a   NM n/a   MIP $8

(KP Photo)

❑ **'67 Mustang,** 2000, Community Chest, yellow body, chrome wheels, opening hood, "Community Chest" in script type in black stripe along side, 1:64 scale
EX n/a   NM n/a   MIP $5

❑ **'69 Chevy Camaro,** 2001, Marvin Gardens, yellow, hard tires, 1:64 scale
EX n/a   NM n/a   MIP $5

❑ **'69 Dodge Daytona,** 2001, St. Charles Place, Moulin Rouge, hard tires, 1:64 scale
EX n/a   NM n/a   MIP $5

(KP Photo)

❑ **'98 Corvette,** 2000, Modern Monopoly, white convertible body, red interior, red rims, 1:64 scale
EX n/a   NM n/a   MIP $5

(KP Photo)

❑ **Cameo Pickup truck,** 2000, Water Works, white body with Water Works symbols, opening hood, game piece included, 1:64 scale
EX n/a   NM n/a   MIP $5

(KP Photo)

❑ **Crown Victoria,** 2000, Go To Jail-Do Not Pass Go, Ford Crown Victoria police car, black and white with Monopoly grahics and red and blue roof lights, 1:64 scale
EX n/a   NM n/a   MIP $5

(KP Photo)

❑ **Dodge Dart,** 2000, Chance, orange body, hard tires, engine in rear, black interior, game piece included, 1:64 scale
EX n/a   NM n/a   MIP $5

❑ **Pontiac Tempest,** 2000, Park Place, royal blue body, silver

chrome wheels, black interior, 1:64 scale
EX n/a   NM n/a   MIP $5

(KP Photo)

❑ **Tahoe,** 2000, White, with B&O Railroad emblems on doors and roof, 1:64 scale
EX n/a   NM n/a   MIP $5

(KP Photo)

❑ **Utility Van,** 2000, Electric Company, white GMC van with Monopoly light bulb graphic, silver chrome wheels, 1:64 scale
EX n/a   NM n/a   MIP $5

(KP Photo)

❑ **Viper: Luxury Tax,** 2000, Luxury Tax. White with Luxury Tax gold ring on hood, Monopoly guy on roof. Game piece (like all models in this series) included, 1:64 scale
EX n/a   NM n/a   MIP $5

MOPAR MUSCLE

❑ **'69 Daytona,** 2001, Honolulu blue, hard tires, chrome rims, photo card, 1:64 scale, Model No. 491
EX n/a   NM n/a   MIP $5

❑ **'69 Dodge Charger,** 2001, Hard tires, 1:64 scale
EX n/a   NM n/a   **MIP** $5

❑ **'69 Dodge Charger,** 2001, Shelby red, hard tires, 1:64 scale
EX n/a   NM n/a   **MIP** $5

❑ **'69 Dodge Charger Daytona,** 2002, Vitamin C orange body, photo card, 1:64 scale
EX n/a   NM n/a   **MIP** $5

❑ **'69 Dodge Charger R/T,** 2002, Sassy grass green body, photo card, 1:64 scale
EX n/a   NM n/a   **MIP** $5

❑ **'69 Dodge Daytona,** 2001, Medium green, hard tires, 1:64 scale
EX n/a   NM n/a   **MIP** $5

❑ **'69 Dodge Daytona,** 2001, Hard tires, 1:64 scale
EX n/a   NM n/a   **MIP** $5

❑ **'69 Dodge Daytona,** 2002, Seaform turquoise, hard tires, chrome rims, photo card, 1:64 scale, Model No. 491
EX n/a   NM n/a   **MIP** $5

❑ **'70 Charger R/T,** 2001, Sunburst yellow, hard tires, chrome rims, photo cards, 1:64 scale, Model No. 488
EX n/a   NM n/a   **MIP** $5

❑ **'70 Cuda,** 2001, Starlight black, hard tires, chrome rims, photo cards, 1:64 scale, Model No. 490
EX n/a   NM n/a   **MIP** $5

❑ **'70 Dodge Charger R/T,** 2002, Starlight black, hard tires, chrome rims, photo card, 1:64 scale, Model No. 488
EX n/a   NM n/a   **MIP** $5

❑ **'70 Plymouth GTX,** 2002, Blue body, photo card, 1:64 scale
EX n/a   NM n/a   **MIP** $5

❑ **'70 Plymouth Hemi Cuda,** 2001, Lemon yellow, hard tires, 1:64 scale
EX n/a   NM n/a   **MIP** $5

❑ **'70 Plymouth Hemi Cuda,** 2001, Hard tires, 1:64 scale
EX n/a   NM n/a   **MIP** $5

❑ **'70 Plymouth Hemi Cuda,** 2002, Plum Crazy body, photo card, 1:64 scale
EX n/a   NM n/a   **MIP** $5

❑ **'70 Plymouth Hemi Cuda,** 2002, Vitamin C orange, hard tires,

chrome rims, photo card, 1:64 scale, Model No. 490
EX n/a   NM n/a   **MIP** $5

❑ **'70 Plymouth Road Runner,** 2001, Sublime, hard tires, 1:64 scale
EX n/a   NM n/a   **MIP** $5

❑ **'70 Plymouth Road Runner,** 2001, Hard tires, 1:64 scale
EX n/a   NM n/a   **MIP** $5

❑ **'70 Plymouth Roadrunner,** 2001, Hemi orange, hard tires, chrome rims, photo card, 1:64 scale, Model No. 492
EX n/a   NM n/a   **MIP** $5

❑ **'70 Plymouth Sport Satellite,** 2002, Candyapple red, hard tires, chrome rims, photo card, 1:64 scale, Model No. 492
EX n/a   NM n/a   **MIP** $5

❑ **'71 Duster 340,** 2001, Sassy grass green, hard tires, chrome rims, photo cards, 1:64 scale, Model No. 489
EX n/a   NM n/a   **MIP** $5

❑ **'71 Plymouth Duster,** 2002, Lemon yellow, hard tires, chrome rims, photo card, 1:64 scale, Model No. 489
EX n/a   NM n/a   **MIP** $5

❑ **'71 Plymouth Duster 340,** 2001, Hard tires, 1:64 scale
EX n/a   NM n/a   **MIP** $5

❑ **'71 Plymouth Duster 340,** 2001, Plum Crazy, hard tires, 1:64 scale
EX n/a   NM n/a   **MIP** $5

❑ **'71 Plymouth Duster 340,** 2002, Panther pink body, photo card, 1:64 scale
EX n/a   NM n/a   **MIP** $5

❑ **'71 Plymouth Hemi GTX,** 2001, Plum Crazy, hard tires, chrome rims, photo card, 1:64 scale, Model No. 487
EX n/a   NM n/a   **MIP** $5

❑ **'71 Plymouth Road Runner,** 2001, Hard tires, 1:64 scale
EX n/a   NM n/a   **MIP** $5

❑ **'71 Plymouth Road Runner,** 2001, Hemi orange, hard tires, 1:64 scale
EX n/a   NM n/a   **MIP** $5

❑ **'71 Plymouth Road Runner,** 2002, Tor-Red body, photo card, 1:64 scale
EX n/a   NM n/a   **MIP** $5

❑ **'72 Plymouth GTX,** 2002, Blue fire, hard tires, chrome rims, photo card, 1:64 scale, Model No. 487
EX n/a   NM n/a   **MIP** $5

MOPAR MUSCLE FIRST SHOTS

❑ **'69 Charger,** 2001, Includes two cars: One with chrome green body, rubber tires, chrome rims. The other is a raw-metal car, a "first shot", 1:64 scale, Model No. 488
EX n/a   NM n/a   **MIP** $6

❑ **'69 Daytona,** 2001, Includes two cars: One with a chrome orange body, rubber tires, chrome rims; the second as a raw die-cast car, 1:64 scale, Model No. 491
EX n/a   NM n/a   **MIP** $6

❑ **'70 Cuda,** 2001, Includes two cars: One with a chrome red body, rubber tires, chrome rims. The second vehicle is a raw die-cast car of the same model, 1:64 scale, Model No. 490
EX n/a   NM n/a   **MIP** $6

❑ **'70 GTX,** 2001, Includes two cars: One with a chrome blue body, real wheels rubber tires, chrome rims. The second car is the same, but in raw die-cast metal, 1:64 scale, Model No. 492
EX n/a   NM n/a   **MIP** $6

❑ **'71 Duster,** 2001, Includes two cars: One with a chrome purple, rubber tires, chrome rims. The other is raw die-cast car of the same model--a "first shot", 1:64 scale, Model No. 489
EX n/a   NM n/a   **MIP** $6

❑ **'71 Road Runner,** 2001, Includes two cars: One with a chrome citron body, real wheels, chrome rims, raw car, 1:64 scale, Model No. 487
EX n/a   NM n/a   **MIP** $6

MUSCLE CARS

❑ **'65 Chevy II Nova,** 1:64 scale
EX n/a   NM n/a   **MIP** $25

❑ **'67 GTO,** 1:64 scale
EX n/a   NM n/a   **MIP** $30

❑ **'68 Chevelle,** 1:64 scale
EX n/a   NM n/a   **MIP** $25

❑ **'70 AAR Cuda,** 1:64 scale
EX n/a   NM n/a   **MIP** $30

❏ **'70 AMC Rebel Machine,** 1:64 scale
EX n/a   NM n/a   MIP $25

❏ **'70 Challenger T/A,** 1:64 scale
EX n/a   NM n/a   MIP $25

❏ **'70 Torino,** 1:64 scale
EX n/a   NM n/a   MIP $25

❏ **'71 Demon,** 1:64 scale
EX n/a   NM n/a   MIP $25

❏ **'73 Charger,** 1:64 scale
EX n/a   NM n/a   MIP $25

MUSCLE CARS USA, 1

❏ **'65 Pontiac GTO Convertible,** 1994, Green body, silver rims, hard tires, 1:64 scale
EX n/a   NM n/a   MIP $6

❏ **'65 Pontiac GTO Convertible,** 1994, Red body, silver Cragar rims, hard tires, 1:64 scale
EX n/a   NM n/a   MIP $6

❏ **'65 Pontiac GTO Convertible,** 1994, Black with light tan interior, silver rims, hard tires, 1:64 scale
EX n/a   NM n/a   MIP $7

❏ **'65 Pontiac GTO Convertible,** 1995, Silver body, chrome wheels, opening hood, hard tires, photo collector coin in pack, 1:64 scale
EX n/a   NM n/a   MIP $5

❏ **'65 Pontiac GTO Convertible,** 1995, Gold body, five-spoke chrome wheels, opening hood, hard tires, photo collector coin in pack, 1:64 scale
EX n/a   NM n/a   MIP $5

❏ **'65 Pontiac GTO Convertible,** 1995, Light blue body, chrome wheels, opening hood, hard tires, photo collector coin in pack, 1:64 scale
EX n/a   NM n/a   MIP $5

❏ **'65 Pontiac GTO Convertible,** 1995, Yellow body, chrome wheels, opening hood, hard tires, photo collector coin in pack, 1:64 scale
EX n/a   NM n/a   MIP $5

❏ **'65 Pontiac GTO Convertible,** 1995, Red body, silver Cragar rims, hard tires, 1:64 scale
EX n/a   NM n/a   MIP $7

❏ **'65 Pontiac GTO Convertible,** 1995, Blue body, silver Cragar rims, hard tires, 1:64 scale
EX n/a   NM n/a   MIP $5

❏ **'65 Pontiac GTO Convertible,** 1996, Light metallic gold body, chrome wheels, opening hood, hard tires, photo collector coin in pack, 1:64 scale
EX n/a   NM n/a   MIP $5

❏ **'65 Pontiac GTO Convertible,** 1996, Olive green body, chrome wheels, opening hood, hard tires, photo collector coin in pack, 1:64 scale
EX n/a   NM n/a   MIP $5

❏ **'69 Mercury Cougar Eliminator,** 1994, Blue body, silver rims, hard tires, 1:64 scale
EX n/a   NM n/a   MIP $6

❏ **'69 Mercury Cougar Eliminator,** 1994, Orange body, chrome Cragar rims, hard tires, 1:64 scale
EX n/a   NM n/a   MIP $5

❏ **'69 Mercury Cougar Eliminator,** 1994, White body, silver rims, hard tires, 1:64 scale
EX n/a   NM n/a   MIP $5

❏ **'69 Mercury Cougar Eliminator,** 1995, Red body, chrome Cragar rims, hard tires, 1:64 scale
EX n/a   NM n/a   MIP $6

❏ **'69 Mercury Cougar Eliminator,** 1995, Green body, chrome rims, hard tires, 1:64 scale
EX n/a   NM n/a   MIP $6

❏ **'69 Mercury Cougar Eliminator,** 1995, Green body, chrome Cragar rims, hard tires, 1:64 scale
EX n/a   NM n/a   MIP $5

❏ **'69 Mercury Cougar Eliminator,** 1995, Yellow body, chrome rims, hard tires, 1:64 scale
EX n/a   NM n/a   MIP $7

❏ **'69 Mercury Cougar Eliminator,** 1995, Black body, chrome Cragar rims, hard tires, 1:64 scale
EX n/a   NM n/a   MIP $7

❏ **'69 Mercury Cougar Eliminator,** 1995, Metallic gold body, chrome rims, hard tires, 1:64 scale
EX n/a   NM n/a   MIP $6

❏ **'69 Mercury Cougar Eliminator,** 1996, Magenta body, chrome rims, hard tires, 1:64 scale
EX n/a   NM n/a   MIP $6

❏ **'69 Mercury Cougar Eliminator,** 1996, Metallic silver body, chrome rims, hard tires, 1:64 scale
EX n/a   NM n/a   MIP $5

❏ **'69 Olds 442,** 1994, Purple body with silver wheels, hard tires, 1:64 scale
EX n/a   NM n/a   MIP $5

❏ **'69 Olds 442,** 1994, Gold metallic body with silver wheels, hard tires, 1:64 scale
EX n/a   NM n/a   MIP $6

❏ **'69 Olds 442,** 1994, Light metallic green with silver wheels, hard tires, 1:64 scale
EX n/a   NM n/a   MIP $5

❏ **'69 Olds 442,** 1995, Black body with chrome wheels, hard tires, 1:64 scale
EX n/a   NM n/a   MIP $6

❏ **'69 Olds 442,** 1995, Silver body with chrome Cragar wheels, hard tires, 1:64 scale
EX n/a   NM n/a   MIP $6

❏ **'69 Olds 442,** 1995, Yellow body with chrome wheels, hard tires, 1:64 scale
EX n/a   NM n/a   MIP $6

❏ **'69 Olds 442,** 1995, Light blue body with silver wheels, hard tires, 1:64 scale
EX n/a   NM n/a   MIP $5

❏ **'69 Olds 442,** 1995, Orange body with chrome wheels, hard tires, 1:64 scale
EX n/a   NM n/a   MIP $6

❏ **'69 Olds 442,** 1995, Green body with chrome Cragar wheels, hard tires, 1:64 scale
EX n/a   NM n/a   MIP $6

❏ **'69 Olds 442,** 1996, Blue body with chrome wheels, hard tires, 1:64 scale
EX n/a   NM n/a   MIP $6

(KP Photo, Angelo Van Bogart collection)

❏ **'69 Olds 442,** 1996, Red with silver wheels, hard tires, 1:64 scale
EX n/a   NM n/a   MIP $5

❏ **'69 Pontiac GTO Judge,** 1994, Black body with silver Cragar rims, hard tires. Like other models in the series, this too, had a gold collector coin with photo of actual car, 1:64 scale
EX n/a   NM n/a   MIP $7

❏ **'69 Pontiac GTO Judge,** 1994, Orange body with silver rims, 1:64 scale
EX n/a   **NM** n/a   **MIP** $7

❏ **'69 Pontiac GTO Judge,** 1994, Yellow with silver rims, 1:64 scale
EX n/a   **NM** n/a   **MIP** $7

❏ **'69 Pontiac GTO Judge,** 1995, Blue body with silver Cragar rims, hard tires. Like other models in the series, this too, had a gold collector coin with photo of actual car, 1:64 scale
EX n/a   **NM** n/a   **MIP** $7

❏ **'69 Pontiac GTO Judge,** 1995, Blue body with silver rims, hard tires. Like other models in the series, this too, had a gold collector coin with photo of actual car, 1:64 scale
EX n/a   **NM** n/a   **MIP** $6

❏ **'69 Pontiac GTO Judge,** 1995, Metallic gold body with silver rims, hard tires. Like other models in the series, this too, had a gold collector coin with photo of actual car, 1:64 scale
EX n/a   **NM** n/a   **MIP** $6

❏ **'69 Pontiac GTO Judge,** 1995, Green body with silver rims, hard tires. Like other models in the series, this too, had a gold collector coin with photo of actual car, 1:64 scale
EX n/a   **NM** n/a   **MIP** $6

❏ **'69 Pontiac GTO Judge,** 1995, White body with silver rims, hard tires. Like other models in the series, this too, had a gold collector coin with photo of actual car, 1:64 scale
EX n/a   **NM** n/a   **MIP** $6

❏ **'69 Pontiac GTO Judge,** 1995, Green body with silver rims, hard tires. Like other models in the series, this too, had a gold collector coin with photo of actual car, 1:64 scale
EX n/a   **NM** n/a   **MIP** $6

❏ **'69 Pontiac GTO Judge,** 1996, Dark red body with silver rims, hard tires. Like other models in the series, this too, had a gold collector coin with photo of actual car, 1:64 scale
EX n/a   **NM** n/a   **MIP** $6

❏ **'69 Pontiac GTO Judge,** 1996, Metallic purple body with silver rims, hard tires. Like other models in the series, this too, had

a gold collector coin with photo of actual car, 1:64 scale
EX n/a   **NM** n/a   **MIP** $6

❏ **'70 Chevy Chevelle SS,** 1994, White body, opening hood, hard tires, silver wheels, 1:64 scale
EX n/a   **NM** n/a   **MIP** $5

❏ **'70 Chevy Chevelle SS,** 1994, Black body, black stripes on hood and trunk, opening hood, hard tires, silver wheels, 1:64 scale
EX n/a   **NM** n/a   **MIP** $5

❏ **'70 Chevy Chevelle SS,** 1994, Gold body, black stripes on hood and trunk, opening hood, hard tires, silver wheels, 1:64 scale
EX n/a   **NM** n/a   **MIP** $5

❏ **'70 Chevy Chevelle SS,** 1995, Light blue body, opening hood, hard tires, silver wheels, 1:64 scale
EX n/a   **NM** n/a   **MIP** $5

❏ **'70 Chevy Chevelle SS,** 1995, Black body, opening hood, hard tires, silver wheels, 1:64 scale
EX n/a   **NM** n/a   **MIP** $5

❏ **'70 Chevy Chevelle SS,** 1995, Yellow body, opening hood, hard tires, silver wheels, 1:64 scale
EX n/a   **NM** n/a   **MIP** $5

❏ **'70 Chevy Chevelle SS,** 1995, Blue body, opening hood, hard tires, silver wheels, 1:64 scale
EX n/a   **NM** n/a   **MIP** $6

❏ **'70 Chevy Chevelle SS,** 1995, Olive green body, opening hood, hard tires, silver wheels, 1:64 scale
EX n/a   **NM** n/a   **MIP** $5

❏ **'70 Chevy Chevelle SS,** 1995, Orange body, opening hood, hard tires, silver wheels, 1:64 scale
EX n/a   **NM** n/a   **MIP** $5

❏ **'70 Chevy Chevelle SS,** 1996, Blue body, opening hood, hard tires, silver wheels, 1:64 scale
EX n/a   **NM** n/a   **MIP** $6

❏ **'70 Chevy Chevelle SS,** 1996, Metallic purple body, white stripes, opening hood, hard tires, silver wheels, 1:64 scale
EX n/a   **NM** n/a   **MIP** $6

❏ **'70 Dodge Super Bee,** 1994, Yellow body with chrome Cragar rims and hard tires, 1:64 scale
EX n/a   **NM** n/a   **MIP** $5

❏ **'70 Dodge Super Bee,** 1994, Green body with silver rims and hard tires, 1:64 scale
EX n/a   **NM** n/a   **MIP** $5

❏ **'70 Dodge Super Bee,** 1994, Purple body with silver rims and hard tires, 1:64 scale
EX n/a   **NM** n/a   **MIP** $5

❏ **'70 Dodge Super Bee,** 1995, Red body with chrome Cragar rims and hard tires, 1:64 scale
EX n/a   **NM** n/a   **MIP** $5

❏ **'70 Dodge Super Bee,** 1995, Orange body with chrome rims and hard tires, 1:64 scale
EX n/a   **NM** n/a   **MIP** $7

❏ **'70 Dodge Super Bee,** 1995, Black body with chrome rims and hard tires, 1:64 scale
EX n/a   **NM** n/a   **MIP** $6

❏ **'70 Dodge Super Bee,** 1995, White body with chrome rims and hard tires, 1:64 scale
EX n/a   **NM** n/a   **MIP** $7

❏ **'70 Dodge Super Bee,** 1995, Blue body with chrome rims and hard tires, 1:64 scale
EX n/a   **NM** n/a   **MIP** $7

❏ **'70 Dodge Super Bee,** 1995, Magenta body with chrome Cragar rims and hard tires, 1:64 scale
EX n/a   **NM** n/a   **MIP** $6

❏ **'70 Dodge Super Bee,** 1996, Metallic gold body with chrome rims and hard tires, 1:64 scale
EX n/a   **NM** n/a   **MIP** $6

❏ **'70 Dodge Super Bee,** 1996, Silver body with chrome rims and hard tires, 1:64 scale
EX n/a   **NM** n/a   **MIP** $7

❏ **'70 Ford Boss 302 Mustang,** 1994, Gold metallic body with wide black stripe on hood, silver wheels, hard tires, 1:64 scale
EX n/a   **NM** n/a   **MIP** $6

❏ **'70 Ford Boss 302 Mustang,** 1994, Yellow with black stripes, silver wheels, hard tires, 1:64 scale
EX n/a   **NM** n/a   **MIP** $7

❏ **'70 Ford Boss 302 Mustang,** 1994, Blue with wide black stripe on hood running into stripes on sides, silver wheels, hard tires, 1:64 scale
EX n/a   **NM** n/a   **MIP** $7

❏ **'70 Ford Boss 302 Mustang,** 1995, Orange body with black stripes, silver wheels, hard tires, 1:64 scale
EX n/a   **NM** n/a   **MIP** $6

❏ **'70 Ford Boss 302 Mustang,** 1995, White body, black stripes, silver chrome rims, hard wheels, photo collector coin (like others in the series), 1:64 scale
EX n/a   NM n/a   MIP $6

❏ **'70 Ford Boss 302 Mustang,** 1995, Metallic purple body with black stripes, silver chrome rims, hard wheels, photo collector coin (like others in the series), 1:64 scale
EX n/a   NM n/a   MIP $6

❏ **'70 Ford Boss 302 Mustang,** 1995, Gold metallic body with wide black stripe on hood, running into stripes along sides, silver wheels, hard tires, 1:64 scale
EX n/a   NM n/a   MIP $7

❏ **'70 Ford Boss 302 Mustang,** 1995, Green body, black stripes, silver chrome rims, hard wheels, photo collector coin (like others in the series), 1:64 scale
EX n/a   NM n/a   MIP $6

❏ **'70 Ford Boss 302 Mustang,** 1995, Red body, black stripes, silver chrome rims, hard wheels, photo collector coin (like others in the series), 1:64 scale
EX n/a   NM n/a   MIP $6

❏ **'70 Ford Boss 302 Mustang,** 1996, Black body with white stripes on hood and sides, silver chrome rims, hard wheels, photo collector coin (like others in the series), 1:64 scale
EX n/a   NM n/a   MIP $6

❏ **'70 Ford Boss 302 Mustang,** 1996, Magenta body, black stripes, silver chrome rims, hard wheels, photo collector coin (like others in the series), 1:64 scale
EX n/a   NM n/a   MIP $5

❏ **'70 Plymouth Superbird,** 1994, Blue body, chrome rims, hard tires, 1:64 scale
EX n/a   NM n/a   MIP $5

❏ **'70 Plymouth Superbird,** 1994, Silver body, hard tires, chrome Cragar rims, 1:64 scale
EX n/a   NM n/a   MIP $5

❏ **'70 Plymouth Superbird,** 1994, Red body, black roof, chrome rims, hard tires, 1:64 scale
EX n/a   NM n/a   MIP $5

❏ **'70 Plymouth Superbird,** 1995, White body, silver wheels, "Plymouth" in white type, black roof, 1:64 scale
EX n/a   NM n/a   MIP $6

❏ **'70 Plymouth Superbird,** 1995, Green body, silver wheels, "Plymouth" in white type, black roof, 1:64 scale
EX n/a   NM n/a   MIP $6

❏ **'70 Plymouth Superbird,** 1995, Orange body, hard tires, chrome Cragar rims, 1:64 scale
EX n/a   NM n/a   MIP $5

(KP Photo, Angelo Van Bogart collection)

❏ **'70 Plymouth Superbird,** 1995, Metallic purple body, silver wheels, "Plymouth" in white type, black roof, 1:64 scale
EX n/a   NM n/a   MIP $5

❏ **'70 Plymouth Superbird,** 1995, Magenta body, silver wheels, "Plymouth" in white type, black roof, 1:64 scale
EX n/a   NM n/a   MIP $6

❏ **'70 Plymouth Superbird,** 1995, Yellow body, hard tires, chrome Cragar rims, 1:64 scale
EX n/a   NM n/a   MIP $6

❏ **'70 Plymouth Superbird,** 1996, Blue body, silver wheels, "Plymouth" in white type, black roof, 1:64 scale
EX n/a   NM n/a   MIP $6

❏ **'70 Plymouth Superbird,** 1996, Green body, silver wheels, "Plymouth" in white type, black roof, 1:64 scale
EX n/a   NM n/a   MIP $5

❏ **'71 Plymouth Hemi Cuda,** 1994, Magenta with black "Hemi" stripe, black scoop on hood, silver wheels, 1:64 scale
EX n/a   NM n/a   MIP $5

❏ **'71 Plymouth Hemi Cuda,** 1994, Green body with black "Hemi" stripe, black scoop on hood, silver wheels, 1:64 scale
EX n/a   NM n/a   MIP $5

❏ **'71 Plymouth Hemi Cuda,** 1994, Orange with black "Hemi" stripe, black scoop on hood, silver wheels, 1:64 scale
EX n/a   NM n/a   MIP $5

❏ **'71 Plymouth Hemi Cuda,** 1995, Red body with black "Hemi" stripe, silver chrome rims, hard tires, 1:64 scale
EX n/a   NM n/a   MIP $5

❏ **'71 Plymouth Hemi Cuda,** 1995, Blue body with black "Hemi" stripe, silver chrome rims, hard tires, 1:64 scale
EX n/a   NM n/a   MIP $5

❏ **'71 Plymouth Hemi Cuda,** 1995, Olive green body with black "Hemi" stripe, silver chrome rims, hard tires, 1:64 scale
EX n/a   NM n/a   MIP $5

❏ **'71 Plymouth Hemi Cuda,** 1995, White body with black "Hemi" stripe, black scoop on hood, silver wheels, 1:64 scale
EX n/a   NM n/a   MIP $5

❏ **'71 Plymouth Hemi Cuda,** 1995, Silver body with black "Hemi" stripe, silver chrome rims, hard tires, 1:64 scale
EX n/a   NM n/a   MIP $5

❏ **'71 Plymouth Hemi Cuda,** 1995, Purple body with black "Hemi" stripe, black scoop on hood, silver wheels, 1:64 scale
EX n/a   NM n/a   MIP $5

❏ **'71 Plymouth Hemi Cuda,** 1996, Black body with white "Hemi" stripe, silver chrome rims, hard tires, 1:64 scale
EX n/a   NM n/a   MIP $5

(KP Photo, Angelo Van Bogart)

❏ **'71 Plymouth Hemi Cuda,** 1996, Yellow with black "Hemi" stripe, black scoop on hood, silver wheels, 1:64 scale
EX n/a   NM n/a   MIP $5

❏ **'72 Chevy Nova SS,** 1994, Black with chrome Cragar wheels, opening hood with hood scoop, silver wheels, hard tires, 1:64 scale
EX n/a   NM n/a   MIP $4

❑ **'72 Chevy Nova SS,** 1994, Silver with silver wheels, opening hood with hood scoop, silver wheels, hard tires, 1:64 scale
EX n/a   NM n/a   MIP $6

❑ **'72 Chevy Nova SS,** 1995, Metallic gold body with silver wheels, opening hood with hood scoop, silver wheels, hard tires, 1:64 scale
EX n/a   NM n/a   MIP $5

❑ **'72 Chevy Nova SS,** 1995, Blue body with silver wheels, opening hood with hood scoop, silver wheels, hard tires, 1:64 scale
EX n/a   NM n/a   MIP $7

❑ **'72 Chevy Nova SS,** 1995, Blue body with silver wheels, opening hood with hood scoop, silver wheels, hard tires, 1:64 scale
EX n/a   NM n/a   MIP $5

❑ **'72 Chevy Nova SS,** 1995, Magenta body with silver wheels, opening hood with hood scoop, silver wheels, hard tires, 1:64 scale
EX n/a   NM n/a   MIP $6

❑ **'72 Chevy Nova SS,** 1995, Green body with silver wheels, opening hood with hood scoop, silver wheels, hard tires, 1:64 scale
EX n/a   NM n/a   MIP $6

❑ **'72 Chevy Nova SS,** 1995, Yellow body with silver wheels, opening hood with hood scoop, silver wheels, hard tires, 1:64 scale
EX n/a   NM n/a   MIP $7

❑ **'72 Chevy Nova SS,** 1995, Red body with silver wheels, opening hood with hood scoop, silver wheels, hard tires, 1:64 scale
EX n/a   NM n/a   MIP $6

❑ **'72 Chevy Nova SS,** 1996, Metallic green body, silver wheels, opening hood with hood scoop, silver wheels, hard tires, 1:64 scale
EX n/a   NM n/a   MIP $6

(KP Photo, Angelo Van Bogart collection)

❑ **'72 Chevy Nova SS,** 1996, White with silver wheels, opening hood with hood scoop, silver wheels, hard tires, 1:64 scale
EX n/a   NM n/a   MIP $5

MUSCLE CARS USA, 2

❑ **'66 Chevy Malibu,** 1996, Teal green body, silver wheels, hard tires, 1:64 scale
EX n/a   NM n/a   MIP $5

❑ **'66 Chevy Malibu,** 1996, Bronze body, silver wheels, hard tires, 1:64 scale
EX n/a   NM n/a   MIP $5

❑ **'66 Chevy Malibu,** 1996, Black body, hard tires, silver wheels, 1:64 scale
EX n/a   NM n/a   MIP $5

❑ **'66 Chevy Malibu,** 1996, Magenta body, silver wheels, 1:64 scale
EX n/a   NM n/a   MIP $5

❑ **'68 Dodge Charger,** 1996, Light gold body, black stripes, opening hood, silver wheels, hard tires, 1:64 scale
EX n/a   NM n/a   MIP $5

❑ **'68 Dodge Charger,** 1996, Green body, silver wheels, opening hood, hard tires, 1:64 scale
EX n/a   NM n/a   MIP $5

❑ **'68 Dodge Charger,** 1996, Red body, opening hood, silver wheels, hard tires, 1:64 scale
EX n/a   NM n/a   MIP $5

(KP Photo, Angelo Van Bogart collection)

❑ **'68 Dodge Charger,** 1996, White body, black stripes, white interior, 1:64 scale
EX n/a   NM n/a   MIP $6

❑ **'68 Ford Shelby GT-350,** 1996, Lime gold body, opening hood, silver wheels, hard tires, 1:64 scale
EX n/a   NM n/a   MIP $5

❑ **'68 Ford Shelby GT-500,** 1996, Black body with white "GT-350" stripe, opening hood, silver wheels, hard tires, 1:64 scale
EX n/a   NM n/a   MIP $6

(KP Photo, Angelo Van Bogart collection)

❑ **'68 Ford Shelby GT-500,** 1996, Light gold, black Shelby stripes along bottom with "GT-350," opening hood, silver wheels, 1:64 scale
EX n/a   NM n/a   MIP $5

❑ **'68 Shelby GT-500,** 1996, White body, black stripes, opening hood, silver wheels, hard tires, 1:64 scale
EX n/a   NM n/a   MIP $5

❑ **'69 Plymouth Roadrunner,** 1996, Silver body, silver wheels, opening hood, hard tires, 1:64 scale
EX n/a   NM n/a   MIP $6

❑ **'69 Plymouth Roadrunner,** 1996, Red body, silver wheels, hard tires, opening hood, 1:64 scale
EX n/a   NM n/a   MIP $5

❑ **'69 Plymouth Roadrunner,** 1996, Turqoise body, hard tires, silver wheels, opening hood, 1:64 scale
EX n/a   NM n/a   MIP $6

(KP Photo, Angelo Van Bogart collection)

❑ **'69 Plymouth Roadrunner,** 1996, Dark metallic blue body, white interior, silver wheels, 1:64 scale
EX n/a   NM n/a   MIP $5

❑ **'69 Pontiac Firebird,** 1996, Red body, opening hood, silver wheels, hard tires, 1:64 scale
EX n/a   NM n/a   MIP $6

❑ **'69 Pontiac Firebird,** 1996, Blue body, opening hood, hard tires, silver wheels, 1:64 scale
EX n/a   NM n/a   MIP $5

❏ **'69 Pontiac Firebird,** 1996, Yellow body, silver wheels, opening hood, hard tires, 1:64 scale
EX n/a   NM n/a   MIP $5

(KP Photo, Angelo Van Bogart collection)

❏ **'69 Pontiac Firebird,** 1996, Dark metallic brown body, white interior, hard tires, 1:64 scale
EX n/a   NM n/a   MIP $6

❏ **'70 Buick GSX,** 1996, Metallic lime body, silver wheels, hard tires, opening hood, 1:64 scale
EX n/a   NM n/a   MIP $6

(KP Photo, Angelo Van Bogart collection)

❏ **'70 Buick GSX,** 1996, Yellow body, black stripes, black spoiler, silver mag wheels, black interior. A "Collector's Edition" model, 1:64 scale
EX n/a   NM n/a   MIP $5

(KP Photo, Angelo Van Bogart collection)

❏ **'70 Buick GSX,** 1996, White variation with black stripes, black spoiler, chrome wheels, 1:64 scale
EX n/a   NM n/a   MIP $5

(KP Photo, Angelo Van Bogart collection)

❏ **'70 Buick GSX,** 1996, An orange variation in the series, white interior, silver wheels, 1:64 scale
EX n/a   NM n/a   MIP $5

(KP Photo, Angelo Van Bogart collection)

❏ **'70 Buick GSX,** 1996, Another variation in this series: black with gold hood, gold stripe, silver wheels, 1:64 scale
EX n/a   NM n/a   MIP $5

❏ **'70 Dodge Challenger,** 1996, Orange body, opening hood, hard tires, silver wheels, 1:64 scale
EX n/a   NM n/a   MIP $6

❏ **'70 Dodge Challenger,** 1996, Yellow body, opening hood, silver wheels, hard tires, 1:64 scale
EX n/a   NM n/a   MIP $6

❏ **'70 Dodge Challenger,** 1996, Sublime body, silver wheels, black hood scoop, 1:64 scale
EX n/a   NM n/a   MIP $6

(KP Photo, Angelo Van Bogart collection)

❏ **'70 Dodge Challenger,** 1996, Blue body, silver wheels, black hood scoop, 1:64 scale
EX n/a   NM n/a   MIP $5

❏ **'72 AMC Javelin AMX,** 1996, Red body, silver wheels, hard tires, 1:64 scale
EX n/a   NM n/a   MIP $5

❏ **'72 AMC Javelin AMX,** 1996, Green body, silver wheels, hard tires, 1:64 scale
EX n/a   NM n/a   MIP $5

❏ **'72 AMC Javelin AMX,** 1996, Purple body, silver wheels, hard tires, 1:64 scale
EX n/a   NM n/a   MIP $5

❏ **'72 AMC Javelin AMX,** 1996, Silver body, chrome wheels, hard tires, 1:64 scale
EX n/a   NM n/a   MIP $5

MUSCLE CARS USA, 3

❏ **'65 Chevy II Nova,** 1998, Black body, silver wheels, hard tires, opening hood, 1:64 scale
EX n/a   NM n/a   MIP $5

❏ **'65 Chevy II Nova,** 1998, Mist blue body, silver wheels, hard tires, 1:64 scale
EX n/a   NM n/a   MIP $5

❏ **'65 Chevy II Nova,** 1998, Tahitian Turquoise body, silver wheels, opening hood, hard tires, 1:64 scale
EX n/a   NM n/a   MIP $5

❏ **'65 Chevy II Nova,** 1998, Rally red body, silver wheels, hard tires, 1:64 scale
EX n/a   NM n/a   MIP $5

❏ **'65 Chevy II Nova,** 1998, Blue body, silver wheels, hard tires, opening hood, 1:64 scale
EX n/a   NM n/a   MIP $5

❏ **'65 Chevy II Nova,** 1998, Evening Orchid (Light pink-tinted metallic silver) body, silver wheels, opening hood, hard tires, 1:64 scale
EX n/a   NM n/a   MIP $5

❏ **'67 GTO,** 1998, Red body, silver wheels, hard tires, 1:64 scale
EX n/a   NM n/a   MIP $6

❏ **'67 GTO,** 1998, Burgundy body, silver wheels, hard tires, 1:64 scale
EX n/a   NM n/a   MIP $6

❏ **'67 GTO,** 1998, Light gold body, silver wheels, hard tires, 1:64 scale
EX n/a   NM n/a   MIP $6

❏ **'67 GTO,** 1998, Blue body, silver wheels, hard tires, 1:64 scale
EX n/a   NM n/a   MIP $6

❏ **'67 GTO,** 1998, Seafoam Turquoise body, silver wheels, hard tires, 1:64 scale
EX n/a   NM n/a   MIP $6

❏ **'67 GTO,** 1998, Starlight black body, white interoir, silver painted grille and trim, silver wheels, hard tires, opening hood, 1:64 scale
EX n/a   NM n/a   MIP $6

❏ **'68 Chevelle,** 1998, Tripoli Turquoise body, silver wheels, hard tires, 1:64 scale
EX n/a   NM n/a   MIP $5

❏ **'68 Chevelle,** 1998, Butternut yellow body, silver wheels, hard tires, 1:64 scale
EX n/a   NM n/a   MIP $5

❏ **'68 Chevelle,** 1998, Tuxedo black body, silver wheels, hard tires, 1:64 scale
EX n/a   NM n/a   MIP $5

❏ **'68 Chevelle,** 1998, Red body, silver wheels, hard tires, 1:64 scale
EX n/a   NM n/a   MIP $5

❏ **'68 Chevelle,** 1998, Wine red body, silver wheels, hard tires, 1:64 scale
EX n/a   NM n/a   MIP $5

(KP Photo, Angelo Van Bogart collection)

❏ **'68 Chevelle,** 1998, Deep green body, black interior, silver wheels, 1:64 scale
EX n/a   NM n/a   MIP $5

❏ **'70 AAR Cuda,** 1998, Vitamin C Orange body, black hood, black stripe, silver wheels, hard tires, 1:64 scale
EX n/a   NM n/a   MIP $5

❏ **'70 AAR Cuda,** 1998, Yellow body, black hood, black stripe, silver wheels, hard tires, 1:64 scale
EX n/a   NM n/a   MIP $5

❏ **'70 AAR Cuda,** 1998, Blue Fire body, black hood, black stripe, silver wheels, hard tires, 1:64 scale
EX n/a   NM n/a   MIP $5

❏ **'70 AAR Cuda,** 1998, Rally red body, black hood, black stripe, silver wheels, hard tires, 1:64 scale
EX n/a   NM n/a   MIP $5

❏ **'70 AAR Cuda,** 1998, Violet body, black hood, black stripe, silver wheels, hard tires, 1:64 scale
EX n/a   NM n/a   MIP $5

❏ **'70 AAR Cuda,** 1998, Bright lime green body, black hood, black stripe, silver wheels, hard tires, 1:64 scale
EX n/a   NM n/a   MIP $5

❏ **'70 AMC Rebel Machine,** 1998, Sonic silver body, silver wheels, hard tires, 1:64 scale
EX n/a   NM n/a   MIP $6

❏ **'70 AMC Rebel Machine,** 1998, Lime Gold body with black hood, silver wheels, hard tires, 1:64 scale
EX n/a   NM n/a   MIP $6

❏ **'70 AMC Rebel Machine,** 1998, Copper body with black hood, silver wheels, hard tires, 1:64 scale
EX n/a   NM n/a   MIP $6

❏ **'70 AMC Rebel Machine,** 1998, White body with blue hood and red and blue stripes, silver wheels, hard tires, 1:64 scale
EX n/a   NM n/a   MIP $6

❏ **'70 AMC Rebel Machine,** 1998, Matador red body, silver wheels, hard tires, 1:64 scale
EX n/a   NM n/a   MIP $6

❏ **'70 AMC Rebel Machine,** 1998, Metallic tan/gold body, silver wheels, hard tires, 1:64 scale
EX n/a   NM n/a   MIP $6

❏ **'70 Challenger T/A,** 1998, Bright blue body with black hood, black spoiler, and black stripe on sides. Silver wheels, hard tires, 1:64 scale
EX n/a   NM n/a   MIP $5

❏ **'70 Challenger T/A,** 1998, Dark green body with black hood, black spoiler, and black stripe on sides. Silver wheels, hard tires, 1:64 scale
EX n/a   NM n/a   MIP $5

❏ **'70 Challenger T/A,** 1998, Sublime body with black hood, black spoiler, and black stripe on sides. Silver wheels, hard tires, 1:64 scale
EX n/a   NM n/a   MIP $5

❏ **'70 Challenger T/A,** 1998, Moulin Rouge (hot pink) body with black hood, black spoiler, and black stripe on sides. Silver wheels, hard tires, 1:64 scale
EX n/a   NM n/a   MIP $5

❏ **'70 Challenger T/A,** 1998, Orange body with black hood, black spoiler, and black stripe on sides. Silver wheels, hard tires, 1:64 scale
EX n/a   NM n/a   MIP $5

❏ **'70 Challenger T/A,** 1998, Bright yellow with black hood, black spoiler, and black stripe on sides. Silver wheels, hard tires, 1:64 scale
EX n/a   NM n/a   MIP $6

❏ **'70 Torino,** 1998, Grabber green body, black hood, silver wheels, hard tires, 1:64 scale
EX n/a   NM n/a   MIP $6

❏ **'70 Torino,** 1998, Bright yellow body, black hood, silver wheels, hard tires, 1:64 scale
EX n/a   NM n/a   MIP $6

❏ **'70 Torino,** 1998, Calypso coral body, black hood, silver wheels, hard tires, 1:64 scale
EX n/a   NM n/a   MIP $6

❏ **'70 Torino,** 1998, Blue metallic body, black hood, silver wheels, hard tires, 1:64 scale
EX n/a   NM n/a   MIP $6

❏ **'70 Torino,** 1998, Grabber orange body, black hood, silver wheels, hard tires, 1:64 scale
EX n/a   NM n/a   MIP $6

❏ **'70 Torino,** 1998, Grabber blue body, black hood, silver wheels, hard tires, 1:64 scale
EX n/a   NM n/a   MIP $5

❏ **'71 Demon,** 1998, Citron yellow body, two wide black stripes on hood, silver wheels, hard tires, 1:64 scale
EX n/a   NM n/a   MIP $5

❏ **'71 Demon,** 1998, Green body, two wide black stripes on hood, silver wheels, hard tires, 1:64 scale
EX n/a   NM n/a   MIP $5

❏ **'71 Demon,** 1998, Plum Crazy body (purple), two wide black stripes on hood, silver wheels, hard tires, 1:64 scale
EX n/a   NM n/a   MIP $5

❏ **'71 Demon,** 1998, Bright blue body, two wide black stripes on hood, silver wheels, hard tires, 1:64 scale
EX n/a   NM n/a   MIP $5

❏ **'71 Demon,** 1998, Orange body, two wide black stripes on hood, silver wheels, hard tires, 1:64 scale
EX n/a   NM n/a   MIP $5

❏ **'71 Demon,** 1998, Panther pink body, two wide black stripes on hood, silver wheels, hard tires, 1:64 scale
EX n/a   NM n/a   MIP $5

❏ **'71 GTO Judge,** 1998, Castilian bronze body, opening hood with scoops, silver wheels, hard tires, 1:64 scale
EX n/a   NM n/a   MIP $5

❏ **'71 GTO Judge,** 1998, Starlight black body, opening hood

with scoops, silver wheels, hard tires, 1:64 scale
EX n/a   **NM** n/a   **MIP** $5

❏ **'71 GTO Judge,** 1998, Shelby red body, opening hood with scoops, silver wheels, hard tires, 1:64 scale
EX n/a   **NM** n/a   **MIP** $5

❏ **'71 GTO Judge,** 1998, Lucerne blue body, opening hood with scoops, silver wheels, hard tires, 1:64 scale
EX n/a   **NM** n/a   **MIP** $5

❏ **'71 GTO Judge,** 1998, Yellow body, opening hood with scoops, silver wheels, hard tires, 1:64 scale
EX n/a   **NM** n/a   **MIP** $5

❏ **'71 GTO Judge,** 1998, Nordic silver body, opening hood with scoops, silver wheels, hard tires, 1:64 scale
EX n/a   **NM** n/a   **MIP** $5

❏ **'73 Charger,** 1998, Green body, white roof, silver wheels, hard tires, 1:64 scale
EX n/a   **NM** n/a   **MIP** $5

❏ **'73 Charger,** 1998, Metallic gray body, white roof, silver wheels, hard tires, 1:64 scale
EX n/a   **NM** n/a   **MIP** $5

❏ **'73 Charger,** 1998, Bright blue body, white roof, silver wheels, hard tires, 1:64 scale
EX n/a   **NM** n/a   **MIP** $5

❏ **'73 Charger,** 1998, Black body, white roof, silver wheels, hard tires, 1:64 scale
EX n/a   **NM** n/a   **MIP** $5

❏ **'73 Charger,** 1998, White body, black roof, silver wheels, hard tires, 1:64 scale
EX n/a   **NM** n/a   **MIP** $5

❏ **'73 Charger,** 1998, Deep red body, white roof, silver wheels, hard tires, 1:64 scale
EX n/a   **NM** n/a   **MIP** $5

MUSCLE CARS USA, 3: WHITE LIGHTNING

(KP Photo)

❏ **'65 Chevy II Nova,** 1998, White body, silver wheels, opening hood, rubber tires, collector coin, 1:64 scale
EX n/a   **NM** n/a   **MIP** $30

(KP Photo)

❏ **'67 GTO,** 1998, White body, black interoir, silver painted grille and trim, silver wheels, rubber tires with "White Lightning" in white type, opening hood, collector coin, 1:64 scale
EX n/a   **NM** n/a   **MIP** $30

(KP Photo)

❏ **'68 Chevelle,** 1998, White body, black interior, silver wheels, rubber tires, 1:64 scale
EX n/a   **NM** n/a   **MIP** $25

(KP Photo)

❏ **'70 AAR Cuda,** 1998, White body, black hood, black stripe, silver wheels, rubber tires with "White Lightning" in white type, collector coin, 1:64 scale
EX n/a   **NM** n/a   **MIP** $30

(KP Photo)

❏ **'70 AMC Rebel Machine,** 1998, White body, silver wheels, rubber tires with "White Lightning" in white type, collector coin, 1:64 scale
EX n/a   **NM** n/a   **MIP** $30

(KP Photo)

❏ **'70 Challenger T/A,** 1998, White body with black hood, black spoiler, and black stripe on sides. Silver wheels, rubber tires with "White Lightning" in white type, collector card, 1:64 scale
EX n/a   **NM** n/a   **MIP** $25

(KP Photo)

❏ **'70 Torino,** 1998, White body, black hood, silver wheels, rubber tires, black interior, collector coin, 1:64 scale
EX n/a   **NM** n/a   **MIP** $25

(KP Photo)

❏ **'71 Dodge Demon,** 1998, White body, two wide black stripes on hood, thin black stripes on sides, "Demon" graphics on sides, silver wheels, rubber tires with "White Lightning" in white type, collector coin, 1:64 scale
EX n/a　　NM n/a　　MIP $30

(KP Photo)

❏ **'71 GTO Judge,** 1998, White body, opening hood with scoops, silver wheels, rubber tires with "White Lightning" in white type, collector coin, 1:64 scale
EX n/a　　NM n/a　　MIP $30

(KP Photo)

❏ **'73 Dodge Charger,** 1998, White body, black roof, silver wheels, rubber tires with "White Lightnings" in white type, collector coin, 1:64 scale
EX n/a　　NM n/a　　MIP $25

MUSCLE CARS USA, 4

❏ **'64 Pontiac GTO,** 2000, Deep blue metallic body, black interior, silver wheels, opening hood, black interior, 1:64 scale, Model No. 096
EX n/a　　NM n/a　　MIP $5

(KP Photo, Angelo Van Bogart collection)

❏ **'64 Pontiac GTO,** 2001, Black body, silver wheels, opening hood, black interior, 1:64 scale, Model No. 096
EX n/a　　NM n/a　　MIP $5

❏ **'64 Pontiac GTO,** 2001, Saddle bronze body, silver and black painted grille and trim, opening hood, hard tires, chrome rims, photo card, 1:64 scale, Model No. 096
EX n/a　　NM n/a　　MIP $5

❏ **'64 Pontiac GTO,** 2001, Saddle bronze body, hard tires, chrome rims, opening hood, photo card, 1:64 scale, Model No. 096
EX n/a　　NM n/a　　MIP $5

❏ **'64 Pontiac GTO,** 2001, Cameo white body, black roof, opening hood, hard tires, chrome rims, silver painted exterior detail, photo card, 1:64 scale, Model No. 096
EX n/a　　NM n/a　　MIP $5

❏ **'64 Pontiac GTO,** 2002, Metallic silver body, hard tires, chrome rims, opening hood, photo card, 1:64 scale, Model No. 096
EX n/a　　NM n/a　　MIP $5

❏ **'67 Cougar,** 2001, Polar white body, chrome five-spoke wheels, opening hood, hard tires, silver-painted trim. Available from the Winter 2001-2002 Johnny Lightning catalog, 1:64 scale, Model No. 095
EX n/a　　NM n/a　　MIP $6

(KP Photo)

❏ **'67 Mercury Cougar,** 2001, Glacier blue metallic with white roof, black grille, blue interior, painted taillights, hard wheels, chrome rims, opening hood, photo card, 1:64 scale, Model No. 095
EX n/a　　NM n/a　　MIP $5

(KP Photo, Angelo Van Bogart collection)

❏ **'67 Olds Cutlass 442,** 2000, Yellow body, black interior, hard tires, opening hood. Listed as a "67 Cutlass" in Summer 2000 "Newsflash" Sneak Peek section, 1:64 scale, Model No. 099
EX n/a　　NM n/a　　MIP $5

❏ **'67 Olds Cutlass 442,** 2001, Snow white body, silver wheels, photo card, hard tires, opening hood, 1:64 scale, Model No. 099
EX n/a　　NM n/a　　MIP $5

❏ **'67 Olds Cutlass 442,** 2001, Metallic gold body, opening hood, hard tires, chrome rims, photo card, 1:64 scale, Model No. 099
EX n/a　　NM n/a　　MIP $5

❏ **'67 Olds Cutlass 442,** 2001, Starlight black body, red interior, opening hood, chrome rims, hard tires, photo card, 1:64 scale, Model No. 099
EX n/a　　NM n/a　　MIP $5

❏ **'67 Olds Cutlass 442,** 2001, Roman red, hard tires, chrome rims, opening hood, photo card, 1:64 scale, Model No. 099
EX n/a　　NM n/a　　MIP $5

❏ **'67 Olds Cutlass 442,** 2002, Aspen green body, black roof, hard tires, chrome rims, photo card, 1:64 scale, Model No. 099
EX n/a　　NM n/a　　MIP $5

❏ **'67 Pontiac Firebird,** 2000, Gold metallic body, silver painted grille and trim, opening hood, silver wheels, hard tires, photo card, 1:64 scale, Model No. 094
EX n/a　　NM n/a　　MIP $5

❏ **'67 Pontiac Firebird 400,** 2001, Cameo white, hard tires, chrome rims, photo card, 1:64 scale, Model No. 094
EX n/a　　NM n/a　　MIP $5

(KP Photo)

❏ **'68 Cougar XR7,** 2000, Black with silver trim, chrome wheels, opening hood, 1:64 scale, Model No. 095
EX n/a   NM n/a   MIP $5

❏ **'68 Mercury Cougar GTE,** 2001, Dark moss green, hard tires, chrome mag wheels, hard tires, opening hood, photo card, 1:64 scale, Model No. 095
EX n/a   NM n/a   MIP $5

❏ **'68 Mercury Cougar GTE,** 2001, Metallic Aspen green body, black roof, opening hood, chrome wheels, hard tires, photo card, 1:64 scale, Model No. 095
EX n/a   NM n/a   MIP $5

❏ **'68 Mercury Cougar GT-E,** 2001, Rally red, hard tires, chrome rims, opening hood, photo card, 1:64 scale, Model No. 095
EX n/a   NM n/a   MIP $5

❏ **'68 Mercury Cougar XR7,** 2002, Dark metallic gold body, hard tires, chrome rims, opening hood, photo card, 1:64 scale, Model No. 095
EX n/a   NM n/a   MIP $5

❏ **'68 Pontiac Firebird,** 2001, Seafoam Turquoise body, silver and black painted grille, opening hood, silver wheels, white interior, hard tires, photo card, 1:64 scale, Model No. 094
EX n/a   NM n/a   MIP $5

❏ **'68 Pontiac Firebird,** 2001, Slate blue body, black roof, hard tires, chrome wheels, opening hood, photo card, 1:64 scale, Model No. 094
EX n/a   NM n/a   MIP $5

❏ **'68 Pontiac Firebird,** 2002, Shelby red body, opening hood, chrome rims, hard tires, chrome rims, photo card, 1:64 scale, Model No. 094
EX n/a   NM n/a   MIP $5

❏ **'68 Pontiac Firebird 400,** 2001, Aspen metallic green with black roof, hard tires, chrome rims, opening hood, photo card, 1:64 scale, Model No. 094
EX n/a   NM n/a   MIP $5

❏ **'69 Chevy Nova,** 2000, Dark metallic green body, silver wheels, hard tires, opening hood, 1:64 scale, Model No. 098
EX n/a   NM n/a   MIP $5

❏ **'69 Chevy Nova SS,** 2001, Garnet red, hard wheels, chrome rims, photo card, 1:64 scale, Model No. 098
EX n/a   NM n/a   MIP $5

❏ **'69 Chevy Nova SS,** 2001, Olympic gold body, chrome rims, hard tires, photo card, opening hood, 1:64 scale, Model No. 098
EX n/a   NM n/a   MIP $5

❏ **'69 Chevy Yenko Nova,** 2002, Calypso coral body, white stripes on opening hood, hard tires, chrome rims, photo card, 1:64 scale, Model No. 098
EX n/a   NM n/a   MIP $5

❏ **'70 Chevy Yenko Nova Deuce,** 2001, Roman red body, black stripe along sides and running up trunk, opening hood, silver rims, hard tires, photo card, 1:64 scale, Model No. 098
EX n/a   NM n/a   MIP $5

❏ **'70 Mercury Cyclone,** 2000, Dark blue body, black stripe, black spoiler, 1:64 scale, Model No. 097
EX n/a   NM n/a   MIP $5

❏ **'70 Mercury Cyclone GT,** 2001, Matador red body, black roof and scoop, opening hood, hard tires, chrome rims, photo card, 1:64 scale, Model No. 097
EX n/a   NM n/a   MIP $5

❏ **'70 Mercury Cyclone GT,** 2001, Starlight black body, chrome rims, hard tires, opening hood, photo card, 1:64 scale, Model No. 097
EX n/a   NM n/a   MIP $5

❏ **'70 Mercury Cyclone Spoiler,** 2001, Grabber orange, hard tires, chrome rims, opening hood, photo card, 1:64 scale, Model No. 097
EX n/a   NM n/a   MIP $5

❏ **'70 Mercury Montego MX Brougham,** 2002, Champagne body, black roof, hard tires, chrome rims, photo card, 1:64 scale, Model No. 097
EX n/a   NM n/a   MIP $5

black roof, hard tires, chrome rims, opening hood, photo card, 1:64 scale, Model No. 094
EX n/a   NM n/a   MIP $5

❏ **'71 Chevy Nova SS,** 2001, Moonglow silver body, black narrow stripe on sides, opening hood, hard tires, chrome rims, photo card, 1:64 scale, Model No. 098
EX n/a   NM n/a   MIP $5

❏ **'71 Mercury Cyclone Spoiler,** 2001, Grabber green body, black spoiler and stripe on sides, chrome rims, opening hood, hard tires, photo card, 1:64 scale, Model No. 097
EX n/a   NM n/a   MIP $5

PEARL HARBOR: DAY OF INFAMY

❏ **CCKW 6x6 GMC Troop Carrier,** 2001, Flat olive drab body with white star on hood and doors
EX n/a   NM n/a   MIP $6

(KP Photo)

❏ **Hickam Field Army Air Corps 1937 Ford Staff Car,** 2001, Olive drab body with white star on hood, "Hickam Field Staff Car" on doors, silver painted grille, olive rims
EX n/a   NM n/a   MIP $6

(KP Photo)

❏ **Wheeler Field Army Air Corps 1940 Ford Pickup,** 2001, Flat olive green body, green rims, opening hood, "Wheeler Field" on doors
EX n/a   NM n/a   MIP $6

(KP Photo)

❏ **Willys US Navy Jeep with top,** 2001, Light gray blue body, olive plastic top, thin jeep tires, opening hood with "U.S.N.," white painted headlights, black painted grille, Model No. 065
EX n/a   NM n/a   MIP $6

(KP Photo)

❏ **Willys US Navy Shore Patrol Jeep,** 2001, Light gray blue body, no top, "Shore Patrol" on windshield, opening hood, thin jeep wheels, Model No. 065
EX n/a   NM n/a   MIP $6

(KP Photo)

❏ **WWII WC-54 Ambulance,** 2001, Flat light gray, red cross emblems on sides and roof, opening hood. The "Pearl Harbor" series is also the third round in the "Lightning Brigade" series
EX n/a   NM n/a   MIP $6

POPULAR HOT RODDING

❏ **'41 Willy's,** 2001, Blue, real wheels, chrome rims, photo card, 1:64 scale, Model No. 439
EX n/a   NM n/a   MIP $4

❏ **'54 Corvette,** 2001, Daytona yellow, real wheels, chrome rims, photo card, 1:64 scale, Model No. 731
EX n/a   NM n/a   MIP $4

❏ **'57 Chevy Bel Air,** 2001, Candyapple red, real wheels, 1:64 scale
EX n/a   NM n/a   MIP $4

❏ **'59 El Camino,** 2001, Aqua, real wheels, chrome rims, photo card, 1:64 scale, Model No. 415
EX n/a   NM n/a   MIP $4

❏ **'64 Chevy Nova,** 2001, Banana yellow, real wheels, 1:64 scale
EX n/a   NM n/a   MIP $4

❏ **'67 Olds Cutlass 442,** 2001, Roman red, real wheels, 1:64 scale
EX n/a   NM n/a   MIP $4

❏ **'68 Chevy Camaro SS,** 2001, Yellow, real wheels, 1:64 scale
EX n/a   NM n/a   MIP $4

❏ **'69 Camaro Z-28,** 2001, Cranberry, real wheels, chrome rims, photo card, 1:64 scale, Model No. 537
EX n/a   NM n/a   MIP $4

❏ **'69 Chevy Camaro,** 2001, Sunburst yellow, real wheels, 1:64 scale
EX n/a   NM n/a   MIP $4

❏ **'69 Chevy Camaro SS,** 2001, GTS blue, real wheels, 1:64 scale
EX n/a   NM n/a   MIP $4

❏ **'70 Nova,** 2001, Orange, real wheels, chrome rims, photo card, 1:64 scale, Model No. 098
EX n/a   NM n/a   MIP $4

❏ **'71 440 Cuda Conv.,** 2001, Hemi-orange, real wheels, chrome rims, photo card, 1:64 scale, Model No. 785
EX n/a   NM n/a   MIP $4

RACE EMERGENCY VEHICLES

❏ **'99 Chevy Silverado Fire Equip.,** 2000, White extended cab body, "Indy Racing League" in blue type, red and and blue swoop graphics with IRL logo on doors and hood, chrome rims, hard tires, black interior, red and black plastic fire equipment in truck bed, 1:64 scale
EX n/a   NM n/a   MIP $6

❏ **'99 Chevy Silverado Fire Equip.,** 2000, White extended cab body, "Indy 500" checkered flag graphics on doors and sides, "Chevrolet" on sides and windshield, large bow tie graphic on hood, silver rims, hard tires, red and black plastic fire equipment in truck bed, 1:64 scale
EX n/a   NM n/a   MIP $6

❏ **'99 Chevy Silverado Oil Dri,** 2000, White standard cab body with "Indy Racing League" in blue type and IRL logos on doors and hood. Red and blue swoop on sides, black interior, oil dry bin attached to tailgate, silver rims, hard tires, 1:64 scale
EX n/a   NM n/a   MIP $6

❏ **'99 Chevy Silverado Oil Dri,** 2000, White standard cab body with "Indy 500" graphics on doors and sides, red Chevy bow tie on hood, oil dry bin on tailgate, silver rims, hard tires, 1:64 scale
EX n/a   NM n/a   MIP $6

❏ **'99 Chevy Silverado Utility Pickup,** 2000, White standard cab body with "Indy Racing League" in blue type, red and blue swoop with IRL logo on doors and hood, silver rims, black interior, hard tires, 1:64 scale
EX n/a   NM n/a   MIP $6

❏ **'99 Chevy Silverado Utility Pickup,** 2000, White standard cab body with "Indy 500" graphics on doors and sides, black interior, Chevy bow tie logo on hood, 1:64 scale
EX n/a   NM n/a   MIP $6

RACING DREAMS

❏ **Army,** '71 Charger, 1:64 scale
EX n/a   NM n/a   MIP $5

❏ **Blizzard,** 1:64 scale
EX n/a   NM n/a   MIP $6

❏ **Coast Guard,** Monte Carlo, 1:64 scale
EX n/a   NM n/a   MIP $6

❏ **Cocoa Puffs,** 1:64 scale
EX n/a   NM n/a   MIP $6

❏ **DQ-Dilly Bar,** '71 Demon, 1:64 scale
EX n/a   NM n/a   MIP $6

❏ **Frosted Flakes,** 1:64 scale
EX n/a   NM n/a   MIP $6

❏ **Fudgsicle,** 1:64 scale
EX n/a   NM n/a   MIP $7

❏ **Grimace,** 1:64 scale
EX n/a   NM n/a   MIP $6

❏ **Hawaiin Punch,** '72 Challenger, 1:64 scale
EX n/a   NM n/a   MIP $6

❏ **Hawaiin Punch,** orange, 1:64 scale
EX n/a   NM n/a   MIP $6

❏ **Hershey's,** '94 Olds, 1:64 scale
EX n/a   NM n/a   MIP $6

❏ **James Bond - Goldfinger,** '71 Vega, 1:64 scale
EX n/a   NM n/a   MIP $6

❏ **Jurrassic Park the Ride,** '94 Daytona, 1:64 scale
EX n/a   NM n/a   MIP $6

❏ **Lucky Charms,** Grand Prix, 1:64 scale
EX n/a   NM n/a   MIP $7

❏ **McDonald's Big Mac,** 1:64 scale
EX n/a   NM n/a   MIP $6

❏ **Monkees (Direct Mail car),** 1:64 scale
EX n/a   NM n/a   MIP $9

❏ **Mooneyes,** '71 Mustang, 1:64 scale
EX n/a   NM n/a   MIP $5

❏ **Mug Rootbeer,** 1:64 scale
EX n/a   NM n/a   MIP $6

❏ **Nintendo-Mario 64,** Grand Prix, 1:64 scale
EX n/a   NM n/a   MIP $7

❏ **Nintendo-Star Fox,** '96 Avenger, 1:64 scale
EX n/a   NM n/a   MIP $6

❏ **Nintendo-Zelda,** 1:64 scale
EX n/a   NM n/a   MIP $6

❏ **Pennzoil,** 1:64 scale
EX n/a   NM n/a   MIP $6

❏ **Pez,** Monte Carlo, 1:64 scale
EX n/a   NM n/a   MIP $8

❏ **Pez,** , 1:64 scale
EX n/a   NM n/a   MIP $9

❏ **Planters-Mr. Peanut,** Thunderbird, 1:64 scale
EX n/a   NM n/a   MIP $7

❏ **Popsicle,** '72 Charger, 1:64 scale
EX n/a   NM n/a   MIP $7

❏ **Reese's-Hershey,** 1:64 scale
EX n/a   NM n/a   MIP $5

❏ **TGI Friday's,** Thunderbird, 1:64 scale
EX n/a   NM n/a   MIP $6

❏ **Trix,** '97 Firebird, 1:64 scale
EX n/a   NM n/a   MIP $6

❏ **Yohsi,** 1:64 scale
EX n/a   NM n/a   MIP $6

RACING MACHINES

❏ **'63 Pontiac Tempest,** 2000, "Tameless Tiger" dragster in orange, 1:64 scale
EX n/a   NM n/a   MIP $4

❏ **'69 AMX,** 2000, AMX "Pete's Patriot" in red, white and blue, 1:64 scale
EX n/a   NM n/a   MIP $5

❏ **'69 Pontiac GTO Judge,** 2000, "The Judge," Arnie Beswick's famous orange super stock, 1:64 scale
EX n/a   NM n/a   MIP $5

❏ **'71 Vega,** 2000, "Wonder Wagon" funny car, yellow and white, 1:64 scale
EX n/a   NM n/a   MIP $4

❏ **'72 Charger,** 2000, Gene Snows funny car in red, white and blue, 1:64 scale
EX n/a   NM n/a   MIP $4

❏ **'94 Daytona,** 1999, NHRA funny car (or "Bunny Car," driven by Bunny Burkett) in purple and magenta, 1:64 scale
EX n/a   NM n/a   MIP $4

❏ **'94 Daytona,** 2000, Roland Leong's "Hawaiian Punch" funny car, red, purple and white, 1:64 scale
EX n/a   NM n/a   MIP $4

❏ **'94 Olds,** 2000, McDonald's funny car in red and white, 1:64 scale
EX n/a   NM n/a   MIP $4

❏ **'96 Saleen Racer,** 2000, Saleen LeMans Mustang, Budget Rental cars racer, white, yellow and black body, 1:64 scale
EX n/a   NM n/a   MIP $4

❏ **'97 Firebird,** 2000, Split Fire Pro Stock car in purple, black and white, 1:64 scale
EX n/a   NM n/a   MIP $4

❏ **'97 Firebird,** 2000, NAPA Dragster funny car, white, blue and yellow body, 1:64 scale
EX n/a   NM n/a   MIP $4

❏ **'98 Avenger,** 1999, Pioneer car, driven by Tom Hoover, blue and black, 1:64 scale
EX n/a   NM n/a   MIP $4

❏ **'98 Avenger,** 2000, Red Line Oil funny car, red, white and blue, 1:64 scale
EX n/a   NM n/a   MIP $4

❏ **'98 Avenger,** 2000, Playing Mantis Bug Car, driven by Jim Dunn, chartreuse body, 1:64 scale
EX n/a   NM n/a   MIP $4

❏ **'98 Avenger,** 2000, Johnny Lightning funny car, driven by Jim Dunn, red and white body. This was a bonus mail-in offer, 1:64 scale
EX n/a   NM n/a   MIP $4

❏ **Camaro Trans Am,** 1999, SCCA Automationdirect.com car in light green, blue and red, driven by Johnny Miller. Includes photo card, 1:64 scale
EX n/a   NM n/a   MIP $4

❏ **Camaro Trans Am,** 1999, Glacier Tek Inc., car in red, 1:64 scale
EX n/a   NM n/a   MIP $4

❏ **IRL Race Car,** 1999, Powerteam, white and red body with number "14" on nose and sides. Model of car driven by Kenny Brack and winner of 1999 Indy 500. Includes photo card, 1:64 scale
EX n/a   NM n/a   MIP $4

❏ **Mustang Trans-Am,** 1999, Preformed Line Products car, metallic purple and white body, number "49" on sides and hood. Driven by Randy Ruhlman, includes photo card, 1:64 scale
EX n/a   NM n/a   MIP $5

❏ **Mustang Trans-Am,** 1999, Homelink car, yellow and black, 1:64 scale
EX n/a   NM n/a   MIP $5

❏ **Viper GTS-R,** 1999, Viper Speed SCCA World Challenge car in metallic blue, driven by Neil Hannemann, includes photo card, 1:64 scale
EX n/a   NM n/a   MIP $4

❏ **Viper GTS-R,** 1999, Team Oreca GT2 championship car in white with blue and red swoop design, 1:64 scale
EX n/a   NM n/a   MIP $4

RACING MACHINES IRL CARS—1999

❏ **IRL Race Car,** Scott Goodyear
EX n/a   NM n/a   MIP $5

❏ **IRL Race Car,** Kenny Brack
EX n/a   NM n/a   MIP $5

❏ **IRL Race Car,** Greg Ray
EX n/a   NM n/a   MIP $5

❏ **IRL Race Car,** Indy Event Car, 1999
EX n/a   NM n/a   MIP $5

❑ **IRL Race Car,** Luyendyk '98 winner car, twin w/1990
EX n/a NM n/a MIP $7

❑ **IRL Race Car,** Eliseo Salazar
EX n/a NM n/a MIP $5

❑ **IRL Race Car,** Arie Luyendyk '99 car
EX n/a NM n/a MIP $5

❑ **IRL Race Car,** Scott Sharp
EX n/a NM n/a MIP $5

❑ **IRL Race Car,** Mark Dismore
EX n/a NM n/a MIP $5

❑ **IRL Race Car,** Billy Boat
EX n/a NM n/a MIP $5

RACING MACHINES IRL CARS—2000

❑ **IRL Race Car,** Robby McGhee, Mall.com #5
EX n/a NM n/a MIP $5

❑ **IRL Race Car,** Greg Ray, Menards #2 1999 and #3 2000 twin
EX n/a NM n/a MIP $5

❑ **IRL Race Car,** Indy Event Car, 2000
EX n/a NM n/a MIP $5

❑ **IRL Race Car,** Robby McGhee, Energizer #55
EX n/a NM n/a MIP $5

❑ **IRL Race Car,** Robbie Buhl, Purex #24
EX n/a NM n/a MIP $5

❑ **IRL Race Car,** Buddy Lazier, Tae Bo #91
EX n/a NM n/a MIP $5

❑ **IRL Race Car,** Mark Dismore, Bryant #28
EX n/a NM n/a MIP $5

❑ **IRL Race Car,** Scott Goodyear, Pennzoil #4
EX n/a NM n/a MIP $5

❑ **IRL Race Car,** Greg Ray, Menards #3
EX n/a NM n/a MIP $5

❑ **IRL Race Car,** Scott Sharp, Delphi #8
EX n/a NM n/a MIP $5

REBEL RODS

❑ **'00 Chevy Silverado,** 2001, Apricot body with multicolored graphics on sides, black hood, chrome wheels, hard tires, decal sheet, 1:64 scale
EX n/a NM n/a MIP $4

❑ **'00 Ford Tow Truck,** 2001, Starlight black with flame tampo, red plastic interior, chrome exposed engine, chrome wheels, hard tires, decal sheet, 1:64 scale
EX n/a NM n/a MIP $4

❑ **'57 Corvette Gasser,** 2002, Yellow body, with stripe running from roof to trunk, chrome engine, silver rims, decal sheet, 1:64 scale
EX n/a NM n/a MIP $4

(KP Photo)

❑ **'57 Vette Gasser,** 2001, Dark metallic blue with silver trim, hard tires, chrome rims, decal sheet, 1:64 scale, Model No. 437
EX n/a NM n/a MIP $4

❑ **'57 Vette Gasser,** 2001, Cameo white body with silver painted grille and trim, hard tires, chrome rims, decal sheet, 1:64 scale, Model No. 437
EX n/a NM n/a MIP $4

❑ **'57 Vette Gasser,** 2002, Emerald City body with white stripe running from roof to trunk, hard wheels, chrome rims, decal sheet, 1:64 scale, Model No. 437
EX n/a NM n/a MIP $4

❑ **'64 GTO,** 2002, Metallic red body, white stripe on roof, number "18" on sides, decal sheet, 1:64 scale
EX n/a NM n/a MIP $4

❑ **'69 Charger Daytona,** 2002, White body, red painted spoiler, chrome engine, decal sheet, 1:64 scale
EX n/a NM n/a MIP $4

❑ **'69 Chevy Nova SS,** 2001, Silver chrome body, number "11" on sides, chrome rims, hard tires, decal sheet, 1:64 scale
EX n/a NM n/a MIP $4

❑ **'69 Dodge Coronet,** 2001, Light green body, exposed engine, chrome wheels, number "12" on sides, hard tires, includes decal sheet to customize, 1:64 scale, Model No. 422
EX n/a NM n/a MIP $4

❑ **'69 Dodge Coronet,** 2002, Orange body with white stripe on trunk, number "12" on sides, hard wheels, chrome rims, decal sheet, 1:64 scale, Model No. 422
EX n/a NM n/a MIP $4

❑ **'70 Dodge Charger R/T,** 2002, Sand Dollar body with black stripe running from roof to trunk, number "17" on sides, black interior, hard wheels, chrome rims, decal sheet, 1:64 scale, Model No. 488
EX n/a NM n/a MIP $4

❑ **'70 Plymouth Cuda,** 2002, Starlight black, hard tires, chrome rims, decal sheet, 1:64 scale
EX n/a NM n/a MIP $4

❑ **'72 Plymouth Road Runner,** 2002, Blue body with white stripe, exposed chrome engine, decal sheet, 1:64 scale
EX n/a NM n/a MIP $4

(KP Photo)

❑ **Cheetah,** 2001, Anthracite (glossy black) body, chrome rims, hard tires, silver chrome engine, decal sheet, 1:64 scale, Model No. 431
EX n/a NM n/a MIP $4

❑ **Cheetah,** 2001, Shelby red, hard tires, chrome rims, decal sheet, 1:64 scale, Model No. 431
EX n/a NM n/a MIP $4

❑ **Cheetah,** 2002, Cameo white with red stripe, hard tires, chrome rims, decal sheet, 1:64 scale, Model No. 431
EX n/a NM n/a MIP $4

❑ **Cheetah,** 2002, Green body, white stripe running from hood to trunk, exposed engine, decal sheet, 1:64 scale
EX n/a NM n/a MIP $4

❑ **Ford F250 Pickup,** 2001, Yellow body with exposed chrome engine, chrome rims, hard tires, decal sheet, 1:64 scale
EX n/a NM n/a MIP $4

(KP Photo)

❑ **King Kitty: '67 Mercury,** 2001, Green with number "14" on sides, decal sheet, silver wheels, 1:64 scale

EX n/a   NM n/a   MIP $4

(KP Photo)

❑ **King Kitty: '67 Mercury,** 2001, Green with number "14" on sides, decal sheet, engine and wheel variation, 1:64 scale

EX n/a   NM n/a   MIP $4

❑ **Nifty 250: '00 Ford F-250 Tow Truck,** 2002, Dark blue body with flame tampo, chrome wheels, hard wheels, chrome rims, decal sheet, 1:64 scale, Model No. 054

EX n/a   NM n/a   MIP $4

❑ **She's On Firebird: '67 Firebird,** 2001, Red body, silver exposed engine, silver painted grille and trim, 1:64 scale

EX n/a   NM n/a   MIP $4

❑ **Super Beetnik: '69 Dodge Super Bee,** 2002, Hot pink body with black stripe, hard wheels, chrome rims, decal sheet, 1:64 scale, Model No. 490

EX n/a   NM n/a   MIP $4

❑ **Super Beetnik: '69 Super Bee,** 2002, Silver chrome body, number "12" on sides, exposed chrome engine, hard tires, decal sheet, 1:64 scale

EX n/a   NM n/a   MIP $4

ROCK N' ROLLERS

❑ **'67 GTO,** 2001, Cherry red, real wheels, CD, "Little GTO" by Ronny and the Daytonas, 1:64 scale, Model No. 222

EX n/a   NM n/a   MIP $8

❑ **Bad Bird,** 2001, Pale orange, real wheels, CD, "Fun, Fun, Fun" by the Beach Boys, 1:64 scale, Model No. 557

EX n/a   NM n/a   MIP $8

❑ **Cobra,** 2001, Blue body with white stripes, silver spoked wheels, rubber tires, CD, "Hey Little Cobra" by the Flip Chords, 1:64 scale, Model No. 426

EX n/a   NM n/a   MIP $8

❑ **Fink Speedwagon,** 2001, Mint green body, black roof, woody sides, real wheels, CD, "Surf City" by Jan and Dean, 1:64 scale, Model No. 436

EX n/a   NM n/a   MIP $8

❑ **Flathead Flyer,** 2001, Passion purple body with orange and red flame tampos, real wheels, CD, "Little Deuce Coupe" by the Beach Boys, 1:64 scale, Model No. 556

EX n/a   NM n/a   MIP $8

SHOW RODS— GEORGE BARRIS

❑ **'41 "Tribute" Ford Phaeton,** White Lightnings edition

EX n/a   NM n/a   MIP $20

❑ **'41 "Tribute" Ford Phaeton,** 1999, Light metallic green body, white plastic roof, mirrored display base, 1:64 scale

EX n/a   NM n/a   MIP $4

❑ **'51 Burgundy Mercury Converible,** White Lightnings edition

EX n/a   NM n/a   MIP $22

(KP Photo, Angelo Van Bogart collection)

❑ **'51 Burgundy Mercury Converible,** 1999, Metallic burgundy body, white plastic roof and interior, silver wheels, whitewall tires, 1:64 scale

EX n/a   NM n/a   MIP $6

❑ **Emperor,** White Lightnings edition

EX n/a   NM n/a   MIP $20

(KP Photo, Angelo Van Bogart collection)

❑ **Emperor,** 1999, Dark pink, white interior, silver wheels, whitewall tires, 1:64 scale

EX n/a   NM n/a   MIP $6

❑ **Fireball 500,** White Lightnings edition

EX n/a   NM n/a   MIP $23

❑ **Fireball 500,** 1999, Red with white hood, flame tampos along sides, swivel platform, 1:64 scale

EX n/a   NM n/a   MIP $6

❑ **Kopper Kart,** White Lightnings edition

EX n/a   NM n/a   MIP $25

(KP Photo)

❑ **Kopper Kart,** 1999, White body with copper-red stripes, "Barris Kustom Autos" on doors, "Kopper Kart" on tailgate, whitewall rubber tires, chrome rims, 1:64 scale, Model No. 754

EX n/a   NM n/a   MIP $6

❑ **Sam Barris—'49 Merc,** White Lightnings edition

EX n/a   NM n/a   MIP $20

(KP Photo)

❑ **Sam Barris—'49 Merc,** 1999, Dark green body, chrome rims, whitewall rubber tires, white interior, mirrored display platform, 1:64 scale, Model No. 751

EX n/a   NM n/a   MIP $5

❏ **Speed Coupe,** White Lightnings edition
EX n/a   NM n/a   MIP $25

(KP Photo, Angelo Van Bogart collection)

❏ **Speed Coupe,** 1999, White with red stripe, "Barris Kustom Autos" on doors, small spoked wheels in front, large Firestones in back, 1:64 scale
EX n/a   NM n/a   MIP $4

❏ **Wildkat,** White Lightnings edition
EX n/a   NM n/a   MIP $22

❏ **Wildkat,** 1999, Brown and gold Ford truck
EX n/a   NM n/a   MIP $4

SHOW RODS—TOM DANIEL SHOW RODS

❏ **Baja Bandito,**
EX n/a   NM n/a   MIP $3

❏ **Desert Fox,** Rommel's Rod
EX n/a   NM n/a   MIP $3

❏ **Dog Catcher,**
EX n/a   NM n/a   MIP $3

❏ **Fast Buck,**
EX n/a   NM n/a   MIP $3

❏ **LA Kid or Daddy's Deuce,**
EX n/a   NM n/a   MIP $3

❏ **Rat Vega or Poison Pinto,**
EX n/a   NM n/a   MIP $3

❏ **Smug Bug,**
EX n/a   NM n/a   MIP $3

❏ **TD's Ride,** CA Street Vette
EX n/a   NM n/a   MIP $4

❏ **Triple T,**
EX n/a   NM n/a   MIP $3

❏ **Wild Bull Surfer,**
EX n/a   NM n/a   MIP $3

SHOWSTOPPERS

❏ **Chuck Wagon,**
EX n/a   NM n/a   MIP $3

❏ **Dodge Material,** 1999, Metallic red, white and blue body,

"Dodge Material" in black-outlined yellow type. Silver painted grille, silver wheels with "Goodyear" rubber tires, 1:64 scale
EX n/a   NM n/a   MIP $4

❏ **Dodge Rebellion,**
EX n/a   NM n/a   MIP $3

❏ **Frank Monaghan,** 1999, Multicolored body with flame tampo, "Frank Monaghan's Dodge" on sides, chrome wheels, 1:64 scale
EX n/a   NM n/a   MIP $3

❏ **Hemi Under Glass,**
EX n/a   NM n/a   MIP $3

❏ **Hemi Xpress,**
EX n/a   NM n/a   MIP $3

❏ **Hurst Hairy Olds,**
EX n/a   NM n/a   MIP $3

❏ **LA Dart,**
EX n/a   NM n/a   MIP $3

❏ **Little Red Wagon,**
EX n/a   NM n/a   MIP $5

❏ **Little Red Wagon,** 1999, Red body, yellow lettering "Little Red Wagon" on sides, silver painted headlights and grille, rubber "Goodyear" tires, 1:64 scale
EX n/a   NM n/a   MIP $4

❏ **Tameless Tiger,**
EX n/a   NM n/a   MIP $3

❏ **Thunder Wagon,** 1999, Blue, white and red body, "Thunder Wagon" in red type on sides, small wheels in front, rubber tires and fat wheels in rear. Like others in this series, package includes a Wheelie-Stand, 1:64 scale
EX n/a   NM n/a   MIP $4

SPECIAL EDITION

❏ **'33 Willys,**
EX n/a   NM n/a   MIP $16

(KP Photo)

❏ **'54 Chevy Panel,** 1995, Black body, with blue "Chevrolet" logo on panel sides, "Greater Seattle

Toy Show 1995" on roof, limited to 5,000 models. Silver chrome wheels, rubber "Firestone" tires, 1:64 scale, Model No. 154
EX n/a   NM n/a   MIP $11

(KP Photo)

❏ **'54 Chevy Panel,** 1995, Pearl metallic white body, with blue "Chevrolet" logo on panel sides, "Greater Seattle Toy Show 1995" on roof, limited to 5,000 models. Silver chrome wheels, rubber "Firestone" tires, 1:64 scale, Model No. 154
EX n/a   NM n/a   MIP $14

❏ **'56 Chevy,**
EX n/a   NM n/a   MIP $15

❏ **'60's VW Van,**
EX n/a   NM n/a   MIP $16

(KP Photo)

❏ **60's VW Van,** 1999, Glossy black body, chrome rims with rubber "Goodyear" tires, "2000 www.diecastwarehouse.com" on sides, "Millenium Bus" on roof. Limited to 10,000, 1:64 scale
EX n/a   NM n/a   MIP $8

❏ **'63 Chevy Impala,**
EX n/a   NM n/a   MIP $15

❏ **'66 Mustang 350H,**
EX n/a   NM n/a   MIP $14

❏ **'69 AMC Hurst SC/Rambler,**
EX n/a   NM n/a   MIP $15

❏ **'70 Cougar Convertible,**
EX n/a   NM n/a   MIP $15

❏ **Bugaboo,**
EX n/a   NM n/a   MIP $15

(KP Photo, Angelo Van Bogart collection)

❑ **Buick Grand National,** 1996, Black with black interior, "Grand National" on sides, silver wheels, 1:64 scale

EX n/a   NM n/a   MIP $22

❑ **Dodge A-100,**

EX n/a   NM n/a   MIP $14

❑ **NSX,**

EX n/a   NM n/a   MIP $16

❑ **Plymouth Prowler,**

EX n/a   NM n/a   MIP $15

(KP Photo)

❑ **The VW Thing,** 1995, Light orange body with black roof, gray plastic interior, silver wheels, black rubber "Firestone" tires, silver metal base. Limited to 5,000 pieces, 1:64 scale, Model No. 159

EX n/a   NM n/a   MIP $12

❑ **VW Concept One,**

EX n/a   NM n/a   MIP $15

SPEED RACER

❑ **Assassin,** 1997, Black body with headlight "eyes." Includes animation cel

EX n/a   NM n/a   MIP $6

❑ **GRX: Fastest Car,** 1997, Gold metallic body. Includes animation cel

EX n/a   NM n/a   MIP $6

❑ **Racer X Shooting Star,** 1997, Yellow body with blue number "9" in white circles on hood and sides. Includes animation cel

EX n/a   NM n/a   MIP $7

❑ **Speed Racer Mach 5,** 1997, White body, number "5" on doors,

silver wheels (can also have silver spoked wheels)

EX n/a   NM n/a   MIP $15

SPEED RACER 2000

❑ **Captain Terror,** 2000, Red body with opening rear hood, black interior, blue number "11" on hood and sides, yellow tailpipes

EX n/a   NM n/a   MIP $5

❑ **Mach 5 Stock Car,** 2000, White body with opening hood, number "5" on doors and roof, yellow interior, silver rims

EX n/a   NM n/a   MIP $6

(KP Photo)

❑ **Racer X Shooting Star,** 2000, Yellow body, black nose, number "9" on sides and hood, chrome rims, opening rear hood. Includes animation cel, 1:64 scale

EX n/a   NM n/a   MIP $5

❑ **Racer X Stock Car,** 2000, Yellow body with opening hood, black plastic interior, number "9" on sides and roof, chrome rims, "Racer X" above doors. Includes animation cel

EX n/a   NM n/a   MIP $6

❑ **Snake Oiler,** 2000, Purple and black body, number "12" on sides, opening hood, black interior

EX n/a   NM n/a   MIP $5

(KP Photo)

❑ **Speed Racer Mach 5,** 2000, White body, opening hood, number "5" on doors, silver wheels (can also have silver spoked wheels). Includes animation cel. This car, like others in the Speed Racer 2000 series was a new release and new casting, differing from the first 1997 models, 1:64 scale

EX n/a   NM n/a   MIP $6

STOCK CAR LEGENDS

❑ **'67 Ford Fairlane,** Mario Andretti

EX n/a   NM n/a   MIP $4

(KP Photo, Angelo Van Bogart collection)

❑ **'67 Ford Fairlane,** 1998, David Pearson car, number "17" and "Holman & Moody" on sides, gold wheels, 1:64 scale

EX n/a   NM n/a   MIP $4

❑ **'69 Daytona,** Bobby Isaac

EX n/a   NM n/a   MIP $4

❑ **'69 Daytona,** Buddy Baker

EX n/a   NM n/a   MIP $4

❑ **'69 Torino Talladega,** David Pearson

EX n/a   NM n/a   MIP $4

❑ **'69 Torino Talladega,** LeeRoy Yarbrough

EX n/a   NM n/a   MIP $4

❑ **'70 Superbird,** Pete Hamilton

EX n/a   NM n/a   MIP $4

❑ **'70 Superbird,** Richard Brooks

EX n/a   NM n/a   MIP $4

❑ **'71 Mercury Cyclone,** Donny Allison

EX n/a   NM n/a   MIP $4

❑ **'71 Mercury Cyclone,** Donny Allison, Purolator

EX n/a   NM n/a   MIP $4

❑ **'71 Plymouth Satellite,** Pete Hamilton

EX n/a   NM n/a   MIP $4

❑ **'71 Plymouth Satellite,** Fred Lorenzen

EX n/a   NM n/a   MIP $4

❑ **'73 Dodge Charger,** Marty Robbins

EX n/a   NM n/a   MIP $4

❑ **'73 Dodge Charger,** Neil Bonnett

EX n/a   NM n/a   MIP $4

❑ **'77 Olds Cutlass,** Cale Yarborough

EX n/a   NM n/a   MIP $4

❑ **'77 Olds Cutlass,** AJ Foyt

EX n/a   NM n/a   MIP $4

❏ **'79 Chevy Monte Carlo,** Darrell Waltrip
EX n/a NM n/a MIP $4

❏ **'79 Chevy Monte Carlo,** Benny Parsons
EX n/a NM n/a MIP $4

❏ **'81 Grand Prix,** Geoff Bodine
EX n/a NM n/a MIP $4

(KP Photo, Bert Lehman collection)

❏ **'81 Grand Prix,** 1998, Rusty Wallace, white with green number "88" on sides and roof. The "Gatorade" car, 1:64 scale
EX n/a NM n/a MIP $9

❏ **'83 Chevy Monte Carlo,** Cale Yarborough
EX n/a NM n/a MIP $4

❏ **'83 Chevy Monte Carlo,** Darrell Waltrip
EX n/a NM n/a MIP $4

❏ **'85 Ford Thunderbird,** Buddy Baker
EX n/a NM n/a MIP $4

❏ **'85 Ford Thunderbird,** Buddy Baker
EX n/a NM n/a MIP $4

STREET FREAKS

❏ **'63 Mustang,** 1:64 scale
EX n/a NM n/a MIP $5

❏ **'63 Mustang,** White Lightnings edition, 1:64 scale
EX n/a NM n/a MIP $20

❏ **'65 Nova,** 1:64 scale
EX n/a NM n/a MIP $5

❏ **'67 GTO,** 1:64 scale
EX n/a NM n/a MIP $5

❏ **'67 GTO,** White Lightnings edition, 1:64 scale
EX n/a NM n/a MIP $20

❏ **'67 Mustang,** White Lightnings edition, 1:64 scale
EX n/a NM n/a MIP $20

❏ **'67 Mustang GT,** 1999, Bright blue body, silver chrome metal engine, chrome rims, black interior, silver painted headlights, 1:64 scale
EX n/a NM n/a MIP $6

❏ **'67 Shelby,** White Lightnings edition, 1:64 scale
EX n/a NM n/a MIP $20

❏ **'67 Shelby,** 1999, Teal green body, silver metal blown engine, chrome five-spoke wheels, silver painted trim, Wheelie-Stand, 1:64 scale
EX n/a NM n/a MIP $5

❏ **'68 Chevelle,** 1:64 scale
EX n/a NM n/a MIP $5

❏ **'68 Chevelle,** White Lightnings edition, 1:64 scale
EX n/a NM n/a MIP $20

❏ **'69 Camaro,** 1:64 scale
EX n/a NM n/a MIP $5

❏ **'69 Mach 1,** White Lightnings edition, 1:64 scale
EX n/a NM n/a MIP $20

❏ **'69 Mach 1,** 1999, Purple body, silver metal blown engine, chrome wheels, black interior, rubber tires, 1:64 scale
EX n/a NM n/a MIP $4

❏ **'70 AAR,** 1:64 scale
EX n/a NM n/a MIP $4

❏ **'70 AMC Rebel Machine,** White Lightnings edition, 1:64 scale
EX n/a NM n/a MIP $20

❏ **'70 AMC Rebel Machine,** 1999, Deep magenta body, silver metal engine, silver painted trim, 1:64 scale
EX n/a NM n/a MIP $4

❏ **'70 Torino,** 1:64 scale
EX n/a NM n/a MIP $4

❏ **'71 Demon,** 1:64 scale
EX n/a NM n/a MIP $5

❏ **'71 GTO Judge,** White Lightnings edition, 1:64 scale
EX n/a NM n/a MIP $20

❏ **'71 GTO Judge,** 1999, Yellow body, silver rims, silver metal engine, 1:64 scale
EX n/a NM n/a MIP $6

❏ **'73 Charger,** 1:64 scale
EX n/a NM n/a MIP $7

❏ **'73 Mach 1,** White Lightnings edition, 1:64 scale
EX n/a NM n/a MIP $20

❏ **'73 Mach 1,** 1999, Red body, silver metal engine, chrome rims, black interior and spoiler, 1:64 scale
EX n/a NM n/a MIP $4

❏ **'76 Cobra,** 1:64 scale
EX n/a NM n/a MIP $4

❏ **'76 Cobra,** White Lightnings edition, 1:64 scale
EX n/a NM n/a MIP $15

❏ **'87 Mustang,** 1:64 scale
EX n/a NM n/a MIP $4

❏ **'87 Mustang,** White Lightnings edition, 1:64 scale
EX n/a NM n/a MIP $15

❏ **'94 Mustang,** 1:64 scale
EX n/a NM n/a MIP $4

❏ **'94 Mustang,** White Lightnings edition, 1:64 scale
EX n/a NM n/a MIP $15

SURF RODS

❏ **'29 Crew Cab: Laguna Longboards,** 2000, Red-brown body with black grille and bed, surfboards on roof, "Laguna Longboards" on sides, 1:64 scale
EX n/a NM n/a MIP $4

❏ **'29 Ford: Torrance Terrors,** 2000, Torrance Terrors, 1:64 scale
EX n/a NM n/a MIP $4

(KP Photo)

❏ **'33 Ford Delivery Van: The Ghostriders,** 2001, Dark blue and black body with silver stripe along sides with "The Ghostriders" on panel section. Red and yellow and blue and white surfboards on roof, opening hood, photo card, chrome five-spoke wheels, hard tires, 1:64 scale, Model No. 566
EX n/a NM n/a MIP $4

(KP Photo)

One of everybody's favorite vehicles—the Batmobile. This version, (267-A1), is a rarity with a matte black finish and no tow hook. It features firing missiles, a front chain cutter and Batman and Robin figures. $550 MIP.

Made for only one year, (1973) this version of the Batmobile (267-C1), features unusual red tires, but includes a tow hook for towing the Batboat on adventures. $400 MIP.

This Aston Martin DB4 came with racing numbers 1, 3 or 7. It was produced by Corgi from 1962-65. $125 MIP.

Two versions of the Bedford Dormobile: the 404-A on the left, and the 404-M (with a mechanical friction motor) on the right. These models had many color variations. Also, look for divided or single windshields on these English vans. $125 MIP each.

Austin Cambridge Saloons: 201-A on the left, and the mechanical 201-M on the right. Produced from 1956-61. The regular version, $120 MIP. The mechanical, $150 MIP.

The Austin A60 Motor School (255-A) car featured a steering mechanism controlled by turning the sign on the roof. It included two figures and a five-language leaflet from the "Corgi School of Motoring." $160 MIP.

Austin A40, 216-A, produced from 1959-62. $100 MIP.

The Bedford Carrimore Low Loader, 1100-A, featured a working winch to bring the cars onto the trailer. Produced from 1958-62. $150 MIP.

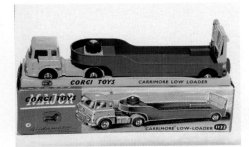

A later version of the Bedford Carrimore Low Loader, 1132-A, with a working ramp, winch and "Glidamatic" spring suspension. $325 MIP.

The first issue of the American La France Ladder Truck, 1143-A. These first models were the most detailed, and included six fireman figures. $150 MIP.

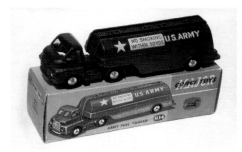

The Bedford Army Fuel Tanker, 1134-A, produced from 1964-65. $375 MIP.

A similar model, the Bedford Mobilgas Tanker, 1110-A. $250 MIP.

The Bedford "Utilecon" Ambulance, produced from 1957-60. $125 MIP.

Ferrari Berlinetta 250LM, (314-A), with an opening hood and detailed engine produced from 1965-72. $75 MIP.

Innovative character toy from Corgi: Basil Brush's car. It included two tapes that let kids hear Basil laughing that played on a soundbox in the car. $200 MIP.

Bedford TK Tipper Truck from 1968-72. $65 MIP.

Bedford Evening Standard Van, $130 MIP.

Austin Mini Van with working rear doors, 1964-67. $100 MIP.

First version of the Bedford Automobile Association Road Service Van with divided windshield, produced from 1957-59. $125 MIP.

The Austin Police Mini Van was packaged like a mini-playset and included a policeman and German Shepard dog, plus a box that doubled as a background. $175 MIP.

The Dodge Kew Fargo Tipper, an English version of a Dodge truck, is a sharp example of a nice heavy model. $85 MIP.

This Dolphin Cabin Cruiser, 104-A, included a driver and outboard motor. The recommended car to tow? The Buick Riviera. $70 MIP.

The Ford Consul Saloon, 200-A, was available in a variety of colors. $120 MIP.

Well detailed models: Ford Thames Airborne Caravan in two color variations. The rear doors opened to show a well-appointed interior included table and Venetian blinds. $95 MIP each.

Excellent play value with this toy: The Ford Thames Wall's Ice Cream Van. Turning a hand crank on the vehicle played the Wall's Ice Cream song. $225 MIP.

The Fiat 1800 was a popular toy for die-cast manufacturers. This Corgi version was available in a variety of colors. $80 MIP.

The ERF 64G Earth Dumper, produced from 1958-67. $85 MIP.

The Austin-Healey Sports Car, 300-A1, was available in two color variations: a red body with cream interior or a cream body with red interior. $125 MIP.

One of Corgi's military models, the Corporal Missile Truck, 1113-A. This model was produced from 1959-62. $600 MIP.

Another character toy: Dougal's Magic Roundabout Car, 807-A. Produced from 1971-74. $175 MIP.

Seeing American vehicles by British die-cast companies is fun. This model, an Impala Police Car, is quite well detailed and even includes two officers. $130 MIP.

This Mustang Fastback featured extra stickers to customize the model. Produced from 1965-69. $85 MIP.

A rarity—this Japanese Airlines Concorde was most likely an import. An interesting choice of livery, considering the actual aircraft was never used by JAL. $700 MIP.

Ecurie Ecosse Transporter, 1126-A, by Corgi, produced from 1961-65. Working tailgate and sliding door. $200 MIP.

ERF Cement Tipper can have plastic or metal filler caps, depending on its time of release. $80 MIP.

The ERF Moorhouse's Jams van was produced from 1958-60. $295 MIP.

Commer Ambulance, 463-A, by Corgi. Like many emergency vehicle toys of the period, there are color variations in this model veering between cream and white. $90 MIP.

The Corvette Stingray, 337-A. The colors on this model firmly place it in the sixties. $95 MIP.

The Constructor Set, GS/24, allowed kids to create their own unique vehicles, a concept very much alive today with the proliferation of die-cast kits on the market. $140 MIP.

The Commer Holiday Mini Bus, a late-sixties vehicle by Corgi. With bathing suits packed in the roof luggage, it looks like this bus is ready for a trip to the shore. $110 MIP.

The Chevrolet Kennel Club Van included a working tailgate and rear window, plus four dogs! $140 MIP.

This Citroen DS 19, 323-A, is ready for the Monte Carlo. $175 MIP.

Chipperfield Circus Land Rover included chimp figures and a revolving clown to announce the arrival of the circus. $175 MIP.

Another Chipperfield Circus vehicle—the Horse Transporter, 1130-A. This model included six horses. $235 MIP.

This Chipperfield Circus Crane Truck, 1121-A, is pictured here with the Chipperfield Circus Cage Wagon that included a set of polar bears or lions. Crane Truck, $225 MIP. Cage Wagon, $140 MIP.

The Chipperfield Circus Mobile Booking Office, produced from 1962-64. A nice addition to the Chipperfield fleet, it included a tin lithographed interior. $325 MIP.

The Cadillac Superior Ambulance, 437-A, in two color schemes. This model featured battery-operated warning lights. $150 MIP.

The second edition of the Chevy Impala, 220-A, had a blue body with a red or yellow interior. The first version is shown here. $125 MIP.

The Car Transporter and Six Cars gift set, 48-A. These sets were fun to receive, and were probably a great way for Corgi to get rid of their excessive stock of car models. $700 MIP.

Another Fordson Power Major Tractor, 55-A, shown with the 61-A Four Furrow Plow. Tractor, $110 MIP. Plow, $35 MIP.

Chevy Impala Fire Chief Car, 482-A. This model was produced with either round or rectangular "Fire Chief" decals on the doors. $130 MIP.

Three versions of this Fordson Power Major Tractor exist, and any one of them can be tough to find—especially with original tracks. $225 MIP.

BMC Mini-Cooper S "Sun/RAC" rally car with jeweled headlights. $350 MIP.

This Vanwall Racing Car, 150-A, was available in three colors; green, red or silver. $120 MIP.

This Renault 1000kg Van is a popular casting in Corgi's French "Collection Heritage" series. The range was started in 1997, and features a great variety of Renault, Peugeot, Berliet commercial vehicles with outstanding graphics. This model is a 2001 release, and retails for about $24 MIP.

The James Bond DB5 is a popular casting that Corgi has employed for years—decades, even. This model includes front machine guns, a bullet shield and of course, and ejector seat. It retails for about $16 MIP.

The BMW Z8 from "The World is Not Enough." The Bond Collection has proven extremely popular with collectors. This 1:36-scale model features side-firing Stinger rockets. $16 MIP.

The Aston-Martin V8 from "The Living Daylights" features side-ejecting skis. $17 MIP.

The Mercedes from "Octopussy" has removable tire that allow it to fit perfectly on it's railroad display section. $16 MIP.

The M151 A1 "Mutt" with Trailer, (50102), part of the Texaco Collection. 1:43-scale, $30 MIP.

This Texaco "deuce and a half" is a highly detailed 1:50-scale model. $45 MIP.

An impressive truck: The Texaco Diamond T980 Ballast and 24-Wheel Low Loader. $89 MIP.

Corgi's "Unsung Heroes" series is a realistic collection of vehicles that really look like they've been in the field. It was a bit of a risk for Corgi to release this series, in part, because of the subject matter—the Vietnam War is still a tough topic—but also because of the painted-on grime and dirt on the models themselves. Generally, collectors want a pristine-looking piece. In this case, though, the series has been quite successful. The M48 A3 "Patton" Battle Tank shown here is an incredibly detailed die-cast model. 1:50-scale, $47 MIP.

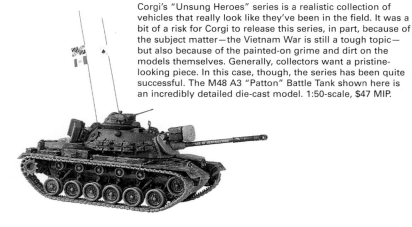

Also from the first "Unsung Heroes" series, (released in 2000), the U.S. Army deuce and a half. 1:50-scale, $45 MIP.

An old favorite from Corgi brought back again—Chitty Chitty Bang Bang. It features a Caracatus Potts figure and extending wings. $35 MIP.

The "Huey Hog," UH-C1 U.S. Army helicopter gunship, 1:48-scale. $50 MIP.

A Northeast Airlines Vickers Viscount in 1:144-scale. $76 MIP.

Part of Corgi's "Aviation Archive" series, the Vaught F4U-1 Corsair "Daphne", as flown by Capt. James N. Cupp. $32 MIP.

The DeHavilland DH-98 Mosquito in D-Day invasion stripes. $45 MIP.

From the "Heroes Under Fire" series—an E-1 Sidemount Pumper shown in markings for the Fairfax, Virginia department. $45 MIP.

A Philadelphia Mack CF Tower with an extending ladder on a pivoting base. 1:50-scale, $65 MIP.

The GM Fishbowl in Chicago Transit Authority colors, from the "Vintage Bus Lines" series. $55 MIP.

From the "Heavy Haulers" collection: A Diamond T980 Girder Trailer and Transformer load, 1:50-scale. $100 MIP.

The decal on the Automobile Association Motorcycle changed depending in which country the vehicle was sold. $70 MIP.

The Missile Servicing Platform, (#667), was a nicely detailed toy with a short production run, starting in 1960 and only running for a couple of years. $270 MIP.

The Panhard Esso Tanker was a French-made toy as part of the Dinky Supertoys line. It was produced from 1954-59. $170 MIP.

Another French-made Dinky, the 32E Berliet Fire Pumper. It included two detachable hose reels. $120 MIP.

The Caravelle S.E. 210, (#60f/891), a French-made Dinky appropriately labeled with "Air France" markings. $230 MIP.

The Vickers Viscount with British European Airways markings. $200 MIP.

An impressive toy, the Super G Constellation Lockheed, produced from 1956-63. $350 MIP.

The BBC-TV Camera truck, produced from 1959-64. $185 MIP.

Another TV crew truck, the ABC-TV Mobile Control Room. It included a camera, cameraman—even a cable! $210 MIP.

The Superior Criterion Ambulance (#277) featured a warning light that actually flashed with the aid of a small battery. $110 MIP.

The white tires really enhance this French-made Delahaye Fire truck, produced from 1955-70. $375 MIP.

The Pinder Circus Truck and Wagon (#881), is a French-made Dinky toy. The animals and labels are still in the package in this example. This model was produced from 1969-71, a short span. $375 MIP.

The Pinder Circus Peugeot and Caravan (#882), are the only other vehicles produced in the Pinder Circus livery by Dinky. It would have been fun to see the line continue, had sales been stronger at the time. $380 MIP.

This BBC-TV Extending Mast vehicle is another great addition to the BBC series Dinky produced. $185 MIP.

A very British vehicle by Dinky: The Royal Mail Van, produced from 1955-61. $180 MIP.

The McLean Tractor-Trailer, (#948), a substantial toy by Dinky produced from 1961-1967. $280 MIP.

The Johnston Road Sweeper, (#449/451), from the 1970s. As the toy was pushed forward, a spring coil turned the brushes in a sweeping motion. $75 MIP.

The D.H. Comet Airliner from 1954-65. $200 MIP.

Pullmore Car Transporter with 794 Loading Ramp. The ramp came separately packaged in the transporter box. $190 MIP.

The French-made Unic Auto Transporter featured a lever that lowered a ramp on the side of the trailer. $300 MIP.

The Healey Sports Boat and Trailer attached to a number of cars in the Dinky lineup. It was produced for only two years: 1960-62. $55 MIP.

The Mersey Tunnel Police Land Rover, produced from 1955-61. $135 MIP.

This Airport Fire Tender by Dinky featured a flashing light. It was produced from 1962-69. $100 MIP.

This Missile Truck from 1959 is a nicely-detailed military model from Dinky. $240 MIP.

The Custom Charger, (#6268), featured an opening hood and detailed engine, and was released in 1969. $250 MIP.

Turbofire, (#6259), was another 1969 release, and featured a tough profile and opening rear hood. $50 MIP.

Mantis, (#6423), had a clever opening canopy and a heavy feel due to its large all-metal baseplate. It was released in 1970. $60 MIP.

The Custom Fleetside, (#6213), was one of the "original sixteen" in Hot Wheels first year of releases. Shown here in two colors, it had an opening tonneau cover. $250 MIP.

The Paddy Wagon, (#6966), is a pretty common vehicle—models in played-with condition are generally missing the lettering on the plastic roof. Or, they are simply are missing the entire roof. $35 MIP.

The McClaren M6A, (#6255), also featured an opening rear hood and detailed engine. This vehicle was released in 1969. $65 MIP.

The Classic '57 T-Bird, (#6252), shown here in a sharp-looking blue, also had the opening hood and detailed engine of many early Hot Wheels. This was a 1969 release. $100 MIP.

Classic '32 Ford Vicky, (#6250), a 1969 release in a chrome red finish. $95 MIP.

The Classic Nomad, (#6404), is a favorite casting among kids and collectors. Look for variations of this vehicle even now. Of course, the first issue from 1970 featured the opening hood and engine detail that many recent versions don't include. $150 MIP.

Twinmill, (#6258), is possibly one of Hot Wheels' most recognizable castings. So popular, it was released in a 1:18-scale version in the 1990s. This model was released in 1969. $50 MIP.

Splittin' Image, (#6261), was another heavy casting with a large unpainted base. The car is a 1969 release. $50 MIP.

The Custom Firebird, (#6212), was another of the "original sixteen" featured in the 1967 catalog. Like most other "stock" models of the time, it had an opening hood and detailed engine and underbody. $250 MIP.

The AMX/2, (#6460) is a sharp-looking casting, but even more so in this dark purple finish. Still from the classic years of Redlines, this model was a 1971 release. $150 MIP.

From the 1967 catalog, the popular Deora, (#6210), featured removable surfboards. Very much in keeping with 1960s California hot rod and surfing culture. $375 MIP.

The coolest way to get to school—the S'Cool Bus, (#6468), a 1971 release (that has been re-released, too). $750 MIP.

This Tow Truck, (#6450), was part of the Heavyweights line of trucks. Featuring identical futuristic cab styles, these vehicles were could be everything from moving vans to garbage haulers. They definitely lived up to their name, too. These are pretty substantial toys. This model is a 1970 release. $80 MIP.

While not part of the Heavyweights series, this truck sure looks like it could be in the second generation of 'em, if such a thing existed. The Hairy Hauler, (#6458), was a 1971 release. $65 MIP.

Referred to as a "California Custom Dream Rod" in the 1967 catalog the Silhouette, (#6209), was another of the "original sixteen" Hot Wheels releases. $90 MIP.

The lime color shown here on the Beatnik Bandit, (#6217), was one of the two paint options originally mentioned in the 1967 catalog. The other color? Aqua. This car has proven to be so popular that it prompted a 1:18-scale version from Mattel in 2002. $45 MIP.

Classic Ford '36 Coupe, (#6253), a detailed little casting with a fun touch—an opening rumble seat. This car was released in 1969. $60 MIP.

A great blue on this Custom El Dorado, (#6218). It naturally featured an opening hood and engine and underbody detail. The other color for the 1968 model? You guessed it—gold—also shown here. $140 MIP each.

The Python, (#6216), was available in orange or red finishes the year it was introduced. Also part of the "original sixteen" as seen in the 1967 catalog. The black "vinyl" roof was a painted flat black finish. $75 MIP.

The King Kuda, (#6411), was a great-looking use of the Custom Barracuda casting. Models of muscle cars and exposed-engine "street machines" are becoming more popular across the board. This car came with extra customizing decals. $100 MIP.

While not in a color of the first year of release, this dark purple Custom T-Bird, (#6207), *was* part of the first sixteen models shown in the 1967 catalog. $165 MIP.

The Jack Rabbit Special, (#6421), was a rare departure from the usual chrome colors seen on early redlines. This car was released in 1970. $55 MIP.

The Custom Volkswagen, (#6220), was another of the "original sixteen" castings featured in the 1967 catalog. $125 MIP.

This sharp-looking dark blue Custom Mustang, (#6206), had an opening hood and detailed engine and underbody. It was also part of the first sixteen castings featured in the 1967 catalog at Hot Wheels' introduction. $425 MIP.

The Torero, (#6260), featured a front-hinged opening hood and great engine detail. It was a 1969 release. $60 MIP.

A reprise of an earlier duo, the Mongoose 2, (#5954), and Snake 2, (#5953), are shown here. Funny cars were almost like getting two toys in one. These cars were 1971 releases—notice the plastic, versus metal, buttons? Mongoose 2, $350 MIP. Snake 2, $275 MIP.

The Demon, (#6401) was a 1970 release. $50 MIP.

The Custom Camaro, (#6208), was originally offered in lime or blue, and featured an opening hood and detailed engine and underbody. It was part of the "original sixteen" releases shown in the 1967 catalog. $450 MIP.

Another vehicle in the first sixteen castings, the Custom Cougar, (#6205), was a sharp-looking toy. And, as can be expected from the first models, it had an opening hood and a detailed engine and underbody. $275 MIP.

The Custom Barracuda, (#6211), was one of Hot Wheels' best castings. An "original sixteen" model, it had an opening hood, detailed engine and realistic underbody. $400 MIP.

The Custom Corvette, another of the "original sixteen" from the1967 catalog. Available first in red or blue, it also featured an opening hood and a detailed engine and underbody. $300 MIP.

The Indy Eagle, (#6263), a 1969 release in two paint guises. $40 MIP.

While a well-known vehicle, the Ford J-Car, (#6214), hasn't proved to be especially popular with collectors. This model was offered initially in white only, but other colors were soon available. It was an "original sixteen" release featured in the 1967 catalog. $70 MIP.

The Chaparral 2G, (#6256), seen with the (often missing) plastic spoiler. $45 MIP.

Another "original sixteen" car from the first Hot Wheels releases, the Hot Heap, (#6219), is generally seen "windshield-free." $65 MIP.

Possibly one of Hot Wheels' most recognizable models, the Red Baron (#6400), was reproduced in various guises and paint types throughout the 1970s. $40 MIP.

The Sand Crab, (#6403), was a popular casting from 1970. $60 MIP.

The Boss Hoss, (#6499), was a chrome finish Club Kit car from 1970. $160 MIP.

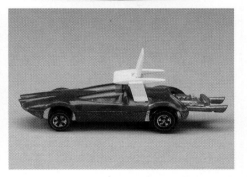

The Swingin' Wing, (#6422), was released in 1970. Like many cars with plastic accessories, the wing is often missing. $75 MIP.

The Baja Bruiser, (#8258), was a 1974 release. Hot Wheels cars from 1973 and later used an enamel paint that was cheaper to produce than the chromed finish of the first models. $85 MIP.

A popular model, the Cockney Cab, (#6466), was a 1971 release. $160 MIP.

Another in the Heavyweights series, this 1971 release, the Fuel Tanker, (#6018), even had removable fuel hoses. A neat addition to sit alongside orange track during races… $200 MIP.

Short Order, (#6176), was a modified 1950s Ford pickup, like the later Baja Bruiser. This model was a 1971 release. $125 MIP.

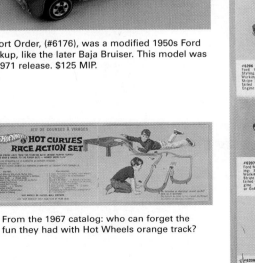

From the 1967 catalog: who can forget the fun they had with Hot Wheels orange track?

A selection of vehicles from the "original sixteen" as they appeared in the 1967 catalog.

The Corgi Juniors 1008-A Popeye Paddle Wagon was a miniature model of the elaborate full-size Corgi vehicle minus the working features. $12 MIP.

The Buick Electra, 7-A, by Husky, produced from 1964-68. $40 MIP.

Two variations of the Citroen Safari—civilian and military ambulances. Both models are quite popular with collectors. Civilian model, $40 MIP. Military model, $30 MIP.

The E.R.F. Cement Lorry by Husky, produced from 1966-69. $30 MIP.

Ford Camper, 35-A, by Husky. A nice model, but as this picture shows, the chromed plastic didn't always hold up to play wear. $30 MIP.

Jaguar E-Type 2+2 by Husky. This is a sharp casting of a truly popular model. Produced from 1968-69. $50 MIP.

Corgi Juniors Kojak Buick Regal, $12 MIP.

Johnny Lightning's Surf Rods series is a colorful, fun collection. Each model is packaged with a LeRoy Grannis snapshot of the beach and surf scene in the 1960s. Most of these models are still available for suggested retail (or less, in some cases) of $5 each.

Two Mercury Cougars from the Rebel Rods series. Notice the differences in wheels, tires and engines? According to the Spring 2002 issue of *Newsflash*, 74 percent of the releases had hard tires, while 25 percent had rubber "Real Wheels" tires. The remaining one percent was split between the two tires also, but as "White Lightning" vehicles. Rebel Rods include decal sheets to customize each model, adding to the fun! Again, these vehicles retail for about $5 each.

Johnny Lightning does a great job creating and re-issuing castings in different series. The "Meat Wagon" on the left and the "Polarlights.com" car on the right are just two examples. Both vehicles are currently selling for around $8-10 a piece.

Another example of Johnny Lightning casting use: the '55 Chevy Nomad. Here are examples from Surf Rods, American Graffiti and Tri-Chevy series, about $5 each.

From "Fright'ning Lightnings" first release in 1995, the "Christine" car, a 1958 Plymouth Fury. The Fright'ning Lightning series was so popular that it was revived two years later. This black edition of "Christine" is about $6, usually found at shows or on the Internet.

A selection of 1950s-era automobiles from more recent series. Johnny Lightning does a nice job with these cars, many featuring opening hoods and rubber tires. Each retails for about $5.

Johnny Lightning covers an impressive group of pop culture icons, including the 1960s hit TV-show, "The Green Hornet." Shown here are two variations of the Green Hornet's car, "Black Beauty." On the left, the standard black version, and on the right, the chrome green Target Exclusive. Each retails for about $5.

The Customizing Kit of the '67 and '68 Camaros has enough pieces to build two complete cars. Shown here, on complete car and another still awaiting the assembly line. The kits allow for quite a bit of flexibility, in this case, about 96 possible variations. These retail for about $11 a piece.

It may have taken over 20 years, but the "Lost Toppers" were finally released. Seen here in a 1970 Topper Toys catalog and in the Playing Mantis die-cast form, the Lost Toppers pictured include: The Skinni Mini, the Beep Heap (or Beep Jeep as it was called in 1970) and Tow'd. Each of these new models includes a collector's card with an illustration of the model. Note that the Skinni Mini and Tow'd are KB Toy exclusives. Retail price: about $5 each.

Whether "in pack" or out of the package, the Dioramas are like mini-playsets. So far, it seems the James Bond Goldfinger and the Starsky and Hutch sets are the most common, with the Monkees being one of the harder-to-find varieties. Normally, though, each diorama retails for about $8.

The VW Collector's Club buses were available in the Winter 2001-2002 catalog. The set of two sold through the club at $14.95, although collectors should expect to pay around $20 for them via online dealers or eBay.

Some of the best-looking and most affordable military die-cast models are being produced by Johnny Lightning. Both of these Jeeps, one from the "Battle of the Bulge" and the other from the "Pearl Harbor" series attest to the attention to detail the company is showing. These examples feature opening hoods, realistic tires and retail for about $5 each.

An orange Studebaker pickup from the "Truckin' America" series shown with two "White Lightning" variations, one in white and the other in pearl. Some of the "Truckin' America" models can still be found on the pegs, but generally, White Lightnings will have to be found at shows or on the Internet. The orange model sells for about $4, but the others usually average around $15-20 each.

Some of the vehicles in the ".com Racers" series. Harder to find are the VW Vans, available with two different wheel types. The models shown, including the eBay Dodge Viper, the Yahoo! IRL car, the CBSsports.com Monte Carlo and the Playing Mantic Pontiac Firebird dragster, are pretty easy to find and average about $5 each or less.

Detail makes the difference on this Mercury Cougar from the "Muscle Cars USA" series. Notice the painted trim, opening hood and sharp finish. About $4-5 retail.

A bit harder to find, but still fun are "White Lightning" variations. They can be all-white renditions of cars and trucks, or simply stock-looking cars (including military vehicles) with subtle differences, like white wheels and rubber tires. The model shown is a close-up of the 1960 Studebaker pickup with an opening hood, white finish, and "White Lightning" printed on rubber tires. Found these days at shows or online, they average about $15-20 MIP.

Another Monopoly series vehicle, the '60 VW Van (Free Parking) is available in regular red and white and chromed red and white editions. The chromed red version shown here is a KB Toys exclusive, and sells at shows for about $6-8.

The Monopoly series vehicles include game pieces with each car. Here, the Reading Railroad 1940 Ford Pickup sits with its Monopoly look alike. This model is fairly common, and retails for about $5 or less.

Combining two collecting fields into one, Johnny Lightning released the United States Postal Service vehicles, each including a real stamp, in 1999. These are pretty common, and can be found at most hobby, toy or discount stores for about $5 each.
Note that this is another use of the 1960s Studebaker truck casting—common with Johnny Lightning. If you really like a particular casting, it can be fun to try and catch its various incarnations in different series.

Two 1954 Chevy Panel trucks created for the 1995 Seattle Toy Show. Production of these models was limited to 5,000 each. About $10 MIP each.

The Woodys and Panels series cars with Mod Squad Woody. Each vehicle retails for about $5.

A use of two castings—a 1950 Mercury station wagon in metallic purple from the Woodys and Panels series, and the same car, a bit more tame, as the "Mod Squad Woody" from the Hollywood on Wheels series. $5 MIP each.

Another vehicle from the .com Racers series—the '60s VW Van. An interesting mix of the sixties and the nineties, this model isn't often seen on the pegs. $8 MIP.

More use of castings—a 1937 Ford Coupe in two versions: one as a Hickam Field Army Staff Car (from the Pearl Harbor series) and the other as a player in the American Graffiti series. $5 MIP each.

One of the "Rock 'N Rollers" series—a car packaged with the song that made it famous—in this case, "Little GTO" by Ronny and the Daytonas. $8 MIP.

This single-vehicle model kit of the Little Red Wagon retails for about $7.

Just some of the fun "extras" that Johnny Lightning packages with their vehicles. Trading cards, decal sheets, collector buttons—neat stuff!

This 1:18-scale BMW 325ti Compact is so incredibly detailed, it can be tough to tell the real thing from the model in this photo. $80 MIP.

Toyota 2000GT '67 Fuji 24-hour rally car in 1:43-scale. $30 MIP.

The Datsun 240Z model from the 1972 Monte Carlo is a 1:43-scale model with an opening hood and detailed engine. $30 MIP.

This Lotus Caterham Super Seven is a beauty. Again, a 1:18-scale model that shows off great detail. $80 MIP.

BMW V12 from the 1999 Le Mans. 1:18-scale, $80 MIP.

Shelby GT350 in 1:43-scale, $30 MIP.

This BMW Z8 in 1:18-scale features some great interior detail that makes you feel like you could drive the car away… $80 MIP.

Another 1:43-scale vehicle, the Shelby Cobra 427C. $30 MIP.

In the Vanguards series, like Days Gone, Lledo is known for a re-use of castings. It's fun to see how different a vehicle can look with just a change of color. About $15 each.

The Tuborg Beer truck is a popular casting with Lledo, used with brands such as 7-Up and Bass Ale. $8 MIP.

The detail for Lledo Vanguards is excellent right down to the packaging, which bears a passing resemblance to vintage Corgi or Dinky boxes. This model is out of production, but still available for about $15 MIP.

This Triumph Herald shows off the detail seen in so many cars in the Vanguards range. In many ways, (due in part to Jack Odell's involvement), Vanguards are almost like a continuation of where Matchbox King Size cars would have gone had they remained "regular wheels" cars. The nostalgic idea behind Vanguards cars, that is, focusing on British models of the fifties and sixties, really brings a collector back to older Matchbox models. $14 MIP.

Another example of great packaging and detail as seen with the Ford Anglia Saloon, one of Lledo's first Vanguards castings. The collector card is a nice touch, and generally, models included license plate options, too. $12 MIP.

This Vanguards set, (#PO1002), from 1996 shows two vintage English vehicles, Ford Anglia Van and a Morris Minor Van, in "Post Office Telephones" livery. This duo is out of production, limited to 5,000 made. It is currently about $45 on the aftermarket.

The Dennis F8 Fire Engine from the Essex Fire brigade. The Dennis F8 is one of Lledo's more popular castings. This one predates the launch of the Vanguards series, and is called a "Days Gone Vanguards." It's currently valued about $7 MIP.

This 1939 Ford Fire Engine was issued in 1999. This casting is now used in Corgi's Showcase lineup as the Milwood, NY Fire Pumper. About $7 MIP.

The Quarry Trucks: 6-1RW, 6-2RW (with two box types) and 6-3RW Euclid Quarry Truck. The models kept increasing in size with each new release. 6-1RW, $75 MIP. 6-2RW, $65 MIP. 6-3RW, $30 MIP.

Studebaker Lark Wagonaire, 42-2RW, shown with box (featuring a red model) and hunter and dog figures attached to their original tree sprue. $65 MIP.

Commer Ice Cream Van, 47-2RW. All three color variations are present in this photo. Left to right: Blue body with square roof decal, cream body with oval roof decal, and rare metallic blue body with square roof decal. Note "striped" side decals on blue versions versus "plain" side decal on cream-colored model. Average for each, $75 MIP.

Color variation on Mercedes Unimog, 49-2RW. Nicely detailed toys, and still fairly common. Red and blue on the left and earlier tan and blue on right. $25 MIP.

Ford Thames Estate Car, 70-1RW. Gray-wheeled version and black-wheeled version, with their respective boxes. $70 MIP each.

International Tractor, K4-1. This photo shows the green metal hubs seen on the first releases of the model. This version, $80 MIP

Transitional Superfast (27-1SF), and regular wheels Mercedes-Benz 230SL, 27-4RW. Beyond the obvious difference in paint, notice how the thin Superfast wheels fit perfectly into the old casting. $25 each.

Color variations seen on the Superfast Skip Truck, 37-3SF. $6 MIP.

Two Ford Cortinas: One regular wheels model, 25-4RW, and one Superfast model, 25-1SF. Colors could change dramatically from regular wheels to transitional models, although rare examples of early Superfast models show old paint schemes. 25-4RW, $17 MIP. 25-1SF, $25-1SF.

More differences in paint and wheels appear on the Volkswagen 1600TL. Superfast versions of this car varied in color, from plum to a pink. Also, wider wheels were added to later Two-Pack editions, changing the casting a bit. 67-2RW, $25 MIP. 67-1SF, $32 MIP.

Here's a regular wheels, 14-4RW, and Superfast, 14-1SF, duo with the same paint scheme: the Iso Grifo. Light blue later replaced dark on the Superfast editions. $25 MIP each.

The Mercury Cougar in regular wheels and Superfast versions. The Cougar was short-lived in its Superfast form—the casting was modified for the 1971 catalog and it was listed as the "Rat Rod Dragster." 62-1SF, $30 MIP. 62-3SF, $15 MIP.

Wheels and grilles differ in these Ford Pickup Trucks. Regular wheels model, 6-4RW, $30 MIP. Superfast model, 6-1SF, $25 MIP.

The Superfast Mercedes Tourer 6-2SF in it's various guises in the 1970s and early 1980s. $14 MIP.

Notice how the casting and color changed over time with these Mercedes 300SE models—the first version of the regular wheels edition is dark green, later changed to blue, and then gold, after 1970. (There were blue editions of the Superfast Mercedes, but they are harder to find, and generally pricey--$100 for mint-in-package at the going rate.) The casting changed again after 1971, sealing the doors and only allowing an opening trunk. This model, like many, lived on in the Two-Pack series as a military staff car. Gold Superfast model, opening or cast doors, $16 MIP. Blue or green regular wheels version, $25 MIP.

Safari Land Rovers over time. The dark green model was first released in 1965, but by 1967, had switched its colors to blue (with red or brown plastic luggage). In 1970 as a Superfast car, it was painted metallic gold. However, like some of the other hard-to-find transitionals, there was a blue Superfast release. Gold Superfast model, 12-1SF, $30 MIP. Blue or green regular wheels version, $25 MIP.

A collection of Police Patrol (20-2SF) Range Rovers in various guises. The most common model is white with an orange stripe that reads "Police" in black lettering. The cars are part of the Rola-Matic series, with a revolving orange or blue light on top. Average $12 MIP each.

Collecting by marque can be a fun way to assemble a miniature fleet of vehicles. The three Superfast Rolls-Royce models shown here are well-detailed pieces with opening trunks or doors. From left to right; Rolls Royce Coupe, 69-1SF, $20 MIP. Rolls Royce Silver Shadow, 24-1SF, $20 MIP. Rolls Royce Mark II, 39-4SF, $9 MIP.

Mercedes-Benz "Binz" Ambulances in regular wheels and Superfast versions. Regular wheels, 3-3RW, $25 MIP. Superfast, 3-1SF, also $25 MIP.

154DICST2 and 153DICST2: The King Size Claas Combine (K9-2) and Fordson Tractor (K11-1) shown in the 1969 catalog and as the real model. Combine, $60 MIP. Fordson Tractor, $70 MIP

The K12-2 Scammell Crane Truck—a hefty model that blended perfectly with other King Size offerings. $50 MIP.

The Ford "Singer" Van, (39-1RW), an early model in the Matchbox lineup from 1958. Notice the lack of interior and window plastic, but nice painted detail—common on 1950s Matchbox cars. $100 MIP for common lighter green models.

The last version of a regular wheels Volkswagen Camper, (34-4RW), from 1969. Notice the top section, which kept the sunroof from the previous edition, but eliminated the windows. $35 MIP.

The DAF Girder Truck (58-3RW), from 1968. Finding models with the girders, much less the box, can be a challenge. $20 MIP.

Another King Size model, the K17-1 Low Loader with Bulldozer. The packaging and box illustrations for these models reached their zenith by the late 1960s. Separate scenes were painted for the inside and back of the box. $150 MIP.

Generally, the plastic figures and removable tires on racecars like the BRM (52-2RW) shown, are missing, so examples in excellent shape can be a real find. $25 MIP.

This Mack Dumper, (28-4RW), is a sharp, robust-looking piece. As with all toy construction vehicles, look for wear in the bed (from hauling loads of pebbles or sand) and dings on the corners. $25 MIP.

These old Lincoln Continentals, (31-3RW), are so squared-off that anything less than mint is bound to have some edgewear. $22 MIP.

Another early regular wheels vehicle, the DUKW, (55-1RW) from 1958. This model featured metal wheels. $60 MIP.

The 10-4RW Pipe Truck is another vehicle that is tough to find with complete accessories. $20 MIP.

The Fire Pumper, (29-3RW), released in 1966, is seen with or without the "Denver" decal on the cab. $22 MIP.

The Mountaineer Dump Truck with Snowplough, (16-3RW), is a great-looking toy truck. Examples with intact decals on the blade are especially nice. $50 MIP.

The Rolls Royce Silver Shadow, (24-3RW), shown with box. Notice the difference between the color on the packaging versus the real thing. Discrepancies like this were common in early catalogs and boxes, as pre-production models and illustrations were sometimes rushed into service to represent the real thing. $25 MIP.

The Honda Motorcycle with Trailer, (38-3RW), was like having two toys in one, although admittedly, the motorcycle is the cool part. $40 MIP.

The Mercury Commuter, (73-3RW), featured "Auto-Steer," which allowed the wheels to steer depending on which direction you pushed down on the vehicle. Of course, this car is also famous for the two dogs in the back, a collie and boxer, their heads peeking out over the tailgate. $25 MIP.

The Ford Galaxie Fire Chief Car in regular wheels (59-3RW) and Transitional Superfast (59-1SF) variations. The Superfast version really sits noticeably, but not outrageously, higher than its regular wheels counterpart. Regular wheels model, $30 MIP. Superfast model, $45 MIP.

The switch from regular wheels to Superfast for the Opel Diplomat is much the same as it was for the Ford Galaxie Fire Chief Car: the color of the model is unchanged, but the Superfast wheels push the vehicle's height up just a bit. Regular wheels version, 36-3RW, $20 MIP Superfast version, 36-1SF, also $20 MIP.

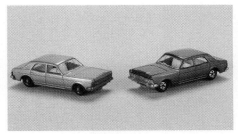

The looks of the Ford Zodiac actually improved with a switch to Superfast wheels—the paint change alone makes a real difference. Regular wheels, 53-3RW, $12 MIP. Superfast version, 53-1SF, $22 MIP.

A transitional Superfast model, the 1-1SF Mercedes Truck, now with metallic gold paint and a yellow canopy. $18 MIP.

As Matchbox went further into the 1970s, the emphasis on "hot rod" vehicles became evident, as seen in this bulldozer, the 12-3SF "Big Bull." $5 MIP.

Three models of the Airport Coach, (65-3SF), are shown here: Qantas, Lufthansa and TWA. Variations like this are fun to collect—it's interesting how much a change in color can alter a vehicle's appearance. $9 MIP each.

The 1976 "Vantastic" (34-2SF), in both of its body variations: the model with the silver exposed engine is more commonplace, while the civilized version is harder to find. Model with exposed engine, $12 MIP. Closed hood version, $22 MIP.

Notice the box art on the Mercury Cougar (62-1SF), still showing the old regular wheels illustrations and "auto-steer" wheels. The "Superfast" logo is just superimposed above the hood. $30 MIP.

The Blue Shark, 61-2SF, was first shown in the 1971 catalog in its concept form with two engines. Variations of this model include different labels and engine colors. $15 MIP.

The Mod Rod, (1-2SF), is an unusual model—available with the standard black wheels or the offbeat red wheels shown. $25 MIP.

The casting on this BMW 3.0 CSL, (45-2SF), is a bit bulky compared to the real vehicle, but it has a tough, wide stance to it. Notice the slight sticker mishap from the factory. $15 MIP.

Two examples of cars and boxes not exactly matching up: at first, most Superfast models were painted in the same colors as their regular wheels predecessors, before new colors could be specified for them. When the Mercedes 300SE was first produced, it was blue just like the regular wheels model before it; likewise, the Ford Cortina was still painted metallic brown when it was first released. The boxes simply reflect those early versions. Each car about $25 MIP.

The 8-Wheel Crane, (30-1SF), wound up a much more colorful vehicle after 1970. It changed from what had been mundane green and yellow to bright red and gold. $45 MIP.

Hi-Tailer, (56-2SF), from 1975, was a heavy casting done up in red, white and blue just in time for the bicentennial. $9 MIP.

The Fire Chief Car, (64-3SF), shows another example of Matchbox's direction toward hot rod vehicles in the mid-1970s. $12 MIP.

The futuristic truck Toe Joe, (74-2SF), was a casting that saw long use—especially in the Two-Pack series. $12 MIP.

The Ford Group Six, (45-1SF), was available in metallic green with number "45" or number "7" label, or in the harder-to-find metallic red with a number "45." The red version was a later release, dating from 1973. $22 MIP.

From 1979, a Ford Cortina 1600GL, (55-4SF), continued Matchbox's history of producing realistic British vehicles. In fact, toward the end of the 1970s, Matchbox seemed to return to an emphasis on realistic cars and trucks and away from the hot rods of the early and mid-1970s. $12 MIP.

This early Matchbox DUKW (55-1RW), from 1958 featured metal wheels and crimped axles. A nice toy of an unusual (and not often done) model. $60 MIP.

Two color variations of the Hot Rod Draguar, (36-2SF), a 1971 release. The futuristic design brings to mind Hot Wheels and Johnny Lightning vehicles of the same period. Vehicles like this marked a real departure for Matchbox. $18 MIP each.

The Londoner, (17-2SF), kept a tradition of double-decker buses by Matchbox alive. A SuperKings version was also released in the early 1970s. This smaller casting continues to be issued by the company. $5 MIP.

Two Superfast Mercury station wagons: the transitional Commuter (73-1SF) with thin wheels—a 1970 release; and the Cougar Villager, (74-3SF), from 1979. Commuter, $25 MIP. Cougar Villager, $11 MIP.

The Volkswagen 1600TL, (67-1SF), is a little harder to find in it's transitional form with thin wheels than it is as a wider-tire version from the Two-Packs, or even from its regular wheel days. $32 MIP.

The Ford Transit, (66-3SF), another very British model, is often seen without its cargo. $12 MIP.

This Rolls Royce Silver Shadow (24-1SF), is practically a direct descendent of the regular wheels edition. $20 MIP.

The detail on the Matchbox Collectibles' 1946 Dodge Power Wagon WDX is particularly striking. $30 MIP.

The Matchbox Collectibles' 1961 International Scout is part of the "First Great 4x4 Collection." $30 MIP.

Also part of the "First Great 4x4 Collection," the 1966 Ford Bronco is a sharp reproduction. It features opening tailgate and rear window, and captures the look of the vehicle quite well. $30 MIP.

The Tucker Torpedo was part of the "Oldies But Goodies Series II," and shows both "Matchbox" and "Dinky" names on the baseplate. $30 MIP.

This 1950 Ford Pumper Unit is incredibly detailed. It is included in the International Fire Engine Collection III. $30 MIP.

"Classic European Economy Cars" was the series that this 1962 Renault 4L called home. It too, shows both "Matchbox" and "Dinky" names on the baseplate. $20 MIP.

From the International Fire Engine Collection I, the 1953 Land Rover. $30 MIP.

The Matchbox-Dinky 1948 Land Rover casting has been re-issued in plenty of incarnations, including models in the Fire Engine Collections and the Great 4x4 collection. This particular model dates to 1990 and carries the markings of the Automobile Association, a British road service. $11 MIP.

Matchbox Collectibles has a strong showing in the 1:64-scale market as well—this VW Transporter is part of the Coca-Cola series. $6 MIP.

Another example of King Size and regular wheels 1-75 series models complimenting each other— the 8-Wheel Tipper Truck. Regular wheels version, 17-4RW, $37 MIP. King Size version, K1-2, $70 MIP.

Matchbox-Dinky/Matchbox Collectibles military vehicles are impressively detailed. They are 1:72-scale and feature rotating turrets. The Wirbelwind Flakpanzer IV is just one of the vehicles based on the Panzer IV platform. Both "Matchbox" and "Dinky" are on the baseplate. $30 MIP.

The Matchbox-Dinky Commer 8cwt Van features appropriate graphics for an RCA dealer in the 1950s. $10 MIP.

The K13-1 Readymix Cement Mixer has close relatives in the regular-wheels 1-75 lineup, but no "little brothers" or exact matches. Wheel variations include silver metal or red plastic, and decals can read "Readymix" or "RMC." $75 MIP.

In honor of the 50th Anniversary of Matchbox, new vehicles appeared in 2002 painted a deep metallic red and emblazoned with "50th Anniversary" logos. These 1:64-scale Volkswagens are two sharp examples. They feature painted headlights and trim, chrome wheels and rubber tires. $5 MIP.

Matchbox Collectibles released 1:43-scale vehicles in honor of their 50th as well. This Ford F-100 shows great attention to detail. $12 MIP.

Two color variations shown on the Mercedes-Benz Unimog, (49-1SF); medium blue and dark red or metallic turquoise and dark red. $25 MIP each.

The Panzer IV, Type H/J is another detailed model from Matchbox Collectibles' Great Tanks of the World Collection. Its color is representative of late-war paint schemes used on the Eastern Front. $30 MIP.

Another use of the Panzer IV casting—this time as short-barreled model in early war dark gray. $30 MIP.

The first Matchbox catalog was a single, folded sheet showing illustrations of 42 models in full color, and was printed in 1957. These days, original catalogs sell for as much as $300.00 (or more) in pristine condition, but there are clearly marked reproductions available, such as the example shown here.

Two Pack, (TP-1), Mercedes Truck and Trailer. Another example of an older casting reused well into the 1970s. $25 MIP.

Front cover and inside pages from the 1970 catalog show the introduction of Superfast models. Notice the mix of regular-wheels vehicles with converted Superfast versions.

Another color variation of the Volkswagen Golf—yellow. $12 MIP.

Three color variations of the Atlas Tipper, (23-2SF), $7 MIP each.

Another grouping of like vehicles by different toy makers. Mercury Cougars from left to right: Johnny Lightnings Rebel Rods, Matchbox Superfast, Johnny Lightnings American Muscle, Hot Wheels First Editions 2002.

Although well-loved, the attention to detail still shows through in this Lone Star "Impy" Super Car model of the Imperial. "Impy" Super Cars lived up to their billing has "having everything:" opening doors, hood and spring suspension were standard. Lone Star toys remain a good investment, and generally aren't too pricey, even mint-in-box. $20 MIP.

Various guises for the WC-54 from left to right: Johnny Lightning U.S. Navy Ambulance from the Pearl Harbor series, Corgi Showcase model from the Texaco series, the same casting, used by Lledo, as a Days Gone model, and another Johnny Lightning Army Ambulance from the Lightning Brigade series.

Another Lone Star, an outstanding Routemaster bus from the early 1970s. The detail on this model is excellent, and the weight of the piece brings to mind earlier Corgi or Dinky models. $15 MIP.

Two views of the Lone Star Rambler Rebel Station Wagon from the Roadmaster series, 1:50-scale. Although the black baseplate of this particular model reads, "Lone Star Roadmasters," some models would say "Tootsietoy." In 1960, Tootsietoy had Lone Star make four vehicles (all with baseplates) that could be marketed under the Tootsietoy name. The arrangement didn't last long, though, and soon they returned to being Lone Star models. $15 MIP.

Lone Star Impy AEC Ladder Fire Truck, 1960s. A nicely-detailed model with a value of $25-$35 MIP.

Two views of the Lone Star "Impy" Super Car model of the Volkswagen Microbus. Again, Lone Star showed amazing detail, with opening doors, rear hatch and rear engine hood. $12 MIP.

This Budgie Coca-Cola Van, (#228), was highlighted with "Coca-Cola" decals and came with fourteen plastic cases of Coke. Like other "crossover" collectibles, both die-cast and Coca-Cola fans seek out this toy. Released from 1959 to 1964, its value range is $250-$350 MIP.

Daimler Ambulance, (#258), by Budgie released in 1963-64. Interesting to see a non-Dinky version of this toy. Value range, $100-$150 MIP.

Tonibell Ice Cream van, (#290), by Budgie. Released in 1963-64, this van, like other ice cream vans, is highly collectible. Note the colorful decals and intact (and often missing) plastic cow on the roof. Value range, $350-$450 MIP.

Morestone A.A. Scout Patrol Motorcycle and Sidecar, was a highly detailed model that assembled from die-cast parts to create a beautiful toy. Released in 1959, its value range is $125-$175 MIP.

Spot-On Ford Zodiac 100SL from 1960. An attractive model with two-tone paint, it also featured battery-operated headlights and taillights. Value range, $125-$175 MIP.

An odd little car, the Meadows Frisky, (#119), a 1960 release from Spot-On, has a value range of $85-$135 MIP.

Another 1:42-scale model, the Spot-On E.R.F. 68G Flat Float with Sides, (#109/3), came with a photo card. Many toys from Spot-On included these cards, and they are required to add to the full resale value ($385-$500 MIP) for the toy. This truck is a 1960 release.

Interesting scale on Spot-On models—1:42. This Jones Crane KL 10/10, (#117), is a highly detailed toy released in 1963. Value range, $285-$365 MIP.

Spot-On A/OG Ford Thames Trader Truck with Arctic Float, (#111), 1962. This toy carries an unassembled garage kit which can be built to form a complete building. Quite a creative toy with much play value. Range, $385-$500 MIP.

Streamline Sedan, (#810), by Mettoy, 1948-1951. The Mettoy company was the parent company of Corgi Toys. These key-wound mechanical die-cast toys were the precursors to the famous Corgi Toy range that debuted in 1956. Value, $140-$180 MIP.

The Mettoy Eight-Wheel Lorry, (#840), another key-wound toy from 1948-1951. Value range, $100-$150 MIP.

Two Jaguar E-Type Roadsters (#926 and #927) by Tekno, released in the 1960s. First a Danish, then Dutch company, Tekno toys are known for superb detail. Each vehicle has a value range of $75-$125 MIP.

Authenticast American LaFrance Aerial Fire Truck and L Mack Pumper Fire Truck, 1950s. These nicely-detailed HO-scale kits were easy to assemble but very difficult to obtain on today's secondary market. $35-$50 MIP each.

Castalloy B Mack Fire Pumper Fire Truck. This HO-scale kit is currently being produced, and while it's a nightmare to build, the finished product is worth the effort. The kit is a re-issue that originally sold in the 1950s. Value, $25 MIP.

Hubley Kiddie Toy Arhens Fox Pumper Fire Truck and Kiddie Toy Ladder Fire truck from 1940. Value range, $75-150 MIP each.

Ladder Fire Truck and Pumper Fire Truck, 1940. These two trucks were produced before and after World War II and are a larger scale than the Kiddie Toys. Most pre-war trucks (like models made by Tootsietoy) were issued with white rubber tires. Value range, $75-$150 MIP each.

Midgetoy American LaFrance Pumper Fire Truck, 1950s. The fender skirts on this model give the toy a very aerodynamic look. Value range, $30-$45 MIP.

This Britains Land Rover, released in 1978, was a popular 1:32-scale model for the company, available as a single vehicle, or as part of a set with a horse trailer. $25 MIP.

Solido is a French company well-known for their military die-cast vehicles. This Sherman tank was issued in 1984 as part of a 40th Anniversary of D-Day series. It included a set of decals, and is valued at $25 MIP.

Another military offering by Solido—a German Tiger tank, also part of the 40th Anniversary of D-Day series. It too, included a set of decals, and is valued at $25 MIP. One reason the prices haven't appreciated dramatically on these tanks is that the casting is still in use by Solido. Still, these are nice, big die-cast vehicles with moving metal treads and a rotating turret.

The Italian company, Bburago makes highly detailed models in 1:24 and 1:18-scale. This 1:24-scale Jaguar retails for about $7 MIP.

Britains produced this Mercedes-Benz Unimog from the late 1970s to the early 1980s. Currently, they are valued at about $20 MIP.

Greyhound Scenicruiser (#769), from the 1950s. This bus was a popular model and available in a variety of paint schemes. Value range, $55-$85 MIP.

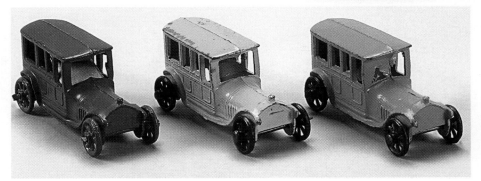

This set of three limousines, (#4528), represent just some of the colors available when the toy was released in 1911. Despite it's antiquity, it's still quite affordable to collectors at about $40 in mint condition.

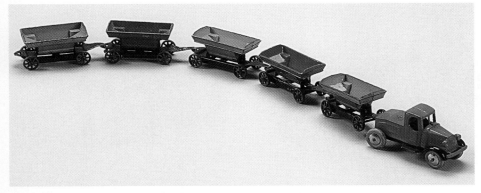

The Contractor Set, (#191), was produced from 1933 to 1941. Although only three tipping trailers were included with the original 1:43-scale set, additional models could be purchased separately. $325 MIP.

A Graham 5-wheel coupe, (#514). A convertible model by way of its painted roof, the Graham series is an elegant, well-constructed set of toys. $160 MIP.

The Tootsietoy Dairy Mack truck and trailer set. This set originally included three trailers, though more could be purchased separately. It makes an impressive display. $175 MIP.

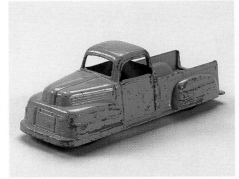

The 1949 model Ford F1 Pickup was produced by Tootsietoy from 1949 to 1960. $25 MIP.

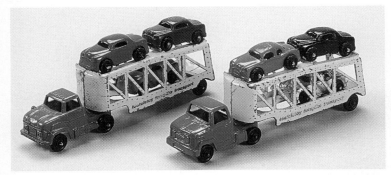

Two versions of the Auto Transport from 1970. These models were once common, but finding an intact toy without much playwear is difficult. Two cab styles were on the market, a Ford or Chevy. Of the two, the Ford seems harder to find, although the difference in price is only a few dollars. Ford model, $32 MIP. Chevy model, $25 MIP.

Two versions of the Wrigley's Gum Railway Express Truck, (#810). The earlier model on the right has a two-piece cab, while the later edition on the left had a simplified one-piece casting. Two-piece version, $175 MIP. One-piece version, $160 MIP.

A Graham Coupe from the "Bild-A-Car" set that featured interchangeable body styles. A set is valued at $130 MIP.

These Oil Tankers, (#253), reflect changes in prewar and postwar models: The model on the left is a prewar version with white tires and a silver-painted tank. After the war, the same vehicles featured black tires and no trim. Either is valued at about $25 MIP.

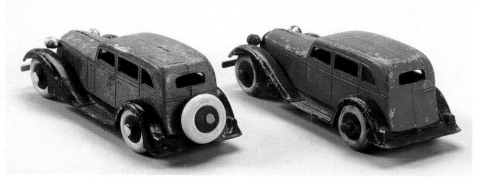

Two Grahams Sedans—a five-wheel and a four-wheel model. Note the white tires often seen on pre-war Tootsietoys. Five-wheel model, $150 MIP. Four-wheel Bild-A-Car Version, $130 MIP for set.

The Tootsietoy Ford Falcon was produced in 1960 to 1961. About $15 MIP.

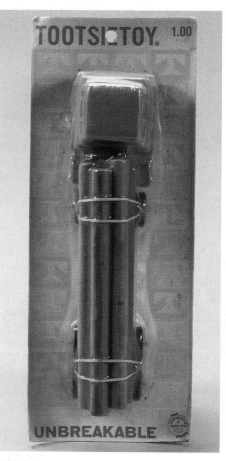

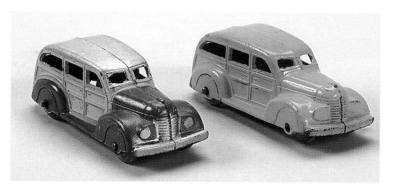

Two versions of the '38 Ford Woody Station Wagon—one, a prewar version with painted wood paneling, and silver grille and roof, and the other in a simple orange finish. About $40 MIP each.

This Chevy Semi-Truck Logger is a rare find, especially in this condition. The mint model is about $130, the mint-in-pack model—about $250.

❑ **'50 Ford F-1: Hermosa Beach Bums 3,** 2000, Deep green-blue body, peace symbol on opening hood, "Hermosa Beach Bums" on doors and hood, silver five-spoke wheels, silver base, two surfboards in truck bed, silver painted grille. Like others in the series, this model comes with a photo card of early '60s snapshots by LeRoy Grannis, 1:64 scale
EX n/a   NM n/a   MIP $4

❑ **'54 Chevy Panel Truck: Waimea Mamas,** 2000, Light purple and green, 1:64 scale
EX n/a   NM n/a   MIP $4

(KP Photo)

❑ **'55 Chevy Cameo Truck: Wave Rockers,** 2002, Starlight black body with pink and white "Wave Rockers" on sides with musical notes, red interior, two surfboards on covered truck bed, opening hood, five-spoke chrome wheels, hard tires, 1:64 scale
EX n/a   NM n/a   MIP $4

(KP Photo)

❑ **'55 Chevy Nomad: County Line Zulus,** 2001, Light and dark blue body with yellow and pink jagged edge design, mask graphics on hood and sides, light green opening hood, "County Line Zulus" on sides and hood, surfboards on roof, gray interior, hard tires, silver chrome five spoke wheels, photo card, 1:64 scale, Model No. 242
EX n/a   NM n/a   MIP $4

(KP Photo)

❑ **'56 Chevy Convertible: South Bay Bandits,** 2001, Red body with gray and black swoop on sides, "South Bay Bandits" in white lettering on sides, hood and trunk, clear windshield, gray interior, two surfboards propped in back seat, hard tires, silver chrome five spoke wheels, photo card, 1:64 scale, Model No. 240
EX n/a   NM n/a   MIP $4

❑ **'57 Chevy Bel Air Convertible,** 2002, Primer red body, hard tires, 1:64 scale
EX n/a   NM n/a   MIP $4

❑ **'59 El Camino: Redondo Gonzos,** 2000, Light purple with white roof, opening hood, "Redondo Gonzos" on hood and sides, chrome rims, silver painted grille, surfboards on back, 1:64 scale
EX n/a   NM n/a   MIP $5

(KP Photo)

❑ **'60s Studebaker Truck: Lava Mamas,** 2002, Flat black, hard tires, surfboards in back, opening hood. Tires in front slightly smaller than rear wheels and tires, 1:64 scale
EX n/a   NM n/a   MIP $4

❑ **'60s VW Thing,** 2002, Snow white body, open top, surfboards, hard tires, 1:64 scale
EX n/a   NM n/a   MIP $4

❑ **'60's VW Van: Huntington Hunnies,** 2000, Orange and blue van with surfer girl silhouette graphics, surfboards on roof, silver wheels, hard tires, 1:64 scale
EX n/a   NM n/a   MIP $7

❑ **'63 Pontiac Tempest,** 2002, Light blue body, hard tires, 1:64 scale
EX n/a   NM n/a   MIP $4

(KP Photo)

❑ **'64 1/2 Mustang: Bikini Beach,** 2001, Pink body with "Bikini Beach" and surfer girl silhouette on sides and opening hood, two surfboards balanced in back seat, hard tires, silver chrome five spoke wheels, photo card, 1:64 scale, Model No. 653
EX n/a   NM n/a   MIP $4

(KP Photo)

❑ **'65 Shelby Cobra: Beach Queens,** 2001, Black with wide yellow stripe, "Beach Queens" with female body silhouette and crown graphics on sides, hard tires, five-spoke chrome wheels, surf boards balanced in front seat, "ROYLT" on license plate, photo card, 1:64 scale, Model No. 426
EX n/a   NM n/a   MIP $4

❑ **'70 Dodge Dart Custom,** 2002, Pale orange body, hard tires, 1:64 scale
EX n/a   NM n/a   MIP $4

(KP Photo)

JOHNNY LIGHTNING / PLAYING MANTIS

❑ **Bad News: Coast Busters,** 2000, Turquoise and black with hot pink stripe along side, "Coast Busters" in pink type on panel section and hood, two surfboards on roof, silver painted grille, chrome six-spoke wheels, red painted taillights, 1:64 scale
EX n/a   **NM** n/a   **MIP** $4

❑ **Bahama Mamas,** 2000, White and lavender body, hard tires, 1:64 scale
EX n/a   **NM** n/a   **MIP** $4

❑ **Banzai Babes,** 2000, White with red stripes along body of car, smaller wheels in front (but not as thin as the "Boys" version), photo card included, 1:64 scale
EX n/a   **NM** n/a   **MIP** $4

❑ **Banzai Boys,** 2000, White with red stripes along body of car, thin spoked wheels in front, fat tires in back, photo card included, 1:64 scale
EX n/a   **NM** n/a   **MIP** $4

❑ **Big Kahunas,** 2000, White and light blue body, hard tires, 1:64 scale
EX n/a   **NM** n/a   **MIP** $4

❑ **Dan Fink Speedwagon,** 2000, Light blue-green woody with black roof, silver rims, hard tires, surfboards on roof, 1:64 scale
EX n/a   **NM** n/a   **MIP** $4

❑ **Emperor: Malibu Babes,** 2000, Red and white, 1:64 scale
EX n/a   **NM** n/a   **MIP** $4

❑ **Haulin' Hearse: Santa Monica Maniacs,** 2000, White and yellow, 1:64 scale
EX n/a   **NM** n/a   **MIP** $4

❑ **Meat Wagon: Cowabunga Boyz,** 2000, White with black spotted Holstein motif, "Cowabunga Boys" in black and white type along sides, 1:64 scale
EX n/a   **NM** n/a   **MIP** $5

❑ **Palos Verde Vixens,** 2000, Salmon pink body, hard tires, 1:64 scale
EX n/a   **NM** n/a   **MIP** $4

❑ **Rumblur: The Hang 10 Men,** 2000, Red body with peace symbol on hood, "The Hang 10 Men" on sides, silver chrome rims, white roof with surfboards, 1:64 scale
EX n/a   **NM** n/a   **MIP** $4

(KP Photo)

❑ **Surf Daddies,** 2000, Green and metallic yellow Cadillac wagon body with "Surf Daddies" on hood and sides, surfboards on roof, chrome rims, 1:64 scale
EX n/a   **NM** n/a   **MIP** $5

(KP Photo)

❑ **T-Bucket: 6-Foot Swells,** 2001, Medium green body with cream plastic interior, blue and white and blue and orange surfboards tucked in seats, "6 Foot Swells" in white type on sides and back tailgate, chrome plastic engine, black fan belts, black grille, hard tires, silver-chrome five spoke wheels, photo card, 1:64 scale, Model No. 562
EX n/a   **NM** n/a   **MIP** $4

TEAM LIGHTNING

(KP Photo)

❑ **Alfred Hitchcock's "Vertigo",** 2000, White "Meat Wagon" casting with Alfred Hitchcock's "Vertigo" design in oval on red and white body, silver five-spoke wheels, 1:64 scale
EX n/a   **NM** n/a   **MIP** $5

❑ **Bad Medicine,** Bela Lugosi's Dracula, 1:64 scale
EX n/a   **NM** n/a   **MIP** $5

(KP Photo)

❑ **Black Beauty, Frankenstude,** 2000, Dark green body with "The Green Hornet" lettering and graphics on hood and sides, 1:64 scale
EX n/a   **NM** n/a   **MIP** $5

❑ **Bugaboo,** Bozo the Clown, 1:64 scale
EX n/a   **NM** n/a   **MIP** $5

❑ **Count Chocula Pro Street,**
EX n/a   **NM** n/a   **MIP** $3

❑ **Crash Bandicoot Viper,** 2000, Light green body with "Crash Bandicoot" ovals on hood, roof and sides. Illustrations of Crash on hood and sides, yellow rims, 1:64 scale
EX n/a   **NM** n/a   **MIP** $5

❑ **Dodge Ram,** Blow Pops, 1:64 scale
EX n/a   **NM** n/a   **MIP** $5

❑ **Munsters '29 Crew Cab,** 2000, Gray and red body with "The Munters" on sides, 1:64 scale
EX n/a   **NM** n/a   **MIP** $5

❑ **Three Stooges Flathead Fly,** 2000, Green and gray body with Larry Fine photo image on hood and sides, 1:64 scale
EX n/a   **NM** n/a   **MIP** $5

❑ **Willys,** 3 Stooges Moe, 1:64 scale
EX n/a   **NM** n/a   **MIP** $5

THUNDER WAGONS

❑ **'33 Ford Delivery,** 2002, 1:64 scale
EX n/a   **NM** n/a   **MIP** $4

❑ **'50s Custom Rambler Wagon,** 2001, Cameo white side tampos, five spoke chrome wheels, hard tires, 1:64 scale
EX n/a   **NM** n/a   **MIP** $4

❑ **'50s Custom Rambler Wagon,** 2002, Blue, white and red body, chrome rims, hard tires, 1:64 scale
EX n/a   NM n/a   MIP $4

❑ **'50s Custom Rambler Wagon,** 2002, Metallic orange body, white roof, hard tires, chrome wheels, 1:64 scale, Model No. 554
EX n/a   NM n/a   MIP $4

❑ **'54 Corvette Nomad,** 2001, Blue Fire body, white roof, chrome five-spoke wheels, hard tires, 1:64 scale
EX n/a   NM n/a   MIP $4

❑ **'54 Corvette Nomad,** 2002, White body with red stripes, chrome rims, hard tires, 1:64 scale
EX n/a   NM n/a   MIP $4

❑ **'54 Corvette Nomad,** 2002, Gold Rush body, white roof, silver painted trim, hard tires, chrome rims, 1:64 scale, Model No. 171
EX n/a   NM n/a   MIP $4

❑ **'55 Nomad,** 2001, Starlight black with flame tampos on sides, chrome five spoke wheels, hard tires, opening hood, 1:64 scale
EX n/a   NM n/a   MIP $4

❑ **'55 Nomad,** 2002, Cobalt blue with flame tampos, hard tires, chrome rims, 1:64 scale, Model No. 242
EX n/a   NM n/a   MIP $4

❑ **'55 Nomad,** 2002, Red scallop over tan/yellow body, chrome rims, 1:64 scale
EX n/a   NM n/a   MIP $4

❑ **'56 Nomad,** 2001, Light green body, five spoke chrome wheels, hard tires, opening hood, 1:64 scale
EX n/a   NM n/a   MIP $4

❑ **'56 Nomad,** 2002, Calypso coral red with yellow flame tampos, hard tires, chrome rims, 1:64 scale, Model No. 243
EX n/a   NM n/a   MIP $4

❑ **'56 Nomad,** 2002, 1:64 scale
EX n/a   NM n/a   MIP $4

(KP Photo)

❑ **'57 Nomad,** 2001, Maverick red body with silver painted trim, chrome five spoke wheels, opening hood, hard tires, 1:64 scale
EX n/a   NM n/a   MIP $4

❑ **'57 Nomad,** 2002, 1:64 scale
EX n/a   NM n/a   MIP $4

❑ **'57 Nomad,** 2002, Starlight black with flame tampos on sides, silver painted trim, chrome five spoke wheels, hard tires, chrome rims, 1:64 scale, Model No. 244
EX n/a   NM n/a   MIP $4

❑ **'60s Custom Chevy Wagon,** 2001, Gold Rush body, black roof, hard tires, chrome five-spoke wheels, 1:64 scale
EX n/a   NM n/a   MIP $4

❑ **'60s Custom Chevy Wagon,** 2002, Cameo white body with black roof, hard tires, chrome rims, 1:64 scale, Model No. 302
EX n/a   NM n/a   MIP $4

THUNDERBIRDS

❑ **'56 Ford Thunderbird Roadster,** 2002, Starlight black, hard tires, chrome rims, 1:64 scale, Model No. 290
EX n/a   NM n/a   MIP $4

❑ **'56 Roadster,** 2002, Fiesta red body, chrome rims, 1:64 scale
EX n/a   NM n/a   MIP $4

❑ **'58 Thunderbird,** 2002, Roman red, hard tires, chrome rims, 1:64 scale, Model No. 295
EX n/a   NM n/a   MIP $4

❑ **'59 Thunderbird,** 2002, Cascade green, hard tires, chrome rims, 1:64 scale, Model No. 295
EX n/a   NM n/a   MIP $4

❑ **'60 Hardtop,** 2002, Indian turquoise body, silver chrome rims, 1:64 scale
EX n/a   NM n/a   MIP $4

❑ **'61 Roadster,** 2002, Dark blue metallic body, silver chrome rims, 1:64 scale
EX n/a   NM n/a   MIP $4

❑ **'61 Thunderbird Convertible,** 2002, Charcoal, hard tires, chrome rims, 1:64 scale, Model No. 292
EX n/a   NM n/a   MIP $4

❑ **'62 Sports Roadster,** 2002, Yellow body, silver chrome rims, 1:64 scale
EX n/a   NM n/a   MIP $4

❑ **'67 Hardtop,** 2002, White body, silver chrome rims, opening hood, 1:64 scale
EX n/a   NM n/a   MIP $4

(KP Photo)

❑ **'67 Thunderbird,** 2002, Glacier blue body, hard tires, chrome five-spoke wheels, black and silver grille, opening hood, dark blue interior, 1:64 scale, Model No. 291
EX n/a   NM n/a   MIP $4

❑ **'68 Hardtop,** 2002, Lime gold body, chrome rims, 1:64 scale
EX n/a   NM n/a   MIP $4

❑ **'68 Thunderbird,** 2002, Lime gold, hard tires, chrome rims, opening hood, 1:64 scale, Model No. 291
EX n/a   NM n/a   MIP $4

TOP FUEL

❑ **'60s Front Engine Top Fuel,** Ramchargers
EX n/a   NM n/a   MIP $3

❑ **'60s Front Engine Top Fuel,** Tommy Ivo
EX n/a   NM n/a   MIP $3

❑ **'60s Front Engine Top Fuel,** Hawaiian
EX n/a   NM n/a   MIP $3

❑ **'60s Front Engine Top Fuel,** Tony Nancy
EX n/a   NM n/a   MIP $5

❑ **'60s Front Engine Top Fuel,** Soapy Sales
EX n/a   NM n/a   MIP $3

❑ **'60s Front Engine Top Fuel,** John Wiebe
EX n/a   NM n/a   MIP $3

❑ **'60s Front Engine Top Fuel,** BB & Mulligan
EX n/a   NM n/a   MIP $3

❑ **'60s Front Engine Top Fuel,** Steve Carbone '71 Dragster
EX n/a   NM n/a   MIP $3

❑ **'60s Front Engine Top Fuel,** Creitz and Donovan
EX n/a   NM n/a   MIP $3

❏ **'60s Front Engine Top Fuel,** Garlits Swamp Rat X
EX n/a   NM n/a   MIP $3

❏ **'60s Front Engine Top Fuel,** Jerry Ruth Dragster
EX n/a   NM n/a   MIP $3

❏ **'70s Rear Engine Car,** Don Garlits "Swamp Rat 19"
EX n/a   NM n/a   MIP $3

❏ **'70s Rear Engine Car,** Jeb Allen "Praying Mantis"
EX n/a   NM n/a   MIP $3

❏ **'70s Rear Engine Car,** Warren Coburn and Miller "Rain For Rent"
EX n/a   NM n/a   MIP $5

❏ **'70s Rear Engine Car,** Tommy Ivo Rod Shop
EX n/a   NM n/a   MIP $3

❏ **'70s Rear Engine Car,** Walton Cerny & Moody
EX n/a   NM n/a   MIP $3

❏ **'70s Rear Engine Car,** Don Garlits
EX n/a   NM n/a   MIP $3

❏ **'70s Rear Engine Car,** Jungle Jim
EX n/a   NM n/a   MIP $3

❏ **'70s Rear Engine Car,** Don Garlits Swamp Rat 24
EX n/a   NM n/a   MIP $3

❏ **'70s Rear Engine Car,** Diamond Jim Annin
EX n/a   NM n/a   MIP $3

❏ **'70s Rear Engine Car,** Benny Osborne
EX n/a   NM n/a   MIP $3

❏ **'70s Rear Engine Car,** Jade Grenade
EX n/a   NM n/a   MIP $3

❏ **'70s Rear Engine Car,** Keeling and Clayton California Charger
EX n/a   NM n/a   MIP $3

TRI-CHEVY

❏ **'55 Chevy Bel Air Convertible,** 2001, Nassau blue body with white trunk and interior, rubber tires, chrome rims, photo card, 1:64 scale
EX n/a   NM n/a   MIP $4

❏ **'55 Chevy Bel Air Convertible,** 2001, Black body with plastic light tan top, rubber tires, chrome rims, 1:64 scale
EX n/a   NM n/a   MIP $4

❏ **'55 Chevy Bel Air Convertible,** 2001, Matador red body, light tan plastic roof, opening hood, chrome rims, rubber tires, photo card, 1:64 scale
EX n/a   NM n/a   MIP $4

❏ **'55 Chevy Bel Air Convertible,** 2001, Matador red, real wheels, chrome rims, 1:64 scale, Model No. 239
EX n/a   NM n/a   MIP $4

(KP Photo)

❏ **'55 Chevy Nomad,** 2000, Skyline blue body, white roof, silver painted bumpers, headlights and grille, white plastic interior, silver engine, opening hood, whitewall rubber tires, chrome rims, photo card, 1:64 scale, Model No. 242
EX n/a   NM n/a   MIP $4

❏ **'55 Chevy Nomad,** 2001, Red body, white roof, opening hood, gold and silver painted grille, rubber tires, chrome rims, 1:64 scale, Model No. 242
EX n/a   NM n/a   MIP $4

❏ **'55 Chevy Nomad,** 2001, Shadow gray body, silver painted grille, rubber tires, 1:64 scale, Model No. 242
EX n/a   NM n/a   MIP $4

❏ **'55 Chevy Nomad,** 2001, Starlight black, chrome wheels, rubber tires, opening hood, photo card, 1:64 scale, Model No. 242
EX n/a   NM n/a   MIP $5

❏ **'56 Chevy Bel Air Convertible,** 2001, Bronze and yellow body, tan roof, opening hood, chrome rims, rubber tires, photo card, 1:64 scale, Model No. 240
EX n/a   NM n/a   MIP $4

❏ **'56 Chevy Bel Air Convertible,** 2001, Light purple-blue and white body, light blue interior, blue cover over spare, rubber tires, chrome rims, 1:64 scale
EX n/a   NM n/a   MIP $4

❏ **'56 Chevy Bel Air Convertible,** 2001, Blue body, white interior, opening hood, rubber tires, chrome rims, photo card, 1:64 scale
EX n/a   NM n/a   MIP $4

❏ **'56 Chevy Bel Air Convertible,** 2001, Forest green and white body, mint green interior, chrome rims, rubber tires, photo card, 1:64 scale
EX n/a   NM n/a   MIP $4

❏ **'56 Chevy Nomad,** 2000, Moonglow silver, real wheels, chrome rims, 1:64 scale, Model No. 243
EX n/a   NM n/a   MIP $4

❏ **'56 Chevy Nomad,** 2001, Skyline blue body, rubber tires, chrome rims, opening hood, photo card, 1:64 scale
EX n/a   NM n/a   MIP $4

❏ **'56 Chevy Nomad,** 2001, Dark gold and yellow body, chrome wheels, rubber tires, photo card, 1:64 scale
EX n/a   NM n/a   MIP $4

❏ **'56 Chevy Nomad,** 2001, Yellow body with black trim, rubber tires, chrome rims, opening hood, 1:64 scale
EX n/a   NM n/a   MIP $4

❏ **'57 Chevy Bel Air,** 2001, Starlight black body, rubber tires, chrome rims, red interior, photo card, 1:64 scale
EX n/a   NM n/a   MIP $5

(KP Photo)

❏ **'57 Chevy Bel Air,** 2001, Royal blue body, white roof and trim, white plastic interior, chrome rims with rubber tires, gold and silver painted grille, gold "Bel-Air" lettering on tailfin, cast, non-opening hood, 1:64 scale
EX n/a   NM n/a   MIP $4

❏ **'57 Chevy Bel Air Convertible,** 2000, Highland green, real wheels, chrome rims, 1:64 scale, Model No. 241
EX n/a   NM n/a   MIP $4

❑ **'57 Chevy Bel Air Convertible,** 2001, Evening orchid body, tan roof, rubber tires, chrome rims, photo card, 1:64 scale
EX n/a   NM n/a   MIP $4

❑ **'57 Chevy Nomad,** 2000, Flat black, real wheels, chrome rims, 1:64 scale, Model No. 244
EX n/a   NM n/a   MIP $4

❑ **'57 Chevy Nomad,** 2001, Red body, red interior, white trim, opening hood, rubber tires, chrome rims, 1:64 scale
EX n/a   NM n/a   MIP $4

❑ **'57 Chevy Nomad,** 2001, Larkspur blue body, white roof, white trim, silver and gold painted grille, opening hood, rubber tires, 1:64 scale
EX n/a   NM n/a   MIP $4

❑ **'57 Chevy Nomad,** 2001, Sierra gold body, white roof, opening hood, chrome wheels, rubber tires, photo card, 1:64 scale
EX n/a   NM n/a   MIP $4

TRUCKIN' AMERICA

❑ **'29 Ford**
EX n/a   NM n/a   MIP $6

❑ **'29 Ford** White Lightnings edition
EX n/a   NM n/a   MIP $20

❑ **'40 Ford**
EX n/a   NM n/a   MIP $4

❑ **'40 Ford,** White Lightnings edition
EX n/a   NM n/a   MIP $20

❑ **'50 Ford F-1**
EX n/a   NM n/a   MIP $4

❑ **'50 Ford F-1** White Lightnings edition
EX n/a   NM n/a   MIP $20

❑ **'55 Chevy Cameo**
EX n/a   NM n/a   MIP $4

❑ **'55 Chevy Cameo,** White Lightnings edition
EX n/a   NM n/a   MIP $20

❑ **'59 El Camino**
EX n/a   NM n/a   MIP $4

❑ **'59 El Camino,** White Lightnings edition
EX n/a   NM n/a   MIP $20

(KP Photo)

❑ **'60's Studebaker,** 1998, Pearl white body, white camper top, gray interior, "White Lightning" on rubber tires, opening hood, silver painted grille and headlights, metal base with series number, 1:64 scale
EX n/a   NM n/a   MIP $20

(KP Photo)

❑ **'60's Studebaker,** 1998, White body, white plastic interior and camper top, "White Lightning" on rubber tires, opening hood, silver painted grille and headlights, metal base with series number, 1:64 scale
EX n/a   NM n/a   MIP $20

(KP Photo)

❑ **'60's Studebaker Champ,** 1998, Blue or orange, black or whitewall tires, white plastic camper top, 1:64 scale
EX n/a   NM n/a   MIP $6

❑ **'71 El Camino**
EX n/a   NM n/a   MIP $4

❑ **'71 El Camino,** White Lightnings edition
EX n/a   NM n/a   MIP $20

❑ **'78 Li'l Red Express**
EX n/a   NM n/a   MIP $6

❑ **'78 Li'l Red Express,** White Lightnings edition
EX n/a   NM n/a   MIP $20

❑ **'91 GMC Syclone**
EX n/a   NM n/a   MIP $7

❑ **'91 GMC Syclone,** White Lightnings edition
EX n/a   NM n/a   MIP $20

❑ **'96 Dodge Ram**
EX n/a   NM n/a   MIP $4

❑ **'96 Dodge Ram,** White Lightnings edition
EX n/a   NM n/a   MIP $20

TRUCKS—KISS ALBUM

❑ **'29 Ford,** KISS The Original Album
EX n/a   NM n/a   MIP $6

❑ **'40 Ford,** KISS Destroyer
EX n/a   NM n/a   MIP $6

❑ **'59 El Camino,** KISS Love Gun
EX n/a   NM n/a   MIP $6

❑ **'71 El Camino,** KISS Unmasked
EX n/a   NM n/a   MIP $6

❑ **'78 Li'l Red Express,** KISS Dressed to Kill
EX n/a   NM n/a   MIP $6

❑ **'91 GMC Syclone,** KISS Dynasty
EX n/a   NM n/a   MIP $6

TRUE GRIT

❑ **Basic Step Van,** 2000, Tootsie Roll
EX n/a   NM n/a   MIP $3

❑ **Basic Step Van,** 2000, Rice Krispies
EX n/a   NM n/a   MIP $3

❑ **Basic Step Van,** 2000, Mooneyes
EX n/a   NM n/a   MIP $3

(KP Photo)

❏ **Chevrolet Delivery Van,** 2000, Dots: yellow body with silver plastic rims, rubber tires, silver and black painted grille, and "DOTS" graphics on sides and front, 1:64 scale
EX n/a   NM n/a   MIP $3

❏ **Utility Van,** 2000, Alvin and the Chipmunks
EX n/a   NM n/a   MIP $3

UNITED STATES POSTAL SERVICE: TRUCK & STAMP COLLECTION

❏ **'29 Ford Model A,** 1999, White with black base, exposed silver chrome engine, rubber tires, 1:64 scale
EX n/a   NM n/a   MIP $5

❏ **'29 Ford Model A,** 1999, Metallic gold body with black base, exposed engine, rubber "Goodyear" tires, stamp in truck bed, 1:64 scale
EX n/a   NM n/a   MIP $5

❏ **'40 Ford F1 Pickup,** 1999, Metallic gold with black base, opening hood, "Special Delivery" in blue type on doors, gold chrome wheels, rubber "Goodyear" tires, silver-painted headlights, stamp in bed, 1:64 scale
EX n/a   NM n/a   MIP $5

(KP Photo)

❏ **'40 Ford F1 Pickup,** 1999, White with black base, opening hood, "Special Delivery" in blue type on doors, black interior, chrome wheels, rubber "Goodyear" tires, silver-painted headlights, stamp in bed. (Model pictured is part of the "Dramatic Dinosaurs" series), 1:64 scale
EX n/a   NM n/a   MIP $5

❏ **'50 Ford F1 Pickup,** 1999, White with black base, opening hood, black interior, chrome wheels, rubber tires, silver-painted headlights, stamp in bed, 1:64 scale
EX n/a   NM n/a   MIP $5

❏ **'50 Ford F1 Pickup,** 1999, Metallic gold with black base, black interior, gold chrome wheels, rubber tires, silver-painted headlights, American flag graphics on doors, stamp in bed, 1:64 scale
EX n/a   NM n/a   MIP $5

❏ **'55 Chevy Cameo Pickup,** 1999, Metallic gold body with black base, opening hood, rubber tires, stamp in bed, 1:64 scale
EX n/a   NM n/a   MIP $5

❏ **'55 Chevy Cameo Pickup,** 1999, White with black base, opening hood, rubber tires, stamp in bed, 1:64 scale
EX n/a   NM n/a   MIP $5

❏ **'59 El Camino,** 1999, White with black base, opening hood, rubber tires, stamp in bed, 1:64 scale
EX n/a   NM n/a   MIP $5

(KP Photo)

❏ **'59 El Camino,** 1999, Metallic gold with black base, opening hood, rubber tires, stamp in bed, 1:64 scale
EX n/a   NM n/a   MIP $5

❏ **'60s Studebaker Champ,** 1999, Metallic with black base, opening hood, rubber "Goodyear" tires, silver painted grille and headlights, "Special Delivery" in blue type behind doors, black interior, stamp in truck bed, 1:64 scale
EX n/a   NM n/a   MIP $5

(KP Photo)

❏ **'60s Studebaker Champ,** 1999, White with black base, opening hood, rubber "Goodyear" tires, silver painted grille and headlights, "Special Delivery" in blue type behind doors, black interior, stamp in truck bed from the "Pre-historic Animals" series, 1:64 scale
EX n/a   NM n/a   MIP $5

❏ **'71 El Camino,** 1999, Metallic gold with black base, American flag graphics on sides, opening hood, gold chrome wheels, rubber tires, stamp in truck bed, 1:64 scale
EX n/a   NM n/a   MIP $5

❏ **'71 El Camino,** 1999, White with black base, opening hood, silver chrome wheels, rubber tires, stamp in truck bed. Within the series, there are five stamp variations: Prehistoric Animals, Space Fantasy, Dramatic Dinosaurs, Space Discovery, Riverboats and Endangered Species, 1:64 scale
EX n/a   NM n/a   MIP $5

❏ **'78 Li'l Red Express,** 1999, Metallic gold with gold chrome wheels, rubber tires, painted wood truck bed, American flags on doors, "Special Delivery", 1:64 scale
EX n/a   NM n/a   MIP $5

❏ **'78 Li'l Red Express,** 1999, White with silver chrome wheels, rubber tires, painted wood truck bed, American flags on doors, "Special Delivery", 1:64 scale
EX n/a   NM n/a   MIP $5

❏ **'91 GMC Syclone,** 1999, White with silver chrome wheels, American flag graphics on sides, rubber tires, stamp in truck bed, 1:64 scale
EX n/a   NM n/a   MIP $5

❏ **'91 GMC Syclone,** 1999, Metallic gold with gold chrome wheels, American flag graphics on sides, rubber tires, stamp in truck bed, 1:64 scale
EX n/a   NM n/a   MIP $5

❏ **'96 Dodge Ram,** 1999, Metallic gold with gold chrome wheels, rubber tires, stamp in truck bed, 1:64 scale
EX n/a   NM n/a   MIP $5

❏ **'96 Dodge Ram,** 1999, White with silver chrome wheels, rubber tires, stamp in truck bed, 1:64 scale
EX n/a   NM n/a   MIP $5

VETTE MAGAZINE

❏ **'54 Chevy Corvette,** 2001, Light yellow, rubber tires, 1:64 scale
EX n/a   NM n/a   MIP $4

❏ **'63 Chevy Corvette,** 2001, Roman red body, rubber tires, 1:64 scale
EX n/a   NM n/a   MIP $4

❏ **'66 Chevy Corvette Convertible,** 2001, Candyapple red body, rubber tires, 1:64 scale
EX n/a   NM n/a   MIP $4

❏ **'82 Chevy Corvette,** 2001, Silver beige, rubber tires, 1:64 scale
EX n/a   NM n/a   MIP $4

❏ **'93 Chevy Corvette,** 2001, Kodak yellow body, rubber tires, 1:64 scale
EX n/a   NM n/a   MIP $4

❏ **'98 Chevy Corvette,** 2001, Dark blue body, rubber tires, 1:64 scale
EX n/a   NM n/a   MIP $4

VIP

❏ **'00 Dodge Truck,** 2001, Otter blue, real wheels, 1:64 scale
EX n/a   NM n/a   MIP $4

❏ **'00 Dodge Viper,** 2001, Shelby red, real wheels, 1:64 scale
EX n/a   NM n/a   MIP $4

❏ **'00 Ford Mustang,** 2001, Daytona yellow, rubber tires, chrome rims, photo card, 1:64 scale, Model No. 235
EX n/a   NM n/a   MIP $4

❏ **'00 Ford Mustang,** 2001, Daytona yellow, real wheels, 1:64 scale
EX n/a   NM n/a   MIP $4

❏ **'00 Jaguar XK8,** 2001, Blue Fire, real wheels, 1:64 scale
EX n/a   NM n/a   MIP $4

❏ **'00 Jaguar XK8,** 2001, Blue Fire, rubber tires, chrome rims, photo card, 1:64 scale, Model No. 237
EX n/a   NM n/a   MIP $4

❏ **'00 Jaguar XK8 (Convertible),** 2001, Blue Fire, rubber tires, chrome rims, photo card, 1:64 scale, Model No. 237
EX n/a   NM n/a   MIP $4

❏ **'00 Mazda Miata**

❏ **'00 Mazda Miata,** 2001, Champagne, real wheels, 1:64 scale
EX n/a   NM n/a   MIP $4

❏ **'00 Miata,** 2001, Champagne body, rubber tires, chrome rims, photo card, 1:64 scale, Model No. 238
EX n/a   NM n/a   MIP $4

❏ **'00 Plymouth Prowler,** 2001, Moonglow silver, real wheels, 1:64 scale
EX n/a   NM n/a   MIP $4

❏ **'00 Prowler,** 2001, Moonglow silver, rubber tires, chrome rims, photo card, 1:64 scale, Model No. 162
EX n/a   NM n/a   MIP $4

❏ **'00 Viper,** 2001, Shelby red, rubber tires, chrome rims, photo card, 1:64 scale, Model No. 234
EX n/a   NM n/a   MIP $4

VOLKSWAGENS

❏ **'01 New Beetle,** 2002, White body, silver wheels, hard tires, photo card, 1:64 scale
EX n/a   NM n/a   MIP $5

❏ **'01 VW New Beetle,** 2002, Maize yellow body, hard wheels, chrome rims, photo card, 1:64 scale, Model No. 274
EX n/a   NM n/a   MIP $5

❏ **'65 21-Window Bus,** 2002, Aqua and white, photo card, 1:64 scale
EX n/a   NM n/a   MIP $5

❏ **'65 Beetle,** 2002, Tan body, silver wheels, hard tires, photo card, 1:64 scale
EX n/a   NM n/a   MIP $5

❏ **'65 Beetle,** 2002, Yellow body, silver wheels, hard tires, photo card, 1:64 scale
EX n/a   NM n/a   MIP $5

❏ **'65 Type 2 Pickup,** 2002, Orange body, silver wheels, hard tires, photo card, 1:64 scale
EX n/a   NM n/a   MIP $5

(KP Photo)

❏ **'65 VW 21 Window Samba Bus,** 2002, Dark red and white body, hard tires, five spoke chrome wheels, tan plastic roof canopy, black painted trim, silver-gray plastic interior, photo card, 1:64 scale, Model No. 276
EX n/a   NM n/a   MIP $5

❏ **'66 VW Beetle,** 2002, Adriatic blue, (dark blue) hard wheels, chrome rims, photo card, 1:64 scale, Model No. 273
EX n/a   NM n/a   MIP $5

(KP Photo)

❏ **'66 VW Beetle,** 2002, Toga white body, (two-tone white and light gray body) hard tires, chrome five-spoke wheels, white interior, silver painted trim, black running boards, photo card, 1:64 scale, Model No. 273
EX n/a   NM n/a   MIP $5

❏ **'66 VW Type 2 Pickup,** 2002, Velvet green, hard wheels, chrome rims, photo card, 1:64 scale, Model No. 277
EX n/a   NM n/a   MIP $5

(KP Photo)

❏ **'98 VW New Beetle,** 2002, Moonglow silver body, white-painted headlights, hard wheels, chrome rims, photo card, 1:64 scale, Model No. 274
EX n/a   NM n/a   MIP $5

❏ **'99 New Beetle Custom,** 2002, Black and red body, silver wheels, hard tires, photo card, 1:64 scale
EX n/a   NM n/a   MIP $5

WACKY WINNERS

❑ **Bad Medicine,**
EX n/a   NM n/a   MIP $4

(KP Photo, Angelo Van Bogart collection)

❑ **Bad News,** 1996, Medium blue, amber windows, five-spoke wheels, hard tires, 1:64 scale
EX n/a   NM n/a   MIP $6

❑ **Badman,**
EX n/a   NM n/a   MIP $7

❑ **Cherry Bomb,**
EX n/a   NM n/a   MIP $5

❑ **Draggin' Dragon,**
EX n/a   NM n/a   MIP $4

❑ **Garbage Truck,**
EX n/a   NM n/a   MIP $4

❑ **Root Beer Wagon,**
EX n/a   NM n/a   MIP $4

❑ **Tijuana Taxi,**
EX n/a   NM n/a   MIP $4

❑ **T'rantula,**
EX n/a   NM n/a   MIP $5

❑ **Trouble Maker,**
EX n/a   NM n/a   MIP $4

WILLYS GASSERS

❑ **'33 - All American Willys,** 2001, Snow white, hard tires, 1:64 scale
EX n/a   NM n/a   MIP $5

❑ **'33 - Hill Bros. Red Baron,** 2001, Candyapple red, hard tires, 1:64 scale
EX n/a   NM n/a   MIP $5

❑ **'33 - Nostalgia Racing Photos.,** 2001, Blue Fire, hard tires, 1:64 scale
EX n/a   NM n/a   MIP $5

❑ **'33 - Prock & Howell,** 2001, Honolulu blue, hard tires, 1:64 scale
EX n/a   NM n/a   MIP $5

❑ **'33 - Souza Bros.,** 2001, Red-orange, hard tires, 1:64 scale
EX n/a   NM n/a   MIP $5

❑ **'33 - Terry Langdon-Davies,** 2001, Reef blue, hard tires, 1:64 scale
EX n/a   NM n/a   MIP $5

(KP Photo)

❑ **'33 Willys - Bel Engine Services,** 2001, Kodak yellow with purple flames, hard tires, chrome rims, photo card, 1:64 scale, Model No. 156
EX n/a   NM n/a   MIP $5

❑ **'33 Willys - Bryson & Sons,** 2001, Red-orange, hard wheels, chrome rims, photo card, 1:64 scale, Model No. 156
EX n/a   NM n/a   MIP $5

❑ **'33 Willys - Wild Bill & Cody,** 2001, Moonglow silver, hard tires, chrome rims, photo card, 1:64 scale, Model No. 156
EX n/a   NM n/a   MIP $5

❑ **'40 - Terry Rose,** 2001, Twilight blue body, hard tires, 1:64 scale
EX n/a   NM n/a   MIP $5

❑ **'41 - Don Montgomery - Rockerhead,** 2001, Starlight black body, hard tires, 1:64 scale
EX n/a   NM n/a   MIP $5

❑ **'41 - J.C. & Mickey Hudgins,** 2001, Bright blue body, hard tires, 1:64 scale
EX n/a   NM n/a   MIP $5

❑ **'41 - Jr. Thompson,** 2001, Rally red, hard tires, 1:64 scale
EX n/a   NM n/a   MIP $5

❑ **'41 - Owen-Dahlin,** 2001, Snow white, hard tires, 1:64 scale
EX n/a   NM n/a   MIP $5

❑ **'41 - Roger Campbell,** 2001, Tor-red, hard tires, 1:64 scale
EX n/a   NM n/a   MIP $5

❑ **'41 Willys - Mary Ann Harmon,** 2001, Starlight black, hard wheels, chrome rims, photo card, 1:64 scale, Model No. 439
EX n/a   NM n/a   MIP $5

❑ **'41 Willys - Wee Willys,** 2001, Wineberry, hard wheels, chrome rims, photo card, 1:64 scale, Model No. 439
EX n/a   NM n/a   MIP $5

❑ **'41 Willys - Willy Fast,** 2001, Great Grape, hard wheels, chrome rims, photo card, 1:64 scale, Model No. 439
EX n/a   NM n/a   MIP $5

❑ **Bones, Dubach, Pisano,** 2002, Candyapple red body, hard tires, chrome rims, photo card, 1:64 scale, Model No. 156
EX n/a   NM n/a   MIP $5

❑ **Cooner Wire,** 2002, Candy Magenta body, hard tires, chrome rims, photo card, 1:64 scale, Model No. 439
EX n/a   NM n/a   MIP $5

❑ **Gary Wright,** 2002, Medium blue metallic, hard tires, chrome rims, photo card, 1:64 scale, Model No. 439
EX n/a   NM n/a   MIP $5

❑ **Hot Rod Willys,** 2002, Kodak yellow body, hard tires, chrome rims, photo card, 1:64 scale, Model No. 439
EX n/a   NM n/a   MIP $5

❑ **Malco - George Montgomery,** 2002, Malco blue body, hard tires, chrome rims, photo card, 1:64 scale, Model No. 156
EX n/a   NM n/a   MIP $5

❑ **Willie's Willys,** 2002, Shelby red body, hard tires, chrome rims, photo card, 1:64 scale, Model No. 156
EX n/a   NM n/a   MIP $5

WOODYS & PANELS

(KP Photo)

❑ **'31 Ford Woody,** 2002, Tan body, painted wood panels, flat black roof and running boards, black interior, chrome engine and wheels, black painted grille, 1:64 scale, Model No. 835
EX n/a   NM n/a   MIP $5

(KP Photo)

❏ **'33 Willys Panel Truck,** 2002, Pale light orange body, silver-painted trim, white-painted headlights, chrome wheels and engine, hard tires, white interior, 1:64 scale, Model No. 837
EX n/a   **NM** n/a   **MIP** $5

(KP Photo)

❏ **'50 Mercury Woody Station Wagon,** 2002, Metallic purple body, painted wood panel sides, chrome five-spoke wheels, hard tires, silver painted grille and headlights, 1:64 scale, Model No. 146
EX n/a   **NM** n/a   **MIP** $5

❏ **'50 Ford F-1,** 2002, Bermuda blue, real wheels, chrome rims, billboard, 1:64 scale
EX n/a   **NM** n/a   **MIP** $7

❏ **'53 Chevy Corvette,** 2001, Cameo white, real wheels, 1:64 scale
EX n/a   **NM** n/a   **MIP** $7

❏ **'61 Jaguar E-Type,** 2002, Glacier blue, real wheels, chrome rims, billboard, 1:64 scale
EX n/a   **NM** n/a   **MIP** $7

❏ **'67 Chevy Camaro RS/SS,** 2001, Snow white, real wheels, 1:64 scale
EX n/a   **NM** n/a   **MIP** $7

❏ **'93 Chevy Camaro Z28,** 2001, Snow white, real wheels, 1:64 scale
EX n/a   **NM** n/a   **MIP** $7

❏ **Firebird,** 2001, 1:64 scale
EX n/a   **NM** n/a   **MIP** $7

❏ **Mustang,** 2001, 1:64 scale
EX n/a   **NM** n/a   **MIP** $7

(KP Photo)

❏ **'40 Ford Panel Truck,** 2002, Bright blue body, flat black running boards, silver-painted grille and trim, white headlights. Highly detailed, 1:64 scale, Model No. 839
EX n/a   **NM** n/a   **MIP** $5

(KP Photo)

❏ **'55 Ford Panel Truck,** 2002, Bright red with yellow and white flames, black interior, flat black running boards, black and silver grille, white-painted headlights, chrome engine and wheels, hard tires. Very detailed, 1:64 scale, Model No. 838
EX n/a   **NM** n/a   **MIP** $5

YESTERDAY & TODAY

❏ **'00 Chevy Corvette Convertible,** 2001, Moonglow silver, real wheels, 1:64 scale
EX n/a   **NM** n/a   **MIP** $7

❏ **'01 Ford F-250 Super Duty Supercab,** 2002, Starlight black, real wheels, chrome rims, billboard, 1:64 scale
EX n/a   **NM** n/a   **MIP** $7

❏ **'01 Jaguar XK8 Roadster,** 2002, Emerald, real wheels, chrome rims, billboard, 1:64 scale
EX n/a   **NM** n/a   **MIP** $7

(KP Photo)

❏ **'41 Chevy Woody Wagon,** 2002, Metallic steel blue body, black interior, flat black roof, painted wood panel sides, five-spoke chrome wheels, hard tires, silver-painted grille and trim, white-painted headlights, 1:64 scale, Model No. 836
EX n/a   **NM** n/a   **MIP** $5

Kyosho Die-Cast

The detail on this 1:18-scale Morris Mini Cooper 1257S is great—opening hood, detailed engine, opening doors, realistic-looking interior and lights.

Known for remote-control cars and planes as much as detailed die-cast models, Kyosho is one of the preeminent companies producing high-end collectible vehicles.

Their lineup of 1:43-scale and 1:18-scale vehicles is impressive to say the least. Kyosho models possibly have more opening and removable features than vehicles by any other company out there. Even the interiors and trunks of many 1:18-scale cars are carpeted, and each vehicle has working steering.

MARKET UPDATE

Kyosho does retire their die-cast vehicles, so there really are limited-edition prices occurring in the aftermarket. Most 1:18-scale models retail for around $80, and any collector of Kyosho can attest to it being money well spent. If anything, it's hard to believe the level of detail you get for the price.

For fans of vintage American cars, Kyosho's 1:18-scale model of the 1948 Tucker Torpedo is hard to beat. This car has been produced by many die-cast manufacturers, but none have the detail that Kyosho features.

The Datsun 240Z '71 Safari No. 11 in 1:18-scale—a tough-looking model car.

Another rally car, the Lancia Stratos HF Rally No. 7 Safari '77.

Collectors of 1:43-scale cars have an extensive range to choose from. Here are two Jaguar E-Types offered by Kyosho.

Another example of detail: Kyosho's BMW X5 in 1:18-scale.

Two 1:43-scale Shelby Series 1 cars.

A classic sports car in 1:18-scale: the Triumph TR3-A.

Right in the driver's seat—front dash detail on the TR3-A.

(Kyosho Photo)

❏ **BMW Z8 Bond Car,** 2001, Silver-gray, with detailed black interior, side rockets, lift-off roof, opening doors, hood and trunk, 1:12 scale, Stock No. KYOV0007, Model No. 08601S

EX n/a **NM** n/a **MIP** $450

(Kyosho Photo)

❏ **BMW Z8 Bond Car,** 2001, This photo shows the side-mounted rockets on the Bond BMW, 1:12 scale, Stock No. KYOV0007, Model No. 08601S

(Kyosho Photo)

❏ **BMW Z8 Bond Car,** 2001, Extreme attention to detail on the piece all-around makes this an incredible model, 1:12 scale, Stock No. KYOV0007, Model No. 08601S

(Kyosho Photo)

❏ **Mazda Miata MX-5,** 2001, Red with gray spoked wheels, black interior, left-hand drive, opening hood and doors, 1:18 scale, Stock No. KYOV0105, Model No. 08051R

EX n/a **NM** n/a **MIP** $80

(Kyosho Photo)

❏ **Mazda Miata MX-5,** 2001, Yellow body with silver-gray wheels, opening hood and doors, charcoal and black interior, left-hand drive, 1:18 scale, Stock No. KYOV0400, Model No. 08051Y

EX n/a **NM** n/a **MIP** $80

(Kyosho Photo)

❏ **Mazda Miata MX-5,** 2001, Interior and dash detail, 1:18 scale, Stock No. KYOV0400, Model No. 08051Y

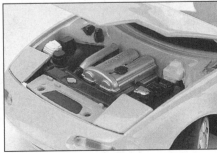

(Kyosho Photo)

❏ **Mazda Miata MX-5,** 2001, Opened hood and engine detail, 1:18 scale, Stock No. KYOV0400, Model No. 08051Y

(Kyosho Photo)

❏ **Mercedes-Benz 300SL,** 2001, Silver exterior, with opening gull-wing doors, opening hood, red interior. Even a "trunk" in the back, 1:18 scale, Stock No. KYOV0107, Model No. 08091S

EX n/a **NM** n/a **MIP** $80

(Kyosho Photo)

❏ **Mercedes-Benz 300SL,** 2001, Red exterior, with opening gull-wing doors, opening hood, red interior with trunk, 1:18 scale, Stock No. KYOV0108, Model No. 08091R

EX n/a **NM** n/a **MIP** $80

(Kyosho Photo)

❏ **Nissan 300ZX Turbo,** 2001, Red exterior, opening doors, highly-detailed black interior, opening hood, silver-gray wheels, 1:18 scale, Stock No. KYOV0109, Model No. 08071R

EX n/a **NM** n/a **MIP** $80

(Kyosho Photo)

❑ **Nissan 300ZX Turbo,** 2001, Yellow exterior, opening doors, highly-detailed black interior, opening hood, silver-gray wheels, left-hand drive, 1:18 scale, Stock No. KYOV0500, Model No. 08071Y
EX n/a **NM** n/a **MIP** $80

(Kyosho Photo)

❑ **Mini Cooper,** 2001, Green exterior, white roof with full sun-roof, white five-spoke wheels, opening hood, hatch and doors. Right-hand drive, 1:18 scale, Stock No. KYOV0143, Model No. 08553G
EX n/a **NM** n/a **MIP** $80

(Kyosho Photo)

❑ **Mini Cooper,** 2001, Red exterior, white roof with full sun-roof, white five-spoke wheels, opening hood, hatch and doors. Right-hand drive, 1:18 scale, Stock No. KYOV0144, Model No. 08553R
EX n/a **NM** n/a **MIP** $80

(Kyosho Photo)

❑ **Mini Cooper,** 2001, Detail showing opening hood and engine detail, 1:18 scale, Stock No. KYOV0144, Model No. 08553R

(Kyosho Photo)

❑ **Mini Cooper,** 2001, Sliding, full-length tinted sun roof, 1:18 scale, Stock No. KYOV0144, Model No. 08553R

(Kyosho Photo)

❑ **Mini Cooper,** 2001, Opening doors--great detail on dash and interior, 1:18 scale, Stock No. KYOV0144, Model No. 08553R

(Kyosho Photo)

❑ **Mini Cooper,** 2001, Opening rear hatch, 1:18 scale, Stock No. KYOV0144, Model No. 08553R

(Kyosho Photo)

❑ **Toyota Supra,** 2001, Black exterior and interior, gray five-spoke wheels, opening doors, trunk and hood, left-hand drive, 1:18 scale, Stock No. KYOV0120, Model No. 08061K
EX n/a **NM** n/a **MIP** $80

(Kyosho Photo)

❑ **Toyota Supra,** 2001, Detail showing opening hood and engine, 1:18 scale, Stock No. KYOV0120, Model No. 08061K

(Kyosho Photo)

❑ **Toyota Supra,** 2001, Red exterior, black interior, gray five-spoke wheels, opening doors, hood and trunk, 1:18 scale, Stock No. KYOV0121, Model No. 08061R
EX n/a **NM** n/a **MIP** $80

(Kyosho Photo)

❑ **Triumph TR3-A,** 2001, White exterior, red interior, right-hand driver, silver spoked wheels and trim, opening hood, doors and trunk, 1:18 scale, Stock No. KYOV0129, Model No. 08031W
EX n/a **NM** n/a **MIP** $80

(Kyosho Photo)

❏ **Triumph TR3-A,** 2001, Detail, showing opening features, 1:18 scale, Stock No. KYOV0129, Model No. 08031W

(Kyosho Photo)

❏ **Shelby Cobra 427S/C,** 2001, Red body with wide white stripes, silver and red spokes, black interior, opening doors, hood and trunk, 1:18 scale, Stock No. KYOV0133, Model No. 08043RW

EX n/a   **NM** n/a   **MIP** $80

(Kyosho Photo)

❏ **Shelby Cobra 427S/C,** 2001, Red body, black interior, white exhaust, chrome and red wheels, silver trim, opening doors, hood and trunk, 1:18 scale, Stock No. KYOV0600, Model No. 08040R

EX n/a   **NM** n/a   **MIP** $80

(Kyosho Photo)

❏ **Shelby Cobra 427S/C: Racing,** 2001, Blue body with white stripe and sponsor graphics, black interior, chrome, gold and black wheels, white exhaust, silver trim,

1:18 scale, Stock No. KYOV0602, Model No. 08041B

EX n/a   **NM** n/a   **MIP** $80

(Kyosho Photo)

❏ **Shelby Cobra 427S/C: Racing,** 2001, Detail of opening hood and engine, 1:18 scale, Stock No. KYOV0602, Model No. 08041B

(Kyosho Photo)

❏ **Shelby Cobra 427S/C: Racing,** 2001, Close-up of opening trunk, 1:18 scale, Stock No. KYOV0602, Model No. 08041B

(Kyosho Photo)

❏ **Shelby Cobra 427S/C: Racing,** 2001, Silver body with black interior, number "6" on doors and hood. Chrome and black wheels, opening hood, doors and trunk, 1:18 scale, Stock No. KYOV0134, Model No. 08041S

EX n/a   **NM** n/a   **MIP** $80

(Kyosho Photo)

❏ **Lotus Caterham Super Seven,** 2001, Green body with yellow stripe on front and hood, silver spoked wheels, black interior with blue seatbelts, black roll bar, silver headlights and trim, 1:18 scale, Stock No. KYOV0139, Model No. 7020GY

EX n/a   **NM** n/a   **MIP** $80

(Kyosho Photo)

❏ **MGB MK-1,** 2001, Red body with black interior, silver spoked wheels, silver trim, opening doors and hood, 1:18 scale, Stock No. KYOV0140, Model No. 08021R

EX n/a   **NM** n/a   **MIP** $80

(Kyosho Photo)

❏ **MGB MK-1,** 2001, Green body with black interior, silver spoked wheels, silver trim, opening doors and hood, 1:18 scale, Stock No. KYOV0141, Model No. 08021G

EX n/a   **NM** n/a   **MIP** $80

(Kyosho Photo)

❏ **MGB MK-1,** 2001, Detail showing the intricate interior of the MGB MK-1, 1:18 scale, Stock No. KYOV0141, Model No. 08021G

(Kyosho Photo)

❑ **MGB MK-1,** 2001, Detail showing opened hood and engine, 1:18 scale, Stock No. KYOV0141, Model No. 08021G

(Kyosho Photo)

❑ **MGB MK-1,** 2001, White body with red interior, silver spoked wheels, silver trim, opening doors and hood, 1:18 scale, Stock No. KYOV0142, Model No. 08021W
EX n/a   **NM** n/a   **MIP** $80

❑ **Morris Mini Cooper 1257S,** 2001, Blue body, white roof with Union Jack graphic, silver wheels and trim. Opening hood and doors, 1:18 scale, Stock No. KYOV0145, Model No. 08101B
EX n/a   **NM** n/a   **MIP** $80

❑ **Morris Mini Cooper 1257S,** 2001, Red body with white roof, white wheels with silver hubcaps, silver trim. Opening hood and doors, 1:18 scale, Stock No. KYOV0147, Model No. 08101R
EX n/a   **NM** n/a   **MIP** $80

(Kyosho Photo)

❑ **Morris Mini Cooper 1257S: Monte Carlo no. "177",** 2001, Red body with white roof, opening doors and hood, white roof rack

with two spares, silver wheels, bumper-mounted rally lights, number "177" on doors, 1:18 scale, Stock No. KYOV0148, Model No. 8102R
EX n/a   **NM** n/a   **MIP** $80

(Kyosho Photo)

❑ **Morris Mini Cooper 1257S: Monte Carlo no. "177",** 2001, Detail showing spares on roof and opening doors and hood, 1:18 scale, Stock No. KYOV0148, Model No. 8102R

(Kyosho Photo)

❑ **Austin Healey 3000MK-1,** 2001, Black and red body, opening doors, hood and trunk, gray wheels with silver hubs, red interior, 1:18 scale, Stock No. KYOV0150, Model No. 08141KR
EX n/a   **NM** n/a   **MIP** $80

(Kyosho Photo)

❑ **Austin Healey 3000MK-1,** 2001, Detail shot showing doors, hood and trunk opened, 1:18 scale, Stock No. KYOV0150, Model No. 08141KR

(Kyosho Photo)

❑ **Austin Healey 100-Six,** 2001, Light yellow body, gray wheels, silver hubs and trim, black interior, opening hood, doors and trunk, 1:18 scale, Stock No. KYOV0151, Model No. 08144Y
EX n/a   **NM** n/a   **MIP** $80

(Kyosho Photo)

❑ **Lamborghini Jota SVR,** 2001, Red body, opening hoods and doors, black interior, chrome and red spoked wheels, 1:18 scale, Stock No. KYOV0155, Model No. 08311R
EX n/a   **NM** n/a   **MIP** $80

(Kyosho Photo)

❑ **Lamborghini Jota SVR,** 2001, Detail showing interior, 1:18 scale, Stock No. KYOV0155, Model No. 08311R

(Kyosho Photo)

❑ **Lamborghini Jota SVR,** 2001, Detail showing opening rear hood, 1:18 scale, Stock No. KYOV0155, Model No. 08311R

(Kyosho Photo)

❑ **Morgan 4/4 Series-II,** 2001, Green body, silver-gray wheels and hubs, opening folding hood, opening doors, green interior, 1:18 scale, Stock No. KYOV0160, Model No. 08111G

EX n/a   NM n/a   MIP $80

(Kyosho Photo)

❑ **Morgan 4/4 Series-II,** 2001, Detail showing opening hood and engine, 1:18 scale, Stock No. KYOV0160, Model No. 08111G

(Kyosho Photo)

❑ **Morgan 4/4 Series-II,** 2001, Detail showing interior and dash, 1:18 scale, Stock No. KYOV0160, Model No. 08111G

(Kyosho Photo)

❑ **Datsun 240Z '72 Monte Carlo no. "5",** 2001, Red exterior with black hood, "Datsun" on hood, number "5" on doors, black wheels, bumper-mounted rally lights. Left-hand drive, 1:18 scale, Stock No. KYOV0168, Model No. 08215B

EX n/a   NM n/a   MIP $80

(Kyosho Photo)

❑ **Datsun 240Z '72 Monte Carlo no. "5",** 2001, Detail showing opening hatch and spares, 1:18 scale, Stock No. KYOV0168, Model No. 08215B

(Kyosho Photo)

❑ **Datsun 240Z '71 Safari no. "11",** 2001, Red body, black hood, side-mounted spotlights, black wheels, opening doors, hood and hatch, number "11" on sides and roof. Right-hand drive, 1:18 scale, Stock No. KYOV0169, Model No. 08215A

EX n/a   NM n/a   MIP $80

(Kyosho Photo)

❑ **Datsun 240Z '71 Safari no. "11",** 2001, Detail showing opening hood and engine, 1:18 scale, Stock No. KYOV0169, Model No. 08215A

❑ **Lancia Stratos HF Rally no. "1," Monte Carlo, 1977,** 2001, White body, red and green stripes, yellow five-spoked wheels, number "1," and "Alitalia" on sides. Opening doors, rear engine hood and front trunk, 1:18 scale, Stock No. KYOV0171, Model No. 08132A

EX n/a   NM n/a   MIP $80

(Kyosho Photo)

❑ **Lancia Stratos HF Rally no. "1," Monte Carlo, 1977,** 2001, Detail showing opened doors and interior of the Stratos, 1:18 scale, Stock No. KYOV0171, Model No. 08132A

(Kyosho Photo)

❑ **Lancia Stratos HF Rally no. "7," Safari, 1977,** 2001, White exterior, re-enforced bumper, yellow wheels, spare on roof, opening doors, rear hood and front trunk, 1:18 scale, Stock No. KYOV0175, Model No. 08135B

EX n/a   NM n/a   MIP $80

(Kyosho Photo)

❑ **Lancia Stratos HF Rally no. "7," Safari, 1977,** 2001, Detail showing "opened up" view of the

Stratos, 1:18 scale, Stock No. KYOV0175, Model No. 08135B

(Kyosho Photo)

❑ **Lancia Rally 037 no. "5," Tour de Corse, 1984,** 2001, White body with Martini racing red and blue stripes, silver-gray wheels, number "5" on sides, opening doors, rear hood and front trunk, 1:18 scale, Stock No. KYOV0178, Model No. 08301A

EX n/a   **NM** n/a   **MIP** $80

(Kyosho Photo)

❑ **Lancia Rally 037 no. "5," Tour de Corse, 1984,** 2001, Detail showing the opening features of the Lancia Rally 037, 1:18 scale, Stock No. KYOV0178, Model No. 08301A

❑ **Nissan Skyline 2000GT-R (KPGC10),** 2001, Silver body, black wheels, black interior, right-hand drive, opening doors, hood and trunk, 1:18 scale, Stock No. KYOV0180, Model No. 08121S

EX n/a   **NM** n/a   **MIP** $80

(Kyosho Photo)

❑ **Nissan Skyline 2000GT-R (KPGC10),** 2001, Detail showing opened doors, dash and interior, 1:18 scale, Stock No. KYOV0180, Model No. 08121S

(Kyosho Photo)

❑ **Nissan Skyline 2000GT-R (KPGC10),** 2001, Opened hood, detailed engine on the Skyline, 1:18 scale, Stock No. KYOV0180, Model No. 08121S

(Kyosho Photo)

❑ **Nissan Skyline 2000GT-R (KPGC10),** 2001, White body, black wheels, black interior, right-hand drive, opening doors, hood and trunk, 1:18 scale, Stock No. KYOV0181, Model No. 08121W

EX n/a   **NM** n/a   **MIP** $80

(Kyosho Photo)

❑ **Nissan Skyline 2000GT-R (KPGC10): Racing,** 2001, White and blue body, number "15" on sides, sponsor graphics including "STP" and "Mobil," black wheels, black interior, 1:18 scale, Stock No. KYOV0183, Model No. 08122B

EX n/a   **NM** n/a   **MIP** $80

(Kyosho Photo)

❑ **Nissan Skyline 2000GT-R (KPGC10): Racing,** 2001, White and red body, number "6" on sides and hood, sponsor graphics including NGK, opening doors, hood and trunk, black wheels, black interior, 1:18 scale, Stock No. KYOV0189, Model No. 08122R

EX n/a   **NM** n/a   **MIP** $80

(Kyosho Photo)

❑ **Nissan Fairlady Z-L 1970,** 2001, Red body, opening doors, hood and trunk, charcoal gray five-spoke wheels, 1:18 scale, Stock No. KYOV0185, Model No. 08211R

EX n/a   **NM** n/a   **MIP** $80

(Kyosho Photo)

❑ **Nissan Fairlady Z-L 1970,** 2001, White body, black interior, black side-mounted rearview mirrors, charcoal-gray five-spoke wheels, opening doors, hood and trunk, 1:18 scale, Stock No. KYOV0186, Model No. 08211W

EX n/a   **NM** n/a   **MIP** $80

(Kyosho Photo)

❑ **Nissan Fairlady Z-L 1970,** 2001, Photo showing opening features, 1:18 scale, Stock No. KYOV0186, Model No. 08211W

(Kyosho Photo)

❑ **Nissan Fairlady Z-L 1970,** 2001, Detail of opened doors, interior and dash, 1:18 scale, Stock No. KYOV0186, Model No. 08211W

(Kyosho Photo)

❑ **Nissan Fairlady Z-L 1970,** 2001, Yellow body, opening hood, doors, and trunk, right-hand drive, 1:18 scale, Stock No. KYOV0195, Model No. 08211Y
EX n/a   **NM** n/a   **MIP** $80

(Kyosho Photo)

❑ **Datsun 240Z,** 2001, Silver body, charcoal-gray five-spoke wheels, opening hood, doors and trunk, left-hand drive, 1:18 scale, Stock No. KYOV0187, Model No. 08214S
EX n/a   **NM** n/a   **MIP** $80

(Kyosho Photo)

❑ **Datsun 240Z,** 2001, Yellow body, charcoal-gray five-spoke wheels, opening doors, hood and trunk, left-hand drive, 1:18 scale, Stock No. KYOV0188, Model No. 08214Y
EX n/a   **NM** n/a   **MIP** $80

(Kyosho Photo)

❑ **Datsun 240Z,** 2001, Opened hood and engine detail, 1:18 scale, Stock No. KYOV0188, Model No. 08214Y

(Kyosho Photo)

❑ **Datsun 240Z,** 2001, Red body, opening hood, doors and trunk, left-hand drive, 1:18 scale, Stock No. KYOV0196, Model No. 08214R
EX n/a   **NM** n/a   **MIP** $80

(Kyosho Photo)

❑ **Nissan Fairlady Z432R,** 2001, Red body, black hood, opening doors, hood and trunk, black interior, right-hand drive, 1:18 scale, Stock No. KYOV0194, Model No. 08213P
EX n/a   **NM** n/a   **MIP** $80

(Kyosho Photo)

❑ **Nissan Fairlady Z432R,** 2001, Detail of opened hood and engine, 1:18 scale, Stock No. KYOV0194, Model No. 08213P

(Kyosho Photo)

❑ **Nissan Fairlady 240ZG 1971,** 2001, White body, detailed black interior, five-spoke wheels, opening hood and doors, 1:18 scale, Stock No. KYOV0197, Model No. 08212W
EX n/a   **NM** n/a   **MIP** $80

(Kyosho Photo)

❑ **Nissan Fairlady 240ZG 1971,** 2001, Maroon body, opening hood and doors, black interior, five-spoke wheels, side-mounted rearview mirrors, headlight covers, right-hand drive, 1:18 scale, Stock No. KYOV0198, Model No. 08212M
EX n/a   **NM** n/a   **MIP** $80

(Kyosho Photo)

❑ **Nissan Fairlady 240ZG 1971,** 2001, Interior detail of 240ZG, 1:18 scale, Stock No. KYOV0198, Model No. 08212M

(Kyosho Photo)

❑ **Acura NSX,** 2001, Black body, opening doors, pop-up headlights, opening rear windshield, silver-gray wheels, black interior, left-hand drive, 1:18 scale, Stock No. KYOV0652, Model No. 08082K
EX n/a   **NM** n/a   **MIP** $80

(Kyosho Photo)

❑ **Acura NSX,** 2001, Red body, opening doors, pop-up headlights, opening rear windshield, silver-gray wheels, black interior, 1:18 scale, Stock No. KYOV0653, Model No. 08082R
EX n/a   **NM** n/a   **MIP** $80

(Kyosho Photo)

❑ **Tucker Torpedo 1948,** 2001, Blue body, off-white interior, opening rear hood, doors and front trunk (includes luggage), whitewall tires, silver hubs, 1:18 scale, Stock No. KYOV0800, Model No. 08201B
EX n/a   **NM** n/a   **MIP** $80

(Kyosho Photo)

❑ **Tucker Torpedo 1948,** 2001, Quite a few opening features on this model, 1:18 scale, Stock No. KYOV0800, Model No. 08201B

(Kyosho Photo)

❑ **Tucker Torpedo 1948,** 2001, Detail of the front trunk that even includes luggage, 1:18 scale, Stock No. KYOV0800, Model No. 08201B

(Kyosho Photo)

❑ **Tucker Torpedo 1948,** 2001, Opening door and interior detail, 1:18 scale, Stock No. KYOV0800, Model No. 08201B

(Kyosho Photo)

❑ **Tucker Torpedo 1948,** 2001, Rear hood and engine, 1:18 scale, Stock No. KYOV0800, Model No. 08201B

(Kyosho Photo)

❑ **Tucker Torpedo 1948,** 2001, Black exterior, silver hubs and trim, opening trunk, doors and hood, whitewall tires, 1:18 scale, Stock No. KYOV0802, Model No. 08201K
EX n/a   **NM** n/a   **MIP** $80

(Kyosho Photo)

❑ **BMW V12 LMR, no. "15," Le Mans, 1999,** 2001, White body with "Dell" and number "15" on front and sides, five-spoke wheels, rear spoiler, 1:18 scale, Stock No. KYOV0895, Model No. 08533A
EX n/a   **NM** n/a   **MIP** $80

(Kyosho Photo)

❏ **BMW V12 LMR, no. "17," Le Mans, 1999,** 2001, White body with "Dell," number "17" and German flag graphic on front and sides, five-spoke wheels, rear spoiler, 1:18 scale, Stock No. KYOV0896, Model No. 08534A
EX n/a NM n/a MIP $80

(Kyosho Photo)

❏ **BMW V12 LMR, no. "17," Le Mans, 1999,** 2001, Detail showing interior of BMW V12 LMR, 1:18 scale, Stock No. KYOV0896, Model No. 08534A

(Kyosho Photo)

❏ **BMW V12 LMR, no. "17," Le Mans, 1999,** 2001, Detail showing front of car, 1:18 scale, Stock No. KYOV0896, Model No. 08534A

(Kyosho Photo)

❏ **BMW 328i Cabriolet,** 2001, Silver body, silver-gray five-spoke wheels, black interior, opening doors and hood, 1:18 scale, Stock No. KYOV0903, Model No. 08504S
EX n/a NM n/a MIP $80

(Kyosho Photo)

❏ **BMW 328i Cabriolet,** 2001, Detail showing opening door and interior, 1:18 scale, Stock No. KYOV0903, Model No. 08504S

(Kyosho Photo)

❏ **BMW 328i Cabriolet,** 2001, Opening hood shows intricate engine detail, 1:18 scale, Stock No. KYOV0903, Model No. 08504S

(Kyosho Photo)

❏ **BMW 328Ci,** 2001, Dark-blue coupe body, opening doors and hood, silver-gray multi-spoked wheels, 1:18 scale, Stock No. KYOV0904, Model No. 08502B
EX n/a NM n/a MIP $80

(Kyosho Photo)

❏ **BMW X5,** 2001, Dark-blue body, silver-gray wheels, opening doors, hood, hatch and tailgate,

1:18 scale, Stock No. KYOV0905, Model No. 08521DB
EX n/a NM n/a MIP $80

(Kyosho Photo)

❏ **BMW X5,** 2001, All four doors open on this model--nice interior detail, too, 1:18 scale, Stock No. KYOV0905, Model No. 08521DB
EX n/a NM n/a MIP $80

(Kyosho Photo)

❏ **BMW Z8,** 2001, Silver-body, red and silver-gray interior, silver-gray multi-spoked wheels, 1:18 scale, Stock No. KYOV0909, Model No. 08511S
EX n/a NM n/a MIP $80

(Kyosho Photo)

❏ **BMW Z8,** 2001, Highly-detailed red and silver-gray interior, 1:18 scale, Stock No. KYOV0909, Model No. 08511S

(Kyosho Photo)

❏ **BMW 2002 tii,** 2001, White body, black interior, opening hood, doors and trunk, silver-gray wheels, 1:18 scale, Stock No. KYOV0911, Model No. 08541W

EX n/a   **NM** n/a   **MIP** $80

(Kyosho Photo)

❏ **BMW 2002 turbo,** 2001, Silver body, blue and red "turbo" stripe along bottom, black grille, black interior, silver and black wheels, 1:18 scale, Stock No. KYOV0912, Model No. 08542S

EX n/a   **NM** n/a   **MIP** $80

(Kyosho Photo)

❏ **BMW 2002 turbo,** 2001, This car features and extremely detailed engine, 1:18 scale, Stock No. KYOV0912, Model No. 08542S

(Kyosho Photo)

❏ **BMW 2002 turbo,** 2001, View of opened trunk and spare, 1:18 scale, Stock No. KYOV0912, Model No. 08542S

(Kyosho Photo)

❏ **BMW 2002 turbo,** 2001, View showing interior and dash detail, 1:18 scale, Stock No. KYOV0912, Model No. 08542S

(Kyosho Photo)

❏ **BMW 325 ti Compact,** 2001, Red body, opening doors, hood and hatch, silver five-spoke wheels, black interior, 1:18 scale, Stock No. KYOV0913, Model No. 08561R

EX n/a   **NM** n/a   **MIP** $80

(Kyosho Photo)

❏ **BMW 325 ti Compact,** 2001, Pistaccio Green body, light tan interior, five-spoke silver wheels, 1:18 scale, Stock No. KYOV0914, Model No. 08561PG

EX n/a   **NM** n/a   **MIP** $80

(Kyosho Photo)

❏ **BMW M3 Convertible,** 2001, Red body, opening doors, hood and trunk, black interior, 1:18 scale, Stock No. KYOV0915, Model No. 08505R

EX n/a   **NM** n/a   **MIP** $80

(Kyosho Photo)

❏ **BMW M3 Coupe,** 2001, Yellow body, silver-gray multi-spoked wheels, black interior, 1:18 scale, Stock No. KYOV0916, Model No. 08503Y

EX n/a   **NM** n/a   **MIP** $80

(Kyosho Photo)

❏ **BMW M3 Coupe,** 2001, Opening features on BMW M3 Coupe include doors, hood and trunk, 1:18 scale, Stock No. KYOV0916, Model No. 08503Y

(Kyosho Photo)

❏ **Lamborghini Jota SVR,** 2001, Red body, chrome and gold multi-spoked wheels, black interior, 1:43 scale, Stock No. KYOV1050, Model No. 03201R

EX n/a   **NM** n/a   **MIP** $30

(Kyosho Photo)

❏ **Lamborghini Jota SVR,** 2001, Opening hood and engine on the Jota SVR, 1:43 scale, Stock No. KYOV1050, Model No. 03201R

(Kyosho Photo)

❏ **Shelby Cobra 427S/C,** 2001, Blue body, chrome, black and gold wheels, black interior, 1:43 scale, Stock No. KYOV1100, Model No. 03011B

EX n/a   **NM** n/a   **MIP** $30

KYOSHO / 1:43 SCALE

(Kyosho Photo)

❑ **Shelby Cobra 427S/C: Racing,** 2001, Blue body, white rally stripes, white exhaust, black interior, chrome, gold and black wheels, 1:43 scale, Stock No. KYOV1104, Model No. 03012A
EX n/a   **NM** n/a   **MIP** $30

(Kyosho Photo)

❑ **Shelby Cobra 427S/C: Racing,** 2001, Silver body, white racing stripes, sponsor graphics, silver, gold and black wheels, white exhaust, 1:43 scale, Stock No. KYOV1106, Model No. 03012S
EX n/a   **NM** n/a   **MIP** $30

(Kyosho Photo)

❑ **Shelby GT350,** 2001, White body, blue stripe, chrome five-spoke wheels, black interior, 1:43 scale, Stock No. KYOV1107, Model No. 03121W
EX n/a   **NM** n/a   **MIP** $30

(Kyosho Photo)

❑ **Shelby GT350: Hertz,** 2001, Black body, gold stripes, chrome and gold wheels, black interior, 1:43 scale, Stock No. KYOV1108, Model No. 03122H
EX n/a   **NM** n/a   **MIP** $30

(Kyosho Photo)

❑ **Shelby GT350: Open,** 2001, White convertible body, blue stripe, black interior, chrome wheels, 1:43 scale, Stock No. KYOV1109, Model No. 03124W
EX n/a   **NM** n/a   **MIP** $30

(Kyosho Photo)

❑ **Shelby GT350: Open,** 2001, Red convertible body, white stripe, black interior, chrome wheels, 1:43 scale, Stock No. KYOV1110, Model No. 03124R
EX n/a   **NM** n/a   **MIP** $30

(Kyosho Photo)

❑ **Shelby Series 1,** 2001, Silver body, red stripes, chrome wheels, black interior, 1:43 scale, Stock No. KYOV1111, Model No. 03131SR
EX n/a   **NM** n/a   **MIP** $30

(Kyosho Photo)

❑ **Shelby Series 1,** 2001, Blue body, white stripes, chrome wheels, black interior, 1:43 scale, Stock No. KYOV1112, Model No. 03131BW
EX n/a   **NM** n/a   **MIP** $30

(Kyosho Photo)

❑ **Caterham Super Seven JPE,** 2001, Yellow and black body, yellow wheels, "Caterham Super Seven" on sides, 1:43 scale, Stock No. KYOV1122, Model No. 03152Y
EX n/a   **NM** n/a   **MIP** $30

(Kyosho Photo)

❑ **Nissan Fairlady 240ZG,** 2001, Maroon body, silver-gray wheels, black interior, opening hood showing engine, 1:43 scale, Stock No. KYOV1125, Model No. 03162M
EX n/a   **NM** n/a   **MIP** $30

(Kyosho Photo)

❑ **Nissan Fairlady 240ZG,** 2001, Detail of opening hood and engine, 1:43 scale, Stock No. KYOV1125, Model No. 03162M

(Kyosho Photo)

❑ **Nissan Fairlady 240ZG,** 2001, White body, opening hood with engine, right-hand drive, 1:43 scale, Stock No. KYOV1126, Model No. 03162W
EX n/a   **NM** n/a   **MIP** $30

(Kyosho Photo)

❏ **Nissan Fairlady Z432R,** 2001, Orange body, black hood, black wheels, side-mounted mirrors, opening hood with engine, 1:43 scale, Stock No. KYOV1127, Model No. 03163P

EX n/a **NM** n/a **MIP** $30

(Kyosho Photo)

❏ **Nissan Fairlady Z-L,** 2001, Yellow body, gray and silver five-spoke wheels, black interior, side-mounted mirrors, opening hood and trunk, 1:43 scale, Stock No. KYOV1128, Model No. 03161Y

EX n/a **NM** n/a **MIP** $30

(Kyosho Photo)

❏ **Nissan Fairlady Z-L,** 2001, White body, black interior, gray and silver hubs, opening hood with engine, 1:43 scale, Stock No. KYOV1131, Model No. 03161W

EX n/a **NM** n/a **MIP** $30

(Kyosho Photo)

❏ **Datsun 240Z,** 2001, Yellow body, black interior, black and chrome wheels, opening hood with engine, left-hand drive, 1:43 scale, Stock No. KYOV1133, Model No. 03164S

EX n/a **NM** n/a **MIP** $30

(Kyosho Photo)

❏ **Nissan Skyline 2000GT-R (KPGC110),** 2001, Dark green body with gold trim, number "73" on sides and hood, "Skyline" on rear quarter panels, gold spoked wheels, right-hand drive, 1:43 scale, Stock No. KYOV1138, Model No. 03112R

EX n/a **NM** n/a **MIP** $30

(Kyosho Photo)

❏ **Toyota 2000GT: Open,** 2001, White convertible body with silver multi-spoked wheels, black interior, 1:43 scale, Stock No. KYOV1155, Model No. 03033W

EX n/a **NM** n/a **MIP** $30

(Kyosho Photo)

❏ **Toyota 2000GT: Time Trial,** 2001, Yellow body with green hood, sponsor graphics on sides, including "Esso," gold and silver wheels, black interior, 1:43 scale, Stock No. KYOV1156, Model No. 03032Y

EX n/a **NM** n/a **MIP** $30

(Kyosho Photo)

❏ **Toyota 2000GT: '67 Fuji 24-hour,** 2001, White body with red swoop and stripe, number "1" on sides, black and silver wheels, black interior and rollbar, 1:43 scale, Stock No. KYOV1157, Model No. 03032F

EX n/a **NM** n/a **MIP** $30

(Kyosho Photo)

❏ **Toyota 2000GT,** 2001, White body with silver and black wheels, black interior, silver trim, 1:43 scale, Stock No. KYOV1158, Model No. 03031W

EX n/a **NM** n/a **MIP** $30

(Kyosho Photo)

❏ **Lancia Stratos Gr.5,** 2001, White body with green and red "Alitalia" graphics, number "539," green wheels, opening rear hood, 1:43 scale, Stock No. KYOV1250, Model No. 03141A

EX n/a **NM** n/a **MIP** $30

(Kyosho Photo)

❏ **Lancia Rally 037: Tour de Corse, 1984,** 2001, White body with blue and red Martini racing stripes, number "5" on sides, silver-gray wheels, 1:43 scale, Stock No. KYOV1252, Model No. 03181A

EX n/a **NM** n/a **MIP** $30

(Kyosho Photo)

❑ **Lancia Rally 037: Tour de Corse, 1984,** 2001, Opening hood with engine, 1:43 scale, Stock No. KYOV1252, Model No. 03181A

(Kyosho Photo)

❑ **Lancia Rally 037: Monte Carlo, 1983,** 2001, White body, blue and red Martini racing stripes, silver-gray wheels, number "1" on sides, 1:43 scale, Stock No. KYOV1253, Model No. 03181B
EX n/a   NM n/a   MIP $30

(Kyosho Photo)

❑ **Shelby Cobra Daytona Coupe,** 2001, Blue body with white stripe, sponsor graphics, silver wheels, white exhaust, 1:43 scale, Stock No. KYOV1300, Model No. 03051A
EX n/a   NM n/a   MIP $30

(Kyosho Photo)

❑ **Shelby Cobra Daytona Coupe,** 2001, Blue body, white stripe, yellow tape over headlights, number "21" on sides and hood, silver wheels, white exhaust, 1:43 scale, Stock No. KYOV1301, Model No. 03051B
EX n/a   NM n/a   MIP $30

(Kyosho Photo)

❑ **Shelby Cobra Daytona Coupe,** 2001, Blue body, white stripe, number "26" on hood and sides, white exhaust, black interior, 1:43 scale, Stock No. KYOV1302, Model No. 03051C
EX n/a   NM n/a   MIP $30

(Kyosho Photo)

❑ **Shelby Cobra Daytona Coupe,** 2001, Red body, white stripe, number "59" on hood and sides, white exhaust, silver wheels, black interior, 1:43 scale, Stock No. KYOV1304, Model No. 03051F
EX n/a   NM n/a   MIP $30

(Kyosho Photo)

❑ **Datsun 240Z: 1971 Safari, no. "11",** 2001, Red body, black hood, right-hand drive, black wheels, opening hood with engine, sponsor graphics, number "11", 1:43 scale, Stock No. KYOV1350, Model No. 03165A
EX n/a   NM n/a   MIP $30

(Kyosho Photo)

❑ **Datsun 240Z: 1972 Monte Carlo, no. "5",** 2001, Red body, black hood, left-hand drive, black wheels, "Datsun" on hood, opening hood with engine, number "5", 1:43 scale, Stock No. KYOV1351, Model No. 03165B
EX n/a   NM n/a   MIP $30

(Kyosho Photo)

❑ **Lotus Europa Special,** 2001, Dark metallic blue body, opening hood with engine, silver and black wheels, 1:43 scale, Stock No. KYOV1499, Model No. 03073B
EX n/a   NM n/a   MIP $30

(Kyosho Photo)

❑ **Jaguar E-type Roadster,** 2001, Silver convertible body, beige interior, silver, multi-spoked wheels, silver trim, 1:43 scale, Stock No. KYOV1599, Model No. 03061S
EX n/a   NM n/a   MIP $30

(Kyosho Photo)

❑ **Jaguar E-type Roadster,** 2001, Red convertible body, beige interior, silver, multi-spoked wheels, silver trim, 1:43 scale, Stock No. KYOV1600, Model No. 03061R
EX n/a   NM n/a   MIP $30

(Kyosho Photo)

❑ **Jaguar E-type Roadster,** 2001, Green convertible body, silver, multi-spoked wheels, silver trim, 1:43 scale, Stock No. KYOV1601, Model No. 03061G
EX n/a   NM n/a   MIP $30

(Kyosho Photo)

❑ **Jaguar E-type Coupe,** 2001, White body, silver, multi-spoked wheels, 1:43 scale, Stock No. KYOV1602, Model No. 03062W

EX n/a   **NM** n/a   **MIP** $30

(Kyosho Photo)

❑ **Jaguar E-type Coupe,** 2001, Red body, silver, multi-spoked wheels, 1:43 scale, Stock No. KYOV1604, Model No. 03062R

EX n/a   **NM** n/a   **MIP** $30

(Kyosho Photo)

❑ **Jaguar E-type Roadster: Racing, no. "15," 1963 Le Mans,** 2001, White body, blue stripes, number "15" on hood and doors, 1:43 scale, Stock No. KYOV1605, Model No. 03063A

EX n/a   **NM** n/a   **MIP** $30

(Kyosho Photo)

❑ **Jaguar E-type Coupe: Racing, no. "10," 1963 Le Mans,** 2001, White body, stripes, number "10" on hood and doors, silver, multi-spoked wheels, 1:43 scale, Stock No. KYOV1606, Model No. 03064A

EX n/a   **NM** n/a   **MIP** $30

Lledo Days Gone Series

This set of three Lledo Days Gone vehicles with Dairy Farm advertisements on the sides is an example of the vehicle groupings Lledo issued in the 1990s. This set is valued at about $15.

Lledo was created in 1982 by Jack Odell, one of the original founders of Matchbox. Odell had been one of the prime movers behind the "Models of Yesteryear" series and had been with Lesney virtually since the beginning, so it's not surprising that many of Lledo's first models look amazingly like Matchbox Models of Yesteryear. When Matchbox was sold to Universal Toys in 1982, Odell wanted to keep jobs in England, so he opened up a plant in Enfield for the die-cast business.

The name for the company stems from Odell's call name on the radioset while with the British Army in World War II. Fighting in the North African desert, he simply reversed his name last name, going by "Lledo." So, year later, when starting his company it seemed appropriate. Hence, Lledo.

Over the years, Lledo has been known for high-quality, yet inexpensive, models. Often, the company makes promotional models with logos for popular brands along the sides.

Part of the Zindart family of companies since December 1999, Lledo and Corgi are now sister companies, and share many castings. In fact, collectors will notice some venerable Lledo Days Gone castings showing up in Corgi's new Showcase series.

These days, Lledo continues to emphasize early 20th century vehicles in its Days Gone line, leaving the (now strictly) 1:43-scale Vanguards range to enter the late '60s and early '70s with some of it's newest releases.

MARKET UPDATE

Lledo vehicles are a bit harder to find in the U.S., but possibly due to the company's relationship with Corgi, more companies are stocking them now than before. The price for each model typically hovers around $7 MIP, but there are hard-to-find promotional issues that bump past the $70 dollar mark and higher.

Another promotional vehicle by Lledo, a Milk Delivery Truck advertising "PG Tips" on the sides. Valued at about $7.

Originally labeled a "Days Gone Vanguards," this 1955 Dennis F8 Fire Engine is a popular casting for Lledo. This series, focusing on 1950s and 1960s vehicles, set the stage for the stand-alone "Vanguards" series that followed in 1996.

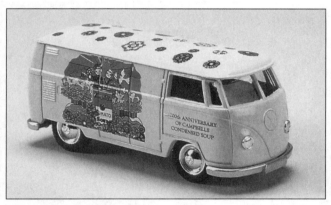

The VW Combi Bus is a staple in the Lledo Days Gone lineup. This model was a promotional piece for Campbell's Soup, available via mail order in 1998.

The Youngers Brewer's Dray from 1999. Horse-drawn vehicles speak to an earlier era of toy-making, and this model would feel right at home with some of Matchbox's first issues.

This old Bentley 4.5L is reminiscent of a Matchbox Model of Yesteryear, most likely also created by Jack Odell.

1934 Dennis Parcels Van with "Cadbury's" advertising on sides. This 1987 issue is typical for the many commercial vehicles in the Days Gone lineup.

This 1942 Dodge 4x4 with "San Jose Fire Dept." on the sides is a well-used casting. Lledo has issued this model as military ambulances, and more recently, Corgi has issued a sharp version of this truck in their Texaco "Showcase" series.

Another mail-away program vehicle, the Bedford Truck. Four vehicles in the Campbell's soup program were offered by Lledo, introducing many in the United States to this British die-cast company.

A 1928 Chevrolet Delivery Van for Tuborgs, the Danish beer. This model has seen use in many liveries, including Coca-Cola and Budweiser.

The Burrell Showman's Steam Loco "Pride of the South," a 2002 release and a definite nod to Matchbox "Models of Yesteryear" vehicles.

This Morris Minor Van is from the "Comic Corner" series. It advertises a British comic book called "The Beezer," which began running the "Space Patrol" strips in the 1960s.

From the 1998 Campbell's Soup series, a Model T Van. There have been over 150 variations of this vehicle, probably because it's a perfect platform for advertising and promotions—much like the real thing.

DAYS GONE VANGUARDS

(KP Photo)

❑ **Dennis F8 Fire Engine: Essex Fire Brigade,** 1993, Red with black roof, brown ladder, red wheels, thin black tires, silver plastic grille, black base. This is a popular casting for Lledo, and quite a few variations in other liveries exist. The packaging reads "Days Gone Vanguards: Fifties and Sixties Classics Collection", Model No. DG60000
EX n/a   **NM** n/a   **MIP** $7

HORSE-DRAWN

(KP Photo)

❑ **Horse-Drawn Brewer's Dray: Youngers,** 1999, Dark blue body with brown plastic barrels, orange spoked wheels, light tan plastic driver, brown horse, "William Younger & Co. No. 1374", Model No. DG10200
EX n/a   **NM** n/a   **MIP** $7

PIONEERS OF AVIATION

(Lledo Photo)

❑ **Fokker DRI Triplane, Jasta 18,** Blue and white with updated black cross markings, white dove insignia near cockpit, Model No. DG116004
EX n/a   **NM** n/a   **MIP** $7

(Lledo Photo)

❑ **Sopwith Camel, No10 Naval Sqdn, RNAS,** White stripes, "Star Paint" on wheels, Royal Navy Air Service color yellow underneath, Model No. DG115001
EX n/a   **NM** n/a   **MIP** $7

(Lledo Photo)

❑ **Sopwith Camel, Royal Flying Corps,** 2001, Silver nose, red props green body, yellow underbody, Model No. DG115000
EX n/a   **NM** n/a   **MIP** $7

(Lledo Photo)

❑ **Stearman Kaydet, USAAF Trainer,** Blue and yellow, US Army Air Force markings, Model No. DG122000
EX n/a   **NM** n/a   **MIP** $7

(Lledo Photo)

❑ **Tiger Moth, RAF Post War Training Scheme,** Yellow tan on black prop, black struts, Model No. DG117001
EX n/a   **NM** n/a   **MIP** $7

(Lledo Photo)

❑ **Tiger Moth, RAF Training Scheme,** Green and yellow with RAF insignia, Model No. DG117003
EX n/a   **NM** n/a   **MIP** $7

ROLLS ROYCE AND BENTLEY COLLECTION

(KP Photo)

❑ **1930 Bentley Blower 4.5 Liter,** 1997, British Racing Green body, white interior, silver plastic grille and windshield, black wheels and tires. One of the many Lledo vehicles that mirrored former Matchbox "Models of Yesteryear" vehicles, Model No. SL46000
EX n/a   **NM** n/a   **MIP** $9

SHOWMANS COLLECTION - NOTTINGHAM GOOSE FAIR

(Lledo Photo)

❑ **AEC Mammoth Ballast (generator load) boxwith drawbar trailer and Dodgems load: R.Edwards & Sons Ltd,** Brown body with red fenders and cab, Model No. DG123003
EX n/a   **NM** n/a   **MIP** $17

(Lledo Photo)

❑ **Burrell Showman's Steam locomotive with drawbar trailer and Box load: Pat Collins,** Black engine, yellow lettering, white roof, Model No. DG151000
EX n/a   **NM** n/a   **MIP** $21

(Lledo Photo)

❑ **Scammell Six Wheeler: Biddall's Fun Fair,** Red and white body with "John Biddall's Cars Fun Fair" on sides, Model No. DG044034
EX n/a   **NM** n/a   **MIP** $8

(Lledo Photo)

❑ **Sentinel Ballast Tractor: G R Tuby & Sons,** Black body with gray fenders, red wheels, Model No. DG106002
EX n/a   **NM** n/a   **MIP** $8

SPECIAL LICENSED EDITIONS

❑ **1928 Chevrolet Van: Campbell's,** 1998, Dark green cab and body with red chassis, black roof, solid black wheels with thin tires, gold plastic grille, "Campbell Soup Co. Tomato" on side panels, "100th Anniversary of Campbell's Condensed Soup" in white type on doors. Vehicle is part of a mail-in offer advertised on Campbell's soup labels, Model No. SL51002
EX $274   **NM** $304   **MIP** $518

(KP Photo)

❑ **Bedford Van: Campbell's,** 1998, Campbell's red body with black fenders and chassis, solid red wheels with thin tires, "Campbell's Soup" label on side panels, "100th Anniversary of Campbell's Condensed Soup" in white type on sides. Another vehicle advertised as a mail-in offer on Campbell's soup labels
EX n/a   **NM** n/a   **MIP** $8

(KP Photo)

❑ **Ford Model T Van: Campbell's,** 1998, Dark blue and orange body with "Condensed Beefsteak Tomato Soup" graphics on side panels, "100th Anniversary of Campbells Condensed Soup" in white type on doors. Gold plastic grille and spoked wheels. Part of a mail-away set advertised on Campbell's soup labels in 1998
EX n/a   **NM** n/a   **MIP** $9

(KP Photo)

❑ **VW Kombi Van: Campbell's,** 1998, Yellow body with 60's-inspired graphics on sides, flower tampos on roof, silver wheels, "100th Anniversary of Campbell's Condensed Soup" in red type on doors. Part of a mail-in offer program advertised on Campbell's soup labels
EX n/a   **NM** n/a   **MIP** $10

STANDARD

❑ **1928 Chevrolet Delivery Truck: Tuborg,** 1996, White body with red chassis and fenders, gold plastic grille, red wheels, thin black tires, green beer cases in truck bed with "Tuborg OI" in yellow lettering, "Tuborgs Bryggerier" on sides, Model No. DG26018
EX n/a   **NM** n/a   **MIP** $8

(KP Photo)

❑ **1934 Dennis Parcels Van: Cadbury's,** 1987, Dark blue body, white roof, white wheels with thin tires, gold plastic grille, "Cadbury's Dairy Milk Chocolate" on sides, Model No. DG16009

EX n/a　　**NM** n/a　　**MIP** $7

(Lledo Photo)

❑ **1934 Model A Ford State Truck - Mobil,** 2002, Red stake truck body, black "Mobil" lettering on sides of bed, Model No. DG020025

EX n/a　　**NM** n/a　　**MIP** $6

(KP Photo)

❑ **1939 Ford Fire Engine: US Navy Airfield, San Diego,** 1999, Gray cab, yellow body with brown plastic ladders, black hose reel, "US Navy Air Station San Diego" on doors, gray wheels, thin black tires, silver plastic grille. This casting matches one used by Corgi Classics in their Showcase series the Milwood, NY Fire Pumper, Model No. DG79002

EX n/a　　**NM** n/a　　**MIP** $9

(Lledo Photo)

❑ **1939 Ford Tanker - BP,** 2002, Green body with black fenders, red tanker section, Model No. DG057006

EX n/a　　**NM** n/a　　**MIP** $6

(KP Photo)

❑ **1942 Dodge 4x4: San Jose Fire Dept.,** 1994, Yellow body, white chassis and fenders, black wheels, spare attached to side, red type reads, "San Jose Fire Dept." on sides and "Airport" on doors. A popular casting for Lledo, with many military and civilian variations, this model also shows up in Corgi's Texaco Showcase lineup, Model No. DG29007

EX n/a　　**NM** n/a　　**MIP** $8

(Lledo Photo)

❑ **Bedford 30cwt - Wynn's,** 2002, Bright red body, white roof, yellow lettering "Wynn's" on sides, silver plastic grille, Model No. DG059030

EX n/a　　**NM** n/a　　**MIP** $6

(Lledo Photo)

❑ **Bedford 30cwt Van - Mr Kipling,** 2002, White body with red panels and roof, Model No. DG063024

EX n/a　　**NM** n/a　　**MIP** $6

(Lledo Photo)

❑ **Bull Nose Morris Van - Royal Mail,** 2002, Red body with black fenders & roof, "Royal Mail" on panel sides, Model No. DG050044

EX n/a　　**NM** n/a　　**MIP** $6

(Lledo Photo)

❑ **Bull Nose Morris Van - The Macallan,** 2002, White body, gold roof, fenders, wheels and grille, Model No. DG050045

EX n/a　　**NM** n/a　　**MIP** $6

(Lledo Photo)

❑ **Burrell Showman's Road Roller - J Dickinson & Sons Ltd,** 2002, Model No. DG126003
EX n/a   NM n/a   MIP $8

(Lledo Photo)

❑ **Burrell Showman's Steam Wagon - Joseph Brewer & Sons Golden Gallopers,** 2002, Bright red, white roof, black stack and trim, Model No. DG125004
EX n/a   NM n/a   MIP $8

(Lledo Photo)

❑ **Chevrolet Van - Royal Mail,** 2002, Red body, silver plastic grille, black fenders and roof, "Royal Mail" and royal crest on panel sides, Model No. DG021054
EX n/a   NM n/a   MIP $6

(Lledo Photo)

❑ **Dennis Delivery Van - Eddie Stobart,** 2002, Red chassis, black body "Eddie Stobart, Ltd. Cumbria" on sides, Model No. DG066025
EX n/a   NM n/a   MIP $6

(Lledo Photo)

❑ **Dennis Delivery Van - Fisher Renwick,** 2002, Dark blue body, white roof, "Fisher Renwick" lettering blue, gold wheels, silver grille, Model No. DG066024
EX n/a   NM n/a   MIP $6

(Lledo Photo)

❑ **Dick Kerr Tram closed top - Bandettes,** 2002, Tram, red body, Model No. DG108004
EX n/a   NM n/a   MIP $6

(Lledo Photo)

❑ **Dick Kerr Tram open top - Woman's Own,** 2002, Red and white body "Woman's Own" on sides, Model No. DG109002
EX n/a   NM n/a   MIP $6

(Lledo Photo)

❑ **Foden Steam Wagon - Tate & Lyle's,** 2002, Red with black plastic canopy, gold stack, Model No. DG091009
EX n/a   NM n/a   MIP $6

(Lledo Photo)

❑ **Ford Model A Van - Balvenie,** 2002, Model No. DG013086
EX n/a   NM n/a   MIP $6

(Lledo Photo)

❑ **Ford Model T Van - Brazil,** 2002, Red spoked wheels, red body, yellow type, Model No. DG006169
EX n/a   NM n/a   MIP $6

(Lledo Photo)

❑ **Ford Model T Van - Glenmorangie,** 2002, Light yellow body, black spoked wheels, brown fenders and roof, Model No. DG006168
EX n/a   NM n/a   MIP $6

(Lledo Photo)

❏ **Fordson 7V Truck - BRS,** 2002, Red body with tan canvas top, red wheels, silver grille, "British Road Service", Model No. DG100008

EX n/a   NM n/a   MIP $6

(Lledo Photo)

❏ **Horse Drawn Delivery Van,** 2002, Red with white roof, black spoked wheels, Model No. DG003019

EX n/a   NM n/a   MIP $6

(Lledo Photo)

❏ **J Dickinson & Sons Ltd Renault Van - Laphroaig,** 2002, White body, black roof & fenders, gold grille, Model No. DG085019

EX n/a   NM n/a   MIP $6

(Lledo Photo)

❏ **Model T Ford Tanker - Dixon's Oil,** 2002, Black with green tank section, red wheels, "Dixon's" on tank, Model No. DG008024

EX n/a   NM n/a   MIP $6

(Lledo Photo)

❏ **Morris LD150 Van Jacobs 1940 Assorted,** 2002, Light blue body, "1940 Jacobs Assorted," on panel sides, black wheels, Model No. DG071020

EX n/a   NM n/a   MIP $6

(Lledo Photo)

❏ **Morris Minor Van - Pickfords,** 2002, Dark blue body, white roof, "Pickfords" on sides, Model No. DG127002

EX n/a   NM n/a   MIP $6

(Lledo Photo)

❏ **Morris Minor Van - Ponds Face Powder,** 2002, Medium blue, black wheels, black grille, Model No. DG127003

EX n/a   NM n/a   MIP $6

(Lledo Photo)

❏ **Morris Parcel Van - Eddie Stobart,** 2002, Sloping roof, red chassis, red wheels, gold plastic grille, Model No. DG052023

EX n/a   NM n/a   MIP $6

(Lledo Photo)

❏ **Morris Parcel Van - Royal Mail,** 2002, Red body, sloping roof, silver grille, "Royal Mail" on sides, Model No. DG052024

EX n/a   NM n/a   MIP $6

(Lledo Photo)

❏ **Morris Van - Regent,** 2002, Red, silver grille, black wheels, "Regent", Model No. DG043034

EX n/a   NM n/a   MIP $6

(Lledo Photo)

LLEDO / DAYS GONE

❏ **Renault Van - Womens Land Army,** 2002, Brown and gold body with poster graphics on panel sides, Model No. DG085020
EX n/a   NM n/a   MIP $6

(Lledo Photo)

❏ **VW Kombi Van - Starlight Matches,** 2002, Red body, yellow signage, black wheels, Model No. DG073017
EX n/a   NM n/a   MIP $6

TRACKSIDE

(Lledo Photo)

❏ **AEC Mammoth with Flatbed Trailer and Brick load: London Brick Co.,** 2002, Red body with brick load, Model No. DG149000
EX n/a   NM n/a   MIP $17

(Lledo Photo)

❏ **Foden S21 Ballast Box: British Railways,** Red body, cream top half of cab, black fenders and chassis, Model No. DG147000
EX n/a   NM n/a   MIP $8

(Lledo Photo)

❏ **Foden S21 with Flatbed Trailer and Cement bags load: Blue Circle Cement,** Yellow cab and bed, blue chassis, cement bags on trailer, Model No. DG150000
EX n/a   NM n/a   MIP $17

(Lledo Photo)

❏ **GUY Pantechnican: BRS,** Green body with "BRS Parcel Services" in white, Model No. DG146000
EX n/a   NM n/a   MIP $8

(Lledo Photo)

❏ **Scammell with artic Low Loader and Transformer load: Fisher Renwick,** Black tractor and trailer, red wheels, blue roof, transformer on trailer, Model No. DG112007
EX n/a   NM n/a   MIP $17

(Lledo Photo)

❏ **Sentinel Ballast Box with Low Loader and Gun barrel load: LNER,** Model No. DG111002
EX n/a   NM n/a   MIP $17

The Ford Anglia 105E from 1999, white and green. The Vanguards models are packaged with a collector card and a bit of history of the vehicle. Also, side-mounted mirrors are included for the collector to attach. The box graphics are definitely in the tradition of older British die-cast toys.

By 1996, Lledo was beginning a new series of 1:43-scale British vehicles from the 1950s and '60s. These models were different than the Days Gone models Lledo had been making in that they were geared toward the collector, and packaged as such. Most were limited to 5,000 pieces, and indeed, models released back in 1996 tend to be harder to find, especially vehicle sets.

For about two years, Lledo created 1:64-scale models of trucks as part of the Cargo Carriers and Cargo Kings range.

After the purchase of Lledo by Zindart in 1999, these models were phased out of production, and the 1:43-scale vehicles are the only Vanguards still produced. Some of the castings have crossed lines back and forth with sister corporation Corgi, and the result has been some fun variations and models you wouldn't have seen in each company's lineup otherwise.

These days, the Vanguards range has expanded into new turf by replicating more British models from the late '60s and early '70s. European Vanguards, models featuring Saabs, Volkswagens and the like are available from die-cast dealers online.

MARKET UPDATE

Vanguards are not as easily found in the United States, although more and more American die-cast dealers are starting to carry them. For the most part, British die-cast dealers and auctions allow collectors to find a varied supply, but it can still be a challenge getting a hold of older British-made models. Usually, a single model is valued around $14 mint in pack, but factoring in overseas shipping can bump up the price a bit..

A 2001 release by Lledo, the Hillman Minx Salford City Police Car. This model has even greater detail than previous versions: photo-etched windshield wipers, more tampo detail, and more painted features on the body. It is seen here without the side-mounted mirrors included in the box.

A gift set by Lledo: the Post Office Telephones set, (PO 1002), from 1996. Like most Lledo Vanguards Gift Sets, this one was limited to 5,000 pieces, making it harder to find now. The detail on both vehicles, a Ford Anglia Van and a Morris Minor Van is well-done, and a history of the vehicles is included.

This Ford Anglia Panel Van is a limited-edition piece of 5,000. The limited edition pieces really do sell out, and over the years they can be harder-to-find. The Anglia van and saloon castings are well-used by Lledo, and are available in virtually every color/label combination.

One of the Vanguards European releases, the Saab 96. These models are just a bit tougher to get a hold of, but most British die-cast shops online carry them.

This Triumph Herald is a great example of the thoroughly British saloons in the Vanguards line. While many of the vehicle names are familiar with any collector of vintage British die-cast, it is almost unusual to see these models being produced now. Great detail on this 1:43-scale car.

From Lledo's new series, "Hidden Treasures," a Ford Transit in need of repair. This series is an interesting choice for Lledo: producing vehicles that look like they've seen heavy use. These models blur the line somewhat between model kit and die-cast model, because these pieces practically demand some customization and diorama-building.

COMMERCIALS

(Lledo Collectibles)

❑ **Austin A35 Van: British Railways,** 2002, Cream and maroon body, silver grille and trim, 1:43 scale, Model No. VA01707
EX n/a   NM n/a   MIP $15

(Lledo Collectibles)

❑ **Austin A40: Thames Valley,** 2002, Red body with black fenders and front quarter panels. Brown plastic step ladder stowed above, "Thames Valley" in gold type on panel sides, 1:43 scale, Model No. VA00316
EX n/a   NM n/a   MIP $15

❑ **Ford 300E Thames Van: Brylcreem,** 2001, Light red and cream colored van with "Brylcreem" lettering and graphics, 1:43 scale, Model No. VA33001
EX n/a   NM n/a   MIP $14

❑ **Ford 300E Thames Van: Evening Standard,** 2001, Red and black van with "Evening Standard," "Central 3000," and "21" tampos on sides, gray wheels, silver hubcaps. Limited edition, 1:43 scale, Model No. VA03303
EX n/a   NM n/a   MIP $15

❑ **Ford 300E Thames Van: Maidstone & District Bus Company,** 2001, Very dark green body with graphics on side panels, 1:43 scale, Model No. VA33002
EX n/a   NM n/a   MIP $15

(KP Photo)

❑ **Ford Anglia Van: Automobile Association,** 1996, Yellow body with plastic signage on roof for "Road Service." Base indicates the model was built in Enfield, England--not seen on baseplates after 1998, 1:43 scale, Model No. VA4001
EX n/a   NM n/a   MIP $15

(KP Photo)

❑ **Ford Anglia Van: Ford Special Products,** 2001, White van with "Ford Special Products" and Ford logos on sides, rear and top of car, white wheels, silver hubcaps, gray or black plastic interior, jewelled headligts. Limited run of 5,000, 1:43 scale, Model No. VA00412
EX n/a   NM n/a   MIP $14

(KP Photo)

❑ **Ford Anglia Van: Jordan's,** 1999, Dark blue-green and cream body with "Jordan's, Maker of Today's Farm Feeds" tampo and windmill graphic on sides, silver-painted details, black plastic interior, 1:43 scale, Model No. VA4010
EX n/a   NM n/a   MIP $14

(KP Photo)

❑ **Ford Anglia Van: RAC,** 1997, Medium blue body, white roof with "RAC Radio Rescue" sign, silver plastic grille, "Radio Rescue" in white type on side panels, gray wheels with silver hubs, thin tires, 1:43 scale, Model No. VA40005
EX n/a   NM n/a   MIP $16

(Lledo Collectibles)

❑ **Ford Anglia Van: Stratford Blue,** 2002, Light-blue body with white top and "Stratford Blue" on panels, 1:43 scale, Model No. VA00414
EX n/a   NM n/a   MIP $15

❑ **Ford Popular Van: Fordson Tractor Sales,** 2001, Orange and dark blue with "Fordson Mobile Parts Sales" in white type on sides and tractor graphic on panel. Orange hubcaps, black wheels, black grille. Limited edition, 1:43 scale, Model No. VA06200
EX n/a   NM n/a   MIP $15

(Lledo Collectibles)

❑ **Ford Transit Diesel,** 2001, Eddie Stobart model, 1:43 scale, Model No. VA06603
EX n/a   NM n/a   MIP $15

LLEDO / VANGUARDS

LLEDO / VANGUARDS

(Lledo Collectibles)

❏ **Ford Transit MKI Van,** 2001, Post Office Telephones service vehicle. This transit van is a continuation of a series of PO Telephone trucks Lledo has released since the launch of the Vanguards line in 1996. Altogether, they would make a sharp set, 1:43 scale, Model No. VA06600

EX n/a **NM** n/a **MIP** $15

(Lledo Collectibles)

❏ **Ford Transit MKI Van, Diesel,** 2002, Blackpool Transport: dark green with logos, silver side mirrors and hubs, 1:43 scale, Model No. VA06607

EX n/a **NM** n/a **MIP** $15

❏ **Ford Transit Van MKI: Evening News,** 2001, Black and yellow "panda" markings van with "Evening News" on sides and sides, plastic signage on top of van, gray wheels, gray hubcaps. Limited edition, 1:43 scale, Model No. VA06601

EX n/a **NM** n/a **MIP** $15

(Lledo Collectibles)

❏ **Ford Transit Van: British Rail,** 2002, Yellow body, "British Rail" on sides in small type, jewelled headlights, 1:43 scale, Model No. VA06612

EX n/a **NM** n/a **MIP** $16

(Lledo Collectibles)

❏ **Land Rover Series II,** 2002, Midland red, white roof, red wheels, green plastic tarp over bed. Nicely detailed piece. This popular casting has also been used in the Corgi lineup, 1:43 scale, Model No. VA07600

EX n/a **NM** n/a **MIP** $15

(Lledo Collectibles)

❏ **Morris Commercial Truck: British Railways,** 2002, Cream and maroon body, silver grille, jewelled headlights, black wheels, 1:43 scale, Model No. VA07500

EX n/a **NM** n/a **MIP** $16

(Lledo Collectibles)

❏ **Morris Minor Van,** 2001, Eddie Stobart, 1:43 scale, Model No. VA01116

EX n/a **NM** n/a **MIP** $15

(Lledo Collectibles)

❏ **Morris Minor Van: British Railways,** 2002, Red body, yellow British Railways lion emblem on panel sides, silver side-mounted mirrors, hubcaps and trim, jewelled headlights, 1:43 scale, Model No. VA01119

EX n/a **NM** n/a **MIP** $16

(Lledo Collectibles)

❏ **Morris Minor Van: Oxford Motor Services,** 2002, Red and black body with white stripe on sides, gold type reads "Oxford Motor Services" on panels, 1:43 scale, Model No. VA01118

EX n/a **NM** n/a **MIP** $15

EURO SERIES

(Lledo Collectibles)

❏ **Ford Consul,** 2002, Ruby red body with gray trim, five-spoke wheels, wide tires, 1:43 scale, Model No. VA05505

EX n/a **NM** n/a **MIP** $16

(Lledo Collectibles)

❏ **Ford Granada: Polizei Saarland,** 2002, White and dark green body, "Polizei" in white lettering, blue dome light, wide tires, 1:43 scale, Model No. VA05204

EX n/a   NM n/a   MIP $16

(Lledo Collectibles)

❏ **Ford Transit MKI CRS,** 2002, Dark green body, silver bar covers over headlights, white wheels, silver hubcaps, blue dome light on roof, 1:43 scale, Model No. VA06608

EX n/a   NM n/a   MIP $16

(Lledo Collectibles)

❏ **Ford Transit Van: Amstelveen Police,** 2002, White body, orange stripes, black "Politie" on front, blue dome lights, 1:43 scale, Model No. VA06611

EX n/a   NM n/a   MIP $16

(Lledo Collectibles)

❏ **Mercedes Benz 300SL,** 2002, Light blue-green convertible, silver trim, bumper and grille, gold hubs, thin tires, 1:43 scale, Model No. VA07800

EX n/a   NM n/a   MIP $16

(Lledo Collectibles)

❏ **Porsche 356,** 2002, Metallic purple-blue body, black convertible roof, silver wheels, 1:43 scale, Model No. VA07900

EX n/a   NM n/a   MIP $16

(Lledo Collectibles)

❏ **Saab 96,** 2002, Savanna beige body, silver grille and bumpers, gray wheels, thin tires, 1:43 scale, Model No. VA07700

EX n/a   NM n/a   MIP $16

(Lledo Collectibles)

❏ **Volkswagen Beetle, split window,** 2002, Green body, silver trim and hubcaps, narrow tires, 1:43 scale, Model No. VA01205

EX n/a   NM n/a   MIP $16

(Lledo Collectibles)

❏ **Volkswagen Camper,** 2002, Red and dark brown body, silver wheels, spare on front, brown interior, 1:43 scale, Model No. VA08100

EX n/a   NM n/a   MIP $16

(Lledo Collectibles)

❏ **Volkswagen LT1 Transporter: Hessen Polizei,** 2002, Dark green body, "Polizei" in white lettering, black wheels, blue dome light, 1:43 scale, Model No. VA08000

EX n/a   NM n/a   MIP $16

HIDDEN TREASURES

(Lledo Collectibles)

❏ **Austin Allegro,** 2002, Glacier white 4-door body, with silver grille and side mirrors, painted-on rust spots, "dirty windshield," dinged-up silver hubcaps, 1:43 scale, Model No. VA04506

EX n/a   NM n/a   MIP $15

(Lledo Collectibles)

❏ **Ford Granada 3.0 Ghia,** 2002, Sebring red body, black hood and roof, silver spoked wheels, rust spots on chrome parts, 1:43 scale, Model No. VA05206

EX n/a   NM n/a   MIP $16

LLEDO / VANGUARDS

(Lledo Collectibles)

❏ **Ford Transit MK1,** 2002, White, with painted "dirt" on sides, hood and top. Graffiti on sides reads, "I wish my bird was as dirty as this van!" Part of a fun new series by Lledo, showing many of their famous vehicles as they appear in real life--less than perfect, 1:43 scale, Model No. VA06609
EX n/a   NM n/a   MIP $15

(Lledo Collectibles)

❏ **Morris 1000 Pick Up,** 2002, Dark purple body, red fenders with paint nicks, dull-chrome bumpers with rust spots, 1:43 scale, Model No. VA08300
EX n/a   NM n/a   MIP $16

(Lledo Collectibles)

❏ **Morris Marina,** 2002, Blaze-colored body with primered front quarter panels and primer spots throughout, silver grille and detailing, dinged-up silver hubcaps, wide tires, 1:43 scale, Model No. VA06304
EX n/a   NM n/a   MIP $15

(Lledo Collectibles)

❏ **Reliant Regal Supervan,** 2002, Three-wheeled van with powder blue body, dirty windshield, paint nicks, 1:43 scale, Model No. VA02204
EX n/a   NM n/a   MIP $16

POLICE VEHICLES

❏ **Austin A60 Cambridge,** 2001, Hertfordshire Constabulary. Black with some pinstriping on sides, blue roof light, white wheels with silver hubs, "police" plates on front grille, red plastic interior. Limited edition, 1:43 scale, Model No. VA04403
EX n/a   NM n/a   MIP $15

(Lledo Collectibles)

❏ **Austin A60 Cambridge,** 2002, Cardiff City Police, plain white body with no police markings, blue roof light, silver hubs and grille, 1:43 scale, Model No. VA04405
EX n/a   NM n/a   MIP $15

(Lledo Collectibles)

❏ **Ford Anglia,** 2002, Liverpool and Bootle Police, plain white body with "Police" in black lettering along sides, 1:43 scale, Model No. VA00120
EX n/a   NM n/a   MIP $15

❏ **Ford Consul,** 2001, West Yorkshire Constabulary. White car with orange stripe, blue roof light on "police" sign, gray spoked wheels. Limited edition, 1:43 scale, Model No. VA05503
EX n/a   NM n/a   MIP $15

(Lledo Collectibles)

❏ **Ford Cortina MKII 1600 GT,** 2002, Lancashire Constabulary: white with orange sides, police shield on doors, "Police" sign on roof with blue dome light, silver hubs, orange wheels, 1:43 scale, Model No. VA04105
EX n/a   NM n/a   MIP $15

(Lledo Collectibles)

❏ **Ford Granada,** 2002, Greater Manchester Police, white body with black hood, orange stripe on sides with Manchester Police Shield, blue dome light mounted on "Police" sign, antennae on roof, five-spoked silver-gray wheels, wide tires, 1:43 scale, Model No. VA05203
EX n/a   NM n/a   MIP $15

❏ **Ford Lotus Cortina MKII,** 2001, Hampshire Constabulary, white car with blue roof light mounted on "Police" sign. Black type "Police" on sides of car. Limited edition, 1:43 scale, Model No. VA04101
EX n/a   NM n/a   MIP $15

(Lledo Collectibles)

❑ **Ford Transit MKI Van,** 2002, Lancashire Constabulary Section Van, light blue and white body with police shield on doors and blue roof light, 1:43 scale, Model No. VA06610

EX n/a   NM n/a   MIP $20

❑ **Ford Transit MKI, Series II Van,** 2001, Lancashire Accident Unit, orange and white with red roof light on "police" sign, fluorescent illuminating lights on each side, "Lancashire Constabulary" on panels of van. Limited edition, 1:43 scale, Model No. VA06602

EX n/a   NM n/a   MIP $15

❑ **Ford Zephyr 4 MKIII,** 2001, Bomb Disposal Unit, red and blue body with blue roof light. Limited edition, 1:43 scale, Model No. VA60001

EX n/a   NM n/a   MIP $15

(Lledo Collectibles)

❑ **Ford Zephyr 6 Mk. III,** 2002, Royal Ulster Constabulary, dark green body with "Police" sign and blue dome light on roof, silver grille and trim, 1:43 scale, Model No. VA04604

EX n/a   NM n/a   MIP $16

(Lledo Collectibles)

❑ **Ford Zephyr 6 MKIII,** 2002, Plymouth City Police car, white body with black doors and "Police" reversed out in white, 1:43 scale, Model No. VA04603

EX n/a   NM n/a   MIP $15

❑ **Ford Zephyr 6, MKIII,** 2001, West Riding Constabulary. Black and white (panda) paint scheme, small blue roof light, siren speakers on front bumper, 1:43 scale, Model No. VA46000

EX n/a   NM n/a   MIP $15

(KP Photo)

❑ **Hillman Minx 111A: Salford City Police,** 2001, Black and white "panda" body markings, Salford City shield on doors. Highly detailed with photo-etched windshield wipers, "Hillman" tampos, jewelled headlights, white wheels with silver hubs, thin tires, 1:43 scale, Model No. VA06801

EX n/a   NM n/a   MIP $16

(Lledo Collectibles)

❑ **Jaguar Mk. II,** 2002, Somerset Constabulary, silver multi-spoked wheels and trim, red dome light, 1:43 scale, Model No. VA08400

EX n/a   NM n/a   MIP $16

(Lledo Collectibles)

❑ **Land Rover Canvas Back Truck,** 2002, Kent Police, black truck with black canvas tarp over truck bed, Kent Police emblem on doors, blue "Police" sign on roof, silver bumpers and grille, black wheels, 1:43 scale, Model No. VA07601

EX n/a   NM n/a   MIP $16

❑ **Mini Van,** 2001, Metropolitan Police, white with orange and yellow stripes, silver hubs, 1:43 scale, Model No. VA14014

EX n/a   NM n/a   MIP $15

❑ **Rover 3500 V8,** 2001, Metropolitan Police, dark blue body, two roof-mounted plastic spotlights, blue roof light, five-spoke wheels. Limited edition, 1:43 scale, Model No. VA06501

EX n/a   NM n/a   MIP $15

(Lledo Collectibles)

❑ **Triumph 2000,** 2002, West Mercia Police, white with orange trunk and doors, "Police" sign and blue dome light on roof, "Police" on doors, silver wheels, 1:43 scale, Model No. VA08201

EX n/a   NM n/a   MIP $16

(Lledo Collectibles)

❑ **Triumph Dolomite Sprint,** 2002, Nottingham Constabulary, white body, black roof, red dome light, "Police" on doors and trunk, silver spoked wheels, 1:43 scale, Model No. VA05306

EX n/a   NM n/a   MIP $16

RACING

❑ **Austin Allegro,** 2001, Patrick Motors. Red with white stripe, gray spoked wheels, rally lights under front bumper. Limited edition, 1:43 scale, Model No. VA04505

EX n/a   NM n/a   MIP $15

❏ **Austin Healy 3000 MKI,** 2001, Historic Rally car. Red with white roof and "Unipart" graphics. Large, silver-spoked wheels. Limited edition, 1:43 scale, Model No. VA57000
EX n/a   **NM** n/a   **MIP** $15

❏ **Broadspeed Dolomite Sprint,** 2001, Andy Rouse 1975 rally edition. Silver with "40" on doors and various company logos, including Leyland and Dunlop. Silver spoked hubcaps. Limited edition, 1:43 scale, Model No. VA05303
EX n/a   **NM** n/a   **MIP** $15

❏ **Ford Lotus Cortina MKII,** 2001, Roger Clark 1967 rally model. White with dark green stipe, number "2" in circle on doors and on hood, gray 8-spoked wheels, rally lights on front bumper. Limited edition, 1:43 scale, Model No. VA04102
EX n/a   **NM** n/a   **MIP** $15

❏ **Hillman Imp Californian,** 2001, 1986 Coronation Rally. Red with white top, "47" on doors, black spoked wheels. Limited edition, 1:43 scale, Model No. VA40002
EX n/a   **NM** n/a   **MIP** $15

❏ **Rover P4,** 2001, Round the World Rally edition, driven by Tony Sinclair and David Hughes. Black and gray with "58" on doors. Limited edition, 1:43 scale, Model No. VA01911
EX n/a   **NM** n/a   **MIP** $15

❏ **Rover P6 2000,** 2001, Roger Clark's rally car, 1965 Monte Carlo. Dark green with white roof and "136" numbering on doors. Plain black wheels, 1:43 scale, Model No. VA27008
EX n/a   **NM** n/a   **MIP** $15

❏ **Triumph Dolomite Sprint,** 2001, British Leyland Works Rally Car. White with black roof, blue, yellow and red striping on hood and around sides, spoked hubs, 1:43 scale, Model No. VA53001
EX n/a   **NM** n/a   **MIP** $15

❏ **Vauxhall Victor F-Series MKI,** 2001, 1959 Kenya Coronation Safari Rally. Dark-red body with white roof, "52" on doors and on front bumper plate. Limited edition, 1:43 scale, Model No. VA38003
EX n/a   **NM** n/a   **MIP** $15

SALOON SETS

❏ **Hillman Imp,** 2002, Hillman Imp, in silver, one of three vehicles in the set including the Hillman Minx and Singer Chamois. Price reflects value of complete set, 1:43 scale, Model No. HI1003A
EX n/a   **NM** n/a   **MIP** $47

❏ **Hillman Minx,** 2002, Second car in the three-car set, 1:43 scale, Model No. HI1003B

(Lledo Collectibles)

❏ **Hillman Singer Chamois,** 2002, Third car in the Hillman set, 1:43 scale, Model No. HI1003C

❏ **Rover P4 100,** 2002, Rover model in Ivory, part of three-vehicle set featuring the P5 in steel blue, and the 3500 in green. Price shown reflects value of complete set, 1:43 scale, Model No. RC1003A
EX n/a   **NM** n/a   **MIP** $47

(Lledo Collectibles)

❏ **Rover P5,** 2002, Second car in the Rover Collection, 1:43 scale, Model No. RC1003B

(Lledo Collectibles)

❏ **Rover P6 3500,** 2002, In Cameron Green, the latest model year car in the Rover Collection. Set of three vehicles price shown, 1:43 scale, Model No. RC1003C
EX n/a   **NM** n/a   **MIP** $47

SALOONS

❏ **Austin 1300 Estate,** 2001, Beige two-door station wagon, light-brown plastic interior, 1:43 scale, Model No. VA05601
EX n/a   **NM** n/a   **MIP** $15

❏ **Austin 1300 Estate,** 2001, Snowberry white body (off-white) with gray wheels and small silver hubcaps, dark gray plastic interior, 1:43 scale, Model No. VA56000
EX n/a   **NM** n/a   **MIP** $14

❏ **Austin 7 Mini,** 2001, Black, limited edition, 1:43 scale, Model No. VA01306
EX n/a   **NM** n/a   **MIP** $15

❏ **Austin A35,** 2001, Old English white, limited edition, 1:43 scale, Model No. VA02306
EX n/a   **NM** n/a   **MIP** $15

(Lledo Collectibles)

❏ **Austin A60 Cambridge,** 2002, Persian blue with snowberry white stripe, light gray interior, silver grille and detailing, 1:43 scale, Model No. VA04406
EX n/a   **NM** n/a   **MIP** $15

(Lledo Collectibles)

❏ **Austin Allegro,** 2002, Brazil Metallic (metallic dark brown) body, sorrel interior, gray wheels with silver hubcaps, silver trim, 1:43 scale, Model No. VA04507
EX n/a   **NM** n/a   **MIP** $16

❏ **Austin Allegro Series I 1500 Super Deluxe,** 2001, Dark blue (Cosmic Blue) four-door, gray wheels, silver hubcaps, limited edition, 1:43 scale, Model No. VA04504

EX n/a   NM n/a   MIP $15

(Lledo Collectibles)

❏ **Ford Anglia,** 2002, Bermuda blue body, Azure white roof and stripe, silver grille and trim, 1:43 scale, Model No. VA00122

EX n/a   NM n/a   MIP $16

❏ **Ford Anglia 105E,** 2001, Blue body with white roof, gray wheels, silver hubcaps, and silver painted pinstripe detail, 1:43 scale, Model No. VA00116

EX n/a   NM n/a   MIP $15

(KP Photo)

❏ **Ford Anglia 105E: White and green,** 1999, Dark-green roof and stripe, white body, white hubs with silver hubcaps, silver-painted detailing, 1:43 scale, Model No. VA0141

EX n/a   NM n/a   MIP $12

(Lledo Collectibles)

❏ **Ford Anglia Super,** 2002, Venetian-gold (light gold) metallic body, silver grille, hubcaps and side mirrors, gray wheels, narrow tires, 1:43 scale, Model No. VA00119

EX n/a   NM n/a   MIP $15

❏ **Ford Capri,** 2001, Monaco red body and ermine white roof, silver hubcaps, gray wheels. This was the first version of the Ford to be called a "Capri.", 1:43 scale, Model No. VA34004

EX n/a   NM n/a   MIP $15

❏ **Ford Consul,** 2001, Yellow body, black plastic interior, limited edition, 1:43 scale, Model No. VA05502

EX n/a   NM n/a   MIP $15

(Lledo Collectibles)

❏ **Ford Cortina MK II GT,** 2001, Ermine white body with black roof, 1:43 scale, Model No. VA04100

EX n/a   NM n/a   MIP $15

(Lledo Collectibles)

❏ **Ford Cortina MKI,** 2002, Goodwood green (dark green), light brown interior, gray wheels with silver-pearl hubs, narrow tires, 1:43 scale, Model No. VA07300

EX n/a   NM n/a   MIP $15

(Lledo Collectibles)

❏ **Ford Cortina MKII GT,** 2001, Ermine white and black, 1:43 scale, Model No. VA04100

EX n/a   NM n/a   MIP $14

(Lledo Collectibles)

❏ **Ford Cortina MKII Super,** 2002, Dragoon red, red wheels, silver hubs, grille and side mirrors, 1:43 scale, Model No. VA04106

EX n/a   NM n/a   MIP $15

❏ **Ford Granada Ghia,** 2001, Roman bonze body, wider, 5-spoke wheels, silver-painted details, limited edition, 1:43 scale, Model No. VA05201

EX n/a   NM n/a   MIP $15

(Lledo Collectibles)

❏ **Ford Granada Ghia,** 2002, Diamond white with black roof, five-spoked wheels, black grille, wide tires, 1:43 scale, Model No. VA05205

EX n/a   NM n/a   MIP $15

❏ **Ford Granada MKI,** 2001, Flame red (bright red) body, spoked hubs, 1:43 scale, Model No. VA52000

EX n/a   NM n/a   MIP $15

(Lledo Collectibles)

❏ **Ford Popular Saloon,** 2002, Dorchester gray, black grille, black wheels, brown interior, silver bumpers, 1:43 scale, Model No. VA07200

EX n/a   **NM** n/a   **MIP** $15

(Lledo Collectibles)

❏ **Ford Zephyr 4 MKIII,** 2001, Lime green, 1962 model, 1:43 scale, Model No. VA06000

EX n/a   **NM** n/a   **MIP** $15

(Lledo Collectibles)

❏ **Ford Zephyr MKII,** 2002, Aqua blue and Ermine white body, silver hubs, thin wheels, 1:43 scale, Model No. VA06101

EX n/a   **NM** n/a   **MIP** $15

(Lledo Collectibles)

❏ **Ford Zodiac Mk. II,** 2002, Two-tone green body, silver grille, wheels and trim, 1:43 scale, Model No. VA06102

EX n/a   **NM** n/a   **MIP** $16

(Lledo Collectibles)

❏ **Hillman Minx,** 2001, Ember red and cream body, silver trim, 1:43 scale, Model No. VA06800

EX n/a   **NM** n/a   **MIP** $15

(Lledo Collectibles)

❏ **Hillman Minx,** 2002, Embassy black body, red interior, silver grille and trim, great detail, 1:43 scale, Model No. VA06804

EX n/a   **NM** n/a   **MIP** $15

(Lledo Collectibles)

❏ **Hillman Minx IIIA,** 2002, Azure blue with pearl-gray roof, gray interior, silver-gray grille and hubs, 1:43 scale, Model No. VA06802

EX n/a   **NM** n/a   **MIP** $15

❏ **Mini Cooper 'S',** 2001, Cream body with black roof and spoked wheels, 1:43 scale, Model No. VA25005

EX n/a   **NM** n/a   **MIP** $15

❏ **Morris 1300 Estate,** 2001, Trafalgar blue, gray interior, 1:43 scale, Model No. VA48000

EX n/a   **NM** n/a   **MIP** $15

(Lledo Collectibles)

❏ **Morris Marina,** 2002, Glacier white body, silver grille and detailing, red interior, 1:43 scale, Model No. VA06303

EX n/a   **NM** n/a   **MIP** $15

(Lledo Collectibles)

❏ **Morris Marina 1800,** 2001, Teal blue, gray hubcaps, silver highlights, 1:43 scale, Model No. VA06300

EX n/a   **NM** n/a   **MIP** $15

(Lledo Collectibles)

❏ **Morris Marina 1800,** 2001, Teal blue, 1:43 scale, Model No. VA06300

EX n/a   **NM** n/a   **MIP** $14

(Lledo Collectibles)

❏ **Morris Minor Convertible,** 2002, Cream body with maroon roof, cream-colored wheels with pearl hubs, narrow, fine-tread tires, 1:43 scale, Model No. VA07100

EX n/a   **NM** n/a   **MIP** $15

❏ **Morris Oxford,** 2001, Medium gray-green, black wheels, silver hubcaps, regular plastic head-lights, 1:43 scale, Model No. VA54000

EX n/a   **NM** n/a   **MIP** $15

(Lledo Collectibles)

❏ **Morris Oxford,** 2002, Damask red, silver grille and trim, 1:43 scale, Model No. VA05402
EX n/a   NM n/a   MIP $16

❏ **Morris Oxford VI,** 2001, Trafalgar blue body with white roof, gray front grille, white multi-spoked wheels, limited edition, 1:43 scale, Model No. VA05401
EX n/a   NM n/a   MIP $15

❏ **Rover 3500 V8,** 2001, Almond body, black roof, silver and black hubcaps, silver-painted highlights and details, 1:43 scale, Model No. VA06500
EX n/a   NM n/a   MIP $15

(Lledo Collectibles)

❏ **Rover 3500 V8,** 2002, Brown with dark brown interior, silver stripe detail along sides, black and silver "flower-petal" hubcaps, 1:43 scale, Model No. VA06505
EX n/a   NM n/a   MIP $15

(Lledo Collectibles)

❏ **Rover P4,** 2002, Ivory body with silver wheels, grille and trim, 1:43 scale, Model No. VA01903
EX n/a   NM n/a   MIP $16

(Lledo Collectibles)

❏ **Rover P5,** 2002, Burgundy body with silver hubcaps, grille and trim, 1:43 scale, Model No. VA06904
EX n/a   NM n/a   MIP $16

(Lledo Collectibles)

❏ **Rover P5,** 2002, Steel blue body, silver-gray trim, 1:43 scale, Model No. VA06903
EX n/a   NM n/a   MIP $16

(Lledo Collectibles)

❏ **Rover P5 MKII,** 2002, Stone gray hood, roof and trunk, juniper green lower panels, gray and black hubs, silver-gray grille, 1:43 scale, Model No. VA06900
EX n/a   NM n/a   MIP $15

(Lledo Collectibles)

❏ **Rover P6 3500,** 2002, Cameron green--available separately or as part of Rover set. Beige interior, silver trim, 1:43 scale, Model No. VA06508
EX n/a   NM n/a   MIP $16

❏ **Singer Chamois Coupe,** 2001, Turquoise blue metallic, jewelled headlights, 1:43 scale, Model No. VA40001
EX n/a   NM n/a   MIP $15

(Lledo Collectibles)

❏ **Triumph 2000,** 2002, Delft blue body, black interior, gray wheels and trim, 1:43 scale, Model No. VA08200
EX n/a   NM n/a   MIP $16

❏ **Triumph Dolomite,** 2001, Yellow with black roof, spoked hubs, black pinstripe, 1:43 scale, Model No. VA53000
EX n/a   NM n/a   MIP $15

❏ **Triumph Dolomite Sprint,** 2001, Brooklands green--a very dark green body with silver-painted detailing, jewelled headlights, spoked hubs. Limited edition, 1:43 scale, Model No. VA05304
EX n/a   NM n/a   MIP $15

(Lledo Collectibles)

❏ **Triumph Herald Convertible,** 2002, Damson body with removable black plastic roof, red plastic interior, silver hubs, 1:43 scale, Model No. VA07400
EX n/a   NM n/a   MIP $15

(Lledo Collectibles)

❑ **Triumph Herald Convertible,** 2002, White body, black convertible roof, gray trim, 1:43 scale, Model No. VA07401
EX n/a **NM** n/a **MIP** $16

(KP Photo)

❑ **Triumph Herald: Two-tone green,** 1999, Dark-green roof and lower panels, light-green hood, nice silver detailing, white wheels, silver hubcaps, 1:43 scale, Model No. VA0105
EX n/a **NM** n/a **MIP** $14

(Lledo Collectibles)

❑ **Vauxhall Cresta,** 2002, Maroon and silver-gray, silver grille and hubcaps, whitewall tires, 1:43 scale, Model No. VA06403
EX n/a **NM** n/a **MIP** $15

(Lledo Collectibles)

❑ **Vauxhall PA Cresta,** 2001, Dusk rose and lilac haze, (two-tone dark and light pink), 1:43 scale, Model No. VA06400
EX n/a **NM** n/a **MIP** $15

(Lledo Collectibles)

❑ **Vauxhall Victor,** 2002, Metallic gray charcoal body, silver grille and trim, light gray interior,, 1:43 scale, Model No. VA03806
EX n/a **NM** n/a **MIP** $16

❑ **Vauxhall Victor F-Series MKI,** 2001, Gypsy Red (bright red), with gray wheels, small silver hubcaps, 1:43 scale, Model No. VA38000
EX n/a **NM** n/a **MIP** $15

SNAPSHOTS IN TIME GIFT SETS

❑ **Annual Inspection,** 2001, MGA and Ford Zephyr cars with Lancashire Constabulary vehicle inspection garage in the background. Includes female and male officer figures. Limited edition, 1:43 scale, Model No. PD2002
EX n/a **NM** n/a **MIP** $47

❑ **Austin A40 Van and Ford Anglia Van,** 2001, Whitbread Beer and Tavern set featuring Austin A40 and Ford Anglia vans in blue with "Whitbread" graphics on panels. Includes two figures with sky background, 1:43 scale, Model No. BD1002
EX n/a **NM** n/a **MIP** $47

(Lledo Collectibles)

❑ **Police Accident Set,** 2001, Includes Ford Transit Van, accident cones, policeman figure and road signs. Nottinghamshire Police Department, 1:43 scale, Model No. VA06606
EX n/a **NM** n/a **MIP** $25

(Lledo Collectibles)

❑ **RAC Set,** 2001, Includes an all-blue RAC Ford Anglia van, phone box and policeman, 1:43 scale, Model No. VA00413
EX n/a **NM** n/a **MIP** $23

❑ **Racing Scene,** 2001, Features two Ford Classic 109E cars, one in pea green and white and one in blue and white with numbers on doors. Cars are racing on a closed track setting with Castrol signage in the background. Based on an actual photo of a Ford public relations exercise in 1961, 1:43 scale, Model No. RD1002
EX n/a **NM** n/a **MIP** $47

❑ **Rally Diorama,** 2001, Features Mini Cooper splashing through an English landscape with a stone bridge and spectators. Limited edition, 1:43 scale, Model No. RD2001
EX n/a **NM** n/a **MIP** $28

❑ **Renfrew & Bute Constabulary,** 2001, Features Rover 200 police car in Renfrew and Bute markings--white care with orange stripe and blue door panel--plus a bronze Jaguar XK120 set before a village scene. Includes officer and female figures. Limited edition, 1:43 scale, Model No. PD1002
EX n/a **NM** n/a **MIP** $47

❑ **Royal Mail Scene,** 2001, Features red Royal Mail Morris Minor van and Mini Van dusted with snow in front of a snow-covered post office and village scene. Includes a postman figure, limited edition, 1:43 scale, Model No. GD1002
EX n/a **NM** n/a **MIP** $47

(Lledo Collectibles)

❏ **Royal Mail Set,** 2001, Mini Van, postman figure and mailbox, limited edition, 1:43 scale, Model No. VA01416
EX n/a   **NM** n/a   **MIP** $23

(Lledo Collectibles)

❏ **Telecommunications Set,** 2001, Features Ford Transit van, figure and telephone box, 1:43 scale, Model No. VA06604
EX n/a   **NM** n/a   **MIP** $25

SPORTS CARS

(Lledo Collectibles)

❏ **Austin Healey,** 2002, Healey blue (a silver-blue) and ivory white convertible body, spoked wheels, nice silver detailing and trim, 1:43 scale, Model No. VA05701
EX n/a   **NM** n/a   **MIP** $15

❏ **Jaguar XK120,** 2002, Suede green body, black interior, silver trim, 1:43 scale, Model No. VA05902
EX n/a   **NM** n/a   **MIP** $16

(Lledo Collectibles)

❏ **MGA Open Top,** 2002, Chariot red, silver-spoked wheels, fine-tread tires, light brown interior, 1:43 scale, Model No. VA05003
EX n/a   **NM** n/a   **MIP** $15

(Lledo Collectibles)

❏ **Sunbeam Alpine,** 2002, White body, silver trim, great exterior and interior detail, 1:43 scale, Model No. VA07001
EX n/a   **NM** n/a   **MIP** $16

(Lledo Collectibles)

❏ **Sunbeam Alpine MKII,** 2002, Carnival red convertible body, black removable top, black plastic interior, silver bumpers, thin-stripe whitewall tires, 1:43 scale, Model No. VA07000
EX n/a   **NM** n/a   **MIP** $15

❏ **Triumph Spitfire MKII,** 2001, Signal red, 1:43 scale, Model No. VA06700
EX n/a   **NM** n/a   **MIP** $15

(Lledo Collectibles)

❏ **Triumph Spitfire MKII Hard Top,** 2002, Royal blue body, silver detailing, black interior, 1:43 scale, Model No. VA06704
EX n/a   **NM** n/a   **MIP** $15

(Lledo Collectibles)

❏ **Triumph Spitfire MKIII Soft Top,** 2002, Jasmine yellow, black roof, black interior, silver grille and trim, whitewall tires, 1:43 scale, Model No. VA06707
EX n/a   **NM** n/a   **MIP** $16

(Lledo Collectibles)

❏ **Triumph Spitfire MKIII Soft Top,** 2002, White convertible body, red interior, red removable top, white wheels, silver hubs, 1:43 scale, Model No. VA06705
EX n/a   **NM** n/a   **MIP** $15

(Lledo Collectibles)

❏ **Triumph TR3A,** 2002, Silverstone gray exterior, red roof, silver multi-spoked wheels and trim, including luggage rack, 1:43 scale, Model No. VA04702
EX n/a   **NM** n/a   **MIP** $16

Maisto Die-Cast

The 1948 Chevrolet Fleetmaster Woody Station Wagon in 1:18-scale. This is one of Maisto's nicest vintage models, with incredible detail, including steering wheels, opening doors, rubber tires and an opening hood.

Maisto is a well-known name among die-cast collectors, but its predecessor was well known, too—Zee Toys. (Or Zylmex, as they were also popularly known).

May Cheong Toy Products is a Hong Kong-based company that made many replica 1:64-scale toy cars in the 1970s and 1980s, branding them "Zylmex" or "Zee Toys." They produced everything from road cars, ("Dynawheels" and "Pacesetters") motorcycles, (Ridge Riders) tanks (Dynamights) and aircraft, (Dyna-Flites).

By the mid-1990s, "Zee Toy" and "Zylmex"-branded toys started to disappear from store shelves. By 1997, the Maisto became more noticeable, producing high-quality die-cast cars in the 1:18 and 1:24-scale sizes that were becoming popular.

Detail is certainly the key when looking at Maisto models. Even their series of pull-back cars focuses on not-usually-seen vehicles. Plus, they even have opening doors, something many die-cast toys lack these days.

MARKET UPDATE

It's really a collectors' market for Maisto die-cast. Their vehicle toys are sold virtually everywhere, and at very reasonable prices. The toy lineup, G.I. Joe, Tonka and pull-back vehicles are very popular with kids. Maisto's Special Edition and Premium Edition 1:18-scale die-cast vehicles are extremely well-detailed models, available at most toy and hobby stores. They are currently priced at an average of $25 each, although smaller models (Mini Coopers, for instance) generally sell for less. The 1:24-scale vehicles are detailed enough to enjoy opening doors and rubber tires, but priced right for everyone to collect.

Some of the Harley-Davidson models and the Tour d'Maisto series truly recall their Zee Toys Ridge Rider and City Cycle series forebears, as do the Tailwinds series of die-cast toy aircraft resemble the Dyna-Flites series.

A close-up of the opening hood and engine on the Fleetmaster wagon.

Pre-Maisto: Zee Toy Alarm Busters 3" cars. They featured flashing LEDs and a siren sound that was activated by pressing down on the car. 1989. They were in the Maisto line until 2001.

From the Tailwinds series—a B25-J Mitchell bomber. Reminiscent of the old Zee toys "Dyna-Flites" series.

Another Zee Toy vehicle, Color Splash cars with thermochromic paint (changes color depending on temperature). Kids were encouraged to dip them in warm water to see a different color. Huge sellers for Zee Toys, introduced in 1989.

The 1969 Ford Torino Talladega (#31616) by Maisto. This highly-detailed 1:18-scale model features opening doors, hood and trunk, and working steering and suspension.

New for 2002—the Lamborghini Murcielago. This 1:18-scale model from the Special Edition series also features the opening hood, doors and trunk that other Maisto vehicles share.

More Zee Toys, the Power Flippers. They were 6"-long all-plastic battery-operated cars. When it hit the wall, it would flip over and come back as a "different" car. A neat idea that didn't work out as well for the company as they would've hoped.

A view of the detailed engine in the '69 Talladega by Maisto.

The Chrysler PT Cruiser, "Hot PT" from the 1:18-scale Cool Cruisers series. A noticeable model in a bright blue finish with silver and yellow flames, working steering, independent suspension and opening doors and tailgate.

The Honda S2000, a 1:18-scale model featuring opening hood, doors and trunk, plus working steering and suspension.

The 1:18-scale 1972 Chevelle SS454 Sport Coupe is another popular casting for Maisto. The details on the car include opening doors, hood and trunk.

Another view of the Chevelle showing steerable wheels, opening hood and detailed engine.

While Maisto makes some great vintage car models, they stay up-to-minute, too. Now, they've made one of the year's coolest cars, the 2002 Ford Focus SVT, in 1:24-scale, with a Sonic Blue body and opening doors and hood.

1:10-SCALE HARLEY-DAVIDSON MOTORCYCLES

(Maisto International, Inc.)

❑ **1999 FLSTF Fat Boy,** Red or silver body, detailed engine, working suspension, 1:10 scale, Model No. 31606

EX n/a   **NM** n/a   **MIP** $38

(Maisto International, Inc.)

❑ **1999 FLSTF Heritage Springer,** Black body with red or blue trim, working suspension, 1:10 scale, Model No. 31605

EX n/a   **NM** n/a   **MIP** $38

1:10-SCALE SPECIAL EDITION MOTORCYCLES

(Maisto International, Inc.)

❑ **BMW R1100R,** Red or dark blue body, silver-gray engine and wheels, black seat, 1:10 scale, Model No. 31601

EX n/a   **NM** n/a   **MIP** $37

(Maisto International, Inc.)

❑ **Honda VT1100C2,** Aqua or red with "Shadow" logo on tank. Chrome fork, wheels and engine, 1:10 scale, Model No. 31602

EX n/a   **NM** n/a   **MIP** $38

(Maisto International, Inc.)

❑ **Moto Guzzi California,** Red and black or yellow and black body, black saddlebags, chrome fork, engine and wheels. Full suspension, 1:10 scale, Model No. 31603

EX n/a   **NM** n/a   **MIP** $37

1:12-SCALE SPECIAL EDITION

(Maisto International, Inc.)

❑ **Cadillac Eldorado Biarritz,** Pink or white body, detailed interior, whitewall tires, adjustable seats and visors, working steering, independent suspension, opening hood, doors and trunk, 1:12 scale, Model No. 33202

EX n/a   **NM** n/a   **MIP** $35

(Maisto International, Inc.)

❑ **Jaguar XJ220,** Silver or dark green body, solid silver-gray wheels, opening hood, doors and trunk, steerable wheels, four-wheel suspension, adjustable seats, detailed interior, 1:12 scale, Model No. 33201

EX n/a   **NM** n/a   **MIP** $35

(Maisto International, Inc.)

❑ **Jaguar XJ220,** Yellow body, yellow and chrome multi-spoked wheels, opening hood, doors and trunk, steerable wheels, four-wheel suspension, adjustable seats, detailed interior, 1:12 scale, Model No. 33203

EX n/a   **NM** n/a   **MIP** $35

1:18-SCALE ASSEMBLY LINE KITS

(Maisto International, Inc.)

❑ **BMW Z8,** Red body, opening trunk, hood and doors. Kit includes metal body, plastic parts and extra wheels to customize. The kits are self-contained, including a screw driver to assemble, and do not need any glue or paint. Additionally, the vehicles are usually in a different color than the regular assembled die-cast vehicles, 1:18 scale, Model No. 39896

EX $4   **NM** $12   **MIP** $18

(Maisto International, Inc.)

❑ **Chevrolet Corvette Z06,** Yellow body, black interior, opening doors, hood and trunk, chrome or silver wheels, 1:18 scale, Model No. 39889
EX n/a   **NM** n/a   **MIP** n/a

(Maisto International, Inc.)

❑ **Chrysler Panel Cruiser,** 2002, Bright blue body, opening doors, hood and rear hatch, chrome or silver six-spoke wheels, 1:18 scale, Model No. 39618
EX n/a   **NM** $1   **MIP** $3

(Maisto International, Inc.)

❑ **Dodge Viper GT2,** White body, blue stripes running from front to rear, silver or chrome multi-spoked wheels, opening doors and hood, 1:18 scale, Model No. 39845
EX $4   **NM** $7   **MIP** $9

(Maisto International, Inc.)

❑ **Honda S2000,** Yellow body, opening doors, hood and trunk, black interior, silver or chrome wheels, 1:18 scale, Model No. 39879
EX n/a   **NM** n/a   **MIP** n/a

(Maisto International, Inc.)

❑ **Mini Cooper,** 2002, Red body, white roof, opening hood, doors and hatch, silver or chrome five-spoke wheels, 1:18 scale, Model No. 39619
EX $68   **NM** $77   **MIP** $94

(Maisto International, Inc.)

❑ **Opel Speedster,** 2002, Silver body, opening hoods and doors, black and gray interior, five-spoke wheels, 1:18 scale, Model No. 39615
EX $152   **NM** $291   **MIP** n/a

(Maisto International, Inc.)

❑ **Volkswagen New Beetle,** Silver body, light gray interior, opening doors, hood and trunk, nicely detailed kit, 1:18 scale, Model No. 39875
EX $3   **NM** $6   **MIP** $8

1:18-SCALE COOL CRUISERS

(Maisto International, Inc.)

❑ **Chrysler PT Cruiser: Cool Cruiser,** Purple body with teal and yellow flame tampo, chrome five-spoke wheels, opening doors and tailgate, working steering, independent suspension, 1:18 scale, Model No. 31046
EX n/a   **NM** n/a   **MIP** $24

(Maisto International, Inc.)

❑ **Chrysler PT Cruiser: Hot PT,** Bright blue body with silver and yellow flames, opening doors and tailgate, working steering, independent suspension, 1:18 scale, Model No. 31046
EX n/a   **NM** n/a   **MIP** $24

(Maisto International, Inc.)

❑ **Chrysler PT Cruiser: Moo Cruiser,** White body with black "Holstein" markings, chrome five-spoke wheels, opening doors and tailgate, working steering, independent suspension, 1:18 scale, Model No. 31046
EX n/a   **NM** n/a   **MIP** $24

(Maisto International, Inc.)

❑ **Chrysler PT Cruiser: PT Woody,** Yellow body, opening doors and tailgate, working steering, independent suspension, chrome five-spoke wheels, wood tampo on sides, 1:18 scale, Model No. 31046
EX n/a   **NM** n/a   **MIP** $24

1:18-SCALE GT RACING

(Maisto International, Inc.)

❑ **Audi R8 Le Mans-Sieger 2000,** Silver body with number "8" on sides and hood, German flag design, silver multi-spoked wheels, red spoiler, working steering, lift-off engine cover, 1:18 scale, Model No. 38899

EX n/a   NM n/a   MIP $25

(Maisto International, Inc.)

❑ **Audi R8 Le Mans-Sieger 2001,** Silver body with number "1" on sides and hood, silver multi-spoked wheels, red spoiler, working steering, lift-off engine cover, 1:18 scale, Model No. 38626

EX n/a   NM n/a   MIP $25

(Maisto International, Inc.)

❑ **Audi R8R Le Mans 1999,** Black and silver body with number "8" on sides and hood, German flag on sides and front, silver spoked wheels, 1:18 scale, Model No. 38881

EX n/a   NM n/a   MIP $25

(Maisto International, Inc.)

❑ **BMW V12 LMR 1999,** White body with number "15" on sides and hood, black spoiler with "Genuine BMW parts" in white type, "Dell" on sides, 1:18 scale, Model No. 38882

EX n/a   NM n/a   MIP $25

❑ **Mercedes-Benz CLK LM,** Silver body with red and blue "D2 Privat" on hood and sides, red number "1" on sides and front, black spoiler, silver spoked wheels, "Warsteiner" across top of windshield, 1:18 scale, Model No. 38868

EX n/a   NM n/a   MIP $25

❑ **Porsche 911 GT1 Le Mans 1998,** White body with black spoiler, "Mobil" on hood and sides, number "26" on sides and front, German flag emblem, gold spoked wheels, removable engine cover, opening doors, working steering, independent suspension, 1:18 scale, Model No. 38864

EX n/a   NM n/a   MIP $25

(Maisto International, Inc.)

❑ **Team Zakspeed Racing Porsche 911 GT1, 1998,** Dark green body with red and white candy stripe design on roof, gold spoked wheels, "Saudi Arabian Airlines" on sides and front, red number "5" on sides and hood. Removable engine cover, opening doors, independent suspension, steerable wheels, 1:18 scale, Model No. 38873

EX n/a   NM n/a   MIP $25

1:18-SCALE HARLEY-DAVIDSON MOTORCYCLES

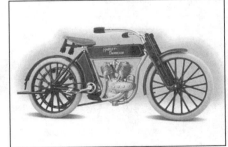
(Maisto International, Inc.)

❑ **1909 Twin 5D V-Twin,** Black body, tan seat, white tires, silver-gray engine. From the Series 7 Collection, 1:18 scale, Model No. 39705

EX n/a   NM n/a   MIP $7

(Maisto International, Inc.)

❑ **1909 Twin 5D V-Twin,** Dark gray body, brown seat, silver-gray engine, white rubber tires, brown spoked wheels. From the Series 5 Collection, 1:18 scale, Model No. 39385

EX n/a   NM n/a   MIP $7

(Maisto International, Inc.)

❑ **1928 JDH Twin Cam,** Olive green body, yellow "Harley-Davidson" lettering on tank. From the Series 11 Collection, 1:18 scale, Model No. 39730

EX n/a   NM n/a   MIP $7

(Maisto International, Inc.)

❑ **1936 EL Knucklehead,** Orange and black body, tan spoked wheels, part of Series 10 Collection, 1:18 scale, Model No. 39724

EX n/a   NM n/a   MIP $7

(Maisto International, Inc.)

❑ **1936 EL Knucklehead,** Black body, silver fenders, yellow spoked wheels, chrome engine. From the Series 7 Collection, 1:18 scale, Model No. 39706

EX n/a   **NM** n/a   **MIP** $7

(Maisto International, Inc.)

❑ **1936 EL Knucklehead,** Dark blue and cream body, black frame, seat and fork. Pale yellow spoked wheels. From the Series 5 Collection, 1:18 scale, Model No. 39386

EX n/a   **NM** n/a   **MIP** $7

(Maisto International, Inc.)

❑ **1942 WLA Flat Head,** Olive green body and wheels, tan cargo pouches and rifle case, flat black and gray engine. From the Series 9 Collection, 1:18 scale, Model No. 39717

EX n/a   **NM** n/a   **MIP** $7

(Maisto International, Inc.)

❑ **1942 WLA Flat Head,** Olive green body, tan saddlebags and rifle case, flat black and gray engine. From the Series 5 Collection, 1:18 scale, Model No. 39387

EX n/a   **NM** n/a   **MIP** $7

(Maisto International, Inc.)

❑ **1948 FL Panhead,** Black body, black seat, chrome wheels and engine, black pipes. From the Series 8 Collection, 1:18 scale, Model No. 39711

EX n/a   **NM** n/a   **MIP** $7

(Maisto International, Inc.)

❑ **1948 FL Panhead,** Black body, silver spoked wheels, part of Series 10 Collection, 1:18 scale, Model No. 39723

EX n/a   **NM** n/a   **MIP** $7

(Maisto International, Inc.)

❑ **1948 FL Panhead,** Red body, black fork, seat and pipes. Silver-gray engine and wheels. From the Series 5 Collection, 1:18 scale, Model No. 39388

EX n/a   **NM** n/a   **MIP** $7

(Maisto International, Inc.)

❑ **1953 74FL Hydra-Glide,** Blue body, black seat, gray engine and wheels. From the Series 11 Collection, 1:18 scale, Model No. 39728

EX n/a   **NM** n/a   **MIP** $7

(Maisto International, Inc.)

❑ **1962 FLH Duo Glide,** Red body, off-white seat, whitewall tires, gray and chrome engine. From the Series 5 Collection, 1:18 scale, Model No. 39389

EX n/a   **NM** n/a   **MIP** $7

(Maisto International, Inc.)

❑ **1962 FLH Duo Glide,** Blue body, white seat, whitewall tires, silver spoked wheels. From the Series 9 Collection, 1:18 scale, Model No. 39718

EX n/a   **NM** n/a   **MIP** $7

(Maisto International, Inc.)

❑ **1968 FLH Electra Glide,** Red, black and cream body, whitewall tires, white seat, gray and silver engine. From the Series 12 Collection, 1:18 scale, Model No. 31737

EX n/a   **NM** n/a   **MIP** $7

(Maisto International, Inc.)

❏ **1978 FLH-80 Electra Glide Special Edition,** Black body with gold trim, from the Series 11 Collection, 1:18 scale, Model No. 39726
EX n/a **NM** n/a **MIP** $7

(Maisto International, Inc.)

❏ **1986 FLST Heritage Softail Evolution,** Dark metallic blue and gray body, chrome and gray engine, gray wheels. From the Series 8 Collection, 1:18 scale, Model No. 39712
EX n/a **NM** n/a **MIP** $7

(Maisto International, Inc.)

❏ **1986 FLST Heritage Softail Evolution,** Orange-red and yellow body, gray and chrome engine, silver spoked wheels. From the Series 5 Collection, 1:18 scale, Model No. 39390
EX n/a **NM** n/a **MIP** $7

(Maisto International, Inc.)

❏ **1993 FLSTN Heritage Softail Nostalgia,** 2002, Black and white body and seat, whitewall tires. From the Series 14 Collection, 1:18 scale, Model No. 31726
EX n/a **NM** n/a **MIP** $7

(Maisto International, Inc.)

❏ **1999 FLHR Road King,** Red body, black trim, chrome engine and wheels. From the Series 6 Collection, 1:18 scale, Model No. 39395
EX n/a **NM** n/a **MIP** $7

(Maisto International, Inc.)

❏ **1999 FLHT Electra Glide Standard,** Black body, thin whitewall tires, chrome engine and wheels. From the Series 6 Collection, 1:18 scale, Model No. 39396
EX n/a **NM** n/a **MIP** $7

(Maisto International, Inc.)

❏ **1999 FLSTS Heritage Springer,** Red body with black fringed saddlebags, chrome and gray engine, whitewall tires. From the Series 6 Collection, 1:18 scale, Model No. 39393
EX n/a **NM** n/a **MIP** $7

(Maisto International, Inc.)

❏ **1999 FXDL Dyna Low Rider,** Black body, yellow "Harley-Davidson" on tank, chrome wheels and engine. From the Series 6 Collection, 1:18 scale, Model No. 39392
EX n/a **NM** n/a **MIP** $7

(Maisto International, Inc.)

❏ **1999 FXSTS Springer Softail,** Dark blue and white body, gray and chrome engine, chrome fork and wheels. From the Series 6 Collection, 1:18 scale, Model No. 39394
EX n/a **NM** n/a **MIP** $7

(Maisto International, Inc.)

❏ **1999 XL 1200C Sportster 1200 Custom,** Silver body, black seat, gray and chrome engine. From the Series 6 Collection, 1:18 scale, Model No. 39391
EX n/a **NM** n/a **MIP** $7

(Maisto International, Inc.)

❏ **2000 FLHRC Road King Classic,** Deep metallic red body, black saddle bags, chrome and gray engine. From the Series 8 Collection, 1:18 scale, Model No. 39709
EX n/a   NM n/a   MIP $7

(Maisto International, Inc.)

❏ **2000 FLSTC Heritage Softail Classic,** Yellow and black body, clear windshield, black saddlebags. In Series 10 Collection, 1:18 scale, Model No. 39722
EX n/a   NM n/a   MIP $7

(Maisto International, Inc.)

❏ **2000 FLSTF Fat Boy,** Silver body, silver (almost solid) wheels, part of Series 10 Collection, 1:18 scale, Model No. 39721
EX n/a   NM n/a   MIP $7

(Maisto International, Inc.)

❏ **2000 FLSTF Fat Boy,** Silver body, silver (almost solid) wheels, part of Series 10 Collection, 1:18 scale, Model No. 39721
EX n/a   NM n/a   MIP $7

(Maisto International, Inc.)

❏ **2000 FLTR Road Glide,** Bright red body, black seat, silver engine and wheels, from the Series 9 Collection, 1:18 scale, Model No. 39716
EX n/a   NM n/a   MIP $7

(Maisto International, Inc.)

❏ **2000 FXD Dyna Super Glide,** Metallic red body, chrome and gray engine, chrome spoked wheels. From the Series 8 Collection, 1:18 scale, Model No. 39708
EX n/a   NM n/a   MIP $7

(Maisto International, Inc.)

❏ **2000 FXDL Dyna Low Rider,** Black body, chrome wheels, fork and engine. From the Series 8 Collection, 1:18 scale, Model No. 39710
EX n/a   NM n/a   MIP $7

(Maisto International, Inc.)

❏ **2000 FXSTB Night Train,** Black body, black engine with chrome pipes, chrome wheels. From the Series 9 Collection, 1:18 scale, Model No. 39715
EX n/a   NM n/a   MIP $7

(Maisto International, Inc.)

❏ **2000 Sportster 1200 Custom,** Black body, chrome wheels, from the Series 10 Collection, 1:18 scale, Model No. 39720
EX n/a   NM n/a   MIP $7

(Maisto International, Inc.)

❏ **2000 XL 1200C Sportster 1200 Custom,** Yellow and black body, chrome engine and wheels, black fenders. From the Series 7 Collection, 1:18 scale, Model No. 39703
EX n/a   NM n/a   MIP $7

(Maisto International, Inc.)

❏ **2001 FLHRC Road King Classic,** Black body and saddle bags.

From the Series 11 Collection, 1:18 scale, Model No. 39729
EX n/a   **NM** n/a   **MIP** $7

(Maisto International, Inc.)

❏ **2001 FLSTS Heritage Springer,** White and red body, black saddle bags, from the Series 11 Collection, 1:18 scale, Model No. 39727
EX n/a   **NM** n/a   **MIP** $7

(Maisto International, Inc.)

❏ **2001 FXDL Dyna Low Rider,** From the Series 12 Collection, 1:18 scale, Model No. 39735
EX n/a   **NM** n/a   **MIP** $7

(Maisto International, Inc.)

❏ **2001 FXDL Dyna Low Rider,** Blue and cream body, chrome and gray engine, part of Series 12 Collection, 1:18 scale, Model No. 31736
EX n/a   **NM** n/a   **MIP** $7

(Maisto International, Inc.)

❏ **2001 FXST Softail Standard,** Silver body, detailed engine, part of Series 11 Collection, 1:18 scale, Model No. 39725
EX n/a   **NM** n/a   **MIP** $7

(Maisto International, Inc.)

❏ **2001 FXSTS Springer Softail,** From the Series 12 Collection, 1:18 scale, Model No. 39731
EX n/a   **NM** n/a   **MIP** $7

(Maisto International, Inc.)

❏ **2001 XL 1200C Sportster,** Black body, gray and chrome engine. From the Series 12 Collection, 1:18 scale, Model No. 31738
EX n/a   **NM** n/a   **MIP** $7

(Maisto International, Inc.)

❏ **2002 FLHRSEI CVO Custom,** 2002, Two-seater with dark metallic blue body and gray flame design. Chrome and gray engine. From the Series 13 Collection, 1:18 scale, Model No. 31740
EX n/a   **NM** n/a   **MIP** $7

(Maisto International, Inc.)

❏ **2002 FLSTF Fat Boy,** 2002, Red body, black seat, gray and chrome engine, (almost solid) chrome wheels. From the Series 13 Collection, 1:18 scale, Model No. 31742
EX n/a   **NM** n/a   **MIP** $7

(Maisto International, Inc.)

❏ **2002 FXDL Dyna Low Rider,** 2002, Silver and black body, chrome engine, fork and wheels. From the Series 14 Collection, 1:18 scale, Model No. 31746
EX n/a   **NM** n/a   **MIP** $7

(Maisto International, Inc.)

❏ **2002 FXDWG CVO Custom,** 2002, Dark metallic purple body, gray and chrome engine, silver-gray five-spoke wheels, tan seat. From the Series 14 Collection, 1:18 scale, Model No. 31745
EX n/a   **NM** n/a   **MIP** $7

MAISTO / MOTORCYCLES

(Maisto International, Inc.)

(Maisto International, Inc.)

(Maisto International, Inc.)

❏ **2002 FXSTB Night Train,** 2002, Black body, flat black engine with chrome exhaust, silver gray wheels, chrome fork. From the Series 13 Collection, 1:18 scale, Model No. 31741
EX n/a   **NM** n/a   **MIP** $7

❏ **Alabama State Trooper,** White body, black seat, blue Alabama State tampos on tank and saddle bags, chrome engine, 1:18 scale, Model No. 39701
EX n/a   **NM** n/a   **MIP** $7

❏ **FLTRSEI Screamin' Eagle Road Glide,** 2002, Black and red body with Eagle graphic, chrome engine and wheels. From Series 14 Collection, 1:18 scale, Model No. 31725R
EX n/a   **NM** n/a   **MIP** $7

(Maisto International, Inc.)

(Maisto International, Inc.)

(Maisto International, Inc.)

❏ **2002 FXSTD Deuce,** 2002, Dark charcoal body, chrome and gray engine, silver-gray wheels. From the Series 13 Collection, 1:18 scale, Model No. 31743
EX n/a   **NM** n/a   **MIP** $7

❏ **Arkansas State Police,** White and black body, chrome engine and wheels, light blue cargo container at rear, blue lights under windshield. From the Series 9 Collection, 1:18 scale, Model No. 39713
EX n/a   **NM** n/a   **MIP** $7

❏ **FXSTD Softail Deuce,** Metallic red body, gray and chrome engine, chrome wheels. From the Series 9 Collection, 1:18 scale, Model No. 39714
EX n/a   **NM** n/a   **MIP** $7

(Maisto International, Inc.)

(Maisto International, Inc.)

(Maisto International, Inc.)

❏ **2002 XL 883R Sportster,** 2002, Orange and black body, black and silver-gray engine, chrome fork and wheels. From Series 14 Collection, 1:18 scale, Model No. 31747
EX n/a   **NM** n/a   **MIP** $7

❏ **Boston Police Department,** White body with blue stripes and "Boston Police" on front and sides. "Special Operations" in blue type. Chrome engine and wheels. From the Series 4 Collection, 1:18 scale, Model No. 39384
EX n/a   **NM** n/a   **MIP** $7

❏ **Michigan State Police,** Blue body, white "State Police" type on front and sides, white cargo container on rear, chrome engine and wheels. From the Series 8 Collection, 1:18 scale, Model No. 39707
EX n/a   **NM** n/a   **MIP** $7

(Maisto International, Inc.)

❑ **Oklahoma Highway Patrol,** Black body, "Oklahoma Highway Patrol" on tank, "State Patrol" on fender, gray wheels, from Series 10 Collection, 1:18 scale, Model No. 39719
EX n/a　　NM n/a　　MIP $7

1:18-SCALE PREMIERE EDITION

(Maisto International, Inc.)

❑ **1948 Chevrolet Fleetmaster Woody,** 1999, Green or burgundy body, wood paneled sides, opening hood and doors, great detail, 1:18 scale, Model No. 36854
EX n/a　　NM n/a　　MIP $22

(Maisto International, Inc.)

❑ **2000 Cadillac DeVille DTS,** Silver or red body, seven-spoke wheels, 1:18 scale, Model No. 36877
EX n/a　　NM n/a　　MIP $24

(Maisto International, Inc.)

❑ **2001 Hummer H2 SUT Concept,** 2002, Red or green body,

opening doors and hood, steerable wheels, independent suspension, 1:18 scale, Model No. 36633
EX n/a　　NM n/a　　MIP $23

(Maisto International, Inc.)

❑ **2003 Hummer H2 SUV,** 2002, Pewter or yellow body, black trim, chrome wheels, opening doors and hood, workable steering, independent wheels suspension, 1:18 scale, Model No. 36631
EX n/a　　NM n/a　　MIP $25

(Maisto International, Inc.)

❑ **Aston Martin DB7 Vantage,** Dark gray body, cream interior, spoked wheels, 1:18 scale, Model No. 36880
EX n/a　　NM n/a　　MIP $27

(Maisto International, Inc.)

❑ **BMW Z8,** Silver, blue or red body, black interior, five-spoke wheels, opening doors, hood and trunk, 1:18 scale, Model No. 36896
EX n/a　　NM n/a　　MIP $24

(Maisto International, Inc.)

❑ **Cadillac Eldorado Biarritz,** Blue or pink body, opening doors and hood, white interior, whitewall tires, 1:18 scale, Model No. 36813
EX n/a　　NM n/a　　MIP $19

(Maisto International, Inc.)

❑ **Chevrolet Impala Police Car,** 2002, Cream and black body with "Tennessee State Trooper" on sides, 1:18 scale, Model No. 36611
EX n/a　　NM n/a　　MIP $24

(Maisto International, Inc.)

❑ **Chevrolet Impala Taxi,** 2002, Yellow body, black wheels, black trim, 1:18 scale, Model No. 36617
EX n/a　　NM n/a　　MIP $22

(Maisto International, Inc.)

❑ **Ford Explorer Sport Trac,** 2002, Dark blue or white body, five-spoke wheels, black interior, black trim, opening doors, hood and tailgate, 1:18 scale, Model No. 36891
EX n/a　　NM n/a　　MIP $22

(Maisto International, Inc.)

❑ **Ford Thunderbird Show Car,** Includes hard top, 1:18 scale, Model No. 36866
EX n/a　　NM n/a　　MIP $24

(Maisto International, Inc.)

❑ **Hummer Hard Top,** Black body with black wheels or silver body with silver wheels, tan interior, black bumpers and trim, 1:18 scale, Model No. 36857
EX n/a   NM n/a   MIP $32

(Maisto International, Inc.)

❑ **Hummer Soft Top,** White or yellow body, plastic soft top, black bumpers and wheels, "Hummer" along bottom on sides, 1:18 scale, Model No. 36859
EX n/a   NM n/a   MIP $35

(Maisto International, Inc.)

❑ **Hummer Station Wagon,** Red body with red wheels or black body with black wheels, black bumpers and trim, 1:18 scale, Model No. 36858
EX n/a   NM n/a   MIP $35

(Maisto International, Inc.)

❑ **Mercedes CLK-GTR Street Version,** Silver body, spoked wheels, spoiler, 1:18 scale, Model No. 36849
EX n/a   NM n/a   MIP $25

(Maisto International, Inc.)

❑ **Mercedes-Benz 300 SLR Coupe "Uhlenhaut",** 2002, Silver body, spoked wheels, gullwing-style doors, 1:18 scale, Model No. 36898
EX n/a   NM n/a   MIP $25

(Maisto International, Inc.)

❑ **Mercedes-Benz 300 SLR Mille Miglia, 1955,** Silver body, spoked wheels, red number "722" on sides and hood, 1:18 scale, Model No. 36887
EX n/a   NM n/a   MIP $25

(Maisto International, Inc.)

❑ **Mercedes-Benz 300 SLR Targa Florio, 1955,** 2002, Silver body, black interior, spoked wheels, number "104" on hood and sides, 1:18 scale, Model No. 36613
EX n/a   NM n/a   MIP $24

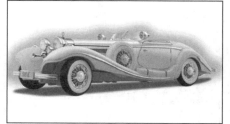

(Maisto International, Inc.)

❑ **Mercedes-Benz 500 K Roadster, 1936,** White body, cream interior, spoked wheels, whitewall tires, 1:18 scale, Model No. 36055
EX n/a   NM n/a   MIP $27

(Maisto International, Inc.)

❑ **Mercedes-Benz 500 K Roadster, 1936,** Red body, cream interior, spoked wheels, whitewall tires, 1:18 scale, Model No. 36862
EX n/a   NM n/a   MIP $25

(Maisto International, Inc.)

❑ **Mercedes-Benz S-Class,** Silver or metallic burgundy body, opening doors, gray seven-spoke wheels, gray interior, 1:18 scale, Model No. 36855
EX n/a   NM n/a   MIP $24

(Maisto International, Inc.)

❑ **Mercedes-Benz SL-Class Convertible,** 2002, Silver or red body, five-spoke wheels, black interior, opening doors, hood and trunk, workable steering, independent suspension, 1:18 scale, Model No. 36623
EX n/a   NM n/a   MIP $24

(Maisto International, Inc.)

❑ **Mercedes-Benz SL-Class Coupe,** 2002, Black or dark metallic blue body, six-spoke wheels, opening doors, hood and trunk, independent suspension, 1:18 scale, Model No. 36624
EX n/a   NM n/a   MIP $24

1:18-SCALE SPECIAL EDITION

(Maisto International, Inc.)

❑ **Mercedes-Benz SLK,** 2002, Red or yellow body, five-spoke wheels, opening doors and hood, black interior, 1:18 scale, Model No. 36838

EX n/a   NM n/a   MIP $26

(Maisto International, Inc.)

❑ **Military Humvee,** Sand and green camouflage body, black wheels, bumper and machine gun, 1:18 scale, Model No. 36874

EX n/a   NM n/a   MIP $25

(Maisto International, Inc.)

❑ **Morgan Aero 8,** 2002, Blue or green body, silver five-spoke wheels, opening doors, hood and trunk, workable steering, independent suspension, 1:18 scale, Model No. 36637

EX n/a   NM n/a   MIP $26

(Maisto International, Inc.)

❑ **Porsche Carrera GT,** 2002, Black or gray body, black interior, five-spoke wheels, opening doors, hood and trunk, adjustable spoiler, workable steering, independent suspension, 1:18 scale, Model No. 36622

EX n/a   NM n/a   MIP $26

(Maisto International, Inc.)

❑ **1956 Chrysler 300B,** 2002, Black, white or dark red body, opening doors, hood and trunk, steerable wheels, 1:18 scale, Model No. 31897

EX n/a   NM n/a   MIP $23

(Maisto International, Inc.)

❑ **1962 Chevrolet Bel-Air,** 2002, Red or white body, opening hood, doors and trunk, workable steering, independent suspension, 1:18 scale, Model No. 31641

EX n/a   NM n/a   MIP $22

(Maisto International, Inc.)

❑ **1965 Chevrolet Corvette,** 2002, Metallic steel blue body, opening doors and hood, workable steering, independent suspension, 1:18 scale, Model No. 31640

EX n/a   NM n/a   MIP $23

(Maisto International, Inc.)

❑ **1965 Pontiac GTO Convertible, Hurst Edition,** Red body, chrome five-spoke wheels, white interior, opening doors, hood and trunk, 1:18 scale, Model No. 31884

EX n/a   NM n/a   MIP $27

(Maisto International, Inc.)

❑ **1965 Pontiac GTO Hurst Edition,** Black hardtop body, chrome five-spoke wheels, opening doors, hood and trunk, 1:18 scale, Model No. 31885

EX n/a   NM n/a   MIP $25

(Maisto International, Inc.)

❑ **1971 Chevrolet Chevelle SS454 Convertible,** Blue body, black interior, opening doors, hood and trunk, working steering, independent suspension, 1:18 scale, Model No. 31883

EX n/a   NM n/a   MIP $24

(Maisto International, Inc.)

❑ **1971 Chevrolet Chevelle SS454 Sport Coupe,** Silver body with black stripes and roof, black interior, opening doors and hood, or black body with silver trim, 1:18 scale, Model No. 31890

EX n/a   NM n/a   MIP $23

(Maisto International, Inc.)

❑ **1972 Chevrolet Chevelle SS454 Convertible,** Red body with wide white stripe, opening doors and hood, white interior, silver five-spoke wheels, 1:18 scale, Model No. 31892

EX n/a   NM n/a   MIP $24

MAISTO / CARS AND TRUCKS

(Maisto International, Inc.)

❏ **1972 Chevrolet Chevelle SS454 Sport Coupe,** Bronze body with black stripes, black roof, white interior, opening doors, hood and trunk, steerable wheels, 1:18 scale, Model No. 31886
EX n/a   NM n/a   MIP $24

(Maisto International, Inc.)

❏ **1996 Corvette,** Dark metallic purple body, light tan interior, opening doors and hood, adjustable seats, working steering, independent suspension, 1:18 scale, Model No. 31830
EX n/a   NM n/a   MIP $25

(Maisto International, Inc.)

❏ **1996 Corvette Coupe,** Red body, opening doors, hood and trunk, adjustable seats, working steering, independent suspension, 1:18 scale, Model No. 31840
EX n/a   NM n/a   MIP $23

(Maisto International, Inc.)

❏ **1999 Mustang GT Convertible,** Black exterior, black interior, five-spoke wheels, opening hood, doors and trunk, working steering, independent suspension, 1:18 scale, Model No. 31861
EX n/a   NM n/a   MIP $24

(Maisto International, Inc.)

❏ **1999 Mustang GT Hardtop,** Silver body, black interior, opening doors, hood and trunk, chrome five-spoke wheels, working steering, independent suspension, 1:18 scale, Model No. 31860
EX n/a   NM n/a   MIP $24

(Maisto International, Inc.)

❏ **2000 SVT Mustang Cobra R,** Red body, black interior, opening doors, hood and trunk, five-spoke wheels, workable steering, independent suspension, 1:18 scale, Model No. 31872
EX n/a   NM n/a   MIP $24

❏ **2002 Ford Thunderbird,** 2002, Black, metallic blue or red body, opening doors, hood and trunk, operating front wheels, 1:18 scale, Model No. 31620
EX n/a   NM n/a   MIP $25

(Maisto International, Inc.)

❏ **Alfa Romeo Spider,** Dark blue body, gray interior, opening doors, hood and trunk, working steering, independent suspension, 1:18 scale, Model No. 31831
EX n/a   NM n/a   MIP $24

(Maisto International, Inc.)

❏ **Alpine Renault 1600S, 1971,** Blue body, gray wheels, black inte-

rior, opening doors, hood and trunk, working steering, independent suspension, 1:18 scale, Model No. 31850
EX n/a   NM n/a   MIP $18

(Maisto International, Inc.)

❏ **Audi Supersportwagen "Rosemeyer",** 2002, Silver body, opening doors, workable steering, independent suspension, 1:18 scale, Model No. 31625
EX n/a   NM n/a   MIP $27

(Maisto International, Inc.)

❏ **Audi TT Roadster,** Black or gray body, opening hood, trunk and doors, silver five-spoke wheels, 1:18 scale, Model No. 31878
EX n/a   NM n/a   MIP $23

(Maisto International, Inc.)

❏ **BMW 325i Convertible,** Blue-green or white body, black roof, (convertible roof actually folds up!), six-spoke silver wheels, adjustable seats, visors and headrests, working steering, independent suspension, 1:18 scale, Model No. 31816
EX n/a   NM n/a   MIP $23

(Maisto International, Inc.)

❑ **BMW 325i Convertible,** White body, roof in down position, black trim, six-spoke silver wheels, adjustable seats and visors, working steering, independent suspension, 1:18 scale, Model No. 31812
EX n/a   NM n/a   MIP $23

(Maisto International, Inc.)

❑ **BMW 502, 1955,** Dark blue body, light tan interior, opening doors, hood and trunk, adjustable seats, working steering, independent suspension, 1:18 scale, Model No. 31817
EX n/a   NM n/a   MIP $25

(Maisto International, Inc.)

❑ **BMW 850i,** Dark blue body, white interior, gray multi-spoked wheels, opening hood, trunk and doors, adjustable seat and visor, working steering, independent suspension, 1:18 scale, Model No. 31805
EX n/a   NM n/a   MIP $25

❑ **Chevrolet Corvette Z06,** 2002, Red, yellow or black body with opening doors and hood, steerable wheels, 1:18 scale, Model No. 31889
EX n/a   NM n/a   MIP $21

(Maisto International, Inc.)

❑ **Chevrolet SSR Concept Convertible Truck,** 2002, Black or pewter body, chrome five-spoke wheels, opening hood and doors, independent suspension, 1:18 scale, Model No. 31639
EX n/a   NM n/a   MIP $24

(Maisto International, Inc.)

❑ **Chevrolet SSR Concept Truck,** 2002, Bright blue, yellow or red body, silver five-spoke wheels, opening doors and hood, detailed engine, 1:18 scale, Model No. 31612
EX n/a   NM n/a   MIP $24

(Maisto International, Inc.)

❑ **Chrysler Panel Cruiser,** 2002, Metallic blue or red body. Opening doors, tailgate and hood, steerable wheels, black interior, independent suspension, 1:18 scale, Model No. 31618
EX n/a   NM n/a   MIP $23

(Maisto International, Inc.)

❑ **Chrysler Pronto Cruiser: Original Concept Version,** Yellow body, opening doors and tailgate, working steering, independent suspension, 1:18 scale, Model No. 31870
EX n/a   NM n/a   MIP $24

(Maisto International, Inc.)

❑ **Chrysler PT Cruiser,** Silver, white, black or dark metallic burgundy body, opening hood, doors and tailgate, steerable wheels, 1:18 scale, Model No. 31895
EX n/a   NM n/a   MIP $17

(Maisto International, Inc.)

❑ **Citroen 15CV 6-cylinder,** Gray body, four opening doors, opening hood, adjustable seats, working steering, independent suspension, 1:18 scale, Model No. 31837
EX n/a   NM n/a   MIP $22

❑ **Citroen 15CV 6-Cylinder, 1952,** Black exterior, four opening doors, adjustable seats, working steering, opening hood and trunk,

independent suspension, 1:18 scale, Model No. 31821
EX n/a   **NM** n/a   **MIP** $25

(Maisto International, Inc.)

❑ **Citroen 2CV, 1952,** Sand colored body, plaid (real fabric) interior upholstery, black trim, gray wheels, thin tires, black base, opening hood and doors, working steering, independent suspension, 1:18 scale, Model No. 31835
EX n/a   **NM** n/a   **MIP** $25

(Maisto International, Inc.)

❑ **Citroen 2CV, 1952, Hardtop,** Gray body, opening doors and hood, working steering, independent suspension, 1:18 scale, Model No. 31834
EX n/a   **NM** n/a   **MIP** $22

(Maisto International, Inc.)

❑ **Dodge Concept Vehicle,** Copper body, opening doors, trunk and hood, steerable wheels, independent suspension, 1:18 scale, Model No. 31851
EX n/a   **NM** n/a   **MIP** $22

(Maisto International, Inc.)

❑ **Dodge Viper GT2,** White body, dark blue stripes running from hood to trunk, silver multi-

spoked wheels, opening doors and hood, adjustable seats, working steering, independent suspension, 1:18 scale, Model No. 31845
EX n/a   **NM** n/a   **MIP** $26

(Maisto International, Inc.)

❑ **Dodge Viper GTS, 1997,** Red body, opening doors, hood and trunk, adjustable seats, working steering, silver five-spoke wheels, independent suspension, 1:18 scale, Model No. 31832
EX n/a   **NM** n/a   **MIP** $26

(Maisto International, Inc.)

❑ **Ford 1969 Torino Talladega,** 2002, Metallic dark blue or maroon body, steerable wheels, opening hood with detailed engine, opening doors, 1:18 scale, Model No. 31616
EX n/a   **NM** n/a   **MIP** $24

❑ **Ford GT90,** White body, blue and chrome wheels, opeing doors and hood, opening rear hatch, working steering, independent suspension, 1:18 scale, Model No. 31827
EX n/a   **NM** n/a   **MIP** $26

❑ **Honda S2000,** Silver or red body, two-tone interior, silver five-spoke wheels, opening doors, hood and trunk, working steering, 1:18 scale, Model No. 31879
EX n/a   **NM** n/a   **MIP** $22

(Maisto International, Inc.)

❑ **Jaguar Mark II, 1959,** Dark green body, four opening doors, working steering, opening trunk and hood, independent suspension, multi-spoked silver wheels, tan interior, 1:18 scale, Model No. 31833
EX n/a   **NM** n/a   **MIP** $23

(Maisto International, Inc.)

❑ **Jaguar S-Type,** Silver blue or pearl body, opening doors, hood and trunk, working steering, independent suspension, 1:18 scale, Model No. 31865
EX n/a   **NM** n/a   **MIP** $23

(Maisto International, Inc.)

❑ **Jaguar XJ220,** Dark green body, silver-gray wheels, opening hood, doors and trunk, adjustable seats and visors, working steering, independent suspension, 1:18 scale, Model No. 31807
EX n/a   **NM** n/a   **MIP** $25

(Maisto International, Inc.)

❑ **Jaguar XK180,** Blue-green body, opening doors, hood and trunk, five-spoke silver wheels, independent suspension, working steering, 1:18 scale, Model No. 31867
EX n/a   **NM** n/a   **MIP** $25

(Maisto International, Inc.)

❑ **Jaguar XK8,** Green body, opening doors and hood, adjustable seats, working steering, independent suspension, 1:18 scale, Model No. 31836
EX n/a   **NM** n/a   **MIP** $22

(Maisto International, Inc.)

❏ **Jaguar XKR,** Red body, cream interior, opening doors, trunk and hood, adjustable seats, independent suspension, 1:18 scale, Model No. 31863
EX n/a   **NM** n/a   **MIP** $25

(Maisto International, Inc.)

❏ **Jaguar X-Type, 2001,** 2002, Metallic silver or red body, opening doors, hood and trunk, workable steering, independent suspension, 1:18 scale, Model No. 31621
EX n/a   **NM** n/a   **MIP** $22

(Maisto International, Inc.)

❏ **Lamborghini Diablo,** Yellow body, black interior, opening doors, hood and trunk, working steering, independent suspension, 1:18 scale, Model No. 31803
EX n/a   **NM** n/a   **MIP** $26

(Maisto International, Inc.)

❏ **Lamborghini Diablo SV,** Black body with large script "SV" on sides, black and silver five-spoke wheels, opening doors, trunk and hood, independent suspension, working steering, 1:18 scale, Model No. 31844
EX n/a   **NM** n/a   **MIP** $26

❏ **Lamborghini Jota,** Bright red body, opening doors and hood,

working steering, independent suspension, black interior, silver-gray wheels, wide rear tires, 1:18 scale, Model No. 31829
EX n/a   **NM** n/a   **MIP** $26

(Maisto International, Inc.)

❏ **Lamborghini Murcielago,** 2002, Available in the following colors: yellow, orange, gray, black, green and light blue. Opening doors, hood and trunk, independent suspension, workable steering, 1:18 scale, Model No. 31638
EX n/a   **NM** n/a   **MIP** $26

(Maisto International, Inc.)

❏ **Lamborghini SE,** Metallic pink-purple body, opening doors and hood, working steering, independent suspension, 1:18 scale, Model No. 31819
EX n/a   **NM** n/a   **MIP** $25

(Maisto International, Inc.)

❏ **Lexus SC 430,** 2002, Silver or red body, cream interior, opening doors, hood and trunk, workable steering, independent suspension, 1:18 scale, Model No. 31629
EX n/a   **NM** n/a   **MIP** $25

(Maisto International, Inc.)

❏ **Mercedes-Benz 190SL, 1955,** Red body, opening doors, hood and trunk, cream interior, working steer-

ing, independent suspension, 1:18 scale, Model No. 31824
EX n/a   **NM** n/a   **MIP** $26

(Maisto International, Inc.)

❏ **Mercedes-Benz 280SE, 1966,** Cream exterior, silver trim, red interior, opening hood, trunk and doors, adjustable seats, working steering, independent suspension, 1:18 scale, Model No. 31811
EX n/a   **NM** n/a   **MIP** $26

(Maisto International, Inc.)

❏ **Mercedes-Benz 300S, 1955,** Black body, cream interior, adjustable seats, working steering, opening hood, doors and trunk, independent suspension, 1:18 scale, Model No. 31806
EX n/a   **NM** n/a   **MIP** $24

(Maisto International, Inc.)

❏ **Mercedes-Benz 500SL,** Silver body, adjustable visors and seats, black interior, opening doors, hood and trunk, working steering, independent suspension, 1:18 scale, Model No. 31801
EX n/a   **NM** n/a   **MIP** $25

(Maisto International, Inc.)

❏ **Mercedes-Benz A-Class,** Pacific blue or red body with opening doors, hood and tailgate, working steering, independent suspension, cream interior, 1:18 scale, Model No. 31841

EX n/a   **NM** n/a   **MIP** $16

(Maisto International, Inc.)

❑ **Mercedes-Benz A-Class, Long Version,** 2002, Ocean blue or red body, opening tailgate, doors and hood, independent suspension and workable steering, 1:18 scale, Model No. 31630

EX n/a   **NM** n/a   **MIP** $18

(Maisto International, Inc.)

❑ **Mercedes-Benz C-Klasse Sportcoupe,** 2002, Silver or dark blue body, black interior, opening doors, hood and trunk, steerable wheels, independent suspension, 1:18 scale, Model No. 31614

EX n/a   **NM** n/a   **MIP** $22

(Maisto International, Inc.)

❑ **Mercedes-Benz ML 55 AMG,** Ruby red body, opening doors and hood, silver five-spoke wheels, black interior, working steering, independent suspension, 1:18 scale, Model No. 31876

EX n/a   **NM** n/a   **MIP** $23

(Maisto International, Inc.)

❑ **Mercedes-Benz ML-Class,** 2002, Dark metallic green or blue body, opening hood and doors, working steering, independent suspension, 1:18 scale, Model No. 31847

EX n/a   **NM** n/a   **MIP** $24

(Maisto International, Inc.)

❑ **Mercedes-Benz SLK,** Silver body with opening hood, doors and trunk, black interior, five-spoke silver wheels, independent suspension, working steering, 1:18 scale, Model No. 31842

EX n/a   **NM** n/a   **MIP** $22

(Maisto International, Inc.)

❑ **Mini Cooper,** 2002, Red, black or green body with white roof or silver with black roof, opening doors, hood and hatch, five-spoke wheels, 1:18 scale, Model No. 31619

EX n/a   **NM** n/a   **MIP** $17

(Maisto International, Inc.)

❑ **Mustang Mach III,** Yellow body, black interior, chrome wheels, opening doors, hood and trunk, adjustable seats and spoiler, working steering, independent suspension, 1:18 scale, Model No. 31815

EX n/a   **NM** n/a   **MIP** $25

(Maisto International, Inc.)

❑ **Opel Speedster,** 2002, Red or dark yellow body, five-spoke wheels, opening doors, 1:18 scale, Model No. 31615

EX n/a   **NM** n/a   **MIP** $23

(Maisto International, Inc.)

❑ **Porsche 550A Spyder,** Silver body with silver wheels, thin tires, opening doors, hood and trunk, independent suspension, working steering, 1:18 scale, Model No. 31843

EX n/a   **NM** n/a   **MIP** $16

(Maisto International, Inc.)

❑ **Porsche 550A Spyder "1000km Race, Buenos Aires, 1958,** Silver body, number "48" on doors and hood, working steering, independent suspension, opening doors, hood and trunk, 1:18 scale, Model No. 31871

EX n/a   **NM** n/a   **MIP** $16

(Maisto International, Inc.)

❑ **Porsche 911 Carrera,** Silver blue body, silver five-spoke wheels, opening hood, doors and trunk, adjustable seats and visors, independent suspension, working steering, 1:18 scale, Model No. 31818

EX n/a   **NM** n/a   **MIP** $25

(Maisto International, Inc.)

❏ **Porsche 911 Carrera,** 2002, Silver or black body, opening doors, hood and trunk, workable steering, independent suspension, 1:18 scale, Model No. 31628
EX n/a   **NM** n/a   **MIP** $25

(Maisto International, Inc.)

❏ **Porsche 911 Speedster,** Red body, black trim, adjustable visors and seats, black and silver five-spoke wheels, opening hood, doors and trunk, working steering, independent suspension, 1:18 scale, Model No. 31802
EX n/a   **NM** n/a   **MIP** $23

(Maisto International, Inc.)

❏ **Porsche 911 Targa,** 2002, Deep blue or red body, black interior, opening doors, hood and trunk, workable steering, independent suspension, 1:18 scale, Model No. 31627
EX n/a   **NM** n/a   **MIP** $27

(Maisto International, Inc.)

❏ **Porsche Boxter: Original Concept Version,** Silver body, red interior, chrome five-spoke wheels, opening hood, trunk and doors, working steering, independent suspension, 1:18 scale, Model No. 31814
EX n/a   **NM** n/a   **MIP** $24

(Maisto International, Inc.)

❏ **Porsche No. 1 Typ 356 Roadster, 1948,** Silver body, opening doors, hood and trunk, working steering, independent suspension, 1:18 scale, Model No. 31853
EX n/a   **NM** n/a   **MIP** $16

(Maisto International, Inc.)

❏ **Smart,** 2002, Blue, stream green or silver body, additional body panels included to customize model, opening doors and tailgate, independent suspension, working steering, 1:18 scale, Model No. 31852
EX n/a   **NM** n/a   **MIP** $17

(Maisto International, Inc.)

❏ **Volkswagen Cabriolet, 1951,** Red or baby blue body, tan interior, whitewall tires, opening trunk, rear hood and doors, adjustable seats, working steering, independent suspension, 1:18 scale, Model No. 31826
EX n/a   **NM** n/a   **MIP** $18

(Maisto International, Inc.)

❏ **Volkswagen Export Sedan, 1951,** Dark green body, opening doors, rear hood and front trunk, working steering, independed sus-

pension, 1:18 scale, Model No. 31820
EX n/a   **NM** n/a   **MIP** $19

(Maisto International, Inc.)

❏ **Volkswagen New Beetle,** Blue, green, red or yellow body, silver six-spoke wheels, working steering and independent suspension, opening hood, trunk and doors, 1:18 scale, Model No. 31875
EX n/a   **NM** n/a   **MIP** $23

1:24-SCALE ASSEMBLY LINE KITS

(Maisto International, Inc.)

❏ **1948 Ford F-1 Pickup,** Red body, opening tailgate and doors, 1:25 scale, Model No. 39935
EX n/a   **NM** n/a   **MIP** $12

(Maisto International, Inc.)

❏ **1966 Chevrolet Chevelle SS396,** 2002, Gloss black body, opening hood and doors, 1:24 scale, Model No. 39960
EX n/a   **NM** n/a   **MIP** $12

(Maisto International, Inc.)

❏ **1970 Boss Mustang,** Yellow body with black stripes, black louvres, spoiler and interior, opening doors and hood, 1:24 scale, Model No. 39943
EX n/a   **NM** n/a   **MIP** $12

(Maisto International, Inc.)

❏ **1995 Dodge Viper RT/10,** 2002, Red body, opening doors, hood and trunk, black interior, silver or chrome wheels, 1:24 scale, Model No. 39915
EX n/a   **NM** n/a   **MIP** $12

(Maisto International, Inc.)

❏ **1997 Chevrolet Corvette,** Silver body, silver or chrome wheels, opening hood and doors, 1:24 scale, Model No. 39940
EX n/a   **NM** n/a   **MIP** $12

(Maisto International, Inc.)

❏ **1999 Ford F-350 Super Duty Pickup,** 2002, Dark green body, black interior and bedliner, opening doors and tailgate, 1:27 scale, Model No. 39937
EX n/a   **NM** n/a   **MIP** $12

(Maisto International, Inc.)

❏ **1999 Ford Mustang Cobra,** Blue body, opening hood and doors, silver or chrome wheels, 1:24 scale, Model No. 39946
EX n/a   **NM** n/a   **MIP** $12

(Maisto International, Inc.)

❏ **2000 Chevrolet SSR Concept,** 2002, Red body, opening doors and hood, silver or chrome wheels, 1:24 scale, Model No. 39212
EX n/a   **NM** n/a   **MIP** $12

(Maisto International, Inc.)

❏ **2002 Ford Thunderbird,** Black body, opening doors and hood, silver or chrome wheels, 1:25 scale, Model No. 39966
EX n/a   **NM** n/a   **MIP** $12

(Maisto International, Inc.)

❏ **'64 Ford Fairlane Thunderbolt,** Light gold body, opening hood and doors, chrome wheels, 1:24 scale, Model No. 39957
EX n/a   **NM** n/a   **MIP** $12

(Maisto International, Inc.)

❏ **Audi TT Roadster,** Charcoal gray body, tan interior, chrome or silver five-spoke wheels, opening doors and trunk, 1:24 scale, Model No. 39978
EX n/a   **NM** n/a   **MIP** $12

(Maisto International, Inc.)

❏ **BMW Z8,** Red body, black interior, opening hood and doors, silver or chrome wheels, 1:24 scale, Model No. 39996
EX n/a   **NM** n/a   **MIP** $12

(Maisto International, Inc.)

❏ **Chevrolet Impala,** 2002, Black and off-white body, "Tennessee State Trooper" on sides, yellow stripe on sides, blue dome light, opening hood and doors, 1:24 scale, Model No. 39211
EX n/a   **NM** n/a   **MIP** $12

(Maisto International, Inc.)

❏ **Chevrolet Silverado,** Red body, black and silver trim, opening doors, 1:27 scale, Model No. 39941
EX n/a   **NM** n/a   **MIP** $12

(Maisto International, Inc.)

❑ **Chysler PT Cruiser,** Purple-blue body, opening doors and tailgate. Kit includes extra wheels (like the 1:18 variety), 1:24 scale, Model No. 39995

EX n/a NM n/a MIP $12

(Maisto International, Inc.)

❑ **Dodge Ram SuperSport (SS/T),** Blue body, white stripes running from hood to bed cover, opening doors and tailgate, black interior, 1:26 scale, Model No. 39930

EX n/a NM n/a MIP $12

(Maisto International, Inc.)

❑ **Dodge Viper GT2,** White body with blue stripes, opening doors, chrome multi-spoked wheels, 1:24 scale, Model No. 39945

EX n/a NM n/a MIP $12

(Maisto International, Inc.)

❑ **Ford Explorer Sport Trac,** Bronze-orange body, opening

doors and tailgate, black interior, 1:25 scale, Model No. 39991

EX n/a NM n/a MIP $12

(Maisto International, Inc.)

❑ **Hummer Softop,** 2002, Red body, red or black wheels, black plastic softop, beige interior, opening doors, 1:27 scale, Model No. 39959

EX n/a NM n/a MIP $12

(Maisto International, Inc.)

❑ **Jaguar XK8,** 2002, Red body, silver or chrome wheels, opening doors and trunk, 1:24 scale, Model No. 39936

EX n/a NM n/a MIP $12

(Maisto International, Inc.)

❑ **Lamborghini Murcielago,** 2002, Yellow body, opening doors and hood, 1:24 scale, Model No. 39238

EX n/a NM n/a MIP $12

(Maisto International, Inc.)

❑ **Mercedes CLK-GTR Street Version,** Silver body, silver or

chrome wheels, opening doors, 1:26 scale, Model No. 39949

EX n/a NM n/a MIP $12

(Maisto International, Inc.)

❑ **Mercedes-Benz SLK,** 2002, Blue body, charcoal interior, silver or chrome five-spoke wheels, opening hood, doors and trunk, 1:24 scale, Model No. 39942

EX n/a NM n/a MIP $12

(Maisto International, Inc.)

❑ **Military Humvee,** 2002, Desert-sand body, black wheels, bumper, exhaust and machine gun. Opening doors and top hatch, 1:27 scale, Model No. 39974

EX n/a NM n/a MIP $12

(Maisto International, Inc.)

❑ **Porsche 911 Carrera,** Silver body, opening hood and doors, 1:24 scale, Model No. 39938

EX n/a NM n/a MIP $12

(Maisto International, Inc.)

❑ **Porsche Boxster,** 2002, Silver body, opening doors and hood, black interior, 1:24 scale, Model No. 39933

EX n/a   **NM** n/a   **MIP** $12

(Maisto International, Inc.)

❑ **Shinoda Boss Mustang,** Red body, "Boss" on hood and side strobe-stripes, black interior, 1:24 scale, Model No. 39934

EX n/a   **NM** n/a   **MIP** $12

(Maisto International, Inc.)

❑ **Volkswagen Beetle,** Blue body, opening front trunk and doors, black running boards, white or silver wheels, 1:24 scale, Model No. 39926

EX n/a   **NM** n/a   **MIP** $12

(Maisto International, Inc.)

❑ **Volkswagen New Beetle,** Flat black body, gray interior, six-spoke wheels, opening hood and doors, 1:25 scale, Model No. 39975

EX n/a   **NM** n/a   **MIP** $12

(Maisto International, Inc.)

❑ **Volkswagen Van "Samba",** Aqua blue and white body, white or silver wheels, opening tailgate and side door, 1:25 scale, Model No. 39956

EX n/a   **NM** n/a   **MIP** $12

1:24-SCALE SPECIAL EDITION

(Maisto International, Inc.)

❑ **1948 Ford F1 Pickup,** Gray-blue or red body, opening doors and tailgate, 1:25 scale, Model No. 31935

EX n/a   **NM** n/a   **MIP** $8

(Maisto International, Inc.)

❑ **1964 Ford Fairlane Thunderbolt,** Maroon body, chrome grille and wheels, opening hood and doors, 1:24 scale, Model No. 31957

EX n/a   **NM** n/a   **MIP** $8

(Maisto International, Inc.)

❑ **1966 Chevrolet Chevelle SS396,** Black or metallic blue body, chrome wheels and grille, opening hood and doors, 1:24 scale, Model No. 31960

EX n/a   **NM** n/a   **MIP** $8

(Maisto International, Inc.)

❑ **1970 Ford Boss Mustang,** Yellow body, black stripe running from hood to sides, black spoiler, chrome wheels, opening doors and hood, 1:24 scale, Model No. 31943

EX n/a   **NM** n/a   **MIP** $8

(Maisto International, Inc.)

❑ **1993 Ford F-150 Pickup,** Green body, opening doors and tailgate, 1:25 scale, Model No. 31911

EX n/a   **NM** n/a   **MIP** $8

(Maisto International, Inc.)

❑ **1994 Mustang GT,** Red or blue body, black interior, opening hood, doors and trunk, adjustable seats, 1:24 scale, Model No. 31905

EX n/a   **NM** n/a   **MIP** $8

(Maisto International, Inc.)

❑ **1995 Dodge Viper RT/10,** Red or black body, black interior, silver wheels, opening hood, doors and trunk, adjustable seats, 1:24 scale, Model No. 31915

EX n/a   **NM** n/a   **MIP** $8

(Maisto International, Inc.)

❑ **1995 Ford Explorer,** Bright blue body, opening doors and tailgate, fold-down rear seat, adjustable front seat, chrome wheels, beige interior, 1:24 scale, Model No. 31909

EX n/a   NM n/a   MIP $8

(Maisto International, Inc.)

❑ **1996 Chevrolet Camaro Z28,** Burgundy or green body, black interior, opening doors and hood, adjustable seats, 1:25 scale, Model No. 31924

EX n/a   NM n/a   MIP $8

❑ **1996 Dodge Viper RT/10,** Red or white with blue stripes, five-spoke wheels, black interior, opening hood, doors and trunk, adjustable seats, 1:24 scale, Model No. 31914

EX n/a   NM n/a   MIP $8

(Maisto International, Inc.)

❑ **1997 Chevrolet Corvette,** Red or blue body, opening doors and hood, black interior, 1:24 scale, Model No. 31940

EX n/a   NM n/a   MIP $8

(Maisto International, Inc.)

❑ **1997 Dodge Viper RT/10,** Blue with white stripes or silver with black stripes, chrome five-spoke wheels, opening hood, doors and trunk, adjustable seats, 1:24 scale, Model No. 31932

EX n/a   NM n/a   MIP $8

(Maisto International, Inc.)

❑ **1997 Ford F-150 Flareside Pickup,** Silver body, black interior, opening doors and tailgate, 1:26 scale, Model No. 31921

EX n/a   NM n/a   MIP $8

(Maisto International, Inc.)

❑ **1999 Ford F-350 Super Duty Pickup,** Red, silver or black body, opening doors and tailgate, 1:27 scale, Model No. 31937

EX n/a   NM n/a   MIP $8

(Maisto International, Inc.)

❑ **1999 Mustang Cobra,** Red or black body, opening hood and doors, silver five-spoke wheels, 1:24 scale, Model No. 31946

EX n/a   NM n/a   MIP $8

(Maisto International, Inc.)

❑ **1999 Mustang GT,** Red or yellow body, silver five-spoke wheels, opening hood and doors, black interior, 1:24 scale, Model No. 31961

EX n/a   NM n/a   MIP $8

(Maisto International, Inc.)

❑ **2002 Acura RS-X,** 2002, Black or blue body, silver six-spoke wheels, opening doors and hood, 1:24 scale, Model No. 31981

EX n/a   NM n/a   MIP $8

(Maisto International, Inc.)

❑ **2002 Buick Rendezvous,** Black blody, opening doors and tailgate, gray interior, silver-gray eight-spoke wheels, 1:24 scale, Model No. 31950

EX n/a   NM n/a   MIP $8

(Maisto International, Inc.)

❑ **2002 Dodge Ram Quad Cab,** 2002, Black body, chrome five-spoke wheels, opening doors, 1:27 scale, Model No. 31963

EX n/a   NM n/a   MIP $8

(Maisto International, Inc.)

❑ **2002 Ford Thunderbird,**
Metallic blue or black body, open-
ing doors and hood, 1:25 scale,
Model No. 31966
EX n/a   NM n/a   MIP $8

(Maisto International, Inc.)

❑ **2002 Subaru Impreza WRX,**
2002, Bright blue body, gold
spoked wheels, opening doors and
hood, 1:24 scale, Model No. 31976
EX n/a   NM n/a   MIP $8

(Maisto International, Inc.)

❑ **Audi TT Roadster,** Black or
dark gray body, silver-gray five-
spoke wheels, black interior, opening doors and trunk, 1:24 scale,
Model No. 31978
EX n/a   NM n/a   MIP $8

(Maisto International, Inc.)

❑ **BMW X5,** Silver, blue or red
body, opening doors and hood,
black interior and trim, 1:24 scale,
Model No. 31954
EX n/a   NM n/a   MIP $8

(Maisto International, Inc.)

❑ **BMW Z8,** Dark blue, silver or
red body, opening hood and
doors, black interior, 1:24 scale,
Model No. 31996
EX n/a   NM n/a   MIP $8

(Maisto International, Inc.)

❑ **Chevrolet 3100 Pickup
(1950),** Dark red or black body,
opening doors and tailgate, 1:25
scale, Model No. 31952
EX n/a   NM n/a   MIP $8

(Maisto International, Inc.)

❑ **Chevrolet Corvette Z06,**
2002, Yellow or red body, opening
hood and doors, black interior, silver-gray wheels, 1:24 scale, Model
No. 31989
EX n/a   NM n/a   MIP $8

(Maisto International, Inc.)

❑ **Chevrolet El Camino, 1965,**
2002, Black or green body, opening
doors and tailgate, 1:24 scale,
Model No. 31977
EX n/a   NM n/a   MIP $8

(Maisto International, Inc.)

❑ **Chevrolet Silverado,** Black or
blue body, opening doors, chrome
wheels, black interior, 1:27 scale,
Model No. 31941
EX n/a   NM n/a   MIP $8

(Maisto International, Inc.)

❑ **Chrysler Prowler,** Dark blue
body, opening hood and doors,
adjustable seats, light gray interior, silver wheels, black grille, 1:24
scale, Model No. 31931
EX n/a   NM n/a   MIP $8

(Maisto International, Inc.)

❑ **Chrysler PT Cruiser,** Black,
white or red body, opening doors
and tailgate, silver five-spoke
wheels, 1:24 scale, Model No. 31995
EX n/a   NM n/a   MIP $8

(Maisto International, Inc.)

❑ **Dodge Caravan,** Burgundy or
green body, silver five-spoke
wheels, sliding side door and
opening tailgate, 1:26 scale, Model
No. 31913
EX n/a   NM n/a   MIP $8

(Maisto International, Inc.)

❑ **Dodge Concept Vehicle,** Copper body, opening doors, hood and trunk, silver five-spoke wheels, 1:24 scale, Model No. 31951
EX n/a   NM n/a   MIP $8

(Maisto International, Inc.)

❑ **Dodge Ram Pickup,** Dark metallic green body, opening doors and tailgate, black grille and trim, 1:26 scale, Model No. 31912
EX n/a   NM n/a   MIP $8

(Maisto International, Inc.)

❑ **Dodge Ram SuperSport (SS/T),** Black or bright red body, opening doors and tailgate, chrome wheels, 1:26 scale, Model No. 31930
EX n/a   NM n/a   MIP $8

(Maisto International, Inc.)

❑ **Dodge Viper GT2,** White body, blue stripes running from hood to trunk, silver multi-spoked wheels, opening doors, 1:24 scale, Model No. 31945
EX n/a   NM n/a   MIP $8

(Maisto International, Inc.)

❑ **Ford Escape,** Yellow or dark metallic blue body, silver five-spoke wheels, opening doors and tailgate, 1:24 scale, Model No. 31948
EX n/a   NM n/a   MIP $8

(Maisto International, Inc.)

❑ **Ford Explorer Sport Trac,** Dark blue or white body, opening doors and tailgate, five-spoke wheels, rubber tires, 1:25 scale, Model No. 31991
EX n/a   NM n/a   MIP $8

(Maisto International, Inc.)

❑ **Ford Focus SVT,** 2002, Sonic blue body, silver-gray five spoke wheels, black interior, opening doors and hood, 1:24 scale, Model No. 31962
EX n/a   NM n/a   MIP $8

(Maisto International, Inc.)

❑ **Honda S2000,** Red or silver body, black interior, silver five-spoke wheels, opening hood and doors, 1:24 scale, Model No. 31979
EX n/a   NM n/a   MIP $8

(Maisto International, Inc.)

❑ **Hummer Four-Door Wagon,** 2002, Black or red body, white roof, opening doors, 1:27 scale, Model No. 31958
EX n/a   NM n/a   MIP $8

(Maisto International, Inc.)

❑ **Hummer Soft Top,** 2002, Yellow or white body, black plastic soft top, opening doors, 1:27 scale, Model No. 31959
EX n/a   NM n/a   MIP $8

(Maisto International, Inc.)

❑ **Humvee,** 2002, Olive body, black machine gun and bumpers, black antenna, opening doors and hatch, 1:27 scale, Model No. 31974
EX n/a   NM n/a   MIP $8

(Maisto International, Inc.)

❑ **Jaguar XJ220,** Green or silver body, opening hood, doors and trunk, adjustable seats, 1:24 scale, Model No. 31907
EX n/a   NM n/a   MIP $8

MAISTO / CARS AND TRUCKS

(Maisto International, Inc.)

❏ **Jaguar XK180,** Blue-green body, opening doors and trunk, silver five-spoke wheels, 1:25 scale, Model No. 31967
EX n/a   **NM** n/a   **MIP** $8

(Maisto International, Inc.)

❏ **Jaguar XK8,** Dark metallic green or blue body, opening hood, doors and trunk, silver wheels, 1:24 scale, Model No. 31936
EX n/a   **NM** n/a   **MIP** $8

(Maisto International, Inc.)

❏ **Lamborghini Diablo,** Red body, opening hood, doors and trunk, black interior, 1:24 scale, Model No. 31903
EX n/a   **NM** n/a   **MIP** $8

(Maisto International, Inc.)

❏ **Lamborghini Jota,** Pink-purple or sky blue body, opening hood, doors and trunk, 1:24 scale, Model No. 31929
EX n/a   **NM** n/a   **MIP** $8

(Maisto International, Inc.)

❏ **Lamborghini SE,** Pink-purple or light green body, black interior, opening hood, trunk and doors, 1:24 scale, Model No. 31919
EX n/a   **NM** n/a   **MIP** $8

(Maisto International, Inc.)

❏ **Mercedes CLK-GTR Street Version,** Silver body, opening doors, mult-spoked wheels, 1:26 scale, Model No. 31949
EX n/a   **NM** n/a   **MIP** $8

(Maisto International, Inc.)

❏ **Mercedes-Benz 500 SL,** Aqua blue body, dark blue bumpers, black interior, opening hood, doors and trunk, adjustable seats, 1:24 scale, Model No. 31901
EX n/a   **NM** n/a   **MIP** $8

(Maisto International, Inc.)

❏ **Mercedes-Benz ML 320,** Dark green or silver body, opening hood and doors, silver five-spoke wheels, 1:24 scale, Model No. 31947
EX n/a   **NM** n/a   **MIP** $8

(Maisto International, Inc.)

❏ **Mercedes-Benz S-Class,** Dark metallic purple or silver blue body, opening hood and doors, adjustable seats, 1:26 scale, Model No. 31955
EX n/a   **NM** n/a   **MIP** $8

(Maisto International, Inc.)

❏ **Mercedes-Benz SLK,** Yellow or red body, opening doors, hood and trunk, adjustable seats, silver wheels, 1:24 scale, Model No. 31942
EX n/a   **NM** n/a   **MIP** $8

(Maisto International, Inc.)

❏ **Peugeot 206cc,** 2002, Blue, silver or orange body, opening doors and hood, 1:24 scale, Model No. 31972
EX n/a   **NM** n/a   **MIP** $8

(Maisto International, Inc.)

❏ **Plymouth Pronto Spyder,** Silver body, red interior, opening doors, 1:24 scale, Model No. 31944
EX n/a   **NM** n/a   **MIP** $8

(Maisto International, Inc.)

❏ **Plymouth Voyager,** Dark blue or white body, black trim, sliding side door, opening tailgate, silver five-spoke wheels, 1:26 scale, Model No. 31928
EX n/a   **NM** n/a   **MIP** $8

(Maisto International, Inc.)

❑ **Porsche 911 Carrera, 1997,** Yellow or red body, opening doors and hood, black interior, silver wheels, 1:24 scale, Model No. 31938
EX n/a   NM n/a   MIP $8

(Maisto International, Inc.)

❑ **Porsche 911 Speedster,** Sky blue body, opening hood, doors and trunk, adjustable seats, 1:24 scale, Model No. 31902
EX n/a   NM n/a   MIP $8

(Maisto International, Inc.)

❑ **Porsche Boxster,** Dark blue or yellow body, opening hood and doors, silver wheels, dark gray interior, 1:24 scale, Model No. 31933
EX n/a   NM n/a   MIP $8

(Maisto International, Inc.)

❑ **Porsche No. 1 Typ 356 Roadster, 1948,** Silver body, opening doors and trunk, 1:24 scale, Model No. 31953
EX n/a   NM n/a   MIP $8

(Maisto International, Inc.)

❑ **Shinoda Boss Mustang,** Black body, opening doors, hood and trunk, silver wheels, strobed "Boss" stripe on sides, 1:24 scale, Model No. 31934
EX n/a   NM n/a   MIP $8

(Maisto International, Inc.)

❑ **Volkswagen Beetle,** Red body, opening front trunk and doors, black and silver trim, 1:24 scale, Model No. 31926
EX n/a   NM n/a   MIP $8

(Maisto International, Inc.)

❑ **Volkswagen New Beetle,** Metallic lime green, red, yellow or blue body, silver six-spoke wheels with "VW" at center, opening hood and doors, 1:25 scale, Model No. 31975
EX n/a   NM n/a   MIP $8

(Maisto International, Inc.)

❑ **Volkswagen Van "Samba",** Red and white or gray-blue and

white body, opening tailgate and side door, chrome trim, 1:25 scale, Model No. 31956
EX n/a   NM n/a   MIP $8

1:32-SCALE SPECIAL EDITION

(Maisto International, Inc.)

❑ **1934 Ford Coupe,** Dark blue body, black fenders and running boards, off-white wheels, opening doors, silver bumpers and grille, 1:32 scale, Model No. 81011
EX n/a   NM n/a   MIP $15

(Maisto International, Inc.)

❑ **1934 Ford Coupe,** Light brown body, black fenders, wheels and running boards, opening doors, silver bumpers and grille, 1:32 scale, Model No. 81011
EX n/a   NM n/a   MIP $15

(Maisto International, Inc.)

❑ **1937 Ford Pickup,** Red body, brown wheels, black fenders and running boards, opening doors, silver bumpers and grille, 1:32 scale, Model No. 81012
EX n/a   NM n/a   MIP $15

(Maisto International, Inc.)

❑ **1937 Ford Pickup,** Dark blue body, red wheels, opening doors, black fenders and running boards, silver bumpers and grille, 1:32 scale, Model No. 81012
EX n/a   **NM** n/a   **MIP** $15

1:43-SCALE CLASSIC COLLECTION

(Maisto International, Inc.)

❑ **2002 Ford Thunderbird,** Black or metallic blue body, silver spoked wheels, black interior, 1:43 scale, Model No. 31507
EX $6   **NM** $8   **MIP** $8

(Maisto International, Inc.)

❑ **Jaguar Mark II,** Green or cream body, chrome spoked wheels, 1:43 scale, Model No. 31503
EX n/a   **NM** n/a   **MIP** $8

(Maisto International, Inc.)

❑ **Jaguar S-Type,** Pearl or silver blue body, silver multi-spoked wheels, 1:43 scale, Model No. 31509
EX n/a   **NM** n/a   **MIP** $8

(Maisto International, Inc.)

❑ **Jaguar XK8,** Dark blue or green body, white interior, chrome wheels, 1:43 scale, Model No. 31501
EX n/a   **NM** n/a   **MIP** $8

(Maisto International, Inc.)

❑ **Mercedes-Benz CLK LM,** Silver body, "Warsteiner" on sides and front, red number "2" on sides and front, black spoiler, 1:43 scale, Model No. 31508
EX n/a   **NM** n/a   **MIP** $10

(Maisto International, Inc.)

❑ **Mercedes-Benz CLK-GTR Street Version,** Silver body, chrome mult-spoked wheels, 1:43 scale, Model No. 31506
EX n/a   **NM** n/a   **MIP** $10

(Maisto International, Inc.)

❑ **Mercedes-Benz S-Class,** Dark blue or silver gray body, silver seven-spoked wheels, black interior, 1:43 scale, Model No. 31505
EX n/a   **NM** n/a   **MIP** $8

2-WHEELERS

(Maisto International, Inc.)

❑ **BMW F 650 GS,** Light metallic blue and silver body, black seat, chrome engine and wheels, 1:18 scale, Model No. 31300TT
EX n/a   **NM** n/a   **MIP** $8

(Maisto International, Inc.)

❑ **BMW R1100R,** Red body, chrome fork, engine and wheels, black seat, 1:18 scale, Model No. 31300SS
EX n/a   **NM** n/a   **MIP** $8

(Maisto International, Inc.)

❑ **BMW R1100RS,** Dark metallic purple and black body, black seat, chrome engine and wheels, 1:18 scale, Model No. 31300QQ
EX n/a   **NM** n/a   **MIP** $8

(Maisto International, Inc.)

❏ **BMW R1200C,** Steel metallic blue body with chrome fork, engine and wheels, black seat, 1:18 scale, Model No. 31300RR
EX n/a   **NM** n/a   **MIP** $8

(Maisto International, Inc.)

❏ **Cagiva GP 500 1994,** 2002, Dark red body, white number "11" on front and sides, black wheels, 1:18 scale, Model No. 31300gp500
EX n/a   **NM** n/a   **MIP** $8

(Maisto International, Inc.)

❏ **Cagiva MITO 125,** 2002, Red and black body, gray engine, "Cagiva" and "MITO" on sides, 1:18 scale, Model No. 31300mito
EX n/a   **NM** n/a   **MIP** $8

(Maisto International, Inc.)

❏ **Cannondale MX400,** Red and white body, yellow "Cannondale" type, silver frame, engine and wheels, 1:18 scale, Model No. 31300yy
EX n/a   **NM** n/a   **MIP** $8

(Maisto International, Inc.)

❏ **Cannondale XC400,** Yellow, white and silver body, chrome wheels, black seat and handlebars, 1:18 scale, Model No. 31300XX
EX n/a   **NM** n/a   **MIP** $8

(Maisto International, Inc.)

❏ **Ducati 748,** Yellow with yellow and chrome wheels, black seat, "748" on sides, 1:18 scale, Model No. 31300f
EX n/a   **NM** n/a   **MIP** $8

(Maisto International, Inc.)

❏ **Ducati MH900E,** Red and silver body, chrome wheels, black seat, 1:18 scale, Model No. 31300a
EX n/a   **NM** n/a   **MIP** $8

(Maisto International, Inc.)

❏ **Ducati Monster 900,** Yellow body, gold frame, chrome engine, wheels and exhaust, black seat, 1:18 scale, Model No. 31300b
EX n/a   **NM** n/a   **MIP** $8

(Maisto International, Inc.)

❏ **Ducati Monsterdark,** Black body, black seat, silver engine, chrome exhaust and fork, black wheels, 1:18 scale, Model No. 31300g
EX n/a   **NM** n/a   **MIP** $8

(Maisto International, Inc.)

❏ **Ducati Supersport 900,** Red body, chrome wheels and exhaust, black seat, 1:18 scale, Model No. 31300d
EX n/a   **NM** n/a   **MIP** $8

(Maisto International, Inc.)

❏ **Ducati Supersport 900FE,** Silver body, black seat, gold frame, chrome engine and exhaust, 1:18 scale, Model No. 31300c
EX n/a   **NM** n/a   **MIP** $8

MAISTO / MOTORCYCLES

(Maisto International, Inc.)

❑ **Honda CBR600F4,** Yellow body with black stripes, silver frame, black wheels and seat,, 1:18 scale, Model No. 31300y

EX n/a   NM n/a   MIP $8

(Maisto International, Inc.)

❑ **Honda CBR600F4i,** 2002, Red body with black stripes and white "F4i" on sides, black three-spoke wheels, 1:18 scale, Model No. 31300f4i

EX n/a   NM n/a   MIP $8

(Maisto International, Inc.)

❑ **Honda CRB600F,** Red and dark blue body, silver frame, black wheels, 1:18 scale, Model No. 31300dd

EX n/a   NM n/a   MIP $8

(Maisto International, Inc.)

❑ **Honda NR,** Red body, chrome wheels, black "NR" behind seat, 1:18 scale, Model No. 31300ee

EX n/a   NM n/a   MIP $8

(Maisto International, Inc.)

❑ **Honda Valkyrie,** Black body with white stripe running from front to rear fender, large chrome engine and exhaust, chrome wheels and fork, 1:18 scale, Model No. 31300CC

EX n/a   NM n/a   MIP $8

(Maisto International, Inc.)

❑ **Honda VT1100C2,** Blue body, black frame, chrome fork and wheels, silver and chrome engine, 1:18 scale, Model No. 31300z

EX n/a   NM n/a   MIP $8

(Maisto International, Inc.)

❑ **Honda XR400R,** Red and white body with number "111" on sides and front, silver wheels and engine, 1:18 scale, Model No. 31300AA

EX n/a   NM n/a   MIP $8

(Maisto International, Inc.)

❑ **Kawasaki KLX250SR,** Lime green body, silver engine, chrome fork and wheels, black seat, 1:18 scale, Model No. 31300ii

EX n/a   NM n/a   MIP $8

(Maisto International, Inc.)

❑ **Kawasaki Ninja ZX-12R,** 2002, Dark blue body, gold wheels, black seat, 1:18 scale, Model No. 31300zx12r

EX n/a   NM n/a   MIP $8

(Maisto International, Inc.)

❑ **Kawasaki Ninja ZX-7R,** Silver body, yellow and black graphics, black wheels and seat, 1:18 scale, Model No. 31300gg

EX n/a   NM n/a   MIP $8

(Maisto International, Inc.)

❏ **Kawasaki Ninja ZX-9R,** Green and silver body, green wheels, black seat, 1:18 scale, Model No. 31300hh
EX n/a   **NM** n/a   **MIP** $8

(Maisto International, Inc.)

❏ **KTM 520SX,** Orange, black and white, chrome wheels, "SX 520" in white type on sides, black fork, silver handlebars, 1:18 scale, Model No. 31300vv
EX n/a   **NM** n/a   **MIP** $8

(Maisto International, Inc.)

❏ **KTM 640 Duke II,** Red and black body, black wheels and fork, "Duke" in black type on sides, 1:18 scale, Model No. 31300uu
EX n/a   **NM** n/a   **MIP** $8

(Maisto International, Inc.)

❏ **Moto Guzzi V10 Centauro,** Red and white body, silver engine, chrome wheels, fork and exhaust, 1:18 scale, Model No. 31300PP
EX n/a   **NM** n/a   **MIP** $8

(Maisto International, Inc.)

❏ **MV Brutale Oro,** 2002, Red, gray, silver and black body, red wheels, 1:18 scale, Model No. 31300mv
EX n/a   **NM** n/a   **MIP** $8

(Maisto International, Inc.)

❏ **MV F4S,** 2002, Red and silver body, "Agusta" in blue type on sides, black wheels, 1:18 scale, Model No. 31300f4s
EX n/a   **NM** n/a   **MIP** $8

(Maisto International, Inc.)

❏ **Peugeot Elyseo 125,** Silver and black body, black handlebars and seat, silver wheels, 1:18 scale, Model No. 31300nn
EX n/a   **NM** n/a   **MIP** $8

(Maisto International, Inc.)

❏ **Peugeot Speedflight,** Yellow, blue and black body, silver wheels, 1:18 scale, Model No. 31300OO
EX n/a   **NM** n/a   **MIP** $8

(Maisto International, Inc.)

❏ **Suzuki GSX1300R,** Silver and purple body, black seat, chrome wheels, 1:18 scale, Model No. 31300KK
EX n/a   **NM** n/a   **MIP** $8

(Maisto International, Inc.)

❏ **Suzuki GSX-R1000,** 2002, Red and silver body, silver frame, black wheels, 1:18 scale, Model No. 31300kk1
EX n/a   **NM** n/a   **MIP** $8

(Maisto International, Inc.)

❏ **Suzuki GSX-R600,** 2002, Black and yellow body, silver frame, black wheels, 1:18 scale, Model No. 31300kk6
EX n/a   **NM** n/a   **MIP** $8

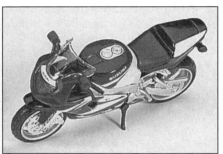

(Maisto International, Inc.)

❑ **Suzuki GSX-R750,** Purple, white and silver body, chrome wheels, silver frame, 1:18 scale, Model No. 31300LL
EX n/a   **NM** n/a   **MIP** $8

(Maisto International, Inc.)

❑ **Triumph Daytona 955i,** Silver body and wheels, black seat, 1:18 scale, Model No. 31300k
EX n/a   **NM** n/a   **MIP** $8

(Maisto International, Inc.)

❑ **Triumph Speed Triple,** Lime body, silver frame, black engine and exhaust, black seat, chrome fork and handlebars, 1:18 scale, Model No. 31300i
EX n/a   **NM** n/a   **MIP** $8

(Maisto International, Inc.)

❑ **Triumph Sprint RS,** Bed body, silver wheels, black seat, 1:18 scale, Model No. 31300j
EX n/a   **NM** n/a   **MIP** $8

(Maisto International, Inc.)

❑ **Triumph T120 Bonneville, 1969,** Red and black body, chrome and silver engine, chrome wheels, black seat, 1:18 scale, Model No. 31300m
EX n/a   **NM** n/a   **MIP** $8

(Maisto International, Inc.)

❑ **Triumph Thunderbird,** Metallic purple and silver body, chrome fork, engine, wheels and exhaust, black seat, 1:18 scale, Model No. 31300h
EX n/a   **NM** n/a   **MIP** $8

(Maisto International, Inc.)

❑ **Triumph Tiger,** Orange body, black engine and seat, red graphics on tank, chrome wheels, 1:18 scale, Model No. 31300L
EX n/a   **NM** n/a   **MIP** $8

(Maisto International, Inc.)

❑ **Triumph TT600,** Yellow body, silver engine, chrome wheels, black seat, 1:18 scale, Model No. 31300n
EX n/a   **NM** n/a   **MIP** $8

(Maisto International, Inc.)

❑ **Yamaha 1000 Thunderace,** Silver and black body, silver wheels, 1:18 scale, Model No. 31300o
EX n/a   **NM** n/a   **MIP** $8

(Maisto International, Inc.)

❑ **Yamaha FZR600R,** Red, white and blue body, red wheels, blue seat, 1:18 scale, Model No. 31300r
EX n/a   **NM** n/a   **MIP** $8

(Maisto International, Inc.)

❑ **Yamaha Road Star,** 2002, Red and silver body, black seat, chrome engine and wheels, 1:18 scale, Model No. 31300rstar
EX n/a   **NM** n/a   **MIP** $8

(Maisto International, Inc.)

❑ **Yamaha Road Star Silverado,** 2002, Black and silver body, chrome engine and wheels, whitewall tires, 1:18 scale, Model No. 31300silver
EX n/a   NM n/a   MIP $8

(Maisto International, Inc.)

❑ **Yamaha TDM850,** Metallic yellow and silver body, "TDM850" on sides of tank, black wheels and seat, 1:18 scale, Model No. 31300w
EX n/a   NM n/a   MIP $8

(Maisto International, Inc.)

❑ **Yamaha TTR250,** 2002, White and purple body, 1:18 scale, Model No. 31300ttr250
EX n/a   NM n/a   MIP $8

(Maisto International, Inc.)

❑ **Yamaha V-Max,** Black body and engine, chrome wheels, exhaust and forks, 1:18 scale, Model No. 31300v
EX n/a   NM n/a   MIP $8

(Maisto International, Inc.)

❑ **Yamaha V-Max,** Black body and engine, chrome wheels, exhaust and forks, 1:18 scale, Model No. 31300v
EX n/a   NM n/a   MIP $8

(Maisto International, Inc.)

❑ **Yamaha YZF-RT,** 2002, Dark blue and white body, black wheels and seat, 1:18 scale, Model No. 31300t
EX n/a   NM n/a   MIP $8

(Maisto International, Inc.)

❑ **Yamaha YZF-RZ,** Red, white and black body, 1:18 scale, Model No. 31300s
EX n/a   NM n/a   MIP $8

ASSEMBLY LINE 4.5" MODEL KITS

(Maisto International, Inc.)

❑ **1953 Ford Pickup,** Dark blue body, blue wheels, white interior, chrome bumpers and grille, hay bales in truck bed, pull-back motor, Model No. 29409
EX n/a   NM n/a   MIP $5

(Maisto International, Inc.)

❑ **1957 Chevrolet Corvette,** Black body, red interior, white trim, chrome wheels and grille, pull-back motor, Model No. 29406
EX n/a   NM n/a   MIP $5

(Maisto International, Inc.)

❑ **1963 Corvette,** Dark blue body, black interior, opening doors, chrome bumper and wheels, pull-back motor, Model No. 29416
EX n/a   NM n/a   MIP $5

(Maisto International, Inc.)

❑ **1978 Corvette,** Red body, black roof, opening doors, chrome

wheels, pull-back motor, Model No. 29419
EX n/a   **NM** n/a   **MIP** $5

(Maisto International, Inc.)

❑ **1991 Chevrolet Corvette,** Yellow body, black interior, silver wheels, opening doors, pull-back motor, Model No. 29407
EX n/a   **NM** n/a   **MIP** $5

(Maisto International, Inc.)

❑ **2000 Chevrolet SSR,** Dark blue body, black interior, chrome wheels, opening doors, pull-back motor, Model No. 29414
EX n/a   **NM** n/a   **MIP** $5

(Maisto International, Inc.)

❑ **Audi TT Roadster,** Deep red body, silver five-spoke wheels, opening doors, black interior, pull-back motor, Model No. 29402
EX n/a   **NM** n/a   **MIP** $5

(Maisto International, Inc.)

❑ **BMW Z8,** Metallic steel blue body, opening doors, black interior, pull-back motor, Model No. 29404
EX n/a   **NM** n/a   **MIP** $5

(Maisto International, Inc.)

❑ **Chrysler GT Cruiser,** Silver body, opening doors, silver five-spoke wheels, pull-back motor, Model No. 29411
EX n/a   **NM** n/a   **MIP** $5

(Maisto International, Inc.)

❑ **Chrysler Panel Cruiser,** Blue body, opening doors, pull-back motor. Each kit includes a screw-driver and is powered by a pull-back motor, Model No. 29424
EX n/a   **NM** n/a   **MIP** $5

(Maisto International, Inc.)

❑ **Chrysler PT Cruiser,** Black body, opening doors, silver five-spoke wheels, pull-back motor, Model No. 29412
EX n/a   **NM** n/a   **MIP** $5

(Maisto International, Inc.)

❑ **Dodge Ram,** Dark blue body, silver grille and wheels, opening doors, pull-back motor, Model No. 29408
EX n/a   **NM** n/a   **MIP** $5

(Maisto International, Inc.)

❑ **Dodge Viper GT2,** Black body with white stripes, opening doors, silver multi-spoked wheels, pull-back motor, Model No. 29422
EX n/a   **NM** n/a   **MIP** $5

(Maisto International, Inc.)

❑ **Ford Explorer,** Red body, light tan interior, chrome grille and wheels, pull-back motor, Model No. 29417
EX n/a   **NM** n/a   **MIP** $5

(Maisto International, Inc.)

❑ **Ford Explorer Sport Trac,** Orange body, black trim, opening front doors, chrome wheels, pull-back motor, Model No. 29413
EX n/a   **NM** n/a   **MIP** $5

MAISTO / CARS AND TRUCKS

(Maisto International, Inc.)

❏ **Ford F-350 Super Duty Pickup,** Red body, opening doors, pull-back motor, Model No. 29420
EX n/a   NM n/a   MIP $5

(Maisto International, Inc.)

❏ **Ford Police Interceptor,** Black and white body with red, clear and blue dome lights, "Highway Patrol" and "K-9 Team" on sides. Pull-back motor, Model No. 29423
EX n/a   NM n/a   MIP $5

(Maisto International, Inc.)

❏ **Honda S2000,** Yellow body, black interior, opening doors, silver wheels, pull-back motor, Model No. 29401
EX n/a   NM n/a   MIP $5

(Maisto International, Inc.)

❏ **Jeepster,** Orange-red body, silver roof and wheels, opening doors, black interior, pull-back motor, Model No. 29403
EX n/a   NM n/a   MIP $5

(Maisto International, Inc.)

❏ **Mercedes-Benz SLK,** Silver body, black interior, opening doors, pull-back motor, Model No. 29418
EX n/a   NM n/a   MIP $5

(Maisto International, Inc.)

❏ **Porsche 911 Carrera, 1997,** Silver body, opening doors, black interior, pull-back motor, Model No. 29421
EX n/a   NM n/a   MIP $5

(Maisto International, Inc.)

❏ **Volkswagen 1303 Cabriolet,** Red body, off-white interior, five-spoke wheels, opening doors, pull-back motor, Model No. 29415
EX n/a   NM n/a   MIP $5

(Maisto International, Inc.)

❏ **Volkswagen New Beetle,** Black body, opening doors, black interior, silver six-spoke wheels, Model No. 29410
EX n/a   NM n/a   MIP $5

POWER RACERS

(Maisto International, Inc.)

❏ **2001 Hummer H2 SUT Concept,** 2002, Metallic green body, silver wheels and grille, opening doors, pull-back motor, Model No. 25001sut
EX n/a   NM n/a   MIP $4

(Maisto International, Inc.)

❏ **2003 Hummer H2 SUV,** 2002, Silver body, black chassis and trim, opening doors, pull-back motor, Model No. 25001suv
EX n/a   NM n/a   MIP $4

(Maisto International, Inc.)

❑ **Acura RS-X,** 2002, Deep blue body, opening doors, silver wheels, pull-back motor, Model No. 25001rsx
EX n/a   NM n/a   MIP $4

(Maisto International, Inc.)

❑ **Chrysler Prowler,** 2002, Purple body, gray trim and wheels, opening doors, pull-back motor. Still seen as "Plymouth Prowler" on store shelves, Model No. 25001l5
EX n/a   NM n/a   MIP $4

(Maisto International, Inc.)

❑ **Clio V6 Renault Sport,** 2002, Blue body, silver multi-spoked wheels, opening doors, black interior, pull-back motor, Model No. 25001clio
EX n/a   NM n/a   MIP $4

(Maisto International, Inc.)

❑ **Dodge Ram Quad Cab,** 2002, Black body, chrome wheels and grille, opening doors, pull-back motor, Model No. 25001quad
EX n/a   NM n/a   MIP $4

(Maisto International, Inc.)

❑ **Jeep Liberty,** 2002, Black body, chrome five-spoke wheels, black interior, pull-back motor, Model No. 25001lib
EX n/a   NM n/a   MIP $4

(Maisto International, Inc.)

❑ **Lexus IS 300,** 2002, Silver body, opening doors, pull-back motor, Model No. 25001300
EX n/a   NM n/a   MIP $4

(Maisto International, Inc.)

❑ **Lexus SC 430,** 2002, Gold body, beige interior, opening doors, pull-back motor, Model No. 25001430
EX n/a   NM n/a   MIP $4

(Maisto International, Inc.)

❑ **Lexus SC 430,** 2002, Gold body, beige interior, opening doors, pull-back motor, Model No. 25001430
EX n/a   NM n/a   MIP $4

(Maisto International, Inc.)

❑ **Mercedes-Benz SL-Class,** 2002, Gloss-black body, opening doors, silver wheels, pull-back motor, Model No. 25001mbsl
EX n/a   NM n/a   MIP $4

(Maisto International, Inc.)

❑ **Mini Cooper,** 2002, Red body, white roof, silver five-spoke wheels, opening doors, pull-back engine, Model No. 25001mini
EX n/a   NM n/a   MIP $4

(Maisto International, Inc.)

❑ **Opel Speedster,** 2002, Yellow body, black interior, silver wheels, opening doors, pull-back motor, Model No. 25001opel
EX n/a   NM n/a   MIP $4

TAILWINDS SERIES

(Maisto International, Inc.)

❑ **A-10 Thunderbolt II,** Gray and dark green camo pattern, Model No. 15061s

EX n/a   **NM** n/a   **MIP** $3

(Maisto International, Inc.)

❑ **A-6E Intruder,** Gray and white with American markings and "Navy" on fuselage, Model No. 15061g

EX n/a   **NM** n/a   **MIP** $3

(Maisto International, Inc.)

❑ **AH-64A Apache,** Dark green body, black rotors and wheels, Model No. 15061x

EX n/a   **NM** n/a   **MIP** $3

(Maisto International, Inc.)

❑ **AV-8B Harrier II,** Gray and green camo pattern, American markings, Model No. 15061h

EX n/a   **NM** n/a   **MIP** $3

(Maisto International, Inc.)

❑ **B-17G Flying Fortress,** Silver body with dark blue stripes, Model No. 15061t

EX n/a   **NM** n/a   **MIP** $3

(Maisto International, Inc.)

❑ **B-24D Liberator,** Silver with dark and light green camo pattern, RAF markings, Model No. 15061dd

EX n/a   **NM** n/a   **MIP** $3

(Maisto International, Inc.)

❑ **B-25J Mitchell,** Light and dark green camo pattern with early star-in-circle U.S. Army Air Corps markings, Model No. 15061w

EX n/a   **NM** n/a   **MIP** $3

(Maisto International, Inc.)

❑ **Bell OH-58A Kiowa,** 2002, Dark green, black rotors and landing skids, Model No. 15061n2

EX n/a   **NM** n/a   **MIP** $3

(Maisto International, Inc.)

❑ **Bell TH-57 Sea Ranger,** 2002, Red and white body, black nose and rotors, "Navy" on tail, Model No. 15061n6

EX n/a   **NM** n/a   **MIP** $3

(Maisto International, Inc.)

❑ **CH-47 Chinook,** Gray and dark-green camo pattern, Royal Marines markings on sides, black rotors, Model No. 15061ee

EX n/a   **NM** n/a   **MIP** $3

(Maisto International, Inc.)

❑ **EF-2000 Eurofighter,** White and silver with delta-style wings, Model No. 15061bb

EX n/a   **NM** n/a   **MIP** $3

(Maisto International, Inc.)

MAISTO / AIRPLANES

❏ **F/A-18C Hornet,** Blue and yellow with "U.S. Navy" on wings, Model No. 15061v

EX n/a   NM n/a   MIP $3

(Maisto International, Inc.)

❏ **F-104 Starfighter,** Orange fuselage with silver wings, "U.S. Air Force" underneath cockpit, Model No. 15061f

EX n/a   NM n/a   MIP $3

(Maisto International, Inc.)

❏ **F-117A Nighthawk,** Flat black with U.S. Air Force markings, Model No. 15061j

EX n/a   NM n/a   MIP $3

(Maisto International, Inc.)

❏ **F-14 Tomcat,** Gray and white camo pattern, Model No. 15061y

EX n/a   NM n/a   MIP $3

(Maisto International, Inc.)

❏ **F-15 Eagle,** Gray-green and light green camo pattern, Model No. 15061q

EX n/a   NM n/a   MIP $3

(Maisto International, Inc.)

❏ **F-16 Fighting Falcon,** White and gray camo pattern, Model No. 15061u

EX n/a   NM n/a   MIP $3

(Maisto International, Inc.)

❏ **F-4J Phantom,** Dark gray with U.S insignia and "Navy" on sides, Model No. 15061p

EX n/a   NM n/a   MIP $3

(Maisto International, Inc.)

❏ **F4U-1D Corsair Fighter,** Blue body, checkerboard design on tail, black propeller, Model No. 15061m

EX n/a   NM n/a   MIP $3

(Maisto International, Inc.)

❏ **F6F Hellcat,** Blue body, white star-in-circle markings, black prop, Model No. 15061n

EX n/a   NM n/a   MIP $3

(Maisto International, Inc.)

❏ **Gee Bee Super Sportster R-1,** 2002, Red and white body with number "11", and silver prop, Model No. 15061n5

EX n/a   NM n/a   MIP $3

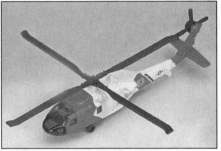
(Maisto International, Inc.)

❏ **HH-60J Jayhawk,** White and orange body, "U.S. Coast Guard" on sides, black nose and rotors, Model No. 15061d

EX n/a   NM n/a   MIP $3

(Maisto International, Inc.)

❏ **KA-52 Alligator,** 2002, Black body and rotors, blue and white markings, Model No. 15061n8

EX n/a   NM n/a   MIP $3

(Maisto International, Inc.)

❏ **MH-53 Pave Low III,** 2002, Tan and gray camo pattern, "Marines" on sides, black rotors, Model No. 15061n7

EX n/a   **NM** n/a   **MIP** $3

(Maisto International, Inc.)

❏ **MIG-29 Fulcrum,** Gray and green camo pattern Soviet red star markings, Model No. 15061e

EX n/a   **NM** n/a   **MIP** $3

(Maisto International, Inc.)

❏ **Mirage 2000C,** Gray and blue camouflage pattern, French insignia, Model No. 15061o

EX n/a   **NM** n/a   **MIP** $3

(Maisto International, Inc.)

❏ **Mitsubishi Zero,** White with blue stripes, black engine cowling, Model No. 15061aa

EX n/a   **NM** n/a   **MIP** $3

(Maisto International, Inc.)

❏ **P-38 Lightning,** 2002, Dark olive with light blue underbody, star-in-circle American insignia, Model No. 1506113

EX n/a   **NM** n/a   **MIP** $3

(Maisto International, Inc.)

❏ **P-47D Thunderbolt,** Green plane with "All American Rescue" and number "2" on fuselage, black propeller, Model No. 15061l

EX n/a   **NM** n/a   **MIP** $3

(Maisto International, Inc.)

❏ **P-61 Black Widow,** Flat black body, crescent moon and red-and-white stripe on tail, Model No. 15061k

EX n/a   **NM** n/a   **MIP** $3

(Maisto International, Inc.)

❏ **RAH-66 Comanche,** Dark green body, "United States Army" in black type on sides, black rotors, Model No. 15061cc

EX n/a   **NM** n/a   **MIP** $3

(Maisto International, Inc.)

❏ **RQ-1 Predator,** White model of experimental unmanned aircraft, Model No. 15061n1

EX n/a   **NM** n/a   **MIP** $3

(Maisto International, Inc.)

❏ **SR-71 Blackbird,** Black body, "U.S. Air Force" on fuselage, Model No. 15061ff

EX n/a   **NM** n/a   **MIP** $3

(Maisto International, Inc.)

❏ **SU-37 Super Flanker,** Yellow and green camo pattern, Soviet red star insignia, Model No. 15061gg

EX n/a   **NM** n/a   **MIP** $3

(Maisto International, Inc.)

❏ **SU-47,** 2002, Dark gray-green with white nose and Soviet red star markings, Model No. 15061n4

EX n/a   **NM** n/a   **MIP** $3

(Maisto International, Inc.)

Matchbox Accessory Packs

The Double-Fronted Store, (A5-1), from 1961. Accessory Packs were generally buildings and static models, but the Bedford Car Transporter managed to sneak into the lineup as it's only vehicle toy.

Matchbox, like Dinky and Corgi, liked to supply kids and collectors with a miniature landscape of buildings and gear. The Accessory Packs line seemed the perfect way to do just that.

Not a large grouping to begin with, the Accessory Packs seem to only keep the name up until 1970 or so. Beyond that, Gift Sets, racing track sets, magnetic "action centers" (playsets that allowed you to move people and livestock around Matchbox vehicles), service stations and even a "Superfast Auto Sales" miniature dealership lot—dominate outside of the regular 1-75 lineup.

As it happens, the last Accessory Pack seems to be the Matchbox Service Ramp, a vehicle lift with plastic oil and grease guns on small hose lines.

MARKET UPDATE

The Accessory Packs, like other extra-vehicular Matchbox toys have higher-but-still collectible mint-in-package values. They're fun to set up with a display of Matchbox vehicles and will more than likely only climb in price, especially models with later, more graphically detailed packages, (which are appealing to die-cast and generally collectors alike.)

This metal "lock-up" garage, (A3-1), of the type seen in so many British towns, could be linked with others to form an entire row. With opening front doors, it made the perfect spot to park a Matchbox car.

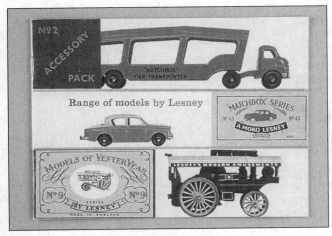

This cover of a 1959 catalog reprint shows the only vehicle to make it into the Accessory Packs line—the A2-1 Bedford Car Transporter.

This time for real: two variations of the Bedford Car Transporter shown here in the more commonly-found blue, and the rare, late-issue gray and red. These trucks are handsome toys, but really quite simple when compared to later Major Packs and King Size releases from Matchbox.

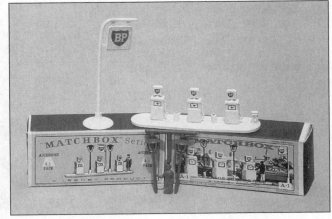

BP Petrol Pumps & Signs: Note the box variations and plastic light posts and service attendant still on tree sprue in foreground.

❑ **A1-1, Esso Pumps and Forecourt Sign,** 1957, Red pump with Esso decals, attendant and sign in white Esso decals on sign, 3-5/8"
EX $35   **NM** $65   **MIP** $110

(KP Photo by Dr. Douglas Sadecky)

❑ **A1-2, B.P. Garage Pumps and Forecourt Sign,** 1963, White pumps and sign with B.P. decals, green plastic attendant and lights, 4-1/2"
EX $25   **NM** $50   **MIP** $90

❑ **A1-3, Car Service Ramp,** 1970, Gold ramp and base, red plastic handles, white control panel, Castrol label
EX $15   **NM** $25   **MIP** $40

(KP Photo by Dr. Douglas Sadecky)

❑ **A2-1, Bedford Car Transporter,** 1957, Blue cab and trailer, black or orange decals on trailer, silver grille and headlights, metal, gray or black plastic wheels. The blue transporter on the left is more common; the red and gray version is a rare, and later, color variation, 6-1/2"
EX $55   **NM** $110   **MIP** $180

(KP Photo)

❑ **A3-1, Metal "Lock-Up" Type Garage,** 1957, Yellow walls, dark red roof, opening green doors, could be joined with other garages to form a complete row, 2-5/8"
EX $30   **NM** $60   **MIP** $100

❑ **A4-1, Road Signs,** 1960, Eight different metal signs with black base and pole, white and black signs, red triangle on top
EX $20   **NM** $45   **MIP** $80

(KP Photo, John Brown Sr. collection)

❑ **A5-1, Double-Fronted Store,** 1961, Cream walls, light green roof and door, pictures of produce in windows, Home Stores label across front
EX $30   **NM** $60   **MIP** $100

Matchbox Major Packs 1957-1966

An impressive toy: the Inter State Double Freighter, (M9-1), shown with variations of packaging. Big trucks and construction vehicles were natural choices for Matchbox in a lineup of larger-scaled models. The graphics for the box on the upper right suggests adventure the way all of the best artwork for Matchbox did.

When Lesney started making die-cast toys, larger models were already a part of the lineup. The success of the Matchbox series (soon to be the 1-75 series) put larger-toy building on hold, but only for a few years.

In 1957, the Matchbox Major Packs series was launched to compete with the ever-popular Dinky and Corgi vehicles. A grouping of larger-sized toys, they included construction, agricultural and commercial models—think of them as "proto-King Size" Matchbox cars.

The line lasted until 1966, when a few of the vehicles were incorporated into the already successful and more memorably-named King Size line. The GMC Tractor with Hopper Train, the Race Car Transporter and the Guy Warrior Car Transporter all made the cut, and by the 1968 catalog, they were firmly part of the King Size pantheon.

MARKET UPDATE

Major Packs are another area of collecting that has grown more popular over the past decade. Mint-in-package prices area formidable for beginning collectors, but even pieces in "good" condition—that is, with some nicks and scratches can be impressive-looking on the shelf.

The Racing Car Transporter, (M6-2), one of the Major Packs that transferred to the King Size lineup in 1966. This truck featured a fold-down ramp and could hold two racing cars from the 1-75 series.

The Dinkum Rear Dumper, (M10-1). The long snout on the cab of this vehicle brings to mind an animal of some kind. Overall, though, it's an elegant casting.

This BP Autotanker (M1-2), is an usual-looking truck these days, but were a common sight along European racetracks in the 1960s. It's interesting to note that because so many British-made toys in the 1960s and 1970s had "BP" on them, no one in America thinks it's odd to finally see a British Petroleum station here in the states.

Another English vehicle, the Ford Thames Cattle Truck, (M7-1), with gray plastic wheels.

The decals on this Davies Tyres truck, (M2-2), are pretty sharp. Finding older toys with intact decals is great, because so many of them would chip off with play.

This Car Transporter, (M8-2), features many King Size traits such as removable plastic wheels on hubs, independent axles and an intricate trailer with quite a few moving parts.

(KP Photo by Dr. Douglas Sadecky)

❑ **M1-1, Caterpillar Earth Mover,** 1957, Yellow tractor, driver, and scraper, unpainted metal wheels, black plastic tires, 4-1/2"
EX $30   NM $65   MIP $125

❑ **M1-2, B.P. Autotanker,** 1961, Green lower body, yellow & white upper body, BP decals, green windshield, black plastic wheels, silver-painted headlights, no interior, 4"
EX $25   NM $50   MIP $90

(KP Photo by Dr. Douglas Sadecky)

❑ **M2-1, Bedford Articulated Walls' Ice Cream Lorry,** 1957, Light-blue cab, silver-painted grille, headlights and bumper, cream trailer with Wall's decals, metal or gray plastic wheels, no interior, 3-7/8"
EX $60   NM $110   MIP $160

(KP Photo by Dr. Douglas Sadecky)

❑ **M2-2, Davies Tyres Truck,** 1961, Orange cab, trailer base, & doors, silver-gray trailer body with Davies Tyres decals, silver grille, headlights, & bumper, gray or black plastic wheels, 4-3/8"
EX $60   NM $110   MIP $160

❑ **M2-3, Articulated Truck Box,** 1961, Silver-gray cab, dark-red trailer, LEP decals, three different color variation of trailer base & doors, 4-3/8"
EX $60   NM $110   MIP $160

❑ **M3-1, 10-Wheel Transporter with Centurion Tank,** 1959, Olive cab, trailer, & tank, black plastic wheels on truck, metal, gray or black plastic wheels on tank, 6-1/8". Also known as "Thornycroft Antar with Sankey 50-ton Tank Transporter and Centurion Mark III Tank
EX $60   NM $110   MIP $160

❑ **M4-1, Ruston-Bucyrus Model 22 RB Excavator,** 1959, Dark red body, yellow base, shovel, & arms, gray or green treads, red or yellow decals
EX $45   NM $100   MIP $150

❑ **M4-2, GMC Tractor with Hopper Train,** 1964, Maroon cab, blue windows, silver headlights & bumper, silver-gray trailers, Fruehauf labels, red plastic wheel with gray or black plastic tires, 11-1/4". This model was incorporated into the King-Size line as K4-1
EX $45   NM $110   MIP $150

❑ **M5-1, Massey-Ferguson Combine Harvester,** 1960, Red body, yellow combines, tan driver, white decals, unpainted metal wheels or various orange/yellow plastic wheel combinations with black plastic tires, 4-3/8"
EX $40   NM $85   MIP $135

❑ **M6-1, 18-Wheel Pickford Scammell Tractor & Transporter,** 1960, Dark-blue tractor and trailer wheel supports, dark-red trailer, white Pickfords decals, black plastic wheels
EX $80   NM $165   MIP $235

(KP Photo by Dr. Douglas Sadecky)

❑ **M6-2, Racing Car Transporter,** 1965, Green body, white interior, clear windows, yellow/white/black decals, red plastic wheels, black plastic tires, 5". Incorporated into the King-Size line as K-5 in two years later
EX $25   NM $45   MIP $80

❑ **M7-1, Ford Thames Cattle Truck,** 1960, Red cab, trailer base, & rear fenders, tan or dark-red trailer body & doors, gray or black plastic wheels
EX $60   NM $110   MIP $160

(KP Photo by Dr. Douglas Sadecky)

❑ **M8-1, Mobilgas Petrol Tanker,** 1960, Red cab & trailer, silver grille, headlights, & bumper, Mobilgas decals, gray or black plastic wheels
EX $75   NM $160   MIP $225

❑ **M8-2, Car Transporter,** 1964, Turquoise cab, orange trailer, white decals & interior, orange plastic wheels with gray plastic tires, tinted windshield, 8-1/2"
EX $25   NM $50   MIP $100

❑ **M9-1, Inter-State Double Freighter,** 1962, Dark-blue cab, silver grille & headlights, gold airhorns, dark-blue or unpainted trailer connector, two different shades of gray trailers & doors possible, yellow or orange Cooper-Jarrett decals, black plastic wheels, 11-3/8
EX $60   NM $120   MIP $180

❑ **M10-1, Whitlock "Dinkum" Rear Dumper,** 1962, Yellow cab, body, & dumper, black & white decals, unpainted metal or red plastic wheels with black plastic tires, 4-1/4"
EX $30   NM $60   MIP $100

Matchbox King Size 1965-1970

The Low Loader with Bulldozer, (K17-1), is like a small playset. Like other truck and vehicle combinations in the King Size line, it tends to have a higher mint-in-package price because of its multiple parts. Note, though, the incorrect spare tire on the trailer on this example. Something to look for, as all of the tires are easily removeable.

British die-cast vehicles have long been dominated by 1:43 and 1:50-scale toys. Dinky and Corgi (as well as Spot-On, Lonestar and others) had a virtual lock on the larger die-cast market until Matchbox expanded its Major Packs line into the King-Size range.

The popularity of King Size Matchbox has grown in the past few years. Items that once were fairly common and not too expensive are easily running past the $50 and $100 dollar price range for mint-in-package examples.

It's easy to understand why—the models are quite well made and are often larger versions of a "little brother" in the 1-75 lineup. Collecting King Size toys with intact boxes can be tricky, as the boxes changed over the years, making some editions double (or more) in price. The boxes aren't just desirable for their favorable impact on the collectibility of the toys, though—they're also mini-paintings showing examples of the real car in action.

The downside to King Size Matchbox toys? Loose tires. Because of shrinking plastic wheels, the black tires on many regular-wheels era King Size toys become extremely loose. Ironically, this condition seems to affect mint-in-package examples more than loose models. Perhaps the played-with versions

adapted to the change in climate. In any case, the "loose-tire syndrome" makes the toy cars (as opposed to the trucks and tractors) even more sought after. Although the tires on a Mercury police car or a Dodge Charger are still removable, they aren't likely to fall off on their own.

After 1972, the last of the regular-wheels era King Size models gave way to "Super Kings" and "Speed Kings" ranges—larger-scale Matchbox toys fitted with Superfast wheels.

MARKET UPDATE

Whether regular wheels collectors are purchasing "bigger brother" editions of their 1-75 Matchbox toys, or 1:43-scale fans are reaching toward vintage vehicles, King Size models have proven increasingly popular over the past 4 or 5 years. Models with boxes are naturally quite desirable, but out-of-box examples are worthwhile investments, given their great detail.

Its fun to find fire and rescue vehicles in good shape. Like construction and military toys, they tended to be played with frequently, meaning lost ladders, stretchers, and dinged-up decals. This Merryweather Fire Engine (K15-1), is a sharp example with intact extension ladder.

The Mercury Commuter Police Car (K23-1) was a late entry in the King Size line. Like other car models in the series, it featured "True Guide" steering, and tightly-fitted black tires.

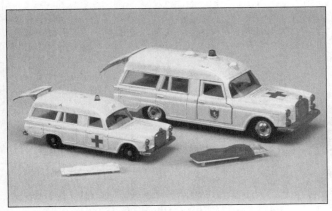

Collecting the King Size model and its smaller counterpart can be fun. Shown here are the Benz "Binz" Ambulance, (3-3RW) and the bigger brother, (K6-2).

This Heavy Breakdown Truck, (K12-1), has seen some play. Earlier versions of this model feature silver metal wheels, versus the red plastic hubs shown here.

Page from the 1969 (1st Edition) Matchbox catalog showing some of the range of King Size vehicles. Notice the Racing Transporter (K5-2) in the upper right corner— it's a former Major Packs model that moved into the King Size lineup in 1966.

The Leyland Tipper, (K4-3), was a popular casting that survived well into the SuperKings era. This model was introduced in the 1969 Second Edition catalog, and replaced the Fruehauf Hopper Train, (K4-2).

MATCHBOX / KING-SIZE

❑ K1-1, Hydraulic Shovel,
1960, Yellow body and front loader, no plastic windows, no interior, gray plastic wheels
EX $30   **NM** $65   **MIP** $95

(KP Photo by Dr. Douglas Sadecky)

❑ K1-2, Foden Tipper Truck,
1964, Red cab and chassis, orange dumper bed with "Hoveringham" decals or labels on sides, red plastic wheels with removable black plastic tires, blue plastic windows, no interior, axle suspension system to roll over bumps, silver metal horns on cab, 4-1/2"

EX $25   **NM** $45   **MIP** $70

❑ K1-3, O & K Excavator, 1970,
Red body with silver excavator arm, red hubs with eight black plastic removable tires, "MH6", "O&K" and white stripe labels on sides, 4-15/16"
EX $15   **NM** $25   **MIP** $35

❑ K2-1, Dumper Truck, 1960,
Blocky red body and chassis with open cab, gray or black plastic tires on green metal hubs, "Muir-Hill" decals
EX $25   **NM** $45   **MIP** $75

(KP Photo by Dr. Douglas Sadecky)

❑ K2-2, KW-Dart Dump Truck,
1964, Yellow articulated body with silver trim on engine and hood. Red hubs with removable black plastic tires, "KW-Dart" decals with arrow graphic, no window plastic, 5-5/8"
EX $30   **NM** $65   **MIP** $95

❑ K2-3, Scammell Heavy Wreck Truck,
1969, White or gold body with red plastic hubs and black removable wheels, silver metal hooks, red towing arm, silver horns on cab roof, "Esso" labels on doors, 4-3/4"
EX $22   **NM** $45   **MIP** $70

(KP Photo by Dr. Douglas Sadecky)

❑ K3-1, Caterpillar Bulldozer,
1960, Yellow body with green rubber treads and unpainted metal or yellow or red plastic roller wheels, cast tow hook, red-painted engine
EX $25   **NM** $50   **MIP** $80

(KP Photo by Dr. Douglas Sadecky)

❑ K3-2, Hatra Tractor Shovel,
1965, Orange-red body with articulating center and lifting loader. Blue-tinted plastic windows, "Hatra" decals on sides of cab, red hubs with black plastic removable tires, 6"
EX $36   **NM** $65   **MIP** $110

❑ K3-3, Massey-Ferguson Tractor and Trailer, 1970, Red
cab and hood with gray engine and base, yellow hubs with removable black plastic tires, white grille, green plastic windows. Trailer with yellow chassis, red dumper bed, yellow hubs with black removable tires. Set measures 8"
EX $17   **NM** $28   **MIP** $60

(KP Photo)

❑ K4-1, International Tractor,
1960, Red body with "McCormick International" and "B-250" decals, green, red or orange hubs with black plastic removable tires, 2-7/8". Early versions with green metal hubs have approx. $80 MIP value
EX $25   **NM** $40   **MIP** $65

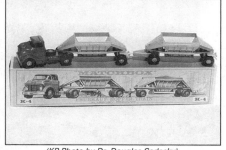

(KP Photo by Dr. Douglas Sadecky)

❑ K4-2, GMC Tractor with Hopper Train, 1967, Red tractor
with two silver hopper trailers, red plastic hubs with black plastic removable wheels, opening chutes, "Fruehauf" decals on each trailer, set measures 11-1/4"
EX $55   **NM** $90   **MIP** $145

(KP Photo)

❑ K4-3, Leyland Tipper, 1969,
Red cab and chassis, silver dumper bed, red hubs with black plastic removable tires, (duals in rear), "Wates" and "LE Transport" labels most common. Amber plastic windows, yellow plastic interior, 4-1/2". Some hard-to-find models with green cabs exist, but have approx. $300 MIP values.

Other models include orange cabs with green dumper beds
EX $12   NM $20   MIP $45

(KP Photo by Dr. Douglas Sadecky)

❏ **K5-1, Tipper Truck,** 1961, Yellow body, silver-painted grille, silver metal or red plastic hubs with black tires, "Foden" decal on sides of hood, 4-1/4". First-version siver-hub models about $80 MIP
EX $25   NM $50   MIP $80

(KP Photo)

❏ **K5-2, Racing Car Transporter,** 1967, Medium-green body, cream plastic interior, clear plastic windows and skylights, red plastic hubs with black removable tires, decals on sides show racing car graphic with "Racing Transporter," "BP," and "LeMans, Sebring, Silverstone, Nurburgring." Silver metal base. Opening tailgate reveals tilting ramp and space for two racing cars, 5". This model entered the King-Size line, after being number M-6 in the Major Packs series
EX $25   NM $50   MIP $80

(KP Photo)

❏ **K5-2, Racing Car Transporter,** View of vehicle showing the ramp and car storage area

❏ **K6-1, Allis-Chalmers Earth Scraper,** 1961, Orange scraper with silver metal or red plastic hubs and black plastic tires. Adjustable scaper bed with springs (sometimes missing) "Allis-Chalmers" decals, 5-7/8"
EX $42   NM $75   MIP $130

(KP Photo)

❏ **K6-2, Mercedes-Benz "Binz" Ambulance,** 1967, White body with blue plastic windows and dome light, black base, red cross decal on hood and shield decals on opening doors, opening rear hatch with white plastic patient and red plastic blanket, silver hubs with black plastic tires, silver metal grille and bumpers, "True Guide" steering, 4-1/8"
EX $12   NM $25   MIP $62

(KP Photo by Dr. Douglas Sadecky)

❏ **K7-1, Curtiss-Wright Rear Dumper,** 1961, Yellow articulated body with silver metal hubs and black plastic tires, tilting dumper bed, "Curtiss-Wright" decals, red-painted engine block, 5-3/4"
EX $40   NM $85   MIP $135

❏ **K7-2, SD Refuse Truck,** 1967, Red cab & chassis, silver rear refuse unit, "Cleansing Service" decals or labels, red plastic wheels with black plastic tires, cream-colored plastic interior, clear plastic windows, 4-5/8"
EX $15   NM $25   MIP $45

(KP Photo by Dr. Douglas Sadecky)

❏ **K8-1, Prime Mover and Transporter with Caterpillar Tractor,** 1962, Orange body & trailer, yellow "Laing" decals, metal towhook, unpainted metal or red plastic wheels with black plastic tires, yellow tractor with green treads and no blade, set measures 12-1/2"
EX $125   NM $180   MIP $275

❏ **K8-2, Car Transporter,** 1967, Green or yellow cab, orange or yellow trailer, orange or red plastic wheels with black plastic tires, "Car Auction Collection" and "Farnborough Meashan" decals on trailer, 8-1/2"
EX $25   NM $45   MIP $70

❏ **K8-3, Caterpillar Traxcavator,** 1970, Various versions of shades of yellow cab, orange shovel & arms, figure, yellow or black wheels with green or black treads, "available mid-1970" in catalog, 4-1/4"
EX $15   NM $25   MIP $35

❏ **K9-1, Diesel Road Roller,** 1962, Green body, red metal rollers, gray or red driver, red "Aveling Barford" decals on sides with white reversed type, 3-3/4"
EX $35   NM $65   MIP $95

(KP Photo)

❏ **K9-2, Claas Combine Harvester,** 1967, Green or red body, red or yellow reels, "Claas" decals or labels, yellow plastic wheels with black plastic tires, 5-1/2"
EX $20   NM $40   MIP $60

❏ **K10-1, Aveling-Barford Tractor Shovel,** 1963, Light-blue body & shovel, red seat, with or without air filter, unpainted metal or red plastic wheels with black plastic tires, 4-1/8"
EX $30   **NM** $60   **MIP** $90

❏ **K10-2, Pipe Truck,** 1967, Yellow cab & trailer chassis, black house-shaped decal on cab doors, gray plastic pipes, red plastic wheels with black plastic tires, later issues had Superfast wheels and pink cab and chassis, 8"
EX $20   **NM** $40   **MIP** $85

(KP Photo)

❏ **K11-1, Fordson Tractor and Trailer,** 1963, Blue tractor body & trailer chassis, light-gray trailer bed, orange metal or plastic wheels with black plastic tires, 6-1/4"
EX $25   **NM** $45   **MIP** $70

❏ **K11-2, DAF Car Transporter,** 1969, Metallic blue cab with gold trailer or yellow cab with orange & yellow trailer, DAF labels, red plastic wheels with black plastic tires or Superfast Wheels, 9"
EX $20   **NM** $50   **MIP** $85

(KP Photo by Dr. Douglas Sadecky)

❏ **K12-1, Heavy Breakdown Wreck Truck,** 1963, Green body, yellow boom, with or without roof lights, unpainted metal or red plastic wheels with black plastic tires, 4-3/4"
EX $25   **NM** $50   **MIP** $75

(KP Photo)

❏ **K12-2, Scammell Crane Truck,** 1970, Yellow cab & crane, red plastic wheels with black plastic tires or orange body & crane with Superfast wheels, 6"
EX $20   **NM** $35   **MIP** $50

(KP Photo by Dr. Douglas Sadecky)

❏ **K13-1, Ready-Mix Concrete Truck,** 1963, Orange body & mixer with unpainted metal or red plastic wheels with black plastic tires, green plastic windows, no interior, "Readymix" or "RMC" decals on mixer barrel, 4-1/2"
EX $25   **NM** $50   **MIP** $80

(KP Photo by Dr. Douglas Sadecky)

❏ **K14-1, Taylor Jumbo Crane,** 1964, Yellow body & crane, green windows, red or yellow weight box, red plastic wheels with black plastic tires, 5-1/4"
EX $25   **NM** $50   **MIP** $75

(KP Photo)

❏ **K15-1, Merryweather Fire Engine,** 1964, Red body, gray extending ladder, red plastic wheels with black plastic tires or Superfast wheels, 6-1/8"
EX $25   **NM** $45   **MIP** $65

(KP Photo by Dr. Douglas Sadecky)

❏ **K16-1, Dodge Tractor with Twin Tippers,** 1966, Green cab & trailer chassis, yellow dumps, Dodge Trucks decals, red plastic wheels with black plastic tires; later issues had yellow cab with blue dump & Superfast wheels, 11-7/8"
EX $70   **NM** $135   **MIP** $200

(KP Photo by Dr. Douglas Sadecky)

❏ **K17-1, Low Loader with Bulldozer,** 1967, Green Ford cab & trailer, red plastic wheels with black plastic tires, red Case bulldozer body, yellow roof & blade, green treads, "Laing" or "Taylor Woodrow" decals or labels, later issues had Superfast wheels and lime-green cab and trailer, 9-1/2"
EX $65   **NM** $100   **MIP** $150

❑ **K18-1, Articulated Horse Box,** 1967, Red Dodge cab with tan trailer, clear windows on trailer, gray ramp, four white horses, red plastic wheels with black plastic tires, later issues had Superfast wheels , 6-5/8"

EX $35   **NM** $55   **MIP** $90

❑ **K19-1, Scammell Tipper Truck,** 1967, Red cab & yellow dump, red plastic wheels with black plastic tires or Superfast wheels, 4-3/4"

EX $20   **NM** $35   **MIP** $50

❑ **K20-1, Tractor Transporter,** 1968, Red Ford cab & trailer, red plastic wheels with black plastic tires, green plastic windows, 3 blue tractors with yellow wheels, later issues had Superfast wheels, 9"

EX $65   **NM** $100   **MIP** $150

❑ **K21-1, Mercury Cougar,** 1968, Gold body, red or white interior, unpainted metal wheels with black plastic tires, 4-1/8". Shown in blue in 1968 catalog, announcing model would be available mid-year

EX $25   **NM** $50   **MIP** $75

❑ **K22-1, Dodge Charger,** 1969, Dark-blue body, light-blue interior, unpainted metal wheels with black plastic tires with "True Guide" steering, 4-1/2". Shown in 1969 catalog, announcing available mid-year

EX $25   **NM** $50   **MIP** $75

(KP Photo)

❑ **K23-1, Mercury Police Car,** 1969, White body, red interior, blue dome lights, police labels, unpainted metal wheels with black plastic tires with "True Guide" steering or Superfast wheels, 4-3/8". Introduced in 1969 catalog as being available mid-year

EX $20   **NM** $35   **MIP** $50

❑ **K24-1, Lamborghini Miura,** 1969, Red body, white interior, unpainted metal wheels with black plastic tires and "True Guide" steering, many color & wheel variations exist, 4"

EX $20   **NM** $35   **MIP** $55

MATCHBOX / KING-SIZE

The first version of the Matchbox Dumper, (2-1RW) dark green with gold-painted grille, metal wheels, and a red dump bed. 1953.

T he Matchbox story began in 1947, when Leslie Smith and Rodney Smith (not related) started a die-casting company called "Lesney," a combination of their two first names. John "Jack" Odell, a die-maker and car enthusiast, joined them from Die-Casting Machine Tools, Ltd. (Years later, in 1982, Odell would found the die-cast company "Lledo"— using his own name spelled backwards.)

After producing die-cast metal parts for electrical products, toy castings began to sneak into the mix as a sideline by 1949. However, it was the Coronation of Queen Elizabeth II in 1953 that gave Lesney its toy-making breakthrough. Odell and Leslie Smith decided to create a miniature version of the young Queen's Coronation Coach, complete with a team of eight horses. It proved to be hugely successful— over one million of the models sold that year.

Also in 1953, Lesney released three miniature die-cast toys: a road roller, a dump truck and a cement mixer. Packaging these little items determined their name—they were sold in imitation matchboxes—the "Matchbox" line was born. Each

year, new models were added to the line, while existing models were dropped, until 75 different vehicles were produced by 1960.

MARKET UPDATE

Matchbox Regular Wheels models continue to sell well. Because so many collectors grew up with these cars, an audience for them is virtually guaranteed. Prices for these vintage toys haven't really leveled off, and the market seems strong. Look for crisp boxes when buying mint-in-package examples, but on sharp-looking pieces without boxes, keep an eye open for complete decals, corner wear and wheel condition. If a car has what appears to be a perfect coat of paint, but worn tires, be aware you might be looking at a re-paint.

As early as 1954, Matchbox models were being imported into the United States by the Fred Bronner Corporation, which gained the exclusive rights in 1956, before being acquired in 1964 and being made a division of Lesney.

Even in the 1950s, children and adults were collecting the toys. They were, after all, amazingly detailed with opening doors and hoods, and featured replica engines and interiors. Plus, they were quite affordable. By 1957, moved to larger facilities—it's third such move. By 1966, an official Collector's Club was formed, publishing a quarterly newsletter, and uniting widespread collectors in Britain and America.

The first great era of the Matchbox 1-75 line—the "regular wheels" period—ended shortly after the advent of Hot Wheels in 1968. By the next year, plans were already in the works for faster, easier-rolling toys that made their debut in the 1970 catalog.

Triumph Motorcycle with Sidecar, (4-3RW), 1960. Motorcycle models have a subset of collectors—not necessarily just interested in Matchbox, any die-cast with two (or in this case, three) wheels is desirable. Crossover collecting like this can mean higher prices for mint-in-box examples than you'd see for regular passenger cars.

Cover of the 1966 Collector's Guide. Catalogs and promotional items are great ways to track collections. The artwork in many of these old booklets is outstanding, and serves as a real compliment to the illustrators of the period.

Daimler Bus, (74-2RW) from 1966. Matchbox introduced an entire generation to British vehicles, making Austins, Fodens, and yes, double-decker buses seem familiar.

The "even-load" Coca-Cola Lorry, (37-2RW) from 1960. An earlier edition featured an "uneven-load" of soda crates.

Finding construction toys in good shape is rewarding, because many of them were used for their intended purposes, i.e. hauling pebbles, sand, cereal, etc... This Mack Dump Truck, (28-4RW) from 1969 is a sharp example.

MATCHBOX / REGULAR WHEELS

❑ **1-1RW, Road Roller,** 1953, One of the first Matchbox offerings, this model had a "steamroller"-style large-roofed cab that matched the large toy produced by Lesney. Green paint on body can vary in shade, red metal wheels and rollers
EX $40   **NM** $75   **MIP** $125

❑ **1-2RW, Diesel Road Roller,** 1955, Second in the series, but first with a smaller cab, roller attachment a little more snug than the first version, red metal wheels and roller, driver available in light and dark tan variations, gold-painted upright tow hook, 2-1/4"
EX $30   **NM** $45   **MIP** $85

❑ **1-3RW, Road Roller,** 1958, Third in the series, this casting kept the driver, but changed the tow hook at rear of the tractor. It still featured red metal wheels and rollers, 2-1/4"
EX $45   **NM** $70   **MIP** $90

(KP Photo)

❑ **1-4RW, Diesel Road Roller,** 1962, Green with orange/red plastic wheels, open window on cab behind driver, tow hook on back. 2-5/8", "Aveling Barford Road Roller" on base near rear wheels
EX $12   **NM** $35   **MIP** $60

(KP Photo, George Cuhaj collection)

❑ **1-5RW, Mercedes-Benz Truck,** 1968, Light pea-green, with orange or yellow plastic canopy, truck could be hitched to a matching trailer, released the same year, 3"
EX $5   **NM** $12   **MIP** $20

❑ **2-1RW, Dumper,** 1953, This first version featured a gold-painted front grille on a green body with red dump bed, 1-1/2"
EX $22   **NM** $40   **MIP** $90

(KP Photo by Dr. Douglas Sadecky)

❑ **2-2RW, Dumper,** 1957, Second casting is larger than first, with less painted detail. First issue with metal wheels, second with gray plastic wheels. Green body, red dumper bed, 2". Pictured here 2-3RW Muir-Hill Dumper
EX $20   **NM** $55   **MIP** $80

(KP Photo, George Cuhaj collection)

❑ **2-3RW, Dumper,** 1961, Short, blocky cab with "Laing" or "Muir-Hill" decal on right-hand door. Red cab with pea-green dumper bed, black plastic wheels, 2-1/8". Although the cab is different, this model is very similar to the K-2 dumper released one year earlier. "Muir-Hill" decal versions can have about $100 MIP value
EX $7   **NM** $12   **MIP** $30

(KP Photo, George Cuhaj collection)

❑ **2-3RW, Dumper,** 1961, Another view of 2-3RW, also sim-

ply called "Dumper" in Matchbox 1966 catalog
EX $7   **NM** $12   **MIP** $30

(KP Photo, George Cuhaj collection)

❑ **2-4RW, Mercedes-Benz Trailer,** 1968, Pea-green trailer released same year as Mercedes-Benz Truck, 1-5RW. Also came with orange or yellow canopy, 3-1/2"
EX $5   **NM** $10   **MIP** $20

(KP Photo by Dr. Douglas Sadecky)

❑ **3-1RW, Cement Mixer,** 1953, Another early Matchbox, this model mirrors one of Lesney's first larger die-cast toys. Variations seem to exist in castings, earlier models measure slightly larger at 1-3/4" length than the later ones, coming in at 1-1/2" length. Orange metal or gray plastic wheels
EX $25   **NM** $55   **MIP** $90

(KP Photo, Tom Michael collection)

❑ **3-2RW, Bedford Tipper Truck,** 1961, Available in red and maroon dumper variations, as well as gray and black plastic wheels, 2-1/2". Gray plastic wheeled version harder to find, about $120 MIP
EX $10   **NM** $20   **MIP** $45

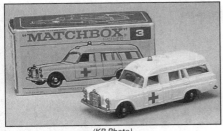

(KP Photo)

❑ **3-3RW, Mercedes-Benz "Binz" Ambulance,** 1968, White or cream body with Red Cross label or decal and plastic patient on stretcher. This was a smaller version of the K-6 ambulance released one year earlier, 2-7/8". Unpainted base with textured surface along sides and near back tailgate
EX $9 **NM** $20 **MIP** $35

(KP Photo)

❑ **3-3RW, Mercedes-Benz "Binz" Ambulance,** 1968, Variation photo showing cream paint and decal version of Mercedes ambulance
EX $6 **NM** $12 **MIP** $20

❑ **4-1RW, Tractor,** 1954, Red Massey-Harris tractor body and fenders; a small version of larger Lesney Massey-Harris toy tractor
EX $35 **NM** $65 **MIP** $95

❑ **4-2RW, Massey-Harris Tractor,** 1957, Red with no fenders. An update on the previous model, this tractor was re-released painted green in 1994 as an anniversary issue. Metal wheel and gray plastic wheel variations, some casting variations with 1-1/2" and 1-3/4" lengths
EX $40 **NM** $75 **MIP** $135

(KP Photo, George Cuhaj collection)

❑ **4-3RW, Triumph Motorcycle w/Sidecar,** 1960, Light metallic

blue with 24-spoke silver wheels and black tires, 2-1/8"
EX $17 **NM** $30 **MIP** $85

(KP Photo, George Cuhaj collection)

❑ **4-3RW, Triumph Motorcycle w/Sidecar,** 1960, Another view of the Triumph Motorcycle w/Sidecar
EX $17 **NM** $30 **MIP** $85

(KP Photo, George Cuhaj collection)

❑ **4-4RW, Dodge Stake Truck,** 1967, Yellow cab and body with green plastic stakes. A popular model, Matchbox made many toy trucks with this Dodge cab style, 2-7/8". Models with blue-green stakes, a very slight color difference, can have about $150 MIP value
EX $6 **NM** $9 **MIP** $19

❑ **5-1RW, Double Decker Bus,** 1954, First of Matchbox's London Buses, this one featured decals that read "Buy Matchbox Series" on the side, 2"
EX $15 **NM** $45 **MIP** $80

(KP Photo, Tom Michael collection)

❑ **5-2RW, Double Decker Bus,** 1958, Second London Bus, casting slightly larger, at 2-1/4" length. "No.

5" cast into front of bus, no interior. Available with metal and gray plastic wheels, with a variety of decals
EX $40 **NM** $80 **MIP** $120

❑ **5-3RW, Routemaster London Bus,** 1961, Red, with gray or black plastic wheels, "Visco-Static" decal most common. No interior in bus, major change from last model: a wider front grille, with cast headlights on front fenders
EX $20 **NM** $45 **MIP** $80

(KP Photo)

❑ **5-4RW, Routemaster London Bus,** 1965, Red body, white plastic interior-first Matchbox model bus to feature one. Like 5-3RW, the "Visco-Static" decals and labels are the most common, 2-3/4"
EX $6 **NM** $12 **MIP** $30

❑ **6-1RW, Quarry Truck,** 1954, Orange body with gray dumper bed. No interior. Most commonly seen with metal wheels, crimped or rounded axles, 2-1/4"
EX $20 **NM** $40 **MIP** $75

❑ **6-2RW, Quarry Truck,** 1959, Yellow body, black plastic wheels most common, red, white and black decal on cab doors, cab extends the full width of the front of truck, appears first in 1959 catalog with black plastic wheels
EX $12 **NM** $30 **MIP** $65

(KP Photo)

❑ **6-3RW, Euclid 10-Wheel Quarry Truck,** 1964, Yellow body, no decals, exposed engine shows on casting, partial cab does not extend across body of truck, 2-5/8"
EX $7 **NM** $15 **MIP** $30

(KP Photo, George Cuhaj collection)

❑ **6-4RW, Ford Pickup,** 1969, Red, with white plastic camper top and white or silver plastic front grille. Featured "Autosteer," a Matchbox innovation making its appearance in the 1969 catalog, that "turns the front wheels in either direction by simple pressure." 2-3/4"
EX $10   NM $20   MIP $30

(KP Photo by Dr. Douglas Sadecky)

❑ **7-1RW, Horse-Drawn Milk Float,** 1954, Orange wagon body, white painted driver, brown horse. Available with metal spoked or gray solid plastic wheels, 2-1/4". Quite a detailed little model
EX $45   NM $60   MIP $120

(KP Photo, George Cuhaj collection)

❑ **7-2RW, Ford Anglia,** 1961, Light blue body, no interior, gray, silver or black plastic wheels, silver painted grille, bumper and headlights, 2-5/8", black painted baseplate, tow hook. Gray plastic wheel versions, about $90 MIP; silver plastic wheel versions, about $55 MIP
EX $15   NM $22   MIP $45

(KP Photo by Dr. Douglas Sadecky)

❑ **7-2RW, Ford Anglia,** 1961, A view of a gray-plastic-wheel version of the Ford Anglia, a harder-to-find variation
EX $20   NM $40   MIP $90

(KP Photo, Tom Michael collection)

❑ **7-3RW, Ford Refuse Truck,** 1967, Red body, gray and silver dumper section, tilts together when dumped, no interior, black plastic wheels, green window plastic, 3"
EX $7   NM $12   MIP $20

❑ **8-1RW, Caterpillar Tractor,** 1955, Yellow or orange with cast driver, silver painted grille. Unpainted roller wheels for treads, 1-1/2". Fully exposed engine under hood. Note: Orange variation harder to find, MIP value can reach over $200; yellow versions with painted drivers also about $200 MIP
EX $20   NM $40   MIP $85

❑ **8-2RW, Caterpillar Tractor,** 1959, Yellow, different casting with engine partially covered by hood, and cast "roller wheels" between two actual turning metal wheels. Driver cast with toy, 1-3/4", green or gray rubber treads
EX $25   NM $65   MIP $90

❑ **8-3RW, Caterpillar Crawler Tractor,** 1961, Yellow body with cast driver, metal or plastic tread wheels, very similar to previous casting, models with silver plastic roller wheels about $90 MIP
EX $20   NM $40   MIP $65

(KP Photo, Tom Michael collection)

❑ **8-4RW, Caterpillar Crawler Tractor,** 1965, Yellow, cast without driver, black plastic roller wheels, 2", gray or black rubber treads
EX $12   NM $22   MIP $30

(KP Photo, George Cuhaj collection)

❑ **8-5RW, Ford Mustang Fastback,** 1966, White, with red interior and tow hook. Black plastic tires on silver wheels. Unique steering lever on driver's side allows front wheels to turn left or right, 2-7/8", orange versions are quite rare, about $300 MIP
EX $12   NM $20   MIP $45

❑ **9-1RW, Fire Escape,** 1955, Red with cast driver, metal wheels, gold-painted trim, 2-1/4", no front bumper in casting
EX $20   NM $45   MIP $80

❑ **9-2RW, Fire Escape,** 1957, Red, cast with driver, metal wheels most common, versions with gray plastic wheels about $400 MIP, front bumper included in casting, 2-1/4"
EX $20   NM $45   MIP $80

(KP Photo)

❑ **9-3RW, Merryweather Marquis Fire Engine,** 1959, Red body with cab, gold ladder, black plastic wheels (first versions had gray plastic wheels), ladder colors can vary, 2-5/8", simply called "Fire Truck" in 1966 catalog

EX $20   **NM** $55   **MIP** $70

(KP Photo, Tom Michael collection)

❑ **9-4RW, Boat and Trailer,** 1967, Plastic blue and white boat with blue die-cast trailer, black plastic wheels. First time a stand-alone trailer makes appearance in regular wheels line

EX $7   **NM** $15   **MIP** $30

❑ **10-1RW, Mechanical Horse and Trailer,** 1955, Red, three-wheeled cab and gray stake-style trailer, metal wheels, 3"

EX $55   **NM** $70   **MIP** $95

(KP Photo by Dr. Douglas Sadecky)

❑ **10-2RW, Mechanical Horse and Trailer,** 1957, Second casting of Scammell Scarab, red three-wheeled cab and light-tan stake-style trailer with fenders. Grille can be painted or unpainted, metal wheels, 3". Appears first in 1957 catalog/flyer

EX $40   **NM** $60   **MIP** $95

(KP Photo, George Cuhaj collection)

❑ **10-3RW, Sugar Container Truck,** 1962, Blue Foden truck body with "Tate & Lyle" decal, with silver, gray, or black plastic wheels (shown). Popular Foden cab design, 2-5/8". Gray-wheeled models tend to have higher MIP values, up to $200

EX $15   **NM** $30   **MIP** $65

(KP Photo, George Cuhaj collection)

❑ **10-3RW, Sugar Container Truck,** 1962, Another view of 10-3RW, showing decal from back of truck

(KP Photo, John Brown Sr. collection)

❑ **10-4RW, Pipe Truck,** 1967, Red Leyland die-cast body, silver grille and baseplate, gray plastic pipes. "Ergomatic Cab" written on baseplate, 3". The Ergomatic cab was a new feature on large British trucks, including Leyland and AEC, beginning in the mid-sixties, so this model reflected the latest advance at time of release

EX $12   **NM** $25   **MIP** $50

❑ **11-1RW, Road Tanker,** 1955, Yellow or red ERF truck body, metal wheels, "Esso" decal on rear of tank, 2", painted side gas tanks, crimped axles

EX $40   **NM** $75   **MIP** $100

❑ **11-2RW, Road Tanker,** 1959, Red ERF truck body, metal wheels, gray or black plastic wheels, variations include silver painted side gas tanks and grilles, slightly larger casting, 2-1/2"

EX $35   **NM** $60   **MIP** $100

(KP Photo by Dr. Douglas Sadecky)

❑ **11-3RW, Jumbo Crane,** 1965, Yellow, red plastic hook, large black plastic wheels in front near cab, small in back-1966 catalog illustration looks more like King Size version, K-14, with what appears to be a die-cast hook. Some with red counterweights, 3". Shown here with 42-3RW Iron Fairy Crane

EX $8   **NM** $15   **MIP** $30

(KP Photo, John Brown Sr. collection)

❑ **11-4RW, Scaffold Truck,** mid-1969, Mercedes-Benz truck, silver body with yellow plastic scaffold sections in stake-style bed. "Builders Supply Company" decal on side, 2-5/8", released late in 1969, just before transition to Superfast

EX $8   **NM** $12   **MIP** $20

(KP Photo, John Brown Sr. collection)

❑ **12-1RW, Land Rover,** 1957, Dark green body with tan driver, metal wheels. No real windshield, just a low flat piece of the casting appearing where the base of a windshield would be. Slight casting variations, some 1-5/8" length, later editions, 1-3/4" length. Silver-painted grille

EX $8   **NM** $40   **MIP** $80

(KP Photo, George Cuhaj collection)

❑ **12-2RW, Land Rover,** 1960, Dark green, black or gray plastic wheels (black more common). Open cab, model shown has bent windshield. "Land-Rover Series II" on black baseplate
EX $15   **NM** $40   **MIP** $75

(KP Photo)

❑ **12-3RW, Safari Land Rover,** 1965, Dark green body, dark brown plastic luggage on top, white interior, white tow hook, black plastic baseplate. First issue of the Safari Land Rover, says "Land Rover Safari" on base, 2-3/4"
EX $8   **NM** $15   **MIP** $25

(KP Photo)

❑ **12-3RW, Safari Land Rover,** 1967, Medium-blue body, light reddish-brown plastic luggage, white plastic interior and tow hook, black plastic baseplate with "Land Rover Safari." Second issue of same casting in blue
EX $8   **NM** $15   **MIP** $25

(KP Photo, Tom Michael collection)

❑ **13-1RW, Wreck Truck,** 1955, Tan Bedford truck with red tow hook and scaffold, metal wheels, silver-painted grille and bumper, 2-1/4"
EX $35   **NM** $50   **MIP** $75

❑ **13-2RW, Wreck Truck,** 1958, Tan Bedford body, red boom section, metal or gray plastic wheels, no interior, slightly smaller than previous casting at 2"
EX $40   **NM** $60   **MIP** $90

(KP Photo, George Cuhaj collection)

❑ **13-3RW, Wreck Truck,** 1961, Red body with metal or plastic tow hook, and gray or black plastic wheels, decal on side of truck says "A.A. & R.A.C. Matchbox Garages Breakdown Service," silver trim on front grille
EX $18   **NM** $45   **MIP** $115

(KP Photo, George Cuhaj collection)

❑ **13-4RW, Wreck Truck,** 1966, Dodge Wreck Truck with yellow cab, green tow bed, red plastic hook, clear red plastic cab light, BP decals or labels, 3", black plastic wheels. Variations with colors

reversed, (green cab and yellow body) are extremely rare. "Dodge Wreck Truck" on green base near rear wheels
EX $7   **NM** $12   **MIP** $30

❑ **14-1RW, Ambulance,** 1956, Cream painted body, metal wheels, Red Cross decal, word "Ambulance" cast in raised letters along side of vehicle, 2"
EX $20   **NM** $45   **MIP** $85

(KP Photo, John Brown Sr. collection)

❑ **14-2RW, Ambulance,** 1958, Daimler with cream or off-white body with metal or gray plastic wheels, Red Cross decal, slightly larger casting at 2-1/4", word "Ambulance" cast in raised letters
EX $18   **NM** $60   **MIP** $90

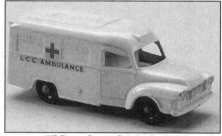

(KP Photo, George Cuhaj collection)

❑ **14-3RW, Lomas Ambulance,** 1962, White body with black plastic wheels and "LCC Ambulance" decals, 2-5/8", referred to simply as "Ambulance" in catalog. "LCC" is an abbreviation for the "London County Council," responsible for designing and building ambulances in the 1950s and 1960s to its own specifications, later adapted by Daimler and other companies
EX $10   **NM** $20   **MIP** $45

(KP Photo, George Cuhaj collection)

14-4RW, Iso Grifo, 1968, Dark blue, almost purple body, light blue plastic interior and tow hook, opening doors, 3", in 1968 catalog, "available in early 1968," steering wheel on right-hand side, black tires on silver wheels, textured baseplate

EX $9   **NM** $17   **MIP** $25

(KP Photo, George Cuhaj collection)

14-4RW, Iso Grifo, Detail photo: shows white tow hook and driver's side door open to British-style steering wheel arrangement

(KP Photo, George Cuhaj collection)

15-1RW, Prime Mover Truck, 1956, Orange body, silver grille and trim, metal wheels. Harder to find editions: yellow body with metal wheels and orange with gray plastic wheels

EX $22   **NM** $45   **MIP** $70

15-2RW, Atlantic Prime Mover, 1959, Orange body, black plastic wheels, spare tire in bed of truck, no interior

EX $25   **NM** $45   **MIP** $80

(KP Photo, George Cuhaj collection)

15-3RW, Dennis Refuse Truck, 1963, Blue body, gray dumper section, red and white decals or labels say "Cleansing Service," and have cross-in-shield

design at center. Black plastic knobby wheels, no interior, 2-1/2"

EX $7   **NM** $14   **MIP** $30

(KP Photo, George Cuhaj collection)

15-4RW, Volkswagen 1500 Saloon, 1968, White Volkswagen Beetle body with "137" decals or labels, black plastic tires on silver wheels, 2-7/8"

EX $7   **NM** $12   **MIP** $25

16-1RW, Transporter Trailer, 1956, Tan, flat bodied trailer with ramp and non-skid surface for vehicles, one axle and metal wheels in front near towbar, two axles with metal wheels on back near ramp, 3", ramp fold up onto trailer body

EX $17   **NM** $30   **MIP** $60

(KP Photo by Dr. Douglas Sadecky)

16-2RW, Atlantic Transporter, 1960, Orange trailer body, black plastic wheels, 4 axles; two at front near drawbar, two at back near ramp, non-skid tire tracks on trailer, pictured here with 15-2RW Atlantic Prime Mover

EX $17   **NM** $40   **MIP** $75

(KP Photo, George Cuhaj collection)

16-3RW, "Mountaineer" Dump Truck w/Snowplough, 1964, Gray cab and body with orange dumper section, snowplow on front with orange and white striped decal, black plastic wheels, 3", gray plastic wheel version about twice MIP value

EX $18   **NM** $30   **MIP** $50

(KP Photo, George Cuhaj collection)

16-3RW, "Mountaineer" Dump Truck w/Snowplough, 1964, Another view of Mountaineer Dump Truck with raised dumper bed

(KP Photo, John Brown Sr. collection)

16-4RW, Case Bulldozer, 1969, Red body with yellow blade and cab, "Available mid-1969" in 1969 1st issue catalog, 2-1/2"

EX $9   **NM** $18   **MIP** $32

17-1RW, Removals Van, 1956, Green, blue or dark red body, metal wheels, "Matchbox Removals Service" decal, green more common color

EX $15   **NM** $60   **MIP** $100

(KP Photo by Dr. Douglas Sadecky)

MATCHBOX / REGULAR WHEELS

❏ **17-2RW, Removals Van,** 1958, Green body, with "Matchbox Removals Service" decal on sides, metal or gray plastic wheels
EX $35   **NM** $75   **MIP** $120

❏ **17-3RW, Metropolitan Taxi,** 1960, Dark red with gray or silver plastic wheels, gray more common, silver can have $130+ MIP value, gray-wheel values shown
EX $25   **NM** $40   **MIP** $75

(KP Photo)

❏ **17-4RW, 8-Wheel Tipper,** 1963, Red Foden body, orange dumper section, black plastic wheels, no interior, 3", "Hoveringham" decal on tipper. A "little brother" to the 8-Wheel Tipper K-1 in the King Size line
EX $9   **NM** $18   **MIP** $37

(KP Photo)

❏ **17-4RW, 8-Wheel Tipper,** 1963, Another view of Foden 8-Wheel Tipper, with hinged gate at back opening when dumper section is tilted up
EX $9   **NM** $18   **MIP** $37

(KP Photo, George Cuhaj collection)

❏ **17-5RW, Horse Box,** 1969, Red AEC (Associated Equipment Company) Ergomatic cab and truck body, green plastic box with gray door, two white plastic horses, black plastic wheels, 2-7/8", "Available mid-1969" in 1969 catalog, 1st edition
EX $8   **NM** $12   **MIP** $25

❏ **18-1RW, Bulldozer,** 1956, Yellow body, tow hook, red blade, metal roller wheels, driver in hat cast as part of toy
EX $18   **NM** $35   **MIP** $85

❏ **18-2RW, Bulldozer,** 1958, Yellow body, tow hook, yellow blade, driver cast into body, metal roller wheels. Engine partially covered on side
EX $25   **NM** $78   **MIP** $110

(KP Photo, John Brown Sr. collection)

❏ **18-3RW, Caterpillar Bulldozer,** 1961, Yellow body, tow hook, yellow blade, driver cast into body, metal or black plastic rollers. Driver shown here is painted, but normally they were the same color as casting
EX $18   **NM** $40   **MIP** $80

❏ **18-4RW, Caterpillar Crawler Bulldozer,** 1964, Yellow body, curving tow hook, no driver, black plastic roller wheels. Casting essentially the same as 18-3, but with flatter blade and no driver
EX $7   **NM** $18   **MIP** $40

(KP Photo, George Cuhaj collection)

❏ **18-5RW, Field Car,** 1969, Yellow body, white plastic interior, generally red wheels with black plastic tires. Many collectors consider this vehicle to be an International Scout model, and in fact the side view bears close resemblance. However, the front grille also looks a bit like a French SINPAR Renault military vehicle (although they were produced in the 1970s). "Available mid-1969" in catalog. Auto-Steer model. 2-5/8"
EX $7   **NM** $11   **MIP** $18

(KP Photo, George Cuhaj collection)

❏ **18-5RW, Field Car,** 1969, View of rear of Field Car, showing spare and tow hook

❏ **19-1RW, Sports Car,** 1956, White or cream body with metal wheels, painted driver, silver grille
EX $45   **NM** $70   **MIP** $150

❏ **19-2RW, MG "A" Sports Car,** 1958, White body, metal or gray plastic wheels, painted driver, can have rounded or crimped axles, silver-painted grille and headlights, 2-1/4"
EX $58   **NM** $85   **MIP** $150

❏ **19-3RW, Aston Martin Racer,** 1961, Green body, white or gray driver, 24-spoke wheels with black plastic tires. Variable number decals on body
EX $45   **NM** $80   **MIP** $165

(KP Photo, Tom Michael collection)

❏ **19-4RW, Lotus Racing Car,** 1966, Green or orange body, white plastic driver, yellow wheels with black plastic tires, No. "3" decal or label, 2-3/4". Green pictured in 1966 catalog, but orange variation included in G-4 Racetrack Set that same year. Driver missing in this photo
EX $11   **NM** $22   **MIP** $50

❑ **20-1RW, Heavy Lorry,** 1956, Dark red ERF truck body, metal or gray plastic wheels, no interior, dropside stake bed appearance with fuel tanks along sides. Can have silver-painted grille, some casting variations, 2-1/4" and 2-5/8"
EX $18   NM $40   MIP $100

❑ **20-2RW, Transport Truck,** 1959, ERF dropside truck with dark blue body, gray or black plastic wheels, "Ever Ready For Life" decal along stake sides, model also called "Heavy Lorry" in 1959 catalog
EX $18   NM $45   MIP $90

(KP Photo by Dr. Douglas Sadecky)

❑ **20-3RW, Taxi Cab,** 1965, Chevrolet Impala Taxi Cab with yellow body, red or white plastic interior, (red is harder to find) black plastic wheels, 3"
EX $11   NM $18   MIP $30

(KP Photo, Colin Bruce collection)

❑ **21-1RW, Bedford Coach,** 1956, Light pea-green body with red and yellow "London to Glasgow" decals above windows, metal wheels
EX $22   NM $40   MIP $68

(KP Photo, George Cuhaj collection)

❑ **21-2RW, Bedford Coach,** 1958, Light pea-green body with red and yellow "London to Glasgow" decal above windows, metal or gray plastic wheels, "Bedford Duple Luxury Coach" on black base, 2-1/2", silver painted grille and front bumper, no interior
EX $25   NM $60   MIP $95

(KP Photo by Dr. Douglas Sadecky)

❑ **21-3RW, Milk Delivery Truck,** 1961, Commer truck with light green body, white or cream plastic cargo and gray or black plastic wheels, 2-1/4", cow or milk bottle decal on cab doors. Both variations shown here
EX $15   NM $35   MIP $65

(KP Photo, George Cuhaj collection)

❑ **21-4RW, Foden Concrete Truck,** 1969, Yellow Foden cab and plastic mixer with orange body, dark green plastic windows, eight black plastic wheels, 3". Worm-gear under second set of wheels turns mixer as truck rolls forward
EX $5   NM $9   MIP $22

❑ **22-1RW, Vauxhall Cresta,** 1956, Red body with white roof, no interior, metal wheels, silver painted grille and bumpers, tow hook
EX $22   NM $40   MIP $62

(KP Photo by Dr. Douglas Sadecky)

❑ **22-2RW, Vauxhall Cresta,** 1958, Different casting than previous version. Longer, more "Chevy-like" body with low tailfins and wraparound front and rear windshields. Many paint variations exist, some pushing MIP price well into the hundreds of dollars. Can have gray or black plastic wheels or metal wheels
EX $30   NM $72   MIP $150

(KP Photo, George Cuhaj collection)

❑ **22-3RW, Pontiac Grand Prix,** 1964, Red body, black plastic wheels, gray plastic interior & tow hook, 3", opening doors, "Pontiac G.P. Sports Coupe" on black painted baseplate
EX $12   NM $22   MIP $45

❑ **23-1RW, Caravan,** 1956, Pale blue body, metal wheels, 2-1/2"
EX $17   NM $30   MIP $75

❑ **23-2RW, Trailer,** 1958, Pale blue-green or lime-green body, metal or gray plastic wheels
EX $22   NM $40   MIP $75

(KP Photo by Dr. Douglas Sadecky)

❏ **23-3RW, Bluebird Dauphine Trailer,** 1960, Metallic tan or green body, opening door, no interior or plastic windows, black or gray plastic wheels. Variations with green bodies are hard to find, and can be quite valuable. More common tan variation prices given below
EX $25   **NM** $40   **MIP** $85

❏ **23-4RW, Trailer Caravan,** 1966, Yellow or pink body, black plastic wheels, white plastic interior, 3", pink more common beginning in 1968 and after. Yellow version about $45 MIP value
EX $9   **NM** $17   **MIP** $30

❏ **24-1RW, Hydraulic Excavator,** 1956, Yellow or orange body with metal wheels; larger two at rear and smaller at front, figure cast as part of body, front dumping bucket
EX $18   **NM** $40   **MIP** $75

❏ **24-2RW, Hydraulic Excavator,** 1959, Yellow body, black or gray plastic wheels, larger at rear or cab, smaller in front near dumper bucket. Figure cast in piece, 2-5/8"
EX $17   **NM** $28   **MIP** $45

(KP Photo, George Cuhaj collection)

❏ **24-3RW, Rolls-Royce Silver Shadow,** 1967, Deep red sedan body, white plastic interior, opening trunk, silver wheels with black plastic tires, clear plastic windshield and windows, unpainted silver metal grille, headlights and front bumper, 3". Black baseplate with "A" near front axle
EX $7   **NM** $11   **MIP** $25

(KP Photo, George Cuhaj collection)

❏ **24-3RW, Rolls-Royce Silver Shadow,** 1967, View of opening trunk on Rolls

❏ **25-1RW, Bedford Dunlop Van,** 1956, Dark blue Bedford panel van, with yellow "Dunlop" decals on sides, no interior or plastic windows
EX $18   **NM** $40   **MIP** $80

(KP Photo by Dr. Douglas Sadecky)

❏ **25-2RW, Volkswagen Sedan,** 1960, Volkswagen 1200 Sedan, blue-silver body, gray plastic wheels, opening rear engine hood, green or clear plastic windows, black base
EX $45   **NM** $65   **MIP** $100

(KP Photo, George Cuhaj collection)

❏ **25-3RW, Petrol Tanker,** 1964, Yellow Bedford cab, green body, white tanker with "BP" decal. Cab tilts to reveal white plastic interior. Black plastic wheels, 3". Called "B.P. Tanker" in 1966 catalog. Blue versions with "Aral" decals on tanker section harder to find, about $200 MIP
EX $8   **NM** $14   **MIP** $25

(KP Photo)

❏ **25-4RW, Ford Cortina,** 1968, Light brown body, cream-colored plastic interior and tow hook, black plastic wheels, "Auto-Steer," textured pattern on unpainted base-

plate near front and rear axles, opening doors, 2-5/8". Interesting to note that its first catalog appearance in 1968 showed a blue car with the subhead "Available in mid-1968." The blue color wouldn't be used until the 1970 Superfast version was released. Yellow roof rack included in 1969 G-4 Race'n Rally Gift Set
EX $6   **NM** $9   **MIP** $17

(KP Photo, Tom Michael collection)

❏ **26-1RW, Ready Mixed Concrete Lorry,** 1957, Orange ERF cab and body with silver-painted grille and side gas tanks, metal or gray plastic wheels, 1-3/4", metal mixer section, four wheels
EX $18   **NM** $45   **MIP** $88

(KP Photo, George Cuhaj collection)

❏ **26-2RW, Ready-Mix Concrete Truck,** 1961, Orange diecast Foden cab and body with plastic orange mixer section. Gray or black plastic wheels, 2-1/2". Six wheels, says "Foden Cement Mixer" on base
EX $9   **NM** $19   **MIP** $40

(KP Photo, George Cuhaj collection)

❑ **26-3RW, GMC Tipper Truck,** 1968, Red cab with green plastic windows, silver-gray tipper bed, green chassis, black plastic wheels with duals at rear, 2-5/8", 1968 catalog shows subhead "Available early 1968" and model with yellow tipper bed
EX $6　　**NM** $10　　**MIP** $18

(KP Photo, George Cuhaj collection)

❑ **26-3RW, GMC Tipper Truck,** 1968, View showing tilting cab and green engine block underneath

❑ **27-1RW, Bedford Low Loader,** 1956, Green Bedford cab with silver trim, tan trailer, metal wheels, 3", no windows or interior
EX $28　　**NM** $48　　**MIP** $90

❑ **27-2RW, Bedford Low Loader,** 1958, Green Bedford cab with silver trim, tan trailer, metal or gray plastic knobby wheels, slightly larger casting at 3-3/4" length. No windows or interior
EX $30　　**NM** $75　　**MIP** $140

(KP Photo, John Brown Sr. collection)

❑ **27-3RW, Cadillac Sixty Special,** 1960, Silver-gray or silver-purple Cadillac body with cream or pink colored roof, plastic windows, no interior and gray or black plastic wheels, red base, tow hook, red-painted taillights and silver-painted trim
EX $28　　**NM** $45　　**MIP** $90

(KP Photo, George Cuhaj collection)

❑ **27-4RW, Mercedes 230SL,** 1966, White Mercedes convertible with red plastic interior, opening doors, black plastic wheels, tow hook, 2-3/4", "Available early 1966" in catalog
EX $7　　**NM** $13　　**MIP** $25

(KP Photo, George Cuhaj collection)

❑ **27-4RW, Mercedes 230SL,** 1966, Rear view of Mercedes convertible showing opening doors and tow hook

(KP Photo by Dr. Douglas Sadecky)

❑ **28-1RW, Bedford Compressor Lorry,** 1956, Orange or yellow Bedford cab and chassis with Caterpillar-type compressor engine on back, painted-silver grille and trim, 1-3/4", metal wheels. Pictured here with 28-2RW Thames Compressor Truck
EX $20　　**NM** $30　　**MIP** $50

(KP Photo, John Brown Sr. collection)

❑ **28-2RW, Ford Thames Compressor Lorry,** 1959, Yellow Ford Thames truck cab and chassis with black plastic wheels, no interior or window plastic, silver headlights and grille
EX $25　　**NM** $40　　**MIP** $60

(KP Photo, George Cuhaj collection)

❑ **28-3RW, Mark Ten Jaguar,** 1964, Light metallic brown body with opening hood, black plastic wheels, black-painted base. Engine can be painted the same as body color or left unpainted, 2-3/4". White plastic interior, clear window plastic, tow hook
EX $12　　**NM** $20　　**MIP** $30

(KP Photo, George Cuhaj collection)

❑ **28-3RW, Mark Ten Jaguar,** 1964, View of opening hood on the Mark Ten Jaguar

(KP Photo, George Cuhaj collection)

❑ **28-4RW, Mack Dump Truck,** 1969, Orange Mack truck body with orange dumper bed, black plastic tires on orange or yellow wheels, 2-5/8", green window plastic, unpainted base
EX $7　　**NM** $18　　**MIP** $25

(KP Photo, George Cuhaj collection)

❑ **28-4RW, Mack Dump Truck,** 1969, View of operating dumper bed. This model first appears in the 1969 1st edition catalog

❏ **29-1RW, Bedford Milk Delivery Van,** 1956, Tan body with white plastic milk bottles and boxes, silver trim, metal or gray plastic wheels, no interior or window plastic, 2-1/4"
EX $18   NM $30   MIP $80

(KP Photo, George Cuhaj collection)

❏ **29-2RW, Austin A55 Cambridge,** 1961, Medium green body with light green roof, gray or black plastic wheels, green window plastic, no interior, black-painted base with tow hook, 2-1/2"
EX $17   NM $30   MIP $72

(KP Photo, John Brown Sr. collection)

❏ **29-3RW, Fire Pumper,** 1966, Red LaFrance fire engine body, white plastic ladders along sides, unpainted base and trim, green window plastic, no interior, blue dome light, black plastic wheels, 3". With or without "Denver" decal
EX $6   NM $11   MIP $22

(KP Photo, George Cuhaj collection)

❏ **30-1RW, Ford Prefect,** 1956, Light sage-green or light brown body with metal or gray plastic wheels, (light blue harder to find, $200 or more MIP). No window plastic or interior, silver-painted grille, headlights and bumpers, red-painted taillights. Tow hook, black-painted base, 2-3/8"
EX $15   NM $40   MIP $80

(KP Photo, George Cuhaj collection)

❏ **30-2RW, Magirus-Deutz Crane Truck,** 1961, Silver cab and truck body with orange boom section and gray or black plastic wheels. Hook can be metal or plastic. Black-painted baseplate under front cab section, 2-3/8"
EX $17   NM $30   MIP $72

(KP Photo, George Cuhaj collection)

❏ **30-3RW, 8-Wheel Crane,** 1965, Medium-dark green body with 8 black plastic wheels, orange crane section, yellow plastic hook, 3"
EX $5   NM $11   MIP $20

❏ **31-1RW, American Ford Station Wagon,** 1957, Yellow body with metal or gray plastic wheels, silver painted bumpers and headlights, no interior or window plastic, 2-5/8". Appears brown in 1957 leaflet catalog
EX $15   NM $40   MIP $78

(Photo by Dr. Douglas Sadecky)

❏ **31-2RW, Ford Fairlane Station Wagon,** 1960, Mint green with pink-white roof, gray or black plastic wheels, silver-painted trim,

tow hook. Yellow-painted versions are harder to find, and can bring higher MIP values (up to $300). Two box variations shown
EX $22   NM $55   MIP $78

(KP Photo)

❏ **31-3RW, Lincoln Continental,** 1964, Dark blue or mint-green body, white plastic interior, clear window glass, opening trunk, 3". Metallic tan versions rare, over $1000 MIP at auction
EX $6   NM $10   MIP $22

(KP Photo by Dr. Douglas Sadecky)

❏ **32-1RW, Jaguar XK140 Coupe,** 1957, Cream body with metal or gray plastic wheels, 2-3/8", called "Fixed Head Coupe" in 1957 catalog/flyer. Silver-painted grille, red-painted taillights
EX $30   NM $45   MIP $70

(KP Photo, John Brown Sr. collection)

❏ **32-2RW, E-Type Jaguar,** 1962, Metallic red body, spoked wheels with gray or black tires, green or clear window plastic, 2-5/8", white plastic interior
EX $20   NM $40   MIP $80

❑ **32-2RW, Leyland Petrol Tanker,** 1968, Medium-green Ergomatic cab and chassis, eight black plastic wheels, white tanker section, "BP" decals or labels, silver or white plastic grille and bumper, 3". A blue and white version with "Aral" labels is harder to find, and can have $120 or more MIP value. "Available early 1968" in catalog
EX $4   NM $7   MIP $15

(KP Photo by Dr. Douglas Sadecky)

❑ **33-1RW, Ford Zodiac,** 1957, A variety of body colors exist for this model: blue, dark green, blue-green, silver, tan & orange and turquoise. Dark green and tan and orange models more common, with around $80-$90 MIP values. 2-5/8"
EX $20   NM $40   MIP $80

(KP Photo, George Cuhaj collection)

❑ **33-2RW, Ford Zephyr 6,** 1962, Blue-green body, white plastic interior, gray or black plastic wheels, silver front grille and headlights, slight tailfins, black painted base, 2-1/2". Some models with black wheels have a lighter blue-green color than earlier versions
EX $8   NM $15   MIP $30

(KP Photo, George Cuhaj collection)

❑ **33-3RW, Lamborghini Miura,** 1969, Yellow or gold body with red or cream plastic interior,

2-3/4", silver wheels with black plastic tires, opening doors. Gold cars with cream interiors (as shown in 1969 catalog) have high MIP values, around $200
EX $4   NM $12   MIP $25

(KP Photo, John Brown Sr. collection)

❑ **34-1RW, Volkswagen Microvan,** 1957, Blue panel van body, no interior, "Matchbox International Express" yellow type decal on sides, with silver-painted bumper and headlights, 2-1/4". Mostly found with metal or gray plastic wheels, decal on side with "Matchbox International Express" in yellow lettering
EX $30   NM $50   MIP $95

(KP Photo)

❑ **34-2RW, Volkswagen Camping Car,** 1962, Light sea-green body, gray or black plastic wheels, opening side doors, top window plastic, camper section interior, 2-5/8"
EX $20   NM $40   MIP $90

(KP Photo)

❑ **34-3RW, Volkswagen Camper,** 1967, Silver body with opening camper section doors, orange plastic interior, yellow win-

dow plastic, raised roof with windows and top window plastic, black plastic wheels, 2-5/8"
EX $10   NM $18   MIP $45

(KP Photo)

❑ **34-3RW, Volkswagen Camper,** 1967, Another view of the Volkswagen Camper
EX $10   NM $18   MIP $45

(KP Photo)

❑ **34-4RW, Volkswagen Camper,** 1969, Silver body, opening doors to camper section, slightly raised roof with window plastic on top but no windows, orange plastic interior, black plastic wheels. Interestingly, the size of this vehicle remained the same since the 1962 release at 2-5/8". Makes first appearance in 1969 catalog
EX $11   NM $17   MIP $35

(Photo by Dr. Douglas Sadecky)

❑ **35-1RW, Marshall Horse Box,** 1957, Red ERF cab with silver-painted grille and headlights, brown horse box with opening side door, metal and gray plastic wheels most common, 2-1/8". Silver plastic wheel version, about $180 MIP; black plastic wheel version, about $135 MIP
EX $15   NM $30   MIP $80

(Photo by Dr. Douglas Sadecky)

❑ **35-2RW, Snow-Trac Tractor,** 1964, Red body with unpainted base, six black tread roller wheels, green window plastic, 2-1/4". White or gray treads, some versions have "Snow-Trac" cast in side of tractor, (as seen in 1968 and 1969 catalogs) others have decal, and some variations have neither, (as seen in the 1966 catalog). Gray-tread models may have slightly higher MIP values, although decal models (based on the tenuous nature of decals) may start to become more desirable

EX $9   **NM** $17   **MIP** $40

(KP Photo)

❑ **35-2RW, Snow-Trac Tractor,** 1964, A plain-sided variation of the Snow-Trac in the condition many of us find them-without treads...

(KP Photo, George Cuhaj collection)

❑ **36-1RW, Austin A 50,** 1957, Blue-green body, no interior, metal or gray plastic wheels, silver-painted grille, headlights and bumper, tow bar, 2-3/8"

EX $20   **NM** $35   **MIP** $75

(KP Photo, George Cuhaj collection)

❑ **36-3RW, Opel Diplomat,** 1966, Gold body, black-painted metal base, white plastic interior and tow hook, opening hood, silver or gray plastic motor, 2-3/4". Pictured in elusive sea-green in 1966 catalog with caption "Available mid 1966." These (possibly) first versions are rarely seen

EX $4   **NM** $10   **MIP** $20

(KP Photo, George Cuhaj collection)

❑ **36-1RW, Opel Diplomat,** 1966, A view of Opel Diplomat with open hood and silver engine

❑ **37-1RW, Coca-Cola Lorry,** 1956, Yellow-orange truck with Coca-Cola decals on sides and back of truck, metal or gray plastic wheels, 2-1/4", no step on the running board on cab, silver-painted trim on running boards, grille. Some versions have "uneven" loads of cast Coca-Cola cases (as seen in 1957 flyer) in the bed of the truck. These typically run about $150 MIP. "Even" load versions in gray plastic wheels comparable MIP price. Even-load metal wheel version prices shown below

EX $30   **NM** $55   **MIP** $95

(KP Photo by Dr. Douglas Sadecky)

❑ **37-2RW, Coca-Cola Lorry,** 1960, Yellow body, black baseplate, "even" cast crate load on bed, Coca-Cola decals on sides and back, 2-1/4", gray or black plastic wheels. Gray plastic wheel versions tend toward higher MIP values, about $110

EX $25   **NM** $40   **MIP** $80

(KP Photo, John Brown Sr. collection)

❑ **37-3RW, Cattle Truck,** 1966, Yellow Dodge cab and chassis, gray plastic cattle box, originally included two white plastic steers, 2-1/2". Introduced in 1966 catalog as a new model, but hadn't yet replaced the #37 Coca-Cola truck in the line-up

EX $4   **NM** $7   **MIP** $15

❑ **38-1RW, Refuse Wagon,** 1957, Silver-gray or dark-gray cab and almost tanker-truck shaped rounded-top bed and "Cleansing Department" decals. Metal or gray plastic wheels. 1957 flyer shows model painted green and without the decals. Casting variations must account for size difference: 2-1/8" and 2-1/2" lengths

EX $18   **NM** $45   **MIP** $85

❑ **38-2RW, Vauxhall Victor Estate Car,** 1963, Yellow station wagon with opening rear hatch, gray, silver or black plastic tires, red or green plastic interiors, clear plastic windows. 2-1/2"

EX $18   **NM** $32   **MIP** $60

(KP Photo, George Cuhaj collection)

❑ **38-3RW, Honda Motorcycle with Trailer,** 1967, Blue-silver Honda motorcycle with kickstand and orange or yellow trailer. Trailer may or may not included labels or decals. 3". As with many motorcycle-related toys, these fairly common models are increasing in value

EX $12   **NM** $25   **MIP** $40

(KP Photo, John Brown Sr. collection)

❑ **39-1RW, "Zodiac" Convertible,** 1957, Pink body, turquoise interior, driver, tow hook. Metal, gray or silver plastic wheels. Casting variations: Model can measure 2-5/8" or 2-1/2". Silver-painted grille, gray-painted headlights, red-painted taillights, light green baseplate

EX $27   **NM** $68   **MIP** $95

(KP Photo by Dr. Douglas Sadecky)

❑ **39-2RW, Pontiac Convertible,** 1962, Purple Pontiac convertible body with gray or silver plastic wheels; yellow body with gray, silver or black plastic wheels. Yellow with black plastic wheels is most common, around $55 MIP. Purple version with silver plastic wheels is hard to find (pictured above and in color section). 2-3/4". Yellow with gray or silver wheels prices shown below

EX $28   **NM** $55   **MIP** $95

(KP Photo)

❑ **39-3RW, Ford Tractor,** 1967, Blue Ford tractor body with yellow die-cast hood, yellow wheels with black plastic tires, 2-1/8", tow hook. Versions of this tractor exist in all-blue, being part of the King Size K-20 set

EX $7   **NM** $16   **MIP** $25

(KP Photo, John Brown Sr. collection)

❑ **40-1RW, Bedford 7-Ton Tipper,** 1957, Red Bedford cab and chassis, tan dumper bed, metal or gray plastic wheels, silver painted trim. Casting variations: Size varies between 2-1/8" and 2-1/4". Shown in all-green color in 1957 flyer

EX $15   **NM** $40   **MIP** $80

(KP Photo, Tom Michael collection)

❑ **40-2RW, Long Distance Bus,** 1961, Blue-silver coach body with tailfins at rear, 3", green window plastic, silver-painted grille. With gray, silver or black plastic wheels. (Gray or silver-wheel versions about $55 MIP value.) Black-wheel version values given below

EX $7   **NM** $15   **MIP** $28

(KP Photo)

❑ **40-3RW, Hay Trailer,** 1967, Blue die-cast trailer body with yellow die-cast stake-ends, often missing. Yellow plastic wheels with black plastic tires, 3-3/8"

EX $3   **NM** $8   **MIP** $12

(KP Photo by Dr. Douglas Sadecky)

❑ **41-1RW, "D" Type Jaguar,** 1957, Green D-type body, metal driver in later catalogs, but not in 1957 flyer, "41" decal, metal or gray plastic tires, 2-1/4". Photo shows 41-1RW and second release with a larger casting, 41-2R

EX $20   **NM** $45   **MIP** $70

❑ **41-2RW, Jaguar Racing Car ("D"-Type),** 1961, Second issue of car featured a green body and tan driver, but came in a variety of wheel types, from more common gray and silver plastic wheels to rare spoked versions and black plastic wheels

EX $25   **NM** $40   **MIP** $80

(KP Photo, George Cuhaj collection)

❑ **41-3RW, Ford G.T.,** 1966, Generally white Ford G.T. bodies with yellow plastic wheels and black plastic tires. Clear window plastic, blue rally stripe on hood with "6" or "9" reversed in white. Visible rear engine, 2-5/8". "Available early 1966" in 1966 catalog. Black base, red plastic interior. Versions with differently-colored wheels or bodies are hard to find

EX $5   **NM** $12   **MIP** $20

(KP Photo by Dr. Douglas Sadecky)

❑ **42-1RW, Bedford "Evening News" Van,** 1957, Mustard-yellow

Bedford panel van body with die-cast billboard on roof and red decal "First With The News" in white type. "Evening News" on panel side of van and "Football Results" in red type decals on each door. Metal, gray or black plastic wheels, (gray and black shown). 2-1/4"
EX $17 **NM** $40 **MIP** $95

(KP Photo, George Cuhaj collection)

❏ **42-2RW, Studebaker Station Wagon,** 1965, Blue body with blue or light blue sliding roof, white plastic interior and tow hook, clear window plastic, white plastic dog and hunter figure included with original (often missing), 3"
EX $15 **NM** $30 **MIP** $65

(KP Photo, George Cuhaj collection)

❏ **42-2RW, Studebaker Station Wagon,** 1965, Another view, showing the sliding rear roof of the Studebaker Station Wagon, 42-2RW

(KP Photo, George Cuhaj collection)

❏ **42-3RW, Iron Fairy Crane,** 1969-70, Red body, yellow crane arm, yellow plastic hook and seat, black plastic wheels, 3". Introduced in 1970 catalog, as a "non-Superfast" toy
EX $4 **NM** $11 **MIP** $18

(KP Photo, George Cuhaj collection)

❏ **43-1RW, Hillman "Minx",** 1958, Blue body, light gray roof, no window plastic or interior, silver-painted grille, metal or gray plastic wheels, 2-1/2", first appears in 1958 catalog
EX $12 **NM** $40 **MIP** $75

(KP Photo, John Brown Sr. collection)

❏ **43-2RW, Aveling-Barford Tractor Shovel,** 1962, Yellow tractor body with cast yellow or red driver and yellow or red bucket, black wheels, 2-5/8". All yellow versions can have $140 MIP value. Model prices for yellow with red bucket and yellow with red driver shown
EX $15 **NM** $30 **MIP** $55

(KP Photo, George Cuhaj collection)

❏ **43-3RW, Pony Trailer,** 1968, Yellow body with clear window plastic on sides and top, gray/brown plastic door, black plastic wheels, 2 white plastic horses, 2-5/8"
EX $6 **NM** $11 **MIP** $25

(KP Photo, John Brown Sr. collection)

❏ **44-1RW, Rolls Royce Silver Cloud,** 1958, Blue metallic Rolls Royce body, metal, gray or silver plastic wheels, crimped axles, no interior, no window plastic, silver-painted grille and bumpers, 2-5/8"
EX $18 **NM** $35 **MIP** $80

(KP Photo, George Cuhaj collection)

❏ **44-2RW, Rolls Royce,** 1962, Metallic tan or metallic silver/gray body, opening trunk, black plastic wheels, white plastic interior, clear window plastic, black base, silver-painted grille, 2-7/8"
EX $12 **NM** $20 **MIP** $40

(KP Photo, George Cuhaj collection)

❏ **44-3RW, Refrigerator Truck,** 1967, Red GMC cab and chassis, green refrigerator box, green window plastic, black plastic wheels, opening rear door on box, 3"
EX $4 **NM** $7 **MIP** $13

(KP Photo, George Cuhaj collection)

❏ **44-3RW, Refrigerator Truck,** 1967, Another view showing box of refrigerator truck

(KP Photo, George Cuhaj collection)

❑ **45-1RW, Vauxhall "Victor",** 1958, Yellow body, silver-painted headlights and grille, can have no windows, clear or green plastic windows. No interior. Metal, gray, silver or black plastic wheels, 2-3/8"
EX $18   **NM** $40   **MIP** $85

(KP Photo by Dr. Douglas Sadecky)

❑ **45-1RW, Vauxhall "Victor",** 1958, Vauxhall Victor models can include green or clear plastic windows, as this one does

(KP Photo, George Cuhaj collection)

❑ **45-2RW, Ford Corsair,** 1965, Cream-yellow body, red plastic interior and tow hook, gray or black plastic wheels, silver-painted grille and headlights, green plastic roof rack and boat (not shown), 2-5/8". Gray-wheeled versions may have higher MIP values
EX $6   **NM** $12   **MIP** $30

(KP Photo, George Cuhaj collection)

❑ **46-1RW, Morris Minor 1000,** 1958, Dark blue or dark green body, metal or gray plastic wheels, black base, no interior, no plastic windows, 2". Dark blue with gray plastic wheels harder to find, with higher MIP values
EX $45   **NM** $65   **MIP** $100

(KP Photo by Dr. Douglas Sadecky)

❑ **46-2RW, Pickford's Removal Van,** 1960, Dark blue or green body, silver-painted grille, no interior, no plastic windows, gray, silver or black plastic wheels, 2-5/8". Decals can have 2 or 3 lines. Many variations of this model exist, although versions with 2-line decals seem hard to find, bumping up the MIP price from what is shown here
EX $30   **NM** $80   **MIP** $150

(KP Photo, George Cuhaj collection)

❑ **46-3RW, Mercedes 300SE,** 1968, Medium blue or green body, white plastic interior, opening doors and trunk, black plastic wheels, unpainted base extends to bumpers and front grille, 2-7/8"
EX $9   **NM** $18   **MIP** $25

(KP Photo)

❑ **46-3RW, Mercedes 300SE,** 1968, Another view of the 46-3RW Mercedes showing opening doors and trunk

(KP Photo by Dr. Douglas Sadecky)

❑ **47-1RW, Trojan "Brooke Bond" Van,** 1958, Red body, metal or gray plastic wheels, decals on van box read "Brooke Bond Tea," tea leaf decal on each door, silver-painted headlights, 2-1/4"
EX $18   **NM** $45   **MIP** $95

(KP Photo, John Brown Sr. collection)

❑ **47-2RW, Commer Ice Cream Van,** 1963, Blue, cream or metallic blue body with white plastic interior, clear plastic windows and black plastic wheels, 2-1/4". Color and decal variations change MIP values considerably. Metallic blue versions with square roof decals are more rare than cream-colored models with plain (non-striped) side decals (see color section)
EX $20   **NM** $45   **MIP** $75

(KP Photo, George Cuhaj collection)

❑ **47-3RW, DAF Tipper Container Truck,** 1969, Green or silver-gray cab and chassis, yellow tipper bed with removable gray top. Red plastic grille and baseplate under cab, black plastic wheels, 3". Makes first appearance in 1969 catalog. Green version higher MIP value, about $40

EX $3   **NM** $8   **MIP** $18

(KP Photo, George Cuhaj collection)

❏ **47-3RW, DAF Tipper Container Truck,** 1969, Another view of truck with raised tipper bed

(KP Photo, Tom Michael collection)

❏ **48-1RW, "Meteor" Sports Boat on Trailer,** 1958, Blue and yellow plastic boat with slight rise for windshield, black die-cast trailer, metal or gray plastic wheels, 2-3/4"

EX $25   **NM** $40   **MIP** $70

(KP Photo, George Cuhaj collection)

❏ **48-2RW, Sports-Boat and Trailer,** 1961, Plastic red and white boat with gold or silver outboard motor, blue die-cast trailer, gray or black plastic wheels, 3-1/2". Boat can come with red deck and white hull or white deck and red hull

EX $12   **NM** $25   **MIP** $60

(KP Photo, John Brown Sr. collection)

❏ **48-3RW, Dumper Truck,** 1967, Red Dodge cab, chassis and dumper bed, silver plastic baseplate, bumper and front grille, black plastic wheels, 3"

EX $3   **NM** $8   **MIP** $18

(KP Photo, George Cuhaj collection)

❏ **49-1RW, Army Half-Track,** 1958, Dark olive-green with star-in-circle U.S. insignia on hood, no interior, metal, gray or black plastic wheels and rollers, gray treads (often missing as they are here) 2-1/2". Known as Army Half-Track and Military Personnel Carrier, this toy stayed in the 1-75 lineup for many years

EX $18   **NM** $30   **MIP** $55

(KP Photo, George Cuhaj collection)

❏ **49-2RW, Mercedes Unimog,** 1967, Two color variations, one tan and blue and the other blue and red, green plastic windows, yellow plastic wheels with black plastic tires, silver-painted grille, tow hook cast, 2-1/2"

EX $8   **NM** $12   **MIP** $25

(KP Photo, George Cuhaj collection)

❏ **49-2RW, Mercedes Unimog,** 1967, Another view of the Mercedes Unimog, blue and red variation (also see color section)

(KP Photo, John Brown Sr. collection)

❏ **50-1RW, Commer Pickup,** 1958, Tan or red and gray body, with metal, gray or black plastic wheels, 2-1/2", silver-painted grille and headlights

EX $25   **NM** $45   **MIP** $60

(KP Photo by Dr. Douglas Sadecky)

❏ **50-1RW, Commer Pickup,** 1958, A view of the red and gray variation of the Commer Pickup with black plastic wheels

EX $40   **NM** $75   **MIP** $150

(KP Photo)

❏ **50-2RW, John Deere-Lanz Tractor,** 1964, Green body, yellow plastic wheels, gray or black plastic tires, cast tow hook, 2-1/8". After

John Deere acquired the German manufacturer Lanz in the 1950s, a variety of toy manufacturers, including Matchbox, produced models of this tractor. Photo shows black-tire version tractor with 51-2RW Tipping Trailer. Note: Gray-tire versions have slightly higher MIP value, about $55

EX $14   **NM** $20   **MIP** $35

(KP Photo, John Brown Sr. collection)

❑ **50-2RW, John Deere-Lanz Tractor,** 1964, A view of the gray-tire version of the John Deere-Lanz tractor-a very detailed model

❑ **50-3RW, Kennel Truck,** 1969, Dark green die-cast body, white or silver plastic grille, green window plastic, truck bed partitioned into four sections, to hold one plastic dog each (included), clear plastic canopy over truck bed, "Auto-Steer" front wheels, black plastic wheels, 2-3/4"

EX $9   **NM** $20   **MIP** $35

❑ **51-1RW, Albion "Portland Cement" Lorry,** 1958, Yellow Albion truck cab and chassis, two decal variations: "Portland Cement" and "Blue Circle Portland Cement." Metal, gray, silver or black plastic wheels, silver-painted trim, tan-painted cement bag load on flatbed, no interior, no window plastic, 2-1/2". Silver plastic wheel versions have about $150 MIP values

EX $18   **NM** $40   **MIP** $80

(KP Photo, George Cuhaj collection)

❑ **51-2RW, Tipping Trailer,** 1964, Green body, yellow wheels, tilting bed, black or gray plastic tires, three yellow barrels, 2-5/8"

EX $8   **NM** $12   **MIP** $25

(KP Photo, George Cuhaj collection)

❑ **51-3RW, 8-Wheel Tipper,** 1969, Orange or yellow Ergomatic AEC cab and chassis with silver-gray tipper bed, 8 black plastic wheels, green plastic windows, no interior, "Douglas" or "Pointer" labels on the sides of tipper bed, 3". Orange models with "Douglas" appear to have higher MIP values, about $40

EX $9   **NM** $16   **MIP** $28

(KP Photo, George Cuhaj collection)

❑ **51-3RW, 8-Wheel Tipper,** 1969, Another view of Tipper truck with bed tilted. As with all miniature construction toys, finding these models in pristine shape can be a bit of a hunt

(KP Photo by Dr. Douglas Sadecky)

❑ **52-1RW, Maserati 4CLT Racecar,** 1958, Yellow or red body with spoked wheels and black tires or solid black plastic wheels. Open cockpit with driver, mostly seen with "52" decal, 2-3/8", silver-painted grille

EX $20   **NM** $35   **MIP** $70

(KP Photo, George Cuhaj collection)

❑ **52-2RW, BRM Racing Car,** 1965, Blue or red body, white plastic driver, yellow wheels, black plastic tires, 2-3/4". Generally carries no. "5" decals on hood and sides

EX $7   **NM** $12   **MIP** $25

❑ **53-1RW, Aston Martin,** 1958, Light green, metal or gray plastic wheels, no interior, no plastic windows, 2-1/2", silver-painted grille

EX $18   **NM** $35   **MIP** $70

(KP Photo, George Cuhaj collection)

❑ **53-2RW, Mercedes-Benz 220SE,** 1963, Red or maroon body, opening doors, white plastic interior, clear plastic windows, 2-3/4", silver, gray or black plastic wheels

EX $10   **NM** $30   **MIP** $55

(KP Photo, Tom Michael collection)

❑ **53-3RW, Ford Zodiac Mk. IV,** 1968, Blue-silver body, opening hood, white plastic interior, clear plastic windows, black plastic wheels, 2-3/4"

EX $3   **NM** $6   **MIP** $12

(KP Photo, Tom Michael collection)

❑ **53-3RW, Ford Zodiac Mk. IV,** 1968, View of Ford Zodiac with opened hood, showing silver plastic engine and a spare tire tucked in front! Opening doors and hoods were always favorite features

(KP Photo, George Cuhaj collection)

❑ **54-1RW, Army Saracen Carrier,** 1958, Olive-green "turtle-shaped" body, six black plastic wheels, rotating turret on top, 2-1/4". One of Matchbox's first military vehicle releases. Like rescue and construction vehicles, military toys tend to be in rough shape, so finding mint or MIP examples can be a little tough
EX $8　　**NM** $18　　**MIP** $40

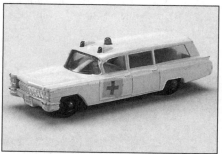

(KP Photo, George Cuhaj collection)

❑ **54-2RW, S&S Cadillac Ambulance,** 1965, White Cadillac ambulance body with red cross decal or label, blue plastic windows, detailed white plastic interior, black plastic wheels, silver-painted grille, red plastic dome lights, 2-7/8"
EX $9　　**NM** $18　　**MIP** $40

(KP Photo)

❑ **55-1RW, D.U.K.W. Amphibian,** 1958, Olive-green body, metal, gray or black plastic wheels, 2-3/4", another in the early military grouping of Matchbox vehicles
EX $15　　**NM** $35　　**MIP** $60

(KP Photo by Dr. Douglas Sadecky)

❑ **55-2RW, Ford Fairlane Police Car,** 1963, Dark or light blue Ford Fairlane with white plastic interior, clear plastic windows, red dome light, silver-painted grille, black plastic wheels. Dark blue version is harder to find; about $300 MIP. Light blue values shown
EX $22　　**NM** $40　　**MIP** $85

(KP Photo, George Cuhaj collection)

❑ **55-3RW, Ford Galaxie Police Car,** 1966, White body, white plastic interior with molded figure, black plastic wheels, red, white and blue stars-in-shield decals, unpainted base, red dome light
EX $17　　**NM** $25　　**MIP** $40

(KP Photo)

❑ **55-4RW, Mercury Police Car,** 1969, White Mercury sedan with white plastic interior, featuring two officers, silver hubs with black plastic tires, blue dome light, clear plastic windows, unpainted base, "Auto-Steer" front wheels, 3-1/16". A new model, this police car was released at the same time as a Mercury station wagon, #73. Both share auto-steer feature and a baseplate, reading "55 or 73"
EX $16　　**NM** $28　　**MIP** $60

❑ **56-1RW, Trolley Bus,** 1958, Red double-decker body with sloped front, no interior; six metal, gray, or black plastic wheels, "Drink Peardrax" decals on sides, flat trolley poles on roof, "OXO" decal on front, 2-5/8". Note that MIP metal wheel versions have sold for $250. Common prices for gray and black wheel versions shown
EX $20　　**NM** $45　　**MIP** $70

(KP Photo, George Cuhaj collection)

❑ **56-2RW, Fiat 1500,** 1965, Pea-green Fiat 1500 sedan with dark or light brown plastic luggage on roof, red plastic interior, silver-painted grille and headlight details, black plastic wheels, 2-5/8", black plastic base. Red versions of this car were included with the G-1 Service Station Gift Set, and are tough to find, usually over $100 mint value. Standard green values shown
EX $4　　**NM** $9　　**MIP** $15

(KP Photo, George Cuhaj collection)

❑ **57-1RW, Wolseley 1500,** 1958, Pale green body, no plastic windows, no interior, silver-painted grille, bumpers and headlights, red-painted taillights, black-painted base, 2-1/8"

EX $20   NM $35   MIP $70

(KP Photo by Dr. Douglas Sadecky)

❑ **57-2RW, Chevrolet Impala,** 1961, Medium-blue body with light-blue top, cast tow hook, clear plastic windows, no interior, silver, gray or black plastic wheels

EX $25   NM $50   MIP $110

(KP Photo, George Cuhaj collection)

❑ **57-3RW, Land Rover Fire Truck,** 1966, Red Land Rover body with "Kent Fire Brigade" and fire dept. insignia decals on sides, blue plastic windows and dome light, white plastic ladder (removable) on top, black plastic wheels, 2-1/2"

EX $6   NM $11   MIP $25

❑ **58-1RW, British European Airways Coach,** 1958, Rounded metal blue bus body, no plastic windows, no interior, gray plastic wheels, "British European Airways" decals, 2-1/2"

EX $30   NM $50   MIP $85

(KP Photo, John Brown Sr. collection)

❑ **58-2RW, Drott Excavator,** 1962, Red or orange body, silver-painted motors on some red variations, orange motor on some orange models, 2-5/8"

EX $15   NM $35   MIP $60

(KP Photo, John Brown Sr. collection)

❑ **58-3RW, DAF Girder Truck,** 1968, Cream-colored cab and chassis, red plastic grille, green plastic windows, no interior, "Available mid-1968" in 1968 catalog, black plastic wheels, 12 red plastic girders, 3"

EX $10   NM $20   MIP $32

(KP Photo, John Brown Sr. collection)

❑ **59-1RW, Ford "Singer" Van,** 1958, Light green Ford Thames van with "Singer" decals on panel sides and "S" logo decals on doors. No plastic windows, no interior, silver-painted grille, gray plastic wheels, 2-1/8". Dark green models seem hard to find, about $250 MIP

EX $35   NM $55   MIP $100

❑ **59-2RW, Ford Fairlane Fire Chief Car,** Red Ford Fairlane casting (same as 55-2RW Ford Fairlane police car) black plastic wheels,

white plastic interior, clear plastic windows

EX $25   NM $45   MIP $80

(KP Photo, Tom Michael collection)

❑ **59-3RW, Ford Galaxie Fire Chief Car,** 1966, Red Ford Galaxie body, white plastic interior with figure cast as part of interior (like police car version) unpainted base and metal grille and headlight section, fire chief decals or labels on side doors and hood, clear plastic windows, white plastic tow hook, blue plastic dome light, 2-7/8"

EX $9   NM $12   MIP $30

(KP Photo, George Cuhaj collection)

❑ **60-1RW, Morris J2 Pick-Up Truck,** 1958, Blue pick-up body, gray, silver or black plastic tires, "Builders Supply Company" decals on sides, silver-painted grille, no plastic windows, no interior, 2-1/4"

EX $18   NM $30   MIP $60

(KP Photo, George Cuhaj collection)

❑ **60-2RW, Site Hut Truck,** 1967, Blue Leyland Ergomatic cab and flatbed chassis, silver plastic grille and headlights, blue plastic windows, no interior, black plastic wheels, plastic yellow hut on back with green roof, 2-1/2"

EX $3   NM $6   MIP $12

(KP Photo, George Cuhaj collection)

❏ **61-1RW, Ferret Scout Car,** 1959, Olive-green, open-cockpit armored car body, tan-colored driver, four black plastic wheels, (one spare on side), 2-1/4"
EX $9   NM $12   MIP $30

(KP Photo, George Cuhaj collection)

❏ **61-2, Alvis Stalwart,** 1967, White body with green plastic windows and green or yellow wheels with black plastic tires. Plastic canopy over bed (not shown), no interior, 2-5/8". Yellow wheels are less common and have approx. $75 MIP values
EX $9   NM $17   MIP $30

(KP Photo, George Cuhaj collection)

❏ **62-1RW, General Service Lorry,** 1959, Olive green body with six black plastic wheels, no plastic windows, no interior
EX $20   NM $32   MIP $60

(KP photo by Dr. Douglas Sadecky)

❏ **62-2RW, TV Service Van,** 1963, Cream colored body with "Rentaset" or "Radio Rentals" decals on sides, red plastic accessories: antenna, 3 TV sets and ladder. No interior, 2-1/2"
EX $20   NM $50   MIP $110

(KP Photo)

❏ **62-3RW, Mercury Cougar,** 1969, Lime-green Mercury Cougar body with unpainted base, silver wheels with removable black plastic tires (like other Mercury models in the line), opening doors, red plastic interior, "auto-steer" front wheels, tow hook, 3"
EX $10   NM $18   MIP $24

(KP Photo, George Cuhaj collection)

❏ **63-2RW, Fire Fighting Crash Tender,** 1964, Block-shaped red body with white plastic ladder (missing in this photo) and white plastic lettering on sides. No plastic windows, no interior, black plastic wheels, 2-3/8"
EX $12   NM $30   MIP $50

(KP Photo, George Cuhaj collection)

❏ **63-2RW, Fire Fighting Crash Tender,** 1964, View of the detailed casting on rear of vehicle

(KP Photo, George Cuhaj collection)

❏ **63-3RW, Dodge Crane Truck,** 1969, Yellow Dodge cab and chassis, red or yellow plastic hook, black grille and headlights, green plastic windows, no interior, six black plastic wheels, swivelling crane section, 3"
EX $6   NM $10   MIP $18

(KP Photo, George Cuhaj collection)

❏ **63-3RW, Service Ambulance,** 1959, Olive green truck-ambulance chassis, black plastic wheels, no interior, no plastic windows, red cross decals on sides
EX $8   NM $22   MIP $50

(KP Photo, George Cuhaj collection)

❏ **64-1RW, Scammell Breakdown Lorry,** 1959, Olive green body, box cab, green, silver or gray hook, six black plastic wheels
EX $25   NM $45   MIP $70

(KP Photo, George Cuhaj collection)

❏ **64-2RW, M.G. 1100,** 1966, Green car body, white plastic interior with driver in front and dog peeking out of rear window, clear plastic windows, black plastic wheels, unpainted base, white plastic tow hook, 2-5/8"

EX $3   **NM** $7   **MIP** $12

(KP Photo, George Cuhaj collection)

❏ **64-2RW, M.G. 1100,** 1966, View of the M.G. and collie peeking out from window. Matchbox included dogs in many later regular wheels models--a fun addition

(KP Photo by Dr. Douglas Sadecky)

❏ **65-RW, Jaguar 3.4 Litre,** 1959, Blue body, no interior, no plastic windows, gray plastic wheels, silver-painted grille. Shown here with 65-2RW Jaguar 3.8 Litre Sedan

EX $18   **NM** $35   **MIP** $65

(KP Photo, George Cuhaj collection)

❏ **65-2RW, Jaguar 3.8 Litre Sedan,** 1962, Red body, opening hood, silver-painted grille and headlights, gray, silver or black plastic wheels, green plastic windows, no interior, 2-5/8"

EX $11   **NM** $20   **MIP** $50

(KP Photo, George Cuhaj collection)

❏ **65-2RW, Jaguar 3.8 Litre Sedan,** 1962, View of gray-wheeled model with open hood-a favorite feature

(KP Photo)

❏ **65-3RW, Combine Harvester,** 1967, Red Claas combine with yellow plastic grain reel and yellow wheels with removable black plastic tires, 3". A popular casting for Matchbox, matching the King-Size model (K-9) version

EX $3   **NM** $7   **MIP** $12

(KP Photo by Dr. Douglas Sadecky)

❏ **66-1RW, Citroen DS19,** 1959, Yellow body, silver-painted grille, no window plastic, no interior, gray plastic wheels

EX $15   **NM** $32   **MIP** $55

(KP Photo by Dr. Douglas Sadecky)

❏ **66-2RW, Harley-Davidson Motorcycle with Sidecar,** 1962, Gold metallic body with spoked wheels, 2-5/8". This piece has escalated in value due to Matchbox and Harley-Davidson collector cross-over

EX $65   **NM** $95   **MIP** $160

(KP Photo, George Cuhaj collection)

❏ **66-3RW, Greyhound Bus,** 1967, Silver-gray body, "Greyhound" decals or labels, yellow plastic windows, white plastic interior, black plastic wheels, 3"

EX $8   **NM** $12   **MIP** $25

(KP Photo, George Cuhaj collection)

❏ **67-1RW, Saladin Armoured Car,** 1959, Olive-green body, rotating turret (gun barrel in photo is broken, a common occurrence with these models) six black plastic wheels, 2-1/4"

EX $11   **NM** $18   **MIP** $30

(KP Photo, George Cuhaj collection)

❑ **67-2RW, Volkswagen 1600 TL,** 1967, Red body, white interior, unpainted base running up into headlights, clear window plastic, opening doors, 2-11/16". One version with snap-on plastic roof rack was included with Race'n Rally G-4 gift set, harder to find

EX $11   NM $17   MIP $25

(KP Photo, George Cuhaj collection)

❑ **67-2RW, Volkswagen 1600 TL,** 1967, Another view of the car showing opening doors and interior

(KP Photo, George Cuhaj collection)

❑ **68-1RW, Austin Mark II Radio Truck,** 1959, Olive-green body, no window plastic, no interior, black plastic wheels

EX $18   NM $35   MIP $65

(KP Photo, George Cuhaj collection)

❑ **68-2RW, Mercedes Coach,** 1966, White and blue-green or white and orange body, clear window

plastic, white plastic interior, black plastic wheels, 2-7/8". Blue-green version harder-to-find with approx. $130 MIP values. More common orange-version values shown

EX $7   NM $11   MIP $15

(KP Photo by Dr. Douglas Sadecky)

❑ **69-1RW, Commer 30 CWT Nestlé's Van,** 1959, Dark red or red van with Nestlé's decals on panel sides, sliding doors, no window plastic, no interior, silver-painted grille, gray plastic wheels

EX $22   NM $40   MIP $90

(KP Photo, George Cuhaj collection)

❑ **69-2RW, Hatra Tractor Shovel,** 1965, Yellow or orange body with black plastic removable tires. Hubs can be yellow or red, 3-1/8". Models with red hubs seem to have higher MIP values, about $90-$125

EX $11   NM $17   MIP $30

(KP Photo, George Cuhaj collection)

❑ **70-1RW, Ford Thames Estate Car,** 1959, Pale blue and yellow van-shaped body with clear or green plastic windows, no interior, silver-painted grille. Gray, silver or black plastic wheels

EX $25   NM $40   MIP $70

(KP Photo, John Brown Sr. collection)

❑ **70-2RW, Grit Spreader,** 1966, Red Ford cab and chassis, yellow hopper section, green plastic windows, no interior, black plastic wheels, silver metal grille, gray or black plastic "pulls" that open bottom chute, 2-5/8"

EX $7   NM $9   MIP $20

❑ **71-1RW, Service Water Truck,** 1959, Olive-green truck chassis with water tank on back, black plastic wheels, spare black plastic tire behind cab, no plastic windows, no interior

EX $28   NM $40   MIP $75

(KP Photo, George Cuhaj collection)

❑ **71-2RW, Jeep Pick-Up Truck,** 1964, Red body, opening doors, black partial base, black plastic wheels, clear plastic windows, silver-painted grille, 2-5/8". Early models came with green plastic interior (shown in 1964 catalog) and are hard to find, about $175 MIP. White plastic interior more common; prices shown

EX $12   NM $22   MIP $40

(KP Photo, George Cuhaj collection)

❑ **71-2RW, Jeep Pick-Up Truck,** 1964, Another view of Jeep Pick-Up Truck showing opening doors

(KP Photo, George Cuhaj collection)

❑ **71-3RW, Ford Heavy Wreck Truck,** 1969, Red cab, green plastic windows and dome light, red plastic hook, black plastic wheels, "Esso" label, white grille extending from white base with "1968" date, 3". A nice, hefty model

EX $12   NM $20   MIP $40

(KP Photo by Dr. Douglas Sadecky)

❑ **72-1RW, Fordson Major Tractor,** 1959, Blue tractor with gray or black plastic tires, and orange hubs in rear and in variations, on front. Silver-painted grille, 2". Gray-tire version and black-tire version with box variations shown

EX $18   NM $30   MIP $75

(KP Photo, George Cuhaj collection)

❑ **72-1RW, Fordson Major Tractor,** 1959, Another variation of the Fordson tractor with orange hubs and black tires, front and rear. This is the version of the tractor that appeared in its last catalog appearance in 1966

EX $18   NM $30   MIP $75

(KP Photo, George Cuhaj collection)

❑ **72-2RW, Standard Jeep,** 1967, Yellow body with upright windshield, black base, red plastic interior and tow hook, black plastic removable tires over yellow hubs, spare tire on back, 2-3/8"

EX $12   NM $20   MIP $40

❑ **73-1RW, RAF Refueller Truck,** 1960, Blue body with RAF decal on top of truck behind cab, no plastic windows, no interior, gray plastic wheels

EX $20   NM $45   MIP $75

(KP Photo)

❑ **73-2RW, Ferrari Racing Car,** 1962, Red racing car body with "73" and Ferrari decals on sides, spoked wheels, white or gray plastic driver, 2-5/8"

EX $20   NM $35   MIP $80

(KP Photo)

❑ **73-3RW, Mercury Commuter,** 1969, Lime green body with clear plastic windows, white plastic interior (including two dogs peeking out of the back), black plastic removable tires with silver hubs, "Auto-Steer" front steering, 3-1/16"

EX $9   NM $12   MIP $25

❑ **74-1, Mobile Refreshment Bar,** 1960, Silver trailer body with opening sides and plastic interior, "Refreshments" decals below side openings, silver or gray plastic

wheels, medium-blue baseplate models about $190 MIP, 2-5/8". Common prices with lighter blue bases shown below

EX $28   NM $45   MIP $95

(KP Photo, George Cuhaj collection)

❑ **74-2RW, Daimler Bus,** 1966, Cream, green or red bodies with white plastic interior, black plastic wheels, "Esso Extra Petrol" decals or labels, 3". First appears in 1966 catalog as new model, "Available mid 1966" with no series number

EX $7   NM $14   MIP $25

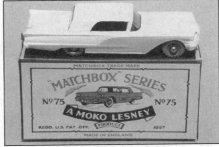

(KP Photo by Dr. Douglas Sadecky)

❑ **75-1RW, Ford Thunderbird,** 1960, Pink and cream 1959 Ford Thunderbird body, green plastic windows, no interior, silver, gray or black plastic wheels

EX $20   NM $50   MIP $90

(KP Photo)

❑ **75-2RW, Ferrari Berlinetta,** 1965, Dark or light green body with white plastic interior and tow hook, clear plastic windows, spoked wheels or silver hubs, (with black plastic removable tires), 2-7/8". Red-colored versions of this model are very rare, about $750 MIP. Common prices shown below

EX $11   NM $18   MIP $40

Matchbox Superfast 1970-1982

This Safari Land Rover, (12-1SF) from 1970 is an example of a transitional Superfast; the casting is the same as its regular wheels predecessor, but the color is now gold, and it is fitted with thin Superfast wheels.

The challenge to Matchbox after the debut of Mattel's Hot Wheels was obvious—make faster cars. The problem was keeping Matchbox cars realistic, so their identity wouldn't be lost in the marketplace. Although new models were added to the 1-75 lineup in time for the 1970 catalog, many of the then-current regular wheels castings were left unchanged, but painted in brighter colors and fitted with new, lighter axles and wheels, which Matchbox dubbed "Superfast."

These transitional Superfast models have a following of their own, being comparatively limited in production. Their thin wheels and light axles generally weren't produced after 1972, and by the 1973 catalog, the 1-75 lineup had changed dramatically, with more fantasy and racing cars.

The 1973 catalog also debuted the "Rola-Matic" series, a fun, wheel-activated mechanism on select cars. For instance, the Ford Mustang "Piston Popper" had a clear plastic engine showing off red pistons that moved up and down as the car was pushed along. The "Stoat" armored car featured a soldier with binoculars that pivoted 360 degrees in search of enemy troops.

MARKET UPDATE

Superfast models are generally quite affordable, and were favorites of kids growing up in the 1970s. Expect to pay a bit more for thin-wheeled transitional Superfast models, due to their crossover appeal to regular wheels collectors, and some harder-to-find color variations. Any muscle-car (Boss Mustang, Dodge Challenger) or Rola-Matic model may start to see increasing aftermarket value.

Throughout the Seventies, Matchbox continued to introduce new models into the 1-75 lineup, moving older models into Gift Sets or Two-Pack series. Castings were still high quality, but it wasn't enough to keep the company British-owned. In 1982, Matchbox was sold to Universal Toys, a Hong-Kong based corporation. Shortly after, castings and variations become dizzying—the same model can have "Made in England," or "Made in Macau" or even "Made in Hong Kong" on its baseplate.

This chapter covers those models made (mostly) in Britain. Superfast models are still quite reasonable, even mint-in-package examples. (The exceptions being a few of the transitionals and some of the blister-packed cars.) With their metal baseplates, solid construction and detailed castings, they make a sharp addition to any collection.

By 1973, Matchbox added more "fantasy" cars to their 1-75 lineup. The Stretcha Fetcha Ambulance (46-2SF) is just one example.

Introduced in 1973, Rola-Matics featured moving parts activated by the rolling wheels of the car. The Ford Capri Hot Rocker (67-2SF) was one of the first entries in that series.

From the 1972 catalog, a spread showing a newer casting, the Hot Rod Draguar, a transitional, the Mercedes 300SE, and one regular wheels holdover, the Ford Tractor.

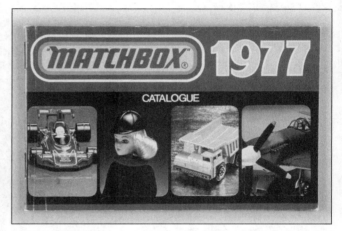

As this 1977 catalog cover shows, Matchbox wasn't just about die-cast cars—it included model kits and dolls as well.

Another transitional, the Ford Cortina, (25-1SF) was available in a new blue finish, although boxes still showed tan examples. The tan Superfast version of the Cortina is tough to find, with about $80 mint-in-package values.

By the late 1970s, model-specific box art, though still around, was being phased out with generic boxes picturing multiple vehicles. This Plymouth Gran Fury Police Car, (10-3SF) was identified only with a stamped name and number on the outside flap.

(KP Photo, George Cuhaj collection)

❑ **1-1SF, Mercedes Truck,**
1970, Gold-colored body, orange
plastic tarp cover, green window
plastic, narrow transitional Superfast wheels, silver plastic grille and
half-baseplate, tow hook cast with
body, 3"

EX $4   **NM** $8   **MIP** $18

(KP Photo, Tom Michael collection)

❑ **1-2SF, Mod Rod,** 1972, Yellow
body, amber window plastic,
exposed silver-plastic engine in
back, red or black Superfast wheels,
"wildcat" label on hood, 2-7/8"

EX $6   **NM** $12   **MIP** $25

(KP Photo)

❑ **1-3SF, Dodge Challenger,**
1976, Red or blue body, white or
red plastic interior, black wheels,
plastic air scoops on hood, blue-
tinted windshield plastic, white
plastic roof, 2-7/8"

EX $5   **NM** $12   **MIP** $18

(KP Photo)

❑ **1-4SF, Dodge Challenger,**
1982, Yellow body, gray base, "Toy-
man" tampos, black plastic roof

❑ **2-1SF, Mercedes Trailer,**
1970, Gold-colored body with
orange plastic canopy, thin transitional wheels, 3-1/2"

EX $5   **NM** $9   **MIP** $20

❑ **2-2SF, Hot Rod Jeep,** 1972,
Pink body, exposed silver plastic
engine with black plastic exhaust
pipes, white plastic seats, lime-
green base and bumpers, 2-5/16"

EX $4   **NM** $7   **MIP** $12

(KP Photo)

❑ **2-3SF, Hovercraft,** 1976, Metallic-green hovercraft body with light
brown plastic base and thin "hidden
wheels" beneath, 3-1/6"

EX $1   **NM** $3   **MIP** $6

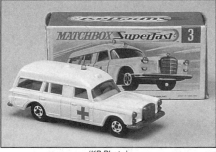
(KP Photo)

❑ **3-1SF, Mercedes-Benz "Binz"
Ambulance,** 1970, White body
with opening hatch and patient on
stretcher, red cross labels, blue window plastic, white plastic interior,
thin transitional wheels, (later
issued with thicker wheels as part of
TP-10 Two-Pack), 2-7/8"

EX $7   **NM** $11   **MIP** $25

(KP Photo)

❑ **3-1SF, Mercedes-Benz
"Binz" Ambulance,** View of
wider-wheel version without
opening rear hatch, included as
part of TP-10

(KP Photo)

❑ **3-2SF, Monterverdi Hai,**
1974, Orange body with number
"3" label on hood, blue window
plastic, thick black wheels, opening doors, 3"

EX $5   **NM** $7   **MIP** $17

(KP Photo)

❑ **3-2SF, Monterverdi Hai,**
1974, Another view of the Monterverdi Hai showing opening doors

(KP Photo, Tom Michael collection)

❑ **3-3SF, Porsche Turbo,** 1979,
Charcoal-gray, red or white exterior
with rally number "14," plastic interior can be yellow, tan or brown,
plastic tow hook, opening doors

EX $1   **NM** $2   **MIP** $5

MATCHBOX / SUPERFAST

❑ **4-1SF, Stake Truck,** 1970, Yellow, or orange-yellow cab and chassis with green window plastic, no interior, green plastic stake-side cargo area, silver metal base, grille and headlights, 2-7/8"
EX $3   **NM** $8   **MIP** $15

(KP Photo, Tom Michael collection)

❑ **4-2SF, Gruesome Twosome,** 1972, Gold with cream interiors and pink or purple window plastic. Two exposed engines, unpainted base, 2-7/8"
EX $2   **NM** $4   **MIP** $11

(KP Photo, Tom Michael collection)

❑ **4-3SF, Pontiac Firebird,** 1976, Blue body with silver plastic interior, amber window plastic, unpainted base and bumpers, 2-7/8"
EX $1   **NM** $3   **MIP** $5

(KP Photo)

❑ **4-4SF, '57 Chevy,** 1981, Red or light purple with unpainted or black base, opening hood with silver plastic engine underneath
EX $1   **NM** $3   **MIP** $5

(KP Photo)

❑ **5-1SF, Lotus Europa,** 1970, Pink or blue body, white plastic interior, opening doors, 2-7/8", thin or thick Superfast wheels. Blue model shown in 1970 catalog, but pink was advertised afterward until model removed from lineup
EX $4   **NM** $9   **MIP** $20

(KP Photo, Tom Michael collection)

❑ **5-1SF, Lotus Europa,** 1970, The pink version of the Lotus Europa, here with thin wheels. This color variation also comes with wide wheels, and generally seems more common

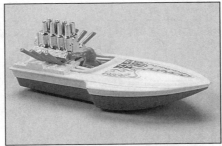
(KP Photo, John Brown Sr. collection)

❑ **5-2SF, Seafire,** 1976, White body with "Seafire" label on front, blue base, blue or orange driver, exposed silver plastic engine with red plastic exhaust pipes. This casting has been used many times by Matchbox, returning in 5-Packs in the 1990s
EX $1   **NM** $3   **MIP** $5

(KP Photo)

❑ **6-1SF, Ford Pick-Up Truck,** 1970, Red body, white plastic camper top, silver or white plastic grille, 2-3/4", black or charcoal base
EX $8   **NM** $15   **MIP** $25

(KP Photo, Tom Michael collection)

❑ **6-2SF, Mercedes Tourer,** 1973, Orange or yellow 350SL body with black plastic top, amber windows, light yellow or cream plastic interior, 3", unpainted base. Later models in light or dark red with white plastic roof, or red or metallic blue with no roof
EX $3   **NM** $7   **MIP** $14

❑ **7-1SF, Ford Refuse Truck,** 1970, Red-orange cab with gray plastic and silver metal garbage dumper bed, 3". The same model as the old regular-wheels version, just with thin or thick Superfast wheels
EX $4   **NM** $8   **MIP** $12

(KP Photo, Tom Michael collection)

❑ **7-2SF, Hairy Hustler,** 1973, Bronze body, with amber windows, number "5" racing labels on front and side, or white body with checkered labels on hood and roof, and red stripes on fenders, black metal base
EX $2   **NM** $4   **MIP** $7

(KP Photo, John Brown Sr. collection)

❑ **7-3SF, Volkswagen Golf,** 1977, Lime green, dark green, yellow or red body, amber window plastic, black plastic, detachable surf boards on roof rack, yellow

plastic interior, black or charcoal base, tow hook
EX $4   NM $7   MIP $12

❑ **8-1SF, Ford Mustang Fast-back,** 1970, White, red or orange-red body, white or red plastic interior (red is harder-to-find), tow hook, 2-7/8". Red models with red plastic interiors are the most rare, selling for around $400 MIB
EX $65   NM $80   MIP $120

❑ **8-2SF, Wildcat Dragster,** 1971, Orange or pink body with silver engine protruding from hood, and "Wild Cat" labels on sides, tow hook, 2-7/8". This is the same casting used on the Mustang Fastback model 8-1SF
EX $3   NM $5   MIP $11

(KP Photo)

❑ **8-3SF, De Tomasa Pantera,** 1975, White body with "8" labels, blue base, red plastic interior, or blue body, tempo "17", black base, 3"
EX $2   NM $4   MIP $10

(KP Photo)

❑ **8-3SF, De Tomasa Pantera,** 1975, A view of the blue version of the Pantera with the "17" tempo

❑ **9-1SF, Boat and Trailer,** 1970, Blue die-cast boat trailer with thin Superfast wheels and plastic blue and white boat, 3-1/2"
EX $4   NM $9   MIP $20

❑ **9-2SF, AMX Javelin,** 1972, Lime-green or blue body (blue included with Twin-Pack #3, Javelin and Pony Trailer), black or silver plastic air scoop, light yellow or white plastic interior, opening doors, tow hook, 3-1/16"
EX $3   NM $6   MIP $10

(KP Photo, Tom Michael collection)

❑ **9-3SF, Ford Escort RS 2000,** 1979, White body with Ford and Shell rally labels, clear window plastic, black base, tan plastic interior
EX $3   NM $5   MIP $8

❑ **10-1SF, Pipe Truck,** 1970, Red or orange cab and chassis, gray or yellow plastic pipes, thin or wide Superfast wheels, silver grille, green window plastic, 3". Red models about $35 MIB, orange model values shown below
EX $7   NM $14   MIP $23

(KP Photo, Tom Michael collection)

❑ **10-2SF, Piston Popper,** 1973, Blue or yellow Mustang Mach I body with silver Rola-Matic engine with red plastic pistons that move as car is rolled along. Yellow plastic interior, unpainted base, 2-7/8"
EX n/a   NM $5   MIP $10

(KP Photo)

❑ **10-3SF, Plymouth Gran Fury Police Car,** 1979, Black and white with "Metro Police" on doors and hood, blue police lights on roof, amber or blue window plastic, unpainted or silver base. Introduced in 1979/80 catalog, it hadn't yet replaced Piston Popper in the lineup
EX $1   NM $4   MIP $7

(KP Photo, George Cuhaj collection)

❑ **11-3SF, Scaffold Truck,** 1970, Silver Mercedes-Benz truck with red plastic base and grille, yellow plastic scaffold sections in back, "Builders Supply Company" labels on sides of truck, green window plastic, no interior, 2-5/8"
EX $4   NM $6   MIP $13

❑ **11-2SF, Flying Bug,** 1973, Red metallic Volkswagen Beetle with Iron Cross label on hood, oversized face with silver helmet peeking up from car, opaque windows, tail-wing and yellow plastic jet engine section on back. Silver or unpainted base, 2-7/8"
EX $4   NM $9   MIP $16

(KP Photo)

❑ **11-3SF, Car Transporter,** 1978, Orange body with black base and light tan/cream car carrying section with red, yellow and blue plastic cars. Dark blue window plastic, no interior
EX $3   NM $5   MIP $9

(KP Photo, Tom Michael collection)

❑ **11-4SF, Cobra Mustang,** 1982, Orange body with opening hood, chrome interior, yellow windows, "The Boss" in white lettering on sides, number "5" on roof. Another in the many variations of the old "Boss Mustang" casting

(KP Photo)

❑ **12-1SF, Safari Land Rover,** 1970, Gold body with white plastic interior, red-brown plastic luggage, tow hook, thin Superfast wheels, 2-3/4". Blue versions of this model exist as Superfasts, but are extremely rare, so prices shown are for gold models only
EX $8   NM $14   MIP $25

(KP Photo, John Brown Sr. collection)

❑ **12-2SF, Setra Coach,** 1971, Metallic yellow and white or burgundy and white with clear or green window plastic, white plastic interior, unpainted base, 3"
EX $3   NM $6   MIP $14

(KP Photo, John Brown Sr. collection)

❑ **12-3SF, Big Bull,** 1975, Orange bulldozer body and rollers, green base and blade, silver plastic engine and trim, 2-1/2"
EX $1   NM $3   MIP $5

(KP Photo)

❑ **66-2SF, Citroen CX Station Wagon,** 1980, Blue body with cream or light yellow plastic interior, clear or blue window plastic, unpainted or silver base
EX $2   NM $5   MIP $10

❑ **13-1SF, Wreck Truck,** 1970, Yellow Dodge cab and tow boom with green bed. "BP" labels on sides, thin Superfast wheels, red window plastic and dome light, no interior, red plastic tow hook, 3". This is another transitional model that is becoming hard to find
EX $17   NM $30   MIP $48

(KP Photo, Tom Michael collection)

❑ **13-2SF, Baja Buggy,** 1972, Lime green body, orange plastic interior, no window plastic, thick Superfast wheels, flower label on hood, silver plastic engine with orange plastic exhaust pipes, 2-5/8"
EX $2   NM $4   MIP $9

(KP Photo)

❑ **13-3SF, Snorkel Fire Engine,** 1977, Red body with blue or amber window plastic, yellow or white snorkel section, unpainted metal base. Models with amber-colored window plastic tend to have higher MIP prices, about $15. This fire engine first appeared in the 1977 catalog with a white snorkel as a new model to watch for, not yet replacing Baha Buggy in the lineup
EX $1   NM $4   MIP $7

(KP Photo)

❑ **14-1SF, Iso Grifo,** 1970, Dark or medium blue with thin Superfast wheels, light blue or white plastic interior, unpainted base, 3"
EX $6   NM $12   MIP $25

❑ **14-2SF, Mini-Ha-Ha,** 1976, Red body with blue opaque window plastic, silver plastic rotary engine protruding through hood, large rear wheels, head with pilot's helmet showing through roof, circular British RAF side labels on doors
EX $3   NM $8   MIP $17

❑ **15-1SF, Volkswagen 1500,** 1970, White, cream or red body with white plastic interior, tow hook, unpainted base, "137" labels on doors, 2-7/8"
EX $7   NM $12   MIP $20

(KP Photo)

❑ **15-2SF, Fork Lift Truck,** 1973, Red body with larger wheels at front, gray or yellow plastic lifting forks on yellow metal or unpainted track, "Lansing Bagnall" or "Hi-Lift" side labels, unpainted, black or green base, 2-3/4"
EX $3   NM $6   MIP $9

(KP Photo)

(KP Photo, John Brown Sr. collection)

MATCHBOX / SUPERFAST

❑ **15-3SF, Hi Ho Silver,** 1981, Silver Volkswagen Beetle (same casting as "Volks Dragon") with "Hi Ho Silver" and "31" tempo. Black base, clear window plastic, red plastic interior, 2-5/8". Having "31" on the roof is an interesting choice of graphic, considering it was the same vehicle casting as the 31-2SF
EX $4   NM $7   MIP $12

(KP Photo by Dr. Douglas Sadecky)

❑ **16-1SF, Case Bulldozer,** 1970, Red with yellow engine, cab and blade and green or black rubber tracks, 2-1/2". This model was released at the same time as the Superfast line-notice that the box has "speed lines" just like the other models
EX $5   NM $8   MIP $15

❑ **16-2SF, Badger,** 1974, Block, metallic bronze-red body with surface detail tools, ladders, etc., and plastic "Rola-Matic" radar. Green window plastic, no interior, six thick wheels, 2-3/4". Later editions in olive green were included as part of TP-14 Two-Pack
EX $4   NM $7   MIP $12

(KP Photo, Tom Michael collection)

❑ **16-3SF, Pontiac Firebird,** 1981, Metallic light or dark tan, Firebird tempo on hood, light tan plastic interior
EX n/a   NM $2   MIP $5

❑ **17-1SF, Horse Box,** 1971, Red or orange AEC Ergomatic cab with green or gray plastic horse box, gray or mustard door, and two white plastic horses, 2-7/8"
EX $3   NM $7   MIP $12

(KP Photo, John Brown Sr. collection)

❑ **17-2SF, The Londoner,** 1973, Red body with "Berger Paints" or "Swinging London Carnaby Street" side labels (most common). White plastic interior, no window plastic, 3". There are many color and label variations of this model, some limited runs that command MIP values over $200. However, prices shown are for the common red-colored "Berger" and "Swinging London" versions
EX $1   NM $3   MIP $8

(KP Photo, Tom Michael collection)

❑ **17-2SF, The Londoner,** 1973, The "Swinging London" version of the The Londoner bus

(KP Photo, Tom Michael collection)

❑ **18-1SF, Field Car,** 1970, Yellow body with tan plastic roof, white plastic interior, no window plastic, unpainted base, spare tire, tow hook, thin or thick wheels, 2-7/8". Other variations as part of Two-Packs in the 1970s, included orange with checked hood label and black plastic roof, olive green with light-tan plastic roof and hood

label, red with light-tan plastic roof and "44" hood label-almost all with black plastic interiors. White editions are harder to find, about $250-300 in MIP condition. Prices shown reflect the more common models listed
EX $7   NM $12   MIP $25

(KP Photo, Tom Michael collection)

❑ **18-1SF, Field Car,** Variation with dark yellow-orange body, black interior, base and roof. Part of Two Pack (TP-8), with Honda motorcycle

❑ **18-2SF, Hondarora,** 1975, Red or orange body with silver or black forks and black seat are the most common, some with gas-tank labels, some without. Olive-drab military models were part of the TP-11 set with the olive-drab field car. 2-1/2"
EX n/a   NM $2   MIP $5

❑ **19-1SF, Lotus Racing Car,** 1970, Dark metallic purple, white plastic driver, wide Superfast wheels, "3" decal on sides, 2-3/4"
EX $9   NM $20   MIP $48

(KP Photo, Tom Michael collection)

❑ **19-2SF, Road Dragster,** 1971, Red or metallic pink body with unpainted base, exposed silver plastic engine, white plastic interior, wide wheels, clear window plastic, "8" labels on hood and roof, 3". Some models have "Wynns" or scorpion labels and are pink or orange-red and harder to find, about $80 MIP
EX $2   NM $5   MIP $10

(KP Photo)

❑ **19-3SF, Cement Truck,** 1977, Red cab and chassis, unpainted metal base, green window plastic, no interior, yellow plastic mixer, with or without black or red stripes, 3"
EX $1   NM $3   MIP $6

(KP Photo)

❑ **20-1SF, Lamborghini Marzal,** 1970, Pink or dark red with amber window plastic, white plastic interior and thin wheels; or pink or orange-pink with thick wheels, 2-3/4"
EX $4   NM $9   MIP $18

(KP Photo)

❑ **20-2SF, Police Patrol,** 1975, White Range Rover with orange stripe "Police" label, frosted window plastic and blue or orange revolving police light (part of the Rola-Matics series). 2-7/8". Other models include orange Site Engineer from Gift Pack #13, olive-drab military ambulance model, and orange Paris-Dakar model, each with approx. $25-$35 MIP value. Common white model values given below
EX $1   NM $4   MIP $8

(KP Photo, Tom Michael collection)

❑ **20-2SF, Police Patrol: Site Engineer,** 1977, Orange body with rotating orange dome light, "Site Engineer" labels on doors, plain metal base. Part of #13 Construction Gift Pack
EX $5   NM $8   MIP $14

(KP Photo)

❑ **20-2SF, Police Patrol: Paris-Dakar Rallye,** 1983, Gold body with black and white checkered label and "Securitie-Rallye Paris Dakar 83" on sides, black base, red rotating dome light
EX $5   NM $9   MIP $13

(KP Photo)

❑ **20-2SF, Police Patrol: County Sheriff,** 1982, White body with blue doors and roof, star design on hood and doors, "County Sheriff" in blue type on sides, blue rotating dome light
EX $3   NM $5   MIP $8

(KP Photo)

❑ **20-2SF, Police Patrol: British Police,** 1983, White body with yellow and black/white checkered "Police" labels on sides. Blue rotating dome light, black base
EX $4   NM $8   MIP $12

❑ **21-1SF, Foden Concrete Truck,** 1971, Yellow cab, orange truck bed with yellow plastic mixer, eight thin wheels, 3"
EX $8   NM $12   MIP $25

(KP Photo)

❑ **21-2SF, Rod Roller,** 1973, Yellow body with red plastic seat, star and flames label on hood, (later editions without black plastic roller wheels, some with red or metallic red hubs on rear, black plastic steering lever, 2-1/2". Prices for metallic red hub versions about $45 MIP
EX $3   NM $8   MIP $17

(KP Photo)

❑ **21-3SF, Renault 5TL,** 1979, Yellow, blue, white or silver-gray body, clear or amber window plastic, tan or red plastic interior, tow hook, 2-1/2". Some yellow models have "Le Car" tempo
EX $2   NM $6   MIP $10

❑ **22-1SF, Pontiac Grand Prix,** 1970, Purple body, thin wheels, silver grille and black base, 3"
EX $12   NM $22   MIP $55

(KP Photo, Tom Michael collection)

❑ **22-2SF, Freeman Inter-City Commuter,** 1971, Purple-red body with white plastic interior,

clear window plastic, unpainted base, some with side labels, 3"
EX $2   NM $4   MIP $8

(KP Photo)

❑ **22-3SF, Blaze Buster,** 1976, Red body with yellow or black plastic ladder, silver plastic interior, amber window plastic, black or silver base, 3-1/16". Black-ladder versions about $25 MIP value
EX $2   NM $4   MIP $7

(KP Photo)

❑ **22-4SF, 4 x 4 Big Foot,** 1982, Silver body, white plastic camper top, blue window plastic, black base, "Big Foot" and "26" tempos on sides and hood
EX $2   NM $5   MIP $12

❑ **23-1SF, Volkswagen Camper,** 1970, Blue or orange body with plastic orange lift-up top reveals white plastic interior, amber or clear window plastic. Some models with sailboat labels on sides, 2-5/8". Military olive-drab versions without lift-up camper top were included as ambulances with TP-12 Two-Pack
EX $9   NM $22   MIP $45

(KP Photo)

❑ **23-2SF, Atlas Tipper,** 1976, Blue body with orange or silver tipper section, wide wheels, amber or clear window plastic, silver or gray plastic interior, 2-3/4". Later versions available with red body
EX $1   NM $3   MIP $7

(KP Photo, Tom Michael collection)

❑ **23-3SF, Ford Mustang GT-350,** 1981, White body, blue Shelby stripes, exposed engine in front, "GT 350" on sides
EX $3   NM $6   MIP $14

(KP Photo)

❑ **24-1SF, Rolls-Royce Silver Shadow,** 1970, Metallic-red body, white plastic interior, clear window plastic, opening trunk, silver metal grille and headlights, black or silver base, 3"
EX $5   NM $9   MIP $20

(KP Photo, Tom Michael collection)

❑ **24-2SF, Team Matchbox,** 1973, Metallic green, red or orange body, "8" or "44" label (included with TP-9, Field Car and Racing Car Two-Pack), white plastic driver, 2-7/8". Metallic green version, about $35 MIP, orange version about $85 MIP. Values for red shown
EX $1   NM $4   MIP $9

(KP Photo, John Brown Sr. collection)

❑ **24-3SF, Diesel Shunter,** 1979, Dark green and red or yellow and red body, no window plastic, labels read "Rail Freight" or "D1496-RF"
EX n/a   NM $2   MIP $5

(KP Photo)

❑ **25-1SF, Ford Cortina GT,** 1970, Metallic tan or blue body, white plastic interior, opening doors, tow hook, 2-5/8". Metallic tan versions, the first of the transitional Superfast models, are harder-to-find and have approx. $70-$80 MIP values
EX $8   NM $12   MIP $25

(KP Photo)

❑ **25-2SF, Mod Tractor,** 1973, Metallic purple body, black base, some with "V" cast on fenders, some without, silver plastic exposed engine, yellow plastic seat, 2-1/4". Harder to find editions have headlights cast in rear fender, about $60 MIP
EX $1   NM $3   MIP $7

(KP Photo, John Brown Sr. collection)

❑ **25-3SF, Flat Car and Container,** 1979, Black or charcoal flat car with tan or red plastic container with "NYK Worldwide Service" labels
EX $1   NM $3   MIP $5

❑ **26-1SF, GMC Tipper Truck,** 1970, Red tipping cab, green engine and base, silver dump bed, green window plastic, no interior, 2-5/8"
EX $5   NM $9   MIP $20

(KP Photo, Tom Michael collection)

❑ **26-2SF, Big Banger,** 1973, Red with dark-blue window plastic, no interior, large silver plastic engine and exhaust pipes, "Big Banger" side labels, 3". Later versions were brown with "Brown Sugar" side labels or white with "Cosmic Blues" tempo
EX $4   NM $9   MIP $18

(KP Photo, Tom Michael collection)

❑ **26-2SF, Brown Sugar,** 1973, The "Brown Sugar" version of the Big Banger with brown body, large silver engine with black scoop and yellow and red "Brown Sugar" labels

❑ **26-3SF, Site Dumper,** 1977, Yellow body with yellow or red dumper bed, or orange body with silver-gray dumper bed, no window plastic, black or brown base, black plastic interior
EX $2   NM $4   MIP $7

(KP Photo)

❑ **27-1SF, Mercedes 230SL,** 1970, Yellow convertible body with black plastic interior, or white body with red plastic interior, clear window plastic, silver base, thin wheels, 2-3/4"
EX $8   NM $12   MIP $25

(KP Photo, Tom Michael collection)

❑ **27-2SF, Lamborghini Countach,** 1973, Pale-orange body with "3" label on hood, or red-orange with "8" tempo and stripes, silver or gray plastic interior, amber or blue window plastic, opening rear hood, 3"
EX $3   NM $7   MIP $16

(KP Photo, John Brown Sr. collection)

❑ **28-1SF, Mack Dump Truck,** 1970, Light-green body and dumper bed, silver base, wide wheels, no interior, amber window plastic, 2-5/8". Olive-drab versions

were released with Case bulldozer in TP-16 Two-Pack
EX $6   NM $10   MIP $22

(KP Photo)

❑ **28-2SF, Stoat,** 1973, Metallic bronze-tan body with rotating (Rola-Matic) soldier holding binoculars. Black base, wide wheels, 2-5/8". Olive-green versions with all-black wheels were included in TP-13 Two-Pack along with an olive version of 73-2SF Weasel armored vehicle
EX $2   NM $6   MIP $12

(KP Photo, Tom Michael collection)

❑ **28-3SF, Lincoln Continental Mk V,** 1979, Red body, white plastic roof, light-yellow or gray interior, silver base. First introduced in the 1979/80 catalog, this model had not yet replaced the Stoat in the lineup, but was due to be "available in your shops later this year"
EX $3   NM $6   MIP $12

❑ **29-1SF, Fire Pumper,** 1970, Red body, blue window plastic and dome light, white plastic ladders and reels, silver base, thin wheels, 3"
EX $12   NM $32   MIP $70

(KP Photo, Tom Michael collection)

MATCHBOX / SUPERFAST

❑ **29-2SF, Racing Mini,** 1971, Orange-red body with yellow "29" labels, clear window plastic, white plastic interior, unpainted silver-gray base and grille, 2-1/4". Also included with TP-6 Two-Pack
EX $5   **NM** $8   **MIP** $16

(KP Photo)

❑ **29-3SF, Shovel-Nose Tractor,** 1977, Yellow body with silver or black plastic engine and interior, shovel can be red or black plastic, 2-7/8". Lime green models with yellow plastic shovels are harder to find, about $65 MIP value. Models with yellow body, black plastic and stripes (as shown) were included in the G-5 Giftset in the 1979/80 catalog. Orange models with red plastic shovels, also about $65 MIP value
EX $5   **NM** $8   **MIP** $16

(KP Photo)

❑ **30-1SF, 8-Wheel Crane,** 1970, Red with gold crane section, red plastic hook, no window plastic, yellow plastic hook, 3"
EX $10   **NM** $20   **MIP** $45

(KP Photo, Tom Michael collection)

❑ **30-2SF, Beach Buggy,** 1971, Pink body with yellow "spatter paint," white or yellow plastic interior and side tanks, no window plastic, 2-9/16". White interior versions have approx. $20 MIP value
EX $4   **NM** $7   **MIP** $12

(KP Photo)

❑ **30-3SF, Swamp Rat,** 1977, Squared-boat body with olive-green deck, tan plastic hull, rotating striped army gunner (Rola-Matic), "Swamp Rat" labels, 3-1/16"
EX $3   **NM** $7   **MIP** $9

❑ **31-1SF, Lincoln Continental,** 1970, Lime-green body with thin wheels, opening trunk, clear window plastic, white plastic interior, 3"
EX $12   **NM** $21   **MIP** $38

❑ **31-2SF, Volksdragon,** 1972, Red Volkswagen Beetle body with clear window plastic, white or yellow plastic interior, silver plastic engine, "eyes" label, unpainted base, 2-5/8"
EX $6   **NM** $10   **MIP** $16

(KP Photo, John Brown Sr. collection)

❑ **31-3SF, Caravan,** 1978, White body with amber or blue window plastic, some with orange stripe with white reversed bird graphic label, unpainted base, light-yellow plastic interior, 2-3/4"
EX $1   **NM** $3   **MIP** $6

(KP Photo)

❑ **32-1SF, Leyland Petrol Tanker,** 1970, Green cab and chassis, white tank, "BP" labels, thin wheels, blue or amber window plastic, no interior, chrome plastic base, 3"
EX $6   **NM** $10   **MIP** $22

(KP Photo, Tom Michael collection)

❑ **32-2SF, Maserati Bora,** 1973, Magenta body with yellow plastic interior, clear window plastic, opening doors, "8" stripe label on hood, lime green, dark green or unpainted base, 3"
EX $3   **NM** $7   **MIP** $13

(KP Photo)

❑ **32-3SF, Field Gun,** 1978, Olive-green with black plastic barrel that fired shells attached to sprue on tan plastic base with soldiers, 3". An interesting piece, in that it included a diarama with the toy. Field Gun was removable from base
EX $3   **NM** $6   **MIP** $11

(KP Photo, George Cuhaj collection)

❏ **33-1SF, Lamborghini Miura,** 1970, Gold body, opening doors, white plastic interior, thin wheels, unpainted base, 2-3/4"
EX $7 **NM** $12 **MIP** $22

❏ **33-2SF, Datsun 126X,** 1973, Yellow body with silver plastic interior, orange base, opening rear hood, amber window plastic, 3". Some versions have black and red flame tempo detail on hood and roof
EX $1 **NM** $4 **MIP** $8

❏ **33-3SF, Police Motorcycle,** 1978, White motorcycle with blue plastic policeman rider, silver plastic engine, "Police" on saddlebags, silver or black wire spoked wheels, 2-7/8". Models included with the K-71 Porsche Polizei set had green plastic riders and detailing
EX $1 **NM** $4 **MIP** $7

❏ **34-1SF, Formula 1 Racing Car,** 1970, Magenta or yellow body, white plastic driver, silver plastic engine, wide wheels, "16" striped label on hood, clear windshield plastic, 2-7/8"
EX $5 **NM** $8 **MIP** $14

(KP Photo, Tom Michael collection)

❏ **34-2SF, Vantastic,** 1976, Modified orange Ford Mustang body, white plastic interior, blue window plastic, early models with large silver plastic engine, later models with closed hood, white base, 2-7/8"
EX $2 **NM** $6 **MIP** $12

(KP Photo, Tom Michael collection)

❏ **34-2SF, Vantastic,** 1976, Earlier and harder-to-find release

without the exposed engine. Number "34" appears on hood

(KP Photo, George Cuhaj collection)

❏ **35-1SF, Merryweather Marquis Fire Engine,** 1970, Red body, blue window plastic, gray plastic reels and instrument panel, white plastic ladder, blue dome lights, "London Fire Service" labels, narrow or wide tires, 3". This model was also included with TP-2 Two-Pack (900 Range). A modified casting was later used for 63-5SF Snorkel Fire Engine
EX $4 **NM** $7 **MIP** $12

(KP Photo, Tom Michael collection)

❏ **35-2SF, Fandango,** 1975, White body with red plastic interior, "35" label with stripe on hood, rotating (Rola-Matic) fan behind driver, clear window plastic, 3". Also red body with red or white plastic interiors, a later release. Versions with white body and red interior and a number "6" label are harder to find, and about $40 MIP
EX $1 **NM** $3 **MIP** $10

(KP Photo, Tom Michael collection)

❏ **36-1SF, Opel Diplomat,** 1970, Metallic green-gold color, opening hood, thin wheels, 2-3/4"
EX $6 **NM** $11 **MIP** $20

(KP Photo, Tom Michael collection)

❏ **36-2SF, Hot Rod Draguar,** 1971, Metallic pink or purple body with white or light yellow plastic interior, clear bubble window plastic, large silver engine, wide wheels, 2-7/8"
EX $5 **NM** $8 **MIP** $18

(KP Photo, Tom Michael collection)

❏ **36-3SF, Formula 5000,** 1977, Orange with blue label number "3" and blue plastic driver, or red with "Texaco" and "Champion" labels and yellow plastic driver, 2-7/8"
EX $1 **NM** $4 **MIP** $8

❏ **37-1SF, Cattle Truck,** 1970, Yellow Dodge cab and chassis, green plastic windows, no interior, gray-brown plastic stake-side bed with two white plastic cows, 2-1/2"
EX $6 **NM** $11 **MIP** $20

(KP Photo, Tom Michael collection)

❏ **37-2SF, Scoopa Coopa,** 1973, Blue or pink body with yellow plastic interior, amber plastic windshield, unpainted base, 2-7/8". Pink models have a daisy-shaped sticker on the roof section, and were shown first in the 1976 catalog
EX $1 **NM** $3 **MIP** $8

MATCHBOX / SUPERFAST

(KP Photo)

❑ **37-3SF, Skip Truck,** 1977, Red cab and chassis, clear or amber plastic windows, yellow bucket, white plastic interior, 2-3/4"
EX $2   **NM** $4   **MIP** $6

❑ **38-1SF, Honda Motorcycle with Trailer,** 1970, Yellow motorcycle trailer with thin wheels and "Honda" labels. Green or pink motorcycle, silver spokes, 3"
EX $7   **NM** $11   **MIP** $19

❑ **38-2SF, Stingeroo,** 1973, Purple chopper-style bike with cream-colored plastic horse head on seat, two wide wheels in rear, one solid wheel in front, purple plastic forks, silver plastic engine, 3-1/8"
EX $6   **NM** $10   **MIP** $22

❑ **38-3SF, Armored Jeep,** 1977, Dark olive-drab with white star emblem on hood, black base and grille, black plastic gun on back (swivels), all-black wide wheels
EX $4   **NM** $7   **MIP** $10

(KP Photo)

❑ **39-1SF, Ford Tractor,** 1970, Blue body with yellow hood and wheels or all-blue body (included with K-20 Tractor Transporter), 2-1/8". This was another regular-wheels holdover into the Superfast era
EX $7   **NM** $16   **MIP** $25

(KP Photo)

❑ **39-2SF, Clipper,** 1973, Metallic magenta body with light metallic green base, yellow plastic interior, flip-up cockpit, and "clicking" exhaust pipes that moved up and down as the car rolled along. One of the first in the Rola-Matics series, 3"
EX $1   **NM** $4   **MIP** $9

(KP Photo)

❑ **39-4SF, Rolls-Royce Mark II,** 1979, Silver body with red plastic interior or metallic red body with yellow plastic interior. Clear window plastic, opening doors, unpainted base, silver grille and headlights. Introduced in the 1979/80 catalog, but had not replaced Clipper in the 1-75 lineup
EX $2   **NM** $5   **MIP** $9

(KP Photo)

❑ **40-1SF, Hay Trailer,** 1970, Blue with yellow wheels and stakeside attachments, 3-3/8". Another holdover from the regular wheels series, this model was replaced in 1972 with the Superfast Guildsman
EX $3   **NM** $8   **MIP** $12

(KP Photo, Tom Michael collection)

❑ **40-2SF, Guildsman,** 1972, Pink with white plastic interior and light-green window plastic, star and flames label on hood; or, red body with white plastic interior

with amber window plastic and "40" label on hood (first appears in 1976 catalog), 3"
EX $4   **NM** $8   **MIP** $16

(KP Photo, John Brown Sr. collection)

❑ **40-3SF, Horse Box,** 1978, Orange cab and chassis, no interior, green window plastic, cream-colored plastic box with light-brown door, two white plastic horses, 2-7/8". This model was reissued in the 1990s with green and blue color variations
EX $2   **NM** $6   **MIP** $10

❑ **41-1SF, Ford GT,** 1970, White or red with red plastic interior, blue stripe and number "6" label on hood, thin or wide wheels
EX $8   **NM** $15   **MIP** $28

(KP Photo, Tom Michael collection)

❑ **41-2SF, Siva Spyder,** 1973, Red body with cream-colored plastic interior, black segment wraps behind cabin, wide wheels, clear window plastic, 3". Blue versions with stars and stripes label motif available in 1976 catalog
EX $3   **NM** $7   **MIP** $12

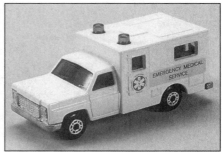

(KP Photo, John Brown Sr. collection)

❑ **41-3SF, Ambulance,** 1979, White body, blue window plastic and dome lights, opening rear doors, unpainted base, white plastic interior, "Emergency Medical Service" or "Ambulance" with red cross labels, 2-1/2"
EX $3   NM $6   MIP $12

❑ **42-1SF, Iron Fairy Crane,** 1971, Red with open cab (no window plastic) yellow plastic interior, yellow crane section with yellow plastic hook, wide wheels, 3". Continued as a regular wheels model, but only for the 1970 catalog, then converted to Superfast
EX $15   NM $25   MIP $45

(KP Photo, Tom Michael collection)

❑ **42-2SF, Tyre Fryer,** 1973, Light or dark-blue body, open cockpit, yellow plastic seat, large silver plastic engine behind driver, large Superfast wheels in rear, wide wheels in front, 3"
EX $2   NM $6   MIP $12

(KP Photo, John Brown Sr. collection)

❑ **42-3SF, Mercedes Container Truck,** 1978, Red cab and chassis, blue window plastic, no interior, unpainted or black base, plastic container with "SeaLand," "NYK" or "Matchbox" labels, 3"
EX $1   NM $3   MIP $6

(KP Photo)

❑ **42-4SF, '57 T-Bird,** 1981, Red body, white interior, clear windshield, silver metal base
EX $1   NM $3   MIP $6

(KP Photo)

❑ **42-4SF, '57 T-Bird,** 1982, Later version with black body, red interior, yellow windshield, plain base
EX $1   NM $3   MIP $7

(KP Photo)

❑ **43-1SF, Pony Trailer,** 1970, Yellow body with green base, clear window plastic, two white plastic horses, narrow wheels, brown plastic door, 2-5/8". Orange version with horse label included with TP-3 Two-Pack
EX $5   NM $8   MIP $15

(KP Photo, Tom Michael collection)

❑ **43-2SF, Dragon Wheels,** 1973, Green Volkswagen Beetle funny-car body hinged to silver plastic and metal base, "Dragon Wheels" labels on sides, 2-7/8"
EX $4   NM $7   MIP $14

(KP Photo, John Brown Sr. collection)

❑ **43-3SF, Steam Loco,** 1979, Red and black body, red base, "4345" labels on sides, 2-11/16"
EX $1   NM $3   MIP $6

(KP Photo, Tom Michael collection)

❑ **44-1SF, Refrigerator Truck,** 1970, Yellow GMC cab and chassis with red refrigeration box, green window plastic, 3". The first release in 1970 was painted like the regular wheels version with red cab and chassis and green refrigeration box. These are hard to find and command approx. $145 MIP values
EX $6   NM $11   MIP $18

❑ **44-2SF, Boss Mustang,** 1973, Yellow body with opening black hood, silver plastic interior, amber plastic window, unpainted base, 3"
EX $3   NM $6   MIP $12

(KP Photo, John Brown Sr. collection)

❑ **44-3SF, Passenger Coach,** 1979, Red body, cream-colored plastic top, green window plastic, black base, "431 & 432" or "GWR" labels, 2-7/8"

(KP Photo, Tom Michael collection)

❏ **45-1SF, Ford Group Six,**
1970, Metallic green body with white plastic interior, silver plastic engine, clear window plastic and number "7" label; or red body with amber-colored windows and number "45" labels, (a later version, first appearing in 1973), 3"
EX $4   **NM** $10   **MIP** $22

(KP Photo)

❏ **45-2SF, B.M.W. 3.0 CSL,** 1975, Orange body with opening doors, yellow plastic interior, amber or blue plastic windows, silver base, "BMW" label on hood, 2-7/8"
EX $3   **NM** $7   **MIP** $15

(KP Photo)

❏ **46-1SF, Mercedes 300SE,**
1970, Gold or blue body, white plastic interior, opening trunk, (some early models with opening doors, too) thin wheels, unpainted base, grille and headlights, 2-7/8". Blue models are hard to find and may command MIP values of $100 or more. Olive-drab staff car versions as part of TP-14 Two-Pack set, about $15 in NM condition
EX $4   **NM** $8   **MIP** $16

(KP Photo, Tom Michael collection)

❏ **46-2SF, Stretcha Fetcha,**
1973, White with blue windows, white plastic interior, red base, "Ambulance" red cross labels, wide wheels, opening rear hatch, 2-3/4"
EX $2   **NM** $4   **MIP** $8

(KP Photo)

❏ **46-3SF, Ford Tractor & Harrow,** 1979, Blue Ford tractor with cab, no window plastic, gray engine block and base, black wheels with or without orange-yellow painted hubs, yellow plastic disk or harrow included (not shown). Also included with hay trailer in TP-11 Two-Pack
EX $1   **NM** $6   **MIP** $14

(KP Photo)

❏ **46-4SF, Hot Chocolate,** 1982, Metallic brown and black funny car body with white stripe. This car was an update on the "Dragon Wheels" funny car
EX $2   **NM** $5   **MIP** $8

❏ **47-1SF, DAF Tipper Container Truck,** 1970, Silver-green cab and chassis, plastic tipping box with removable top, red plastic grille and partial base, green plastic windows, no interior, 3". A Superfast update of the regular wheels model
EX $6   **NM** $10   **MIP** $22

(KP Photo, Tom Michael collection)

❏ **47-2SF, Beach Hopper,** 1973, Blue with pink "spatter" paint, brown plastic interior, tan plastic driver that "hops" as car moves along (a Rola-Matic model), wide wheels, sun label on hood, 2-5/8"
EX $2   **NM** $5   **MIP** $9

(KP Photo)

❏ **47-3SF, Pannier Locomotive,** 1979, Green body, "GWR" labels, metallic brown base. This model had not yet replaced the Beach Hopper in the 1-75 catalog lineup, but was introduced as being available later in the year
EX $2   **NM** $5   **MIP** $8

(KP Photo)

❏ **47-4SF, Jaguar SS,** 1982, Red body, silver grille, headlights and windshield, light-brown plastic interior, wide wheels
EX $1   **NM** $4   **MIP** $7

MATCHBOX / SUPERFAST

❏ **48-1SF, Dumper Truck,** 1970, Blue Dodge cab and chassis, yellow dumper bed, green plastic windows, no interior, silver plastic grille, bumper and partial base, 3". A Superfast version of the 48-3RW regular wheels model
EX $10   NM $18   MIP $32

❏ **48-2SF, Pi-Eyed Piper,** 1973, Blue body, oversized plastic engine on hood, number "8" label on roof, silver exhaust pipes along sides, no interior, blue plastic windows, 2-1/2"
EX $5   NM $8   MIP $20

❏ **48-3SF, Sambron Jack Lift,** 1978, Yellow body with yellow plastic lifting forks, no window plastic, 3-1/16"
EX $2   NM $4   MIP $7

(KP Photo, Tom Michael collection)

❏ **49-1SF, Unimog,** 1970, Blue or metallic blue-green with red base, green plastic windows, wide wheels, 2-1/2". Another update of a regular wheels model, in the 1-75 lineup until 1973. An olive-drab version with a plastic container for artillery shells in the bed was part of the TP-13 Two-Pack in 1979
EX $7   NM $12   MIP $25

❏ **49-2SF, Chop Suey,** 1973, Magenta seat, red plastic fork, yellow plastic bull's head on handlebars, silver plastic engine, black roller-style wheels, 2-7/8"
EX $5   NM $9   MIP $17

❏ **49-3SF, Crane Truck,** 1977, Yellow body with swiveling crane section, extendable crane arm, red plastic hook, six wide wheels, 3"
EX $3   NM $6   MIP $12

❏ **50-1SF, Kennel Truck,** 1970, Dark-green Ford truck body, with four white plastic dogs and clear plastic canopy over bed. Green plastic window, no interior, thin wheels, 2-3/4"
EX $8   NM $17   MIP $40

(KP Photo, Tom Michael collection)

❏ **50-2SF, Articulated Truck,** 1973, Short yellow cab with green plastic windows and blue trailer with yellow plastic chassis, wide wheels, 3". Some have arrow labels, some do not. Notice the difference in the wheels on the trailer.
EX $1   NM $4   MIP $7

(KP Photo, George Cuhaj collection)

❏ **51-1SF, 8-Wheel Tipper,** 1971, Yellow AEC cab and chassis, silver tipper bed, green plastic windows, no interior, "Pointer" labels, silver grille and headlights and partial base, 3"
EX $8   NM $18   MIP $40

(KP Photo)

❏ **51-2SF, Citroen SM,** 1973, Dark red metallic body, opening doors, unpainted base, white plastic interior and tow hook, clear plastic windows, 2-7/8". In 1976, the paint scheme changed to blue with a red stripe and number "8" on roof
EX $4   NM $7   MIP $12

(KP Photo)

❏ **51-3SF, Combine Harvester,** 1979, Red with yellow reel and auger, black Superfast wheels, Superfast wheels with yellow hubs or regular wheels, 2-7/8"
EX $1   NM $3   MIP $7

(KP Photo)

❏ **52-1SF, Dodge Charger Mk III,** 1970, Metallic red or metallic lime-green body with black plastic interior, lift-up canopy, wide wheels, 3". Early red models also featured "hood scoop" labels
EX $4   NM $7   MIP $18

(KP Photo)

❏ **52-2SF, Police Launch,** 1977, White body with blue plastic base and two blue plastic officers, labels on sides read "Police," silver metal horns on cabin roof, dark-blue plastic windows, thin wheels, 3-1/16"
EX $1   NM $4   MIP $7

MATCHBOX / SUPERFAST

(KP Photo, Tom Michael collection)

❑ **53-1SF, Ford Zodiac Mk IV,** 1970, Metallic green body, opening hood, silver engine with spare tire, white plastic interior, clear plastic windows, 2-3/4"
EX $7 **NM** $10 **MIP** $22

(KP Photo, Tom Michael collection)

❑ **53-2SF, Tanzara,** 1973, Orange body, amber plastic windows, opening rear hood shows silver plastic engine, wide wheels, silver plastic interior, unpainted base, 3". Models in 1976 had a bicentennial color scheme; white with red and blue stripes and number "53" on hood
EX $2 **NM** $4 **MIP** $7

(KP Photo)

❑ **53-3SF, CJ6 Jeep,** 1978, Red body, tan plastic roof, yellow plastic interior, unpainted metal base
EX $3 **NM** $7 **MIP** $12

(KP Photo by Dr. Douglas Sadecky)

❑ **54-1SF, Cadillac Ambulance,** 1970, White body, blue plastic windows, white plastic interior, red cross labels, white or silver-painted grille, narrow wheels, 2-7/8". Shown here with its regular wheels predecessor
EX $12 **NM** $22 **MIP** $40

(KP Photo, Tom Michael collection)

❑ **54-2SF, Ford Capri,** 1971, Red with black hood or all pink with white plastic interior, unpainted base, opening hood, wide wheels, 2-7/8". All-red models were included with boat and trailer in TP-5 Two-Pack starting in 1977
EX $2 **NM** $5 **MIP** $11

(KP Photo)

❑ **54-3SF, Personnel Carrier,** 1978, Olive-green with tan plastic troops and gun, black base, wide wheels, 3"
EX $3 **NM** $7 **MIP** $12

(KP Photo, Tom Michael collection)

❑ **55-1SF, Police Car,** 1970, White Mercury sedan, clear windows, white plastic interior with molded figures, police label on hood, shield labels on doors, blue or red dome light, thin wheels, 3-1/16"
EX $8 **NM** $17 **MIP** $30

(KP Photo, Tom Michael collection)

❑ **55-2SF, Mercury Police Car,** 1971, White station wagon body with blue or red dome lights, thin or wide wheels, unpainted base and grille, clear plastic windows, 3-1/16". Early versions had shield labels on doors and "Police" label on hood. Versions from 1973 to 1975 had only arrow-shaped red "Police" label. This car was a minor casting variation of the Mercury Commuter 73-1SF
EX $7 **NM** $15 **MIP** $27

(KP Photo, Tom Michael collection)

❑ **55-3SF, Hellraiser,** 1976, White body with red plastic interior, silver plastic rear engine, clear windshield, wide wheels, stars and stripes label on hood. Or, blue body and white plastic interior, stars and stripes label, 3"
EX $2 **NM** $5 **MIP** $12

(KP Photo, Tom Michael collection)

❑ **55-4SF, Ford Cortina 1600 GL,** 1979, Metallic gold with clear plastic windows, opening doors, unpainted base, red plastic interior. Introduced in 1979/80 catalog, but not yet part of the 1-75 lineup
EX $2 **NM** $6 **MIP** $12

(KP Photo, George Cuhaj collection)

❑ **56-1SF, BMC 1800 Pininfa-rina,** 1970, Metallic gold or orange body, thin or wide wheels, opening doors, clear plastic windows, unpainted base, white plastic interior, 2-3/4". Later models modified the casting of the rear wheel wells to accommodate the wider Super-fast wheels that became standard by 1973. This was a new model in the 1-75 lineup, not an adapted regular wheels casting like many others in 1970. Orange body versions about $16 MIP

EX $4   **NM** $7   **MIP** $12

(KP Photo)

❑ **56-2SF, Hi-Tailer,** 1975, White body with yellow or blue plastic driver, silver plastic rear engine, red, white and blue striped label with "5, Team Matchbox and MB," 3"

EX $2   **NM** $4   **MIP** $9

❑ **56-3SF, Mercedes 450 SEL,** 1979, Blue body, opening doors, light-yellow plastic interior, clear plastic windows, unpainted base. Introduced in 1979/80 catalog, had not yet replaced Hi-Tailer in the 1-75 lineup

EX $1   **NM** $3   **MIP** $6

❑ **57-1SF, Eccles Caravan,** 1970, Cream or light-yellow trailer body with four thin wheels, stripe and flower label on sides, red or orange plastic roof, green or light-yellow plastic interior, 3-1/16". Like many models, the Eccles Caravan continued on in a Two-Pack set, the TP-4 Holiday Set

EX $4   **NM** $7   **MIP** $16

❑ **57-2SF, Wild Life Truck,** 1973, Yellow body, red plastic windows, "Ranger" label on hood with ele-phant illustration, silver plastic grille, wide wheels, red plastic lion circles in truck bed as it is pushed along (Rola-Matic), no interior, clear plastic canopy over truck bed

EX $4   **NM** $7   **MIP** $14

❑ **58-1SF, DAF Girder Truck,** 1970, Off-white or lime-green cab and chassis, red plastic girders, red plastic grille and partial base, green window plastic, no interior, 3". Off-white versions aren't real common and have approx. $65 MIP value

EX $6   **NM** $11   **MIP** $20

(KP Photo, Tom Michael collection)

❑ **58-2SF, Woosh-N-Push,** 1973, Yellow body with open cock-pit, red plastic interior, silver plas-tic exhaust, number "2" label on back of roof; or metallic red body, cream plastic interior, number "8" label with stars and stripes on roof (1976 version), 3"

EX $2   **NM** $4   **MIP** $8

(KP Photo)

❑ **58-3SF, Faun Dumper,** 1977, Yellow body and dumper bed, black base, red plastic windows, 2-3/4"

EX $1   **NM** $3   **MIP** $5

(KP Photo, Tom Michael collection)

❑ **59-1SF, Ford Galaxie Fire Chief Car,** 1970, Red body, white plastic interior and tow hook, clear plastic windows, thin wheels, shield labels on doors, blue dome light, 2-7/8". Oddly, this model dropped from the lineup for one year and returned, briefly, for 1972

EX $12   **NM** $22   **MIP** $45

❑ **59-1SF, Mercury Fire Chief Car,** 1971, Red sedan body with white plastic interior (early ver-sions with two figures), unpainted base, blue dome light, thin or wide wheels, shield and fire chief labels or fire helmet labels, also included in TP-10 Two-Pack with a dual dome light arrangement

EX $4   **NM** $8   **MIP** $16

(KP Photo, Tom Michael collection)

❑ **59-3SF, Planet Scout,** 1976, Metallic green with lime-green or red with yellow body, silver plastic interior, yellow plastic windows, wide wheels, 2-3/4"

EX $2   **NM** $4   **MIP** $8

❑ **60-1SF, Truck with Site Office,** 1970, Blue Leyland truck with Ergomatic cab, yellow plastic hut with green plastic roof, thin wheels, green plastic windows, sil-ver plastic grille and partial base, 2-1/2"

EX $6   **NM** $10   **MIP** $22

❑ **60-2SF, Lotus Super Seven,** 1972, Orange or yellow body with unpainted base, black plastic inte-rior, clear plastic windshield, ghost and flame label on hood, or checker pattern with "60" along length of car, 2-7/8"

EX $5   **NM** $9   **MIP** $16

❑ **60-3SF, Holden Pick-Up,** 1978, Red with yellow plastic motorcycles in bed and yellow plastic interior, unpainted base, checkered label with "500" on hood, 3-1/16"

EX $4   **NM** $7   **MIP** $14

❑ **60-4SF, Piston Popper,** 1982, Yellow body with "Piston Popper" on hood and number "60" on sides. Unpainted metal base, red Rola-Matic pistons like the earlier version

(KP Photo, George Cuhaj collection)

❑ **61-1SF, Alvis Stalwart,** 1970, White body, with yellow plastic canopy (not shown) green plastic wheels with removable black tires, "BP Exploration" labels on sides, 2-5/8". Olive-green versions were included with TP-16 Two-Pack in 1979

EX $9   **NM** $17   **MIP** $30

(KP Photo)

❑ **61-2SF, Blue Shark,** 1972, Blue body with unpainted base, white plastic driver, silver plastic rear engine, black plastic exhaust pipes, clear plastic windshield, "86" or Scorpion label (harder to find, about $50 MIP), 3"

EX $3   **NM** $8   **MIP** $15

❑ **61-3SF, Wreck Truck,** 1979, Red truck body, black base, red plastic windows and dome lights, no interior, white towing arms with red plastic hooks

EX $3   **NM** $6   **MIP** $10

(KP Photo)

❑ **62-1SF, Mercury Cougar,** 1970, Lime-green body with red plastic interior and tow hook, opening doors, 3"

EX $9   **NM** $16   **MIP** $25

❑ **62-2SF, Rat Rod Dragster,** 1971, Light-green body, clear plastic windows, red plastic interior, exposed engine through hood, "Rat Rod" labels on sides, 3". A reworking of the Mercury Cougar casting

EX $5   **NM** $8   **MIP** $18

(KP Photo, Tom Michael collection)

❑ **62-2SF, Renault 17TL,** 1974, Red body with opening doors, white plastic interior, blue plastic windows, some with stripe and number "6" label, some without, 3". A version with "Fire" labels was included in the G-12 Rescue Gift Set in the 1977 catalog

EX $2   **NM** $5   **MIP** $12

(KP Photo, Tom Michael collection)

❑ **62-3SF, Chevy Corvette,** 1982, Black body with yellow and orange stripes running from hood to trunk, white plastic interior, plain base with side-pipes

EX $2   **NM** $5   **MIP** $8

❑ **62-1SF, Dodge Crane Truck,** 1970, Yellow body with rotating crane section, yellow plastic hook, black base, green plastic windows, no interior, 3"

EX $6   **NM** $11   **MIP** $20

(KP Photo)

❑ **63-2SF, Freeway Gas Tanker,** 1974, Short red cab with black base and wide wheels, white plastic

tanker trailer with red chassis, "Burmah" labels on tanker section, 3-1/8". Also available in yellow and white Shell versions, blue and white Aral versions and red and white Chevron version (part of TP-17 Two-Pack). As with regular wheels editions, the German-issue Aral version is harder to find, about $25 MIP. There is also an olive-green version with TP-14 with "High Octane" labels on the sides

EX $2   **NM** $4   **MIP** $8

(KP Photo, Tom Michael collection)

❑ **63-2SF, Freeway Gas Tanker,** 1974, A view showing the more popular edition with the "Burmah" labels and red cab

❑ **64-1SF, MG 1100,** 1970, Blue body, white plastic interior with dog and driver, tow hook, thin wheels, silver base, 2-5/8"

EX $9   **NM** $22   **MIP** $40

(KP Photo, Tom Michael collection)

❑ **64-2SF, Slingshot Dragster,** 1972, Pink or blue body with dual silver plastic engines and red exhaust pipes, label on hood with number "9" and flames, white plastic driver, 3"

EX $4   **NM** $7   **MIP** $15

(KP Photo, Tom Michael collection)

❑ **64-3SF, Fire Chief Car,** 1976, Red body with blue plastic windows, silver air scoops on hood, silver base, "Fire Chief" labels with shield on sides, 3"

EX $3   **NM** $5   **MIP** $12

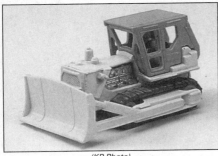

(KP Photo)

❑ **64-4SF, Caterpillar Bulldozer,** 1981, Yellow die-cast body with yellow plastic blade and unpainted base and engine. Cab can be tan or black, and later models have "CAT" and "C" logos on sides near cab

EX $2   **NM** $4   **MIP** $7

(KP Photo, John Brown Sr. collection)

❑ **64-4SF, Caterpillar Bulldozer,** The black cab and "CAT" logos appeared on later versions of the bulldozer

(KP Photo)

❑ **65-1SF, Combine Harvester,** Red with yellow plastic reel and front wheels with removable black plastic tires, 3". This model was another holdover from the regular wheels lineup, first introduced in 1967, but remaining until 1973

EX $3   **NM** $7   **MIP** $12

❑ **65-2SF, Saab Sonnet,** 1974, Blue body with plastic lift-up rear hatch, light-yellow plastic interior, wide wheels, unpainted base, 2-7/8"

EX $4   **NM** $7   **MIP** $15

(KP Photo, Tom Michael collection)

❑ **65-3SF, Airport Coach,** 1978, Metallic blue body, white roof, yellow plastic windows, off-white interior, "British Airways," "American Airlines" or "Lufthansa" labels on sides are most common, 3-1/16". German versions with "Schulbus" labels are harder to find, about $45 MIP. Other variations include: Red body, white top with "TWA" or "Qantas" labels

EX $4   **NM** $6   **MIP** $9

(KP Photo, Tom Michael collection)

❑ **65-3SF, Airport Coach,** 1978, Version with red body, white top and "TWA" labels

(KP Photo, Tom Michael collection)

❑ **65-3SF, Airport Coach,** 1978, Version with red body, white top and "Qantas" labels

(KP Photo by Dr. Douglas Sadecky)

❑ **66-1SF, Greyhound Bus,** 1971, Silver with yellow plastic windows, thin wheels, blue and white Greyhound labels on sides, 3". Shown here in an interesting blister-pack/box combo that Matchbox tried out in the late 1960s and early 1970s. MIP value approx $60 for this combo, regular MIP values shown

EX $9   **NM** $16   **MIP** $30

(KP Photo, Tom Michael collection)

❑ **66-2SF, Mazda RX 500,** 1972, Early releases were orange with white base, opening rear engine hood, silver plastic interior with purple windows, 2-7/8". Later versions were red with white base and racing tempo "77" on hood with yellow windows

EX $3   **NM** $5   **MIP** $9

(KP Photo)

❑ **66-3SF, Ford Transit,** 1978, Orange truck with dropside bed and plastic cargo crates, unpainted base, blue/green plastic windows, light-yellow plastic interior, 2-3/4"

EX $4   **NM** $7   **MIP** $12

MATCHBOX / SUPERFAST

(KP Photo)

❑ **67-1SF, Volkswagen 1600 TL,** 1970, Pink or purple body, opening doors, white plastic interior, clear windows, unpainted base, thin or wide wheels (wide wheels version included in G-2 Transporter Gift Set), 2-11/16"
EX $8   **NM** $17   **MIP** $32

(KP Photo, Tom Michael collection)

❑ **67-2SF, Hot Rocker,** 1973, Ford Capri body with open hood and oversized "hopping" engine (part of Rola-Matics series). Wide wheels, unpainted base. Available in lime-green and red paint variations, 3"
EX $3   **NM** $5   **MIP** $9

(KP Photo, Tom Michael collection)

❑ **67-3SF, Datsun 260Z,** 1979, Pinkish-red or silver body with yellow plastic or red interior, opening doors, black base, 3". Silver model has red and black stripes on sides and hood with "Datsun 2+2" in black type
EX $3   **NM** $6   **MIP** $10

(KP Photo, Tom Michael collection)

❑ **68-1SF, Porsche 910,** 1970, Red body with thin or wide wheels, cream or light-yellow plastic interior, clear windows, number "68" label on hood, 3"
EX $4   **NM** $8   **MIP** $17

(KP Photo)

❑ **68-2SF, Cosmobile,** 1976, Blue or red body, silver plastic trim and interior, yellow base, wide wheels, 2-7/8"
EX $2   **NM** $5   **MIP** $8

❑ **68-3SF, Chevy Van,** 1979, Orange with blue and red stripes along sides, blue plastic windows, silver base. Introduced in the 1979/80 catalog, but hadn't yet replaced the Cosmobile in the 1-75 lineup
EX $1   **NM** $4   **MIP** $7

(KP Photo, George Cuhaj collection)

❑ **69-1SF, Rolls-Royce Coupe,** 1970, Blue body, clear windshield, brown plastic interior, thin wheels, opening trunk, tow hook, 3-1/16"
EX $6   **NM** $11   **MIP** $20

(KP Photo, Tom Michael collection)

❑ **69-2SF, Turbo Fury,** 1973, Red body, clear windshield, number "69" label on hood, white plastic driver, fans on rear of car rotate when pushed (Rola-Matics series), and front of vehicle same style as Blue Shark, 3"
EX $1   **NM** $4   **MIP** $7

(KP Photo, Tom Michael collection)

❑ **69-3SF, Security Truck,** 1979, Red armored truck with white "Wells Fargo" type on sides, blue windows and dome light, unpainted base, wide wheels, white roof, 2-7/8"
EX $5   **NM** $9   **MIP** $14

❑ **70-1SF, Grit Spreader,** 1971, Red Ford cab and chassis, yellow hopper section, no interior, thin wheels, green windows, 2-5/8"
EX $5   **NM** $10   **MIP** $18

(KP Photo)

❑ **70-2SF, Dodge Dragster,** 1972, Pink funny-car Dodge Charger body, silver engine, black or unpainted base, red plastic struts to hold body, snake labels along sides, 3". A preview drawing of this model is seen in the 1971 catalog under the heading "watch out for these 4 new models"
EX $6   **NM** $11   **MIP** $20

❑ **70-3SF, Self-Propelled Gun,** 1977, Green with black plastic gun that fires and recoils while rolled along (Rola-Matics series). Tan treads, black roller wheels, 2-5/8"
EX n/a   **NM** n/a   **MIP** $8

(KP Photo, Tom Michael collection)

❑ **70-4SF, Ferrari 308 GTB,** 1981, Red, may or may not have "Ferrari" on sides and emblem on hood, black base

❑ **71-1SF, Ford Heavy Wreck Truck,** 1970, Red cab and towing crane, red plastic hook, white bed with "Esso" labels on sides, green windows and dome light, white grille, 3". Olive-green versions with all-black wheels were included in 1978's TP-16 Two-Pack
EX $11   NM $17   MIP $32

❑ **71-2SF, Jumbo Jet,** 1973, Motorcycle with blue seat and handlebars, black roller-style wheels, silver plastic engine, red elephant head on handlebars, 2-3/4"
EX $6   NM $9   MIP $18

(KP Photo, Tom Michael collection)

❑ **71-3SF, Cattle Truck,** 1978, Red or metallic gold with plastic yellow or cream stake bed, black plastic cattle, blue or green windows, 2-7/8". Also included in the 1979 TP-19 Two-Pack in red with a matching trailer and plastic cattle
EX $2   NM $5   MIP $8

❑ **72-1SF, Standard Jeep,** 1970, Yellow body with red plastic seats, black bumpers, spare tire on back, 2-3/8". An update of the 72-2RW Standard Jeep, but in this case the spare couldn't actually be used
EX $8   NM $12   MIP $30

❑ **72-2SF, SRN Hovercraft,** 1972, White top with black plastic base and "SRN6" with British flag labels on sides, red plastic propeller, thin wheels in underside of hull, blue plastic windows, 3-1/16"
EX $1   NM $2   MIP $5

❑ **72-3SF, Bomag Road Roller,** 1979, Yellow body with red plastic interior and engine, black plastic roller, silver or yellow hubs. Introduced in 1979/80 catalog, but hadn't yet replaced the SRN Hovercraft in the 1-75 lineup
EX $1   NM $4   MIP $7

(KP Photo)

❑ **72-4SF, Maxi Taxi,** 1982, Yellow Ford Capri body with Rola-Matic engine that hops when car is moved, an update of the Hot Rocker model. Checkered taxi tampos and rates on sides, "Maxi Taxi" on roof, black base

(KP Photo)

❑ **73-1SF, Mercury Commuter,** 1970, Metallic lime-green body with thin wheels, clear windows, white plastic interior with dogs looking out the back, unpainted base, 3-1/16". By 1972, this car had changed to red with a bull's head label on the hood and luggage rack grooves on the roof, with approx. $16 MIP value. Prices for green model shown
EX $6   NM $14   MIP $25

(KP Photo)

❑ **73-1SF, Mercury Commuter,** View showing back of car, with dogs still making an appearance out the back window

❑ **73-2SF, Weasel,** 1973, Medium metallic-green armored vehicle with black turret that turns as the car is rolled (Rola-Matics series), wide wheels, all-black or with silver hubs, 2-7/8". Olive-green versions were issued as part of TP-13 Two-Pack
EX $2   NM $5   MIP $8

❑ **74-1SF, Daimler Bus,** 1970, Red or pink body, white plastic

interior, thin or wide wheels, "Esso Extra Petrol" and Esso logo labels on sides, 3"
EX $5   NM $11   MIP $20

(KP Photo, Tom Michael collection)

❑ **74-2SF, Toe Joe,** 1974, Metallic lime-green body with green plastic towing arms and red plastic hooks, yellow windows, unpainted base, 3". Versions with yellow bodies and red towing arms with black plastic hooks were included with the Racing Mini in TP-6 Two-Pack
EX $3   NM $6   MIP $12

(KP Photo, Tom Michael collection)

❑ **74-3SF, Mercury Cougar Villager,** 1979, Lime-green or blue body, pale yellow interior, unpainted base, opening tailgate, 3-1/16"
EX $2   NM $5   MIP $11

❑ **75-1SF, Ferrari Berlinetta,** 1970, Red with white plastic interior, thin wheels, unpainted base, 2-7/8". Some early models were produced in green, echoing the regular wheels editions, but they are rare and can have $350 MIP values
EX $12   NM $22   MIP $40

❑ **75-2SF, Alfa Carabo,** 1971, Pink with yellow or white base, models in 1976 had yellow stripes running across top of car. White plastic interior, clear windows, 3"
EX $2   NM $5   MIP $11

❑ **75-3SF, Seasprite Helicopter,** 1977, White body, red base, blue windows, regular wheels landing gear, black plastic rotor, "Rescue" labels on tail section, 2-7/8"
EX $4   NM $6   MIP $9

Matchbox Collectibles

Matchbox is celebrating its 50th Anniversary this year with a variety of metallic-red vehicles in 1:64, 1:43 and even 1:18-scales.

Originally based on Yesteryears and Dinky Matchbox castings—you'll often find both "Dinky" and "Matchbox" on the baseplates—the lineup now known as "Matchbox Collectibles" has grown to include 1:76, 1:64 and 1:43-scale vehicles of every variety.

At first, many of the 1:43-scale cars were offered only in sets—it was up to retailers later to decide to sell the models individually. Each set had it's own theme: "Classic European Economy Cars," "Cars of the Rich and Infamous," "Great Tanks of the World" and so on. They are still organized into such themes, but as a rule, they're available separately for those who want to select their favorites from each grouping.

Over the past couple of years, Matchbox Collectibles has marketed their lineup in toy and discount stores at prices that encourage younger or casual collectors. They have expanded their licensed products to include sharp 1:64-scale representations of vintage cars featuring Coca-Cola graphics, and have a variety of models celebrating their 50th Anniversary.

MARKET UPDATE

Most of the models listed in this chapter are still available from hobby or gifts and collectibles stores. However, the aftermarket—dealers, eBay, online shops, etc—can offer great prices. The bottom line is that it's a buyer's market for Matchbox Collectibles vehicles.

A close-up of the 1962 Volkswagen Beetle. Sharp detail—even rubber tires!

A "Matchbox-Dinky" 1948 Land Rover from 1990. This casting has been the basis for many Matchbox Collectibles Land Rovers since.

Another Volkswagen—a 1967 Transporter in commemorative Coca-Cola graphics. This 1:64-scale model is available at most toy and discount retailers.

This German Panther tank is a well-detailed model from the "Great Tanks of the World" series. The baseplates read "Dinky" and "Matchbox."

From the "Great Tanks" series, a short-barreled Panzer Mark IV.

The casting for this GMC panel truck has been used often—you'll find it dressed in Coca-Cola graphics in plenty of stores—but this model Military Ambulance was actually limited to 5,000 pieces. A nice heavy-feeling vehicle, its notable for being an American military ambulance with right-hand drive.

Incredible detail is a given with Matchbox Collectible's "International Fire Engines" series. This 1950 Ford Pumper Unit has plenty of appealing attachments.

The 1966 Ford Bronco from the "First Great 4x4s" series is a sharp casting that captures that square stance and build of the original. The tailgate and rear window open, too—a nice touch.

The Scania Post Bus is a holdover from Matchbox's "Models of Yesteryear" lineup. This casting has been issued in a variety of guises, including as a halftrack mail-delivering model.

Recognize the casting for this "U.K. Pheasant Club" Land Rover? It's the same as the Automobile Association Land Rover from 1990.

The 1957 Chevy Nomad from the "Automobilia—1957 Chevy Collection" is a well-detailed 1:43-scale model. The Nomad is a favorite with die-cast manufacturers, and collectors who specialize on this make and model won't have trouble finding replicas in a variety of scales.

The Tucker Torpedo is another vintage American car model. This 1:43-scale car is part of the first "Oldies but Goodies" series.

50TH ANNIVERSARY SERIES

❑ **1923 Mack AC Fire Pumper,** Metallic red and silver body, silver wheels, black interior, "50th Anniversary" logo on doors, 1:43 scale
EX n/a   NM n/a   MIP $12

❑ **1933 Ford Coupe,** Metallic red body, silver exposed engine, black-painted grille, white headlights, rubber "Goodyear/Eagle" tires, "50th Anniversary" logo on trunk
EX n/a   NM n/a   MIP $6

❑ **1939 Bedford,** Metallic red body, silver trim and tank, black plastic firehose, "Matchbox 50th" logo on doors, 1:43 scale
EX n/a   NM n/a   MIP $12

❑ **1953 Ford F-100 Fire Truck,** Metallic red body, silver trim and wheels, "Matchbox 50th" logo on doors, 1:43 scale
EX n/a   NM n/a   MIP $12

❑ **1955 Cadillac Fleetwood,** Metallic red body, white roof, silver trim, whitewall rubber tires, silver hubs
EX n/a   NM n/a   MIP $6

❑ **1955 Chevy Bel-Air Convertible,** White and metallic red body, white interior, silver trim, white-painted headlights, "50th Anniversary" logo on trunk, rubber "Goodyear/Eagle" tires
EX n/a   NM n/a   MIP $6

❑ **1962 Volkswagen Beetle,** Metallic red body, white roof, off-white interior, silver hubs, rubber "Goodyear/Eagle" tires, white-painted headlights, silver bumpers, tow hook, "50th Anniversary" logo on rear engine hood, 1:58 scale
EX n/a   NM n/a   MIP $6

❑ **1967 Volkswagen Bus,** Metallic red body, white and silver painted bumpers, silver hubs, rubber "Goodyear/Eagle" tires, "50th Anniversary" logo on sides, cream interior, 1:58 scale
EX n/a   NM n/a   MIP $6

❑ **Dennis Sabre Fire Engine,** Metallic red and silver body, gray plastic ladder on roof, blue plastic windows, silver hubs, rubber tires, "50 Anniversary" logo on sides
EX n/a   NM n/a   MIP $6

AUTOMOBILIA: 1957 CHEVY COLLECTION

❑ **1957 Chevy Bel Air,** Silver pink body with white hardtop, 1:43 scale, Model No. DYG02/SA-M
EX n/a   NM n/a   MIP $25

❑ **1957 Chevy Convertible,** Red body with red and white interior, silver plastic highlights and exterior detail, 1:43 scale, Model No. DY027/SB-M
EX n/a   NM n/a   MIP $30

❑ **1957 Chevy Corvette,** White hardtop with blue-gray trim, about 4" long, 1:43 scale, Model No. CCV03/SA-M
EX n/a   NM n/a   MIP $30

❑ **1957 Chevy Nomad,** Black body, white roof, black and white interior, silver bumpers and exterior highlights, silver hubcaps, whitewall tires, 1:43 scale, Model No. VCV01-M
EX n/a   NM n/a   MIP $30

❑ **1957 Chevy Pick-Up,** Light-blue body with white roof, blue wheels and black tires, silver exterior highlights, 1:43 scale, Model No. YRS05/SA-M
EX n/a   NM n/a   MIP $30

AUTOMOBILIA: AMERICAN MUSCLE CARS I

❑ **1967 Pontiac GTO,** Blue body, black roof, silver trim and wheels, blue interior, 1:43 scale, Model No. YMC03-M
EX n/a   NM n/a   MIP $30

❑ **1968 Camaro,** Black with red stripe trim, red interior, chrome wheels, 1:43 scale, Model No. YMC06-M
EX n/a   NM n/a   MIP $30

❑ **1970 Chevelle SS 454,** Red hardtop with black rally stripes, five-spoke wheels, black interior, 1:43 scale, Model No. YMC01-M
EX n/a   NM n/a   MIP $30

❑ **1970 Mustang Boss 429,** Orange with black scoop, louvres and spoiler. Five-spoke chrome wheels, black interior, 1:43 scale, Model No. YMC05-M
EX n/a   NM n/a   MIP $30

❑ **1970 Roadrunner Hemi,** Metallic bronze-green with black stripe on hood, black interior, hood scoop, Goodyear tires, 1:43 scale, Model No. YMC04-M
EX n/a   NM n/a   MIP $30

❑ **1971 Cuda 440 6 Pack,** Yellow with black spoiler, trim and interior, 1:43 scale, Model No. YMC02-M
EX n/a   NM n/a   MIP $30

AUTOMOBILIA: AMERICAN MUSCLE CARS II

❑ **1966 Chevy Chevelle,** Red body, silver five-spoke wheels, black roof, black and red interior, 1:43 scale, Model No. YMC08-M
EX n/a   NM n/a   MIP $30

❑ **1966 Ford Fairlane,** Dark blue body with white plastic interior, silver wheels and trim, white stripe along bottom sides, 1:43 scale, Model No. YMC09-M
EX n/a   NM n/a   MIP $30

❑ **1969 Dodge Challenger,** Blue with white rally stripes on sides, five-spoke wheels, white interior, 1:43 scale, Model No. YCM10-M
EX n/a   NM n/a   MIP $30

❑ **1970 Oldsmobile 442,** Whte convertible body with two wide blue stripes on hood, and stripe detail along sides. Silver five-spoke wheels, 1:43 scale, Model No. YMC11-M
EX n/a   NM n/a   MIP $30

❑ **1970 Plymouth GTX,** Lime green body, wide slick tires on rear, smaller on front, hood scoop, white stipe detail on sides, 1:43 scale, Model No. YMC07-M
EX n/a   NM n/a   MIP $30

❑ **1971 Dodge Charger,** Red body with black roof and black stripe. Six-spoke wheels, 1:43 scale, Model No. YMC12-M
EX n/a   NM n/a   MIP $30

AUTOMOBILIA: CARS OF THE RICH AND INFAMOUS

❑ **1930 Duesenberg Model J,** Red towncar body with white Landau roof and interior, silver spoked

wheels, whitewall tires, Model No. DYM35182
EX n/a   NM n/a   MIP $35

❏ **1931 Mercedes-Benz 770,** Deep blue-black boey with gray stripe and roof, gray interior, silver solid wheels and trim, Model No. DYM35185
EX n/a   NM n/a   MIP $35

❏ **1931 Stutz Bearcat,** Yellow convertible body, black fenders, whitewall spoked wheels and tires, brown interior, Model No. DYM35179
EX n/a   NM n/a   MIP $35

❏ **1933 Cadillac 452 Towncar,** Deep green with open driver's cockpit, closed tan Landau-style roof over passenger seats, silver 24-spoke wheels, whitewall tires, silver trim, Model No. DYM35181
EX n/a   NM n/a   MIP $35

❏ **1937 Cord 812,** Dark blue body with white plastic roof and interior, silver wheels and grille, Model No. DYM35178
EX n/a   NM n/a   MIP $35

❏ **1938 Lincoln Zephyr,** Champagne-colored covertible body, brown interior, whitewall tires and silver hubs, Model No. DYM35180
EX n/a   NM n/a   MIP $35

AUTOMOBILIA: CLASSIC EUROPEAN ECONOMY CARS

(KP Photo)

❏ **1962 Renault 4L,** Light blue body, cream wheels with silver hubcaps, black sunroof, off-white interior. This was another model in the Matchbox Collectibles line to use older Dinky castings. Often "Dinky" is seen in parallel with "Matchbox" on the baseplates of these models, 1:43 scale, Model No. VEM07-M
EX n/a   NM n/a   MIP $20

AUTOMOBILIA: CORVETTE COLLECTION

❏ **1953 Chevrolet Corvette,** Light-blue body with white trim and roof, silver wheels and grille, whitewall tires, 1:43 scale, Model No. CCV03-M
EX n/a   NM n/a   MIP $30

❏ **1957 Chevrolet Corvette Convertible,** White body with red interior, silver hubs, whitewall tires, 1:43 scale, Model No. CCV06-M
EX n/a   NM n/a   MIP $30

❏ **1963 Chevrolet Corvette Stingray,** Silver-blue body, spoked wheels, black interior, 1:43 scale, Model No. CCV05-M
EX n/a   NM n/a   MIP $30

❏ **1969 Chevrolet Corvette Convertible 427,** Yellow convertible body with black interior, spoked wheels, black interior, 1:43 scale, Model No. CCV01-M
EX n/a   NM n/a   MIP $30

❏ **1993 Chevrolet Corvette 40th Anniversary Edition,** Black body with silver wheels, gray plastic interior, 1:43 scale, Model No. CCV02-M
EX n/a   NM n/a   MIP $30

❏ **1997 Chevrolet Corvette Coupe,** Red body, bronze five-spoke wheels, gray interior, 1:43 scale, Model No. CCV04-M
EX n/a   NM n/a   MIP $30

AUTOMOBILIA: GOLDEN AGE OF SPORTS CARS

❏ **1962 Mercedes-Benz 300 SL,** Dark blue convertible body, red interior, silver trim, blue hubcaps with Mercedes-Benz symbol, 1:43 scale, Model No. DY0033/A-M
EX n/a   NM n/a   MIP $35

❏ **1973 MGB GT V8,** Red body, silver highlights, red interior, silver wheels, plain black tires, "V8" on front panels, 1:43 scale, Model No. DY019/B-M
EX n/a   NM n/a   MIP $30

AUTOMOBILIA: GRAND MARQUIS

❏ **1931 Stutz Bearcat,** Red body, black fenders and running

boards, silver spoked wheels, beige interior, Model No. YY014AC-M
EX n/a   NM n/a   MIP $35

❏ **1935 Mercedes-Benz 540K,** Black convertible body with red interior, silver-spoked wheels, silver grille, bumpers and windshield, Model No. YY020AD-M
EX n/a   NM n/a   MIP $35

❏ **1938 Hispano Suiza,** Dark blue body with black plastic top, gold-spoked wheels, whitewall tires, gray interior, Model No. YY017AD-M
EX n/a   NM n/a   MIP $35

❏ **1938 Lincoln Zephyr,** Red convertible body, silver hubcaps and whitewall tires, light tan interior, silver bumpers and highlights, 1:43 scale, Model No. YY064/B-M
EX n/a   NM n/a   MIP $35

AUTOMOBILIA: OLDIES BUT GOODIES I

(KP Photo)

❏ **1948 Tucker Torpedo,** Green body with silver hubcaps and grille, whitewall tires, off-white interior, 1:43 scale, Model No. DYG07-M
EX n/a   NM n/a   MIP $30

❏ **1953 Buick Skylark,** Light yellow body with silver trim, yellow and beige interior, whitewall tires, 1:43 scale, Model No. DYG04-M
EX n/a   NM n/a   MIP $20

❏ **1955 Ford Thunderbird,** Light-blue body with white roof and blue and white interior, 1:43 scale, Model No. DYG08-M
EX n/a   NM n/a   MIP $30

❏ **1956 Chevrolet Corvette,** Black body with white trim, red interior, silver wheels and grille, 1:43 scale, Model No. DYG06-M
EX n/a   NM n/a   MIP $30

❏ **1957 Chevy Bel Air Coupe,** Red body, white roof, red and black interior, silver trim, wheels and grille, whitewall tires, 1:43 scale, Model No. DYG02-M

EX n/a   NM n/a   MIP $30

(KP Photo)

❏ **1957 Studebaker Golden Hawk,** Teal green body with white trim on tailfins, silver hubs, whitewall tires. Another re-issue of an older Dinky and "Matchbox Dinky" casting, 1:43 scale, Model No. DYG03-M

EX n/a   NM n/a   MIP $30

❏ **1959 Cadillac Coupe de Ville,** Black convertible body, red interior, whitewall tires, 1:43 scale, Model No. DYG05-M

EX n/a   NM n/a   MIP $30

❏ **1967 Ford Mustang Fastback,** Black body with silver/gray highlights, black interior, silver wheels, 1:43 scale, Model No. DYG01-M

EX n/a   NM n/a   MIP $30

AUTOMOBILIA: OLDIES BUT GOODIES II

❏ **1947 Chrysler Town and Country,** Tan convertible body with wood panel sides, checked interior design, silver hubcaps and grille, plain black tires, 1:43 scale, Model No. DYG10-M

EX n/a   NM n/a   MIP $20

❏ **1955 Chevrolet Bel Air,** Red body with white roof and trunk, silver hubs and grille, whitewall tires, 1:43 scale, Model No. DYG16-M

EX n/a   NM n/a   MIP $20

❏ **1956 Ford Fairlane,** Blue and white body with blue roof, white and blue interior, white hubcaps, whitewall tires, silver grille, 1:43 scale, Model No. DYG12-M

EX n/a   NM n/a   MIP $20

❏ **1959 Chevy Impala,** White convertible body with silver trim and grille, red interior, whitewall tires, 1:43 scale, Model No. DYG09-M

EX n/a   NM n/a   MIP $30

AUTOMOBILIA: STARS OF THE SILVER SCREEN

❏ **1953 Buick Skylark,** Blue convertible body with white and blue interior, spoked hubs, plain black tires, gray stripe trim, 1:43 scale, Model No. DY029/B-M

EX n/a   NM n/a   MIP $30

❏ **1956 Chevrolet Corvette,** Red with off-white trim, red interior, 1:43 scale, Model No. DY023/A-M

EX n/a   NM n/a   MIP $30

❏ **1957 Chevrolet Convertible,** Blue convertible body with blue and white interior, silver trim, grille and hubs, 1:43 scale, Model No. DY027/B-M

EX n/a   NM n/a   MIP $30

EMERGENCY: AMBULANCE SERIES I

❏ **1912 Ford Model T Van,** Off-white/gray body with red 12-spoke wheels, red cross and "American Ambulance Field Service" tampos on sides, 1:48 scale, Model No. YYM39057

EX n/a   NM n/a   MIP $30

❏ **1937 GMC Van,** Red and white body with "Mercy Hospital" tampos on sides, red wheel covers, red dome light. Interestingly, this model has right-hand drive steering, 1:43 scale, Model No. YYM38058

EX n/a   NM n/a   MIP $30

❏ **1955 Holden FJ Van,** Gray body with red fenders, "Melbourne District Ambulance" on panels, red cross on doors, silver sirens and red lights on roof, 1:43 scale, Model No. YYM38061

EX n/a   NM n/a   MIP $30

❏ **1959 Mercedes L408,** White body with raised roof, "Ambulance" and red cross on sides and front cab. Roof lights on top corners. Silver-gray wheels, duals in rear, 1:43 scale, Model No. YYM38062

EX n/a   NM n/a   MIP $30

❏ **Citroen Type H Van,** Red and white with blue dome light, white doors with red cross tampos, panels read "Amubulance" and "Hopitaux", 1:43 scale, Model No. YYM38059

EX n/a   NM n/a   MIP $30

❏ **Ford E83W 10CWT Van,** White with black fenders and roof, red dome light, silver hubcaps, red cross on doors and "Ambulance" on sides. Same base model as YFE18-M Ford Pumper Unit, 1:43 scale, Model No. YYM38060

EX n/a   NM n/a   MIP $30

EMERGENCY: INTERNATIONAL FIRE ENGINE COLLECTION: SERIES I

❏ **1932 Ford Model AA Fire Engine,** Red body, white and tan hoses, brown ladder, silver grille and details, 1:43 scale, Model No. YFE06-M

EX n/a   NM n/a   MIP $29

❏ **1932 Mercedes Ladder Truck,** Red truck, gold wheels and grille, extending ladder on pivot base, 1:50 scale, Model No. YFE05-M

EX n/a   NM n/a   MIP $28

❏ **1933 Cadillac V16 Fire Engine,** Red body, silver wheels, brown ladder on roof. Extremely detailed hose reels, gauges and pumps, 1:43 scale, Model No. YFE03-M

EX n/a   NM n/a   MIP $28

❏ **1939 Bedford Tanker Truck,** Red body, white hoses, silver hubs, 1:43 scale, Model No. YFE04-M

EX n/a   NM n/a   MIP $28

(KP Photo)

❏ **1953 Land Rover and Trailer,** Red Land Rover Series I with red

trailer. Brown ladder on roof, hose reel in bed, 1:43 scale, Model No. YFE02-M
EX n/a   NM n/a   MIP $29

EMERGENCY: INTERNATIONAL FIRE ENGINE COLLECTION: SERIES II

❏ **1930 Ford Model A Battalion Chief,** Red pickup truck body, silver multi-spoked hubs, black canvas roof, "Fire Chief" on doors and "F.D.N.Y." on sides, spotlights in bed, Model No. YFE12-M
EX n/a   NM n/a   MIP $27

❏ **1932 Ford Model AA,** Red, open cab truck with silver hubs, black side-mounted ladder, silver grille, Model No. YFE09-M
EX n/a   NM n/a   MIP $29

❏ **1936 Leyland Cub,** Red body with yellow pinstripe detailing, black roof. Fully extending black ladder on rolling wheels, silver hubs, white hoses, Model No. YFE08
EX n/a   NM n/a   MIP $28

❏ **1937 GMC Rescue Van,** Red body, white fenders and running boards, "Rescue Squad" in yellow type on sides, brown ladder, silver grille and hubs, Model No. YFE10-M
EX n/a   NM n/a   MIP $28

❏ **1938 Mercedes Wagon,** Red and white body, black ladder, silver panel section, silver hubs, Model No. YFE07-M
EX n/a   NM n/a   MIP $30

EMERGENCY: INTERNATIONAL FIRE ENGINE COLLECTION: SERIES III

❏ **1939 Bedford Truck,** Red body, large spotlight on cab roof, brown side-mounted ladder, silver grille, black base, "City of Manchester Fire Brigade" on doors, Model No. YFE17-M
EX n/a   NM n/a   MIP $29

(KP Photo)

❏ **1947 Citroen Type H Van,** Red Citroen van, tan ladder on silver roof rack, blue dome light, "Longueville" on sides, Model No. YFE13-M
EX n/a   NM n/a   MIP $28

❏ **1948 Dodge Route Canteen,** Red and white van, "Springfield Fire Brigade Auxillary" on sides, blue dome light, silver grille and hubs, Model No. YFE16-M
EX n/a   NM n/a   MIP $29

(KP Photo)

❏ **1950 Ford Pumper Unit,** Red Ford with black fenders towing red supply and pumper trailer. Brown ladder on roof, white hose on trailer, black base. British Ford trucks kept much of the same styling after World War II as they had before., 1:43 scale, Model No. YFE18-M
EX n/a   NM n/a   MIP $29

❏ **1953 Ford Pickup,** Red body, tan hoses on reels in bed, "Garden City F.D. No. 1" on doors, Model No. YFE14-M
EX n/a   NM n/a   MIP $28

EMERGENCY: INTERNATIONAL FIRE ENGINE COLLECTION: SERIES IV

❏ **1904 Merryweather,** Red body, red bench-style seat, gold tanks and trim, black grille and hand crank, Model No. YFE19-M
EX n/a   NM n/a   MIP $38

❏ **1906 Waterous,** Red with white tires, black chair-style seats, white hose, gold steering wheel and trim, Model No. YFE23-M
EX n/a   NM n/a   MIP $38

❏ **1907 Seagrave AC53,** White body, brown pinstripe detail, open cab with chair-style seats, gold tanks and trim, Model No. YFE21-M
EX n/a   NM n/a   MIP $38

❏ **1912 Benz,** Red, open cab body, black fenders and running boards, white hoses on reels, brown ladder, red spoked wheels, Model No. YFE20-M
EX n/a   NM n/a   MIP $38

❏ **1916 Ford Model T,** Red with black seats, black hose wraps around vehicle, side-mounted ladder, Model No. YFE22-M
EX n/a   NM n/a   MIP $38

EMERGENCY: INTERNATIONAL FIRE ENGINE COLLECTION: SERIES V

❏ **1932 Ford Model AA 1 Ton,** Green body with black roof, "White Mountain National Forest" on doors, "Prevent Forest Fires" on sides, white hoses, Model No. YYM35190
EX n/a   NM n/a   MIP $38

❏ **1937 GMC Ambulance,** White body, red fenders and running board, silver roof rack with gear and supplies, "Ambulance" in red type on panel sides, Model No. YYM35192
EX n/a   NM n/a   MIP $38

❏ **1938 Bedford Airport Rescue,** Red body, black roof on cab, black fenders, silver tank in bed, "Bristol Aeroplane Co. Ltd." on sides, Model No. YYM35191
EX n/a   NM n/a   MIP $38

❏ **1941 Chevrolet 3100 Pickup: US Army,** Dark olive green with white stars on doors and hood, white hoses on reels in bed, Model No. YYM35189
EX n/a   NM n/a   MIP $38

❏ **1952 Land Rover: Royal Navy,** Dark blue body, white wheels, knobby tires, tan ladder. This truck is decked out with gear for every contingency, 1:43 scale, Model No. YYM35188

EX n/a   **NM** n/a   **MIP** $38

❑ **1954 Ford F-100 Civil Defense Truck,** White with black hood and "Rescue Service" with Civil Defense logo on doors. Silver hubs, tan ladder, 1:43 scale, Model No. YYM35187

EX n/a   **NM** n/a   **MIP** $38

EMERGENCY: INTERNATIONAL FIRE ENGINE COLLECTION: SERIES VI

❑ **1932 Ford AA High Pressure Truck,** White open cab truck, two nozzles in bed, black interior, silver six-spoked wheels, Model No. YYM37634

EX n/a   **NM** n/a   **MIP** $38

❑ **1932 Mercedes L5 Light Truck,** Dark green body, gold instrument panels on sides, five roof-mounted spotlights, Model No. YYM37632

EX n/a   **NM** n/a   **MIP** $38

❑ **1936 Leyland Cub Open Top Ladder,** Red body, gray extended ladder, black hoses on reels, black grille, Model No. YYM37635

EX n/a   **NM** n/a   **MIP** $38

❑ **1946 Dodge Power Wagon Brush/Field Truck,** White red fenders, black base, fire-fighting apparatus in bed, black grille, Model No. YYM37636

EX n/a   **NM** n/a   **MIP** $38

❑ **1948 GMC COE Tanker/Pumper,** White body, red front and fenders, silver side-mounted ladders, silver hubs, red dome light, Model No. YYM37631

EX n/a   **NM** n/a   **MIP** $38

EMERGENCY: VINTAGE CITY POLICE

❑ **1912 Ford Model T Van: Dallas,** Black body with "Dallas Police" on side panels. Silver spoke wheels, Model No. DYM38019

EX n/a   **NM** n/a   **MIP** $30

❑ **1926 Ford Model T: New York City,** Green body with black roof and interior, white police shields on doors, 12-spoke silver wheels, "New York City Police Department" on panel sides, Model No. DYM38024

EX n/a   **NM** n/a   **MIP** $30

❑ **1933 Cadillac: Salt Lake City,** Black body with white side panels, silver hubs and grille, red dome lights, "Accident Prevention Bureau", Model No. DYM38021

EX n/a   **NM** n/a   **MIP** $30

❑ **1957 Chevy Bel Air: Atlanta,** Black and white body with red dome light, "Atlanta Police" shields on doors, Model No. DYM38023

EX n/a   **NM** n/a   **MIP** $30

❑ **1966 Ford Fairlane: Miami,** White body with green doors, red dome light, black interior, silver hubs and grille, Model No. DYM38020

EX n/a   **NM** n/a   **MIP** $30

❑ **1970 Plymouth GTX: Denver,** White body with blue stripes and Denver Police shield on doors. Red dome light on roof, black interior, Model No. DYM38022

EX n/a   **NM** n/a   **MIP** $30

HI BEAM: AUSTIN POWERS

(KP Photo)

❑ **Jaguar E-Type, "Shaguar",** E-type covertible with Union Jack paint, silver spoked wheels and black plastic interior, 1:43 scale, Model No. DYM37905

EX n/a   **NM** n/a   **MIP** $34

HI-BEAM: AUSTIN POWERS

❑ **Volkswagen Beetle Concept Convertible,** Rainbow, stars and swirls psychedelic-painted Beetle convertible with six-spoke wheels and gray interior, 1:43 scale, Model No. DYM37094

EX n/a   **NM** n/a   **MIP** $34

HI-BEAM: CHRISTMAS THEMES

❑ **1930 Ahrens Fire Engine with Santa,** Large, red open-cab fire engine with Santa and Coca-Cola bottles in back with sign "Season's Greetings from Coca-Cola." Highly detailed, about 7-1/2" long, Model No. YYM35193

EX n/a   **NM** n/a   **MIP** $90

❑ **1932 Ford Model AA with Santa,** Small fire truck with red cab and body, Mr. & Mrs. Claus riding in back, Model No. YSC04-M

EX n/a   **NM** n/a   **MIP** $40

❑ **1932 Ford Model AA with Snowy Carolers,** Dark green truck body, open stake bed with snowmen in back, gold grille and wheels, Model No. YY062A/B-M

EX n/a   **NM** n/a   **MIP** $40

❑ **1967 Ford Mustang Fastback,** Red with two wide, white stripes running from hood to back, silver spoked wheels, Model No. SY016/D-M

EX n/a   **NM** n/a   **MIP** $30

❑ **1968 Ford Mustang Cobra,** Red and white Ford Mustang with white interior, silver wheels, Model No. MB298/SC-M

EX n/a   **NM** n/a   **MIP** $30

HI-BEAM: GREAT TANKS OF THE WORLD

❑ **Churchill MK IV,** Olive green body with British armoured division markings on front, 1:72 scale, Model No. DYM37584

EX n/a   **NM** n/a   **MIP** $30

(KP Photo)

❑ **Panther IV Type A,** Tan camo pattern, long barrel, rotating turret, 1:72 scale, Model No. DYM37581

EX n/a   **NM** n/a   **MIP** $30

(KP Photo)

❏ **Panzer IV Type F1,** Dark gray with short barrel, black cross markings, 1:72 scale, Model No. DYM37580

EX n/a   NM n/a   MIP $30

(KP Photo)

❏ **Panzer IV Type H/J,** Tan camo pattern, anti-tank shell skirts, "Grislybar" and bear tampo on turret, black cross markings, 1:72 scale, Model No. DYM37586

EX n/a   NM n/a   MIP $30

❏ **Sherman M4 A3 Tank, 76mm,** Dark green with white star and "USA" tampos, black 50 cal. machine gun on turret, 1:72 scale, Model No. DYM37579

EX n/a   NM n/a   MIP $30

❏ **T-34/76 Russian Tank,** Olive green body with Cyrillic writing and red star on turret, 1:72 scale, Model No. DYM37583

EX n/a   NM n/a   MIP $30

(KP Photo)

❏ **Wirbelwind Flak PZ IV,** Four-barrel anti-aircraft cannon in octagonal open turret on Panzer IV

chassis, tan camo pattern, black cross markings, 1:72 scale, Model No. DYM37582

EX n/a   NM n/a   MIP $30

HI-BEAM: LIMITED EDITION EXCLUSIVES

❏ **1913 Fowler Showman's Engine,** Red and black steam tractor with white canopy. A reissue of the old Models of Yesteryear Y9-1 Fowler's Showman's Engine, Model No. YY019B/SC-M

EX n/a   NM n/a   MIP $45

❏ **1918 Crossley Floral,** Blue body, tan roof, gold wheels and grille, potted flower cargo, black fenders and running boards, "Sherwood Florist" type on sides, Model No. YY013/SA-M

EX n/a   NM n/a   MIP $40

❏ **1922 Scania Vabis Postbus,** Red body with white roof, black roof rack with mailbags, gold spoked wheels, tread attachments to rear, ski attachments to front, Model No. YYM36793

EX n/a   NM n/a   MIP $45

❏ **1931 Diddler Tramcar: Coke,** Red and yellow body with black roof and trucks. Coca-Cola signage and logos, Model No. YYM37797

EX n/a   NM n/a   MIP $50

❏ **1931 Mercedes-Benz 770,** Red body, black top, silver wheels and running boards, Model No. YY053/SA-M

EX n/a   NM n/a   MIP $30

❏ **1932 Mercedes-Benz L5 Truck,** Dark green cab and open bed with stacked plastic produce and straw bales. Yellow type on sides, "O'Neill Family Produce--New England Farms." Gray spoked wheels, Model No. YY032A/SA-M

EX n/a   NM n/a   MIP $40

❏ **1935 Auburn Speedster 851,** White convertible body with red interior, silver spoked wheels and highlights, Model No. DYM38179

EX n/a   NM n/a   MIP $30

❏ **1937 GMC Ambulance: US Army,** Dark olive green, red cross emblems on roof and panel sides,

white star-in-circle design on doors and hood, right-hand drive. Limited to 5,000 pieces, Model No. YY0345CM

EX n/a   NM n/a   MIP $60

❏ **1946 Delahaye Type-145,** Light pearly-green, dark green fenders, silver spoked wheels, whitewall tires, beige interior, Model No. DY014/SA-M

EX n/a   NM n/a   MIP $50

❏ **Ford Aeromax Tractor-Trailer: Jack Daniels,** Black and gray cab with Jack Daniels label graphic on sleeper compartment. Black trailer with gray edging, "Jack Daniels--Quality Tennessee Sour Mash Whiskey" on sides, silver wheels, Model No. DYM36097

EX n/a   NM n/a   MIP $45

❏ **Hispano-Suiza,** Bronze and tan body with gold-spoked wheels, off-white interior, Model No. YY017A/SA-M

EX n/a   NM n/a   MIP $35

❏ **Horsedrawn Wagon: Budweiser,** White wagon with gray draught horse. Brown crates of beer in back of wagon, Model No. YYM36791

EX n/a   NM n/a   MIP $50

HI-BEAM: MILITARY PLANES

❏ **F-4-U Corsair,** Dark blue body with light gray paint and torpedo underneath. Black propeller, number "86" under cockpit, Model No. DYM92099

EX n/a   NM n/a   MIP $30

❏ **Grumman Hellcat,** Dark blue body with checkerboard pattern white and blue tail and wingtips. Dark blue torpedo, number "59" under cockpit, Model No. DYM92101

EX n/a   NM n/a   MIP $30

❏ **P-38 Lightning,** Silver with European theater black and white invasion stripes, yellow propeller noses, full bomb load, Model No. DYM92108

EX n/a   NM n/a   MIP $30

❏ **P-40 Curtiss,** Olive green body, eyes and mouth design on nose, red nose, star-in-circle ensignia on wings, Model No. DYM92107

EX n/a   NM n/a   MIP $30

❑ **P-51 Mustang,** Silver body with red nose and tail, number "7" under cockpit, Model No. DYM92098

EX n/a   NM n/a   MIP $30

❑ **Spitfire,** Tan and olive camo pattern, light blue-gray underneath wings and fuselage, Model No. DYM92106

EX n/a   NM n/a   MIP $30

HI-BEAM: U.S. POSTAL SERVICE VEHICLES

❑ **1912 Ford Model T Truck,** Dark green and black body, "U.S. Mail" and "I Want You For the U.S. Army" Uncle Sam poster on sides, 12-spoke wheels, Model No. YYM38237

EX n/a   NM n/a   MIP $30

❑ **1932 Ford Model AA 1-1/2 Ton Truck,** Dark green and black body, "Air Mail" on stake bed section with canopy, "U.S. Mail" on doors, Model No. YYM38239

EX n/a   NM n/a   MIP $30

❑ **1937 GMC Postal Van,** Blue body with white top and red stripe, wartime "We Can Do It!" poster on panel sides, silver hubs, silver grille, Model No. YYM38240

EX n/a   NM n/a   MIP $30

❑ **1948 Dodge Route Van,** White, blue and red body with "U.S. Mail" and forest fire poster graphics on panel sides, silver hubs, bumper and trim, Model No. YYM38241

EX n/a   NM n/a   MIP $30

❑ **1961 International Scout 80,** Blue body with white roof, red stripe, Zip Code logo on doors, gray hubs, black interior, Model No. YYM38242

EX n/a   NM n/a   MIP $30

LICENSES: ANHEUSER-BUSCH TRACTOR TRAILERS

❑ **Ford Aero Tractor Trailer: O'Doul's,** Yellow and green cab with green O'Doul's trailer. Silver grille and wheels, Model No. DYM36674

❑ **Kenworth Aero Tractor Trailer: Busch,** White, yellow and blue cab with red, white and blue Busch beer trailer with mountains graphics, Model No. DYM36675

❑ **Kenworth Tractor Trailer: Michelob,** Red and black Cabover Kenworth with Anheuser-Busch logo on sides towing amber and black Michelob trailer, Model No. DYM36671

EX n/a   NM n/a   MIP $25

❑ **Peterbilt Tractor Trailer: Bud Ice,** Dark blue cab with yellow and red stripes and Anheuser-Busch logo on sides. Blue trailer with Bud Ice graphic, including the penguins! Gold wheels and highlights, Model No. DYM36677

❑ **Peterbilt Tractor Trailer: Budweiser,** Red and white conventional cab with red trailer and cooling bottle on ice graphic, 1:100 scale, Model No. DYM36670

EX n/a   NM n/a   MIP $25

LICENSES: BUDWEISER SPORTS CARS

❑ **1957 Chevrolet Bel Air Hardtop,** Blue body with red roof, Budweiser log and bowling graphics on sides, red and black interior, Model No. DYM37600

❑ **1959 Cadillac Coupe DeVille,** Black convertible with whitewall tires, yellow and red interior, Michelob and golf graphics on sides, Model No. DYM37597

❑ **1964 Mustang,** White Mustang convertible with blue stripes and "Bud Light" on doors with cowboy graphic on sides, Model No. DYM37619

❑ **1968 Volkswagen Beetle,** Multicolored Beetle with red fenders, white sides with Budweiser logo and bowling graphic, yellow interior, Model No. DYM37622

❑ **1969 Dodge Charger,** Red body with yellow roof and rally stripes, "Bud Racing" on doors with checkered flag graphic, silver wheels and grille, Model No. DYM37598

❑ **1971 Plymouth Barracuda,** Yellow and blue body with red interior, Budweiser logo with fishing graphic on sides, silver wheels and grille, Model No. DYM37599

LICENSES: BUDWEISER VINTAGE TRUCKS

❑ **1926 Ford Model TT,** Mostly black body with red fenders and roof, white doors with Anheuser-Busch logo, vintage Budweiser ad graphic on panel section, Model No. YVT03-M

EX n/a   NM n/a   MIP $30

❑ **1933 Diamond T,** Red with white fenders and roof, stake bed with "Budweiser--King of Bottled Beer" sign, red six-spoke wheels, Model No. YVT01-M

EX n/a   NM n/a   MIP $30

❑ **1937 Dodge Airflow,** Red cab, white fenders, mostly white panel bed with "Anheuser-Busch Budweiser--Everywhere" on sides, Model No. YVT02-M

EX n/a   NM n/a   MIP $30

❑ **1940 Ford Pickup,** Black body with red fenders, hood and roof, "Budweiser" on front fenders, Anheuser-Busch eagle on doors, gold wheels and grille, 1:43 scale, Model No. YVT05-M

EX n/a   NM n/a   MIP $30

❑ **1948 GMC Cabover (C.O.E.),** Red body and panel van section with Budweiser label graphics, white sides to cab with eagle on doors, 1:50 scale, Model No. YVT06-M

EX n/a   NM n/a   MIP $30

❑ **1955 Chevrolet 3100,** Red and white body--white fenders, red hood and pickup truck bed, red wheels. Budweiser and Eagle graphics on sides and doors, 1:43 scale, Model No. YVT04-M

EX n/a   NM n/a   MIP $30

LICENSES: CLASSIC 50's AUTOMOBILIA COLLECTION

❑ **1939 Peterbilt: Michelin,** Blue and white cab with yellow stripe and Michelin Man graphic on doors. Blue trailer with "Michelin" in white type and Michelin Man graphic, Model No. DYM35269

EX n/a   NM n/a   MIP $30

MATCHBOX / COLLECTIBLES

❏ **1939 Peterbilt: Pep Boys,** Red cab with light blue fenders, matching trailer with "Pep Boys" graphic, "Manny, Mac & Jack" images. Red wheels, Model No. DYM35267
EX n/a   NM n/a   MIP $30

❏ **1939 Peterbilt: Sinclair,** Red and black cab with "Sinclair" on doors, red and black trailer with dinosaur graphic and "Sinclair-- mellowed a hundred million years" in gold type, Model No. DYM35270
EX n/a   NM n/a   MIP $30

❏ **1956 Mack: Champion,** Dark blue cab with orange fenders with orange and silver trailer. Large Champion spark plug graphics on trailer with "More Power, More Speed" copy, Model No. DYM35268
EX n/a   NM n/a   MIP $30

❏ **1956 Mack: Penzoil,** Yellow cab with black fenders, yellow trailer with black stripes, Penzoil logo and "Ask For It" slogan. Yellow wheels, Model No. DYM35265
EX n/a   NM n/a   MIP $30

❏ **1956 Mack: Texaco,** Green cab with red fenders with Texaco star logo on doors. Green trailer with "Fire Chief Gasoline" and Texaco and fireman hat logo, Model No. DYM35266
EX n/a   NM n/a   MIP $30

LICENSES: COCA-COLA SERIES I

❏ **1912 Ford Model T,** Yellow and red body with signs on panels that read, "Ice Cold Coca-Cola Sold Here." Red sign on roof, "Delicious and Refreshing," gold 12-spoke wheels, 1:43 scale, Model No. YPC04-M
EX n/a   NM n/a   MIP $30

❏ **1930 Ford Model A,** Black body with red fenders and running boards, red pickup bed, yellow roof. Circle Coca-Cola logos on doors, gold wheels, 1:43 scale, Model No. YPC05-M
EX n/a   NM n/a   MIP $30

❏ **1932 Ford Model AA,** Yellow and red body with open bed and stacked Coca-Cola cases. Gold wheels and grille, 1:43 scale, Model No. YPC06-M
EX n/a   NM n/a   MIP $30

❏ **1937 GMC Van,** Red van with black fenders, running boards and roof. "Special Delivery" in white type on doors. Coca-Cola lettering on panels, yellow sign on roof reads "Nine Million Drinks A Day", 1:43 scale, Model No. YPC02-M
EX n/a   NM n/a   MIP $30

❏ **1957 Chevy Pickup,** Yellow and red pickup with stake bed and two Coke machines in back. "Vending Service and Repair" on fenders and "The Coca-Cola Company…it's the real thing…" on stakes, 1:43 scale, Model No. YPC01-M
EX n/a   NM n/a   MIP $30

LICENSES: COCA-COLA SERIES II

❏ **1932 Mercedes-Benz L5,** Red cab, yellow panel section, white fenders and roof. "The Drink That Makes the Pause Refreshing" on side panels, Model No. YYM96506
EX n/a   NM n/a   MIP $30

❏ **1937 Dodge Airflow,** Red and black cab, white panel section with black roof. Coke machine graphic on side with "Coca-Cola Goes Along" slogan, Model No. YYM96505
EX n/a   NM n/a   MIP $30

❏ **1948 GMC COE,** Red and yellow chassis and panel section with graphic of electric Coke cooler and "What You Want is Coke" lettering. Silver wheels and grille, 1:50 scale, Model No. YYM96504
EX n/a   NM n/a   MIP $30

❏ **Ford Model AA,** Red cab with white fenders, roof and stake bed with yellow panel section and "Best Friend Thirst Ever Had" on sides, Model No. YYM96507
EX n/a   NM n/a   MIP $30

❏ **Ford Model TT,** Red cab, white panel section, black roof, silver 12-spoke wheels, "Around the Corner from Everywhere" on sides, , Model No. YYM96509
EX n/a   NM n/a   MIP $30

❏ **Morris Light Van,** Red Morris "Bullnose" van with yellow fenders and running boards, "Coca-Cola" on doors, and "The Pause that Refreshes" on sides. Silver-

spoke wheels, Model No. YYM95608
EX n/a   NM n/a   MIP $30

LICENSES: COKE CRUISERS

❏ **1953 Corvette,** Red with yellow stripes, Coca-Cola logo on doors, "Dependable as Sunshine" on front fenders, 1:43 scale, Model No. CCV06/B-M
EX n/a   NM n/a   MIP $30

❏ **1955 Ford Thunderbird,** Black with red roof, Coke bottle graphic on sides, Coca-Cola logo in yellow on doors, red and black interior, 1:43 scale, Model No. DYG08/B-M
EX n/a   NM n/a   MIP $30

❏ **1957 Chevrolet Bel Air,** Yellow convertible body with silver trim, red and black interior, bottle graphic with Coca-Cola logo on doors, "Sign of Good Taste" on front panels, 1:43 scale, Model No. DYG02/B-M
EX n/a   NM n/a   MIP $30

❏ **1967 Pontiac GTO,** Red with black roof, Coke bottle cap graphic on doors, yellow pinstripe along sides, yellow interior, 1:43 scale, Model No. YMC03/B-M
EX n/a   NM n/a   MIP $30

❏ **1968 Chevrolet Camaro,** Black and yellow body with Coca-Cola logo on front panels, two bottles graphic on doors, "It's Twice Time" over rear wheels, 1:43 scale, Model No. YMC06/B-M
EX n/a   NM n/a   MIP $30

❏ **1970 Ford Boss Mustang,** Yellow body with sideways bottle graphic along sides of car, "It's the Real Thing" on front panels, red scoops, 1:43 scale, Model No. YMC05/B-M
EX n/a   NM n/a   MIP $30

LICENSES: COKE VINTAGE SMALL TRACTOR TRAILERS

❏ **1939 Peterbilt: Baseball,** Red cab with yellow fenders, white trailer with boy baseball player holding Coke and "Baseball and Coke grew up together" underneath, Model No. DYM96656
EX n/a   NM n/a   MIP $55

❏ **1939 Peterbilt: Bowling,** Red cab with Coca-Cola logo on doors, trailer shows vintage Coke sign and 50s bowling alley scene, Model No. DYM96654

EX n/a   NM n/a   MIP $55

❏ **1939 Peterbilt: Sprite Boy,** White cab with red fenders and Coca-Cola logo on doors, mostly red trailer with graphics showing line of full Coke glasses, "Sprite" boy, and "Come In… We Have Coca-Cola", Model No. DYM96658

EX n/a   NM n/a   MIP $55

LICENSES: GAS & OIL TANKERS

❏ **DAF: British Petroleum,** Green, white and yellow cab; green, white and yellow tanker trailer with "BP" logo, Model No. CCY13-M

EX n/a   NM n/a   MIP $45

❏ **Ford Aeromax: Sunoco,** Blue cab with silver trim; gray tanker trailer with Sunoco logo and "Ultra 94 Octane." Silver wheels, Model No. CCY10-M

EX n/a   NM n/a   MIP $45

❏ **Kenworth: Mobil,** Gray cab with silver trim; gray tanker trailer with Mobil Pegasus logo and "Mobil" blue and red lettering, Model No. CCY12-M

EX n/a   NM n/a   MIP $45

❏ **Peterbilt: Texaco,** Black cab with red stripes and Texaco star logo; silver tanker trailer with black stripe, Texaco star logo, "Texaco" and "Take it to the Star" on sides, Model No. CCY09-M

EX n/a   NM n/a   MIP $45

LICENSES: GREAT BEERS OF THE WORLD

❏ **1910 Renault Type AG: Kronenbourg,** Model No. YGB07-M

EX n/a   NM n/a   MIP $30

❏ **1912 Ford Model T Van: Yuengling,** Red body with black fenders and running boards, blue roof, gold spoked wheels and grille, "Yuengling's--America's Oldest Brewery Since 1829" and bald eagle design on sides, Model No. YGB19-M

EX n/a   NM n/a   MIP $30

❏ **1912 Ford Model T: Anchor Steam,** Model No. YGB13-M

EX n/a   NM n/a   MIP $30

❏ **1917 Yorkshire: Lowenbrau,** Model No. YGB12-M

EX n/a   NM n/a   MIP $30

❏ **1918 Atkinson Steam Wagon: Swan,** Dark green van body with red roof, red spoked wheels, black chassis, silver stack at front of cab, "The Swan Brewery Co. LTD" on panel sides, Model No. YGB03-M

EX n/a   NM n/a   MIP $30

❏ **1918 Atkinson: Beamish,** Model No. YGB22-M

EX n/a   NM n/a   MIP $30

❏ **1920 Mack AC: Tsingtao,** Green cab and sides, canopy roof over bed with Chinese characters, "Tsingtao Beer" on sides of truck, red wheels and pinstriping, Model No. YGB23-M

EX n/a   NM n/a   MIP $30

❏ **1922 Foden: Whitbread,** Model No. YGB11-M

EX n/a   NM n/a   MIP $30

❏ **1926 Ford Model T Truck: Becks,** Light tan body, red roof, red spoked wheels, black interior, dark green fenders, silver grille, "Beck & Co. Expertbrauerei, Bremen", Model No. YGB02-M

EX n/a   NM n/a   MIP $30

❏ **1927 Talbot Van: South Pacific Lager,** Red body, white roof, red spoked wheels, "South Pacific Export Lager" with bird of logo on side panels, Model No. YGB10-M

EX n/a   NM n/a   MIP $30

❏ **1929 Garrett Steam Wagon: Flowers,** Light tan body, red and black chassis, red wheels, "Flowers Fine Ales" with Shakespeare portrait on sides, (the brewery was located in Stratford-upon-Avon), Model No. YGB15-M

EX n/a   NM n/a   MIP $30

❏ **1929 Morris Courier Van: Fuller's,** Dark green van body with red fenders and running boards, gold spoked wheels, red roof, "Fuller's" on sides, Model No. YGB04-M

EX n/a   NM n/a   MIP $30

❏ **1930 Ford Model A Van: Castlemaine,** Yellow body with red spoked wheels and red roof, "Castlemaine" on panel sides, Model No. YGB01-M

EX n/a   NM n/a   MIP $30

❏ **1931 Morris Van: Cascade,** Dark brown body with yellow fenders, wheels and roof, "Cascade Premium Lager" on panel sides, Model No. YGB18-M

EX n/a   NM n/a   MIP $30

❏ **1932 Ford AA: Corona,** Blue body with white top over bed and "Corona Extra" on sides, gold wheels and grille, Model No. YGB16-M

EX n/a   NM n/a   MIP $30

❏ **1932 Ford AA: Stroh's,** Red body with "Stroh's Bohemian Beer" and logo on sides, gold wheels and grille, Model No. YGB20-M

EX n/a   NM n/a   MIP $30

❏ **1932 Ford Model AA: Carlsberg,** Dark green body with tan roof on cab and tan canvas cover over bed. Red wheels, black fenders and running boards, silver grille, Model No. YGB05-M

EX n/a   NM n/a   MIP $30

❏ **1932 Mercedes L5 Truck: Henninger Brau,** White cab and truck bed, red chassis, silver wheels, red plastic tarp cover, barrels in truck bed--nice detail. "Henninger Brau" on white stake bed section, "HB" on red tarp, Model No. YGB17-M

EX n/a   NM n/a   MIP $30

❏ **1932 Mercedes L5 Truck: Holsten,** White cab and stake bed truck with tan canopy featuring Holsten Brauerei knight-on-horseback design. Red spoked wheels, "Holsten Bier" on stake sides, Model No. YGB06-M

EX n/a   NM n/a   MIP $30

❏ **1932 Mercedes-Benz LS: DAB,** White body, black roof on cab and panel section, "Das Bier von Weltruf--DAB Pils" on sides, DAB logo on doors, silver wheels and grille, Model No. YGB21-M

EX n/a   NM n/a   MIP $30

❏ **1933 Mack Truck: Moosehead,** Model No. YGB09-M

EX n/a   NM n/a   MIP $30

❏ **1937 GMC Van: Steinlager,** Dark green body with red Stein-

lager sign logos on sides, red wheels, "Product of New Zealand" with Steinlager logos on doors, Model No. YGB08-M
EX n/a   NM n/a   MIP $30

❑ **1939 Bedford: Tooheys,** Blue body with black fenders and chassis, "Tooheys" signs on sides, barrels in back, silver wheels and grille, Model No. YGB24-M
EX n/a   NM n/a   MIP $30

LICENSES: GREAT SPIRITS COLLECTION

❑ **1910 Renault AG: Dewar's,** Pale yellow and pink body with black roof, fenders and running boards, black interior, "Dewar's Blended Scotch Whiskey" on side panels, Model No. YYM37792
EX n/a   NM n/a   MIP $30

❑ **1926 Ford Model TT: Bacardi,** Pink and pale yellow body with black fenders and chassis, gold-spoked wheels and grille. "The world's greatest rums--Barcardi" with barrel graphic on sides, Model No. YYM37789
EX n/a   NM n/a   MIP $30

❑ **1929 Morris Light Van: Beefeater,** White body with red roof, fenders and running boards, silver-gray wheels and grille, Union Jack design on hood and "Beefeater--the spirit of London" on side panels, Model No. YYM37793
EX n/a   NM n/a   MIP $30

❑ **1929 Morris Light Van: Cutty Sark,** Yellow body with black fenders, running boards and roof. Sign on cab reads, "Berry Bros. & Co." and side panels feature Cutty Sark logo, Model No. YYM37791
EX n/a   NM n/a   MIP $30

❑ **1937 Dodge Airflow: Jack Daniel's,** Black and white body with "Jack Daniel's Tennessee Whiskey" on side panels. Silver wheels, grille and headlights, Model No. YYM37790
EX n/a   NM n/a   MIP $30

❑ **1948 GMC COE: Jim Beam,** Black and yellow-orange body with "Jim Beam" on panel sides, silver wheels and grille, Model No. YYM37788
EX n/a   NM n/a   MIP $30

LICENSES: HERSHEY'S SMALL TRACTOR TRAILERS

❑ **Ford: Season's Greetings,** Red cab and trailer with snowman and Hershey's Miniatures graphics, Model No. DYM92173
EX n/a   NM n/a   MIP $30

❑ **Kenworth: Happy Easter,** Blue Kenworth Aerodyne tractor with silver stacks, trailer with "Easter Greetings" and Easter bunny enjoying Hershey's bars on sides, Model No. DYM92168
EX n/a   NM n/a   MIP $30

❑ **Kenworth: Mother's Day,** White cab, white trailer with "To Mother" Hershey's Kisses advertising with flowers background, silver wheels and grille, Model No. DYM92169
EX n/a   NM n/a   MIP $30

❑ **Mack: Tricks or Treat,** Black and orange cab and trailer with witch and black cat graphics and "Tricks or Treat" on sides, silver wheels and trim, Model No. DYM92172
EX n/a   NM n/a   MIP $30

❑ **Peterbilt: Hershey's Valentine Greetings,** Black cab with yellow and black trailer with black banner design and heart graphic, Model No. DYM92167
EX n/a   NM n/a   MIP $30

❑ **Peterbilt: Independence Day,** Pinkish-cream cab and trailer with vintage "Hershey's Chocolate" advertising on sides, Model No. DYM92171
EX n/a   NM n/a   MIP $30

LICENSES: INTERNATIONAL BREWMASTERS

DAF: Holsten Pils, Green cab, green and yellow trailer, silver wheels, "Holsten Pils" on trailer, Model No. CCY08-M
EX n/a   NM n/a   MIP $25

❑ **Ford: Dos Equis,** Black cab and trailer, Dos Equis logo and beer bottle graphics, 7", Model No. CCY02/B-M
EX n/a   NM n/a   MIP $30

❑ **Mack CH600: Labatts,** Blue cab and trailer with silver wheels and trim. Trailer shows open bottle of Labatt's pouring out beer, Model No. CCY05/C-M
EX n/a   NM n/a   MIP $30

❑ **Peterbilt: Budweiser,** Red cab and trailer, "Budweiser King of Beers" on sides, silver wheels, grille and trim, 1:100 scale, Model No. CCY06/B-M
EX n/a   NM n/a   MIP $25

❑ **Scania: Castlemaine XXXX,** White cab with silver trailer showing photos of Castlemaine and ice cubes, Model No. CCY07/B-M
EX n/a   NM n/a   MIP $30

❑ **Scania: Skol Lager,** White cab, amber trailer (photo close-up of beer in background) red "Skol" lettering, silver wheels, Model No. CCY07-M
EX n/a   NM n/a   MIP $25

LICENSES: INTERNATIONAL WORKHORSES

❑ **1929 Scammell 100 Ton,** Green cab, black hood and fenders, "Great Western Railway" on sides of flatbed, sandbag load in bed, , Model No. YYM36861
EX n/a   NM n/a   MIP $30

❑ **1937 Diamond T,** Yellow cab and body, black roof and fenders, "Caterpillar" on sides, yellow spoked wheels, Model No. YYM36835
EX n/a   NM n/a   MIP $30

❑ **1937 Dodge Airflow Tanker,** Red body and wheels, "Texaco" on tank, Texaco star logo on doors, silver grille and bumpers, Model No. YYM36834
EX n/a   NM n/a   MIP $37

❑ **1937 International Stake Bed,** Black cab, brown stakeside bed, red wheels, "Harley-Davidson" on sides, silver trim, Model No. YYM36833
EX n/a   NM n/a   MIP $30

❑ **1948 GMC Dump Truck,** White cab, black fenders and dumper bed, silver-gray wheels, "U.S. Steel" on sides of bed, Model No. YYM36836
EX n/a   NM n/a   MIP $30

LICENSES: KINGS OF THE ROAD

❑ **Ford Aeromax: Consolidated Freight,** White cab with red and green stripes and "CF" on sleeper section. Red wheels, silver bumper, tanks and grille. White trailer with red and green stripes and "CF" logo, 1:100 scale, Model No. DYM38008
EX n/a   NM n/a   MIP $30

❑ **Ford Aeromax: Overnite,** Dark blue and silver cab with "Overnite" diamond logo on doors. Gray trailer with "Overnite" diamond and silver wheels, 1:100 scale, Model No. DYM38009
EX n/a   NM n/a   MIP $30

❑ **Ford Aeromax: Roadway,** Blue and orange cab with "Roadway" on doors, silver wheels, tanks and grille. White trailer with "Roadway" on sides, 1:100 scale, Model No. DYM38007
EX n/a   NM n/a   MIP $30

LICENSES: NORTH AMERICAN BREWMASTERS

❑ **Ford Aeromax: Red Dog,** Red cab; white trailer with Red Dog label, large Red Dog graphic with paw prints and "You are your own dog", Model No. CCY02-M
EX n/a   NM n/a   MIP $20

❑ **Kenworth: Corona,** Dark blue, white and yellow conventional cab with blue, white and yellow trailer featuring Corona label graphic, Model No. CCY04-M
EX n/a   NM n/a   MIP $20

❑ **Kenworth: Moosehead,** Black cabover with "Moosehead Beer" on sleeper section; black trailer with bottles and "The Moose is Loose" on sides, Model No. CCY03-M
EX n/a   NM n/a   MIP $20

❑ **Peterbilt: Miller Genuine Draft,** Black cab with red and bronze stripes; trailer with close-up photo of Miller Genuine Draft labels, Model No. CCY01-M
EX n/a   NM n/a   MIP $20

❑ **Peterbilt: Pabst Blue Ribbon,** White and red cab with PBR logo on doors, trailer shows cans with "PBR me ASAP!" slogan, Model No. CCY06-M
EX n/a   NM n/a   MIP $20

WORK HORSES: 1930'S & 1940'S PICKUPS

❑ **1934 International-Harvester C-Series,** Red body with black running boards, opening tailgate, red multi-spoked wheels, 1:43 scale, Model No. YTC06-M
EX n/a   NM n/a   MIP $30

❑ **1938 Studebaker Coupe Express K-Model,** Yellow body, opening tailgate, yellow wheels with silver hubcaps, black running boards, 1:43 scale, Model No. YTC05-M
EX n/a   NM n/a   MIP $30

❑ **1939 Reo Speed Delivery Vehicle,** Cream-colored body, red grille, red stripe on sides of cab and hood, red wheels with silver hubcaps, black step boards, 1:43 scale, Model No. YTC04-M
EX n/a   NM n/a   MIP $30

❑ **1940 Ford Pickup Truck,** Red body, whitewall tires, opening tailgate, 1:43 scale, Model No. YTC03-M
EX n/a   NM n/a   MIP $30

❑ **1941 Chevrolet Model AK 1/2 Ton,** Blue body, black fenders and running board, silver grille, 1:43 scale, Model No. YTC01-M
EX n/a   NM n/a   MIP $30

❑ **1946 Dodge Power Wagon WDX,** Dark green body with black fenders and running board. A civilian update of the Power Wagon used by the Army during World War II, 1:43 scale, Model No. YTC02-M
EX n/a   NM n/a   MIP $30

WORK HORSES: AMERICAN GIANTS

❑ **1953 Ford: Parts and Service,** Red body with "Genuine Ford Parts" blue oval logos on doors, blue engine block cargo in bed, silver hubs, 1:43 scale, Model No. YIS06-M
EX n/a   NM n/a   MIP $30

❑ **1954 Ford: Pennsylvania Railroad,** Red body with orange dome light on roof, track inspection roller trucks at front and rear, twin silver spotlights near cab, Pennsilvania Railroad logo on doors, 1:43 scale, Model No. YIS05-M
EX n/a   NM n/a   MIP $30

❑ **1955 Chevy Pickup: Harley-Davidson,** Black body with Harley-Davidson logo on doors, stake bed with "Genuine Parts" in black lettering, cargo in back, 1:43 scale, Model No. YIS01-M
EX n/a   NM n/a   MIP $30

❑ **1955 Ford: Caterpillar,** Yellow body with black roof and "Peoria Tractor & Equipment Co." on doors and Caterpillar logo on rear fenders. Tractor tire cargo load in bed, 1:43 scale, Model No. YIS02-M
EX n/a   NM n/a   MIP $30

❑ **1956 Chevy Pickup: Chevrolet Service,** Light blue body with Chevrolet logo on doors, "Genuine Parts" on fenders, engine block cargo load in back, 1:43 scale, Model No. YIS03-M
EX n/a   NM n/a   MIP $30

❑ **1957 Chevy Pickup: American Airlines,** White body with blue roof, orange dome light, American Airlines logos on doors, blue hubs, luggage cargo in bed, 1:43 scale, Model No. YIS04-M
EX n/a   NM n/a   MIP $30

WORK HORSES: EVOLUTION OF THE 4x4

❑ **1947 Jeep CJ2A,** Olive-green civilian version of Jeep, with khaki softtop roof and black interior, 1:43 scale, Model No. YYM35055
EX n/a   NM n/a   MIP $30

❑ **1948 Dodge Power Wagon,** Red body with black fenders and running board, opening tailgate, 1:43 scale, Model No. YYM35053
EX n/a   NM n/a   MIP $30

❑ **1948 Land Rover Series I,** Green body with tan softtop roof, knobby tires, spare on hood, 1:43 scale, Model No. YYM35054
EX n/a   NM n/a   MIP $30

❑ **1961 International Scout 80,** Pale yellow body with white roof, black interior, black wheels with silver hubcaps, opening rear tailgate, 1:43 scale, Model No. YYM35056
EX n/a   NM n/a   MIP $30

❑ **1966 Ford Bronco,** Dark green with white roof, white interior, opening rear tailgate and hatch, silver hubcaps, gray bumpers, 1:43 scale, Model No. YYM35057
EX n/a   NM n/a   MIP $30

❑ **1969 Chevrolet K/5 Blazer,** Orange body with white roof, dark gray interior, 1:43 scale, Model No. YYM35058
EX n/a   NM n/a   MIP $30

Work Horses: Great Outdoors

❑ **1946 Dodge Power Wagon,** Yellow body with red fenders and "White Tail Reserve" graphics on doors, 1:43 scale, Model No. YYM38051
EX n/a   NM n/a   MIP $30

❑ **1947 Jeep CJ2A,** Red body with silver windshield and rollbars, "Bass Heaven" and "Lake Harpon" in yellow type, fishing rods strapped to top of rollbars, gray interior, 1:43 scale, Model No. YYM38053
EX n/a   NM n/a   MIP $30

❑ **1948 Land Rover,** View of rear of vehicle showing hunting dog and gear, 1:43 scale, Model No. YYM38052
EX n/a   NM n/a   MIP $30

❑ **1948 Land Rover,** Dark blue and red body with rollcage-mounted spotlights, "UK Pheasant Club" on sides, Retriever graphic on doors, dog figure in back, knobby tires, silver wheels, winch and bumpers, 1:43 scale, Model No. YYM38052
EX n/a   NM n/a   MIP $30

❑ **1961 International Scout 80,** Blue body with white top, gray roof rack with red canoe, "Matura Brown Trout--Queenstown, New Zealand" on doors, black interior, 1:43 scale, Model No. YYM38054
EX n/a   NM n/a   MIP $30

❑ **1966 Ford Bronco,** White body with green top and green trim, "Marlin Adventures" on doors, fishing poles and cooler on gray roof rack, 1:43 scale, Model No. YYM38055
EX n/a   NM n/a   MIP $30

❑ **1969 Chevrolet K/5 Blazer,** Silver and blue body with "Mallard Acres--Chesapeake Bay, Maryland" on doors. Yellow boat on roof rack, 1:43 scale, Model No. YYM38056
EX n/a   NM n/a   MIP $30

Work Horses: Highway Commanders

❑ **Freightliner,** White and green cabover with gray grille and wheels, 1:58 scale, Model No. KS195/A-M
EX n/a   NM n/a   MIP $40

❑ **Kenworth,** Medium blue conventional tractor with red stripes along sides, silver grille, stacks and wheels, 1:58 scale, Model No. KS194/A-M
EX n/a   NM n/a   MIP $40

❑ **Peterbilt,** Dark green conventional tractor with silver grille, wheels and highlights, 1:58 scale, Model No. KS193/A-M
EX n/a   NM n/a   MIP $40

Work Horses: Road Service Collection

❑ **1953 Ford F100: Flying A Tire Service,** Black body with white roof, silver wheels, set of tires and compressor in bed of truck, Flying A logo on doors, "Joe's Roadside Service" on front fenders, 1:43 scale, Model No. YRS02-M
EX n/a   NM n/a   MIP $30

❑ **1954 Ford F100: Sinclair Snow Plow,** Dark green body with yellow snowplow blade on front, Sinclair dinosaur logo on doors, chains on rear tires, gas cans and other gear in bed, 1:43 scale, Model No. YRS04-M
EX n/a   NM n/a   MIP $30

❑ **1955 Chevy 3100: AAA Towing,** Red body with gray towing boom, red dome light, red wheels, "Emergency AAA Service" on doors, "Fred's Service" on rear fenders, "24 HR. Towing" on sides of hood, 1:43 scale, Model No. YRS01-M
EX n/a   NM n/a   MIP $30

❑ **1956 Chevy 3100: Mobil Battery,** Blue body with modified bumper, Mobilgas logo on doors, battery charging gear in back, opening tailgate, 1:43 scale, Model No. YRS03-M
EX n/a   NM n/a   MIP $30

❑ **1956 Ford F100: Red Crown,** White truck body with black roof and tonneau cover over bed. "Santa Fe" and Red Crown Gasoline logo on doors, "Radio Dispatched" with radio tower graphic on rear fenders, 1:43 scale, Model No. YRS06/BM
EX n/a   NM n/a   MIP $30

❑ **1957 Chevy 3100: Dixie Gas,** Pale yellow body with black roof and stakeside bed with "Ray's Service" and Dixie Gasoline logo on doors, 1:43 scale, Model No. YRS05-M
EX n/a   NM n/a   MIP $30

Work Horses: Small Town Pickups

❑ **1934 International Pickup,** Pale yellow body with black fenders and running boards, yellow spoked wheels, bales and sacks in truck bed, "Wilson's Grain and Feed" on doors, 1:43 scale, Model No. YYM38039
EX n/a   NM n/a   MIP $30

❑ **1939 REO Pickup,** Dark green body with "Stone Brick and Masonry--Forgione" on doors, load of bricks in back, silver hubcaps, 1:43 scale, Model No. YYM38041
EX n/a   NM n/a   MIP $30

❑ **1940 Ford Pickup,** Dark purple body with black running boards and fenders, lumber in truck bed, "Murdock Lumber and Millwork" on doors, 1:43 scale, Model No. YYM38040
EX n/a   NM n/a   MIP $30

❑ **1941 Chevrolet Pickup,** Bright medium-blue body with milk cans in truck bed, and "Kent's Dairy--Grade A Milk" on doors, 1:43 scale, Model No. YYM38042
EX n/a   NM n/a   MIP $30

❑ **1948 Holden Pickup,** Yellow body with black tonneau cover over bed, "Mr. Fixit Handyman Service & Repairs" on doors, "Service At Your Door" on sides, 1:43 scale, Model No. YYM38035
EX n/a   NM n/a   MIP $30

❑ **1953 Ford F100 Pickup,** Bright orange-red body with "Custer Dry Goods" on doors, ladder and bags in back, spotlights near doors on cab, 1:43 scale, Model No. YYM38038

EX n/a   NM n/a   MIP $30

WORK HORSES: STEAM POWERED VEHICLES I

❏ **1829 Stephenson's Rocket,** Yellow and black model of the early train "Rocket." white stack, gold piston, Model No. YAS01-M

EX n/a   NM n/a   MIP $29

❏ **1894 Aveling & Porter Steam Roller,** Blue and black body with gold-colored highlights, "Bluebell" on sides, "Alconbury-Huntingdon" and "P.B. Coulson & Sons" on canopy, Model No. YAS03-M

EX n/a   NM n/a   MIP $29

❏ **1905 Fowler/Showman's Engine,** Red steam engine, white canopy with "John Hoadley's Mammoth Fair" on sides, black and gold smokestack, Model No. YAS05-M

EX n/a   NM n/a   MIP $29

❏ **1917 Yorkshire Steam Wagon,** Black and red body, red spoked wheels, silver stack, stones in truck bed, Model No. YAS04-M

EX n/a   NM n/a   MIP $29

❏ **1918 Atkinson Logger,** Green cab and bed, red chassis, silver stack through cab, logs on back, Model No. YAS06-M

EX n/a   NM n/a   MIP $29

❏ **1922 Foden Coal Truck,** Cream-colored body with red chassis and roof, gold-colored stack in front, red spoked wheels, coal load in back, Model No. YAS02-M

EX n/a   NM n/a   MIP $29

WORK HORSES: STEAM POWERED VEHICLES II

❏ **1912 Burrel Traction Engine,** Model No. YAS08-M

EX n/a   NM n/a   MIP $29

❏ **1917 Yorkshire Steam Lorry,** Red-brown body with black chassis, white lettering on sides, "1087 Great Western Railway Co.", white spoked wheels, railroad ties load in truck bed, Model No. YAS11-M

EX n/a   NM n/a   MIP $29

❏ **1918 Atkinson Steam Wagon,** Yellow cab and bed, black chassis, solid yellow wheels, silver boiler and stack, bricks, wheelbarrow and shovel on flatbed, "City of Westminster Works, Sewers & Highways" on sides, Model No. YAS10-M

EX n/a   NM n/a   MIP $29

❏ **1922 Foden Steam Wagon,** White body, black roof, black interior, gold stack in front, yellow spoked wheels, barrel load in truck bed, "R. Brett & Sons" letting on sides, Model No. YAS12-M

EX n/a   NM n/a   MIP $29

❏ **1929 Fowler Crane Engine,** Black engine, canopy, wheels and crane boom, yellow stripe highlighted trim, gray "tires", Model No. YAS07-M

EX n/a   NM n/a   MIP $29

❏ **1930 Garrett Steam Truck with Barrels,** Dark blue cab, bed and chassis, pipe section load, pale yellow lettering, "Rainford Potteries Ltd." on sides, red spoked wheels, Model No. YAS09-M

EX n/a   NM n/a   MIP $29

WORK HORSES: TROLLEYS, TRAMS AND BUSES

❏ **1923 Scania Post Bus: Stockholm,** Dark blue body, gold wheels and grille, white roof with "Kaffe DG Rich" sign, "Stockholm Automobil Trafik Aktiebolag" in white type on sides, Model No. YET04

EX n/a   NM n/a   MIP $20

WORK HORSES: VINTAGE BIG RIG CABS

❏ **1939 Peterbilt,** Blue cab, white doors and bumper, black hood, blue and silver wheel rims, black interior, silver grille, 1:50 scale, Model No. DYM35216

EX n/a   NM n/a   MIP $40

❏ **1948 Diamond T,** Red and black cab, black chassis, red wheels, silver grille and stacks, beige interior, 1:50 scale, Model No. DYM35217

EX n/a   NM n/a   MIP $40

Paul's Model Art Minichamps

Mercedes-Benz 03500 Bus, from 1954. The details on this model include removable cloth roof section, realistic chrome luggage racks, mesh cargo holds above seats and authentic colors.

Minichamps, or "Paul's Model Art Minichamps" as they are known, are impressive die-cast vehicles, and specialize in vehicles you usually don't see other companies producing. (Don't look for any '57 Chevys in their lineup.)

The company was founded in Aachen, Germany in 1990, by Paul Lang, the first model being an Audi V8 Quattro. While they focus primarily on 1:43-scale vehicles, they have more recently branched out and are creating 1:18-scale editions of Formula 1 cars, WRC cars and European and Japanese trucks and road cars.

Most of Minichamps vehicles are produced in limited editions, (the Ford Focus WRC, Rally Finland, for instance, is one of 1,008 pieces), so they do actually have some exclusivity. More and more American die-cast dealers are selling Minichamps models, and there is a brisk trade in them on eBay.

MARKET UPDATE

Most of Minichamps' 1:43-scale vehicles retail for around $30, a bit more for Formula 1 cars. Because the American market for such vehicles is limited, the prices are generally stable. However, since the supply is likewise limited, you can have a tough time finding the model you're looking for, especially if it's a few years old.

New 1:18-scale models are priced similarly to other high-end die-cast collectible models—expect to pay about $70 for each model— sometimes more. Of course, the payoff is great detail and a die-cast car that you're unlikely to find on another collector's shelf.

This Magirus S 6500 Aerial Ladder from 1955 features a working extension ladder and levelers.

Minichamps is known for making highly-detailed models of European vehicles. This Boehringer Unimog 70200, from 1949 is just one example.

Another modern and popular model produced by Minichamps: The 2001 Mini Cooper. This 1:43-scale model shows plenty of detail—especially with a sunroof.

A more classically-styled vehicle, the 1964 Porsche 911, a 1:43-scale model.

Like many military vehicle models, both metal and plastic, this late-version Jagdpanther is built to 1:35-scale.

Minichamps is famous for their Formula 1 race car models. This Williams Ford FW 07 (driven by A. Jones in 1979) is another offshoot in their lineup of 1:43-scale cars.

Modern road cars are also a specialty for Minichamps. This 1:43-scale Volvo V70 XC almost looks like it could drive out of the showroom. This model is available in black or silver.

A not-so-new vehicle, the Opel Rekord Caravan P1. This model of a bulky, 1958 station wagon is obviously foreign, but oddly familiar, in a 1950s-old-car way.

1:12/1:18-SCALE

❏ **BMW F 650 Cross, 1997,** Dark metallic gray body, black seat, gray engine, 1:18 scale, Model No. 182 026660

EX n/a   NM n/a   MIP $48

❏ **BMW F 650 ST, 1997,** Red with black seat, silver engine, silver wheels, 1:18 scale, Model No. 182 026650

EX n/a   NM n/a   MIP $48

❏ **BMW R 1100 S, 1997,** Black with red seat, silver gray wheels, silver engine, 1:18 scale, Model No. 182 027000

EX n/a   NM n/a   MIP $48

❏ **BWM R32, 1923,** Black and silver body, tan seat, silver engine, 1:18 scale, Model No. 182 027100

EX n/a   NM n/a   MIP $48

1:12-SCALE

❏ **BSA Goldstar DB 34, 1956,** 2002, Black with silver engine, 1:12 scale, Model No. 122 130000

EX n/a   NM n/a   MIP $99

❏ **Ducati 996 R Superbike 2001 Imola Team Ducati Infostrada,** 2002, Troy Bayliss. Silver bike with Shell logo and number "21" on front and behind seat, 1:12 scale, Model No. 122 011271

EX n/a   NM n/a   MIP $63

❏ **Ducati 996 R Superbike 2001 Team Ducati Infostrada,** Ruben Xaus. Red and white with Shell logo and number "11" on front and behind seat, 1:12 scale, Model No. 122 011211

EX n/a   NM n/a   MIP $63

❏ **Ducati 996 R Superbike 2001 Team Ducati Infostrada,** Troy Bayliss. Red bike with Shell logos and number "21" on front and behind seat, 1:12 scale, Model No. 122 011221

EX n/a   NM n/a   MIP $63

❏ **Ducati 996 R Superbike 2001 Team Ducati Infostrada,** Carl Fogarty. Red bike with Shell logo and number "1" on front and behind seat, 1:12 scale, Model No. 122 001201

EX n/a   NM n/a   MIP $63

❏ **Ducati 996 R Superbike 2001 Team Ducati L&M,** Ben Bostrom. Red, white and blue with number

"155" on front and behind seat, 1:12 scale, Model No. 122 011255

EX n/a   NM n/a   MIP $63

(Minichamps Photo)

❏ **Ducati 996 Superbike 2001 Team GSE-Racing,** 2002, Neil Hodgson. Orange, white and blue bike with "Hitachi" on sides and number "100" on front and behind seat, 1:12 scale, Model No. 122 011200

EX n/a   NM n/a   MIP $63

❏ **Ducati 996 Superbike, 2001 Team Reve-Racing,** 2002, John Reynolds, blue and yellow bike with "Red Bull" graphics, 1:12 scale, Model No. 122 011203

EX n/a   NM n/a   MIP $63

❏ **Ducati 996, Street Version,** 2002, Red body, black seat, charcoal wheels, "996" on sides, 1:12 scale, Model No. 122 120000

EX n/a   NM n/a   MIP $63

❏ **Ducati Monster (620, 750, 900) I.E.,** 2002, Yellow and charcoal body, black seat, white muffler, 1:12 scale, Model No. 122 120102

EX n/a   NM n/a   MIP $63

❏ **Ducati Monster S4 Anthracite,** 2002, Charcoal body, orange wheels, white muffler, 1:12 scale, Model No. 122 120121

EX n/a   NM n/a   MIP $63

❏ **Ducati Monster S4 Fogarty,** 2002, Red and gray with Ducati emblem on tank, 1:12 scale, Model No. 122 120130

EX n/a   NM n/a   MIP $63

(Minichamps Photo)

❏ **Honda NSR 500, 500 CC GP 2000,** 2002, Team Nastro Azzuro: Valentino Rossi. Yellow and blue with number "46" on front and behind seat, 1:12 scale, Model No. 122 006146

EX n/a   NM n/a   MIP $63

(Minichamps Photo)

❏ **Honda NSR 500, 500 CC GP 2001,** 2002, Team West Honda Pons: Alex Barros. Green and white with "Alex" on sides and number "4" on front and behind seat, 1:12 scale, Model No. 122 016104

EX n/a   NM n/a   MIP $63

❏ **Honda NSR 500, 500 CC GP 2001,** 2002, Team West Honda Pons: Loris Capirossi. Black with "elf" in white type and number "65" on front and behind seat, 1:12 scale, Model No. 122 016165

EX n/a   NM n/a   MIP $63

❏ **Honda NSR 500, 500 CC GP 2001,** 2002, Team Repsol YPF Honda 2001: Tohru Ukawa. Dark blue and yellow with number "11" on front and on sides behind seat, 1:12 scale, Model No. 122 016111

EX n/a   NM n/a   MIP $63

❏ **Honda NSR 500, 500 CC GP 2001,** 2002, Team Repsol YPF Honda: Alex Riville. Dark blue and yellow with number "28" in white type on front and sides behind seat, 1:12 scale, Model No. 122 016128

EX n/a   NM n/a   MIP $63

❏ **Honda NSR 500, 500 CC GP 2001,** 2002, Team Nastro Azzuro: Valentino Rossi. Dark blue and yellow with number "46" on front and sides behind seat, 1:12 scale, Model No. 122 016146

EX n/a   NM n/a   MIP $63

❏ **Kawasaki Z1 900 Super 4, 1972,** 2002, Yellow and black body, black seat, silver engine, 1:12 scale, Model No. 122 164100

EX n/a   NM n/a   MIP $99

❑ **McLaren F1 Dark Blue Metallic,** 1:12 scale, Model No. 530 133128
EX n/a   NM n/a   MIP n/a

❑ **Muench TTS, 1966-81,** 2002, Blue body, black seat, wide rear wheel, silver engine, 1:12 scale, Model No. 122 011000
EX n/a   NM n/a   MIP $99

❑ **Norton Commando, 1968,** 2002, Green body, black seat, silver engine, 1:12 scale, Model No. 122 132000
EX n/a   NM n/a   MIP $99

❑ **Suzuki RGV-Gamma 500 CC GP 2000,** 2002, Team Telefonica Movistar: Kenny Roberts. Dark blue with yellow checkered flag design, number "2" on front and behind seat, 1:12 scale, Model No. 122 006202
EX n/a   NM n/a   MIP $63

❑ **Suzuki RGV-Gamma 500 CC GP 2001,** 2002, Team Telefonica Movistar: Sete Gibernau. Dark blue with number "15" on front and behind seat, 1:12 scale, Model No. 122 016215
EX n/a   NM n/a   MIP $63

❑ **Suzuki RGV-Gamma 500 GP 2001,** 2002, Team Telefonica Movistar: Kenny Roberts. Dark blue with yellow number "1" on front and behind seat, 1:12 scale, Model No. 122 016201
EX n/a   NM n/a   MIP $63

❑ **Triumph Bonneville 650 T120, 1959,** 2002, White and red tank, white fenders, silver engine, 1:12 scale, Model No. 122 133000
EX n/a   NM n/a   MIP $99

(Minichamps Photo)

❑ **Yamaha YZR 500, 500 CC GP 2000,** 2002, Team Marlboro Yamaha: Max Biaggi. Red and black with "Yamaha" in white type, Michelin man graphics and number "4" on front and behind seat, 1:12 scale, Model No. 122 006304
EX n/a   NM n/a   MIP $63

❑ **Yamaha YZR 500, 500 CC GP 2001,** 2002, Team Marlboro Yamaha: Carlos Checa. Red with white number "7" on front and sides behind seat, 1:12 scale, Model No. 122 016307
EX n/a   NM n/a   MIP $63

❑ **Yamaha YZR 500, 500 CC GP 2001,** 2002, Team Gauloises Yamaha Tech 3: Olivier Jacque. Blue and yellow with number "19" on front and sides behind seat, 1:12 scale, Model No. 122 016319
EX n/a   NM n/a   MIP $63

❑ **Yamaha YZR 500, 500 CC GP 2001,** 2002, Team Gauloises Yamaha Tech 3: Shinja Nakano. Blue and yellow with orange number "56" on front and sides behind seat, 1:12 scale, Model No. 122 016356
EX n/a   NM n/a   MIP $63

❑ **Yamaha YZR 500, 500 CC GP 2001,** 2002, Team Antena 3 Yamaha: Norifumi Abe. Red, black and white with number "6" on front and sides, 1:12 scale, Model No. 122 016306
EX n/a   NM n/a   MIP $63

❑ **Yamaha YZR 500, 500 CC GP 2001,** 2002, Team Antena 3 Yamaha: Jose Luis Cardoso. Red, white and black with number "10" on front and on sides behind seat, 1:12 scale, Model No. 122 016310
EX n/a   NM n/a   MIP $63

❑ **Yamaha YZR 500, 500 CC GP 2001,** 2002, Team Marlboro Yamaha: Max Biaggi. Red bike with number "3" on front and behind seat, 1:12 scale, Model No. 122 016303
EX n/a   NM n/a   MIP $63

1:18/1:43-SCALE

❑ **Jack Set 3 Figurines 2 Jacks/1 Signboard,** 1:18 scale, Model No. 318 100024
EX n/a   NM n/a   MIP $38

❑ **Jack Set: 3 Figurines 2 Jacks/ 1 Signboard,** 1:43 scale, Model No. 343 100024
EX n/a   NM n/a   MIP $27

❑ **McLaren Ford M23: D. Hulme 1973,** 2002, 1:43 scale, Model No. 530 734307
EX n/a   NM n/a   MIP $40

❑ **McLaren Ford M23: E. Fittipaldi 1974,** 2002, 1:43 scale, Model No. 530 744305
EX n/a   NM n/a   MIP $38

❑ **McLaren Ford M23: J. Hunt 1976,** 2002, 1:18 scale, Model No. 530 761811
EX n/a   NM n/a   MIP $116

(Minichamps Photo)

❑ **McLaren Ford M23: J. Hunt 1976,** 2002, 1:43 scale, Model No. 530 764311
EX n/a   NM n/a   MIP $40

❑ **McLaren Ford M23: J. Mass 1976,** 2002, 1:18 scale, Model No. 530 761812
EX n/a   NM n/a   MIP $116

(Minichamps Photo)

❑ **McLaren Ford M23: J. Mass 1976,** 2002, 1:43 scale, Model No. 530 764312
EX n/a   NM n/a   MIP $40

(Minichamps Photo)

❑ **McLaren Ford M23: P. Revson 1973,** 2002, 1:43 scale, Model No. 530 734308
EX n/a   NM n/a   MIP $40

(Minichamps Photo)

❑ **McLaren Honda MP4-7: G. Berger 1992,** 2002, 1:18 scale, Model No. 530 921802
EX n/a   NM n/a   MIP $75

❑ **Porsche 917/20 "Pink Pig",** Joest and Kauhsen, 24-hour Le Mans, 1971. Light pink body with names and dashed lines in red. Detailed interior, opening doors, removable rear body section, incredible engine detail, working steering, engine sound. Comes in a presentation box with history of vehicle, limited to 9,999 pieces, 1:18 scale, Model No. 186 716923
EX n/a   NM n/a   MIP $138

❑ **Porsche 917/20 "Pink Pig",** Joest and Kauhsen, 24-hour Le Mans, 1971. Light pink body with names and dashed lines in red, number "23" on front, sides and rear. Comes in a presentation box with history of vehicle, limited to 10,001 pieces, 1:43 scale, Model No. 430 716923
EX n/a   NM n/a   MIP $73

❑ **Porsche 917/30,** M. Donohue Can-Am Champion 1973. Dark blue and yellow with "Sunoco" on spoiler and front, number "6" on front and sides. Comes in a presentation box with a history of the car. Limited to 9,999 pieces, 1:43 scale, Model No. 436 736006
EX n/a   NM n/a   MIP $76

❑ **Porsche 917/30,** M. Donohue Can-Am Champion 1973. Dark blue and yellow with yellow and blue rims, "Sunoco" on spoiler and front. Great detail, including removable rear body, opening doors, intricate engine and interior detailing, and working steering. Like its 1:43-scale counterpart, it too comes in a presentation box with a history of the vehicle. Limited to 9,999 pieces, 1:18 scale, Model No. 186 736006
EX n/a   NM n/a   MIP $138

❑ **Refueller Set: 2 Figurines 1 Fuel Rig,** 1:43 scale, Model No. 343 100021
EX n/a   NM n/a   MIP $27

❑ **Refueller Set: 2 Figurines 1 Fuel Rig,** 1:18 scale, Model No. 318 100021
EX n/a   NM n/a   MIP $38

❑ **Tire Change Set: 3 Figurines 1 Front Wheel,** 1:43 scale, Model No. 343 100022
EX n/a   NM n/a   MIP $27

❑ **Tire Change Set: 3 Figurines 1 Front Wheel,** 1:18 scale, Model No. 318 100022
EX n/a   NM n/a   MIP $38

❑ **Tire Change Set: 3 Figurines 1 Rear Wheel,** 1:43 scale, Model No. 343 100023
EX n/a   NM n/a   MIP $27

❑ **Tire Change Set: 3 Figurines 1 Rear Wheel,** 1:18 scale, Model No. 318 100023
EX n/a   NM n/a   MIP $38

1:18-SCALE

❑ **Alfa Romeo 2000 Spider 1970,** Red convertible body, opening doors, hood and trunk, working steering and realistic operating suspension, 1:18 scale, Model No. 180 120930
EX n/a   NM n/a   MIP $75

❑ **Alfa Romeo Giulia 1300 Super 1970,** Red four-door body, opening doors, hood and trunk, tan interior, working steering, detailed engine and interior, gray grille, bumpers and trim, 1:18 scale, Model No. 180 120901
EX n/a   NM n/a   MIP $75

❑ **Alfa Romeo Giulia 1300 Super 1971,** Ochre, 1:18 scale, Model No. 180 120900
EX n/a   NM n/a   MIP $75

❑ **Alfa Romeo Giulia 1600 1970: Carabinieri,** Black body with white roof, blue dome light, "Carabinieri" in white type on sides, four opening doors, opening hood and trunk, light tan interior, detailed engine, 1:18 scale, Model No. 180 120990
EX n/a   NM n/a   MIP $75

❑ **Alfa Romeo Giulia 1600, 1970: Polizia,** 2002, Black body with white roof, "Carabinieri" in white type on sides, 1:18 scale, Model No. 180 120991
EX n/a   NM n/a   MIP $75

❑ **Arrows Asiatech A22,** J. Verstappen. Orange and black with "Orange" on sides and spoiler, silver wheels, sponsor graphics, number "14" on nose, 1:18 scale, Model No. 100 010014
EX n/a   NM n/a   MIP $75

❑ **Arrows Asiatech A22,** E. Bernoldi. Orange and black, "Orange" on sides and spoiler, silver wheels, sponsor graphics, number "15" on nose, 1:18 scale, Model No. 100 010015
EX n/a   NM n/a   MIP $75

(Minichamps Photo)

❑ **Bar Honda 03,** 2002, J. Villeneuve. White with black and red circle graphics, Red "Honda" type, "Look Alive" on spoiler, number "10" in black circle on nose of car, black wheels, "Bridgestone" tires, 1:18 scale, Model No. 100 010010
EX n/a   NM n/a   MIP $75

(Minichamps Photo)

❑ **Bar Honda 03,** 2002, O. Panis. White with red and black graphics, "Honda" in red type, number "9" on reversed out in white type from black circle on nose, black wheels, "Bridgestone" tires, 1:18 scale, Model No. 100 010009
EX n/a   NM n/a   MIP $75

❑ **Benetton BMW B186: G. Berger 1986,** 1:18 scale, Model No. 181 860020
EX n/a   NM n/a   MIP n/a

❑ **Benetton Renault B201,** 2002, Fisichella and Giancarlo, 2001, 1:18 scale, Model No. 100 010007
EX n/a   NM n/a   MIP $75

❏ **BMW 1600 Cabriolet 1967,** 2002, Orange, 1:18 scale, Model No. 100 021030
EX n/a   NM n/a   MIP $75

❏ **BMW 2000 TII Touring 1971,** 2002, Light Blue Metallic, 1:18 scale, Model No. 100 021010
EX n/a   NM n/a   MIP $75

❏ **BMW 3.0 CSL, 1972,** Silver coupe body, black interior, opening trunk, hood and doors, silver spoked wheels, working steering, detailed engine, 1:18 scale, Model No. 180 029020
EX n/a   NM n/a   MIP $75

❏ **BMW 320I GR.5 "Jaegermeister" DRM Eifelrennen '77 Div. 2 Winner: H.J. Stuck,** 2002, 1:18 scale, Model No. 180 772115
EX n/a   NM n/a   MIP $80

❏ **BMW 320I GR.5 "Warsteiner" DRM 1977: Joerg Obermoser,** 1:18 scale, Model No. 180 772105
EX n/a   NM n/a   MIP $80

❏ **BMW 320I GR.5 'Fruit Of The Loom' DRM 1977: P. Schneeberger,** 2002, 1:18 scale, Model No. 180 772108
EX n/a   NM n/a   MIP $80

(Minichamps Photo)

❏ **BMW CSL 3.5,** 2002, IMSA 1976 Winner, 24-hour Daytona. White body and spoiler, red and light and dark blue stripes, silver spoked wheels, number "59" on hood and sides. Opening hood, trunk and doors, detailed engine and interior, working steering, 1:18 scale, Model No. 180 762959
EX n/a   NM n/a   MIP $80

❏ **BMW CSL 3.5 GR. 5 "Gosser Bier" Nuerburgring 1000KM Winners: Quester/Krebs,** 2002, 1:18 scale, Model No. 180 762007
EX n/a   NM n/a   MIP $80

❏ **BMW CSL 3.5 GR. 5 'Hermetite',** 2002, 1:18 scale, Model No. 180 762004
EX n/a   NM n/a   MIP $80

❏ **BMW CSL 3.5 IMSA Winners: Redman/Moffat/Posey/Stuck Sebring 12 HRS. 1975,** 2002, 1:18 scale, Model No. 180 752925
EX n/a   NM n/a   MIP $80

❏ **BMW M1 "Muenchen" Le Mans 24 HRS. 1981: Danner/Von Bayern/Oberndorfer,** 2002, 1:18 scale, Model No. 180 812971
EX n/a   NM n/a   MIP $80

❏ **BMW M1 Denim Team GS Sport Procar Series 1980: Heyer, Hans,** 2002, 1:18 scale, Model No. 180 802981
EX n/a   NM n/a   MIP $80

❏ **BMW M1, "Kreistelefonbuch",** Team Winkelhock Procar Series, 1979: M. Winkelhock. Yellow body with "Kreis telefonbuch" on sides, front, roof and spoiler in black type. Opening doors and rear hood, detailed engine and interior, black wheels, "Dunlop" tires, working steering, 1:18 scale, Model No. 180 792981
EX n/a   NM n/a   MIP $80

(Minichamps Photo)

❏ **BMW M1, Carte De France,** 2002, Team BMW France, 24-hour Le Mans: D. Quester 1980. Pink, white, green and blue all-over map graphics (carte), number "83" on front and sides, silver wheels. Opening doors and rear hood, detailed engine and interior, working steering, 1:18 scale, Model No. 180 802983
EX n/a   NM n/a   MIP $80

❏ **BMW M3 "Blauplunkt" DTM Norisring 1987 Winner: Olaf Manthey,** 2002, 1:18 scale, Model No. 180 872024
EX n/a   NM n/a   MIP $80

❏ **BMW M3 "Jagermeister" DTM Avus 1988: M. Ketterer,** 2002, 1:18 scale, Model No. 180 882039
EX n/a   NM n/a   MIP $80

❏ **BMW M3 Street 1987,** 2002, Black, 1:18 scale, Model No. 180 020300
EX n/a   NM n/a   MIP $75

❏ **BMW Z1 1988,** 2002, Black, 1:18 scale, Model No. 180 020100
EX n/a   NM n/a   MIP $75

❏ **Brabham BMW BT52: N. Piquet 1983,** 1:18 scale, Model No. 181 830005
EX n/a   NM n/a   MIP $100

❏ **Fiat X1/9, 1974,** 2002, Red, 1:18 scale, Model No. 100 121660
EX n/a   NM n/a   MIP $75

❏ **Ford Capri 1969,** Red body, opening doors, hood and trunk, working steering, detailed engine and interior, 1:18 scale, Model No. 180 089001
EX n/a   NM n/a   MIP $75

❏ **Ford Capri 1969,** Light Green Metallic, 1:18 scale, Model No. 180 089000
EX n/a   NM n/a   MIP $75

❏ **Ford Capri RS 1970,** Yellow body with black hood, silver-gray spoked wheels, opening hood and doors, detailed engine and interior, working steering, 1:18 scale, Model No. 180 089070
EX n/a   NM n/a   MIP $75

❏ **Ford Ranger, 1999,** Red body, opening doors, hood and tailgate, black bedliner, silver-gray six spoke wheels, gray interior, 1:18 scale, Model No. AC8 089100
EX n/a   NM n/a   MIP $75

❏ **Ford Sierra Cosworth "LUI" DTM 1988: Manuel Reuter,** 1:18 scale, Model No. 100 888005
EX n/a   NM n/a   MIP $80

❏ **Ford Sierra Cosworth "Speedware" DTM 1988 Champion: Klaus Ludwig,** 1:18 scale, Model No. 100 888018
EX n/a   NM n/a   MIP $80

❏ **Jordan 191,** 2002, A. De Cesaris, 1991. Green and blue, with "7up" behind driver and "Fujifilm" logo on sides, 1:18 scale, Model No. 100 910031
EX n/a   NM n/a   MIP $80

❏ **Jordan 191: M. Schumacher 1991,** 2002, 1:18 scale, Model No. 100 910032
EX n/a   NM n/a   MIP $80

(Minichamps Photo)

❏ **London Taxi, 1989,** 2002, Black body, opening hood and rear doors, gray trim, folding seats and interior detail, working steering, detailed engine, 1:18 scale, Model No. 180 136000
EX n/a   NM n/a   MIP $75

(Minichamps Photo)

❏ **Lotus Honda 99T: S. Nakajima 1987,** 2002, 1:18 scale, Model No. 180 870011
EX n/a   NM n/a   MIP $75

❏ **Lotus Renault 97T,** 1985, 1:18 scale, Model No. 540 851812
EX n/a   NM n/a   MIP n/a

❏ **Lotus Renault 98T,** 1986, 1:18 scale, Model No. 540 861812
EX n/a   NM n/a   MIP n/a

❏ **Lotus Renault 98T,** J. Dumfries, 1986, 1:18 scale, Model No. 180 860011
EX n/a   NM n/a   MIP $75

❏ **McLaren Ford M23,** 2002, World Champion: Emerson Fittipaldi, 1974. Red and white with "Texaco" on sides, front and spoiler and number "5" on sides and front, 1:18 scale, Model No. 530 741805
EX n/a   NM n/a   MIP $116

❏ **McLaren Mercedes MP4-16: D. Coulthard 2001,** 1:18 scale, Model No. 530 011804
EX n/a   NM n/a   MIP $75

❏ **McLaren Mercedes MP4-16: M. Hakkinen 2001,** 1:18 scale, Model No. 530 011803
EX n/a   NM n/a   MIP $75

❏ **Morris Minor 1959,** 2002, Light Blue, 1:18 scale, Model No. 100 137000
EX n/a   NM n/a   MIP $75

❏ **Morris Minor Cabriolet 1959,** 2002, Black, 1:18 scale, Model No. 100 137030
EX n/a   NM n/a   MIP $75

❏ **Morris Minor Traveller 1959,** 2002, White, 1:18 scale, Model No. 100 137010
EX n/a   NM n/a   MIP $75

(Minichamps Photo)

❏ **Opel GT 1900 1968,** 2002, Red body, detailed black interior, working steering, opening doors and hood, 1:18 scale, Model No. 180 049022
EX n/a   NM n/a   MIP $75

❏ **Opel GT/J 1900, 1971,** Yellow body, detailed black interior, opening hood and doors, working steering, moveable headlights, 1:18 scale, Model No. 180 049021
EX n/a   NM n/a   MIP $75

❏ **Opel Kadett C Coupe 1973,** 2002, Green, 1:18 scale, Model No. 180 045620
EX n/a   NM n/a   MIP $75

❏ **Opel Rekord P1 Caravan, 1958,** Metallic medium blue and white body, opening hood, tailgate and doors, working steering, highly detailed engine and interior, 1:18 scale, Model No. 180 043210
EX n/a   NM n/a   MIP $75

(Minichamps Photo)

❏ **Opel Rekord P1, 1958,** 2002, Light red body, white roof, red and white detailed interior, opening hood, trunk and doors, silver bumpers, working steering, 1:18 scale, Model No. 180 043201
EX n/a   NM n/a   MIP $75

❏ **Opel Rekord P1, 1958-60,** Turquoise blue body, opening doors, hood and trunk, black wheels, silver bumpers and trim, 1:18 scale, Model No. 180 043200
EX n/a   NM n/a   MIP $75

❏ **Opel Team Holzer: J. Winkelhock,** 1:18 scale, Model No. AC8 004804
EX n/a   NM n/a   MIP $75

❏ **Opel Team Holzer: U. Alzen,** 1:18 scale, Model No. AC8 004803
EX n/a   NM n/a   MIP $75

❏ **Opel V8 Coupe Opel Team Phoenix,** M. Reuter DTM 2000, white and yellow with "Opel Service" on sides and hood, sponsor graphics, opening doors and hood, detailed engine and interior, working steering, 1:18 scale, Model No. AC8 004807
EX n/a   NM n/a   MIP $75

❏ **Porsche 904 GTS,** Team Pon GT Class Winner: Koch and Gerhards 1000km Nurburgring, 1964. Orange body, silver rims, number "45" on front, sides and rear hood. Opening doors and front and rear hoods. Detailed engine and interior, working steering, 1:18 scale, Model No. 180 646745
EX n/a   NM n/a   MIP $80

❏ **Porsche 904 GTS 1964,** Blue, 1:18 scale, Model No. 180 067721
EX n/a   NM n/a   MIP $75

❏ **Porsche 904 GTS 1964,** Silver body and rims, opening trunk, doors and rear hood, detailed engine and interior, working steering, 1:18 scale, Model No. 180 067722
EX n/a   NM n/a   MIP $75

❏ **Porsche 904 GTS Team Cassel,** Cassel and Chuck 2000km Daytona, 1964. Silver body, number "50" on front, sides and rear hood, silver rims, opening doors, front and rear hoods, detailed interior and engine, working steering, 1:18 scale, Model No. 180 646750
EX n/a   NM n/a   MIP $75

❏ **Porsche 904 GTS Team Veulliet: Buchet/Ligier GT Class Winner 24H Le Mans 1964,** 2002, 1:18 scale, Model No. 180 646734
EX n/a   NM n/a   MIP $80

❑ **Porsche 906: Her-rmann/Linge Class Winners Daytona 24 HRS. 1966,** 2002, 1:18 scale, Model No. 100 666115
EX n/a   NM n/a   MIP $80

❑ **Porsche 956L,** 2002, M. Andretti 3rd Place, 24-hour Le Mans, 1983. Blue body, "Ken-wood" on sides, front and rear hood. Opening doors, removable rear hood section. Detailed engine and interior, working steering, 1:18 scale, Model No. 180 836921
EX n/a   NM n/a   MIP $80

❑ **Porsche 956L 1986 "Stars & Stripes": Follmer/Morton,** 2002, 1:18 scale, Model No. 180 866508
EX n/a   NM n/a   MIP $80

(Minichamps Photo)

❑ **Prost Acer AP04,** L. Burti. Dark blue with red patch, "Prost" on sides, "Acer" behind driver, number "23" on nose, silver wheels, "Michelin" tires, 1:18 scale, Model No. 100 010123
EX n/a   NM n/a   MIP $75

❑ **Prost Acer AP04,** J. Alesi. Dark blue with red patch, "Prost" on sides, "Acer" behind driver, number "22" on nose, silver wheels, 1:18 scale, Model No. 100 010022
EX n/a   NM n/a   MIP $75

❑ **Prost Acer AP04,** 2002, H.H. Frentzen., 1:18 scale, Model No. 100 010122
EX n/a   NM n/a   MIP $75

❑ **Sauber Petronas C20,** K. Raikkonen. Dark blue and aqua green, with "Petronas" on sides and Red Bull graphics behind driver, silver and black wheels, number "17" on nose, 1:18 scale, Model No. 100 010017
EX n/a   NM n/a   MIP $75

❑ **Sauber Petronas C20,** N. Heidfeld. Dark blue and aqua green, silver and black wheels, "Petronas"

on sides, number "16" on nose, 1:18 scale, Model No. 100 010016
EX n/a   NM n/a   MIP $75

❑ **Tempo 3-Wheeler Box 1952: Phoenix Reifen,** Blue body with "Phoenix Reifen" in white type on box sides, black chassis, working steering, detailed engine and interior, opening hood and rear cargo door, 1:18 scale, Model No. 180 099040
EX n/a   NM n/a   MIP $54

❑ **Tempo 3-Wheeler Truck,** Green/Gray, 1:18 scale, Model No. 180 099020
EX n/a   NM n/a   MIP $54

❑ **Volvo P1800 ES, 1971,** 2002, Light metallic blue, 1:18 scale, Model No. 100 171610
EX n/a   NM n/a   MIP $75

❑ **VW 1600 TL 1969,** 2002, Light Blue, 1:18 scale, Model No. 100 051020
EX n/a   NM n/a   MIP $75

❑ **VW 1600L 1969,** 2002, Cream-colored body, 1:18 scale, Model No. 100 051000
EX n/a   NM n/a   MIP $75

❑ **VW 1600L Variant 1969,** 2002, Red body, 1:18 scale, Model No. 100 051010
EX n/a   NM n/a   MIP $75

❑ **Williams F1 BMW FW23,** J.P. Montoya. Dark blue and white, "Compaq" on sides and spoiler, number "6" on sides and nose, 1:18 scale, Model No. 100 010006
EX n/a   NM n/a   MIP $75

❑ **Williams F1 BMW FW23,** R. Schumacher. Dark blue and white with "Compaq" on sides and spoiler, "Allianz" behind driver, silver wheels, number "5" on sides and nose, 1:18 scale, Model No. 100 010005
EX n/a   NM n/a   MIP $75

❑ **Williams Renault FW 18,** D. Hill, 1996, 1:18 scale, Model No. 180 960005
EX n/a   NM n/a   MIP $75

❑ **Williams Renault FW 19,** J. Villeneuve, 1997, 1:18 scale, Model No. 180 970003
EX n/a   NM n/a   MIP $75

1:35-SCALE

❑ **German 88 MM Flak 37 With Trailer,** 2002, 1:35 scale, Model No. 350 011080
EX n/a   NM n/a   MIP $99

❑ **Leopard 2,** 2002, Dark olive green, Iron Cross emblems on turret, 1:35 scale, Model No. 350 011000
EX n/a   NM n/a   MIP $99

❑ **M4 A3 Sherman,** Dark olive green, black treads, white star-in-circle design on turret, silver .50 cal. machine gun, tan cargo boxes attached at rear, white star on front, 1:35 scale, Model No. 350 040000
EX n/a   NM n/a   MIP $99

❑ **M48 A3,** 2002, Olive green, white star emblems, 1:35 scale, Model No. 350 041000
EX n/a   NM n/a   MIP $99

❑ **M60 A1,** 2002, Olive green, 1:35 scale, Model No. 350 041100
EX n/a   NM n/a   MIP $99

(Minichamps Photo)

❑ **Panzerkampfwagen V Jagd-panther Late Version, Winter Camouflage,** 2002, White and gray camouflage pattern, number "121" and black cross emblems on sides, dark gray treads, 1:35 scale, Model No. 350 019021
EX n/a   NM n/a   MIP $99

❑ **Panzerkampfwagen V Jagd-panther, Late Version,** Tan and green camouflage pattern, num-ber "113" and black cross emblems on sides, silver cable and tools attached to body, gunmetal gray treads, 1:35 scale, Model No. 350 019020
EX n/a   NM n/a   MIP $99

(Minichamps Photo)

❑ **Panzerkampfwagen V Panther Ausf.G, Late Version,** 2002, Two-tone green camouflage pattern, silver-gray treads, silver hook and cable attached to sides, silver MG34 machine gun on turret, 1:35 scale, Model No. 350 019001
EX n/a   NM n/a   MIP $99

(Minichamps Photo)

❑ **Panzerkampfwagen VI Tiger I, Late Version,** 2002, Afrika Korps sand color, silver MG34 on turret, silver cables on sides and deck. Black cross emblems on turret and body, 1:35 scale, Model No. 350 010000
EX n/a   NM n/a   MIP $99

❑ **SD.KFZ.251/1 Half Truck,** 2002, Personnel carrier model, 1:35 scale, Model No. 350 011270
EX n/a   NM n/a   MIP $99

❑ **SD.KFZ.7 8-Ton Semi Track Personnel Carrier,** 2002, Canvas roof, 1:35 scale, Model No. 350 011170
EX n/a   NM n/a   MIP $99

(Minichamps Photo)

❑ **T34/76, 1943 Production model,** 2002, Olive green with black treads, white "3A" and Cyrillic writing on turret. Silver cable and brown box attached to side, 1:35 scale, Model No. 350 020000
EX n/a   NM n/a   MIP $99

1:43-SCALE

(Minichamps Photo)

❑ **Alfa Romeo 147 2001,** 2002, Two-door hatch, blue metallic body, silver gray spoked wheels, black interior, 1:43 scale, Model No. 430 120001
EX n/a   NM n/a   MIP $35

(Minichamps Photo)

❑ **Alfa Romeo 156 Sportwagon, 2000,** 2002, Grey metallic four-door body, five-circle gray wheels, black interior, 1:43 scale, Model No. 430 120711
EX n/a   NM n/a   MIP $35

❑ **Alfa Romeo 156, 1997,** Light blue four-door body, gray wheels, gray interior, 1:43 scale, Model No. 430 120704
EX n/a   NM n/a   MIP n/a

❑ **Alfa Romeo 156, 1998,** Blue metallic body, gray interior, silver-gray wheels, 1:43 scale, Model No. 430 120702
EX n/a   NM n/a   MIP $35

(Minichamps Photo)

❑ **Alfa Romeo Alfasud, 1972,** 2002, Medium blue body, silver hubcaps, reddish-tan interior, four-doors, 1:43 scale, Model No. 400 120100
EX n/a   NM n/a   MIP $35

❑ **Alfa Romeo Alfetta GT Coupe, 1976,** 2002, Red body, black and silver grille, silver wheels, 1:43 scale, Model No. 400 120120
EX n/a   NM n/a   MIP $35

❑ **Alfa Romeo Tipo 33 Stradale, 1968,** Red body, red interior, opening rear hood, individually numbered limited edition of 9,999. Presentation box with history of car, 1:43 scale, Model No. 436 120920
EX n/a   NM n/a   MIP $80

❑ **Alpine Renault A 110, 1963,** Red body with silver gray rims, 1:43 scale, Model No. 430 113602
EX n/a   NM n/a   MIP $35

❑ **Alpine Renault A 442B,** 2002, Winner 24-hour Le Mans, 1978, Pironi and Didier. Orange and black with "elf," "Michelin" and "Renault" on body, number "2" on sides and front, 1:43 scale, Model No. 430 781102
EX n/a   NM n/a   MIP $48

❑ **Alpine Renault A 443,** 2002, 24-hour Le Mans, 1978, Depailler and Patrick. Yellow, white and black body with "Renault" and "elf" on front and sides, silver wheels, number "1" on front and sides, 1:43 scale, Model No. 430 781101
EX n/a   NM n/a   MIP $48

❑ **Arrows Asiatech A22,** J. Verstappen. Orange and black body and wheels, "Orange" on sides and spoiler, "Chello" behind driver, number "14" on nose, 1:43 scale, Model No. 400 010014
EX n/a   NM n/a   MIP $35

❑ **Arrows Asiatech A22,** E. Bernoldi. Orange and black body and wheels, sponsor graphics, "Orange" on sides and spoiler, number "15" on nose, 1:43 scale, Model No. 400 010015
EX n/a   NM n/a   MIP $35

❑ **Arrows Asiatech A22 "Nose Wing",** E. Bernoldi, Monaco 1st. practice. Orange and black with front and rear spoilers, black and orange wheels, "Orange" on sides and rear spoiler, number "15" on nose, 1:43 scale, Model No. 400 010115
EX n/a   NM n/a   MIP $48

❑ **Arrows Asiatech A22 "Nose Wing",** J. Verstappen, Monaco, 1st practice. Front and rear spoilers, orange and black body, "Orange" on sides and on rear spoiler, number "14" on nose, 1:43 scale, Model No. 400 010114
EX n/a   NM n/a   MIP $48

❑ **Audi 100 Coupe S, 1970,** Orange body, black interior, silver wheels and trim, 1:43 scale, Model No. 430 019121
EX n/a   NM n/a   MIP $35

(Minichamps Photo)

❑ **Audi 50 1974,** 2002, Blue body, black interior, gray wheels, black grille, 1:43 scale, Model No. 430 010401
EX n/a   NM n/a   MIP $35

❑ **Audi 60 1970,** 2002, Red with silver trim, 1:43 scale, Model No. 400 011300
EX n/a   NM n/a   MIP $35

❑ **Audi 60 Variant 1970,** 2002, Cream, 1:43 scale, Model No. 400 011310
EX n/a   NM n/a   MIP $35

❑ **Audi A2, 2000,** Black body, six-spoke wheels, tan interior, 1:43 scale, Model No. 430 019002
EX n/a   NM n/a   MIP $35

❑ **Audi A2, 2000,** Dark blue metallic, six-spoke wheels, tan interior, 1:43 scale, Model No. 430 019001
EX n/a   NM n/a   MIP n/a

(Minichamps Photo)

❑ **Audi A2, 2000,** 2002, Bright blue body, gray interior, six-spoke wheels, 1:43 scale, Model No. 430 019004
EX n/a   NM n/a   MIP $35

❑ **Audi A3 4-Door 2000,** Green metallic body, five-spoke silver gray hubs, 1:43 scale, Model No. 430 010301
EX n/a   NM n/a   MIP $35

(Minichamps Photo)

❑ **Audi A4 Avant, 2001,** 2002, Dark gray metallic body, silver gray five-spoke wheels, 1:43 scale, Model No. 430 010110
EX n/a   NM n/a   MIP $35

❑ **Audi A4, 2000,** Green metallic four-door body, five spoke wheels, black interior, 1:43 scale, Model No. 430 010100
EX n/a   NM n/a   MIP $35

❑ **Audi A4, 2000,** Blue metallic body, black interior, 1:43 scale, Model No. 430 010101
EX n/a   NM n/a   MIP $35

(Minichamps Photo)

❑ **Audi A6 Avant, 2001,** 2002, Blue metallic body, charcoal gray interior, silver roof rack, silver multi-spoke wheels, 1:43 scale, Model No. 430 010210
EX n/a   NM n/a   MIP $35

(Minichamps Photo)

❑ **Audi A6, 2001,** 2002, Black four-door body, gray nine-spoke wheels, 1:43 scale, Model No. 430 010200
EX n/a   NM n/a   MIP $35

❑ **Audi A8, 1994,** Red metallic body, tan interior, five-spoke wheels, 1:43 scale, Model No. 430 013005
EX n/a   NM n/a   MIP n/a

❑ **Audi Allroad Quattro, 2000,** Silver body, dark gray interior, sun roof, five-spoke wheels, 1:43 scale, Model No. 430 010011
EX n/a   NM n/a   MIP $35

(Minichamps Photo)

❑ **Audi Allroad Quattro, 2000,** 2002, Dark blue body, silver five-spoke wheels and trim, charcoal interior, 1:43 scale, Model No. 430 010012
EX n/a   NM n/a   MIP $35

❑ **Audi Quattro,** 2002, Roehrl and Geistdoerfer, Rally Monte Carlo, 1984. White with yellow stripes on sides, white five-spoke wheels, number "1" on sides, 1:43 scale, Model No. 430 841901
EX n/a   NM n/a   MIP $48

(Minichamps Photo)

❏ **Audi Quattro,** 2002, Blomquist and Cederberg, Rally Sweden, 1982. White and blue body with yellow stripes, "Sanyo" on sides, hood and roof, number "4" on sides, 1:43 scale, Model No. 430 821904
EX n/a　　NM n/a　　MIP $48

(Minichamps Photo)

❏ **Audi Quattro,** 2002, Mouton and Pons, Rally Portugal, 1982. White body with red, gray and black stripes, "Audi" logo on hood, number "7" on sides, 1:43 scale, Model No. 430 821907
EX n/a　　NM n/a　　MIP $48

❏ **Audi Quattro,** 2002, S. Blomquist, Rally Monte Carlo, 1984., 1:43 scale, Model No. 430 841907
EX n/a　　NM n/a　　MIP $48

(Minichamps Photo)

❏ **Audi Quattro,** 2002, Mikkola and Hertz, Rally Monte Carlo, 1984. White body with yellow stripes, "Audi" logo on hood and roof, number "4" on sides, white five-spoke wheels, 1:43 scale, Model No. 430 841904
EX n/a　　NM n/a　　MIP $48

(Minichamps Photo)

❏ **Audi Quattro,** 2002, Mouton and Pons, Rally Tour De Corse, 1981. Dark green with black hood and doors and yellow stripes. "BP" on hood and roof, number "15" on sides, 1:43 scale, Model No. 430 811915
EX n/a　　NM n/a　　MIP $48

❏ **Audi Quattro 1981,** Black body, Audi graphics along bottom of doors, rear spoiler, 1:43 scale, Model No. 430 019421
EX n/a　　NM n/a　　MIP $35

❏ **Audi R8,** 2002, Road Atlanta Petit Le Mans, 2001: Herbert and Wallace. White body with red and blue color patches, American flag on front, number "38" on front and sides, "Audisport North America" on spoiler, 1:43 scale, Model No. 400 010938
EX n/a　　NM n/a　　MIP $50

(Minichamps Photo)

❏ **Audi R8 Audi Sport North America 2nd Place 24H Le Mans 2001: Aiello/Capello/Pescatori,** 2002, 1:43 scale, Model No. 400 011202
EX n/a　　NM n/a　　MIP $48

(Minichamps Photo)

❏ **Audi R8 Audi Sport Team Joest Winners 24H Le Mans 2001: Biela/Kristensen/Pirro,** 1:43 scale, Model No. 400 011201
EX n/a　　NM n/a　　MIP $48

❏ **Audi R8 Team Champion 24H Le Mans 2001: Herbert/Kelleners/Theys,** 1:43 scale, Model No. 400 010903
EX n/a　　NM n/a　　MIP $48

❏ **Audi R8S,** 2002, Team Johansson 24-hour Le Mans, 2001: Stefan Johansson. Light blue body with red stripes, spoked wheels, number "4" on front and sides, 1:43 scale, Model No. 400 010904
EX n/a　　NM n/a　　MIP $48

❏ **Audi RS4, 2000,** Black metallic body, white spoked wheels, black interior, sunroof, 1:43 scale, Model No. 430 019310
EX n/a　　NM n/a　　MIP $35

❏ **Audi TT Coupe, 1998,** White, charcoal interior, gray six-spoke wheels, 1:43 scale, Model No. 430 017224
EX n/a　　NM n/a　　MIP $35

(Minichamps Photo)

❏ **Audi TT Roadster, 1999,** 2002, Red convertible body, dark gray interior, six-spoke wheels, 1:43 scale, Model No. 430 017232
EX n/a　　NM n/a　　MIP $35

❏ **Audi TT-R Team ABT "Sportsline",** DTM 2001: M. Ekstroem. Yellow body with red "Halleroder" on sides, roof and front, Swedish flag graphics by rear wheels on sides, silver spoked wheels, black grille, number "22" on sides and hood, 1:43 scale, Model No. 400 011122
EX n/a　　NM n/a　　MIP $48

(Minichamps Photo)

❏ **Audi TT-R Team ABT "Sportsline",** 2002, DTM 2001: L. Aiello. Yellow body, blue swoop on sides near bottom with "PlayStation 2" in white lettering, silver wheels, "Halleroder" in red type on hood, sides and roof, number "19" on hood and sides, 1:43 scale, Model No. 400 011119
EX n/a　　NM n/a　　MIP $48

(Minichamps Photo)

❏ **Audi TT-R Team ABT "Sportsline",** 2002, DTM 2001: Ch. Abt. Yellow body with blue on bottom sides and "PlayStation2" in white lettering. Red "Halleroder" type on sides, hood and roof, number "18" on sides and hood, black spoiler, silver wheels, 1:43 scale, Model No. 400 011118
EX n/a   **NM** n/a   **MIP** $48

(Minichamps Photo)

❏ **Audi TT-R Team ABT "Sportsline",** 2002, DTM 2001: M. Tomczyk. Yellow body with black spoiler, "Halleroder" in red lettering on roof, hood and sides, number "23" on front and sides, German flag graphic near rear wheels, 1:43 scale, Model No. 400 011123
EX n/a   **NM** n/a   **MIP** $48

❏ **Auto Union 1000 SP Coupe, 1958,** 2002, Cream-white body, silver grille and hubs, tailfins. This model bears resemblance to a Ford Thunderbird of the period, 1:43 scale, Model No. 400 011020
EX n/a   **NM** n/a   **MIP** $35

❏ **Auto Union 1000 SP Roadster, 1961,** 2002, Red convertible body, silver grille and hubs, 1:43 scale, Model No. 400 011030
EX n/a   **NM** n/a   **MIP** $35

❏ **Autobianchi A112, 1974,** 2002, Green body, gray wheels, 1:43 scale, Model No. 400 121100
EX n/a   **NM** n/a   **MIP** $35

(Minichamps Photo)

❏ **Bar 01 Supertec Testcar: J. Villeneuve 1999,** 2002, 1:43 scale, Model No. 430 990120
EX n/a   **NM** n/a   **MIP** n/a

❏ **Bar Honda 03,** O. Panis. White with red circle graphics, "Look Alive" on spoiler, "Honda" in red type, number "9" in small black circle on nose, black wheels, "Bridgestone" tires, 1:43 scale, Model No. 400 010009
EX n/a   **NM** n/a   **MIP** $35

❏ **Bar Honda 03,** J. Villeneuve. White with black and red circle graphics, "Look Alive" on spoiler, "Honda" in red type, number "10" in small black circle on nose, black wheels, Bridgestone tires, 1:43 scale, Model No. 400 010010
EX n/a   **NM** n/a   **MIP** $35

❏ **Benetton BMW B186: G. Berger 1986,** 1:43 scale, Model No. 430 860020
EX n/a   **NM** n/a   **MIP** $35

❏ **Benetton BMW B186: T. Fabi 1986,** 1:43 scale, Model No. 430 860019
EX n/a   **NM** n/a   **MIP** $35

❏ **Benetton Renault B201,** 2002, G. Fisichella. Light and dark blue body with "elf" on sides and "Fisico" behind driver in white type, black wheels, 1:43 scale, Model No. 400 010107
EX n/a   **NM** n/a   **MIP** $38

❏ **Benetton Renault B201,** 2002, J. Button, Indianapolis. Limited edition of 2,811 pieces, 1:43 scale, Model No. 400 010108
EX n/a   **NM** n/a   **MIP** $38

❏ **Benetton Renault B201,** 2002, Fisichella and Giancarlo, 2001, 1:43 scale, Model No. 400 010007
EX n/a   **NM** n/a   **MIP** $35

❏ **Benetton Renault B201,** 2002, Button and Jenson team, 2001, 1:43 scale, Model No. 400 010008
EX n/a   **NM** n/a   **MIP** $35

❏ **BMW 2002 Turbo 1974,** White, with black interior, blue and red stripe along sides, black grille, 1:43 scale, Model No. 430 022200
EX n/a   **NM** n/a   **MIP** $35

(Minichamps Photo)

❏ **BMW 318 I Compact, 2001,** 2002, Black body, gray interior, sunroof, five-spoke wheels, opening hood with detailed engine, 1:43 scale, Model No. 431 020071
EX n/a   **NM** n/a   **MIP** $38

(Minichamps Photo)

❏ **BMW 3231, 1975,** 2002, Green metallic body, multi-spoked wheels, black and silver trim, 1:43 scale, Model No. 430 025474
EX n/a   **NM** n/a   **MIP** $35

❏ **BMW 325 Ti Compact, 2001,** Red with silver five-spoked wheels, black interior, sunroof, 1:43 scale, Model No. 431 020070
EX n/a   **NM** n/a   **MIP** $38

❏ **BMW 328 CI Coupe, 1999,** Gold body, silver multi-spoked wheels, opening hood with detailed engine, tan interior, 1:43 scale, Model No. 431 028322
EX n/a   **NM** n/a   **MIP** $38

❏ **BMW 328 I Cabriolet, 2000,** Dark blue metallic body, charcoal interior, silver multi-spoked wheels, opening hood with detailed engine, 1:43 scale, Model No. 431 028031
EX n/a   **NM** n/a   **MIP** $38

❏ **BMW 328 I Touring, 1999,** Red body, seven-spoke wheels, black interior, black trim, 1:43 scale, Model No. 431 028312
EX n/a   **NM** n/a   **MIP** $38

(Minichamps Photo)

❑ **BMW 635 CSI "AC Schnitzer",** 2002, DTM 1988: A. Goeser. Black body with silver diagonal pinstripes, "AC Schnitzer" on sides, number "13." Red and silver five-spoke wheels, black grille, 1:43 scale, Model No. 430 882613
EX n/a   NM n/a   MIP $48

(Minichamps Photo)

❑ **BMW 740 I, 2001,** 2002, Silver body and wheels, black interior, sunroof, opening hood with detailed engine, 1:43 scale, Model No. 431 020200
EX n/a   NM n/a   MIP $38

❑ **BMW CSL 3.5,** 2002, IMSA Sebring 12 hours. '75 Winners: Redman, Moffat, Posey and Stuck. Number "25", 1:43 scale, Model No. 430 752925
EX n/a   NM n/a   MIP $48

❑ **BMW M1,** Procar 1980 'Basf': H.J. Stuck. Red body with white "radio wave" graphics and BASF logos. Number "80" on sides and hood, 1:43 scale, Model No. 430 802580
EX n/a   NM n/a   MIP $48

❑ **BMW M1,** "Carte De France" 24-hour Le Mans 1980: Pironi, Quester and Mignot. Blue and white map graphics on body, number "83" on hood and sides, 1:43 scale, Model No. 430 802583
EX n/a   NM n/a   MIP $48

❑ **BMW M1,** Procar 1979: D. Pironi. White body with wide, diagonal red, dark and light blue stripes. Silver wheels, black spoiler, 1:43 scale, Model No. 430 792505
EX n/a   NM n/a   MIP $48

❑ **BMW M3 "Blaupunkt",** 2002, DTM Norisring 1987 Winner: Olaf Manthey. White body with "Blaupunkt" in black type, silver wheels, number "24", 1:43 scale, Model No. 430 872024
EX n/a   NM n/a   MIP $48

❑ **BMW M3 "Jagermeister",** 2002, DTM Avus 1988: M. Ketterer. Orange body, "Jagermeister" in Gothic script on sides, silver wheels, number "39", 1:43 scale, Model No. 430 882039
EX n/a   NM n/a   MIP $48

❑ **BMW M3 Cabriolet, 2001,** Red convertible body, black interior, silver multi-spoked wheels, opening hood with detailed engine, 1:43 scale, Model No. 431 020030
EX n/a   NM n/a   MIP $38

❑ **BMW M3 Cabriolet, 2001,** 2002, Glossy blue convertible body, blue and black interior, silver multi-spoked wheels, opening hood with detailed engine, 1:43 scale, Model No. 431 020031
EX n/a   NM n/a   MIP $38

❑ **BMW M3 Coupe, 2000,** Black body, silver multi-spoked wheels, black interior, 1:43 scale, Model No. 431 020020
EX n/a   NM n/a   MIP $38

(Minichamps Photo)

❑ **BMW M3 Coupe, 2000,** 2002, Yellow body, charcoal interior, silver multi-spoked wheels, sunroof, 1:43 scale, Model No. 431 020021
EX n/a   NM n/a   MIP $38

❑ **BMW M3, 1987,** 2002, Black body, silver wheels, 1:43 scale, Model No. 430 020300
EX n/a   NM n/a   MIP $35

(Minichamps Photo)

❑ **BMW X5, 1999,** 2002, Dark green metallic body, light gray interior, gray-silver five spoke wheels, opening hood with detailed engine, 1:43 scale, Model No. 431 028474
EX n/a   NM n/a   MIP $38

❑ **BMW Z3 Roadster 2.8, 1997,** Black body, five-spoke wheels, dark tan interior, 1:43 scale, Model No. 430 024331
EX n/a   NM n/a   MIP $35

❑ **BMW Z3 Roadster, 1999,** Yellow body, black interior, multi-spoked wheels, silver trim, 1:43 scale, Model No. 430 028234
EX n/a   NM n/a   MIP $35

❑ **BMW Z8, 1999,** Dark metallic blue convertible body, black interior, silver trim and five-spoked wheels, opening hood and detailed engine, 1:43 scale, Model No. 431 028740
EX n/a   NM n/a   MIP $38

(Minichamps Photo)

❑ **Boehringer Unimog 70200, 1949,** 2002, Green body, gray-green canvas roof, orange wheels, "Unimog" in white type along sides and on hood, 1:43 scale, Model No. 439 030260
EX n/a   NM n/a   MIP $48

❑ **Brabham Alfa Romeo BT46: N. Lauda 1978,** 1:43 scale, Model No. 430 780001
EX n/a   NM n/a   MIP $35

❑ **Brabham Judd BT60,** 2002, Damon Hill, 1992. Blue body, red nose, white spoiler, 1:43 scale, Model No. 430 920007
EX n/a   NM n/a   MIP $38

❑ **Brabham Judd BT60: E. Van De Poele 1992,** 2002, 1:43 scale, Model No. 430 920008
EX n/a   NM n/a   MIP $38

❑ **Brabham Judd BT60: G. Amati 1992,** 2002, 1:43 scale, Model No. 430 920097
EX n/a   NM n/a   MIP $38

(Minichamps Photo)

❑ **Buessing 8000 S Blue Canvas Truck Spedition Dachser, 1950,** 2002, Dark blue cab and body, black fenders and chassis, gray canvas top over truck bed, 1:43 scale, Model No. 439 079021
EX n/a　　NM n/a　　MIP $65

❑ **Buessing D2U Double-Deck Bus, 1955,** 2002, Cream body, detailed interior, silver trim, 1:43 scale, Model No. 439 071080
EX n/a　　NM n/a　　MIP $80

(Minichamps Photo)

❑ **Chaparral 2D 1000KM Nuerburgring 1966: PH. Hill/Bonner,** 2002, 1:43 scale, Model No. 436 661407
EX n/a　　NM n/a　　MIP $76

(Minichamps Photo)

❑ **Chaparral 2D 24H LeMans 1966: PH. Hill/Bonner,** 2002, 1:43 scale, Model No. 436 661409
EX n/a　　NM n/a　　MIP $76

(Minichamps Photo)

❑ **Chaparral 2F 24H Le Mans 1967: Jennings/Johnson,** 2002, 1:43 scale, Model No. 430 671408
EX n/a　　NM n/a　　MIP $48

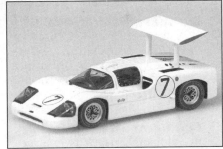

(Minichamps Photo)

❑ **Chaparral 2F 24H Le Mans 1967: P. Hill/Bonner,** 2002, 1:43 scale, Model No. 430 671407
EX n/a　　NM n/a　　MIP $48

(Minichamps Photo)

❑ **Chaparral 2H Can Am Edmonton 1969: J. Surtees,** 2002, 1:43 scale, Model No. 436 691407
EX n/a　　NM n/a　　MIP $76

(Minichamps Photo)

❑ **Chaparral 2J Can Am 1970: V. Elford,** 2002, 1:43 scale, Model No. 436 701466
EX n/a　　NM n/a　　MIP $76

❑ **Chevrolet Corvette C5R Team Corvette,** Pilgrim, Collins and Freon 24-hour Le Mans 2000. Yellow and white body, gray multi-spoked wheels, number "64" on sides and front, 1:43 scale, Model No. AC4 001464
EX n/a　　NM n/a　　MIP $48

❑ **Chevrolet Corvette C5R, Alms "Petit Le Mans",** Pilgrim, Collins and Freon 2001 GTS Class Winners. Yellow body, American flag design running from hood to trunk, "United We Stand" in black type on spoiler, number "4" on sides and front, 1:43 scale, Model No. AC4 011404
EX n/a　　NM n/a　　MIP $50

❑ **Chevrolet Corvette C5R, Team Corvette,** Parnett, O'Connel and Fellows GTS Class, Winner, 24-hour Le Mans 2001. All-yellow body and spoiler, number "63" on sides and front, 1:43 scale, Model No. AC4 011463
EX n/a　　NM n/a　　MIP $48

❑ **Chevrolet Corvette C5R, Team Corvette,** Pilgrim, Collins and Freon 24-hour Daytona 2000. Yellow and white body, number "4" on sides, roof and hood, 1:43 scale, Model No. AC4 001404
EX n/a　　NM n/a　　MIP $48

❑ **Chevrolet Corvette C5R, Team Corvette,** Fellows, Kneifel and Bell, 24-hour Le Mans 2000. Yellow and white body, gray spoked wheels, number "63" on sides and front, 1:43 scale, Model No. AC4 001463
EX n/a　　NM n/a　　MIP $48

❑ **Chevrolet Corvette C5R, Team Corvette,** Pilgrim, Collins and Freon 24-hour Le Mans 2001. Yellow body, yellow and black spoiler, gray multi-spoked wheels, number "64" on sides and front, 1:43 scale, Model No. AC4 011464
EX n/a　　NM n/a　　MIP $48

❑ **Chevrolet Corvette C5R, Team Corvette,** Fellows, Kneifel and Bell 24-hour Daytona 2000. Yellow and white body, gray spoked wheels, number "3" on sides, roof and hood, 1:43 scale, Model No. AC4 001403
EX n/a　　NM n/a　　MIP $48

❑ **Chrysler Viper GTS-R,** 2002, Team Larbre 24-hour Le Mans, 2001: Christophe Bouchout. White body with wide black and red stripes, "Chereau" on sides, number "58" on sides and front, 1:43 scale, Model No. 400 011458
EX n/a　　NM n/a　　MIP $48

❑ **Chrysler Viper GTS-R Equipe De France FFSA 24H Le Mans 2001: Terrien/Cochet/Dayraut,** 1:43 scale, Model No. 400 011457
EX n/a   NM n/a   MIP $48

(Minichamps Photo)

❑ **Citroen SM, 1970,** 2002, Gold metallic body, silver wheels and trim, dark tan interior, 1:43 scale, Model No. 400 111020
EX n/a   NM n/a   MIP $35

(Minichamps Photo)

❑ **De Lorean DMC 12,** 2002, 1:43 scale, Model No. 436 140020
EX n/a   NM n/a   MIP $80

(Minichamps Photo)

❑ **DKW Junior De Luxe, 1961,** 2002, Dark red, white roof, light yellow wheels with silver hubcaps, 1:43 scale, Model No. 400 011500
EX n/a   NM n/a   MIP $35

❑ **Dodge Viper GTS, 1993,** Red body, dark gray interior, silver-gray three-spoke wheels, 1:43 scale, Model No. 430 144032
EX n/a   NM n/a   MIP $35

❑ **Dodge Viper GTS-R,** Team Chamberlain 24H Daytona 2000: Messley, Seiler, Brun and Hugenholtz, 1:43 scale, Model No. 430 001446
EX n/a   NM n/a   MIP $48

❑ **Dodge Viper, 1993,** Red body, dark gray interior, silver five-spoke wheels, 1:43 scale, Model No. 430 144022
EX n/a   NM n/a   MIP $35

❑ **European-Minardi PS01,** 2002, Alex Yoong, 2001. Black car with "European Avaition" sides and spoiler, "Magnum" graphics behind driver, 1:43 scale, Model No. 400 010120
EX n/a   NM n/a   MIP $38

❑ **Fiat Barchetta, 1999,** Black body, black interior, silver-gray five-spoke wheels, 1:43 scale, Model No. 430 121932
EX n/a   NM n/a   MIP $35

(Minichamps Photo)

❑ **Fiat Barchetta, 1999,** 2002, Orange body, orange and black interior, silver five-spoke wheels, 1:43 scale, Model No. 430 121934
EX n/a   NM n/a   MIP $35

(Minichamps Photo)

❑ **Fiat X1/9, 1972,** 2002, Red metallic body, orange tan interior, gray wheels, black "strobe" stripe along sides, removable roof, detailed interior, 1:43 scale, Model No. 430 121661
EX n/a   NM n/a   MIP $35

❑ **Ford Capri II 1974,** 2002, Yellow, 1:43 scale, Model No. 400 081200
EX n/a   NM n/a   MIP $35

❑ **Ford Capri RS 3100,** 2002, DRM Norisring '75 Div. 1 Winner: J. Mass., 1:43 scale, Model No. 430 758031
EX n/a   NM n/a   MIP $48

❑ **Ford Capri, 1969,** Brown metallic body, tan interior, silver and black wheels, silver trim, 1:43 scale, Model No. 430 085507
EX n/a   NM n/a   MIP $35

❑ **Ford Cougar, 1998,** Black body, silver six-spoke wheels, charcoal interior, sunroof, 1:43 scale, Model No. 430 088022
EX n/a   NM n/a   MIP $35

❑ **Ford Escort 1968,** 2002, Yellow, 1:43 scale, Model No. 400 081000
EX n/a   NM n/a   MIP n/a

❑ **Ford Escort I RS 1600 Twin Cam,** 2002, Silver body and wheels, rally lights attached to front bumper, 1:43 scale, Model No. 400 688100
EX n/a   NM n/a   MIP $50

❑ **Ford Escort RS Cosworth, 1992,** Red body and spoiler, gray interior, five-spoke wheels, 1:43 scale, Model No. 430 082104
EX n/a   NM n/a   MIP $35

(Minichamps Photo)

❑ **Ford Fiesta, 2001,** 2002, Black body, silver-gray multi-spoke wheels, gray interior, 1:43 scale, Model No. 400 081100
EX n/a   NM n/a   MIP $35

❑ **Ford Focus RS WRC,** McRae and Grist, Rally Monte Carlo, 2001. White body with red and blue stripe down hood and roof, red and blue swoop toward rear of car, "Ford" oval on hood and sides, number "4" on sides, white five-spoke wheels, 1:43 scale, Model No. 430 018904
EX n/a   NM n/a   MIP $48

❑ **Ford Focus WRC,** Sainz and Moya, Rally Monte Carlo, 2000. White body with red and light and dark blue swoop toward back of car. White five-spoke wheels, "Ford" oval on hood, roof and sides, number "6" on sides, 1:43 scale, Model No. 430 008906
EX n/a   NM n/a   MIP $48

(KP Photo)

❑ **Ford Focus WRC,** Solberg and Mills, Rally Finland, 2000. White body with light and dark blue letters from the word "focus" overlapping around car. "Ford" oval on roof, number "16" on sides, 1:43 scale, Model No. 430 008996
EX n/a   NM n/a   MIP $48

❑ **Ford Focus WRC Team,** 2002, A1 Ring Rally, 2001: Baumschlager and Wicha. Dark blue with Red Bull graphics on sides and front, number "4", 1:43 scale, Model No. 430 008907
EX n/a   NM n/a   MIP $48

❑ **Ford Focus, 1998,** Light green metallic four-door hatch, five-spoke silver wheels, charcoal interior, 1:43 scale, Model No. 430 087021
EX n/a   NM n/a   MIP $35

❑ **Ford Galaxy, 2000,** blue-green metallic body, blue interior, five-spoke wheels, black trim and roof rack, 1:43 scale, Model No. 430 089500
EX n/a   NM n/a   MIP $35

❑ **Ford Galaxy, 2000,** Black body, gray interior, five spoke wheels, 1:43 scale, Model No. 430 089501
EX n/a   NM n/a   MIP $35

❑ **Ford Mondeo Turnier, 2001,** Red metallic body, light gray interior, five-spoke wheels, black trim and roof rack, 1:43 scale, Model No. 430 080011
EX n/a   NM n/a   MIP $35

❑ **Ford Mondeo, 1997,** Deep metallic red body, six-spoke wheels, charcoal interior, 1:43 scale, Model No. 430 086301
EX n/a   NM n/a   MIP $35

❑ **Ford Mondeo, 2001,** Silver body, charcoal interior, 1:43 scale, Model No. 430 080071
EX n/a   NM n/a   MIP $35

❑ **Ford Mondeo, 2001,** Black metallic body, charcoal interior, 1:43 scale, Model No. 430 080001
EX n/a   NM n/a   MIP $35

❑ **Ford Mustang Cabriolet, 1994,** Red convertible body, black and gray interior, three-spoke wheels, 1:43 scale, Model No. 430 085632
EX n/a   NM n/a   MIP $35

❑ **Ford Puma, 1998,** Dark green metallic body, black interior, five-spoke wheels, 1:43 scale, Model No. 430 086524
EX n/a   NM n/a   MIP $35

❑ **Ford RS 200,** 2002, Rally Sweden 1986: Kalle Grundel. White with blue stripe design on back, number "8" on sides, 1:43 scale, Model No. 430 868008
EX n/a   NM n/a   MIP $48

(Minichamps Photo)

❑ **Ford RS 200, 1986,** 2002, White body, gray multi-spoked wheels, tan interior, 1:43 scale, Model No. 430 080200
EX n/a   NM n/a   MIP $35

❑ **Ford Sierra Cosworth,** 2002, Winner 24H Nuerburgring 1987: K. Niedzwiedz. Number "67" and "Texaco" on sides, 1:43 scale, Model No. 430 878067
EX n/a   NM n/a   MIP $48

❑ **Ford Sierra Cosworth "Speedware",** 2002, DTM 1988: Champion: Klaus Ludwig. White body, "Speedware" along sides, gold and silver spoked wheels, number "18", 1:43 scale, Model No. 430 888018
EX n/a   NM n/a   MIP $48

❑ **Ford Sierra Cosworth 'Lui',** 2002, DTM 1988: M. Reuter., 1:43 scale, Model No. 430 888005
EX n/a   NM n/a   MIP $48

❑ **Ford Sierra RS 500 Cosworth 'Wuerth' DTM 1988,** 2002, Armin Hahne. Whtie with red "Wuerth" logos on sides and hood, number "25", 1:43 scale, Model No. 430 888025
EX n/a   NM n/a   MIP $48

❑ **Ford Taunus 1970,** 2002, White, 1:43 scale, Model No. 400 081300
EX n/a   NM n/a   MIP $35

❑ **Ford Taunus Coupe 1970,** 2002, Light Blue Metallic, 1:43 scale, Model No. 400 081320
EX n/a   NM n/a   MIP $35

❑ **Ford Taunus P5 1964,** 2002, White, 1:43 scale, Model No. 400 081400
EX n/a   NM n/a   MIP $35

❑ **Ford Taunus P5 Coupe 1964,** 2002, Silver, Model No. 400 081420
EX n/a   NM n/a   MIP $35

❑ **Ford Taunus P5 Turnier, 1964,** 2002, Light blue body, silver trim, 1:43 scale, Model No. 400 081410
EX n/a   NM n/a   MIP $35

❑ **Ford Taunus Turnier 1970,** 2002, Light Grey, 1:43 scale, Model No. 400 081310
EX n/a   NM n/a   MIP $35

❑ **Ford Taunus, 1960,** Turquoise body, silver trim and hubcaps, turquoise and white interior, 1:43 scale, Model No. 430 085106
EX n/a   NM n/a   MIP $35

❑ **Ford Transit Bus, 2000,** Dark metallic red bus body with high roof, gray interior, silver wheels, 1:43 scale, Model No. 430 089400
EX n/a   NM n/a   MIP $48

❑ **Ford Transit Delivery Van High Roof, 2000,** Dark metallic red van, gray interior, silver wheels, 1:43 scale, Model No. 430 089300
EX n/a   NM n/a   MIP $48

❑ **Ford Transit Double Cabin, 2000,** Red metallic extended cab truck with silver truck bed and silver wheels, 1:43 scale, Model No. 430 089100
EX n/a   NM n/a   MIP $48

❑ **Ford Transit Single Cabin 2000,** Red metallic cab with silver truck bed, black trim, silver wheels, 1:43 scale, Model No. 430 089000
EX n/a   NM n/a   MIP $48

(Minichamps Photo)

❑ **Ford Transit Tourneo, 2001,** 2002, Red minibus body, gray interior, black trim, silver wheels, 1:43 scale, Model No. 400 081210
EX n/a   NM n/a   MIP $48

❑ **Henschel HS 140 Canvas Truck, 1953,** 2002, White body and canvas with red chassis, fenders and wheels, 1:43 scale, Model No. 439 171020
EX n/a   NM n/a   MIP $65

(Minichamps Photo)

❑ **Honda RA099: J. Verstappen 1999,** 2002, 1:43 scale, Model No. 436 990099
EX n/a   NM n/a   MIP $65

❑ **Jordan Set 1991/92,** 2002, Limited edition of 3,999 pieces, 1:43 scale, Model No. 402 109192
EX n/a   NM n/a   MIP $105

❑ **Jordan Set 1993/94,** 2002, Limited edition of 3,666 pieces, 1:43 scale, Model No. 402 109394
EX n/a   NM n/a   MIP $105

❑ **Jordan Set 1995/96,** 2002, Limited edition of 3,666 pieces, 1:43 scale, Model No. 402 109596
EX n/a   NM n/a   MIP $105

❑ **Jordan Set 1997/98,** Limited edition of 3,666 pieces, 1:43 scale, Model No. 402 109798
EX n/a   NM n/a   MIP $105

❑ **Jordan Set 1999/2000,** 2002, Limited edition of 3,999 pieces, 1:43 scale, Model No. 402 109900
EX n/a   NM n/a   MIP $105

❑ **Krupp Titan Blue Canvas Truck Spedition Dachser, 1950,** Blue and black cab and body, "Dachser Spedition" in Gothic type along sides, gray canvas cover on truck bed, 1:43 scale, Model No. 439 069021
EX n/a   NM n/a   MIP $65

(Minichamps Photo)

❑ **Lamborghini 350 GT, 1964,** 2002, Blue metallic body, silver spoked wheels, black interior, silver trim, 1:43 scale, Model No. 430 103200
EX n/a   NM n/a   MIP $35

(Minichamps Photo)

❑ **Lamborghini 400 GT 2+2, 1964,** 2002, Silver-blue body, silver mult-spoked wheels, silver trim, 1:43 scale, Model No. 430 103300
EX n/a   NM n/a   MIP $35

(Minichamps Photo)

❑ **Lamborghini Countach LP400, 1974,** 2002, Lime-metallic gold body, silver rims, black interior, 1:43 scale, Model No. 430 103100
EX n/a   NM n/a   MIP $35

(Minichamps Photo)

❑ **Lexus SC430 Cabriolet, 2001,** 2002, Black convertible body, silver rims, black interior, 1:43 scale, Model No. 400 166130
EX n/a   NM n/a   MIP $35

❑ **Lincoln Continental L.B. Johnson, 1964,** Black body, sunroof, light gray interior, silver bumpers and trim, American and Presidential flags in front, presentation packaging, 1:43 scale, Model No. 436 086101
EX n/a   NM n/a   MIP $60

❑ **Lincoln Continental Presidental Parade Vehicle X-100: J.F. Kennedy 1961,** Black convertible body with black interior, American and Presidential flags in front, JFK, Jackie and other figures in car, presentation packaging, 1:43 scale, Model No. 430 086100
EX n/a   NM n/a   MIP $60

❑ **Lotus Ford 72: E. Fittipaldi 1970,** 1:43 scale, Model No. 430 700024
EX n/a   NM n/a   MIP $38

❑ **Lotus Ford 79: R. Peterson 1978,** 1:43 scale, Model No. 430 780006
EX n/a   NM n/a   MIP $35

❑ **Magirus Deutz S 3500 Medium Pumper, 1955,** 2002, Red body, black fenders and running boards, blue dome lights, 1:43 scale, Model No. 439 141070
EX n/a   NM n/a   MIP $99

(Minichamps Photo)

❑ **Magirus S 6500 Aerial Ladder, 1955,** 2002, Red body with black roof, white fenders, silver extension ladder, black levellers, 1:43 scale, Model No. 439 140071
EX n/a   NM n/a   MIP $99

❑ **MAN F8 Canvas Truck 1953,** 2002, Green and red, 1:43 scale, Model No. 439 070020
EX n/a   NM n/a   MIP $65

❑ **March BMW 792,** 2002, European F2 Championship: Keke Rosberg, 1979. White body, number "7" on sides and front, 1:43 scale, Model No. 400 790097
EX n/a   NM n/a   MIP $38

❑ **March BMW 792,** 2002, European F2 Championship: Manfred Hoettinger, 1979. Orange body with "Jagermeister" in white script on sides and front, number "26" on front and sides, 1:43 scale, Model No. 400 790026
EX n/a   NM n/a   MIP $38

❑ **March BWM 792,** 2002, European F2 Championship, Teo Fabi, 1979. White body, red and blue stripes, number "4" on sides and front, 1:43 scale, Model No. 400 790004

EX n/a　　**NM** n/a　　**MIP** $38

❑ **March Ford-Cosworth DFV 751: "Beta",** 2002, Winner, GP Austrian: Vittorio Brambilla, 1975. Orange body with "Goodyear" on spoiler, "Beta" on nose, number "9" on sides and front, 1:43 scale, Model No. 430 750009

EX n/a　　**NM** n/a　　**MIP** $40

❑ **March Ford-Cosworth DFV 761,** 2002, Jaegermeister GP of Germany, Hans-Joachim Stuck, 1976. Dark yellow body, "Jagermeister" on sides and front, number "34" on sides and front, 1:43 scale, Model No. 430 760034

EX n/a　　**NM** n/a　　**MIP** $40

❑ **Maybach Zeppelin, 1932,** Gray open-top body, dark gray-green fenders and running boards, two spares on sides, presentation packaging, 1:43 scale, Model No. 436 039401

EX n/a　　**NM** n/a　　**MIP** $48

❑ **Mazda 787 B,** 2002, Winner, 24-hour Le Mans 1981: Volker Weidler. Green and red body with colors divided by white stripes. "Renown" and number "55" on sides and front. Limited to 9,999 pieces, individually numbered. Comes in a presentation gift box, 1:43 scale, Model No. 436 911655

EX n/a　　**NM** n/a　　**MIP** $76

❑ **McLaren Chevrolet M8D: D Hulme Can-Am Champion '70,** 2002, 1:43 scale, Model No. 530 704305

EX n/a　　**NM** n/a　　**MIP** $48

❑ **McLaren Chevrolet M8D: P. Gethin Can-Am 1970,** 2002, 1:43 scale, Model No. 530 704397

EX n/a　　**NM** n/a　　**MIP** $48

❑ **McLaren Ford M19 Sunoco: M. Donohue 1971,** 1:43 scale, Model No. 530 714310

EX n/a　　**NM** n/a　　**MIP** $38

❑ **McLaren Ford-Cosworth DFV M19,** 2002, GP Monaco: Dennis Hulme, 1971. Orange body, black engine behind driver, number "9" on sides and front,

"McLaren Cars" on sides below driver, 1:43 scale, Model No. 530 714309

EX n/a　　**NM** n/a　　**MIP** $38

❑ **McLaren M8A,** 2002, Team McLaren Can Am Series Champion 1968: Dennis Hulme. Orange body, chrome exhaust behind driver, number "5" on sides and front, 1:43 scale, Model No. 530 684305

EX n/a　　**NM** n/a　　**MIP** $48

❑ **McLaren M8A,** 2002, Team McLaren Can Am Series Champion 1968: Bruce McLaren. Orange body, number "4" on sides and front, 1:43 scale, Model No. 530 684304

EX n/a　　**NM** n/a　　**MIP** $45

❑ **McLaren M8B,** 2002, Team McLaren Can Am Series Champion, 1969: Dennis Hulme. Orange body with spoiler, number "5" on front and sides, "Goodyear" on front, 1:43 scale, Model No. 530 694305

EX n/a　　**NM** n/a　　**MIP** $48

❑ **McLaren M8D,** 2002, Team McLaren Can Am Series 1970: Dan Gurney. Orange body, black spoiler, number "48" on sides and front, 1:43 scale, Model No. 530 704307

EX n/a　　**NM** n/a　　**MIP** $48

❑ **McLaren M8F,** 2002, Can Am 1971: Denny Hulme. Orange body, number "5" on sides and front, "McLaren Cars" on sides, 1:43 scale, Model No. 530 714305

EX n/a　　**NM** n/a　　**MIP** $48

❑ **McLaren M8F: P. Revson Can-Am Champion 1971,** 2002, 1:43 scale, Model No. 530 714307

EX n/a　　**NM** n/a　　**MIP** $48

❑ **McLaren Mercedes MP4-16 + Mercedes-Benz CLK DTM: M. Hakkinen,** 2002, 1:43 scale, Model No. 402 014303

EX n/a　　**NM** n/a　　**MIP** $88

❑ **McLaren Mercedes MP4-16: D. Coulthard 2001,** 1:43 scale, Model No. 530 014304

EX n/a　　**NM** n/a　　**MIP** $35

❑ **McLaren Mercedes MP4-16: M. Hakkinen 2001,** 1:43 scale, Model No. 530 014303

EX n/a　　**NM** n/a　　**MIP** $35

❑ **McLaren MP4: A. De Cesaris 1981,** 1:43 scale, Model No. 530 814308

EX n/a　　**NM** n/a　　**MIP** $35

❑ **McLaren MP4: J. Watson Winner GP England 1981,** 1:43 scale, Model No. 530 814307

EX n/a　　**NM** n/a　　**MIP** $35

❑ **McLaren Tag Turbo MP4/2,** 2002, GP England, 1986: Prost. White body with wide diagonal red stripes on sides, red chevron design on front, "McLaren" on nose, sides and spoiler. Shell logo behind driver, number "1" on nose, 1:43 scale, Model No. 530 864301

EX n/a　　**NM** n/a　　**MIP** $38

❑ **McLaren Tag Turbo MP4/2C,** 2002, GP England, 1986: Rosberg. White body with red chevron design on nose, red diagonal stripes on body, "McLaren" on front and sides, number "2" on nose, 1:43 scale, Model No. 530 864302

EX n/a　　**NM** n/a　　**MIP** $38

❑ **Melkus RS 1000, 1972,** White body, blue stripes, black interior, silver rims, 1:43 scale, Model No. 430 010121

EX n/a　　**NM** n/a　　**MIP** $35

(Minichamps Photo)

❑ **Mercedes-Benz 03500 Bus, 1954 'Fernreisen',** 2002, Light and dark green body, incredibly detailed tan interior with silver luggage racks, folded back canvas roof, silver wheel covers and trim, 1:43 scale, Model No. 439 360004

EX n/a　　**NM** n/a　　**MIP** $65

❑ **Mercedes-Benz 1113 Aerial Ladder, 1966,** 2002, Red and white body with silver ladder, 1:43 scale, Model No. 439 031070

EX n/a　　**NM** n/a　　**MIP** $99

(Minichamps Photo)

❑ **Mercedes-Benz 190 SL Cabriolet, 1955,** 2002, Blue body, dark blue interior, white cover over folded-down convertible top, blue and silver hubcaps, silver trim, 1:43 scale, Model No. 430 033137

EX n/a   NM n/a   MIP $35

❑ **Mercedes-Benz 200 T, 1980,** Light pea-green body, green interior, green and silver hubcaps, silver roof rack and trim, 1:43 scale, Model No. 430 032224

EX n/a   NM n/a   MIP $35

❑ **Mercedes-Benz 300 SEL 6.3, 1968,** Dark maroon-red body, silver and dark red hubcaps, silver trim, black interior, 1:43 scale, Model No. 430 039102

EX n/a   NM n/a   MIP $35

❑ **Mercedes-Benz 300 SEL 6.3, 1968,** Pearl-silver metallic body, gray interior, silver trim, 1:43 scale, Model No. 430 039104

EX n/a   NM n/a   MIP $35

❑ **Mercedes-Benz 300 SL,** 24-hour Le Mans, 1952 Helferich and Niedermayer. Silver body, silver wheels, number "20" on sides and hood, 1:43 scale, Model No. 432 003311

EX n/a   NM n/a   MIP $38

❑ **Mercedes-Benz 300 SLR,** 24-hour Le Mans, 1955: Fangio and Moss. Silver body, silver spoked rims, number "19" in white circle on sides and hood, 1:43 scale, Model No. 432 553000

EX n/a   NM n/a   MIP $38

❑ **Mercedes-Benz 320 E Cabriolet, 1990,** Deep magenta-red body, black interior, silver-gray rims, 1:43 scale, Model No. 430 003515

EX n/a   NM n/a   MIP $35

❑ **Mercedes-Benz 320 E, 1990,** Silver metallic body, charcoal interior, silver trim, 1:43 scale, Model No. 430 003215

EX n/a   NM n/a   MIP $35

❑ **Mercedes-Benz 320 TE,** Dark red metallic station wagon (break) body with gray trim, 1:43 scale, Model No. 430 003315

EX n/a   NM n/a   MIP n/a

❑ **Mercedes-Benz 450 SEL 6.9, 1974,** Silver-/light green metallic body, black and silver trim, 1:43 scale, Model No. 430 039202

EX n/a   NM n/a   MIP $35

❑ **Mercedes-Benz 450 SEL 6.9, 1974,** Dark orange body, light gray interior, silver hubs and trim, 1:43 scale, Model No. 430 039204

EX n/a   NM n/a   MIP $35

❑ **Mercedes-Benz 560 SEL, 1989,** Black body, tan interior, gray trim, 1:43 scale, Model No. 430 039304

EX n/a   NM n/a   MIP $35

❑ **Mercedes-Benz 560 SEL, 1989,** Blue metallic body, gray trim, black interior, gray wheels, 1:43 scale, Model No. 430 039302

EX n/a   NM n/a   MIP $35

❑ **Mercedes-Benz 600 SEC, 1992,** Silver body, black interior, silver trim, black grille, 1:43 scale, Model No. 430 032603

EX n/a   NM n/a   MIP n/a

❑ **Mercedes-Benz Atego Box Truck, 1997 'Exel Logistics',** Silver cab and body, "Exel" in blue type on box. Black chassis, gray wheels, 1:43 scale, Model No. 439 380042

EX n/a   NM n/a   MIP $55

❑ **Mercedes-Benz Atego Box Truck, 1997 'Hammer-Time Shuttle',** White cab and body with sun-burst graphics on box and "Time Shuttle by Hammer." Black chassis, gray wheels, 1:43 scale, Model No. 439 380041

EX n/a   NM n/a   MIP $55

❑ **Mercedes-Benz Atego Canvas Truck, 1997, Dachser',** Dark blue cab and body, black chassis, bright yellow canvas cover, "Dachser" on yellow cover in blue type, 1:43 scale, Model No. 439 380022

EX n/a   NM n/a   MIP $55

❑ **Mercedes-Benz C111 / II 1970,** Orange metallic body, presentation box with history of automobile, limited edition of 9,999 pieces, 1:43 scale, Model No. 436 030060

EX n/a   NM n/a   MIP $80

❑ **Mercedes-Benz C36 AMG, 1993,** Pale yellow body, dark gray interior, silver-gray hubs, 1:43 scale, Model No. 430 032161

EX n/a   NM n/a   MIP $35

❑ **Mercedes-Benz C-Class Sports Coupe, 2001,** Red body, black interior, silver five-spoke wheels, sunroof, 1:43 scale, Model No. 430 030000

EX n/a   NM n/a   MIP $35

(Minichamps Photo)

❑ **Mercedes-Benz C-Class Sports Coupe, 2001,** 2002, Light lime-green metallic body, charcoal interior, silver-gray five-spoke wheels, 1:43 scale, Model No. 430 030001

EX n/a   NM n/a   MIP $35

❑ **Mercedes-Benz C-Class T-Model, 2001,** Black station wagon body, light gray interior, silver seven-spoke wheels, silver trim, 1:43 scale, Model No. 430 030110

EX n/a   NM n/a   MIP $35

(Minichamps Photo)

❑ **Mercedes-Benz C-Class T-Model, 2001,** 2002, Blue metallic station wagon body, light gray interior, silver seven-spoke wheels, 1:43 scale, Model No. 430 030111

EX n/a   NM n/a   MIP $35

❑ **Mercedes-Benz C-Class, 1993,** Dark green metallic body, tan interior, silver rims, 1:43 scale, Model No. 430 032104

EX n/a   NM n/a   MIP $35

❑ **Mercedes-Benz CL-Coupe, 1999,** Purple-blue metallic body, gray interior, silver five-spoke wheels, 1:43 scale, Model No. 430 038025

EX n/a   NM n/a   **MIP** $35

❑ **Mercedes-Benz CLK "D2" Team AMG,** DTM 2001 Champion: B. Schneider. Silver body with black spoiler, red and blue "D2" on sides and hood, silver wheels, "Vodafone" and number "1" on sides and hood, silver wheels, 1:43 scale, Model No. 400 013101

EX n/a   NM n/a   **MIP** $48

❑ **Mercedes-Benz CLK "D2" Team AMG,** DTM 2001: P. Dumbreck. Silver body with red and blue "D2" on sides and hood, black spoiler, "Vodafone" and number "2" on sides and hood, silver wheels, 1:43 scale, Model No. 400 013102

EX n/a   NM n/a   **MIP** $48

❑ **Mercedes-Benz CLK "Eschmann" Team Manthey,** DTM 2001: P. Huismann. Dark blue body, black spoiler, "Eschmann Stahl" in white type on sides, roof and hood, silver wheels, number "10" on sides and hood, 1:43 scale, Model No. 400 013110

EX n/a   NM n/a   **MIP** $48

❑ **Mercedes-Benz CLK "Eschmann" Team Manthey,** DTM 2001: B. Maylaender. Dark blue body with "Eschmann Stahl" in white type on sides, roof and hood, silver wheels, black spoiler, number "9" on sides and hood, 1:43 scale, Model No. 400 013109

EX n/a   NM n/a   **MIP** $48

❑ **Mercedes-Benz CLK "Original-Teile" Team Persson,** DTM 2001: Ch. Albers. White and gray body with nuts, bolts and springs graphics, blue nose "bursting through" design (looks like torn-away paper), silver wheels, black spoiler, "Original-Teile" on sides, number "15" on sides and hood, 1:43 scale, Model No. 400 013715

EX n/a   NM n/a   **MIP** $48

❑ **Mercedes-Benz CLK "Original-Teile" Team Persson,** DTM 2001: T. Jaeger. White and gray hardware, gears, springs graphics, blue nose, "Original-Teile" on sides, number "14" on sides and front, silver wheels, 1:43 scale, Model No. 400 013714

EX n/a   NM n/a   **MIP** $48

❑ **Mercedes-Benz CLK "Service 24h" Team Rosberg,** DTM 2001: P. Lamy. Dark blue with sun and stars graphics, black spoiler, "Service 24h" on hood, roof, and sides, number "24" on hood and sides, Benz graphic on roof, silver wheels, 1:43 scale, Model No. 400 013724

EX n/a   NM n/a   **MIP** $48

❑ **Mercedes-Benz CLK "Service 24h" Team Rosberg,** DTM 2001: D. Turner. Dark blue body with sun and stars graphics, "Service 24h" on sides, hood and roof, number "42" on sides and hood, black spoiler, silver wheels, 1:43 scale, Model No. 400 013742

EX n/a   NM n/a   **MIP** $48

❑ **Mercedes-Benz CLK "Warsteiner" Team AMG,** DTM 2001: U. Alzen. Black body with silver "Warsteiner" on sides, hood and roof, silver wheels, number "5" on hood and sides, 1:43 scale, Model No. 400 013105

EX n/a   NM n/a   **MIP** $48

❑ **Mercedes-Benz CLK "Warstiner" Team AMG,** DTM 2001: M. Faessler. Gloss black body with "Warsteiner" in silver type on sides, roof and hood, silver wheels, number "6" on sides and hood, 1:43 scale, Model No. 400 013106

EX n/a   NM n/a   **MIP** $48

❑ **Mercedes-Benz CLK Test Car Team AMG,** 2002, DTM 2001: Manuel Reuter. With figurine., 1:43 scale, Model No. 400 013791

EX n/a   NM n/a   **MIP** $48

❑ **Mercedes-Benz E-Class Cabriolet, 1994,** Blue metallic body, gray trim, light tan interior, silver hubs, 1:43 scale, Model No. 430 033531

EX n/a   NM n/a   **MIP** $35

❑ **Mercedes-Benz E-Class Coupe, 1994,** Dark blue-purple metallic body with gray trim, gray interior, silver hubs, 1:43 scale, Model No. 430 033520

EX n/a   NM n/a   **MIP** $35

(Minichamps Photo)

❑ **Mercedes-Benz L 3500 Canvas Truck, Deutsche Bundesbahn, 1954,** 2002, Dark green body, black fenders, chassis and wheels, light tan canvas top over truck bed, light tan lettering on sides, "Deutsche Bundesbahn", 1:43 scale, Model No. 439 350022

EX n/a   NM n/a   **MIP** $48

(Minichamps Photo)

❑ **Mercedes-Benz L 3500 Tipper Truck, 1954,** 2002, Bright blue body and tipper section, red chassis and wheels. Operating tipper with spare wheel underneath, 1:43 scale, Model No. 439 350004

EX n/a   NM n/a   **MIP** $55

(Minichamps Photo)

❑ **Mercedes-Benz SL-Class, 2001,** 2002, Blue metallic body, charcoal interior, seven-spoke hubs, 1:43 scale, Model No. 400 031030

EX n/a   NM n/a   **MIP** $35

(Minichamps Photo)

❑ **Mercedes-Benz Sprinter Break, 2001,** 2002, Turquoise minibus body with gray interior, silver-gray hubcaps, 1:43 scale, Model No. 400 031110

EX n/a   NM n/a   **MIP** $48

(Minichamps Photo)

❑ **Mercedes-Benz Sprinter Van, 2001 "Nobis",** 2002, Dark brown with "Nobis Printen" graphics on panel sides, 1:43 scale, Model No. 400 031160
EX n/a   NM n/a   MIP $48

❑ **Mercedes-Benz Travego Bus, 2000,** 2002, Ivory body with tinted windows, 1:43 scale, Model No. 439 030180
EX n/a   NM n/a   MIP n/a

(Minichamps Photo)

❑ **Mercedes-Benz Unimog 401 1950,** 2002, Blue-gray body, gray-green canvas roof over cab, orange wheels, black chassis, "Unimog" in white type on sides and hood, 1:43 scale, Model No. 439 030200
EX n/a   NM n/a   MIP $48

(Minichamps Photo)

❑ **Mercedes-Benz Vaneo, 2001,** 2002, Black metallic van body, charcoal interior, silver wheels, 1:43 scale, Model No. 400 031200
EX n/a   NM n/a   MIP $35

❑ **Mercedes-Benz W196 GP,** Reims, 1954: K. Kling. Silver body, red interior, silver spoked wheels, red number "20" on front and sides, 1:43 scale, Model No. 432 543020
EX n/a   NM n/a   MIP $38

❑ **Mercedes-Benz W196 GP,** Reims, 1954: H. Lang. Silver body, silver spoked wheels, red number "22" on sides and hood, 1:43 scale, Model No. 432 543022
EX n/a   NM n/a   MIP $38

❑ **MGB Cabriolet 1962,** Black body, tan interior, silver spoked wheels and trim, 1:43 scale, Model No. 430 131030
EX n/a   NM n/a   MIP $35

❑ **MGB Soft Top, 1962,** Cream body, black roof, whitewall tires, silver spoked wheels and silver luggage rack and trim, 1:43 scale, Model No. 430 131040
EX n/a   NM n/a   MIP $35

❑ **Minardi European PS01,** 2002, Alex Yoong, Indianapolis 2001. Black body with "European Aviation" on sides and spoiler, small American flags on nose, 1:43 scale, Model No. 400 010220
EX n/a   NM n/a   MIP $38

❑ **Minardi European PS01,** 2002, Tarso Marques, 2001. Black with "European Avaition" on sides and spoiler, 1:43 scale, Model No. 400 010021
EX n/a   NM n/a   MIP $35

❑ **Minardi European PS01,** 2002, F. Alonso, 1:43 scale, Model No. 400 010020
EX n/a   NM n/a   MIP $35

❑ **Minardi European PS01,** 2002, Testcar, C. Albers, 1:43 scale, Model No. 400 010121
EX n/a   NM n/a   MIP $38

❑ **Minardi European PS01,** 2002, Fernando Alonso, Indianapolis 2001. Black body with "European Aviation" on sides and spoiler, yellow "Magnum" graphic behind driver, small American flags on nose, 1:43 scale, Model No. 400 010221
EX n/a   NM n/a   MIP $38

(Minichamps Photo)

❑ **Mini Cooper, 2001,** 2002, Dark blue metallic body, white roof with full sunroof, white five-spoke wheels, opening hood with detailed engine, 1:43 scale, Model No. 431 138100
EX n/a   NM n/a   MIP $38

❑ **Mitsubishi Pajero LWB, 1991,** Black body, cream trim, gray-blue interior, spoked wheels, 1:43 scale, Model No. 430 163471
EX n/a   NM n/a   MIP $38

❑ **Mitsubishi Pajero SWB, 1991,** Blue metallic two-door model with white trim, light gray interior, silver wheels, 1:43 scale, Model No. 430 163370
EX n/a   NM n/a   MIP $38

❑ **NSU 1000L, 1964,** Dark blue body, cream wheels with silver hubcaps, silver bumpers and trim, gray interior, 1:43 scale, Model No. 430 015202
EX n/a   NM n/a   MIP $35

❑ **NSU Ro80, 1972,** Dark green four-door body, silver wheels, trim and bumpers, 1:43 scale, Model No. 430 015404
EX n/a   NM n/a   MIP $35

(Minichamps Photo)

❑ **NSU Ro80, 1972,** 2002, Silver body and wheels, black interior, chrome bumpers and trim, 1:43 scale, Model No. 430 015405
EX n/a   NM n/a   MIP $35

(Minichamps Photo)

❑ **NSU Spider, 1964,** 2002, Silver convertible body, red interior, cream wheels with silver hubcaps, chrome bumpers and trim, 1:43 scale, Model No. 430 019231
EX n/a   **NM** n/a   **MIP** $35

❑ **NSU Sport Prinz, 1959,** Silver body, cream wheels with silver hubcaps, chrome bumpers and trim, 1:43 scale, Model No. 430 019220
EX n/a   **NM** n/a   **MIP** $35

(Minichamps Photo)

❑ **NSU Sport Prinz, 1964,** 2002, Blue-green body (very close to a VW 1600 TL), off-white interior, cream wheels with silver hubcaps, silver trim and bumpers, 1:43 scale, Model No. 430 019221
EX n/a   **NM** n/a   **MIP** $35

❑ **NSU TT, 1967,** Blue metallic body, blue interior, silver-gray rims, 1:43 scale, Model No. 430 015302
EX n/a   **NM** n/a   **MIP** $35

❑ **Opel Admiral, 1969,** Light silver-green metallic body, tan interior, silver hubcaps, bumpers and grille, thin whitewall tires, 1:43 scale, Model No. 430 046061
EX n/a   **NM** n/a   **MIP** $35

❑ **Opel Agila, 2000,** Red body, black trim and roof rack, six-spoke wheels, 1:43 scale, Model No. 430 049001
EX n/a   **NM** n/a   **MIP** $35

❑ **Opel Astra Cabriolet, 2001,** Silver convertible body, red interior, silver six-spoke wheels, 1:43 scale, Model No. 430 049130
EX n/a   **NM** n/a   **MIP** $35

(Minichamps Photo)

❑ **Opel Astra Cabriolet, 2001,** 2002, Red convertible body, black interior, gray six-spoke wheels, 1:43 scale, Model No. 430 049131
EX n/a   **NM** n/a   **MIP** $35

❑ **Opel Blitz Canvas Truck, 1955,** 2002, Blue, 1:43 scale, Model No. 439 051020
EX n/a   **NM** n/a   **MIP** $48

❑ **Opel Commodore A, 1968,** Deep green metallic body with black roof, tan interior, silver hubcaps, bumpers and trim, 1:43 scale, Model No. 430 046160
EX n/a   **NM** n/a   **MIP** $35

❑ **Opel Corsa, 2000,** Silver body, black trim, black interior, seven-spoke wheels, 1:43 scale, Model No. 430 040301
EX n/a   **NM** n/a   **MIP** $35

❑ **Opel Coupe, 2000,** Dark maroon-red body, tan interior, silver-gray six-spoke wheels, 1:43 scale, Model No. 430 049124
EX n/a   **NM** n/a   **MIP** $35

❑ **Opel Diplomat, 1968,** 2002, Black body, silver spoked hubcaps, thin whitewall tires, 1:43 scale, Model No. 430 046070
EX n/a   **NM** n/a   **MIP** $35

❑ **Opel Kadett A Caravan, 1962,** Grey two-door station wagon body, thin whitewall tires with plain silver hubcaps, gray interior, silver bumpers and trim, 1:43 scale, Model No. 430 043010
EX n/a   **NM** n/a   **MIP** $35

❑ **Opel Kadett C Caravan, 1977,** Dark maroon-red two-door station wagon with gray rims, 1:43 scale, Model No. 430 045614
EX n/a   **NM** n/a   **MIP** $35

(Minichamps Photo)

❑ **Opel Kadett C Coupe Sport Special,** 2002, Dark metallic purple body and spoiler, blue, black and silver interior with rollbar, gray five-spoke wheels, sponsor stickers in windows, 1:43 scale, Model No. 430 045625
EX n/a   **NM** n/a   **MIP** $35

❑ **Opel Kapitaen, 1951,** Medium green body, off-white interior, black wheels with silver hubcaps, silver chrome bumpers, grille and trim, 1:43 scale, Model No. 430 043304
EX n/a   **NM** n/a   **MIP** $35

❑ **Opel Kapitaen, 1959,** Bright medium blue body, white roof, white interior, silver hubcaps, grille, bumpers and trim, 1:43 scale, Model No. 430 040001
EX n/a   **NM** n/a   **MIP** $35

❑ **Opel Kapitaen, 1969,** Glossy black four-door with silver hubcaps, bumpers, grille and trim, 1:43 scale, Model No. 430 046001
EX n/a   **NM** n/a   **MIP** $35

❑ **Opel Olympia 1952,** 2002, Grey, 1:43 scale, Model No. 430 040401
EX n/a   **NM** n/a   **MIP** $35

(Minichamps Photo)

❑ **Opel Olympia Cabriolet, 1952,** 2002, Dark gray-blue body, silver hubcaps, grille and trim, open-top body with gray interior, 1:43 scale, Model No. 430 040430
EX n/a   **NM** n/a   **MIP** $35

(Minichamps Photo)

❏ **Opel Rekord A Caravan, 1962,** 2002, Red body, silver bumpers and trim, silver hubcaps, 1:43 scale, Model No. 400 041010
EX n/a   NM n/a   MIP $35

(Minichamps Photo)

❏ **Opel Rekord A Coupe, 1963,** 2002, Blue metallic body, blue interior, chrome rims, thin whitewall tires, silver grille, bumpers and trim, 1:43 scale, Model No. 400 041020
EX n/a   NM n/a   MIP $35

(Minichamps Photo)

❏ **Opel Rekord A, 1962,** 2002, Silver body with black roof, tan interior, silver hubcaps, bumpers and trim, thin whitewall tires, 1:43 scale, Model No. 400 041000
EX n/a   NM n/a   MIP $35

❏ **Opel Rekord C Caravan, 1966,** Pale blue body, black and silver grille, thin whitewalls, chrome hubcaps, bumpers and roof rack, 1:43 scale, Model No. 430 046114
EX n/a   NM n/a   MIP $35

❏ **Opel Rekord C Coupe, 1966,** Bright red body, black interior, silver grille, hubcaps and body, 1:43 scale, Model No. 430 046124
EX n/a   NM n/a   MIP $35

❏ **Opel Rekord C, 1966,** Dark blue body, tan interior, silver trim, bumpers and hubcaps, 1:43 scale, Model No. 430 046104
EX n/a   NM n/a   MIP $35

(Minichamps Photo)

❏ **Opel Rekord Caravan P1, 1958,** 2002, Turquoise and white station wagon body, turquoise wheels with silver hubcaps, white and turquoise interior, silver grille, bumpers and trim, 1:43 scale, Model No. 430 043260
EX n/a   NM n/a   MIP $35

❏ **Opel Rekord P1 Caravan, 1958,** Dark red and white body, white interior, silver bumpers, grille, and trim, 1:43 scale, Model No. 430 043218
EX n/a   NM n/a   MIP $35

❏ **Opel Rekord P2 Caravan, 1960,** Dark gray body, white interior, black wheels with silver hubcaps, roof rack and trim, white painted area under roof rack, 1:43 scale, Model No. 430 040210
EX n/a   NM n/a   MIP $35

❏ **Opel Rekord P2, 1960,** White two-door body, black wheels with silver hubcaps, white interior, silver bumpers, grille and trim, 1:43 scale, Model No. 430 040200
EX n/a   NM n/a   MIP $35

❏ **Opel V8 Coupe "Oase" Opel Team Phoenix,** DTM 2001: M. Bartels. Yellow body with light green stripe with "Oase" in white type on hood and sides, light green and black spoiler, silver wheels, number "11" on sides, 1:43 scale, Model No. 400 014111
EX n/a   NM n/a   MIP $48

(Minichamps Photo)

❏ **Opel V8 Coupe "Sat 1 ja" Opel Euroteam,** 2002, DTM 2001: A. Menu. White body with red and blue rising sun graphics, "Sat 1 ja" on sides, roof and hood, number "16" on sides and hood, silver wheels, black spoiler, 1:43 scale, Model No. 400 014116
EX n/a   NM n/a   MIP $48

(Minichamps Photo)

❏ **Opel V8 Coupe "Service Fit" Opel Team Phoenix,** 2002, DTM 2001: M. Reuter. Yellow body with white hood, rear fenders and trunk, "Service Fit" on sides and hood, number "7" on sides and hood, 1:43 scale, Model No. 400 014107
EX n/a   NM n/a   MIP $48

(Minichamps Photo)

❏ **Opel V8 Coupe "Sport Bild" Opel Team Holzer,** 2002, DTM 2001: J. Winkelhock. Red body with "Sport Bild" on sides, roof and rear quarter panels, black spoiler, silver wheels, number "3" on sides and hood, 1:43 scale, Model No. 400 014103
EX n/a   NM n/a   MIP $48

❏ **Opel V8 Coupe 'P.M. Magazin' Opel Team Holzer,** DTM 2001: T. Scheider. Black body and spoiler, red hood and doors with white "P.M. Magazin," number "4" on sides and hood, silver wheels, "Wissen kommt an." on sides, 1:43 scale, Model No. 400 014104
EX n/a   NM n/a   MIP $48

❏ **Opel V8 Coupe Team Mamerow,** DTM 2001: P. Mamerow. White and blue body, black spoiler, "www.arsios.de" on sides, number "20" on sides and hood, silver-gray wheels, 1:43 scale, Model No. 400 014820
EX n/a   NM n/a   MIP $48

(Minichamps Photo)

❏ **Opel V8 Coupe Test Car With Figurine DTM 2001: V. Strycek,** 2002, 1:43 scale, Model No. 400 014190
EX n/a   NM n/a   MIP $48

(Minichamps Photo)

❏ **Opel V8 Coupe Test Car With Figurine Opel Team Holzer DTM 2000: V. Strycek,** 2002, 1:43 scale, Model No. 430 004890
EX n/a   NM n/a   MIP $48

(Minichamps Photo)

❏ **Opel V8 Coupe Test Car With Figurine Team Phoenix DTM Presentation 2001: B. Schneider,** 2002, 1:43 scale, Model No. 400 014897
EX n/a   NM n/a   MIP $48

❏ **Opel V8 Coupe, Opel Euroteam,** DTM 2001: H. Haupt. White with blue and red, "ATS" on sides and hood, black spoiler, number "17" on hood and sides, silver spoked wheels, 1:43 scale, Model No. 400 014817
EX n/a   NM n/a   MIP $48

❏ **Opel V8 Coupe, Opel Team Phoenix,** DTM 2001: Y. Olivier. White and yellow with green arrow designs on sides and roof, silver spoked wheels, number "8" on sides and hood, 1:43 scale, Model No. 400 014808
EX n/a   NM n/a   MIP $48

(Minichamps Photo)

❏ **Opel Vivaro, 2001,** 2002, Blue metallic minibus body, black trim, gray wheels, white interior, 1:43 scale, Model No. 430 040511
EX n/a   NM n/a   MIP $46

(Minichamps Photo)

❏ **Opel Vivaro, 2001,** 2002, Dark magenta-red metallic van body with gray interior, charcoal trim, silver-gray wheels, 1:43 scale, Model No. 430 040561
EX n/a   NM n/a   MIP $48

❏ **Opel Zafira, 1999,** Silver station wagon/minivan body with black trim and roof rack, gray five-spoke wheels, 1:43 scale, Model No. 430 048002
EX n/a   NM n/a   MIP $35

❏ **Panoz Esperante GTR,** Wallace, Weaver and Leitzinger 24-hour Le Mans, 1997. White body with blue, green and red color patches, "Toad Car Security" on sides, number "54" on sides and hood, 1:43 scale, Model No. AC4 978954
EX n/a   NM n/a   MIP $48

❏ **Panoz Esperante GTR,** Lagorce, Bernard and Bovillon 24-hour Le Mans, 1997. Black body with yellow flames behind rear wheels, "Motorola" on spoiler, sides and front, French flags on sides and hood, number "52", 1:43 scale, Model No. AC4 978952
EX n/a   NM n/a   MIP $48

❏ **Panoz Esperante GTR,** Brabham, Mc Carthy and Bundy 24-hour Le Mans, 1997. White body with blue, green and red color patches, "Toad Car Security" on sides, number "55" on sides and hood, 1:43 scale, Model No. AC4 978955
EX n/a   NM n/a   MIP $48

❏ **Panoz LMP,** Magnussen, O'Connell and Angelleli 24-hour Le Mans, 1999. Silver and black body, "Visteon" on spoiler and sides, American flag on sides and front, number "11", 1:43 scale, Model No. AC4 998811
EX n/a   NM n/a   MIP $48

❏ **Panoz LMP,** Brabham, Bernard and Leitzinger 24-hour Le Mans, 1999. Silver and black body, "Visteon" on spoiler and sides, American flag on front and sides, number "12," gray multi-spoked wheels, 1:43 scale, Model No. AC4 998812
EX n/a   NM n/a   MIP $48

❏ **Peugeot 306, 1998,** Gold metallic body with black trim and multi-spoked wheels, 1:43 scale, Model No. 430 112870
EX n/a   NM n/a   MIP n/a

❏ **Peugeot 306, 1998,** Dark blue metallic body with black trim and multi-spoked wheels, 1:43 scale, Model No. 430 112871
EX n/a   NM n/a   MIP n/a

❏ **Peugeot 406 Coupe, 1997,** Dark gray body, tan interior, six-spoke wheels, sunroof, 1:43 scale, Model No. 430 112626
EX n/a   NM n/a   MIP $35

❏ **Peugeot 504 Cabriolet, 1974,** 2002, Black convertible body, gray wheels, 1:43 scale, Model No. 400 112130
EX n/a   NM n/a   MIP $35

❏ **Peugeot 504 Coupe, 1974,** 2002, Light silver-green metallic body, 1:43 scale, Model No. 400 112120
EX n/a   NM n/a   MIP $35

(Minichamps Photo)

❏ **Porsche 356 A Speedster, 1956,** 2002, Yellow body, gray wheels, silver hubcaps, bumpers and trim, black interior, 1:43 scale, Model No. 430 065535
EX n/a   NM n/a   MIP $35

❏ **Porsche 356 C Cabriolet 1965,** Blue-green body, white interior, gray cover over folded-down roof, silver hubcaps, bumper and trim, 1:43 scale, Model No. 430 062334
EX n/a   NM n/a   MIP $35

(Minichamps Photo)

❏ **Porsche 356 C Cabriolet, 1965,** 2002, Black body, gray cover over folded-down top, silver hubcaps, red interior, 1:43 scale, Model No. 430 062335
EX n/a   NM n/a   MIP $35

❏ **Porsche 356 C Coupe, 1965,** Red body, silver hubs and trim, 1:43 scale, Model No. 430 062322
EX n/a   NM n/a   MIP n/a

(Minichamps Photo)

❏ **Porsche 356 C Coupe, 1965,** 2002, Gray body, silver hubs and trim, 1:43 scale, Model No. 430 062324
EX n/a   NM n/a   MIP $35

❏ **Porsche 908/80,** 2002, Technocar Team Joest 24-hour Le Mans 1981: Reinhold Joest. White body with small illustrations of forklifts all over, number "14" on sides and front, 1:43 scale, Model No. 430 816714
EX n/a   NM n/a   MIP $48

❏ **Porsche 908/80,** 2002, Team Joest Sports Class Winners 1000KM Nuerburgring 1981: J. Mass., 1:43 scale, Model No. 430 816701
EX n/a   NM n/a   MIP $48

(Minichamps Photo)

❏ **Porsche 911 4S, 2001,** 2002, Black body, dark gray interior, silver-gray five-spoke wheels, 1:43 scale, Model No. 400 061070
EX n/a   NM n/a   MIP $35

❏ **Porsche 911 Cabriolet, 1983,** Red body, black interior, silver and black wheels, black trim, 1:43 scale, Model No. 430 062031
EX n/a   NM n/a   MIP $35

(Minichamps Photo)

❏ **Porsche 911 Cabriolet, 1983,** 2002, Gray-blue metallic convertible body, black interior, black and silver wheels, black trim, 1:43 scale, Model No. 430 062032
EX n/a   NM n/a   MIP $35

(Minichamps Photo)

❏ **Porsche 911 Cabriolet, 2001,** 2002, Blue metallic convertible body, dark tan interior, silver-gray multi-spoked hubs, 1:43 scale, Model No. 400 061030
EX n/a   NM n/a   MIP $35

❏ **Porsche 911 Carrera RSR,** 2002, Team Kremer 1000KM Monza 1973: Kremer and Schickentanz. Black body with "Samson" on sides, front and roof, number "84", 1:43 scale, Model No. 430 736984
EX n/a   NM n/a   MIP $48

❏ **Porsche 911 Carrera RSR 2.8,** 2002, Sebring 12 HRS. 1973 Winners: Gregg. Yellow body, five-spoke wheels, "59" on sides, 1:43 scale, Model No. 430 736999
EX n/a   NM n/a   MIP $48

❏ **Porsche 911 Carrera RSR Coupe, 1973,** White body with red "Carrera" stripe along sides, red and silver wheels, 1:43 scale, Model No. 430 736900
EX n/a   NM n/a   MIP $35

❏ **Porsche 911 GT2 Coupe, 2001,** Red body and spoiler, silver five-spoke hubs, 1:43 scale, Model No. 430 060120
EX n/a   NM n/a   MIP $35

(Minichamps Photo)

❏ **Porsche 911 GT2 Coupe, 2001,** 2002, Yellow body and spoiler, black interior, silver-gray five-spoke wheels, 1:43 scale, Model No. 430 060121
EX n/a   NM n/a   MIP $35

(Minichamps Photo)

❑ **Porsche 911 GT3,** 2002, Green metallic body and spoiler, silver chrome spoked wheels, tan interior, 1:43 scale, Model No. 430 068005
EX n/a NM n/a MIP $35

(Minichamps Photo)

❑ **Porsche 911 GT3-R Team Warmup 24H Le Mans 2001: Ligonnet/Alphand/Marques,** 2002, 1:43 scale, Model No. 400 016974
EX n/a NM n/a MIP $48

❑ **Porsche 911 GT3RS,** 2002, Daytona Grand Am Finale 2001: Jeanette, Bartkiw and Minkin. Red with pink stripes in diagonal criss-cross pattern, number "76", red and silver spoked wheels, 1:43 scale, Model No. 400 016976
EX n/a NM n/a MIP $50

❑ **Porsche 911 GT3-RS Team Freisinger 24 H Le Mans 2001: Jeannette/Dumas/Haezebrouck,** 1:43 scale, Model No. 400 016977
EX n/a NM n/a MIP $48

❑ **Porsche 911 GT3-RS Team Orbit 24H Daytona 2001: Baron/Buitoni/Hindery/Petty,** 1:43 scale, Model No. 400 016943
EX n/a NM n/a MIP $48

(Minichamps Photo)

❑ **Porsche 911 GT3-RS Team Seikel Motorsport GT Class Winner 24H Le Mans 2001: Rosa/Babini/Drudi,** 2002, 1:43 scale, Model No. 400 016983
EX n/a NM n/a MIP $48

❑ **Porsche 911 GT3-RS Team White Lightning GT Class Winner 24H Daytona 2001: Pobst/Luhr/Fitzgerald/Menzel,** 1:43 scale, Model No. 400 016931
EX n/a NM n/a MIP $48

❑ **Porsche 911 Targa, 1965,** 2002, Purple body, black interior, silver trim, silver and black rims, 1:43 scale, Model No. 400 061160
EX n/a NM n/a MIP $35

❑ **Porsche 911 Targa, 1977,** 2002, Green metallic open-top body with light tan interior, silver-gray spoked wheels, 1:43 scale, Model No. 400 061260
EX n/a NM n/a MIP $35

❑ **Porsche 911 Targa, 1990,** 2002, Black body with open top, dark tan interior, silver-gray spoked wheels, 1:43 scale, Model No. 400 061360
EX n/a NM n/a MIP $35

(Minichamps Photo)

❑ **Porsche 911 Targa, 2001,** 2002, Red body, gray interior, gray multi-spoked wheels, "Targa" in black script on rear of car, 1:43 scale, Model No. 400 061060
EX n/a NM n/a MIP $35

❑ **Porsche 911 Turbo, 1977,** Lime green metallic with black trim, checkered-plaid interior, green and silver wheels, 1:43 scale, Model No. 430 069005
EX n/a NM n/a MIP $35

❑ **Porsche 911 Turbo, 1990,** Dark green metallic body, gray five-spoke hubs, gray interior, 1:43 scale, Model No. 430 069105
EX n/a NM n/a MIP $35

❑ **Porsche 911 Turbo, 1995,** Red body, dark gray interior, silver-gray five-spoke wheels, 1:43 scale, Model No. 430 069205
EX n/a NM n/a MIP $35

❑ **Porsche 911 Turbo, 1999,** Dark metallic purple body, with light gray interior and silver-gray five-spoke wheels, 1:43 scale, Model No. 430 069305
EX n/a NM n/a MIP $35

(Minichamps Photo)

❑ **Porsche 911, 1964,** 2002, Blue-green body, black interior, silver hubcaps and trim, 1:43 scale, Model No. 430 067126
EX n/a NM n/a MIP $35

(Minichamps Photo)

❑ **Porsche 911, 2001,** 2002, Dark gray metallic body, gray interior, multi-spoked silver gray wheels, 1:43 scale, Model No. 400 061020
EX n/a NM n/a MIP $35

❑ **Porsche 917K,** Team Neuhaus Interseries Champion 1970: J. Neuhaus. Blue and yellow body, black wheels, number "12" on front and sides, 1:43 scale, Model No. 430 706712
EX n/a NM n/a MIP $48

❑ **Porsche 917K Gulf Team Wyer Winners 24H Daytona 1970: Rodriguez/Kinnunen,** 1:43 scale, Model No. 430 706702
EX n/a NM n/a MIP $48

❑ **Porsche 936,** 2002, "Warsteiner" DRM 1983: V. Bayern., 1:43 scale, Model No. 430 836703
EX n/a NM n/a MIP $48

❑ **Porsche 936/81 "Jules",** 2002, Team Porsche Winner 24-hour Le Mans. 1981: Jacky Ickx. White body, with orange along bottom, "Jules" in script lettering, number "11", 1:43 scale, Model No. 430 816911
EX n/a NM n/a MIP $48

(Minichamps Photo)

❑ **Porsche 936/81 'Jules' 24H Le Mans 1981: Mass/Schuppan/Haywood,** 2002, 1:43 scale, Model No. 430 816912
EX n/a   NM n/a   MIP $48

❑ **Porsche 956K,** "Warsteiner" DRM 1983: B. Wollek. White and gold body, Dunlop tires, number "1", 1:43 scale, Model No. 430 836601
EX n/a   NM n/a   MIP $48

❑ **Porsche Carrera GT, 2000,** Black body and interior, silver-gray five-spoke wheels, 1:43 scale, Model No. 430 060230
EX n/a   NM n/a   MIP $35

❑ **Porsche Carrera RSR 3.0,** 2002, "Jagermeister" Nuerburgring: Kelleners, Heyer and Wollek, 1975. Red body, "Jagermeister" in Gothic script along sides, number "4", 1:43 scale, Model No. 430 756954
EX n/a   NM n/a   MIP $48

❑ **Porsche Carrera RSR 3.0,** 2002, "Samson" Imola 1000KM: Heyer and Keller, 1974. Black with "Samson" on hood and sides, number "14", 1:43 scale, Model No. 430 746952
EX n/a   NM n/a   MIP $48

❑ **Porsche Carrera RSR 3.0,** 2002, "Lista": A. Lienhard 1974. Red and white body, "Lista" on hood, number "210" on sides, 1:43 scale, Model No. 430 746910
EX n/a   NM n/a   MIP $48

❑ **Porsche Carrera RSR 3.0 "Wallys Jeans" Nuerburgring,** 2002, K. Siewertsen, 1975. Blue body with stitching graphics, "Wallys Jeans" on sides and hood, number "6", 1:43 scale, Model No. 430 756906
EX n/a   NM n/a   MIP $48

❑ **Prost Acer AP04,** J. Alesi. Dark blue body with red patch, "Prost" on sides, "Acer" behind

driver, number "22" on nose, 1:43 scale, Model No. 400 010022
EX n/a   NM n/a   MIP $35

❑ **Prost Acer AP04,** L. Burti. Dark blue with red patch on sides, "Prost" on sides, "Acer" behind driver, silver wheels, number "23" on nose, 1:43 scale, Model No. 400 010123
EX n/a   NM n/a   MIP $35

❑ **Prost Acer AP04,** 2002, Heinz Harald Frentzen, 2001. Dark blue with "Prost" and "Acer" in white type, silver wheels, number "22" on nose, 1:43 scale, Model No. 400 010122
EX n/a   NM n/a   MIP $35

❑ **Prost-Acer AP04,** 2002, Thomas Enge, 2001. Dark blue with "Prost" on sides and "Acer" behind driver, 1:43 scale, Model No. 400 010223
EX n/a   NM n/a   MIP $38

(Minichamps Photo)

❑ **Renault 16, 1965,** 2002, White four-door with silver trim and hubcaps, 1:43 scale, Model No. 400 113100
EX n/a   NM n/a   MIP $35

❑ **Renault 8 Gordini, 1964,** Dark yellow body with two white stripes running from hood to trunk. Silver gray wheels and trim, 1:43 scale, Model No. 430 113552
EX n/a   NM n/a   MIP $35

❑ **Saab 900 Cabriolet, 1995,** Red body, black interior, black trim, three-spoke hubs, 1:43 scale, Model No. 430 170532
EX n/a   NM n/a   MIP $35

❑ **Saab 900, 1995,** Black body, blue-gray interior, sunroof, multi-spoked hubs, 1:43 scale, Model No. 430 170500
EX n/a   NM n/a   MIP $35

❑ **Saab 900, 1995,** Red body, tan interior, black trim, multi-spoked hubs, black spoiler, 1:43 scale, Model No. 430 170501
EX n/a   NM n/a   MIP $35

❑ **Saab 9-3 1999,** Bright blue four-door, blue-gray interior, black trim and spoiler, three-spoke wheels, 1:43 scale, Model No. 430 170800
EX n/a   NM n/a   MIP $35

❑ **Saab 9-3 Cabriolet, 1999,** Bright metallic blue body, black interior, six-spoke wheels, 1:43 scale, Model No. 430 170830
EX n/a   NM n/a   MIP $35

(Minichamps Photo)

❑ **Saab 9-3 Cabriolet, 1999,** 2002, Silver convertible body, black interior, black trim, six-spoke silver wheels, 1:43 scale, Model No. 430 170831
EX n/a   NM n/a   MIP $35

❑ **Saab 9-5, 1999,** Red station wagon body, black trim and roof rack, tan interior, three-spoke wheels, 1:43 scale, Model No. 430 170811
EX n/a   NM n/a   MIP n/a

❑ **Sauber Petronas C20,** K. Raikkonen, GP Malaysia. Blue and aqua green with "Petronas" on sides, Mayasian flag behind driver. Limited to 1,444 pieces, 1:43 scale, Model No. 400 010117
EX n/a   NM n/a   MIP $38

❑ **Sauber Petronas C20,** N. Heidfeld, GP Malaysia. Blue and aqua green with "Petronas" on sides, Mayalsian flag behind driver. Limited to 1,444 pieces, 1:43 scale, Model No. 400 010116
EX n/a   NM n/a   MIP $38

❑ **Sauber Petronas C20,** K. Raikkonen. Blue and aqua green with "Petronas" on sides, number "17" on nose, 1:43 scale, Model No. 400 010017
EX n/a   NM n/a   MIP $35

❑ **Sauber Petronas C20,** N. Heidfeld. Blue and aqua green with "Petronas" on sides, number "16" on sides, 1:43 scale, Model No. 400 010016
EX n/a   NM n/a   MIP $35

❑ **Seat Arosa, 1997,** Medium metallic green body, blue-gray interior, multi-spoke wheels, 1:43 scale, Model No. 430 057101
EX n/a   NM n/a   MIP $35

❑ **Seat Toledo, 1999,** Metallic steel gray body, silver five-spoke wheels, black grille and trim, 1:43 scale, Model No. 430 058401
EX n/a   NM n/a   MIP $35

(Minichamps Photo)

❑ **Setra S8 Bus 1953 'Der Walser',** 2002, Two-tone green, 1:43 scale, Model No. 439 030081
EX n/a   NM n/a   MIP $65

(Minichamps Photo)

❑ **Setra S8 Bus, 1953,** 2002, Red and cream body, detailed light-red interior with silver mesh luggage racks, silver trim and ladder, silver and wood-tone luggage rack on roof. Ladder folds up into driving position, 1:43 scale, Model No. 439 030080
EX n/a   NM n/a   MIP $65

❑ **Smart City Cabriolet, 2000,** Yellow-green and black open-top body, yellow-green interior, six-spoke wheels, 1:43 scale, Model No. 430 039005
EX n/a   NM n/a   MIP $35

(Minichamps Photo)

❑ **Smart City Cabriolet, 2001,** 2002, Black open-top body, yellow and black interior, six-spoke wheels, 1:43 scale, Model No. 430 039006
EX n/a   NM n/a   MIP $35

❑ **Toyota Celica SS II, 1994,** Black body, gray interior, five-spoke wheels, 1:43 scale, Model No. 430 166620
EX n/a   NM n/a   MIP $35

❑ **Toyota Celica SS II, 1994,** Red body, gray interior, silver-gray five-spoke wheels, 1:43 scale, Model No. 430 166622
EX n/a   NM n/a   MIP $35

❑ **Toyota Celica, 2000,** Black body, charcoal interior, silver-gray five-spoke hubs, 1:43 scale, Model No. 430 168921
EX n/a   NM n/a   MIP $35

(Minichamps Photo)

❑ **Toyota Corolla 5-Door, 2001,** 2002, Dark metallic green body, charcoal interior, silver-gray multi-spoked wheels, 1:43 scale, Model No. 400 166170
EX n/a   NM n/a   MIP $35

(Minichamps Photo)

❑ **Toyota Corolla, 2001,** 2002, Dark metallic blue hatchback with charcoal interior and multi-spoked silver-gray wheels, 1:43 scale, Model No. 400 166100
EX n/a   NM n/a   MIP $35

❑ **Toyota GT-One Team Toyota Motorsports 24-hour Le Mans 1999,** Katayama, Tsuchiya and Suzuki, 1:43 scale, Model No. 430 991603
EX n/a   NM n/a   MIP $48

❑ **Toyota GT-One Team Toyota Motorsports 24-hour Le Mans 1999,** Brundle, Collard and Sospiri, 1:43 scale, Model No. 430 991601
EX n/a   NM n/a   MIP $48

❑ **Toyota GT-One Team Toyota Motorsports 24-hour Le Mans, 1999,** Boutsen, McNish and Kelleners, 1:43 scale, Model No. 430 991602
EX n/a   NM n/a   MIP $48

❑ **Toyota MR 2, 2000,** Black convertilble body, black interior, silver-gray five-spoke wheels, 1:43 scale, Model No. 430 166961
EX n/a   NM n/a   MIP $35

❑ **Toyota Rav 4, 2000,** Dark teal-green metallic body, gray interior, silver-gray five-spoke wheels, 1:43 scale, Model No. 430 166000
EX n/a   NM n/a   MIP $35

(Minichamps Photo)

❑ **Toyota Rav 4, 2000,** 2002, Black two-door body with gray interior and silver-gray five-spoke wheels, 1:43 scale, Model No. 430 166001
EX n/a   NM n/a   MIP $35

❑ **Toyota Yaris TS, 2001,** Black two-door hatch body, black interior, sunroof, silver-gray five-spoke wheels, 1:43 scale, Model No. 430 166060
EX n/a   NM n/a   MIP $35

(Minichamps Photo)

❑ **Toyota Yaris TS, 2001,** 2002, Medium metallic blue body, charcoal interior, six-spoke wheels, 1:43 scale, Model No. 430 166061
EX n/a   NM n/a   MIP $35

MINICHAMPS / TRIUMPH

❏ **Triumph TR6, 1968,** British Racing Green convertible body, black interior and roof cover, silver bumpers and rims, 1:43 scale, Model No. 430 132571
EX n/a   NM n/a   MIP $35

❏ **Triumph TR6, 1968,** Red convertible body, tan interior and roof cover, silver bumpers and rims, 1:43 scale, Model No. 430 132572
EX n/a   NM n/a   MIP $35

(Minichamps Photo)

❏ **Truck Trailer Canvas, 1946,** 2002, Bright blue body, red chassis, gray canvas cover, 1:43 scale, Model No. 439 159092
EX n/a   NM n/a   MIP $48

❏ **Truck Trailer Canvas, 1946 Spedition Dachser,** Dark blue body with "Dachser Spedition" on sides, black chassis, gray wheels, 1:43 scale, Model No. 439 159091
EX n/a   NM n/a   MIP $48

❏ **Tyrrell Ford 003: F. Cevert 1971,** 1:43 scale, Model No. 430 710009
EX n/a   NM n/a   MIP $35

❏ **Tyrrell Ford 006: F. Cevert 1973,** 1:43 scale, Model No. 430 730006
EX n/a   NM n/a   MIP $35

❏ **Tyrrell Ford 006: J. Stewart 1973,** 1:43 scale, Model No. 430 730005
EX n/a   NM n/a   MIP $35

❏ **Tyrrell Ford P34,** 2002, Ronnie Peterson, 1977. Dark blue and white six-wheeled racer with "elf" in white on front and sides, number "3" on front and sides, "Goodyear" on spoiler, 1:43 scale, Model No. 430 770103
EX n/a   NM n/a   MIP $35

❏ **Tyrrell Ford P34,** 2002, Patrick Depailler, 1977. Dark blue and white body, "elf" and number "4" in white type on front and sides, "Goodyear" on spoiler, 1:43 scale, Model No. 430 770104
EX n/a   NM n/a   MIP $35

❏ **Tyrrell Ford P34 6-Wheeler: P. Depailler 1976,** 1:43 scale, Model No. 430 760004
EX n/a   NM n/a   MIP $35

❏ **Tyrrell Ford P34 FNCB: P. Depailler 1977,** 1:43 scale, Model No. 430 770004
EX n/a   NM n/a   MIP $35

❏ **Volvo 121 Amazon,** Light gray two-door body with silver bumpers, trim and hubs, 1:43 scale, Model No. 430 171001
EX n/a   NM n/a   MIP $35

❏ **Volvo 121 Amazon Station Wagon,** Dark blue body, blue interior, silver chrome bumpers, grille, hubs and trim, 1:43 scale, Model No. 430 171011
EX n/a   NM n/a   MIP $35

❏ **Volvo P1800 ES, 1971,** Dark green body, gray rims, 1:43 scale, Model No. 430 171616
EX n/a   NM n/a   MIP $35

❏ **Volvo P1800 S Coupe, 1969,** Metallic silver body, red interior, chrome grille, bumpers and trim, 1:43 scale, Model No. 430 171626
EX n/a   NM n/a   MIP $35

❏ **Volvo S40, 2000,** Red metallic body with sunroof, black trim, multi-spoked silver-gray wheels, 1:43 scale, Model No. 430 171100
EX n/a   NM n/a   MIP $35

(Minichamps Photo)

❏ **Volvo S40, 2000,** 2002, Bright blue four-door body with sunroof, black trim, silver-gray multi-spoked wheels, 1:43 scale, Model No. 430 171101
EX n/a   NM n/a   MIP $35

❏ **Volvo S60, 2000,** Metallic silver-blue body with sunroof, black trim, black interior, silver spoked wheels, 1:43 scale, Model No. 430 171260
EX n/a   NM n/a   MIP $35

(Minichamps Photo)

❏ **Volvo S60, 2000,** 2002, Gold metallic body with black trim, silver-gray wheels, 1:43 scale, Model No. 430 171261
EX n/a   NM n/a   MIP $35

❏ **Volvo S70, 2000 "Politie" (Dutch Police),** White body with red and blue stripe/check design on hood and sides. Blue dome light toward back of roof on driver's side. "Politie" in blue type on rear doors, five-spoke wheels, 1:43 scale, Model No. 430 171891
EX n/a   NM n/a   MIP $35

❏ **Volvo V40, 2000,** Red station wagon with sunroof, black interior, silver-gray multi-spoke wheels, black trim, 1:43 scale, Model No. 430 171110
EX n/a   NM n/a   MIP $35

(Minichamps Photo)

❏ **Volvo V40, 2000,** 2002, Black station wagon with sunroof, black interior, silver-gray multi-spoked wheels, 1:43 scale, Model No. 430 171111
EX n/a   NM n/a   MIP $35

❏ **Volvo V70 XC, 2000,** 2001, Black station wagon body with dark tan interior, six-spoke silver-gray wheels, 1:43 scale, Model No. 430 171270
EX n/a   NM n/a   MIP $35

(Minichamps Photo)

❑ **Volvo V70 XC, 2000,** 2002, Metallic silver station wagon with black trim and roof rack, silver-gray six-spoke wheels, 1:43 scale, Model No. 430 171271
EX n/a　　NM n/a　　MIP $35

❑ **Volvo V70, 2000,** Black body, silver grille, black interior, silver-gray multi-spoke wheels, 1:43 scale, Model No. 430 171210
EX n/a　　NM n/a　　MIP $35

(Minichamps Photo)

❑ **Volvo V70, 2000,** 2002, Silver station wagon with black trim and roof rack, silver-gray multi-spoke wheels, 1:43 scale, Model No. 430 171211
EX n/a　　NM n/a　　MIP $35

(Minichamps Photo)

❑ **VW - Porsche 914/4, 1970,** 2002, Red open-top body, black and white interior, silver rims and bumpers. An interesting combination of body styles, 1:43 scale, Model No. 430 065665
EX n/a　　NM n/a　　MIP $35

❑ **VW 1200 Export, 1951 (Beetle),** 2002, Black body, silver hubcaps and trim, 1:43 scale, Model No. 400 051200
EX n/a　　NM n/a　　MIP $38

❑ **VW 1302 Cabriolet, 1970,** Green convertible body, green interior, black roof cover, black running boards, silver hubcaps, black and silver bumpers, 1:43 scale, Model No. 430 055037
EX n/a　　NM n/a　　MIP $35

❑ **VW 1302, 1970 (Beetle),** Medium metallic olive-green body, black running boards, black and silver bumpers, silver hubcaps, white interior, 1:43 scale, Model No. 430 055004
EX n/a　　NM n/a　　MIP $35

❑ **VW 1302, 1970 (Beetle),** Blue metallic body, black running boards, white interior, silver and black bumpers, silver trim, 1:43 scale, Model No. 430 055002
EX n/a　　NM n/a　　MIP $35

❑ **VW 1303 Cabriolet, 1972,** Green convertible body, black interior, cream roof cover, five-spoke hubs, black running boards, black and silver bumpers, 1:43 scale, Model No. 430 055136
EX n/a　　NM n/a　　MIP $35

❑ **VW 1303 Cabriolet, 1972,** White convertible body, black interior and roof cover, gray five-spoke wheels, silver and black bumpers, black running boards, 1:43 scale, Model No. 430 055137
EX n/a　　NM n/a　　MIP $35

(Minichamps Photo)

❑ **VW 1303, 1972 (Beetle),** 2002, Red body, black running boards, silver and black bumpers, silver hubcaps, 1:43 scale, Model No. 430 055106
EX n/a　　NM n/a　　MIP $35

❑ **VW 1600 TL, 1966,** Light blue body, silver trim, bumpers and hubcaps, 1:43 scale, Model No. 430 055321
EX n/a　　NM n/a　　MIP $35

❑ **VW 1600 TL, 1966,** 2001, Dark blue body, silver trim, bumpers and hubcaps
EX $6　　NM $22　　MIP n/a

❑ **VW 1600 Variant, 1966,** Dark green two-door station wagon with white interior, silver trim and hubcaps, single headlights, 1:43 scale, Model No. 430 055311
EX n/a　　NM n/a　　MIP $35

❑ **VW 1600, 1966,** White, "notchback" coupe body, silver trim, bumpers and hubcaps, 1:43 scale, Model No. 430 055302
EX n/a　　NM n/a　　MIP $35

❑ **VW 181, 1969,** Orange body, orange and black interior, orange wheels. The civilian update to the Kubelwagen, known as the "Thing" in America, 1:43 scale, Model No. 430 050030
EX n/a　　NM n/a　　MIP $35

(Minichamps Photo)

❑ **VW 181, 1969,** 2002, Army olive green. An updated version of the Kubelwagen, civilian models were known in the U.S. as the VW "Thing." The olive model probably represents a type used by the West German Bundeswehr, 1:43 scale, Model No. 430 050031
EX n/a　　NM n/a　　MIP $35

(Minichamps Photo)

❑ **VW 411 Le 1969,** 2002, Blue, 1:43 scale, Model No. 400 051100
EX n/a　　NM n/a　　MIP $35

(Minichamps Photo)

❑ **VW 411 LE Variant, 1969,** Dark green two-door station wagon body, tan interior, silver trim and hubcaps, twin headlights, longer "snout" than the 1600 Variant, 1:43 scale, Model No. 400 051110
EX n/a　　NM n/a　　MIP $35

❑ **VW Golf Cabriolet, 1999,** Dark green metallic convertible body, light tan interior, multi-spoked silver-gray wheels, 1:43 scale, Model No. 430 058331
EX n/a　　NM n/a　　MIP $35

❑ **VW Golf Variant, 1999,** Black metallic station wagon body, gray interior, silver-gray multi-spoked wheels, 1:43 scale, Model No. 430 056010
EX n/a　　NM n/a　　MIP $35

❑ **VW Golf, 1997,** Gold metallic four-door body, black and gold interior, silver-gray multi-spoked wheels, 1:43 scale, Model No. 430 056008
EX n/a　　NM n/a　　MIP $35

(Minichamps Photo)

❑ **VW Golf, 1997,** 2002, Dark metallic blue body, black interior, silver multi-spoked wheels, 1:43 scale, Model No. 430 056009
EX n/a　　NM n/a　　MIP n/a

(Minichamps Photo)

❑ **VW Karmann Ghia 1600, 1966,** 2002, Turquoise body with white roof, white interior, 1:43 scale, Model No. 430 050221
EX n/a　　NM n/a　　MIP $35

(Minichamps Photo)

❑ **VW Karmann Ghia Cabriolet, 1957,** 2002, White convertible body, tan and green body, silver trim, 1:43 scale, Model No. 430 051039
EX n/a　　NM n/a　　MIP $35

❑ **VW Karmann Ghia Coupe, 1957,** Snow blue body (silver-pearl blue), blue-green interior, silver chrome trim and hubcaps, 1:43 scale, Model No. 430 051022
EX n/a　　NM n/a　　MIP $35

❑ **VW Lupo, 1998,** Black body, gray interior, six-spoke silver-gray wheels, 1:43 scale, Model No. 430 058102
EX n/a　　NM n/a　　MIP $35

(Minichamps Photo)

❑ **VW Lupo, 1998,** 2002, Bright yellow body, yellow and light gray interior, black grille, silver-gray six-spoked wheels, 1:43 scale, Model No. 430 058104
EX n/a　　NM n/a　　MIP $35

(Minichamps Photo)

❑ **VW New Beetle, 1999,** 2002, Dark blue body, black interior, silver-gray six-spoke wheels, 1:43 scale, Model No. 430 058004
EX n/a　　NM n/a　　MIP $35

❑ **VW Polo, 1974,** Red body, red interior, gray rims, 1:43 scale, Model No. 430 050500
EX n/a　　NM n/a　　MIP $35

(Minichamps Photo)

❑ **VW Polo, 1974,** 2002, Yellow body, gray interior, gray rims, 1:43 scale, Model No. 430 050501
EX n/a　　NM n/a　　MIP $35

(Minichamps Photo)

❑ **VW Scirocco, 1974,** 2002, Bright yellow body, black interior, black grille, silver rims, 1:43 scale, Model No. 430 050421
EX n/a　　NM n/a　　MIP $35

❑ **Wartburg A 311 Cabriolet, 1958,** Red and white body with tan interior and folded back roof, silver grille, hubcaps and bumpers, 1:43 scale, Model No. 430 015931
EX n/a　　NM n/a　　MIP $35

(Minichamps Photo)

❑ **Wartburg A 311 Cabriolet, 1958,** 2002, Blue convertible body with red interior, silver bumpers, grille, hubcaps and trim. Folded-back roof, 1:43 scale, Model No. 430 015932
EX n/a　　NM n/a　　MIP $35

❑ **Wartburg A 311 Coupe, 1958,** Gray and white body with gray interior, silver bumpers, grille and trim, 1:43 scale, Model No. 430 015920
EX n/a　　NM n/a　　MIP $35

(Minichamps Photo)

❑ **Wartburg A 311, 1958,** 2002, Black four-door with gray trim, 1:43 scale, Model No. 430 015904
EX n/a　　NM n/a　　MIP $35

❏ **Williams F1 BMW FW23,** R. Schumacher. White and dark blue body with "Compaq" on sides and spoiler, "Allianz" behind driver, number "5" on nose, 1:43 scale, Model No. 400 010005
EX n/a　　NM n/a　　MIP $35

❏ **Williams F1 BMW FW23,** J.P. Montoya, GP Mayalsia. Dark blue and white body, "Compaq" on sides and spoiler, number "6" on nose, silver wheels, 1:43 scale, Model No. 400 010026
EX n/a　　NM n/a　　MIP $38

❏ **Williams F1 BMW FW23,** J.P. Montoya. Dark blue and white, "Compaq" on sides and rear spoiler, silver spoked wheels, number "6" on nose, 1:43 scale, Model No. 400 010006
EX n/a　　NM n/a　　MIP $35

❏ **Williams F1 BMW FW23,** 2002, J.P. Montoya, 1st GP victory, GP Italy, 1:43 scale, Model No. 400 010126
EX n/a　　NM n/a　　MIP $38

❏ **Williams F1 FW21 Michelin: J. Muller Testcar 2000,** 1:43 scale, Model No. 430 990098
EX n/a　　NM n/a　　MIP $35

(Minichamps Photo)

❏ **Williams Ford FW 07: A. Jones 1979,** 2002, 1:43 scale, Model No. 430 790027
EX n/a　　NM n/a　　MIP $38

❏ **Williams Ford FW 08C: J. Laffite 1983,** 1:43 scale, Model No. 430 830002
EX n/a　　NM n/a　　MIP n/a

❏ **Williams Ford FW 08C: K. Rosberg 1983,** 1:43 scale, Model No. 430 830001
EX n/a　　NM n/a　　MIP $35

(Minichamps Photo)

❏ **Williams Ford FW07: C. Regazzoni 1979,** 2002, 1:43 scale, Model No. 430 790028
EX n/a　　NM n/a　　MIP $38

❏ **Williams Ford FW08,** 2002, Derek Daly, 1982. White body with red and blue stripes, "Saudia" on sides, number "5" on sides and front, 1:43 scale, Model No. 430 820095
EX n/a　　NM n/a　　MIP $35

❏ **Williams Ford FW08 World Champion,** 2002, Keke Rosberg, 1982. White body with red and blue stripes, "Saudia" on sides and number "6" on sides and front, 1:43 scale, Model No. 430 820006
EX n/a　　NM n/a　　MIP $35

1:8/1:18/1:43-SCALE

❏ **Williams Renault FW16,** 1994, 1:18 scale, Model No. 540 941802
EX n/a　　NM n/a　　MIP n/a

❏ **Williams Renault FW16,** 1994, 1:43 scale, Model No. 430 940002
EX n/a　　NM n/a　　MIP $35

1:8/1:18-SCALE

❏ **McLaren Ford MP4-8: 1993,** 1:18 scale, Model No. 540 931808
EX n/a　　NM n/a　　MIP n/a

❏ **McLaren Honda MP4-4: A. Senna World Champion 1988,** 1:18 scale, Model No. 540 881812
EX n/a　　NM n/a　　MIP n/a

❏ **McLaren Honda MP4-5: 1989,** 1:18 scale, Model No. 540 891801
EX n/a　　NM n/a　　MIP n/a

❏ **McLaren Honda MP4-5B: A. Senna World Champion 1990,** 1:18 scale, Model No. 540 901827
EX n/a　　NM n/a　　MIP n/a

❏ **McLaren Honda MP4-6: A. Senna World Champion 1991,** 1:18 scale, Model No. 540 911801
EX n/a　　NM n/a　　MIP n/a

❏ **McLaren Honda MP4-7: 1992,** 1:18 scale, Model No. 540 921801
EX n/a　　NM n/a　　MIP n/a

1:8/1:43-SCALE

❏ **McLaren Ford MP4-8: Ayrton's 41st GP Win GP Australia 1993,** 1:43 scale, Model No. 540 414341
EX n/a　　NM n/a　　MIP n/a

1:8-SCALE

(Minichamps Photo)

❏ **Arrows Supertec A21,** 2002, J. Verstappen, 2000. Orange and black body with number "19" on nose and "Orange" on sides, top and spoiler, 1:8 scale, Model No. 080 000019
EX n/a　　NM n/a　　MIP n/a

(Minichamps Photo)

❏ **Arrows Supertec A21,** 2002, P. De La Rosa, 2000. Orange and black with sponsor graphics, "Orange" on sides, top and spoiler, 1:8 scale, Model No. 080 000018
EX n/a　　NM n/a　　MIP $2440

❏ **Benetton Ford B192,** 2002, M. Schumacher 1992, GP SPA-Francorchamps, 1:8 scale, Model No. 080 920019
EX n/a　　NM n/a　　MIP $2440

❏ **Benetton Ford B193,** 2002, M. Schumacher, 1993, GP Portugal, 1:8 scale, Model No. 080 930005
EX n/a　　NM n/a　　MIP $2440

(Minichamps Photo)

❏ **Lotus Honda 99T,** 2002, A. Senna, 1987. Yellow with "Lotus" and "elf" in blue type, Honda sponsor graphics, Goodyear/Eagle tires, black wheels, 1:8 scale, Model No. 080 870812
EX n/a　　NM n/a　　MIP $2375

Racing Champions NASCAR

A small sample of Racing Champions' 1:64-scale NASCAR die-cast vehicles.

Racing Champions (now Racing Champions/Ertl, although the two are generally marketed separately) began as a single line of 1:64-scale die-cast stock cars in 1989. NASCAR's popularity was growing, and Bob Dods, Boyd Meyer and Peter Chung thought the time was right to form a company based on selling racing-related items-everything from die-cast cars and banks to trading cards.

Originally based in Glen Ellyn, Illinois, the company now sells about 2,000 different styles of racing vehicles in different scales—1:64, 1:43, 1:24 and 1:18—ranging in price from about $5 to $65. Rarities and extremely limited editions, of course, sell for much more on the aftermarket.

In 1999, Racing Champions acquired Ertl, giving the company a much greater market. Now, Racing Champions/Ertl encompasses the world of plastic and die-cast model kits, racing and road vehicles, and, naturally, agricultural vehicles. The combination of the two companies makes it one of the largest die-cast manufacturers in the world.

MARKET UPDATE

Fans of NASCAR will always love the sport, but the interest for these models seems to have peaked, making it buyers market. Collecting NASCAR die-cast is driver-based, making it different than collecting by toy manufacturer, i.e., Corgi, Dinky, Matchbox, etc. That is, most collectors are picking up models because of the name associated with the car—Bill Elliott, Terry Labonte, Jeff Gordon. The earlier models will retain value, but the newer ranges will really depend on the popularity of a driver, sponsor fluctuations and Winston Cup Standings.

580

ALLEN, JR., GLENN

❏ **#99 Luxaire,** 1997, stock car, 1:64-scale
EX n/a   NM n/a   MIP $5

❏ **#99-Luxaire,** 1996, team transporter, 1:64-scale
EX n/a   NM n/a   MIP $20

❏ **#99-Luxaire,** 1996, team transporter, 1:87-scale
EX n/a   NM n/a   MIP $8

❏ **#99-Luxaire,** 1997, stock car, 1:24-scale
EX n/a   NM n/a   MIP $15

ALLEN, LOY

❏ **#19-Healthsource,** 1996, stock car, 1:24-scale
EX n/a   NM n/a   MIP $25

❏ **#19-Healthsource,** 1996, stock car, 1:64-scale
EX n/a   NM n/a   MIP $15

ANDRETTI, JOHN

❏ **#37-Kmart,** 1996, stock car, 1:24-scale
EX n/a   NM n/a   MIP $20

❏ **#37-Kmart,** 1996, stock car, 1:64-scale
EX n/a   NM n/a   MIP $7

❏ **#37-Kmart/Little Caesars,** 1996, team transporter, 1:64-scale
EX n/a   NM n/a   MIP $25

❏ **#37-Kmart/Little Caesars,** 1996, premier stock car, 1:64-scale
EX n/a   NM n/a   MIP $7

❏ **#37-Kmart/Little Caesars,** 1996, stock car, 1:64-scale
EX n/a   NM n/a   MIP $7

BARFIELD, RON

❏ **#94-New Holland,** 1997, stock car, 1:24-scale
EX n/a   NM n/a   MIP $15

❏ **#94-New Holland,** 1997, stock car, 1:64-scale
EX n/a   NM n/a   MIP $5

BENDER, TIM

❏ **#17-Kraft,** 1997, stock car, 1:64-scale
EX n/a   NM n/a   MIP $5

BENSON, JR., JOHNNY

❏ **#30-Pennzoil,** 1996, premier stock car w/opening hood, 1:64-scale
EX n/a   NM n/a   MIP $12

❏ **#30-Pennzoil,** 1996, team transporter w/two stock cars, 1:64-scale
EX n/a   NM n/a   MIP $25

❏ **#30-Pennzoil,** 1996, team transporter w/stock car, 1:64-scale
EX n/a   NM n/a   MIP $25

❏ **#30-Pennzoil,** 1996, team transporter, 1:64-scale
EX n/a   NM n/a   MIP $15

❏ **#30-Pennzoil,** 1996, team transporter w/mini stock car, 1:87-scale
EX n/a   NM n/a   MIP $8

❏ **#30-Pennzoil,** 1996, premier stock car w/opening hood, 1:18-scale
EX n/a   NM n/a   MIP $30

❏ **#30-Pennzoil,** 1996, stock car w/opening hood, 1:24-scale
EX n/a   NM n/a   MIP $50

❏ **#30-Pennzoil,** 1996, stock car, 1:24-scale
EX n/a   NM n/a   MIP $20

❏ **#30-Pennzoil,** 1997, stock car, 1:64-scale
EX n/a   NM n/a   MIP $5

❏ **#30-Pennzoil,** 1997, stock car, 1:24-scale
EX n/a   NM n/a   MIP $15

❏ **#30-Pennzoil,** 1997, team transporter w/mini stock car, 1:144-scale
EX n/a   NM n/a   MIP $2

❏ **#30-Pennzoil,** 1997, team transporter w/mini stock car, 1:87-scale
EX n/a   NM n/a   MIP $10

❏ **#30-Pennzoil,** 1997, team transporter, 1:64-scale
EX n/a   NM n/a   MIP $22

❏ **#30-Pennzoil,** 1997, team transporter w/two stock cars, 1:64-scale
EX n/a   NM n/a   MIP $25

❏ **#30-Pennzoil,** 1997, stock car, Pinnacle Series, 1:64-scale
EX n/a   NM n/a   MIP $6

❏ **#30-Pennzoil,** 1997, team transporter w/stock car, 1:64-scale
EX n/a   NM n/a   MIP $25

❏ **#30-Pennzoil/Preview Edition,** 1997, stock car, 1:64-scale
EX n/a   NM n/a   MIP $5

❏ **#30-Pennzoil/Preview Edition,** 1997, stock car, 1:24-scale
EX n/a   NM n/a   MIP $20

BESSEY, JOE

❏ **#9-Delco Remy,** 1996, premier stock car w/opening hood, 1:18-scale
EX n/a   NM n/a   MIP $30

❏ **#9-Delco Remy,** 1996, stock car w/opening hood, 1:24-scale
EX n/a   NM n/a   MIP $25

❏ **#9-Delco Remy,** 1996, stock car, 1:24-scale
EX n/a   NM n/a   MIP $20

❏ **#9-Delco Remy,** 1996, stock car, 1:64-scale
EX n/a   NM n/a   MIP $5

❏ **#9-Delco Remy/Preview Edition,** 1996, stock car, 1:24-scale
EX n/a   NM n/a   MIP $20

❏ **#9-Delco Remy/Preview Edition,** 1996, stock car, 1:64-scale
EX n/a   NM n/a   MIP $5

❏ **#9-Power Team,** 1997, stock car, 1:24-scale
EX n/a   NM n/a   MIP $15

❏ **#9-Power Team,** 1997, stock car, 1:64-scale
EX n/a   NM n/a   MIP $5

BODINE, BRETT

❏ **#11-Frontier,** 1997, stock car, 1:24-scale
EX n/a   NM n/a   MIP $15

❏ **#11-Frontier,** 1997, team transporter, 1:64-scale
EX n/a   NM n/a   MIP $22

❏ **#11-Frontier,** 1997, team transporter w/stock car, 1:64-scale
EX n/a   NM n/a   MIP $25

❏ **#11-Frontier,** 1997, team transporter w/two stock cars, 1:64-scale
EX n/a   NM n/a   MIP $25

❏ **#11-Frontier,** 1997, stock car, 1:64-scale
EX n/a   NM n/a   MIP $5

❏ **#11-Frontier,** 1997, team transporter w/mini stock car, 1:144-scale
EX n/a   NM n/a   MIP $3

❏ **#11-Frontier,** 1997, team transporter w/mini stock car, 1:87-scale
EX n/a   NM n/a   MIP $10

❑ **#11-Lowe's,** 1996, stock car, 1:64-scale
EX n/a   NM n/a   MIP $4

❑ **#11-Lowe's,** 1996, premier stock car w/opening hood, 1:64-scale
EX n/a   NM n/a   MIP $8

❑ **#11-Lowe's,** 1996, stock car, 1:24-scale
EX n/a   NM n/a   MIP $20

❑ **#11-Lowe's,** 1996, stock car w/opening hood, 1:24-scale
EX n/a   NM n/a   MIP $25

❑ **#11-Lowe's,** 1996, team transporter w/mini stock car, 1:87-scale
EX n/a   NM n/a   MIP $8

❑ **#11-Lowe's,** 1996, team transporter, 1:64-scale
EX n/a   NM n/a   MIP $15

❑ **#11-Lowe's,** 1996, team transporter w/stock car, 1:64-scale
EX n/a   NM n/a   MIP $25

❑ **#11-Lowe's,** 1996, team transporter w/two stock cars, 1:64-scale
EX n/a   NM n/a   MIP $25

❑ **#11-Lowe's,** 1996, premier team transporter w/stock car, 1:64-scale
EX n/a   NM n/a   MIP $20

❑ **#11-Lowe's 50th Anniversary,** 1996, stock car, 1:64-scale
EX n/a   NM n/a   MIP $15

❑ **#11-Lowe's Gold,** 1996, stock car, 1:24-scale
EX n/a   NM n/a   MIP $40

❑ **#11-Lowe's/Preview Edition,** 1996, team transporter, 1:64-scale
EX n/a   NM n/a   MIP $15

❑ **#11-Lowe's/Preview Edition,** 1996, team transporter w/mini stock car, 1:87-scale
EX n/a   NM n/a   MIP $8

❑ **#11-Lowe's/Preview Edition,** 1996, team transporter w/stock car, 1:64-scale
EX n/a   NM n/a   MIP $25

❑ **#11-Lowe's/Preview Edition,** 1996, stock car, 1:24-scale
EX n/a   NM n/a   MIP $20

BODINE, GEOFF

❑ **#7 QVC,** 1997, stock car, Pinnacle Series, 1:64-scale
EX n/a   NM n/a   MIP $6

❑ **#7-QVC,** 1996, team transporter w/mini stock car, 1:87-scale
EX n/a   NM n/a   MIP $8

❑ **#7-QVC,** 1996, stock car, 1:64-scale
EX n/a   NM n/a   MIP $5

❑ **#7-QVC,** 1996, premier stock car w/opening hood, 1:64-scale
EX n/a   NM n/a   MIP $10

❑ **#7-QVC,** 1996, premier stock car w/opening hood, 1:18-scale
EX n/a   NM n/a   MIP $30

❑ **#7-QVC,** 1996, team transporter, 1:64-scale
EX n/a   NM n/a   MIP $15

❑ **#7-QVC,** 1996, stock car, 1:24-scale
EX n/a   NM n/a   MIP $20

❑ **#7-QVC,** 1997, stock car, 1:64-scale
EX n/a   NM n/a   MIP $5

❑ **#7-QVC,** 1997, stock car, 1:24-scale
EX n/a   NM n/a   MIP $15

❑ **#7-QVC,** 1997, premier stock car w/opening hood, 1:64-scale
EX n/a   NM n/a   MIP $8

❑ **#7-QVC,** 1997, roaring racer stock car w/real engine sounds, 1:64-scale
EX n/a   NM n/a   MIP $25

❑ **#7-QVC,** 1997, team transporter w/stock car, 1:64-scale
EX n/a   NM n/a   MIP $25

❑ **#7-QVC,** 1997, team transporter, 1:64-scale
EX n/a   NM n/a   MIP $20

❑ **#7-QVC,** 1997, team transporter w/mini stock car, 1:87-scale
EX n/a   NM n/a   MIP $10

❑ **#7-QVC,** 1997, team transporter w/mini stock car, 1:144-scale
EX n/a   NM n/a   MIP $5

❑ **#7-QVC/Chrome,** 1997, premier stock car w/opening hood, 1:64-scale
EX n/a   NM n/a   MIP $8

❑ **#7-QVC/Preview Edition,** 1997, team transporter w/mini stock car, 1:144-scale
EX n/a   NM n/a   MIP $2

❑ **#7-QVC/Preview Edition,** 1997, team transporter w/mini stock car, 1:87-scale
EX n/a   NM n/a   MIP $10

❑ **#7-QVC/Preview Edition,** 1997, team transporter, 1:64-scale
EX n/a   NM n/a   MIP $20

BODINE, TODD

❑ **#36-Stanley Tools,** 1997, team transporter, 1:64-scale
EX n/a   NM n/a   MIP $20

❑ **#36-Stanley Tools,** 1997, team transporter w/mini stock car, 1:87-scale
EX n/a   NM n/a   MIP $11

❑ **#36-Stanley Tools,** 1997, team transporter w/mini stock car, 1:144-scale
EX n/a   NM n/a   MIP $3

❑ **#36-Stanley Tools,** 1997, stock car, 1:64-scale
EX n/a   NM n/a   MIP $5

BOWN, JIM

❑ **#51-Lucks,** 1996, premier stock car w/opening hood, 1:18-scale
EX n/a   NM n/a   MIP $30

❑ **#51-Lucks,** 1996, stock car w/opening hood, 1:24-scale
EX n/a   NM n/a   MIP $25

❑ **#51-Lucks,** 1996, stock car, 1:64-scale
EX n/a   NM n/a   MIP $4

❑ **#57-Matco Tools,** 1996, premier stock car w/opening hood, 1:18-scale
EX n/a   NM n/a   MIP $40

❑ **#57-Matco Tools,** 1996, premier stock car w/opening hood, 1:64-scale
EX n/a   NM n/a   MIP $12

BRADBERRY, GARY

❑ **#19-Child Support Recovery,** 1997, stock car, 1:24-scale
EX n/a   NM n/a   MIP $15

BURTON, JEFF

❑ **#99 Exide,** 1997, stock car, Pinnacle Series, 1:64-scale
EX n/a   NM n/a   MIP $6

❑ **#99-Exide,** 1996, team transporter, 1:64-scale
EX n/a   NM n/a   MIP $20

❑ **#99-Exide,** 1996, stock car, 1:24-scale
EX n/a   NM n/a   MIP $20

❑ **#99-Exide,** 1996, stock car, 1:64-scale
EX n/a   NM n/a   MIP $5

❏ **#99-Exide,** 1998, team transporter, 1:64-scale
EX n/a   NM n/a   MIP $8

❏ **#99-Exide,** 1998, team transporter w/mini stock car, 1:87-scale
EX n/a   NM n/a   MIP $10

❏ **#99-Exide,** 1998, stock car, 1:24-scale
EX n/a   NM n/a   MIP n/a

❏ **#99-Exide,** 1998, premier stock car, 1:64-scale
EX n/a   NM n/a   MIP $6

❏ **#99-Exide,** 1998, premier stock car w/opening hood, 1:64-scale
EX n/a   NM n/a   MIP $8

❏ **#99-Exide,** 1998, stock car, 1:64-scale
EX n/a   NM n/a   MIP $4

❏ **#99-Exide Chrome,** 1998, stock car, 1:64-scale
EX n/a   NM n/a   MIP $4

❏ **#99-Exide/Preview Edition,** 1998, stock car, 1:64-scale
EX n/a   NM n/a   MIP $4

❏ **#9-Track Gear,** 1998, team transporter w/mini stock car, 1:87-scale
EX n/a   NM n/a   MIP $10

❏ **#9-Track Gear,** 1998, stock car, 1:64-scale
EX n/a   NM n/a   MIP $4

BURTON, WARD

❏ **#22-MBNA,** 1996, team transporter, 1:64-scale
EX n/a   NM n/a   MIP $20

❏ **#22-MBNA,** 1996, team transporter w/mini stock car, 1:87-scale
EX n/a   NM n/a   MIP $8

❏ **#22-MBNA,** 1996, premier stock car w/opening hood, 1:18-scale
EX n/a   NM n/a   MIP $30

❏ **#22-MBNA,** 1996, stock car, 1:24-scale
EX n/a   NM n/a   MIP $20

❏ **#22-MBNA,** 1996, premier stock car w/opening hood, 1:64-scale
EX n/a   NM n/a   MIP $12

❏ **#22-MBNA,** 1996, stock car, 1:64-scale
EX n/a   NM n/a   MIP $15

❏ **#22-MBNA/Preview Edition,** 1996, stock car, 1:24-scale
EX n/a   NM n/a   MIP $20

❏ **#22-MBNA/Preview Edition,** 1996, stock car, 1:64-scale
EX n/a   NM n/a   MIP $15

COMBS, RODNEY

❏ **#43-Lance Snacks,** 1996, team transporter, 1:64-scale
EX n/a   NM n/a   MIP $20

❏ **#43-Lance Snacks,** 1996, team transporter w/mini stock car, 1:87-scale
EX n/a   NM n/a   MIP $8

❏ **#43-Lance Snacks,** 1996, stock car, 1:64-scale
EX n/a   NM n/a   MIP $5

❏ **#43-Lance Snacks,** 1997, team transporter, 1:64-scale
EX n/a   NM n/a   MIP $20

❏ **#43-Lance Snacks,** 1997, team transporter w/mini stock car, 1:87-scale
EX n/a   NM n/a   MIP $10

❏ **#43-Lance Snacks,** 1997, team transporter w/mini stock car, 1:144-scale
EX n/a   NM n/a   MIP $3

❏ **#43-Lance Snacks,** 1997, stock car, 1:64-scale
EX n/a   NM n/a   MIP $5

COPE, DERRIKE

❏ **#12-Badcock,** 1996, stock car, 1:64-scale
EX n/a   NM n/a   MIP $12

❏ **#12-Mane 'N Tail/Preview Edition,** 1996, team transporter w/two stock cars, 1:64-scale
EX n/a   NM n/a   MIP $25

❏ **#12-Mane 'N Tail/Preview Edition,** 1996, team transporter w/stock car, 1:64-scale
EX n/a   NM n/a   MIP $25

❏ **#12-Mane 'N Tail/Preview Edition,** 1996, team transporter, 1:64-scale
EX n/a   NM n/a   MIP $15

❏ **#12-Mane 'N Tail/Preview Edition,** 1996, team transporter w/mini stock car, 1:87-scale
EX n/a   NM n/a   MIP $8

❏ **#12-Mane 'N Tail/Preview Edition,** 1996, stock car, 1:24-scale
EX n/a   NM n/a   MIP $20

❏ **#36 Skittles,** 1997, stock car, Pinnacle Series, 1:64-scale
EX n/a   NM n/a   MIP $6

❏ **#36-Skittles,** 1997, team transporter w/two stock cars, 1:64-scale
EX n/a   NM n/a   MIP $25

❏ **#36-Skittles,** 1997, premier stock car w/opening hood, 1:64-scale
EX n/a   NM n/a   MIP $8

❏ **#36-Skittles,** 1997, stock car, 1:24-scale
EX n/a   NM n/a   MIP $15

❏ **#36-Skittles,** 1997, stock car w/opening hood, 1:24-scale
EX n/a   NM n/a   MIP $25

❏ **#36-Skittles,** 1997, team transporter w/mini stock car, 1:144-scale
EX n/a   NM n/a   MIP $3

❏ **#36-Skittles,** 1997, team transporter w/mini stock car, 1:87-scale
EX n/a   NM n/a   MIP $10

❏ **#36-Skittles,** 1997, team transporter, 1:64-scale
EX n/a   NM n/a   MIP $20

❏ **#36-Skittles,** 1997, stock car, 1:64-scale
EX n/a   NM n/a   MIP $5

❏ **#36-Skittles,** 1997, team transporter w/stock car, 1:64-scale
EX n/a   NM n/a   MIP $30

❏ **#36-Skittles/Premier Gold,** 1997, premier stock car w/opening hood, 1:18-scale
EX n/a   NM n/a   MIP $400

❏ **#36-Skittles/Premier Gold,** 1997, premier stock car w/opening hood, 1:24-scale
EX n/a   NM n/a   MIP $85

COPE, MIKE

❏ **#58-Penrose,** 1996, stock car, 1:64-scale
EX n/a   NM n/a   MIP $5

CRAVEN, RICKY

❏ **#25-Hendrick Motorsports,** 1997, stock car, 1:24-scale
EX n/a   NM n/a   MIP $15

❏ **#25-Hendrick Motorsports,** 1997, stock car, 1:64-scale
EX n/a   NM n/a   MIP $5

❏ **#2-DuPont,** 1996, premier stock car w/opening hood, 1:18-scale
EX n/a   NM n/a   MIP $30

❏ **#2-DuPont,** 1996, stock car w/opening hood, 1:24-scale
EX n/a   NM n/a   MIP $25

❑ **#2-DuPont,** 1996, stock car, 1:24-scale
EX n/a   NM n/a   MIP $20

❑ **#2-DuPont,** 1996, premier stock car w/opening hood, 1:64-scale
EX n/a   NM n/a   MIP $12

❑ **#2-DuPont,** 1996, stock car, 1:64-scale
EX n/a   NM n/a   MIP $5

❑ **#2-DuPont Teflon/Preview Edition,** 1996, premier stock car w/opening hood, 1:18-scale
EX n/a   NM n/a   MIP $30

❑ **#2-DuPont Teflon/Preview Edition,** 1996, stock car, 1:64-scale
EX n/a   NM n/a   MIP $5

❑ **#2-DuPont Teflon/Preview Edition,** 1996, stock car w/opening hood, 1:24-scale
EX n/a   NM n/a   MIP $25

❑ **#2-DuPont Teflon/Preview Edition,** 1996, stock car, 1:24-scale
EX n/a   NM n/a   MIP $20

❑ **#2-Raybestos,** 1997, team transporter, 1:64-scale
EX n/a   NM n/a   MIP $20

❑ **#2-Raybestos,** 1997, team transporter w/mini stock car, 1:87-scale
EX n/a   NM n/a   MIP $12

❑ **#2-Raybestos,** 1997, team transporter w/mini stock car, 1:144-scale
EX n/a   NM n/a   MIP $5

❑ **#2-Raybestos,** 1997, stock car, 1:24-scale
EX n/a   NM n/a   MIP $15

❑ **#2-Raybestos,** 1997, stock car, 1:64-scale
EX n/a   NM n/a   MIP $5

❑ **#41-Hendrick,** 1996, stock car, 1:64-scale
EX n/a   NM n/a   MIP $5

❑ **#41-Hendrick,** 1996, premier stock car w/opening hood, 1:64-scale
EX n/a   NM n/a   MIP $12

❑ **#41-Hendrick,** 1996, stock car, 1:24-scale
EX n/a   NM n/a   MIP $18

❑ **#41-Kodak,** 1996, stock car, 1:64-scale
EX n/a   NM n/a   MIP $5

DALLENBACH, WALLY

❑ **#15-Hayes Modems,** 1996, team transporter, 1:64-scale
EX n/a   NM n/a   MIP $25

❑ **#15-Hayes Modems,** 1996, team transporter w/mini stock car, 1:87-scale
EX n/a   NM n/a   MIP $8

❑ **#15-Hayes Modems,** 1996, premier stock car w/opening hood, 1:18-scale
EX n/a   NM n/a   MIP $40

❑ **#15-Hayes Modems,** 1996, stock car, 1:24-scale
EX n/a   NM n/a   MIP $50

❑ **#15-Hayes Modems,** 1996, premier stock car w/opening hood, 1:64-scale
EX n/a   NM n/a   MIP $18

❑ **#46-First Union,** 1997, team transporter w/two stock cars, 1:64-scale
EX n/a   NM n/a   MIP $25

❑ **#46-First Union,** 1997, team transporter w/stock car, 1:64-scale
EX n/a   NM n/a   MIP $25

❑ **#46-First Union,** 1997, team transporter, 1:64-scale
EX n/a   NM n/a   MIP $20

❑ **#46-First Union,** 1997, team transporter w/mini stock car, 1:87-scale
EX n/a   NM n/a   MIP $10

❑ **#46-First Union,** 1997, team transporter w/mini stock car, 1:144-scale
EX n/a   NM n/a   MIP $2

❑ **#46-First Union,** 1997, stock car, 1:24-scale
EX n/a   NM n/a   MIP $15

❑ **#46-First Union,** 1997, roaring racer stock car w/real engine sounds, 1:64-scale
EX n/a   NM n/a   MIP $23

❑ **#46-First Union,** 1997, premier stock car w/opening hood, 1:64-scale
EX n/a   NM n/a   MIP $8

❑ **#46-First Union,** 1997, stock car, 1:64-scale
EX n/a   NM n/a   MIP $5

DILLON, MIKE

❑ **#72-Detroit Gasket,** 1997, team transporter w/mini stock car, 1:144-scale
EX n/a   NM n/a   MIP $5

❑ **#72-Detroit Gasket,** 1997, stock car, 1:24-scale
EX n/a   NM n/a   MIP $15

❑ **#72-Detroit Gasket,** 1997, stock car, 1:64-scale
EX n/a   NM n/a   MIP $5

ELLIOTT, BILL

❑ **#94-Mac Tonight,** 1997, team transporter w/mini stock car, 1:87-scale
EX n/a   NM n/a   MIP $15

❑ **#94-Mac Tonight,** 1997, stock car, 1:64-scale
EX n/a   NM n/a   MIP $5

❑ **#94-Mac Tonight,** 1997, premier stock car w/opening hood, 1:64-scale
EX n/a   NM n/a   MIP $8

❑ **#94-Mac Tonight,** 1997, roaring racer stock car w/real engine sounds, 1:64-scale
EX n/a   NM n/a   MIP $30

❑ **#94-Mac Tonight,** 1997, team transporter w/mini stock car, 1:144-scale
EX n/a   NM n/a   MIP $4

❑ **#94-Mac Tonight,** 1997, team transporter, 1:64-scale
EX n/a   NM n/a   MIP $25

❑ **#94-Mac Tonight,** 1997, stock car, 1:24-scale
EX n/a   NM n/a   MIP $20

❑ **#94-McDonalds,** 1996, stock car, 1:64-scale
EX n/a   NM n/a   MIP $5

❑ **#94-McDonalds,** 1996, team transporter w/stock car, 1:64-scale
EX n/a   NM n/a   MIP $25

❑ **#94-McDonalds,** 1996, team transporter, 1:64-scale
EX n/a   NM n/a   MIP $20

❑ **#94-McDonalds,** 1996, team transporter w/mini stock car, 1:87-scale
EX n/a   NM n/a   MIP $8

❑ **#94-McDonalds,** 1996, premier stock car w/opening hood, 1:18-scale
EX n/a   NM n/a   MIP $30

❑ **#94-McDonalds,** 1996, stock car w/opening hood and display stand, 1:24-scale
EX n/a   NM n/a   MIP $30

❑ **#94-McDonalds,** 1996, stock car, 1:24-scale
EX n/a   NM n/a   MIP $20

❏ **#94-McDonalds,** 1996, premier stock car w/opening hood, 1:64-scale
EX n/a   NM n/a   MIP $12

❏ **#94-McDonalds,** 1996, premier team transporter w/premier stock car, 1:64-scale
EX n/a   NM n/a   MIP $25

❏ **#94-McDonalds,** 1996, team transporter w/two stock cars, 1:64-scale
EX n/a   NM n/a   MIP $25

❏ **#94-McDonalds,** 1997, premier team transporter w/premier stock car, 1:64-scale
EX n/a   NM n/a   MIP $25

❏ **#94 McDonald's,** 1997, stock car, Pinnacle Series, 1:64-scale
EX n/a   NM n/a   MIP $6

❏ **#94-McDonalds,** 1997, team transporter w/two stock cars, 1:64-scale
EX n/a   NM n/a   MIP $25

❏ **#94-McDonalds,** 1997, team transporter w/stock car, 1:64-scale
EX n/a   NM n/a   MIP $32

❏ **#94-McDonalds,** 1997, team transporter, 1:64-scale
EX n/a   NM n/a   MIP $20

❏ **#94-McDonalds,** 1997, team transporter w/mini stock car, 1:87-scale
EX n/a   NM n/a   MIP $15

❏ **#94-McDonalds,** 1997, stock car w/opening hood and display stand, 1:24-scale
EX n/a   NM n/a   MIP $30

❏ **#94-McDonalds,** 1997, team transporter w/mini stock car, 1:144-scale
EX n/a   NM n/a   MIP $4

❏ **#94-McDonalds,** 1997, roaring racer stock car w/real engine sounds, 1:64-scale
EX n/a   NM n/a   MIP $25

❏ **#94-McDonalds,** 1997, stock car, 1:24-scale
EX n/a   NM n/a   MIP $20

❏ **#94-McDonalds,** 1997, stock car, 1:64-scale
EX n/a   NM n/a   MIP $5

❏ **#94-McDonalds,** 1997, premier stock car w/Pinnacle collector card, opening hood, display stand and serial numbers, 1:64-scale
EX n/a   NM n/a   MIP $12

❏ **#94-McDonalds/Hurry Back,** 1996, stock car, 1:64-scale
EX n/a   NM n/a   MIP $5

❏ **#94-McDonalds/Hurry Back,** 1996, stock car, 1:24-scale
EX n/a   NM n/a   MIP $20

❏ **#94-McDonalds/Premier Gold,** 1997, premier stock car w/opening hood, painted interior and serial number on chassis, 1:24-scale
EX n/a   NM n/a   MIP $90

❏ **#94-McDonalds/Premier Gold,** 1997, premier stock car w/opening hood, painted interior and serial number on chassis, 1:18-scale
EX n/a   NM n/a   MIP $400

❏ **#94-McDonalds/Preview Edition,** 1996, stock car, 1:64-scale
EX n/a   NM n/a   MIP $4

❏ **#94-McDonalds/Preview Edition,** 1996, stock car, 1:24-scale
EX n/a   NM n/a   MIP $20

❏ **#94-McDonalds/Preview Edition,** 1997, stock car, 1:24-scale
EX n/a   NM n/a   MIP $15

❏ **#94-McDonalds/Preview Edition,** 1997, premier stock car w/opening hood, 1:64-scale
EX n/a   NM n/a   MIP $8

❏ **#94-McDonalds/Preview Edition,** 1997, stock car, 1:64-scale
EX n/a   NM n/a   MIP $5

❏ **#94-Monopoly,** 1996, stock car, 1:24-scale
EX n/a   NM n/a   MIP $25

❏ **#94-Monopoly,** 1996, stock car w/opening hood and display stand, 1:24-scale
EX n/a   NM n/a   MIP $30

❏ **#94-Monopoly,** 1996, premier stock car w/opening hood, 1:64-scale
EX n/a   NM n/a   MIP $12

❏ **#94-Monopoly,** 1996, team transporter w/stock car, 1:64-scale
EX n/a   NM n/a   MIP $25

❏ **#94-Monopoly,** 1996, premier stock car w/opening hood, 1:18-scale
EX n/a   NM n/a   MIP $30

FEDEWA, TIM

❏ **#40-Kleenex,** 1996, stock car, 1:64-scale
EX n/a   NM n/a   MIP $5

❏ **#40-Kleenex,** 1997, stock car, 1:64-scale
EX n/a   NM n/a   MIP $5

❏ **#40-Kleenex/Preview Edition,** 1996, team transporter, 1:64-scale
EX n/a   NM n/a   MIP $20

❏ **#40-Kleenex/Preview Edition,** 1996, stock car, 1:24-scale
EX n/a   NM n/a   MIP $20

❏ **#40-Kleenex/Preview Edition,** 1996, stock car, 1:64-scale
EX n/a   NM n/a   MIP $5

FOSTER, JIMMY

❏ **#11-Speedvision,** 1997, team transporter w/two stock cars, 1:64-scale
EX n/a   NM n/a   MIP $30

❏ **#11-Speedvision,** 1997, team transporter w/stock car, 1:64-scale
EX n/a   NM n/a   MIP $30

❏ **#11-Speedvision,** 1997, team transporter, 1:64-scale
EX n/a   NM n/a   MIP $22

❏ **#11-Speedvision,** 1997, team transporter w/mini stock car, 1:87-scale
EX n/a   NM n/a   MIP $10

❏ **#11-Speedvision,** 1997, team transporter w/mini stock car, 1:144-scale
EX n/a   NM n/a   MIP $3

❏ **#11-Speedvision,** 1997, stock car, 1:64-scale
EX n/a   NM n/a   MIP $5

FULLER, JEFF

❏ **#47-Sunoco,** 1996, team transporter, 1:64-scale
EX n/a   NM n/a   MIP $25

❏ **#47-Sunoco,** 1996, premier stock car w/opening hood, 1:18-scale
EX n/a   NM n/a   MIP $30

❏ **#47-Sunoco,** 1996, stock car w/opening hood and display stand, 1:24-scale
EX n/a   NM n/a   MIP $40

❏ **#47-Sunoco,** 1996, stock car, 1:64-scale
EX n/a   NM n/a   MIP $10

❏ **#47-Sunoco,** 1997, stock car, 1:24-scale
EX n/a   NM n/a   MIP $15

❏ **#47-Sunoco,** 1997, roaring racer stock car w/real engine sounds, 1:64-scale
EX n/a   NM n/a   MIP $22

❏ **#47-Sunoco,** 1997, stock car, 1:64-scale
EX n/a NM n/a MIP $5

❏ **#47-Sunoco/Preview Edition,** 1996, team transporter w/two stock cars, 1:64-scale
EX n/a NM n/a MIP $30

❏ **#47-Sunoco/Preview Edition,** 1996, team transporter w/stock car, 1:64-scale
EX n/a NM n/a MIP $30

❏ **#47-Sunoco/Preview Edition,** 1996, team transporter, 1:64-scale
EX n/a NM n/a MIP $25

❏ **#47-Sunoco/Preview Edition,** 1996, team transporter w/mini stock car, 1:87-scale
EX n/a NM n/a MIP $10

❏ **#47-Sunoco/Preview Edition,** 1996, stock car w/opening hood and display stand, 1:24-scale
EX n/a NM n/a MIP $20

❏ **#47-Sunoco/Preview Edition,** 1996, stock car, 1:24-scale
EX n/a NM n/a MIP $20

❏ **#47-Sunoco/Preview Edition,** 1996, stock car, 1:64-scale
EX n/a NM n/a MIP $5

GANNON, KEVIN

❏ **#32 Chevy,** 1996, stock car, 1:24-scale
EX n/a NM n/a MIP $20

❏ **#32 Ford,** 1996, stock car, 1:24-scale
EX n/a NM n/a MIP $20

GLENN, JR., ALLEN

❏ **#24-DuPont,** 1996, premier stock car w/opening hood, 1:64-scale
EX n/a NM n/a MIP $15

❏ **#24-DuPont,** 1996, stock car, 1:64-scale
EX n/a NM n/a MIP $30

❏ **#24-DuPont,** 1996, stock car, 1:24-scale
EX n/a NM n/a MIP $40

❏ **#24-DuPont,** 1996, stock car w/opening hood and display stand, 1:24-scale
EX n/a NM n/a MIP $40

❏ **#24-DuPont,** 1996, premier stock car w/opening hood, 1:18-scale
EX n/a NM n/a MIP $40

❏ **#24-DuPont,** 1996, team transporter w/mini stock car, 1:87-scale
EX n/a NM n/a MIP $20

❏ **#24-DuPont,** 1996, team transporter, 1:64-scale
EX n/a NM n/a MIP $25

❏ **#24-DuPont,** 1996, team transporter w/stock car, 1:64-scale
EX n/a NM n/a MIP $25

❏ **#24-DuPont,** 1996, premier team transporter w/premier stock car, 1:64-scale
EX n/a NM n/a MIP $30

❏ **#24-DuPont,** 1997, team transporter w/mini stock car, 1:144-scale
EX n/a NM n/a MIP $15

❏ **#24-DuPont,** 1997, stock car, 1:24-scale
EX n/a NM n/a MIP $25

❏ **#24-DuPont,** 1997, stock car, 1:64-scale
EX n/a NM n/a MIP $10

❏ **#24-DuPont Chrome,** 1996, stock car bank w/opening hood, 1:24-scale
EX n/a NM n/a MIP $40

❏ **#24-DuPont/Preview Edition,** 1996, stock car, 1:24-scale
EX n/a NM n/a MIP $20

❏ **#24-DuPont/Preview Edition,** 1997, team transporter w/mini stock car, 1:144-scale
EX n/a NM n/a MIP $15

❏ **#24-DuPont/Preview Edition,** 1997, stock car, 1:24-scale
EX n/a NM n/a MIP $25

❏ **#24-DuPont/Preview Edition,** 1997, premier stock car w/opening hood, 1:64-scale
EX n/a NM n/a MIP $8

❏ **#24-DuPont/Preview Edition,** 1997, stock car, 1:64-scale
EX n/a NM n/a MIP $5

❏ **#99-Luxaire,** 1996, stock car, 1:24-scale
EX n/a NM n/a MIP $20

GORDON, JEFF

(KP Photo, Bert Lehman collection)

❏ **#1-Baby Ruth,** 1993, White body, "Baby Ruth" on sides and hood (along with Ford oval), number "1" on sides and roof, black wheels, 1:64-scale
EX n/a NM n/a MIP $10

❏ **#24-DuPont,** 1991, Orange-red and dark blue body with rainbow stripes, yellow number "24" on sides and roof, "DuPont" oval on sides and hood, black wheels, 1:64-scale
EX n/a NM n/a MIP $12

GORDON, ROBBY

❏ **#40-Coors,** 1997, premier team transporter w/premier stock car, 1:64-scale
EX n/a NM n/a MIP $25

❏ **#40-Coors,** 1997, team transporter w/stock car, 1:64-scale
EX n/a NM n/a MIP $25

❏ **#40-Coors,** 1997, stock car, 1:64-scale
EX n/a NM n/a MIP $5

❏ **#40-Coors/Premier Gold,** 1997, premier stock car w/opening hood, painted interior and serial number on chassis, 1:18-scale
EX n/a NM n/a MIP $410

❏ **#40-Coors/Premier Gold,** 1997, premier stock car w/opening hood, painted interior and serial number on chassis, 1:24-scale
EX n/a NM n/a MIP $45

❏ **#40-Sabco,** 1997, team transporter w/two stock cars, 1:64-scale
EX n/a NM n/a MIP $25

❏ **#40-Sabco,** 1997, team transporter w/stock car, 1:64-scale
EX n/a NM n/a MIP $25

❏ **#40-Sabco,** 1997, team transporter, 1:64-scale
EX n/a NM n/a MIP $20

❏ **#40-Sabco,** 1997, team transporter w/mini stock car, 1:87-scale
EX n/a NM n/a MIP $10

❏ **#40-Sabco,** 1997, team transporter w/mini stock car, 1:144-scale
EX n/a NM n/a MIP $3

❏ **#40-Sabco,** 1997, stock car, 1:24-scale
EX n/a NM n/a MIP $15

❏ **#40-Sabco,** 1997, roaring racer stock car w/real engine sounds, 1:64-scale
EX n/a NM n/a MIP $25

❑ **#40-Sabco,** 1997, premier stock car w/opening hood, 1:64-scale
EX n/a   NM n/a   MIP $8

❑ **#40-Sabco,** 1997, stock car, 1:64-scale
EX n/a   NM n/a   MIP $5

GREEN, DAVID

❑ **#96 Caterpillar,** 1997, stock car, Pinnacle Series, 1:64-scale
EX n/a   NM n/a   MIP $6

❑ **#96-Busch,** 1996, stock car, 1:24-scale
EX n/a   NM n/a   MIP $35

❑ **#96-Busch,** 1996, premier stock car w/opening hood, 1:64-scale
EX n/a   NM n/a   MIP $12

❑ **#96-Busch,** 1996, stock car, 1:64-scale
EX n/a   NM n/a   MIP $12

❑ **#96-Busch Chrome,** 1996, stock car bank w/opening hood, 1:24-scale
EX n/a   NM n/a   MIP $200

❑ **#96-Caterpillar,** 1997, team transporter, 1:64-scale
EX n/a   NM n/a   MIP $20

❑ **#96-Caterpillar,** 1997, premier stock car w/opening hood, 1:64-scale
EX n/a   NM n/a   MIP $14

❑ **#96-Caterpillar,** 1997, premier stock car w/Pinnacle collector card, opening hood, display stand and serial numbers, 1:64-scale
EX n/a   NM n/a   MIP $12

❑ **#96-Caterpillar,** 1997, roaring racer stock car w/real engine sounds, 1:64-scale
EX n/a   NM n/a   MIP $20

❑ **#96-Caterpillar,** 1997, stock car, 1:24-scale
EX n/a   NM n/a   MIP $15

❑ **#96-Caterpillar,** 1997, stock car w/opening hood and display stand, 1:24-scale
EX n/a   NM n/a   MIP $20

❑ **#96-Caterpillar,** 1997, premier stock car w/opening hood, 1:18-scale
EX n/a   NM n/a   MIP $40

❑ **#96-Caterpillar,** 1997, stock car bank w/opening hood and display stand, 1:24-scale
EX n/a   NM n/a   MIP $35

❑ **#96-Caterpillar,** 1997, stock car, 1:64-scale
EX n/a   NM n/a   MIP $5

❑ **#96-Caterpill0**

❑ **ar,** 1997, team transporter w/mini stock car, 1:87-scale
EX n/a   NM n/a   MIP $13

❑ **#96-Caterpillar,** 1997, team transporter w/stock car, 1:64-scale
EX n/a   NM n/a   MIP $25

❑ **#96-Caterpillar,** 1997, team transporter w/two stock cars, 1:64-scale
EX n/a   NM n/a   MIP $25

❑ **#96-Caterpillar,** 1997, premier team transporter w/premier stock car, 1:64-scale
EX n/a   NM n/a   MIP $25

❑ **#96-Caterpillar,** 1997, team transporter w/mini stock car, 1:144-scale
EX n/a   NM n/a   MIP $2

GREEN, JEFF

❑ **#29-Cartoon Network,** 1997, team transporter, 1:64-scale
EX n/a   NM n/a   MIP $20

❑ **#29-Cartoon Network,** 1997, team transporter w/mini stock car, 1:87-scale
EX n/a   NM n/a   MIP $11

❑ **#29-Cartoon Network,** 1997, team transporter w/mini stock car, 1:144-scale
EX n/a   NM n/a   MIP $3

❑ **#29-Cartoon Network,** 1997, stock car, 1:24-scale
EX n/a   NM n/a   MIP $15

❑ **#29-Cartoon Network,** 1997, stock car, 1:64-scale
EX n/a   NM n/a   MIP $5

GRISSOM, STEVE

(KP Photo, Bert Lehman collection)

❑ **#29-Cartoon Network: Stock Rods Series,** 1996, White '57 Chevy Bel Air body with number "29" on sides and roof, Tom and Jerry on hood, PowerPuff girls on sides, silver wheels, thin tires, silver grille, 1:64-scale
EX n/a   NM n/a   MIP $5

❑ **#29-Hanna Barbera Flintstones,** 1996, stock car, 1:24-scale
EX n/a   NM n/a   MIP $20

❑ **#29-Hanna Barbera Flintstones,** 1996, stock car w/opening hood and display stand, 1:24-scale
EX n/a   NM n/a   MIP $25

❑ **#29-Hanna Barbera Flintstones,** 1996, premier stock car w/opening hood, 1:18-scale
EX n/a   NM n/a   MIP $30

❑ **#29-Hanna Barbera Flintstones,** 1996, team transporter w/mini stock car, 1:87-scale
EX n/a   NM n/a   MIP $8

❑ **#29-Hanna Barbera Flintstones,** 1996, team transporter, 1:64-scale
EX n/a   NM n/a   MIP $25

❑ **#29-Hanna Barbera Flintstones,** 1996, team transporter w/stock car, 1:64-scale
EX n/a   NM n/a   MIP $25

❑ **#29-Hanna Barbera Flintstones,** 1996, premier team transporter w/premier stock car, 1:64-scale
EX n/a   NM n/a   MIP $20

❑ **#29-Hanna Barbera Flintstones,** 1996, stock car, 1:64-scale
EX n/a   NM n/a   MIP $10

❑ **#29-WCW,** 1996, stock car, 1:24-scale
EX n/a   NM n/a   MIP $20

❑ **#29-WCW,** 1996, premier stock car w/opening hood, 1:64-scale
EX n/a   NM n/a   MIP $12

❑ **#29-WCW,** 1996, stock car w/opening hood and display stand, 1:24-scale
EX n/a   NM n/a   MIP $25

❑ **#29-WCW,** 1996, premier stock car w/opening hood, 1:18-scale
EX n/a   NM n/a   MIP $30

❑ **#29-WCW,** 1996, team transporter w/mini stock car, 1:87-scale
EX n/a   NM n/a   MIP $8

❏ **#29-WCW,** 1996, team transporter, 1:64-scale
EX n/a   NM n/a   MIP $20

❏ **#29-WCW,** 1996, team transporter w/stock car, 1:64-scale
EX n/a   NM n/a   MIP $25

❏ **#29-WCW,** 1996, team transporter w/two stock cars, 1:64-scale
EX n/a   NM n/a   MIP $25

❏ **#29-WCW,** 1996, premier team transporter w/premier stock car, 1:64-scale
EX n/a   NM n/a   MIP $25

❏ **#29-WCW,** 1996, stock car, 1:64-scale
EX n/a   NM n/a   MIP $10

HAMILTON, BOBBY

❏ **#43-STP 1972 Blue Pontiac on 1996 Pontiac body,** 1996, stock car, 1:64-scale
EX n/a   NM n/a   MIP $10

❏ **#43-STP 1979 Blue/Red Pontiac on 1996 Pontiac body,** 1996, stock car, 1:64-scale
EX n/a   NM n/a   MIP $10

❏ **#43-STP 1984 Blue/Red Pontiac on 1996 Pontiac body,** 1996, stock car, 1:64-scale
EX n/a   NM n/a   MIP $10

❏ **#43-STP 1996 Silver Pontiac,** 1996, premier team transporter w/premier stock car, 1:64-scale
EX n/a   NM n/a   MIP $25

❏ **#43-STP 1996 Silver Pontiac,** 1996, team transporter, 1:64-scale
EX n/a   NM n/a   MIP $20

❏ **#43-STP 1996 Silver Pontiac,** 1996, team transporter w/mini stock car, 1:87-scale
EX n/a   NM n/a   MIP $8

❏ **#43-STP 1996 Silver Pontiac,** 1996, premier stock car w/opening hood, 1:18-scale
EX n/a   NM n/a   MIP $40

❏ **#43-STP 1996 Silver Pontiac,** 1996, stock car, 1:24-scale
EX n/a   NM n/a   MIP $25

❏ **#43-STP 1996 Silver Pontiac,** 1996, premier stock car w/opening hood, 1:64-scale
EX n/a   NM n/a   MIP $15

❏ **#43-STP 1996 Silver Pontiac,** 1996, stock car, 1:64-scale
EX n/a   NM n/a   MIP $20

HOUSTON, TOMMY

❏ **#6-Suburban Propane,** 1996, stock car, 1:24-scale
EX n/a   NM n/a   MIP $20

❏ **#6-Suburban Propane,** 1996, stock car, 1:64-scale
EX n/a   NM n/a   MIP $5

IRVAN, ERNIE

❏ **#28 Havoline,** 1997, stock car, Pinnacle Series, 1:64-scale
EX n/a   NM n/a   MIP $6

(KP Photo, Bert Lehman collection)

❏ **#28 Havoline: Stock Rods Series,** 1997, White and black '57 Ford Ranchero body with gold number "28" on roof and sides, opening tailgate, silver hubcaps, thin black tires, "Havoline" on hood and sides, Texaco star on hood, 1:64-scale
EX n/a   NM n/a   MIP $5

❏ **#28-Texaco,** 1996, team transporter w/two stock cars, 1:64-scale
EX n/a   NM n/a   MIP $25

❏ **#28-Texaco,** 1996, team transporter w/stock car, 1:64-scale
EX n/a   NM n/a   MIP $25

❏ **#28-Texaco,** 1996, team transporter, 1:64-scale
EX n/a   NM n/a   MIP $20

❏ **#28-Texaco,** 1996, team transporter w/mini stock car, 1:87-scale
EX n/a   NM n/a   MIP $8

❏ **#28-Texaco,** 1996, stock car w/opening hood and display stand, 1:24-scale
EX n/a   NM n/a   MIP $30

❏ **#28-Texaco,** 1996, stock car, 1:24-scale
EX n/a   NM n/a   MIP $20

❏ **#28-Texaco,** 1996, premier stock car w/opening hood, 1:64-scale
EX n/a   NM n/a   MIP $12

❏ **#28-Texaco,** 1996, stock car, 1:64-scale
EX n/a   NM n/a   MIP $4

❏ **#28-Texaco,** 1997, team transporter w/stock car, 1:64-scale
EX n/a   NM n/a   MIP $28

❏ **#28-Texaco,** 1997, stock car, 1:64-scale
EX n/a   NM n/a   MIP $5

❏ **#28-Texaco,** 1997, premier stock car w/opening hood, 1:64-scale
EX n/a   NM n/a   MIP $10

❏ **#28-Texaco,** 1997, premier stock car w/Pinnacle collector card, opening hood, display stand and serial numbers, 1:64-scale
EX n/a   NM n/a   MIP $15

❏ **#28-Texaco,** 1997, roaring racer stock car w/real engine sounds, 1:64-scale
EX n/a   NM n/a   MIP $30

❏ **#28-Texaco,** 1997, stock car, 1:24-scale
EX n/a   NM n/a   MIP $15

❏ **#28-Texaco,** 1997, team transporter w/mini stock car, 1:144-scale
EX n/a   NM n/a   MIP $15

❏ **#28-Texaco,** 1997, team transporter, 1:64-scale
EX n/a   NM n/a   MIP $22

❏ **#28-Texaco,** 1997, team transporter w/mini stock car, 1:87-scale
EX n/a   NM n/a   MIP $13

❏ **#28-Texaco Anneversary,** 1997, stock car, 1:24-scale
EX n/a   NM n/a   MIP $30

❏ **#28-Texaco/Preview Edition,** 1997, stock car, 1:64-scale
EX n/a   NM n/a   MIP $5

❏ **#28-Texaco/Preview Edition,** 1997, stock car, 1:24-scale
EX n/a   NM n/a   MIP $15

JARRETT, DALE

(KP Photo, Bert Lehman collection)

❏ **#18-Interstate Batteries,** 1991, Green and black Chevy body with red number "18" on sides and

roof, black wheels, "Good-year/Eagle" tires, 1:64-scale
EX n/a   NM n/a   MIP $4

❏ **#32-Gillette,** 1997, roaring racer stock car w/real engine sounds, 1:64-scale
EX n/a   NM n/a   MIP $22

❏ **#32-Gillette,** 1997, stock car, 1:24-scale
EX n/a   NM n/a   MIP $15

❏ **#32-Gillette,** 1997, team transporter w/mini stock car, 1:144-scale
EX n/a   NM n/a   MIP $5

❏ **#32-Gillette,** 1997, team transporter w/mini stock car, 1:87-scale
EX n/a   NM n/a   MIP $11

❏ **#32-Gillette,** 1997, team transporter, 1:64-scale
EX n/a   NM n/a   MIP $20

❏ **#32-Gillette,** 1997, team transporter w/stock car, 1:64-scale
EX n/a   NM n/a   MIP $25

❏ **#32-Gillette,** 1997, stock car, 1:64-scale
EX n/a   NM n/a   MIP $5

❏ **#32-White Rain,** 1997, team transporter w/two stock cars, 1:64-scale
EX n/a   NM n/a   MIP $25

❏ **#88-Ford Quality Care,** 1996, stock car, 1:24-scale
EX n/a   NM n/a   MIP $20

❏ **#88-Ford Quality Care,** 1996, premier stock car w/opening hood, 1:64-scale
EX n/a   NM n/a   MIP $12

❏ **#88-Ford Quality Care,** 1996, stock car w/opening hood and display stand, 1:24-scale
EX n/a   NM n/a   MIP $30

❏ **#88-Ford Quality Care,** 1996, premier stock car w/opening hood, 1:18-scale
EX n/a   NM n/a   MIP $30

❏ **#88-Ford Quality Care,** 1996, team transporter w/mini stock car, 1:87-scale
EX n/a   NM n/a   MIP $8

❏ **#88-Ford Quality Care,** 1996, team transporter, 1:64-scale
EX n/a   NM n/a   MIP $20

❏ **#88-Ford Quality Care,** 1996, team transporter w/stock car, 1:64-scale
EX n/a   NM n/a   MIP $25

❏ **#88-Ford Quality Care,** 1996, team transporter w/two stock cars, 1:64-scale
EX n/a   NM n/a   MIP $25

❏ **#88-Ford Quality Care,** 1996, premier team transporter w/premier stock car, 1:64-scale
EX n/a   NM n/a   MIP $25

❏ **#88-Ford Quality Care,** 1996, stock car, 1:64-scale
EX n/a   NM n/a   MIP $12

JONES, BUCKSHOT

❏ **#00-Aquafresh,** 1997, stock car, 1:64-scale
EX n/a   NM n/a   MIP $5

KELLER, JASON

❏ **#57-Halloween Havoc,** 1996, stock car, 1:24-scale
EX n/a   NM n/a   MIP $20

❏ **#57-Halloween Havoc,** 1996, stock car, 1:64-scale
EX n/a   NM n/a   MIP $5

❏ **#57-Slim Jim,** 1996, stock car, 1:64-scale
EX n/a   NM n/a   MIP $5

❏ **#57-Slim Jim,** 1996, premier stock car w/opening hood, 1:18-scale
EX n/a   NM n/a   MIP $30

❏ **#57-Slim Jim,** 1997, team transporter w/stock car, 1:64-scale
EX n/a   NM n/a   MIP $25

❏ **#57-Slim Jim,** 1997, team transporter, 1:64-scale
EX n/a   NM n/a   MIP $20

❏ **#57-Slim Jim,** 1997, team transporter w/mini stock car, 1:87-scale
EX n/a   NM n/a   MIP $10

❏ **#57-Slim Jim,** 1997, team transporter w/mini stock car, 1:144-scale
EX n/a   NM n/a   MIP $5

❏ **#57-Slim Jim,** 1997, stock car, 1:24-scale
EX n/a   NM n/a   MIP $15

❏ **#57-Slim Jim,** 1997, stock car, 1:64-scale
EX n/a   NM n/a   MIP $5

❏ **#57-Slim Jim/Preview Edition,** 1996, stock car w/opening hood and display stand, 1:24-scale
EX n/a   NM n/a   MIP $25

❏ **#57-Slim Jim/Preview Edition,** 1996, stock car, 1:24-scale
EX n/a   NM n/a   MIP $20

❏ **#57-Slim Jim/Preview Edition,** 1996, stock car, 1:64-scale
EX n/a   NM n/a   MIP $5

KENSETH, MATT

(KP Photo, Bert Lehman collection)

❏ **#17-DeWalt,** 1998, Black and yellow Monte Carlo with number "17" on sides and roof, black wheels, "Firestone/Eagle" tires, gray interior, 1:64-scale
EX n/a   NM n/a   MIP $5

(KP Photo, Bert Lehman collection)

❏ **#17-DeWalt,** 1999, From "The Originals" series. Black and yellow Monte Carlo with number "17" on sides and roof, "DeWalt" on hood and sides, gray interior, 1:24-scale
EX n/a   NM n/a   MIP $18

(KP Photo, Bert Lehman collection)

❏ **#17-Dewalt Ford/Preview Edition,** 2000, View of car with cover, 1:64-scale
EX n/a   NM n/a   MIP $5

(KP Photo, Bert Lehman collection)

❑ **#17-Dewalt Ford/Preview Edition,** 2000, Yellow and black car with "17" on roof and sides. Includes cloth cover, 1:64-scale
EX n/a   NM n/a   MIP $5

(KP Photo, Bert Lehman collection)

❑ **#17-DeWalt: Stock Rods Series,** 1998, Black and yellow '49 Mercury body with number "17" on sides and roof, gray wheels with thin black tires, silver bumpers, 1:64-scale
EX n/a   NM n/a   MIP $5

(KP Photo, Bert Lehman collection)

❑ **#17-Lycos,** 1998, Black Monte Carlo body with white number "17" on sides and roof, "Lycos" on sides and hood, black wheels, "Goodyear/Eagle" tires, 1:64-scale
EX n/a   NM n/a   MIP $5

LABONTE, BOBBY

❑ **#18 Interstate Battery,** 1997, stock car, Pinnacle Series, 1:64-scale
EX n/a   NM n/a   MIP $6

❑ **#18-Interstate,** 1996, premier stock car w/opening hood, 1:18-scale
EX n/a   NM n/a   MIP $30

❑ **#18-Interstate,** 1996, stock car, 1:64-scale
EX n/a   NM n/a   MIP $4

❑ **#18-Interstate,** 1996, stock car, 1:24-scale
EX n/a   NM n/a   MIP $25

❑ **#18-Interstate,** 1996, team transporter w/mini stock car, 1:87-scale
EX n/a   NM n/a   MIP $8

❑ **#18-Interstate,** 1996, team transporter, 1:64-scale
EX n/a   NM n/a   MIP $20

❑ **#18-Interstate,** 1996, team transporter w/stock car, 1:64-scale
EX n/a   NM n/a   MIP $30

❑ **#18-Interstate,** 1996, premier stock car w/opening hood, 1:64-scale
EX n/a   NM n/a   MIP $12

❑ **#18-Interstate,** 1996, team transporter w/two stock cars, 1:64-scale
EX n/a   NM n/a   MIP $30

❑ **#18-Interstate,** 1997, stock car w/opening hood and display stand, 1:24-scale
EX n/a   NM n/a   MIP $20

❑ **#18-Interstate,** 1997, team transporter w/stock car, 1:64-scale
EX n/a   NM n/a   MIP $25

❑ **#18-Interstate,** 1997, team transporter w/two stock cars, 1:64-scale
EX n/a   NM n/a   MIP $25

❑ **#18-Interstate,** 1997, team transporter w/mini stock car, 1:87-scale
EX n/a   NM n/a   MIP $10

❑ **#18-Interstate,** 1997, team transporter w/mini stock car, 1:144-scale
EX n/a   NM n/a   MIP $5

❑ **#18-Interstate,** 1997, premier stock car w/opening hood, 1:18-scale
EX n/a   NM n/a   MIP $45

❑ **#18-Interstate,** 1997, premier stock car w/opening hood, 1:64-scale
EX n/a   NM n/a   MIP $8

❑ **#18-Interstate,** 1997, team transporter, 1:64-scale
EX n/a   NM n/a   MIP $30

❑ **#18-Interstate,** 1997, premier stock car w/Pinnacle collector card, opening hood, display stand and serial numbers, 1:64-scale
EX n/a   NM n/a   MIP $12

❑ **#18-Interstate,** 1997, roaring racer stock car w/real engine sounds, 1:64-scale
EX n/a   NM n/a   MIP $25

❑ **#18-Interstate,** 1997, stock car, 1:24-scale
EX n/a   NM n/a   MIP $15

❑ **#18-Interstate,** 1997, stock car, 1:64-scale
EX n/a   NM n/a   MIP $5

❑ **#18-Interstate/Premier Gold,** 1997, premier stock car w/opening hood, painted interior and serial number on chassis, 1:18-scale
EX n/a   NM n/a   MIP $340

❑ **#18-Interstate/Preview Edition,** 1996, team transporter, 1:64-scale
EX n/a   NM n/a   MIP $20

❑ **#18-Interstate/Preview Edition,** 1996, team transporter w/mini stock car, 1:87-scale
EX n/a   NM n/a   MIP $8

❑ **#18-Interstate/Preview Edition,** 1996, team transporter w/stock car, 1:64-scale
EX n/a   NM n/a   MIP $30

❑ **#18-Interstate/Preview Edition,** 1996, team transporter w/two stock cars, 1:64-scale
EX n/a   NM n/a   MIP $30

❑ **#18-Interstate/Preview Edition,** 1996, stock car, 1:24-scale
EX n/a   NM n/a   MIP $25

❑ **#18-Interstate/Preview Edition,** 1997, stock car, 1:64-scale
EX n/a   NM n/a   MIP $5

❑ **#18-Interstate/Preview Edition,** 1997, stock car, 1:24-scale
EX n/a   NM n/a   MIP $20

❑ **#18-Interstate/Preview Edition,** 1997, premier stock car w/opening hood, 1:64-scale
EX n/a   NM n/a   MIP $8

❑ **#44-Shell,** 1996, stock car, 1:64-scale
EX n/a   NM n/a   MIP $10

❑ **#44-Shell,** 1996, premier stock car w/opening hood, 1:64-scale
EX n/a   NM n/a   MIP $25

❏ **#44-Shell,** 1996, stock car, 1:24-scale
EX n/a   NM n/a   **MIP** $30

❏ **#44-Shell,** 1996, team transporter w/mini stock car, 1:87-scale
EX n/a   NM n/a   **MIP** $8

❏ **#44-Shell,** 1996, team transporter, 1:64-scale
EX n/a   NM n/a   **MIP** $25

LABONTE, TERRY

❏ **#5 Kellogg's,** 1997, stock car, Pinnacle Series, 1:64-scale
EX n/a   NM n/a   **MIP** $8

❏ **#5-Bayer,** 1996, stock car, 1:24-scale
EX n/a   NM n/a   **MIP** $30

❏ **#5-Bayer,** 1996, premier stock car w/opening hood, 1:64-scale
EX n/a   NM n/a   **MIP** $12

❏ **#5-Bayer,** 1996, stock car w/opening hood and display stand, 1:24-scale
EX n/a   NM n/a   **MIP** $35

❏ **#5-Bayer,** 1996, premier stock car w/opening hood, 1:18-scale
EX n/a   NM n/a   **MIP** $30

❏ **#5-Bayer,** 1996, team transporter, 1:64-scale
EX n/a   NM n/a   **MIP** $30

❏ **#5-Bayer,** 1996, stock car, 1:64-scale
EX n/a   NM n/a   **MIP** $4

❏ **#5-Bayer,** 1997, stock car, 1:64-scale
EX n/a   NM n/a   **MIP** $5

❏ **#5-Bayer,** 1997, stock car, 1:24-scale
EX n/a   NM n/a   **MIP** $25

❏ **#5-Bayer,** 1997, team transporter w/mini stock car, 1:144-scale
EX n/a   NM n/a   **MIP** $6

❏ **#5-Bayer,** 1997, team transporter w/mini stock car, 1:87-scale
EX n/a   NM n/a   **MIP** $13

❏ **#5-Bayer,** 1997, team transporter, 1:64-scale
EX n/a   NM n/a   **MIP** $20

❏ **#5-Bayer/Preview Edition,** 1996, stock car, 1:24-scale
EX n/a   NM n/a   **MIP** $20

❏ **#5-Bayer/Preview Edition,** 1996, stock car, 1:64-scale
EX n/a   NM n/a   **MIP** $5

❏ **#5-Kellogg's,** 1996, team transporter w/two stock cars, 1:64-scale
EX n/a   NM n/a   **MIP** $35

❏ **#5-Kellogg's,** 1996, team transporter w/mini stock car, 1:87-scale
EX n/a   NM n/a   **MIP** $8

❏ **#5-Kellogg's,** 1996, team transporter, 1:64-scale
EX n/a   NM n/a   **MIP** $30

❏ **#5-Kellogg's,** 1996, team transporter w/stock car, 1:64-scale
EX n/a   NM n/a   **MIP** $35

❏ **#5-Kellogg's,** 1996, stock car, 1:24-scale
EX n/a   NM n/a   **MIP** $20

❏ **#5-Kellogg's,** 1996, stock car w/opening hood and display stand, 1:24-scale
EX n/a   NM n/a   **MIP** $35

❏ **#5-Kellogg's,** 1996, stock car, 1:64-scale
EX n/a   NM n/a   **MIP** $5

❏ **#5-Kellogg's,** 1997, team transporter w/mini stock car, 1:87-scale
EX n/a   NM n/a   **MIP** $13

❏ **#5-Kellogg's,** 1997, team transporter, 1:64-scale
EX n/a   NM n/a   **MIP** $25

❏ **#5-Kellogg's,** 1997, team transporter w/stock car, 1:64-scale
EX n/a   NM n/a   **MIP** $25

❏ **#5-Kellogg's,** 1997, team transporter w/two stock cars, 1:64-scale
EX n/a   NM n/a   **MIP** $30

❏ **#5-Kellogg's,** 1997, premier team transporter w/premier stock car, 1:64-scale
EX n/a   NM n/a   **MIP** $25

❏ **#5-Kellogg's,** 1997, stock car w/opening hood and display stand, 1:24-scale
EX n/a   NM n/a   **MIP** $35

❏ **#5-Kellogg's,** 1997, stock car, 1:24-scale
EX n/a   NM n/a   **MIP** $20

❏ **#5-Kellogg's,** 1997, stock car, 1:64-scale
EX n/a   NM n/a   **MIP** $5

❏ **#5-Kellogg's,** 1997, premier stock car w/Pinnacle collector card, opening hood, display stand and serial numbers, 1:64-scale
EX n/a   NM n/a   **MIP** $15

❏ **#5-Kellogg's,** 1997, premier stock car w/opening hood, 1:64-scale
EX n/a   NM n/a   **MIP** $12

❏ **#5-Kellogg's,** 1997, team transporter w/mini stock car, 1:144-scale
EX n/a   NM n/a   **MIP** $5

❏ **#5-Kellogg's,** 1997, roaring racer stock car w/real engine sounds, 1:64-scale
EX n/a   NM n/a   **MIP** $25

❏ **#5-Kellogg's Ironman,** 1996, premier stock car w/opening hood, 1:64-scale
EX n/a   NM n/a   **MIP** $12

❏ **#5-Kellogg's Ironman,** 1996, stock car, 1:64-scale
EX n/a   NM n/a   **MIP** $15

❏ **#5-Kellogg's Tony the Tiger,** 1997, team transporter w/mini stock car, 1:87-scale
EX n/a   NM n/a   **MIP** $13

❏ **#5-Kellogg's Tony the Tiger,** 1997, stock car, 1:64-scale
EX n/a   NM n/a   **MIP** $8

❏ **#5-Kellogg's Tony the Tiger,** 1997, team transporter w/mini stock car, 1:144-scale
EX n/a   NM n/a   **MIP** $5

❏ **#5-Kellogg's Tony the Tiger,** 1997, team transporter, 1:64-scale
EX n/a   NM n/a   **MIP** $25

❏ **#5-Kellogg's Tony the Tiger,** 1997, team transporter w/stock car, 1:64-scale
EX n/a   NM n/a   **MIP** $25

❏ **#5-Kellogg's Tony the Tiger,** 1997, team transporter w/two stock cars, 1:64-scale
EX n/a   NM n/a   **MIP** $25

❏ **#5-Kellogg's Tony the Tiger,** 1997, stock car, 1:24-scale
EX n/a   NM n/a   **MIP** $30

❏ **#5-Kellogg's/Premier Gold,** 1997, premier stock car w/opening hood, painted interior and serial number on chassis, 1:24-scale
EX n/a   NM n/a   **MIP** $125

❏ **#5-Kellogg's/Preview Edition,** 1996, team transporter, 1:64-scale
EX n/a   NM n/a   **MIP** $25

❏ **#5-Kellogg's/Preview Edition,** 1996, stock car w/opening hood and display stand, 1:24-scale
EX n/a   NM n/a   **MIP** $20

❏ **#5-Kellogg's/Preview Edition,** 1996, stock car, 1:24-scale
EX n/a   NM n/a   **MIP** $20

❏ **#5-Kellogg's/Preview Edition,** 1996, stock car, 1:64-scale
EX n/a   NM n/a   MIP $5

❏ **#5-Kellogg's/Preview Edition,** 1997, team transporter w/mini stock car, 1:87-scale
EX n/a   NM n/a   MIP $13

❏ **#5-Kellogg's/Preview Edition,** 1997, stock car, 1:64-scale
EX n/a   NM n/a   MIP $5

❏ **#5-Kellogg's/Preview Edition,** 1997, premier stock car w/opening hood, 1:64-scale
EX n/a   NM n/a   MIP $10

❏ **#5-Kellogg's/Preview Edition,** 1997, team transporter w/mini stock car, 1:144-scale
EX n/a   NM n/a   MIP $5

❏ **#5-Kellogg's/Preview Edition,** 1997, team transporter, 1:64-scale
EX n/a   NM n/a   MIP $25

❏ **#5-Kellogg's/Preview Edition,** 1997, stock car, 1:24-scale
EX n/a   NM n/a   MIP $15

LAJOIE, RANDY

❏ **#74-Fina,** 1996, team transporter, 1:64-scale
EX n/a   NM n/a   MIP $2

❏ **#74-Fina,** 1996, team transporter w/mini stock car, 1:87-scale
EX n/a   NM n/a   MIP $8

❏ **#74-Fina,** 1996, stock car, 1:64-scale
EX n/a   NM n/a   MIP $5

❏ **#74-Fina,** 1997, stock car, 1:24-scale
EX n/a   NM n/a   MIP $25

❏ **#74-Fina,** 1997, roaring racer stock car w/real engine sounds, 1:64-scale
EX n/a   NM n/a   MIP $25

❏ **#74-Fina,** 1997, stock car, 1:64-scale
EX n/a   NM n/a   MIP $5

LEPAGE, KEVIN

❏ **#88-Hype,** 1997, team transporter w/two stock cars, 1:64-scale
EX n/a   NM n/a   MIP $25

❏ **#88-Hype,** 1997, team transporter w/stock car, 1:64-scale
EX n/a   NM n/a   MIP $25

❏ **#88-Hype,** 1997, team transporter, 1:64-scale
EX n/a   NM n/a   MIP $20

❏ **#88-Hype,** 1997, team transporter w/mini stock car, 1:87-scale
EX n/a   NM n/a   MIP $10

❏ **#88-Hype,** 1997, team transporter w/mini stock car, 1:144-scale
EX n/a   NM n/a   MIP $3

❏ **#88-Hype,** 1997, stock car, 1:24-scale
EX n/a   NM n/a   MIP $15

❏ **#88-Hype,** 1997, stock car, 1:64-scale
EX n/a   NM n/a   MIP $5

LITTLE, CHAD

❏ **#23-John Deere,** 1996, stock car bank w/opening hood and display stand, 1:24-scale
EX n/a   NM n/a   MIP $40

❏ **#23-John Deere,** 1996, stock car, 1:64-scale
EX n/a   NM n/a   MIP $5

❏ **#23-John Deere,** 1996, premier stock car w/opening hood, 1:64-scale
EX n/a   NM n/a   MIP $12

❏ **#23-John Deere,** 1996, stock car w/opening hood and display stand, 1:24-scale
EX n/a   NM n/a   MIP $40

❏ **#23-John Deere,** 1996, team transporter w/mini stock car, 1:87-scale
EX n/a   NM n/a   MIP $12

❏ **#23-John Deere,** 1996, team transporter, 1:64-scale
EX n/a   NM n/a   MIP $20

❏ **#23-John Deere,** 1996, team transporter w/stock car, 1:64-scale
EX n/a   NM n/a   MIP $25

❏ **#23-John Deere,** 1996, team transporter w/two stock cars, 1:64-scale
EX n/a   NM n/a   MIP $25

❏ **#23-John Deere,** 1996, stock car, 1:24-scale
EX n/a   NM n/a   MIP $30

❏ **#23-John Deere Dealer Special,** 1996, stock car, 1:64-scale
EX n/a   NM n/a   MIP $12

❏ **#23-John Deere Dealer Special,** 1996, team transporter, 1:64-scale
EX n/a   NM n/a   MIP $25

❏ **#23-John Deere Dealer Special,** 1996, team transporter w/stock car, 1:64-scale
EX n/a   NM n/a   MIP $30

❏ **#23-John Deere Dealer Special,** 1996, premier stock car w/opening hood, 1:64-scale
EX n/a   NM n/a   MIP $18

❏ **#97 John Deere,** 1997, stock car, Pinnacle Series, 1:64-scale
EX n/a   NM n/a   MIP $6

❏ **#97-John Deere,** 1997, team transporter w/two stock cars, 1:64-scale
EX n/a   NM n/a   MIP $25

❏ **#97-John Deere,** 1997, premier stock car w/opening hood, 1:64-scale
EX n/a   NM n/a   MIP $10

❏ **#97-John Deere,** 1997, premier stock car w/Pinnacle collector card, opening hood, display stand and serial numbers, 1:64-scale
EX n/a   NM n/a   MIP $12

❏ **#97-John Deere,** 1997, roaring racer stock car w/real engine sounds, 1:64-scale
EX n/a   NM n/a   MIP $25

❏ **#97-John Deere,** 1997, stock car, 1:24-scale
EX n/a   NM n/a   MIP $20

❏ **#97-John Deere,** 1997, stock car w/opening hood and display stand, 1:24-scale
EX n/a   NM n/a   MIP $25

❏ **#97-John Deere,** 1997, team transporter w/mini stock car, 1:144-scale
EX n/a   NM n/a   MIP $5

❏ **#97-John Deere,** 1997, team transporter w/mini stock car, 1:87-scale
EX n/a   NM n/a   MIP $12

❏ **#97-John Deere,** 1997, team transporter, 1:64-scale
EX n/a   NM n/a   MIP $25

❏ **#97-John Deere,** 1997, team transporter w/stock car, 1:64-scale
EX n/a   NM n/a   MIP $25

❏ **#97-John Deere,** 1997, stock car, 1:64-scale
EX n/a   NM n/a   MIP $8

❏ **#97-Sterling Cowboy,** 1996, stock car w/opening hood and display stand, 1:24-scale
EX n/a   NM n/a   MIP $25

❏ **#97-Sterling Cowboy,** 1996, stock car, 1:24-scale
EX n/a   NM n/a   MIP $20

❏ **#97-Sterling Cowboy,** 1996, premier stock car w/opening hood, 1:64-scale
EX n/a　　NM n/a　　MIP $10

❏ **#97-Sterling Cowboy,** 1996, stock car, 1:64-scale
EX n/a　　NM n/a　　MIP $15

❏ **#97-Sterling Cowboy,** 1996, premier stock car w/opening hood, 1:18-scale
EX n/a　　NM n/a　　MIP $30

MARCIS, DAVE

❏ **#71-Prodigy,** 1996, premier stock car w/opening hood, 1:64-scale
EX n/a　　NM n/a　　MIP $20

MARKHAM, CURTIS

❏ **#63-Lysol,** 1996, team transporter, 1:64-scale
EX n/a　　NM n/a　　MIP $20

❏ **#63-Lysol,** 1996, team transporter w/mini stock car, 1:87-scale
EX n/a　　NM n/a　　MIP $8

❏ **#63-Lysol,** 1996, stock car, 1:24-scale
EX n/a　　NM n/a　　MIP $20

❏ **#63-Lysol,** 1996, stock car, 1:64-scale
EX n/a　　NM n/a　　MIP $5

❏ **#63-Lysol/Preview Edition,** 1996, team transporter, 1:64-scale
EX n/a　　NM n/a　　MIP $25

❏ **#63-Lysol/Preview Edition,** 1996, team transporter w/mini stock car, 1:87-scale
EX n/a　　NM n/a　　MIP $8

❏ **#63-Lysol/Preview Edition,** 1996, stock car, 1:24-scale
EX n/a　　NM n/a　　MIP $20

MARLIN, STERLING

❏ **#4 Kodak,** 1997, stock car, Pinnacle Series, 1:64-scale
EX n/a　　NM n/a　　MIP $6

❏ **#4-Kodak,** 1996, premier stock car w/opening hood, 1:18-scale
EX n/a　　NM n/a　　MIP $30

❏ **#4-Kodak,** 1996, premier stock car w/opening hood, 1:64-scale
EX n/a　　NM n/a　　MIP $12

❏ **#4-Kodak,** 1996, team transporter w/mini stock car, 1:87-scale
EX n/a　　NM n/a　　MIP $8

❏ **#4-Kodak,** 1996, team transporter, 1:64-scale
EX n/a　　NM n/a　　MIP $15

❏ **#4-Kodak,** 1996, team transporter w/stock car, 1:64-scale
EX n/a　　NM n/a　　MIP $25

❏ **#4-Kodak,** 1996, team transporter w/two stock cars, 1:64-scale
EX n/a　　NM n/a　　MIP $20

❏ **#4-Kodak,** 1996, stock car, 1:64-scale
EX n/a　　NM n/a　　MIP $4

❏ **#4-Kodak,** 1997, stock car, 1:64-scale
EX n/a　　NM n/a　　MIP $5

❏ **#4-Kodak,** 1997, team transporter w/stock car, 1:64-scale
EX n/a　　NM n/a　　MIP $25

❏ **#4-Kodak,** 1997, team transporter w/two stock cars, 1:64-scale
EX n/a　　NM n/a　　MIP $25

❏ **#4-Kodak,** 1997, team transporter w/mini stock car, 1:87-scale
EX n/a　　NM n/a　　MIP $13

❏ **#4-Kodak,** 1997, team transporter w/mini stock car, 1:144-scale
EX n/a　　NM n/a　　MIP $3

❏ **#4-Kodak,** 1997, stock car w/opening hood and display stand, 1:24-scale
EX n/a　　NM n/a　　MIP $25

❏ **#4-Kodak,** 1997, stock car, 1:24-scale
EX n/a　　NM n/a　　MIP $15

❏ **#4-Kodak,** 1997, premier stock car w/Pinnacle collector card, opening hood, display stand and serial numbers, 1:64-scale
EX n/a　　NM n/a　　MIP $11

❏ **#4-Kodak,** 1997, team transporter, 1:64-scale
EX n/a　　NM n/a　　MIP $20

❏ **#4-Kodak,** 1997, roaring racer stock car w/real engine sounds, 1:64-scale
EX n/a　　NM n/a　　MIP $22

❏ **#4-Kodak Back to Back,** 1996, team transporter w/stock car, 1:64-scale
EX n/a　　NM n/a　　MIP $25

❏ **#4-Kodak Back to Back,** 1996, stock car bank w/opening hood and display stand, 1:24-scale
EX n/a　　NM n/a　　MIP $25

❏ **#4-Kodak Back to Back,** 1996, premier stock car w/opening hood, 1:18-scale
EX n/a　　NM n/a　　MIP $30

❏ **#4-Kodak Back to Back,** 1996, stock car, 1:24-scale
EX n/a　　NM n/a　　MIP $25

❏ **#4-Kodak/Preview Edition,** 1996, team transporter, 1:64-scale
EX n/a　　NM n/a　　MIP $25

❏ **#4-Kodak/Preview Edition,** 1996, stock car, 1:64-scale
EX n/a　　NM n/a　　MIP $4

❏ **#4-Kodak/Preview Edition,** 1996, team transporter w/mini stock car, 1:87-scale
EX n/a　　NM n/a　　MIP $8

❏ **#4-Kodak/Preview Edition,** 1996, team transporter w/stock car, 1:64-scale
EX n/a　　NM n/a　　MIP $25

❏ **#4-Kodak/Preview Edition,** 1996, team transporter w/two stock cars, 1:64-scale
EX n/a　　NM n/a　　MIP $25

❏ **#4-Kodak/Preview Edition,** 1996, stock car, 1:24-scale
EX n/a　　NM n/a　　MIP $20

❏ **#4-Kodak/Preview Edition,** 1997, stock car, 1:64-scale
EX n/a　　NM n/a　　MIP $5

❏ **#4-Kodak/Preview Edition,** 1997, stock car, 1:24-scale
EX n/a　　NM n/a　　MIP $20

❏ **#4-Kodak/Preview Edition,** 1997, premier stock car w/opening hood, 1:64-scale
EX n/a　　NM n/a　　MIP $8

❏ **#4-Kodak-Gold,** 1997, roaring racer stock car w/real engine sounds, 1:64-scale
EX n/a　　NM n/a　　MIP $30

(KP Photo, Bert Lehman collection)

❏ **#8 Raybestos,** 1992, Ford stock car with blue and white body, number "8" on sides and roof, black wheels, 1:64-scale
EX n/a　　NM n/a　　MIP $7

MARTIN, MARK

❏ **#60-Winn Dixie,** 1996, premier stock car w/opening hood, 1:18-scale
EX n/a   NM n/a   **MIP** $30

❏ **#60-Winn Dixie,** 1996, stock car, 1:64-scale
EX n/a   NM n/a   **MIP** $10

❏ **#60-Winn Dixie,** 1997, roaring racer stock car w/real engine sounds, 1:64-scale
EX n/a   NM n/a   **MIP** $35

❏ **#60-Winn Dixie,** 1997, team transporter w/mini stock car, 1:144-scale
EX n/a   NM n/a   **MIP** $8

❏ **#60-Winn Dixie,** 1997, team transporter w/mini stock car, 1:87-scale
EX n/a   NM n/a   **MIP** $15

❏ **#60-Winn Dixie,** 1997, stock car, 1:64-scale
EX n/a   NM n/a   **MIP** $8

❏ **#6-Valvoline,** 1996, premier stock car w/opening hood, 1:64-scale
EX n/a   NM n/a   **MIP** $10

❏ **#6-Valvoline,** 1996, stock car, 1:64-scale
EX n/a   NM n/a   **MIP** $18

❏ **#6-Valvoline,** 1996, stock car, 1:24-scale
EX n/a   NM n/a   **MIP** $20

❏ **#6-Valvoline,** 1996, stock car w/opening hood and display stand, 1:24-scale
EX n/a   NM n/a   **MIP** $35

❏ **#6-Valvoline,** 1996, team transporter w/mini stock car, 1:87-scale
EX n/a   NM n/a   **MIP** $10

❏ **#6-Valvoline,** 1996, team transporter, 1:64-scale
EX n/a   NM n/a   **MIP** $20

❏ **#6-Valvoline,** 1996, team transporter w/stock car, 1:64-scale
EX n/a   NM n/a   **MIP** $25

❏ **#6-Valvoline,** 1996, team transporter w/two stock cars, 1:64-scale
EX n/a   NM n/a   **MIP** $25

❏ **#6-Valvoline,** 1996, premier team transporter w/premier stock car, 1:64-scale
EX n/a   NM n/a   **MIP** $25

❏ **#6-Valvoline,** 1997, team transporter w/mini stock car, 1:87-scale
EX n/a   NM n/a   **MIP** $15

❏ **#6-Valvoline,** 1997, premier stock car w/Pinnacle collector card, opening hood, display stand and serial numbers, 1:64-scale
EX n/a   NM n/a   **MIP** $20

❏ **#6-Valvoline,** 1997, roaring racer stock car w/real engine sounds, 1:64-scale
EX n/a   NM n/a   **MIP** $35

❏ **#6-Valvoline,** 1997, stock car, 1:24-scale
EX n/a   NM n/a   **MIP** $20

❏ **#6-Valvoline,** 1997, stock car w/opening hood and display stand, 1:24-scale
EX n/a   NM n/a   **MIP** $30

❏ **#6-Valvoline,** 1997, team transporter w/mini stock car, 1:144-scale
EX n/a   NM n/a   **MIP** $8

❏ **#6-Valvoline,** 1997, stock car, 1:64-scale
EX n/a   NM n/a   **MIP** $8

❏ **#6-Valvoline,** 1997, team transporter, 1:64-scale
EX n/a   NM n/a   **MIP** $25

❏ **#6-Valvoline,** 1997, team transporter w/stock car, 1:64-scale
EX n/a   NM n/a   **MIP** $25

❏ **#6-Valvoline,** 1997, premier team transporter w/premier stock car, 1:64-scale
EX n/a   NM n/a   **MIP** $30

❏ **#6-Valvoline,** 1997, stock car, Pinnacle Series, 1:64-scale
EX n/a   NM n/a   **MIP** $6

❏ **#6-Valvoline,** 1997, team transporter w/two stock cars, 1:64-scale
EX n/a   NM n/a   **MIP** $30

❏ **#6-Valvoline/Premier Gold,** 1997, premier stock car w/opening hood, painted interior and serial number on chassis, 1:18-scale
EX n/a   NM n/a   **MIP** $425

❏ **#6-Valvoline/Premier Gold,** 1997, premier stock car w/opening hood, painted interior and serial number on chassis, 1:24-scale
EX n/a   NM n/a   **MIP** $120

❏ **#6-Valvoline/Preview Edition,** 1996, stock car, 1:64-scale
EX n/a   NM n/a   **MIP** $5

❏ **#6-Valvoline/Preview Edition,** 1996, stock car, 1:24-scale
EX n/a   NM n/a   **MIP** $20

❏ **#6-Valvoline/Preview Edition,** 1997, stock car, 1:64-scale
EX n/a   NM n/a   **MIP** $8

❏ **#6-Valvoline/Preview Edition,** 1997, team transporter, 1:64-scale
EX n/a   NM n/a   **MIP** $25

❏ **#6-Valvoline/Preview Edition,** 1997, team transporter w/mini stock car, 1:87-scale
EX n/a   NM n/a   **MIP** $15

❏ **#6-Valvoline/Preview Edition,** 1997, team transporter w/mini stock car, 1:144-scale
EX n/a   NM n/a   **MIP** $8

❏ **#6-Valvoline/Preview Edition,** 1997, stock car, 1:24-scale
EX n/a   NM n/a   **MIP** $18

❏ **#6-Valvoline/Preview Edition,** 1997, premier stock car w/opening hood, 1:64-scale
EX n/a   NM n/a   **MIP** $10

MAST, RICK

❏ **#1-Hooters,** 1997, team transporter w/stock car, 1:64-scale
EX n/a   NM n/a   **MIP** $25

❏ **#75 Remington,** 1997, stock car, Pinnacle Series, 1:64-scale
EX n/a   NM n/a   **MIP** $6

❏ **#75-Remington,** 1997, team transporter w/mini stock car, 1:144-scale
EX n/a   NM n/a   **MIP** $5

❏ **#75-Remington,** 1997, stock car, 1:64-scale
EX n/a   NM n/a   **MIP** $5

❏ **#75-Remington,** 1997, premier stock car w/opening hood, 1:64-scale
EX n/a   NM n/a   **MIP** $8

❏ **#75-Remington,** 1997, premier stock car w/Pinnacle collector card, opening hood, display stand and serial numbers, 1:64-scale
EX n/a   NM n/a   **MIP** $13

❏ **#75-Remington,** 1997, stock car, 1:24-scale
EX n/a   NM n/a   **MIP** $15

❏ **#75-Remington,** 1997, team transporter w/mini stock car, 1:87-scale
EX n/a   NM n/a   **MIP** $10

❏ **#75-Remington,** 1997, team transporter, 1:64-scale
EX n/a   NM n/a   MIP $20

❏ **#75-Remington,** 1997, team transporter w/stock car, 1:64-scale
EX n/a   NM n/a   MIP $25

❏ **#75-Remington,** 1997, team transporter w/two stock cars, 1:64-scale
EX n/a   NM n/a   MIP $25

❏ **#75-Remington,** 1997, premier team transporter w/premier stock car, 1:64-scale
EX n/a   NM n/a   MIP $25

❏ **#75-Remington,** 1997, roaring racer stock car w/real engine sounds, 1:64-scale
EX n/a   NM n/a   MIP $25

❏ **#75-Remington/Premier Gold,** 1997, premier stock car w/opening hood, painted interior and serial number on chassis, 1:18-scale
EX n/a   NM n/a   MIP $300

❏ **#75-Remington/Preview Edition,** 1997, stock car, 1:64-scale
EX n/a   NM n/a   MIP $5

❏ **#75-Remington/Preview Edition,** 1997, stock car w/opening hood and display stand, 1:24-scale
EX n/a   NM n/a   MIP $20

❏ **#75-Remington/Preview Edition,** 1997, stock car, 1:24-scale
EX n/a   NM n/a   MIP $15

❏ **#75-Remington/Preview Edition,** 1997, premier stock car w/opening hood, 1:64-scale
EX n/a   NM n/a   MIP $8

MAYFIELD, JEREMY

❏ **#37-Kmart,** 1997, team transporter, 1:64-scale
EX n/a   NM n/a   MIP $20

❏ **#37-Kmart,** 1997, team transporter w/mini stock car, 1:87-scale
EX n/a   NM n/a   MIP $10

❏ **#37-Kmart,** 1997, team transporter w/mini stock car, 1:144-scale
EX n/a   NM n/a   MIP $3

❏ **#37-Kmart,** 1997, stock car, 1:24-scale
EX n/a   NM n/a   MIP $15

❏ **#37-Kmart,** 1997, roaring racer stock car w/real engine sounds, 1:64-scale
EX n/a   NM n/a   MIP $22

❏ **#37-Kmart,** 1997, premier stock car w/Pinnacle collector card, opening hood, display stand and serial numbers, 1:64-scale
EX n/a   NM n/a   MIP $12

❏ **#37-Kmart,** 1997, premier stock car w/opening hood, 1:64-scale
EX n/a   NM n/a   MIP $8

❏ **#37-Kmart,** 1997, stock car, 1:64-scale
EX n/a   NM n/a   MIP $5

❏ **#Kmart,** 1997, stock car, Pinnacle Series, 1:64-scale
EX n/a   NM n/a   MIP $6

McLAUGHLIN, MIKE

❏ **#34-Royal Oak,** 1996, team transporter w/mini stock car, 1:87-scale
EX n/a   NM n/a   MIP $8

❏ **#34-Royal Oak,** 1996, premier stock car w/opening hood, 1:18-scale
EX n/a   NM n/a   MIP $30

❏ **#34-Royal Oak,** 1996, stock car, 1:24-scale
EX n/a   NM n/a   MIP $20

❏ **#34-Royal Oak,** 1996, premier stock car w/opening hood, 1:64-scale
EX n/a   NM n/a   MIP $12

❏ **#34-Royal Oak,** 1996, stock car, 1:64-scale
EX n/a   NM n/a   MIP $10

❏ **#34-Royal Oak,** 1997, team transporter w/two stock cars, 1:64-scale
EX n/a   NM n/a   MIP $30

❏ **#34-Royal Oak,** 1997, team transporter w/stock car, 1:64-scale
EX n/a   NM n/a   MIP $30

❏ **#34-Royal Oak,** 1997, team transporter, 1:64-scale
EX n/a   NM n/a   MIP $20

❏ **#34-Royal Oak,** 1997, team transporter w/mini stock car, 1:87-scale
EX n/a   NM n/a   MIP $11

❏ **#34-Royal Oak,** 1997, team transporter w/mini stock car, 1:144-scale
EX n/a   NM n/a   MIP $5

❏ **#34-Royal Oak,** 1997, stock car, 1:64-scale
EX n/a   NM n/a   MIP $5

MOISE, PATTY

❏ **#14-Purex/Dial,** 1996, team transporter w/two stock cars, 1:64-scale
EX n/a   NM n/a   MIP $25

❏ **#14-Purex/Dial,** 1996, team transporter w/stock car, 1:64-scale
EX n/a   NM n/a   MIP $25

❏ **#14-Purex/Dial,** 1996, team transporter, 1:64-scale
EX n/a   NM n/a   MIP $15

❏ **#14-Purex/Dial,** 1996, team transporter w/mini stock car, 1:87-scale
EX n/a   NM n/a   MIP $8

❏ **#14-Purex/Dial,** 1996, stock car, 1:64-scale
EX n/a   NM n/a   MIP $5

❏ **#14-Purex/Dial/Preview Edition,** 1996, stock car, 1:24-scale
EX n/a   NM n/a   MIP $20

❏ **#14-Purex/Dial/Preview Edition,** 1996, stock car, 1:64-scale
EX n/a   NM n/a   MIP $5

MUSGRAVE, TED

❏ **#16 Primestar,** 1997, stock car, Pinnacle Series, 1:64-scale
EX n/a   NM n/a   MIP $6

❏ **#16-Family Channel,** 1996, team transporter w/two stock cars, 1:64-scale
EX n/a   NM n/a   MIP $25

❏ **#16-Family Channel,** 1996, team transporter w/stock car, 1:64-scale
EX n/a   NM n/a   MIP $25

❏ **#16-Family Channel,** 1996, team transporter, 1:64-scale
EX n/a   NM n/a   MIP $15

❏ **#16-Family Channel,** 1996, team transporter w/mini stock car, 1:87-scale
EX n/a   NM n/a   MIP $8

❏ **#16-Family Channel,** 1996, premier stock car w/opening hood, 1:18-scale
EX n/a   NM n/a   MIP $30

❏ **#16-Family Channel,** 1996, stock car, 1:24-scale
EX n/a   NM n/a   MIP $20

❏ **#16-Family Channel,** 1996, premier stock car w/opening hood, 1:64-scale
EX n/a   NM n/a   MIP $12

❏ **#16-Family Channel,** 1996, stock car, 1:64-scale
EX n/a   NM n/a   MIP $5

❏ **#16-Family Channel/Preview Edition,** 1996, stock car, 1:24-scale
EX n/a   NM n/a   MIP $20

❏ **#16-Family Channel/Preview Edition,** 1996, stock car, 1:64-scale
EX n/a   NM n/a   MIP $5

❏ **#16-Family Channel/Preview Edition,** 1996, team transporter w/mini stock car, 1:87-scale
EX n/a   NM n/a   MIP $8

❏ **#16-Family Channel/Preview Edition,** 1996, team transporter, 1:64-scale
EX n/a   NM n/a   MIP $15

❏ **#16-Primestar,** 1997, stock car, 1:64-scale
EX n/a   NM n/a   MIP $5

❏ **#16-Primestar,** 1997, team transporter w/two stock cars, 1:64-scale
EX n/a   NM n/a   MIP $25

❏ **#16-Primestar,** 1997, team transporter w/stock car, 1:64-scale
EX n/a   NM n/a   MIP $25

❏ **#16-Primestar,** 1997, team transporter, 1:64-scale
EX n/a   NM n/a   MIP $20

❏ **#16-Primestar,** 1997, team transporter w/mini stock car, 1:87-scale
EX n/a   NM n/a   MIP $10

❏ **#16-Primestar,** 1997, team transporter w/mini stock car, 1:144-scale
EX n/a   NM n/a   MIP $2

❏ **#16-Primestar,** 1997, stock car, 1:24-scale
EX n/a   NM n/a   MIP $15

❏ **#16-Primestar,** 1997, roaring racer stock car w/real engine sounds, 1:64-scale
EX n/a   NM n/a   MIP $25

❏ **#16-Primestar,** 1997, premier stock car w/Pinnacle collector card, opening hood, display stand and serial numbers, 1:64-scale
EX n/a   NM n/a   MIP $13

❏ **#16-Primestar,** 1997, premier stock car w/opening hood, 1:64-scale
EX n/a   NM n/a   MIP $8

❏ **#16-Primestar,** 1997, premier team transporter w/premier stock car, 1:64-scale
EX n/a   NM n/a   MIP $25

NEMECHEK, JOE

❏ **#42-Bell South,** 1997, team transporter w/two stock cars, 1:64-scale
EX n/a   NM n/a   MIP $25

❏ **#42-Bell South,** 1997, premier stock car w/opening hood, 1:64-scale
EX n/a   NM n/a   MIP $8

❏ **#42-Bell South,** 1997, premier stock car w/Pinnacle collector card, opening hood, display stand and serial numbers, 1:64-scale
EX n/a   NM n/a   MIP $12

❏ **#42-Bell South,** 1997, roaring racer stock car w/real engine sounds, 1:64-scale
EX n/a   NM n/a   MIP $22

❏ **#42-Bell South,** 1997, stock car, 1:24-scale
EX n/a   NM n/a   MIP $15

❏ **#42-Bell South,** 1997, team transporter w/mini stock car, 1:144-scale
EX n/a   NM n/a   MIP $5

❏ **#42-Bell South,** 1997, team transporter w/mini stock car, 1:87-scale
EX n/a   NM n/a   MIP $10

❏ **#42-Bell South,** 1997, team transporter, 1:64-scale
EX n/a   NM n/a   MIP $20

❏ **#42-Bell South,** 1997, stock car, 1:64-scale
EX n/a   NM n/a   MIP $5

❏ **#42-Bell South,** 1997, team transporter w/stock car, 1:64-scale
EX n/a   NM n/a   MIP $25

❏ **#87 Bell South,** 1997, stock car, Pinnacle Series, 1:64-scale
EX n/a   NM n/a   MIP $6

❏ **#87-Bell South,** 1997, roaring racer stock car w/real engine sounds, 1:64-scale
EX n/a   NM n/a   MIP $22

❏ **#87-Bell South,** 1997, stock car, 1:24-scale
EX n/a   NM n/a   MIP $15

❏ **#87-Bell South,** 1997, stock car, 1:64-scale
EX n/a   NM n/a   MIP $5

❏ **#87-Burger King,** 1997, stock car, 1:64-scale
EX n/a   NM n/a   MIP $5

❏ **#87-Burger King,** 1997, premier stock car w/opening hood, 1:64-scale
EX n/a   NM n/a   MIP $8

❏ **#87-Burger King,** 1997, stock car, 1:24-scale
EX n/a   NM n/a   MIP $15

❏ **#87-Burger King,** 1997, team transporter w/mini stock car, 1:87-scale
EX n/a   NM n/a   MIP $11

❏ **#87-Burger King,** 1997, team transporter, 1:64-scale
EX n/a   NM n/a   MIP $20

OLSEN, MIKE

❏ **#61-Little Trees,** 1996, stock car, 1:64-scale
EX n/a   NM n/a   MIP $6

PARSONS, PHIL

❏ **#10-Channellock,** 1996, team transporter, 1:64-scale
EX n/a   NM n/a   MIP $15

❏ **#10-Channellock,** 1996, stock car, 1:64-scale
EX n/a   NM n/a   MIP $4

❏ **#10-Channellock,** 1997, team transporter w/two stock cars, 1:64-scale
EX n/a   NM n/a   MIP $25

❏ **#10-Channellock,** 1997, team transporter w/stock car, 1:64-scale
EX n/a   NM n/a   MIP $25

❏ **#10-Channellock,** 1997, team transporter, 1:64-scale
EX n/a   NM n/a   MIP $22

❏ **#10-Channellock,** 1997, team transporter w/mini stock car, 1:87-scale
EX n/a   NM n/a   MIP $10

❏ **#10-Channellock,** 1997, team transporter w/mini stock car, 1:144-scale
EX n/a   NM n/a   MIP $2

❏ **#10-Channellock,** 1997, stock car, 1:24-scale
EX n/a   NM n/a   MIP $15

❏ **#10-Channellock,** 1997, stock car, 1:64-scale
EX n/a   NM n/a   MIP $5

PEARSON, LARRY

❑ **#92-Stanley Tools,** 1996, premier stock car w/opening hood, 1:18-scale
EX n/a NM n/a MIP $30

❑ **#92-Stanley Tools,** 1996, premier stock car w/opening hood, 1:64-scale
EX n/a NM n/a MIP $10

PETTY, KYLE

❑ **#49-NWO,** 1997, team transporter w/stock car, 1:64-scale
EX n/a NM n/a MIP $25

❑ **#49-NWO,** 1997, team transporter, 1:64-scale
EX n/a NM n/a MIP $22

❑ **#49-NWO,** 1997, team transporter w/mini stock car, 1:87-scale
EX n/a NM n/a MIP $10

❑ **#49-NWO,** 1997, team transporter w/mini stock car, 1:144-scale
EX n/a NM n/a MIP $6

❑ **#49-NWO,** 1997, stock car, 1:24-scale
EX n/a NM n/a MIP $35

❑ **#49-NWO,** 1997, stock car, 1:64-scale
EX n/a NM n/a MIP $10

PRESSLEY, ROBERT

❑ **#29 Cartoon Network,** 1997, stock car, Pinnacle Series, 1:64-scale
EX n/a NM n/a MIP $6

❑ **#29-Cartoon Network,** 1997, roaring racer stock car w/real engine sounds, 1:64-scale
EX n/a NM n/a MIP $25

❑ **#29-Cartoon Network,** 1997, stock car, 1:64-scale
EX n/a NM n/a MIP $5

❑ **#29-Cartoon Network,** 1997, premier stock car w/Pinnacle collector card, opening hood, display stand and serial numbers, 1:64-scale
EX n/a NM n/a MIP $15

❑ **#29-Cartoon Network,** 1997, stock car, 1:24-scale
EX n/a NM n/a MIP $15

❑ **#29-Cartoon Network,** 1997, team transporter w/mini stock car, 1:144-scale
EX n/a NM n/a MIP $3

❑ **#29-Cartoon Network,** 1997, team transporter w/mini stock car, 1:87-scale
EX n/a NM n/a MIP $11

❑ **#29-Cartoon Network,** 1997, team transporter, 1:64-scale
EX n/a NM n/a MIP $24

❑ **#29-Cartoon Network,** 1997, team transporter w/stock car, 1:64-scale
EX n/a NM n/a MIP $25

❑ **#29-Cartoon Network,** 1997, team transporter w/two stock cars, 1:64-scale
EX n/a NM n/a MIP $25

❑ **#29-Cartoon Network,** 1997, premier team transporter w/premier stock car, 1:64-scale
EX n/a NM n/a MIP $30

❑ **#29-Cartoon Network,** 1997, premier stock car w/opening hood, 1:64-scale
EX n/a NM n/a MIP $8

❑ **#29-Cartoon Network/Preview Edition,** 1997, stock car, 1:64-scale
EX n/a NM n/a MIP $5

❑ **#29-Cartoon Network/Preview Edition,** 1997, team transporter, 1:64-scale
EX n/a NM n/a MIP $24

❑ **#29-Cartoon Network/Preview Edition,** 1997, team transporter w/mini stock car, 1:87-scale
EX n/a NM n/a MIP $11

❑ **#29-Cartoon Network/Preview Edition,** 1997, team transporter w/mini stock car, 1:144-scale
EX n/a NM n/a MIP $3

❑ **#29-Cartoon Network/Preview Edition,** 1997, stock car w/opening hood and display stand, 1:24-scale
EX n/a NM n/a MIP $20

❑ **#29-Cartoon Network/Preview Edition,** 1997, stock car, 1:24-scale
EX n/a NM n/a MIP $20

❑ **#29-Cartoon Network/Preview Edition,** 1997, premier stock car w/opening hood, 1:64-scale
EX n/a NM n/a MIP $8

REEVES, STEVIE

❑ **#7-Clabber Girl/Preview Edition,** 1996, stock car, 1:24-scale
EX n/a NM n/a MIP $20

❑ **#7-Clabber Girl/Preview Edition,** 1996, stock car, 1:64-scale
EX n/a NM n/a MIP $5

❑ **#96-Clabber Girl,** 1996, team transporter, 1:64-scale
EX n/a NM n/a MIP $20

❑ **#96-Clabber Girl,** 1996, stock car, 1:64-scale
EX n/a NM n/a MIP $5

RUDD, RICKY

❑ **#10 Tide,** 1997, stock car, Pinnacle Series, 1:64-scale
EX n/a NM n/a MIP $6

❑ **#10-Tide,** 1996, stock car, 1:64-scale
EX n/a NM n/a MIP $4

❑ **#10-Tide,** 1997, stock car, 1:64-scale
EX n/a NM n/a MIP $5

❑ **#10-Tide,** 1997, premier stock car w/opening hood, 1:64-scale
EX n/a NM n/a MIP $8

❑ **#10-Tide,** 1997, premier stock car w/Pinnacle collector card, opening hood, display stand and serial numbers, 1:64-scale
EX n/a NM n/a MIP $12

❑ **#10-Tide,** 1997, roaring racer stock car w/real engine sounds, 1:64-scale
EX n/a NM n/a MIP $22

❑ **#10-Tide,** 1997, stock car, 1:24-scale
EX n/a NM n/a MIP $15

❑ **#10-Tide,** 1997, stock car w/opening hood and display stand, 1:24-scale
EX n/a NM n/a MIP $20

❑ **#10-Tide/Mountain Spring,** 1997, stock car, 1:64-scale
EX n/a NM n/a MIP $5

❑ **#10-Tide/Mountain Spring,** 1997, stock car, 1:24-scale
EX n/a NM n/a MIP $18

❑ **#10-Tide/Mountain Spring,** 1997, roaring racer stock car w/real engine sounds, 1:64-scale
EX n/a NM n/a MIP $22

❑ **#10-Tide/Premier Gold,** 1997, premier stock car w/opening hood, painted interior and serial number on chassis, 1:18-scale
EX n/a NM n/a MIP $340

❑ **#10-Tide/Premier Gold,** 1997, premier stock car w/opening hood, painted interior and serial number on chassis, 1:24-scale
EX n/a NM n/a MIP $60

❏ **#10-Tide/Preview Edition,** 1996, team transporter w/mini stock car, 1:87-scale
EX n/a   NM n/a   MIP $8

❏ **#10-Tide/Preview Edition,** 1996, team transporter w/stock car, 1:64-scale
EX n/a   NM n/a   MIP $25

❏ **#10-Tide/Preview Edition,** 1996, premier stock car w/opening hood, 1:64-scale
EX n/a   NM n/a   MIP $10

❏ **#10-Tide/Preview Edition,** 1996, stock car, 1:24-scale
EX n/a   NM n/a   MIP $20

❏ **#10-Tide/Preview Edition,** 1996, premier stock car w/opening hood, 1:18-scale
EX n/a   NM n/a   MIP $30

❏ **#10-Tide/Preview Edition,** 1996, team transporter w/mini stock car, 1:87-scale
EX n/a   NM n/a   MIP $8

❏ **#10-Tide/Preview Edition,** 1996, team transporter, 1:64-scale
EX n/a   NM n/a   MIP $15

❏ **#10-Tide/Preview Edition,** 1996, team transporter w/two stock cars, 1:64-scale
EX n/a   NM n/a   MIP $25

❏ **#10-Tide/Preview Edition,** 1997, stock car, 1:64-scale
EX n/a   NM n/a   MIP $5

❏ **#10-Tide/Preview Edition,** 1997, stock car, 1:24-scale
EX n/a   NM n/a   MIP $18

❏ **#1-DeWalt,** 1997, team transporter w/stock car, 1:64-scale
EX n/a   NM n/a   MIP $25

❏ **#1-DeWalt,** 1997, team transporter w/two stock cars, 1:64-scale
EX n/a   NM n/a   MIP $25

SAUTER, JAY

❏ **#40-First Union,** 1996, stock car, 1:24-scale
EX n/a   NM n/a   MIP $20

❏ **#40-First Union,** 1996, stock car, 1:64-scale
EX n/a   NM n/a   MIP $7

SCHRADER, KEN

❏ **#25-Budweiser,** 1996, premier stock car w/opening hood, 1:18-scale
EX n/a   NM n/a   MIP $50

❏ **#25-Budweiser,** 1996, stock car, 1:64-scale
EX n/a   NM n/a   MIP $5

❏ **#25-Hendrick Motorsports,** 1996, stock car, 1:24-scale
EX n/a   NM n/a   MIP $40

❏ **#25-Hendrick Motorsports,** 1996, premier stock car w/opening hood, 1:64-scale
EX n/a   NM n/a   MIP $15

❏ **#33-Generic,** 1997, stock car, 1:24-scale
EX n/a   NM n/a   MIP $15

❏ **#33-Generic,** 1997, roaring racer stock car w/real engine sounds, 1:64-scale
EX n/a   NM n/a   MIP $22

❏ **#33-Generic,** 1997, stock car, 1:64-scale
EX n/a   NM n/a   MIP $5

❏ **#52-AC Delco,** 1996, stock car w/opening hood and display stand, 1:24-scale
EX n/a   NM n/a   MIP $25

❏ **#52-AC Delco,** 1996, stock car, 1:24-scale
EX n/a   NM n/a   MIP $20

❏ **#52-AC Delco,** 1996, premier stock car w/opening hood, 1:64-scale
EX n/a   NM n/a   MIP $12

❏ **#52-AC Delco,** 1996, stock car, 1:64-scale
EX n/a   NM n/a   MIP $5

❏ **#52-AC Delco/Preview Edition,** 1996, stock car, 1:24-scale
EX n/a   NM n/a   MIP $20

❏ **#52-AC Delco/Preview Edition,** 1996, stock car, 1:64-scale
EX n/a   NM n/a   MIP $5

SHEPARD, MORGAN

❏ **#75-Remington,** 1996, team transporter, 1:64-scale
EX n/a   NM n/a   MIP $20

❏ **#75-Remington,** 1996, stock car w/opening hood and display stand, 1:24-scale
EX n/a   NM n/a   MIP $35

❏ **#75-Remington,** 1996, stock car, 1:24-scale
EX n/a   NM n/a   MIP $30

❏ **#75-Remington,** 1996, stock car, 1:64-scale
EX n/a   NM n/a   MIP $10

SKINNER, MIKE

❏ **#31-Realtree,** 1996, premier stock car w/opening hood, 1:18-scale
EX n/a   NM n/a   MIP $90

❏ **#31-Realtree,** 1996, stock car w/opening hood and display stand, 1:24-scale
EX n/a   NM n/a   MIP $70

❏ **#31-Realtree,** 1996, stock car, 1:24-scale
EX n/a   NM n/a   MIP $90

❏ **#31-Realtree,** 1996, premier stock car w/opening hood, 1:64-scale
EX n/a   NM n/a   MIP $30

❏ **#31-Realtree,** 1996, stock car, 1:64-scale
EX n/a   NM n/a   MIP $25

SPEED, LAKE

❏ **#9-Spam,** 1996, stock car, 1:24-scale
EX n/a   NM n/a   MIP $22

❏ **#9-Spam,** 1996, stock car, 1:64-scale
EX n/a   NM n/a   MIP $5

❏ **#9-Spam/Preview Edition,** 1996, stock car, 1:24-scale
EX n/a   NM n/a   MIP $20

❏ **#9-Spam/Preview Edition,** 1996, stock car, 1:64-scale
EX n/a   NM n/a   MIP $5

❏ **#9-University of Nebraska,** 1997, premier stock car w/opening hood, 1:64-scale
EX n/a   NM n/a   MIP $25

STRICKLIN, HUT

❏ **#8 Circuit City,** 1997, stock car, Pinnacle Series, 1:64-scale
EX n/a   NM n/a   MIP $6

❏ **#8-Circuit City,** 1997, team transporter w/stock car, 1:64-scale
EX n/a   NM n/a   MIP $25

❏ **#8-Circuit City,** 1997, team transporter, 1:64-scale
EX n/a   NM n/a   MIP $20

❏ **#8-Circuit City,** 1997, team transporter w/mini stock car, 1:87-scale
EX n/a   NM n/a   MIP $10

❏ **#8-Circuit City,** 1997, team transporter w/mini stock car, 1:144-scale
EX n/a   NM n/a   MIP $5

❑ **#8-Circuit City,** 1997, stock car, 1:24-scale
EX n/a   NM n/a   **MIP** $15

❑ **#8-Circuit City,** 1997, roaring racer stock car w/real engine sounds, 1:64-scale
EX n/a   NM n/a   **MIP** $22

❑ **#8-Circuit City,** 1997, premier stock car w/Pinnacle collector card, opening hood, display stand and serial numbers, 1:64-scale
EX n/a   NM n/a   **MIP** $12

❑ **#8-Circuit City,** 1997, stock car, 1:64-scale
EX n/a   NM n/a   **MIP** $5

❑ **#8-Circuit City/Preview Edition,** 1997, team transporter, 1:64-scale
EX n/a   NM n/a   **MIP** $20

❑ **#8-Circuit City/Preview Edition,** 1997, team transporter w/mini stock car, 1:87-scale
EX n/a   NM n/a   **MIP** $10

❑ **#8-Circuit City/Preview Edition,** 1997, team transporter w/mini stock car, 1:144-scale
EX n/a   NM n/a   **MIP** $5

TRICKLE, DICK

❑ **#90-Heilig Meyers,** 1997, stock car, 1:24-scale
EX n/a   NM n/a   **MIP** $15

❑ **#90-Heilig Meyers,** 1997, stock car, 1:64-scale
EX n/a   NM n/a   **MIP** $5

WALLACE, KENNY

❑ **#81-Square D,** 1996, team transporter w/two stock cars, 1:64-scale
EX n/a   NM n/a   **MIP** $25

❑ **#81-Square D,** 1996, team transporter w/stock car, 1:64-scale
EX n/a   NM n/a   **MIP** $25

❑ **#81-Square D,** 1996, team transporter, 1:64-scale
EX n/a   NM n/a   **MIP** $20

❑ **#81-Square D,** 1996, team transporter w/mini stock car, 1:87-scale
EX n/a   NM n/a   **MIP** $8

❑ **#81-Square D,** 1996, stock car w/opening hood and display stand, 1:24-scale
EX n/a   NM n/a   **MIP** $30

❑ **#81-Square D,** 1996, stock car, 1:24-scale
EX n/a   NM n/a   **MIP** $20

❑ **#81-Square D,** 1996, stock car, 1:64-scale
EX n/a   NM n/a   **MIP** $5

WALLACE, MIKE

❑ **#90-Duron Paint,** 1996, stock car, 1:24-scale
EX n/a   NM n/a   **MIP** $20

❑ **#90-Duron Paint,** 1996, stock car, 1:64-scale
EX n/a   NM n/a   **MIP** $5

❑ **#90-Helig Meyers,** 1996, team transporter, 1:64-scale
EX n/a   NM n/a   **MIP** $20

❑ **#90-Helig Meyers,** 1996, team transporter w/mini stock car, 1:87-scale
EX n/a   NM n/a   **MIP** $8

❑ **#90-Helig Meyers/Preview Edition,** 1996, team transporter w/two stock cars, 1:64-scale
EX n/a   NM n/a   **MIP** $25

❑ **#90-Helig Meyers/Preview Edition,** 1996, team transporter w/stock car, 1:64-scale
EX n/a   NM n/a   **MIP** $25

❑ **#90-Helig Meyers/Preview Edition,** 1996, team transporter, 1:64-scale
EX n/a   NM n/a   **MIP** $20

❑ **#90-Helig Meyers/Preview Edition,** 1996, team transporter w/mini stock car, 1:87-scale
EX n/a   NM n/a   **MIP** $8

❑ **#90-Helig Meyers/Preview Edition,** 1996, stock car, 1:24-scale
EX n/a   NM n/a   **MIP** $20

❑ **#90-Helig Meyers/Preview Edition,** 1996, stock car, 1:64-scale
EX n/a   NM n/a   **MIP** $5

❑ **#91-Spam,** 1997, team transporter, 1:64-scale
EX n/a   NM n/a   **MIP** $20

❑ **#91-Spam,** 1997, team transporter w/mini stock car, 1:144-scale
EX n/a   NM n/a   **MIP** $4

❑ **#91-Spam,** 1997, stock car, 1:24-scale
EX n/a   NM n/a   **MIP** $15

❑ **#91-Spam,** 1997, roaring racer stock car w/real engine sounds, 1:64-scale
EX n/a   NM n/a   **MIP** $22

❑ **#91-Spam,** 1997, stock car, 1:64-scale
EX n/a   NM n/a   **MIP** $5

WALLACE, RUSTY

(KP Photo, Bert Lehman collection)

❑ **#2-'64 Ford Mustang/Stock Rods series,** 1996, White and blue body, silver wheels, number "2" on sides and roof, silver-painted grille, opening hood, 1:64-scale
EX n/a   NM n/a   **MIP** $6

(KP Photo, Bert Lehman collection)

❑ **#2-Ford Motorsport,** 1992, Black body with yellow number "2" on roof and sides, 1:64-scale
EX n/a   NM n/a   **MIP** $5

(KP Photo, Bert Lehman collection)

❑ **#2-Ford Motorsport,** 1994, Black body with yellow number "2" on roof and sides, 1:64-scale
EX n/a   NM n/a   **MIP** $5

❑ **#2-Miller,** 1997, stock car w/opening hood and display stand, 1:24-scale
EX n/a   NM n/a   **MIP** $30

❑ **#2-Miller,** 1997, stock car, 1:64-scale
EX n/a   NM n/a   **MIP** $10

❑ **#2-Miller,** 1997, stock car, 1:24-scale
EX n/a   NM n/a   MIP $25

❑ **#2-Miller,** 1997, stock car bank w/opening hood and display stand, 1:24-scale
EX n/a   NM n/a   MIP $60

❑ **#2-Miller,** 1997, team transporter, 1:64-scale
EX n/a   NM n/a   MIP $22

❑ **#2-Miller,** 1997, premier stock car w/opening hood, 1:64-scale
EX n/a   NM n/a   MIP $8

❑ **#2-Miller/Premier Gold,** 1997, premier stock car w/opening hood, painted interior and serial number on chassis, 1:18-scale
EX n/a   NM n/a   MIP $400

❑ **#2-Miller/Premier Gold,** 1997, premier stock car w/opening hood, painted interior and serial number on chassis, 1:24-scale
EX n/a   NM n/a   MIP $55

❑ **#2-Penske,** 1997, team transporter w/stock car, 1:64-scale
EX n/a   NM n/a   MIP $30

❑ **#2-Penske,** 1997, stock car, 1:64-scale
EX n/a   NM n/a   MIP $5

❑ **#2-Penske,** 1997, premier stock car w/opening hood, 1:64-scale
EX n/a   NM n/a   MIP $8

❑ **#2-Penske,** 1997, roaring racer stock car w/real engine sounds, 1:64-scale
EX n/a   NM n/a   MIP $22

❑ **#2-Penske,** 1997, stock car, 1:24-scale
EX n/a   NM n/a   MIP $15

❑ **#2-Penske,** 1997, team transporter w/mini stock car, 1:144-scale
EX n/a   NM n/a   MIP $6

❑ **#2-Penske,** 1997, team transporter w/mini stock car, 1:87-scale
EX n/a   NM n/a   MIP $12

❑ **#2-Penske,** 1997, team transporter, 1:64-scale
EX n/a   NM n/a   MIP $20

❑ **#2-Penske,** 1997, team transporter w/two stock cars, 1:64-scale
EX n/a   NM n/a   MIP $30

❑ **#2-Penske Racing,** 1997, premier stock car w/opening hood, 1:64-scale
EX n/a   NM n/a   MIP $8

❑ **#2-Penske Racing,** 1997, stock car, 1:64-scale
EX n/a   NM n/a   MIP $5

❑ **#2-Penske Racing,** 1997, team transporter w/mini stock car, 1:87-scale
EX n/a   NM n/a   MIP $12

❑ **#2-Penske Racing,** 1997, premier team transporter w/premier stock car, 1:64-scale
EX n/a   NM n/a   MIP $25

❑ **#2-Penske Racing,** 1997, team transporter w/stock car, 1:64-scale
EX n/a   NM n/a   MIP $28

❑ **#2-Penske Racing,** 1997, team transporter, 1:64-scale
EX n/a   NM n/a   MIP $20

❑ **#2-Penske Racing,** 1997, stock car, 1:24-scale
EX n/a   NM n/a   MIP $15

❑ **#2-Penske/Preview Edition,** 1997, stock car, 1:64-scale
EX n/a   NM n/a   MIP $5

(KP Photo, Bert Lehman collection)

❑ **#2-Pontiac,** 1991, Black stock car body, number "2" on roof and sides, "Pontiac" on sides and hood, black wheels, 1:64-scale
EX n/a   NM n/a   MIP $6

(KP Photo, Bert Lehman collection)

❑ **#66-'84 Chevy Camaro/Short Track Champions,** 1992, Red and yellow body, silver wheels, number "66" on sides and roof, "Alugard" on hood, 1:64-scale
EX n/a   NM n/a   MIP $4

WALTRIP, DARRELL

❑ **#17-Western Auto,** 1996, stock car, 1:64-scale
EX n/a   NM n/a   MIP $4

❑ **#17-Western Auto,** 1996, team transporter w/two stock cars, 1:64-scale
EX n/a   NM n/a   MIP $25

❑ **#17-Western Auto,** 1996, team transporter w/stock car, 1:64-scale
EX n/a   NM n/a   MIP $25

❑ **#17-Western Auto,** 1996, team transporter, 1:64-scale
EX n/a   NM n/a   MIP $15

❑ **#17-Western Auto,** 1996, team transporter w/mini stock car, 1:87-scale
EX n/a   NM n/a   MIP $8

❑ **#17-Western Auto,** 1996, premier stock car w/opening hood, 1:18-scale
EX n/a   NM n/a   MIP $30

❑ **#17-Western Auto,** 1996, stock car, 1:24-scale
EX n/a   NM n/a   MIP $20

❑ **#17-Western Auto Anniversary/Chrome Version,** 1997, stock car, 1:64-scale
EX n/a   NM n/a   MIP $10

❑ **#17-Western Auto Anniversary/Chrome Version,** 1997, team transporter w/mini stock car, 1:144-scale
EX n/a   NM n/a   MIP $8

❑ **#17-Western Auto Anniversary/Chrome Version,** 1997, premier stock car w/opening hood, 1:64-scale
EX n/a   NM n/a   MIP $12

❑ **#17-Western Auto Anniversary/Chrome Version,** 1997, stock car, 1:24-scale
EX n/a   NM n/a   MIP $25

❑ **#17-Western Auto Chrome,** 1996, stock car bank w/opening hood, 1:24-scale
EX n/a   NM n/a   MIP $20

❑ **#17-Western Auto/Blue Version,** 1997, premier stock car w/opening hood, 1:64-scale
EX n/a   NM n/a   MIP $8

❑ **#17-Western Auto/Blue Version,** 1997, stock car, 1:64-scale
EX n/a   NM n/a   MIP $5

❏ **#17-Western Auto/Blue Version,** 1997, stock car, 1:24-scale
EX n/a   NM n/a   MIP $15

❏ **#17-Western Auto/Blue Version,** 1997, roaring racer stock car w/real engine sounds, 1:64-scale
EX n/a   NM n/a   MIP $25

❏ **#17-Western Auto/Preview Edition,** 1996, team transporter, 1:64-scale
EX n/a   NM n/a   MIP $15

❏ **#17-Western Auto/Preview Edition,** 1996, stock car, 1:64-scale
EX n/a   NM n/a   MIP $4

❏ **#17-Western Auto/Preview Edition,** 1996, team transporter w/mini stock car, 1:87-scale
EX n/a   NM n/a   MIP $8

❏ **#17-Western Auto/Preview Edition,** 1996, team transporter w/stock car, 1:64-scale
EX n/a   NM n/a   MIP $25

❏ **#17-Western Auto/Preview Edition,** 1996, team transporter w/two stock cars, 1:64-scale
EX n/a   NM n/a   MIP $25

❏ **#17-Western Auto/Preview Edition,** 1996, stock car, 1:24-scale
EX n/a   NM n/a   MIP $20

WALTRIP, MICHAEL

❏ **#12-MW Windows,** 1996, team transporter, 1:64-scale
EX n/a   NM n/a   MIP $25

❏ **#12-MW Windows,** 1996, team transporter w/mini stock car, 1:87-scale
EX n/a   NM n/a   MIP $8

❏ **#12-MW Windows,** 1996, stock car, 1:64-scale
EX n/a   NM n/a   MIP $5

❏ **#21 Citgo,** 1997, stock car, Pinnacle Series, 1:64-scale
EX n/a   NM n/a   MIP $6

❏ **#21-Citgo,** 1996, team transporter w/stock car, 1:64-scale
EX n/a   NM n/a   MIP $25

❏ **#21-Citgo,** 1996, team transporter, 1:64-scale
EX n/a   NM n/a   MIP $20

❏ **#21-Citgo,** 1996, team transporter w/mini stock car, 1:87-scale
EX n/a   NM n/a   MIP $8

❏ **#21-Citgo,** 1996, stock car bank w/opening hood and display stand, 1:24-scale
EX n/a   NM n/a   MIP $30

❏ **#21-Citgo,** 1996, stock car, 1:24-scale
EX n/a   NM n/a   MIP $20

❏ **#21-Citgo,** 1996, stock car, 1:64-scale
EX n/a   NM n/a   MIP $5

❏ **#21-Citgo,** 1996, team transporter w/two stock cars, 1:64-scale
EX n/a   NM n/a   MIP $25

❏ **#21-Citgo,** 1997, stock car, 1:64-scale
EX n/a   NM n/a   MIP $5

❏ **#21-Citgo,** 1997, premier stock car w/opening hood, 1:64-scale
EX n/a   NM n/a   MIP $8

❏ **#21-Citgo,** 1997, premier stock car w/Pinnacle collector card, opening hood, display stand and serial numbers, 1:64-scale
EX n/a   NM n/a   MIP $12

❏ **#21-Citgo,** 1997, roaring racer stock car w/real engine sounds, 1:64-scale
EX n/a   NM n/a   MIP $25

❏ **#21-Citgo,** 1997, stock car, 1:24-scale
EX n/a   NM n/a   MIP $15

❏ **#21-Citgo,** 1997, team transporter w/mini stock car, 1:144-scale
EX n/a   NM n/a   MIP $5

❏ **#21-Citgo,** 1997, team transporter w/mini stock car, 1:87-scale
EX n/a   NM n/a   MIP $11

❏ **#21-Citgo,** 1997, team transporter, 1:64-scale
EX n/a   NM n/a   MIP $20

❏ **#21-Citgo/Preview Edition,** 1996, stock car, 1:64-scale
EX n/a   NM n/a   MIP $5

❏ **#21-Citgo/Preview Edition,** 1996, stock car, 1:24-scale
EX n/a   NM n/a   MIP $20

❏ **#21-Citgo/Preview Edition,** 1997, stock car, 1:24-scale
EX n/a   NM n/a   MIP $20

❏ **#21-Citgo/Preview Edition,** 1997, stock car, 1:64-scale
EX n/a   NM n/a   MIP $5

(KP Photo, Bert Lehman collection)

❏ **#30-Country Time,** 1990, Yellow body, "Maxwell House" and "Country Time" labels on sides and hood, white number "30" on sides and roof, silver wheels with "Racing Champions" on tires, 1:64-scale
EX n/a   NM n/a   MIP $7

Tootsietoy
Prewar and Postwar years

The first Tootsietoy vehicle, the Limousine, a 1911 toy offered in a variety of colors.

Tootsietoy is one of the venerable names in toy collecting, probably because of the longevity of the brand. Tootsietoy's first releases were "limousines" in 1911, available in a range of colors. A few years later, a Model T Ford became the first toy modeled after a specific car. The fact that so many models still exist in great condition is a real testament to their play value.

Originally the company was known as Dowst and Company, then Dowst Brothers. The Tootsietoy name came later in the 1920s and was trademarked by 1924. Ted Dowst is seen as a prime motivator behind the company's interest in toy production, and the pieces made during his tenure from 1906 to 1945 are some of the most noteworthy and collectible. The Graham series, (models with three-piece construction introduced in 1933) the LaSalles (four-piece vehicles introduced in 1935) and the Funnies series (featuring Moon Mullins and other contemporary comic figures from 1932) are seen as some of the best bets for collectors.

MARKET UPDATE

Vintage toys from the prewar period will always hold interest (and most likely, monetary value) for collectors, but the appeal of models from the postwar period is on the rise. There's an authenticity about the old (and not so old) Tootsietoys that gives them a mystique and nostalgia that anyone can relate to.

Two versions of the 1949 Ford F1 Pickup: with and without cast tailgates.

Two Mack Coal trucks, first issued in 1925. Notice the differences in castings with one truck showing a chain-driven rear axle and later version omitting it completely.

A set of Special Delivery Vans from the Camelback Van Series from 1937. Notice the white rubber tires on these models—very typical for 1930s-era Tootsietoys.

Two Mack Railway Express Co. delivery trucks: on the right, an older two-piece cab and on the left, the newer single-piece cab. Both vehicles, especially with intact decals, are sought after by Tootsietoy collectors.

Three models of the Ford V8 Pickup truck. Notice the cracks in the white rubber tires in the example on the far left—not unusual for the material or the age, but something to look for when collecting.

A set of prewar and postwar Mack fire trucks. Great detail on the three prewar examples on the left, a little less (which is not unusual) on the postwar hook and ladder on the far right.

Prewar and postwar versions of the Boattail Roadster. Generally, black wheels will help define a vehicle as a postwar issue of a casting that spans both periods.

More difference in detail between prewar and postwar models: more painted features, along with white rubber wheels, are pretty solid determiners of prewar vehicles. The changes to the Insurance Patrol Fire Engine are quite noticeable here.

TOOTSIETOY / PREWAR

MISCELLANEOUS PREWAR TOOTSIETOYS

❑ **Ford Model A Delivery Van,** 1931, "US Mail," sold in sets only
EX $38   NM $56   MIP $75

❑ **Racer w/Driver,** 1927, Model No. 23
EX $35   NM $60   MIP $80

❑ **Buick Touring Car,** 1925, Model No. 464
EX $28   NM $42   MIP $55

(KP Photo, John Brown Sr. collection)

❑ **Limousine,** 1911, This was the first car Tootsietoy produced, and was available in a variety of colors. Spoked wheels, Model No. 4528
EX $24   NM $32   MIP $40

❑ **Ford Model T Tourer,** 1914, Model No. 4570
EX $35   NM $50   MIP $65

❑ **Ford Model T Pickup,** 1916, Model No. 4610
EX $35   NM $50   MIP $70

❑ **Sedan,** 1923, marked "Yellow Cab", Model No. 4629
EX $15   NM $25   MIP $60

❑ **Buick Coupe,** 1924, Model No. 4636
EX $23   NM $34   MIP $45

❑ **Army Long-Range Cannon,** 1931, Model No. 4642
EX $13   NM $18   MIP $25

(KP Photo, John Brown Sr. collection)

❑ **Caterpillar Tractor,** 1931, Body colors include: red, blue, green or yellow. Gray treads, cast driver, Model No. 4646
EX $30   NM $45   MIP $60

❑ **Fageol Safety Coach,** 1927, Model No. 4651
EX $30   NM $45   MIP $65

❑ **Hook & Ladder Fire Engine,** 1927, Model No. 4652
EX $39   NM $52   MIP $75

❑ **Water Tower Fire Engine,** 1927, Model No. 4653
EX $38   NM $56   MIP $75

(KP Photo, John Brown Sr. collection)

❑ **Huber Star Farm Tractor,** 1927, Assorted-colored body, black chassis and engine, metal wheels, Model No. 4654
EX $40   NM $65   MIP $95

❑ **Ford Model A Coupe,** 1928, Model No. 4655
EX $20   NM $30   MIP $40

❑ **Ford Model A Sedan,** 1929, Model No. 4665
EX $20   NM $30   MIP $40

(KP Photo, John Brown Sr. collection)

❑ **Oil Tank Truck,** 1936, Available in assorted colors, white wheels, Model No. 120
EX $23   NM $34   MIP $45

(KP Photo, John Brown Sr. collection)

❑ **LaSalle Sedan,** Casting covers white or black wheels, no paint on grille or trim. Despite the release date, item was re-issued during postwar period. Postwar issue shown, Model No. 230
EX $15   NM $20   MIP $30

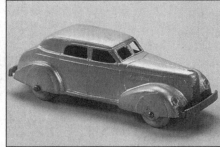

(KP Photo, John Brown Sr. collection)

❑ **LaSalle Sedan,** Casting covers white wheels, silver-painted grille. Despite the release date, item was re-issued during postwar period. Prewar issue shown here, Model No. 230
EX $15   NM $25   MIP $35

(KP Photo, John Brown Sr. collection)

❑ **Chevy Coupe,** Red body, casting covering white or black wheels. Despite the release date, item was re-issued during postwar period, Model No. 231
EX $15   NM $20   MIP $30

(KP Photo, John Brown Sr. collection)

❑ **Buick Roadmaster Touring Coupe,** Assorted color body, casting covers white rubber wheels. Silver painted headlights and grille. Despite the release date, item was re-issued during postwar period, Model No. 232
EX $15   NM $20   MIP $30

(KP Photo, John Brown Sr. collection)

❑ **Boattail Roadster,** Assorted color body, casting covers black wheels. Despite the release date, item was re-issued during postwar period. Postwar version shown here, Model No. 233
EX $12   **NM** $18   **MIP** $27

(KP Photo, John Brown Sr. collection)

❑ **Boattail Roadster,** Assorted color body, casting covers white rubber tires. Despite the release date, item was re-issued during postwar period. Prewar version shown here, Model No. 233
EX $15   **NM** $20   **MIP** $30

(KP Photo, John Brown Sr. collection)

❑ **GMC Box Truck,** Red body, silver painted grille, headlights and bumper. Despite the release date, item was re-issued during postwar period. Prewar version shown here, Model No. 234
EX $20   **NM** $25   **MIP** $35

(KP Photo, John Brown Sr. collection)

❑ **Oil Tank Truck,** Both versions shown here: one with the silver trim and white wheels in pre-war issue and one without in postwar colors. Despite the release date, item was re-issued during postwar period, Model No. 235
EX $13   **NM** $18   **MIP** $25

(KP Photo, John Brown Sr. collection)

❑ **Hook and Ladder Fire engine,** Red body with silver-painted grille, bumper and rear ladder section. Cast driver, white rubber tires. Despite the release date, item was re-issued during postwar period, Model No. 236
EX $20   **NM** $30   **MIP** $40

(KP Photo, John Brown Sr. collection)

❑ **Insurance Patrol Fire Engine,** Postwar re-issue: all-red body, black rubber tires, Model No. 237
EX $15   **NM** $25   **MIP** $35

(KP Photo, John Brown Sr. collection)

❑ **Insurance Patrol Fire Engine,** Red body, silver-painted grille and rear nozzle section, white rubber tires. Despite the release date, item was re-issued during postwar period, Model No. 237
EX $15   **NM** $25   **MIP** $35

(KP Photo, John Brown Sr. collection)

❑ **Hose Wagon Fire Engine,** Red body, no silver-painted trim, white rubber tires. Despite the release date, item was re-issued during postwar period, Model No. 238
EX $20   **NM** $30   **MIP** $40

(KP Photo, John Brown Sr. collection)

❑ **'38 Ford Paneled Station Wagon,** 1940, Reddish-brown body, silver grille, silver roof, black wheels. Despite the release date, item was re-issued during postwar period, Model No. 239
EX $20   **NM** $30   **MIP** $40

(KP Photo, John Brown Sr. collection)

❑ **'38 Ford Paneled Station Wagon,** 1947, Orange body, casting covers white rubber wheels, no separate colors for grille or wood panels, postwar re-issue, Model No. 239
EX $12   **NM** $22   **MIP** $30

❑ **Wrigley GMC Box Truck,** Model No. 1010
EX $55   **NM** $80   **MIP** $110

❑ **Massey-Ferguson Farm Tractor,** 1941, w/driver, Model No. 1011
EX $200   **NM** $300   **MIP** $400

❏ **Small Ford Sedan or Coupe,** 1937, 111 or 112, and Camping Trailer, Model No. 1043
EX $35   **NM** $53   **MIP** $70

(KP Photo, John Brown Sr. collection)

❏ **Roamer House Trailer w/door and tin bottom,** 1937, Various colors available, blue shown here. Doors are often missing from play wear from these models, so finding one intact is quite nice. White rubber tires on hubs, tin trailer tongue, Model No. 1044
EX $275   **NM** $420   **MIP** $580

❏ **Paneled Station Wagon,** Model No. 1046
EX $43   **NM** $64   **MIP** $85

❏ **Army Supply Truck,** Model No. 4634
EX $33   **NM** $50   **MIP** $65

(KP Photo, John Brown Sr. collection)

❏ **Armored Car,** 1938, Dark green body, black rubber wheels, (white on prewar model) silver-painted machine gun, "US Army" in raised cast lettering on sides, Model No. 4635
EX $33   **NM** $50   **MIP** $65

❏ **Renault Tank,** 1931, w/treads, Model No. 4647
EX $23   **NM** $34   **MIP** $45

❏ **Steamroller,** 1931, Model No. 4648
EX $65   **NM** $95   **MIP** $125

❏ **Farm Tractor,** Army Field Battery Set #5071, Model No. 4654
EX $58   **NM** $86   **MIP** $115

❏ **Bluebird Dayton Record Car,** 1932, Model No. 4666
EX $30   **NM** $45   **MIP** $55

❏ **Farm Set,** 1928, w/Ford Truck and Tractor, Huber Star Box Trailer, and Huber Star Scraper-Raker, Model No. 7003
EX $135   **NM** $205   **MIP** $275

5091 Funnies Series (1932)

❏ **Andy Gump Roadster,** Model No. 5101
EX $225   **NM** $340   **MIP** $450

❏ **Andy Gump Roadster,** Axles set so Andy Gump "bobs" as he drives, Model No. 5101X
EX $175   **NM** $265   **MIP** $350

❏ **Uncle Walt Roadster,** Model No. 5102
EX $225   **NM** $340   **MIP** $450

(KP Photo, John Brown Sr. collection)

❏ **Uncle Walt Roadster,** Green body, red painted rims, gold grille, black painted tires, silver painted cast figure of Walt moves as car is pushed along, Model No. 5102X
EX $175   **NM** $265   **MIP** $350

❏ **Smitty Motorcyle,** mechanical, Model No. 5103X
EX $225   **NM** $340   **MIP** $450

❏ **Smitty Motorcyle,** Model No. 5103
EX $175   **NM** $265   **MIP** $350

❏ **Moon Mullins Police Wagon,** Model No. 5104
EX $175   **NM** $265   **MIP** $350

❏ **Moon Mullins Police Wagon,** Mechanical toy, Moon moves as car is pushed along, Model No. 5104X
EX $225   **NM** $340   **MIP** $450

❏ **Kayo Ice Wagon,** Model No. 5105
EX $175   **NM** $265   **MIP** $350

❏ **Kayo Ice Wagon,** mechanical, Model No. 5105X
EX $225   **NM** $340   **MIP** $450

❏ **Uncle Willie rowboat,** Model No. 5106
EX $175   **NM** $265   **MIP** $350

❏ **Uncle Willie rowboat,** Mechanical toy, Uncle Willie and Mamie move as boat is pushed along, Model No. 5106X
EX $225   **NM** $340   **MIP** $450

Airplanes

❏ **Army DC-4 Transport,** 1941,
EX $40   **NM** $75   **MIP** $110

❏ **Dive-Bomber Waco Biplane,** 1937,
EX $50   **NM** $95   **MIP** $140

❏ **United DC-4 Supre Mainliner,** 1941,
EX $35   **NM** $65   **MIP** $95

❏ **U.S. Army Northrup Alpha Pursuit Plane,** 1936, Model No. 119
EX $25   **NM** $50   **MIP** $75

❏ **Lockheed Electra,** 1937, twin-engine, Model No. 125
EX $25   **NM** $50   **MIP** $75

❏ **TWA DC-2,** 1937, Model No. 717
EX $30   **NM** $60   **MIP** $90

❏ **U.S. Navy Waco C-Model Biplane,** 1937, Model No. 718
EX $45   **NM** $85   **MIP** $125

❏ **Crusader,** 1937, twin boom, twin engine, Model No. 719
EX $35   **NM** $70   **MIP** $100

❏ **Curtis P-40 Pursuit,** 1941, silver, Model No. 721
EX $70   **NM** $140   **MIP** $200

❏ **USN Los Angeles Dirigible,** 1937, Model No. 1030
EX $45   **NM** $85   **MIP** $125

❏ **Bleriot Plane,** 1910, Model No. 4482
EX $40   **NM** $80   **MIP** $120

❏ **Ford Tri-Motor,** 1932, Model No. 4649
EX $45   **NM** $85   **MIP** $125

❏ **Biplane,** 1926, open-spoke tires, Model No. 4650
EX $45   **NM** $85   **MIP** $125

❏ **Autogyro,** 1934, Model No. 4659
EX $40   **NM** $80   **MIP** $120

❏ **Aerodawn,** 1928, rubber tires, Model No. 4660
EX $30   NM $55   MIP $80

❏ **Aerodawn,** 1928, metal tires, Model No. 4660
EX $30   NM $60   MIP $85

CAMELBACK DELIVERY VAN SERIES (1937), 3" VEHICLES

❏ **Lewis's,** Model No. 123
EX $135   NM $205   MIP $275

❏ **McLeans,** Model No. 123
EX $145   NM $215   MIP $285

❏ **Miller & Rhoads,** Model No. 123
EX $145   NM $215   MIP $285

❏ **Shepards,** Model No. 123
EX $145   NM $215   MIP $285

(KP Photo, John Brown Sr. collection)

❏ **Special Delivery,** Silver-painted body, white rubber wheels, "Special Delivery" in script type cast on panel sides, Model No. 123
EX $25   NM $38   MIP $50

❏ **Wieboldt's,** Model No. 123
EX $145   NM $215   MIP $285

DEPRESSION-YEARS MINIATURES (1931)

❏ **Buick Marquette Coupe,** 1931,
EX $10   NM $15   MIP $20

❏ **Buick Marquette Sedan,** 1931,
EX $10   NM $15   MIP $20

❏ **Mack Insurance Patrol Fire Truck,** 1931,
EX $25   NM $35   MIP $45

❏ **Buick Marquette Roadster,** Model No. 102
EX $13   NM $19   MIP $25

❏ **Mack Tank Truck,** 1932, Model No. 105
EX $25   NM $40   MIP $55

❏ **Low Wing Monoplane,** 1932, w/propeller, tin wings, Model No. 106
EX $35   NM $55   MIP $70

❏ **High Wing Monoplane,** 1932, w/propeller, tin wings, Model No. 107
EX $35   NM $55   MIP $70

❏ **Caterpillar tractor w/tread,** 1932, Model No. 108
EX $23   NM $34   MIP $45

❏ **Ford Stake Truck,** 1932, Model No. 109
EX $20   NM $30   MIP $40

❏ **Bluebird Dayton Racer,** 1932, Model No. 110
EX $25   NM $40   MIP $55

FEDERAL DELIVERY VAN SERIES (1924)

❏ **Grocery,** Model No. 4630
EX $35   NM $55   MIP $85

❏ **Bakery,** Model No. 4631
EX $50   NM $80   MIP $105

❏ **Market,** Model No. 4632
EX $35   NM $60   MIP $75

❏ **Laundry,** Model No. 4633
EX $45   NM $65   MIP $95

❏ **Milk,** most common in series, Model No. 4634
EX $25   NM $40   MIP $55

❏ **Florist,** rarest in series, Model No. 4635
EX $95   NM $175   MIP $225

FORD V8 SERIES (1935), 3" VEHICLES

(KP Photo, John Brown Sr. collection)

❏ **Ford Pickup Truck,** 1936, Assorted colors, white rubber wheels, Model No. 121
EX $18   NM $26   MIP $35

❏ **'34 Sedan,** Model No. 111
EX $30   NM $45   MIP $60

❏ **'35 Sedan,** Model No. 111
EX $15   NM $23   MIP $30

❏ **'34 Coupe,** Model No. 112
EX $33   NM $49   MIP $65

❏ **'35 Coupe,** Model No. 112
EX $18   NM $26   MIP $35

(KP Photo, John Brown Sr. collection)

❏ **'34 Wrecker,** 1934-35, Earlier model with separately-cast bumper and grill, gray hubs with white tires, assorted color body, Model No. 113
EX $40   NM $60   MIP $75

(KP Photo, John Brown Sr. collection)

❏ **'35 Wrecker,** 1935-36, Later model with single-piece cab (bumper and grille part of casting) and different hook configuration. Also, all-rubber white wheels rather than the tires and hubs of the previous model, Model No. 113
EX $35   NM $50   MIP $68

❏ **'34 Convertible Coupe,** Model No. 114
EX $40   NM $60   MIP $80

❏ **'35 Convertible Coupe,** Model No. 114
EX $30   NM $45   MIP $60

❏ **'34 Convertible Sedan,** Model No. 115
EX $40   NM $60   MIP $80

❏ **'35 Convertible Sedan,** Model No. 115
EX $30   NM $45   MIP $60

❏ **'35 Roadster,** Model No. 116
EX $23   NM $34   MIP $45

❑ '35 Roadster Fire Chief Car, Model No. 117
EX $50   NM $75   MIP $100

(KP Photo, John Brown Sr. collection)

❑ **DeSoto Airflow Sedan,** Four-door model, assorted colors, white rubber tires, Model No. 118
EX $27   NM $40   MIP $55

GM SERIES (1927)

❑ **Buick Roadster,** Model No. 6001
EX $30   NM $45   MIP $60

❑ **Buick Coupe,** Model No. 6002
EX $28   NM $41   MIP $55

❑ **Buick Brougham,** Model No. 6003
EX $28   NM $41   MIP $55

❑ **Buick Sedan,** Model No. 6004
EX $28   NM $41   MIP $55

❑ **Buick Touring Car,** Model No. 6005
EX $50   NM $75   MIP $100

❑ **Buick Screenside Delivery truck,** Model No. 6006
EX $35   NM $53   MIP $70

❑ **Cadillac Roadster,** Model No. 6101
EX $40   NM $60   MIP $80

❑ **Cadillac coupe,** Model No. 6102
EX $40   NM $60   MIP $80

❑ **Cadillac Brougham,** Model No. 6103
EX $40   NM $60   MIP $80

❑ **Cadillac Sedan,** Model No. 6104
EX $40   NM $60   MIP $80

❑ **Cadillac Touring Car,** Model No. 6105
EX $60   NM $90   MIP $120

❑ **Cadillac Screenside Delivery Truck,** Model No. 6106
EX $48   NM $71   MIP $95

❑ **Chevrolet Roadster,** Model No. 6201
EX $33   NM $50   MIP $65

❑ **Chevrolet Coupe,** Model No. 6202
EX $33   NM $50   MIP $65

❑ **Chevrolet Brougham,** Model No. 6203
EX $33   NM $50   MIP $65

❑ **Chevrolet Sedan,** Model No. 6204
EX $33   NM $50   MIP $65

❑ **Chevrolet Touring Car,** Model No. 6205
EX $55   NM $83   MIP $110

❑ **Chevrolet Screenside Delivery Truck,** Model No. 6206
EX $35   NM $53   MIP $70

❑ **Oldsmobile Roadster,** Model No. 6301
EX $38   NM $55   MIP $75

❑ **Oldsmobile Coupe,** Model No. 6302
EX $35   NM $53   MIP $70

❑ **Oldsmobile Brougham,** Model No. 6303
EX $35   NM $53   MIP $70

❑ **Oldsmobile Sedan,** Model No. 6304
EX $35   NM $53   MIP $70

❑ **Oldsmobile Touring Car,** Model No. 6305
EX $55   NM $83   MIP $110

❑ **Oldsmobile Screenside Delivery Truck,** Model No. 6306
EX $45   NM $68   MIP $90

❑ **No-Name Roadster,** Model No. 6401
EX $55   NM $83   MIP $110

❑ **No-Name Coupe,** Model No. 6402
EX $55   NM $83   MIP $110

❑ **No-Name Brougham,** Model No. 6403
EX $55   NM $83   MIP $110

❑ **No-Name Sedan,** Model No. 6404
EX $55   NM $83   MIP $110

❑ **No-Name Touring Car,** Model No. 6405
EX $75   NM $113   MIP $150

❑ **No-Name Screenside Delivery Truck,** Model No. 6406
EX $65   NM $95   MIP $125

GRAHAM SERIES (1933), 4" VEHICLES

(KP Photo, John Brown Sr. collection)

❑ **Bild-A-Car Coupe,** 1933, Four wheel model--part of an innovative set containing 60 pieces, including bodys, chassis, tires and axles that allowed kids to invent their own car combinations
EX $65   NM $95   MIP $130

❑ **Bild-A-Car Roadster,** four wheel
EX $85   NM $130   MIP $175

(KP Photo, John Brown Sr. collection)

❑ **Bild-A-Car Sedan,** 1933, Four wheel model. Part of Grahams set of interchangeable pieces, including body styles, chassis' colors, tires and axles. Vehicle shown has no spare tires on either trunk or sides
EX $65   NM $95   MIP $130

(KP Photo, John Brown Sr. collection)

❑ **Commercial Tire & Supply Co. Van,** Mustard tan body with dark brown fenders and running boards, white rubber tires, "Commercial Tire & Supply Co." in script raised type along panel sides
EX $80   NM $115   MIP $160

(KP Photo, John Brown Sr. collection)

❑ **Roadster,** 1933, Five wheel model with trunk-mounted spare. Color variations include: red and black, light and dark blue, light and dark green, yellow and brown. White rubber tires, nickeled grille, headlights and front bumper, Model No. 511

EX $80   **NM** $125   **MIP** $165

❑ **Coupe,** five wheel, Model No. 512
EX $70   **NM** $110   **MIP** $145

(KP Photo, John Brown Sr. collection)

❑ **Sedan,** 1933, Five wheel model (trunk-mounted spare). Color variations include: red and black, light and dark blue, light and dark green, yellow and brown. White rubber tires, nickeled grille and headlights, Model No. 513
EX $75   **NM** $115   **MIP** $150

(KP Photo, John Brown collection)

❑ **Convertible Coupe,** 1933, Five wheel model (one spare on trunk). A "convertible" by right of the differently-painted roof, the color range for this model is: Red, black and khaki, Light blue, dark blue and khaki, Light brown, dark brown and khaki, and green, red and khaki. White rubber tires, nick-

eled grille, headlights and bumper, Model No. 514
EX $80   **NM** $120   **MIP** $160

(KP Photo, John Brown Sr. collection)

❑ **Convertible Sedan,** 1933, Five wheel model (trunk-mounted spare). Color variations inlcude: red, black and khaki, light blue, dark blue and khaki, dark brown, light brown and khaki, green, red and khaki. Nickeled grille, headlights and front bumper. Again, a "convertible" model because of its khaki-painted roof, Model No. 515
EX $80   **NM** $120   **MIP** $160

❑ **Towncar,** five wheel, Model No. 516
EX $88   **NM** $130   **MIP** $175

(KP Photo, John Brown Sr. collection)

❑ **Roadster,** 1933, Six wheel model with two side-mounted spares. Color variations include: orange-yellow and brown, red and black, light and dark blue, light and dark green. Nickeled grille, bumper and headlights, white rubber tires, Model No. 611
EX $80   **NM** $125   **MIP** $165

(KP Photo, John Brown Sr. collection)

❑ **Coupe,** 1933, Six wheel model (spares on both sides). The coupe differed from the six wheel convertible (0614) in that it had a solid

color for the roof and body. White rubber tires. Colors include: red and black, light and dark green, light and dark blue, yellow and brown, Model No. 612
EX $72   **NM** $110   **MIP** $145

(KP Photo, John Brown Sr. collection)

❑ **Sedan,** 1933, Six wheel model (spares on both sides). Colors include: Light and dark blue, red and black, light and dark green, or yellow and brown. Nickeled grille, headlights and bumpers, Model No. 613
EX $70   **NM** $110   **MIP** $145

❑ **Convertible Coupe,** six wheel, Model No. 614
EX $80   **NM** $120   **MIP** $160

❑ **Convertible Sedan,** six wheel, Model No. 615
EX $80   **NM** $120   **MIP** $160

(KP Photo, John Brown Sr. collection)

❑ **Towncar,** 1933, Six wheel model (spares on each side). Color variations include: blue with darker blue fenders, green with darker green fenders, and red and black. Nickeled grille and headlights, white rubber tires, Model No. 616
EX $80   **NM** $120   **MIP** $160

(KP Photo, John Brown Sr. collection)

❏ **Wrecker,** 1933, Body colors in white, red or yellow. Black fenders, running boards and chassis. White rubber tires, nickeled grille, headlights and bumper, Model No. 806
EX $75   NM $110   MIP $150

(KP Photo, John Brown Sr. collection)

❏ **Tootsietoy Dairy Delivery Van,** 1933, Cream-white body, black fenders and running boards, white rubber tires, raised lettering on panel sides, "Tootsietoy Dairy," silver grille, Model No. 808
EX $75   NM $110   MIP $150

(KP Photo, John Brown Sr. collection)

❏ **Ambulance,** White body, fenders and running boards, raised and painted red cross symbol on sides, silver grille, Model No. 809
EX $75   NM $110   MIP $150

(KP Photo, John Brown Sr. collection)

❏ **Army Ambulance,** Light and dark green camouflage pattern on body, dark green fenders and running boards, white tires, painted and raised (cast) red cross symbol on sides, silver grille and headlights, Model No. 809
EX $75   NM $110   MIP $150

JUMBO SERIES (1936), 6" VEHICLES

❏ **Torpedo Cross-Country Greyhound Bus,**
EX $25   NM $55   MIP $80

❏ **Auburn Torpedo Roadster,** Model No. 1016
EX $23   NM $34   MIP $45

❏ **Torpedo Coupe,** Model No. 1017
EX $20   NM $30   MIP $40

❏ **Torpedo Sedan,** Model No. 1018
EX $20   NM $30   MIP $40

❏ **Torpedo Pickup Truck,** Model No. 1019
EX $20   NM $30   MIP $40

❏ **Torpedo Wrecker,** Model No. 1027
EX $23   NM $34   MIP $45

❏ **Greyhound Bus,** w/tin bottom, Model No. 1045
EX $55   NM $50   MIP $70

❏ **Trans-America Bus,** 1941, sold only in sets, Model No. 1045
EX $90   NM $130   MIP $175

LaSALLE SERIES (1935), 4" VEHICLES

(KP Photo, John Brown Sr. collection)

❏ **Coupe,** 1935, Nicely detailed castings, separate grille and headlights, separate running boards and fenders. Like the Grahams series, convertible models were defined by khaki roofs, Model No. 712
EX $115   NM $180   MIP $240

(KP Photo, John Brown Sr. collection)

❏ **Sedan,** 1935, Sharply detailed castings. One color for body, another for separately cast fenders and running boards, Model No. 713
EX $115   NM $180   MIP $240

❏ **Convertible Coupe,** Model No. 714
EX $125   NM $205   MIP $265

❏ **Convertible Sedan,** 1935, Khaki-painted roof differentiates this model as a convertible. Separate grille and headlight casting, separate fenders and running boards. White rubber tires on hubs, Model No. 715
EX $125   NM $205   MIP $265

LINCOLN SERIES (1935), 4" VEHICLES

❏ **Zephyr and Roamer House Trailer,** Non wind-up version, Model No. 180
EX $555   NM $740   MIP $925

(KP Photo, John Brown Sr. collection)

❏ **Zephyr and Roamer House Trailer,** Includes wind-up Zephyr and Roamer Trailer (1044) with opening door (often missing). The only motorized Tootsietoy of the period, Model No. 180
EX $680   NM $890   MIP $1200

(KP Photo, John Brown Sr. collection)

❏ **Briggs-Lincoln prototype ("Doodlebug"),** Very close to the Zephyr casting, but no trace of a wind-up motor. Separate grille, bumper and headlight casting. Hubs with white rubber tires, Model No. 716
EX $75   NM $95   MIP $125

(KP Photo, John Brown Sr. collection)

❑ **Zephyr,** 1937, Detail view showing wind-up motor underneath car, Model No. 6015
EX $285   **NM** $375   **MIP** $500

(KP Photo, John Brown Sr. collection)

❑ **Zephyr,** 1937, Featured a unique wind-up motor, white rubber tires, silver grille and bumper, Model No. 6015
EX $285   **NM** $375   **MIP** $500

❑ **Zephyr,** Non-wind-up model. Still has the same hubs with white rubber tires, but you can see a place in the casting for the wind-up key, Model No. 6015
EX $165   **NM** $245   **MIP** $325

❑ **Zephyr Wrecker,** An unusual car and a rare find with a wind-up motor, Model No. 6016
EX $350   **NM** $525   **MIP** $700

❑ **Wrecker,** Model No. 6016
EX $250   **NM** $230   **MIP** $350

MACK DELIVERY TRUCKS AND VANS (1933), 4" VEHICLES

(KP Photo, John Brown Sr. collection)

❑ **City Fuel Company Coal Truck,** 1937, This rare four wheel version has white rubber tires, Model No. 804
EX $60   **NM** $95   **MIP** $130

(KP Photo, John Brown Sr. collection)

❑ **City Fuel Company Coal Truck,** 1933, This ten-wheel version is more common. Rubber tires, black fenders and running boards, Model No. 804
EX $75   **NM** $115   **MIP** $150

❑ **Delivery Motorcycle,** adapted from 5103, Model No. 807
EX $85   **NM** $125   **MIP** $175

❑ **Commercial Tire & Supply Co. Van,** Model No. 810
EX $112   **NM** $168   **MIP** $225

(KP Photo, John Brown Sr. collection)

❑ **Railway Express Co., Wrigley's Gum,** 1935, One-piece cab (later) version. Dark green body with Wrigley's advertment on truck bed. White rubber tires, Model No. 810
EX $75   **NM** $110   **MIP** $160

(KP Photo, John Brown Sr. collection)

❑ **Railway Express Co., Wrigley's Gum,** Earlier, two-piece cab version. Dark green cab, lighter green body with black fenders and running boards, Wrigley's advertisement on truck bed, white rubber tires, Model No. 810
EX $80   **NM** $120   **MIP** $175

MACK FIRE TRUCK SERIES (1937), 4" VEHICLES

(KP Photo, John Brown Sr. collection)

❑ **Hook and Ladder,** Red body, silver grille, white rubber tires, three gold-painted ladders, Model No. 1040
EX $35   **NM** $50   **MIP** $70

(KP Photo, John Brown Sr. collection)

❑ **Hose Car,** Red body, silver-painted grille and fire hose. Nozzle on swivelling base, white rubber tires, blue painted driver, Model No. 1041
EX $35   **NM** $55   **MIP** $75

(KP Photo, John Brown collection)

❑ **Insurance Patrol,** Open end red body with silver grille, fenders and truck bed. Blue painted driver, white rubber tires, Model No. 1042
EX $30   **NM** $45   **MIP** $60

❑ **Insurance Patrol,** With ladder and rear fireman, Model No. 1042
EX $35   **NM** $55   **MIP** $75

MACK TRACTOR-TRAILERS, 1:43-SCALE (1931)

(KP Photo, John Brown collection)

❑ **Auto Transport,** 1941, Yellow cab and trailer holds three 1940s Buicks in tilted position, Model No. 187
EX $275   **NM** $415   **MIP** $550

❑ **Auto Transport four-car Hauler,** 1933, w/101-103 Buicks and 109 Ford, Model No. 190X
EX $115   **NM** $170   **MIP** $225

(KP Photo, John Brown Sr. collection)

❑ **Auto Transport three-car Hauler,** 1931, Red cab and trailer with three cars. (Originally, three Buicks. The Ford Stake truck was standard with the 190X transporter). White rubber tires, Model No. 190
EX $115   **NM** $145   **MIP** $180

(KP Photo, John Brown Sr. collection)

❑ **Contractor Set,** 1933, Red cab Mack AC hauling three spoke-wheeled tipper trailers. The original packaging for this model was an 11-1/2" box! Cab shown just hauling one of the three included with set, Model No. 191
EX $75   **NM** $100   **MIP** $150

❑ **Tootsietoy Dairy Tanker,** 1933, Yellow two-piece cab with black fenders and running boards, three trailers with white tanks, yellow chassis, Model No. 192
EX $120   **NM** $160   **MIP** $200

(KP Photo, John Brown Sr. collection)

❑ **Tootsietoy Dairy Tanker,** All-yellow one-piece cab, three trailers with white tanks, yellow chassis and "Tootsietoy Dairy" in black lettering. Shown with one of three included trailers. Additional trailers could be purchased separately from toy stores, Model No. 192
EX $85   **NM** $125   **MIP** $175

❑ **Auto Transport,** one-piece cab, three '35 Fords, Model No. 198
EX $125   **NM** $200   **MIP** $275

❑ **Auto Transport,** two-piece cab, three '35 Fords, Model No. 198
EX $150   **NM** $250   **MIP** $350

(KP Photo, John Brown Sr. collection)

❑ **Express Stake Semi-Trailer,** 1935, Later editions featured a one-piece cab and single wheels all-around. No paint on the raised letters, "Express" as the earlier version, Model No. 801
EX $55   **NM** $80   **MIP** $105

(KP Photo, John Brown Sr. collection)

❑ **Express Stake Semi-Trailer,** 1933, Two-piece cab with black chassis and black paint on "Express" lettering on trailer. Colors range from orange, red, sand or green. Also features dual wheels, dropped from the later versions, Model No. 801
EX $80   **NM** $105   **MIP** $135

❑ **Domaco Tank Semi-Trailer,** two-piece cab, Model No. 802
EX $90   **NM** $120   **MIP** $150

(KP Photo, John Brown Sr. collection)

❑ **Domaco Tank Semi-Trailer,** 1935, Orange-red one-piece cab towing tanker trailer with light green tank and red-orange chassis. Black type on tanker reads, "Domaco Gasoline and Oils", Model No. 802
EX $60   **NM** $90   **MIP** $120

(KP Photo, John Brown Sr. collection)

❑ **Long Distance Hauling Semi-Trailer,** 1933, Two-piece cab with trailer, rubber dual wheels on cab and trailer. Colors range from orange, sand, red and green. All have black fenders, running boards and chassis. Raised "Long Distance Hauling" type on trailer painted black, Model No. 803
EX $85   **NM** $130   **MIP** $175

❑ **Tootsietoy Dairy Semi-Trailer,** 1933, dual tires, Model No. 805
EX $70   **NM** $105   **MIP** $140

❑ **Tootsietoy Dairy Semi-Trailer,** single tires, Model No. 805
EX $60   **NM** $90   **MIP** $120

MACK TRUCKS, 1:72-SCALE (1925)

❑ **Interchangeable Truck Set,** Model No. 170
EX $50   NM $65   MIP $80

(KP Photo, John Brown Sr. collection)

❑ **Stake Truck,** Assorted colors, rubber or black metal tires, Model No. 4638
EX $23   NM $34   MIP $45

(KP Photo, John Brown Sr. collection)

❑ **Coal Truck,** Assorted colors, rubber or metal tires, Model No. 4639
EX $25   NM $40   MIP $55

(KP Photo, John Brown Sr. collection)

❑ **Tank Truck,** Assorted colors, with or without rubber wheels, Model No. 4640
EX $25   NM $40   MIP $55

(KP Photo, John Brown Sr. collection)

❑ **Anti-Aircraft Gun Army Truck,** 1931, Another in the Mack truck line, the gun rotates on a swivel base, Model No. 4643
EX $25   NM $38   MIP $50

❑ **Searchlight Army Truck,** 1931, This Mack truck was available with or without rubber tires. The searchlight, cleverly done, was a mirror, Model No. 4644
EX $25   NM $40   MIP $55

❑ **US Mail Air Mail Service,** 1931, Model No. 4645
EX $35   NM $55   MIP $75

❑ **A&P Trailer Truck,** 1929, Model No. 4670
EX $100   NM $150   MIP $200

❑ **American Railway Express Trailer Truck,** 1929, Model No. 4670
EX $115   NM $170   MIP $225

❑ **Overland Bus Lines,** 1929, Model No. 4680
EX $45   NM $65   MIP $95

MIDGET SERIES/ CRACKER JACKS (1936), 1" VEHICLES

❑ **Boxed Set,** eight piece, Model No. 510
EX $75   NM $100   MIP $150

❑ **Boxed Set,** ten piece set, Model No. 510
EX $90   NM $130   MIP $175

❑ **Boxed Set,** twelve piece, Model No. 610
EX $100   NM $150   MIP $200

(KP Photo, John Brown Sr. collection)

❑ **Bus,** Like others in the series, wheels are part of casting. The open windows are a nice touch, though, Model No. 1628
EX $8   NM $12   MIP $19

(KP Photo, John Brown Sr. collection)

❑ **Stake Truck,** Ford V-8-looking front grille and stake sides to truck bed. Assorted colors
EX $10   NM $15   MIP $20

(KP Photo, John Brown Sr. collection)

❑ **Wrecker,** Model No. 1629
EX $7   NM $10   MIP $14

(KP Photo, John Brown Sr. collection)

❑ **Racer,** Blue car, a tiny version of the Large Bluebird Racer, Model No. 1630
EX $5   NM $7   MIP $10

(KP Photo, John Brown Sr. collection)

TOOTSIETOY / PREWAR

❑ **DeSoto Airflow Sedan,** Assorted colors, Model No. 1631
EX $5   NM $7   MIP $10

(KP Photo, John Brown Sr. collection)

❑ **Zephyr Railcar,** Assorted colors, modelled after the larger Zephyr Railcar, #117, Model No. 1632
EX $7   NM $10   MIP $14

(KP Photo, John Brown Sr. collection)

❑ **Fire Engine,** Red body, cast driver, Model No. 1634
EX $7   NM $10   MIP $14

(KP Photo, John Brown Sr. collection)

❑ **Delivery Van,** Assorted colors body, Model No. 1635
EX $6   NM $9   MIP $12

(KP Photo, John Brown Sr. collection)

❑ **Army Tank,** Assorted colors, Model No. 1666
EX $4   NM $6   MIP $8

(KP Photo, John Brown Sr. collection)

❑ **Armored Car,** Model No. 1667
EX $6   NM $9   MIP $12

MINIATURE SHIPS

❑ **Fleet,** 1941, nine-piece carded battleship assortment: USS Idaho, USS Indiana, USS Tennessee, USS Texas, USS New Mexico, USS Maryland, USS Arizona, USS New York, USS Pennsylvania, Model No. 1405
EX $50   NM $75   MIP $100

❑ **Naval Defense,** 1941, fourteen-piece carded assortment, Model No. 1408
EX $70   NM $105   MIP $140

❑ **Sea Champions,** 1946, five-piece carded set contains two No. 1638 battleships, one No. 1618 submarine, one No. 1619 destroyer, and one No. 1620 aero carrier, Model No. 1811
EX $30   NM $45   MIP $60

REO OIL TRUCK SERIES (1938), DISTINCTIVE 6" TRUCKS

❑ **Standard,** Model No. 1006
EX $35   NM $55   MIP $80

❑ **Sinclair,** Model No. 1007
EX $35   NM $55   MIP $80

❑ **Texaco,** Model No. 1008
EX $35   NM $55   MIP $80

❑ **Shell,** Model No. 1009
EX $40   NM $60   MIP $90

MACK FIRE TRUCK SERIES (1937), 4" VEHICLES

(KP Photo, John Brown Sr. collection)

❏ **Hook and Ladder,** A re-release of pre-war version 1040, note the wheel covers (over black wheels) added to the casting, and less paint variety overall, Model No. 1040
EX $30   NM $45   MIP $65

MISCELLANEOUS POSTWAR TOOTSIETOYS

(KP Photo, John Brown Sr. collection)

❏ **1931 Ford B Hot Rod,** 1960, Red body, black wheels, sharp casting
EX $8   NM $12   MIP $20

❏ **1938 Buick Y Experimental Convertible**
EX $20   NM $30   MIP $40

❏ **1940 Ford Special Deluxe Convertible,** 1960
EX $20   NM $30   MIP $401

❏ **1940 Ford V-8 Hot Rod,** 1960
EX $15   NM $22   MIP $30

❏ **1941 Chrysler Windsor Convertible**
EX $20   NM $30   MIP $40

❏ **1941 International Army Ambulance**
EX $24   NM $34   MIP $50

❏ **1941 International K1 Panel Truck**
EX $22   NM $32   MIP $45

(KP Photo, John Brown Sr. collection)

❏ **1941 White Army Half Track,** Dark green body covering black rubber wheels. Cast raised lettering on sides, "USA W-60118"
EX $10   NM $16   MIP $25

❏ **1942 Chrysler Thunderbolt Experimental Roadster**
EX $22   NM $32   MIP $40

❏ **1946 International K11 Oil Tanker,** Texaco
EX $25   NM $40   MIP $65

❏ **1946 International K11 Oil Tanker,** Sinclair
EX $25   NM $35   MIP $55

❏ **1946 International K11 Oil Tanker,** Shell
EX $25   NM $40   MIP $65

❏ **1946 International K11 Oil Tanker,** Standard
EX $25   NM $35   MIP $55

❏ **1947 Chevrolet Fleetmaster Coupe**
EX $13   NM $19   MIP $25

❏ **1947 Hudson Streamlined Pickup**
EX $22   NM $32   MIP $45

❏ **1947 Kaiser Sedan**
EX $28   NM $37   MIP $50

❏ **1947 Mack L-Line Dump Truck**
EX $14   NM $25   MIP $35

❏ **1947 Mack L-Line Fire Pumper**
EX $25   NM $40   MIP $65

❏ **1947 Mack L-Line Stake Truck**
EX $22   NM $32   MIP $45

❏ **1947 Mack L-Line Wrecker**
EX $14   NM $25   MIP $35

❏ **1947 Offenhauser Race Car**
EX $13   NM $19   MIP $25

❏ **1947 Offenhauser Race Car, on trailer**
EX $15   NM $22   MIP $30

(KP Photo, John Brown Sr. collection)

❏ **1947 Studebaker Champion Coupe,** Assorted colors, casting covers black wheels. A rare find in these postwar models
EX $25   NM $35   MIP $55

(KP Photo, Johnn Brown Sr. collection)

❏ **1947 Willys Jeepster,** 1949, Yellow body, black wheels, wheel covers over rear wheels
EX $10   NM $15   MIP $20

❏ **1948 Buick Super Estate Wagon**
EX $27   NM $42   MIP $65

❏ **1948 Cadillac 60 Special Four-door Sedan**
EX $18   NM $26   MIP $35

❏ **1948 GMC 3751 Greyhound Diesel Bus**
EX $25   NM $35   MIP $55

❏ **1949 Buick Roadmaster Four-door Sedan**
EX $20   NM $34   MIP $45

❏ **1949 Ford Custom Convertible**
EX $10   NM $15   MIP $25

❏ **1949 Ford Custom Four-door Sedan**
EX $10   NM $15   MIP $25

(KP Photo, John Brown Sr. collection)

❑ **1949 Ford F1 Pickup,**
Assorted colors, casting fits over
black plastic wheels
EX $10   NM $15   MIP $25

❑ **1949 Ford F6 Oil Tanker**
EX $13   NM $19   MIP $25

❑ **1949 Ford F6 Oil Tanker,**
Shell
EX $25   NM $35   MIP $55

❑ **1949 Ford F6 Stake Truck**
EX $15   NM $22   MIP $30

❑ **1949 Indianapolis No. 3
Race Car**
EX $10   NM $15   MIP $25

❑ **1949 Mercury Fire Chief
Sedan**
EX $22   NM $32   MIP $45

❑ **1949 Mercury Four-door
Sedan**
EX $15   NM $24   MIP $35

❑ **1949 Oldsmobile 88
Convertible**
EX $20   NM $30   MIP $40

❑ **1950 Chevrolet Army
Ambulance**
EX $15   NM $24   MIP $35

❑ **1950 Chevrolet Deluxe
Panel**
EX $14   NM $21   MIP $28

❑ **1950 Chevrolet Deluxe
Panel Truck**
EX $10   NM $15   MIP $25

(KP Photo, John Brown Sr. collection)

❑ **1950 Chevrolet Fleetline
Deluxe Sedan,** Two door model.
Casting covers black wheels,
assorted colors
EX $10   NM $15   MIP $25

❑ **1950 Chrysler Windsor Convertible**
EX $70   NM $95   MIP $125

❑ **1950 Dodge Pickup**
EX $15   NM $22   MIP $30

❑ **1950 Ford F6 Oil Tanker,**
Sinclair
EX $25   NM $35   MIP $55

(KP Photo, John Brown Sr. collection)

❑ **1950 Jeep CJ3,** Civilian model
in a variety of colors. Shown here
next to military version in green.
Both have black wheels, civilian
model without treads, earlier edition
EX $5   NM $7   MIP $14

❑ **1950 Jeep CJ3 Army**
EX $9   NM $15   MIP $22

(KP Photo, John Brown Sr. collection)

❑ **1950 Plymouth Special
Deluxe Sedan,** Four door model,
assorted colors, black wheels
EX $10   NM $15   MIP $25

❑ **1950 Pontiac Cheftain
Deluxe Coupe Sedan**
EX $20   NM $30   MIP $40

❑ **1950 Pontiac Fire Chief
Chieftain Sedan**
EX $22   NM $32   MIP $45

❑ **1950 Twin Coach Bus,** Red
body, casting covers black wheels
EX $14   NM $23   MIP $34

❑ **1951 Buick Le Sabre Experimental Roadster**
EX $25   NM $38   MIP $55

❑ **1951 Ford F6 Oil Tanker,**
Standard
EX $25   NM $35   MIP $55

❑ **1952 Ford F6 Oil Tanker,** Texaco
EX $25   NM $35   MIP $55

❑ **1952 Ford Mainline Four-
door Sedan**
EX $12   NM $21   MIP $32

❑ **1952 Lincoln Capri Two-
door Hardtop**
EX $28   NM $37   MIP $50

❑ **1952 Mercury Custom
Sedan,** four door
EX $15   NM $22   MIP $30

❑ **1953 Chrysler New Yorker
Sedan,** four door
EX $18   NM $28   MIP $45

❑ **1954 American La France
Pumper**
EX $10   NM $15   MIP $25

❑ **1954 Buick Century Estate
Wagon**
EX $20   NM $34   MIP $45

❑ **1954 Buick Special Experimental Coupe**
EX $23   NM $38   MIP $50

❑ **1954 Cadillac 62 Sedan,** four
door
EX $20   NM $30   MIP $40

❑ **1954 Ford Ranch Wagon**
EX $8   NM $12   MIP $20

❑ **1954 Ford Ranch Wagon**
EX $15   NM $24   MIP $35

❑ **1954 Jaguar XK120 Roadster**
EX $8   NM $12   MIP $20

❑ **1954 MG Roadster**
EX $10   NM $20   MIP $30

❑ **1954 MG Roadster**
EX $8   NM $12   MIP $20

(KP Photo, John Brown Sr. collection)

❑ **1954 Nash Metropolitan
Convertible,** Assorted colors,
casting covers black wheels
EX $30   NM $40   MIP $55

❑ **1954-55 Chevrolet Corvette Roadster**
EX $15   NM $22   MIP $30

(KP Photo, John Brown Sr. collection)

❑ **1955 Chevrolet Bel Air Sedan,** Four door casting, assorted colors, black wheels
EX $8   NM $12   MIP $20

(KP Photo, John Brown Sr. collection)

❑ **1955 Ford Customline V-8 Sedan,** Two door model, assorted colors, black plastic wheels
EX $8   NM $12   MIP $20

(KP Photo, John Brown Sr. collection)

❑ **1955 Ford Thunderbird Coupe,** Assorted colors, black plastic wheels
EX $7   NM $11   MIP $18

❑ **1955 Ford Thunderbird Coupe**
EX $20   NM $30   MIP $40

❑ **1955 Mack B-Line Cement Mixer,** axle-driven drum
EX $30   NM $40   MIP $55

❑ **1955 Mack B-Line Cement Mixer**
EX $22   NM $32   MIP $45

❑ **1955 Mack L-Line Stake Truck,** 1958, w/"Tootsietoy" tin cover
EX $50   NM $75   MIP $100

❑ **1955 Oldsmobile 98 Holiday Hardtop,** two-door
EX $15   NM $24   MIP $35

❑ **1956 Austin-Healey 100-5 Roadster**
EX $20   NM $30   MIP $40

❑ **1956 Caterpillar Bulldozer**
EX $20   NM $30   MIP $40

❑ **1956 Caterpillar Road Scraper**
EX $18   NM $26   MIP $35

❑ **1956 Chevrolet Cameo Pickup**
EX $13   NM $19   MIP $25

❑ **1956 Dodge D100 Panel Truck**
EX $23   NM $38   MIP $50

❑ **1956 Ferrari Racer**
EX $18   NM $28   MIP $45

❑ **1956 Ford C600 Oil Tanker**
EX $8   NM $12   MIP $20

❑ **1956 Jaguar XK140 Coupe**
EX $15   NM $22   MIP $30

❑ **1956 Lancia Racer**
EX $18   NM $27   MIP $45

❑ **1956 Mercedes 190SL Coupe**
EX $10   NM $20   MIP $30

❑ **1956 Packard Patrician Sedan,** four door
EX $28   NM $37   MIP $50

❑ **1956 Porsche Spyder Roadster**
EX $10   NM $20   MIP $30

❑ **1956 Triumph TR3 Roadster**
EX $7   NM $11   MIP $18

(KP Photo, John Brown Sr. collection)

❑ **1957 Ford F100 Styleside Pickup,** Assorted colors, orange most common. Black plastic wheels
EX $5   NM $7   MIP $14

❑ **1957 Ford Fairlane 500 Convertible**
EX $8   NM $12   MIP $20

❑ **1957 GMC Greyhound Scenicruiser Bus**
EX $22   NM $32   MIP $45

❑ **1957 Jaguar Type D**
EX $8   NM $12   MIP $20

(KP Photo, John Brown Sr. collection)

❑ **1957 Plymouth Belvedere,** Two-door hardtop model, assorted colors, black wheels
EX $8   NM $12   MIP $20

❑ **1959 Ford Country Sedan Station Wagon**
EX $10   NM $20   MIP $30

❑ **1959 Oldsmobile Dynamic 88 Convertible**
EX $14   NM $25   MIP $35

❑ **1959 Pontiac Star Chief Sedan,** four door
EX $10   NM $16   MIP $25

❑ **1960 Chevrolet El Camino Pickup,** w/camper and boat
EX $17   NM $32   MIP $50

❑ **1960 Chevrolet El Camino Pickup**
EX $12   NM $22   MIP $30

❑ **1960 Chrysler Windsor Convertible**
EX $13   NM $19   MIP $25

❑ **1960 Ford Country Sedan Station Wagon**
EX $8   NM $12   MIP $20

(KP Photo)

❑ **1960 Ford Falcon Sedan,** Two-door body, black wheels
EX $5   NM $8   MIP $15

❑ **1960 International Metro Van,** rare
EX $100   NM $125   MIP $150

❑ **1960 Jeep CJ5,** w/snow-plow
EX $25   NM $35   MIP $55

❑ **1960 Jeep CJ5**
EX $9   NM $18   MIP $25

❑ **1960 Rambler Super Cross-Country Wagon**
EX $15   NM $24   MIP $35

❑ **1960 Studebaker Lark Custom Convertible**
EX $9   NM $16   MIP $22

❑ **1960 Volkswagen 113**
EX $10   NM $20   MIP $30

❑ **1960 Volkswagen Bug**
EX $7   NM $11   MIP $18

❑ **1962 Ford C600 Oil Tanker Truck**
EX $20   NM $30   MIP $40

❑ **1962 Ford Country Sedan Station Wagon**
EX $8   NM $18   MIP $25

❑ **1962 Ford Econoline Pickup**
EX $20   NM $30   MIP $40

❑ **1969 Ford LTD Hardtop,** two door, last of the larger-size die-cast Tootsietoys
EX $13   NM $19   MIP $25

(KP Photo, John Brown Sr. collection)

❑ **Army Cannon,** Four wheel version. Dark green body, black wheels, trailer hookups at both ends
EX $10   NM $15   MIP $25

❑ **Army Cannon,** six wheel
EX $12   NM $21   MIP $30

❑ **U-Haul Trailer**
EX $4   NM $6   MIP $8

❑ **U-Haul Trailer**
EX $5   NM $10   MIP $15

'47 INTERNATIONAL K5 TRACTOR-TRAILERS

❑ **Auto Transporter,** scaled to match 6" vehicles
EX $30   NM $42   MIP $55

❑ **Machinery Hauler,** scaled to match 6" vehicles
EX $30   NM $42   MIP $55

❑ **Shipping Van,** "Tootsietoy Trucking," scaled to match 6" vehicles
EX $27   NM $37   MIP $50

❑ **Utility Truck,** scaled to match 6" vehicles
EX $27   NM $37   MIP $50

'47 MACK L-LINE TRACTOR-TRAILERS (1954)

❑ **Hook and Ladder,** scaled to match 6" vehicles
EX $35   NM $55   MIP $75

❑ **Log Hauler,** scaled to match 6" vehicles
EX $35   NM $55   MIP $75

❑ **Machinery Hauler,** scaled to match 6" vehicles
EX $35   NM $55   MIP $75

❑ **Oil Tanker,** Tootsietoy Line, scaled to match 6" vehicles
EX $50   NM $75   MIP $125

❑ **Oil Tanker,** scaled to match 6" vehicles
EX $32   NM $50   MIP $70

❑ **Pipe Truck**
EX $35   NM $55   MIP $75

❑ **Shipping Van,** Tootsietoy Line, scaled to match 6" vehicles
EX $50   NM $50   MIP $75

❑ **Shipping Van,** Tootsietoy Coast to Coast, scaled to match 6" vehicles
EX $37   NM $57   MIP $80

❑ **Stake Truck,** closed sides, scaled to match 6" vehicles
EX $35   NM $55   MIP $75

❑ **Stake Truck,** open sides, scaled to match 6" vehicles
EX $50   NM $70   MIP $115

'55 MACK B-LINE TRACTOR-TRAILERS (1960)

❑ **Auto Transport,** scaled to match 6" vehicles
EX $30   NM $42   MIP $65

❑ **Boat Transport,** scaled to match 6" vehicles
EX $28   NM $40   MIP $60

❑ **Hook and Ladder,** scaled to match 6" vehicles
EX $28   NM $40   MIP $60

❑ **Log Hauler,** scaled to match 6" vehicles
EX $28   NM $40   MIP $60

❑ **Machinery Hauler,** scaled to match 6" vehicles
EX $28   NM $40   MIP $60

❑ **Oil Tanker,** "Mobil," scaled to match 6" vehicles
EX $32   NM $50   MIP $70

❑ **Oil Tanker,** "Tootsietoy Line," scaled to match 6" vehicles
EX $40   NM $60   MIP $80

❑ **Pipe Truck,** scaled to match 6" vehicles
EX $28   NM $40   MIP $60

❑ **Shipping Van,** scaled to match 6" vehicles
EX $28   NM $40   MIP $60

❑ **Stake Truck,** closed sides, scaled to match 6" vehicles
EX $28   NM $40   MIP $60

❑ **Utility Truck,** scaled to match 6" vehicles
EX $25   NM $35   MIP $55

'58 INTERNATIONAL RC180 TRACTOR-TRAILERS (1962)

❑ **Auto Transport,** metal trailer scaled to match 6" vehicles
EX $42   NM $65   MIP $85

❑ **Auto Transport,** plastic trailer, scaled to match 6" vehicles
EX $24   NM $32   MIP $45

❑ **Boat Transport,** plastic trailer, scaled to match 6" vehicles
EX $24   NM $32   MIP $45

❑ **Machinery Hauler,** scaled to match 6" vehicles
EX $25   NM $35   MIP $55

❑ **Shipping Van,** "Dean Van Lines," plastic trailer, scaled to match 6" vehicles
EX $40   NM $60   MIP $80

'59 CHEVROLET TRACTOR-TRAILERS (1965)

❑ **Auto Transport,** scaled to match 6" vehicles
EX $50   NM $75   MIP $125

❑ **Hook and Ladder,** scaled to match 6" vehicles
EX $50   NM $75   MIP $125

❑ **Log Hauler,** scaled to match 6" vehicles
EX $45   NM $70   MIP $100

❑ **Machinery Hauler,** scaled to match 6" vehicles
EX $45   NM $70   MIP $100

❑ **Oil Tanker,** scaled to match 6" vehicles
EX $45   NM $70   MIP $100

AIRPLANES

❑ **Beechcraft Bonanza,** 1948
EX $8   NM $16   MIP $25

❑ **Boeing 707,** 1958
EX $18   NM $35   MIP $55

❑ **Coast Guard Seaplane,** 1950
EX $50   NM $100   MIP $150

❑ **F-86 Sabre Jet,** 1956, single casting
EX $7   NM $13   MIP $20

❑ **F-86 Sabre Jet,** 1950, two-casting body
EX $8   NM $16   MIP $25

❑ **Lockheed Constellation,** 1951
EX $45   NM $90   MIP $135

❑ **P-38 Fighter,** 1950, twin boom, twin engine
EX $40   NM $75   MIP $110

❑ **P-39 Fighter,** 1947
EX $50   NM $100   MIP $150

❑ **P-80 Shooting Star,** 1948
EX $10   NM $20   MIP $30

❑ **Twin-Engine Convair,** 1950, twin engine
EX $35   NM $65   MIP $95

CLASSIC SERIES (1960)

❑ **1906 Cadillac Coupe,** w/plastic wheels
EX $8   NM $12   MIP $18

❑ **1907 Stanley Steamer Runabout,** w/plastic wheels
EX $8   NM $12   MIP $18

❑ **1912 Ford Model T Touring Car,** w/plastic wheels
EX $8   NM $12   MIP $18

❑ **1919 Stutz Bearcat,** w/plastic wheels
EX $8   NM $12   MIP $18

❑ **1921 Mack Dump Truck,** w/plastic wheels
EX $10   NM $15   MIP $25

❑ **1929 Ford Model A Coupe,** w/plastic wheels
EX $8   NM $12   MIP $18

HO POCKET SERIES (1960)

❑ **Cadillac**
EX $8   NM $15   MIP $20

❑ **Dump Truck**
EX $10   NM $15   MIP $22

❑ **Ford Sunliner Convertible,** w/midget racer Trailer
EX $12   NM $22   MIP $35

❑ **Ford Sunliner Convertible,** w/boat trailer
EX $10   NM $18   MIP $30

❑ **Ford Wrecker Truck**
EX $10   NM $15   MIP $22

❑ **Metro Van,** various
EX $8   NM $15   MIP $20

❑ **Metro Van,** Railway Express
EX $10   NM $17   MIP $25

❑ **Rambler Station Wagon,** w/U-Haul trailer
EX $10   NM $18   MIP $30

❑ **Township School Bus**
EX $10   NM $17   MIP $25

LITTLE TOUGHS/MIDGET SERIES (1970)

❑ **American La France Aerial Ladder Truck**
EX $5   NM $8   MIP $12

❑ **American La France Ladder Truck**
EX $4   NM $6   MIP $10

(KP Photo, John Brown Sr. collection)

❑ **Auto Transport Semi-Cab and Trailer,** Red Ford cab, yellow trailer, black plastic wheels. Includes three cars. Raised cast lettering on trailer reads, "tootsietoy turnpike transport"
EX $15   NM $20   MIP $32

(KP Photo, John Brown Sr. collection)

❑ **Auto Transport Semi-Cab and Trailer,** Red Chevy cab, yellow trailer, black plastic wheels. Includes three cars. Raised cast lettering on trailer reads, "tootsietoy turnpike transport"
EX $12   NM $17   MIP $25

❑ **Cement Truck**
EX $6   NM $8   MIP $12

❑ **Coast to Coast Shipping Semi-cab and Van**
EX $12   NM $17   MIP $25

❑ **Dump Truck**
EX $6   NM $8   MIP $12

❑ **Heavy duty Hydraulic Crane**
EX $8   NM $12   MIP $17

❑ **Logging Semi-cab and Trailer**
EX $6   NM $8   MIP $12

❑ **Mobil Semi-cab and Tanker**
EX $10   NM $15   MIP $20

❑ **Shipping Semi-cab and Van**
EX $6   NM $8   MIP $12

❑ **Shuttle Truck,** 1967
EX $2   NM $3   MIP $4

Index
by Toy Manufacturer

Index by Car Manufacturer/type